# The Basilica of Saint John Lateran to 1600

The archbasilica of Saint John Lateran is the world's earliest cathedral. A Constantinian foundation pre-dating Saint Peter's in the Vatican, it remains the seat of the bishop of Rome, the pope, to this day. This volume brings together scholars of topography, archaeology, architecture, art history, geophysical survey and liturgy to illuminate this profoundly important building. It takes the story of the site from the early imperial period, when it was occupied by elite housing, through its use as a barracks for the emperor's horse guards to Constantine's revolutionary project and its development over 1,300 years. Richly illustrated throughout, this innovative volume includes both broad historical analysis and accessible explanations of the cutting-edge technological approaches to the site that allow us to visualise its original appearance.

LEX BOSMAN is Professor of Architectural History at the University of Amsterdam, with a special interest in Early Christian and Medieval Architecture. He has been a fellow of the Royal Netherlands Institute in Rome and Scholar in Residence at the Istituto Universitario Olandese di Storia dell'Arte in Florence. He is the author of many publications, including *The Power of Tradition: Spolia in the Architecture of St. Peter's in the Vatican* (2004).

IAN P. HAYNES is Professor of Archaeology at Newcastle University, specialising in Roman Archaeology. He has directed twelve field projects in five countries and in 2019 was awarded an ERC Advanced Grant for a five-year investigation of SE Rome. He is the author or editor of eight books including *Blood of the Provinces* (2013).

PAOLO LIVERANI was Curator for Classical Antiquities at the Vatican Museum and is now Professor of Ancient Topography at the University of Florence. He is the author of eight books, including *The Vatican Necropoleis* (2010).

**British School at Rome Studies**

*Series editors*
Barbara Borg
*Chair of Publications of the British School at Rome*

Rosamond McKitterick
*Chair of the Faculty of Archaeology, History and Letters and member of the Council of the British School at Rome*

Stephen J. Milner
*Director of the British School at Rome*

British School at Rome Studies builds on the prestigious and long-standing *Monographs* series of the British School at Rome. It publishes volumes on topics that cover the full range of the history, archaeology and art history of the western Mediterranean both by the staff of the BSR and its present and former members, and by members of the academic community engaged in top-quality research in any of these fields.

*Roman Port Societies: The Evidence of Inscriptions*
Edited by Pascal Arnaud and Simon Keay

*Rome in the Eighth Century: A History in Art*
John Osborne

*Rome, Pollution and Propriety: Dirt, Disease and Hygiene in the Eternal City from Antiquity to Modernity*
Edited by Mark Bradley, with Kenneth Stow

*Old Saint Peter's, Rome*
Edited by Rosamond Mckitterick, John Osborne, Carol M. Richardson and Joanna Story

*The Punic Mediterranean: Identities and Identification from Phoenician Settlement to Roman Rule*
Edited by Josephine Crawley Quinn and Nicholas C. Vella

*Turin and the British in the Age of the Grand Tour*
Edited by Paola Bianchi and Karin Wolfe

# The Basilica of Saint John Lateran to 1600

*Edited by*

L. BOSMAN
Universiteit van Amsterdam

I. P. HAYNES
Newcastle University

P. LIVERANI
Università degli Studi di Firenze

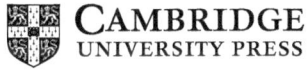

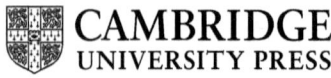

Shaftesbury Road, Cambridge CB2 8EA, United Kingdom

One Liberty Plaza, 20th Floor, New York, NY 10006, USA

477 Williamstown Road, Port Melbourne, VIC 3207, Australia

314–321, 3rd Floor, Plot 3, Splendor Forum, Jasola District Centre, New Delhi – 110025, India

103 Penang Road, #05–06/07, Visioncrest Commercial, Singapore 238467

Cambridge University Press is part of Cambridge University Press & Assessment, a department of the University of Cambridge.

We share the University's mission to contribute to society through the pursuit of education, learning and research at the highest international levels of excellence.

www.cambridge.org
Information on this title: www.cambridge.org/9781108813709

DOI: 10.1017/9781108885096

© The British School at Rome 2020

This publication is in copyright. Subject to statutory exception and to the provisions of relevant collective licensing agreements, no reproduction of any part may take place without the written permission of Cambridge University Press & Assessment.

First published 2020
First paperback edition 2023

*A catalogue record for this publication is available from the British Library*

*Library of Congress Cataloging-in-Publication data*
Names: Bosman, Lex, editor. | Haynes, Ian P., editor. | Liverani, Paolo, editor. | Lateran Basilica (Conference) (2016 : British School at Rome)
Title: The Basilica of Saint John Lateran to 1600 / edited by L. Bosman, Universiteit van Amsterdam; I.P. Haynes, University of Newcastle upon Tyne; P. Liverani, Università degli Studi di Firenze, Italy.
Description: Cambridge ; New York : Cambridge University Press, 2020. | Series: British School at Rome studies | Includes bibliographical references and index.
Identifiers: LCCN 2020004191 (print) | LCCN 2020004192 (ebook) | ISBN 9781108839761 (hardback) | ISBN 9781108885096 (ebook)
Subjects: LCSH: Basilica di S. Giovanni in Laterano – History – Congresses. | Basilicas – Italy – Rome – History – Congresses. | Caelian Hill (Italy) – History – Congresses. | Rome (Italy) – Buildings, structures, etc. – Congresses.
Classification: LCC NA5620.S4 B37 2020 (print) | LCC NA5620.S4 (ebook) | DDC 720.9456/32–dc23
LC record available at https://lccn.loc.gov/2020004191
LC ebook record available at https://lccn.loc.gov/2020004192

ISBN   978-1-108-83976-1   Hardback
ISBN   978-1-108-81370-9   Paperback

Cambridge University Press & Assessment has no responsibility for the persistence or accuracy of URLs for external or third-party internet websites referred to in this publication and does not guarantee that any content on such websites is, or will remain, accurate or appropriate.

# Contents

*List of Figures* [*page* viii]
*List of Contributors* [xxiv]
*Acknowledgements* [xxv]
*List of Abbreviations* [xxvii]

1 The Lateran Basilica to 1600 [1]
   IAN P. HAYNES, PAOLO LIVERANI AND LEX BOSMAN

2 The Evolution of the Lateran: From the *Domus* to the Episcopal Complex [6]
   PAOLO LIVERANI

3 At the Foot of the Lateran Hill, from Via Sannio to Viale Ipponio: Archaeological Investigations Prior to the Construction of Metro Line C [25]
   ROSSELLA REA AND NICOLETTA SAVIANE

4 Ground-Penetrating Radar Survey in the Saint John Lateran Basilica Complex [52]
   SALVATORE PIRO, IAN P. HAYNES, PAOLO LIVERANI AND DANIELA ZAMUNER

5 The First Residential Phases of the Lateran Area and a Hypothesis to Explain the So-Called Trapezoidal Building [71]
   GIANDOMENICO SPINOLA

6 The Castra Nova and the Severan Transformation of Rome [91]
   IAN P. HAYNES AND PAOLO LIVERANI

7 Andrea Busiri Vici and the Excavations of 1876: A Reassessment of the Archaeological Evidence [114]
   SABINA FRANCINI

8 Visualising the Constantinian Basilica [134]
   LEX BOSMAN, PAOLO LIVERANI, IWAN PEVERETT AND IAN P. HAYNES

9 Constantine's *Spolia*: A Set of Columns for San Giovanni in Laterano and the Arch of Constantine in Rome [168]
LEX BOSMAN

10 The Constantinian Basilica in the Early Medieval *Liber Pontificalis* [197]
ROSAMOND MCKITTERICK

11 The Lateran Baptistery in the Fourth and Fifth Centuries: New Certainties and Unresolved Questions [221]
OLOF BRANDT

12 The Nymphaeum of Pope Hilarus [239]
PAOLO LIVERANI AND IAN P. HAYNES

13 Examples of Medieval Construction Techniques in the Basilica of San Giovanni in Laterano [250]
LIA BARELLI

14 The Medieval Portico of Saint John Lateran [276]
ANNA MARIA DE STROBEL AND NICOLETTA BERNACCHIO

15 MATER ET CAPUT OMNIUM ECCLESIARUM: Visual Strategies in the Rivalry between San Giovanni in Laterano and San Pietro in Vaticano [294]
CAROLA JÄGGI

16 The Remodelling of San Giovanni in Laterano by Pope Nicholas IV: Transept, Apse and Façade [318]
PETER CORNELIUS CLAUSSEN

17 *Furtum Sacrilegum*: The 'Holy Heads' of Peter and Paul and Their Reliquaries in the Lateran [345]
DANIELA MONDINI

18 Reconsidering the Traces of Gentile da Fabriano and Pisanello in the Lateran Basilica [379]
ANDREA DE MARCHI

19 The Rite of the Reconciliation of Penitents at the Lateran Basilica [400]
JOHN F. ROMANO

20 The New Passion Relics at the Lateran, Fifteenth to Sixteenth Centuries: A Translocated Sacred Topography [428]
NADJA HORSCH

21 The East Façade of the Complex of Saint John Lateran in the Modern Era [466]
ALESSANDRO IPPOLITI

22 The Book of Acts in the Constantinian Basilica: Cardinal Cesare Baronio and the *Navata Clementina* in San Giovanni in Laterano [492]
FILIP MALESEVIC

*Bibliography* [523]
*Index* [572]

# Figures

1.1 Overview of the Lateran area. [*page* 3]
2.1 Map of Rome. [7]
2.2 Archaeological map of the Lateran: 1. Pottery fragments from the Orientalising period; 2. Chamber tombs of the middle Republican age; 3. Votive offerings (second half of the fourth and third centuries BC); 4. Corsini chapel; 5. So-called Saint Augustine fresco: 6. Cellars under the oratory of Santissimo Sacramento. [8]
2.3 Paolo Anesi (Rome, 1697–1773), *View of the Lateran Basilica from the East.* [9]
2.4 Plan of the Lateran area during the renovation works in 1965: Roman walls on the alignment of the Via Tusculana between the Lateran cloister and the seminary. [10]
2.5 Marble fountain near the western corner of the Pallottines' Garden. [20]
2.6 Marble fountain, plan of the excavation. [21]
2.7 Pallottines' Garden, remains of a street. [21]
2.8 Corsini Throne, Corsini Gallery, Rome. [22]
2.9 Plan of the Scala Santa sanctuary: in the middle of the eastern foundation of the Sancta Sanctorum Lauer's tunnel. To the south (n. 5), the oratory of Ss.mo Sacramento. [23]
2.10 Plan of Lauer's tunnel in the foundation of the Sancta Sanctorum: z. is the so-called Saint Augustine. [23]
2.11 Cross section north–south of the Scala Santa sanctuary. [24]
3.1 The itinerary of the Metro Line C along the Aurelian Walls. [26]
3.2 Station of San Giovanni. River bank (third century BC). [27]
3.3 The landscape before human interventions. [29]
3.4 Amba Aradam Ipponio station: the building partially excavated inside the perimeter of the station. [30]

3.5  Overview of the complex. [31]
3.6  Overview from west. [32]
3.7  Above: plan and distribution of the billets. [34]
3.8  Museum Het Valkhof, Nijmegen: the interiors of the billets. [35]
3.9  Barracks plan: Davison's typology F. [36]
3.10 Plan of other barracks from Rome and plan of the Ipponio barracks. [37]
3.11 The barracks on the Caelian and the Ipponio barracks. [38]
3.12 The structures found in the gardens of Via Sannio. [40]
3.13 Stratigraphic section of the shaft of the gardens of Via Sannio with the Aurelian Walls to the left. [42]
3.14 Plan of the portico dating to the Julio-Claudian period from the gardens of Via Sannio. [44]
3.15 Structures dating to the first half of the third century BC from the shaft of the gardens of Via Sannio. [45]
3.16 Plan of phase 1 of the Julio-Claudian portico from the shaft of the gardens of Via Sannio. [47]
3.17 Wall in *opus mixtum* (northwestern internal end) and its lining, part of the Julio-Claudian portico from the shaft of the gardens of Via Sannio. [48]
3.18 Plan of phase 2 of the Julio-Claudian portico from the shaft of the gardens of Via Sannio. [49]
3.19 Plan of phase 3 of the Julio-Claudian portico from the shaft of the gardens of Via Sannio. [49]
3.20 Overview of the portico and gardens from the shaft of the gardens of Via Sannio. [50]
4.1  Plan showing location of survey areas outside the basilica. [56]
4.2  Anomalies located with 400 MHz antenna at the estimated depth of 0.88 m (19–22 ns, twt), individuated in areas A1 and B1. [58]
4.3  Anomalies located with 400 MHz antenna at an estimated depth of 1.75 m (41–45 ns, twt), individuated in areas A1 and B1. [60]
4.4  Anomalies located with 70 MHz antenna at an estimated depth of 6.0 m, individuated in Areas A1 and B1. [62]
4.5  Anomalies located at an estimated depth of 1.35 m (30–34 ns, twt), individuated in the area A2, B2 and C2. [63]

4.6 Anomalies located at an estimated depth of 2.0 m (47–50 ns, twt), individuated in Areas A2, B2 and C2. [65]

4.7 Anomalies located at the estimated depth of 2.0 m (38–42 ns twt), individuated in the area inside the basilica. [67]

4.8 Anomalies located at an estimated depth of 4.2 m (80–84 ns twt), individuated inside the basilica. [68]

5.1 The Lateran area. 1. Domus of Titus Sextius Lateranus; 2. Suburban villa (Plautius Lateranus?); 3. Villa of Lucius Lusius Petellinus; 4. Villa of Lucius Piso. [73]

5.2 The suburban villa under the basilica: 1. Corridor; 2. Staircase between the terraces; 3. Court; 4. *Cubicula*; 5. Room excavated in 1890. [74]

5.3 The excavations of the Trapezoidal Insula in 1876. 1. The basin located in the *peristilium* near the Via Tusculana; 2. Underground room of second phase. [75]

5.4 Pompeii, the Villa of Diomedes and Rome, the Lateran Villa. [76]

5.5 The east side of the suburban villa. Suburban villa under the basilica and the *castra*. [77]

5.6 An infill in the lower terracing and the elevation of the pillars. [81]

5.7 The *castra* of Vindobona and the Castra Nova Equitum Singularium. [89]

6.1 Plan showing location of historical excavations in the area of the Castra Nova. [93]

6.2 The inverted Ionic capital recovered in the *principia* with inscriptions recording the *collegium* of the *curatores*. [95]

6.3 Section of Lateran Project laser scan showing the foundations of one of the Castra Nova's elongated barrack-like buildings. [99]

6.4 Concept model of the Castra Nova complex c. AD 215 looking east. [104]

6.5 Visualisation of an office room in the *principia* of the Castra Nova c. AD 310. [107]

6.6 The complex, multi-phase wall of Saint Venanzio preserves elements of the walls of the original third-century bath complex. [111]

6.7 Concept model showing the spatial relationship between the Constantinian basilica and its predecessor, the Castra Nova. [112]

7.1  A cross-section illustrating the plan for the mechanical relocation of the Constantinian apse along with the rearrangement of the underground archaeological area. [115]
7.2  A. Busiri Vici, 8 August 1876. West side view of the excavation area. [117]
7.3  A. Busiri Vici, plan of the excavations in the area of the apse, 1877. [119]
7.4  Northeastern corner of the courtyard of the Trapezoidal Insula. [120]
7.5  Detail of the 1876 illustration by Busiri Vici featuring the basin below the mosaic flooring. [121]
7.6  Detail of the 1876 illustration by Busiri Vici showing the rooms discovered in the southeastern portion of the excavation. [122]
7.7  Detail of the 1876 illustration by Busiri Vici describing the wall typologies found during the excavation. [124]
7.8  Detail of the 1876 photograph by Busiri Vici showing the northern perimeter wall seen from the southwestern side. [126]
7.9  Virginio Vespignani, 13 May 1877, 1:100 scale drawing of the excavation area. Detail of the eastern portion of the Trapezoidal Insula. [127]
7.10  Detail of the 1876 illustration by Busiri Vici showing the eastern portion of the Trapezoidal Insula. [127]
7.11  Southeastern portion of the Trapezoidal Insula. [128]
7.12  Detail of the 1876 illustration by Busiri Vici showing the western portion of the Trapezoidal Insula. [129]
7.13  Detail of the 1876 photograph by Busiri Vici showing the western portion of the Trapezoidal Insula. [129]
7.14  Detail of the 1876 illustration by Busiri Vici showing the northeastern corner of the Trapezoidal Insula. [130]
7.15  Detail of the 1876 illustration by Busiri Vici showing the basin discovered between the B and C walls of the *castra*. [131]
7.16  The sector to the east of the Constantinian apse. [132]
8.1  Filippo Gagliardi fresco, San Martino ai Monti (*c.* 1651). [135]

8.2  Image derived from laser scan under the basilica floor showing column foundation surrounded by modern conservation work. [140]
8.3  Working document showing overlay of modern basilica plan on 2D slice of laser-scan data of foundations. [141]
8.4  Initial internal concept model based largely on survey results, plans and the Gagliardi fresco showing simple place-holder details such as columns. [143]
8.5  Concept models showing various interpretations of roof design and pitch. [144]
8.6  Notated drawing showing thoughts and amendments from one of the later workshops. [146]
8.7  The so-called spandrel in the Lateran basilica. [149]
8.8  The Constantinian Basilica as visualised by the team. [149]
8.9  Chandelier, Musée du Louvre, Department of Egyptian Antiquities. [153]
8.10 Various types of lights used in the reconstruction of the basilica on the basis of the *Liber Pontificalis*. [154]
8.11 Saint John Lateran, Altar of the Holy Sacrament with the four bronze columns from the Constantinian *fastigium*. [157]
8.12 Battista Panzera, *Saint Angelus from Jerusalem Preaching in the Lateran*, engraving, 1598, Franciscan Museum, Rome. [159]
8.13 Francesco Contini, plan of the church and palace of the Lateran. [160]
8.14 Hypothetical reconstruction of the *fastigium*. [163]
8.15 The blocks of the *solea* during Josi's excavations. [163]
8.16 The blocks of the *solea* during Josi's excavations. [164]
8.17 One of the blocks of the *solea* preserved in the cistern under the *principia*. [165]
8.18 Cross-section with the reconstruction of the chancel fixed on the foundation block. [166]
8.19 Axonometric model of the Lateran basilica. [166]
9.1  San Giovanni in Laterano, interior to the west. [172]
9.2  Niche in southern nave wall, flanked by columns of *verde antico*. [175]
9.3  San Giovanni in Laterano, fragment of red granite column in excavation area. [177]

9.4  San Giovanni in Laterano, westernmost niche on north side of the nave, with *verde antico* columns, and one column shaft of red granite under the triumphal arch.   [180]
9.5  San Giovanni in Laterano, two *giallo antico* columns supporting the organ tribune in the north transept.   [182]
9.6  Detail of *giallo antico* column on the right side under the organ tribune.   [184]
9.7  Westernmost end of aisles on the south side, with colonnade as continuation of row of green marble columns between inner and outer aisles.   [188]
9.8  San Giovanni in Laterano, longitudinal section.   [188]
9.9  Plan of foundations in southwestern part, with indication of wall B.   [189]
9.10  Plan of basilica with foundations and rising walls preserved.   [190]
9.11  Image of GPR survey by Salvatore Piro.   [191]
9.12  Ground plan of fourth-century basilica.   [193]
9.13  Open axonometric view of southwestern part of the basilica.   [193]
11.1  Drawings of the Lateran baptistery prepared by Spencer Corbett for the *Corpus Basilicarum Christianarum Romae*.   [222]
11.2  Plan of the excavations 1924–6 inside the Lateran baptistery.   [223]
11.3  Plan of the foundation wall and of the lowest part of the brick building.   [225]
11.4  Wall paintings beneath the Lateran baptistery.   [226]
11.5  One of the walls of the Lateran baptistery with traces of two ancient windows.   [227]
11.6  The two phases of the outer walls of the Lateran baptistery: Constantine and fifth century.   [228]
11.7  The wall of the Lateran baptistery towards the chapel of Santa Croce.   [230]
11.8  Plan of the Lateran baptistery and the surrounding chapels.   [231]
11.9  The preserved and visible remains of the Constantinian walls of the Lateran baptistery; 3D model visualized in Meshlab.   [232]
11.10  Wall decoration of the Lateran baptistery in a drawing by Giuliano di Sangallo around 1500.   [233]

11.11  Wall decoration of the Lateran baptistery in an anonymous drawing from the early seventeenth century. [234]
11.12  The vestibule of the Lateran baptistery. [235]
11.13  Outside of the left apse of the vestibule of the Lateran baptistery. [237]
12.1  Plan of the area around the baptistery. Intact walls are marked in black. The oratory of Santa Croce lies to the northwest of the baptistery; the area we identify with the nymphaeum of Pope Hilarus lies north-northeast of the baptistery and directly north of the chapel of San Giovanni Evangelista. [240]
12.2  Porphyry basin used as baptismal font, Santa Maria Maggiore. [244]
12.3  Laser-scan point-cloud data rotated to view from northeast with later intrusive features digitally removed. [245]
12.4  Cistern, fountain and 'steps' viewed from the northeast. [245]
12.5  Mosaic floor positioned at base of 'steps' shown in Fig. 12.4. [246]
12.6  *Opus sectile* floor. [247]
12.7  Structures associated with the putative nymphaeum viewed from the northeast. [248]
12.8  The northwest wall of the twelfth/thirteenthcentury fountain, seen from the northeast. [249]
13.1  Above, details with the east portico and south area of the same, from the plan of the Lateran complex of Francesco Borromini, *c.* 1647; down, the same details from the plan drawn by Giuseppe Marchetti for the Holy Year 1725. [253]
13.2  On the left, hypothetical reconstruction of the portico of Sergius II (844–7) in front of Lateran basilica, plan and elevation; on the right, hypothetical reconstruction of the portico of Leo IV (847–55) in the complex of the Santi Quattro Coronati at Rome. [254]
13.3  Above, Lateran baptistery. Fresco by Andrea Sacchi depicting the façade of the Lateran basilica (*c.* 1644) and detail of the same; below, anonymous sketch of the southern section of the east portico of the Lateran basilica during the demolition of the chapel of Saint Thomas in 1647. [255]

*List of Figures*  xv

13.4 Above, detail of survey of the east façade of the Lateran complex designed by Francesco Righi, *c.* 1647, and detail of the same; in the middle, engraving of the Lateran basilica façade and detail; below, view from east of the Lateran basilica of Hendrik van Lint, datable between 1700 and 1732, and detail. [256]

13.5 Southern section of Sergian portico at the conclusion of the construction site, highlighting the construction techniques. [262]

13.6 The east tower view from the roof of the nave. [263]

13.7 Above, plans of the east and west towers; below, plan of the north arm of the transept with the addition of towers between the existing walls. [265]

13.8 Survey of the inner walls of the towers with indication of materials. [266]

13.9 East tower: above, detail of the transition between the courtain of bricks and the courtain of *tufelli*; below, details of mortar joints of central pier and an inner wall. [267]

13.10 Above, on the left, view of staircase of east tower and, on the right, detail of the vaults of west tower with centring holes; below, on the left, detail of vaults of east tower and, on the right, steps of east tower with marks in the form of an 'H'. [268]

13.11 Synthetic model of construction phases of northern end of the transept. [273]

14.1 The portico of the basilica of San Lorenzo fuori le Mura. [277]

14.2 The main façade of the medieval archbasilica as depicted in Ciampini, *De sacris aedificiis*. [278]

14.3 Fragments of the architrave of the medieval archbasilica, now in the cloister of the complex. [279]

14.4 The frieze of the medieval archbasilica as depicted in Ciampini, *De sacris aedificiis*. [280]

14.5 The frieze of the portico of San Lorenzo fuori le Mura. [281]

14.6 The inscription-signature of Nicolaus de Angelo in Ciampini's etching. [282]

14.7 The *Easter Candlestick* in the basilica of San Paolo fuori le Mura. [283]

14.8 Two columns in yellow marble supporting the organ of the transept. [285]
14.9 The Arch of Constantine in an etching by Bonaventura van Overbeek (1660–1705), published in 1708. [290]
14.10 The column now located in the rightmost side of the northern façade of the Arch of Constantine. [291]
14.11 The five columns from the Cosmatesque portico seem to have been reused in the Loggia delle Benedizioni of the new façade of the archbasilica. [292]
14.12 The coat of arms of Pope Pius XII at the centre of the modern pavement of the archbasilica. [293]
15.1 Cartouche with inscription on the eighteenth-century façade of San Giovanni in Laterano. [295]
15.2 Plan of Saint Peter's (detail of the northern part of the transept with the *piscina* of the baptistery and the chapels of Saint John the Evangelist (no. 32), Saint John the Baptist (no. 30) and the Holy Cross (no. 35). [302]
15.3 Drawing of the wooden *arca* commissioned by Pope Leo III (795–816). [305]
15.4 Giotto: Fresco in Saint Francis, Assisi, showing Saint Francis acting as a support for the collapsing Lateran basilica (= Roman Church). [307]
15.5 Late Antique porphyry sarcophagus from the mausoleum of Helena, reused in 1154 for the burial of Pope Anastasius IV. In the Lateran basilica. [310]
15.6 The medieval façade of San Giovanni in Laterano with the twelfth-century portico. [311]
15.7 Seventeenth-century drawings of the twelfth-century mosaics of the Lateran portico. [312]
15.8 Remaining fragments of the twelfth-century inscription of the Lateran portico, today in the cloister of San Giovanni in Laterano. [313]
16.1 San Giovanni in Laterano: Saint Francis, and Nicholas IV, renewed apse mosaic. [319]
16.2 Assisi, San Francesco, upper church. Saint Francis supports the porch of San Giovanni in Laterano. Detail of the *Dream of Innocent III* scene within the Saint Francis cycle, probably by Giotto. [321]

*List of Figures* xvii

16.3 San Giovanni in Laterano, Saviour, apse mosaic. Photo before 1880 of the original mosaic of 1292. [322]
16.4 San Giovanni in Laterano, apse with ambulatory before 1875 from the west. [323]
16.5 San Giovanni in Laterano, ground plan of apse with ambulatory, before 1880, by Busiri Vici. [324]
16.6 San Giovanni in Laterano, drawing of the eastern façade, seventeenth century. [325]
16.7 San Giovanni in Laterano, reconstruction sketch of the eastern façade, *c.* 1300. [326]
16.8 San Giovanni in Laterano, reconstruction of the Constantinian basilica by de Blaauw, apse and western parts [327]
16.9 San Giovanni in Laterano, view from the north. Anonymous drawing, *c.* 1540. [328]
16.10 San Giovanni in Laterano, traces of a Constantinian door and window in the northern aisle. [330]
16.11 San Giovanni in Laterano, plan of the southwestern parts of the basilica. Black indicates the Constantinian foundations, diagonal black/white indicates the foundations of the transverse wing. [331]
16.12 San Giovanni in Laterano, Marten van Heemskerck, view from the Lateran field with the papal palace und the façade of the north transept of the basilica, *c.* 1536. [332]
16.13 San Giovanni in Laterano, scheme of transept, transvers wings and cloister. [337]
16.14 San Giovanni in Laterano, south wall of transept. [339]
16.15 San Giovanni in Laterano, east wall of south transept. [340]
16.16 San Giovanni in Laterano, ground plan. Reconstruction of the medieval basilica, detail with transept. [341]
16.17 San Giovanni in Laterano, cross-section of the basilica and eastern transept tower. [342]
16.18 Rome, Santi Quattro Coronati, palace (Torre Magno) from the east with buttress. [343]
16.19 San Giovanni in Laterano, south wall of transept with buttresses. [344]
17.1 San Giovanni in Laterano, main altar tabernacle by Giovanni di Stefano, 1370. [346]

List of Figures

17.2 San Giovanni in Laterano, the reliquaries of the 'Holy Heads' of Peter and Paul, enclosed in the tabernacle; Giuseppe Valadier and Workshop, 1804. [347]

17.3 The 'Holy Heads' of Paul and Peter, reliquaries endowed by the French pope Urban V and the French king Charles V, 1369. [348]

17.4 Portrait medallion of Paul on the left bronze door of the reliquary altar endowed by Innocent III in the former chapel of Saint Lawrence in the Lateran Palace (Sancta Sanctorum). [351]

17.5 Papal seal of Paschal II (1099–1118) with the portraits of Paul and Peter. [352]

17.6 The Lateran tabernacle during the ostention of the 'Holy Heads', detail from a fresco representing the Encounter of Saint Francis, Dominicus and the Carmelitan Saint Angelus, by Giacomo Ligozzi, c. 1600, Florence, Ognissanti, first cloister. [355]

17.7 San Giovanni in Laterano, Cappella del Coro, former Colonna chapel, late Gothic reliquary bust of Paul, painting, oil on canvas, c. 1585. [356]

17.8 San Giovanni in Laterano, Cappella del Coro, former Colonna chapel, late Gothic reliquary of Peter, painting, oil on canvas, c. 1585. [357]

17.9 The reliquary busts of Peter and Paul from behind. [360]

17.10 The reliquary bust of Saint Agatha, Catania Cathedral, signed by Giovanni di Bartolo, 1376. [362]

17.11 The Lateran tabernacle with a balcony-like stage (western side). [364]

17.12 Andreuccio da Peroscia (?) stealing ecclesiastical goods (?); copy of a lost fresco cycle, dated 1364, formerly in the north transept of the Lateran basilica. [367]

17.13 Andreuccio da Peroscia being punished with incandescent irons; copy of a lost fresco cycle, dated 1364, formerly in the north transept of the Lateran basilica. [368]

17.14 Execution of Andreuccio da Peroscia; copy of a fresco cycle, dated 1364, formerly in the north transept of the Lateran basilica. [369]

17.15 Coat of arms belonging to the lost fresco cycles in the north transept of the Lateran basilica. [370]

17.16 Cappocciola and Garofalo stealing the jewels from the reliquary busts of Peter and Paul in the tabernacle of the Lateran; copy of a fresco cycle (1438–40), formerly in the north transept of the Lateran basilica. [371]

17.17 The public removal from office and degradation of the three clergymen at the main altar of Santa Maria di Aracoeli; copy of a fresco cycle (1438–40), formerly in the north transept of the Lateran basilica. [373]

17.18 The exposure of the three culprits in the pillory on the Campo dei Fiori; copy of a fresco cycle (1438–40), formerly in the north transept of the Lateran basilica. [374]

17.19 The dragging and public execution of the sacrilegious thieves on the Lateran square in front of the Annibaldi tower; copy of a fresco cycle (1438–40), formerly in the north transept of the Lateran basilica. [375]

18.1 Saint John Lateran, general view of the fragment of the foliated frieze by Gentile da Fabriano at the top of the northern wall of the nave. [382]

18.2 Saint John Lateran, fragment of the foliated frieze by Gentile da Fabriano at the top of the northern wall of the nave. [383]

18.3 Saint John Lateran, fragment of the foliated frieze by Gentile da Fabriano at the top of the northern wall of the nave. [384]

18.4 Saint John Lateran, fragment of the foliated frieze by Gentile da Fabriano at the top of the northern wall of the nave. [385]

18.5 Saint John Lateran, fragment of the foliated frieze by Gentile da Fabriano (detail of the raised plaster at the top of the northern wall of the nave). [386]

18.6 Saint John Lateran, relief from Gentile da Fabriano's frescos at the top of the northern wall of the nave, workshop of Francesco Borromini. [387]

18.7 Saint John Lateran, fragment of the foliated frieze by Gentile da Fabriano (detail of the azurite on the layer of red *morellone* altered to malachite). [388]

18.8 Saint John Lateran, fragment of the foliated frieze by Gentile da Fabriano (detail of the incisions of arches related to the original curvature of the scroll). [388]

18.9 Saint John Lateran, fragment of the foliated frieze by Gentile da Fabriano (detail of the vertex of the moulding surrounding a window and overlapping the horizontal foliated frieze). [389]

18.10 Saint John Lateran, relief of the foliated frieze at the end of the northern wall of the nave. [390]

18.11 *Head of a Prophet* (Solomon? Also believed to represent Charlemagne) by Gentile da Fabriano. [391]

18.12 *Fragment of the Head of a Prophet* by Gentile da Fabriano. [392]

18.13 Proposal for the sequence of the episodes painted by Gentile da Fabriano (1427) and Pisanello (1431–2) on the northern wall of the nave in Saint John Lateran. [394]

18.14 Pisanello, *Woman's Head* (from a lost fresco with the *Preaching of the Baptist*?). [398]

20.1 The 'new relics' marked in the so-called archive plan, workshop of Domenico Fontana (?), 1585–6, etching, Rome, Archivio Capitolare Lateranense [430]

20.2a Two octagonal pillars 'from Pilate's palace', cloister of San Giovanni in Laterano. [431]

20.2b Detail of a column shaft with iron ring. [431]

20.3a The *mensura Christi*, cloister of San Giovanni in Laterano. [433]

20.3b Close-up of the upper part of the *mensura Christi*. [433]

20.4 The Pilate doors in the upper corridor of the Scala Santa building. [434]

20.5 The Scala Santa with pilgrims. [436]

20.6a The 'split column', cloister of San Giovanni in Laterano. [437]

20.6b Detail of a shaft with foliage and maenad relief. [438]

20.7 Hans Burgkmair, central panel of the triptych *San Giovanni in Laterano*, from a series of seven altar pieces dedicated to the Principal Roman Churches, oil on wood, 1502. [441]

20.8 The interior of Pilate's palace with the Scala Santa, the doorframes and a porphyry slab. Detail from Piero della Francesca, *Flagellation of Christ*, c. 1456–7, tempera on wood. [499]

20.9 *Die gewisse und wahrhafte Läng unsers Herrn Jesu Christi* ('the true length of Our Lord Jesus Christ'), paper amulet,

Germany, fifteenth century. Freistadt (Upper Austria). [452]

20.10 Jeronimo Nadal, *Evangelicae Historiae Imagines Jeronimo Nadal, Imagines evangelicae historiae*, Antwerp, 1593, p. CXVIII. [460]

20.11 Bernardino Amico, Reconstruction of Pilate's palace in Jerusalem with the Scala Santa, 1620. [462]

20.12a Görlitz (Saxonia), interior of the Holy Cross chapel, before 1520. 'Golgotha' setting with the three holes of the crosses and a ditch for Christ's blood. [462]

20.12b Görlitz, ground plan of the Holy Cross chapel. [463]

20.13a Görlitz, Holy Cross chapel, table with three dice in a repository – an adaptation of the *mensura Christi*? [463]

20.13b Detail of the repository. [463]

21.1 Fra' Paolino da Venezia, *Roma di Fra' Paolino da Venezia*, Rome, 1320. [467]

21.2 Alessandro Strozzi, *Roma nei secoli IV/V*, detail, Rome, 1474. [467]

21.3 Leonardo Bufalini, *Roma nei secc. IV/XV: zona del Celio*, Rome, 1551. [468]

21.4 Marten van Heemskerck, *Il palazzo lateranense e la basilica*, Rome, 1535–8. [469]

21.5 Antonio Lafrèry, *Veduta delle sette chiese di Roma*, Rome, 1575. [471]

21.6 Mario Cartaro, *Roma nel sec. XVI: Zona di Porta Maggiore e del Colosseo*, Rome, 1576. [472]

21.7 Stefano du Pèrac, *Roma nel sec. XVI: Zona dell'Anfiteatro Castrense e di Porta Latina*, Rome, 1577. [473]

21.8 Historical reconstruction of *coritore novo* through building costs: plans and façades. [475]

21.9 Historical reconstruction of *coritore novo* through building costs: sections and façade. [476]

21.10 Domenico Fontana's survey of the Palazzo Apostolico: façades. [478]

21.11 Domenico Fontana's survey of the Palazzo Apostolico: plans. [479]

21.12 Filippino Lippi, *Disputa di S. Tommaso d'Aquino con gli eretici*, Rome, 1488. [481]

21.13 Marten van Heemskerck, *Il palazzo lateranense e la basilica*, Rome, 1535–8. [483]

21.14 First scholar of Francesco Borromini, *Alzato di S. Giovanni in Laterano*, Rome, 1647. [484]

21.15 Francesco Borromini and scholars, *Pianta del complesso di S. Giovanni in Laterano*, Rome, 1646. [485]

21.16 Giovan Battista Falda, *Roma nel sec. XVII: Zona di S. Giovanni in Laterano e delle Terme di Caracalla*, Rome, 1676. [486]

21.17 Filippo Juvarra, *Progetto per la facciata e la piazza di S. Giovanni in Laterano*, Rome, 1715–16? [488]

21.18 Paolo Anesi, *Veduta della basilica di S. Giovanni in Laterano*, Rome, 1697–1773. [488]

21.19 Anonymous, *Pianta di progetto della piazza da realizzare davanti alla Basilica di S. Giovanni in Laterano*, Rome, eighteenth century. [490]

21.20 Paul Marie Letarouilly, *Veduta della facciata principale della Basilica e del Palazzo di S. Giovanni in Laterano*, Rome, 1841. [491]

22.1 Giovanni Battista de' Cavalieri, *Constantine the Great's Vision of the Cross*, in *Ecclesiae anglicanae trophaea* (1584). [495]

22.2 Pier Paolo Olivieri et al., Altar of the Blessed Sacrament, transept, San Giovanni in Laterano. [498]

22.3 Cesare d'Arpino, *Ascension of Christ*, 1601, transept, San Giovanni in Laterano. [499]

22.4 Bernardino Cesari, *Triumphal Entry of Constantine the Great into Rome*, 1598–1600, fresco, transept, San Giovanni in Laterano. [500]

22.5 Cesare Nebbia, *Constantine the Great's Dream of the Apostles Peter and Paul*, 1598–1600, transept, San Giovanni in Laterano. [501]

22.6 Paris Nogari, *The Discovery of Sylvester on Mount Soratte*, 1598–1600, transept, San Giovanni in Laterano. [502]

22.7 Cristoforo Roncalli, *Pope Sylvester Baptises Constantine the Great*, 1598–1600, transept, San Giovanni in Laterano. [503]

22.8 Paris Nogari, *Foundation of the Lateran*, 1598–1600, transept, San Giovanni in Laterano. [504]

22.9 Giovanni Battista Ricci, *The Consecration of the Main Altar*, 1598–1600, transept, San Giovanni in Laterano. [505]

22.10 Paris Nogari, *The Miraculous Apparition of the Volto Santo*, 1598–1600, transept, San Giovanni in Laterano. [506]
22.11 Giovanni Baglione, *Constantine the Great's Donation to the Lateran*, 1598–1600, transept, San Giovanni in Laterano. [507]
22.12 Altar and *confessio* chapel in Cardinal Baronio's titular church of Santi Nereo e Achilleo. [516]

# Contributors

Lia Barelli, Sapienza Università di Roma, Italy
Nicoletta Bernacchio, Sovrintendenza di Roma Capitale, Italy
Lex Bosman, Universiteit van Amsterdam, the Netherlands
Olof Brandt, Pontificio Istituto di Archeologia Cristiana, Rome, Italy
Peter Cornelius Claussen, Universität Zürich, Switzerland
Andrea De Marchi, Università degli studi di Firenze, Italy
Anna Maria De Strobel, Independent Scholar, Italy
Sabina Francini, Musei Vaticani, Vatican City
Ian P. Haynes, Newcastle University, UK
Nadja Horsch, Universität Leipzig, Germany
Alessandro Ippoliti, Università degli Studi di Ferrara, Italy
Carola Jäggi, Universität Zürich, Switzerland
Paolo Liverani, Università degli studi di Firenze, Italy
Filip Malesevic, Université de Fribourg, Switzerland
Rosamond McKitterick, University of Cambridge, UK
Daniela Mondini, Università della Svizzera italiana, Switzerland
Iwan Peverett, New Visions, UK
Salvatore Piro, Consiglio Nazionale delle Ricerche, Italy
Thea Ravasi, Newcastle University, UK
Rossella Rea, Parco Archeologico del Colosseo, Rome, Italy
John Romano, Benedictine College in Atchison, Kansas, USA
Nicoletta Saviane, Società Land, Italy
Giandomenico Spinola, Musei Vaticani, Vatican City
Daniella Zamuner, Consiglio Nazonale delle Ricerche, Italy

# Acknowledgements

The editors and authors of this volume would like to extend their thanks to the following colleagues for their contribution to its production.

It has been an extraordinary privilege to research the story of the archbasilica of Saint John Lateran and to work in the archaeological area beneath the cathedral. None of the analysis below ground would have been possible without the kind support of Dr Barbara Jatta, director of the Vatican Museums, the colleagues of the Vatican Museums' Department of Greek and Roman Antiquities who have contributed to this volume and Dr Leonardo Di Blasi of the same department. For his gracious permission to conduct research inside the Archbasilica, we are indebted to Mons. Natalino Zagotto, Capitolo della Basilica di S. Giovanni in Laterano. The help of Stefano Porfiri and Roberto Rosselli, both of the archbasilica, is also very gratefully acknowledged. In and around the basilica grounds, the insight, expertise and technical assistance of colleagues from the Servizi Tecnici del Governatorato, notably the director, Don Rafael Garcia de la Serrana Villalobos, Ing. Enrico Sebastiani and Ing. Silvio Scripanti, has been of the greatest possible importance.

The idea for a volume on Saint John Lateran developed from conversations with Professor Christopher Smith, then director of the British School at Rome. He also secured the generous funding that made the initial conference in September 2016 possible, and has been of tremendous support throughout. Our thanks go to the generous anonymous donor, a major supporter of the British School at Rome, whose gift made all the difference to taking this work forward. The British School's ongoing support, both from Christine Martin and Stefania Peterlini in the organisation of the launch conference, and subsequently through the director, Professor Stephen Milner, has been indispensable. We also wish to extend our thanks to Professor Barbara Borg, the BSR's chair of publications, and to the two anonymous readers whose reports on the volume were so useful to us as editors.

Further thanks are due to the Royal Netherlands Institute in Rome (KNIR) for supporting the conference in 2016, lodging several of the speakers and hosting a reception for conference delegates. We are also grateful to the Netherlands Institute for Advanced Study (NIAS) for a fellowship for Lex and for facilitating an early and formative residential seminar on visualisation, and to the many colleagues who have joined us in discussion on so many aspects of this journey. In particular, we thank Dr Patricia Lulof, and Professor Drs Bram Kempers, Ralf Behrwald, Sible de Blaauw and Bernard Frischer. Ian would like to thank the Fellows of Peterhouse, Cambridge for electing him a Visiting Fellow to pursue work on this volume. He also acknowledges with gratitude the hospitality of the McDonald Institute of Archaeology at the University of Cambridge during the same period. As directors of the Lateran Project, Paolo and Ian would also like to acknowledge their debt to the many colleagues otherwise unnamed in this volume whose sheer hard work and technical expertise played a vital role in the extensive survey work undertaken at the Lateran. In this context we would especially wish to honour the work of Dr Sabrina Amaducci, Dave and Denise Heslop, Stephen Kay, Dr Antonio Garcia Lopez, Adriano Morabito (and our colleagues at Roma Sotterranea) and Alex Turner.

The compilation of the volume has been a substantial task, and we are most grateful for the expertise and assistance of three colleagues in particular, all of them accomplished archaeologists in their own right. Dr Thea Ravasi has contributed to multiple aspects of the finished volume and prepared many of the technical illustrations. Dr Evan Scherer has played an invaluable role in further proofreading and the building of the bibliography. Dr Giacomo Savani further contributed extensively to both editing and the translation of key texts.

# Abbreviations

| | |
|---|---|
| *AE* | *L'Année Épigraphique* (Paris, 1888–) |
| ASV | Archivo Segreto Vaticano |
| BAV | Biblioteca Apostolica Vaticana |
| BiASA | Biblioteca di Archeologia e Storia dell'Arte |
| Blaauw, *CD* | S. de Blaauw, *Cultus et decor: liturgia e architetuttura nella Roma tardoantica e medieval*, 2 vols. (Vatican City, 1994) |
| *CBCR* | R. Krautheimer, S. Corbett and A. Frazer, *Corpus Basilicarum Christianarum Romae*, 5 vols. (Vatican City, 1937–77) |
| CCCM | Corpus Christianorum, Continuatio Mediaevalis |
| CCSL | Corpus Christianorum, Series Latina |
| *CIL* | Deutsche Akademie der Wissenschaften zu Berlin (ed.), *Corpus Inscriptionum Latinarum*, 17 vols. (Berlin 1862–93) |
| CSEL | Corpus Scriptorum, Ecclesiasticorum Latinorum |
| *DNO* | S. Kansteiner, K. Hallof, L. Lehmann and B. Seidensticker and K. Stemmer (eds.), *Der Neue Overbeck*, 5 vols. (Berlin, 2014) |
| *ICUR* | G. B. de Rossi (ed.), *Inscriptiones Christianae Urbis Romae*, 2 vols. (Rome, 1857–88) |
| *ILCV* | E. Diehl (ed.), *Inscriptiones Latinae Christianae Veteres* (Berlin, 1924) |
| *ILS* | H. Dessau (ed.), *Inscriptiones Latinae Selectae*, 3 vols. (Berlin, 1892–1916) |
| *LP* | L. Duchesne (ed.), *Le Liber Pontificalis: Texte, introduction et commentaire*, 2 vols. (Paris, 1886-92); additions and corrections, C. Vogel (ed.) (Paris, 1957), cited subsequently as *LP*, I, II with *vita* number and chapter (where relevant) |
| *LTUR* | E. M. Steinby (ed.), *Lexicon Topographicum Urbis Romae*, 6 vols. (Rome, 1993–2000) |
| *LTURS* | A. La Regina (ed.), *Lexicon Topographicum Urbis Romae Suburbium*, 5. vols. (Rome, 2001-8) |
| MLCT | Monumenta Liturgica Concilii Tridentinini |
| *MEFRA* | *Mélanges de l'École Française de Rome. Antiquité* |

| | |
|---|---|
| MGH | Monumenta Germaniae Historica |
| PBSR | *Papers of the British School at Rome* |
| PIR | Deutsche Akademie der Wissenschaften zu Berlin (ed.), *Prosographia Imperi Romani*, 8 vols. (1933–2015) |
| PL | J.-P. Migne (ed.), *Patrologia Latina*, 217 vols. (Paris, 1841–65) |
| PLRE | A. H. M. Jones, J. R. Martindale and J. Morris (eds.), *The Prosography of the Later Roman Empire*, 3 vols. (Cambridge, 1972–92) |
| RAC | *Rivista di Archeologia Cristiana* |
| RE | *Realencyclopädie des classischen Altertumswissenschaft* |
| RIC | H. Mattingly and E. A. Syndenham, *The Roman Imperial Coinage*, 10 vols. (London, 1923–94) |
| RJBH | *Römisches Jahrbuch der Bibliotheca Hertziana* |

# 1 | The Lateran Basilica to 1600

IAN P. HAYNES, PAOLO LIVERANI AND LEX BOSMAN

The archbasilica of Saint John Lateran occupies a uniquely important place in world history. The first public building erected for Christian worship and the pope's own cathedral, it shaped figuratively and literally the reach and form of Christendom. Its location, in the south-east of Rome, is associated with many of the defining events of Late Antique and medieval Christianity. A summary history would note the synod of 313, convened at the so-called Domus Faustae to condemn Donatism even before the basilica's completion; synods of 649 against Monothelitism and 769 against Iconoclasm; and five ecumenical councils, each of profound importance, between 1123 and 1512. Intertwined with authoritative statements on Church governance from the palace and *patriarchium* next to it came a steady stream of teachings on proper form and liturgical practice as articulated within its walls.

It is this rich pedigree that the title *Sancrosancta Lateranenis ecclesia omnium Urbis et Orbis ecclesiarum mater et caput* displayed on the building's magnificent eighteenth-century eastern façade proclaims. Yet despite its greater antiquity and unquestioned dominance to the high Middle Ages, Saint John Lateran has lost its prominence in public perception, and perhaps even scholarly attention, to Saint Peter's in the Vatican. Competition between these two great churches is one of the great themes in the evolution of ecclesial Rome, and is indeed attested in that self-same declaration that the Lateran church is *mater et caput*, mother and head, of the world's churches. With the hindsight of history, we can read in the proclamation in which it originated, a bull issued by Gregory XI (1370–8) from distant Avignon, a claim to pre-eminence that was becoming increasingly tenuous. Despite Gregory's assertion that the Lateran was 'our home above all other churches in Rome and in all the world' and his emphasis that it played a more important role than Saint Peter's, 'the church and basilica of the Prince of Apostles in the city of Rome', the Lateran basilica was in a strikingly dilapidated state. It would, of course, have taken more than structural deterioration to end the dominance of this fine basilica, which had rebounded from devastation before and was to be magnificently remodelled again. Yet the Avignon years were to mark another shift of fundamental importance: following the end of the long schism the pope's residence and the seat of Church government moved from the Lateran to the Vatican.

In offering an end date for this volume of 1600 we are mindful of the comparative history of the two churches and their associated buildings, but we end our collection then for reasons particular to the Lateran. Our sister volume in the BSR/CUP series, *Old St Peter's, Rome*, naturally took as its end point the wholesale destruction of the fourth-century Saint Peter's, and the creation in the sixteenth and seventeenth centuries of a radically different structure. Crucially, the Lateran basilica's history unfolded differently. Twice sacked in the fifth century, devastated by an earthquake in 896, severely fire damaged in 1308 and again in 1360, augmented already under Constantine with a separate baptistery, and further supplemented at various times by adjacent oratories, libraries and a nymphaeum, the building's appearance certainly changed many times, yet crucially its essential structure endured. There was no radical Renaissance rebuild. When the time came for major refurbishment and remodelling at the Lateran, papal priorities post-Reformation meant that this monument's tangible testimony to the antiquity of Rome's Christian tradition was seen in a different light. Francesco Borromini's brilliant three-year-long remodelling of the archbasilica of Saint John Lateran, completed in October 1649, was marked by innovation, but underpinned by an emphasis on conservation. Preserving elements of the earliest basilica was a priority. Though the degree to which this was achieved is debated further within this volume, one cannot simply speak of an 'Old' Saint John Lateran and a 'New' one.

Rather than ending with the transformation wrought by Borromini, our volume ends in the Holy Year 1600. A visitor to the Lateran prior to the building projects that culminated then would have still been able to see many traces of Constantine's basilica; key elements of the *spolia* that characterised its variegated interior still occupied the positions where their fourth-century builders had placed them. Even the recently completed commissions of Pope Clement VIII (1592–1605), the refurbishment of the archbasilica transept and its magnificent pictorial cycle, harked back to earlier times. Adorned with scenes depicting the basilica's founder, Constantine, the cycle speaks to the interconnectedness of Clement's aspirations for a revival of Church authority with restoration of the archbasilica itself. The fundamental connection between the two lies at the heart of Freiberg's study of the Lateran in 1600.[1]

---

[1] J. Freiberg, *The Lateran in 1600: Christian Concord in Counter-Reformation Rome* (New York, 1995).

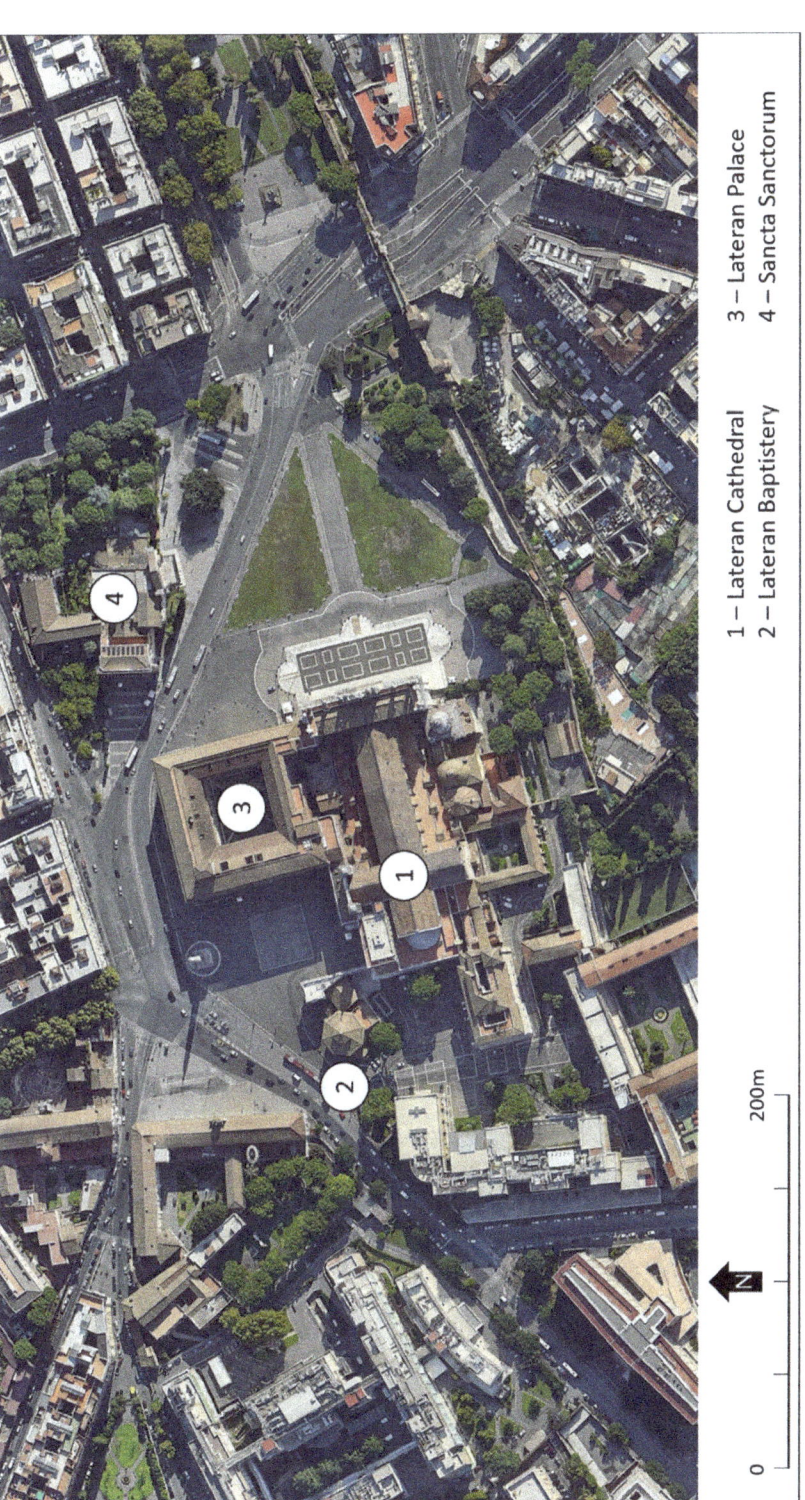

Fig. 1.1 Overview of the Lateran area (T. Ravasi, modified from Google Earth Image Landsat/Copernicus, IBCAO, US Geographical Survey).

1 – Lateran Cathedral
2 – Lateran Baptistery
3 – Lateran Palace
4 – Sancta Sanctorum

Perhaps less obvious, initially, will be our starting point for this volume. To understand the location and significance of the Lateran archbasilica, we believe that it is necessary to go back beyond the building's Constantinian foundation, and to look at the history of the Lateran quarter itself. Aspects of this history, such as the origins of the quarter's name, or the location of the Domus Faustae, have certainly been much debated. Chapters in this volume address both these issues and, as the reader will see, the volume seeks to go beyond them to situate the Lateran basilica's emergence within the broader transformation of Rome. The site of the foundation was at once pragmatic and symbolic, for it took over the newly available site of the Castra Nova of the *equites singulares*, the imperial horse guards who had formed a vital part of the force that had unsuccessfully opposed Constantine at the critical battle of Milvian Bridge (312). The platform on which the fort had been constructed provided a prominent space in an area of Rome which had, from the reign of Septimius Severus onwards, become increasingly valued by the successive emperors. The alignment of the basilica to the east, towards the Sessorian palace, a complex greatly developed under Constantine, further underscores the attraction of a setting looking south-east, away from the traditional heart of the city.

Consecrated by Pope Sylvester I (314–35), in either 318 or 324, the basilica has been known by several names over the centuries. Reference to it as the Basilica Aurea, or Golden Basilica, current in the sixth century, recalled its lavish interiors, but the earliest reference to a dedication, to the Saviour, appears in the seventh century.[2] Bede, writing in the eighth century, refers to it as the Basilica of Saint John, known as the Basilica Constantiniana.[3] And the Saviour and two Saint Johns are honoured in the church's formal title today: *Archibasilica Sanctissimi Salvatoris et Sanctorum Iohannes Baptista et Evangelista in Laterano*. That we cannot fully reconstruct the process and pattern of the basilica's many dedications underscores how much there is that remains unknown and contested in its history.

How should we approach study of this remarkable building about which so much has been written, but so much remains uncertain? We acknowledge with pleasure the foundational work of previous scholars, of Krautheimer for his pioneering work on the Constantinian basilica,[4] for example, and de

---

[2] Readers are directed to McKitterick's careful analysis of Lateran dedication, Chapter 10 in this volume.

[3] Bede, *De temporum ratione*, c, 66 in C. Jones (ed.), *Bedae Venerabilis Opera. Pars VI: Opera didascalica 2 (De temporum ratione)* (Corpus Christianorum Series Latina 123B) (Turnhout, 1977), 509: 'Constantinus fecit Romae, ubi baptizatus est basilicam beati Johannis baptistae, quae appellatur Constantiniana.'

[4] CBCR V.

Blaauw for his illumination of *Cultus et decor*,⁵ but we also look to the future. This volume brings together a body of work which collectively marks a major expansion in the range and depth of research into the Lateran. In bringing together the contributions that make up this volume, we wish to stress the many different disciplinary approaches that may be fruitfully applied. Studies of the archaeology, architecture, art, history, topography and liturgy all have a vital role to play and are all represented within these pages; bringing these approaches together is essential to advance new thinking. Our aim has also been to foreground the latest research and, in doing so, provide what we hope will prove an essential point of reference for scholars. Complete and even coverage, however, must remain elusive; we acknowledge that some aspects are better represented than others. While the Lateran palace and the *patriarchium* are bound up with that of the basilica, we can only engage with them partially here and direct colleagues to other important forthcoming research.⁶

The attentive reader will also note another aspect of our approach which we trust will reward close reading. The bringing together of diverse contributors and specialist expertise has strengthened the case for some hypotheses, but it has also highlighted differences of scholarly opinion over others. In the richly stimulating conference held at the British School at Rome to discuss the Lateran which laid the foundations for this book,⁷ and in subsequent extended correspondence with and between our authors, we have sought to ensure that all have been exposed to such differences of opinion and responded to them. In several cases it has not been possible to resolve these differences to the satisfaction of all, and of course the contributors' right to argue their case their way is respected. Ensuring that difference in opinion emerges clearly from these pages is, in our opinion, every bit as essential for future research as is identifying areas where we argue that a new consensus has been achieved.

---

⁵ S. de Blaauw, *Cultus et decor: Liturgia e Architettura nella Roma Tardoantica e Medievale: Basilica Salvatoris, Sanctae Mariae, Sancti Petri*, 2 vols. (Studi e testi 355) (Vatican City, 1994).

⁶ The work of P. Cornelius Claussen, *Die Kirchen der Stadt Rom im Mittelalter 1050–1300: S. Giovanni in Laterano* (Corpus Cosmatorum II, 2) (Forschungen zur Kunstgeschichte und Christlichen Archäologie 21) (Stuttgart, 2008); P. Lauer, *Le palais de Latran: Étude historique et archéologique* (Paris, 1911); M. Luchterhandt, 'Päpstlicher Palastbau und höfisches Zeremoniell unter Leo III', in C. Stiegemann and M. Wemhoff (eds), *799: Kunst und Kultur der Karolingerzeit: Karl der Große und Papst Leo III. in Paderborn* (Mainz, 1999), 109–22; and M. Luchterhandt, 'Rom und Achen: Die Karolinger und der päpstliche Hof um 800', in F. Pohle (ed.), *Karl der Grose/Charlemagne: Orte der Macht* (Aachen, 2014), 104–13 remain important points of reference, but we draw the reader's attention particularly to forthcoming monographs by Manfred Luchterhandt and John Osborne.

⁷ The Lateran Basilica, 19–21 September 2016.

## 2 | The Evolution of the Lateran: From the *Domus* to the Episcopal Complex

PAOLO LIVERANI

Despite its relatively peripheral position on the slopes of the Caelian hill on the edge of the area enclosed by the Aurelian Wall, the Lateran area has a special significance in the urban history of Rome (Fig. 2.1). This part of the city was occupied by the sumptuous *domus* and three forts: the Castra Peregrina under Santo Stefano Rotondo; the Castra Priora; and Castra Nova of the *equites singulares*, the imperial horse guard. The area finally became an urban nexus of growing importance when Constantine razed the Severan Castra Nova and built the basilica of the Saviour – today Saint John Lateran – for the bishop of Rome. An episcopal residence was added to the basilica and its baptistery shortly after their construction.

Our knowledge of this area in ancient times is both extraordinarily rich and unsatisfactory (Fig. 2.2). On the one hand, we have several indications in the literary sources – albeit not unproblematic ones – and a wealth of archaeological remains – though often from old excavations or preliminary publications.[1] On the other hand – especially for the early Christian period and the early Middle Ages – we have a very fragmentary knowledge of the basilica and the residence of the bishop, known as the *patriarchium* from the eighth century onwards. In this context, the Lateran Project aims to document the Lateran structures and to read them in a critical way from both a topographical and historical point of view.

Before we analyse in detail the monumental structures, phases and historical development of the area, it is useful to summarise the general problems, which constitute the starting point for investigation, paying particular attention to the literary and epigraphic sources, in order to update the overall picture in the light of the latest hypotheses.

In Antiquity the area now occupied by the Lateran complex had a different orography from that of today: it was a hill connected to the

---

[1] The extraordinary synthesis by Colini remains fundamental (A. M. Colini, *Storia e topografia del Celio nell'antichità* (Memorie della Pontificia Accademia Romana di Archeologia 7) (Vatican City, 1944)); a very important update for the western part of the Caelian hill is C. Pavolini, *Archeologia e Topografia della regione II (Celio): Un aggiornamento sessant'anni dopo Colini* (*LTUR*, Supplementum III) (Rome, 2006). For the Lateran area, see F. Consalvi, *Il Celio Orientale: Contributi alla carta archeologica di Roma Tav. VI settore H* (Rome, 2009).

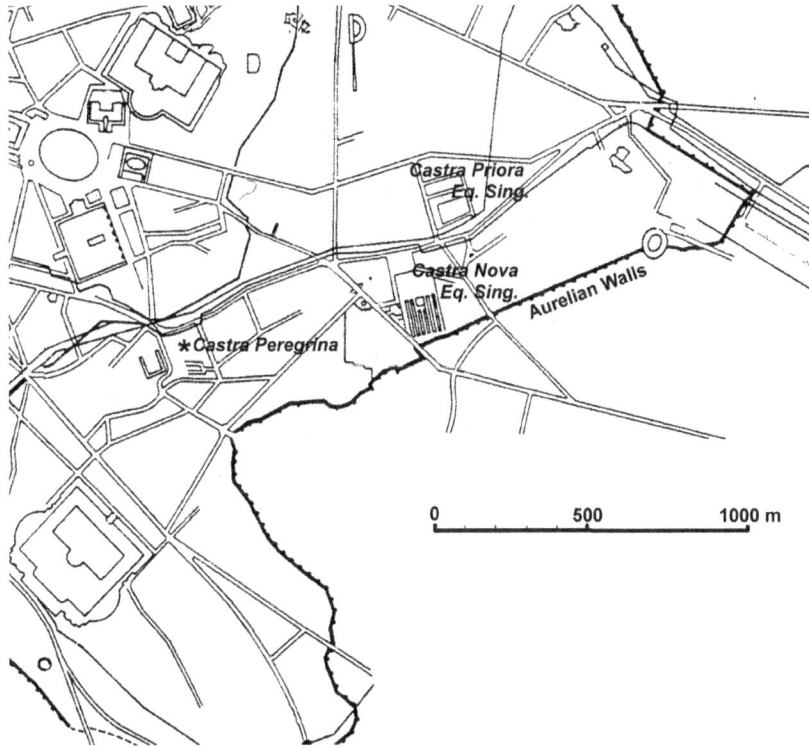

Fig. 2.1 Map of Rome.

north to the remaining part of the Caelian, with much more pronounced boundaries on the other three sides. To the south, a strong difference in level was evened out in the first century with substructures, later incorporated into the Aurelian Walls. To the west was a street, the Via Tusculana according to Colini,[2] which descended to the valley below on a path currently no longer traceable on the ground, to cross the Lateran *posterula*, a minor gate. To the east, the Via Asinaria passed through the homonymous gate with a sharp rise that has only been softened, but that appears as a steep descent supported by massive walls in seventeenth-century drawings and paintings (Fig. 2.3).[3]

---

[2] Colini, *Storia e topografia del Celio*, 321–2, fig. 261.

[3] M. D'Onofrio, 'Il Patriarchio nascosto', in P. Liverani (ed.), *Giornata di studio tematica dedicata al Patriarcato Lateranense: Atti della giornata tematica dei Seminari di Archeologia Cristiana (École française de Rome, 10 maggio 2001)* (*MEFRA* 116, 1) (special issue) (Rome, 2004), 141–60, at p. 149 fig. 6; P. Liverani, 'L'episcopio lateranense dalle origini all'Alto Medioevo', in S. Balcon, F. Baratte, J.-P. Caillet and D. Sandron (eds.), *Des domus ecclesiae aux palais épiscopaux* (Bibliothèque de l'Antiquité tardive 23) (Turnhout, 2012), 119–31, at p. 129 fig. 8. To the bibliography listed in this article, add M. Bona Castellotti (ed.), *Quadreria dell'Arcivescovado* (Milan, 1999), 293 n. 318 (view by Paolo Anesi, before 1732); M. N. Boisclair, *Gaspar Dughet, sa vie et son oeuvre (1615–1675)* (Paris, 1986), 277 n. 350 fig. 385 (view attributed to Gaspar Dughet).

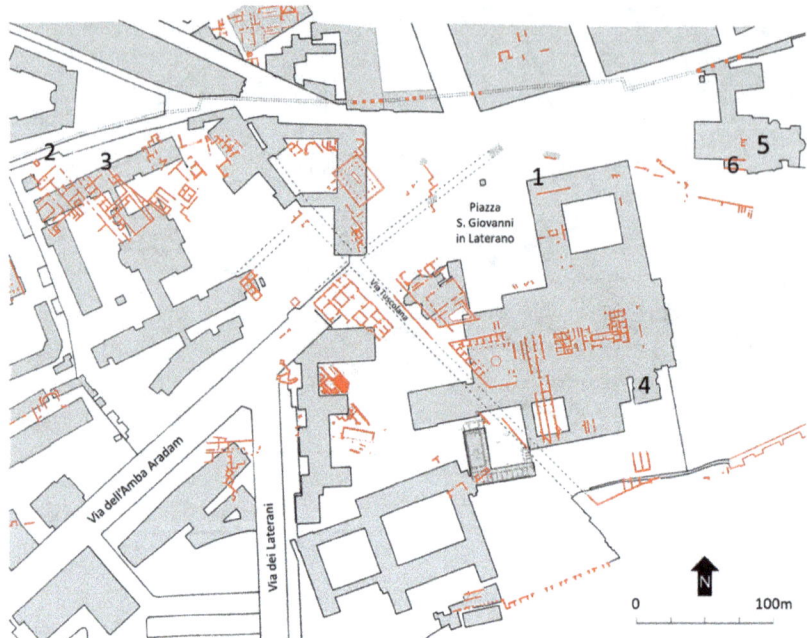

**Fig. 2.2** Archaeological map of the Lateran: 1. Pottery fragments from the Orientalising period; 2. Chamber tombs of the middle Republican age; 3. Votive offerings (second half of the fourth and third centuries BC); 4. Corsini chapel; 5. So-called Saint Augustine fresco: 6. Cellars under the oratory of Santissimo Sacramento (Image: T. Ravasi. Adapted from Liverani, *Laterano 1*).

The top of the hill was located at the front of the basilica, while the slope went down to the west, towards the current apse. On this side, the remains of various structures below the basilica and the baptistery are oriented with the Via Tusculana. The construction of the Castra Nova by Septimius Severus abandoned this orientation in favour of the one that prevailed further east: this new alignment was used first by the Castra Nova, then by the Constantinian basilica, and finally by the modern city. Further evidence for street alignments before Septimius Severus derives from some unpublished excavations of 1965. During renovation works in the Lateran area some walls were found along the expected alignment of the Via Tusculana (Fig. 2.4),[4] in the former garden of

---

[4] *L'Attività della Santa Sede* (1965), 867, 'Cortile adiacente al Chiostro': near the western corner, at the depth of 5.75 m, the remains of a square-shaped marble fountain (1.04 m on each side, Figs 2.5–2.6) was found against a brick wall. To the west was a great marble entablature of the age of Domitian (G. Spinola, 'Sculture, rilievi, decorazione, architettonica, iscrizioni e reperti ceramici', in P. Liverani (ed.), *Laterano 1: Scavi sotto la basilica di S. Giovanni in Laterano*, vol. I: *Materiali* (Vatican City, 1998), 17–114, at p. 47 n. 183 fig. 139; P. Pensabene, *Roma su Roma: Reimpiego architettonico, recupero*

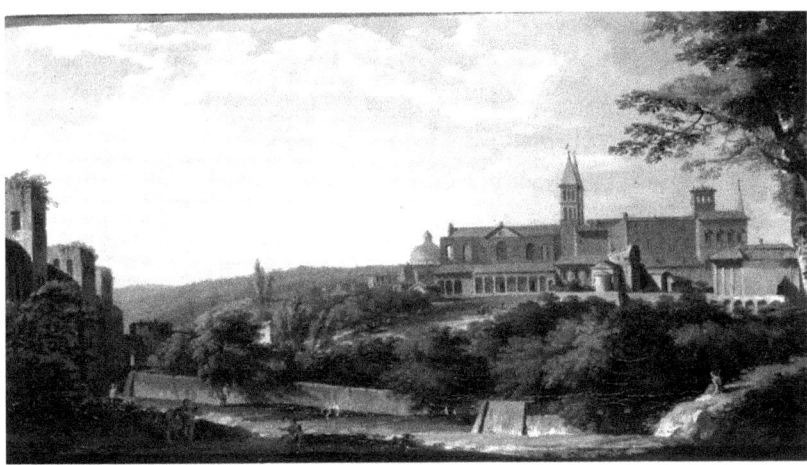

Fig. 2.3 Paolo Anesi (Rome, 1697–1773), *View of the Lateran Basilica from the East* (Photo: Diocesan Museum, Milan).

the Pallottine Fathers, now an open space for flower beds and parking between the Lateran cloister and the seminary.

The first evidence for settlement in the area dates back to the end of the Orientalising period. However, the only remains consist of pottery sherds, probably from the backfill of construction cuts. They were found during restoration works in the cellars at the northwest corner of the Lateran palace (see Fig. 2.2.1).[5] Considering the state of conservation and the types of pottery, these sherds probably derived from burials along the Via Tusculana. A few hundred metres to the northwest (see Fig. 2.2.2), Valnea Scrinari identified chamber tombs of the middle Republican age gravitating towards the same street.[6] Votive offerings dated between

---

*dell'antico e trasformazioni urbane tra il III e il XIII secolo* (Monumenti di antichità cristiana ser. II, vol. XXII) (Vatican City, 2015), 272. Upon the fountain were several blocks in travertine and peperino, forming a rough pavement. Along the north-eastern side of the courtyard were the remains of a street (Fig. 2.7); an entire column shaft and some similar fragments were found together. Not far from this point, a lion statue in *Bardiglio* marble was brought to light (Spinola, 'Sculture', 24 n. 26 fig. 39). A skeleton was lying in the same courtyard, along its east–west diagonal on the side of a brick wall. See also Archivio Storico Musei Vaticani, plan SRA 7.4; A. Schiavo, *Restauri e nuove opera nella zona extraterritoriale lateranense (1961–1968)* (Vatican City, 1968), 84, figs. 101–3.

[5] F. Buranelli and S. Le Pera Buranelli, 'Rinvenimenti arcaici sotto il Palazzo Apostolico Lateranense', in M. Pallottino (ed.), *Etrusca et italica: Scritti in ricordo di Massimo Pallottino I* (Pisa, 1997), 79–115.

[6] V. S. M. Scrinari, 'Tombe a camera sotto via S. Stefano Rotondo', *Bullettino della Commissione archeologica comunale di Roma* 81 (1968–9), 17–24; E. Lissi Caronna, 'Terrecotte da una tomba repubblicana in via S. Stefano Rotondo', in Musei Capitolini, *Roma Medio repubblicana. Aspetti*

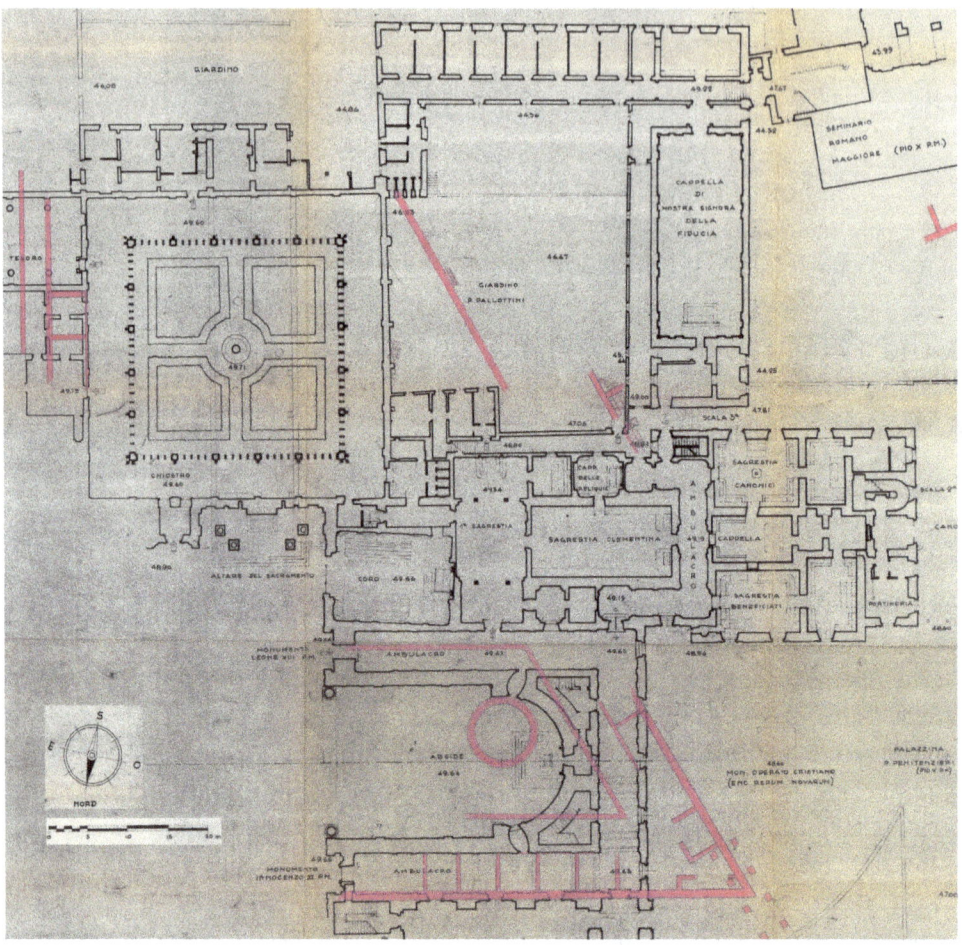

**Fig. 2.4** Plan of the Lateran area during the renovation works in 1965: Roman walls on the alignment of the Via Tusculana between the Lateran cloister and the seminary.

the second half of the fourth and the third centuries BC attest to a small cult place in the area of the modern hospital of Saint John (see Fig. 2.2.3).[7]

Under the basilica, however, the structures exposed through successive explorations date mostly to the imperial period: the earliest evidence was brought to light during Josi's investigations under the nave, where a large number of fragments of painted plaster were recovered

culturali di Roma e del Lazio nei secoli IV e III a.C. (Rome, 1973), 241–6, nos. 373–7, plates LIII–LV; V. S. M. Scrinari, *Il Laterano imperiale II: Dagli 'horti Domitiae' alla cappella cristiana* (Vatican City, 1995), 17–30.

[7] Scrinari, *Il Laterano imperiale II*, 30–40.

from secondary contexts. The oldest of these can be dated to the Augustan age, and probably represents the backfill from earlier diggings, which reached layers deeper than those excavated at that time.[8] In the past I have dated to the late Flavian age the structures of the *domus* in the eastern half of the basilica, but more recent studies have tended to offer an earlier date.[9]

The last element to consider in this brief overview derives from eighteenth-century excavations, acknowledging the problems involved in using evidence from such a source. This concerns the discoveries made in 1732 during the construction of the Corsini chapel (see Fig. 2.2.4), the first in the left outer aisle of the church, and perhaps during the simultaneous building of Galilei's façade. Colini[10] collected the antiquarian sources, and little can be added to his work.[11] The Corsini chapel lies astride two of the barrack ranges of the Castra Nova, southeast of the *principia*. Some of the finds clearly originated from the *castra*, as in the case of a statue base and an altar dedicated in AD 200 for the imperial Severan family.[12] A number of sculptures were also found, but unfortunately they are difficult to date on the basis of the descriptions in the excavation reports: an exception is the so-called Commodus, now considered to be a second- or third-century portrait on account of its beard, though possibly a philosopher portrait of earlier date. The other portraits and sculptures are mostly lost or unidentified: among them is an inscribed herm with the signature of Myron,[13] which seems more likely for a *domus* than a military setting. We should also note the famous 'Corsini Throne'[14] (Fig. 2.8), an early imperial model carved in Luna marble in archaising style, inspired by the thrones used in Etruria from the Orientalising period until the fourth century BC. According to

---

[8] E. M. Moormann and S. T. A. M. Mols, 'Le pitture romane: Frammenti e resti in situ', in Liverani (ed.), *Laterano 1*, 115–34, plates I–XV.

[9] On the issue, see Spinola, Chapter 5 in this volume.

[10] Colini, *Storia e topografia del Celio*, 347–8; G. De Luca, *I monumenti antichi di Palazzo Corsini in Roma* (Rome, 1976), 6 nn. 5 and 7, 7 nn. 9 and 11, 93.

[11] F. Valesio, *Diario di Roma*, ed. G. Scano, 5 vols. (Milan, 1979), V, 454–6, 516; J. Raspi Serra, F. de Polignac and A. Themelly, 'Cronologia: 1726–1732', in J. Raspi Serra (ed.), *Idea e Scienza dell'antichità: Roma e l'Europa 1700–1770* (Eutopia II, 1) (Rome, 1993), 105–50, at p. 143 (26 and 29 March), 145 (1 July), 147 (21 July); J. Raspi Serra (ed.), *Il primo incontro di Winckelmann con le collezioni romane: Ville e Palazzi di Roma, 1756* (Quaderni di Eutopia 6.2) (Rome, 2003), 162–3 nn. 1–2 fig. 1.

[12] CIL VI 225–6; De Luca, *I monumenti antichi di Palazzo Corsini*, 125 n. 68, plate CIV.

[13] CIL VI 29796; E. Loewy, *Inschriften Griechischer Bildhauer* (Leipzig, 1885), 319 n. 488a; I. Calabi Limentani, *Studi sulla società romana: Il lavoro artistico* (Milan, 1958), 160 n. 59; P. Stewart, *The Social History of Roman Art* (Cambridge, 2008), 22. Not considered in DNO.

[14] De Luca, *I monumenti antichi di Palazzo Corsini*, 93–100 n. 54, plates LXXXI–LXXXV.

Francesco Cancellieri,[15] the throne was found at a depth of nearly 20 feet – just under 4.5 m – that is, probably below the level of the Severan structures; hence, we have evidence of a wealthy *domus* of the early imperial age. We cannot make many more conclusions from the eighteenth-century discoveries: the description of the findings contemporary to the excavations is, in fact, too generic and the history of the Corsini sculpture collection insufficiently known, so we can neither recognise the works of art mentioned by the reports nor even be sure that they entered the collection in their entirety. Those who work systematically with Roman collections know the caution needed to propose convincing identifications on evidence such as this. We have to leave aside, then, the fascinating but baseless hypothesis attributing the Throne to Plautius Lateranus[16] or even to his family tomb.[17]

We must now address the different sources for the *domus* in the Lateran area: the attestations are numerous, and many agree on key points.[18] It is most worthwhile, therefore, to focus on the most difficult problem: to what precisely do the terms *aedes Lateranorum* and/or *Laterani* used by ancient writers refer? This debate is entwined with all major topographical issues of the Lateran, and its solution has significant consequences for the overall picture.

In short: we know that the *aedes Lateranorum* equates to the dwelling of the consul-designate for the year AD 65, Plautius Lateranus. They were confiscated because of Plautius' involvement in the Pisonian conspiracy against Nero, as we learn from a famous passage of Juvenal.[19] Furthermore,

---

[15] F. Cancellieri, *Il mercato, il lago dell'Acqua Vergine ed il palazzo panfiliano nel Circo Agonale detto volgarmente Piazza Navona* (Rome, 1811), 246, unnumbered footnote.

[16] M. Torelli, 'La "Sedia Corsini", monumento della genealogia etrusca dei Plautii', in M.-M. Mactoux and E. Geny (eds.), *Mélanges Pierre Lévêque*, vol. V: *Anthropologie et société* (Besançon, 1990), 355–67. This author draws his conclusions on the basis of a quick reconstruction of the Lateran topography, but he does not seem to be aware of all the complex issues involved. In any case, if Plautius' house was in the Lateran area, it would not be located under the Corsini chapel, but below the medieval *patriarchium*.

[17] G. Colonna, 'Roma arcaica, i suoi sepolcri e le vie per i Colli Albani', in A. Pasqualini (ed.), *Alba Longa: Mito, storia, archeologia. Atti dell'incontro di studi Roma-Albano Laziale 27-29 gennaio 1994* (Rome, 1996), 335–54, at pp. 352–3.

[18] An overview is in P. Liverani, 'Le proprietà private nell'area lateranense fino all'età di Costantino', *MEFRA* 100, 2 (1988), 891–915; P. Liverani, 'L'area lateranense in età tardo antica e le origini del Patriarchio', in Liverani (ed.), *Giornata di studio*, 17–49.

[19] Juv. 10.15–18: 'Temporibus diris igitur iussuque Neronis / Longinum et magnos Senecae praedivitis hortos / clausit, et egregias Lateranorum obsidet aedes / tota cohors: rarus venit in coenacula miles' ('Hence it was, in those terrible times, that on Nero's orders / Longinus' house and the over-rich Seneca's spacious park / were closed, and in the Lateran family's splendid mansion besieged / by an entire company. A soldier rarely enters an attic', trans. in N. Rudd (ed. and trans.), *Juvenal: The Satires* (Oxford, 1991)). See Tac. *Ann.* 15.49.3.

we know that Septimius Severus gave sumptuous *domus* to some of his closest collaborators.[20] The most faithful of them was T. Sextius Lateranus, who received one of the most beautiful:[21] the Aedes Laterani, cited six more times in texts ranging from the second half of the fourth century to the early fifth. Usually the sources concerning both Plautius' and Sextius' *domus* have been interpreted as referring to the same house. Elsewhere, instead, I have proposed treating them independently of each other,[22] arguing that the *domus* of Sextius gave its name to the Lateran, a toponym used up to the present day, while the evidence placing that of Plautius in this area is weaker, since the passage of Saint Jerome[23] normally used for this purpose is problematic. In any case, the Aedes Laterani became the seat of the bishop of Rome no later than the early fifth century, as explained below.

Some recent contributions have touched on the issue, preferring to maintain the identification of the two *domus* with one another, but without new arguments.[24] Much more detailed is an important philological contribution by Christian Gnilka,[25] which needs a thorough discussion. The

---

[20] Ps.-Aur. Vict. *Epit.* 20.6: 'Lateranum Cilonem Anullinum Bassum ceterosque alios ditaret aedibus quoque memoratu dignis, quarum praecipuas videmus Parthorum quae dicuntur ac Laterani.'

[21] In the past (P. Liverani, 'Domus Faustae', *LTUR* II, 97–9) I have translated the passage as follows: 'he enriched Lateranus, Cilo, Anullinus, Bassus, and several others, and with buildings worthy of note: among them the House of the Parthians – also named "House of Lateranus" – looks outstanding'. Gnilka (C. Gnilka, 'Aedes Laterani', *Zeitschrift für Papyrologie und Epigraphik* 188 (2014), 70–80, at pp. 70–1 n. 2), on the other hand, has shown that the text should be translated in a different way: 'among them the House of the Parthians and the House called of Lateranus appear outstanding'.

[22] Liverani, 'Le proprietà private nell'area lateranense', 899; the distinction was suggested by Colini, *Storia e topografia del Celio*, 372–3.

[23] Jer. *Ep.* 77.4.

[24] Manacorda (D. Manacorda, 'Il Laterano e la produzione ceramica a Roma: aspetti del paesaggio urbano', in A. Leone, D. Palombi and S. Walker (eds.), *Res Bene Gestae: Ricerche di storia urbana su Roma antica in onore di Eva Margareta Steinby* (Rome, 2007), 195–204) considers the *aedes Lateranorum* and *Laterani* as equivalent or indistinguishable: in his view, the main argument for unifying the two houses is the passage of the *Historia Augusta* (*Hist. Aug. Marc.* 1.7) where Annius Verus' house is located near the *aedes Laterani*. According to this interpretation, it was anachronistic for the fourth-century writer to give a contemporary reference, instead of referring to the second-century topographical setting. It is difficult to follow this argument, as the best evidence is to the contrary: it seems extremely unlikely that the late author anachronistically gave as topographic reference for a late second-century situation a first-century *domus*, which had been confiscated and had perhaps changed its name. On the contrary, it is quite natural for him to have updated his reference to be understood by contemporary readers. Consalvi (*Il Celio Orientale*, 84–91) tries to maintain the identity between the *aedes* of Plautius and that of Sextius and to save the indication of Saint Jerome's letter (Jer. *Ep.* 77.4: see below). He accepts that this house was the first nucleus of the bishop's palace, but places it in the area later occupied by the Apostolic palace of Sixtus V.

[25] Gnilka, 'Aedes Laterani'.

crucial point is the passage of Jerome, written around 400, in which the saint describes the penance of the noble Fabiola 'in basilica quondam Laterani, qui Cesariano truncatus est gladio':[26] usually translated as 'in the basilica which formerly belonged to that Lateranus, who perished by the sword of Caesar'. There is a clear allusion to Plautius Lateranus, but the expression 'basilica quondam Laterani' is difficult to interpret. The basilica was dedicated to the Saviour but was called *ecclesia* or *basilica Salvatoris* only from the seventh century;[27] in the fourth and fifth centuries the current name was rather *ecclesia* or *basilica Lateranensis*, and it was only in the late fifth century that the name *basilica Costantiniana* appeared,[28] that is when there was no more danger of confusing it with the Constantinian civil basilica on the Via Sacra.

The expression 'basilica quondam Laterani' then designates the Basilica Lateranensis, which took its name from the adjacent Aedes Laterani, whose name Jerome associates with Plautius Lateranus. Of the general meaning, therefore, there is no discussion: less clear, however, is the exact interpretation of the terms. If we translate the passage literally 'the former Lateranus' basilica', how do we explain the relationship with Plautius Lateranus? On this basis, I suggested that Jerome had considered the basilica as standing on the site of Plautius Lateranus' home.[29] On the other hand, we know the church was built by Constantine on the site of the Castra Nova, and therefore I had considered Jerome's definition as a mistake. Christian Gnilka, however, prefers to trust to Jerome's reliability, considering that he was well informed on the Roman situation given his familiarity with the city and Pope Damasus.[30] The German philologist hypothesises instead a corruption of the text, and assumes an ellipsis implying the word *aedibus*. We should then read 'in basilica <in> (aedibus) quondam Laterani, qui Cesariano truncatus est gladio'. The proposal is certainly ingenious, but at this point we must return from the philology to the topography. The understanding of the text requires, first of all, a philological study, but

---

[26] Jer., *Ep.* 77.4.
[27] Ecclesia Salvatoris: *LP* 76, 3; 76, 8 Martinus I (649–55); Basilica Salvatoris: De Locis Sanctis Martyrum (*c.* 635–42; see R. Valentini and G. Zucchetti, *Codice topografico della città di Roma*, 4 vols. (Fonti per la Storia d'Italia 90) (Rome, 1940–53), II, 118); *LP* 86, 10 Sergius I (687–701).
[28] Lateran Council of 487: G. D. Mansi, *Sacrorum conciliorum nova et amplissima collectio 7* (Florence, 1762), 1171C; in the *Liber Pontificalis* (96, 18), the name Basilica Constantini appears only much later, since the life of Stephanus III (768–72).
[29] Liverani, 'L'area lateranense in età tardo antica', 20–2; Liverani, 'L'episcopio lateranense', 121–3.
[30] Gnilka, 'Aedes Laterani', 74–6 n. 7.

must then confront the extra-linguistic referent, before returning again to the text, according to the principle of the hermeneutic circle.

In order to justify his proposal, Gnilka is forced to consider *aedes Laterani* as a place name designating a neighbourhood rather than a particular *domus*.[31] This reading, however, cannot be substantiated: on the contrary, all the attestations refer to a specific *domus*.[32] The expression 'in basilica <in> (aedibus) quondam Laterani', therefore, would fall in the same contradictions raised by the text without correction. The only alternative, already advanced by Gnilka as second-best solution, is then to read: 'in basilica <ad> (aedibus) quondam Laterani', i.e. 'in the basilica near the former Lateranus' *aedes*'.

If we accept such a restoration, then we have to reconsider the possibility that Plautius' *aedes Lateranorum* of the Neronian age coincide with the Severan and Late Antique *aedes Laterani*.[33] This identification, however, retains some difficulties of a more general nature: first of all, we would have to believe that Plautius' *aedes Lateranorum*, although joined to the imperial property after the confiscation of Nero, and despite the fact that their owner suffered the *damnatio memoriae*, would keep their original name for about 130 years – that is, for at least four generations, until they were reassigned by Septimius Severus to Sextius Lateranus. Secondly, no family relationship existed between the Sextii and Plautii until the Severan age; and, in any case, the *cognomen* Lateranus is attested only once among the Plautii, while it has a strong significance for the Sextii: it recalls the first

---

[31] Gnilka, 'Aedes Laterani', 75–6. See also 79 n. 9b.

[32] The same is true also for the 'Lactearius de domum Laterani' (ICUR V, 14583; P. Liverani, 'Dalle *aedes Laterani* al Patriarchio lateranense', *RAC* 75 (1999), 521–49, at pp. 534–5; Gnilka, 'Aedes Laterani', 79 n. 9c). Lactearius is a unicum, but we can consider it as a secondary form of *lactarius*: he who prepares (or sells) milk cakes (A. Hug, 'Lactarius 2', *RE* XII.1, col. 361 (1924); H. von Petrikovits, *Das Handwerk in vor- und frühgeschichtlicher Zeit I* (Abhandlungen der Akademie der Wissenschaften zu Göttingen, Philologisch-Historische Klasse 122) (Göttingen, 1981), 100). The attestation of a craft or an office specified by the expression *de domu* or *de domo* (*alicuius*) is not a generic indication of the district where the work is done – as Gnilka believes – but rather it designates the house or the administration where the person served: we know several examples in Rome, *CIL* VI 8654: 'Albanus Caesar a supel(l)ect(ile) de domu Tiberiana'; 8663: 'Symphorus tesserarius servus Caesaris de domo Gelotiana'; 22471: 'Metrodorus de domu Eruci Clari'; Pozzuoli, *CIL* X 1745: 'T(iti) Flavi Aug(usti) / lib(erti) Primigeni / supra velarios / de domu Aug(usti); ICUR III, 8286 Sempron[i –] / [d]e domo [–]'; Bolsena, *CIL* XI 2720: 'Haevelpisti / Beneaccipioni / collegius Dia/nes(ium) de domu / publica'; Salona, *CIL* III 14906: 'Arca Marcell/(a)e de domo Valeri / def(ensoris)'. The *lactearius*, therefore, was a pastry cook who worked for the owner of the *aedes Laterani* and, if they were the seat of the Roman bishop, he was the first papal pastry cook.

[33] Not only does Jerome's corrected passage avoid the topographical difficulties, but the reading of Ps.-Aur. Vict., *Epit.* 20.6 (discussed above, nn. 20–1) solves another difficulty, as the *aedes Parthorum* and *Laterani* are different houses.

plebeian consul in 366 BC, the L. Sextius Sextinus Lateranus who the year before, as tribune of the people, had, together with C. Licinius Calvus Stolo, proposed the Licinian Rogations, which opened to the plebeians access to the highest magistracy of Rome.[34] Therefore, it seems quite unlikely that Septimius Severus would grant his friend Sextius the *domus* as a 'compensation' – so to say – for the wrong suffered four generations before by a distant great-uncle of a secondary lineage. Also, if we accept Gnilka's correction, we cannot free ourselves from the suspicion that Jerome's statement was due to a combination of scholarly reconstructions of events, inspired by Plautius' enduring reputation as a champion of the senatorial opposition. Certainly this reputation, burnished by Tacitus' consecration[35] and even more by Juvenal,[36] the best-selling poet in Rome at that time,[37] was well known to Jerome.[38]

Summing up: although we can no longer categorically rule out continuity between the two houses, such an identification requires a correction of the text and the overcoming of some historical difficulties not to be underestimated. Therefore, it should be considered with caution as a hypothesis yet to be definitively proved rather than as an established fact.

As mentioned earlier, the Aedes Laterani, in their Late Antique phase, became the seat of the bishop of Rome at a time difficult to determine precisely. It is better to present the evidence of the sources starting from the clearest attestation and to trace back towards those that are older and more difficult to interpret. We have a note by Theoderich,[39] in the record of the Roman synod of 501, dedicated to the charges against Pope Symmachus and his administration of properties of the Roman Church. The Gothic king writes 'de arca vero vel de domo Lateranensi', 'about the administration indeed or the Lateran house', using the two definitions almost as synonyms, where the latter is evidently the seat of the bishop of Rome. A century earlier, however, in 402 or 403 Prudentius[40] was writing about crowds of the faithful flocking towards the 'aedes Laterani: unde sacrum

---

[34] In imperial times we know two more Sextii Laterani: T. Sextius Magius Lateranus cos. 94 (*PIR* S 472) and T. Sextius Lateranus cos. 154 (*PIR* S 468).

[35] Tac. *Ann.* 15.49.3.   [36] Juv. 10.15–18.

[37] Amm. Marc. 28.4.14; A. D. E. Cameron, 'Literary allusions in the *Historia Augusta*', *Hermes* 92 (1964), 363–77.

[38] N. Adkin, 'Juvenal and Jerome', *Classical Philology* 89 (1994), 69–72; N. Adkin, 'Jerome, Seneca, Juvenal', *Revue belge d'archéologie et d'histoire de l'art* 78 (2000), 119–28, at pp. 124–8.

[39] MGH, AA XII, 426: 'De arca vero vel de domo Lateranensi, prout iudicatum fuerit, eidem synhodus reddat'. See below.

[40] Prudent. c. Symm. 1.585–6: 'Omnis qui . . . / coetibus aut magnis Laterani adcurrit ad aedes, / unde sacrum referat regali chrismate signum' (All the multitude that . . . hasten in great companies to the house of Lateranus to get the sacred sign of the royal anointing).

referat regali chrismate signum' (to get the holy sign of the royal anointing). The information that catechumens flock to the seat of the bishop of Rome[41] is important even if it opens a problem hitherto neglected. Usually the text is meant as an allusion to the rite of baptism and confirmation, but how could we justify that baptism was taking place in the papal residence instead of the Constantinian baptistery? Gnilka tried to give an answer to this problem by considering the baptistery part of the Aedes Laterani.[42] Such a proposal, however, cannot be accepted if we consider the issue from a topographical point of view: the Aedes Laterani stood in front of the basilica or, more precisely, to the north-east, in a place corresponding to the early medieval *patriarchium*, while the baptistery was behind its apse. Therefore, there is no link between the two nuclei, which were separated by the basilica. Furthermore, in the *Liber Pontificalis* the baptistery is described separately from the basilica and as being economically independent of it, with diligently listed revenues amounting to 10,234 *solidi* every year.[43] All the more reason, then, to believe that the baptistery was considered as a building independent from the bishop's palace. We therefore can propose an alternative explanation, arguing that Prudentius alluded to the sacrament of confirmation as distinct from baptism and conferred in a hall of the episcopal palace. In fifth-century Rome, indeed, baptism and confirmation were distinct rites, the latter being reserved to the bishop, as is clearly attested at this time by Pope Innocent I.[44] A century later John the Deacon[45] distinguished between the first baptismal

---

[41] Liverani, 'Dalle *aedes Laterani*', 523–4.

[42] Gnilka, 'Aedes Laterani', 79. For the chronology and interpretation of the baptistery see now O. Brandt, 'Il Battistero lateranense da Costantino a Ilaro: Un riesame degli scavi', *Opuscula Romana* 22-3 (1997–8), 7–65; O. Brandt and F. Guidobaldi, 'Il Battistero lateranense: Nuove interpretazioni delle fasi strutturali', *RAC* 84 (2008), 189–282; O. Brandt, *Battisteri oltre la pianta: Gli alzati di nove battisteri paleocristiani in Italia* (Vatican City, 2012), 33–85.

[43] *LP* 34, 13–15.

[44] Innocentius I, *Ep. ad Decentium* 6 (*PL* 20 c. 555A): 'Nam presbyteris, sive extra episcopum sive praesente episcopo cum baptizant, chrismate baptizatos ungere licet, sed quod ab episcopo fuerit consecratum non tamen frontem ex eodem oleo signare, quod solis debetur episcopis, cum tradunt Spiritum Paracletum.' See J. P. Bouhot, *La confermazione sacramento della comunione ecclesiale* (Turin, 1970), 47–54 (original edition in French: *La confirmation, sacrement de la communion ecclésiale* (Lyon, 1968)); L. Padovese, *La cristologia di Aurelio Clemente Prudenzio* (Analecta Gregoriana 219) (Rome, 1980), 61 n. 63; V. Saxer, *Les rites de l'initiation chrétienne du IIe au VIe siècle: Esquisse historique et signification d'après leurs principaux témoins* (Spoleto, 1988), 643–7.

[45] Joh. Diaconus, *Ep. ad Senarium* 6 (*PL* 59, 403A–C; A. Wilmart (ed.), 'Epistola de Iohannis Diaconi ad Senarium', in *Analecta Reginensia, Studi e Testi* 59 (Vatican City, 1933), 170–9, at p. 174). See also Leo Magnus, *Sermo* 4, 1 (444 AD), CCL 138, 16–17 (*PL* 54, 149): 'Omnes enim in Christo regeneratos, crucis signum efficit reges, Spiritus Sancti unctio consecrat sacerdotes, ut praeter istam specialem nostri ministerii servitutem universi spiritales et rationabiles christiani

anointing performed by the priest on the breast of the catechumen with the 'oil of consecration' and the post-baptismal one ('sacri chrismatis unctio') by the bishop on the head: 'ut intellegat baptizatus regnum in se ac sacerdotale convenisse mysterium' (so that the baptised person may understand that in his person a kingdom and a priestly mystery have met). The correspondence between Prudentius' definition and John the Deacon's terminology for the confirmation is evident.

Finally, we must examine a much-debated text: the story told by Optatus, bishop of Milevi, in 365 concerning the Donatist schism and the synod convened in 313 by Constantine in Rome to seek a solution. The Synod Fathers 'convenerunt in domum Faustae in Laterani':[46] these few words raise numerous textual, historical and topographical problems. The text normally used in the discussion is 'in domum Faustae in Laterano', which is hard to justify since the toponym *Lateranum* appeared only in the eleventh century.[47] Gnilka correctly pointed out that the codices' reading is 'in Laterani', which he interprets as a colloquial and elliptical form implying 'in (aedibus) Laterani'.[48] The proposal should certainly be accepted because it is the most logical and economical one from a philological point of view, in that it clarifies the text without needing further corrections.

Here we confront the historical problem: a long tradition of studies has suggested that Fausta was Constantine's wife. According to this reconstruction, the emperor hosted the synod in a family property; later he gave the bishop the *domus*, which became his residence. Ernest Nash,[49] however, had stressed that Fausta was absent from Rome from the age of five or six

agnoscant se regii generis et sacerdotalis officii esse consortes' ('All who have been regenerated in Christ are made kings by the sign of the cross and consecrated priests by the anointing of the Holy Spirit. Apart the particular service that our ministry entails, all Christians who live spiritual lives according to reason recognize that they have a part in the royal race and the priestly office'), trans. in J. P. Freeland (ed.), *St Leo the Great: Sermons* (Fathers of the Church Patristic Series 93) (Washington, DC, 1996)).

[46] Opt. Mil. 1.23.
[47] First attestation in Lupus Protospatarius, *Chronicon*: G. H. Pertz (ed.), MGH, SS, 5 (Hanover, 1844), 59 ad a. 1046, 61 ad a. 1083. See Liverani, 'Dalle *aedes Laterani*', 526 and Tab. 2; Liverani, 'L'area lateranense in età tardo antica', 22 n. 17.
[48] Gnilka, 'Aedes Laterani', 72–4. The first to note the inaccuracy of the commonly accepted text in Optatus editions (in Laterano) was Fried (J. Fried, *'Donation of Constantine' and 'Constitutum Constantini': The Misinterpretation of a Fiction and Its Original Meaning* (Berlin, 2007), 81), but his proposal is unlikely from a philological point of view. Unfortunately, the chapter this author dedicated to Late Antiquity (VI a: *The Palatium Lateranense*) is so full of inaccuracies, confusion and anachronisms that it does not deserve comment.
[49] E. Nash, 'Convenerunt in domum Faustae in Laterano: Optati Milevitani 1.23', *Römische Quartalschrift für Altertumskunde und für Kirchengeschichte* 71 (1976), 1–21. The presence of Fausta in Rome for the celebration of Constantine's vicennalia in 326 remains hypothetical and in any case too late for our discussion; even more fragile is the hypothesis linking Fausta to the

years, so that a house would be registered instead in her father's name, Emperor Maximian, or her mother's, Eutropia. For this reason, we could consider Optatus' Fausta rather to be a private person. Unfortunately, the epigraphic evidence for Roman noble women in the fourth century is much less extensive than in previous centuries, and we do not know of other candidates. However, since the *cognomen* Faustus frequently recurs in the Anicia family,[50] among the noblest of the period and one of the first to convert to Christianity, we could assume that our Fausta was a member of this family. Gnilka, on the contrary, prefers to maintain the identification with the empress, because Optatus' definition would be less significant for his readers in case of a private Fausta. The argument is interesting and useful, but it should be turned upside down: Fausta's low fame has prompted Optatus to add as explanation *in (aedibus) Laterani*, using a name much better known in his day. Otherwise, it would be difficult to explain the double locative.

A last objection against the identification of Fausta with the empress derives from her history: after Constantine executed his wife, her memory was banned. It seems difficult to believe, therefore, that a property could retain her name thereafter.[51]

Finally, it remains to consider the archaeological evidence we can attribute to the Aedes Laterani and the first papal palace. Leaving aside for the moment the results of GPR investigations carried out in front of the façade of the basilica, which need a thorough and separate discussion, we can recall that in 1900 Philippe Lauer excavated a tunnel under the Sancta Sanctorum chapel, the last surviving element of the bishop's medieval palace (see Figs 2.2.5, 2.9–2.10). The French archaeologist intercepted several Roman walls[52] and brought to light the famous fresco depicting a father of the church, perhaps of the sixth century: the so-called Saint Augustine,[53] hypothetically interpreted as overseeing the Lateran *scrinium*, the archive and library.

A little further south, in the basement of the oratory of Santissimo Sacramento, a vaulted room is still accessible (see Figs 2.2.6, 2.10–2.11)

---

Basilica Apostolorum (last discussion in A. M. Nieddu, *La Basilica Apostolorum sulla via Appia e l'area cimiteriale circostante* (Vatican City, 2009), 139).

[50] *PLRE* I Faustus 8, Flavianus 8, Paulinus 16–17, Paulinianus. See Liverani, 'Domus Faustae'; Liverani, 'Dalle *aedes Laterani*', 525; Liverani, 'L'area lateranense in età tardo antica', 22–3; Liverani, 'L'episcopio lateranense', 123; for the Anicii family, see *PLRE* II, 1133.

[51] A. Barbero, *Costantino il vincitore* (Rome, 2016), 332.

[52] P. Lauer, 'Les fouilles du *Sancta Sanctorum* au Latran', *Mélanges de l'École Française de Rome* 20 (1900), 251–87; see Colini, *Storia e topografia del Celio*, 361–4.

[53] F. Bisconti, 'L'affresco del S. Agostino', in Liverani (ed.), *Giornata di studio*, 51–78.

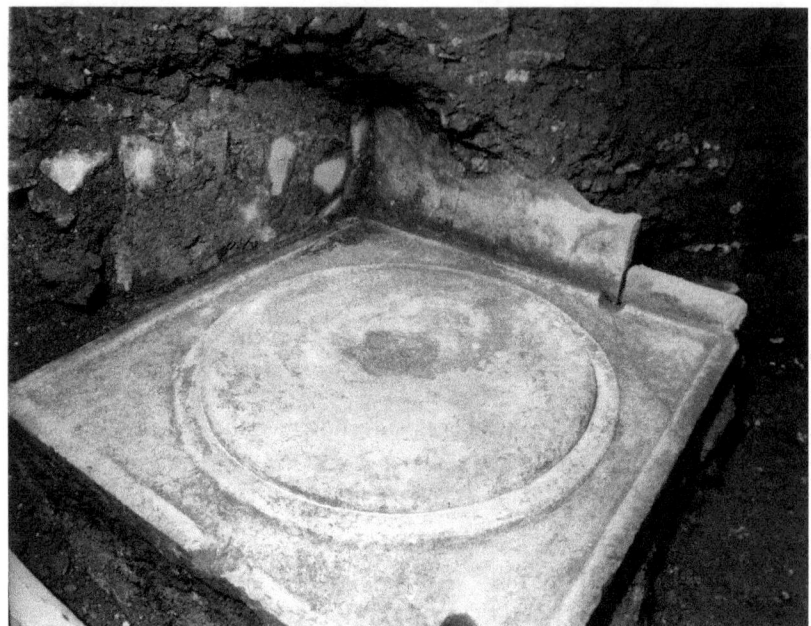

Fig. 2.5 Marble fountain near the western corner of the Pallottines' Garden (Photo: Vatican Museum – Scavi e Ricerche Archeologiche GL VIII.1).

with a fresco decoration from the Hadrianic period.[54] To the north of the Scala Santa, several sculptures now preserved in the Vatican Museums came to light during the construction of the monastery of the Passionist Fathers in 1852. One year later, a few metres to the south, a head of Marcus Aurelius was found, together with a sculptural group portraying Mithras killing the bull. Again, in the same area a fourth-century mosaic – once part of the decoration of a bath and now lying in one of the Raphael Rooms in the Vatican – came to light.[55] The evidence – although scattered and fragmentary – is compatible with an important *domus* of the imperial age prolonging its life into early Christian times, as demonstrated by the Saint Augustine fresco: in short, we could identify these structures with the Aedes Laterani.

---

[54] B. Bertani, 'I sotterranei della sede dell'Arciconfraternita lateranense del Ss. Sacramento', *Alma Roma* 27, 3–4 (1986), 79–96; L. Donadono, 'In margine alle celebrazioni sistine. La Scala Santa (1586–1853): nuove acquisizioni', *Roma Moderna e Contemporanea* 2, 1 (1994), 249–66, at pp. 254–5 n. 23; Consalvi, *Il Celio Orientale*, 80, 109 n. 35.

[55] P. Liverani, 'Discoveries at the Scala Santa: The excavations of 1852–54', in I. Bignamini (ed.), *Archives and Excavations: Essays on the History of Archaeological Excavations in Rome and Southern Italy from the Renaissance to the Nineteenth Century* (Archaeological Monographs of the British School at Rome) (London, 2004), 203–20; D'Onofrio, 'Il Patriarchio nascosto'.

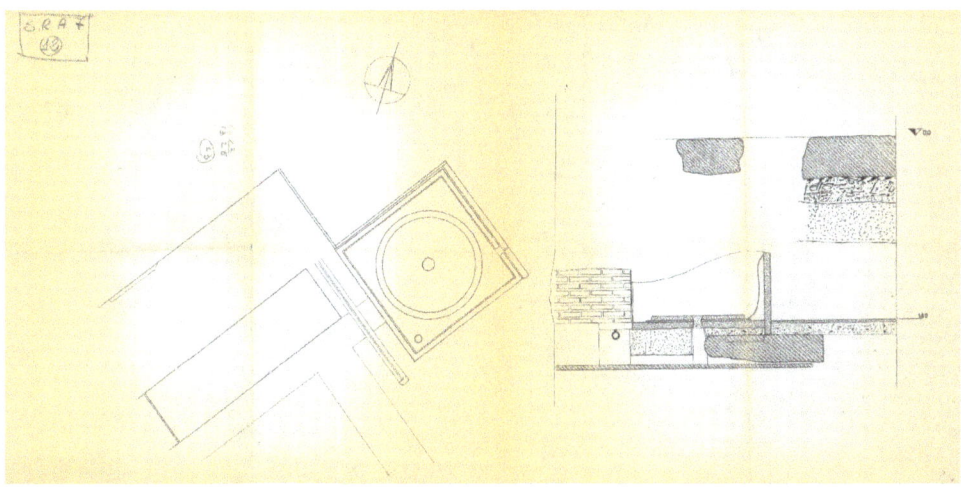

**Fig. 2.6** Marble fountain, plan of the excavation (Archivio Storico Musei Vaticani, plan SRA 7.12).

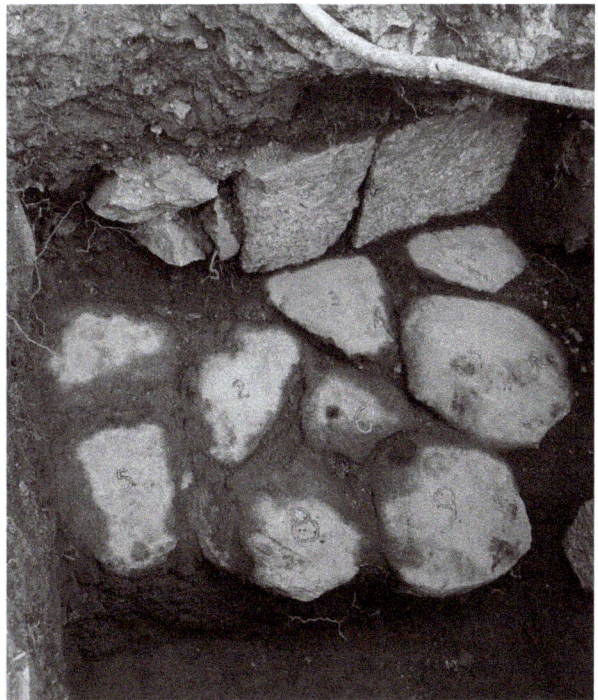

**Fig. 2.7** Pallottines' Garden, remains of a street (Photo: Vatican Museum – Scavi e Ricerche Archeologiche GL VIII 26).

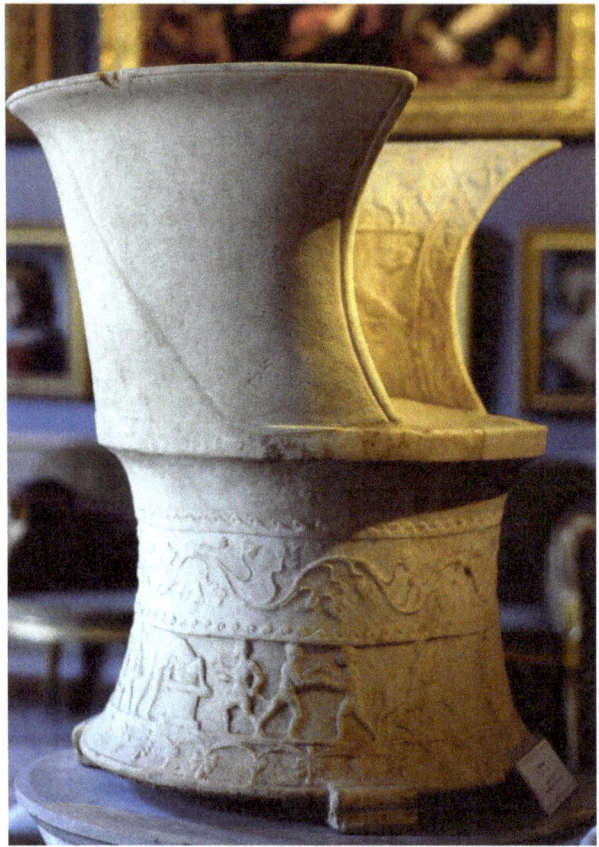

Fig. 2.8 Corsini Throne, Corsini Gallery, Rome (Photo: author).

To conclude, we can synthesise our results: there is literary and archaeological evidence of various private properties in the Lateran area in the early imperial age. The topography of the district underwent a remarkable evolution after the construction of the barracks of the imperial horse guards of Septimius Severus between AD 193 and 196. This event, however, did not radically change the residential character of the neighbourhood. The name of the area derived from the rich dwelling that Septimius Severus gave to one of his closest collaborators: Titus Sextius Lateranus. His connection with the house of Plautius Lateranus, the conspirator of the age of Nero, is not clear, and we have no certainty that the two *domus* are connected, despite what is often claimed. In any case, Sextius Lateranus' house stood in front of the basilica, and during the fourth century became the seat of the bishop of Rome. In the Middle Ages the house grew up until it was transformed into the complex of the *patriarchium*. The religious and

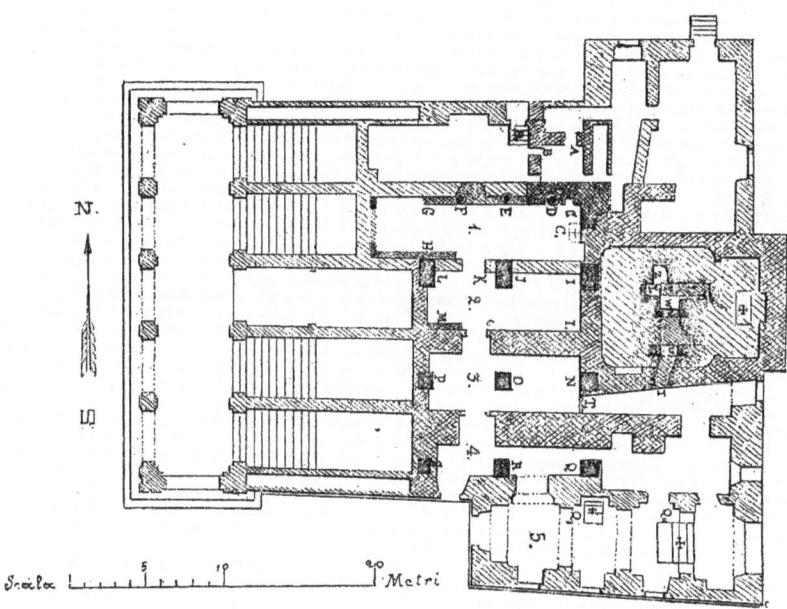

**Fig. 2.9** Plan of the Scala Santa sanctuary: in the middle of the eastern foundation of the Sancta Sanctorum Lauer's tunnel. To the south (n. 5), the oratory of Ss.mo Sacramento (from Lauer, 'Les fouilles du *Sancta Sanctorum* au Latran').

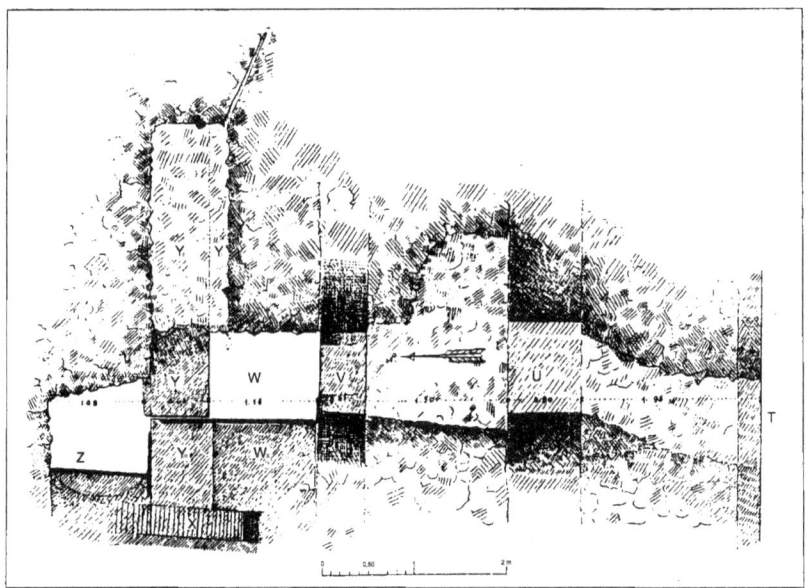

**Fig. 2.10** Plan of Lauer's tunnel in the foundation of the Sancta Sanctorum: z. is the so-called Saint Augustine (from Lauer, 'Les fouilles du *Sancta Sanctorum* au Latran').

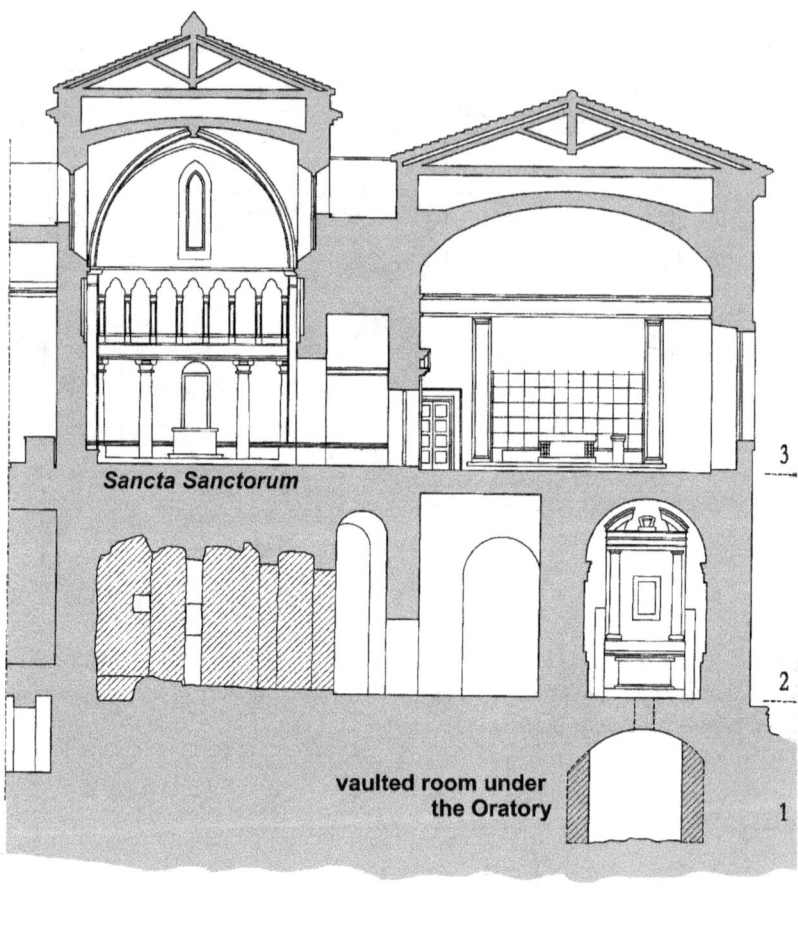

**Fig. 2.11** Cross-section north–south of the Scala Santa sanctuary (after D'Onofrio, 'Il Patriarchio nascosto').

political importance of this building and the basilica preserved the toponym Lateran until today, although none of today's Roman citizens connects it to Sextius, the late second-century general and friend of Septimius Severus.

# 3 | At the Foot of the Lateran Hill, from Via Sannio to Viale Ipponio: Archaeological Investigations Prior to the Construction of Metro Line C

ROSSELLA REA AND NICOLETTA SAVIANE

## Introduction

Metro Line C runs from the Pantano terminus through the southeastern suburbs of Rome. Near Via Casilina Vecchia its course runs steadily closer to the external perimeter of the Aurelian Walls before cutting it near Porta Matronia (Fig. 3.1).

The results of the archaeological investigations carried out along Via La Spezia and Via Sannio, published as a series of preliminary reports, show evidence of intense human activity before the construction of the Aurelian Walls. These reports record different types of land use in different settings, but it is hard to get a broader understanding of the overall topography from them.[1] This is because the excavations examined areas selected for building development rather than covering a large, connected area. It is also because there is a lack of archaeological data from nearby areas, where the exceptionally deep foundations of modern buildings have obliterated or obscured archaeological evidence. Furthermore, there is little evidence from the areas inside the Walls to the east of the Porta Asinaria, at the beginning of Viale Carlo Felice. Yet the archaeological evidence suggests that the river banks – here tentatively identified with the Aqua Crabra or one of its branches[2] – were farmed from the third century BC, as were most of the areas excavated so far. The river worked as a catalyst in this sense, and imposing embankments to control its floods were

---

This chapter was translated from the Italian by Dr Giacomo Savani.

[1] Via La Spezia produced a tuff quarry abandoned and filled in during the third century. It also produced agricultural features from the first to the fifth centuries AD near the Lodi metro stop (see R. Rea (ed.), *Cantieristica archeologica e opere pubbliche: La linea C della metropolitana di Roma* (Rome, 2011)). Part of a large farm dating from the first century AD was excavated near San Giovanni stop (see R. Rea, 'Archeologia nel suburbio di Roma: La stazione S. Giovanni della Linea C della Metropolitana', in A. F. Ferrandes and G. Pardini (eds.), *Le regole del gioco: Tracce archeologi racconti: Studi in onore di Clementina Panella* (Rome, 2016), 425–42). A marble workshop dating to the Hadrianic period was found in the gardens of Via Sannio, near Porta Asinaria (see M. Martines, 'Un laboratorio di marmi fuori Porta Asinaria: Scavi Metro C 2006–2007', *Bollettino di Archeologia Online* 6 (2015), 1–24). Rea wrote the introduction and section on Amba Aradam in this paper, Saviane the section on the via Sannio.

[2] Rea, 'Archeologia nel suburbio di Roma', 425.

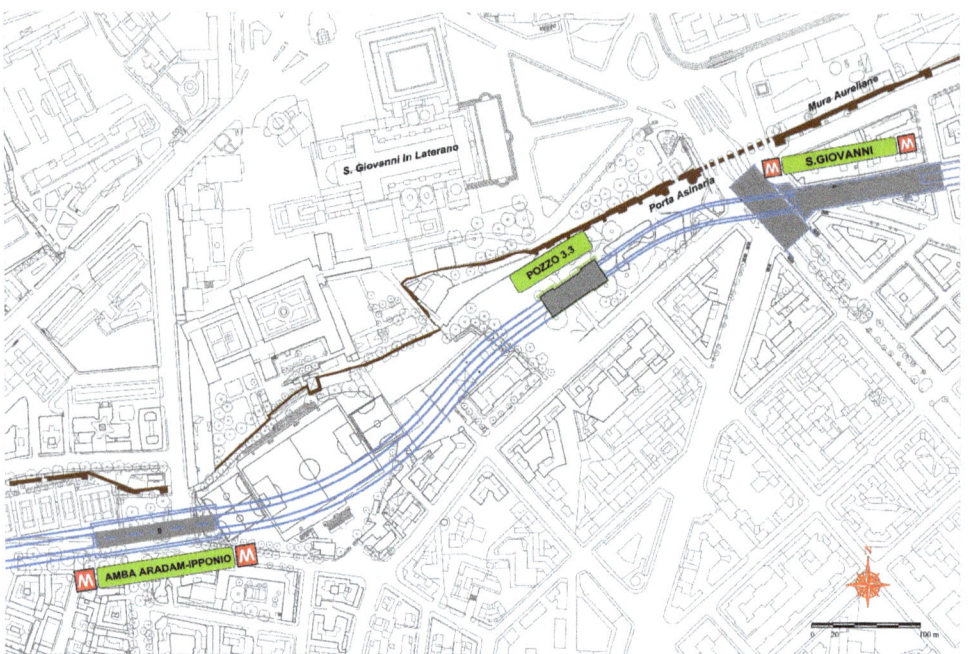

**Fig. 3.1** The itinerary of the Metro Line C along the Aurelian Walls. The stations of San Giovanni and Amba Aradam Ipponio, and Shaft 3.3 are highlighted.

built in the third century BC. These allow us to indirectly reconstruct the original river bed (Fig. 3.2). Things started to change in the second half of the first century BC; the land use became diversified and the complexity of the landscape increased. This process continued up until the construction of the Aurelian Walls, which effectively created intra-mural and extra-mural areas, now linked only by roads that passed through gates and posterns. From the last quarter of the third century AD land use takes a more homogeneous form, mainly characterised by agricultural and funerary use. The construction of the Aurelian Walls modified and, in places, substantially reduced the width of the river bed. It was not until the twelfth century that we can find a more structured land use like the one in place during the Republican period, which continued until the nineteenth century.[3]

This is the picture that has emerged from rescue archaeology carried out in this area. We do not have stratigraphic continuity between archaeological sites of the imperial period located inside and outside the area later to be occupied by the Aurelian Walls. The different height of layers should not be

---

[3] R. Rea, 'Roma: Progettazione e realizzazione della Linea "C" della metropolitana', in *Arqueologia, Patrimonio y Desarrollo Urbano. Problematica y Soluciones* (Girona, 2010), 181–98.

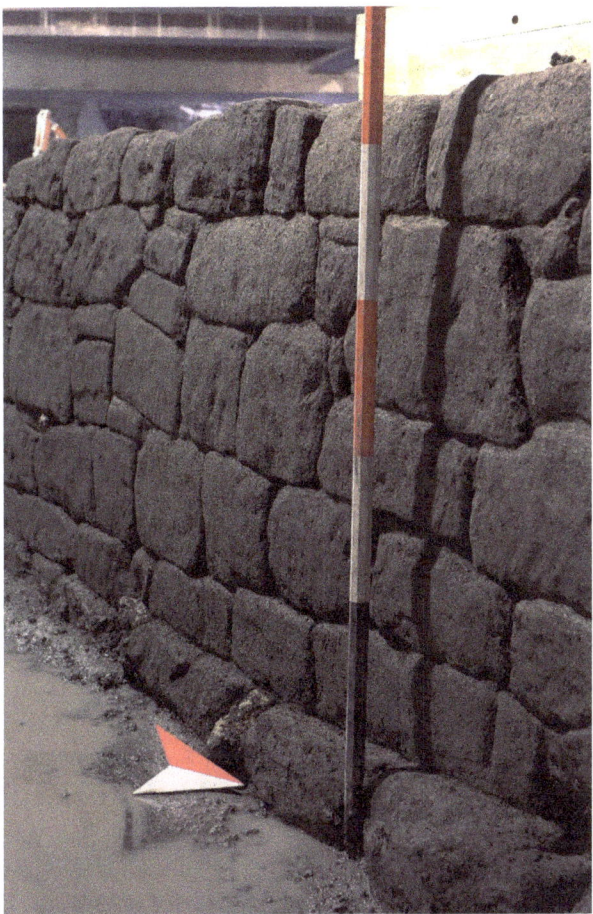

Fig. 3.2 Station of San Giovanni. River bank (third century BC). SSABAP Roma

interpreted a priori as an indication of different land use. A dense urban fabric is suggested by structures later incorporated into the Walls and still emerging around them,[4] with architectonical solutions being employed to compensate for variations in the ground height. In some cases, however, these variations had an impact on the settlement development: the farm of San Giovanni, for instance, was built in the first century AD at the foot of a hill.[5]

While recent investigations carried out in the gardens of Via Sannio at the foot of the Lateran hill have opened new perspectives on the topographic relationship of this area with the hill itself, the excavations in Viale

[4] See A. M. Colini, *Storia e topografia del Celio nell'antichità* (Memorie della Pontificia Accademia Romana di Archeologia 7) (Vatican City, 1944).
[5] Rea, 'Archeologia nel suburbio di Roma', 433–41.

Ipponio have shed new light on the function of the large area between the southern slope of the Caelian and the Lateran hill.

## The Amba Aradam–Ipponio Station

The station in Viale Ipponio lies around 15 m away from the Aurelian Walls. The excavation covers an area of 3,348 m² and approximately 30 m deep from modern ground surface to virgin (natural) soil. About 2,000 m² had been investigated at the time the buildings discussed in this chapter were uncovered, and work had exposed surface areas dating to the first century BC (c. 9 m deep). The archaeology of this area was previously unknown, with the exception of some structures discovered in 1999–2000 between Via Farsalo and Via Illiria. These were found between 25.23 and 23.85 m above sea level[6] and were oriented in the same direction as the barrack-like Ipponio complex discussed below.

Variations in the ancient ground level have been reconstructed comparing orthometric heights obtained via borings. These were quite significant, ranging between 12 and 18 m above sea level (Fig. 3.3). A depression (12 m above sea level at its deepest point) was identified near the northwest corner of the station, and has been identified as part of a basin that lies between the southern slope of the Caelian and modern Piazzale Metronio.

Five macro-phases (dating from the first to the twentieth centuries AD) have been recognised at the site so far, a chronology that matches the data from Via Sannio and Via La Spezia.[7] A Roman building was located beneath the post-classical and modern deposits. This building reached its greatest extent during the first half of the second century AD, covering an area of 1753 m². Its floor levels varied between 22 and 23.70 m above sea level (Fig. 3.4). The complex, only partially excavated, extends beyond the station, and only its eastern limit seems to have been identified so far.

Analysis of this complex suggests that it was built in accordance with ground morphology: the ground sloped south–north and east–west towards the depression near the northwest corner of the station. The stream identified in Via Sannio flowed to the north of the site. The complex was therefore built on different levels, gently sloping towards the stream (east–west). The instability of the ground required frequent later interventions.

---

[6] F. Montella, 'Via Latina: Quartiere Metronio. Insediamenti abitativi a nord della via Latina', *Bullettino della Commissione Archeologica Comunale di Roma* 109 (2008), 281–99.

[7] See Rea, 'Archeologia nel suburbio di Roma', 433–41.

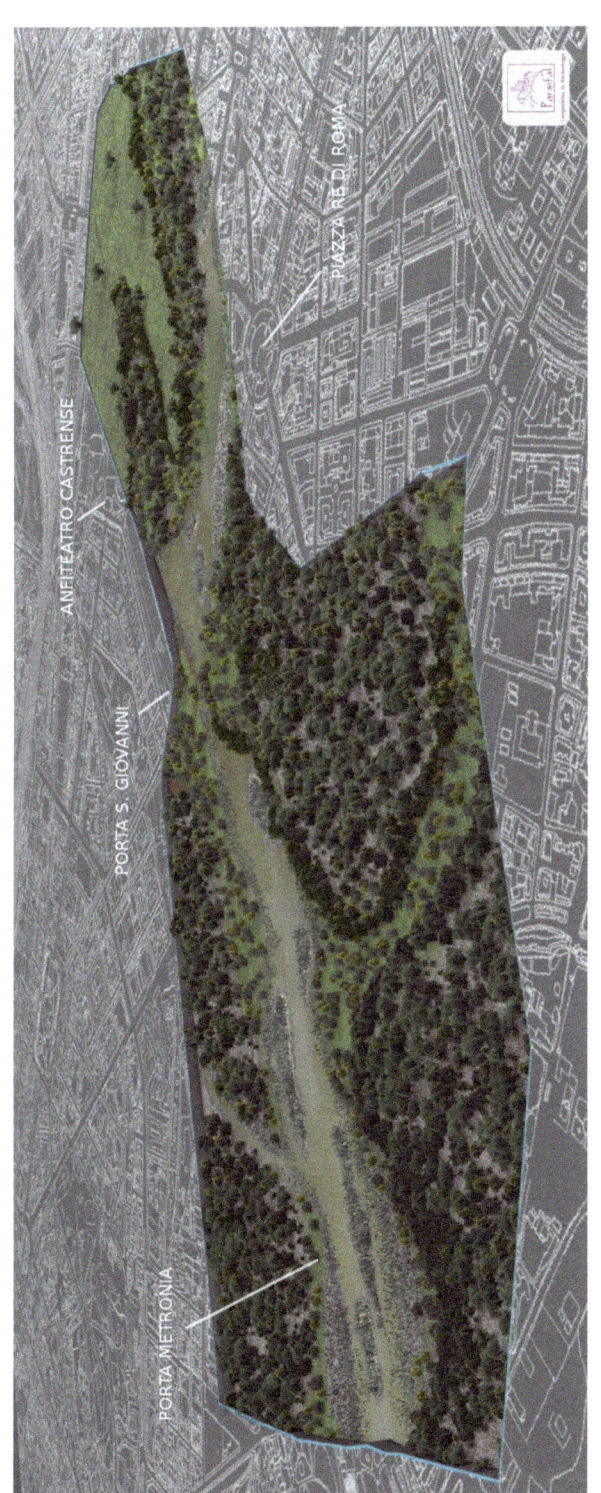

Fig. 3.3 The landscape before human interventions.

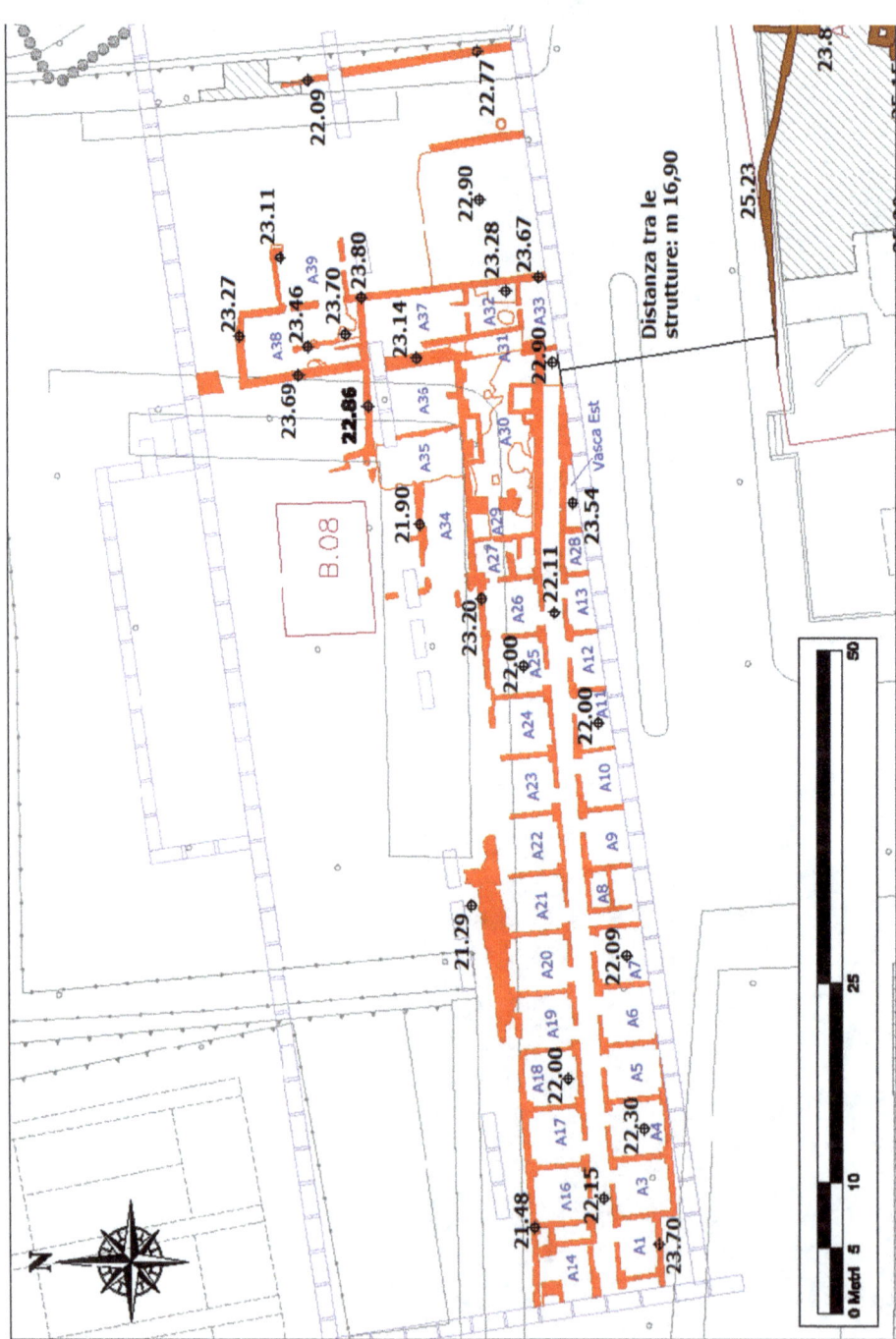

Fig. 3.4 Amba Aradam Ipponio station: the building partially excavated inside the perimeter of the station. Heights and numbers of the rooms are indicated.

The excavated building revealed a long corridor linking thirty-four rooms; the southern ones were gradually cut off by the perimeter of the station (Figs 3.5–3.6). To the northeast, three other rooms have been located at a lower level than the corridor, but their investigation has been temporarily suspended. Finally, another wing with at least six rooms was orthogonally attached to the east side of the building, at a higher height than the corridor. Forty-three rooms have been identified to date. At the eastern end of the site there was a large open space, divided into two sections by long rectilinear walls.

The complex was built in the second half of the first century AD, and was subsequently modified during the second and third centuries. It is possible to attempt an analysis of how the complex was used at the beginning of the second century, during the Trajanic period. Works at the site continued apparently without interruption, and the building reached its final layout in the Hadrianic period. The dating of the Hadrianic phase is suggested by the presence of several stamped bricks preserved *in situ*. Two different stamps of the *figlinae Sulpicianae*, dating between 129 and 139,[8] have been found in the same brickwork.

The two parts of the building had different characteristics (see Fig. 3.5): the southern part included the corridor and the rooms linked to it, twenty-four of which had a square plan (4 x 4 m, 16 m² each); the northern one, only partially excavated, lay at a lower level than the southern rooms. The corridor was 1.50 m wide. It had a mortar floor that started to gently slope towards the southwest (from 22.15 m to 22.90 m, with a difference in height

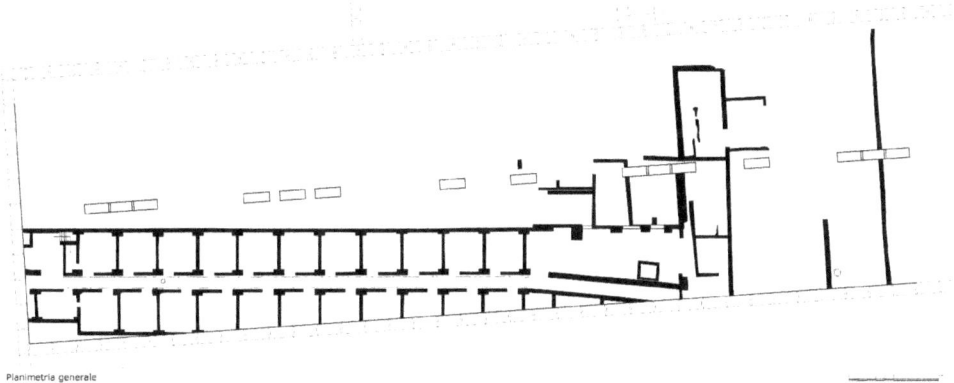

Fig. 3.5 Overview of the complex. To the right, the possible eastern boundary of the building.

[8] *CIL* XV 585b, 395b.

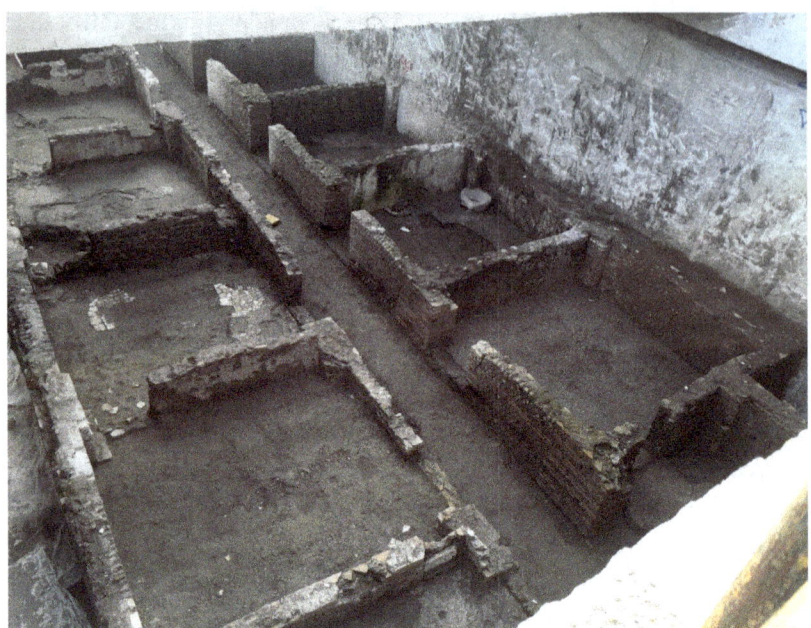

**Fig. 3.6** Overview from west. To the right, we can see where the rooms are cut by the perimeter of the station. SSABAP Roma

of 0.75 m) soon after Rooms A26 and A13 (see Fig. 3.5). The twenty-four rooms were built at the same time over an area of 672 m². They faced each other and were aligned along the corridor, to which they were linked via staggered doors of the same size, originally equipped with marble thresholds. Most of the rooms were constructed in *opus mixtum* with panels in *cubilia* (7 x 7 cm) and horizontal courses of irregular tuff blocks. The linking structures against which the partition walls between rooms were leaning were in *opus vittatum*, made of tuff blocks alternated with bricks. The walls were between 0.30 and 0.45 m thick. Part of the perimetral structures and those in *opus vittatum* were 0.60 m thick.

The back side of the rooms to the north of the corridor, originally underground, consisted of exposed brick walls made of horizontal courses of irregular tuff blocks. Segmental arches with brick voussoirs were used to support the weight of the walls.

Two rooms (A14 and A30), located at the western and eastern end of the complex, had peculiar characteristics (see Fig. 3.4). The door in Room A14 was wider and connected with stairs to the upper floor), with a fountain in front of it. Room A30 had windows, allowing for lighting and aeration of the rooms at a lower height. Under its *opus spicatum* floor, there was a drain sloping east–west, in line with the slope of the ground, linked to two brick-made shafts. There was also a brick-made fountain/pool in this room.

In the Hadrianic period a new wing was added to the east side of the building and the open space to the east of the complex was reorganised (see Figs 3.4–3.5). The new rooms, between 0.38 and 0.80 m higher than the corridor, were also built in *opus mixtum*. They had a rectangular plan (8.45 x 4.50 m, *c.* 38 m²) and floors made of *opus spicatum*, *bipedales* or *opus signinum*. These types of flooring suggest that these rooms were service areas. The corridor extends beyond the western end of the excavated area, bending to the south in line with the new wing, which also continues beyond the excavated area.

Due to the incomplete state of the excavations, it is not possible to identify the doors that linked the rooms in the new wing and those between them and the two eastern areas, which were separated by a wall. The first one had a simple mortar floor over a substantial preparation layer. The second one was probably a green area, located between the former and the complex's eastern boundary. The lower part of the boundary wall, identified along the entire width of the excavation (31 m), was built in *opus reticulatum*. It dates to the first building phase and was subsequently modified and reused. During the Hadrianic phase the door between the corridor and Room A30 was blocked, while a new entrance was opened on corridor A31. The access to the corridor from Rooms A27 and A28 onwards was also blocked and two blocks of stone, probably the base for a gate, were placed alongside these two rooms. The eastern part of the building was therefore intentionally separated from the twenty-four rooms to the west of the complex.

Mosaic floors have been recovered from five rooms on the northern line of rooms. Only the one in Room A25 is complete. The rooms were decorated internally with wall paintings characterised by geometric motifs (rectangular frames) on a background of different colours (white, red, yellow); some sections retain faint traces of floral motifs. The east pool was built between the end of the second and the third centuries at a higher level than the corridor, with a difference in height of about 1.50 m (see Fig. 3.5). From the second half of the third century, during the construction of the Aurelian Walls, part of the complex was reorganised, and the rest was demolished.

The plan of the building and its position in the topography of the Caelian hill suggest that it was most likely designed as barracks (Fig. 3.7). The complex was 59.43 m long (200 Roman feet) and 11.32 m wide (around 40 Roman feet). The ratio between length and width was 5:1. Each of the twenty-four rooms of the barracks could have hosted four people, with

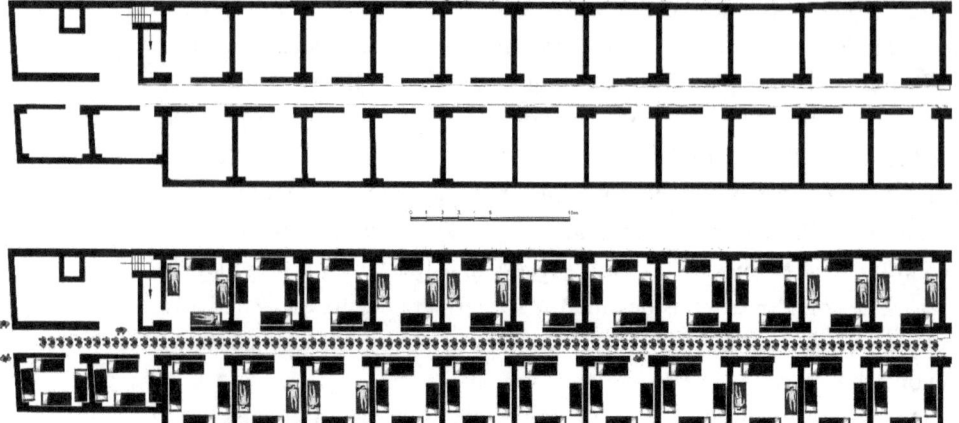

Fig. 3.7 Above: plan and distribution of the billets. Below: scheme of the billets and the corridor, with the ninety-six occupants of the rooms in single file.

a grand total of about a hundred people (ninety-six), corresponding to a *centuria*. The building had an upper floor, and the number of people would have been then around 200, corresponding to two *centuriae*. If we were to argue that the complex hosted a cohort of 500 people, then we might hypothesise the presence of a similar building, perhaps further to the south, and of a third one with only one floor.

The centre-to-centre distance between doors was 2.50 m, enough to accommodate a line of four individuals occupying the same room, spaced with a distance of an arm's length between them. If we envisage that the rooms were planned in a modular way to accommodate the soldiers of the *centuria*, it could be argued that such an arrangement would have allowed them to leave the two-storey building quickly and in an orderly manner whenever needed. Those living in the upper floor would have used the stairs in Room 14, which had a door large enough to facilitate the exiting of a large group of people. Another flight of stairs was probably symmetrically located to the eastern end of the complex.

Each room could host a maximum of four beds, and there was enough space in the corridor for 100 people in single file (see Fig. 3.7). The front wall of each room was of the right size for a bed to be placed to the right of the door, which was almost certainly single-leaf and opened in the opposite direction. A similar solution was adopted in the reconstruction of the *castrum* of Nijmegen, where three bunk beds and a single bed have been

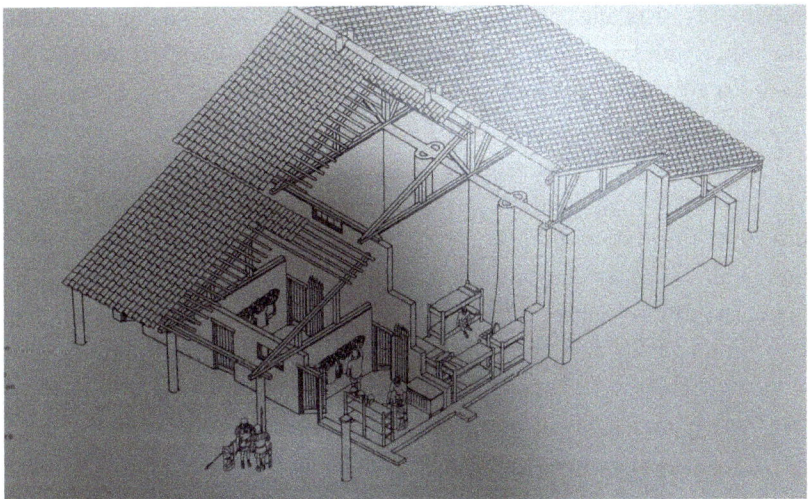

Fig. 3.8 Museum Het Valkhof, Nijmegen: the interiors of the billets.

envisioned for each room (Fig. 3.8).[9] The billets were separated from the rest of the complex by a gate at the eastern end of the corridor.

The standard plan of Roman barracks up until the fourth century was introduced in the Claudio-Neronian period, although some of its characteristics can be found in buildings of the earlier Augustan and Tiberian periods. While variations due to topographical differences and availability of building materials did occur, the spatial and functional balance between the different components of these complexes tended to be maintained, regardless of the size of the barracks. These buildings were overall similar and homogeneously organised.

This topic has been widely explored by scholars. In 1989 Davison carried out a complete analysis of all known Roman barracks,[10] including three sites in Italy: Ostia, Albano and Rome. He claims that differences in the plans of these buildings could be explained exclusively by variations in their function. While the presence of stables might suggest a cavalry barracks, a 'standard' set of stables has not yet been identified and it is not always possible to identify them. Furthermore, without official documents it is extremely difficult to distinguish between legionary and auxiliary barracks, and between barracks hosting different auxiliary units. Military installations included billets, quarters for the officers, taverns, ovens, latrines,

---

[9] A. Koster, K. Peterse and L. Swinkels, *Romeins Nijmegen boven het maaiveld* (Nijmegen, 2002); L. Swinkels and A. Koster, *Nijmegen, oudste Stad van Nederland* (Nijmegen, 2005).

[10] D. P. Davison, *The Barracks of the Roman Army from the 1st to 3rd Centuries A.D.* (British Archaeological Reports International Series 472) (Oxford, 1989).

warehouses, washing facilities, storerooms, waste pits, kitchens, stables, and other buildings such as infirmaries/hospitals. While complexes on the *limes* had to be self-sufficient, barracks in Rome seemingly included only essential facilities.

Davison states that the surface occupied by billets in cohorts' barracks was between 140 and 300 m². The size of a single billet varied between 14 and 29 m², most commonly between 21 and 25 m². Smaller examples were almost always located in installations believed to have been occupied by auxiliary infantry units. Davison distinguishes three groups of billets according to their size: those between 25 and 100 m² were part of small barracks; between 125 and 525 m² of medium-size barracks, the most common ones usually hosting auxiliary troops; and between 650 and 800 m² were part of large barracks. Legionary *castra*, which varied between 675 and 850 m², were part of the latter group.

Following Davison's categories, the barracks of Viale Ipponio, where the twenty-four rooms at the ground floor alone cover 672 m², should be included among the large complexes. The size of each room was 16 m², with 7 m² available to each soldier. The plan of the building can be included in Davison's typology F (Fig. 3.9). Given the particular conditions in Rome, however, we should be cautious in assuming that these general categories apply.

The site of Viale Ipponio did not produce any evidence that could help us to identify this complex more precisely. The Regionary Catalogues, generally dated to the fourth century, do not mention abandoned

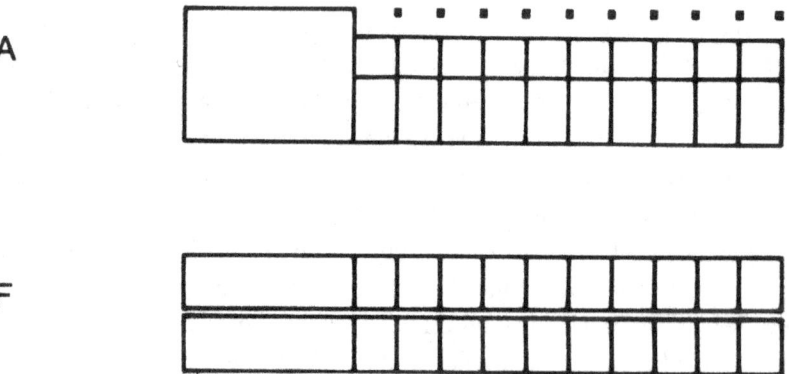

**Fig. 3.9** Barracks plan: Davison's typology F.

complexes, and this one was mostly ruinous at the time. The excavation revealed only part of the complex, including some of the billets and purpose service area. While further work is required, it is already clear that the complex extended far beyond the site of the station.

This is not the place to examine in detail all the barracks of Rome.[11] Figure 3.10, however, shows the plans of the main barracks discovered in the city, and similarities can be recognised between the billets at the Ipponio site and those of the Castra Peregrinorum.

We should now briefly discuss the topographical context of the site (Fig. 3.11). The Caelian is well known for the presence of barracks: the barracks of the fifth Cohort of *Vigiles*, built under Trajan and functioning at least until the beginning of the third century; the Castra Peregrina, also dating to the Trajanic period and in use until the second half of the third century; the Castra Nova Equitum Singularium, dating to the Severan period, now lying under the archbasilica of Saint John Lateran and discussed elsewhere in this

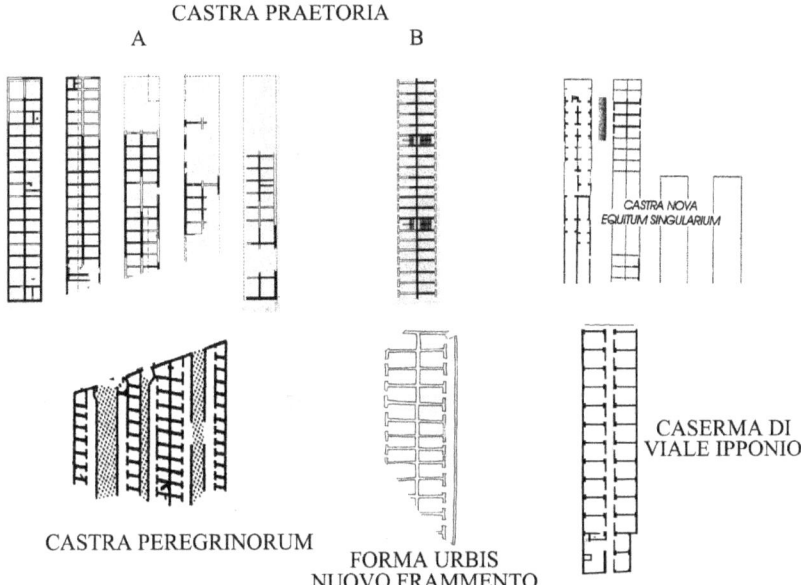

Fig. 3.10 Plan of other barracks from Rome and plan of the Ipponio barracks. In the centre, a new fragment of the Forma Urbis shows the barracks of the fifth Cohort of *Vigiles* on the Caelian hill (Meneghini, 'La Forma Urbis severiana').

---

[11] About the Castra Nova and the barracks of the fifth Cohort of *Vigiles*, see D. Colli, M. Martines and S. Palladino, 'Roma: Viale Manzoni, via Emanuele Filiberto. L'ammodernamento della linea A della Metropolitana: Nuovi spunti per la conoscenza della topografia antica', *Journal of Fasti Online* (2009), 1–26, at pp. 14–16; R. Meneghini, 'La Forma Urbis severiana: Storia e nuove scoperte', in R. Meneghini and R. Rea (eds.), *La biblioteca infinita* (Milan, 2014), 327–36.

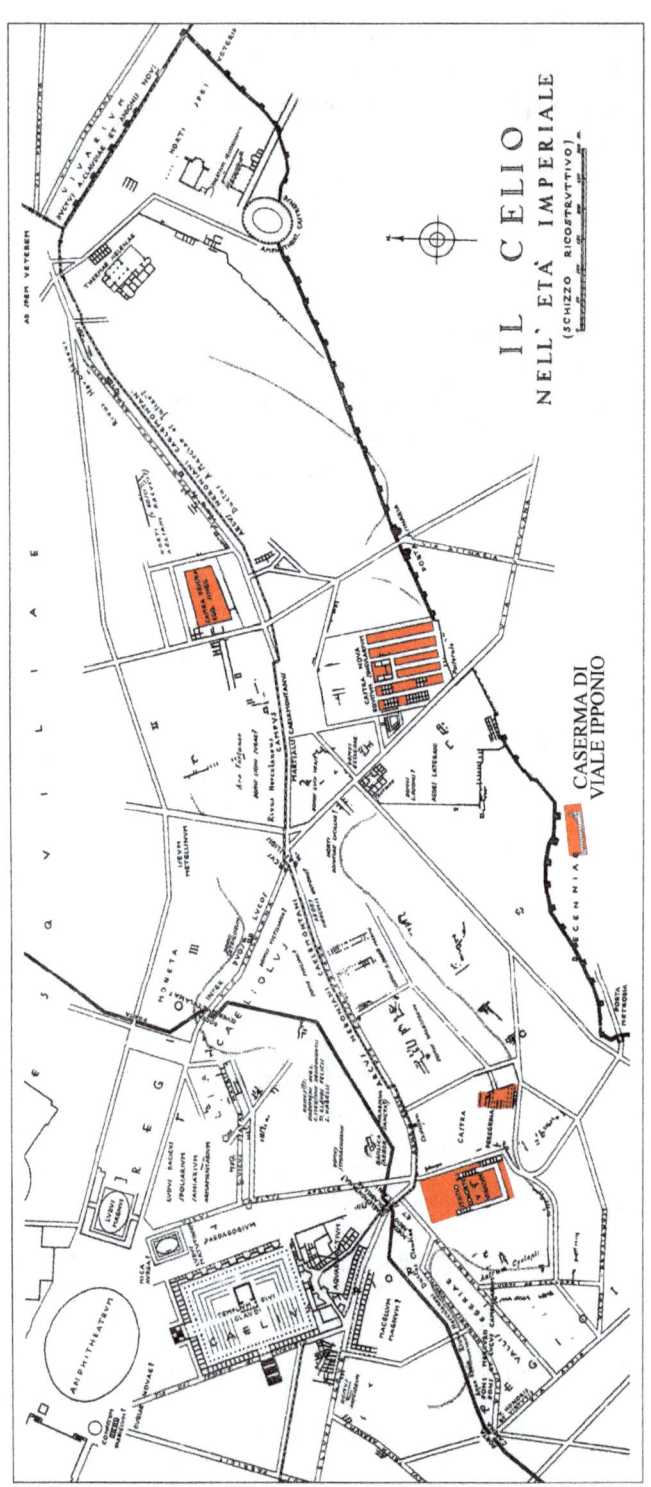

Fig. 3.11 The barracks on the Caelian and the Ipponio barracks (After Colini, *Storia e topografia del Celio*).

volume; and the Castra Priora Equitum Singularium, in use from the early second century, through the third and probably into the fourth century, built between Regio II and V and now under Via Tasso–Via Emanuele Filiberto and Via Statilia. The Ipponio barracks, completed in the Hadrianic period, should now be added to the list. Most of these sites – four out of five – were built under Trajan and Hadrian. All these barracks were close to the Campus Caelemontanus, which has been identified with the Campus Lateranensis (near Piazza San Giovanni in Laterano) and with the Campus Martialis, an area perhaps dedicated to military exercises of the *equites* or even of other units.[12]

The area between Porta Maggiore and the Lateran (Regio V) transformed by Maecenas' reclamation into a residential quarter of large private houses, in time became home to military facilities, such as the Castra Priora.[13] Elagabalus built the Castrensis amphitheatre, which was large enough to host 3,500 people[14] and is comparable to the amphitheatres at Carnuntum in Austria and Aquincum in Hungary. In 1998 Federico Guidobaldi suggested a link between this amphitheatre and the Castra Priora and Nova, but this building might have also been used by soldiers from other barracks nearby during the first half of the third century AD.[15]

The area between Porta Maggiore and San Giovanni is believed to have been the centre of the system of imperial proprieties in the eastern *suburbium* of Rome. It is possible that this system included also the area of Via Sannio and, more likely, the area of Viale Ipponio where the barracks have been found.[16]

## The Shaft in the Gardens of Via Sannio

A multifunctional shaft (Shaft 3.3) was dug in the gardens of Via Sannio to serve Metro Line C of Rome (route T3: San Giovanni–Fori Imperiali

---

[12] Colli, Martines and Palladino, 'Roma', 1–2.
[13] M. Barbera, 'Un anfiteatro di corte: Il Castrense', in A. La Regina (ed.), *Sangue e Arena* (Milan, 2001), 127–45.
[14] D. Colli, S. Palladino, C. Paterna and F. Zisa, 'Le campagne di scavo nell'anfiteatro Castrense a Roma: Nuove acquisizioni', *Bullettino della Commissione Archeologica Comunale di Roma* 98 (1997), 249–82, esp. p. 255.
[15] F. Guidobaldi, 'Il Tempio di Minerva e le strutture adiacenti: Settore privato del *Sessorium* costantiniano', *RAC* 74 (1998), 485–518; M. Barbera, 'Dagli *Horti Spei Veteris* al *Palatium Sessorium*', in S. Ensoli and E. La Rocca (eds.), *Aurea Roma: Dalla città pagana alla città Cristiana* (Florence, 2000), 104–12.
[16] Barbera, 'Dagli *Horti Spei Veteris*'.

Colosseo; see Fig. 3.1). Rescue excavations were carried out over an area of approximately 1,440m2 between August 2014 and July 2016;[17] previous investigations had been undertaken in 2006–7 in the an area northeast of the site (Fig. 3.12).[18]

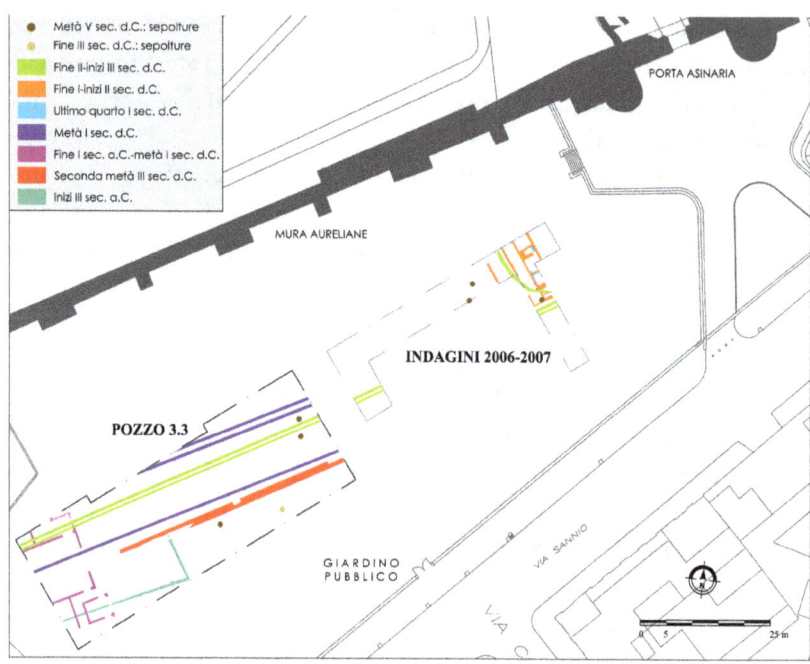

Fig. 3.12 The structures found in the gardens of Via Sannio.

[17] The site was excavated under the direction of R. Rea of the Soprintendenza speciale for the Colosseum and the central archaeological area of Rome, in collaboration with F. Montella and S. Morretta of the same Soprintendenza. Fieldwork, coordinated by N. Saviane, was carried out by M. A. Castagna, M. Carcieri, E. Civitelli, A. Di Feo, V. Forte, C. Frontani, A. Iannaccone, F. R. Paolillo and A. Sebastiani for Land s.r.l.–Indagini Territoriali e Archeologiche (technical supervisor: R. Leonardi). M. Casalini was in charge for the materials analysis. Photographic recording of the site was realised by M. Letizia and T. Letizia, video recording by B. Fruttini. Topographic surveys were executed by A. Caioli, field drawings by A. Di Feo, C. Frontani, F. R. Paolillo, N. Saviane. I would like to thank all my colleagues for their valuable contribution to this project. I would also like to thank R. Rea for letting me publish these new, if partial, data from the excavations.

[18] The excavations in 2006–7 had to stop at around 23 m above sea level due to the presence of an aquifer. Preliminary test pits were carried out prior to the construction of Metro Line C in 1999. See R. Rea, 'Indagini archeologiche 1999–2009 lungo le Mura Aureliane: Da via Casilina vecchia a Porta Metronia. L'evoluzione del paesaggio', in R. Egidi, F. Filippi and S. Martone (eds.), *Archeologia e infrastrutture: Il tracciato fondamentale della linea C della metropolitana di Roma: Prime indagini archeologiche* (Bollettino d'Arte Serie 7) (Rome, 2010), 221–42; Martines, 'Un laboratorio di marmi'.

The stratigraphy of the excavation, 16 m thick, ranges from modern buildings down to the middle Republican period (Fig. 3.13). The material from the upper 4.5 m dates to the beginning of the twentieth century and is linked to the construction of the Appio-Tusculano quarter (see Fig. 3.13, in light grey). Immediately underneath there were strata from the second half of the seventeenth and the nineteenth centuries, showing a slow rising of the ground level and evidence for agricultural use in the area outside the Aurelian Walls (see Fig. 3.13, in dark grey). This agricultural use is attested by planting-holes and recorded in contemporary maps (max. thickness: 2.50 m, between about 29 and 26.50 m above sea level).[19] No activity dating between the seventh and the sixteenth centuries has been recorded. Written sources, the earliest of which dates to the papacy of Callixtus II (1119–24),[20] and ancient maps indicate a stream called Aqua Mariana or Aqua Crabra, perhaps named in memory of the Ancient Aqua Crabra mentioned by Cicero, Frontinus and Procopius.[21] While this stream was not identified during the excavations, small signs of erosion, accumulation of clay and sandy loam sediments in the southern sector of the site, as well as evidence of earth and masonry canalisation works, suggest its proximity.

The evidence from the fourth–sixth centuries is limited, mostly consisting of layers of levelling between 1 and 2 m thick, lying between 27 and 26 m above sea level. These layers reveal a north–south slope, which increases towards the southern end of the excavated area, possibly due to its proximity to the stream. A channel following a sinuous course dating to the fourth century passes through the site and was obliterated in the late fourth–early fifth centuries, when the Aurelian Walls were rebuilt by Honorius. Finally, three burials dating to the middle of the fifth century were located, contemporary with another three burials excavated in 2006–7 (see Fig. 3.12).[22]

A 1 m stratum of debris has been interpreted as backfill soil from the construction of the Aurelian Walls in the second half of the third century (see Fig 3.13, in sky blue). The same slope seen in the Late Antique layers of levelling can be seen here, and its surface is likely to have been the grade

---

[19] Agricultural areas can be recognised in the maps drawn by F. De Paoli in 1623, by G. B. Nolli in 1748 and A. Fornari in 1852 (A. P. Frutaz, *Le piante di Roma* (Rome, 1962), tables 302, 408, 512).

[20] R. Motta, 'Il canale della Marana o Acqua Mariana', in D. Mancioli and G. Pisani Sartorio (eds.), *Gli Acquedotti Claudio e Aniene Nuovo nell'area della Banca d'Italia in via Tuscolana* (Rome, 2001), 91–101.

[21] Rea, 'Archeologia nel suburbio di Roma'.

[22] These burials were excavated under the direction of W. Pantano. Four of these were simple inhumation burials and two were *enchytrismòs* burials. The funerary assemblage from one of them included a small ceramic jug; another one had two bone objects, a hairpin and a dice (see Martines, 'Un laboratorio di marmi'). Other burials have been found near the excavations of San Giovanni Metro C Station (see Rea, 'Archeologia nel suburbio di Roma').

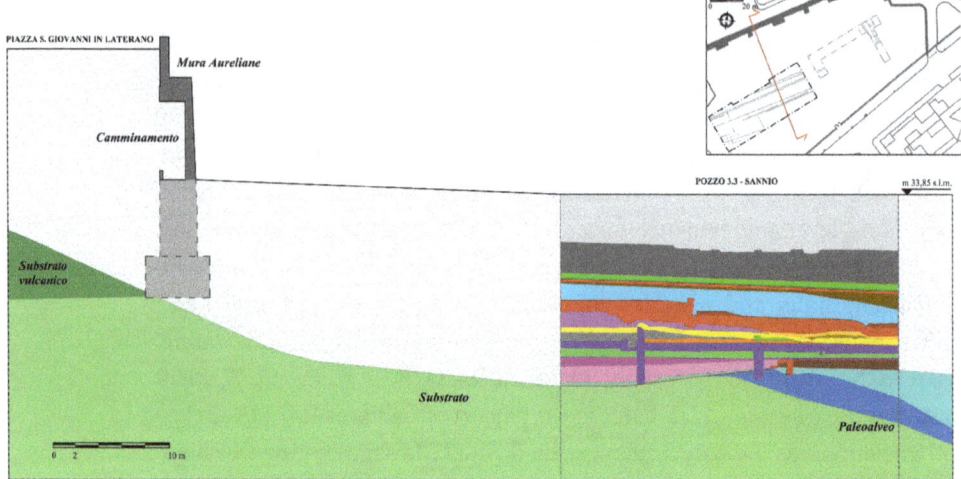

Fig. 3.13 Stratigraphic section of the shaft of the gardens of Via Sannio with the Aurelian Walls to the left.

plane of the Walls, previously identified by analysing a core from the inside of these fortifications.[23]

Further down we found a wall in *opus vittatum*, mostly ruinous, dating to the early Severan period (running northeast–southwest, 0.6 m wide). This structure was first located during the preliminary excavations in 2006–7 to the northeast of Shaft 3.3 (see Fig. 3.12, in green).[24] It was at least 110 m long, with a maximum height of 2 m. A channel, with masonry abutment and tile floor, was found to the southeast of it.[25] The wall seems to have been built to terrace the sloping land, with a difference of 1.50 m between the uphill (on the side of the Walls: 25.30 m above sea level) and downhill planking levels (on the side of Via Sannio: 23.85 m above sea level; see Fig. 3.13, in red). Planting-holes and post-holes with irregular distribution were found in the latter area, together with a narrow trench. This ran parallel to the wall and might have hosted a water pipe in *tubuli* or *fistulae*. A northeast–southwest track with carriage ruts was located 15 m from the wall, near the southern end of the excavation. A structure on the uphill side

---

[23] This was 28.68 m above sea level. See L. Asor Rosa, E. M. Loreti, R. Motta, F. Pacetti and N. Saviane, 'Piazza di Porta S. Giovanni: Riscoperta di un tratto di Mura Aureliane (2013–2015)', *Bullettino della Commissione Archeologica Comunale di Roma* 115 (2015), 211–20.

[24] Rea, 'Indagini archeologiche 1999–2009'; Martines, 'Un laboratorio di marmi'.

[25] A stamp (*CIL* XV 1, no. 773) from a brick fragment dates to 198–211 CE. See E. M. Steinby, 'La cronologia delle figlinae doliari urbane dalla fine dell'età repubblicana fino all'inizio del III sec', *Bollettino della Commissione Archeologica Comunale di Roma* 84 (1974–5), 7–132, at pp. 43–4.

of the wall, possibly part of a garden, was identified in the 2006–7 excavations (see Fig. 3.12, in green). These structures are contemporary with the construction of the Castra Nova Equitum Singularium on top of the Lateran hill, the cavalry barracks built by Septimius Severus. We know that the latter donated to his friend T. Sextius Lateranus the Aedes Parthorum, later known as Aedes Laterani. The location of this complex near the archbasilica has been possible owing to the discovery in the seventeenth century of two lead *fistulae* stamped with the name of Sextius Lateranus.[26]

The construction of the wall in *opus vittatum* pre-dates a sequence of ground surfaces dating between the late Flavian and the early Antonine periods, each of which preserves a track running northeast–southwest on its southeast side.[27] The oldest of these surfaces (see Fig. 3.13, in yellow), dating to the late Flavian period, contains three parallel rows of almost 300 *ollae perforatae*[28] running northeast–southwest across and beyond the excavated area. Some rooms dating between the end of the first and the early second century were identified during the preliminary excavations in 2006–7 (see Fig. 3.12, in orange).[29] These rooms, linked to a corridor running northwest–southeast, were part of a building with at least two storeys, of which only the southeastern end is known. They were probably part of marble workshops, the floor surface of which lay 23.80 m above sea level. The construction of this building post-dates the levelling of two structures in *opus mixtum*. A fragment of *opus signinum* (23.50 m above sea level) dates the latter structures to the Flavian period, on the basis of a comparison with the heights recorded in the excavation of the shaft. The 'Garden of the *ollae*'

---

[26] P. Liverani identified the Aedes Laterani with the remains discovered near the Sancta Sanctorum (P. Liverani, 'L'episcopio lateranense dalle origini all'Alto Medioevo', in S. Balcon, E. Baratte, J.-P. Caillet and D. Sandron (eds.), *Des 'domus ecclesiae' aux palais épiscopaux: Actes du colloque tenu à Autun du 26 au 28 novembre 2009* (Bibliothèque de l'Antiquité tardive 23) (Turnhout, 2012), 119–31). See also P. Liverani, 'Le proprietà private nell'area lateranense fino all'età di Costantino', *MEFRA* 100, 2 (1988), 891–915; V. S. M. Scrinari, *Il Laterano imperiale I: Dalle 'Aedes Laterani' alla 'Domus Faustae'* (Vatican City, 1991); P. Liverani, 'Introduzione topografica', in P. Liverani (ed.), *Laterano 1: Scavi sotto la Basilica di S. Giovanni in Laterano*, vol. I: *Materiali* (Vatican City, 1998), 6–16; P. Liverani, 'Dalle *Aedes Laterani* al patriarchio lateranense', *RAC* 75 (1999), 521–49; I. Haynes, P. Liverani, S. Piro, I. Peverett and G. Spinola, 'Progetto Laterano: Primi risultati', *Atti della Pontificia Accademia Romana di Archeologia (Serie III)* 86 (2013–14), 125–44; and Liverani, Chapter 2 in this volume.

[27] There are three different tracks, one over the other, located at 21.77 m, 22 m and 22.35 m above sea level, respectively.

[28] About these vessels and their significance, see E. Macaulay Lewis, 'The role of *ollae perforatae* in understanding horticulture, planting techniques, garden design, and plant trade in the Roman world', in J.-P. Morel, J. Tesserras and J. C. Matamala (eds.), *The Archaeology of Crop Fields and Gardens* (Bari, 2006), 207–19.

[29] Rea, 'Indagini archeologiche 1999–2009'; Martines, 'Un laboratorio di marmi'.

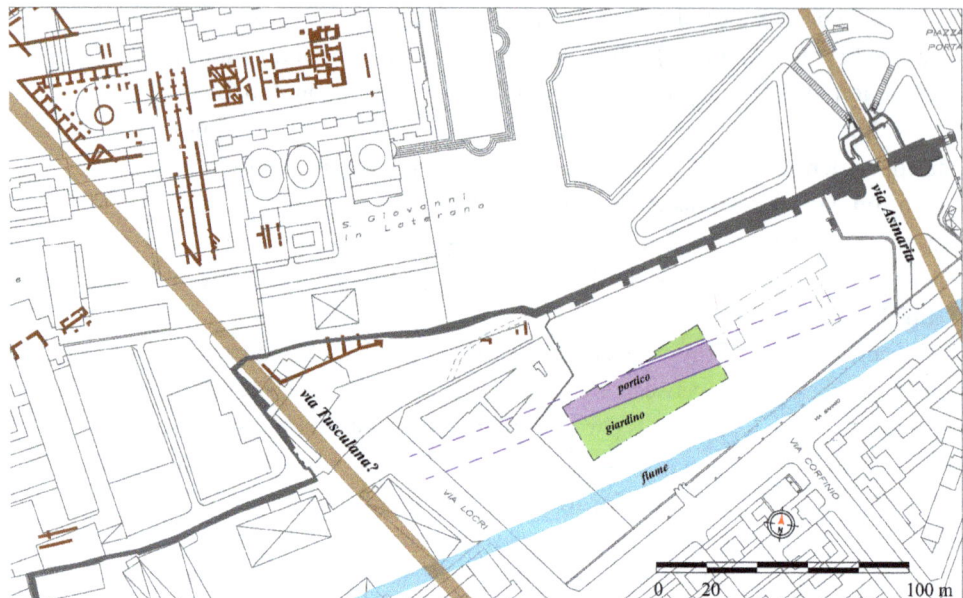

**Fig. 3.14** Plan of the portico dating to the Julio-Claudian period from the gardens of Via Sannio.

overlays the remains of a portico, located near a green area. Three phases of the latter have been recognised, from the mid-first century AD and the Flavian period (Fig. 3.14). We will discuss them in more detail later on.

The construction of the portico levelled a complex built in *opus reticulatum* with tuff blocks, identified to the southwest of the excavated area (see Fig 3.12, in purple; Fig. 3.15). Only the northeastern end of this building is known. It was modified several times between the early and mid-first century AD.[30] Room 1 was part of the earliest phase, a heated room equipped with *suspensurae*. During a following phase, a set of rooms (Rooms 2–8) with earth floors were added to the structure. They were built around an open courtyard (Room 3). Room 2 was a portico with columns and pilasters in *opus testaceum*. Later structures with rectangular hollows, possibly flowerpots, were found leaning against them. The skeleton of an equine was located in Room 2, dating to the last phase of the complex.[31] Outside the building there was a masonry water pipe with three different phases (see Fig. 3.15, in azure).

---

[30] This building was contemporaneous with a farm of the Augustan period (abandoned at the end of the first century CE) found during the construction of the San Giovanni Metro C Station (see Rea, 'Archeologia nel suburbio di Roma').

[31] This burial was recorded by L. Brancazi.

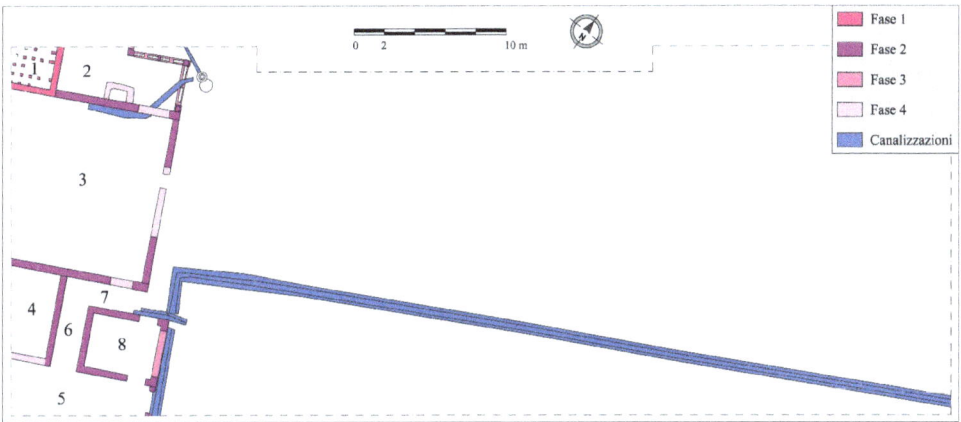

Fig. 3.15 Structures dating to the first half of the third century BC from the shaft of the gardens of Via Sannio.

Underneath these rooms there was a homogeneous backfill layer (mid-first century BC) covering a sunken area, dug in the second half of the third century BC perhaps to collect water. Only the southeastern end of this feature has been identified, where a masonry structure in *èmplekton* runs northeast–southwest (see Fig. 3.12, in red). This was built in roughly squared blocks of tuff of the 'cappellaccio' type (1.35 m wide; higher height: 20.30 m above sea level), only one course of which survives on both sides. Between the two sides there was a difference in height of around 0.60 m (lower height: 19.50 m above sea level; higher height: 20.10 m above sea level). To the southeast of this structure there was a rectangular trench filled with clay, probably to waterproof it (0.60 m wide and 1.10 m high). The bottom of the sunken area lies above archaeologically sterile ground (lower height: 18 m above sea level) and does not include sediments indicating running water. Instead, it is covered by a layer of clay rich in gastropoda, suggesting stagnant water. This might have been a basin for collecting water, running alongside the river.[32] The tuff blocks of the embankment were found scattered in the sunken area, perhaps following a violent flood event or the voluntary dismantlement of the structure. The embankment of Via Sannio is related to the one recorded during the

---

[32] Inside the excavated area, the basin covers an area of 800 m² (max. length: 62.50 m; max. width: 17.50 m). Its minimal estimated capacity was 890,000 litres of water (assuming that the water level touched the first course of tuff blocks). Based on borings in the area outside the shaft, the basin was probably between 21 m and 24 m wide, and it extended for at least 56 m to the northeast of the site. According to this reconstruction, the basin would have covered at least 2,500 m², hosting 2,780,000 litres of water.

excavation of the San Giovanni Metro C Station. No lateral trenches were found there, and the structure was broader, but it dated to the same period and was constructed with the same building technique.[33]

Two perpendicular structures in blocks of tuff, perhaps parts of fences, pre-date the construction of the embankment. They date to the early third century BC and their ground surface lay approximately 19.20 m above sea level (see Fig. 3.12, in sea green). These are the oldest structures identified during the excavation, and lie on natural fillings of a palaeo-channel of the river Tiber dating to the Holocene. This palaeo-channel ran northeast-southwest and cut Pleistocenic volcanic deposits, including those of the Lateran hill.[34] The northern river bank was located during the excavation between 19.10 m and 12.90 m above sea level (see Fig 3.13).[35] The upper fills of the channel were of natural origin but contained isolated artefacts; the latest of these dated to the fourth century BC at the latest. The archaeologically sterile alluvial will was observed at 17 m above sea level.

Following this general introduction to the site and its stratigraphy, we will now discuss in more detail the portico built in the mid-first century AD (Phase 1; see Fig. 3.13, in dark blue; Figs 3.14, 3.16). The building faced northeast-southwest and was 9.30 m wide. While its length inside the shaft site was 63 m, it certainly continued beyond the limits of the excavated area both towards the northeast and southwest. The building was enclosed to the northwest by a wall in *opus mixtum* with panels in *opus reticulatum* and courses in *opus mixtum* of bricks and *tufelli* with a saw-tooth pattern.[36] When excavated, the structure was 1.60 m high, but collapsed material found nearby suggests an original height of at least 3.20 m. A dwarf wall in *opus reticulatum*, interpreted as a colonnade's base, enclosed the southeast side of the portico (0.78 m wide; 0.26 m high). Two fragments of columns in African marble (diameter of the lower scape: 0.68 m; diameter of the shaft: 0.60 m) might have come from this colonnade. The dwarf wall underlay a narrow wall in *opus testaceum*, of which three courses survived, with empty spaces for the columns.[37] The portico was

---

[33] Rea, 'Archeologia nel suburbio di Roma'.

[34] R. Funiciello, A. Praturlon and G. Giordano, *La geologia di Roma dal centro storico alla periferia* (Florence, 2008), unnumbered table.

[35] To the south of the excavation, the cut of the ditch was recorded through coring down to a minimum height of 9 m above sea level.

[36] The wall was 35 m long and 0.58 m wide. The brickwork was very regular: the side of each *cubilium* was 7–7.5 cm; the small blocks of tuff were 15–28 cm long and 7.5–8.5 cm thick; the bricks used to form the courses were of a light yellow-pinkish colour and 16–26 cm long. Those used just above the foundations were 13–50 cm long. The mortar was of a light brown-greyish colour and was made with lime and crumbled brown volcanic material, with inclusions.

[37] The structure is cut by blocks of travertine dating to the following phase, located about 4.70 m from one another. Both the structures enclosing the portico were built over foundations in *opus*

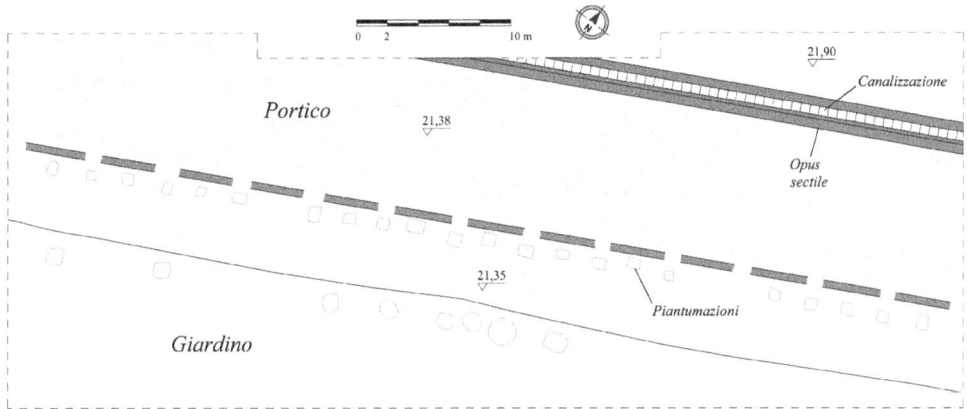

Fig. 3.16 Plan of Phase 1 of the Julio-Claudian portico from the shaft of the gardens of Via Sannio.

paved with a concrete screed 0.15 m thick. *Arriccio* were identified in its northwestern wall and holes for iron cramps (two of which survived *in situ*) to attach the *opus sectile* decorations to it were recorded (Fig. 3.17).[38]

Outside the portico, on the northwest side, a masonry channel was found (see Fig. 3.16). It was lined with *bipedales*, almost all with the same stamp: T. CLAVDI▲/SABINI▲.[39] This feature seems to have been built to drain the soil and protect the building from water streaming down from the Lateran hill, as the drainage holes in the northwestern parapet of the pipe suggest. In the area outside the portico the ground surface (21.90 m above sea level, c. 0.50 m above the internal floor of the building) was paved with fragments of crumbled tuff.

To the southeast, the portico faced a garden. For 4.50 m the area near the building was paved with a thin concrete screed (5 cm thick). A series of quadrangular planting-holes (side: 0.7–1 m; see Fig. 3.16) were found near the portico, probably located in front of the columns and between intercolumniations. A row of larger circular ditches was identified approximately

*caementicium* made with mortar and pieces of tuff. The upper part of these foundations was laid directly in the preparatory trench ('cavo libero') while their lower part was laid in a mould made of wooden boards ('cavo armato'). The height of the two foundations is different due to the composition of the soil they overlay (northwestern foundations: 3 m; southeastern foundations: 1.80 m).

[38] Marks left over the *arriccio* seem to suggest that the lower part of the wall was covered with plates (0.30 m high). The surface of the wall was carved horizontally by a cut (0.60 m above the floor), probably to facilitate the lining of the wall. The holes for the cramps were mostly placed on three horizontal rows. Two of them still contained two iron cramps and others had fragments of marble.

[39] CIL XV, 1, 933a; at the end of the first line there is an arrow, at the end of the second one a palmette. The stamp dates to the mid-first century AD. See E. M. Steinby, 'I bolli laterizi dell'Area sacra di Largo Argentina', in F. Coarelli, I. Kajanto, U. Nyberg and M. Steinby (eds.), *L'Area sacra di Largo Argentina I* (Rome, 1981) 298–332, at p. 318, no. 71.

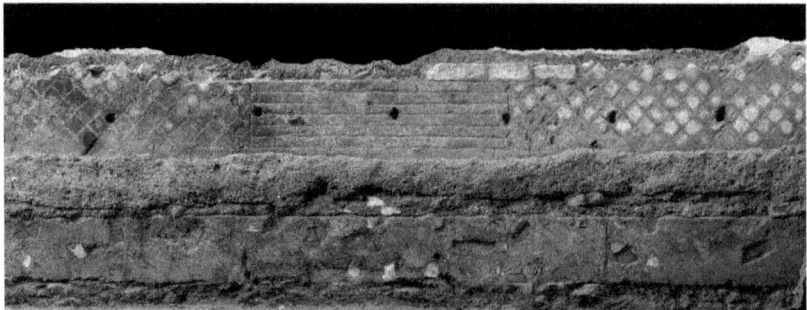

**Fig. 3.17** Wall in *opus mixtum* (northwestern internal end) and its lining, part of the Julio-Claudian portico from the shaft of the gardens of Via Sannio. SSABAP Roma

5.50 m to the southeast, perhaps dug to house trees.[40] Outside the excavated area, southeast of the portico, the pre-existing stream probably continued to flow (see Fig. 3.14).

Soon after its construction the portico was modified, and its marble decoration removed (Phase 2; see Fig. 3.13, in orange; Fig. 3.18). The inner floor was raised, and its centre showed traces of ruts, probably left by carriage wheels (height: 21.70 m above sea level). To the southeastern side were now brick columns (diameter: 0.88 m) on brick square bases (side: 0.90 m) placed over blocks of travertine, perhaps to substitute the marble columns of the previous phase.[41] These blocks were linked by a structure in *opus latericium*, which incorporated the one from the previous phase. The marble decoration was removed also from the wall enclosing the northwest side of the portico and substituted by a new lining (see Fig. 3.17). Only the undercoat survived, but this was likely the base for decorated plaster, as suggested by many fragments of wall painting recovered from the abandonment layer of the building. The planting-holes near the portico were now filled in and covered by a pozzolana floor with a low trench, perhaps for planting.

The portico building was further modified before its final abandonment (Phase 3; see Fig. 3.19). During this third phase, a new wall in *opus*

---

[40] The stratigraphy would also allow for the possibility that these ditches were dug during the following phase. The filling of these ditches has been sampled and the pollen recovered has been analysed by F. Di Rita. Both arboreal (*Quercus, Pinus, Cupressaceae*) and herbaceous plants (mostly *Chenopodiaceae*, with some *Cichirioideae, Poaceae, Fabaceae, Apiaceae, Caryophyllaceae*; the percentage of *Centaurea, Cyperaceae, Ranunculaceae, Brassicaceae* was very low) have been identified.

[41] Only the first course of bricks of one of the columns survived. All the brick bases survived in the northeastern area of the site. Over the blocks of travertine there were square marks, slightly raised circular areas and cavities, usually employed to house elements of stone. These marks seem to suggest some sort of reuse more than a different building phase.

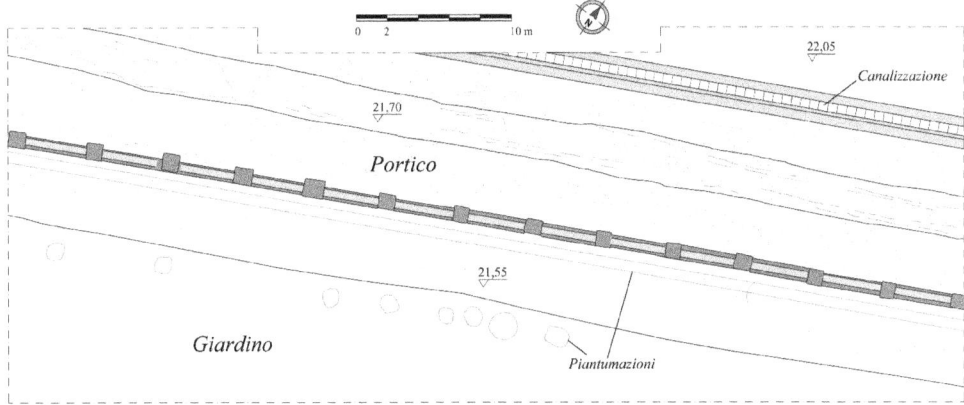

**Fig. 3.18** Plan of Phase 2 of the Julio-Claudian portico from the shaft of the gardens of Via Sannio.

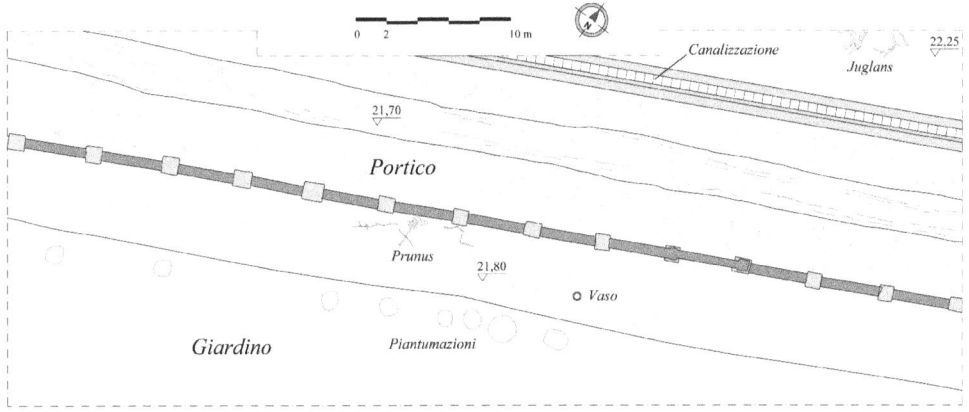

**Fig. 3.19** Plan of Phase 3 of the Julio-Claudian portico from the shaft of the gardens of Via Sannio.

*latericium* was built, lying over the blocks of travertine of the southeastern side. In places, this feature was lying over the brick columns of the previous phases, while elsewhere these were substituted by brick semi-columns or lesenes, jutting out towards both the inside and outside of the portico. The northwestern internal wall received a new lining and was probably painted. The internal floor seems to have remained unchanged.

The ground surface of the garden was 0.25 m above the previous phase and produced a cylindrical vase in Pentelic marble (see Fig. 3.20).[42] Its foot was decorated with fillet and trefoil Lesbian *kyma* and its lip with fillet and Ionian *kyma*. The body was decorated with racemes linked by a ribbon tie

[42] External diameter: 54 cm; internal diameter: 40 cm. It was 54 cm high and 45 cm deep.

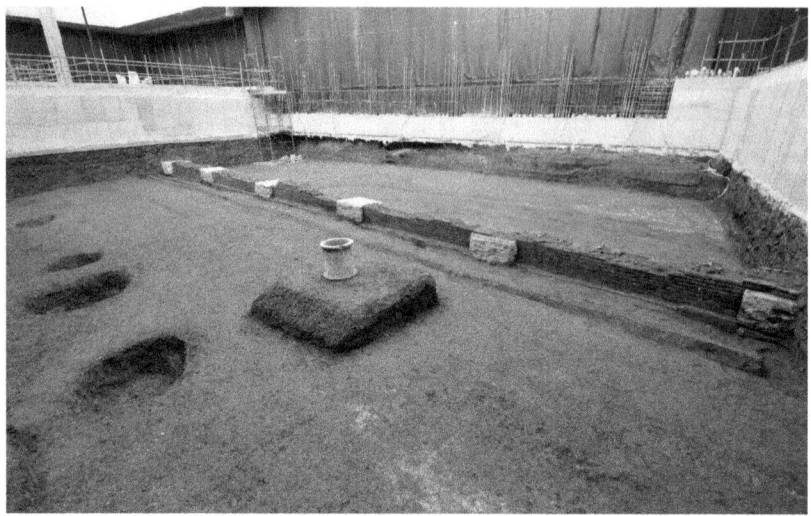

**Fig. 3.20** Overview of the portico and gardens from the shaft of the gardens of Via Sannio. SSABAP Roma

to a nail.[43] A stump of *Prunus* (peach tree or plum tree; see Fig. 3.19) was found near the portico and two stumps of *Juglans regia* (walnut tree) and roots of *Buxus sempervirens* (box) and *Rubus* (blackberry or raspberry bush)[44] were identified in the area to the uphill side of the portico. It is possible that the plants located in the circular trenches to the southeast were still in place during this phase.

Materials from layers contemporary to Phase 1 date it to the mid-first century AD. Furthermore, the foundations of the building overlay the rooms in *opus reticulatum* dated to the first half of the first century AD. This chronology is confirmed by the brick stamps on the canalization to the northwest of the area. Phases 2 and 3 cannot be dated through excavated materials, but the stratigraphic sequence suggests that their *terminus ante quem* was the construction of the 'Garden of the *ollae*', dating to the late Flavian period. Built under Claudius, the portico was then robbed and partially rebuilt twice, perhaps between the Neronian and early Flavian period. It was subsequently destroyed and built over in the late Flavian period.

The topography of the area where the portico building was found during the excavations for Shaft 3.3 may be characterised as follows: as noted above,

---

[43] A. Coletta is now studying this vase. It has been provisionally dated between the second and the first centuries BC, perhaps a luxury item imported from Attica.

[44] The study of these stumps and roots has been coordinated by N. Macchioni (CNR IVALSA, Sesto Fiorentino).

the portico ran northeast–southwest, at the foot of the Lateran hill. It faced a garden near a river close to modern Via Sannio. The river had flowed through the area since before intensive human settlement began. The portico was probably part of a complex of many blocks, a typical form for the *horti*. The topography of this area can help us in reconstructing the size of this complex: it was probably enclosed by the Via Tusculana to the west; the river to the south; Via Asinaria to the east; and the Lateran hill to the north, where the residential quarters might have been located. This would have been in line with the classic 'terracing system'.[45] The complex was therefore probably part of the 'belt' of *horti* developed from the late Republican period onwards around and beyond the Servian Walls.

We know of several properties dating to the Julio-Claudian period in the Lateran area. Juvenal mentions the 'egregiae Lateranorum aedes',[46] the position of which is still debated. They originally belonged to Plautius Lateranus, but were militarily occupied and expropriated by Nero in 65 after the Pisonian conspiracy and Plautius' death.[47] The house of the Calpurni Pisoni was also probably located in this area, as suggested by the finding of a lead *fistula* inscribed *L. Piso[nis]* between Via Tusculana and Via Amba Aradam (during the excavation of the 'Lateran baths').[48] This complex was also most likely expropriated by Nero. A similar fate has been hypothesised for the *horti Torquatiani*, located further to the east and seemingly owned by D. Iunius Torquatus Silanus (nephew of Augustus and consul in 53), who was forced by Nero to take his own life in 64.[49]

---

[45] Some structures in *opus reticulatum* with side scarfs of tuff blocks were recorded by Colini to the northwest of the portico near Via Tusculana, later incorporated into the Aurelian Walls. See Colini, *Storia e topografia del Celio*, 343 and fig. 282. Two *domus*, dating to the late first–early second centuries, were found under the Castra Nova Equitum Singularium. The excavations carried out by Josi beneath the archbasilica produced a group of fragments of wall painting and marble dating to the first half of the first century AD, together with contemporary brick stamps. See Colini, *Storia e topografia del Celio*, 343–77; Liverani, 'Introduzione topografica'.

[46] Juv. 10.15–18.

[47] Liverani, 'Le proprietà private nell'area lateranense'; Scrinari, *Il Laterano imperiale II*; Liverani, 'Introduzione topografica'; Liverani, 'Dalle *Aedes Laterani* al patriarchio lateranense'; Haynes et al., 'Progetto Laterano' (2013–14).

[48] Colini, *Storia e topografia del Celio*, 338.

[49] Frontinus (*Aq.* 1.5.65) seems to suggest that the eastern boundary of these *horti* was in an area called *ad Spem veterem*, near Porta Maggiore. See S. B. Platner and T. Ashby, *A Topographical Dictionary of Ancient Rome* (London, 1929), 272–3; D. Mancioli, 'Horti Torquatiani', *LTUR* III, 85–6. F. Fraioli, 'Regione V. *Esquiliae*', in A. Carandini (ed.), *Atlante di Roma antica* (Milan, 2012), 323–41, at p. 331 and table III) proposes that their boundary was near Via Tusculana, including the area of the archbasilica.

# 4 | Ground-Penetrating Radar Survey in the Saint John Lateran Basilica Complex

SALVATORE PIRO, IAN P. HAYNES, PAOLO LIVERANI AND
DANIELA ZAMUNER

## Introduction

An exceptional building in its own right, the archbasilica of Saint John Lateran also lies within an area of intense archaeological interest. As explored elsewhere in this volume, extensive excavations beneath the basilica have revealed its Constantinian phases, together with elements of the Severan Castra Nova and still earlier elite residences. Further investigations in the vicinity have exposed not only some of the earliest elements of the basilica's baptistery, but also part of the oratory of Santa Croce, itself overlying a major bath complex of the Severan period. An integral element of the Lateran Project's attempt to characterise these features better and to set them within the topography of the Lateran area has been a programme of ground-penetrating radar (GPR) survey. This chapter outlines the methods employed in that survey and considers some of the key results to emerge. Advanced interpretation of GPR results is best undertaken in conjunction with material derived from a range of other sources and specialist fields; discussion of relevant material is, therefore, incorporated into the interpretation of survey data by area.

Given the complexity of the archaeological deposits beneath and around the archbasilica the team sought to focus GPR work on the following questions:

1. Private residences of the imperial period: Could the extent and layout of any of these buildings be identified? What might radar reveal about road systems and property boundaries?
2. The Castra Nova: How far might it be possible to identify the wall circuit of the *castra*? How did it relate to the buildings around it? What did it replace when it was constructed in AD 193–6?
3. The archbasilica: How much could be learnt about the form of the Constantinian basilica? What could GPR reveal about the later structural history of the building?

4. The *patriarchium*: Could the layout and extent of the buildings cleared by Sixtus V be identified?

These concerns in turn determined the areas selected for GPR survey, but always the team remained conscious that other features could emerge in any data sample which would in turn require further analysis.

## Ground-Penetrating Radar Survey: Methodology

Ground-Penetrating Radar (GPR) survey is an electromagnetic impulsive method well suited for shallow-depth investigations because GPR can supply sub-surface profiles grouped in vertical radar sections. When the transmitter-receiver antenna is pulled along the surface of a site signals are sent with a highly directive radiation pattern into the ground and echoes are returned from targets in the ground.

The radar signal emitted is a pulse of electromagnetic radiation with nominal frequency value in the range 15–2500 MHz (1 MHz=$10^6$ Hz). The velocity of an electromagnetic wave in air is 30 cm/ns (1ns=$10^{-9}$s), meaning that it travels 30 cm per nanosecond, a nanosecond being a thousand-millionth/billionth of a second, but in soils the velocity is less, typical values there are in the range 5–15 cm/ns. Depending on the impedance and heterogeneity of the media they encounter, radar pulses can be reflected towards the surface or attenuated and diffused, and thus quickly totally dissipated. When reflected echoes emerge, the received signal can be correlated with the transmitted one and the delay of arrivals – that is to say, the travel time in the ground – is a function of velocity. The vertical scale in radargrams is proportional to the two-way travel time (twt): it can be transformed into a depth scale if the wave-propagation velocity is known. In general, wave-propagation velocity is affected by the dielectric constant ($\varepsilon_r$) and by the magnetic susceptibility ($\mu$) of the media through which it passes, while electric conductivity ($\sigma$) contributes to wave attenuation (signal power loss) and reflection.

When interpreting GPR survey results, it is important to be aware of both the limits imposed by attenuation and resolving power. Resolving power, or the ability to locate small objects, is affected by various factors. The wavelength used affects the ability of the GPR to identify thin layers or isolated features. Resolution is more than $\lambda/2$ and the depth of horizontal interfaces can be determined to about $\lambda/10$ ($\lambda$=the wavelengths of the GPR signal). In order to get a better resolution of sub-surface features, higher-frequency antennas could be used, but their use increases attenuation, while low-frequency antennas have a coarser resolution but their penetration depth is very much better. Not all features respond equally well to GPR survey, and it is important to be aware of this fact when interpreting the data. A pit with a well-defined edge will produce a better reflection than one with a less clear boundary, for example. Walls and foundations are also good reflectors. Typical archaeological applications of GPR are the search for graves, buildings and the identification of anthropic soil transformations.

The increasing necessity for detailed three-dimensional resolution of shallow-depth structures makes 3D GPR acquisition one of the most important remote-sensing tools. The advantages of 3D surveying are documented for mapping geological features as well as archaeological investigations, where higher horizontal and vertical resolution is required. High-resolution acquisition techniques, using a sub-meter profile spacing interval, have been successfully applied in locating sub-surface archaeological structures.[1]

One of the most useful ways to represent GPR data sets collected along closely spaced parallel profiles is to display the data in horizontal maps of recorded reflection amplitudes measured across the survey grid. These maps, referred to as amplitude time slices, allow easy visualisation of the location, depth, size and shape of radar anomalies buried in the ground. The maps can be created at various reflection time levels within a data set to show radar structures at a specified time (depth) across a surveyed site. Mapping the energy in the reflected radar returns across a survey grid can help to create useful information that can sometimes be shown to mirror the general archaeological site plan result obtained from invasive excavation.

The raw reflection data acquired by GPR is nothing more than a collection of many individual traces along 2D transepts within a grid. Each of those reflection traces contains a series of waves that vary in amplitude depending on the amount and intensity of energy reflection at buried interfaces. When these traces are plotted sequentially in standard 2D profiles, the specific amplitudes within individual traces that contain important reflection information are usually difficult to visualise and interpret. In areas where the stratigraphy is complex and buried features are difficult to discern, however, amplitude time-slice analysis is one of the most efficient post processes which can be applied to the raw data to extract

---

[1] D. Goodman and S. Piro, *GPR Remote Sensing in Archaeology* (Berlin, 2013).

the 3D shapes of buried remains.[2] Due to velocity changes across the area and with depth, a slice map made across a constant level time window will not represent a level slice in terms of depth in the ground. Horizontal time slices must therefore be considered only approximate depth slices. Without very detailed velocity control throughout a grid, it is impossible to construct perfectly horizontal depth slices.

To compute horizontal time slices, the software employed compares amplitude variations within traces that were recorded within a defined time window. When this is done, both positive and negative amplitudes of reflections are compared to the norm of all amplitudes within that window. No differentiation is made between positive and negative amplitudes in this analysis, only the magnitude of amplitude deviation from the norm. Low-amplitude variations within any one slice denote little sub-surface reflection, and therefore indicate fairly homogeneous material. High amplitudes indicate significant sub-surface discontinuities and, in many cases, indicate the presence of buried features. Once all this has been done data are interpolated and gridded on a regular mesh. A high-to-low amplitude scale is normally presented as part of the legend of each map, but without specific units because, in GPR, reflected wave amplitudes are usually arbitrary.

For work in the Lateran area, a decision was made to use a SIR3000 (GSSI) radar equipped with a 400 MHz (GSSI) bistatic antenna with constant offset and a 70 MHz (Subecho Radar) monostatic antenna to survey targeted areas both within and beyond the basilica. The survey areas selected are shown in Fig. 4.1.

Areas A1 and B1 lie in the Piazza Giovanni Paolo II. They were selected to address questions about the private residences of the imperial period, and the northwestern area of the Castra Nova. Areas A2, B2 and C2 lie to the east in the Piazza San Giovanni in Laterano; they were chosen to address questions about the Castra Nova and *patriarchium*. Survey under the floor of the archbasilica was – by contrast – primarily designed to address questions about the building's structural history, but it was also hoped that it might reveal elements of earlier structures, such as the Castra Nova and its predecessors.

Horizontal spacing between parallel profiles at the site was 0.5 m, employing the two antennas. The methodology employed was designed to enhance the signal-to-noise ratio for each scan. Radar reflections along the transects were recorded continuously across the ground at 40 scan $s^{-1}$ (i.e.

---

[2] Goodman and Piro, *GPR Remote Sensing*.

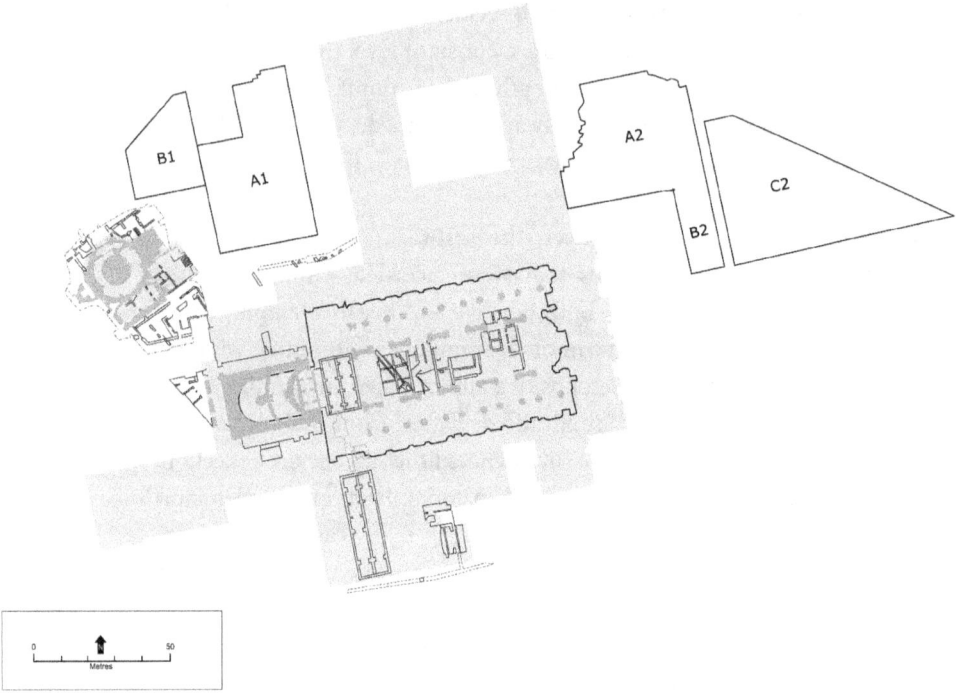

**Fig. 4.1** Plan showing location of survey areas outside the basilica (image: T. Ravasi).

40 scans per second);[3] horizontal stacking was set to three scans (i.e. each stored scan is the result of the average of the three scans taken at that point).

In the area outside the basilica a total of 777 adjacent profiles were collected across the site alternatively in forward and reverse directions employing the GSSI cart system equipped with an odometer. All radar reflections within the 90 ns for 400 MHz antenna and 195 ns for 70 MHz antenna (two-way-travel) time window were recorded digitally in the field as 16 bit data and 512 samples per radar scan.

Inside the basilica a total of 192 adjacent profiles across the four naves, the north transept and the entrance were collected alternatively in forward and reverse directions employing the GSSI cart system equipped with odometer. All radar reflections within the 120 ns for 400 MHz antenna (two-way-travel) time window were recorded digitally in the field as 16 bit data and 512 samples per radar scan. Nominal microwave velocities of about 8 cm/ns and 10 cm/ns, respectively outside and inside the basilica, were determined from fitting hyperbolas to the raw field

---

[3] Goodman and Piro, *GPR Remote Sensing*.

data. This was used in estimating a penetration depth from the GPR survey.

All the GPR data were processed in GPR-SLICE v7.0 Ground Penetrating Radar Imaging Software.[4] The basic radargram signal processing steps included: (i) post-processing pulse regaining; (ii) DC drift removal; (iii) data resampling; (iv) band pass filtering; (v) migration; and (vi) background filtering.

In order to generate a planimetric vision of all possible anomalous bodies the time-slice representation technique was applied using all processed profiles.[5] Time-slice data sets were generated by spatially averaging the squared wave amplitudes of radar reflections in the horizontal as well as the vertical. The squared amplitudes were averaged horizontally every 0.25 m along the reflection profiles 3 ns (for 400 MHz antenna) and 6 ns (for 70 MHz antenna) time windows (with a 10 per cent overlapping of each slice). The resampled amplitudes were gridded using the inverse distance algorithm with a search radius of 0.75 m.

## Data Analysis: Piazza Giovanni Paolo II: Areas A1 and B1

GPR amplitude maps generated from the profiles collected with 400 MHz antenna have been analysed with particular reference to the 19–22 ns, 25–28 ns, 30–34 ns, 41–45 ns, 47–50 ns and 58–61 ns (two-way-time) time windows, corresponding to averaged estimated depths of 0.88 m, 1.1 m, 1.3 m, 1.7 m, 2.0 m and 2.4 m respectively. This chapter presents a selection of GPR time slices of particular interest.

Fig. 4.2 shows the anomalies located at the estimated depth of 0.88 m (19–22 ns, twt), individuated in areas A1 and B1. At this depth, the area is characterised by many strong reflections due to the presence of utilities (6–7) and elements of possible structures (1–2–3–4–5).

The size of the anomalies are approximate: (1) strong anomaly with linear orientation and dimension x: 13.0 m; y: 3.5 m; (2) anomaly with semi-circular shape 9.0 m in diameter and 2.5 m long; (3) anomaly with average dimension of x: 2.0 m; y: 7.0 m; (4) two parallel anomalies with average dimension x: 2.0 m; y: 7.0 m; (5) anomalies with different size and dimension 13.0 m x 17.0 m; (6) and (7) – anomalies reflecting the presence of modern utilities of different dimensions.

---

[4] D. Goodman, *GPR-Slice 7.0, Manual* (www.gpr-survey.com, 2016).
[5] Goodman and Piro, *GPR Remote Sensing*.

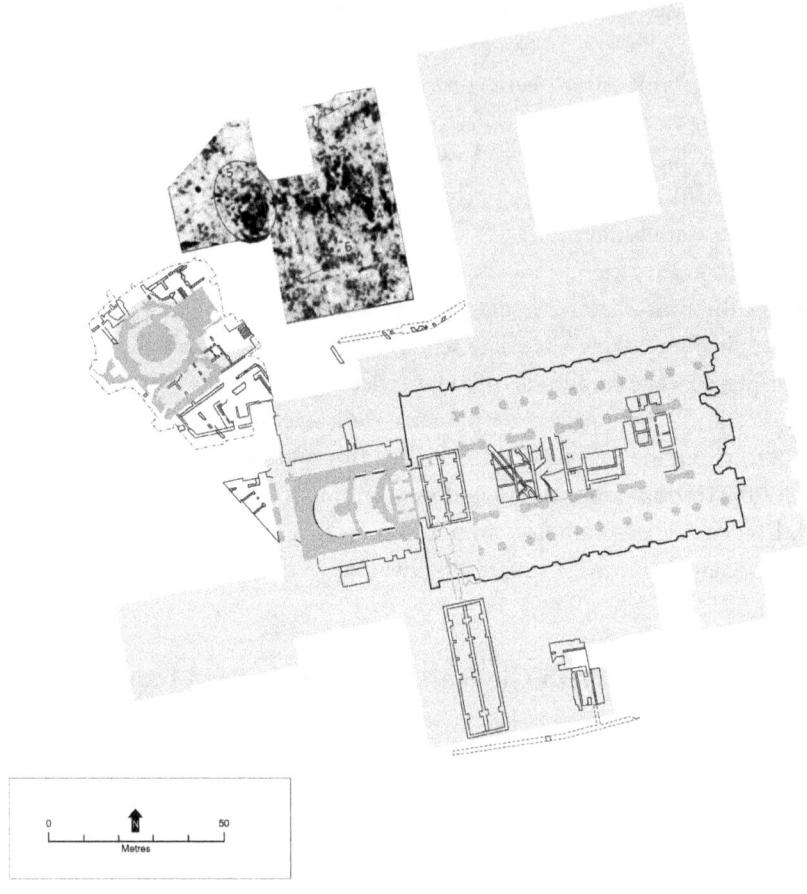

Fig. 4.2 Anomalies located with 400 MHz antenna at the estimated depth of 0.88 m (19–22 ns, twt), individuated in areas A1 and B1 (image: T. Ravasi).

Any attempt to interpret these anomalies must be mindful of the conditions in which they have been formed. They lie at a relatively shallow depth, a time depth of 0.88 m in an area where GPR can detect archaeological anomalies with confidence to at least 6.7 m. Crucially, however, the transects cover an area which has probably been clear of major structures for much of the last two millennia. While our understanding of the historical remodelling of the Caelian's slopes is still incomplete, it is probable that this part of the hill formed a natural plateau, occupied in part by the ancient Campus Caelemontanus. From the late seventh century this largely open area came to be referred to as the Campus Lateranensis, a nomenclature which again suggests a space largely free of buildings. The open character of the plateau seems to have endured through the centuries. In the absence of maps prior to the early modern period, we are obliged to consider the evidence of early engravings. Our earliest examples date only a few decades prior to Pope Sixtus V's remodelling, but nonetheless also show the area where the transects lie as largely devoid of major buildings. The earliest of these sources, Marten van Heemskerck's view of the Lateran palace drawn from the northwest around 1535, shows an open space, as does the celebrated map of the seven churches of Rome produced by Antoine Lafrery in 1575.[6] Two illustrations offered in Francino's 1588 guide to Rome further indicate that the space was uninterrupted by buildings.[7] That traces of more ancient and medieval features here may be closer to the modern ground surface than elsewhere in the Lateran quarter is also a product of the lack of building work thereafter.

Having discounted anomalies (6) and (7), which represent modern utilities, we can now consider the anomalies shown in Fig. 4.2. High-amplitude responses, such as those generated by anomalies (1), (3) and (4), indicate the presence of structural features, most likely walls. These anomalies either run parallel to or at right angles to the course of one of the best attested ancient roads in the area, the Via Tusculana, west of the basilica. Dating the structures represented by these anomalies is of course difficult; orientations such as these can endure for millennia, but consideration may be given also to the fact that, 170 m southeast of this site, walls on these alignments were excavated underneath the platform of the Castra Nova. Might these features too reflect pre-Severan activity? We should add that there are no anomalies in this area that can be plausibly connected with the Castra Nova itself.

Anomalies (1), (2) and (5) also appear in the next time slice featured, at an estimated depth of 1.75 m, and are therefore discussed further below.

Fig. 4.3 shows anomalies located at an estimated depth of 1.75 m (41–45 ns, twt), individuated in the same area as Fig. 4.2 (i.e. areas A1 and B1). At this depth the anomalies can be confirmed in terms of location and size, but with reduced intensity. The size of the anomalies, indicated below, are approximate: (1) this anomaly, also visible in Fig. 4.2, is still present with dimension of x: 19.5 m; y: 3.0 m, (2) this anomaly is still present with an average dimension of 230 m², (5) the corresponding anomaly is present

---

[6] M. van Heemskerck, *View of the Lateran Palace*, Berlin, Kupferstichkabinett inv. 79D2A, fol. 12.
[7] G. Francino, *Le cose maravigliose dell'alma citta' di Roma* (Venice, 1588), offers two illustrations. One is a somewhat stylised illustration heavily influenced by Lafrery's own engraving, showing the area immediately prior to the installation of the Obelisk of Thutmose III/IV. The other is a more technically accurate drawing showing it thereafter. Both again illustrate the open character of what has become a piazza.

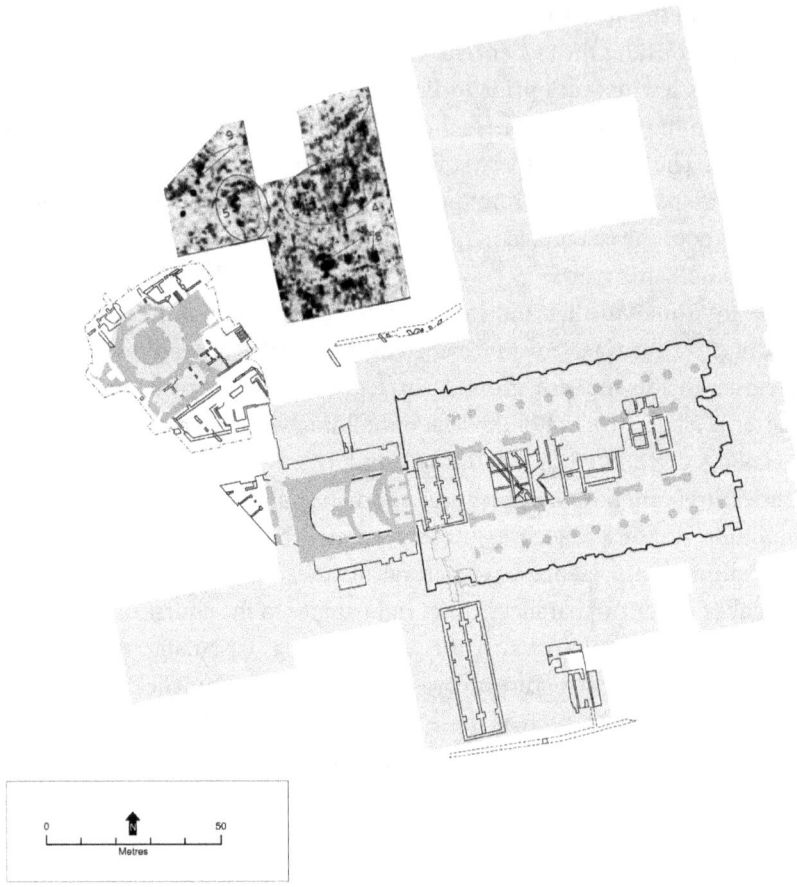

Fig. 4.3 Anomalies located with 400 MHz antenna at an estimated depth of 1.75 m (41–45 ns, twt), individuated in areas A1 and B1 (image: T. Ravasi).

with dimension of 125 m², (8) two parallel anomalies, of the same dimensions x: 1.7 m; y: 3 m, (9) shows two new anomalies with an average surface of 30 m².

As noted above, several features continue to appear at this depth. Anomaly (1), identified as a wall above, continues strongly. Anomaly (2) appears with far greater clarity now and can be seen to be regular in form; note in particular the rectangular space. The same feature was also identified in time slices at 0.9 m and 1.4 m (not shown). The alignment of the building approximates more closely to that of the *castra*, basilica and palace, than to the orientation of the Via Tusculana and the pre-Severan residences. Both the depths and location indicate that it must pre-date our earliest depictions of the Lateran area. The northeast/southwest wall of anomaly (2) does not extend beyond anomaly (4), suggesting that the two may in fact be in phase with one another.

Anomaly (5) was first detected in the 0.88 m time slices. Already traces of corners were visible. At this depth, the anomaly appears to have resolved into a distinct shape, which may represent the corner of a structure disturbed in later building. Interestingly, the anomaly is oriented on the same lines as the Severan *castra* baths; it also appears at approximately the same depth as excavated remains of those baths.

The results of the GPR survey at this depth can be compared with profiles collected with 70 MHz antenna. GPR amplitude maps derived from the profiles collected with 70 MHz antenna were analysed. Attention focused on time windows corresponding to the averaged estimated depths of 1.7 m, 2.1 m, 2.6 m, 3.0 m, 3.8 m, 4.7 m and 6.0 m respectively. Fig. 4.4 shows the anomalies located at an estimated depth of 6.0 m. At this depth, the area is characterised by anomalies contained in two sectors: 1 – is characterised (portion visible) by dimension x: 1.4 m; y: 13.0 m and x: 14.0 m; y: 10.0 m; 2 – is characterised by dimension (portion visible) x: 17.0 m; y: 3.5 m.

Anomaly (1) running north–south correlates with the line Lateran Project team members believe is the most likely course of the *castra* wall, but the apparent right-angle return is notably further south than scholars have previously proposed for the extremity of the *castra*.[8] It is possible therefore that this corner merely represents a section of wall with a building abutting it, or that, given its depth, it represents an earlier structure predating the *castra*.

To the south anomaly (2) indicates an area of high amplitude, a concentration that may perhaps be associated with a large area of debris. It is hard to offer further archaeological interpretation of the results from the 70 MHz antenna without additional investigation.

## Data Analysis: Piazza San Giovanni in Laterano – Areas A2, B2 and C2

East of the archbasilica, in areas A2, B2 and C2, GPR survey detected different patterns of development. This area is of particular interest because it housed a substantial part of the *patriarchium*. Fig. 4.5 shows the anomalies located at an estimated depth of 1.35 m (30–34 ns, twt), individuated in the areas A2, B2

---

[8] See Haynes and Liverani, Chapter 6 in this volume.

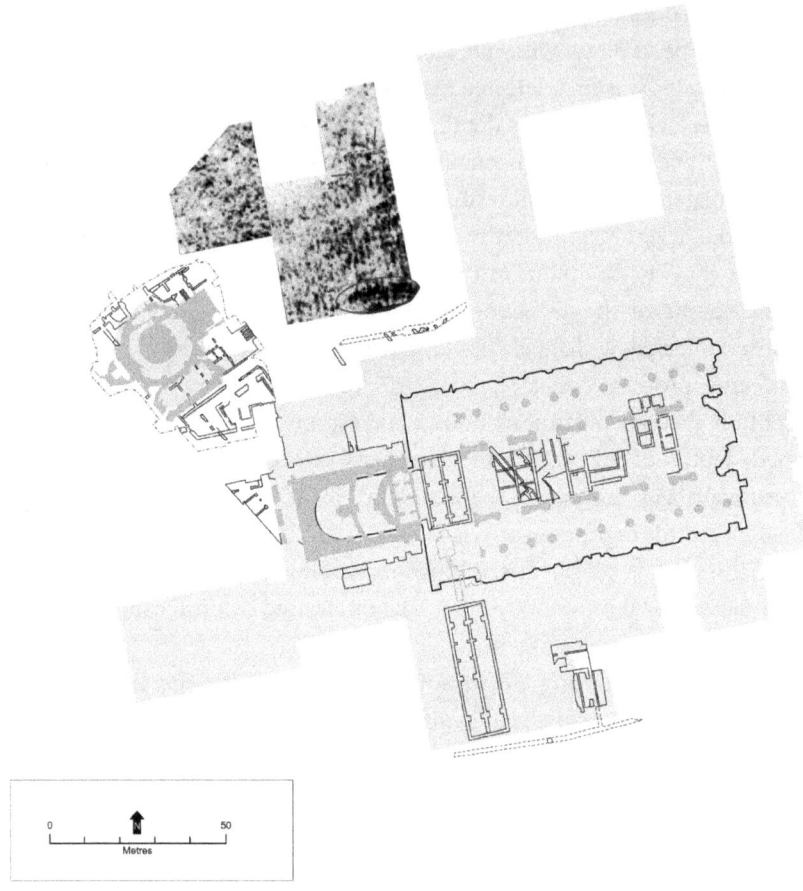

Fig. 4.4 Anomalies located with 70 MHz antenna at an estimated depth of 6.0 m, individuated in Areas A1 and B1 (image: T. Ravasi).

and C2. At this depth, the area is characterised by many strong reflections due to the presence of utilities (1) and structural elements (2–3–4–5–6–7).

The sizes of the anomalies, indicated below, are again an approximation based on the best possible evaluation of the radar signals. The anomalies at (1) indicate the presence of utilities (pipes and gully-holes). Anomalies (2) and (3) must be considered together; they are characterised by structures located perpendicular to each other inside an area with a total surface of 960 m². A sequence of squared features, 1.0 m apart from one another, emerge in association with anomaly (3). Feature (4) represents a linear anomaly with a low intensity x: 40.4 m; y: 2.0 m, (5) is an anomaly with a squared shape 3.7 m x 4.5 m, (6) is an anomaly with a dimension averaging 2.3 m x 4.2 m. Zone (7) is characterised by small anomalies.

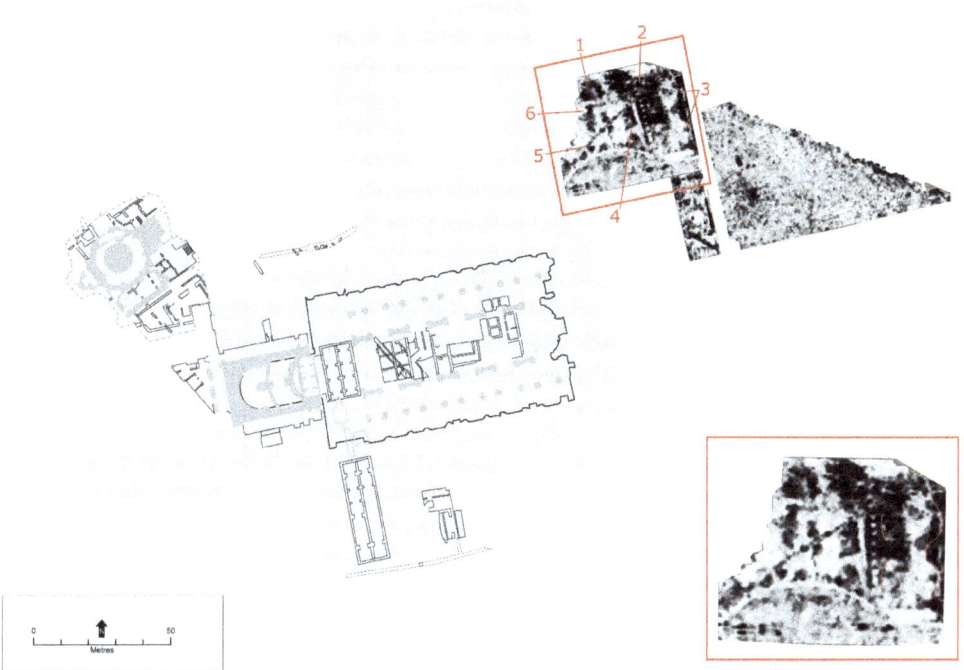

**Fig. 4.5** Anomalies located at an estimated depth of 1.35 m (30–34 ns, twt), individuated in the area A2, B2 and C2 (image: T. Ravasi).

Anomaly (3) suggests the presence of a substantial apse. Its shape and location immediately call to mind the celebrated *triclinium* built on the order of Pope Leo III (795–816) and completed by AD 800. The building was demolished along with most other elements of the old Lateran palace during the remodelling of the area by Sixtus V in 1586. Leo's *triclinium*, celebrated in the *Liber Pontificalis* for its marvellous size,[9] may have inspired Charlemagne's great hall at Aachen.[10] Certainly its form, and that of the eleven-apsed council hall Leo ordered built to the west soon after, echoed the palaces of contemporary monarchs. Unsurprisingly, therefore, the use of such architecture and the decor known to have accompanied it has been extensively discussed by those studying the papacy's claims to temporal power at this time. Copies of the mosaics that once adorned the *triclinium* were built into a tribunal next to the

---

[9] *LP* II, 3–4.
[10] B. Ward-Perkins, 'Constantinople: A city and its ideological territory', in G. P. Brogiolo, N. Gauthier and N. Christie (eds.), *Towns and their Territories between Late Antiquity and the Early Middle Ages* (Leiden, 2000), 325–46, at p. 340.

Scala Santa in 1743, 50 m east of what we believe to have been the building's original location.

If anomalies (2) and (3) relate to Leo's *triclinium* this discovery would have important implications. Some of the most important recent work on reconciling surviving sources for the building has been undertaken by Luchterhandt. He rightly stresses that producing an accurate reconstruction of the *patriarchium* in the time of Leo III represents a major challenge,[11] before presenting his own proposed plan and axonometric view of the complex.[12] Our GPR survey could be read to suggest that the position of the *triclinium*, and thus of some other elements of the complex, lay on a rather different alignment, somewhat to the southwest of that envisioned by Luchterhandt. Unfortunately, there are further challenges that confront scholars seeking to resolve this issue. Paolo Anesi's (1697–1773) depiction of the area indicates that there was a substantial partially exposed substructure between the Sancta Sanctorum and the papal palace, some elements of which may be associated with Leo III's *triclinium*, others from a still earlier period. Together these would have constituted a substantial feature, but no traces of it appear in the results of our georadar survey. The most likely explanation for the absence of a major anomaly here is that the subsequent re-engineering of the Caelian hill in modern times destroyed the substructure and much besides.[13]

Feature (5), a long and irregular anomaly running northeast–southwest is best explained as modern given its relationship to other features, but it does not correspond to known utilities in the area. The faint (negative – white) semi-circle in the southern part of the data just below (5) reflects work undertaken to raise the ground surface as it approached the entrance to the basilica from the north.

Fig. 4.6 shows the anomalies located at an estimated depth of 2.0 m (47–50 ns, twt), in the same area. As above, many strong reflections resulting from the presence of utilities/gully-holes (1) and structures (2-3-4-5-6) characterise the area at this depth. Feature (2) elements, also visible at an estimated depth of 1.35 m, are still present, but the corresponding anomalies at (3) have resolved themselves into three anomalies with perpendicular orientation, with an average dimension of x: 16.0 m; y: 1.7 m.

---

[11] M. Luchterhandt, 'Päpstlicher Palastbau und höfisches Zeremoniell unter Leo III', in C. Stiegemann and M. Wemhoff (eds.), *Kunst und Kultur der Karolingerzeit: Karl der Große und Leo III. in Paderborn* (Mainz,1999), 109–22, at p. 109.

[12] Luchterhandt, 'Päpstlicher Palastbau', 111 fig. 4, 113 fig. 6.

[13] P. Liverani, 'L'episcopio lateranense dalle origini all'Alto Medioevo', in S. Balcon-Berry, E. Baratte, J.-P. Caillet and D. Sandron (eds.), *Des 'domus ecclesiae' aux palais épiscopaux: Actes du colloque tenu à Autun du 26 au 28 novembre 2009* (Bibliothèque de l'Antiquité tardive 23) (Turnhout, 2012), 119–31.

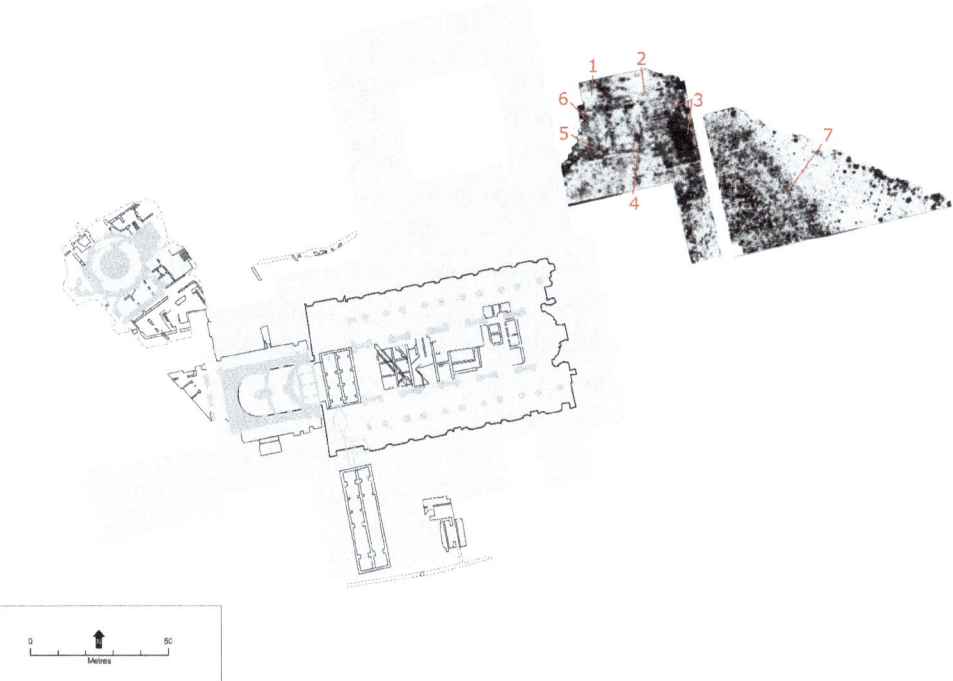

**Fig. 4.6** Anomalies located at an estimated depth of 2.0 m (47–50 ns, twt), individuated in Areas A2, B2 and C2 (image: T. Ravasi).

There are also two anomalies with dimension x: 2.0 m; y: 22.7 m. The area of (5) and (6) is characterised by small reflections. Diffused anomalies at (7) may reflect both the presence of collapsed structures and the undulating topography of the ground. The light-grey area is characterised by reflected signals corresponding to an expanse of subsoil with high attenuation.

Though at an estimated depth of 2.0 m, and therefore only approximately, 0.65 m below Fig. 4.5, the anomalies shown in Fig. 4.6 present a rather different picture. While most of the features shown above continue, this time slice offers sharper definition. The southern edge of feature (3) is much clearer, though the apsidal element is no longer visible. We may be seeing the lower part of that building's foundations. To the west, a square/semi-rectangular structure with a mid-north–south dividing wall emerges at (4–5–6). It is difficult to reconcile this complex with any known elements of the *patriarchium*, and it certainly appears very different in plan to the Casa dei Penitenzieri, known to have occupied the area adjacent to the *triclinium* prior to the demolition of both structures by Sixtus V. How much earlier in date it was is impossible to state at this stage, however.

## Data Analysis: The Survey inside the Basilica

For the purposes of this survey, the interior of the archbasilica was subdivided into eight sectors. The same GPR system was used as was employed for the exterior transects, albeit here fitted with the 400 MHz antenna only. Time-slice data sets were generated by spatially averaging the squared wave amplitudes of radar reflections in the horizontal as well as the vertical. The squared amplitudes were averaged horizontally every 0.25 m along the reflection profiles 4 ns (for 400 MHz antenna) time windows with a 5 per cent overlapping of each slice. The resampled amplitudes were gridded using the inverse distance algorithm with a search radius of 0.75 m. GPR amplitude maps related to the profiles collected with 400 MHz antenna have been analysed, focusing on the 3–7 ns, 10–14 ns, 17–21 ns, 24–28 ns, 38–42 ns, 52–56 ns, 59–63 ns, 66–70 ns, 73–77 ns, 80–84 ns, 87–91 ns and 94–97 ns twt slices. These correspond to averaged estimated depths of 0.4 m, 0.7 m, 1.0 m, 1.4 m, 2.0 m, 2.5 m, 3.0 m, 3.5 m, 4.0 m, 4.5 m, 5.0 m and 5.5 m respectively.

Anomalies located at the estimated depth of 2.0 m (38–42 ns twt), individuated in the area inside the basilica are shown in Fig. 4.7. At this depth, reflection of radar signals from the centre of the ceiling must be taken into consideration. As with the survey results above, the nature of GPR data prevents us offering anything more than approximate sizes for the anomalies, but it is possible to offer a broad characterisation as follows: (a1) linear anomalies, with dimensions 1.0 x 4.0 m, (a2) an area explored in excavations in 1934–8 (to the west) and 1977 (to the east) and partially backfilled, (a3) two anomalies with an average dimension of x: 4.0 m; y: 1.6 m. Two other anomalies, (a4) an isolated feature 4.3 x 3.5 m and (a5) an anomaly of 4.7 x 3.4 m, are noted here but their interpretation will be held over to the discussion of the 4.2 m time slice (Fig. 4.8).

The GPR results here offer an important complement to the analysis of exposed archaeology beneath the nave. Anomalies (a1) can be observed beneath every aisle, on both the north and south sides of the basilica, at regular intervals. Their course connects columns on each side of each aisle, suggesting that they served to underpin the columns. Their presence almost certainly relates to the substantial remodelling of the basilica interior by Borromini commissioned by Pope Innocent X in 1646; a process that had significant implications for the arrangement of the aisle columns. Here, therefore, GPR analysis appears to illuminate seventeenth-century engineering practice.

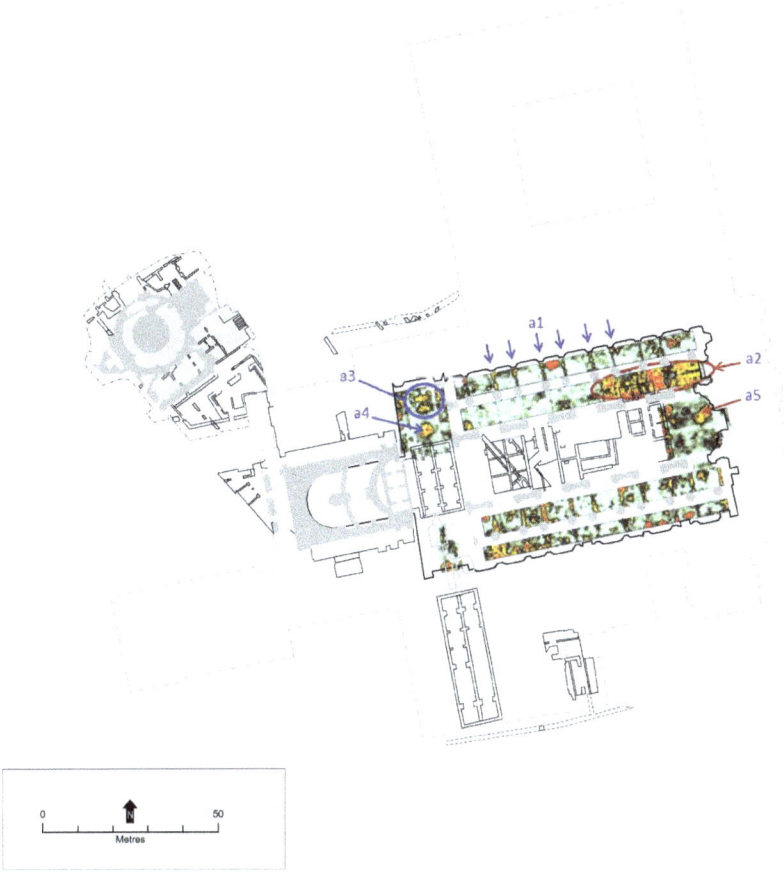

**Fig. 4.7** Anomalies located at the estimated depth of 2.0 m (38–42 ns twt), individuated in the area inside the basilica (image: T. Ravasi).

A rather different process accounts for the substantial anomaly (a2). This corresponds to the northern end of two separate phases of intervention, the works of Josi in the 1930s and by the Servizi Tecnici del Governatorato SCV in 1977. The highly distinct response reflects the fact that this area was not backfilled prior to the reinstatement of the basilica floor. Traces of anomalies corresponding to (a1) can be seen, suggesting that this work left this underpinning intact.

Of particular interest to the Lateran Project team was the major anomaly at (a3). This can be observed in GPR survey results to a depth approximating to around 6 m below the basilica floor. The position is of considerable importance as it occupies the same spot beneath the north transept as does an area extensively investigated by Krautheimer and Corbett in the late

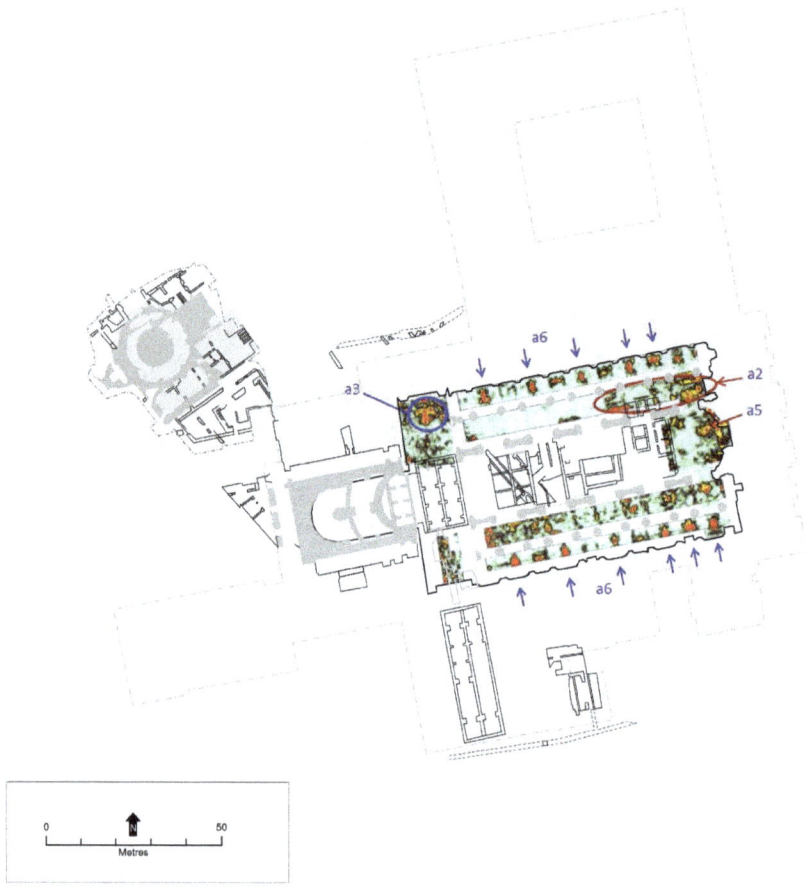

**Fig 4.8** Anomalies located at an estimated depth of 4.2 m (80–84 ns twt), individuated inside the basilica (image: T. Ravasi).

1950s beneath the southern transept.[14] Krautheimer and Corbett found a Constantinian wall (Wall B) intersecting earlier Severan features at this point, and as these features are still accessible beneath the cathedral floor, members of the Lateran team have been able to re-examine it at length. Krautheimer interpreted Wall B as evidence for the foundations of an original 'aisle-transept', an understanding that Bosman, working with the Lateran team on the visualisation of the original building, contests. The presence of a mirror feature underneath the north transept allows for a new and different view of the initial layout and spatial structure of the basilica in the early fourth century to that advanced by Krautheimer.[15]

---

[14] *CBCR* V, 30 with fig. 16, 32–3 figs. 21, 23, 24, 25a and b.
[15] See Bosman, Chapter 9 in this volume.

Anomalies located at an estimated depth of 4.2 m (80–84 ns twt), individuated in the area inside the basilica, are shown in Fig. 4.8. At this depth, too, the area is characterised by many strong reflections due to the presence of several different structural elements, but several of the most important concentrations noted above can still be seen.

The results suggest the continuity of some phenomena observed in the last figure. At (a2) a few linear anomalies related to subsurface structures remain, possibly representing twentieth-century excavations, while at (a3) a clearer picture emerges; two anomalies can be seen, orientated perpendicular to each other and with an approximate size of x: 4.3 m; y: 1.6 m and 1.7 x 4.7 m. The relationship of the (a3) anomalies with one another is paralleled in the archaeologically observable relationship of Krautheimer's Constantinian Wall B to the Severan in the southern transept. Lying alongside the distinct anomaly (a5) which was already observable at depth of 2.0 m (see Fig. 4.7) lies a second anomaly 1.6 x 10.8 m. The relationship of these two features to one another and the depth at which they are recorded may indicate that they are related to buildings of the *castra*; they certainly share the same orientation. A series of anomalies (a6) averaging 1.6 x 3.0 m lie below and between the positions occupied by the anomaly group (a1) documented at 2.0 m, but their role and character remains unclear. It is possible that they too are related to the works undertaken by Borromini in the seventeenth century, but if so their function and character are unclear.

## Conclusions

Ground Penetrating Radar has played, and will continue to play, an important role in archaeological and architectural survey. Its potential should always be considered when setting a research agenda for sites on this scale. Certainly the GPR surveys at the Lateran have produced significant and fruitful results. The use of 400 and 70 MHz antenna has enabled observations to depths of up to 3.4 and 6.7 m respectively in the area around the basilica, while the 400 MHz antenna has detected anomalies up to 5.5 m beneath its floors.

The location, depth, shape and size of a range of buried structures has been determined by GPR, but their interpretation is by no means straightforward. Multiple very different sources must be considered when weighing potential interpretations. Yet even with the advantages of the Lateran site – the access to sub-surface features revealed by earlier fieldwork and the range of historical documents depicting the basilica and its environs through the centuries – there are still notable gaps in our knowledge that oblige us to qualify many of our interpretations with a note of caution. The sheer challenge of maintaining a cathedral and indeed a major thoroughfare for over 1,700 years has meant that multiple interventions capable of generating notable anomalies will have taken place, only a few of which will have been documented. And while our understanding of the natural shape of the Caelian hill continues to develop, not least through ongoing GPR research, it remains limited – restricting our capacity to extrapolate the rough date of features from their relative depth.

Our quest to illuminate certain key themes by GPR has proved only partially successful. Work on our first aim, to learn more about private residences of the imperial period, has yielded strong evidence for structural elements that may be associated with them. It also provided indications that property boundary and road orientations archaeologically attested around the Via Tusculana continued further east.

Elements of the Castra Nova have remained notably elusive, however, even though GPR survey across the archbasilica floor may have identified some further elements of the fort's interior. The wall that once surrounded the *castra* cannot be traced with confidence, even in those areas where we believe we know the line it followed, though interestingly one feature, identified 6 m below the modern ground surface, corresponds exactly with this projected course. We must expect that the Constantinian builders would have had to dismantle some of the fort wall's circuit, a necessity not only given changing patterns of access, but also perhaps to assert the site's transformation from the military stronghold of the new emperor's predecessor to its new function. It was not unrealistic to hope for some trace of the wall's foundations, but we must acknowledge that they are not currently discernible in the survey area. The maxim absence of evidence is not evidence of absence should be recalled here, as in other such surveys.

Yet there are consolations. GPR in the A1, B1 does reveal a series of features that surely attest to the extent of a series of building orientations archaeologically observable northeast of the *castra*/basilica site, while the discoveries to the east in A2, B2 are especially noteworthy. The possibility that elements of Leo's *triclinium* can be identified raises significant questions for students studying the topography of the *patriarchium*'s many parts. Within the basilica, the GPR survey has yielded results of fundamental importance to our interpretation of the Constantinian phase, while at the same time apparently illuminating the engineering procedures that literally underpinned Borromini's transformative programme of works.

# 5 | The First Residential Phases of the Lateran Area and a Hypothesis to Explain the So-Called Trapezoidal Building

GIANDOMENICO SPINOLA

It is worthwhile to re-examine a number of structures excavated in the nineteenth and twentieth centuries in the light of the most recent archaeological studies[1] in order to advance hypotheses about the development of the Lateran area. Data now available make it possible to present a series of observations on the first houses located in the area underneath the nave of the basilica, and to attempt to clarify the function of the so-called Trapezoidal Building that lies today beneath the basilica's apse.

This chapter argues that, with regard to the first extensive building in the area, it is possible to identify parts of an Augustan-age suburban villa, most likely a single property positioned between the Via Tusculana and Via Asinaria. The first, residential, part of this complex can only be partially seen below the structures of the Castra Nova Equitum Singularium and the so-called Trapezoidal Building. These residential quarters lay to the west in the direction of the main road (Via Tusculana) and shared its alignment. The eastern half of the complex was less lavishly appointed; it was structured around a pillared courtyard (lying below the point where the *principia* of the Castra Nova was subsequently built), oriented along a suburban roadway and probably in close proximity to the *pars rustica* of the villa. In the second half of the second century AD, following a series of intermediate phases which transformed the western portion, the eastern half of the complex was remodelled through a number of operations, including the raising of the

---

This chapter was translated from the Italian by Dr Alexander Agostini.

[1] I. P. Haynes, P. Liverani, G. Spinola and S. Piro, 'The Lateran Project', *PBSR* 80 (2012), 369–71; I. P. Haynes, P. Liverani, S. Piro and G. Spinola, 'The Lateran Project: Interim report on the July 2012 and January 2013 seasons (Rome)', *PBSR* 81 (2013), 360–3; I. P. Haynes, P. Liverani, G. Spinola, S. Piro and I. Peverett, 'Progetto Laterano: Primi risultati', *Rendiconti della Pontificia Accademia Romana di Archeologia* 86 (2014), 1–19; I. P. Haynes, P. Liverani, G. Spinola, S. Piro, I. Peverett and A. Turner, 'The Lateran Project: Interim report for the January 2014 Season (Rome)', *PBSR* 82 (2014), 331–5; I. P. Haynes, P. Liverani, I. Peverett, G. Spinola and A. Turner, 'The Lateran Project: Interim report for 2015–2016 seasons (Rome)', *PBSR* 84 (2016), 311–16; G. Spinola, 'Nuove ipotesi per l'area sotto la basilica lateranense: La *villa suburbana* e il possibile *valetudinarium* dei Castra Nova Equitum Singularium', *Bolletino dei Monumenti, Musei e Gallerie Pontificie* 35 (2017), 61–92.

northeastern terrace; this contributed to the enlargement of the lavish residential part of the complex that in the meantime had taken on the form of a large *domus* located on the margins of Rome's urban boundaries.

The so-called Trapezoidal Building, adjacent to and contemporary with the main nucleus of the Severan *castra*, interpreted in the past as lodgings for the officers of the *equites* and recently imagined as a *macellum*, might, it is suggested here, instead be reinterpreted – on the basis of its plan, infrastructure and decorative apparatus – as the *castra*'s *valetudinarium*.

## The Suburban Villa

The first significant residential phase that can be identified in the area consists of a building complex arranged on different levels and identifiable as part of a suburban villa on the basis of its plan and urban location (Fig. 5.1). This first phase is characterised by walls in *opus incertum* and *opus quasi reticulatum*, with short lines in brickwork, mainly of *opus testaceum*, and angles in tuff blocks, recognisable as a first version of *opus mixtum*, uncommon in Rome, but in this case ascribable, as we shall see, to the Augustan age.[2] This technique was used especially in the lower eastern terracing, while other walls in *reticulatum*, with angles in *opus testaceum*, pertain to the corridors of the upper terracing (Fig. 5.2).

[2] In Rome as in Ostia, Tivoli, southern Latium and Campania, the use of *opus quasi reticulatum* and *reticulatum* with lines first in stone (see M. Tonbrägel, 'Considerazioni sull'origine dell'opus incertum: il caso delle ville repubblicane di Tivoli', in F. M. Cifarelli (ed.), *Tecniche costruttive del tardo ellenismo nel Lazio e in Campania: Atti del Convegno (Segni, 3 dicembre 2011)* (Rome, 2013), 33–42), and then in brickwork, is attested from the first century BC (see G. Lugli, *La tecnica edilizia romana* (Rome, 1957), plate CLI, fig. 1; F. Coarelli, 'Architettura sacra e architettura privata nella tarda repubblica', in École française de Rome (ed.), *Architecture et société: De l'archaïsme grec à la fin de la République. Actes du Colloque international organise par le Centre national de la recherche scientifique et l'École française de Rome (Rome 2-4 décembre 1980)* (Rome, 1983), 191–217, at pp. 201–2; M. A. Tomei, '*Domus* oppure *lupanar*? I materiali dallo scavo Boni della "casa repubblicana" a ovest dell'Arco di Tito', *MEFRA* 107 (1995), 549–619; J.-P. Adam, *L'arte di costruire presso i Romani* (Milan 2006), 143–7; C. Ebanista, 'Il complesso archeologico dei Santi Quaranta: Archeologia e storia', in M. Rotili (ed.), *Benevento nella Tarda Antichità: Dalla diagnostica archeologica in contrada Cellarulo alla ricostruzione dell'assetto urbano* (Naples, 2006), 179–210; H. Broise and V. Jolivet, *Pincio 1. La villa Médicis et le couvent de la Trinité-des-Monts à Rome: Réinvestir un site antique* (Rome, 2009), 162–7; M. Buonfiglio, 'M. E. Blake e lo sviluppo dell'*opus testaceum* a Roma: Il "caso" del Teatro di Marcello', *Musiva & Sectilia* 7 (2010), 109–22; M. Buonfiglio, 'L'utilizzo di laterizi nella costruzione augustea del Teatro di Marcello', in E. Bukowiecki, R. Volpe and U. Wulf-Rheidt (eds.), *Il laterizio nei cantieri imperiali: Roma e il Mediterraneo: Atti del I Workshop 'Laterizio' (Roma, 27-28 Novembre 2014)*, Archeologia dell'Architettura 20 (special issue) (2015), 13–19; P. Tomassini, '"Scavare" negli Archivi: La domus tardo-repubblicana e giulio-claudia sotto al Caseggiato delle Tabernae Finestrate di Ostia (IV, V, 18): Nuove e vecchie scoperte', *Journal of Fasti Online* (2016), 1–12.

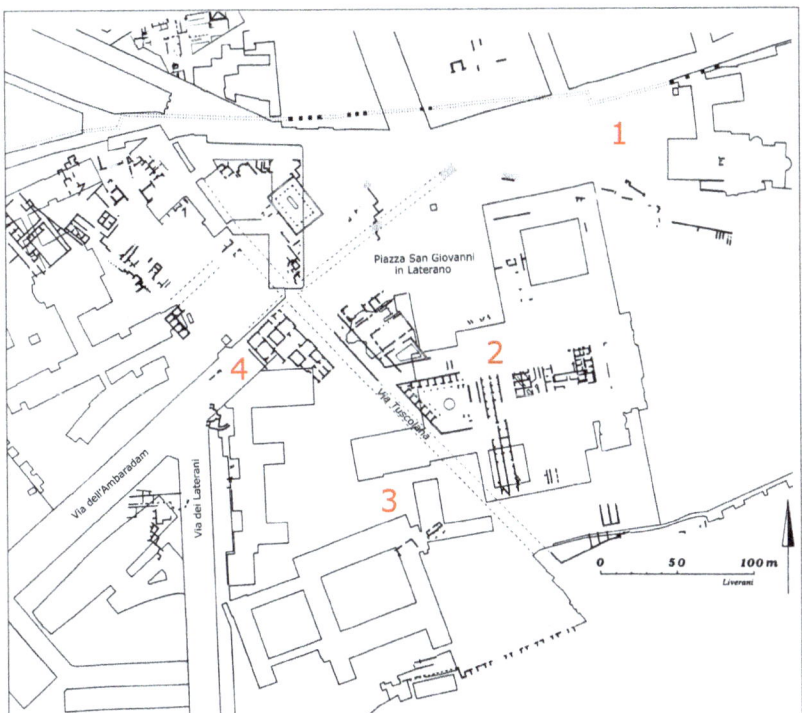

**Fig. 5.1** The Lateran area. 1. *Domus* of Titus Sextius Lateranus; 2. Suburban villa (Plautius Lateranus?); 3. Villa of Lucius Lusius Petellinus; 4. Villa of Lucius Piso (Image: T. Ravasi. Adapted from Liverani (ed.), *Laterano 1*).

The layout of the villa develops from an entrance area set on a roadway identified as a portion of the Via Tusculana. Of this section – on the basis of the plans, drawings and documentation by Andrea Busiri Vici[3] – only a large open area with an extensive pool basin is discernible, perpendicularly oriented to the road alongside a number of rooms set to the east and following the same direction. The location of these rooms is further identifiable due to patterns of subsidence in the mosaic courtyard of the Trapezoidal Building. Indeed, all these structures, which were discovered in 1875–6, lay beneath this courtyard, which dates to the Severan period (Fig. 5.3).[4] The area in question may be identified as a large *peristilium*, constituting a monumental entrance to the

---

[3] See Francini, Chapter 7 in this volume.
[4] These rooms were certainly present when the successive restructuring took place, described by Busiri Vici (see Francini) as delimitated by walls in *opus latericium*, although it is not possible to ascertain whether the restoration pertains to rooms already present in the first phase. Pit testing conducted in the nineteenth century below the mosaic flooring seems, in fact, to be limited only to small and scarcely below-soil portions of the undulated Severan mosaic.

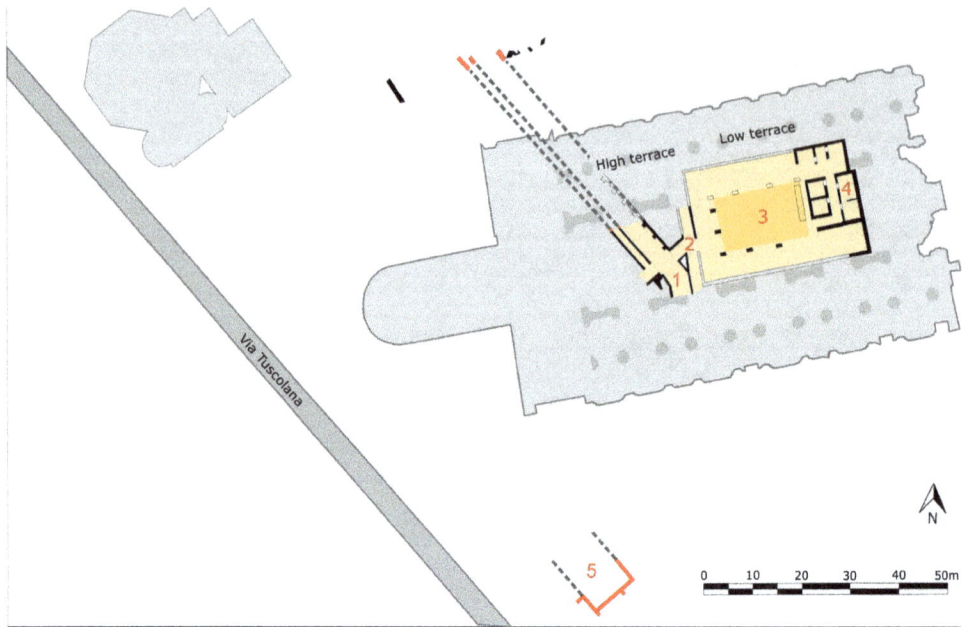

**Fig. 5.2** The suburban villa under the basilica: 1. Corridor; 2. Staircase between the terraces; 3. Court; 4. *Cubicula*; 5. Room excavated in 1890 (Image: T. Ravasi).

residence, overlooked by the most luxurious rooms, and in the style of other suburban villas such as the Pompeian Villa of Diomedes (Fig. 5.4).[5] The successive development of the *castra*, especially with the excavation of cellars under the westernmost range of *castra* buildings, led to the obliteration of some of the residential structures to the east of the *peristilium*. Further east, where the *castra* buildings did not have cellars, some elements were preserved up to a height of 3 m when they were buried beneath the fort platform. At one point, two adjoining corridors can be seen (see Fig. 5.5). The first is quite narrow and at a slightly higher level than the one located in the entrance area, whereas the second, connected to the first (at least in the second phase) by way of a small marbled staircase, is wider and partially set against the hillside. Both run parallel to the route of the Via Tusculana. Beyond these corridors to the east the alignment of the residence changes – possibly reflecting the presence of a suburban roadway located downhill – and it takes on the orientation that

[5] H. Dessales, J. Ponce, M. Carrive, J. Cavero, J. Dubouloz, É. Letellier, F. Marchand-Beaulieu, F. Monier, A. Péron, A. Tricoche and Y. Ubelmann, 'Pompéi: Villa de Diomède', in *Chronique des activités archéologiques de l'École française de Rome, Les cités vésuviennes, mis en ligne le 02 février 2015* (Rome, 2015), 1–15; H. Eristov, 'Décors méconnus de la Villa de Diomède', in T. Ganschow, M. Steinhart and D. Berges (eds.), *Otium: Festschrift für Volker Michael Strocka* (Remshalden, 2005), 75–86.

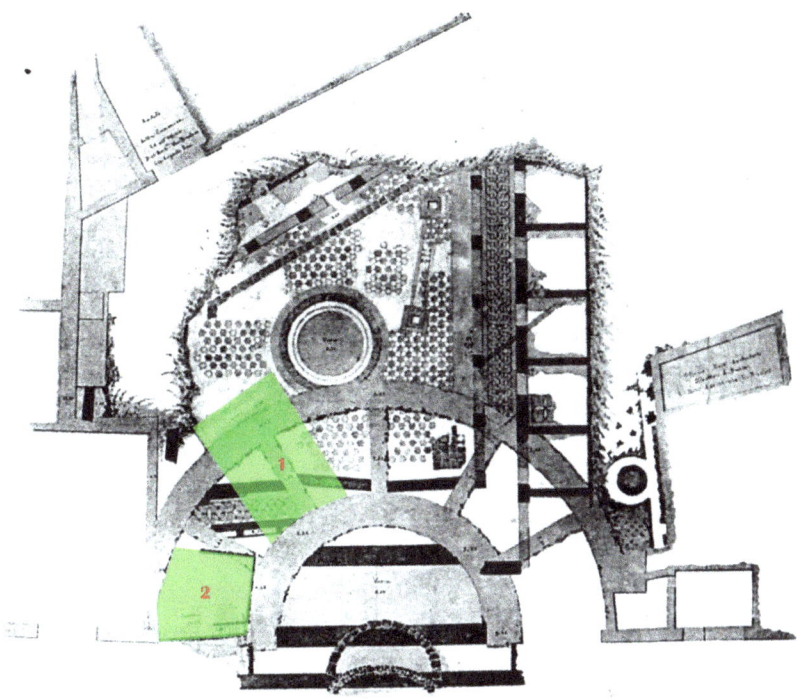

**Fig. 5.3** The excavations of the Trapezoidal Insula in 1876. 1. The basin located in the *peristilium* near the Via Tusculana; 2. Underground room of second phase (Image: T. Ravasi, adapted from a plan by Busiri Vici published in Morbidelli, *L'abside di S. Giovanni in Laterano*).

the *castra* and then the basilica would subsequently assume. A staircase leads to the summit of the hill, set 3 m above, where it was possible to gain access to the lower eastern terrace that was presumably accessible by way of two slanting staircases.

The lower terrace featured a rectangular porticoed courtyard with tuff block pillars (see Fig. 5.2). On the side opposite to the entrance, the porticoed courtyard is characterised by a series of rooms arranged on two floors and lacking any form of decoration or distinctive element that might help in identifying their original function. The lower floor appears to be occupied by rooms with back walls built directly against the hillside, whereas the upper floor is characterised by rooms with large windows (late Antonine in date) set high up the wall. These structural details indicate that the hill rose slightly towards the east. The structure, building technique and layout would suggest that the lower terracing operated as a secondary area of the villa, possibly a private area or service quarter, definitely less luxurious than the one near the Via Tusculana.

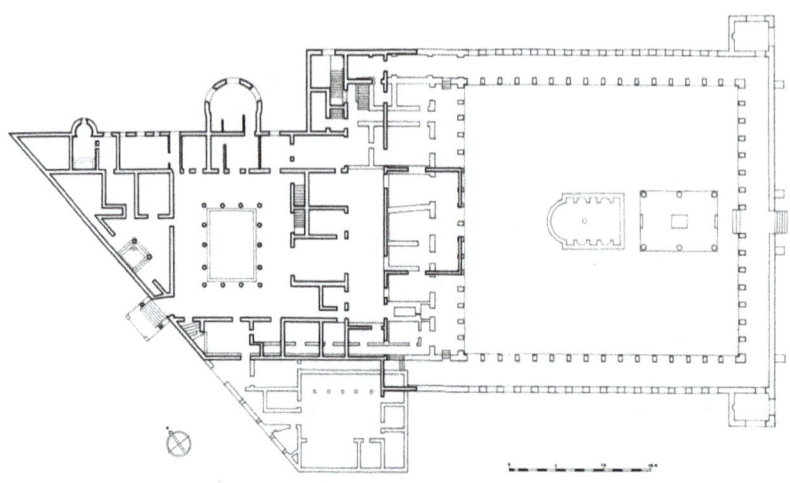

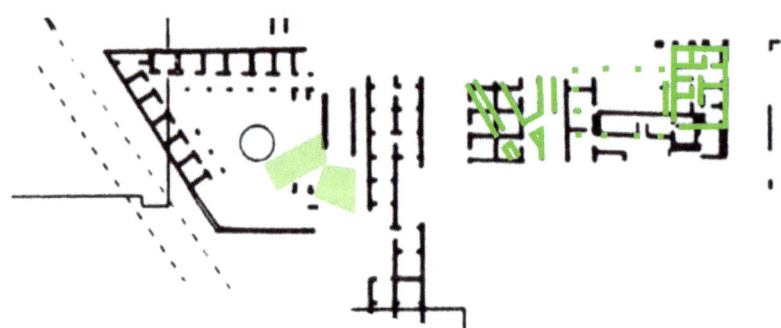

Fig. 5.4 Pompeii, the Villa of Diomedes and Rome, the Lateran Villa (Image: T. Ravasi. The plan of the Villa of Diomedes is adapted from Maiuri and Pane, *La casa di Loreio Tiburtino*).

The structural development of the villa along two terraces – corresponding also to two different quarters of the residence – divided by a triangular area set at a higher level – appears to be determined by the orography of the hill. The first terrace – with the more public-facing elements – develops at the front along the Via Tusculana and up to the wider corridor, the latter set against the hillside bank and maintaining approximately the same floor level. Climbing two staircases, from this sector one arrives at the summit of the hill. There – near the vertex of an open triangular area (whose shape is determined by the change in orientation)[6] – a wide passage is present, from where it is possible to reach the lower terrace, presumably connected by steps and set at a height that is not dissimilar to the one of the previous large terrace (see Fig. 5.5). Here a secondary quarter is located, possibly more private and domestic. Still further eastwards, on an irregular slope towards the valley along which runs the Via Asinaria, and more peripherally, one must imagine the presence of another terrace, possibly functioning as garden or the *pars rustica* of the villa.

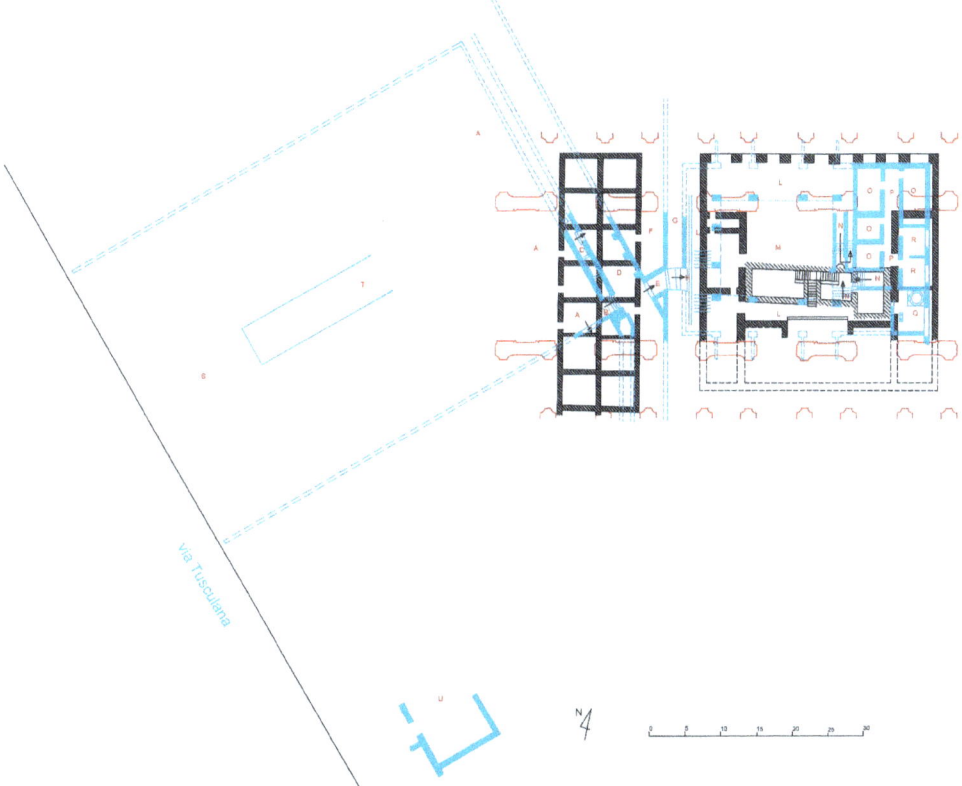

**Fig. 5.5** The east side of the suburban villa. Suburban villa (sky blue) under the basilica (red) and the *castra* (black): A 'Noble rooms' area; B Staircase between two corridors; C Low corridor; D High corridor; E Vaulted staircase; F Open area; G Passage between the high and low terraces; H Staircase; L Portico; M Court; N Staircase; O Underground rooms; P Corridor; Q Room with kiln; R *Cubicula*; S Entrance area; T Peristyle with large basin; U Room excavated in 1890 (Image: L. di Blasi, adapted from Colini, *Storia e topografico del Celio*).

---

[6] The size of this upper terracing is not calculable, but it certainly tends to extend in a north/westerly direction.

Ceramic material, fixtures, sculptures, architectural and pictorial decorations, recovered over the course of a number of excavations undertaken at different times in the area, can all be linked to this first phase.[7] In particular, a *terminus ante quem* can be provided for the wall structures by the numerous fresco fragments featuring garden scenes.[8] These are comparable, for example, to the ones dating to the Augustan period from the Villa of Livia at Prima Porta, or to the Casa della Farnesina, the auditorium of Maecenas – in Rome – and to those in the Pompeian houses of the Bracciale d'Oro, of the Menandro, of the Cubicoli Floreali, and of the Frutteto. Other panels show fresco fragments featuring large yellow, red and black brushstrokes enclosing figurative elements, with stylistic characteristics that can be chronologically associated to Pompeian and Roman works dating to between AD 20 and 40.[9]

Some of the excavations conducted in 1958–9 and 1963 between the baptistery and the Lateran palace, and between the latter and the Scala Santa, brought to light various rooms that might be related to the large villa or to other nearby ones. Walls in *opus mixtum*, comprised of *reticulatum*, tuff blocks and bricks and generically dated to the early empire, were found, along with a mosaic featuring a labyrinthine pattern and crenellated cornice, dated to the first half of the first century BC, and a polychrome mosaic composed of small *tesserae*.[10]

---

[7] Naturally, one cannot be certain of the pertinence of the material, presently preserved in the *antiquarium* of the excavations (see G. Spinola, 'Sculture, rilievi, decoazione, architettonica, iscrizioni e reperti ceramici', in P. Liverani (ed.), *Laterano 1: Scavi sotto la Basilica di S. Giovanni in Laterano*, vol. I: *Materiali* (Vatican City, 1998), 17–114, at pp. 112–14). A good-quality piece such as the Corsini Throne, however, must be added to the aforementioned material. This consists of an eclectic neo-Attic work from the first imperial age found in 1732–4 alongside a number of portraits below the Corsini chapel in the Lateran basilica, corresponding to the area of the lower terracing, but possibly pertaining to a more ancient sepulchral edifice (see *CIL* VI, 29796; P. Liverani, 'Introduzione topografica', in Liverani (ed.), *Laterano 1*, 6–16, at p. 15, with previous bibliography). In the same fashion, possibly in relation to another not too far away edifice – the Iseum Metellinum – is a series of Augustan-age Egyptian-style fixtures (see G. Spinola, 'Alcune sculture egittizzanti nell'area lateranense: Nuove testimonianze dell'Iseum Metellinum?' *Bollettino dei Monumenti, Musei e Gallerie Pontificie* 21 (2001), 75–101).

[8] E. M. Moormann and S. T. A. M. Mols, 'Le pitture romane: Frammenti e resti in situ', in Liverani (ed.), *Laterano 1*, 115–32, at pp. 119, 121–2 and 130, nos. 44–66, 88, figs. 425–31.

[9] Moormann and Mols, 'Le pitture romane', 117–18 and 120–1, nos. 1, 5, 25, 75, 78, figs. 410, 417, 435, 437.

[10] F. Castagnoli, A. M. Colini, C. Buzzetti and G. Pisano Sartorio (eds.), 'Notiziario di scavi, scoperte e studi intorno alle Antichità di Roma e Campagna Romana 1946–1960: Prima parte', *Bullettino della Commissione archeologica Comunale di Roma* 83 (1972–3), 5–156, at p. 53; M. Nota Santi, 'La zona del Laterano', *Archeologia Laziale* 1 (1978), 2–5; K. Werner, *Mosaiken aus Rom: Polychrome Mosaikpavimente und Emblemata aus Rom und Umgebung* (Würzburg, 1994), 68–9, K21.

A series of works in *opus mixtum* composed of *reticulatum* and bricks are attributable to a second construction phase, chronologically ascribable to between the second half of the first century AD and the first half of the second century AD.[11] In the entrance area towards the Via Tusculana, near the pool basin, is a room built in *opus mixtum*. This room was later connected (perhaps with the construction of the Trapezoidal Building) by way of a staircase to another room in *opus testaceum* and set at the same height as the Severan floor. These rooms share a different alignment to the road network here. Certainly, a portion of the wall structures of the other rooms, which we can argue run below the Severan mosaic of the Trapezoidal Building's courtyard, are likely to date to this phase.

In this period, a radical change can be seen in the rooms set immediately to the east of the entrance area and in proximity to the summit of the hill, divisible into two chronologically close micro-phases. The narrower corridor was connected to the wider one by way of a marble staircase and a number of passageways, the wall of the latter being first reinforced by closing a number of the openings and, later on, by placing a series of pillars against it so as to further buttress it against at the hillside at its rear. A second staircase with vaulted ceiling was built between the pillared corridor and the summit of the upper terrace, in order to aggrandise the passage to the east in the direction of the lower terrace. At the end of this last micro-phase, the wall surfaces were enriched by the addition of an elaborate decorative scheme, still for the most part preserved, and composed of a marble base (removed during the successive works for the construction of the *castra*) and a series of frescoes, roughly dated to AD 120–40.[12]

In this case too, the elements associated with the second construction phase are quite numerous; noteworthy are a number of precious Corinthian-like pillar capitals, for the most part lyre-shaped or with a double S design, dated to AD 110–20.[13] The capitals were found during the excavations conducted by Enrico Josi in 1934–6, whose work focused mainly in the area of the lower terrace, although one cannot exclude the possibility that their original location was in one or more of the large public rooms that appear to have lain between the entrance area and the corridors.

---

[11] A number of frescoes mounted on panels can be considered as wall decorations from the Flavian period: see Mormann and Mols, 'Le pitture romane', 121 and 122. Other archaeological material preserved during the excavations is also dated to the second half of the first century AD (see Spinola, 'Sculture', 112).

[12] Mormann and Mols, 'Le pitture romane', 123–7, figs. 446–58.

[13] Spinola, 'Sculture', 51–84, figs. 149–57, 159–60, 216–62, 289–93.

The Severan infills, in fact, especially in the lower terrace, featured large mounds of marble material (still preserved to this day) of various origin (sculptures, marble slabs, domestic and funerary architectural elements), probably found by workmen during the construction of the *castra* and set aside for a possible future reuse that never took place.[14]

A restructuring of the residence in the second half of the second century AD, probably during the reign of Commodus, is visible only in the sector of the eastern terrace, which, together with a large infill, is set at the same height as the summit of the hill (Fig. 5.6). At this point the area featuring the domestic quarters assumes a more striking appearance, in line with the residential area near the Via Tusculana. The levelling by way of an infill of just less than 3 m entailed the raising of the pillared courtyard to the height of rooms that previously corresponded to the first floor; the rooms that had occupied the ground floor were almost all fully buried.[15]

Of these rooms on the eastern side of the courtyard, two *cubicula* with frescoed decorations and mosaic flooring,[16] together with an oven room which remained isolated and at the level of the complex prior to the infill,[17] remain well preserved.[18]

---

[14] It is believed that the fresco fragments mounted on 102 cement panels were originally found by Josi in 1934–8 in the area that initially featured domestic functions, precisely in the *cubicula*, the oven room and the last of the rooms used later on as cisterns. Despite this topographic collocation, one cannot exclude the possibility that following the late Flavian refurbishments conducted in the residential portion of the villa – and whether or not these were due to a fire – a number of decorative renovations were conducted, entailing the removal of a large portion of the walls along with their pictorial apparatus, and successively re-employed in raising the floor level of the residential area along with the *pars rustica* of the lower terrace. Moreover, many of the fresco fragments present identical pictorial portions to those still *in situ* in the residential quarters (the corridors of the upper terrace), whereas – in the other area excavated by Josi (corresponding to the lower terrace) – these fragments can only derive from spaces buried during the second half of the second century AD (the courtyard and adjacent rooms), the two *cubicula* differently frescoed in the Antonine period and the nearby space converted as an oven room.

[15] With the construction of the *castra*, the porticoed courtyard would have been converted into an open area of the *principia*, under which three rooms would have been employed as cisterns.

[16] Moormann and Mols, 'Le pitture romane', 127–30, figs. 459–68. Both the frescoes and the two different mosaic floorings find valid comparisons with examples dating to the end of the second and the beginning of the third century AD (see for example G. Becatti, *Scavi di Ostia*, IV: *Mosaici e pavimenti marmorei* (Rome, 1961), 201, nos. 381–83; P. Liverani and G. Spinola, *Mosaici in bianco e nero dal tratto vaticano della necropoli della via Trionfale: Aiscom, Atti del V Colloquio* (Ravenna, 1999), 220–1 fig. 3).

[17] Important evidence on the chronology of the elevation of the lower terrace is provided by five stamps set in the interior surface of the oven (*CIL* XV, 199) and dated to the end of the second century AD, but associated with others (*CIL* XV, 198) from the same *figlina* – the Veteris – dated to the reign of Commodus, together with another from AD 147–61.

[18] A recent survey (March 2016) – conducted by the author together with Claudia Valeri, Eleonora Ferrazza, Leonardo Di Blasi and Sabina Francini, whom I thank – helped distinguish the sockets

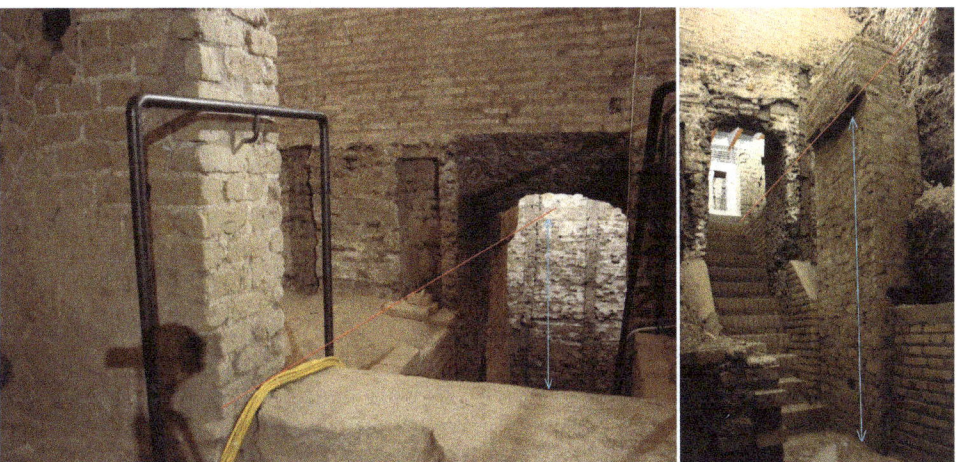

Fig. 5.6 An infill in the lower terracing and the elevation of the pillars (photo: author).

Ultimately, the restoration works that took place during the Flavian and Trajano-Hadrianic period affected only the more public part of the villa, whereas the Commodian-era activities were aimed at enhancing the quarter occupying the eastern terrace. During the second century AD, and due to the city's urban expansion, the complex appears to have taken on the form of a great urban *domus*, possibly with the loss of its *pars rustica* and its lowlands. This last private construction phase was short-lived. Only a few years later – between AD 194 and 196 – Septimius Severus had the Castra Nova Equitum Singularium built over it.

At this point it is possible to re-examine, on the basis of previous studies, some general observations on the private properties located in the area of the Lateran. The discovery in the vicinity of the Lateran of a number of lead *fistulae* displaying the name of the owner of the dwelling that the water system supplied allows us to define – although somewhat generically – the location of some of these properties. In 1873 – to the west of the baptistery, along the present-day Via Amba Aradam – a *fistula* was found inscribed with the name 'L. Piso[nis]', which would suggest linking the dwelling to the Calpurnii Pisoni, a residence confiscated by Nero in the wake of the conspiracy by Gaius Calpurnius Piso in AD 65.[19] Two other *fistulae* feature the name of Lucius Lusius Petellinus,[20] the first found in the 1800s below an

---

for the beams of the original flooring first level, along with those connected to the floor pertaining to the late Antonine phase, set around 25 cm above, and following the interment of a portion of the ground-level rooms.

[19] *CIL* XV, 7513.
[20] *CIL* XV, 7488; W. Eck, 'Domus: L. Lusius Petellinus', in *LTUR* II, 134; Spinola, 'Sculture', 87 n. 437.

edifice generally located in the vicinity of the Lateran basilica, the second discovered during the 1964 excavations for the enlargement of the house of the canons. These topographical indications allow us to place the two residences opposite the villa below the basilica and on the other side of the Via Tusculana: the Pisoni to the northwest, in the area later occupied by the so-called Severan baths, and the Lusi Petellini to the southwest, in the area towards the Lateran University and the Pontifical Roman Major Seminary. The place where two *fistulae* with the name 'Sextius Lateranus' were found in 1595 is not precisely located, although it appears as generically identifiable with the area corresponding to the square of Saint John Lateran towards the front of the basilica and the Scala Santa.[21]

The idea that Septimius Severus wanted to compensate his friend and consul Titus Sextius Lateranus for the past Neronian requisition of an ancestor's place of residence by donating another dwelling in the area of the Lateran, the Aedes Parthorum, interpreted as the remodelling of the house of Plautius Lateranus following the requisition, and as reported by various sources, has been the object of numerous studies that cannot be pursued further in the present work.[22]

Doubts on this historical interpretation stem mainly from the difference in the gentilitial name of the two individuals with the same *cognomen* of Lateranus: Titus Sextius Lateranus, a general of Septimius Severus and consul in AD 197, and Plautius Lateranus, designated consul involved in the AD 65 conspiracy. Their degree of relationship, although probable, does not in fact appear direct, and is made even more elusive by the chronological distance that separates them.[23]

It is possible, however, to observe that at least there is no unresolvable topographical and chronological incompatibility in following the hypothesis

---

[21] *CIL* XV, 7536; P. Liverani, 'Domus: Laterani', in *LTUR* II, 127.

[22] See A. M. Colini, *Storia e topografia del Celio nell'antichità* (Memorie della Pontificia Accademia Romana di Archeologica 7) (Vatican City, 1944), 372–5; P. Liverani, 'Le proprietà private nell'area lateranense fino all'età di Costantino', *MEFRA* 100, 2 (1988), 891–915; V. Santa Maria Scrinari, *Il Laterano in età imperial I: Dalle 'Aedes Laterani' alla 'Domus Faustae'* (Vatican City, 1991); Liverani, 'Introduzione topografica'; P. Liverani, 'Dalle *Aedes Laterani* al Patriarchio lateranense', *RAC* 75 (1999), 521–49; Liverani, 'Domus: Laterani', 248–9; P. Liverani, 'L'area lateranense in età tardo antica e le origini del patriarchio', *MEFRA* 116 (2004), 17–49, at pp. 20–3, 28–30, 34, 37, 48; D. Manacorda, 'Il Laterano e la produzione ceramica a Roma: Aspetti del paesaggio urbano', in A. Leone, D. Palombi and S. Walker (eds.), *Res Bene Gestae: Ricerche di storia urbana su Roma antica in onore di Eva Margareta Steinby* (Rome, 2007), 195–204; F. Consalvi, *Il Celio Orientale: Contributi alla carta archeologica di Roma Tav. VI settore H* (Rome, 2009), 84–91; C. Gnilka, 'Aedes Laterani', *Zeitschrift für Papyrologie und Epigraphik* 188 (2014), 70–80. See also Liverani, Chapter 2 in this volume.

[23] If this were the case, then the former would be a maternal great-uncle of the latter, who lived 130 years earlier.

regarding the pre-existence of this donation. I believe, in fact, that it can be reasonably affirmed that below the Lateran basilica, and before the construction of the Castra Nova Equitum Singularium, only a single large suburban villa is present, at least from the Augustan age, and not two different *domus* dating to the second half of the first century AD – a single grand residence, because from that very first phase the terraces characterised by residential structures appear to be connected to one another. It is identifiable as a suburban villa because it is located near the city, but on the outskirts of the populated centre, set on the fringes of the Regio II Caelimontium – between the so-called Servian Walls and the suburban route which the Aurelian Walls would later follow. Indirect traces of tombs that may have stood in the vicinity, probably along the Via Tusculana, can be found in the funerary material from the early to mid-imperial period, currently preserved in the *antiquarium* of the excavations. The building technique, the employment of early imperial construction methods, would be consistent with completion in the Augustan age, as would the decorative style of the numerous frescoed panels recovered. Therefore, at least for what can be observed *in situ*, there are no topographical, planimetric or chronological elements that can lead us to exclude the possibility that the tragic effects of the requisition by Nero in AD 65 actually took place in the great suburban villa.

Naturally, 'non-exclusion' cannot be considered as evidence of veracity; however, the reliability of ancient sources might be reconsidered. From a verse in one of Juvenal's Satires (10.15–18),[24] in which the 'egregiae Lateranorum aedes' are mentioned, it is possible to deduce that this must have been a complex of enormous size, and quite possibly larger than the area subsequently occupied by the Castra Nova Equitum Singularium, as recognisable from the evidence below the basilica. It is probable that at the beginning of the first century AD the suburban area of the Lateran was quite unoccupied and divided into large properties, and that the villa consisted of a single large property between the Via Tusculana and the Via Asinaria. Consequently, irrespective of the possible Neronian transfer of the structure into imperial ownership and its improbable renaming as Aedes Parthorum,

---

[24] Juv. 10.15–18: 'Temporis diris igitur iussuque Neronis Longinus et magnos Senecae praedivitis hortos clausit et egregias Lateranorum obsidet aedes tota cohors: rarus venit in coenacula miles' ('So during the Reign of Terror, at Nero's command, Longinus was banished, Seneca – grown too wealthy – lost his magnificent gardens, storm-troopers besieged the Lateranus' ancestral mansion. Garrets are very seldom the object of military raids', trans. A. Agostini in E. Barelli (ed.), *Satire: Testo latino a fronte*, 6th edn. (Classici greci e latini) (Milan, 1976)). The size of these residences can be inferred by the number of troops employed to surround and pillage them: a full cohort comprised 600 soldiers.

the Severan-age consul might have received as a gift only the northeastern portion of the Lateran residential complex towards the Via Asinaria, an area that was not a part of the structure of the barracks.[25] From the passage of Pseudo-Victor, it is clear that Titus Sextius Lateranus received a splendid residence as a gift from Septimius Severus, not just a plot of land on which to build.[26] What residence could this be if not part of the one we see continuing below the structure of the *castra* and the Lateran basilica?

The chronological sequence of the phases found in the villa below the basilica offer us other indicative analogies. After the first recorded phase of the villa, specifically the Augustan one (with successive Tiberian-age decorations), on the terraces of the 'residential' sector that descend towards the main front on the Via Tusculana, it is possible to observe a series of complete Flavian-period restorations that would strongly suggest a radical change in layout rather than a simple change in the function of many of the rooms. Consequently, I believe that the new wall structures attest to an imposing transformation of the villa, at least in the residential area. All this might have taken place in the wake of a destructive event which the sources of the *egregiae Lateranorum aedes* describe as Nero's besieging and marauding troops.

Furthermore, the possible presence of the Calpurnii Pisoni in the area of the Lateran might have favoured the presence, in the vicinity, of a residence of an 'allied' family from the same political faction.[27] Other ancient sources from different periods – such as Tacitus[28] and St

---

[25] According to the most recent studies (Liverani and Gnilka), the area in question would be the one on which the Patriarch's palace was built during the early Middle Ages.

[26] Ps.-Aur. Vict. *Epit*. 20.6: 'Lateranum Cilonem Anullinum Bassum ceterosque alios ditaret aedibus quoque memoratu dignis, quarum praecipuas videmus Parthorum quae dicuntur ac Laterani' ('[Septimius Severus] enriched Lateranus, Cilo, Anullinus, Bassus and several others with buildings worthy of note, particular examples of which we see are called the House of the Parthians and (the House?) of Lateranus', trans A. Agostini in J.-L. Gauville (ed.), *Abbreviated Histories: The Case of the Epitome de Caesaribus (AD 395)* (Montreal, 1995), 14.

[27] See Colini, *Storia e topografia del Celio*, 273. A similar case seems to have reoccurred on the Caelian hill many centuries later with the residence of Quintus Aurelius Symmachus and the *domus* of Gaudentius. At the end of the fourth century AD the powerful Symmachus, a noteworthy member of the pagan faction, had in Gaudentius not only a representative and spokesman in the Senate, but possibly also a neighbour; see G. Spinola, 'Il dominus Gaudentius e l'Antinoo Casali: Alcuni aspetti della fine del paganesimo da una piccola domus sul Celio?', *MEFRA* 104, 2 (1992), 953–79; G. Spinola, 'La domus di Gaudentius', in C. Pavolini, A. Carignani, F. Pacetti, G. Spinola, M. Vitti, 'La topografia antica della sommità del Celio', *Mitteilungen des Deutschen Archäologischen Instituts Römische Abteilung* 100 (1993), 443–505, at pp. 473–83.

[28] Tac. *Ann*. 15.49.3: 'et Lucanus Annaeus Plautiusque Lateranus [consul designatus] vivida odia intulere. Lucanum propriae causae accendebant, quod famam carminum eius premebat Nero prohibueratque ostentare, vanu adsimulatione: Lateranum consulem designatum nulla iniuria, sed amor rei publicae sociavit' ('Violent hatred was brought in Lucan and Plautius Lateranus. Lucan's animosity was personal. For Nero had the impudence to compete with Lucan as a poet, and had impeded his reputation by vetoing his publicity. Lateranus joined from no personal

Jerome[29] – mention this historical event; in particular, the passage from one of the epistles of Saint Jerome, the only one to clearly associate the area of the basilica to the house of Plautius Lateranus, presents an uncertain philological interpretation and consequently a controversial judgement on its level of accuracy. This, however, does not present as so univocally negative as to exclude this association.[30] As with Tacitus and Juvenal, the sources dating to the first decades of the second century AD attest to the tragic events – and presumably also the places – connected to the Pisonian conspiracy, which also saw the end of Plautius Lateranus. These events might have remained embedded in the collective memory for quite some time, especially with regard to Nero, a controversial and much unloved figure.

In the event of a Neronian requisition, the villa would have been remodelled a few years later to fulfil another function, with substantial works and the conversion of different areas, regardless of the fact that this portion of the house near the Via Tusculana had been damaged by fire or other traumatic events. The transferal of different large suburban private properties to the imperial demesne either through a legacy or a falling out of favour with the imperial family for political, financial or family reasons, and their subsequent transformation, was a common practice during the first and middle imperial age.[31] Examples of this are the cases of the Horti of Maecenas, the Horti Tauriani, Calyclani, Lamiani, Sallustiani, and the

---

grievance; his motive was patriotism', trans A. Agostini in the Latin Library (ed.), www.thelatinlibrary.com/tacitus/tac.ann15.shtml.

[29] Jer. *Ep.* 77.4, concerning the appeal for pardon from the noble Fabiola, he indicates the place 'in basilica (in or ad? aedibus) quondam Laterani, qui Cesariano truncatus est gladio' ('in the basilica which formerly belonged to that Lateranus who perished by the sword of the Caesar', trans. A. Agostini in Liverani, 'L'area lateranense in età tardo antica').

[30] The theory according to which St Jerome had erroneously associated the area of the basilica with that of the home of Plautius Lateranus, having confused the two Laterans, is a possibility, supported by logical considerations, but must not be considered as axiomatic, seeing that Jerome had studied and also lived in Rome, where he operated as the cultured and severe secretary of Pope Damasus – becoming a candidate for his succession – so theoretically he must have been well acquainted with the documents that are the basis of his Roman narrative.

[31] See V. S. M. Scrinari, 'Contributo all'urbanistica tardo antica sul Campo Laterano', in N. Duval (ed.), *Actes du XIe congrès International d'archéologie chrétienne* (Rome, 1989), 2201–20, at pp. 2207–8; G. Messineo, 'Ville a Tor di Quinto e nelle tenute di Grottarossa e Acquatraversa', in B. S. Frizell and A. Klynne (eds.), *Roman Villas around the Urbs: Interaction with Landscape and Environment. Proceedings of a Conference Held at the Swedish Institute in Rome, September 17–18, 2004* (Rome, 2005), 1–5; C. Ricci, 'Il principe in villa: Residenze imperiali in Italia e servizi di sicurezza', *Cahiers du Centre Gustave Glotz* 15 (2004), 317–41, at pp. 319 and 326; M. Barbera, S. Barrano, G. de Cola, S. Festuccia, L. Giovannetti, O. Menghi and M. Pales, 'La villa di Caligola: Un nuovo settore degli Horti Lamiani scoperto sotto la sede dell'ENPAM a Roma', *Journal of Fasti Online* (2010), 1–5.

Horti Luculliani, along with the Villa of Valerio Asiatico; in particular, the Horti of Caius Sallustius Crispus Passienus and the Horti Pallentiani were expropriated or bought by Agrippina Minor and Nero. A different matter is the possible renaming of the residence as Aedes Parthorum. The aforementioned passage of the Pseudo-Victor regarding this residence has long been the object of different interpretations (dividing or associating the Aedes Parthorum and the Domus Parthorum), the most recent preferring to topographically detach it altogether from the area of the house offered as a gift to Titus Sextius Lateranus and from the area of the Lateran in general.[32]

## The So-Called Trapezoidal Building

The so-called Trapezoidal Building has also been the subject of various interpretations regarding its function and its relationship to the Castra Nova Equitum Singularium. It is clear that its construction is contemporary to that of the *castra*. For practical building purposes – such as the passage of construction material along the Via Tusculana – a large raised terrace was first built over structures of the previous residence, followed by the completion of the central area – with the *strigae*, the *principia* and the infrastructure of the fort – and the final construction of the Trapezoidal Building, along with a bath complex set at the same level and directly up against the Via Tusculana. I argue that the imposing supporting structures of the terracing of the *castra* must not be read as an enclosing wall for the completion of the barracks. Though they separate the barrack buildings from the Trapezoidal Building (passages between the two buildings have been surmised but still not located), I believe that the terrace served only to address a notable difference in height between the Via Tusculana and the levelled and raised surface occupied by the central buildings of the *castra*. Furthermore, it appears to me as probable that the western entrance to the *castra* opened directly on this main roadway with an adequate access door to the military complex, between the Trapezoidal Building and the bathhouse, at the end of a possible sloping internal pathway between the terrace

---

[32] P. Liverani, 'Domus: Parthorum', in *LTUR* II, 152–3; C. Taffetani, 'Il complesso della c.d. Domus Parthorum: Nuova interpretazione delle fasi costruttive', in D. Manacorda and R. Santangeli Valenzani (eds.), *Il primo miglio della via Appia a Roma* (Rome, 2011), 39–45; M. Ceci, 'La cosidetta Domus Parthorum: Vecchie e nuove ipotesi per l'aula absidata', *Bullettino della Commissione archeologica Comunale di Roma* 115 (2014), 354–9; Gnilka, 'Aedes Laterani', 70–1.

passageway and the connection to the Via Tusculana; the existence of an internal route appears to be corroborated by those elements set against the earth, such as the reinforcement of a number of relieving arches, and the walls in the lower portion of the northern rooms of the same *insula*, visible in nineteenth-century photos.[33] In a far better state of conservation are the rooms at the back of the western portico, which maintain the original decorations dating to the early Severan period, of discrete but not superb quality, with floorings in black-and-white mosaics featuring geometric motifs and frescoed walls decorated by red-and-yellow cornices and panels.[34]

The photographs of the excavations conducted in 1876–7 for the construction of the Lateran's new apse and the documentation by Busiri Vici appear very useful in offering an interpretation on the function of the Trapezoidal Insula, a function compatible with the adjacent complex of the *castra* (see Fig. 7.2).

Integrating this documentation with what is currently visible *in situ*, it is possible to affirm that on the mosaic flooring of the Trapezoidal Insula courtyard there is no trace either of the foundations or the raised portion of a pillared *tholos* for a *macellum*, as conjectured from the presence of a circular structure in the middle of the courtyard.[35]

From the photographs and the notes of that period it is instead easily possible to identify a basin decorated with marble slabs, these last comprised of three oblique sections (also decorated in marble) that overlap, reaching a depth of 1.25 m. At the bottom of the basin a drainage channel should be present, connected to a well (1.5 m to the east), and then on to a sewer set 1.2 m below the bottom of the basin and directed towards what is presumably the main sewer underneath the outside road (Via Tusculana). All this would appear to indicate an ornamental fountain at the centre of an elegant courtyard decorated by a geometric mosaic,[36] a flooring that was never replaced or restored in over 120 years (if this were in fact a *macellum*, restorations would have been inevitable because of the wear caused by the passage of wagons), but restored only in the vicinity of the well and in some other small parts (see Busiri Vici's fig. 3). The side rooms which still hold traces of frescoes and mosaic floorings (although not

---

[33] See Francini, Chapter 7 in this volume.
[34] For the mosaics see also Becatti, *Mosaici*, 201, no. 381. For the frescoes, see S. Falzone, *Scavi di Ostia*, XIV: *Le pitture delle insulae (180–250 circa d.C.)* (Rome, 2004), 182–3, 192–5 fig. 96.
[35] The circular structure appears in nineteenth-century drawings and is still marked *in situ* by a circle of modern bricks set in the Severan mosaic.
[36] Comparable to similar examples from the end of the second and beginning of the third century AD: see Becatti, *Mosaici*, 182, no. 336; Liverani and Spinola, *Mosaici*, 221–fig. 5.

of high quality) do not show any traces of the infrastructures necessary in a warehouse. Consequently, for an edifice that is built at least on two floors – due to the presence of large relieving arches – which does not connect directly with the Via Tusculana (a necessity for any edifice with a commercial function), I would without a doubt exclude an original use as a *macellum*, but would rather imagine a function directly connected to the life of the *castra* with which – as said before – it shares the chronology and possibly also the construction work.

As mentioned previously, in the past the Trapezoidal Building was seen as the residence of the officers of the *equites*, with annexed *schola*, and to be fair the structure of this building shows numerous planimetric and decorative affinities with the collegial seats and coeval *scholae*,[37] but this hypothesis presents some difficulties. First, its position within the *castra* appears as too off-centre;[38] furthermore, it seems that a similar function was fulfilled by some of the rooms around the courtyard of the *principia*, where four dedications to emperors from members of the *schola* of the *equites* were found.[39]

A number of structures present in the Trapezoidal Building might instead contribute to the identification of the building. To start with, in two rooms at the western corner of the edifice – in a second phase during the Severan age, and shortly after the building of the site – a small *fullonica* is installed.[40] The *fullonica*, which occupies the terminal portion of the western corridor of the courtyard portico, is set in an irregularly shaped room, with a basin in mortar and *cocciopesto*, along with (not very accurate) traces of restoration on the mosaic flooring around it;[41] near the basin, in another internal room, we find an *opus signinum* floor marked by channels, with walls showing traces of a wooden framework for the *saltus fullonicus*. Probably the *fullonica* was originally elsewhere – presumably in the same edifice – and in a second phase (not much after the previous one) was transferred to the western corner of the Trapezoidal Building. The

[37] See for example J. Ströger, *Rethinking Ostia: A Spatial Enquiry into the Urban Society of Rome's Imperial Port-Town* (Leiden, 2011), 229–56.
[38] See M. Albana, 'Aspetti della burocrazia militare nell'alto impero', *Annali della Facoltà di Scienze della Formazione, Università degli Studi di Catania* 12 (2013), 3–39, at pp. 8–10.
[39] Spinola, 'Sculture', 88–92, nos. 440–3. A statue base and an altar dedicated in AD 200 to the imperial family (*CIL* VI, 225 and 226), and pertaining to the *castra*, were also found during the excavations below the Corsini chapel (1732) in the Lateran basilica.
[40] A similar structure, obtained from *tabernae* and service areas, is also present in the officers' quarters of the barracks of the *Vigiles* at Ostia. Here, however, the function as a lavatory for the *Vigiles* is clear.
[41] The mosaic that surrounds the basin is stylistically similar to others from the Trapezoidal Insula dating to the Severan period.

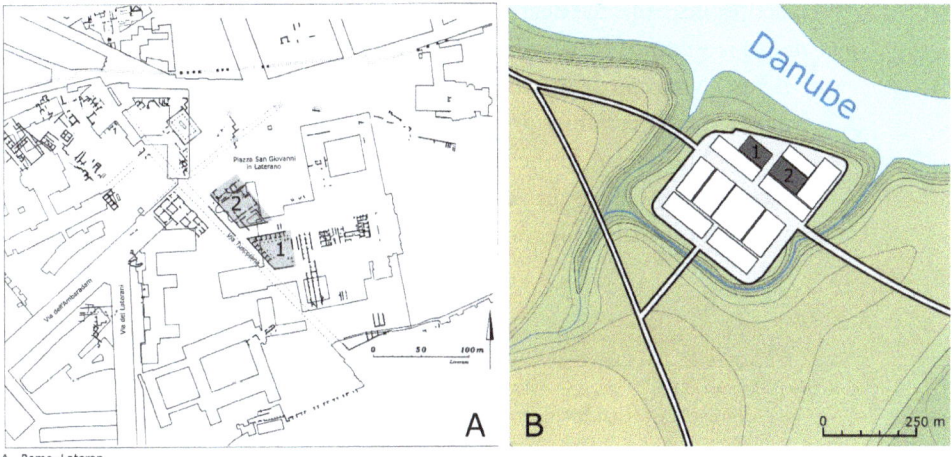

A. Rome, Lateran
B. Vindobona (around AD250)
1. *Valetudinarium*
2. Baths

**Fig. 5.7** The *castra* of Vindobona and the Castra Nova Equitum Singularium (Image: T. Ravasi; the plan of Vindobona is adapted from 'Vindobona 250–300', Wikipedia, available at commons.wikimedia.org/wiki/File:Vindobona_250–300.svg. The plan of the Lateran quarter is adapted from Liverani (ed.), *Laterano 1*).

position of the Trapezoidal Building itself – together with the general layout and distribution of the rooms – is well suited to hypothesise the presence of a *valetudinarium*, the sanatorium of the barracks. There are numerous and substantial comparisons with *valetudinaria* from other barracks, which, as in the present case, are often built on the margins of military complexes – in proximity to one of the doors – and near a bathhouse, the latter equally connected to the *castra*. The excavation of these edifices, however, leaves some margin of uncertainty: their definitive identification of these is not always well documented, nor is the planimetry and distribution of the rooms clearly defined (Fig. 5.7).[42] The small *fullonica* of the Trapezoidal Insula, however, appears to confirm such an identification, fulfilling a hygienic and sanitary function which was absolutely necessary for medical purposes.

The presence of a *valetudinarium* in the Castra Nova Equitum Singularium is not documented epigraphically, but there are three

---

[42] See for example the similar structure of the Vindobona *castra* (Vienna): M. Kronberger, *Siedlungschronologische Forschungen zu den canabae legionis von Vindobona: Die Gräberfelder* (Monographien der Stadtarchäologie Wien Band 1) (Vienna, 2005). See also A. Alonso Alonso, 'Fuentes literarias y epigraficas para el estudio de los valetudinaria urbanos en el mundo romano', *Classica et Christiana* 9, 1 (2014), 11–34, esp. p. 16.

inscriptions from the nearby Castra Priora that mention two *optio valetudinari* (administrative officers) and one *medicus castrorum* for the *equites*.[43] One can deduce that in Rome, if the *valetudinarium* of the *equites singulares* was certainly present in the Castra Priora, the same structure could not be absent in the more modern and functional Castra Nova; the Trapezoidal Building appears as an edifice with all the necessary characteristics to fulfil such a function.

---

[43] *CIL* VI, 31145, 31172; M. P. Speidel, *Die Denkmäler der Kaiserreiter: Equites Singulares Augusti* (Beihefte der Bonner Jahrbücher 50) (Cologne, 1994), 14 and 23, 43–4, no. 9, 70–1, no. 42, 203–4, no. 268; C. Ricci, '*Pro bona valetudine*: Considerazioni sul personale addetto all'infermeria e sui valetudinaria a Roma', *Humanitas* 70, 3 (2015), 355–66.

# 6 | The Castra Nova and the Severan Transformation of Rome

IAN P. HAYNES AND PAOLO LIVERANI

The Constantinian basilica was not the first imperial foundation on the Lateran site. Over a century before Constantine, Septimius Severus remodelled this area of the Caelian with the creation of the Castra Nova of the *equites singulares Augusti*, the 'New Fort' of the imperial horse guards. This development was in turn integral to a larger imperial agenda, advanced by Severus in his self-proclaimed role as *Restitutor Urbis*. As this chapter will argue, study of the Castra Nova is integral not only to the story of the basilica, but also to new thinking of the transformation of Rome from the early empire to Late Antiquity. To appreciate the fort's significance, it is necessary to understand the salient features of its construction, its physical and strategic place in the city, and the way in which its demolition in turn prepared the way for the basilica.

Investigating the Castra Nova has been integral to the research agenda of the Lateran Project, an initiative discussed further elsewhere in this volume.[1] In addition to conducting a comprehensive survey of exposed surviving architectural elements and a programme of ground-penetrating radar analysis,[2] project members have exhaustively reviewed evidence for

---

[1] I. P. Haynes, P. Liverani, A. Turner and T. Ravasi, 'Roma si trasforma: Gli scavi di San Giovanni in Laterano e l'evoluzione della città eterna tra II e VI sec. d.C.', *Forma Urbis* 17, 6 (2011), 36–44; I. P. Haynes, P. Liverani, G. Spinola and S. Piro, 'The Lateran Project', *PBSR* 80 (2012), 369–71; I. P. Haynes, P. Liverani, S. Piro and G. Spinola, 'The Lateran Project: Interim report on the July 2012 and January 2013 seasons (Rome)', *PBSR* 81 (2013), 360–3; I. P. Haynes, P. Liverani, S. Piro, I. Peverett and G. Spinola, 'Progetto Laterano: Primi risultati', *Rendiconti della Pontificia Accademia Romana di Archeologia* 86 (2014), 1–19; I. P. Haynes, P. Liverani, I. Peverett, G. Spinola and A. Turner, 'The Lateran Project: Interim report for 2015–2016 seasons (Rome)', *PBSR* 84 (2016), 311–16; I. P. Haynes, P. Liverani, D. Heslop, I. Peverett, G. Spinola and A. Turner, 'The Lateran Project: Interim report for the 2016–2017 seasons (Rome)', *PBSR* 85 (2017), 317–20. See also Liverani and Haynes, Chapter 12 in this volume. We note with appreciation the contribution of our many colleagues in the Lateran Project to recording of the Castra Nova and to discussions on its form. We would especially like to thank Alex Turner, Dave Heslop, Iwan Peverett for his work on concept drawings and rendered images, and Dr Thea Ravasi for her work on site plans.

[2] S. Piro, I. P. Haynes, P. Liverani and D. Zamuner, 'Integrated archaeological and geophysical investigations to study the area of S. Giovanni in Laterano basilica (Rome, Italy)', in C. Einwogerer, W. Neubauer, R. B. Salisbury and I. Trinks (eds.), *Archaeological Prospection: Proceedings of the 10th International Conference* (Vienna, 2013), 203–5; S. Piro, I. P. Haynes, P. Liverani and D. Zamuner, 'GPR investigation to map the subsoil of the St John Lateran Basilica (Rome)', *Bollettino di Geofisica Teorica ed Applicata* 58, 4 (2018), 431–44. See also Piro, Haynes, Liverani and Zamuner, Chapter 4 in this volume.

elements of the structure identified in previous excavations. Wherever possible, these elements have then been geo-referenced, thus allowing the development of a comprehensive plan of the whole area. Crucially, the systems of 3D recording used by the Lateran Project allow not only the for the reconciliation of different elements of the *castra* with one another, but also with structures that were contemporary with it, the luxurious residences that preceded them, and the basilica that succeeded all.

It will be appreciated that earlier interventions at the site varied significantly in form, scale, motive and documentation. Liverani's introduction to research at the Lateran brings together most of what is known about the site's exploration and study prior to the Lateran Project.[3] Several points should be stressed here, however. First, we should note that there are no explicit references to structural remains likely to be associated with the *castra* before the modern era, though work in and around the cathedral would have meant that they would have been encountered relatively frequently. The surviving floor surfaces of the *castra* lie on average 1.45 m below the current basilica floor. Grave cuts in and around the cathedral would inevitably have disturbed some older structural elements. Some early interventions can be identified archaeologically, even though it is impossible to date them with precision. An area of the excavations currently used to display decorative architectural elements and inscriptions and which may have been a cistern for the *castra*, for example, appears to have been reused in the late medieval/early modern period. Stairs lead up from its interior through the courtyard of one of the Castra buildings to a small hatch in the cathedral floor. Elsewhere, concrete piles attest cases where early modern engineers bolstered points on the cathedral floor by digging through to the partially preserved first century AD walking surfaces several metres below. The latter interventions may be attributable to works required by Borromini's grand transformation of the Lateran basilica interior in the mid-seventeenth century.

Documented major works which will have disturbed the remains of the *castra* and its associated structures are known from the eighteenth century onwards, but the quality of archaeological information derived from them ranges widely. Fig. 6.1 draws on the work of Liverani to show the locations of these investigations superimposed on an outline of the plan of the cathedral as it is today. Works in the area now occupied by the Corsini chapel in 1732, and at the western end of the cathedral in 1876, are discussed

---

[3] P. Liverani, 'Introduzione topografica', in P. Liverani (ed.), *Laterano 1: Scavi sotto la Basilica di S. Giovani in Laterano*, vol. I: *Materiali* (Vatican City, 1998), 6–16.

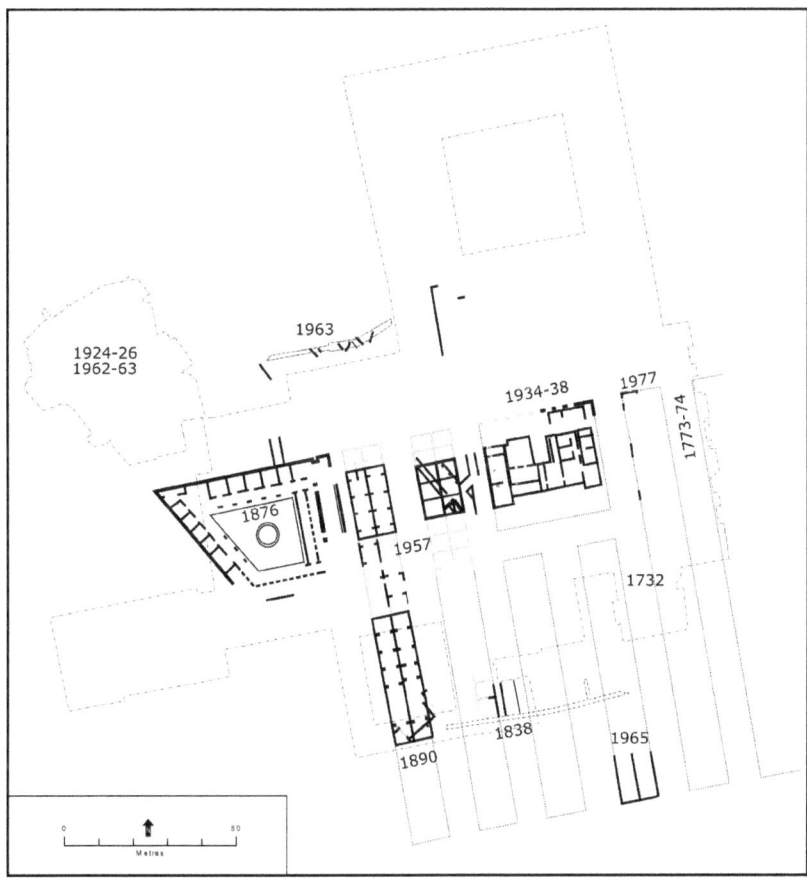

**Fig. 6.1** Plan showing location of historical excavations in the area of the Castra Nova (image: T. Ravasi, adapted from Liverani, 'Introduzione topografica').

in separate chapters in this volume.[4] Further significant interventions took place in 1890 and exposed a substantial stretch of the *castra* basement, an area still used for storage by the Cathedral Estates Office. Several later observations identified walls, which, though only very briefly described, may from their form and orientation be associated with the *castra*.[5]

Of all the excavations to have taken place beneath the basilica, the most important for our understanding of the Castra Nova were assuredly those undertaken by Enrico Josi between 1934 and 1938 during the restoration of the

---

[4] For the eighteenth-century works in advance of the building of the Corsini chapel, see esp. Liverani, Chapter 2 in this volume; for the late nineteenth-century relocation of the apse and associated works see Francini, Chapter 7 in this volume.

[5] For a comprehensive introduction to the investigation of the site, see Liverani, 'Introduzione topografica'.

cathedral's floor. Josi himself only produced a report of the first season of excavation, offering just brief notes on the others.[6] Despite a search by Lateran Project team members, it has not proved possible to find Josi's original field notes, but, thanks to the Pontifical Commission of Sacred Archaeology, photographs taken during his excavations have been recovered. These were accompanied by brief annotations, ambiguous in places, which were confined to identifying the places where the pictures were taken. The essential point of reference for these excavations is, therefore, the report published by Colini in 1944, which sought to bring together the whole programme of works.[7] Colini's account contains much of value, but analysis by the Lateran Project team demonstrates that his appraisal was handicapped by his inability to access all the area Josi had exposed. This, and the possibility that he may not have participated in the excavations himself, must be kept in mind while reading his analysis.[8] Though the basements of the *castra* would have been accessible to him, Colini would only have been able to reach the Severan floor levels of the complex with ladders and/or scaffolding once the cathedral floor was reinstated in 1938. Gaps in the limited plans in his report suggest that Colini was unable to see some key features when he completed it, and that he did not therefore access these areas, but fortunately members of the Lateran Project have been able to do so, and to comprehensively plot them. They now form an integral part of the Lateran Project's 3D digital model of the 4,167 m$^2$ space below the cathedral floor, a model generated from over 4.5 billion readings with the Faro Focus laser scanner.

In addition to the vital structural evidence recovered by Josi and discussed further below, seven inscriptions of importance for the story of the *castra* have been found in the Lateran area. The first two are relatively well known; both adorn the same, inverted, Ionic capital found in what we must now interpret as the *principia* (headquarters building) of the fort (Fig. 6.2). They refer to the *collegium* of the *curatores*, a professional association of junior cavalry officers which had a *schola*, a dedicated meeting-room, in the *castra*'s headquarters. The inscriptions were carved almost six years apart, on 1 January AD 197 and 10 June AD 203 respectively.[9] The date of the first is of interest as it reveals how

---

[6] E. Josi, 'Scoperte nella Basilica costantiniana al Laterano, Rome', *RAC* 11 (1934), 335–8; for references to individual notes and reports, see A. M. Colini, *Storia e topografia del Celio nell'antichità* (Memorie della Pontificia Accademia Romana di Archeologia 7) (Vatican City, 1944), 343 n. 103.

[7] Colini, *Storia e topografia del Celio*.

[8] Liverani has noted the possibility, as yet unconfirmed, that Italo Gismondi, the architect who drew the plans for Colini's 1944 report, may nonetheless have worked with Josi during some of the excavations.

[9] AD 197 inscription: *AE* 1935, 156 = 1954, 83 = 1968, 8b; Colini, *Storia e topografia*, 353 and 353 fig. 298; Josi, 'Scoperte nella Basilica', 347–8 and 349 fig. 8; G. Spinola, 'Sculture, rilevi,

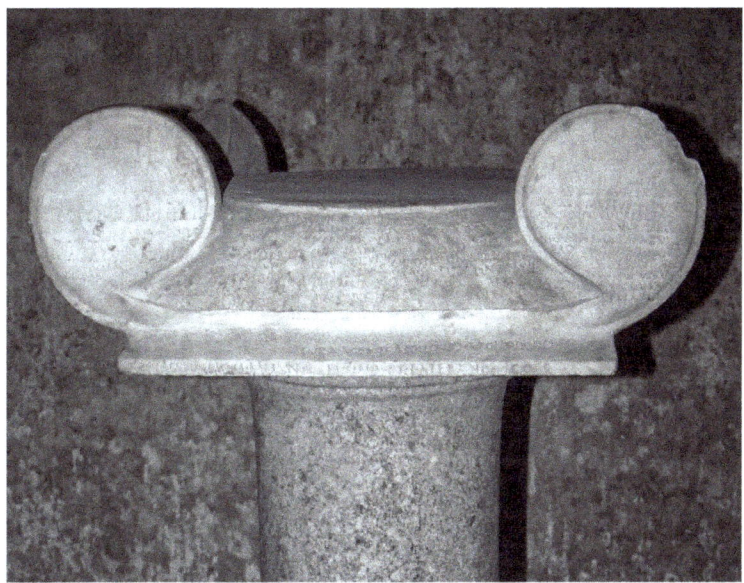

**Fig. 6.2** The inverted Ionic capital recovered in the *principia* with inscriptions recording the *collegium* of the *curatores* (Lateran Project).

soon after Severus' arrival as emperor in Rome the *castra* was completed. That a group of *curatores* was able to meet and set up such an elaborate dedication on the spot demonstrates that the New Fort was fully functional by this time. Lest this be considered insufficient proof that the *equites singulares* were fully in occupation by this early date, we might note the discovery of three other dedications set up by the occupants of the Castra Nova during this period.[10] These are recorded as being discovered during work in preparation for the building of the Corsini chapel in 1732, in an area where traces of what appear to be barrack ranges were unearthed.[11]

Two other inscriptions, found in the *principia* area, offer proof of the longevity of the Castra Nova. They are carved on white marble statue bases dedicated to Diocletian and Maximian respectively.[12] Their presence in this part of the fort is consistent with the practice of setting up statues honouring emperors known from other *principia* around the empire. Crucially

---

decorazione architettonica, iscrizioni e reperti ceramici', in Liverani (ed.), *Laterano 1*, 17–114, at p. 88, no. 441. AD 203 inscription: *AE* 1935, 157 = 1954, 83.

[10] These inscriptions date from AD 197(*CIL* VI, 224); AD 200 (*CIL* VI, 225) and AD 202 (*CIL* VI, 226).

[11] Colini, *Storia e topografia*, 356 n. 134; R. Venuti, *Osservazioni sopra un'antica iscrizione aggiunta al Museo Corsini* (Rome, 1733).

[12] Diocletian: Spinola, 'Sculture', 88, no. 440; Maximian: Spinola, 'Sculture', 89, no. 442.

too, they indicate that this practice continued here through to the Tetrarchy, right through to the final years of the *equites singulares*.

With these essential preliminaries noted, it is now possible to turn back to the structural archaeology of the complex to appreciate the construction, use and demolition of the Castra Nova. We will start with the evidence for the construction, and the remarkable transformation of the Caelian that it reveals.

The area selected for the site of the Castra Nova was already occupied by extensive residences of the highest quality. Whether these properties were confiscated or bought up by the emperor, or whether they were already imperial properties at the time, remains uncertain. The quality of their workmanship would certainly allow for the latter possibility; in some areas traces of walls have been identified that would have been marble clad to a height of at least 6 m – a level of investment without parallel in Rome beyond known imperial palaces. Large areas of these residences had been re-planned and redecorated around AD 120–40, a process clearly demonstrated by some new construction works, the installation of new drains (containing ten stamped bricks of Hadrianic date) and frescoes stylistically consistent with Hadrianic fashion.[13] Works on the *castra* obliterated large swathes of this lavish property but, crucially, ended up burying and thus preserving others.

The builders of Rome's forts and fortresses are often wrongly perceived as unimaginative drudges working to fixed formulae, churning out multiple installations of limited variety or originality. Yet while certain broad assumptions often anchored the range of designs in use, military planners could and did show impressive flexibility. This is notably true where they operated in built-up areas, where comprehensive transformation had necessarily to sit alongside other long-established elements of the cityscape. In this case, the builders of the Castra Nova found it necessary to reshape natural features too. The decision was made to construct substantial brick and concrete substructures against the Caelian hill's western and southern slopes to support a substantial fort platform.

It is possible to reconstruct the construction process of the Castra Nova in considerable detail, more detail indeed than that known for any other fort in the Roman Empire. The first task for building parties was to prepare the site prior to the construction of the fort's substructure. Walls belonging

---

[13] Brick-stamp forms represented follow CIL XV, 374 (c. AD 123), 1029c (AD 123), 277 (AD 126) and 652 (AD 123–41). For Hadrianic dating of the fresco designs, see E. M. Moormann and S. T. A. M. Mols, 'Le pitture Romane: Frammenti e resti in situ', in Liverani (ed.), *Laterano 1*, 115–32, at pp. 126, 130.

to the existing properties were for the most part torn down only so far as was necessary to prevent them obstructing the level chosen for the fort platform. At the same time the fine marble panels that had adorned the walls, some over 1.8 m wide and perhaps as high as 3 m each, were removed. It is conceivable that some of this material was re-used in the decoration of the *castra*, a possibility considered further below. Uniquely, for a fort site, we have graffiti left by gangs responsible for the new building process.[14] Scratched on the wall plaster at a point subsequently rendered almost inaccessible by the construction of the *castra*'s brick basement are the letters COH III, a reference to a third Cohort.[15] Precisely which third Cohort is referred to remains ambiguous; Severus' disbandment of Praetorian Guard units at this time may make it seem unlikely that they were involved,[16] though the guard was, of course, rapidly reformed after this celebrated event. Two other possibilities may be considered: one is that others of Rome's 'armed and belted men',[17] the Urban Cohorts or the *Vigiles*, were employed on the tasks. The basic process of stripping walls and breaking them down did not in itself necessarily require higher-level engineering support. The other possibility is that the work was conducted by men from the *Legio II Parthica* stationed 25 km outside Rome at Albano. This is certainly feasible, and the legion would have been fully capable of delivering the entire programme of site preparation and construction, but the possibility should be weighed against the knowledge that *Legio II Parthica* would have been heavily engaged in building its own fortress at the same time. What is worth noting, though, is that while the teams were composed of military men, in this case at least those responsible for the COH III graffito did not include members of the intended garrison, the *equites singulares*; the term cohort is never for cavalry formations.

---

[14] The closest parallel, if it can be called that, would be the remarkable poems left by the centurions of Bu Njem (see J. N. Adams, 'The poets of Bu Njem: Language, culture and the centurionate', *Journal of Roman Studies* 89 (1999), 109–34), but even these are different in form and attest the literary pretensions of officers, rather than the records of ordinary soldiers.

[15] Haynes et al., 'The Lateran Project: Interim report on the July 2012 and January 2013 seasons (Rome)', 361.

[16] Dio Cass. 75.1.1–2.

[17] The phrase originates with Juvenal (*Sat.* 16.48: 'ast illis quos arma tegunt et balteus ambit'). Coulston has usefully adopted the phrase as a shorthand for the miscellaneous military and para-military formations in and around Rome: J. C. N. Coulston, '"Armed and Belted Men": The soldiery in imperial Rome', in J. C. N. Coulston and H. Dodge (eds.), *Ancient Rome: The Archaeology of the Eternal City* (Oxford University School of Archaeology Monograph 54) (Oxford, 2000), 76–118, at p. 76.

Graffiti found in the immediate vicinity of the COH III graffito and apparently contemporary with it consist mainly of personal names, all consistent with the range of names found in guard units in Severan Rome.[18] There is, however, one text which relates to measurements and is therefore better explained as an auditing device. Scraped onto a surface that had supported one of the marble slabs adorning the pre-Severan residence prior to its destruction were the letters and numbers ILX SE (*or* SII) P CC. As Tomlin observes in his reading, the text ILX *se(mis) p(ondo) CC* or '59 $^1$/2 weight 200', specifies neither what is being weighed nor what measure of weight is employed. The most likely possibility here is that the graffito refers to the resources being stripped from the buildings at this early stage in their demolition.[19]

The next phase of site preparation consisted of the construction of concrete and brick basements and building foundations together with the installation of drainage. In the southwest of the *castra*, the most extensively investigated area, but also the area where slopes of the Caelian were most radically remodelled, we can trace the brick foundations down to at least 3.5 m below the Severan walking surface. There were some notable differences in the way in which the foundations of the long barrack-like buildings were constructed. In the westernmost example, the area was cleared to allow for the creation of a brick-faced concrete-vaulted basement. This range was built up from the pre-existing ground surface, and the gaps between the basement walls and the adjacent elements of the *castra* rebuilt. This arrangement is without ready parallel in the architecture of Roman forts, but it makes excellent use of the pre-existing slope to provide valuable additional space to the occupants in what remains a densely built up area. Access to the basement was via steps at the northern end, and in the first phase of the building light wells (subsequently blocked up) provided illumination.

Adjacent to this building lay another barrack-like structure, but in this case brick- and stone-built coffers underlay the walls of each of the compartments (*contubernia*) of the building above. The coffers thus echoed in plan the chambers they supported, enclosing an area 4.75 x 4.8 m. Those supporting the external load-bearing walls of the buildings were built in brick, while those underpinning internal floors and partitions were constructed in *opus listatum*, incidentally the earliest datable attestation of this method in the Roman metropolis.[20] Fig. 6.3, a digital model generated from the Lateran Project's laser scan survey, shows part of the foundations of one of the Castra Nova's elongated barrack-like buildings. Sections of the walls

---

[18] R. S. O. Tomlin, 'Castra Nova Graffiti Report', Lateran Project, unpublished working document (2017).

[19] Tomlin, 'Castra Nova'.   [20] Colini, *Storia e topografia*, 353.

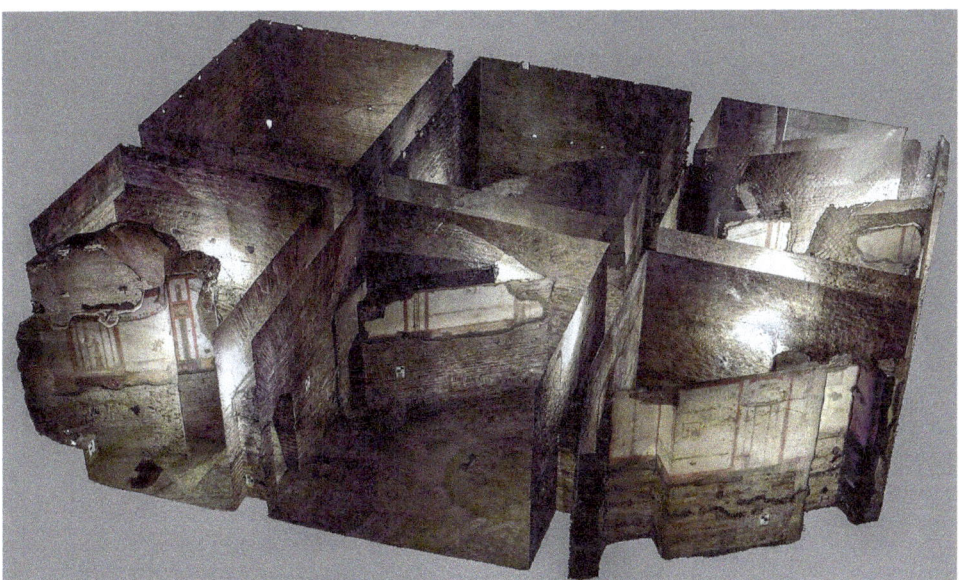

**Fig. 6.3** Section of Lateran Project laser scan showing the foundations of one of the Castra Nova's elongated barrack-like buildings. Sections of the walls of the luxurious residence that preceded the *castra* can be seen between the square brick foundations (Lateran Project).

of the luxurious residence that preceded the *castra* can be seen between the square brick coffer foundations of the fort buildings.

Most imposing of all the buildings in the *castra* would have been the above-mentioned *principia* or headquarters building. The lowest levels of sub-structures accessible lie beneath the offices that ran around the *principia* courtyard. They consist of concrete foundations originally set in timber formwork, above which are set sub-structure walls in finished masonry. While the ranges of offices flanking *principia* courtyards are frequently visualised as one storey in height, it is clear that such footings could have sustained a much higher elevation here. Traces of monumental foundations can be discerned at the edge of the excavations to the south, the area which was almost certainly occupied by the basilican hall of the *principia* complex, but it has never been possible to venture beyond this point.[21]

Complementing the scale of the foundations is a very fine set of drains, which carve through the once elegantly clad walls of the residential houses. Their progress exemplifies the radical transformation of the site, as luxurious frescoes gave way to the passage of sewage. Though research on the bath complex and Trapezoidal Building which lay to the west of the barrack

---

[21] Colini, *Storia e topografia*, 353.

buildings is still ongoing, a case can be made that both were built on land prepared at the time the fort was built, and that the builders took a similar approach to the clearance of their sites as well as the construction of their foundations and drainage.[22] The difference is that both the bath complex and Trapezoidal Building were built into the slope of the Caelian hill at a markedly lower level than the *castra* terrace.[23]

Before embarking on a discussion of the layout and appearance of the Castra Nova, it is useful to make a couple of preliminary observations. First, for all the remodelling of the Caelian that the fort's construction entailed, certain long-standing routes through this part of the city were maintained. The Via Tusculana, for example, clearly retained the route it had followed since at least the late first century BC and would essentially have constrained the fort corner to the southwest. Second, the fort builders, conscious as they must have been of the demands of any cavalry contingent on good water supply, would have paid careful attention to the existing aqueducts and springs in the area. The Claudio-Neronian aqueduct (Arcus Neroniani/Arcus Caelimontani), which passes through the Lateran, was substantially strengthened in AD 201, though whether this was in recognition of the fort's needs can be debated.[24]

---

[22] *Contra* G. Pelliccioni, *Le nuove scoperte sulle origini del battistero lateranense* (Memorie della Pontificia Accademia Romana di Archeologia 12.1) (Vatican City, 1973). While Pelliccioni believed that there was a pre-Severan bath complex at this location, Dr Thea Ravasi of the Lateran Project has observed that the brick-stamp evidence would be more consistent with the construction of the complex during the Severan period. While work might have begun at the same time as the *castra*, she notes that the presence of brick stamps from the sole reign of Caracalla strongly suggests that the complex would not have been completed until after the Castra Nova was in operation. This observation raises interesting questions about the relationship between baths and *castra*.

The date of the construction of the Trapezoidal Building is more ambiguous. Colini (Colini, *Storia e topografia*, 351) is firmly of the view that it pre-dates the *castra*, arguing that what can now be seen is all that remains of a larger building now sealed beneath it. Busch (A. W. Busch, *Militär in Rom: Militärische und paramilitärische Einheiten im kaiserzeitlichen Stadtbild* (Palilia 20) (Wiesbaden, 2011), 79) also holds that it should not be interpreted as part of the *castra* phase, while Spinola (Spinola, 'Sculture', 17) argues conversely that it must be interpreted this way. Unfortunately, crucial stratigraphic relationships were either cut or obscured in later development. The present state of research on this building leaves the authors of this chapter unconvinced that any firm argument about its functional relationship to the *castra* can be reached. We do not, however, believe that the design of the Trapezoidal Building itself indicates that it must post-date the planning of the *castra*. Its layout is designed to fit into the area contained by the substructure of the *castra*, the Via Tusculana and the continuation of the *via principalis*.

[23] The pavement of the baths lies 3.54 m below the lowest point on the *castra* terrace, while the courtyard of the Trapezoidal Building lies 4.56 m below the same terrace.

[24] For the reinforcement of the aqueduct, see A. Claridge, *Rome: An Oxford Archaeological Guide* (Oxford, 2010), 344. The suggestion that the *castra*'s needs may have been part of the rationale for the reinforcement of the aqueduct must, however, be set first against the possibility that the original structure was under-engineered even for its intended purpose, the fact that the *castra* was in use for at least eight years before the date of the known Severan rebuild (AD 201) and the requirements of much further reaching but rather later programme of Severan building work in the area.

Whatever the case, it is clear that while the fort was built in what was once a decidedly suburban space, it was constructed in an area that was increasingly densely occupied and where its planners had to integrate their work within urban infrastructure.

In so far as current evidence – itself limited to the southern and central part of the fort – allows us to tell, the complex retained the same essential configuration from its establishment some time between 193 and 196, to its abandonment around 312. Certain repairs and adaptations can be observed in the western basement range, but with one small exception these suggest continuity rather than change. The exception, probably of no more than local significance, is that the light wells into the basement were bricked over some time before the Castra Nova's destruction.

A long-standing concern for students of the topography of Rome has been to determine the extent of the fort.[25] There can be little doubt that this *castra*, like those others once found in the eastern part of the city, would have had a circuit of walls.[26] Indeed, it is just possible that the fort wall and gate depicted on the late second- or third-century tombstone of the horse guard trooper Aurelius Mestrius are those of the Castra Nova, though it is equally possible that it depicts the neighbouring fort of the horse guards, the Castra Priora.[27] The problem is that traces of the wall circuit on the ground have remained elusive. The very real possibility must remain that the Constantinian transformation of this area saw the wholesale demolition of the circuit. Brief antiquarian observations on the northern side[28] have been provisionally interpreted as evidence for the northern edge of the *castra* based on their monumentality, orientation and location in relation to buildings known from the fort interior, but it has not been possible to verify this interpretation.

In the absence of further direct evidence for the *castra* wall circuit, Lateran Project team members have made taken two other approaches to the problem. The first, conducted in conjunction with colleagues from ITABC-CNR, has been to conduct a major ground-penetrating radar

---

[25] Colini, *Storia e topografia*, 357.
[26] The walls of the Castra Praetoria, still standing today, were to prove necessary for the Praetorian Guard throughout their history, and there is little reason to doubt whether other guard units would have acted differently. Fort walls are not only provided to offer security to military personnel, they are also seen as an essential to their proper control, an aspect of their use too often overlooked (S. James, *Rome and the Sword* (London, 2011), 166).
[27] This possibility was first advanced in print by Speidel (M. P. Speidel, *Die Denkmäler der Kaiserreiter: Equites Singulares Augusti* (Beihefte der Bonner Jahrbücher 50) (Cologne, 1994), 326–7 n. 595.
[28] Colini, *Storia e topografia*, 349 plate XIX.21, 357.

survey across the Lateran quarter, an exercise discussed further elsewhere in this volume.[29] The second has been to study the floor levels and wall thicknesses exposed beneath the foundations of the Constantinian basilica. Though the radar work has proved fruitful and interesting in many respects, it has proved impossible to identify elements of the wall circuit with certainty. The second approach has led team members to slightly different conclusions.

The ground surface of the barrack-like buildings and the *principia* lay much higher than the baths and Trapezoidal Building immediately to the west.[30] The former results from the Severan construction of the platform described above, the latter the construction of a level space at the same date. Nor can there be any doubt that the western wall of the Constantinian basilica, and the apse that was such a significant part of it broadly exploited the step in the hillside that resulted from the Severan works. The apse foundations were built directly onto the floor of Trapezoidal Building; the floors of the basilica were however set 1.45 m above the Severan floor.[31] Running parallel to the western wall of the basilica, traces of a broader wall can be observed encased within the later walls of an underground storeroom. The position of this broader wall section runs along the edge of the platform.

Does this preserve the line of the *castra* wall? We argue here that it does. It is one thing to argue, as our colleague Giandomenico Spinola does, that the baths and the Trapezoidal Building are contemporary with one another and with the construction of the fort, but another to argue that both lay within the circuit of walls. If, as seems probable, the complex was constructed for the *equites singulares* it would almost certainly have been constructed, as virtually all such bath complexes were, as an extra-mural feature.[32] Smaller baths were accommodated inside forts, but baths of this size, capacious enough to serve an entire unit, were almost always built outside unless, as with remote outposts, the security situation demanded otherwise. The fire risk was deemed too great to warrant their inclusion within the wall circuit. That this standard practice was observed at this time in this region is further demonstrated by the location of the contemporary fortress baths at Castra Albana.[33]

There is one further vital clue to the size of the Castra Nova, and that is the location of the *principia* itself. For all the considerable variation found

---

[29] See Piro, Haynes, Liverani and Zamuner, Chapter 4 in this volume.   [30] See above, n. 22.
[31] By contrast, the floor of the cathedral lies 6.6 m above the floor of the Trapezoidal Building.
[32] The proximity of the baths to the *castra* makes it highly probable that these baths served the *equites singulares* stationed there (Busch, *Militär in Rom*, 78; Pelliccioni, *Le nuove scoperte*, 38, 59).
[33] Substantial baths have also been identified inside the Castra Albana, but the main baths there lay outside the fortress's walls.

in Roman forts and fortresses in the Roman west, one point was consistent – as the headquarters, the *principia* occupied the centre of the installation. This was more than just an administrative expedient; the chapel of the standards within the *principia* was home to the spiritual heart of the resident unit. The place where the standards were planted determined the laying out of all other elements.

Fig. 6.4 shows our concept model of the Castra Nova complex as it appeared around AD 215 looking east. It reflects accurately all the known structural elements of the Castra Nova, but also – more problematically – accounts for those areas where, despite relatively recent investigations, no such elements have been identified. While the well-known adage that absence of evidence is not evidence for absence scarcely needs repeating here, enough is known of the survival of superstructure in some areas to suggest that the fact that it has not been observed in others must be incorporated in the visualisation.

While the visualisation represents our best understanding of the *castra*'s likely appearance, it is not without its problems. Though not more densely packed than some contemporary forts, a product arguably of the need to fit the *castra* into a settled area, it is relatively cramped. We might expect more space rather than less given that the occupants of this fort were an elite force, though it should be noted that the size of individual rooms does seem to be larger.[34] The biggest problem, though, is that under no circumstances could a fort of such a size, even with its buildings so relatively densely packed together, have accommodated a cavalry unit of milliary strength. Commentators on the *equites singulares* have frequently argued that Severus doubled the horse guard to a notional strength of 2,000, by creating a second milliary unit (associated with the Castra Nova) to complement and offset the pre-existing guard, a thousand-strong based in the Castra Priora.[35] Even allowing for the

---

[34] The compartments within the barrack-like buildings (averaging 4.7 m$^2$) would have been substantially larger than the average, 3.6 m$^2$ area, allocated to cavalry barrack compartments in the provinces (N. Hodgson and P. T. Bidwell, 'Auxiliary barracks in a new light: Recent discoveries on Hadrian's Wall', *Britannia* 35 (2004), 121–57, at p. 133).

[35] For the argument that the horse guard was doubled to a paper strength of 2,000 under Severus, see M. P. Speidel, *Riding for Caesar: The Roman Emperors' Horse Guards* (Boston, 1994); Coulston, '"Armed and Belted Men"', fig. 5.8. Busch (Busch, *Militär in Rom*, 72, n. 352) notes that Speidel (Speidel, *Riding for Caesar*) appears to be the source of this figure, but that in his earlier work on the *equites singulares* (M. P. Speidel, *Die Equites Singulares Augusti: Begleittruppe der römischen Kaiser des 2. und 3. Jahrhunderts* (Antiquitas I, 11) (Bonn, 1965), 16), he had argued that the force was around five hundred strong and would have thus reached only about a thousand men when doubled under Severus. No explanation is given for this change in calculation, though it is possible that Speidel's view change may be linked to his reappraisal of the famous Hadrianic epitaph of Soranus 'foremost among a thousand Batavi' as one of a small number of literary epitaphs associated with the *equites singulares* (*CIL* III, 3676 = *ILS* 2558;

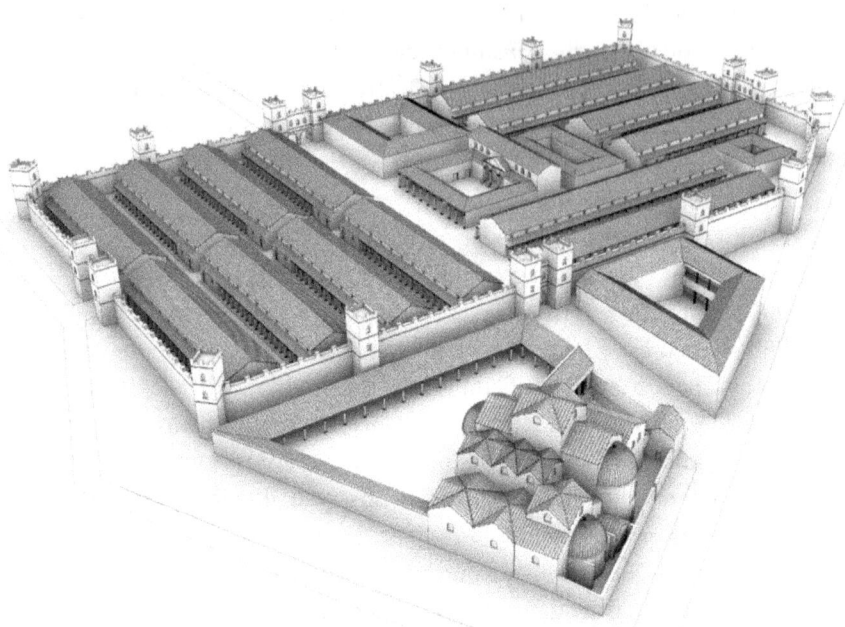

Fig. 6.4 Concept model of the Castra Nova complex c. AD 215 looking east. The fort was in operation by AD 197 but work on the bath complex appears to have continued after AD 211 into the sole reign of Caracalla. The date of the Trapezoidal Building, shown adjacent to the baths in the foreground, remains uncertain (Peverett and Haynes).

fact that milliary cavalry units consisted of rather fewer than a thousand riders, milliary *alae* in the provincial armies are normally reckoned at between 720 and 860 men,[36] the area plausibly occupied by the Castra Nova is too small to accommodate such a number. Milliary *alae* are believed to have consisted of twenty-four *turmae* (troops of cavalry thirty-two to thirty-six strong), and the barrack configuration shown here, the most generous allocation conceivable, could accommodate no more than fourteen such *turmae*, quite possibly less. A further comparison reinforces the basic point: the extensively studied cavalry fort at Aalen in Germany, home to the *ala II Flavia milliaria*, occupied

---

Speidel, *Riding for Caesar*, 46 and 174 n. 56; M. P. Speidel, 'Lebensbeschreibungen traianisch-hadrianischer Gardereiter', in K. Vössing (ed.), *Biographie und Prosopographie: Internationales Kolloquium zum 65. Geburtstag von Anthony R. Birley* (Historia Einzelschrift 178) (Stuttgart, 2005), 73–89, at pp. 73–80). If this view is correct, it follows that the horse guard was already a thousand strong before Severus.

[36] I. P. Haynes, *Blood of the Provinces: The Roman Auxilia and the Making of Provincial Society from Augustus to the Severans* (Oxford, 2013), 53, table 3.1.

6.07 ha, while the visualisation of the Castra Nova shown here would have occupied 2.53 ha.[37]

Before reflecting further on the implications of this, it is important to note another complication. It is not clear that all that have thus far been described rather awkwardly as 'barrack-like' structures functioned as barracks for soldiers and riders. Leaving aside the often-forgotten fact that whatever function architects have in mind for a building when they plan it, it can still be left empty for a period or used for a different purpose, the very design of the structure itself challenges a simple interpretation. Recent work on cavalry forts in the provinces has offered at least a partial answer to the question as to where horses were stabled in cavalry forts.[38] Cavalry barracks would appear to have accommodated troopers on one long side of the block and their horses on the other. The loss of floors from the barrack-like structures in the Castra Nova, most likely ripped up for stone during the destruction of the barracks for the construction of the Constantinian basilica, makes analysis of the rooms' use harder. But the openings on both long sides appear in the surviving buildings appear to be the same, suggesting perhaps that both sides housed similar occupants, rather than indicating a contrast between equine and pedestrian access. In short, there may have been still fewer mounts in the complex than even the limited number of barrack-like buildings might suggest.[39]

Though this might in turn indicate that the larger estimates of the strength of the Severan *equites singulares* are simply wrong, other explanations are possible. If it were accepted that the unit headquartered at the Castra Nova was of milliary size, the implication would be that a significant proportion of its strength must have been quartered elsewhere even when elements were not accompanying the emperor on campaign. This is of course in any event quite likely. Leaving aside multiple parallels with the horse guards of later

---

[37] Busch (Busch, *Militär in Rom*, 80 n. 420) reaches a similar conclusion and also draws this comparison, even though she made her calculations before the Lateran Project and therefore without the benefit of the Lateran survey data and this concept model. Her figure of a maximum size of 2.6 ha was reached separately from our own estimates but is impressively close to it.

[38] C. S. Sommer, '"Where did they put the horses?" Überlegungen zu Aufbau und Starke römischer Auxiliartruppen und deren Unterbringung in den Kastellen', in W. Czysz, C. M. Hüssen, H. P. Kuhnen, C. S. Sommer and G. Weber (eds.), *Provincialrömische Forschungen: Festschrift für Günter Ulbert zum 65. Geburtstag* (Rahden, 1995), 149–68; Hodgson and Bidwell, 'Auxiliary barracks in a new light'.

[39] Very few cavalry barrack door openings have been identified with confidence, as the doors and walls have seldom survived on both sides. Recent work at Vindolanda, where such features have been identified, suggests, however, that doors for horses ranged from 1.1 to 1.35 m wide, in contrast with those for people, which tended to have openings 0.8 m wide (Dr Andrew Birley, pers. com.)

sovereigns, which frequently kept contingents of riders on security and ceremonial duties close to their monarch while accommodating the main body further afield, the situation in Rome would support such an arrangement. First, there would need to be contingents at the imperial palaces themselves. Second, given the growth in importance of the Sessorian palace under the Severans, some kind of security would have been required to the east of the Caelian, most likely beyond the line later taken by the Aurelian Wall. While much attention has rightly been given to the presence of a cemetery of the *equites singulares* on the site later occupied by the basilica of Saint Peter and Saint Marcellinus and the mausoleum of Saint Helena, more attention might be given to what this means. Though not impossibly far away from the known forts of the *equites singulares*, it is far from being the most convenient distance from them. Was its location partly chosen because it lay closer to an unknown station of the horse guards positioned within the imperial estate east of the Sessorian, but close enough to provide appropriate security against approaches to the palace from that quarter?

While other locations where horse guards were stationed around Rome must remain a matter of conjecture, what is certain is that both the Castra Priora and the Castra Nova served as headquarters for the two distinctive elements of the *equites singulares*. This much is clear not only from the soldiers' own epitaphs and diplomas, which frequently state whether they were from the C.P. or C.N. force, but also emerges from the archaeology. The 'grand hall' of the Castra Priora on the Via Tasso, which was vividly described by Lanciani,[40] and which yielded a fine collection of regimental dedications, is most plausibly explained as the basilican hall of that unit's *principia*. Even more clear is that the *principia* of the Castra Nova lies under today's archbasilica of Saint John Lateran.

What more can these remains tell us? A peculiarity of the excavated areas of the Castra Nova as we see them today is that though threshold stones often remain *in situ*, and several major sections of street side guttering survived, much of the original flooring has been removed, most probably by builders working on the Constantinian basilica. There are two exceptions, however: a small stretch of stone-paved flooring flanked by gutters survived between the two surviving barrack-like buildings, while traces of a tessellated floor laid over a deep earth backfill was preserved in one of the *principia* offices.

The survival of decorative elements within the *principia* allows us to visualise the opulence of the complex with a high confidence. Fig. 6.5

---

[40] R. Lanciani, *The Ruins and Excavations of Ancient Rome: A Companion Book for Students and Travellers* (Cambridge, 1897), 338.

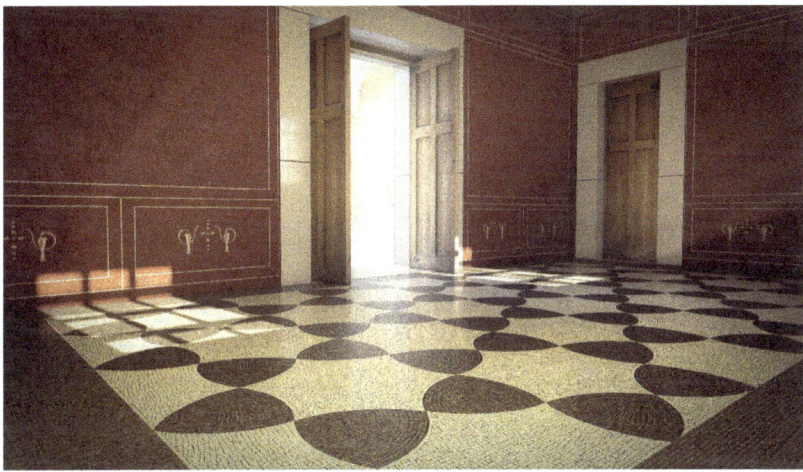

**Fig. 6.5** Visualisation of an office room in the *principia* of the Castra Nova *c.* AD 310. The red wall plaster appears to have replaced an earlier decorative scheme, but otherwise the room retained its original late second-century form and floor (Peverett and Haynes).

depicts an office room in the *principia* of the Castra Nova as it may have appeared around AD 310. The red wall plaster may have replaced an earlier decorative scheme, but otherwise the room retained its original late second-century form and floor. In addition to tessellated floor design, the lower decorative panels of several plastered walls survive. These in turn show where the marble door frames of entry points to each of the offices would have been fastened. In the courtyard, fragments of green marble attest to what would have been a lavishly appointed space. The surviving remains do not permit us to determine the level of decoration applied to other buildings within the complex, however, and scholars have rightly hesitated to endorse the assumptions Lanciani made about the opulent material found in excavations at the Corsini chapel.[41] While material from the *castra* was recovered there in 1732, some of the material clearly came from beneath the level of the fort. Yet, given what Lanciani saw in the hall at the Castra Nova's twin site, the Castra Priora, and given what is known of the opulence of the Castra Praetoria – home to twenty-six documented tessellated floors,[42] it is likely that the complex was lavishly appointed. Fragments of fine marble and porphyry have been found in the basement of the westernmost range of barrack-like buildings in positions that make it

---

[41] Lanciani, *Ruins and Excavations*, 338. Both Liverani (Chapter 2 in this volume) and Busch (*Militär in Rom*, 83) note that significant elements of the material recovered in the eighteenth century would have pre-dated the *castra* phase.

[42] Busch, *Militär in Rom*, 70.

most likely that they originated in the fort, rather than from pre-Severan residences or the Constantinian basilica.[43]

Seen in a Severan context, the construction of this elaborate fort with its lavish headquarters on the Caelian points to two themes. First, it is another, very conspicuous, marker of the link between imperial power and military power, a leitmotif of Severus' reign, and one further associated by contemporaries with the increasingly alien face of Roman soldiers in Rome. While in reality Rome's armies had long been intensely cosmopolitan, and while indeed representatives of their diverse ranks would have made their way to the Caelian from at least the time of Trajan, when the Castra Priora and the Castra Peregrina, a base for personnel travelling through Rome, were established, the Castra Nova added to a mix famously lamented by Dio.[44] The presence of large numbers of men from the Danubian provinces is clearly attested in their ranks, at precisely the time when recruitment to guard units from Italy and neighbouring provinces was suspended and/or decreasing. M. Aurelius Bithus, a trooper from the *equites singulares*, epitomises the change. As his epitaph states, he was from the C(astra) N(ova).[45] Not only is his Thracian origin recorded on the inscription, but he is depicted on his tombstone in the guise of the Thracian Hero, a Danubian divinity extensively worshipped by members of the horse guards. Bithus' contemporaries at the Castra Priora honoured the god too; he appears on the altars recovered from their hall on the Via Tasso. At one level, therefore, the evidence from these forts, situated a few short minutes' trot from the Senate House, strongly suggests that Dio's concerns about a growing and alien military presence at the heart of empire were well founded. They also, however, show what this meant in bricks and mortar – as not only the numbers of armed and belted men in Rome grew,[46] but the very shape of the city was transformed to accommodate them.

For all that Severus valued military power, however, it is clear from both his propaganda and his building programmes that he did not simply wish to be seen as a war leader. Severan coinage from AD 200 onwards represents the emperor as *Restitutor Urbis*, restorer of the city.[47] His programme for Rome has recently been usefully examined by Lusnia, who has drawn attention to its scale and ambition, and noted its importance in revitalising

---

[43] The possibility must remain that the substantial structure encountered by Vacca in 1594 during works under the archbasilica was in fact part of the *castra*. The description of niches partially paved with porphyry could well describe a major building within that complex. See Colini, *Storia e topografia*, 354 n. 129; F. Vacca, *Memorie di varie antichità trovate in diversi luoghi della città di Roma* (Rome, 1594), 120.

[44] Dio Cass. 75.2.6.  [45] *CIL* VI, 3195.  [46] Coulston, "'Armed and Belted Men'", fig. 5.8.

[47] For example, *RIC* IV, part 1, 113, no. 168a.

Rome after the great fire of AD 192. The Castra Nova is included in her comprehensive appraisal, but we would argue that her treatment of it does not convey the full importance of the site.[48] Not only is the New Fort part of the transformation of Rome into an increasingly militarised space, it is also sits both geographically and temporally at a vital point within that transformation. As Severus enters Rome as a victorious commander of armies, he anchors his powers and plans here, before he embarks on the extensive programme of civil works which are then foregrounded in his persona as *Restitutor Urbis*. The *castra* is one of the first of the new Severan buildings precisely because it is so important to his vision of power and governance. No less importantly, as has been noted above, it must be set not only in the context of the restoration of the historic core of the city, but also with a view to a new future for Rome's eastern extremities. The Castra Nova, the Castra Priora and, after the Praetorian Guard is once again operational, the Castra Praetoria partially demarcate a new east, and the new east, with its confiscations and schemes for the Sessorian palace, takes on an imperial form that will endure well into the reign of Constantine.

Indeed, in the years that followed the establishment of the Castra Nova, the area that stretched from the Lateran to what became the Porta Maggiore witnessed a range of developments, many of which were of dazzling opulence. A well-established tendency for luxury residences with roots in the *horti* found here from the first century continued, but an increasing amount of residential space seems to have been held by members of the imperial house and imperial favourites. The development of the Sessorian is perhaps the most conspicuous element of this tendency, but other structures must be linked to this phenomenon. Emperors had incorporated circuses into their *horti* before, but Caracalla's decision to build a circus here still larger than the Circus Maximus reflects how imperial investment further transformed the area. Even the construction of the Aurelian Wall in

---

[48] S. S. Lusnia, *Creating Severan Rome: The Architecture and Self-Image of L. Septimius Severus (AD 193–211)* (Collection Latomus 345) (Leuven, 2014). See also Racine (F. Racine, 'Review of Lusnia 2014 Creating Severan Rome', *Bryn Mawr Classical Review* Blog 2015.06.23 (2015) (http://bmcr.brynmawr.edu/2015/2015-06-23.html) (last viewed 9 April 2018)), who makes a similar point in his review of Lusnia: 'These structures were not just built and restored for practical purposes, as Lusnia details, but were also in dialogue with other monuments either thematically or through the rhythms of city life. The new camp of the *equites singulares*, to take just one example, is seen here only as a product of the government's involvement in changing or preserving the physical aspect of the city. But the new, expanded military camp was also a monumental symbol of the emperor's military persona, in sync with the martial themes proclaimed in celebrations, on coins and on monuments discussed in previous chapters. Together with the newly renovated praetorian camp, it also framed Rome's eastern neighbourhoods and was furthermore within striking distance of the new Sessorian palace.'

the 270s, which cut through Caracalla's circus, reaffirmed rather than reversed the trends emerging under Severus. And, so far as we can see from the archaeological evidence, the Castra Nova endured unaffected, while the Sessorian grew steadily in grandeur.

As noted above, dedications found within the Castra Nova demonstrate that the fort was still in active use into the Tetrarchy, and the academic consensus remains that it would have been in use when, in AD 312, the *equites singulares* joined the forces that rode out to confront Constantine at the Milvian Bridge.[49] Constantinian victory meant an end to the old imperial guard units of the capital, which abruptly disappear from history. The implications of this at the Castra Nova site are clear and dramatic. An old symbol of imperial power is replaced with new symbols of a new order bound up with a new emperor, a cathedral and a baptistery.

The gift of the site to the Church had many advantages. It required neither purchase nor confiscation. It lay close to an area further developed by Constantine and in convenient proximity to the Sessorian palace. As his architects were subsequently to demonstrate in the construction of Saint Peter's, they were as capable of re-engineering the topography of the city for their monuments as Severus' architects had been. Yet, it is hard to escape the conclusion that the great platform of the Castra Nova presented itself as a ready-made opportunity, fit to sustain a massive building at this location, one which might dominate the land southeast of the city. Imperial demolition teams once again worked their way across the site. An essential preliminary, once more, would have been to strip the buildings of finer materials and architectural elements. Fragments of broken columns and capitals that may have adorned the *castra* appear in the basilica's foundations, while smaller pieces of porphyry – which would appropriate to an imperial guard barracks – have been found in the backfill on the barrack basements. It seems highly likely, though it cannot be proven, that many of the more intact elements of the *castra* were used in the ornamentation of the church itself.

Thereafter, the *castra* superstructure was levelled. Walls of its interior buildings were cut down until they projected no more than 1.4 m above the ground surface of the Severan platform. The site was then backfilled. Some elements of the superstructure of the bath complex to the west survived, however, and can still be seen today in the walls of the chapel of Saint Venanzio adjoining the Lateran baptistery (Fig. 6.6). Construction of the cathedral would have begun with the apse, and while its construction

---

[49] For the end of the guard, see Zos. 2.17, 2; M. P. Speidel, 'Maxentius and his "equites singulares" in the battle of the Milvian Bridge', *Classical Antiquity* 5, 2 (1986), 253–62; Busch, *Militär in Rom*, 75.

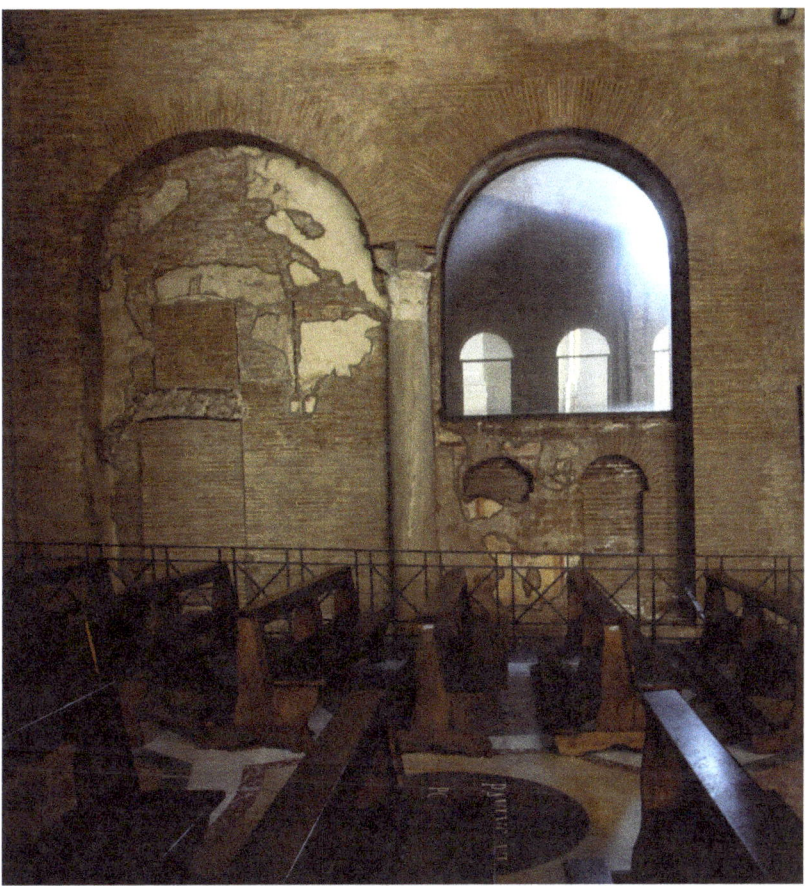

**Fig. 6.6** The complex, multi-phase wall of Saint Venanzio preserves elements of the walls of the original third-century bath complex (Lateran Project).

would have necessitated the destruction of the Trapezoidal Building, it was placed to exploit the terracing originally created by the builders of the *castra*. The effect was that the bulk of the apse projected west of the edge of the former fort's platform, while the floor of the basilica itself lay on a surface of rubble and backfill up to 1.46 m thick stretched across the platform itself.

It is striking that the basilica was built in such a way that it occupied the same space as that previously occupied by the central range of the *castra*'s buildings, the most imposing structures in what must have been a very grand complex indeed. The *principia*, discussed above, would have been designed to impress, but the basilica built above its ruins would have dwarfed its predecessor. Fig. 6.7 superimposes our concept model of the

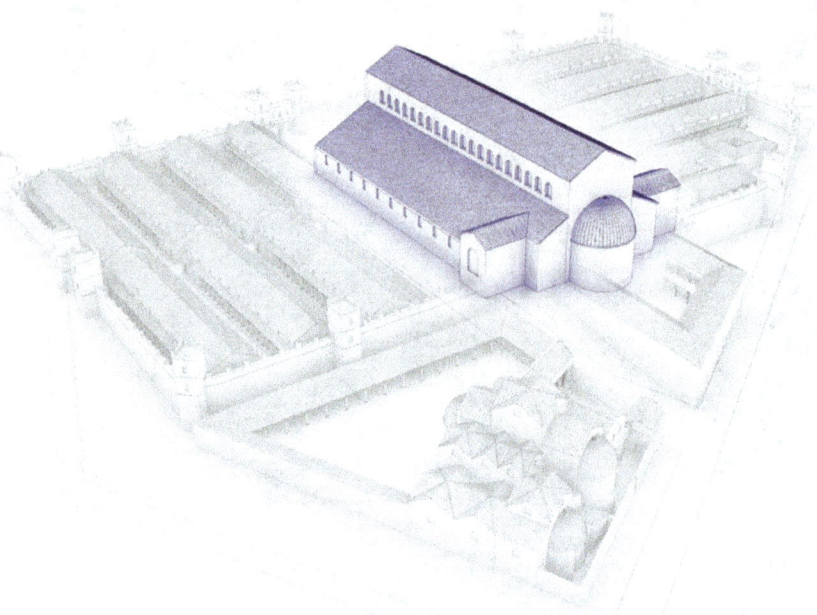

Fig. 6.7 Concept model showing the spatial relationship between the Constantinian basilica and its predecessor, the Castra Nova (Peverett and Haynes, incorporating model developed by Bosman, Liverani, Peverett and Haynes).

Constantinian basilica upon its predecessor, the Castra Nova, to show the relative size and location of the two complexes. If our understanding of the site is correct, the main axis of Constantine's basilica essentially bisects the site on which the *castra* lay, a decision that is unlikely to have been incidental to the message conveyed by the new installation. Given this it might be tempting to assume that elements of the basilica layout exploited some of the pre-existing walls of the *castra* and its interior buildings, but, they do not appear to have done so. While the use of the fort platform framed the general orientation of the basilica, detailed analysis shows a variance of 2.8° between the axis of its nave and the line of the main west–east route through the *castra*, the *via principalis*. Across the breadth of the building, this would have appeared as a marked difference in alignment.

This divergence in alignment does not change the essential point that both symbolically and physically the Castra Nova provided the foundations for Constantine's Lateran basilica. The fort's fundamental importance in the Severan transformation of Rome, a transformation that stressed the centrality of military force to imperial power, but which also ushered in a series of enduring additions to the fabric of the city and its palaces, meant that it lay at an ideal spot for the great Constantinian project that was to give the world its first cathedral. Minutes from the Forum to the west, and from the Sessorian palace to the east, the Lateran was the perfect location for an enduring monument to the God whose divine favour underpinned the new regime.

# 7 | Andrea Busiri Vici and the Excavations of 1876: A Reassessment of the Archaeological Evidence

SABINA FRANCINI

On 16 June 1846, Giovanni Maria Mastai Ferretti ascended to the Holy See, taking the papal name Pius IX. His pontificate would prove to be one of the longest in the history of the Church: thirty-two years, filled with transformative events leading to the establishment of the Kingdom of Italy and consequently the end of the papacy's temporal power. These circumstances informed the decisions made by Pius IX, and his successor, Leo XIII, with regard to the Lateran complex. In this sense, the demolition of the apse and the Portico Leoniano in order to build a new and grandiose presbytery can be seen as essentially a political decision. Following the proclamation of Rome as capital of the Kingdom of Italy, it was necessary for the pontiff to reaffirm his presence in the city by all possible means, including the restoration and enhancement of religious edifices.

In 1874 a number of cracks were noted in the apsidal conch of the basilica, indications of structural damage considered threatening to the structure's stability. This led to the decision to investigate the condition of the wall structures and the edifice's foundations.[1] For this very purpose, in 1876 Pius IX created a commission to supervise the works that would be conducted on the apse; the commission was presided over by the Secretary of State, Cardinal Giacomo Antonelli, along with the architects Francesco Fontana and Antonio Sarti, Andrea Busiri Vici (nominated director of the works) and, among others, Monsignor Vincenzo Tizzani as representative of the Lateran Chapter.[2]

The works, begun in the same year and focused on the sector to the west of the apse and the Portico Leoniano, brought to light not only the foundations of the basilica and portico, but also the remains of a pre-existing edifice, the

---

I would like to thank the architect Saverio Busiri Vici in allowing me to view the original tables by Andrea Busiri Vici held in his private archive, and also for having personally taken them to the Vatican Museums so that I might photograph them with all necessary care. My thanks also to Dott.ssa Barbara Jatta, director of the Vatican Museums, for the valuable advice and suggestions. This chapter was translated from the Italian by Dr Alexander Agostini.

[1] The story of the Lateran apse, from its construction to its demolition, has been thoroughly scrutinized by Monica Morbidelli: M. Morbidelli, *L'Abside di S. Giovanni in Laterano: Una vicenda controversa* (Rome, 2010).

[2] Morbidelli, *L'Abside di S. Giovanni in Laterano*, 81–9.

so-called Trapezoidal Building/Insula. As the works progressed, a series of disagreements began to emerge between members of the commission regarding the fate of the apse and its mosaic decoration, executed by Jacopo Torriti in 1291. As director of the works since 1876, Busiri Vici endeavoured to find solutions that would reconcile the various parties involved. His attempts to resolve diverse approaches are attested by the different proposals he laid out, from the plain enlargement of the presbytery to the much more elaborate but brilliantly envisaged relocation of the apse. This last proposal also included a plan for the subterranean portion of the basilica that considered leaving in plain view the recently discovered ancient structures (Fig. 7.1).[3]

This is not the place to recount the events that occurred between 1874 and 1886, the year in which the new apse was inaugurated. Suffice it to recall that on different occasions during these years animated and violently discordant voices were raised concerning the ongoing works, articulating the indignation of both the Italian and the wider European

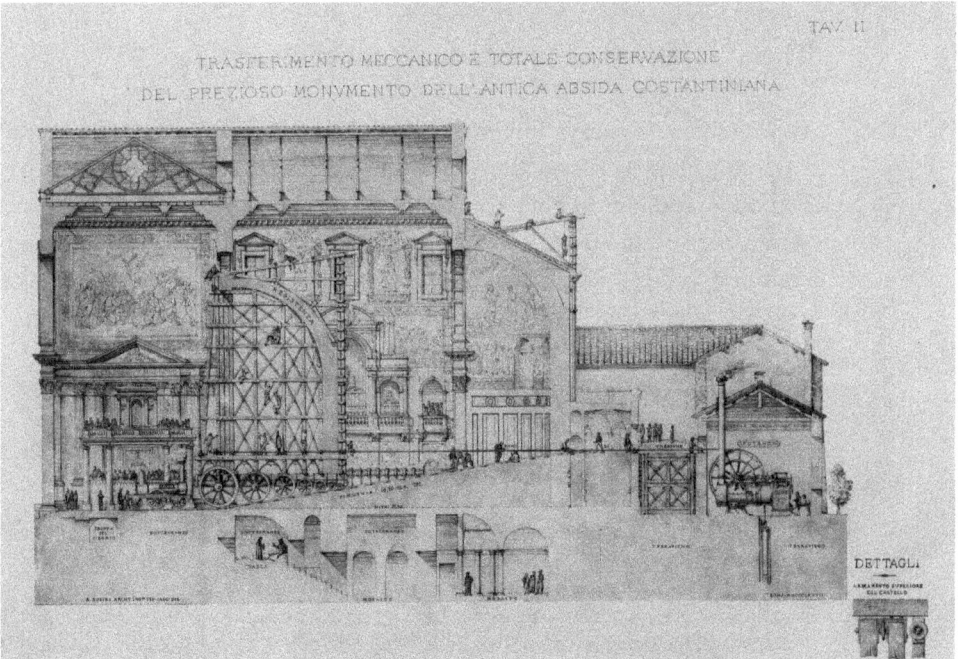

**Fig. 7.1** A cross-section illustrating the plan for the mechanical relocation of the Constantinian apse along with the rearrangement of the underground archaeological area (Busiri Vici, *L'obelisco vaticano*).

---

[3] Morbidelli, *L'Abside di S. Giovanni in Laterano*, 141–7.

academic world with regard to the probable destruction of the apse and Torriti's precious mosaic. These controversies did not, however, halt the inexorable destruction of the apse and the ill-fated 'restoration' and relocation of the mosaic.

Andrea Busiri Vici's direction of the works at the Lateran was brusquely terminated on 7 May 1877, at which time he was replaced by Virginio Vespignani.[4] This pattern of succession allows us to understand better the reasons behind the discrepancies in the documentation currently in our possession: Busiri Vici's papers were highly detailed and factual; Vespignani's were by contrast notably simplified.[5] It is to the latter that the debatable conservation project of the recently discovered structures must be attributed; this consisted of the complete razing of the raised portions of the walls, the obliteration of a number of structures with the foundation pillars of the new apse, the use of terracotta bricks to define the contours of the destroyed features, and the employment of pitch to cover gaps in the mosaics.

## The Excavations Conducted by Andrea Busiri Vici[6]

In March 1876 excavation works began in the area to the west of the Lateran's apse to assess the solidity of the foundations of the Portico Leoniano and the basilica's apse.[7] Preliminary work revealed the presence, below the medieval and modern infills, of a mosaic flooring composed of black-and-white *tesserae*. From March to July 1876 the ancient structures were freed from the infills, and although not

---

[4] ASV, Palazzo Ap., titoli IX, 268, fol. 258. In a letter sent to Virginio Vespignani, Cardinal Giovanni Simeoni, secretary of state upon the death of Cardinal Antonelli and new president of the Lateran Committee, informed Vespignani of his nomination as the new director of the works. See also Morbidelli, *L'Abside di S. Giovanni in Laterano*, 149.

[5] Two original table-plates executed by Vespignani in 1877 and preserved at the Fondo Lanciani of the BiASA of Palazzo Venezia show the archaeological features that were brought to light from the area of Lateran apse as well as the contours of the new presbytery's future foundations: BiASA, *Collezione Lanciani, Roma XI*, 43, nos. 1, 11.

[6] Andrea Busiri was born in Rome in 1818, the son of Giulio Cesare Busiri and Barbara, only daughter of the architect Andrea Vici, from whom Andrea would inherit, as part of a bequest, his second surname. Accordingly, Andrea was raised in a cultured environment that allowed him to acquire solid historical and technical notions. Nominated first architect of the Fabbrica di San Pietro, he followed the planning and construction of numerous edifices of the papal state, as well as the restoration of numerous churches: S. Busiri Vici, *L'architettura di Saverio Busiri Vici e cenni su alcuni altri architetti della sua famiglia: Volume primo 1651-1974* (Rome, 1974), 21-6; Morbidelli, *L'Abside di S. Giovanni in Laterano*, 79-81.

[7] ASV, Segreteria di Stato, Spoglio Leone XIII, busta X, VIII, fol. 55.

requested by the committee, Andrea Busiri Vici proceeded with accurate graphic and photographic documentation of the excavation. The documents produced by Busiri Vici that will be examined here are:

A black-and-white photograph taken by Busiri Vici himself[8] on 8 August 1876, addressed to Rodolfo Lanciani, at the time president of the Commissione Archeologica Comunale,[9] and currently located in the Fondo Lanciani at the BiASA of Piazza Venezia.[10] The photograph, taken from the western side, shows the area during the excavations, contained to the east by the yet-to-be-demolished Portico Leoniano and with the remains of the so-called Trapezoidal Building/Insula visible in the foreground (Fig. 7.2).

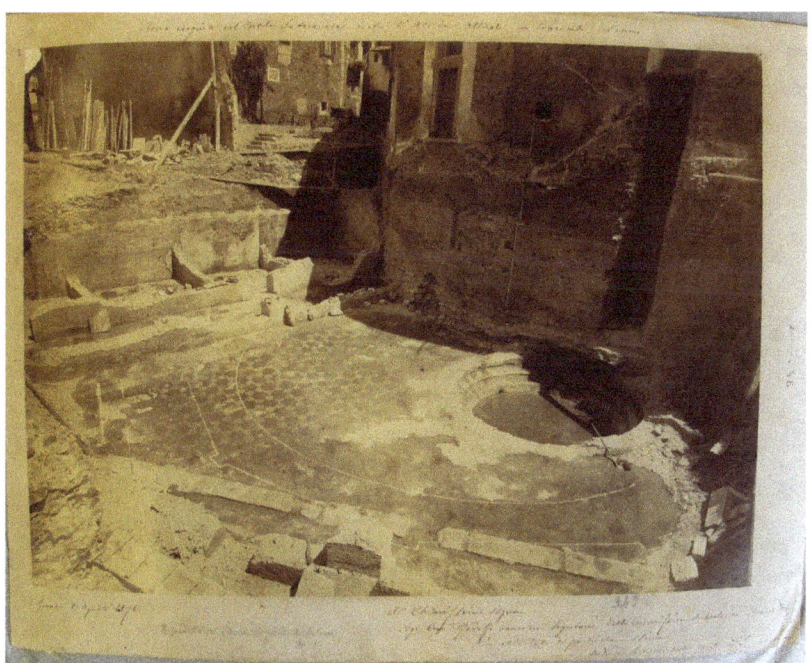

**Fig. 7.2** A. Busiri Vici, 8 August 1876. West-side view of the excavation area (BiASA, *Collezione Lanciani, Roma XI*, 43).

---

[8] The photograph is not signed, but it is likely that it was taken by Busiri Vici, who was accustomed to undertake all the drawn and photographic documentation of his works on his own or with the help of his son Carlo.

[9] These indications are transcribed on the photograph's edge by Busiri Vici himself.

[10] BiASA, *Collezione Lanciani, Roma XI*, 43, no. 5.

- An illustration on paper drawn by Andrea Busiri Vici in 1877, using black Indian ink for the base of the picture and watercolours for the details of the exposed walls.[11] The plate illustrates the discoveries that took place in the western portion of the basilica during the 1876 works directed by the architect (Fig. 7.3). The feature's height, transcribed in red Indian ink, is calculated from the floor of the nineteenth-century basilica of Saint John Lateran. In the illustration's lower part details of the wall structures and decorative apparatus are drawn both in Indian ink and watercolour. The original transcripts describe the nature of the excavated infills, accompanied by a brief list of the materials found in them, along with the results of a coring test conducted in the area of the Trapezoidal Building; in the closing part Busiri specifies that in his project of expanding the apse, approved by the Accademia di San Luca in 1876, such finds would have remained visible and accessible[12] (see Fig.7.1).

Through the documentation produced by Andrea Busiri Vici, it is possible to identify the structures destroyed in later demolition as well as archaeological elements omitted from successive studies. The findings encompass a wide-ranging time span, from the first century AD to the early medieval period, divisible into four distinct phases:

1. Structures that pre-date the construction of the Trapezoidal Building and the *castra*.
2. Structures that are associated with the *castra* and the Trapezoidal Building.

---

[11] The table, titled *Arcibasilica–Lateranense, Domus–Lateranorum, scoperte nelle escavazioni fatte per i grandi lavori e restauri dell'anno MDCCCLXXVI*, together with the other tables of the project, would have been part of the *Album*, set in the appendix of the folder: A. Busiri Vici, *Il Laterano nel Pontificato di Pio IX, Progetti del Nuovo Coro, Presbiterio e dipendenze dell'Arcibasilica Lateranense, grandi lavori finora eseguiti, scoperta dell'antica casa dei Laterani, rilievi dell'Absida e Portico leonino, restauro dell'Absida costantiniana, suo trasferimento meccanico e conservazione* (Rome, 1868/78). The numerous preserved copies do not include the illustrated tables. It is probable that the architect thought of publishing the tables in the near future, but desisted after losing the position as director of works. The only preserved original copy, presented here, is kept, along with the other original tables on the Lateran projects, in Saverio Busiri Vici's private archive. The original on paper measuring 70 x 100 cm is the only one with handwritten comments and observations by the author. From these originals derive the poorly legible photographic copies preserved in the Vatican Apostolic Library along with the copies in the archive of Clemente and Antonello Busiri Vici. Some excellent reproductions in black and white are published in a limited number of copies in the volume: A. Busiri Vici, *L'obelisco vaticano nel terzo centenario della sua erezione* (Rome, 1886).

[12] The project for an enlargement of the apse and the rearrangement of the underground area was presented in a working paper titled 'Trasferimento meccanico e totale conservazione del prezioso monumento dell'antica absida costantiniana.' See Busiri Vici, *L'obelisco vaticano*, table II.

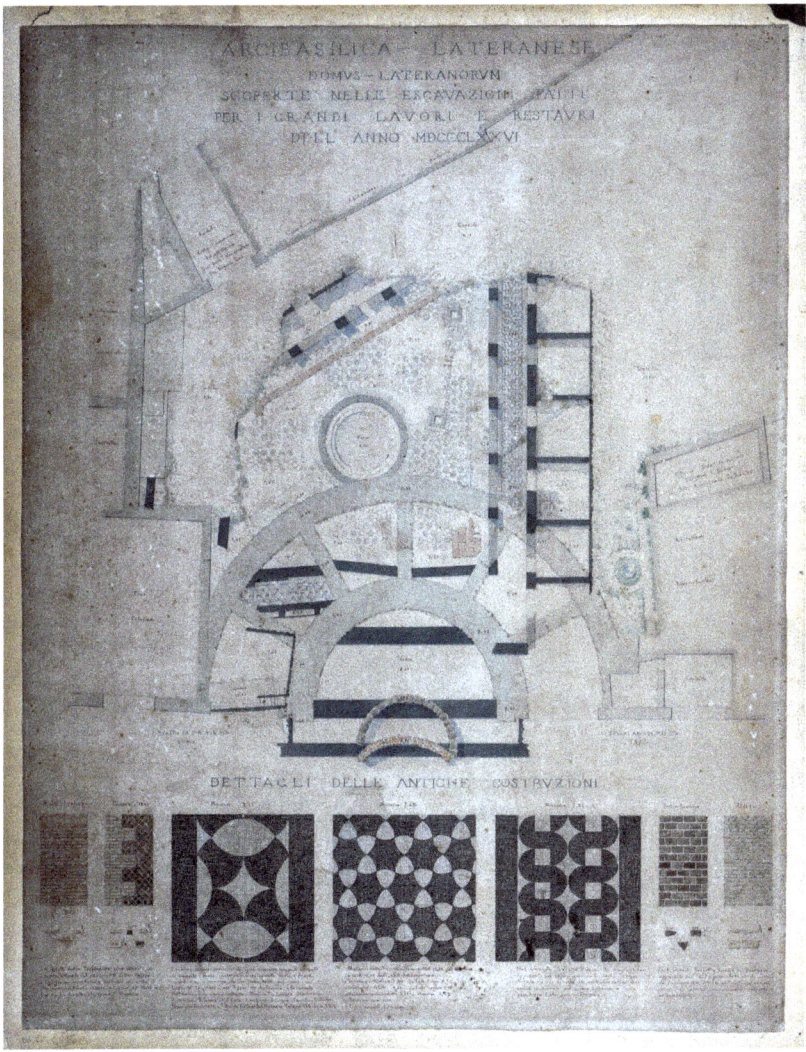

**Fig. 7.3** A. Busiri Vici, plan of the excavations in the area of the apse, 1877 (Private archive, Saverio Busiri Vici).

3. The Constantinian Basilica del Salvatore.[13]
4. Early medieval structures.

---

[13] For this construction phase and the successive building of the Portico Leoniano in the fifth century AD, the nineteenth-century documentation has been impeccably interpreted and published by Lia Barelli and Monica Morbidelli: L. Barelli and M. Morbidelli, '"Ad imitazione, e somiglianza di quello che v'era anticamente": Il restauro del'abside di San Giovanni in Laterano a Roma al tempo di Nicola IV (1288–1292)', in V. Franchetti Pardo (ed.), *Arnolfo di Cambio e la sua epoca. Costruire, scolpire, dipingere, decorare (Atti del Convegno, Firenze–Colle di Val d'Elsa, 7–10 marzo 2006)* (Rome, 2006), 197–208; see also Morbidelli, *L'Abside di S. Giovanni in Laterano*, 37–44.

## Structures that Pre-Date the Construction of the Trapezoidal Building

The presence of walled structures below the mosaic flooring of the Trapezoidal Building can be seen in the floor itself. Subsidence, corresponding to underlying voids or, more likely, partial infills, are clearly visible, while the high points in the sunken floor indicate the presence of walls associated with earlier structures (Fig. 7.4).

This observation is also confirmed by Busiri Vici's report, which acknowledges that the wall faces in coarse-laid brickwork were found below the Trapezoidal Building's courtyard floor.[14] A coring test was conducted upon Busiri's instructions to verify the extent and nature of the stratigraphy below the mosaics; the results were recorded in red Indian ink on the illustration under consideration (see Fig. 7.3), and also transcribed in the final report.[15] Below the mosaic flooring and its preparatory

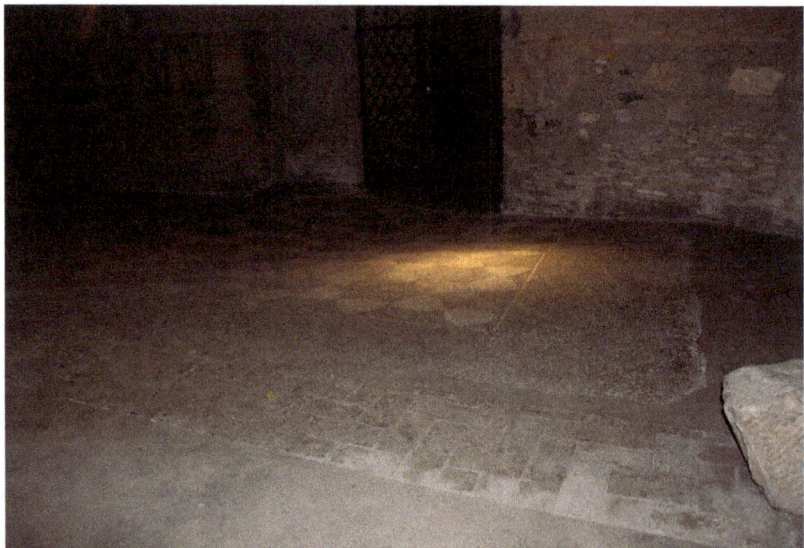

**Fig. 7.4** Northeastern corner of the courtyard of the Trapezoidal Insula: detail showing the depressions in the mosaic flooring corresponding to below-ground cavities or infills.

---

[14] Busiri Vici, *Il Laterano nel Pontificato*, 5–6: '... infatti i sottomuramenti ... del portico Leoniano ... poggiano sull'antico pavimento a mosaico, di opera posteriore ai Laterani, poiché sotto questo sonovi altri muri antichi a cortina ... further on he adds: ... è poi da notarsi che mentre gli antichi muri tanto inferiori che superiori al mosaico sono in laterizio con paramento a cortina, e quelli del Portico Leoniano in quadrelle di pietra di tufo ...'.

[15] Busiri Vici, *Il Laterano nel Pontificato*, 6.

layer, the core revealed 0.80 m thick infills consisting of rubble, building debris and fragmented ceramic building material covering archaeologically sterile strata. It can be assumed that structures measuring 0.80 m high faced in coarse-laid brickwork and founded on sterile volcanic soil survive below the mosaic floor. It is not possible to ascertain the exact location of all of these features, but it is likely that these were connected to other structures that pre-date the *castra* and the Trapezoidal Building. Indeed, in the southeastern corner of the courtyard below the mosaic flooring a great rectangular-shaped cistern was drawn by Busiri, with a southwest–northeast orientation, and with a ground level 2.50/2.75 m below the courtyard's mosaic flooring (Fig. 7.5).

The architect also describes the structure's form, noting that the great cistern, coated with hydraulic mortar, continues in a northeasterly direction, below the foundations of the Portico Leoniano, the apse and the

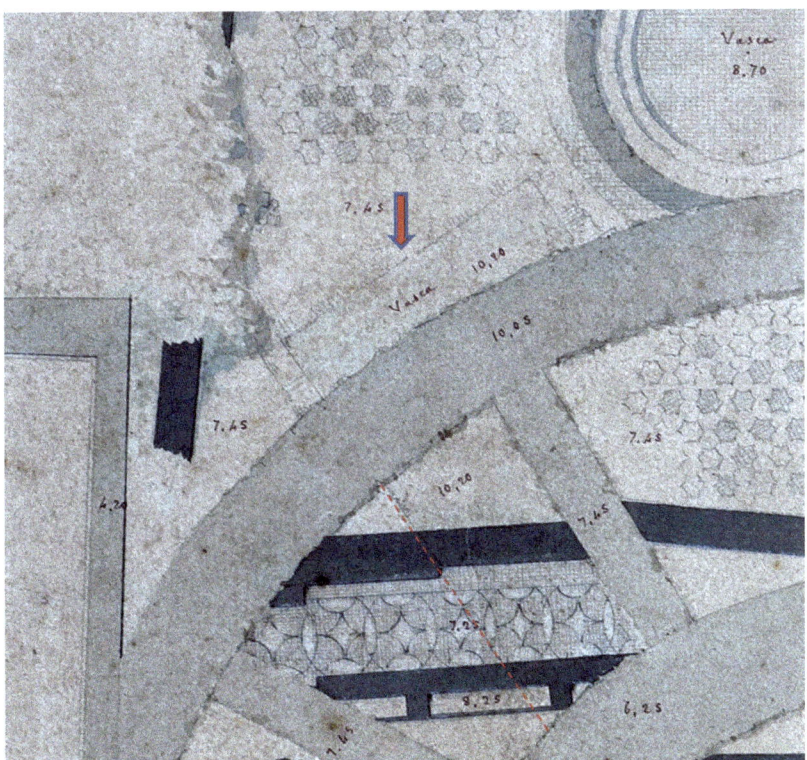

**Fig. 7.5** Detail of the 1876 illustration by Busiri Vici (see fig. 3) featuring the basin below the mosaic flooring. A traced outline indicates the southeastern limit of the structure.

perimeter walls of the Trapezoidal Building.[16] From this it can be deduced that it pre-dates the construction of these edifices. A further structure can be considered as pertaining to buildings that preceded the construction of the Trapezoidal Building. This structure takes on the form of two superimposed rooms, connected by way of a staircase and situated to the east of the Trapezoidal Building's eastern wall in close proximity to the southeastern boundary of the 1876 excavation (Fig. 7.6). The upper level (A)

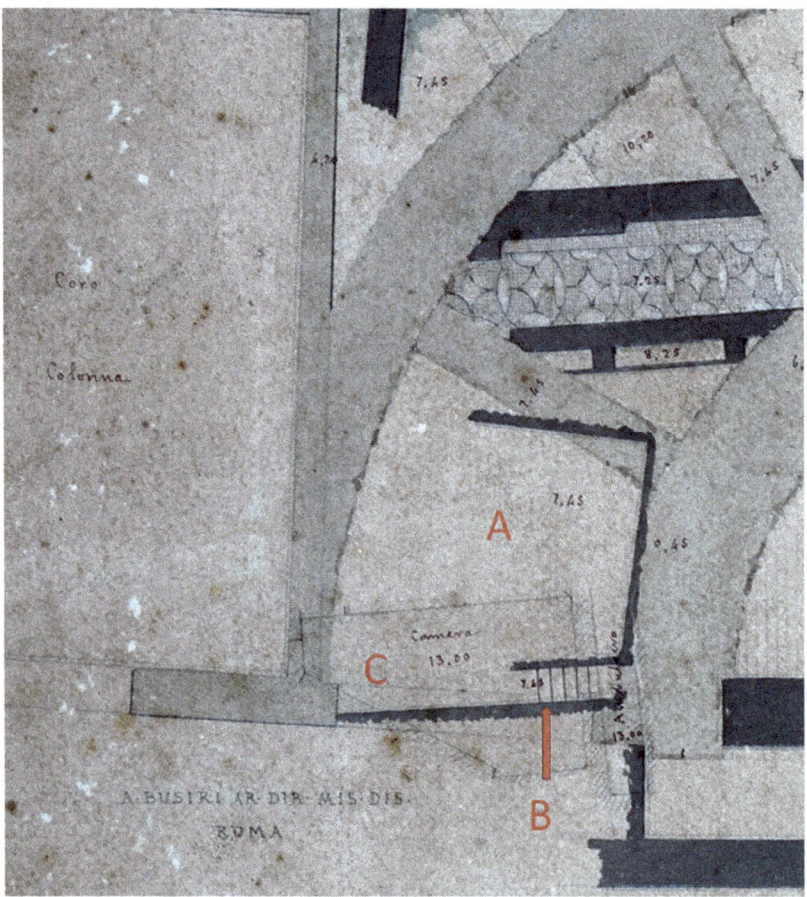

**Fig. 7.6** Detail of the 1876 illustration by Busiri Vici (see fig. 3) showing the rooms discovered in the southeastern portion of the excavation: A. room with surrounding wall facings in *opus testaceum*; B. staircase connecting to the lower room; C. enclosed area located below room A with wall facings in *opus mixtum*.

---

[16] Busiri Vici, *Il Laterano nel Pontificato*, 5; E. Stevenson, 'Scoperte di antichi edifizi al Laterano', *Annali dell'Istituto di corrispondenza Archeologica* 49 (1877), 332–84, at p. 338.

much larger and irregularly shaped, was identified by Busiri at 7.45 m beneath the floor level of the basilica; according to Stevenson the structure possessed wall facings in *opus latericium*.[17] Through a staircase (B) it was possible to gain access to the second room (C) set 5.50 m below the upper level (A) of the structure (12.95 m below the floor of the basilica). This building had a vaulted ceiling and wall facings in *opus mixtum*, as depicted in Busiri's drawing (see Figs 7.3, 7.7).[18] It is clear, therefore, that there were brick-faced buildings in this sector of the Lateran prior to the building of the *castra* and its annexes, that these were razed during the construction of the fort, and that a great cistern possibly pertaining to a suburban villa lies underneath the basilica. Another structure built in good-quality *opus mixtum* (visible in Busiri's drawing) might be considered as part of this vast residential complex, and is possibly attributable to late Flavian restorations of the same suburban villa.[19] We can ascribe this phase to between the second half of the first century AD and the last decade of the second century AD. Separate consideration must be made for the room in *opus latericium* seen by Stevenson and drawn by Busiri, which, for a number of reasons, is more likely associated with the great construction phase that witnessed the construction of the Trapezoidal Building and the *castra*.

## Castra Nova Equitum Singularium and the Trapezoidal Building

Between the end of the second and the beginning of the third century AD, the wall structures now below the courtyard of the Trapezoidal Building were razed and the rooms topped with a 0.85 m thick infill, as indicated by the coring test conducted by Busiri Vici mentioned above.[20] The Trapezoidal Building was built above them, while the room in *opus mixtum*

---

[17] Stevenson, 'Scoperte di antichi edifizi al Laterano', 338.
[18] Busiri Vici, *Il Laterano nel Pontificato*, 6. Together with the summary description of the two rooms, Busiri Vici reports the finding in the lower room of a terracotta Victory, a subject similar to an antefix fragment of a winged Victory currently in the Antiquarium of the Lateran excavations: see G. Spinola, 'Sculture, rilevi, decorazione architettonica, iscrizioni e reperti ceramici', in P. Liverani (ed.), *Laterano i: Scavi sotto la Basilica di S. Giovanni in Laterano*, vol. I: *Materiali* (Vatican City, 1998), 17–114, at p. 79 n. 398.
[19] Colini also mentions the presence of wall fragments in *opus reticulatum* in the area located within the apse and between its wall and one of the nearby barracks, which he reconnects to the room in mixed work seen by Busiri Vici: A. M. Colini, *Storia e topografia del Celio nell'antichità* (Memorie della Pontificia Accademia Romana di Archeologia 7) (Vatican City, 1944), 342 n. 54. The remains of these walls are currently no longer visible. See also Spinola, Chapter 5 in this volume.
[20] See above, n. 14.

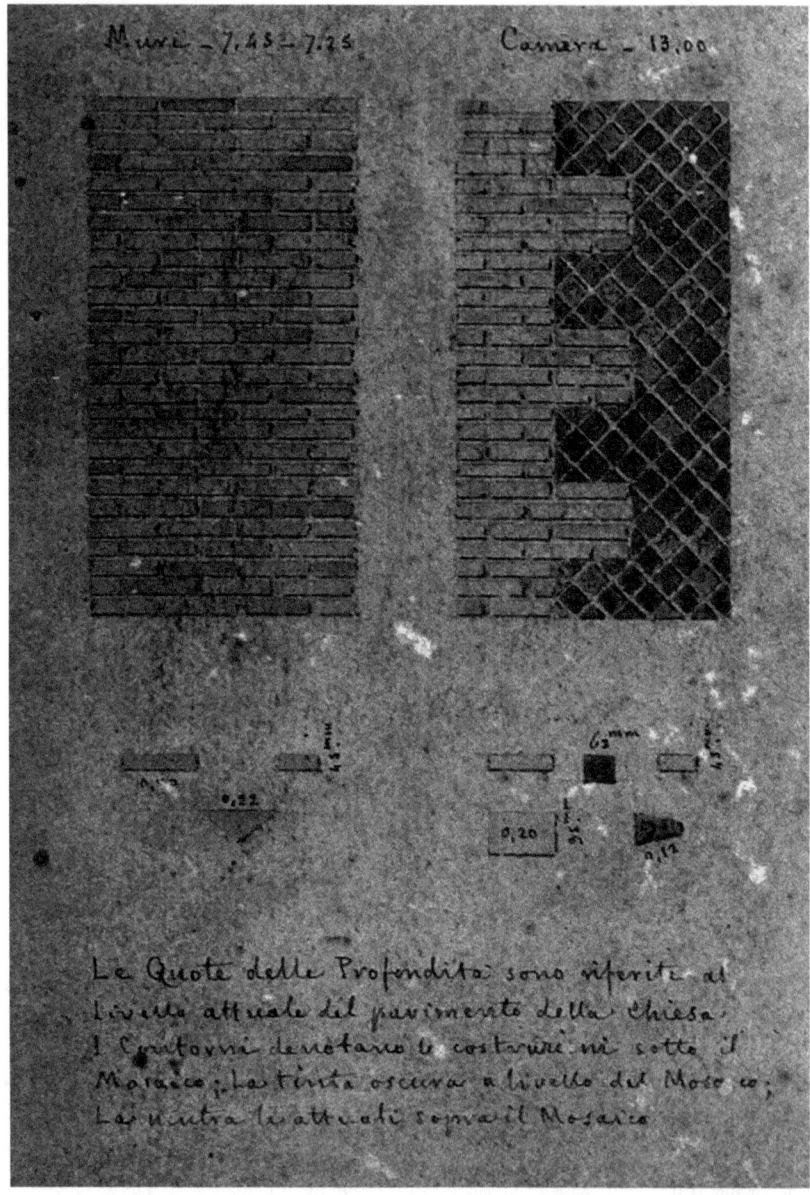

**Fig. 7.7** Detail of the 1876 illustration by Busiri Vici (see fig. 3) describing the wall typologies found during the excavation.

located to the southeast was connected by way of a staircase to an upper level characterised by wall facings in brickwork.[21] The Trapezoidal

---

[21] On the plan by Busiri Vici it is specified that this room was discovered 7.45 m below the basilica's flooring, and at the same height as the mosaic decorating the floor of the Trapezoidal Building's courtyard. It is probable that it therefore belonged to the same construction phase.

Building was located in an area bounded to the west by the original path of the Via Tusculana, to the east by the structures of the *castra*, and probably to the north by a second (interior?) passageway that divided it from the thermal areas discovered below the baptistery. The structure was composed of a large trapezoidal-shaped courtyard, paved with a mosaic in black and white *tesserae* with hexagonal motifs characterised by curved sides (see Fig. 7.3); a great marbled basin was visible in the centre, narrowing towards its bottom portion by way of three steps and reaching a depth of 1.45 m from the mosaic flooring. Two manhole covers, connected to one another by way of a sewer drain, were visible in the courtyard.[22] A pillared portico with a back corridor with mosaic flooring, featuring virtually rectangular shaped rooms characterised by plastered walls in red-and-yellow square designs and, at points, mosaic flooring, ran along the north, west and probably south side.[23] The north side, as we will see, was formed of a continuous wall, demolished by Vespignani, but whose trace remains in the nineteenth-century drawings. The portico was decorated, other than by the mosaic in the courtyard, with a black-and-white mosaic featuring a wave-like design, in the southern part of the site. The same mosaic design was also employed in the western part of the portico; indeed, it is the only portion still visible, while the rooms that looked out on the courtyard had mosaic floors with different motifs of types popular from the Antonine to the Severan periods (Fig. 7.3). The location, the relationship of the structures with the *castra*, together with the decorative apparatus, allow us to date the building to the last decade of the second century AD.[24]

Analysing the photographs and planimetry together with the notes of Busiri Vici, it is possible to acquire useful information for a better understanding of the processes involved in the building of the edifice along with some of its structural characteristics.

The photograph from 1876 clearly shows the features of the Trapezoidal Building's southern perimeter (Fig. 7.8). The wall presents a facing in brickwork, although in the south portion a clear thickening is visible, set at a wall height of 1.50 m, presumably built as a support and set against the bare earthen surface in the northern wall face. The hypothetical presence of

---

[22] The water drainage system is well described by Stevenson: Stevenson, 'Scoperte di antichi edifizi al Laterano', 337.

[23] The south side is not visible in the plan and photograph by Busiri because in 1876 that sector was interred. It is probable that the southern enclosure of the edifice was discovered during the continuation of the digs under Francesco Vespignani, and from him partially demolished and partially incorporated in the foundation of the basilica's new presbytery.

[24] See Spinola, Chapter 5 in this volume.

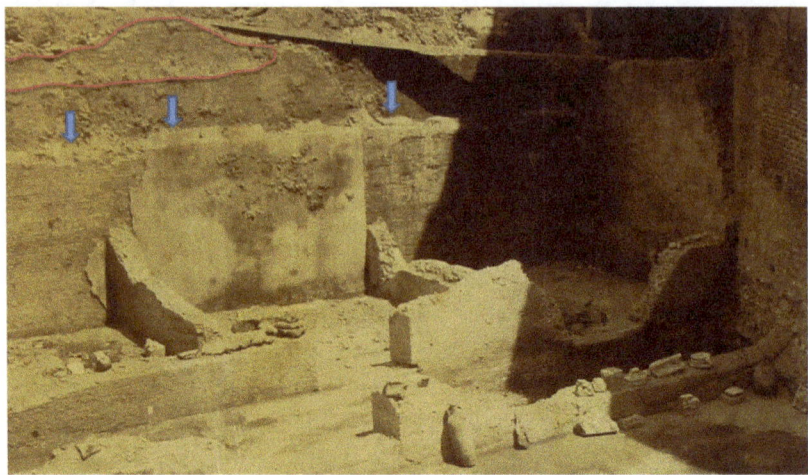

**Fig. 7.8** Detail of the 1876 photograph by Busiri Vici (see fig. 2) showing the northern perimeter wall seen from the southwestern side.

a passageway with an east–west grading running along the southern perimeter of the Insula would probably explain the need to consolidate the south wall at least up to a certain height. The eastern perimeter of the edifice is no longer visible, and, unlike the other walls demolished in the nineteenth century, not even the contours, delineated in red bricks during Vespignani's restoration, remain. The wall was however seen during the 1876 works and drawn in plan by both Vespignani and Busiri (Figs 7.9–7.10); in the latter's plan the layout of the structure appears as anomalous, constituted by three dividing walls with an extremely irregular arrangement.[25] The accuracy adopted in executing the plan allows us to exclude some form of mistake in the plan itself, but would rather suggest that the eastern perimeter wall had been damaged or partially destroyed during the construction of the Constantinian apse. From this it would follow that Busiri saw the wall in a state of collapse or in its original form during the 1800s. Therefore, we can determine that there was no portico here, but rather that a continuous wall was present on the eastern side, flanked to the east by a mosaic paved corridor in black-and-white *tesserae* set in a geometric pattern. Stevenson, probably following Busiri's drawing, describes the corridor ending, at least in its southern portion, with frescoed niches.[26] Upon closer examination of the point where the eastern perimeter

[25] Vespignani drew the wall as perfectly in line with a north–south direction but, as we have already mentioned, his drawing is overly simplified and omits a number of details when compared to Busiri's.

[26] Stevenson, 'Scoperte di antichi edifizi al Laterano', 338.

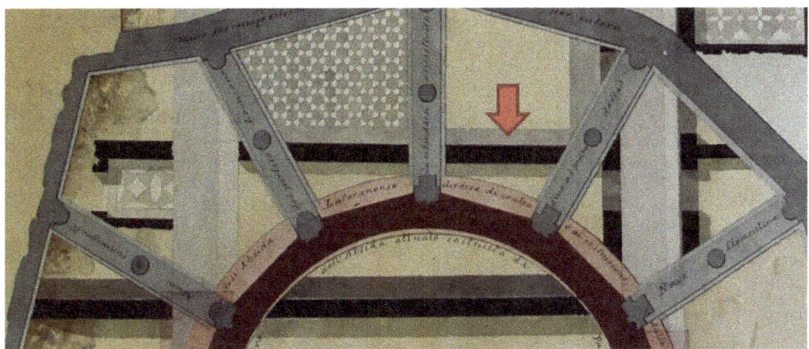

**Fig. 7.9** Virginio Vespignani, 13 May 1877, 1:100 scale drawing of the excavation area. Detail of the eastern portion of the Trapezoidal Insula (BiASA, Collezione Lanciani, Roma XI, no. 11).

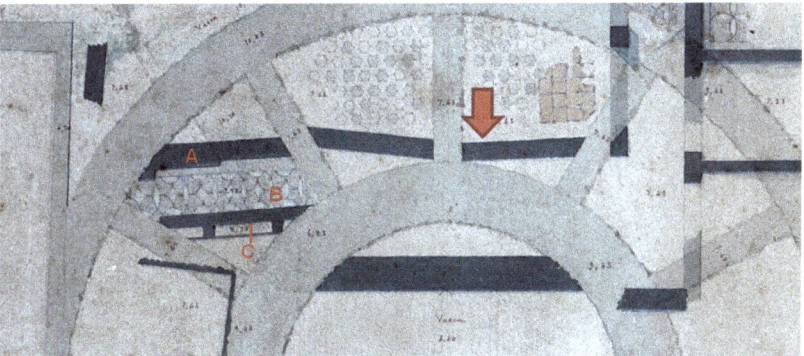

**Fig. 7.10** Detail of the 1876 illustration by Busiri Vici (see fig. 3) showing the eastern portion of the Trapezoidal Insula (arrow and letter marked) with the eastern perimeter wall of the structure (A), the corridor (B) and the niches (C).

is enclosed by the foundation of the Constantinian apse, there are (currently) traces of a white plastering with red bands, the direction of which would suggest the presence of a niche or perhaps a stair (Fig. 7.11).

A series of features appear to post-date the initial layout of the Trapezoidal Building. None of these is visible today, all having been destroyed or covered by Vespignani's foundations. Two structures, or rather infrastructures, currently no longer visible, are indicated in orange watercolour: these correspond to a line of tuff rock blocks[27] positioned parallel to the west side of the portico so as to appear as set directly on the

---

[27] Stevenson describes the structure as 'a wall made up of small tuff rocks' (Stevenson, 'Scoperte di antichi edifizi al Laterano', 338). In Busiri's report there is no trace of these elements but in the drawing a line of bricks appears to be recognisable.

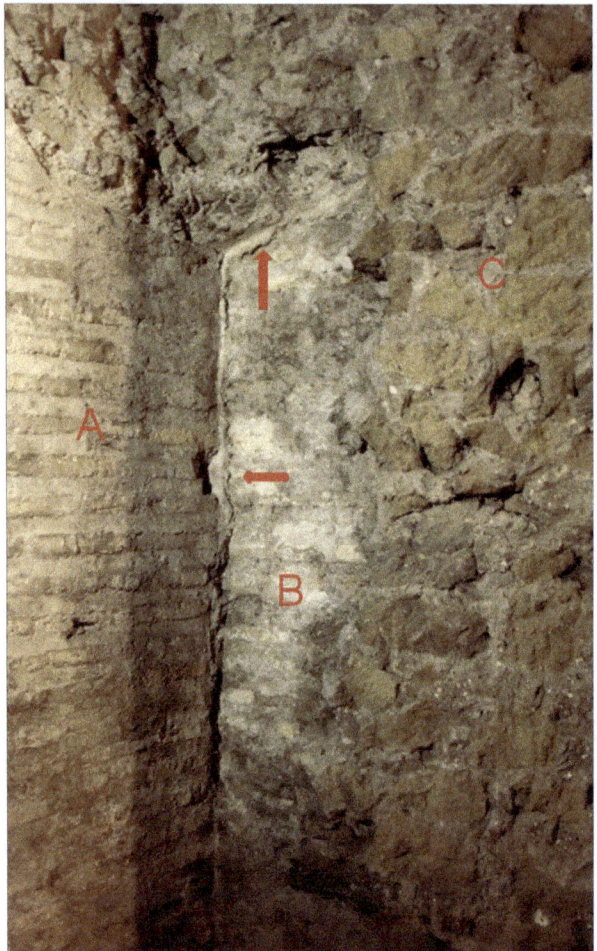

**Fig. 7.11** Southeastern portion of the Trapezoidal Insula: A. wall facing in *opus latericium* pertaining to the foundations of the Constantinian apse; B. wall facings in in *opus latericium* pertaining to the niched wall of the Trapezoidal Insula; C medieval (?) wall. The red arrows indicate the remains of the plaster-painted decoration.

mosaic floor (Figs 7.12–7.13). In the northeast corner of the courtyard a quadrangular-shaped floor is drawn, formed by bipedal bricks laid out flat. These probably rested directly on the mosaic and were completely removed during Vespignani's rearrangement with the clear intention of bringing to light the entire surface of the mosaic (Fig. 7.14). As for the open area of the Trapezoidal Building, we can note the presence of a number of elements, ignored by Vespignani both in the documentation and in the arrangement, pre-dating (although we do not know by how much) the construction of that building and possibly tied to new functional requirements.[28]

To the east of the Trapezoidal Buiding, on a terrace, there stood the barracks of the *equites singulares*. The two structures were certainly part of a single complex, constituted by buildings with different functions. The 1876 works exposed only the westernmost limit of the actual

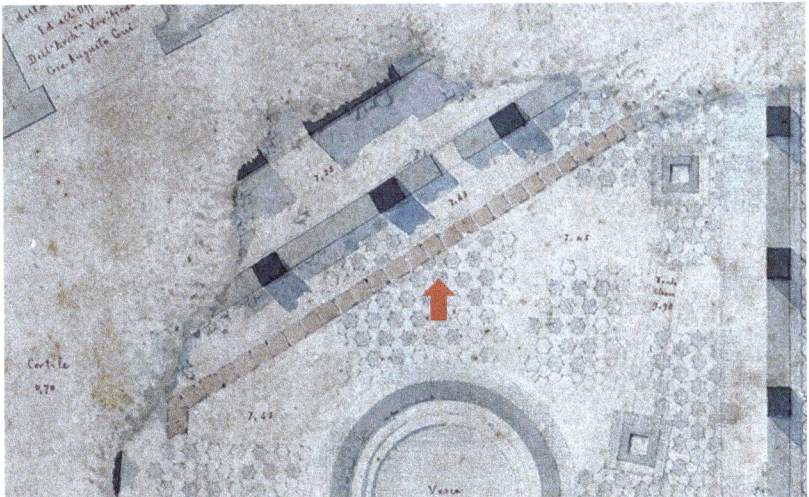

**Fig. 7.12** Detail of the 1876 illustration by Busiri Vici (see fig. 3): western portion of the Trapezoidal Insula. The red arrow marks the structure in tuff blocks.

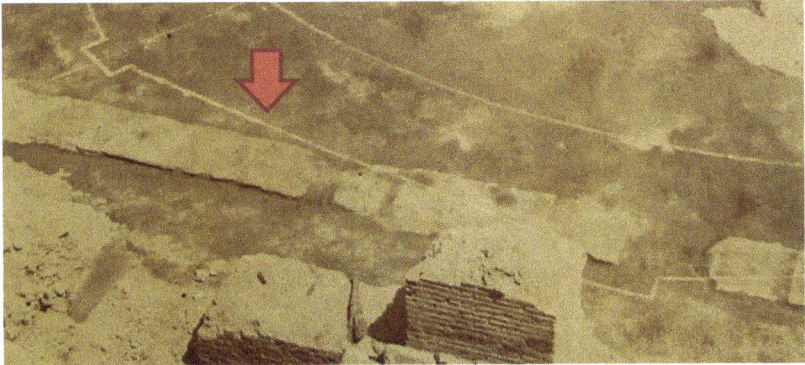

**Fig. 7.13** Detail of the 1876 photograph by Busiri Vici (see fig. 2): western portion of the Trapezoidal Insula. The red arrow marks the structure in tuff blocks.

---

[28] See Spinola, Chapter 5 in this volume.

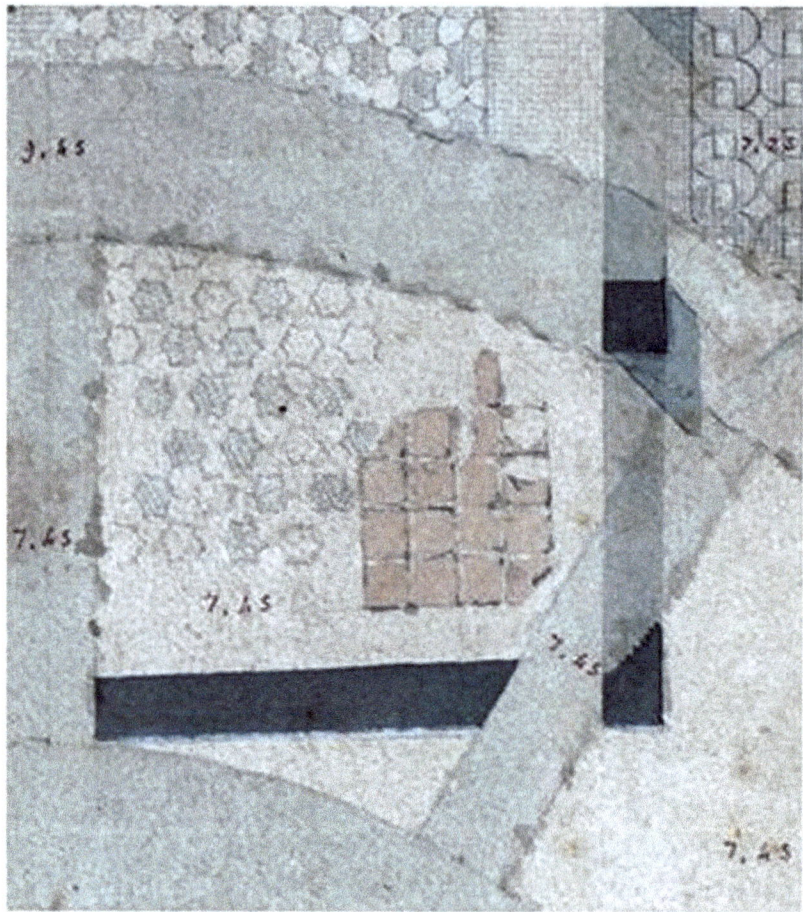

Fig. 7.14 Detail of the 1876 illustration by Busiri Vici (see fig. 3): northeastern corner of the Trapezoidal Insula. Quadrangular-shaped flooring in bricks.

encampment, seeing that the excavations of the *strigae* building post-dates Busiri's documentation. It is possible, however, to extrapolate some data from the small portion included in the planimetry. Busiri's plan records the presence of a great basin or cistern, between the B and C walls of the *castra*, at a point 4.50 m below the basilica's floor (Fig. 7.15).[29] Busiri himself included this discovery in his project for the arrangement of the subterranean area. It is still possible to see, at the height recorded by Busiri, brickwork facings similar to those used in the *castra*, covered by a thick layer of hydraulic mortar. These appear

[29] The doorway was seen also by Krautheimer, who interpreted it as a cistern: *CBCR* V, 30.

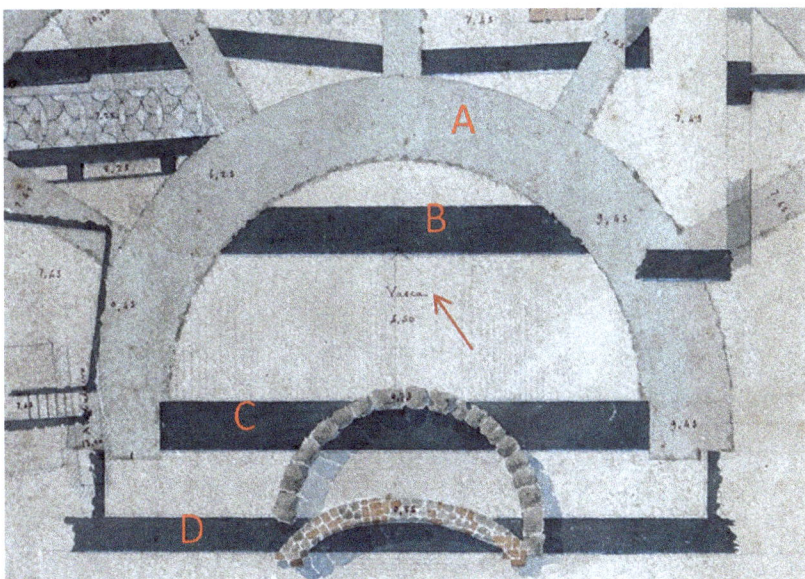

**Fig. 7.15** Detail of the 1876 illustration by Busiri Vici (see fig. 3): basin discovered between the B and C walls of the *castra*.

in the rooms adjacent to the modern passageway opened in the walls of the A apse and the *castra* B and C – on the western face of wall C (Fig. 7.16). It is not possible to establish the typology of the pavements and probable openings for the adduction or drainage of water, but they do not seem to represent traces of an actual cistern which would require much more complex construction elements than the ones found. In any case it can be supposed that it belonged to the life of the *castra* because the wall-building technique can be ascribed to the Severan phase of the encampment; its positioning on the limit of the western fortified portion would seem favourable for service areas, for the sheltering of livestock, for the conservation of liquids and for the storage of foodstuffs.

## Possible Early Medieval Structures

A white cloth envelope kept in the Vatican Apostolic Library contains an account in which Busiri reports the finding, during the 1876 excavations, of two semi-circular structures in tuff blocks connected to the presbytery area. These were discovered at a height of 0.73/

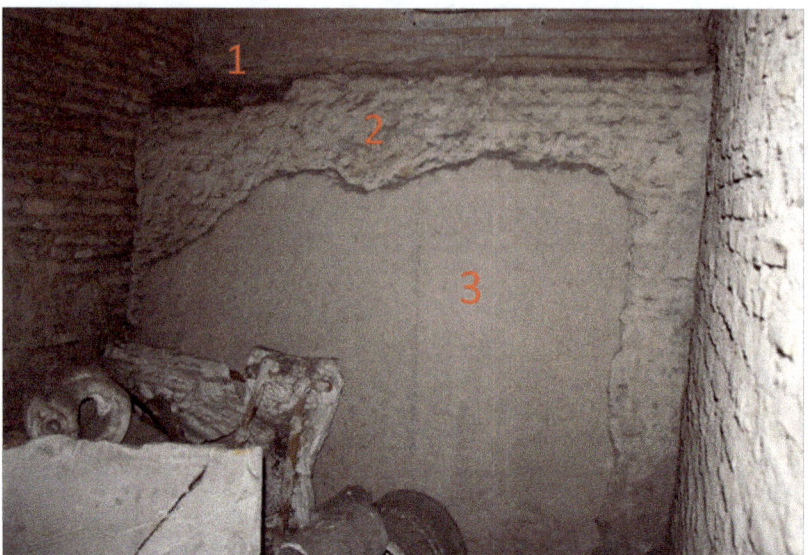

**Fig. 7.16** The sector to the east of the Constantinian apse: 1. Western wall face of the *castra* C wall; 2. Brickwork cover; 3. Hydraulic mortar.

0.85 m below the pavement of the central nave;[30] the discovery is recorded on the 1876 table (see Fig. 7.3). Busiri interprets the two small apses as part of a first oratory that preceded the construction of the basilica, thus giving credence to a fictional tradition according to which Saint Peter celebrated Mass at the Lateran.[31] It is obvious that dating these structures to such an early period is not possible seeing that there are no other sources to support the presence of a religious structure preceding the construction of the basilica dedicated to the Saviour. The height at which these were found would suggest that these were placed above the walls of the *castra* and a few centimetres below the Constantinian floor. It is thus possible to hypothesise that

---

[30] 'Pianta antica della Sacrosanta Papale Arcibasilica Lateranense Cattedrale Romana', Roma, Studio Andrea Busiri-Vici 18/11/1899. BAV, Indirizzi Leone XIII, 1161–1162. The documents were seen also by Tamburini: F. Tamburini, *Andrea Busiri Vici (1818–1911): Architetto-ingegnere del Capitolo Lateranense: Le sue scoperte, i suoi progetti e le polemiche* (Archivium Historiae Pontificiae 34) (Rome, 1996), 245–68. This finding is also mentioned by Stevenson: Stevenson, 'Scoperte di antichi edifizi al Laterano', 347 table T.

[31] BAV, Indirizzi Leone XIII, 1161–2. The only tradition regarding Peter and the Lateran is cited by Bonizone from Sutri in the last decades of the eleventh century, in which he recorded that the altar in the Lateran was the Eucharistic table on which Peter the Apostle celebrated Mass: Blaauw, *CD* I, 234.

the two structures were tied to a medieval reorganisation of the presbytery.

In 1899 Andrea Busiri Vici set out some of the discoveries made in 1876 before his direction of the work at the Lateran was interrupted. It is probable that with this final report the architect sought to reaffirm the importance of the structures that had unfortunately been destroyed in the enlargement of the presbytery area. In fact, it is particularly thanks to the drawings and photographs he made during his work that it is possible to understand better the structures that were concealed or obliterated by the building works that followed, allowing us to further illuminate the topography of the area prior to the construction of the Constantinian apse.

# 8 | Visualising the Constantinian Basilica

LEX BOSMAN, PAOLO LIVERANI, IWAN PEVERETT AND IAN P. HAYNES

## Introduction: Visualisation and Provocation

It is now almost 370 years since the first known attempt to recapture the original appearance of Constantine's Lateran basilica. Work in advance of Borromini's great remodelling of the cathedral's interior informed Filippo Gagliardi's imagining of its ancient appearance in a well-known fresco at San Martino ai Monti painted around 1651 (Fig. 8.1).[1] Operating in the aftermath of the Reformation, both Borromini and Gagliardi were acutely conscious of the Lateran basilica as a powerful monument to the antiquity of Roman Christianity – and their work sought to respect and recall the building's Constantinian roots.

Alongside its historic importance as the first cathedral, the structure lies at the heart of debates on the evolution of the basilica form, the evolution of church architecture, the monumentalising of imperial propaganda, the role of *spolia* in Late Antique buildings and the interplay between space and liturgy. In short, how we see the Lateran basilica under Constantine has profound implications for these debates, and indeed, the way we see it is in turn influenced by them. This chapter offers both a new methodological approach to visualising the basilica and a discussion of the sources vital to any assessment of its original appearance.

In the last few decades, several attempts to reconstruct the earliest appearance of the basilica have been made. A series of axonometric illustrations by Richard Krautheimer, drafted successively by Corbett, Lampl, Waddy and Lloyd, drew on a rich range of archival material and archaeological

---

While the team have worked together closely during the visualisation process and in the production of this chapter, different colleagues took responsibility for individual sections. Bosman wrote the section on the decisions made in the architectural reconstruction. His work on the *spolia*, elaborated further in a separate chapter in this volume, also played a vital role in the visualisation. Liverani authored the sections on lighting, the *fastigium* and the *solea*. Peverett was responsible for 'Building the visualisation' with Haynes as well as undertaking technical modelling. Haynes produced the introduction, visualisation and provocation and concluding text.

[1] The value of the fresco as a source for the original basilica was discussed by R. Krautheimer, S. Corbett and A. K. Frazer, *CBCR* V, 64. As we note below, there are several areas where we have found the depiction in the fresco to be inaccurate and misleading.

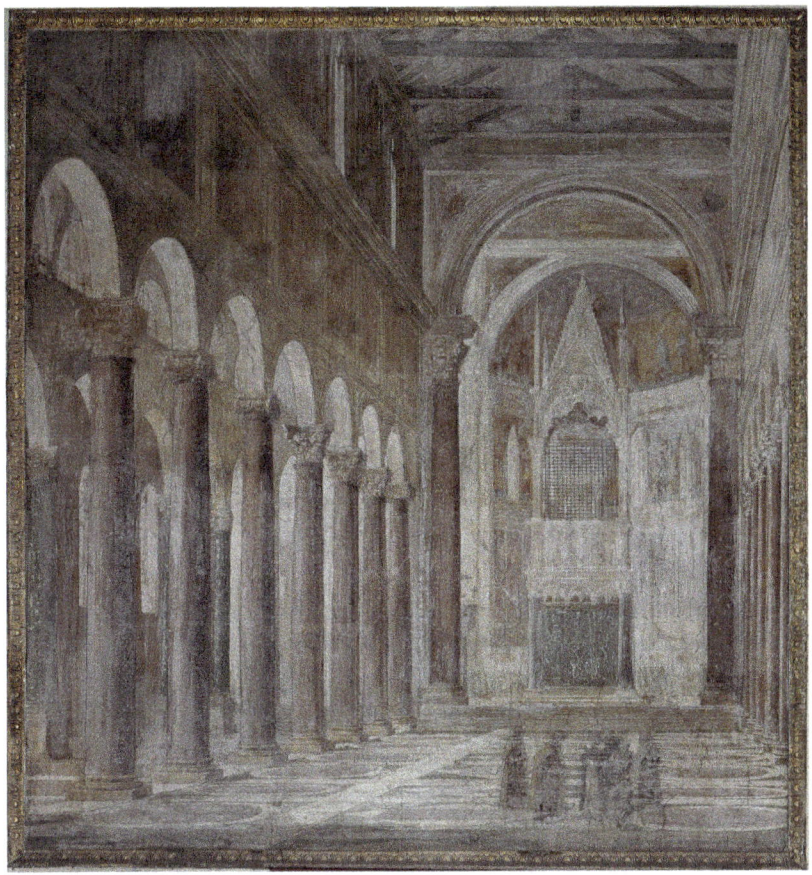

Fig. 8.1 Filippo Gagliardi fresco, San Martino ai Monti (*c.* 1651) (Copyright Scala Archive).

observation.[2] What Krautheimer had envisaged as the 'final' reconstruction was published in 1967,[3] a decade before the fifth volume of his celebrated *Corpus Basilicarum Christianarum Romae* (*CBCR*) with its detailed treatment of the Lateran sources. Complementing the plans were vivid and

---

[2] Krautheimer and Corbett (R. Krautheimer and S. Corbett, 'The Constantinian basilica of the Lateran', *Antiquity* 34, 135 (1960), 201–6, at p. 205 fig. 3) described it as a 'tentative sketch reconstruction of the western part of the original basilica'; Lampl in R. Krautheimer, *Early Christian and Byzantine Architecture* (Harmondsworth, 1965), 25 fig. 8; Waddy in R. Krautheimer, S. Corbett, R. Malmstrom and R. Stapleford, 'La basilica costantiniana al Laterano: Un tentativo di ricostruzione', *RAC* 43 (1967), 125–54, at p. 144 fig. 11; Lloyd in *CBCR* V, 82 fig. 80.

[3] Krautheimer et al., 'La basilica costantiniana al Laterano'. Krautheimer described this model as his 'final' reconstruction in a paper delivered at Dumbarton Oaks in 1966 (R. Krautheimer, 'The Constantinian basilica', *Dumbarton Oaks Papers* 21 (1967), 115–40, at p. 119 n. 7).

colourful descriptions of the basilica's original interior, erudite compilations that again drew on documentary sources, the study of what were believed to be surviving elements of the building in Borromini's new scheme, and reflection on archaeological evidence yielded in successive excavations.

Krautheimer's team's 'final' reconstruction was in fact further developed in what was to be their ultimate version, published in the *CBCR*, and taken further again by de Blaauw in 1994 in his *Cultus et decor*.[4] De Blaauw's version incorporated a depiction of the *fastigium* attested in the *Liber Pontificalis*,[5] and of a *solea* based on the discovery of a series of stone blocks in Josi's 1937 excavations.[6] His work stresses an essential point. Any attempt to understand liturgical practice in the new ecclesial spaces enabled by the adaptation of the basilican form must incorporate not just a study of the structural form, but also the interior layout. Brandenburg generated a further axonometric illustration, drawing on the same principles in 2004.[7]

Each of these images built on previous attempts, but as 2D illustrations they sometimes concealed key structural elements. Thus, the ultimate illustration produced by Krautheimer's team, drafted by Waddy and revised by Lloyd, does not allow the viewer to see the intersection of apse, lateral structures and nave/aisles. De Blaauw's equally important figure with a cut-away axonometric showing the possible interpretation of the *fastigium* and *solea* leaves unresolved some of those elements concealed in Krautheimer's team's illustrations. The detailed reconstruction drawing by Brandenburg does not show the structure in this part of the basilica either. In contrast, the method adopted by the team here to model the building in its entirety on both a macro-level (structure and layout) and a micro-level (for example, decorative scheme and lighting systems) in 3D made it impossible to conceal these and other relationships.

Given the importance of Constantine's Lateran basilica and the repeated attempts that have been made to picture both its interior and exterior, it is vital to acknowledge the objections that may be raised to any attempts to represent its original appearance. The archbasilica's long history has been marked by sackings, natural disasters, fires and episodes of neglect. Does enough of the fabric of the original structure survive to undertake a credible visualisation?

---

[4] Blaauw, *CD* (original edition in Dutch: *Cultus et decor: Liturgie en architectuur in laatantiek en middeleeuws Rome: Basilica Salvatoris, Sanctae Mariae, Sancti Petri* (Delft, 1987)).

[5] *LP* 34, 9–10.

[6] A. M. Colini, *Storia e topografia del Celio nell'antichità* (Memorie della Pontificia Accademia Romana di Archeologia 7) (Vatican City, 1944), 353, 359; *CBCR* V, 43–4; Blaauw, *CD* I, 127–8; I. P. Haynes, P. Liverani, S. Piro and G. Spinola, 'The Lateran Project: interim report on the July 2012 and January 2013 seasons (Rome)', *PBSR* 81 (2013), 360–3, at pp. 361–2.

[7] H. Brandenburg, *Die frühchristlichen Kirchen Roms vom 4. bis zum 7. Jahrhundert: Der Beginn der abendländischen Kirchenbaukunst* (Regensburg, 2004), 261.

Archaeological investigation has certainly revealed direct evidence for the devastation of the cathedral's interior. An unpublished report from the 1937 works records that the excavators encountered 'enorme quantità di resti carbonizzati', including charred ceiling beams, burnt brick, decorative elements and parts of funerary monuments, when they removed the basilica floor.[8] The accompanying collapse of parts of the superstructure was so devastating, the report goes on to state, that it broke through the ceiling of at least one subterranean vault, depositing still more debris into the chasm it opened. Unfortunately, it is now impossible to determine the date(s) of this disaster archaeologically with precision; the material associated with it was not further documented and its whereabouts are unknown.

Among historically documented disasters, the event with the most catastrophic impact on the structure would appear to have been the great earthquake of AD 896. According to his biographer, and indeed his own inscriptions, Pope Sergius III had to rebuild the whole basilica from the bottom upwards as the earthquake was so devastating that it was difficult to see where the building's walls had previously stood.[9] While the capacity of earthquakes to wreak such havoc must be acknowledged, there are strong reasons to doubt that it would have erased all traces of the Constantinian structure. Not only do these claims about Sergius III's reconstruction sound suspiciously like 'laudatory exaggerations', as the authors of the *CBCR* note,[10] the excavations noted above also found intact substructures pre-dating the destruction events they so vividly documented. In fact, while building phases, sometimes concealed under later works, can be difficult to date with precision, crucial structural details of relevance to the basilica's Constantinian form can be identified. As readers will observe, though we may differ from our predecessors on important points of detail, the authors of this chapter therefore share with them the conviction that enough survives to visualise the building's plan and elevation.[11]

The decorative scheme and internal fittings present their own problems of interpretation, examples of which are offered below. Though the employment of *spolia* was common well before Constantine, its extensive use is widely acknowledged as a characteristic of his building programmes in Rome, and the Lateran reflects this practice. The detailed study of

---

[8] Unpublished report by the Ufficio Tecnico Vaticano and Pontificia Commissione di Archeologia Sacra 1937, 'Lavori nel pavimento o sottosuolo dell'arcibasilica lateranense', 3; BAV, Arte e arch 1.92; see *CBCR* V, 43–4.
[9] *CBCR* V, 11 with references.    [10] *CBCR* V, 91.
[11] The fullest evaluation of later rebuilding and their implications for the Constantinian fabric may be found in *CBCR* V, 91–2.

architectural elements still to be seen in the Lateran today has thus played a vital role in generating the visualisations to be seen within this chapter. And finally, and perhaps most controversially, we have the vivid account of the basilica's fittings offered by the *Liber Pontificalis* and used in powerful evocations of the cathedral's earlier interior by successive scholars.[12] As this volume demonstrates, healthy debate about the interpretation of these accounts continues, and specialists disagree not only as to how they should be interpreted but also whether they reflect fourth-century reality at all.[13]

The models of the Constantinian basilica offered in this chapter result from a happy convergence of research over recent years. The Lateran Project sought from its inception to provide a detailed structural analysis of the substantial area excavated beneath the modern floor of the basilica. Crucially, this area preserves the foundations of the Constantinian church and yielded, in partially documented fieldwork conducted by Josi, traces of stone blocks interpreted as supports for a *solea*.[14] Kind permission of Monsignor Natalino Zagotto, the Camerlengo of the Lateran Chapter, enabled Project members to pursue the Project's programme of laser scanning and ground-penetrating radar into the archbasilica, allowing the generation of an integrated digital model of the entire complex. This harmonised with ongoing work by Lex Bosman on the *spolia* within the architecture of the Lateran basilica, work which had profound implications for the study of the building's earliest internal configuration.[15] Together therefore, the authors were able to collaborate in generating a visualisation of the earliest phases of the Lateran.

Visualisation is advanced here as an essential element in the analysis of this important site. As the authors of the *London Charter* understood in their ground-breaking protocol on the making of visual research outcomes of cultural heritage sites 'transparent', images have a tremendous power that can – unharnessed – do great harm to understanding.[16] We can never literally reconstruct the Lateran basilica of Constantine, too much is missing, but we can offer a visualisation that brings together in a manner more precise than words what our shared understanding of its appearance would have been. The 2D images in this chapter are derived from our 3D models, models that were

---

[12] *LP* 33, 9–12.
[13] For questions about the historical accuracy of the *Liber Pontificalis*, see especially McKitterick, Chapter 10 in this volume and P. Liverani, 'Osservazioni sul libellus delle donazioni costantiniane nel Liber Pontificalis', *Athenaeum* 107 (2019), 169–217.
[14] Unpublished report by the Ufficio Tecnico Vaticano and Pontificia Commissione di Archeologia Sacra 1937 'Lavori nel pavimento o sottosuolo dell' arcibasilica lateranense', 3; BAV, Arte e arch 1.92; *CBCR* V, 43–4.
[15] For a detailed discussion of Bosman's analysis of the *spolia*, see Chapter 9 in this volume.
[16] See www.londoncharter.org.

themselves generated with architectural modelling software. Building visualisation in this manner has advantages over conventional plan drawings; it ensures not only that the building depicted has demonstrable architectural integrity, but also that the implications of the structure envisioned must be everywhere reconciled. This form of modelling forces the modeller to address, if not necessarily definitively resolve, areas of ignorance and uncertainty, rather than to conceal them by the adoption of a single perspective.

Best practice, as outlined in the *London Charter*, demands that visualisations should be complemented by detailed justification of the scheme adopted.[17] This is not only an ethical obligation and a vehicle to present data with greater granularity, it is also a dynamic process; it serves an ongoing dialogue. Discussions with the team on sketches contributed to the development of concept models (architecturally robust line drawings), themselves catalysts for further discussion. Thereafter rendered visualisations (photo realistic outputs) have been developed, which have been – and continue through these pages to be – exposed to the critical appraisal of other colleagues. As debate on the Constantinian basilica advances, we continue to develop these visualisations, using them in turn to engage with different research questions, for example in the analysis of the acoustics of early churches.[18] In generating these models the team understands visualisation as *provocation*, a stimulus to ever more refined critical dialogue, and in this spirit the chapter elaborates on the technical methods and steps used in the processes we adopted, as well as on the source material that underpins our interpretation. We begin therefore by outlining the technical processes employed to build the visualisation, before summarising and evaluating the data vital to discussion of four key aspects of the basilica's early appearance: its architectural form, lighting, *fastigium* and *solea*.

## Building the Visualisation

While indebted to the work of earlier scholars, the foundations of this attempt to visualise the complex are underpinned by a range of data which were unavailable to them, generated by the Lateran Project. Krautheimer made many important observations in the large area of excavations beneath the floor of the modern cathedral, and had produced several important

---

[17] H. Denard, *The London Charter for the Computer-Based Visualisation of Cultural Heritage*, 2.1 edn (London, 2009), 7–8.
[18] Gianluca Foschi, 'The Role of Musical Properties in Early Churches', Ph.D. thesis (Newcastle University, forthcoming).

plans, but a comprehensive survey in such conditions could not have been undertaken with the resources then available to him. The Lateran Project's survey, which created one of the largest subterranean laser-scan data sets in archaeology and integrated it with a further survey of the cathedral interior, also incorporates a programme of photogrammetry, ortho-rectified photography and ground-penetrating radar survey.[19] This data set also utilised a full set of survey results for each target to tie it together and to enhance accuracy, measured from a survey network created throughout the site with Leica Scan Stations. The Faro Focus 3D scanner was chosen for the laser-scanning survey as it is small and light, fast and accurate over short distances, and allowed the team to reach places that would have been inaccessible using other scanners available at the time (Fig. 8.2).

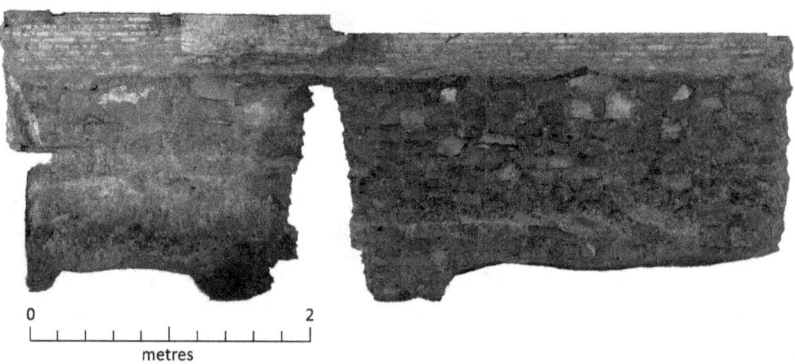

**Fig. 8.2** Image derived from laser scan under the basilica floor showing column foundation surrounded by modern conservation work. The scan survey allowed the team to identify the original locations of many columns with sub-millimetre accuracy (Lateran Project).

---

[19] I. P. Haynes, P. Liverani, A. Turner and T. Ravasi, 'Roma si trasforma: Gli scavi di San Giovanni in Laterano e l'evoluzione della città eterna tra II e VI sec. d.C.', *Forma Urbis* 17, 6 (2011), 36–44; I. P. Haynes, P. Liverani, G. Spinola and S. Piro, 'Archaeological fieldwork reports: The Lateran Project', *PBSR* 80 (2012), 369–71; Haynes et al., P. Liverani, S. Piro and G. Spinola, 'The Lateran Project: Interim report on the July 2012 and January 2013 seasons (Rome)'; I. P. Haynes, P. Liverani, S. Piro, I. Peverett and G. Spinola, 'Progetto Laterano: Primi risultati', *Rendiconti della Pontificia Accademia Romana di Archeologia* 86 (2014), 1–19; I. P. Haynes, P. Liverani, I. Peverett, G. Spinola and A. Turner, 'The Lateran Project: interim report for 2015–2016 seasons (Rome)', *PBSR* 84 (2016), 311–16; I. Haynes, P. Liverani, D. Heslop, I. Peverett, G. Spinola and A. Turner, 'The Lateran Project: Interim report for the 2016–2017 seasons (Rome)', *PBSR* 85 (2017), 317–20; S. Piro, I. P. Haynes, P. Liverani and D. Zamuner, 'Integrated archaeological and geophysical investigations to study the area of S. Giovanni in Laterano basilica (Rome, Italy)', in C. Einwogerer, W. Neubauer, R. B. Salisbury and I. Trinks (eds.), *Archaeological Prospection: Proceedings of the 10th International Conference* (Vienna, 2013), 203–5. See also Piro, Haynes, Liverani and Zamuner, Chapter 4 in this volume.

This process took four successive seasons to complete, with the fourth season including the scanning of the basilica above ground as it appears today. This accurate data set, quite literally, became the foundation on which the 3D model was created. After all the individual scans had been registered together into a complete point cloud for the site, the point-cloud data was imported into AutoCAD drafting software, where the team could accurately analyse relationships and text hypotheses. Accurate plans were created using archival data such as historical building plans, and subsequent academic research, verified and adjusted based on the cutting-edge digital surveying and documentation techniques, available to us through the use of laser scanning. The same point-cloud data, and plans, were then imported into the 3D modelling package, 3D Studio Max, to become the base layer over which the structure and detail was built virtually (Fig. 8.3).

A significant challenge in building the Lateran model was that the intention was to create the first accurate digital interpretation of the building in its entirety. As the model and photorealistic renders would be academic outputs, it was imperative that every detail was included and modelled; this required repeated cross-referencing to the archival documentation at each stage.

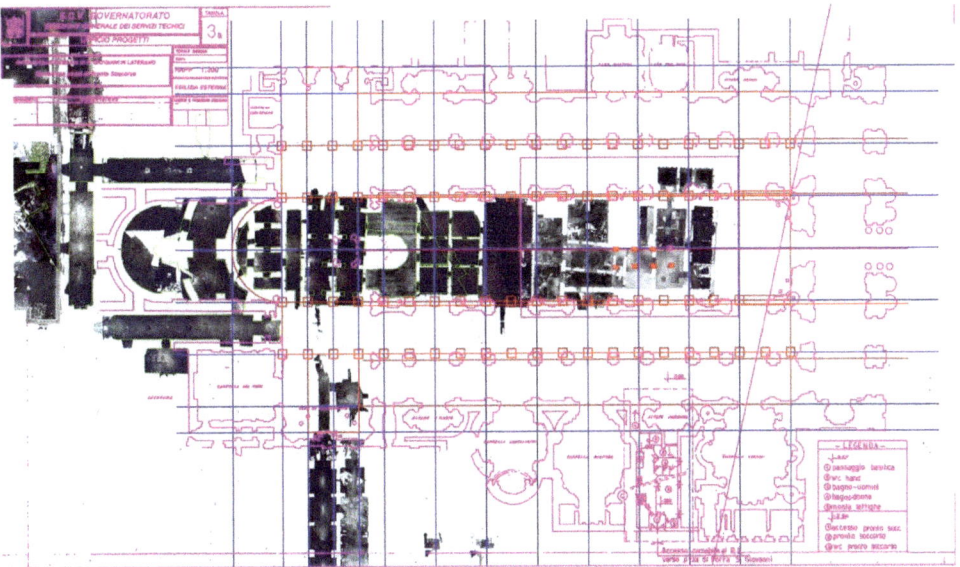

**Fig. 8.3** Working document showing overlay of modern basilica plan on 2D slice of laser-scan data of foundations. The marking-up shows initial interpretations of column spacing and location. (Lateran Project data superimposed on plan of Servizi Tecnici del Governatorato)

Recent developments in technology and software, as well as advances in modelling processes and the utilisation of specialist plug-ins, have improved workflow and enabled projects of this complexity. In normal digital-modelling projects it is no longer necessary to be overly concerned about the number of faces (or polygons) in a scene, nor to rely on storing sections of the model in external files, that are loaded in remotely when the image is created (or rendered), in a process called external referencing. In addition to the primary emphasis here on the generation of an accurate model, a major consideration for the project team was how they could produce a model that in the future may be usable by other researchers. To produce such a model, however, demanded a reduction in the use of those plug-ins that would normally greatly ease the modelling process. A traditional visualisation project might rely on the use of parametric plug-ins, such as Itoo Software's Railclone, a plug-in that allows the modeller to set a series of parameters so that then just drawing a spline (a 3D line used in modelling) or face, the model will in effect draw itself. The greater ease of such an approach can be demonstrated with the example of modelling a terracotta tiled roof. Modelling one roof tile and one ridge tile and drawing a spline for the pitch and another one for the length would suffice to auto-generate the model. Such parametric plug-ins not only save modelling time, they also make the model much easier to 'handle' and navigate around in a 3D application. As the model created for the Lateran Project is designed to sustain further research, however, the more time-consuming method of copying individual elements repeatedly was necessary. A similarly painstaking method of producing the model's chain-hung chandeliers was necessary, and proved even more complicated to generate.

Clearly the creation of complex models is easier if one seeks to produce the final model from the outset. Returning to it, adapting it and amending details is time consuming. Nevertheless, we saw that experimentation and dialogue within the model building as an opportunity to refine our deepening understanding of the form and construction of the basilica. To minimise 'abortive' work and additional time within this process we employed a macro- to micro-modelling strategy. Initial work understanding and drafting up plans and sections in 2D was followed by simple massing of the building in 3D. For example, place-holder cylinders were used to represent columns, with detail, capitals and plinths, added once we were convinced that the location and proportions were accurate to known column bases, intercolumniation and known or existing column sizes. It is important to note here that many black-and-white 'concept models' of this type were generated before the first rendered models were produced (Fig. 8.4).

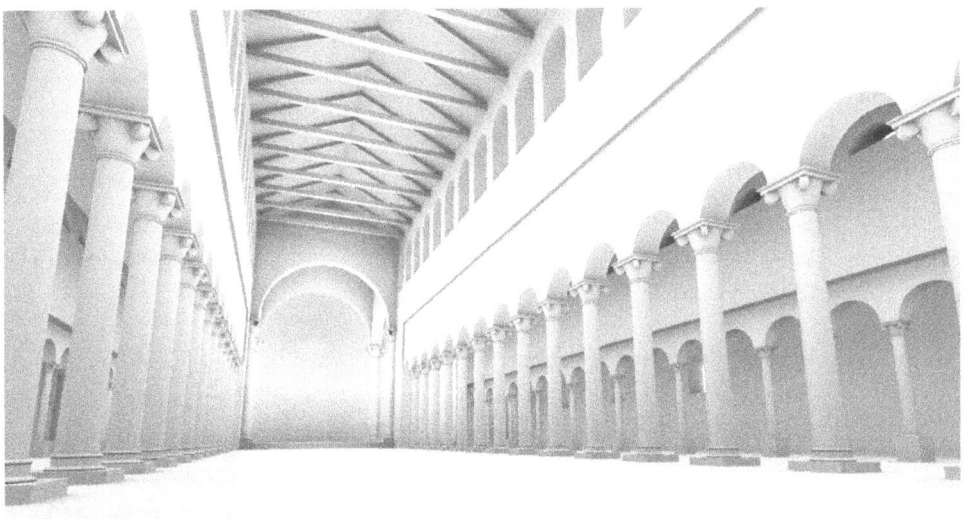

**Fig. 8.4** Initial internal concept model based largely on survey results, plans and the Gagliardi fresco showing simple place-holder details such as columns (The Authors).

Rendered models, incorporating as they do lighting, colour and texture, are necessarily more time consuming to produce and so were only generated in the later stages of analysis for advanced discussion between team members.

Extensive research on the basilica's ground plan led naturally to discussion of the roof structure. Previous researchers had suggested that the basilica had a single-roofed or double-roofed aisles and even proportions of aisle width and heights that suggested what we believed to be unusually steep roof pitches. The discussions and decisions taken on the roof arrangement were not taken in isolation, or based purely on previous researchers' interpretations, but as the model was a full 3D representation the interface and junction of the different elements could be analysed internally and externally at the same time (Fig. 8.5).

Once the overall form was settled the detail could be added, each element of which drew on extensive research. A first consideration was the lighting scheme within the Constantinian basilica. Lighting would have been of central importance to the basilica, playing a crucial role in defining and illuminating sacred space. The fall of light would also have had fundamental implications for the way visitors encountered the many-coloured interior, adorned as it was with lavish marbles and granites, many of which were *spolia*. Clearly, calculations about the roof pitches, ceiling heights and intercolumniation were integral to discussion of illumination. Thereafter,

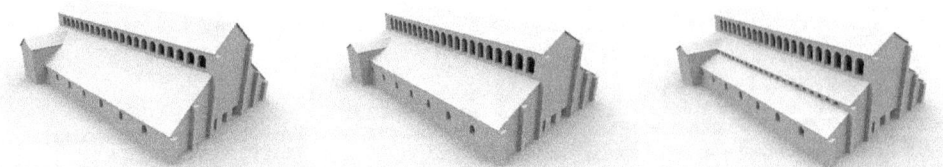

**Fig. 8.5** Concept models showing various interpretations of roof design and pitch. These models were used to investigate the viability of written descriptions produced by earlier commentators (The Authors).

though, the textual evidence for lighting needed to be evaluated. Life 34 in the *Liber Pontificalis* ostensibly details some of the elaborate lighting furnishings, presenting them as part of an imperial endowment under Constantine. As noted elsewhere in this volume, there are lively debates about the degree to which the remarkably specific elements detailed in the *Liber* were present in the original basilica. Nevertheless, the concept model of the basilica interior generated by the team revealed that the internal spaces created through the arrangement of columns and ceilings corresponded very effectively with the number of points of illumination suggested in the *Liber* account.

A detailed discussion of this account and our interpretation of it follows below, but from a visualisation perspective it is important to note the technical challenge it presented. The lighting set-up was a huge undertaking to get right, to achieve the sense of a lamp- and candle-lit space. The decision was made to accurately simulate the lighting with individual light sources for each flame, rather than one overall light source for each chandelier. This obviously increased render times for the final image substantially. It does, however, allow the visualisation to be used in advanced research in the use of light in early ecclesiastical buildings, a field in which digital modelling has already been employed.[20]

A further challenge lay in the convincing modelling of the opulent use of materials within the basilica. Historic descriptions of the space, and *spolia* incorporated into Borromini's remodelled archbasilica, gave an indication of the materials used – various marbles and granites, gold, silver and bronze – and the materials were recreated as accurately as possible for the model to shine and reflect the light, the polished finishes acting as partially mirrored surfaces, reflecting literally the opulent feel and the

---

[20] For an important archaeological study of light in early churches, see Nesbitt's pioneering work on modelling Byzantine churches: C. Nesbitt, 'Space, Light and Experience in Middle Byzantine Churches', Ph.D. thesis (Newcastle University, 2007).

majestic impression the original building must have instilled. Attention to detail of the lights, material finishes and smoke in the upper nave were thus integral to our quest to not only create an accurate representation of the building, but to turn the model into a compelling visualisation/provocation of the architecture and all this implies: experience, space and light.

And at all stages, the idea of generating viable architectural models as a provocation or instrument to challenge different hypotheses has been at the heart of the project, but the process has in turn generated its own challenges. The fact that members of the core team were operating out of four countries meant that for the dynamic process of challenging hypotheses to work, good communication was essential. Images help because they require greater specificity than written description. Regular discussion and emails were supplemented by a series of extremely productive workshops, where, surrounded by the relevant archival material, the process of analysis and examination of detail and form could take place. These workshops were essential in overcoming and resolving numerous problematic areas, as well as refining elements. Modelling was undertaken assessing various hypotheses, trying and retrying options, and all the time referencing any decisions that were taken against the appropriate data. This was fundamental to the successful outcome of the project and a key point to take would be that the architecturally trained illustrator or visualiser is an important addition in interpreting and understanding the design. The traditional approach of bringing in an illustrator at the end of the project to draw up a final picture would have made the understanding of the form and interpretation of the design much more difficult. The team approach of complementary skillsets working collaboratively from the outset was key to the successful delivery of this project (Fig. 8.6).

## Choices Made in the Architectural Reconstruction

Throughout its existence of around 1,800 years, a large number of restorations, additions and other alterations have taken place, gradually changing the substance of the original building as constructed from 312 onwards. First indications pointing to these changes can be found in the walls. In the actual church building the interior walls are plastered, thus hiding the substance of the walls themselves, which in turn means that the thickness of the original Constantinian walls remains unknown. The upper parts of the nave walls can be examined in the space above the wooden ceiling, but these parts show changes made in the later Middle Ages as well as in the seventeenth century. In the interior the significant

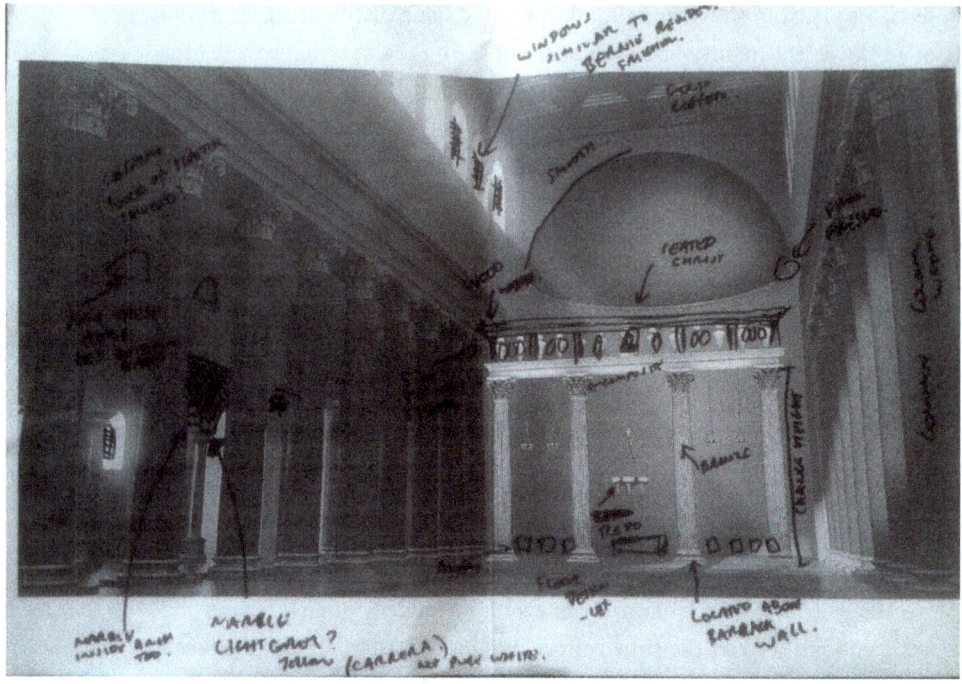

**Fig. 8.6** Notated drawing showing thoughts and amendments from one of the later workshops (The Authors).

alterations which were realised during Borromini's campaign have left the division in the nave and four side-aisles intact, but resulted in newly constructed large piers, which in turn erased the possibility to examine the fourth-century layout. In other words: the ways to come close to the structure, materials, measurements and details of the Constantinian basilica are limited. Parts of the Constantinian foundations of the nave and aisles are visible in the archaeological area underneath the church; those parts were vital in the newly built model on the basis of scanning and GPS-fixed data. In essence the general ground plan published by Krautheimer and his team was confirmed. The position of the nave columns was checked and confirmed; in our model they have the same position as in Krautheimer's reconstruction. The blocks on top of which the bases and column shafts were placed are still in position, and several of them can be examined in the archaeological area.[21]

---

[21] *CBCR* V, 35–6, 75–6, 78–9.

As noted above, the basis for most modern reconstructions of the basilica has been the one made by Richard Krautheimer and his collaborators and students. Although the early Christian basilica of Saint Peter's was torn down in the sixteenth and seventeenth centuries, quite detailed information about the architecture and its details exists, which Krautheimer often used as a point of reference for the Lateran basilica. In many instances he used a comparison in size of both buildings, with Saint Peter's being the larger of the two, resulting in a proportion of 6:5. Confronted with a lack of source material Krautheimer often relied on this ratio.[22] We feel it is more consistent to use architectural examples contemporaneous with the Basilica Constantiniana or preceding it in time, however, than using buildings from later years and periods as models. This choice results in differences in several aspects of the reconstructed building, for instance in our choice to omit windows in the apse. We are certain that windows were made in the apse at a later time, but we have no indication of their existence in the earliest phase.

Previous research by Richard Krautheimer and other scholars made clear that the seventeenth-century nave piers were built on the same west–east axial lines as the colonnades of the original basilica were positioned. The width between the piers gives a clear indication of the accuracy with which the basilica was first constructed; the width of the nave as measured between the piers is a stable 16.99 m.[23] Together with the laser-scan-derived model this gave us a solid base for the ground plan and to build the reconstruction upon. An important and new element in our reconstruction is the continuation towards the west of the colonnades between the inner and the outer aisles, the specifics of which are described in another chapter.[24] This reconstruction changes the ground plan and thus the spatial organisation of the early Christian basilica.

The roof that covered the nave and the side-aisles has puzzled previous researchers. Based on the Gagliardi fresco, the side-aisles have been reconstructed with roofs, separated by walls dividing the inner from the outer aisles and with half-circular windows. De Blaauw and Brandenburg chose to reconstruct single roofs covering both aisles on either side, although the half-circular windows remained. We have chosen to discard the fresco by Gagliardi, since it is highly unreliable in

---

[22] *CBCR* V, 74, 83.   [23] As measured digitally by Lex Bosman on 27 January 2016.

[24] Bosman, Chapter 9 in this volume.

many of the specifics of the architecture, and therefore have omitted the half-circular windows.

Confronted with a lack of certainty about the classical orders of the capitals in both nave and aisles, we base the choice for Ionic in the nave on the oldest mention of that order in a written source, even though it dates from the seventeenth century.[25] Krautheimer, Brenk and others took Gagliardi as their point of departure to reconstruct a variety of orders, but for us the inaccuracies in the fresco are sufficient to suggest that Gagliardi is an unreliable source for this particular point.[26]

The colours and materials of the column shafts are discussed in another contribution in this volume.[27] Whereas it was generally assumed that the interior was very colourful, with marble revetment on part of the walls and pavement, we propose a reconstruction of these elements not as historical truth, but as an arguable approximation of a historical situation. The black-and-white photograph published by Krautheimer and others, showing a small part of the remains of the Constantinian pavement, does not provide a real model for a reconstruction.[28] Two major basilicas preceding the Lateran basilica had coloured marble pavements which have been reconstructed quite thoroughly: the Basilica of Maxentius and the Basilica Ulpia.[29] On the basis of these two large floors we reconstructed the pavement of the Lateran Basilica. Coming from reconstructions in black-and-white drawings, the interior in our reconstruction, rich with colours, may be overwhelming, but it is crucial to bear in mind that with colours we approach the fourth-century situation much more closely than with black-and-white lines.

The height of the marble revetment on the walls is unknown; the so-called spandrel shows that at least at the height of the spandrel the walls were covered with thin slabs of marble, as was already recognised by Krautheimer (Fig. 8.7). When taken together with our interpretations of

---

[25] An., 'Relazione dello stato nel quale si trovava la Basilica Lateranense', in P. Lauer, *Le palais de Latran: Étude historique et archéologique* (Paris, 1911), 585–93, at p. 585. Thanks to Peter Cornelius Claussen for pointing this problem out to us again.

[26] *CBCR* V, 79–80; B. Brenk, 'Spolien und ihre Wirkung auf die Ästhetik der *varietas*: Zum Problem alternierender Kapitelltypen', in J. Poeschke (ed.), *Antike Spolien in der Architektur des Mittelalters und der Renaissance* (Munich, 1996), 49–92, at pp. 54–5.

[27] Bosman, Chapter 9 in this volume.

[28] *CBCR* V, 43; P. C. Claussen, *Die Kirchen der Stadt Rom im Mittelalter 1050–1300, Bd. 2: S. Giovanni in Laterano* (Corpus Cosmatorum II, 2) (Forschungen zur Kunstgeschichte und Christlichen Archäologie 21) (Stuttgart, 2008), 179.

[29] C. M. Amici, *Foro di Traiano: Basilica Ulpia e biblioteche* (Rome, 1982), 16; C. M. Amici, 'From project to monument', in C. Giavarini (ed.), *The Basilica of Maxentius: The Monument, Its Materials, Construction, and Stability* (Rome, 2005), 21–74, at p. 71, n. 16.

*Visualising the Constantinian Basilica* 149

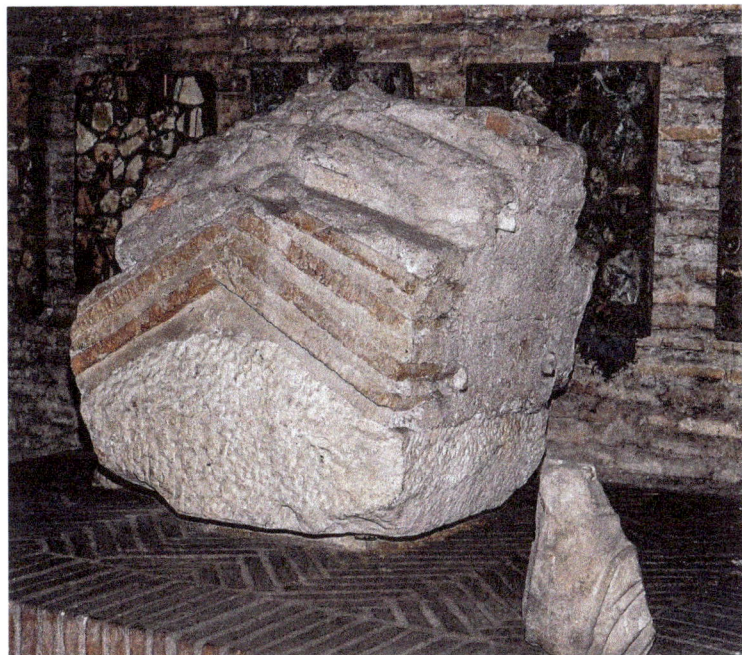

Fig. 8.7 The so-called spandrel in the Lateran basilica (Photo L. Bosman).

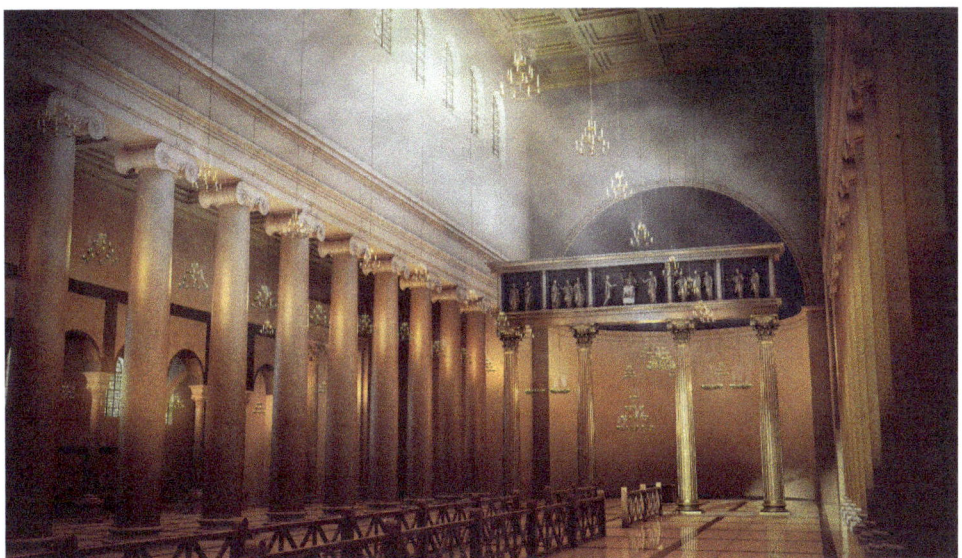

Fig. 8.8 The Constantinian Basilica as visualised by the team (Bosman, Liverani, Haynes, Peverett).

the lighting, *fastigium* and the *solea*, discussed below, we arrive at the visualisation/provocation model shown in Fig. 8.8.

## Lighting the Basilica

The lighting of the basilica is a complex and fascinating subject. The *Liber Pontificalis* devotes a long and detailed section to this topic. The economic resources that the emperor made available for this purpose were very significant, and consisted of the annual income of six or seven farms located between Latium and Campania.[30] The text is as follows:[31]

*Camaram ex auro purissimo*

*et farum ex auro purissimo, qui pendet sub fastidium, cum delfinos L ex auro purissimo, pens. lib. L cum catenas, quae pens. lib. XXV;*

---

[30] LP 34, 12:
   Quibus constituit in servitio luminum:
   
   massa Gargiliana, territurio Suessano, praest. sol. CCCC
   massa Bauronica, territurio Suessano, praest. sol. CCCLX;
   massa Auriana, territurio Laurentino, praest. sol. D;
   massa Urbana, territurio Antiano, praest. sol. CCXL;
   [massa Sentiliana, territurio Ardeatino, praest. sol. CCXL; (only in the codices of the III class)]
   massa Castis, territurio Catenense, praest. sol. mille;
   massa Trapeas, territurio Catinense, praest. sol. MDCL.
   
   For these he assigned to provide for the lights:
   
   the estate Gargiliana, territory of Suessa, revenue 400 solidi;
   the estate Bauronica, territory of Suessa, revenue 360 solidi;
   the estate Auriana, territory of Laurentum, revenue 500 solidi;
   the estate Urbana, territory of Antium, revenue 240 solidi;
   [the estate Sentiliana, territory of Ardea, revenue 240 solidi;]
   the estate Castis, territory of Catina, revenue 1000 solidi;
   the estate Trapeas, territory of Catina, revenue 1650 solidi. Translation by Davis.

[31] LP 34, 10–11; we use the text as revised by Herman Geertman (H. Geertman, *Hic fecit basilicam: Studi sul* Liber Pontificalis *e gli edifici ecclesiastici di Roma da Silvestro a Silverio* (Leuven, 2004), 176), according to the codices of the first class. Note that the *camera* is the ceiling of the basilica and thus has no relation with the *fastigium*: see H. Geertman, 'Il *fastigium* Lateranense e l'arredo presbiteriale: una lunga storia', in H. Geertman (ed.), *Atti del Colloquio Internazionale Il Liber Pontificalis e la storia material: Roma, 21-22 febbraio 2002* (Mededelingen van het Nederlands Instituut te Rome, Antiquity 60-1 (2001-2)) (Assen, 2003), 29–44, repr. in Geertman, *Hic fecit basilicam*, 133–48; P. Liverani, '"Camerae" e coperture delle basiliche paleocristiane', *Mededelingen van het Nederlands Instituut te Rome* 60-1 (2001-2), 13–27. Davis's translation was corrected accordingly.

*coronas IIII ex auro purissimo, cum delfinos XX, pens. sing. lib. quindenas cameram basilicae ex auro trimita in longum et in latum lib. D.*

*(...)*
*Ornamentum in basilica:*

*farum cantharum ex auro purissimo, ante altare, in quo ardet oleus nardinus pisticus, cum delfinos LXXX, pens. lib. XXX;*
*farum cantharum argenteum, cum delfinos XX, qui pens. lib. L, ubi ardet oleus nardinus pisticus;*
*fara canthara argentea in gremio basilicae XXXXV, pens. sing. lib. XXX, ubi ardet oleus suprascriptus;*
*parte dextera basilicae, fara argentea XL, pens. sing. lib. XX;*
*fara cantara in leva basilicae argentea XXV, pens. sing. lib. XX;*
*cantara cirostata in gremio basilicae argentea L, pens. sing. lib. XX;*
*metretas III ex argento purissimo, pens. sing. lib. CCC, portantes medemnos X;*
*candelabra auricalca numero VII, ante altaria, qui sunt in pedibus X, cum ornatu ex argento interclusum sigillis prophetarum, pens. sing. lib. CCC.*

Ceiling of the finest gold

1. and a light (*farum*) of the finest gold hanging beneath the *fastigium*, with fifty dolphins of the finest gold, weighing 50 lb, with chains weighing 25 lb.
2. 4 crowns (*coronae*) of the finest gold, with twenty dolphins, each weighing 15 lb;
   the ceiling of the basilica, of gold-foil in both directions, 500 lb;
   (...)

**Adornment in the Basilica**
3. a chandelier (*farum cantharum*) of the finest gold in front of the altar, in which pure nard-oil is burnt, with eighty dolphins, weighing 30 lb;
4. a silver chandelier (*farum cantharum*) with twenty dolphins, weighing 50 lb, in which pure nard-oil is burnt;
5. forty-five silver chandeliers (*fara canthara*) in the body of the basilica, each weighing 30 lb, in which the same oil is burnt;
6. forty silver lights (*fara*) on the right of the basilica, each weighing 20 lb;

7. twenty-five silver chandeliers (*fara canthara*) on the left of the basilica, each weighing 20 lb;
8. fifty silver candlestick chandeliers (*cantara cirostata*) in the body of the basilica, each weighing 20 lb;

three *metretae* of finest silver each weighing 300 lb, capacity 10 *medimni*;

9. seven brass candelabra in front of the altars, 10 ft in size, adorned with medallions of the prophets inlaid with silver, each weighing 300 lb.[32]

This passage has been carefully analysed by Herman Geertman,[33] but we can integrate his results with archaeological evidence related to lighting in the early Christian and Byzantine basilicas,[34] and with an examination of the terminology. In the Lateran there were four types of lights: 1. the *farum* or *farum cantharum*, which was particularly prestigious; 2. the *corona* (crown); 3. the *cantharum cirostatum*; and 4. the *candelabrum*. The first three types hung from the ceiling, the last rested on the ground. The *farum* and the crown had oil lamps, while the *cantharum cirostatum* and the *candelabrum* clearly had candles.

Dolphins in large numbers decorated the *canthara* of the *fara*. As can be seen from extant examples, the number of dolphins indicates how many glass lamps each light bore. This in turn demonstrates that some of these *fara* were exceptionally large. To get an idea of the dimensions, we can take the specimen in the Louvre (Fig. 8.9).[35] This example consists of a cylinder surmounted by twelve removable branches in the form of dolphins holding glass lamps. Due to its shape, we can think that this light corresponds to the *corona*. The diameter is about 0.5 m: if we use the same shape of the chandelier and the same size of the glass lamps to calculate the size of the largest light in the Lateran basilica – that in front of the altar with eighty dolphins (no. 4) – we should imagine a circle of more than 3 m in diameter, which seems to be excessive.[36] On the other hand, we know that in Saint

---

[32] In the translation the records of the various lights or groups of lights are numbered to facilitate the reference during the discussion.

[33] Geertman, 'Il *fastigium* Lateranense'.

[34] M. L. Fobelli, *Un tempio per Giustiniano: Santa Sofia di Costantinopoli e la descrizione di Paolo Silenziario* (Rome, 2005); L. Bouras and M. G. Parani, *Lighting in Early Byzantium* (Washington, DC, 2008); F. R. Stasolla, 'Dal tramonto all'alba: strumenti e tecniche di illuminazione nell'alto medioevo', in *Il fuoco nell'Alto Medioevo* (Settimane di studio del Centro italiano di studi sull'alto medioevo 60) (Spoleto, 2013), 857–8.

[35] D. Bénazeth, *L'art du métal au début de l'ère chrétienne* (Paris, 1992), 124, 144, 145, 146, 147, 156.

[36] See also H. Geertman, 'Le biografie del Liber Pontificalis dal 311 al 535: Testo e commentario', *Mededelingen van het Nederlands Instituut te Rome* 60-1 (2001–2), 138–355, at p. 185 n. 48.

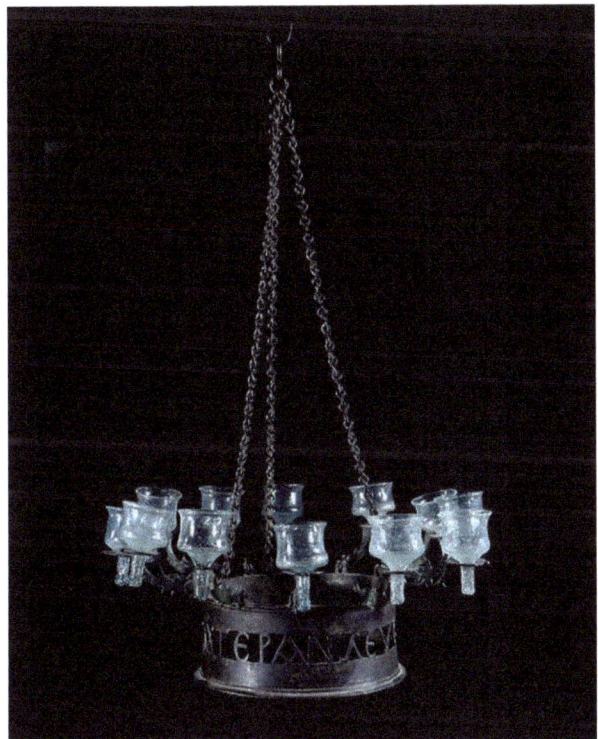

Fig. 8.9 Chandelier, Musée du Louvre, Department of Egyptian Antiquities, Inv. E 11916-3 (Photo © Musée du Louvre, dist. RMN-Grand Palais/Christian Larrieu).

Sophia in Constantinople there were lights hanging from the ceiling (*polycandela* according to the Greek terminology) that Paul the Silentiary describes as consisting of more concentric discs or circles.[37] Some further lights were placed on the cornice and are described as pine-tree or cypresses, or as 'trees of flaming vegetation'.[38] On this basis Maria Luigia Fobelli[39] proposed a reconstruction of these last features with a krater as a base.

[37] Paul. Silent., *Descr. Soph.* 835–8: 'In a smaller, inner circle you will find a second crown bearing lights along its rim, while in the very centre another noble disc rises shining in the air' (trans. C. Mango, *The Art of the Byzantine Empire, 312–1453: Sources and Documents*, 2nd edn (Toronto, 1986), 90.
[38] Paul. Silent., *Descr. Soph.* 871–81: on the cornice 'there is also ... a path full of light, glittering with bright clusters; these one might compare to the mountain-reared pine tree or to the cypress of tender foliage. Pointed at the summit, they are ringed by circles [which] gradually widen down to the lowest curve that surround the base of the trunk; and upon them have grown fiery flowers. Instead of a root, bowls of silver have been affixed beneath these trees of flaming vegetation' (trans. Mango, *The Art of the Byzantine Empire*, 91). Paul. Silent., *Descr. Amb.* 195–200: 'fixed upon the rim you may see trees with fiery clusters, glittering afar with flowers of flame from their silver branches. Nor does each sapling shoot up at random, but it rises in the form of a regular cone with many loops until it comes to a sharp point' (trans. Mango, *The Art of the Byzantine Empire*, 94).
[39] Fobelli, *Un tempio per Guistiniano*, 197 fig. 28.

It is interesting to note that this shape was already described in connection with a Hellenistic specimen in the temple of the Palatine Apollo by Pliny the Elder,[40] who refers to 'lamp-holders ... suspended from the ceiling ... with their lights arranged to look like apples hanging on trees'. This detail does not surprise, considering the function of the chandeliers, whose general shape survived until modern times.

With this 'Christmas tree' shape in mind, we can come back to the terminology and meaning of *farum cantharum*. First the *cantharum*: Geertman – on the basis of an internal analysis of the documents of the *Liber Pontificalis*, interpreted the term as denoting hanging lights.[41] We can confirm this idea: Virgil the Grammarian in the seventh century states that *cantharum* (in the neuter form, not in the masculine *cantharus*) is the *camara domus*: the 'ceiling of the house'.[42] Furthermore, if we consider the form of the ancient *farus* – the lighthouse of Alexandria – which is described as a tower with three tiers, we easily understand the reason for this name, which fits perfectly with the shape we hypothesised. Our reconstruction of the various types of lights is proposed in Fig. 8.10.

It remains to discuss the disposition of the lighting in the basilica, an argument which is also relevant in justifying the visualisation of the interior

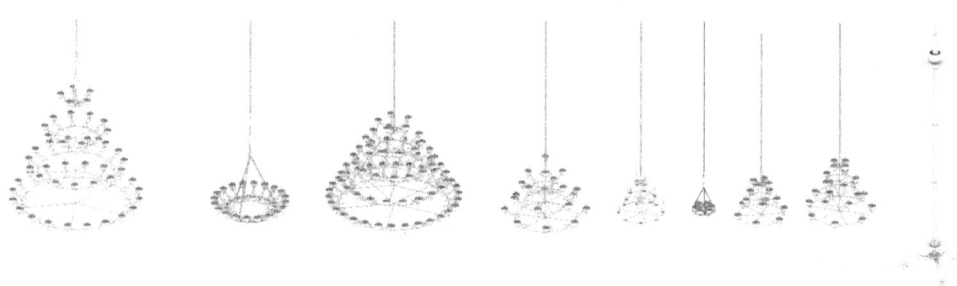

**Fig. 8.10** Various types of lights used in the reconstruction of the basilica on the basis of the *Liber Pontificalis* (Peverett).

---

[40] Plin. *HN* 34.14: 'placuere et lychnuchi pensiles in delubris aut arborum mala ferentium modo lucentes, quale est in templo Apollinis Palatini quod Alexander Magnus Thebarum expugnatione captum in Cyme dicaverat eidem deo' (also lamp-holders were popular suspended from the ceiling in temples or with their lights arranged to look like apples hanging on trees, like the specimen in the temple of Apollo of the Palatine which had been part of the booty taken by Alexander the Great at the storming of Thebes and dedicated by him to the same deity at Cyme': trans. in Pliny the Elder, *Naturalis Historia*, ed. H. Rackham (Loeb Classical Library) (Cambridge, MA, 1952)).

[41] Geertman, *Hic fecit basilicam*, 55.

[42] Verg. Gramm., *Epit*.5.13, Polara (ed.), 62, l. 316. For *camara*, see Liverani, '"Camerae" e coperture'.

of the church as proposed at Fig. 8.8. Our analysis would suggest that the description of lights in the *Liber Pontificalis* indicates the following distribution within the basilica:

1–2: The *farum* and the four *coronae* hung from the *fastigium*.
3–4: The *farum cantharum ante altare* must be considered together with the *farum cantharum argenteum*: we could hypothesise the former hung from the ceiling between the apse and the altar, the latter in front of the altar itself.[43]
  5: We distributed the forty-five *fara canthara argentea* in the nave (*in gremio basilicae*) twenty on each side in the intercolumniations, five in the apse on the chord.
6–7: The difference between the forty lights in the right aisles (*parte dextera basilicae*) and the twenty-five in the left (*in leva basilicae*) was explained arguing it reflected the division between women (to the left) and men (to the right),[44] but even accepting this hypothesis it is difficult to understand the reasons more precisely. According to another guess[45] the left side of the basilica (facing south) could better profit from the sunlight, but this is not true for the liturgies in the evening or at night. In the reconstruction we considered twenty-five lights for each side, inserting them in the intercolumniations of the aisles: the remaining fifteen were distributed in the northernmost aisle, but we admit that this is a very speculative hypothesis.
  8: The fifty *cantara cirostata* were uniformly distributed among the nave and the aisles; the southernmost aisles are the only ones remaining without lights.
  9: The seven *candelabra* are obviously connected with the seven altars for the offerings.

## Visualising the *Fastigium*

Among the furnishing elements of the basilica, two issues deserve particular attention: the *fastigium* and the *solea*. There is a vast body

---

[43] For the meaning of *ante altare* see C. Pietri, *Roma christiana: Recherches sur l'Église de Rome, son organisation, sa politique, son idéologie de Miltiade à Sixte III (311–440)* (Rome, 1976), 100 n. 4; H. Geertman, 'L'illuminazione della basilica paleocristiana secondo il Liber Pontificalis', *RAC* 64 (1988), 135–60. *Contra* J. Romano, *Liturgy and Society in Early Medieval Rome* (Farnham, 2014), 32 n. 47 (but for a later period).

[44] L. Duchesne (ed.), *Le Liber Pontificalis: Texte, introduction et commentaire I* (Rome, 1886), 191 n. 34; Pietri, *Roma christiana*, 323 n 24; Geertman, 'L'illuminazione'.

[45] Geertman, 'L'illuminazione'.

of literature on the *fastigium*,[46] and we have its description in the *Liber Pontificalis*; moreover, four columns and one capital, reused in the altar of Holy Sacrament (Fig. 8.11), have been identified as part of it.[47] The

[46] M. Teasdale Smith, 'The Lateran *fastigium*: A gift of Constantine the Great', *RAC* 46 (1970), 149–75; U. Nilgen, 'Das *Fastigium* in der Basilica Constantiniana und vier Bronzesäulen des Lateran', *Römische Quartalschrift für christliche Altertumskunde und Kirchengeschichte* 72 (1977), 1–31; *CBCR* V, 66–7; J. Engemann, 'Der Skulpturenschmuck des "Fastigiums" Konstantins I. nach dem Liber Pontificalis und der "Zufall der Überlieferung"', *RAC* 69 (1993), 179–203; P. Liverani, 'Le colonne e il capitello in bronzo d'età romana dell'altare del Ss. Sacramento in Laterano: Analisi archeologica e storica', *Rendiconti: Atti della Pontificia accademia romana di archeologia* 75 (1992–3), 75–99; M. Sannibale, 'Le colonne e il capitello in bronzo d'età romana dell'altare del SS. Sacramento in Laterano: Analisi tecnica', *Rendiconti: Atti della Pontificia accademia romana di archeologia* 75 (1992-3), 101–25; Blaauw, *CD* I, 117–27, 176–8, 249–54; S. de Blaauw, 'Das *Fastigium* der Lateranbasilika: Schöpferische Innovation, Unikat oder Paradigma?' in B. Brenk (ed.), *Innovation in der Spätantike (Kolloquium Basel 6.-7. Mai 1994)* (Wiesbaden, 1996), 53–65; S. de Blaauw, 'Imperial connotations in Roman church interiors: The significance and effect of the Lateran *fastigium*', in R. J. Brandt and O. Steen (eds.), *Imperial Art as Christian Art-Christian Art as Imperial Art: Expression and Meaning in Art and Architecture from Constantine to Justinian (International Conference Rome 1999)* (Acta ad archaeologiam et artium historiam pertinentia 15) (Rome, 2001), 137–46; Geertman, 'Il *fastigium* Lateranense'; L. A. Hughes, 'Illusive idols and the Constantinian aesthetic: A note on the Lateran *fastigium*', *Latomus* 70, 2 (2011), 478–92; F. Marcattili, 'Tetrastyla: Ipotesi sull'origine del ciborio d'altare', *RAC* 87–88 (2011-2014), 147–74, at pp. 160–4; P. Liverani, 'Spätantike Ehrenstatuen zwischen Distanz und Dialog', in D. Boschung and C. Vorster (eds.), *Leibhafte Kunst: Statuen und kulturelle Identität* (Paderborn, 2015), 93–121, at pp. 101–2; O. Brandt, 'L'improbabile legame delle colonne di bronzo al Laterano con il *fastigium* costantiniano', *RAC* 92 (2016), 117–36; A. F. Bergmeier, 'Vom Kultbild zur Kirche: Veränderte Materialisierungsformen von Heiligkeit in der Spätantike', in A. F. Bergmeier, K. Palmberger and J. E. Sanzo (eds.), *Erzeugung und Zerstörung von Sakralität zwischen Antike und Mittelalter* (Distant Worlds Journal Special Issues 1) (Heidelberg, 2016), 63–79, at pp. 71–4.

[47] The identification was proposed by Nilgen (Nilgen, 'Das *Fastigium* in der Basilica') and de Blaauw (Blaauw, *CD* I) is generally accepted, with the exception of Brandt (Brandt, 'L'improbabile legame'), who points out that the *Liber Pontificalis* does not mention the bronze columns, but only the silver decoration. No other source mentions the columns before Sergius III (904–11: *LP* 122, 1; L. Duchesne (ed.), *Le Liber Pontificalis: Texte, introduction et commentaire II* (Rome, 1892), 236). According to Brandt they could possibly be identified with the four bronze columns mentioned by Servius on the Capitol (ad Verg. G. 3.29; see D. Palombi, 'Columnae rostratae Augusti', in *LTUR* I, 308). Brandt prefers to interpret the four columns as part of a Carolingian *pergula*, a well-attested type for that period in Roman churches. This theory is not, however, convincing. Notwithstanding the fact that the traditional identification remains hypothetical, it is to be preferred to the new one for several reasons: 1. The *fastigium* is an architectural crown, therefore the columns were not the *fastigium* itself, but only its support. 2. The *Liber* exclusively lists the precious metals (gold and silver), and there is absolutely no bronze in the Lateran list. 3. An *argumentum e silentio* is always weak: the Arch of Titus was never mentioned in the ancient sources before Middle Ages either. 4. The Capitoline columns were of Augustan date, but the only surviving capital of the Lateran columns is dated to the first half of the second century (Liverani, 'Le colonne e il capitello'). 5. The Capitoline columns were *rostratae*, and therefore of a type different from the Lateran ones. 6. It is very difficult to believe that such huge bronze columns outside the basilica escaped melting until the Carolingian period. 7. Lastly, there is a methodological reason to prefer the attribution of the columns to the Constantinian *fastigium*: with one hypothesis we can explain both the *fastigium* and the columns. A single hypothesis with greater explanatory capacity is always preferable to two different, unconnected theories.

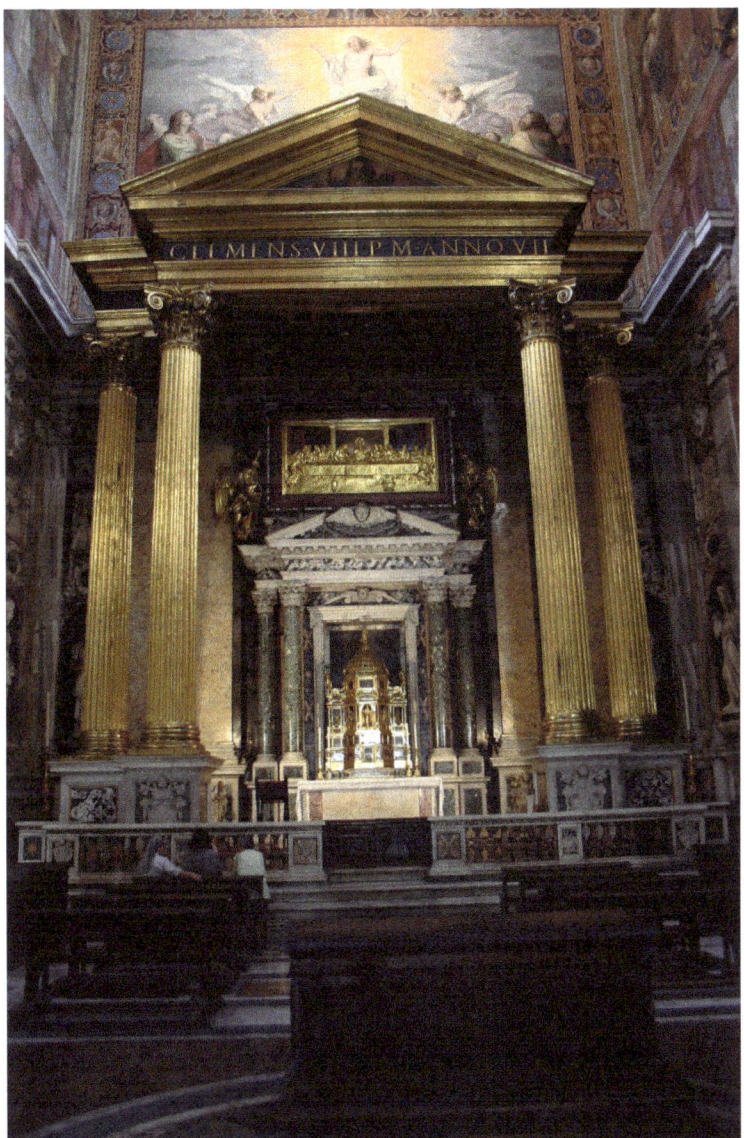

Fig. 8.11 Saint John Lateran, Altar of the Holy Sacrament with the four bronze columns from the Constantinian *fastigium* (Photo: P. Liverani).

*fastigium*'s shape and position has been clarified by Sible de Blaauw. It was a sort of *pergula* that framed and separated the presbytery from the nave. The *Descriptio Lateranensis Ecclesiae*[48] in the twelfth century places it *inter chorum et altare*, thus in front of the altar on the side of

[48] 'Descriptio Lateranensis Ecclesiae', in R. Valentini and G. Zucchetti (eds.), *Codice topografico della città di Roma* (Fonti per la Storia d'Italia 90), 4 vols. (Rome, 1940–53), III, 326–73, at p. 338.

the nave. Further evidence derives from an engraving by Battista Panzera[49] (Fig. 8.12) dated 1598 and Contini's plan[50] (Fig. 8.13). Both place the *fastigium* between the medieval altar and the triumphal arch, thus on the line of the foundation of the external eastern wall of the first wing of the Castra Nova. Earlier sources offer no reason to suggest a different location, and the position some scholars assumed for it in the apse[51] has no evidence and clashes with the results of the nineteenth-century excavations by Busiri Vici[52] (see Fig. 7.13), who discovered in that place two semi-circular foundations, possibly related to medieval phases of a *synthronon*, incompatible with such a reconstruction.[53]

The discussion, however, is still open about the decoration of its summit. According to the *Liber Pontificalis*'s description of the *fastigium*[54] the front

---

[49] S. Prosperi Valenti Rodinò, *L'immagine di San Francesco nella Controriforma* (Rome, 1982), 187 n. 119; J. Freiberg, *The Lateran and Clement VIII* (New York, 1988), 205 fig. 185, with further bibliography. The engraving portrays Saint Angelus from Jerusalem preaching in the Lateran (1216) in the presence of Saint Francis and Saint Dominic. It is the model of the better-known fresco in the portico of Ognissanti Church in Florence, attributed to Jacopo Ligozzi and dated around 1600 (M. Bacci, 'Jacopo Ligozzi e la sua posizione nella pittura fiorentina', *Proporzioni* 4 (1963), 46–84, at pp. 62–3, 80 nn. 36–7).

[50] G. Severano, *Memorie sacre delle sette chiese di Roma*, 2 parts (Rome, 1630), part I, pl. in front of p. 534 n. 17; see also pp. 506, 523.

[51] For the last proposal of this type following Nilgen (Nilgen, 'Das *Fastigium* in der Basilica'), see F. Bisconti, 'Programmi figurativi', in S. Ensoli and E. La Rocca (eds.), *Aurea Roma: Dalla città pagana alla città cristiana* (Rome, 2000), 184–90, at p. 186 fig. 4.

[52] A. Busiri Vici, *Il Laterano nel Pontificato di Pio IX, Progetti del Nuovo Coro, Presbiterio e dipendenze dell'Arcibasilica Lateranense, grandi lavori finora eseguiti, scoperta dell'antica casa dei Laterani, rilievi dell'Absida e Portico leonino, restauro dell'Absida costantiniana, suo trasferimento meccanico e conservazione* (Rome, 1868/1878), plate 20; A. Busiri Vici, *L'obelisco vaticano nel terzo centenario della sua erezione* (Rome, 1886), plate V; Lauer, *Le palais de Latran*, plate II; M. Morbidelli, *L'abside di S. Giovanni in Laterano: Una vicenda controversa* (Rome, 2010), plate 60. See also E. Stevenson, 'Scoperte di antichi edifizi al Laterano', *Annali dell'instituto di corrispondenza Archeologica* 49 (1877), 332–84, at pp. 338–9 plate T, structures L and M: 'piccole tribune concentriche L, M ... paiono prive di relazione con la fabbrica di Costantino, e probabilmente spettano a lavori fatti posteriormente nell'interno dell'abside'.

[53] Liverani, 'Le colonne e il capitello', 96–7.

[54] *LP* 34, 9–10: 'Fastidium argenteum battutilem, qui habet in fronte Salvatorem sedentem in sella, in pedibus V, pens. lib. CXX, et XII apostulos, qui pens. sing. in V pedibus libras nonagenas, cum coronas, argento purissimo; item a tergo respiciens in absida Salvatorem sedentem in throno, in pedibus V, ex argento purissimo, pens. lib. CXL, et angelos IIII ex argento, qui pens. sing. in pedibus V lib. CV, cum gemmis alabandinis in oculos, tenentes hastas; fastidium ipsum pens. lib. MMXXV ex argento dolaticium' (version of the codes of the classes I–II; trans. Davis).

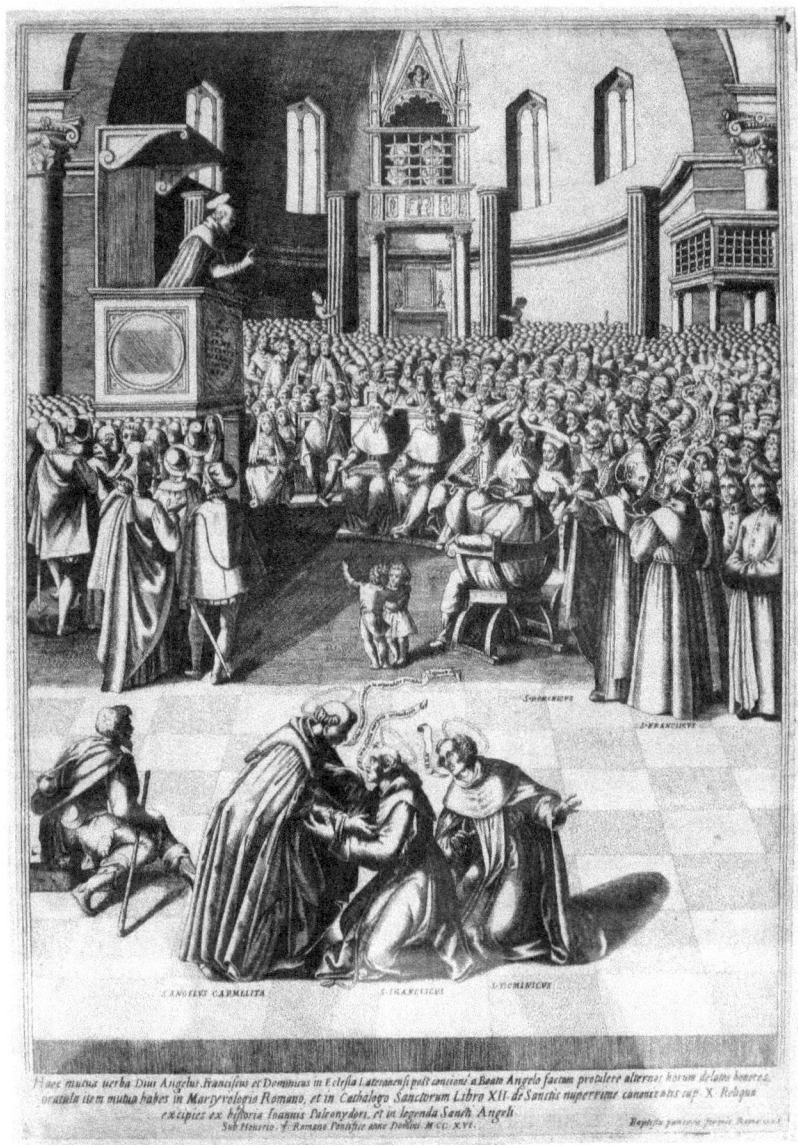

**Fig. 8.12** Battista Panzera, *Saint Angelus from Jerusalem Preaching in the Lateran*, engraving, 1598, Franciscan Museum, Rome, inv. no. 0676/38 (Photo: Franciscan Museum).

has the Saviour seated on a chair, 5 ft in size (1.48 m), weighing 120 lb (39.29 kg), and twelve apostles each 5 ft and weighing 90 lb (29.47 kg) with crowns of finest silver; for someone in the apse looking at it from behind, it has the Saviour sitting on a throne, 5 ft in size, of finest silver weighing 140

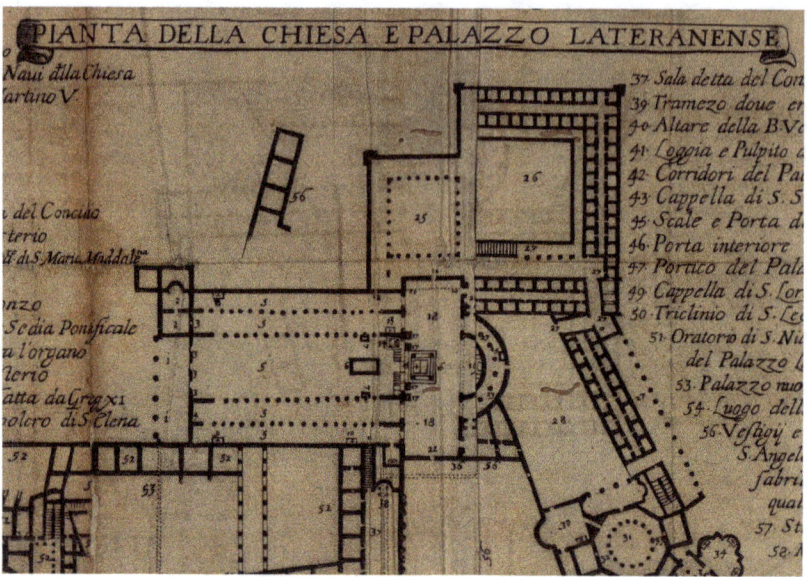

**Fig. 8.13** Francesco Contini, plan of the church and palace of the Lateran, in Severano, *Memorie sacre*. At no. 17 the four bronze columns (Photo: P. Liverani).

lb (45.84 kg), and four spear-carrying silver angels, each 5 ft and weighing 105 lb (34.38 kg), with almandine gemstones for eyes.

The weights are not excessive if we compare them with the honorary statue erected on top of the Columna Palmata in the Roman Forum for Claudius Gothicus, which according to the *Historia Augusta*[55] weighed in at 1,500 lb of silver (about 490 kg) and thus was perhaps 5 m high.

The difficulties in the reconstruction are both theoretical and practical. The first have been clearly shown by Josef Engemann:[56] we do not have any iconographic comparison for this period with the group of angels with rods or spears on either side of Christ; indeed, this image appears only in the sixth century. The subject is better explored elsewhere[57] because it has methodological implications, but it suffices to recall a few points here. The hypothesis that this part of the description of the *fastigium* was inserted in the sixth century is unlikely, if we consider the structure of the archival document from which the *Liber Pontificalis* draws and, more generally, the structure of the lives of the Late Antique and early medieval popes.[58]

---

[55] SHA, *Claud.* 3.2–5. P. Liverani, 'Osservazioni sui rostri del Foro Romano in età tardoantica', in A. Leone, D. Palombi and S. Walker (eds.), *Res bene gestae: Ricerche di storia urbana su Roma antica in onore di Eva Margareta Steinby* (Rome, 2007), 169–93, at pp. 179–80.
[56] Engemann, 'Skulpturenschmuck'.  [57] Liverani, 'Osservazioni sul libellus', 192–5.
[58] Geertman, 'Le biografie'.

Moreover, early Christian monumental cycles are almost entirely lacking for the fourth and fifth centuries, and we can only draw with great caution from funerary art that does not necessarily show the same development. Even if we remain within funerary art, indeed, we observe an iconographic and chronological gap between the frescoes of the catacombs and the sarcophagi.[59] To clarify the argument with an example, it would be very difficult to reconstruct the iconography of the Ara Pacis on the basis of the frescoes of Pompeii.

Second, the beginning of the fourth century was a period of great innovation and creativity, when new typological and iconographic solutions were designed, not all of which had immediate success in the following years.[60] The background for the *fastigium* – which clearly appears as an innovative monument – was as civic imperial rather than religious early Christian art, which at this period did not have a vocabulary and a monumental repertoire. Perhaps we should rather consider models such as the frescoes of the Imperial Cult Room of Luxor,[61] or the reliefs of the Arch of Galerius at Thessaloniki,[62] with images of the emperor between soldiers and court dignitaries. The very idea of the *fastigium* has no precise models: in a broader sense it is reminiscent of the imperial column-monuments (the so-called *Säulenmonumente*)[63] that were popular

---

[59] J. Dresken Weiland, *Bild, Grab und Wort: Untersuchungen zu Jenseitsvorstellungen von Christen des 3. und 4. Jahrhunderts* (Regensburg, 2010).

[60] P. Liverani, 'Il monumento e la voce', in O. Brandt and V. Fiocchi Nicolai (eds.), *Costantino e i Costantinidi: l'innovazione costantiniana, le sue radici e i suoi sviluppi. Atti del XIV Congresso Internazionale di Archeologia Cristiana* (Vatican City, 2016), 393–405.

[61] I. Kalavrezou-Maxeiner, 'The Imperial Chamber at Luxor', *Dumbarton Oaks Papers* 29 (1975), 225–51; J. Deckers, 'Die Wandmalerei in Kaiserkultraum von Luxor', *Jahrbuch des Deutschen Archäologischen Instituts* 94 (1979), 600–52; S. McFadden, 'The Luxor temple paintings in context: Roman visual culture in Late Antiquity', in M. Jones and S. McFadden (eds.), *Art of Empire: the Roman Frescoes and Imperial Cult Chamber in Luxor Temple* (New Haven, 2015), 105–33, at pp. 118–26.

[62] H. P. Laubscher, *Der Reliefschmuck des Galeriusbogens in Thessaloniki* (Archäologische Forschungen 1) (Berlin, 1975), 69–78, frieze B II 21, plates 45.1, 51, 58–60.1.

[63] M. Jordan-Ruwe, *Das Säulenmonument: Zur Geschichte der erhöhten Aufstellung antiker Porträtstatuen* (Asia Minor Studien 19) (Bonn, 1995); P. Baumann, 'Ein spätantikes Säulenmonument am Jerusalemer Nordtor? Zu einem Detail auf der Mosaiklandkarte von Madaba/Jordanien', *Das Münster: Zeitschrift für christliche Kunst und Kunstwissenschaft* 53 (2000), 38–46; S. Heidemann, 'The evolving representation of the early Islamic Empire and its religion on coin imagery', in A. Neuwirth, N. Sinai and M. Marx (eds.), *The Qur'ān in Context: Historical and Literary Investigations into the Qur'ānic Milieu* (Leiden, 2010), 149–95, at p. 180 n. 84; Liverani, 'Spätantike Ehrenstatuen', 101–2.

from the Tetrarchic age onwards. We can also mention the honorary columns of the Rostra and the Roman Forum,[64] or the *tetrapyla* and *tetrakiona* in the provinces.[65]

The practical difficulties, on the other hand, arise rather from the possibility of distinguishing between the two sides of the decoration: to prevent the two images overlapping on the skyline of the *fastigium* in a confused way, it seems necessary to assume a partition – perhaps in wood – between the two series of sculptures, and possibly an architectural framework to give greater prominence to the figures, as de Blaauw proposed (Fig. 8.14).

## Reconstructing the *Solea*

The *solea* has long been debated: this term – or rather, the term *ruga* – refers to the fence at the center of the nave that forms a corridor reserved for celebrants.[66] The oldest archaeologically attested example in Rome is in the basilica of San Lorenzo in Damaso.[67] During Josi's excavations in the Lateran basilica, a series of reused blocks came to light, in two parallel rows along the middle of the nave (Fig. 8.15). They were equipped with a central hole to

[64] P. Verduchi, 'Lavori ai rostri del Foro Romano: L'esempio dell'Umbilicus', *Rendiconti: Atti della Pontificia accademia romana di archeologia* 55–56 (1982–3), 329–40; P. Verduchi, 'Le tribune rostrate', in A. M. Bietti Sestieri (ed.), *Roma: Archeologia nel centro 1. L'area archeologica centrale* (Rome, 1985), 29–33; C. F. Giuliani and P. Verduchi, *L'area centrale del Foro Romano* (Florence, 1987), 148–63 n. 24, 166–73 nn. 25–31, 174–7 n. 32, 184–7; P. Verduchi, 'Colonne onorarie (Forum Romanum)', *LTUR* I, 294–5; P. Verduchi, 'Columna Phocae', *LTUR* I, 307; P. Verduchi, 'Rostra Augusti', *LTUR* IV, 214–17; P. Verduchi, 'Rostra Diocletiani', *LTUR* IV, 217–18; Liverani, 'Osservazioni sui rostri'.

[65] W. Thiel, 'Tetrakiona: Überlegungen zu einem Denkmaltypus tetrarchischer Zeit im Osten des römischen Reiches', *Antiquité tardive* 10 (2002), 299–326; W. Thiel, 'Die "Pompeius-Säule" in Alexandria und die Vier-Säulen-Monumente Ägyptens: Überlegungen zur tetrarchischen Repräsentationskultur in Nordafrika', in D. Boschung and W. Eck (eds.), *Die Tetrarchie: Ein neues Regierungssystem und seine mediale Präsentation* (Wiesbaden, 2006), 249–322.

[66] F. Guidobaldi, 'Struttura e cronologia delle recinzioni liturgiche nelle chiese di Roma dal VI al IX secolo', in S. de Blaauw (ed.), *Arredi di culto e disposizioni liturgiche a Roma da Costantino a Sisto IV (Atti del colloquio internazionale – Roma, 3–4 dic. 1999)* (Mededelingen van het Nederlands Instituut te Rome 59) (Rome, 2000), 81–99; for the Middle Ages, see V. Saxer, 'Recinzioni liturgiche secondo le fonti letterarie', in de Blaauw (ed.), *Arredi di culto e disposizioni liturgiche a Roma da Costantino a Sisto IV*, 71–9. Recent synthesis in O. Brandt, 'The archaeology of Roman ecclesial architecture and the study of Early Christian liturgy', in J. Day and M. Vinzent (eds.), *Early Roman Liturgy to 600* (Studia Patristica 71) (Leuven, 2014), 21–52, at pp. 45–52.

[67] M. Pentiricci, 'Lo scavo: Periodi 8–9', in C. L. Frommel and M. Pentiricci (eds.), *L'antica basilica di San Lorenzo in Damaso: Indagini archeologiche nel Palazzo della Cancelleria (1988–1993)* (Rome, 2009), 235–65, at pp. 247–50; R. Krautheimer and M. Pentiricci, 'La basilica di S. Lorenzo nei secoli IV–X (periodi 8–9)', in Frommel and Pentiricci (eds.), *L'antica basilica di San Lorenzo in Damaso*, 267–76, at pp. 275–6.

## Visualising the Constantinian Basilica 163

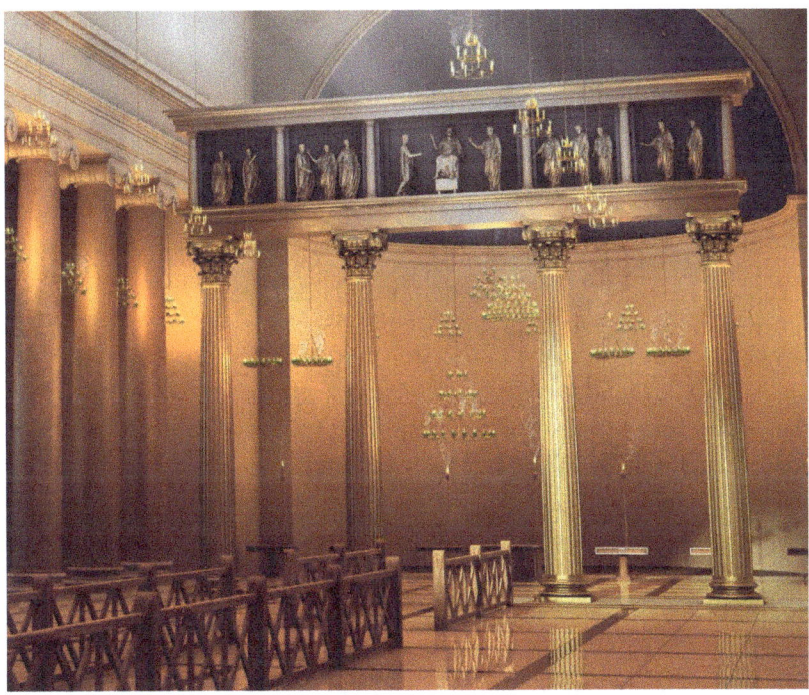

Fig. 8.14 Hypothetical reconstruction of the *fastigium* (Bosman, Liverani, Peverett).

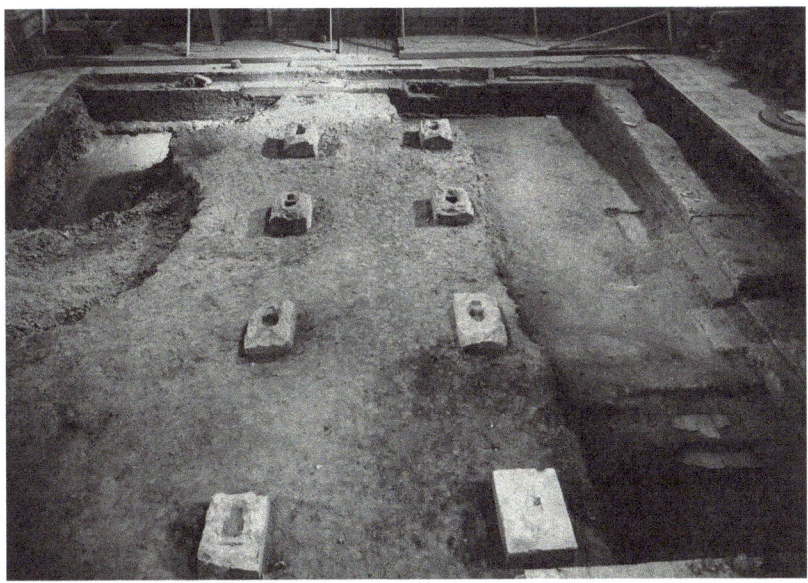

Fig. 8.15 The blocks of the *solea* during Josi's excavations (Pontifical Commission for Sacred Archaeology, neg. LAT C 016).

support the pillars, which in turn held up chancels delimiting the *solea* itself.[68] On the basis of a new analysis of the blocks and the photographic documentation of the excavation,[69] we can propose some interesting observations. First of all, it is finally possible to place the blocks in the first half of the nave with sufficient precision. One unpublished picture (Fig. 8.16) clearly shows that the only block whose upper surface is preserved is placed exactly under the floor level of Pope Martin V, and it therefore retains the height of the Constantinian floor. The tops of the remaining blocks have been deliberately and systematically damaged with a sledgehammer: during the Middle Ages it was necessary to lower them to superimpose a new pavement; but their size, weight and depth made it impossible to remove them. From this we deduce that the blocks were placed in the Constantinian floor, integrated with its design, and possibly following the columns of the nave. It is also important to examine the holes and traces of embedding. At the centre of each block (Fig. 8.17) is a square through-hole either side of which, along the main axis, are two

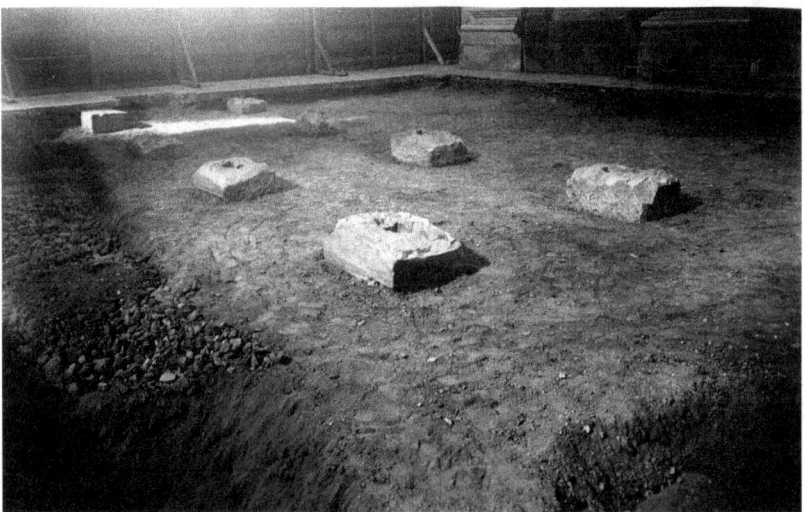

**Fig. 8.16** The blocks of the *solea* during Josi's excavations: the block on the left upper corner lies immediately under the pavement of Pope Martin V (Pontifical Commission for Sacred Archaeology, neg. LAT C 018).

---

[68] The blocks were found in a part of the excavation which is not normally accessible, at the ground floor of the *principia* of the *castra*: I. Haynes, P. Liverani, I. Peverett, S. Piro and G. Spinola, 'Progetto Laterano: Primi risultati', *Atti della Pontificia accademia romana di archeologia (Serie III)* 86 (2013–14), 125–44, at pp. 139–40.

[69] We are deeply indebted to the Pontifical Commission for Sacred Archaeology, which generously put at our disposal the entire photographic campaign of Josi excavations.

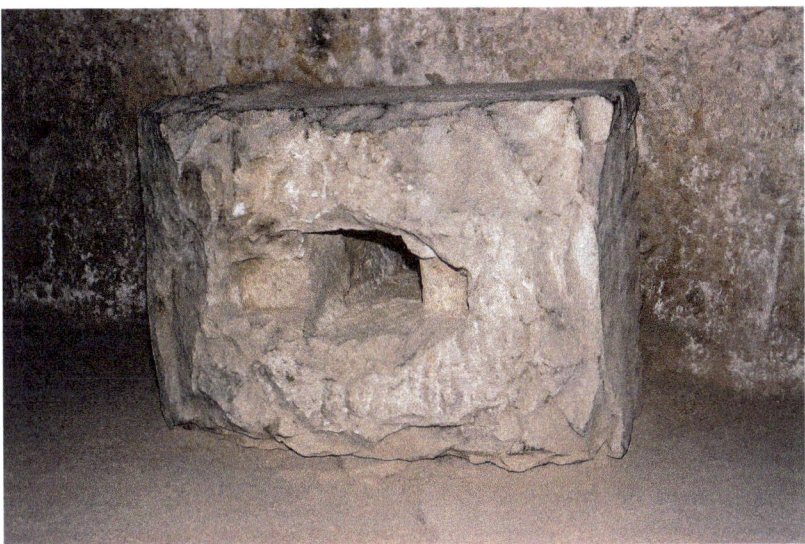

Fig. 8.17 One of the blocks of the *solea* preserved in the cistern under the *principia* (Photo: L. Bosman).

smaller and shallower square sockets. We can therefore envision a central pillar or upright with two chancels – in wood or metal – attached on both sides connecting two successive pillars. We may recall here that Eusebius of Caesarea's description of the basilica of Tyre mentions lattice-work barriers of wood between the altar and the lay people.[70] The smaller sockets would secure the feet of the chancels (Fig. 8.18). The system is similar to that of the wooden chancels in use in the basilica today. Particularly revealing are the traces on the two blocks at the western end of the rows (Fig. 8.15, first line of blocks): here the central hole has only one smaller socket on the side towards the next eastern pillar. This means that the barrier of the *solea* must have stopped, opening a passage to allow people to cross the basilica. The location of this point corresponds to the seventh column from the entrance. This means first of all that we have to reconstruct a *solea* starting from the beginning of the nave up to the *fastigium*, and then that there was probably a second opening further along the nave (Fig. 8.19), a situation very similar to that hypothesised by de Blaauw in his axonometric reconstruction.[71] In short, we can conclude that very probably the blocks of the *solea* must be part of the original Constantinian project.

---

[70] Euseb. *Hist. eccl.* 10.4.44: τοῖς ἀπὸ ξύλου περιέφραττε δικτύοις. See also 10.4.39.
[71] Blaauw, *CD* I, figs. 1–2. As a secondary hypothesis we could imagine that the pillars corresponding to the seventh column marked the beginning of the *solea*.

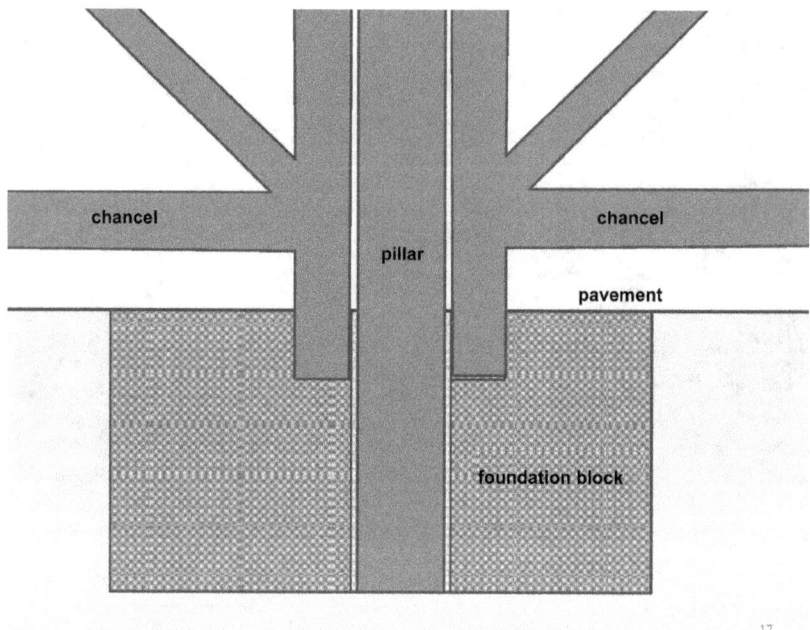

**Fig. 8.18** Cross-section with the reconstruction of the chancel fixed on the foundation block (P. Liverani).

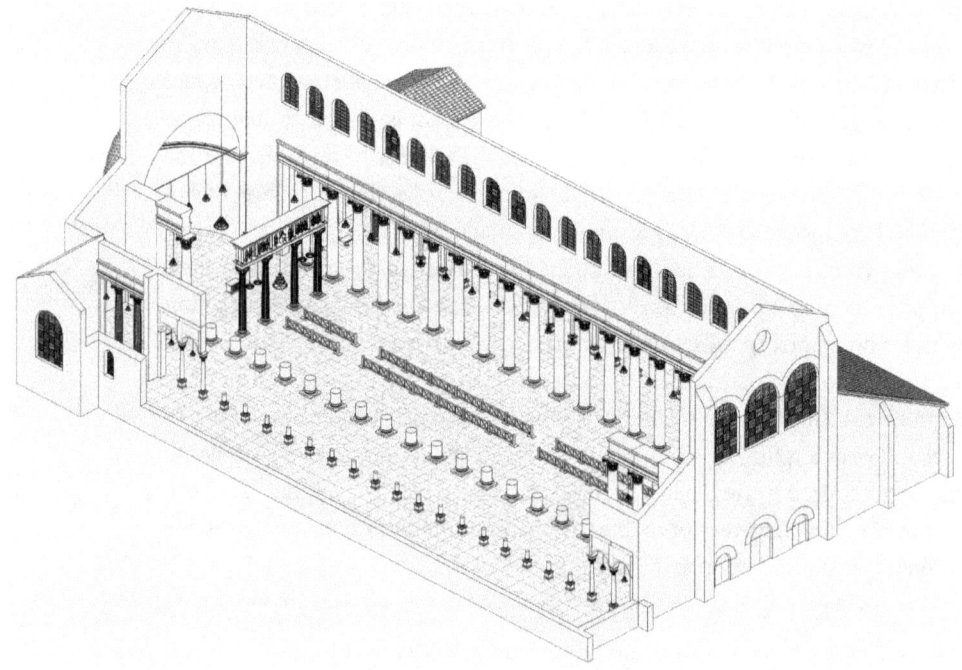

**Fig. 8.19** Axonometric model of the Lateran basilica (Bosman, Liverani, Peverett).

## Conclusion

Building this visualisation of Constantine's Lateran basilica has been an education. The use of architectural modelling techniques to construct it has posed questions of team members that have not been explicitly engaged with before. Similarly, the reconciliation of different hypotheses within a single model has forced participants to challenge the extent of their expertise in diverse aspects of the cathedral and of the culture that led to its creation. We have found the experience rewarding and challenging, and recommend it to others as a way of driving forward debate and understanding.

In making the arguments that underpin the model explicit, we hope too that we have gone some way towards meeting the expectations of those far-seeing colleagues who drafted the first *London Charter*. We also trust that we have produced secure foundations for those who wish to take forward the debates in which this basilica plays a central role. Constantine's Lateran basilica is fundamental to understanding the evolution of the basilica form and church architecture, the rules that determined the interplay between space and liturgy, and to the character and form of imperial propaganda at a pivotal moment in Late Antiquity. It is also of course, a building of intense interest in its own right. If this visualisation serves also as a provocation, as a means of stimulating still more research into its character, form, history and significance, we will be delighted.

9 | Constantine's *Spolia*: A Set of Columns for San Giovanni in Laterano and the Arch of Constantine in Rome

LEX BOSMAN

As the first large church to be built after Constantine had defeated his Roman opponent Maxentius, the Basilica Constantiniana was built in late 312 and the following years. It is generally assumed that work for the building of the church for the bishop of Rome was begun very soon after the famous battle which ended on 28 October 312 near the Milvian Bridge just north of Rome. From the moment when Constantine took control of Rome several connected decisions were made which led to the construction of the Basilica Constantiniana. Some kind of cooperation between the bishop of Rome and his entourage on the one hand and Constantine and his court on the other must have been brought about in order to establish the direct or indirect involvement of Constantine. On a more practical level, a suitable place had to be found where the first official church of the Christian community of Rome could be raised, and the material necessary for the construction work had to be obtained. The support of the emperor Constantine was vital for the prestige of the Christian community, quite apart from the different kinds of financial support that could be obtained from him.

As the site for the church of the bishop of Rome the area in the south-eastern part of Rome was chosen, where a rather large military complex had existed since the late second century. This particular military force was dismissed by Constantine, as these *equites singulares* had fought on the side of his rival, Maxentius.[1] The military camp had thus become superfluous,

My research was supported by grants from the Netherlands Organization for Scientific Research, and the Royal Netherlands Institute in Roma (KNIR). Thanks to a fellowship at the Netherlands Institute for Advanced Study in the Humanities and Social Sciences (NIAS) February–June 2015 I was able to bring my thoughts on these topics together. I would like to thank Paolo Liverani for his indispensable help in and around San Giovanni in Laterano and for the encouraging discussions, and Sible de Blaauw, Cornelius Claussen, Ingo Herklotz and Ian Haynes for their helpful comments.

[1] P. Liverani, 'Introduzione topografica', in P. Liverani (ed.), *Laterano 1: Scavi sotto la basilica di S. Giovanni in Laterano*, vol. I: *Materiali* (Vatican City, 1998), 6–16, at pp. 11, 15; P. Liverani, 'Dalle *Aedes Laterani* al patriachio lateranense', *RAC* 75 (1999), 521–49, at p. 523; J. R. Curran, *Pagan City and Christian Capital: Rome in the Fourth Century* (Oxford, 2000), 95–6, 115.

and the area could be used for other purposes. This *castra* of the *equites singulares* was demolished until the level upon which the building of the church could begin. Perhaps somewhat surprisingly, not many parts of the foundation of the *castra* were used for the construction of the Basilica Constantiniana, but the direction of the basilica was largely determined by the foundations of the *castra*. Those parts of the military complex that obstructed the building of the church were torn down, but most of the foundation was left standing since it didn't interfere with the construction of the church. It would seem likely then that at least some of the building material of the older *castra* was reused for the construction work of the Basilica Constantiniana.[2] Since the early Christian basilica was radically remodelled in the seventeenth century, not much of the fourth-century church apart from the spatial division remains visible in the actual building.

Several important elements of the building of this large church have been discussed in the literature, such as the choice – or, better still, the adoption – of the architectural type of the basilica, the liturgical layout, the part played by the newly converted emperor Constantine in the project and in specific parts of it, and several other questions. In the architecture of Late Antiquity, no other building types can be found to have been used by Christians to organise their religious meetings. The basilica in general was mainly used as a large space for different kinds of gatherings, such as marketplaces or law courts. The possibility of emphasising the longitudinal direction, the relatively simple kind of construction work in building a basilica and the lack of direct associations with pagan religious uses may have favoured the adoption of the basilica for Christian use. Another positive element may have been the strong association in Rome itself of large new basilicas with ruling emperors. Equally important, however, must have been the fact that no other suitable building type existing in Late Antique Roman architecture would have met the demands of the Christian community. Thus, it would seem fair to state that no deliberate choice had to be made for a specific building type when the planning for the construction of the Basilica Constantiniana began, immediately after Constantine's conquest of Rome. Since the Christian of the newly built basilica differed from that of non-Christians without however establishing a new building type as such, it might be best to speak of the 'church basilica' instead of the 'Christian basilica'. The long-established type of the basilica

---

[2] *CBCR* V, 1–44, 71–90; P. Liverani, 'L'area lateranense in età tardoantica e le origine del patriarchio', *MEFRA* 116 (2004), 17–49; H. Brandenburg, *Die frühchristlichen Kirchen in Rom vom 4. bis zum 7. Jahrhundert: Der Beginn der abendländischen Kirchenbaukunst* (Regensburg, 2004), 20–37.

was merely adapted for use by Christians as a large assembly hall and a space suited for the public worship of the Christian God.[3] Several important changes can be grasped, however, in Constantinian architecture for Christian use. Instead of an attractive and striking exterior which in many previous cases showed an open structure to welcome people inside, basilicas for use by Christians were rather austere on the outside while showing rich decoration in the interior. Large windows allowed for better lighting in the basilicas, and the use of lights helped to emphasise the interior decoration and finish.[4]

Research in the fields of Archaeology and Architectural History, together with studies of the liturgical uses of this church, have led to a reconstruction of the Basilica Constantiniana that is generally accepted. It was constructed as a large, five-aisled basilica 100 m in length, built on top of the former Castra Nova Equitum Singularium. Most likely the exterior of the basilica was relatively simple and not equipped with decorative elements. In the interior the architecture breathed another atmosphere, however, with the nave communicating with the inner aisles by means of rows of nineteen columns supporting architraves, while the inner aisles were separated from the outer aisles by rows of twenty-one smaller columns, with arches instead of architraves. The nave and the inner aisles ended at the westernmost wall, whereas the outer aisles ended some 9 m further towards the east. The main altar was situated towards the west, at a short distance from the apse, at the end of the building on that side. Small and relatively low rooms were built on either side of the space of the

---

[3] See L. Bosman, *The Power of Tradition: Spolia in the Architecture of St. Peter's in the Vatican* (Hilversum, 2004), 27–8. The important suggestion to speak of a 'church basilica' was made by J. Christern, 'Die "Gerichtsbasilika" beim Forum von Tipasa (Neuaufnahme), ihre Funkton und die Frage nach den Vorbildern für den basilikalen Kirchenbau', in O. Feld and U. Peschlow (eds.), *Studien zur spätantiken und byzantinischen Kunst: Friedrich Wilhelm Deichmann gewidmet* (Bonn, 1986), 163–204, at p. 195 n. 81. See also S. de Blaauw, 'Kultgebäude (Kirchenbau)', *Reallexikon für Antike und Christentum* (Stuttgart, 2007), XXII, 227–393, at pp. 239–47, 263–4, 286–99; D. Kinney, 'The church basilica', *Acta ad Archaeologiam et Artium Historiarum Pertinentia* 15 (2001), 115–27; Brandenburg, *Die frühchristlichen Kirchen*, 30–2; J. B. Ward-Perkins, 'Constantine and the origins of the Christian basilica', in J. B. Ward-Perkins (ed.), *Studies in Roman and Early Christian Architecture* (London, 1994), 447–68 (article first published in 1954); R. Krautheimer, 'Die konstantinische Basilika', in R. Krautheimer, *Ausgewählte Aufsätze zur Europäischen Kunstgeschichte* (Cologne, 1988), 40–80 (article first published in 1967).

[4] F. Guidobaldi, 'Caratteri e contenuti della nuova architettura dell'età costantiniana', *RAC* 80 (2004), 233–76; H. Brandenburg, 'Prachtentfaltung und Monumentalität als Bauaufgaben frühchristlicher Kirchenbaukunst', in J. Gebauer (ed.), *Bildergeschichte: Festschrift Klaus Stähler* (Möhnesee, 2004), 59–76; S. de Blaauw, 'Le origine e gli inizi dell'architettura cristiana', in S. de Blaauw (ed.), *Storia dell' architettura italiana*, vol. I: *Da Costantino a Carlo Magno* (Milan, 2010), 22–53, at pp. 32–3, 50–2.

main altar, where much later a transept would be built. Modern reconstructions are generally based on those published by Richard Krautheimer during his research in Rome in the twentieth century.[5]

It is generally assumed that *spolia* were used for the columns in the nave and side-aisles of the Basilica Constantiniana. Earlier scholars described the use of *spolia* as a necessity which was forced by the serious economic decline of the Roman Empire in Late Antiquity. Other authors have argued that the choice of *spolia* may have been deliberate, as part of attempts to create a new kind of Christian aesthetics. The efforts to incorporate an older tradition in the new buildings and the need to show a certain *varietas* are also mentioned as possible factors of importance to explain the use of *spolia* in the Basilica Constantiniana and Saint Peter's, the construction of which may have begun around 320.[6] Even though the building of the church of San Giovanni in Laterano – as the Basilica Constantiniana was named later – is still largely existent, the material remains of the columns in the nave and in the side-aisles are scarce. Therefore, it is important to discuss the basis for the material reconstruction of the rows of columns. In the discussion about the use of *spolia* columns by Constantine two other columns should be included. I will argue that these two columns of the yellow *giallo antico* marble that have supported the organ since the late sixteenth century belonged to the original architectural structure of the Basilica Constantiniana as it was built in the first quarter of the fourth century.

---

[5] *CBCR* V, 1–89; Blaauw, *CD* I, 109–29.

[6] D. Kinney, 'The concept of "spolia"', in C. Rudolph (ed.), *A Companion to Medieval Art: Romanesque and Gothic in Northern Europe* (Malden, 2006), 233–52. For different explanations of the use of *spolia* in early Christian architecture, see F. W. Deichmann, 'Die Architektur des Konstantinischen Zeitalters', in F. W. Deichmann, *Rom, Ravenna, Konstantinopel, Naher Osten: Gesammelte Studien zur spätantiken Architektur, Kunst und Geschichte* (Wiesbaden, 1982), 117–18; B. Brenk, 'Spolia from Constantine to Charlemagne: aesthetics versus ideology', *Dumbarton Oaks Papers* 41 (1987), 103–9, at p. 105; P. Pensabene and C. Panella, 'Reimpiego e progettazione architettonica nei monumenti tardo-antichi di Roma', *Atti della Pontificia accademia romana di archeologia: Rendiconti* 66 (1993–4), 111–283, at pp. 128–30 and 135–6; B. Lindros Wohl, 'Constantine's use of spolia', in J. Fleischer, J. Lund and M. Nielsen (eds.), *Late Antiquity: Art in Context* (Acta Hyperborea, Danish Studies in Classical Archaeology) (Copenhagen, 2001), 85–115; M. Fabricius Hansen, *The Eloquence of Appropriation: Prolegomena to an Understanding of Spolia in Early Christian Rome* (Rome, 2003); Bosman, *The Power of Tradition*, 140–2; L. Bosman, 'Spolia in the fourth-century basilica', in R. McKitterick, J. Osborne, C. M. Richardson and J. Story (eds.), *Old Saint Peter's, Rome* (British School at Rome Monograph Series) (Cambridge, 2013), 65–80. For the building dates of Saint Peter's, see: R. Krautheimer, 'The building inscriptions and the dates of construction of Old St. Peter's: A reconsideration', *RJBH* 25 (1989), 1–23, at pp. 16, 21–2; Brandenburg, *Die früchristlichen Kirchen*, 94.

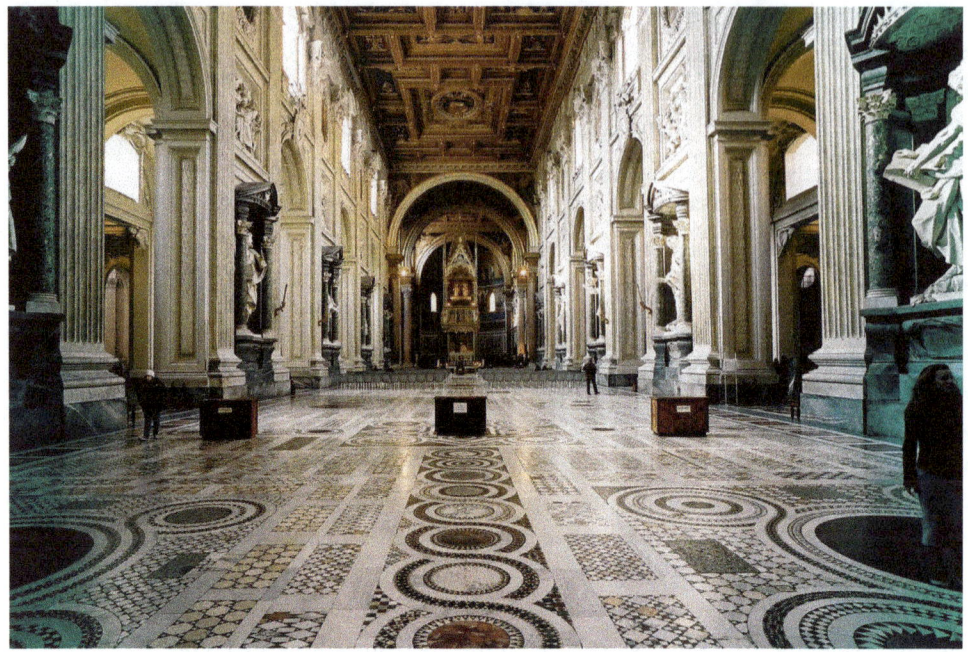

**Fig. 9.1** San Giovanni in Laterano, interior to the west (Photo: L. Bosman).

The interior of the present-day church of San Giovanni in Laterano has been decidedly influenced by the large-scale remodelling which was undertaken in the seventeenth century under Pope Innocent X (1644–55) by Francesco Borromini, which makes an appreciation of the original architectural layout, the liturgical arrangement and the interior decoration very difficult (Fig. 9.1). During this extensive building campaign in the seventeenth century the last of the columns standing in the nave and in the aisles were removed and replaced by large rectangular piers. Under Pope Nicholas IV (1288–92) the large transept had been built, as a result of which three pairs of nave columns had been removed from the western part of the church, if they had not been removed already at some point before that time. In the early Middle Ages, an earthquake in 896 must have brought much damage to the basilica, while in 1308 and 1361 fires had severely damaged the building. As a result of this, the original thirty-eight nave columns had suffered accordingly. According to Malmstrom sixteen pairs of columns of the original nineteen were still in position at the end of the thirteenth century, since with the building of the transept in 1291 three pairs had been taken out. After the damage caused by the fire of August 1361, twenty-two Constantinian columns were removed and replaced by twenty octagonal brick piers, while another two were enveloped in piers. This would leave only eight columns standing, from which another two were removed in 1492, to be used in the triumphal arch.[7] Since Panvinio described seven columns as being visible in 1560, this reconstruction cannot be correct, as Claussen remarked more recently. Of those seven visible columns another two were apparently removed between 1560 and 1645. The remaining five columns would then have been taken out during Borromini's restructuring of the church. More recently Roca de Amicis has come to slightly different conclusions, which were corrected and refined again by Claussen. On the north side the first and fourth column were still visibly standing, while the fifth was partly showing; the first and second column on the south side were still intact and here the fourth was partly hidden by an enveloping brick pier.[8]

Between the inner and outer side-aisles rows of twenty-one green marble columns of considerably shorter proportions were used in the fourth century, adding forty-two columns to the thirty-eight in the nave. Descriptions of San Giovanni in Laterano mention both the number and the material of the columns. In 1588 Pompeo Ugonio mentioned forty-two columns of 'pietra verde Laconica', and other descriptions confirm this information about the green marble columns of *verde antico*. It should be noted however that the number of green marble columns had been reduced by the time Borromini entered the scene, since three of the columns in the northernmost side-aisle had been removed during the pontificate of Sixtus V to enable the building of a new entrance to the Lateran Palace. According to an account of 18 May 1590 two of these three columns were reused somewhere else in the church, while the third one was brought to the church of Santa Susanna. Also, ten of the green marble columns were apparently allotted to the *fabbrica* of San Agnese in 1653 by Pope Innocent X.[9] Several of the green

---

[7] R. E. Malmstrom, 'The building of the nave piers at S. Giovanni in Laterano after the fire of 1361', *RAC* 43, 2 (1967), 155–64.

[8] A. Roca de Amicis, 'Considerazioni sulla basilica Lateranense prima del rifacimento borrominiano', in G. Villetti, R. Bozzoni and G. Carbonara (eds.), *Saggi in onore di Renato Bonelli*, 2 vols. (Rome, 1992), I, 345–54; A. Roca De Amicis, *L'Opera di Borromini in San Giovanni in Laterano: Gli anni della fabbrica (1646–1650)* (Rome, 1995), 14, 27–9. See G. Simoncini, *Roma: Le trasformazioni urbane nel quattrocento*, 2 vols. (Florence, 2004), I, 51–2, 89, II, 67, 100; P. C. Claussen, *Die Kirchen der Stadt Rom im Mittelalter 1050–1300. Bd. 2 S. Giovanni in Laterano* (Corpus Cosmatorum II, 2) (Forschungen zur Kunstgeschichte und Christlichen Archäologie 21) (Stuttgart, 2008), 174–7.

[9] P. Ugonio, *Historia delle stationi di Roma* (Rome, 1588), fol. 40v; O. Panvinio, *De praecipuis urbis Romae sanctioribusque; basilicis, quas Septem ecclesias vulgo vocant, Liber* (Rome, 1570), 116; P. Lauer, *Le Palais de Latran: Étude historique et archéologique* (Paris, 1911), 576, 586; G. Baglione, *Le nove chiese di Roma*, ed. L. Barroero (Rome, 1990 [1639]), 128; Roca de Amicis, 'Considerazioni sulla basilica Lateranense', 352; K. Zollikofer, *Berninis Grabmal für Alexander VII: Fiktion und Repräsentation* (Worms, 1994), 109. See P. Pensabene, *Roma su Roma:*

marble columns from the side-aisles were repaired for use as the niches in the piers of the nave designed by Borromini, and several others were brought in from an excavation site elsewhere, apparently to replace missing or qualitatively less columns.[10] In the actual church twenty-four *verde antico* columns flank the statues of apostles designed by Borromini, and ten more of the green columns are visible in several monuments and in the altar of the Holy Sacrament (Fig. 9.2). The length of these columns in the apostle niches in the piers must have been 12 Roman feet (3.57 m), slightly reduced as a result of repairs and adjustments made when they were reused in the seventeenth century.[11] The originally intended diameter of these columns was 1.5 Roman feet (0.44 m), which gave the columns a regular proportion of diameter versus shaft length of 1:8. Large fragments of columns of the same material and with the same diameter are still present in Rome, for instance in front of the former temple of Divus Julius and the temple of Castor.

Written sources of the kind mentioned above are not very clear about the material of the columns in the nave. For the reconstruction of the church building of the early fourth century it is crucial to understand which elements have been used by Richard Krautheimer and others for their reconstructions. In a manuscript (*c.* 1588) Pompeo Ugonio remarked that the nave was supported by thirty columns of 'marmo numidico', which is the yellow *giallo antico*.[12] This remark led to some insecurity among the authors of the *Corpus Basilicarum Christianarum Romae* when they were preparing the text on San Giovanni in Laterano. In a draft for his text, Krautheimer included the remark that several or perhaps all of the

*Reimpiego architettonico, recupero dell'antico e trasformazioni urbane tra il III e il XIII secolo* (Monumenti di antichità cristiana ser. II, vol. XXII) (Vatican City, 2015), 130. On *verde antico*, see G. Borghini, *Marmi antichi*, 3rd edn (Rome, 1998), 292–3.

[10] K. Güthlein, 'Quellen aus dem Familienarchiv Spada zum römischen Barock. 2. Folge', *Römisches Jahrbuch für Kunstgeschichte* 19 (1981), 179–243, at pp. 181, 184 with contracts of 1646 to repair and polish several *verde antico* columns; in 1659 two *verde antico* columns of 16 *palmi*, which is 12 ancient Roman feet, were found at an excavation and subsequently bought by the pope to be used in San Giovanni. See I. Herklotz, 'Excavations, collectors and scholars in seventeenth-century Rome', in I. Bignamini (ed.), *Archives and Excavations: Essays on the History of Archaeological Excavations in Rome and Southern Italy from the Renaissance to the Nineteenth Century* (London, 2004), 55–88, at pp. 74–5, Catalogue 48.

[11] Bibliotheca Hertziana, *Nachlass Richard Krautheimer* 54/2, letter of John Herrmann to Richard Krautheimer of 10 January 1968 about the green marble columns in the niches with apostle statues. According to Herrmann's research, the shaft lengths varied between 3.51 m (11.79 Roman feet) and 3.55 m (11.92 Roman feet). For the standard lengths of Roman column shafts, see M. Wilson Jones, *Principles of Roman Architecture* (New Haven, 2000), 147–50, 155–6. I use the measurement of 0.297587 m for 1 Roman foot.

[12] Lauer, *Le Palais de Latran*, 576 with edition of Ugonio's MS for *Historia delle stationi di Roma* in BAV XXX, 66. For *giallo antico*, see Borghini, *Marmi antichi*, 214–15.

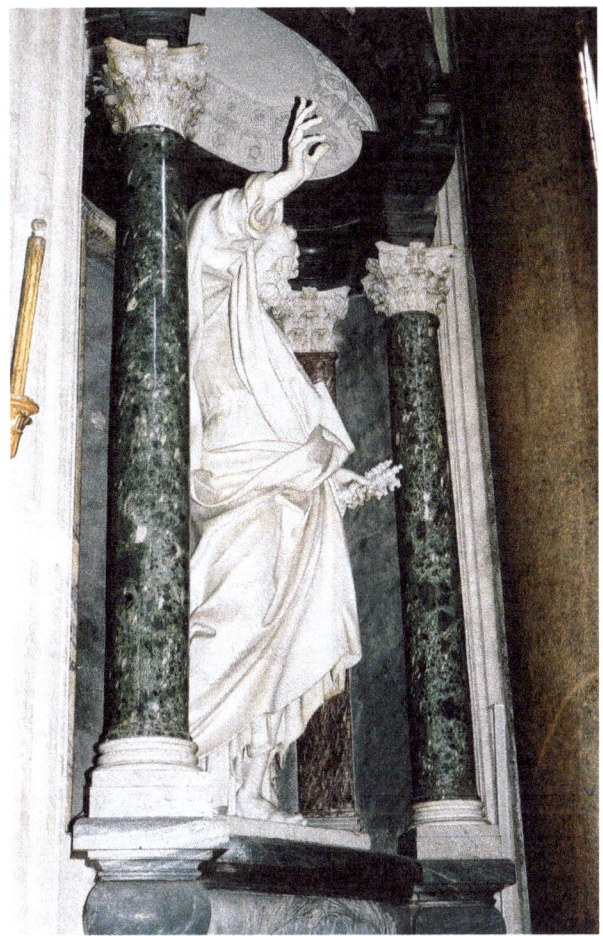

Fig. 9.2 Niche in southern nave wall, flanked by columns of *verde antico* (Photo: L. Bosman).

original column shafts could have been of the yellow *giallo antico*, referring to Ugonio's text. Apparently, he discussed this matter with his colleagues, since Spencer Corbett wrote about it in a letter to Krautheimer, in which he mentioned that Ugonio didn't use the same remark in the printed text; apparently Ugonio was mistaken, and corrected the mistake in the printed version of his text. A remark of the same nature was eventually included in the *Corpus*.[13] For Krautheimer, two arguments were crucial in the reconstruction of the material of the original columns. The first is the assumption

---

[13] Bibliotheca Hertziana, *Nachlass Richard Krautheimer* 55/3, typescript Krautheimer, and letter of Spencer Corbett to Krautheimer of 15 October 1959, *CBCR* V, 68–9.

that the two columns of red granite supporting the triumphal arch since the end of the fifteenth century were taken from the nave, which would mean that they are the only two original nave columns still standing upright in San Giovanni in Laterano. The second argument is the finding of a fragment of a column during excavations in July 1959, underneath the south transept arm.

Stefano Infessura (c. 1440–before 1500) seems to be the oldest written source for the assumption that Pope Innocent VIII (1484–92) used two columns from the nave to support the newly built triumphal arch between the nave and the transept. But although Infessura did mention the construction of the triumphal arch and the use of two large columns, he did not include any remark about the origin of those columns: 'reparavitque ecclesiam Sancti Ioannis Lateranensis, videlicet ante tribunam refecit totum tectum, et ibi praeparavit duas grossas columnas cum lapidibus marmoreis pro faciendo ibi arcu, quod morte praeventus non fecit'.

Much later Marangoni stated that the two columns of red granite supporting the triumphal arch were taken from the nave.[14] He must have used an older source no longer known or based his remark on oral tradition. Judging from the fact that in the fourteenth century two fires had seriously damaged the interior of San Giovanni and that as a result of the fire of 1361 three columns had fallen, the hypothesis that the two columns of red granite under the triumphal arch could be taken from the nave columns after this fire might seem questionable. After all, they aren't broken, nor do they show too much damage. Apart from that, an older triumphal arch resting on columns should by no means be excluded; a few remarks in written sources may be interpreted as pointing to such a structure.[15]

The finding of a fragment of a column in 1959 is the other argument used by Krautheimer for the reconstruction of the material for the nave column shafts. This concerns a fragment of red granite, which according to Krautheimer could have had the same diameter, 1.10 m, as the two columns under the triumphal arch.[16] However, the evidence of this fragment is not as plain as one might think. In the excavation area, underneath the south transept of San Giovanni, no fragment of a red granite column can still be found. The only fragment lying around in that part of the archaeological area is a fragment of a column of grey granite. To complicate matters

---

[14] S. Infessura, *Diario della città di Roma di Stefano Infessura scriba senato*, ed. O. Tommasini (Fonti per la storia d'Italia 5) (Rome, 1890), 7, 279–80; G. Marangoni, *Delle cose gentilesche e profane trasportate ad uso, e adornamento delle chiese* (Rome, 1744), 373.

[15] Claussen, *Die Kirchen der Stadt Rom*, 144.  [16] *CBCR* V, 44.

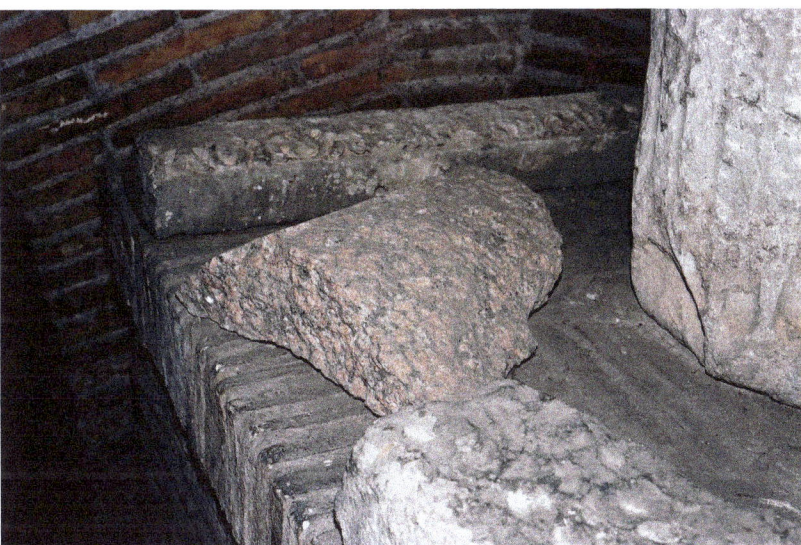

Fig. 9.3 San Giovanni in Laterano, fragment of red granite column in excavation area (Photo: L. Bosman).

somewhat more, Krautheimer mentioned the finding of a column fragment in a typescript for the 'Note Lateranensi II', but called it grey granite rather than the red granite which was mentioned later in the *Corpus* for the very same fragment.[17] However, elsewhere in the excavation area, a fragment of a red granite column is at hand (Fig. 9.3). Since the curves of both column fragments are at least partly available, it was possible for me to measure these curves and to reconstruct the original circumference of the columns.[18] In the light of so few pieces of evidence for the reconstruction of the material of the columns of the nave, this could be vital to either support or reject Krautheimer's conjecture. The grey granite fragment turned out to have had an original diameter of 0.70–0.75 m, which does

---

[17] Bibliotheca Hertziana, *Nachlass Richard Krautheimer* 55/9, p. 6 (Italian version), and 55/10, p. 3, English version: 'The fragment of a column shaft, suggesting a diameter of roughly 1 m for the column, may well have come from this colonnade, even though its material, gray granite, is very different from the yellow numidian marble of the columns which in Panvinio's time were still visible in the nave.' However, in the articles published with the title 'Note Lateranensi' the column fragment was not mentioned. See E. Josi, R. Krautheimer and S. Corbett, 'Note Lateranensi', *RAC* 33, 1–4 (1957), 79–98; E. Josi, R. Krautheimer and S. Corbett, 'Note Lateranensi', *RAC* 34, 1–4 (1958), 59–72.

[18] Thanks to Paolo Liverani, I was able to study the finds underneath San Giovanni on several occasions. On 30 November 2004 and on 7 June 2006 I studied both fragments in detail. The curvature of the two column fragments were reproduced with a plaster cast on a protective foil. The curves were then reconstructed to their original complete circumference, from which other measurements can be deduced.

not come close to the diameter of around 1.20 m. of the two existing columns of red granite supporting the triumphal arch.[19] However, the fragment of red granite does show a reconstructed diameter of 1.26 m, which equals 4.2 Roman feet. Since the reconstruction is based on a relatively small part of the original curve of the column circumference, one can assume that the original diameter was closer to 4 feet, resulting in a shaft length of 32 feet, or slightly more. The measures of both large red granite columns of the triumphal arch are too close to these findings to be accidental. Both columns have a lower diameter of 1.22 m and, measured just above the profile, the diameter in both cases is 1.16 m.[20] When the measures of the red granite column fragment are compared with those of the two columns of red granite supporting the triumphal arch, Krautheimer's hypothesis can be corroborated. The length of these column shafts is 9.36 m.[21] The column fragment of red granite mentioned in the *Corpus* points to the same measures as found in the two large columns supporting the triumphal arch. It seems fair then to conclude that all three columns were proportioned with a diameter of 4 feet (= 1.19 m) and a length of 32 feet (= 9.53 m).

That the two columns of red granite under the triumphal arch and the column fragment of the same material show the same circumference and (reconstructed) dimensions and proportions still does not prove that they originate from the early Christian nave of San Giovanni in Laterano, nor that the early Christian nave was built on columns of red granite. One of the contracts of 1647 relating to the partial rebuilding of the church by Borromini deals with a granite column enveloped in a newly built large pier. Part of 'una Colonna di granito orientale' had to be cut away in order to properly finish the niche of this particular pier.[22] Even if the expression 'granito orientale' does not positively identify the granite as red, that option

[19] The reconstructed diameter of 0.70–0.75 m points to a diameter of 2.5 Roman feet (= 0.74 m). With a proportion of 1:8 the approximated length of the shaft has been put at 20 Roman feet, which is a shaft length often used in Roman antiquity. See Wilson Jones, *Principles of Roman Architecture*, 147–50, 155–6; P. Barresi, 'Il ruolo delle colonne nel costo degli edifici publici', in M. de Nuccio and L. Ungaro (eds.), *I marmi colorati della Roma imperiale* (Rome, 2002), 69–81, at pp. 69–72.

[20] Measured on 7 June 2006, and again on 27 January 2016, this time with laser. The circumference of 3.70 m of the southern column in the triumphal arch corroborates the comparison with the findings of the northern column of the triumphal arch and of the column fragment.

[21] Measured on several occasions (e.g. 27 January 2016). Pensabene and Panella, 'Reimpiego e progettazione architettonica', 168 mention 9.44 m; *CBCR* V, 44 mentions 9.60 m, but 9.44 m is mentioned at p. 79. The surprisingly slender proportions of the shafts mentioned by *CBCR* V, 79 were apparently based on a mistake; the real proportions of 1:8 of these column shafts is nothing out of the ordinary.

[22] Güthlein, 'Quellen aus dem Familienarchiv Spada', 182, no. 56.

seems more plausible than the possibility that grey granite was meant. Since the brick piers had been considerably lower than the original columns, only the third column (numbered from the eastern entrance) on either side could possibly have been left standing and therefore have become visible in the niche of the newly constructed piers, the first pair of large piers upon entering the basilica from the east. On a plan by Borromini (Vienna Albertina, AZ Rom 374) only the third column on the north side is indicated, so this one may have been the column meant in the contract. Taking these facts into consideration, it only seems fair to attach some value to the fact that so far only columns and a fragment of a column of red granite have become available for the reconstruction of the original rows of columns in the nave. No columns or fragments of a different kind of granite or marble have surfaced until now, which allows some conclusions about the reconstruction by Krautheimer. The available evidence supports the reconstruction of the nave of San Giovanni in Laterano with two rows of nineteen columns of red granite, with a diameter of 4 Roman feet (1.19 m) and a shaft length of 32 feet (9.53 m). The columns of the side-aisles and those of the nave were thus used in the peculiar proportion of 1:2.66 (Fig. 9.4).

It has become customary to describe the nave columns of San Giovanni in Laterano as varying in 'material and size'.[23] The famous seventeenth-century fresco by Filippo Gagliardi in San Martino ai Monti is the main source for this assumption, after which the situation at Saint Peter's is mentioned as yet another example of and parallel to this situation. Detailed study does not, however, allow for this hypothesis, since arguments fail for both San Giovanni and Saint Peter's to consider nave colonnades with column shafts of different lengths. The shafts of the nave columns in Saint Peter's measured 30 Roman feet, and there is no reason to assume that in San Giovanni several column shafts had a length that differed from the (red) granite shafts of 32 feet discussed so far.[24] This may be quite important in the debate on the use of *spolia* in Late Antiquity. When the choice of the column shafts in the Basilica Salvatoris and in Saint Peter's in the Vatican can no longer be reduced to the use of disparate material because the means and the material to build in a proper, 'classical' way were absent,

---

[23] *CBCR* V, 79–80; Brenk, 'Spolia from Constantine to Charlemagne', 104–6; Blaauw, *CD* I, 114; B. Brenk, 'Spolien und ihre Wirkung auf die Ästhetik der *varietas*: Zum Problem der alternierenden Kapitelltypen', in J. Poeschke (ed.), *Antike Spolien in der Architektur des Mittelalters und der Renaissance* (Munich, 1996), 49–92, at pp. 54–5.

[24] Bosman, *The Power of Tradition*, 39–41.

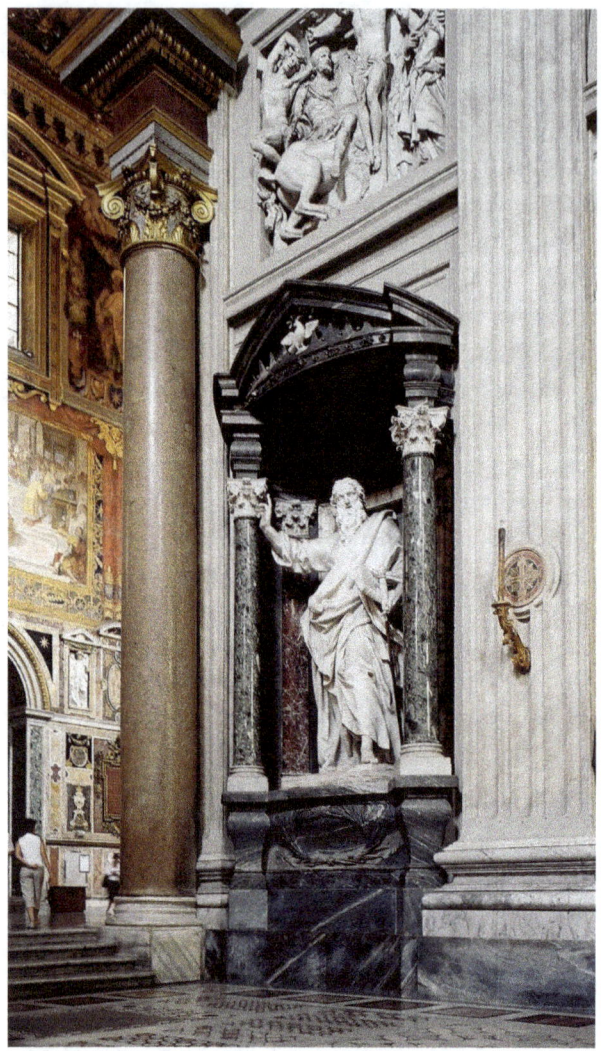

**Fig. 9.4** San Giovanni in Laterano, westernmost niche on north side of the nave, with *verde antico* columns, and one column shaft of red granite under the triumphal arch. (Photo: L. Bosman)

the element of choice, especially with reference to the colour of the columns, gets more emphasis again.[25]

In the description of the material of the columns in the nave of San Giovanni in Laterano mention was made of Pompeo Ugonio, because he

---

[25] D. Kinney, 'Spolia: Damnatio and renovatio memoriae', *Memoirs of the American Academy in Rome* 42 (1997), 117–48, at pp. 125–8.

wrote about columns of the yellow *giallo antico*, which he himself later discarded as a mistake. An anonymous text from the first decade of the sixteenth century describes the church as being 'tutto de spoglie', but the specific material isn't mentioned. The idea that *spolia* were used is also expressed by others, such as Severano.[26] Even though it is more than likely that Ugonio was mistaken about the colour of the columns it would still be interesting to understand why he specifically mentioned the yellow kind of marble rather than any other kind, since red granite columns aren't easily mistaken for yellow marble ones. I assume he must have seen columns of this kind of material somewhere in the church, and mixed them up with the ones in the nave. Indeed, a pair of columns of *giallo antico* is supporting the organ above the entrance to the actual church in the north transept (Fig. 9.5). This arrangement is already adequately described by Giovanni Baglione in 1639: upon entering the church through the transept entrance rebuilt by Pope Sixtus V towards the end of the sixteenth century 'vi sono due colonne di marmo gialle con ordine composito di finissimo pulimento che sostengono un cornicione superbamente lavorato di marmo, e sopra la cornice vi posa un organo'. Rasponi mentioned the same, but without reference to the material. He does however mention the coat of arms of Pope Clement VIII (1592–1605), thereby indicating correctly that this pope was responsible for the placement of the organ against the north transept wall. This formed part of the campaign of remodelling and decorating the transept, which was then often referred to as the 'nave Clementina'.[27] The origin of these two fluted columns is not entirely clear, but can partly be retraced and reconstructed.

In 1597–8 these two columns were taken from the still extant portico on the eastern side of the church to be placed inside the church in the north transept. When Ugonio wrote about yellow marble columns, the two columns were still in use in the portico. Several written sources document their replacement by granite columns.[28] So until 1597 two *giallo antico*

---

[26] A. Fantozzi (ed.), *Nota d'anticaglie et spoglie et cose maravigliose et grande sono nella cipta de Roma da vederle volentieri* (Rome, 1994), 24; G. Severano, *Memorie sacre delle sette chiese di Roma* (Rome, 1630), 507.

[27] Baglione, *Le nove chiese di Roma*, 120; C. Rasponi, *De Basilica et Patriarchio Lateranense libri V* (Rome, 1656), 40. See J. Freiberg, *The Lateran in 1600: Christian Concord in Counter-Reformation Rome* (New York, 1995), 72. The material of these columns also mentioned by F. Corsi, *Delle pietre antiche: Trattato*, 3rd edn (Rome, 1845), 296.

[28] I. Herklotz, 'Der mittelalterliche Fassadenportikus der Lateranbasilika und seine Mosaiken: Kunst und Propaganda am Ende des 12. Jahrhunderts', *RJBH* 25 (1989), 27–95, at pp. 41–2; Freiberg, *The Lateran in 1600*, 298; I. Herklotz, *Gli eredi di Costantino: Il papato, il Laterano e la propaganda visiva nel XII secolo* (La corte dei papi 6) (Rome, 2000), 160; Archivio della Fabbrica di S. Pietro, 3 D 163 Conti, f. 43r: 21 okt. 1597, with instruction of Pope Clement VIII to bring

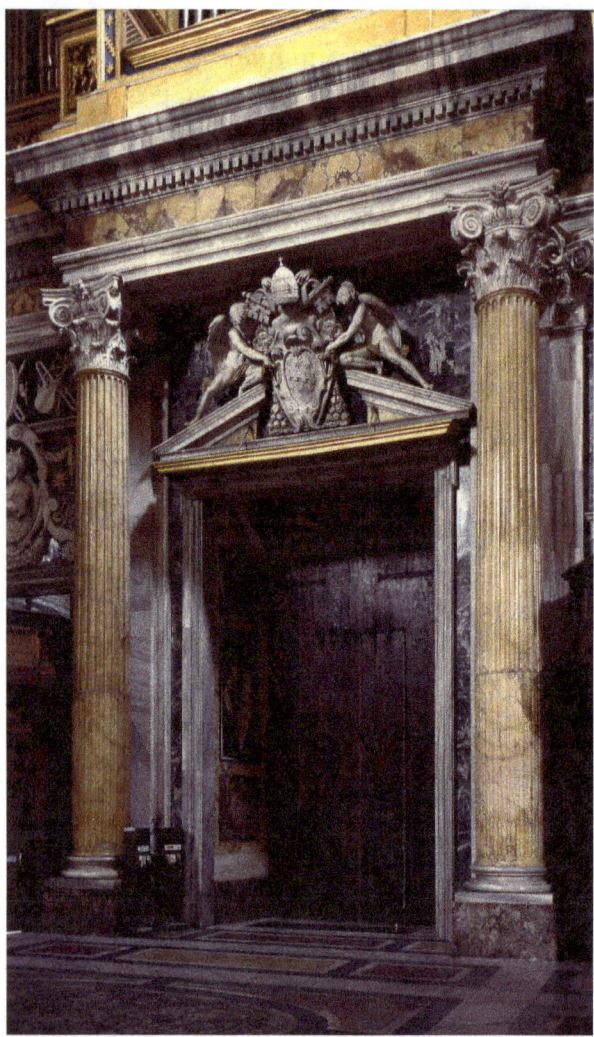

**Fig. 9.5** San Giovanni in Laterano, two *giallo antico* columns supporting the organ tribune in the north transept (Photo: L. Bosman).

columns formed part of the supporting structure of the portico of San Giovanni in Laterano. In fact, three of the columns in the portico were fluted; the third one was of white marble. This is corroborated by references of Panvinio and others; the print by Ciampini which shows the façade in 1693 only has the second column from the right as a fluted one, which

a granite column from the *fabbrica* of Saint Peter's to San Giovanni in Laterano to be placed 'sotto il Portico vecchio' to replace one of the *giallo antico* columns; Lauer, *Le palais de Latran*, 617, with reference to a document in Archivio di Stato Roma, payment 15 November 1597, for the transportation of a granite column to San Giovanni 'per sotto il portico di S. Giovanni'.

confirms that the two fluted *giallo antico* columns in this portico had been taken away almost a century earlier.[29]

The portico in front of the east façade of San Giovanni in Laterano is likely to have been constructed during the last twenty years of the twelfth century by Master Nicolaus de Angelo; according to some authors 1188–98 is the most likely period, but approximately 1180–1200 seems to give a fair date for the portico.[30] This implies that the six columns of this portico, including the two of *giallo antico* marble, cannot have been acquired after this period. Therefore, at this point of my investigation it seems reasonable to consider two options concerning the origin of these columns: the two fluted columns of *giallo antico* were either acquired toward the end of the twelfth century from somewhere in or around Rome, or they had become available in or around San Giovanni in Laterano at that period, having been previously used in another architectural setting.

In this context it is interesting to analyse the proportions of the two extant columns as well as the way they were dressed. With a shaft length of some 7.10 m and a diameter of 0.90 m these columns possess standard proportions of a length of 24 Roman feet (7.14 m), a diameter of 3 feet (0.89 m) and a corresponding proportion of diameter and shaft length of 1:8.[31] The columns show the regular number of twenty-four flutings (Fig. 9.6). A comparison of these proportions to those of other architectural monuments points to only a few specific examples. Two of these monuments are particularly interesting since they show columns with the same proportions, while one of these two monuments has columns shafts of exactly the same material. The first of these monuments is the well-known *fastigium* in San Giovanni in Laterano, which was donated by the emperor Constantine and which must have been a construction based on the four bronze columns that are still extant in the south transept in the altar of the Holy Sacrament. The Arch of Constantine is the other, even more crucial, monument.

---

[29] Herklotz, *Gli eredi di Costantino*, 160; Lauer, *Le palais de Latran*, 434, 585 containing edition of O. Panvinio, *De sacrosancta basilica, baptisterio et patriarchio Lateranensi*, 411–90, who mentioned three fluted columns in the portico, and description of San Giovanni under pope Innocent X.

[30] P. C. Claussen, *Magistri Doctissimi Romani: Die römischen Marmorkünstler des Mittelalters* (Wiesbaden, 1987), 22–6; Herklotz, 'Der mittelalterliche Fassadenportikus', 37–40; Herklotz, *Gli eredi di Costantino*, 161; Claussen, *Die Kirchen der Stadt Rom*, 77.

[31] With the help of P. Liverani, one of the two columns supporting the organ was measured on 10 April 2003. Digital measurements of both *giallo antico* column shafts on 26 January 2016 confirmed my earlier findings.

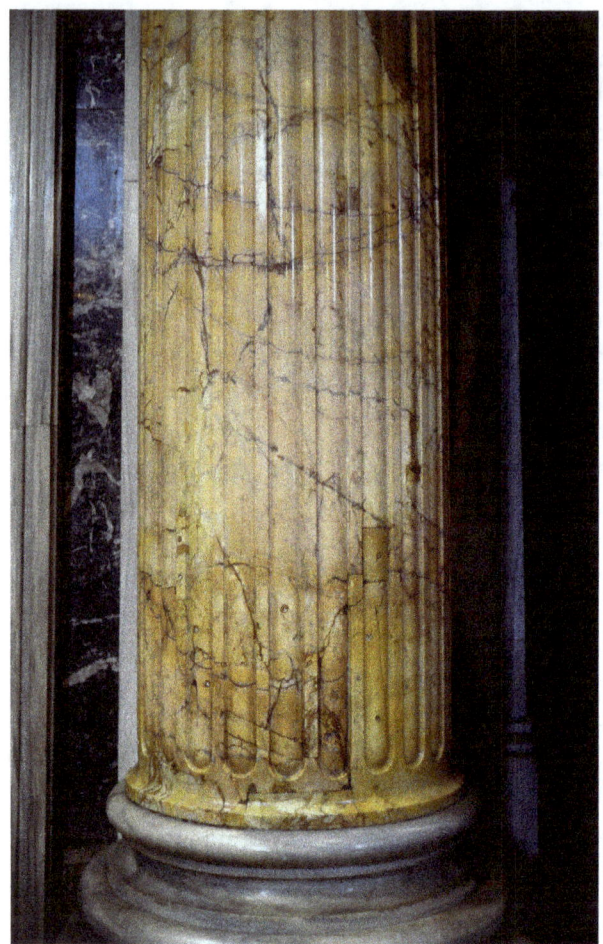

Fig. 9.6 Detail of *giallo antico* column on the right side under the organ tribune (Photo: L. Bosman).

It is well known that the architectural elements as well as the relief sculptures of the Arch of Constantine are *spolia* from different periods, not necessarily assembled for ideological reasons.[32] On both long sides of this monument four columns of *giallo antico* had originally been used, seven of which still exist in their original positions. Although large fluted columns of *giallo antico* marble can be found in various places in Rome, column shafts of exactly the same dimensions are not available elsewhere.

[32] See P. Liverani, 'Reimpiego senza ideologia: La lettura antica degli spolia dall'arco di Costantino all'età carolingia', *Mitteilungen des Deutschen Archäologischen Instituts, Römische Abteilung* 111 (2004), 383–433; P. Liverani, 'L'arco di Costantino', in A. Donati and G. Gentili (eds.), *Costantino il Grande: La civiltà antica al bivio tra Occidente e Oriente* (Rimini, 2005), 65–9.

In the area of the Forum of Augustus and the Forum of Trajan fragments of *giallo antico* columns can be found, but never with the same dimensions as the set on the Arch of Constantine and those in San Giovanni. The admirable nineteenth-century connoisseur of ancient marbles and granites Faustino Corsi had already made similar observations when he noted that the largest columns of *giallo antico* in Rome could be seen in the Pantheon, in San Giovanni in Laterano and on the Arch of Constantine.[33] The columns in the interior of the Pantheon measure 30 Roman feet, however, the same dimension as the four columns of *giallo antico* in the transept of the basilica of Saint Peter's in the Vatican.

The tentative conclusions about the *giallo antico* columns thus far can be summed up as follows. Two fluted columns supporting the organ in San Giovanni in Laterano since 1597–8 were taken from the eastern portico, which dates from the period around 1180–1200. The implication is that the yellow columns were available in San Giovanni at least from this period. But since the same kind of column shafts were used in the Arch of Constantine it is fair to assume that the *giallo antico* columns in San Giovanni in Laterano and those in the Arch of Constantine originate from the same stock, which was available for a selected group of high-end commissions in the first half of the fourth century. As Wilson Jones observed regarding the Arch of Constantine: 'There cannot have been that many possibilities for obtaining a finer set than this one: eight fluted two-part monoliths of *giallo antico*.'[34] Considering all this, the likelihood that the yellow columns were obtained in the period after the Basilica Constantiniana had been constructed and before they formed part of the late twelfth-century eastern portico – between about 320 and about 1180 – can virtually be excluded. I argue that these columns of *giallo antico* were brought to the Basilica Constantiniana during the period of its construction in the years following 312. From the original set of columns, eight were designated for use in the Arch of Constantine and (at least) two were brought to the Basilica Constantiniana. The choice for these columns was of vital importance for the Arch of Constantine, since the design of this monument depended largely on the length of the marble column shafts of 24 Roman feet. Although it is difficult to establish, the columns may have been produced in the period from Hadrian to Septimius Severus, between around 117 and 217.[35]

---

[33] Corsi, *Delle pietre antiche*, 90; F. Corsi, *Delle pietre antiche di Faustino Corsi Romano*, ed. C. Napoleone (Milan, 2001), 39.
[34] Wilson Jones, *Principles of Roman Architecture*, 124.
[35] Wilson Jones, *Principles of Roman Architecture*, 124; M. Wilson Jones, 'Genesis and Mimesis: The design of the Arch of Constantine in Rome', *Journal of the Society of Architectural*

A fundamental element of course is where in the Basilica Constantiniana and how these yellow marble columns may have been used originally. Several possibilities can be suggested, but they are not equally likely. In theory, three different solutions for the use of the columns can be proposed, necessitating the assumption that not two but four of these columns had originally been available; either the original set of *giallo antico* columns counted four shafts, or a combination of two yellow columns and two of another kind of marble had been used. Of the three possible places where four columns of *giallo antico* had been used in the first quarter of the fourth century, the eastern façade and a possible atrium there would offer a likely use. One might suppose that the Basilica Constantiniana was fitted with an atrium or portico. Even though many of the buildings commissioned by or built with the active support of Constantine showed different layouts, a common feature of many of them is the sequence of an atrium, a longitudinal basilica and a crowning element, which could differ – from the transept with apse in Saint Peter's to the polygonal structure in Bethlehem. This would make it likely that the Basilica Constantiniana possessed an atrium with a monumental entrance as well.[36] But unfortunately nothing about such a portico or atrium is known, leaving a reconstruction of it in the realm of desirables.

The second possible use for the yellow columns could theoretically have been as part of the famous *fastigium*, de Blaauw's reconstruction of which has been widely accepted until now. But his reconstruction, based on a careful reading of the text in the *Liber Pontificalis* – which happens to be the only written source for the reconstruction of the *fastigium* – also shows that this fascinating monument could not have been a structure resembling a ciborium. Since the illumination of the altar is mentioned separately in the *Liber Pontificalis* and another lamp is mentioned as hanging from the *fastigium* it has become clear that the *fastigium* could not have been placed above the altar. Even though the length of the *giallo antico* column shafts is exactly the same as that of the four bronze column shafts (24 Roman feet), that does not take away the objections against a ciborium-like reconstruction in which four marble columns (including the two of *giallo antico*) would have

---

Historians 59 (2000), 50–77, at pp. 63–4. For a different kind of analysis of the Arch of Constantine not based on the length of the column, see P. Cicerchia, 'L'Analisi metrologica', in *Adriano: Architettura e progetto* (Tivoli, 2000), 131–5; P. Cicerchia, 'Considerazioni metrologiche sull'arco', in M. L. Conforto (ed.), *Adriano e Costantino: Le due fasi dell'arco nella valle del Colosseo* (Milan, 2001), 61–77.

[36] *CBCR* V, 85; Blaauw, *CD* 0, 113. See Guidobaldi, 'Caratteri e contenuti'; de Blaauw, 'Le origine e gli inizi', 33.

been used as well.[37] So this possibility must be ruled out as well. Silver statues were placed on top of the *fastigium*: a seated Salvator and twelve apostles were placed towards the nave, and a Salvator enthroned and four angels were facing the apse of the basilica. Theoretically a reconstruction of the *fastigium* with eight columns instead of only the four bronze ones seems possible. One might imagine a counterpart resting on the four yellow marble shafts immediately behind the structure with the bronze columns. Such a structure would allow for a separate placement of the statues facing the nave, and the five other statues facing the apse. However, this would turn the *fastigium* into a double structure, which makes one wonder why just a single element was mentioned. The description in the Liber Pontificalis treats the *fastigium* as an object with a front and a reverse, which seems to rule out a reconstruction of it as a monument with four sides, stretching out in some depth. The previously mentioned problem with the mention of the lights in the Liber Pontificalis applies for this idea as well. Thus, to imagine the *fastigium* as a double structure, but with lamps hanging only from one of its elements, seems rather unlikely.[38]

The third possibility seems much more likely. Since the rows of nave columns originally ran along both sides of the space for the main altar, one could imagine that four *giallo antico* columns (or the two yellow ones and two other columns) functioned likewise as the continuation of the rows of the much smaller green columns between the inner and the outer aisles. Between the piers that probably terminated the arcades of green columns on the west side and the west wall enough space was available to position two columns on both the northern and the southern side (Fig. 9.7). Of course, such a construction would have resulted in a different architecture, because

---

[37] Blaauw, CD, 117–27; S. de Blaauw, 'Das *Fastigium* der Lateranbasilika: Schöpferische Innovation, Unikat oder Paradigma?' in B. Brenk (ed.), *Innovation in der Spätantike (Kolloquium Basel 6.-7. Mai 1994)* (Wiesbaden, 1996), 53–65; S. de Blaauw, 'Imperial connotations in Roman church interiors: The significance and effect of the Lateran *fastigium*', in R. J. Brandt and O. Steen (eds.), *Imperial Art as Christian Art–Christian Art as Imperial Art: Expression and Meaning in Art and Architecture from Constantine to Justinian (International Conference Rome 1999)* (Acta ad archaeologiam et artium historiam pertinentia 15) (Rome, 2001), 137–46; H. Geertman, 'Nota sul *Liber Pontificalis* come fonte archeologica', in H. Geertman, *Hic fecit basilicam: Studi sul* Liber Pontificalis *e gli edifice ecclesiastici di Roma da Silvestro a Silverio* (Leuven, 2004) (article first published in 1989), 78–82, with the relevant text from the Liber Pontificalis; H. Geertman, 'Il *fastigium* Lateranense e l'arredo presbiteriale: una lunga storia', in H. Geertman (ed.), *Atti del Colloquio Internazionale Il Liber Pontificalis e la storia materiale. Roma, 21-22 febbraio 2002* (Mededelingen van het Nederlands Instituut te Rome, Antiquity (2001–2002), 60–61) (Assen, 2003), 29–44, repr. in Geertman, *Hic fecit basilicam*, 133–48.

[38] Well analysed by Geertman, 'Nota sul *Liber Pontificalis*, 78–82, and Blaauw, CD I, 119–21.

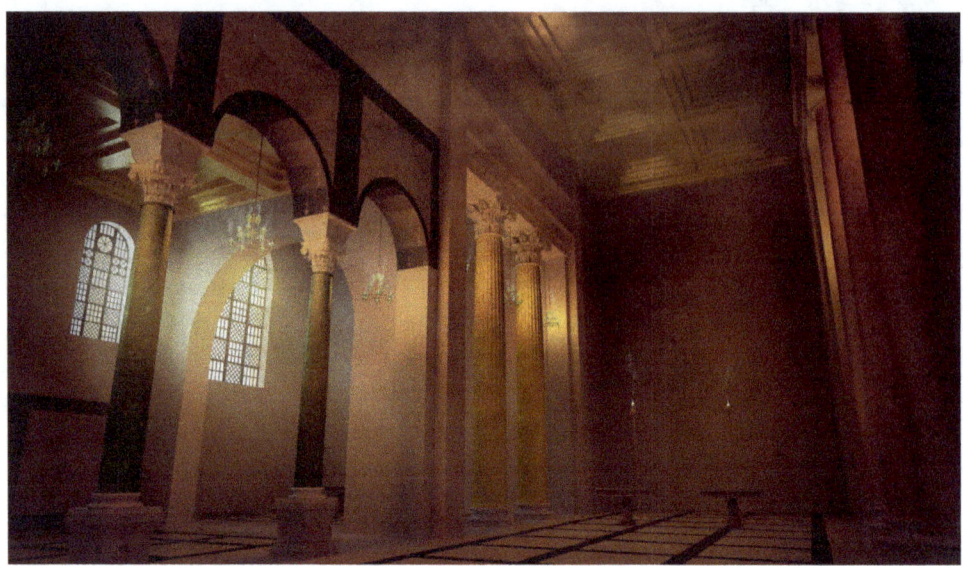

**Fig. 9.7** Westernmost end of aisles on the south side, with colonnade as continuation of row of green marble columns between inner and outer aisles (Reconstruction by Lex Bosman; 3D model and image by Iwan Peverett).

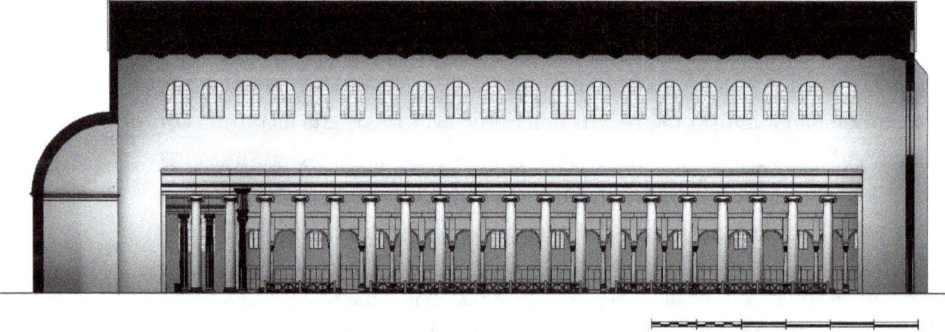

**Fig. 9.8** San Giovanni in Laterano, longitudinal section (Reconstruction by Lex Bosman, Paolo Liverani and Iwan Peverett; 3D model and image by Iwan Peverett).

the continuation of the wall that was supported by the small green columns would have been extended further to the west. Although in a way the arcades with green marble columns would be continued, the difference in height of the column shafts is such that this implies a very different way of shaping and experiencing space (Fig. 9.8). With twice the length of the *verde antico* columns, the 24-foot *giallo antico* shafts would still fit well in the wall if it was stretched to end at the west wall of the basilica. An architrave supported

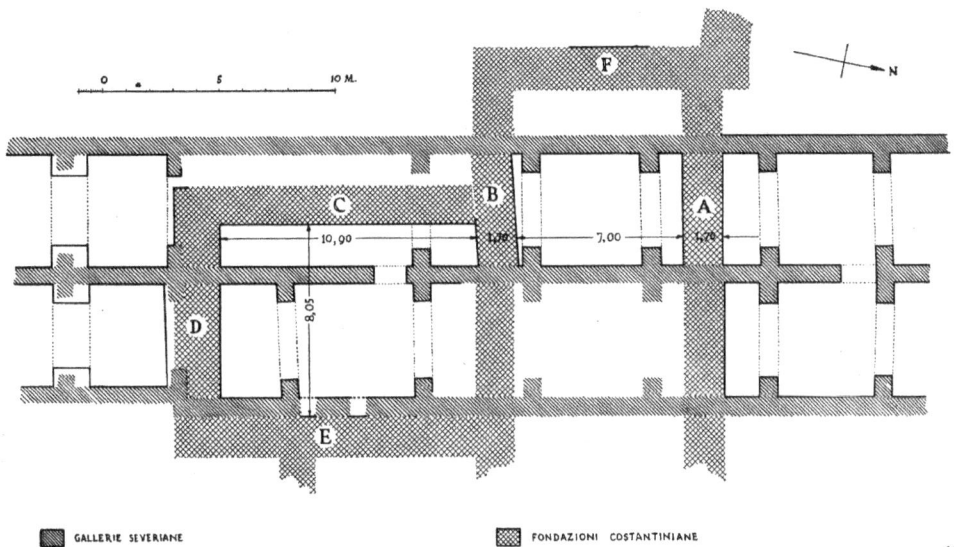

**Fig. 9.9** Plan of foundations in southwestern part, with indication of wall B (Drawing by Spencer Corbett, used in Josi et al., 'Note Lateranensi' and in *CBCR V*).

by the marble columns is more likely than arches. This reconstruction is based on the archaeological evidence of the continuation of the foundation of the arcades between the aisles, a wall mentioned by Krautheimer as wall B and appearing on ground plans (Figs 9.9, 9.10). This foundation wall B has hitherto been neglected in the literature. Only Claussen has mentioned the possibility of a structure on top of foundation wall B as well, correctly pointing out the strange L-shaped spaces at the western end of the aisles in the reconstruction of the ground plan which has become widely accepted.[39] In his first reconstructions of San Giovanni, Krautheimer proposed as one of the possibilities that wall B might have carried a colonnade parallel to that of the nave; the differences in the structure of this wall and the foundation wall A of the southern nave colonnade could be explained by the different weights carried by the two walls.[40] Confronted with the lack of archaeological research in the north transept, the GPR research in that area undertaken by Salvatore Piro was important. From a depth of about 2.5 to

---

[39] Josi, Krautheimer and Corbett, 'Note Lateranensi' (1958), 63–6; *CBCR* V, 29–32, esp. figs. 15, 21, 22; Claussen, *Die Kirchen der Stadt Rom*, 26 and 166 with n. 682. Claussen and I came to this hypothesis independently of each other; Claussen did not make a reconstruction of his hypothesis and did not include the yellow marble column shafts.

[40] Josi, Krautheimer and Corbett, 'Note Lateranensi' (1957), 91–2; Josi, Krautheimer and Corbett, 'Note Lateranensi' (1958), 64–6.

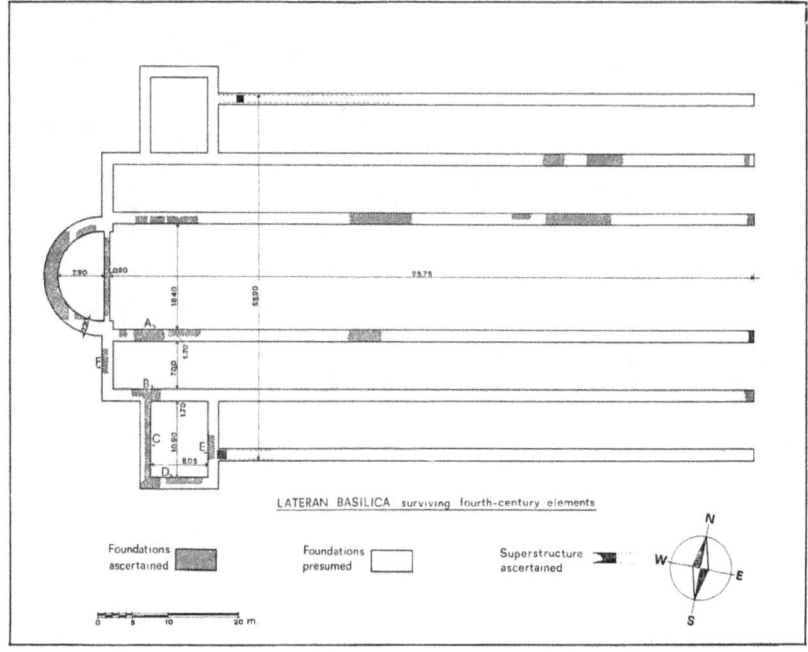

Fig. 9.10 Plan of basilica with foundations and rising walls preserved (Drawing by Spencer Corbett and L. Micchini, in *CBCR V*).

about 6 m a structure could be identified which seems to be the northern counterpart of the foundation wall B (Fig. 9.11).[41]

The consequences of a medieval date for the transept in this reconstruction option should be considered. Claussen has elaborated the arguments for a thirteenth-century date for the transept, which had been put forward earlier by Malmstrom and Krautheimer. The transept was constructed during the pontificate of Pope Nicholas IV (1288–92); moreover, Nicholas IV is generally held to be responsible for the rebuilding of both the apse and the surrounding ambulatory.[42] It is not at all unlikely, however, that an earlier transept-like structure had been realised.[43] A consequence of a reconstruction of the yellow columns (or two yellow and two other columns) as the prolongation of the

---

[41] Salvatore Piro conducted his research in the north transept on 26 January 2016. See his contribution in Chapter 4 of this volume.

[42] Malmstrom, 'The building of the nave piers', 162; *CBCR* V, 91; Blaauw *CD* I, 230–3; Claussen, *Die Kirchen der Stadt Rom*, 143–55.

[43] See Claussen, *Die Kirchen der Stadt Rom*, 140, 144, 166–7; P. C. Claussen, 'Nikolaus IV: Als Erneuerer von S. Giovanni in Laterano und S. Maria Maggiore in Rom', in M. Verhoeven, L. Bosman and H. van Asperen (eds.), *Monuments and Memory: Christian Cult Buildings and Constructions of the Past. Essays in Honour of Sible de Blaauw* (Architectural Crossroads. Studies in the History of Architecture 3) (Turnhout, 2016), 53–67, at pp. 57–9.

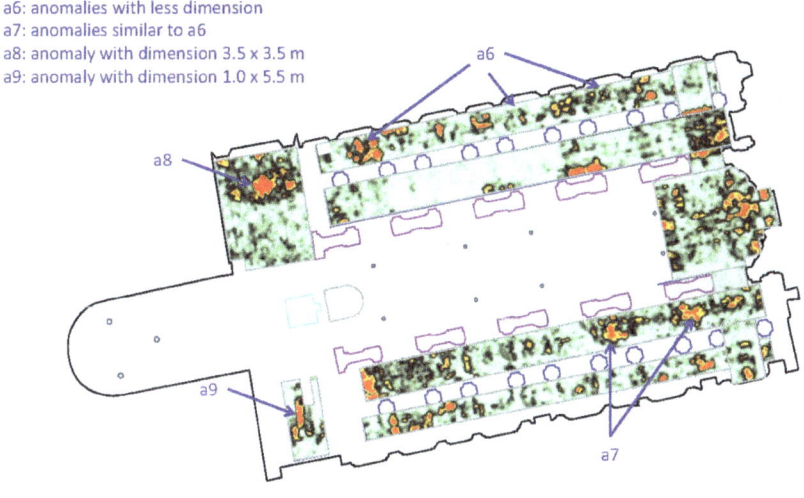

Fig. 9.11 Image of GPR survey by Salvatore Piro, depth 5–6 m. Note anomaly a8 (Image: Lateran Project, S. Piro).

rows of green columns between the side-aisles would be that at least a hundred years before the building campaign of Pope Nicholas IV began, or even much earlier, serious changes had been undertaken in the area of the later medieval transept. Since the *giallo antico* column shafts were incorporated in the portico at the east entrance in the period 1180–1200, such a renovation or partial rebuilding of the spaces directly to the north and to the south of the main altar area in the first half of the twelfth century is very likely. These changes would have been of such consequence that the architecture of this part of the basilica was not just modified but radically changed. Sible de Blaauw argued that the western part of San Giovanni was thoroughly altered in the first half of the twelfth century: on the south side of the southwestern annex of the basilica a portico was constructed as part of the renewal of the convent buildings, and the presbytery may have been arranged with a few steps raised from the original floor level in such a way that the annexes were incorporated in a narrow transept-like space. These building activities may very well be dated to the time of Pope Anacletus II, around 1135.[44]

---

[44] S. de Blaauw, 'A mediaeval portico at San Giovanni in Laterano: The basilica and its ancient conventual building', *PBSR* 58 (1990), 299–313; Blaauw, *CD* 0, 221–33, 265; Claussen, *Die*

In this reconstruction of a partial rebuilding of the west wall that ended the inner aisles, the interior space must have been altered as well. For the removal of the four columns of *giallo antico* (or a combination of two yellow with two other columns) opened this area on either side of the main altar, and it is equally feasible that during this campaign of restructuring the western parts of the Lateran basilica two or even three pairs of columns of red granite were removed from the nave, as was briefly suggested earlier. The original presbytery, which was clearly defined in the fourth century by the *fastigium* to the east, by the apse to the west and by the colonnades towards both the north and south sides may as a result of this have been opened up and for the first time have been conceived as one large space, as a narrow kind of transept. If my reconstruction of the course of things holds water, two of the alleged four yellow columns may have been damaged beyond repair. That would leave two of these marble columns available for later use, and between about 1135 and 1180 they must have been kept in reserve for later reuse. Considering all this it seems more likely that around 1135 not only were the four yellow marble columns taken away from their original position, but two pairs of red granite columns as well, as a result of which the roof of the nave and side-aisles must have been rebuilt in a different form as well. Although rather small with its width of some 9 m on its northern and southern parts, a first continuous space was created to substitute the fourth-century structure.

My reconstruction of the yellow marble columns as supports of the continuation of the colonnade between the inner and outer side aisles changes our understanding of the fourth-century church of the bishop of Rome in several ways (Fig. 9.12). Where the main altar area was a clearly defined space, in previous reconstructions the areas immediately to the west of the four aisles appears to have been much less well defined. Both inner aisles would house several altars, but the spaces on the west side of both outer aisles appeared in the reconstructions of the ground plan almost like left-over areas. With the arcades of two (yellow) marble columns each, which divided these areas on either side of the main altar in two much more clearly delimited spaces, the ground plan of the western part of the Lateran basilica may be better understood (Fig. 9.13). The areas for the altars are

*Kirchen der Stadt Rom*, 140–3, 155, 255, 313. De Blaauw also argued that the medieval transept should be dated to the first half of the twelfth century, as opposed to the papacy of Nicholas IV, but he later withdrew this hypothesis: see S. de Blaauw, 'Reception and renovation of early Christian churches in Rome, c. 1050–1300', in C. Bolgia, R. McKitterick and J. Osborne (eds.), *Rome across Time and Space: Cultural Transmission and the Exchange of Ideas c. 500–1400* (Cambridge, 2011), 151–66, at pp. 161–2.

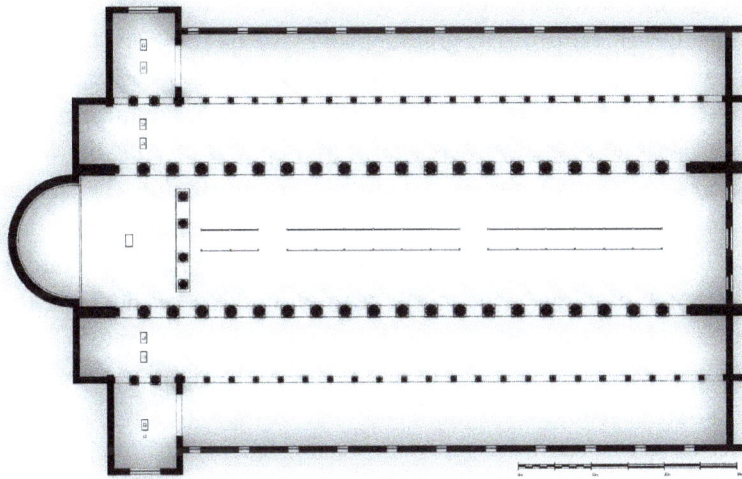

**Fig. 9.12** Ground plan of fourth-century basilica (Reconstruction by Lex Bosman, Paolo Liverani and Iwan Peverett).

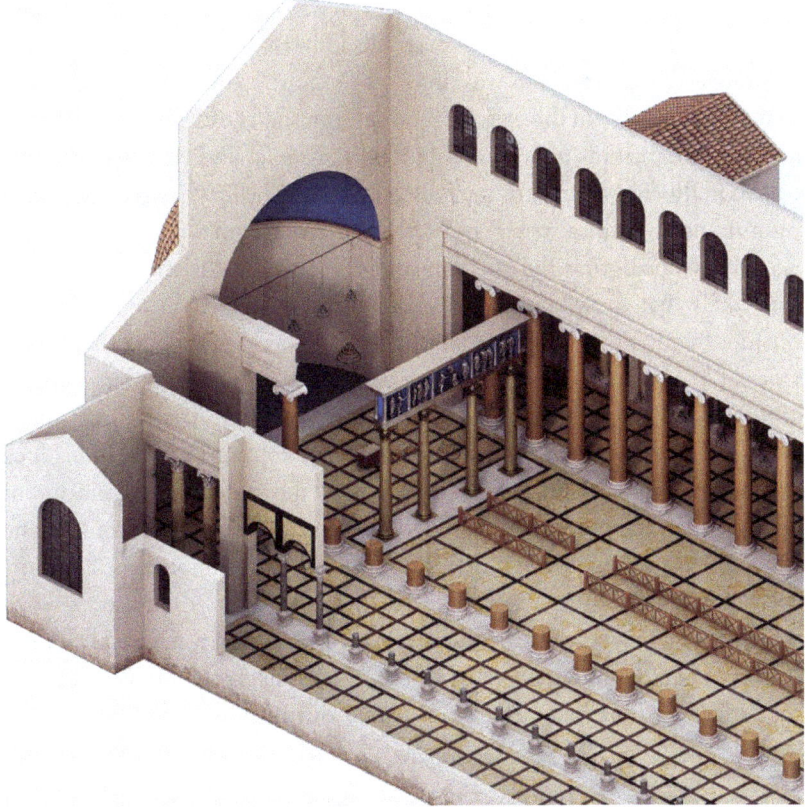

**Fig. 9.13** Open axonometric view of southwestern part of the basilica (Reconstruction by Lex Bosman; 3D model and image by Iwan Peverett).

well organised and the spaces that are the continuation of the outer aisles are equally well defined. The ground plan of the Basilica Salvatoris is now much more in accordance with what we know of other basilicas, since it underscores in a very clear way the really exceptional ground plan of the slightly later Saint Peter's, where a large transept was inserted between the large area of the nave and aisles and the apse. Apparently, the particular function of that part of the basilica – to not only shelter but to monumentalise the sepulchre of Saint Peter – sets this structure clearly apart from all other church basilicas of the fourth century. In other basilicas – whether Christian or non-Christian – the aisles terminate in a wall or a colonnade, which coincides with the situation in the Basilica Salvatoris, where all four aisles are stretched from the east wall to the west wall. The seven *altaria* where the Christians from the seven regions could leave their offerings were placed in the western part of the inner aisles, or perhaps they were spatially more equally divided over the western parts of the outer and inner aisles.[45] In my reconstruction of the ground plan it does not seem very likely that the spaces stretching out to the north and south beyond the outer aisle walls were closed off in an architectural way (with a wall or an arcade), since no piece of foundation has been found in that area on the south side (no archaeological research was done on the north side of the transept).

As for the matter of the origin of the column shafts, it seems likely that in the Basilica Constantiniana a combination of *spolia* and new material was applied in the first quarter of the fourth century. The forty-two *verde antico* column shafts feature a widely used standard length of 12 Roman feet (3.57 m). Considering the number and the unity of the material, it may seem likely that these shafts were taken from stockpiles; I am inclined to consider them as material from an earlier high-level building, perhaps even imperial.[46] Although the *giallo antico* columns possess a shaft length of 24 Roman feet (7.14 m), which is another often-used standard dimension, it remains difficult to decide whether or not these columns were *spolia*. Since no other examples of such shafts with exactly the same dimensions and of the same material are known besides the eight in the Arch of Constantine and the two (possibly four) in San Giovanni in Laterano, these columns may not originate from a stockpile but from the demolished Castra Nova Equitum Singularium. In the foundation of the northern nave wall several fragments of older material were reused; it seems likely that they were taken from material that had become available during the demolition of the

---

[45] See Blaauw, *CD* I, 143–6.

[46] Thanks to Matthias Bruno for helpful discussions and comments about the origins and dates of the *verde antico* as well as the *giallo antico* column shafts.

*castra*. A small fragment of a fluted column may be of particular interest here. The fragment indicates a fluted white marble column shaft, with flutings of around 0.08 m wide and with dents of around 0.025 m. Since the fluting is not filled, it is a fragment of the higher part of the shaft. However small the fragment may be, it may without much trouble be reconstructed as part of a column shaft with a standard length of 24 Roman feet (7.14 m) and a diameter of 3 Roman feet (0.89 m).[47] Hypothetical as it may be, this could be an interesting and welcome indication of the reuse of good marble columns from the *castra*. The yellow marble columns may have been considered more precious and therefore were chosen to be reused in the Basilica Constantiniana and in the Arch of Constantine. Other column shafts and trabeations were probably treated less carefully during the demolition of the *castra*; at least part of such architectural elements ended up as construction material in the foundation walls. As to the thirty-eight columns of *granito rosso* with shafts of 32 feet it is interesting to note that this is not a standard length. This may indicate that these shafts were originally ordered for a specific building. After the demolition of such a building the shafts were stored to be used later, or perhaps the shafts were delivered but the intended building was never constructed.[48] Indicative of the appreciation of the material is the fact that new column shafts and *spolia* were used together. It is not important whether the shafts were new or had been used before, but the richness of the material expressed by the colours was a decisive element.[49]

Also, the use of the *giallo antico* marble adds to the colourful and rich interior decoration of the Basilica Constantiniana, in which the main architectural elements of the columns played a very prominent part. To the red of the nave colonnades and the sparkling green of the columns in the side-aisles the bright yellow was added as yet another element, enhancing the importance of the area where the altars were located. This use of coloured marbles is completely in agreement with present-day understanding of the use of coloured materials in Late Antique and early Christian architecture. As part of this colourful interior decoration the gilded ceiling

---

[47] Measured 30 November 2004. Width of the fluting plus one dent is 10.5 cm, which gives a circumference of 24 x 10.5 = 2.52 m (8.46 Roman feet). A circumference of 8.46 feet gives a diameter of 2.7 feet (= 0.8 m). Since the fragment is from the higher part of the shaft, the lower diameter was slightly larger. Therefore, a diameter of 3 feet (0.89 m) is most likely, as is the matching length of 24 feet.

[48] Bosman, *The Power of Tradition*, 49–50.

[49] Bosman, 'Spolia in the fourth-century basilica', 72–80.

of the area with the main altar should be mentioned as well.[50] Together with the red granite column shafts flanking the area of the main altar, various other elements thus jointly underlined the importance of the westernmost area of the basilica: the bronze columns bearing the *fastigium* on the east side, the (four) bright yellow columns marking the transition from the aisles to the area with the main altar and the *altaria* for offerings, and the gilded ceiling above. As the outcome of deliberate choices, the eighty-four red, yellow and green columns in the Basilica Constantiniana contributed to display the high level of the commission to construct a large church for the bishop and the Christian community of Rome, under active support of the emperor Constantine. The same kind of richness in architectural elements would some eight or ten years later be chosen to adorn the basilica of Saint Peter's on the Vatican hill.[51]

---

[50] Bosman, *The Power of Tradition*, 52–6, 139–42; Geertman, 'Nota sul *Liber Pontificalis*, 80–2; P. Liverani, '"Camerae" e coperture delle basiliche paleocristiane', *Mededelingen van het Nederlands Instituut te Rome* 60–61 (2001–2), 13–27, at pp. 16–17.

[51] Bosman, *The Power of Tradition*, 19–46. See also D. Kinney, 'Bearers of meaning', *Jahrbuch für Antike und Christentum* 50 (2007), 139–53, at pp. 144–45, 151–3.

# 10 | The Constantinian Basilica in the Early Medieval *Liber Pontificalis*

ROSAMOND MCKITTERICK

The remarkable text known as the *Liber Pontificalis* is a serial biography of the popes from Saint Peter, the first bishop of Rome, to the end of the ninth century. It offers very particular representations of both the popes and the transformation of the city of Rome, as well as very far from disinterested narrative strategies in its deployment of information.[1] The *Liber Pontificalis* consequently played a major role in reorienting perceptions of Rome and the Roman past in the early Middle Ages. It is because of the influence subsequently exerted and enjoyed by the *Liber Pontificalis* that its text and the messages it conveyed are so important; it shaped historical understanding and knowledge in ways that still need to be fully explored. Saint Peter's basilica, and its various functions as one key focus of the stational liturgy, venue for councils, pilgrimage site, art treasure, papal necropolis and holy place, are especially prominent in the text, not least in enhancing and promoting papal authority.[2] Further, the narrative strategies deployed by the authors of the *Liber Pontificalis* in relation to Saint Paul and the imperial basilica of San Paolo fuori le Mura contrive to highlight the dominance of Saint Peter.[3] By contrast, the text of the *Liber Pontificalis* at first sight says disappointingly little about the Constantinian basilica, now known as Saint John Lateran. Nevertheless, what the *Liber Pontificalis* does say is instructive in relation to the text's production history as well as to its dominant themes. In this chapter, therefore, I shall consider the peculiarities of the basilica's representation in the

---

[1] T. F. X. Noble, 'A new look at the Liber *Pontificalis*', *Archivium Historiae Pontificiae* 23 (1985), 347–58; D. Mauskopf Deliyannis, 'The Roman *Liber Pontificalis*, papal primacy and the Acacian Schism', *Viator* 45 (2014), 1–16; R. McKitterick, 'La place du *Liber Pontificalis* dans les genres historiographiques du haut moyen âge', in F. Bougard and M. Sot (eds.), *Liber, gesta, histoire: Écrire l'histoire des évêques et des papes de l'antiquité au XXe siècle* (Turnhout, 2009), 23–36. See also R. McKitterick, *Rome and the Invention of the Papacy: The Liber Pontificalis* (Cambridge, 2020).

[2] R. McKitterick, 'The representation of Old Saint Peter's basilica in the *Liber Pontificalis*', in R. McKitterick, J. Osborne, C. M. Richardson and J. Story (eds.), *Old Saint Peter's, Rome* (British School at Rome Monograph Series) (Cambridge, 2013), 95–118.

[3] R. McKitterick, 'Narrative strategies in the *Liber Pontificalis*: The case of St Paul, *doctor mundi, doctor gentium*, and San Paolo fuori le Mura', *Rivista di Storia del Cristianesimo* 10 (2013), 115–30.

*Liber Pontificalis* and their possible implications in relation to the representation of Rome as a Christian city, and of the popes as its rulers. I shall not be concerned with the details of the development of the Lateran palace recorded in the *Liber Pontificalis*, for these have already been the subject of Antonella Ballardini's comprehensive discussion in the Settimane di Spoleto volume for 2015.[4]

Initially compiled during the Gothic wars in the middle of the sixth century in deliberate emulation of the style of Roman imperial biography, and as a dramatic Christianisation of Roman history,[5] the *Liber Pontificalis* was subsequently extended in the seventh, eighth and ninth centuries.[6] In these sections there is again a strong political agenda designed to assert the popes' upholding of Christian orthodoxy and the particularities of the pope's role in Rome and the western church, as well as in relation to Byzantium.[7] Like the compiler of the first section of the *Liber Pontificalis*, the authors of the later extensions, whether Life by Life or in batches of Lives,[8] have been located within the papal administration.[9] Despite this plurality of authorship and the potential for many different perspectives, the *Liber Pontificalis* contrives to offer a notable 'thematic and narrative

---

[4] A. Ballardini, '"In antiquissimo ac venerabili Lateranensi palatio": La residenza dei pontefici secondo il *Liber Pontificalis*', in *Le corti nell'alto Medioevo* (Settimane di Studio del Centro italiano di studi sull'alto medioevo 62) (Spoleto, 2014), 889–928. See also F. A. Bauer, *Das Bild der Stadt Rom im Frühmittelalter: Papststiftungen im Spiegel des Liber Pontificalis von Gregor dem Dritten bis zu Leo dem Dritten* (Wiesbaden, 2004), 61–80.

[5] R. McKitterick, 'Roman texts and Roman history in the early Middle Ages', in C. Bolgia, R. McKitterick and J. Osborne (eds.), *Rome across Time and Space: Cultural Transmission and the Exchange of Ideas c. 400–1400* (Cambridge, 2011), 19–34; German version: R. McKitterick, 'Die Überlieferung eines bestimmten Bildes der Stadt Rom im frühen Mittelalter: der *Liber Pontificalis*', in H. Finger (ed.), *Gedenkschrift Josef Semmler* (Cologne, 2012), 33–46.

[6] The standard edition of the *Liber Pontificalis* is that of L. Duchesne, *Le Liber Pontificalis*, 2 vols. (Paris, 1886 and 1892) (hereafter *LP* I and *LP* II). See also T. Mommsen (ed.), *Liber Pontificalis* (MGH, Gesta Pontificum Romanorum 1, 1) (Berlin, 1898), the new edition of Lives 33–48 supplied by H. Geertman, 'Le biografie del *Liber Pontificalis* dal 311 al 535: Testo e commentario', in H. Geertman (ed.), *Atti del Colloquio Internazionale Il Liber Pontificalis e la storia materiale: Roma, 21-22 febbraio 2002* (Mededelingen van het Nederlands Instituut te Rome, Antiquity 60-1 (2001–2)) (Assen, 2003), 285–356, and an updated schematic version of Lives 1–48 in H. Geertman, 'La genesi del *Liber Pontificalis* romano: Un processo di organizzazione della memoria', in Bougard and Sot (eds.), *Liber, gesta, histoire*, 37–107. See also H. Geertman's fundamental studies: *More veterum: Il Liber Pontificalis e gli edifice ecclesiastici di Roma nella tarda antichita e nell'alto medioevo* (Archaeologia Traiectina 10) (Groningen, 1975), and the papers reprinted in *Hic fecit basilicam: Studi sul Liber Pontificalis e gli edifici ecclesiastici di Roma da Silvestro a Silverio* (Leuven, 2004).

[7] See R. McKitterick, 'The papacy and Byzantium in the seventh and early eighth-century sections of the *Liber Pontificalis*', *PBSR* 84 (2016), 241–73.

[8] C. Gantner, 'The Lombard recension of the *Liber Pontificalis*', *Rivista di Storia del cristianesimo* 10 (2013), 65–114.

[9] Geertman, 'La genesi del *Liber Pontificalis*'.

consistency'.[10] This is all the more striking when the peculiarities of the manuscript transmission of the *Liber Pontificalis* are taken into account. The text in various stages of completion and in a number of redactions, labelled 'A'–'E' by their editor Duchesne, survive, apart from three earlier Italian fragments from the sixth and seventh centuries, first of all in manuscripts from the late eighth and early ninth centuries, all but one of which were written north of the Alps in the Frankish kingdoms ruled by the Carolingians. Only from the eleventh century are there a number of Italian copies, mostly belonging to the 'E' family.[11]

These extant manuscripts appear to attest not only to the episodic production and continuation of the *Liber Pontificalis*, but also to its circulation in increasingly augmented form at different points in its history. These production episodes can be shown to correspond to particularly crucial moments in the history of the early medieval papacy.[12] The layout of the text, moreover, and what scribes chose to highlight, has the potential to illuminate attitudes to particular aspects of the text. The earliest portion of the text, compiled around 535, contains biographies of the first fifty-nine or sixty popes, from Peter to Agapitus (or possibly Silverius). Certainly, the reconstruction of the history of the bishops before the conversion of Constantine fulfils aspects of the letter, allegedly from Jerome to the Pope Damasus, concocted to form a preface to the text. It was designed to make it seem, however improbably, that Jerome was the author of the *Liber Pontificalis*.

This 'letter preface' states that Damasus had asked for an 'orderly account of the history enacted in [your] see from the reign of the Apostle Peter down to [his] own time, so that in humility I may learn which of the bishops of your see deserved the crown of martyrdom and which of them is reckoned to have transgressed against the canons of the apostles'.[13]

---

[10] R. McKitterick, 'Liturgy and history in the early Middle Ages', in M. Fassler, K. Bugyis and A. Kraebel (eds.), *Music, Liturgy, and the Shaping of History (800–1500)* (York, 2017), 23–40.

[11] *LP* I, clxiv–ccvi; useful summary in R. Davis (ed.), *The Lives of the Eighth-Century Popes* (Translated Texts for Historians 13) (Liverpool, 1992), xv–xviii.

[12] L. Duchesne, *Étude sur le* Liber Pontificalis (Paris, 1877); McKitterick, 'The papacy and Byzantium', 268–72. On the later sections, see F. Bougard, 'Composition, diffusion et réception des parties tardives du *Liber Pontificalis* romain (VIIIe–IXe siècles)', in Bougard and Sot (eds.), *Liber, gesta, histoire*, 127–52.

[13] *LP* I, p. 117: 'ut actus gestorum a beati Petri apostoli principatum usque ad vestra tempora, quae gesta sunt in sedem tuam, nobis per ordinem enarrare digneris; quatenus nostra humilitas sentire cognoscat, qui meruit de episcoporum supradictae sedis martyrio coronari, vel qui contra canones apostolorum excessisse cognoscatur', trans. in R. Davis, *The Book of Pontiffs (Liber Pontificalis): The Ancient Biographies of the First Ninety Roman Bishops to AD 715* (Liverpool Translated Texts for Historians 6), rev. 3rd edn (Liverpool, 2010), 1. All the English translations from the *Liber Pontificalis* quoted in this chapter are by Raymond Davis.

Consequently the text, as well as being a papal recasting of imperial serial biography, could be seen as a continuation of the Acts of the Apostles. At another level, all the Lives before the first reference to the 'Constantinian basilica' or Lateran, provide a summary portrait of a city where Christians lived while their religion was that of a minority sect, sometimes tolerated and sometimes persecuted. It is also of course heavily slanted not only to promote the status of the 'monarch bishop' among the many Christian groups in Rome,[14] but also to write the early Christian history of Rome as if it solely concerned the bishop.[15] Of the thirty-three popes before Sylvester, twenty-four were recorded in the *Liber Pontificalis* as martyrs: Saint Peter, Linus, Cletus, Clement, Evaristus, Alexander (along with priest Eventius and deacon Theodulus), Sixtus I, Telesphorus, Anicetus, Victor, Callistus, Pontian, Anteros, Fabian, Cornelius, Lucius, Stephen I, Sixtus II, Felix I, Eutychian, Gaius, Marcellinus, Marcellus and Xystus II. There is very little substance to any of these early Lives, though the overall effect is to emphasise the cult of Saint Peter and the apostolic succession of the bishops of Rome. The author padded out what was little more than a list of names, probably reconstructed from some martyr's passion narratives, possible *fasti* and the lists in the Calendar of 354. These were augmented, it is supposed, by letter registers and accounts in the papal offices as well as Jerome's Latin version and extension of Eusebius's *Chronicon*.[16] The author of the *Liber Pontificalis* provided an invented chronology both for liturgical innovations from Peter onwards[17] and for the progressive steps taken to organise the clergy within the city made by the succession of

---

[14] A. Brent, *Hippolytus and the Roman Church in the Third Century: Communities in Tension before the Emergence of a Monarch Bishop* (Supplements to *Vigiliae Christianae* 31) (Leiden, 1995). See also J. R. Curran, *Pagan City and Christian Capital: Rome in the Fourth Century* (Oxford, 2000); G. D. Dunn (ed.), *The Bishop of Rome in Late Antiquity* (Farnham, 2016); M. Vinzent, 'Rome', in M. M. Mitchell and F. M. Young (eds.), *Cambridge History of Christianity*, vol. I: *Origins to Constantine* (Cambridge, 2006), 397–414.

[15] I have discussed the representation of the early Christian community in the *Liber Pontificalis* more fully in R. McKitterick, 'The *Liber Pontificalis* and the transformation of Rome from pagan to Christian city in the early Middle Ages', in M. Kahlos, K. Ritari and J. Stenger (eds.), *Being Pagan, Being Christian in Late Antiquity and the Early Middle Ages* (London, forthcoming).

[16] Jerome's Latin translation and continuation of Eusebius's *Chronicon* as a resource for the authors of the *Liber Pontificalis* is considered in R. McKitterick, 'Transformations of the Roman past and Roman identity in the early Middle Ages', in C. Gantner, R. McKitterick and S. Meeder (eds.), *The Resources of the Past in Early Medieval Europe* (Cambridge, 2015), 225–44.

[17] On early Roman liturgy, see J. Day and M. Vinzent (eds.), *Early Roman Liturgy to 600* (Studia Patristica 71) (Leuven, 2014), especially P. Bradshaw, 'What do we *really* know about the earliest Roman liturgy?', 7–20; O. Brandt, 'The archaeology of Roman ecclesiastical architecture and the study of early Christian liturgy', 21–52; M. Humphries, 'Liturgy and laity in Late Antique Rome: Problems, sources and social dynamics', 171–86.

bishops, inserted at various points into the third-century biographies. As we shall see, an imaginative history of the earliest Christian churches in Rome was a culmination of this reconstruction. Each biography also adds formulaic notes on the ordinations of deacons, priests and bishops, and the popes' places of burial.

Solid information about the individual popes is meagre, though the burial places may indicate some social standing and wealth or lack thereof.[18] A significant claim is made for Anacletus, who allegedly constructed and arranged the memorial of Saint Peter, as it was by Saint Peter he had been made a priest, and other burial places where bishops could be laid; there he too was buried close to Saint Peter's body.[19]

Zephyrinus (198–217) was said to have had his own cemetery in which he was buried, close to the cemetery of Callixtus. Pope Callixtus (217–22), however, established a cemetery on the Via Appia, and some of his predecessors and successors were buried there, even though he himself was buried in the cemetery of Calepodius.[20] Other cemeteries mentioned, such as that of Praetextatus in which Urban I was buried, indicate that these bishops had substantial landowners among their congregations.[21] A note of personal if not institutional wealth appears in the Life of Urban I (222–30), who is said to have provided twenty-five silver patens for the ministry.[22] That Fabian is said to have ordered many works in the cemeteries may indicate a papal or even institutional means to pay for labour. Although the father of the bishop is always named, except for Dionysius, whose ancestry the authors 'were unable to trace' (*cuius generationum non potuimus repperire*), only in the case of Gaius is there an imperial connection: he was born in Dalmatia of the family of Diocletian. Gaius nevertheless was martyred for his faith.[23]

---

[18] S. de Blaauw, 'Die Gräber der frühen Päpste', in B. Schneidmüller, S. Weinfurter, M. Mattheus and A. Wieczorek (eds.), *Die Päpste: Amt und Herrschaft in Antike, Mittelalter und Renaissance* (Regensburg, 2016), 77–99; J.-C. Picard, 'Étude sur l'emplacement des tombes des papes du IIIe au Xe siècle', *Mélanges d'archéologie et d'histoire* 81 (1960), 725–82; M. Borgolte, *Petrusnachfolge und Kaiserimitation: Die Grablegen der Päpste, ihre Genese und Traditionsbildung* (Göttingen, 1989).

[19] *LP* I, Life 5, 125: 'Hic memoriam beati Petri construxit et conposuit, dum presbyter factus fuisset a beato Petro, seu alia loca ubi episcopi reconderentur sepulturae, ubi tamen et ipse sepultus est, iuxta corpus beati Petri', trans. in Davis, *The Book of Pontiffs*, 3.

[20] *LP* I, Lives 16 and 17, 139 and 141.

[21] *LP* I, Life 18, 143; See R. Behrwald, 'Senatoren als Stifter der Kirche im Spätantiken Rom', in M. Verhoeven, L. Bosman and H. van Asperen (eds.), *Monuments and Memory: Christian Cult Buildings and Constructions of the Past: Essays in Honour of Sible de Blaauw* (Architectural Crossroads. Studies in the History of Architecture 3) (Turnhout, 2016), 162–76.

[22] *LP* I, Life 18, 143.   [23] *LP* I, Lives 26 and 29, 157 and 164.

Even supposing these details to be reliable, therefore, there is little to suggest that the bishops of Rome were of high social rank or wealth, or that the Christian community in Rome was large, prosperous or well organised. There are few indications of actual buildings in the Lives up to the time of Constantine's conversion, apart from the handful of references to cemeteries, and the claims that Pope Callixtus (217–22) built 'the basilica across the Tiber' and that Felix I (268–73) built a basilica on the Via Aurelia, though the latter is a piece of information also allocated, rather more plausibly, to Felix II (355–65).[24]

This lack of status, relative poverty, meagreness of information, and the bishops' exposure to sheer violence all apparently changed with the Life of Pope Sylvester (314–35) and his alleged baptism of the emperor Constantine. Suddenly the church in Rome has buildings, estates and treasure, and a new topography of the city is described. It is as a pivot of this dramatic transformation that the Lateran needs to be seen, for it becomes a crucial part of the new material establishment of the Christian Church in Rome claimed by the *Liber Pontificalis*. In reality there were no sudden and dramatic changes or construction of new buildings in the second decade of the fourth century, nor did Roman Christians so rapidly move from smaller domestic settings for private worship to large monumental buildings.[25] Most of the fourth- and fifth-century basilicas in Rome are post-Constantinian, and only two of the new religious sites created, namely, the Lateran basilica and baptistery complex and the church of Santa Croce in the Sessorian palace, were constructed within the walls of the city.[26] The sixth-century compiler may have found it quite difficult to project back to a period two centuries earlier where the topography and organisation with which they had become familiar simply did not exist. It is in keeping with the text as a whole, however, that this compression of time and credit is deliberate. The apparent wish to fit the chronology of construction into Sylvester's pontificate in relation to the reign and patronage of Constantine creates a pointed picture not only of

---

[24] *LP* I, Life 17, 141: 'Hic fecit basilicam trans Tiberim', trans in Davis, *The Book of Pontiffs*, 7; *LP* I, Lives 27 and 38, 158 and 211. The attribution to Pius I of the construction of Santa Pudenziania in the Life of Pius I is a later addition, only in the eleventh-century manuscript Biblioteca Apostolica Vaticana, Vat. lat. 3764: *LP* I, Life 11, 132 and Duchesne's n. 8, p. 133.

[25] K. Bowes, *Private Worship, Public Values and Religious Change in Late Antiquity* (Cambridge, 2008); A. Cerruto, 'Oratori ed edifici di culto minori di Roma tra il IV secolo ed primi decenni del V', in F. Guidobaldi and A. Guiglia Guidobaldi (eds.), *Ecclesiae Urbis: Atti del congresso internazionale di studi sulle chiese di Roma IV–X secolo 1* (Vatican City, 2002), 397–418.

[26] Brandt, 'The archaeology of Roman ecclesial architecture'; H. Brandenburg, *Die frühchristlichen Kirchen in Rom vom 4. bis zum 7. Jahrhundert: Der Beginn der abendländischen Kirchenbaukunst* (Regensburg, 2004); *CBCR*, esp. vol. V; Davis, *The Book of Pontiffs*, xxviii–xli.

the time and scale of this construction work, but also of papal prominence in attracting such massive and unprecedented imperial patronage. The temptation to regard these infuriatingly unspecific details as evidence of Constantine's own intentions and accomplishments in relation to his promotion of Christianity in the Roman world should in any case be resisted.[27] Their purpose was different.

In Life 34 Pope Sylvester himself, in great contrast to all his predecessors, is credited with building a church, on the estate of one of his priests, named Equitius, which Constantine then endowed with rich gifts, including revenue-yielding estates, mostly in the Sabine territory. Life 34 also gives Sylvester the credit for issuing a decree about the whole church (*de omni ecclesia*) and convening the Synod of Nicaea. The statement of orthodoxy at Nicaea, in contrast to the role of Constantine recounted in Rufinus' Latin translation and continuation of the *Ecclesiastical History* of Eusebius, thus becomes a papal rather than an imperial achievement. In the *Liber Pontificalis* Constantine is then presented as advising Sylvester to assemble a synod in Rome. It is at this synod that many very particular rules about clerical behaviour, dress and public conduct in relation to the law were agreed. In stark contrast to the portraits of his predecessors, the *Liber Pontificalis* emphasises how Pope Sylvester exerted authority in many different spheres. The text continues with a wealth of information about the new churches of Rome. This is prefaced with the statement that 'in Sylvester's time the emperor Constantine built these churches and adorned them'.[28] The earliest manuscripts, moreover – that is, those written in Francia in the late eighth and ninth centuries as well as the north Italian manuscript, Lucca, Biblioteca capitolare Feliniana MS 490 – clearly present the building of churches in the same paragraph as the account of papal ecclesiastical organisation and attention to orthodoxy. The churches are not set out in orderly lists as in Duchesne's edition.

It is thus in this context of consolidation of the Christian Church, all claimed as taking place in the time of Pope Sylvester, that the imperial building, lavish adornment and generous endowment with estates and revenues of both the Constantinian basilica and the baptistery are recorded. There is no reference to any place or reason for the building of the Constantinian basilica. All the others in the long list of constructions, however – that is, Saint Peter's, San Paulo fuori le Mura, Sant'Agnese,

---

[27] See, for example, R. Krautheimer, *Rome: Profile of a City, 312–1308* (Princeton, 1980) and C. Odahl, 'The Christian basilicas of Constantinian Rome', *The Ancient World* 1 (1995), 3–28.

[28] *LP* I, Life 34, 170–87, at p. 172 (c. 9): 'Huius temporibus fecit Constantinus aug. basilicas istas quas et ornavit', trans. in Davis, *The Book of Pontiffs*, 15.

Santi Petri et Marcellini, Santa Croce in Gerusalemme – are all mentioned as churches built in places that are already holy because of proximity to a particular martyr's shrine, burial or execution site, such as Saint Peter, Saint Paul, or Saints Peter and Marcellinus. Whatever the truth or not of the claims that these were imperial foundations in the time of Constantine or later, some of them are also stated to have had a special link with the emperor's family. Thus, the Lateran baptistery was referred to as the site where Constantine had been baptised.[29]

The *Liber Pontificalis* offers possibly later landmarks in terms of buildings that may not have existed at the time of the construction of the mausolea in stating that the mausoleum of Constantine's mother Helena was close to Santi Petri e Marcellini, and the place where his sister and daughter were baptised is cited for Sant' Agnese. The basilica in the Sessorian palace is made instantly into a holy place by the gift of 'some of the wood of our Lord Jesus Christ's Holy Cross'.[30] For most of the churches established outside Rome at Ostia, Albano, and Capua, the dedication makes reference to the saints Peter, Paul, John the Baptist or all the Apostles. The *Liber Pontificalis* chose not to mention that the *Domus Faustae* on the Lateran site had been a base for Sylvester's predecessor Miltiades to preside over a synod in 313 to discuss the Donatists, as recorded by Optatus of Milevi around 384. Whether this is indeed to be identified as the core of the later Lateran basilica is in any case uncertain.[31]

For the churches of Saint Peter and Saint Paul the revenues include renders in kind (an instance of the classic way to lessen the impact of inflation). Yet the relative scale of the endowment credited to the emperor Constantine is also indicative of points that the authors of the *Liber*

---

[29] *LP* I, Life 34, 170–87, at p. 174 (c. 13): 'Fontem sanctum, ubi baptizatus est Augustus Constantinus'.

[30] *LP* I, Life 34, 179 (c. 22): 'ubi etiam de ligno sanctae crucis domini nostri Iesu Christi', trans. in Davis, *The Book of Pontiffs*, 20. On the Sessorian palace see the brief comments and further references in D. Oosten, 'The mausoleum of Helena and the adjoining basilica *Ad duos lauros*: Construction, evolution and reception', in Verhoeven et al. (eds.), *Monuments and Memory*, 137–43.

[31] See Liverani, Chapter 2 in this volume. Duchesne (*LP* I, 190 n. 28) rehearses the fourth-century witnesses to the existence of a church by 366 and that Damasus was ordained there. See also E. T. Nash, '*Convenerunt in domum Faustae in Laterano*: Optati Milevitani 1.23', *Römische Quartalschrift für Altertumskunde und für Kirchengeschichte* 71 (1976), 1–21; W. Pohlkamp, '*Privilegium ecclesiae romanae pontifici contulit*: Zur Vorgeschichte der Konstantinischen Schenkung', in H. Fuhrmann (ed.), *Fälschungen im Mittelalter*, 5 vols. (Hanover, 1988), II, 413–90; W. Pohlkamp, 'Textfassungen, literarische Formen und geschichtliche Funktionen der römischen Silvester-Akten', *Francia* 19 (1992), 115–96; M. Edwards, *Constantine and Christendom. The Oration to the Saints. The Greek and Latin Accounts of the Discovery of the Cross. The Edict of Constantine to Pope Silvester* (Translated Texts for Historians 39) (Liverpool, 2003). See also below 219–20 on the 'Donation of Constantine'.

*Pontificalis* wanted to make. A crude comparison, in terms of gold, silver, brass, value of spices and revenues from estates, in which the weight in pounds of the gold, silver, and brass vessels and ornaments, together with the weight of spices and other products, are simply added up, is instructive.

The Lateran received 1,135 lbs of gold, 18,893 lbs of silver, 2,100 lbs of brass, 150 lbs of spices and 4,390 solidi in revenues, all from estates in Italy. The baptistery was separately endowed with 97 lbs of gold; 3838 lbs of silver, 200 lbs of balsam. To this should be added revenues from estates within Rome itself, in Italy, Sicily, Africa and Greece (Crete). These can be set out in a comparative table as follows:

|  | Gold | Silver | Brass | Revenues | Spices/oil |
| --- | --- | --- | --- | --- | --- |
| Lateran | 1,135 | 18,893 | 2,100 | 4,390 s. | 150 |
| Baptistery | 97 | 3,838 |  | 8,855 s. | 200 |
| TOTAL | 1,230 | 22,731 | 2,100 | 13,245 s. | 350 |
| Saint Peter's | 272 | 1,985 |  | 3,708 s. | 3,575 |
| San Paolo | 150 | ? | ? | 4,070 s. | 1,530 |

There is a striking difference in both commodities and revenues granted to these three foundations. Even taking into account that far less gold and silver but far more precious oils and spices, or specified renders in kind, are stipulated for Saint Peter's and San Paolo, it is clear that the *Liber Pontificalis* presented Constantine's gifts to the Lateran and baptistery as far more munificent than those to any of the other new foundations attributed to him. In the case of Saint Peter's and San Paolo, the text also records the sealing of the bodies of the apostles in copper or bronze and the enclosure and embellishment of the tombs. In the church in the Sessorian palace – that is, Santa Croce in Gerusalemme – there is also a note of the placing of the relic of the Holy Cross.[32]

It would be too easy to think that these differences are only invented figures out of a wish to assert status, though there may be an element of that as well. In any case, given the determined promotion of the cult of Saint Peter within the text, this is not a satisfactory explanation. Art and architectural historians have of course speculated furiously about the precise appearance and disposition of all the gifts, statues and ornaments mentioned, but the *Liber Pontificalis* author seems at this point simply to be

---

[32] See previous note. See also J.-W. Drijvers, 'Helena Augusta, Cross and Myth: Some new reflections', *Millennium* 8 (2011), 125–74; E. Ó Carragáin, 'Interactions between liturgy and politics in Old Saint Peter's, 670–741: John the Archcantor, Sergius I and Gregory III', in McKitterick et al. (eds.), *Old Saint Peter's, Rome*, 177–89.

offering an indication, with hindsight, of his understanding of the process by which Constantine gave the Christian community and the Church both financial security and the prestige of imperial patronage. The text stresses above all, therefore, the new material base provided for the Church in Rome. In addition to the great number of massive holy shrines he created in honour of Peter and Paul, the text stresses that it is the emperor who provided the bishop of Rome with a base, a church with rich ornaments and revenues, and a functional building to assist the process of conversion, namely the baptistery. The *Liber Pontificalis* does not spell all this out, save in one phrase in relation to the Constantinian basilica, where the text says that the revenues from the estates are to provide for 'the lights' (*quibus constituit in servitio luminarum*), that is, a specific provision relating to the conduct of the liturgy in the basilica.[33]

It would be reasonable to conclude that the *Liber Pontificalis* author wished to present the papal version of Constantine's support of the Church in the new world where Christianity was both a legal and imperially favoured religion. Here there was now an organised priesthood that needed to be maintained, not least to fulfil its proselytising mission. On this reading, the extra endowment could indeed reflect a recognition of the necessity in the Lateran's case for provision to be made for the upkeep of the bishop and his clergy, much as, within the Roman pagan religious context, temples and priests also had had to be maintained. The other church buildings, because they were essentially shrines, did not require such a large clerical staff. Yet what this endowment may primarily indicate is the wish to emphasise the substantial imperial contribution to the cost of the episcopal establishment and administration within Rome.[34]

These endowments have recently been subjected to a refreshingly sceptical analysis by Federico Montinaro. In addition to the other anachronisms in the *Liber Pontificalis* account that Ralf Behrwald has identified, Montinaro has argued that the list of the landed wealth of estates in Italy, Africa and Egypt, allegedly presented to this new ecclesiastical foundation by Constantine, contains a toponym, namely, the estate of Baldarus/Walzarus, which point to Africa under Vandal rule. This, as well as the formulation of the lists of gifts themselves in a manner inconsistent with Late Antique documentary practice, has led Montinaro to suggest that the donations reflect not what Constantine gave in the fourth century but rather a summary of the property of the Roman Church in the sixth and

---

[33] *LP* I, 173.
[34] Here I echo the reasonable conjecture of Davis, *The Book of Pontiffs*, xxx: 'in all likelihood we have here the imperial endowment of the bishopric itself'.

seventh centuries, 'only a part of which may have been acquired through imperial generosity'.³⁵ I should like to push Montinaro's conclusion two steps further. First, we should think of these lists of estates, revenues and renders in kind not just as sixth-century records but also as claims made by the papacy. These claims were both an essential part of the text's overall aim to promote papal status and authority and assert rights to the revenues and estates. Second, if the estates are more probably of the sixth century, then the same should surely be said of the descriptions of the fabric, decorations, lights and liturgical vessels in all the churches mentioned in Life 34, not least the Constantinian basilica itself.

A further, though less compelling, aspect of Montinaro's argument was to compare the lists in the late eighth-century redactions of the *Liber Pontificalis* with the Felician and Cononian epitomes that Duchesne long ago suggested were remnants of the first edition of the *Liber Pontificalis*. Whether they should really be so described cannot be discussed here,³⁶ but if they are not in fact preliminary versions of the *Liber Pontificalis*, this would weaken Montinaro's point. Certainly, both epitomes are markedly less interested in the endowments. The Felician epitome omits the bulk of them as well as the details of the donations. The Cononian epitome has more details, but the figures given for revenues and pounds of gold and silver comprising the church ornaments are very much lower than those in the later redaction. The supposed second edition as defined by Duchesne, and reproduced in most of the surviving manuscripts, offers far higher values and revenues. Montinaro interpreted this as a tendency deliberately to increase the quantity and value of Constantine's gifts to enhance the impression of imperial generosity.³⁷ Readers of the *Liber Pontificalis*, especially those of the eighth- and ninth-century manuscript copies, are thereby given a picture of impressive imperial support for the Church and

---

³⁵ F. Montinaro, 'Les fausses donations de Constantin dans le *Liber Pontificalis*', *Millennium* 12 (2015), 203–29.

³⁶ See Geertman, 'La genesi del *Liber Pontificalis*', 44–5; A. A. Verardi, 'La genesi del *Liber Pontificalis* alla luce delle vicende della città di Roma tra la fine del V e gli inizi del VI secolo: Una proposta', *Rivista di Storia del cristianesimo* 10 (2013), 7–28; A. A. Verardi, *La memoria legittimante: Il Liber Pontificalis e la chiesa di Roma del secolo VI* (Nuovi Studi Storici 99) (Rome, 2016). There are other problems, in addition to those discussed by Verardi, with the current definition of the 'first edition' and the Cononian and Felician recensions: see M. Simperl, 'Ein gallischer Liber Pontificalis: Bermerkungen zur text- und Überlieferungsgeschichte des sogeanannten Caralogus Felicianus', *Römische Quartalschrift* 111 (2016), 272–87; R. McKitterick, 'Perceptions of Rome and the papacy in late Merovingian Francia: The Cononian recension', in S. Esders, Y. Fox, Y. Hen, and L. Sarty (eds.), *East and West in the Early Middle Ages: The Merovingian Kingdoms in Mediterranean Perspective* (Cambridge, 2019), 165–86.

³⁷ For the texts of the Felician and Cononian epitomes see *LP* I, 47–113.

the pope's wealth. Ideologically papal status is enhanced, whatever the truth of the figures: the popes now replace the emperors in Rome, assisted materially by the emperors themselves.[38]

There is a handful of references to further embellishments and rich imperial gifts to the Lateran, notably in the time of Valentinian III, who replaced the silver *fastigium* (allegedly removed by barbarians) and weighing 1,610 lbs, at Pope Sixtus III's request.[39] A regular feature of later biographies throughout the text is the record of papal gifts to the churches of Rome. Some of these include the Constantinian basilica. Thus 'after the Vandal disaster', Leo I (440–61)

> replaced all the consecrated silver services throughout all the *tituli*, by melting down six water jars, two at the Constantinian basilica, two at the basilica of St Peter, two at St Paul's, which the emperor Constantine had presented, each weighing 100 lb. From these he replaced all the consecrated vessels (i.e. 600 lbs silver) ... he renewed St Peter's basilica and the apse vault; and he renewed St Paul's after the divine fire. He also constructed the ceiling in the Constantinian basilica.[40]

The contribution made by Pope Hilarus (461–8) was rather more substantial, for he built three oratories in the baptistery of the Constantinian basilica to Saint John the Baptist, Saint John the Evangelist, and the Holy Cross. Gifts including a piece of wood from the True Cross as well as silver and gold vessels and silver doors in both the baptistery and the Constantinian basilica are recorded, totalling 290 lbs of gold and 266 lbs of silver in the latter.[41] The gifts Gelasius (492–6) made to many churches, on the other hand, are lavish and listed in detail in the *Liber Pontificalis*, but none is recorded to the Constantinian basilica.[42] Other papal gifts, of decoration of various kinds, silver and gold vessels, silk veils or curtains, are referred to from time to time in the later seventh- and eighth-century

---

[38] See McKitterick, *Rome and the invention of the papacy*.

[39] *LP* I, Life 46, 233 (c. 4).

[40] *LP* I, Life 47, 239 (c. 6): 'Hic renovavit post cladem Wandalicum omnia ministeria sacrata argentea per omnes titulos, conflatas hydrias VI basilicae Constantinianae, duas basilicae beati Petri apostoli, duas beati Pauli apostoli, quas Constantinus Augustus obtulit, qui pens. sing. lib. Centenas; de quas omnia vasa renovavit sacrata. Hic renovavit basilicam beati Petri apostoli et beati Pauli post ignem divinum renovavit. Fecit vero cameram in basilica Constantiniana.' Davis, *The Book of Pontiffs*, 37 translates 'camera' as 'apse vault'; I follow Paolo Liverani in offering 'ceiling' instead. As Paolo Liverani has pointed out, 'camera' is a difficult term to interpret in architectural terms: see P. Liverani, '"Camerae" e coperture delle basiliche paleocristiane', *Mededelingen van het Nederlands Instituut te Rome* 60–61 (2001–2), 13–27, especially pp. 17–18. See also Herman Geertman's edition of Lives 33–48, 'Le biografie del liber Pontificalis dal 311 al 525', at p. 332 and n. 187.

[41] *LP* I, Life 48, 242–5.  [42] *LP* I, Life 51, 255 (c. 5).

sections of the *Liber Pontificalis*, such as the gifts of John IV (640–2),[43] and of Hadrian I (772–4). The latter apparently carried out major restoration work on the fabric of the basilica as well as adorning it with rich silk hangings and gifts of silver and gold vessels.[44]

It is in the ninth-century sections that the Lives of Leo III and Sergius II contain the most detailed lists of embellishments, in the form of new church furniture, liturgical vessels, ornaments, hangings, glass windows, canopies, railings and pictures, to the churches of Rome, not least the Constantinian basilica and the baptistery.[45] Gifts to the Constantinian basilica even emerge by the middle of the ninth century as a conventional way for a pope to mark the beginning of his pontificate, for this is mentioned in extravagant terms in the Life of Sergius II (844–7): 'At the very start of his pontificate, burning with love from on high he completed a work of wondrous beauty in the Saviour's basilica called Constantinian.'[46] Similarly, Benedict III (855–8), 'at the very start of his pontificate boiling with love from on high in the Saviour's basilica called Constantinian he provided an icon of wondrous beauty of the Redeemer our Lord Jesus Christ himself, trampling the lion and serpent underfoot of fine silver swathed in gold, weighing sixteen and a half pounds'.[47]

## The Function of the Constantinian Basilica

So far, the text has only yielded indications of the status of the Constantinian basilica implied in the narrative of initial foundation and subsequent endowments. It is necessary now to see what the *Liber Pontificalis* might indicate about the function of the Constantinian basilica. This emerges only very gradually in the course of the text, and mostly only

---

[43] *LP* I, Life 74, 330 (c. 2).   [44] *LP* I, Life 97, 500, 507, 510–11 (cc. 49, 70, 84).
[45] *LP* II, Life 98 Leo III, 3, 9, 14, 25 (cc. 8, 31, 51, 82). See also Gregory IV, *LP* II, Life 103, 81 and 82 (cc. 37 and 41).
[46] *LP* II, Life 104, 91 (c. 19): 'In primo quidem pontificatus sui exordio, superno amore exardescans, in basilica Salvatoris quae Constantiniana nuncupatur mire pulchritudinis opus explevit', trans. in R. Davis (ed.), *The Lives of the Ninth-Century Popes (Liber Pontificalis)* (Translated Texts for Historians 20) (Liverpool, 1995), 83.
[47] *LP* II, Life 106, 144 (c. 21): 'In primo quidem pontificatus sui exordio, superno exardescans amore, in basilica Salvatoris quae Constantiniana dicitur, ipsius redemproris domini nostri Iesu Christi mire pulchritudinis ex agento purissimo auroque perfusam fecit iconam, leonem draconemque pedibus conculcantem, pens. Lib. XVI semis', trans. in Davis (ed.), *The Lives of the Ninth-Century Popes*, 177. Pope Nicholas I does not use the phrase, but the record of gifts comes immediately after the elaborate chapters on the festivities accompanying his consecration: *LP* II, Life 107, 152–3 (cc. 11–14).

from the later seventh century onwards. It is there too that the references to the episcopal residence, *patriarchum* or *episcopium*, are to be found in ever greater abundance including, for example, references to the reception of the emperor Constans II by Pope Vitalian (657–72) when the emperor bathed and dined at the Lateran palace and, much later, the Frankish emperor Charlemagne feasted with Pope Hadrian (772–95) in the Lateran.[48] In the seventh- and eighth-century continuations, moreover, the Constantinian basilica itself is portrayed as beginning to play a larger role in both Roman politics and the Roman liturgy.

Even in the early years recorded in the sixth-century portion of the *Liber Pontificalis*, the Constantinian basilica appears to be given a role in determining legitimacy in cases of disputed papal election. The Life of Liberius (352–66) records how his place was taken by Felix when Liberius himself was exiled by the emperor Constantius for refusing to agree to the Arian heresy. Liberius was only reinstated in Rome when he relented to the extent of agreeing to share communion with the heretics. As an indication of his restored status he held the basilicas of Saint Peter and Saint Paul and the Constantinian basilica.[49] Rather less ambiguously, Eulalius, rival candidate for the see to Boniface I, was ordained in the Constantinian basilica, whereas Boniface was ordained in that of Julius (thought to be the original designation of the church that became Santa Maria in Trastevere[50]). The dispute reached the ears of Galla Placidia and her son the emperor Valentinian III, then resident at Ravenna, who reported it to the emperor Honorius, who was in Milan. The *Liber Pontificalis* records that the emperor asked both contenders to leave the city, but Eulalius, relying on the fact that he had been ordained in the Constantinian basilica, dared to enter the city and perform miracles and celebrate Easter in the Constantinian basilica, while Boniface celebrated the Easter baptism in the normal way at the basilica of the martyr Saint Agnes.[51]

This prompted the emperors to decide in Boniface I's favour, though the people of Rome still wanted Eulalius back. Here it is implied that Eulalius was discarded simply because of disobedience to the emperor, despite his

---

[48] *LP* I, Life 78, 343 (cc. 2 and 3) and *LP* I, Life 97, 498 (c. 40).

[49] *LP* I, Life 37, 207–8. The career of Felix is notably confused. Life 37 records that Felix was exiled to his estate where he died in peace on 29 July, but this is contradicted by Life 38 of Felix (355–65), *LP* I, 211, which says he was martyred and beheaded by Constantius.

[50] See D. Trout, *Damasus of Rome: The Epigraphic Poetry* (Oxford, 2015), 6.

[51] *LP* I, Life 44, 227: 'Veniens autem dies proximus Paschae praesumpsit Eulalius, eo quod ordinatus fuisset in basilica Constantiniana, et introivit in urbem et baptizavit et celebravit Pascha in basilica Constantiniana; Bonifatius vero sicut consuetudo erat, celebravit baptismum Paschae in basilica beatae martyris Agnae', trans. in Davis, *The Book of Pontiffs*, 32.

own and the Roman people's perception that he was the rightful pope. The Constantinian basilica also played a significant role in the Dioscoran schism. Again, the ordination in the Constantinian basilica had the people's support but Boniface II (530–2), ordained like Boniface I in the Basilica of Julius, was actually the one who was recognised as the legitimate pope in due course.[52] In the Laurentian schism, consecration and occupation in the Constantinian basilica this time appeared to work in favour of Symmachus, the rival candidate, for Laurence was ordained in Santa Maria Maggiore.[53]

By writing the Constantinian basilica as a venue for papal consecration into the history of the basilica in this way, the *Liber Pontificalis* may have been an instrument of a campaign to make the Constantinian basilica an essential location in the papal election process. It is certainly not the only time it can be seen to be a contribution to an argument.[54] Certainly, by the eighth century the election process appears to have settled into a pattern. When the details of the process are described (apparently more likely to be in the context of a disrupted election process), the election takes place in the Constantinian basilica, the candidate is then installed in the Lateran palace, and thereafter consecration is performed, usually by the bishops of Porto, Ostia and Albano, in Saint Peter's basilica.[55]

As the bishop's seat and church, the Constantinian basilica also became a regular venue for synods and judicial gatherings. An early instance in the sixth-century portion of the text is the reference to Gelasius, who had had a bonfire of Manichaean books in front of the doors of Santa Maria Maggiore, whereas both Symmachus and Hormisdas burnt the books judged to be heretical before the doors of the Constantinian basilica.[56]

It is in the entries from the middle of the seventh century onwards that the Constantinian basilica's functions emerge more clearly. It is not until the disgraceful episode of Maurice the Cartularius and his plundering of the Lateran *episcopium* recorded in the Life of the three-month pope Severinus (May–August 640) that the Lateran emerges in the text as the episcopal residence beside the basilica and baptistery.[57] The residence itself also had many oratories created within the complex of buildings in the course of the

---

[52] *LP* I, Life 57, 281.
[53] *LP* I, Life 53, 260 (c. 2). For full commentary, see E. Wirbelauer, *Zwei Päpste in Rom: Der Konflikt zwischen Laurentius und Symmachus (498–514): Studien und Texte* (Quellen und Forschungen zur antiken Welt 16) (Munich, 1993).
[54] See K. Blair-Dixon, 'Memory and authority in sixth-century Rome: The *Liber Pontificalis* and the *Collectio Avellana*', in K. Cooper and J. Hillner (eds.), *Religion, Dynasty, and Patronage in Early Christian Rome, 300–900* (Cambridge, 2007), 59–76.
[55] Compare *LP* I, Life 35, 202 (c. 2), Life 94, 441 (c. 3), Life 96, 468 (cc. 3–4), 470–1 (cc. 10–11).
[56] *LP* I, Life 51, 255 (c. 1), Life 53, 261 (c. 5), Life 54, 270–1 (c. 9).   [57] *LP* I, Life 73, 328.

seventh and eighth centuries. It is Pope Martin, however, who seems to have established the official standing of the Lateran in relation to papal authority by making it the venue for synodal proceedings and judicial process. These too become a feature of the seventh-, eighth- and ninth-century sections, the most famous being the Lateran Synod of 649 convened by Pope Martin (649–54; †655 in exile),[58] the ritual deposition of Pope Constantine II by his successor Stephen III at the Synod of Rome in 769[59] and the arraignment of John of Ravenna during the pontificate of Pope Nicholas I.[60]

The Constantinian basilica was also the venue for Charlemagne and Hadrian to meet after Charlemagne's conquest of the Lombard kingdom: 'That same Holy Saturday [Charlemagne and Pope Hadrian] entered the Saviour's basilica close to the Lateran together where his Excellency the king with all his [followers stayed] while the thrice-blessed pontiff celebrated the sacrament of holy baptism.'[61]

The *Liber Pontificalis* does not include an account of the baptism of Charlemagne's son Pippin in 781: this is recorded in Frankish sources, not least the famous Godescalc Lectionary.[62] The *Liber Pontificalis* does, however, record gifts Charlemagne made to the basilica a few years later during the reign of Pope Leo III, which also specify their use in the liturgy of the basilica: 'In the Saviour our Lord's basilica called Constantinian Charlemagne presented a cross with jacinths which the bountiful pontiff assigned for the litany procession as the pious emperor suggested; an altar with silver columns and canopy; a gospel book with a cover of fine gold adorned with jewels weighing .. [sic!] lb.'

This cross, incidentally, was stolen sometime after the reign of Paschal I, and only restored by Leo IV.[63]

---

[58] *LP* I, life 76, 366–7 (c. 3); For the text of the Lateran Council of 649 in translation with full commentary see R. Price, with contributions by P. Booth and C. Cubitt, *The Acts of the Lateran Synod of 649* (Translated Texts for Historians 61) (Liverpool, 2014).

[59] *LP* I, Life 96, 475–7 (cc. 18–24) and notes at pp. 483–4. See also R. McKitterick, 'The *damnatio memoriae* of Pope Constantine II (767–768)', in R. Balzaretti, J. Barrow and P. Skinner (eds.), *Italy and Medieval Europe: Papers for Chris Wickham on the Occasion of His 65th Birthday* (Past and Present Supplementary series) (Oxford, 2018), 231–49.

[60] *LP* II, Life 107, 179–80 (c. 31–4).

[61] *LP* I, Life 97, 497 (c. 39): 'In eodem sabbato sancto in basilica Salvatoris iuxta lateranis pariter ingressi, ibidem ipse excellentissimus rex cum omnibus suis quousque sacrosancti baptissmatis sacramentum antedictus ter beatissimus pontifex caelebravit', trans. in Davis (ed.), *The Lives of the Eighth-Century Popes*, 140.

[62] Paris, Bibliothèque nationale de France, MS n.a.lat. 1203, fol. 125r. See the partial facsimile in F. Crivello, C. Denoël and P. Orth, *Das Godescalc-Evangelistar: Eine Prachthandschrift für Karl den Großen* (Darmstadt, 2011), 31.

[63] *LP* II, Life 98 (c. 25): 'Item, in basilica Salvatoris domini nostri, quae appellatur Constantiniana, obtulit crucem cum gemmis yacinctinis, quam almificus pontifex in letania, procedere

## Liturgy and the Constantinian Basilica

The Constantinian basilica's place in the liturgy of Rome is too large a topic to be dealt with here, though John Romano addresses aspects of it in his chapter in this volume. The *Liber Pontificalis* yields very particular instances, however, of the way in which the liturgical functions of the Constantinian basilica and of the baptistery were steadily augmented, and does this in three ways. I only have space to offer a few examples.

First of all, there are indications of provision being made for liturgical observance by a succession of popes, partly by the building of oratories, and partly by establishing communities of monks to perform the offices. I have already referred to the oratories created in the basilica by Pope Hilarus (461–8). These were dedicated to Saint John the Baptist, Saint John the Evangelist and the Holy Cross. Hilarus is also said to have built the oratory of St Stephen in the Lateran baptistery and to have 'built two libraries in the same place'.[64] Hilarus is also credited with 'arranging services' to circulate around the established stations and donating gold and silver vessels for liturgical use which were to be stored at the Constantinian basilica and at Saint Mary's, quite apart from the extraordinary gifts of liturgical vessels and lights to other churches in Rome.[65] His pontificate appears to have been a crucial one in the construction of the history of the Roman liturgy in Rome by the *Liber Pontificalis* authors. The most far-reaching provisions, however, were made from the eighth century onwards.

Gregory III (731–41), for example,

> renewed the monastery of SS John the Evangelist, John the Baptist and St Pancras founded of old alongside the Saviour's church; through excessive neglect it had been abandoned by every monastic order. On this monastery he conferred estates and gifts, and he restored to this place, paying the price for it, whatever he had found to be alienated from it. He established there a community of monks and an abbot to perform every day the sacred offices of divine praise, as arranged for daytime and night time, just like the offices at

---

constituit, secundum petitionem ipsius piissimi imperatoris; immo et altare cum columnis argenteis et ciburio; verum etiam et evangelium cum battaci ex auro mundissimo, in gemmis ornatum, pens. [] lib', trans. in Davis (ed.), *The Lives of the Eighth-Century Popes*, 192. Compare *LP* II, Life 105, 110 (c. 17).

[64] *LP* I, Life 48, 242–3 and 245 (cc. 2, 6 and 12): 'Fecit autem et bibliothecas II in eodem loco', trans. in Davis, *The Book of Pontiffs*, 40.

[65] *LP* I, Life 48, 244–5 (c. 11).

St Peter's, in the Saviour our Lord Jesus Christ's basilica called the Constantinian, close to the Lateran.[66]

Hadrian I (722–95) specified still more liturgical offices as part of a major restoration of the Constantinian basilica:

> He laid down that they [the monks of the onetime Pope Honorius's monastery] should celebrate the office – matins, prime, terce, sext, none and vespers – in the Saviour's basilica also called Constantinian close to the Lateran Patriarchate, in two choirs one, the monks of St Pancras' monastery located there who formerly used to chant on their own antiphonally; the other the monks of the just mentioned monastery of SS Andrew and Bartholomew called that of pope Honorius. In this way they would diligently chant their Psalms of pious praise, re-echoing with chants in hymn singing and God-pleasing choirs, and render glorious melody to the Lord in this venerable pontiff's name, composing his memorial in song for ever.[67]

Leo III (795–816) is also credited with contributions to the liturgical rituals of the Constantinian basilica with the processional litanies from Santa Maria Maggiore to the Constantinian basilica in the three days before Ascension Day,[68] and Paschal I (817–24) required that the resident community of the Santi Sergius and Bacchus monastery 'should day and night chant praises and hymns melodiously to the only God and his saints

---

[66] *LP* I, Life 92, 419 (c. 10): 'Simili autem modo renovavit monasterium sanctorum Iohannis Evangelistae, Ioannis Baptiste et sancti Pancratii secus ecclesiam Salvatoris antiquitus institutum, quod ab omni ordine monachico extiterat nimia incuria distitutum, in quo predia et dona contulit, et quae invenerat de ipso monasterio alienata, reddito pretio, in eumdem locum restituit. Ubi et congregationem monachorum et abbatem constituit ad persolvenda cotidie sacra officia laudis divine in basilica Salvatoris domini nostri Iesu Christi quae Constantiniana nuncupatur, iuxta Lateranis, diurnis nocturnisque temporibus ordinata, iuxta instar officiorum beati Petri apostoli.' In *LP* I, Life 92, 421 (c. 16), it is noted that Gregory also provided altar cloths in the Saviour's, God's mother's Saint Peter's, Saint Paul's, and Saint Andrew's churches. Trans. in Davis (ed.), *The Lives of the Eighth-Century Popes*, 24, and compare p. 28.

[67] *LP* I, Life 97, 503 (c. 68): 'Hic autem ter beatissimus et apostolicus vir, dum per almissima exquisitione sua reperuisset monasterium quondam Honorii papae in nimia desolatione per quandam neglegentiam evenire, divina inspiratione motus, a noviter eum aedificavit atque ditavit; et abbatem cum ceteros monachos regulariter ibidem vita degentes ordinavit. Et constituit eos in basilica Salvatoris quae et Constantiniana iuxta Lateranense patriarchio posita officio celebrari, hoc est matutino, ora prima et tertia, sexta seu nona, etiam et vespertina ab uno choro, qui dudum singulariter in utrosque psallebant, monachi monasterii sancti Pancratii ibidem posito, et ab altero choro monachi iamfati monasterii sancti Andreae et Bartholomei qui appellatur Honorii papae, quatenus piis laudibus naviterque psallentes, hymniferis Deique letis resonent cantibus, reddentes Domino glorificos melos pro sepius memorati venerandi pontificis nomen, scilicet in saecula memorialem eius pangentes carminibus', trans. in Davis (ed.), *The Lives of the Eighth-Century Popes*, 157.

[68] *LP* II, Life 98, 7 (c. 22) and 12 (c. 43). See also *LP* II, Life 98, 504–5 (c. 62) for the repair of the Claudian aqueduct.

in the Saviour our Lord Jesus's Christ's venerable church close to the Lateran'.[69]

Second, there is the clear relationship that developed in the eighth century between the clerical training ground and *scola cantorum* within the Lateran and the implications this has for the performance of the liturgy in the basilica.[70] Thus Gregory II, Paul I, Stephen II, Stephen III and in the ninth-century Leo III, Paschal I, Valentine, Sergius II, Leo IV, Benedict III, Nicholas I, Hadrian II and Stephen V were all brought up and educated within the Lateran palace. The Life of Paschal I (817–24) provides the most detailed indication of what this education might have entailed:

> From his earliest youth he was bound over to the worship of God and at the holy church's patriarchate he was imbued with the study of God's saving scripture. Spiritually trained both in psalm chanting and in the sacred pages of the New and Old Testaments elegant and perfect in all goodness, he was made subdeacon and afterwards honourably consecrated priest ... So he frequently applied himself to talking of the things of God with religious and holy monks as an unremitting duty by day and night and he humbly and becomingly throve on prayers, vigils and daily fasting.[71]

Third, there are a few indications that the holiness of the basilica was enhanced not only by liturgical observance but also by the installation of relics and the embellishment of altars. The oratories of the Lateran palace may also be part of this augmentation of honour accorded particular saints, though whether any relics were associated with these at the very early stage cannot be determined.[72] Close to the basilica itself and in the building once separate that

---

[69] *LP* II, Life 100, 58 (c. 22): 'Soli Deo sanctisque illius laudes et hymnos nocte dieque modulanter in venerabili ecclesia Salvatoris domini nostri Iesu Christi sita iuxta Lateranis decantent instituit', trans. in Davis (ed.), *The Lives of the Ninth-Century Popes*, 21 and n. 71. See also G. Ferrari, *Early Roman Monasteries: Notes for the History of Monasteries and Convents from the V through the X Century* (Studi di antichità cristiana 23) (Vatican City, 1957), 294–6.

[70] See C. Page, *The Christian West and Its Singers: The First Thousand Years* (New Haven, 2010) and compare the Life of Sergius II (844–7): *LP* II, Life 104, 92 (c. 24).

[71] *LP* II, Life 100, 52 (c. 1): 'Qui a primevo etatis suae divino cultu mancipatus atque sacrosantae ecclesiae patriarchio studiis divinae salutiferaeque Scrupturae inbutus, tam in psalterio quamque in sacris paginibus nove et veteris Testamenti spiritaliter eruditus, elegans atque in omni bonitate perfectus, subdiaconus quidem factus et postmodum presbiter honorifice consecratus est ... In colloquia ergo divinis frequentius cum religiosis ac sanctis monachis sedula observatione die noctuque insistebat; et in orationibus ac vigiliis cotidianisque ieiuniis humiliter atque honeste vigebat', trans. in Davis (ed.), *The Lives of the Ninth-Century Popes*, 5. Compare *LP* II, Life 104, 86 (c. 2).

[72] For discussion, see R. M. Jensen, 'Saints' relics and the consecration of church buildings in Rome', *Studia Patristica* 71 (2014), 153–70 and J. M. H. Smith, 'Care of relics in early medieval Rome', in O. Phelan and V. Garver (eds.), *Rome and Religion in the Medieval World: Studies in Honor of Thomas F. X. Noble* (Farnham, 2014), 179–207.

is now a chapel adjoining the baptistery there are some indications of the installation of relics. Thus John IV (640–2) 'built a church for the martyrs Saints Venantius, Anastasius, Maurus and many other martyrs whose relics he had ordered to be brought from the Dalmatias and Histrias; he deposited them in that church close to the Lateran font and the oratory of St John the Evangelist; he decorated it and presented it with many gifts'.[73]

After the dramatic rediscovery of a True Cross fragment in a neglected corner of St Peter's basilica, moreover, Sergius I introduced the Feast Day of the Exaltation of the Holy Cross: 'From this day for the salvation of the human race, this is kissed and worshipped by all Christian people on the day of the Exaltation of the Holy Cross in the basilica of the Saviour called Constantinian.'[74]

## The Dedication to the Saviour

The lack of a specific dedication for the Constantinian basilica is all the more striking. It is not until the seventh-century portion and the convening of the Lateran Synod of 649 that the dedication to the Saviour is mentioned, though it becomes the constant and consistent epithet in the *Liber Pontificalis* thereafter; not once does it refer to the basilica as dedicated to Saint John. The association with the Saviour and Jesus Christ might be thought to be supported by the number of times the Cross and representations of Christ are mentioned in connection with the basilica. Thus one of the gifts Constantine gave to the basilica, the extraordinary 'hammered silver *fastigium*' on the front of which was the Saviour',[75] discussed elsewhere in this volume,[76] may be a further indication of this dedication to the Saviour. Incidentally, Pope Sixtus III (432–40) asked the emperor Valentinian to replace this silver *fastigium* in the Constantinian basilica

---

[73] *LP* I, Life 74, 330 (c. 2): 'Eodem tempore fecit ecclesiam beatis martyribus Venantio, Anastasio, Mauro et aliorum multorum martyum, quorum reliquias de Dalmatias et Histrias adduci praeceperat, et recondit eas in ecclesia suprascripta, iuxta fontem Lateranensem, iuxta oratorium beati Johannis evanglistae, quam ornavit et diversa dona optulit', trans. in Davis, *The Book of Pontiffs*, 64–5.

[74] *LP* I, Life 86, 374 (c. 10): 'Qui etiam ex die illo pro salute humani generis ab omni populo christiano, die exaltationis sanctae crucis, in basilicam salvatoris quae appellatur Constantiniana osculatur et adoratur', trans. in Davis, *The Book of Pontiffs*, 83.

[75] *LP* I, Life 34, 172 (c. 9): 'fastidium argenteum battutilem qui habet in fronte salvatorem, sedentem in sella', trans. in Davis, *The Book of Pontiffs*, 15.

[76] See Chapter 8 in this volume, and compare H. Geertman, 'Il *fastigium* lateranense e l'arredo presbiteriale: Una lunga storia', in Geertman (ed.), *Il Liber Pontificalis e la storia materiale*, 29–44.

with a new one weighing 1,610 lbs because the original had allegedly 'been removed by the barbarians'.[77] Much later, in the reign of Zacharias (741–52) in the middle of the eighth century, a figure of the Saviour was placed by Zacharias in front of the doors of the basilica.[78] In the later ninth century Life of Nicholas I (858–67) there is a reference to the 'fine silver crosses which hang before the figure of the substance of our Lord Jesus Christ's flesh' in the 'Saviour's basilica'.[79]

## The Dedication to Saint John

Whether the obvious association between the baptistery and Saint John the Baptist was extended to include the basilica cannot be determined. There are, of course, the oratories established in the baptistery in the later fifth century by Pope Hilarus mentioned above, dedicated to Saint John the Baptist, Saint John the Evangelist and the Holy Cross, and alluded to again in the ninth-century Life of Leo III (795–816). Perhaps these oratories played a more prominent liturgical role and served to heighten perceptions of these particular saints as the patrons of the Constantinian basilica in the eyes of contemporaries.[80] The earliest reference to the Lateran as dedicated to a Saint John appears to be in the world chronicle which forms chapter 66 of Bede's *De temporum ratione*, completed around 725 and circulated in Francia by the end of the eighth century. Under the year 4290, that is, AD 416, Bede wrote: 'In Rome where he was baptized, Constantine built the basilica of St John, known as the Constantinian basilica.'[81]

A possibly independent development is to be found in early Frankish liturgical books. Whereas the Godescalc Lectionary dated 781 from the court school of Charlemagne only mentions *ad Lateranis* for the particular stations, the 'Phillipps Sacramentary' (Berlin, Deutsche Staatsbibliothek, Phillipps 1667) dated around 800 seems to be the earliest, on fol. 23r, to give the title Saint John to the Lateran when providing details about the stational

---

[77] *LP* I, Life 46, 233 (c. 4): 'quod a barbaris sublatum fuerat', trans. in Davis, *The Book of Pontiffs*, 35.
[78] *LP* I, Life 93, 432 (c. 18).
[79] *LP* II, Life 107, 153 (c. 12), trans. in Davis (ed.), *The Lives of the Ninth-Century Popes*, 209.
[80] *LP* II, Life 98, 9–10 (c. 31).
[81] Bede, *De temporum ratione*, c, 66, in C. Jones (ed.), *Bedae Venerabilis Opera. Pars VI. Opera didascalica 2 (De temporum ratione)* (Corpus Christianorum Series Latina 123B) (Turnhout, 1977), 509: 'Constantinus fecit Romae, ubi baptizatus est basilicam beati Johannis baptistae, quae appellatur Constantiniana', trans. in F. Wallis, *Bede: The Reckoning of Time* (Translated Texts for Historians 29) (Liverpool, 1999), 212.

liturgy. Both the Godescalc Lectionary and the Phillipps Sacramentary are assumed to derive from a Roman list that arrived in Francia in the late seventh century and whose earliest witness is the Würzburg *comes*.[82] The Würzburg *comes*, however, like the Godescalc Lectionary, does not mention any Saint John, but simply refers to the stations for Easter Eve and the first Sunday after Easter as *ad Lateranis*.[83] The reference to Saint John may therefore be a later eighth- or early ninth-century Carolingian addition.

Another possible source is information from pilgrim itineraries. The reference in the short list known as the *Ecclesiae quae intus Romae habentur*: 'Basilica Constantiniana quae et Saluatorius; ipsa quoque et sancti Johannis dicitur' was cited long ago by Krautheimer, following de Rossi, as an indication that there was an association with a Saint John for the Constantinian basilica by the seventh century, for the text is usually dated after 638.[84] But that text survives only in a late eighth-century Frankish codex (Vienna, Nationalbibliothek Cod. 795) associated with Arn of Salzburg and corrected and extended by the Salzburg scribe Baldo in the early ninth century. There is thought to be a slight indication that the *Notitia ecclesiarum urbis Romae*, fol.187v line 17–fol. 191r in the same codex might have been copied from an insular exemplar,[85] but the list headed *Ecclesiae quae intus Rome habentur* in any case acts as an appendix to this text in the manuscript and is written by a different scribe.[86]

The first text on Roman topography in that volume, moreover, the *Notitia ecclesiarum urbis Romae*, includes information about the oratory of Petronilla in the Basilica of Saint Peter that relates to the middle of the eighth century.[87] Although the core of this text describing the ecclesiastical topography of Rome may be as early as de Rossi supposed, it is more likely

---

[82] E.g. Paris, Bibliothèque nationale de France, n.a. lat. 1203, fols. 26v, 48r, 63r, 67r, 70v.

[83] Würzburg Universitätsbibliothek, M.p. th. f.62, fols. 1v, 5v, 123, 13r. See H. Thurn, *Comes Romanus Wirziburgensis: Facsimileausgabe d es Codex M.p.th.f.62 der Universitäts-Bibliothek Würzburg* (Graz, 1968).

[84] *CBCR* V, 10; G. B. de Rossi, *Roma sotteranea Christiana*, 3 vols. (Rome, 1864), I, 128–57; P. Geyer and O. Cuntz (eds.), *Itineraria et alia geographica* (Corpus Christianorum Series Latina 175) (Turnhout, 1965), 321.

[85] B. Bischoff, *Die sudostdeutschen Schreibschulen und Bibliotheken in der Karolingerzeit.2. Die vorwiegend Österreichischen Diözesen* (Wiesbaden, 1980), 115–19, 199 n. 108.

[86] Vienna, Österreichische Nationalbibliothek Cod. 795, fol. 191v. See the facsimile F. Unterkircher (ed.), *Alkuin-Briefe und andere Traktate: Im Auftrage des Salzburger Erzbischofs Arn um 799 zu einem Sammelband vereinigt: Codex Vindobonensis 795 der Österreichischen Nationalbibliothek* (Codices selecti 20) (Graz, 1969).

[87] Geyer and Cuntz (eds.), *Itineraria*, 310. See R. McKitterick, *Perceptions of the Past in the Early Middle Ages* (Notre Dame, IN, 2006), 42–6; M. Diesenberger, 'Rom als virtueller Raum der Märtyrer: Zur gedanklichen Aneignung der Roma suburbana in bayerischen Handschriften um 800', in E. Vavra (ed.), *Imaginäre Räume* (Krems, 2004), 43–68.

that the list of churches inside Rome reflects Arn's own record of the holy sites and thus the current understanding of their names derived from his visit to Rome in 787. The dedication to John is also the way a Frankish pilgrim in the early ninth century described the Lateran.[88]

It may therefore be the Anglo-Saxon and Frankish pilgrims, perhaps because of their perception of the prominence of the oratories of Saint John the Evangelist and Saint John the Baptist in the basilica, as well as the proximity of the baptistery, when they prayed in the Constantinian basilica, who thought of Saint John in association with the basilica as a whole.[89]

## Conclusions

I have argued in this chapter that the initial foundation story in Life 34 of Sylvester has to be read in the context of sixth-century claims made by the popes about their position in Rome. Further, it is the *Liber Pontificalis*' later seventh- and eighth-century sections that draw attention to the various functions of both the Constantinian basilica and the entire Lateran complex, and enhance thereby the central role of the Lateran in relation to the pope's authority and activities as bishop.

It is worth considering briefly, therefore, what the intentions of later additions to the history of the popes may have been. They undoubtedly position the popes in relation to the eastern Roman emperors in a very particular way. The Lombard kings and exarchs of Ravenna are also constant presences in the text in the earlier part of the eighth century. From the time of Pope Stephen II, the popes also have to reckon with the Frankish rulers.

It is a commonplace that the gifts listed in Life 34 of the *Liber Pontificalis* contributed to the construction of the notorious 'Donation of Constantine' or *Constitutum Constantini* in the middle of the eighth century.[90] The Donation describes the Lateran as Constantine's palace, states that he had received the cure for leprosy at the hands of Sylvester and stresses that

> within our Lateran palace to that same Lord God Jesus Christ our Saviour we have built from the foundations a church along with a baptistery and as

---

[88] G. Walser (ed.), *Die Einsiedler Inschriftsammlung und der Pilgerführer durch Rom (Codex Einsidlensis 326)* (Stuttgart, 1987), 152–3, 189, 194–5.

[89] On Anglo-Saxon pilgrims generally see A. Thacker, 'Rome: The pilgrim's city in the seventh century', in F. Tinti (ed.), *England and Rome in the Early Middle Ages: Pilgrimage, Art, and Politics* (Turnhout, 2014), 89–139.

[90] See Montinaro, 'Les fausses donations de Constantin', 203.

to its foundations know you also that on our own shoulders we have carried extremely heavy baskets of earth, equal to the number of the twelve apostles. This sacred church as we determine is to be named, honoured, venerated and proclaimed as the head and summit of all the churches throughout the whole world, just as we have determined through our other imperial decrees.

The Donation further refers to 'the palace of our dominion, the Lateran, which is set above and excels all other palaces in all the lands of the world' and insists on the parallels between the clergy and their eminence within an imperial hierarchy.[91]

I suggest therefore that the *Liber Pontificalis*' eighth-century sections in particular are part of the same vainglorious and extravagant enterprise as this notorious papal forgery of the 760s. Both the eighth-century Lives in the *Liber Pontificalis* and the *Constitutum Constantini* were after all probably written by the same group of notaries within the papal administration.[92] Both witness to the papal officials' creative use of their resources to promote the pope's interests. On this reading, and in conjunction with the *Constitutum Constantini*, the very particular presentation of the Constantinian basilica throughout the text of the *Liber Pontificalis*, widely circulated throughout western Europe from the end of the eighth century onwards, acquires even greater significance.

---

[91] *Constitutum Constantini*: H. Fuhrmann (ed.), *Das Constitutum Constantini: Text* (MGH Fontes Iuris Germanici Antiqui in usum scholarium ex Monumentis Germaniae Historicis separatim editi 10) (Hanover, 1968), 84–5 (c. 13) and 87 (c. 14): 'Construxisse nos intro palatium nostrum Lateranense eidem salvatori nostro domino deo Iesu Christo ecclesiam a fundamentis cum baptisterio, et duodecim nos sciatis de eius fundamentis secundum numerum duodecim apostolorum cophinos terra onustatos propriis asportasse humeris; quam sacrosanctam ecclesiam caput et verticem omnium ecclesiarum in universo orbe terrarum dici, coli, venerari et praedicari sancimus, sicut per alia nostra imperialia decreta statuimus . . . Palatium imperii nostri Lateranense, quod omnibus in toto orbe terrarum praefertur atque praecellet palatiis', trans. in Edwards, *Constantine and Christendom*, 107, 109. Note that on p. 113 Edwards observes the use of the rare word *divalia* (sanctioned by God) which is also used by the *LP* author.

[92] R. M. Pollard, 'The language and style of the *Codex epistolaris Carolinus*, and their affinities with other papal documents', in R. McKitterick, R. M. Pollard, R. Price and D. van Espelo, *Codex epistolaris carolinus* (Translated Texts for Historians) (Liverpool, 2021).

# 11 | The Lateran Baptistery in the Fourth and Fifth Centuries: New Certainties and Unresolved Questions

OLOF BRANDT

Richard Krautheimer never included the Lateran baptistery[1] in his *Corpus Basilicarum Christianarum Romae*, which was published in five monumental volumes between 1937 and 1977 in the English edition, 1937 and 1980 in Italian. The fifth volume, published in English in 1977, deals with the major basilicas: the Lateran basilica, Saint Peter's and Saint Paul's. The section dedicated to the Lateran basilica[2] deals only with the basilica itself and not with its baptistery. One could argue that Krautheimer had a good reason for that: the baptistery is not a basilica and would not fit in a *Corpus basilicarum*. In the same way, Krautheimer left out Santa Costanza from the chapter on Sant'Agnese in the first volume, published in 1937. But we know from Krautheimer himself that he originally intended to include the baptistery in the *Corpus*. Otherwise it is difficult to explain why he had asked his collaborator, the architect Spencer Corbett, to prepare the plans and sections of the building in the 1960s. These original drawings are preserved in the archive of the Pontificio Istituto di Archeologia Cristiana together with other original drawings of the *Corpus* (Fig. 11.1).

The reason for leaving out the baptistery was rather that Krautheimer was waiting for the publication of the excavations and restorations carried out in the early 1960s around the baptistery. However, when the publication by Giovanni Pelliccioni eventually arrived,[3] Krautheimer was puzzled by its conclusions,[4] and spent some of his last years reflecting on the different phases of the baptistery and trying to convince Spencer Corbett to work with him again. Not even Krautheimer's long life gave him enough time to resolve the problem, and the world was left without his final opinion on the Lateran baptistery. This fact forces humility on anyone

---

[1] O. Brandt and F. Guidobaldi, 'Il Battistero Lateranense: Nuove interpretazioni delle fasi strutturali', *RAC* 84 (2008), 189–282; O. Brandt, *Battisteri oltre la pianta: Gli alzati di nove battisteri paleocristiani in Italia* (Vatican City, 2012), 33–85.
[2] *CBCR* V, 1–92.
[3] G. Pelliccioni, *Le nuove scoperte sulle origini del battistero lateranense* (Memorie della Pontificia Accademia Romana di Archeologia 12.1) (Vatican City, 1973).
[4] R. Krautheimer, *Architettura paleocristiana e bizantina* (Turin, 1986), 99, 107.

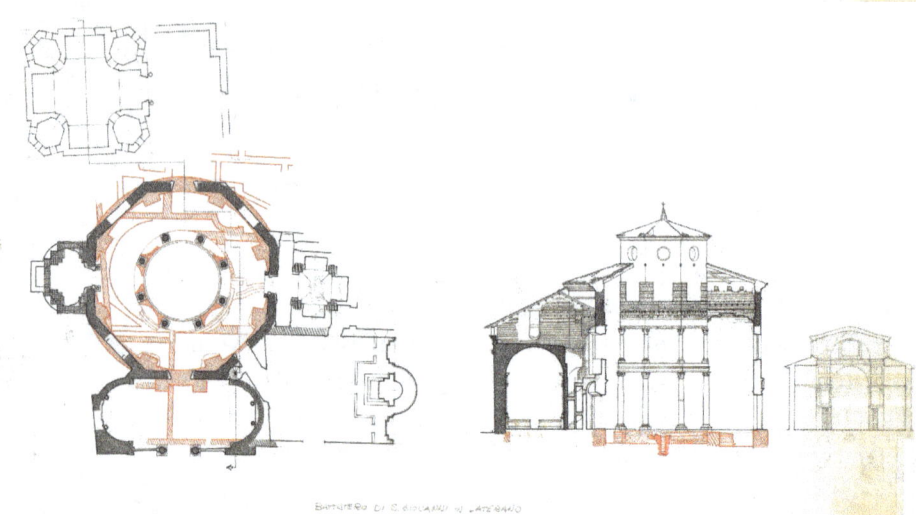

**Fig. 11.1** Drawings of the Lateran baptistery prepared by Spencer Corbett for the *Corpus Basilicarum Christianarum Romae* (Pontificio Istituto di Archeologia Cristiana).

who studies the Lateran baptistery, and an acceptance that it is an extremely difficult building to understand, especially in its first phase.

Why is it so difficult? The Lateran baptistery is one of the very few ancient buildings that are still standing, so it would seem easier to understand than many other, less preserved, buildings. However, what stands there today is, more or less, the fifth-century phase, while we know from the sixth-century *Liber Pontificalis* that the building was founded in the first half of the fourth century by Constantine.[5]

The fifth-century phase can be attributed to the Popes Sixtus III (432–40) and Hilarus (461–8) with the help of the *Liber Pontificalis*[6] and inscriptions[7]. The big problem is how to reconstruct the fourth-century phase.

The first excavations, which were carried out inside the baptistery in 1924–6 (Fig. 11.2),[8] revealed that the octagonal brick building stood on a circular foundation wall of tufa blocks. This was confirmed by later excavations around the baptistery in 1962–4. This led Giovanni Battista Giovenale in 1929[9] and Giovanni Pelliccioni in 1973[10] to conclude that the

---

[5] *LP* 34, 13–15.   [6] *LP* 46, 7, 48, 2–5.   [7] See below.

[8] G. B. Giovenale, *Il Battistero Lateranense nelle recenti indagini della Pontificia Commissione di Archeologia Sacra* (Studi di antichità cristiana 1) (Rome, 1929); Brandt and Guidobaldi, 'Il Battistero Lateranense', 198–206.

[9] Giovenale, *Il Battistero Lateranense*.   [10] Pelliccioni, *Le nuove scoperte*.

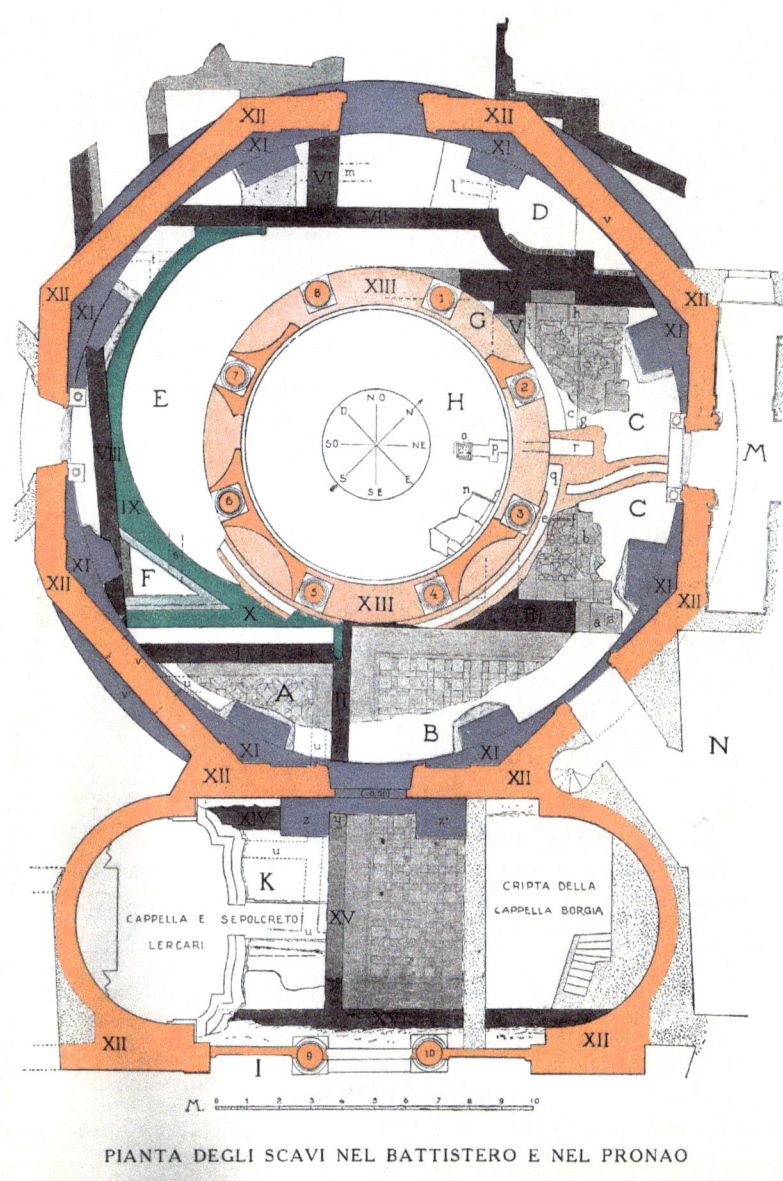

PIANTA DEGLI SCAVI NEL BATTISTERO E NEL PRONAO

Fig. 11.2 Plan of the excavations 1924–6 inside the Lateran baptistery (Giovenale, *Il battistero lateranense*, table I).

circular foundation was that of a demolished fourth-century building of circular shape. Giovenale thought that Constantine's circular baptistery was replaced by an octagonal one by Pope Sixtus III in the fifth century, when that pope erected the eight porphyry columns which still surround the font, according to the *Liber Pontificalis*. More than forty years later, Pelliccioni reconstructed a much more complicated series of phases, but the fundamental idea remained the same. What Krautheimer had to deal with was the idea that Constantine's baptistery was circular. He questioned this idea,[11] but was not able to carry out the necessary research.

The idea that Constantine's baptistery was circular has been radically challenged by the research carried out by the Pontificio Istituto di Archeologia Cristiana during the last twenty years, coordinated for the most part by myself and Federico Guidobaldi. This research has involved many institutions: the Vatican Museums, of course, which are responsible for the building, but also several Swedish institutions, especially the Swedish Institute of Classical Studies in Rome, the Swedish National Heritage Board and Lund University. During this work, Federico and I have had the pleasure of working with colleagues and students from the Pontificio Istituto, of different nationalities, and from Sweden.

The work is far from finished, but it has produced some interesting results. Some of these are observations and conclusions, and some are questions where more research is needed. Our current understanding is outlined below.

The plan: the plan of the first, Constantinian phase was octagonal (Fig. 11.3), although the octagonal brick building stood on a circular foundation wall. The lowest part of the brick building is octagonal on the outside, just above the circular foundation. What had confused earlier scholars was the fact that on the inside, the few bricks that are visible above the foundation wall and beneath the floor of the baptistery follow the circular shape of the foundation. This was interpreted as the remains of a circular brick building. But the octagonal shape on the outside and the circular shape of the inside must belong to the same phase. The circular shape on the inside continues for only a few bricks' height up to the ancient floor level. Above that, the brick structure is octagonal also on the inside.

The date: This octagonal building belongs to the last part of Constantine's reign. This was already known from the *Liber Pontificalis*.[12] It mentions donations to the baptistery in the eastern part of the empire, which Constantine would only have been able to donate after 324. These donations to the baptistery in the *Liber* are separated from those to the basilica,[13] which seems to have been built earlier than the baptistery. New observations seem to confirm this late Constantinian date. The paintings of the last phase of the building, which was partially demolished for the construction of the

[11] Krautheimer, *Architettura paleocristiana*, 99, 107.   [12] *LP* 34, 13.   [13] *LP* 34, 9–12.

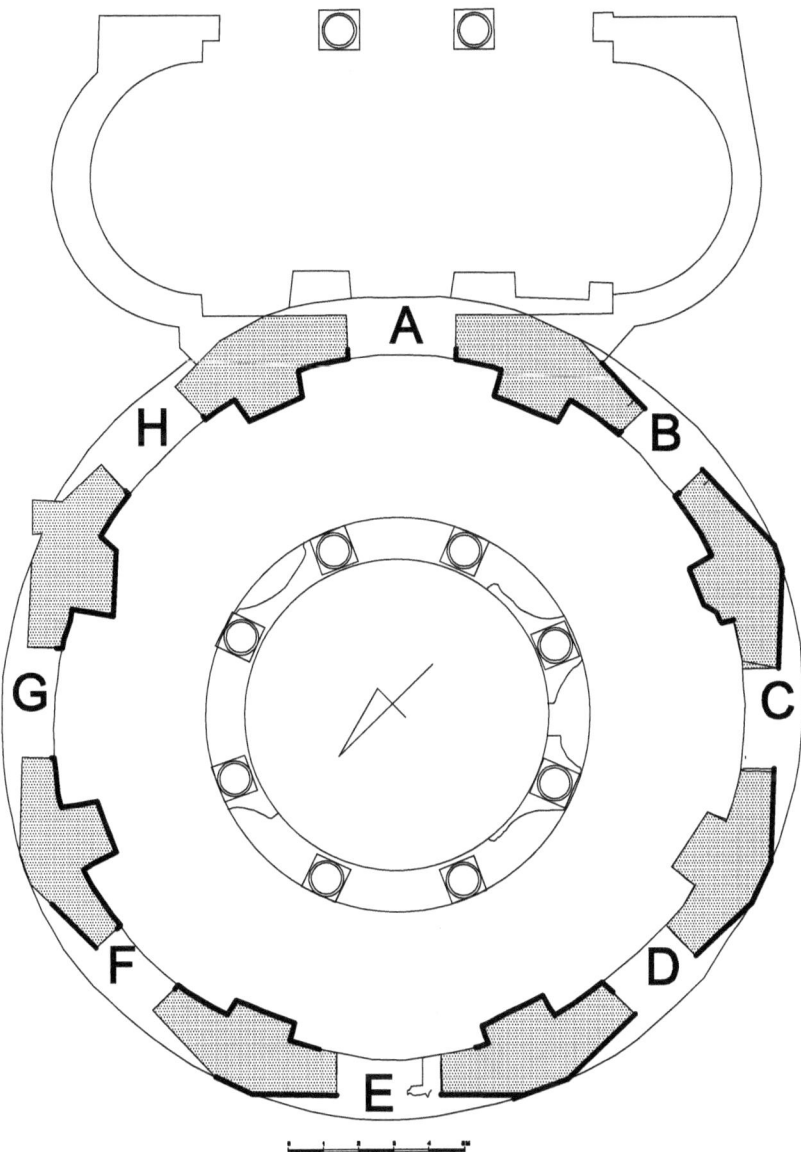

**Fig. 11.3** Plan of the foundation wall and of the lowest part of the brick building (By the author).

baptistery, with diagonal square shapes imitating *opus sectile* (Fig. 11.4), are similar to those found beneath Santa Maria Maggiore, which have recently been dated to the fourth century by Eric Moormann and Stephan Mols[14].

---

[14] S. T. A. M. Mols and E. M. Moormann, 'L'edificio romano sotto S. Maria Maggiore a Roma e le sue pitture: Proposta per una nuova lettura', *Mitteilungen des Deutschen Archäologischen Instituts. Römische Abteilung* 116 (2010), 469–506, at pp. 472–3.

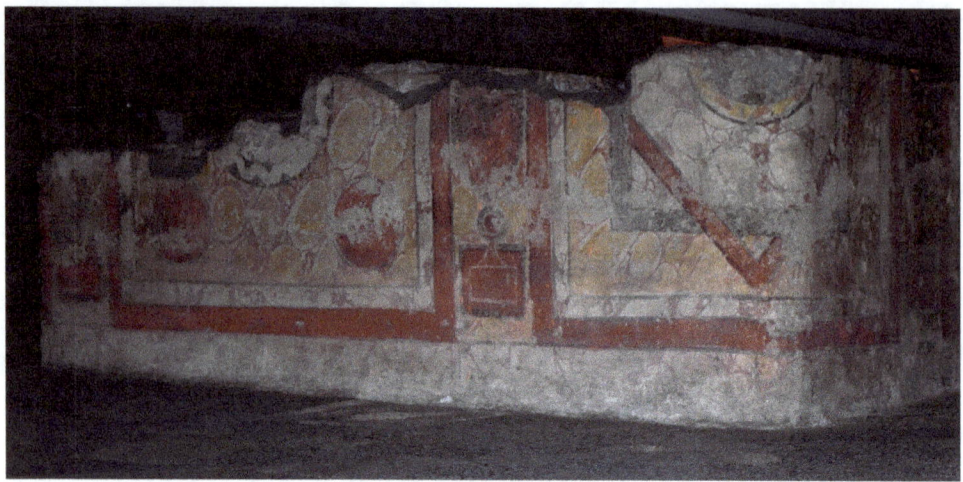

Fig. 11.4 Wall paintings beneath the Lateran baptistery (By the author).

This seems to make improbable a date too early in the fourth century for the building of the baptistery. On the other hand, the brick wall of the octagonal building can hardly have been built after the fourth century. Five bricks and five mortar layers measure 29–31.5 cm, which fits better in the fourth century.[15]

The preserved height of Constantine's baptistery: it was only in 1966 that the plaster was removed from the standing walls. Before that, scholars could not even be sure that the ancient building was still standing. The removal of the plaster made much new information available concerning the upper parts of the building and its phases. This information was not yet known during the excavations of 1924–6 and 1962–4. This explains why the publications of those excavations by Giovenale and Pelliccioni are more concerned with the plan than with the standing walls of the building. Although Pelliccioni's book was not published until 1973, it seems to have been written immediately after the end of the excavations in 1964, because it does not take into account all this new information available from 1966. Krautheimer did however incorporate that information. He noticed[16] that two rows of ancient windows could be seen (Fig. 11.5) and thought of something similar in the palace basilica of Trier.

The problem is that the two windows were too different in size and too close, and must have belonged to two different phases. This is an extremely

---

[15] T. L. Heres, *A Proposal for a Dating System of Late-Antique Masonry Structures in Rome and Ostia* (Amsterdam, 1982), 186.

[16] Krautheimer, *Architettura paleocristiana*, 99.

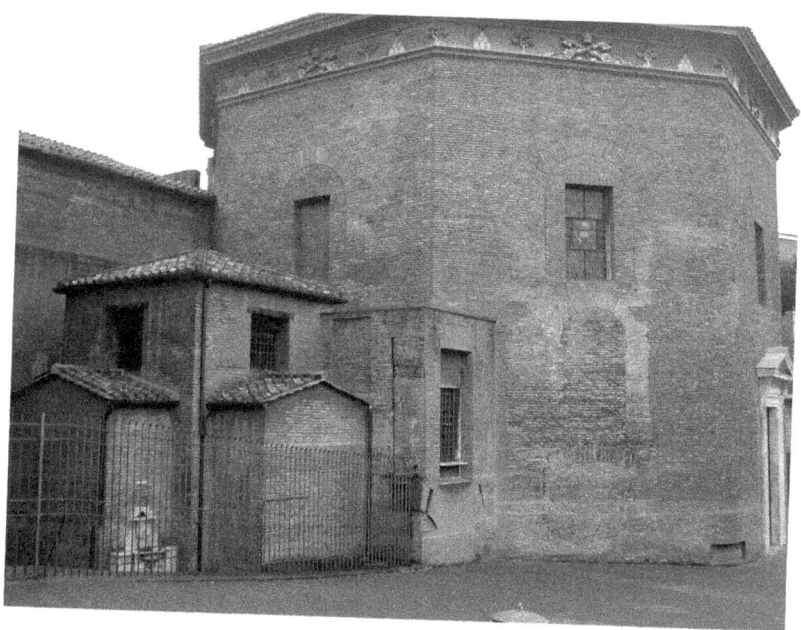

**Fig. 11.5** One of the walls of the Lateran baptistery with traces of two ancient windows (By the author).

important observation. One of the most important questions which our research has tried to answer is where the walls of the first phase end and those of the second phase begin. Up to which height is Constantine's baptistery still preserved?

It seems that the border between the two phases can be observed quite clearly in the corners of the building, which are built differently in the upper and lower parts of the building. In the lower part of the corner, some bricks embrace the corner, while this feature is lacking in the upper part, where diagonally cut bricks meet exactly in the corner. This leads to the conclusion that the original wall is preserved to the height of 9.2 m, approximately 2 m higher than the window of the first phase (Fig. 11.6).

These are the most important observations concerning the original phase of the Lateran baptistery. Others concern the fifth-century phase. The walls of this phase are preserved to a height of around 12.2 m, which is just above the arches of the upper windows. This means that the part of the wall – which seems ancient – above that height probably belongs to a later phase, which has not yet been identified. The upper part of the outer walls, with the big upper windows, was built together with the vestibule: Pelliccioni had noticed that the walls of the vestibule were built

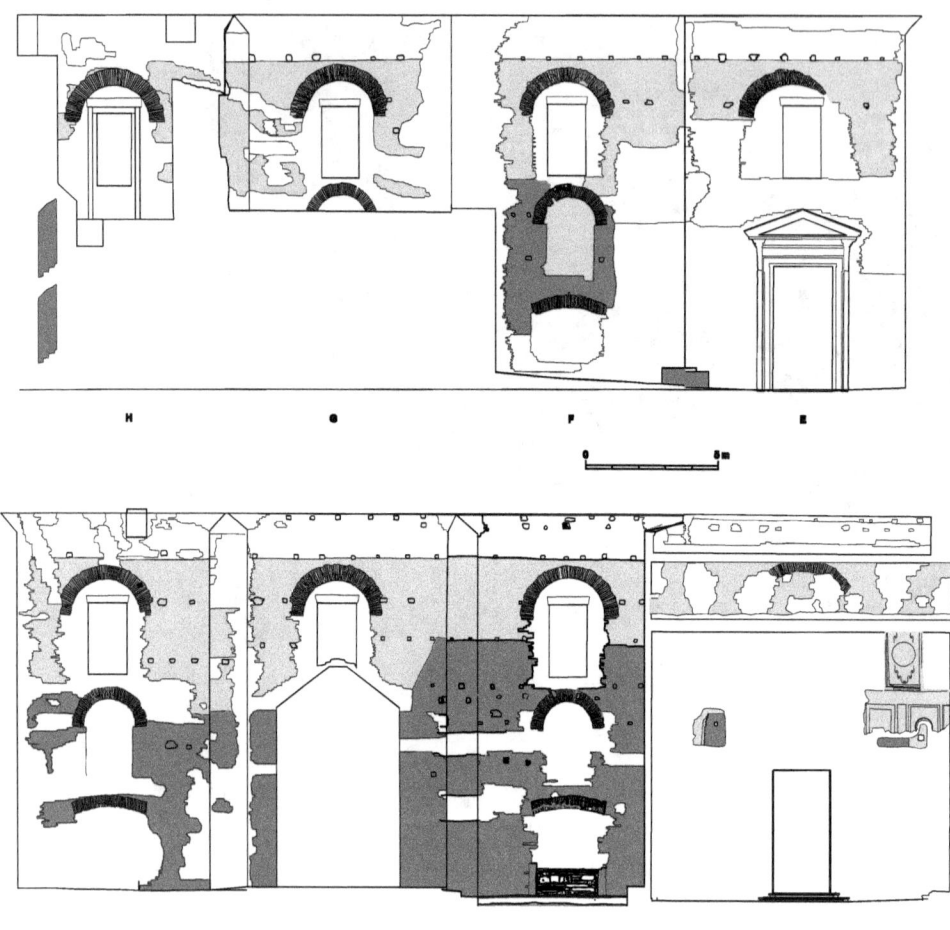

**Fig. 11.6** The two phases of the outer walls of the Lateran baptistery: Constantine (dark grey) and fifth century (light grey) (By the author).

together with the upper part of the octagonal building.[17] Giovenale, on the other hand, noticed that the vestibule shows the same reused marble architrave as the *baldacchino* above the eight porphyry columns around the font, which are attributed to Sixtus III by the *Liber Pontificalis*.[18] Not only the vestibule but also the upper part of the baptistery thus seem to have been built by Sixtus III. However, it now seems that Sixtus was not alone in this project.

One single fifth-century reconstruction begun by Sixtus III and completed by Hilarus: the *Liber* then states that Pope Hilarus added the chapels

---

[17] Pelliccioni, *Le nuove scoperte*, 101–4.   [18] *LP* 46, 7.

that surround the baptistery: the two small, cross-shaped chapels of San Giovanni Evangelista and San Giovanni Battista, and the bigger, cross-shaped chapel of Santa Croce, united to the baptistery by a courtyard with a portico. Those of Sixtus III and Hilarus would seem to be two separated phases. But Federico Guidobaldi has made an observation which points to the contrary. He noticed that while all the upper windows are well centred on their walls, that on the wall towards Santa Croce is quite off-centre, clearly on purpose, as if it was avoiding something (Fig. 11.7); our theory is that this is the portico of Santa Croce. But this would mean that the builders of the wall with the window knew about Santa Croce. Santa Croce and the upper part of the octagon were part of the same project. That is why we have proposed[19] viewing the fifth-century reconstructions as one single project, even if it may have taken some time to finish it: begun by Sixtus III, it was finished by Hilarus thirty years later.

A baptistery signed by Hilarus: while the fifth-century phase is often attributed to Sixtus III, it is striking that his name does not appear, even though the theologically dense verse inscription on the *baldacchino* above the font must be his, according to the *Liber Pontificalis*. On the other hand, Hilarus left several inscriptions in the building. Above the entrance to the chapel of San Giovanni Evangelista there is an inscription[20] where Hilarus thanks Saint John the Evangelist – *liberatori suo* – for saving him during the second Council of Ephesus. This expression is reminiscent of how Galla Placidia earlier in the same century thanked the same saint for saving her and her children during the sea trip from Constantinople to Ravenna, in an inscription[21] in the basilica of San Giovanni Evangelista in Ravenna. Hilarus also signed the baptistery in a lost inscription transcribed in the Sylloge of Lorsch,[22] which is quite obscure, but may mean that this pope built the upper part of the building (*quantum culminis nunc videtur*).

The chronology of Santa Croce: among the chapels attributed to Hilarus by the *Liber Pontificalis*, the chapel of Santa Croce was demolished by Sixtus V in the late sixteenth century, but it was well documented by Renaissance drawings. Krautheimer observed that the architecture of the chapel was so refined that he believed it to be a second-century building which had been reused and at least partially redecorated in the fifth century.[23] However, in the excavations made around the baptistery in 1962–4, parts of the foundations of Santa Croce were excavated although not identified. It has been possible to identify them

---

[19] Brandt and Guidobaldi, 'Il Battistero Lateranense'. [20] *ILCV* 980.
[21] *CIL* XI, 276e; *ILCV* 20e. [22] *ICUR* II, 147, 12.
[23] R. Krautheimer, *Rome: Profile of a City, 312–1308* (Princeton, 1980), 50.

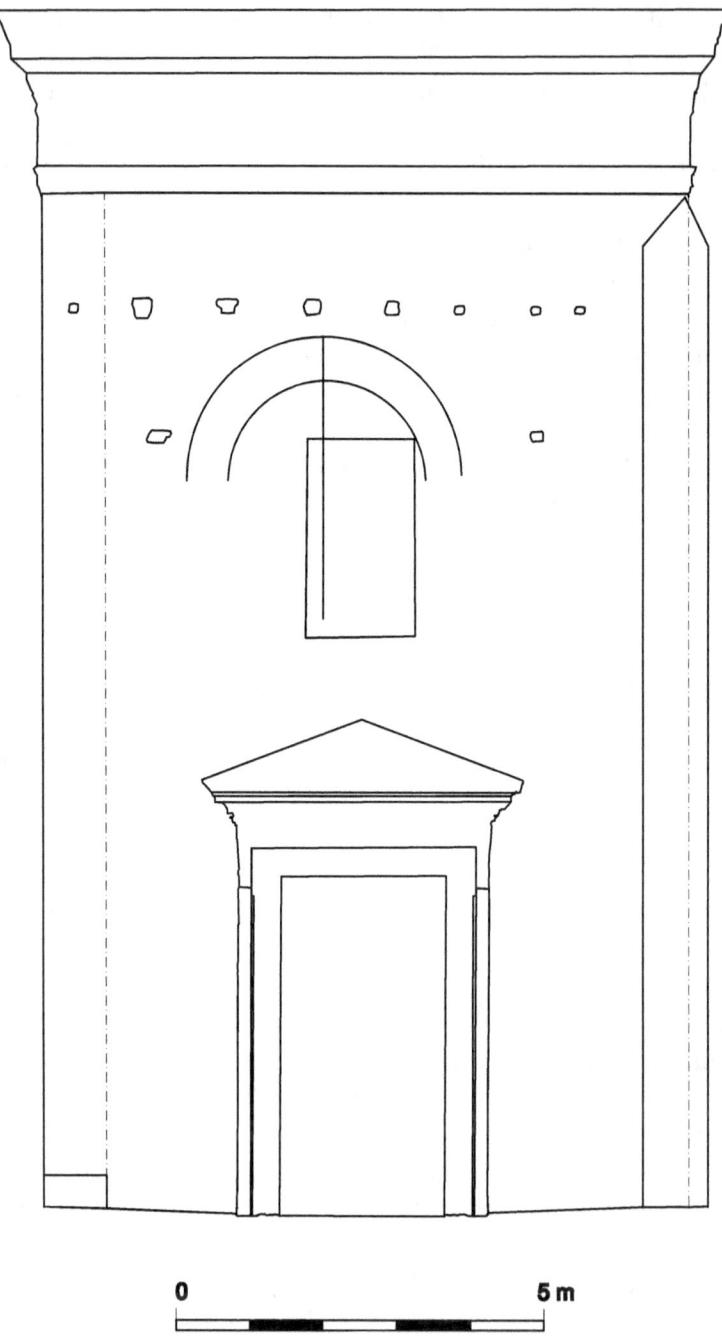

**Fig. 11.7** The wall of the Lateran baptistery towards the chapel of Santa Croce (By the author).

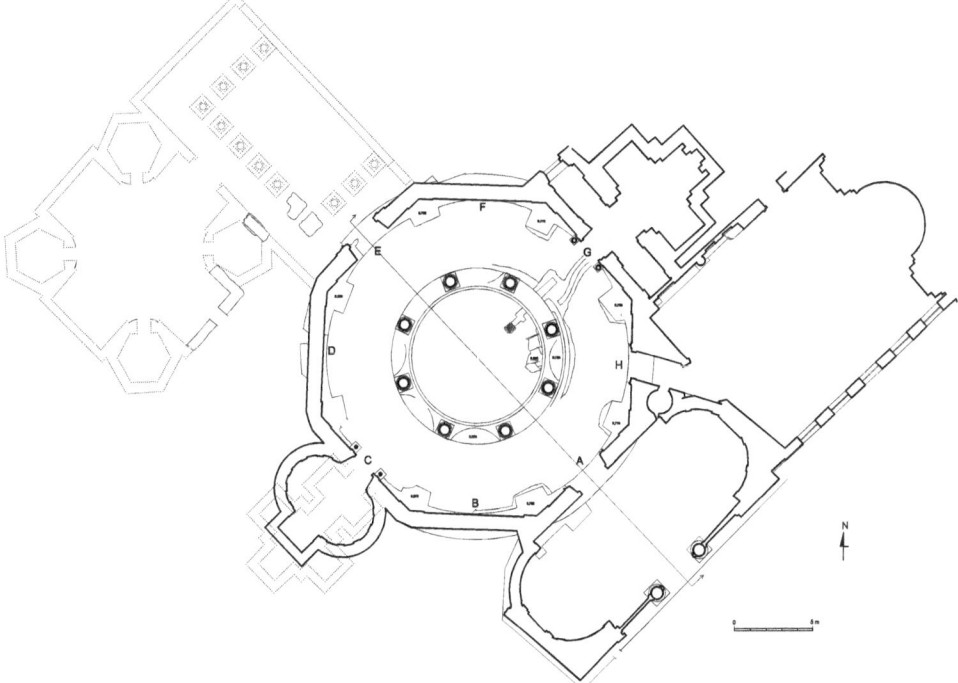

Fig. 11.8 Plan of the Lateran baptistery and the surrounding chapels (By the author).

(Fig. 11.8)[24] because their form and position correspond exactly to the plan of Santa Croce on Renaissance drawings. It is evident that the foundation walls were built from the higher ground level which was raised for the construction of the baptistery in the fourth century, and the possibility that they can have been built in the second century, when the ground level in the area was much lower, must be excluded. Interestingly, Krautheimer's judgement seems to have been shaped by the very old idea that Late Antique buildings with a refined architecture must have been reused Classical buildings.

This is more or less where we are today with ongoing research. This is now continuing with the help of 3D documentation (Fig. 11.9) created in collaboration with the Swedish National Heritage Board, Lund University, the Museum Kulturen in Lund and the Humanities Lab at Lund University.[25] So far this 3D documentation has been used especially in an effort to reconstruct

---

[24] O. Brandt, 'L'Oratorio della Santa Croce', in P. Liverani (ed.), *Giornata di studio tematica dedicata al Patriarcato Lateranense: Atti della giornata tematica dei Seminari di Archeologia Cristiana (École française de Rome, 10 maggio 2001)* (*MEFRA* 116, 1) (special issue) (Rome, 2004), 79–93.

[25] I wish to thank the Swedish colleagues for this stimulating collaboration: Hanna Menander, Håkan Thorén, Gunilla Gardelin and Carolina Larsson. So far, three reports have been published in pdf; they can be found at www.raa.se or on the individual pages of the participants on Academia.edu.

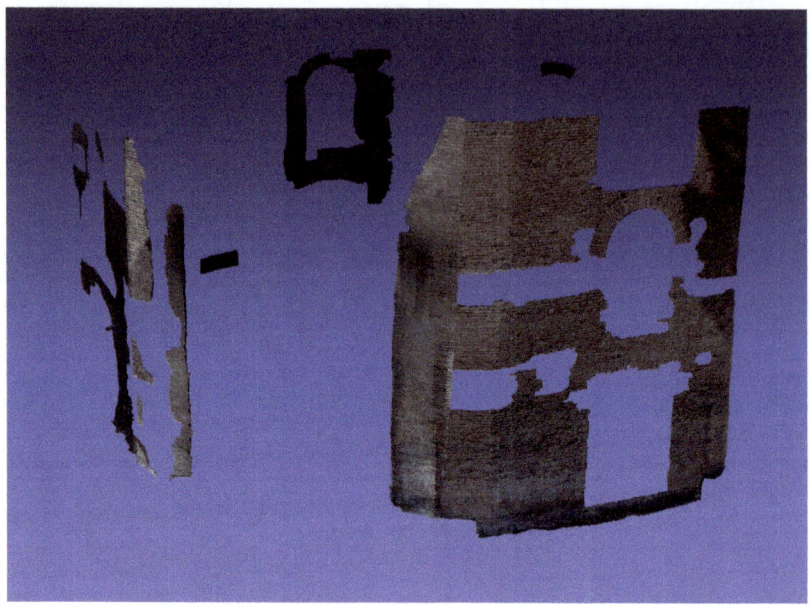

**Fig. 11.9** The preserved and visible remains of the Constantinian walls of the Lateran baptistery; 3D model visualised in Meshlab (By the author).

the fifth-century wall decoration, which is known from drawings made before the redecoration in the seventeenth century. A drawing by Giuliano di Sangallo from around 1500 (Fig. 11.10) shows the entire height of the fifth-century *opus sectile* wall decoration, while a coloured drawing from the early seventeenth century (Fig. 11.11) shows that the upper parts had been modified together with the windows and that the lower parts of the walls were clad with *pavonazzetto* marble. The work on the reconstruction has also given occasion to reflect on how the wall decoration affected the illumination. The wall decoration in the octagon was dominated by the bright *pavonazzetto* marble, and the overall effect may have been brighter than that of the walls in the vestibule.

This is what has been done so far. There are still many questions, which need further study and reflection. Why is the Constantinian wall so high above the windows? The walls of the first phase are preserved about 2 m above the windows of the first phase. That is surprising, considering that in Roman architecture the windows were usually placed as high as possible. A wall above a window usually contained and protected something. An eloquent example is the low position of the windows of the Orthodox baptistery in Ravenna. The high portion of wall above the window requires

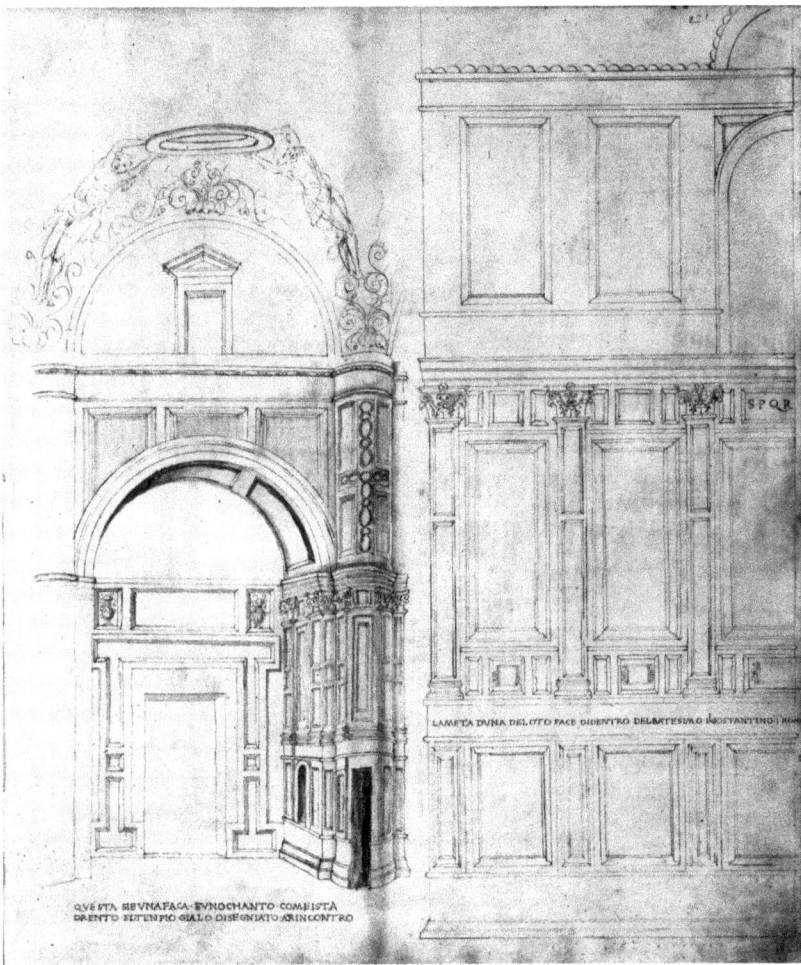

Fig. 11.10 Wall decoration of the Lateran baptistery in a drawing by Giuliano di Sangallo around 1500 (Vat. Lat. 4424 f33; © Biblioteca Apostolica Vaticana).

an explanation. It could possibly indicate the presence of a barrel vault, similar to that in the mausoleum of Santa Costanza in Rome.

This leads to the most important question concerning the first phase: how was the building covered? The answer depends on whether the inner space was divided or not. The baptistery may already have had an inner colonnade in the first phase. This has also been assumed by the authors of recent reconstruction drawings published by some scholars, such as Fabrizio Bisconti[26] and Hugo

---

[26] F. Bisconti, 'L'iconografia dei battisteri paleocristiani', in *Atti dell'VIII Congresso Nazionale di Archeologia Cristiana* (Bordighera, 2001), 405–40, at p. 406 fig. 1.

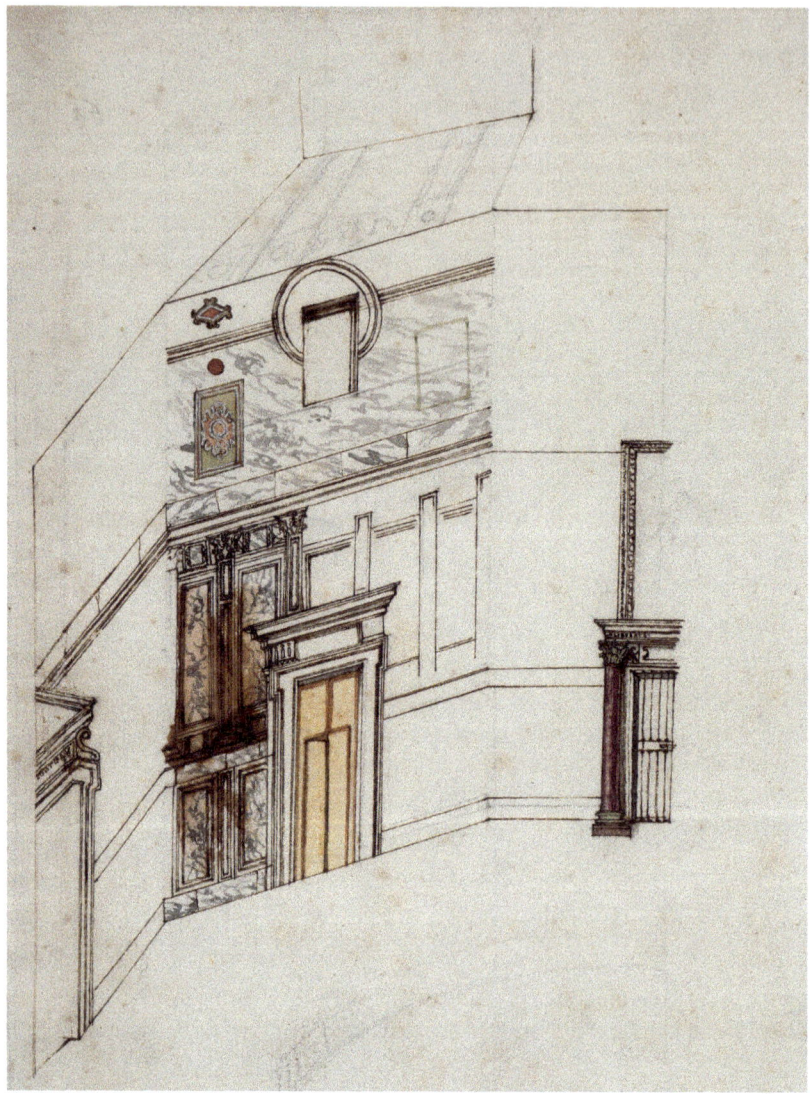

**Fig. 11.11** Wall decoration of the Lateran baptistery in an anonymous drawing from the early seventeenth century (Barb. lat. 4333. f.69v; © Biblioteca Apostolica Vaticana).

Brandenburg.[27] The hypothesis is not new, because it is exactly what the *Liber Pontificalis* seems to say when it states that Sixtus III erected the eight porphyry columns 'quas a Constantino Augusto fuerant congregatas'.[28] The possibility that the high wall above the window could be explained by a vault could point

---

[27] H. Brandenburg, *Le prime chiese di Roma IV–VII secolo* (Milan, 2013), 288.  [28] *LP* 46, 7.

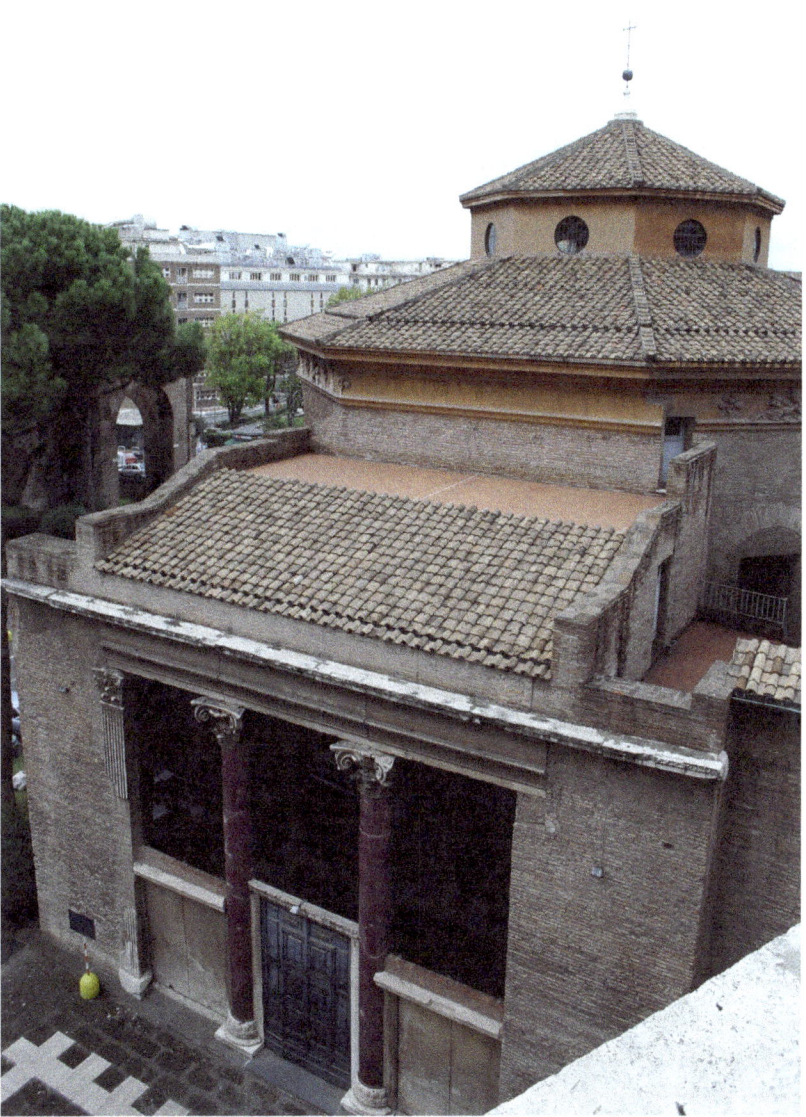

**Fig. 11.12** The vestibule of the Lateran baptistery (By the author).

in the same direction. A vault would, of course, be possible only if it could rest on columns or pillars which divided the inner space in a central room and an octagonal corridor. Such an arrangement seems probable but is, at least so far, entirely hypothetical.

Although new information about the first phase has been obtained, the above discussion about the roof of the building shows that much vital information is still lacking. In spite of this, it is necessary to explore the position of what is known about the first phase of the Lateran baptistery in the wider context of Late Antique architecture. Today's emphasis on archaeological research on standing structures must not make us forget that the study of an ancient building is never complete without a discussion on the place of that particular building in the history of architecture, and thus in the history of human culture.

Why was the fifth-century phase higher than the original phase? Perhaps the reason can be found in the porphyry columns of the vestibule (Fig. 11.12). They were too high for the original building, and it may well be that the opportunity, in the fifth century, to employ these enormous columns led to the decision to raise the entire building to make them fit. It is striking that these columns are not mentioned by the *Liber Pontificalis*, which is always careful to mention particular columns. The eight smaller porphyry columns are mentioned; the spiral columns erected around the tomb of Saint Peter in the Vatican are mentioned; and there are many other examples. Another interesting omission concern the four columns of gilded bronze in the Lateran basilica which many scholars, beginning with Ursula Nilgen,[29] believe to have been a part of the Constantinian *fastigium*.[30] I consider the silence of the *Liber Pontificalis* as a strong argument against their belonging to the Constantinian basilica.[31] But, then, how should the silence on the porphyry columns of the vestibule of the baptistery be explained? Perhaps it has to do with the fact that they are not monolithic: in both columns, the upper part is an addition. But the point is that the addition of these two columns may explain why it was necessary to raise the building. This, in turn, made it necessary to add a second storey to the eight porphyry columns, creating a two-storey *baldacchino*, which, as far as I know, is unique in Late Antique architecture,[32] and which makes the fifth-century phase of the Lateran baptistery a building that has never been copied elsewhere, although it has much in common with the different kinds of octagonal baptisteries all around the Mediterranean.

---

[29] U. Nilgen, 'Das *Fastigium* in der Basilica Constantiniana und vier Bronzesäulen des Lateran', *Römische Quartalschrift für christliche Altertumskunde und Kirchengeschichte* 72 (1977), 1–31.

[30] *LP* 34, 9.

[31] O. Brandt, 'L'improbabile legame delle colonne di bronzo al Laterano con il *fastigium* costantiniano', *RAC* 92 (2016), 117–36.

[32] O. Brandt, *La Croce e il capitello: Le chiese paleocristiane e la monumentalità* (Vatican City, 2016), 60, 66.

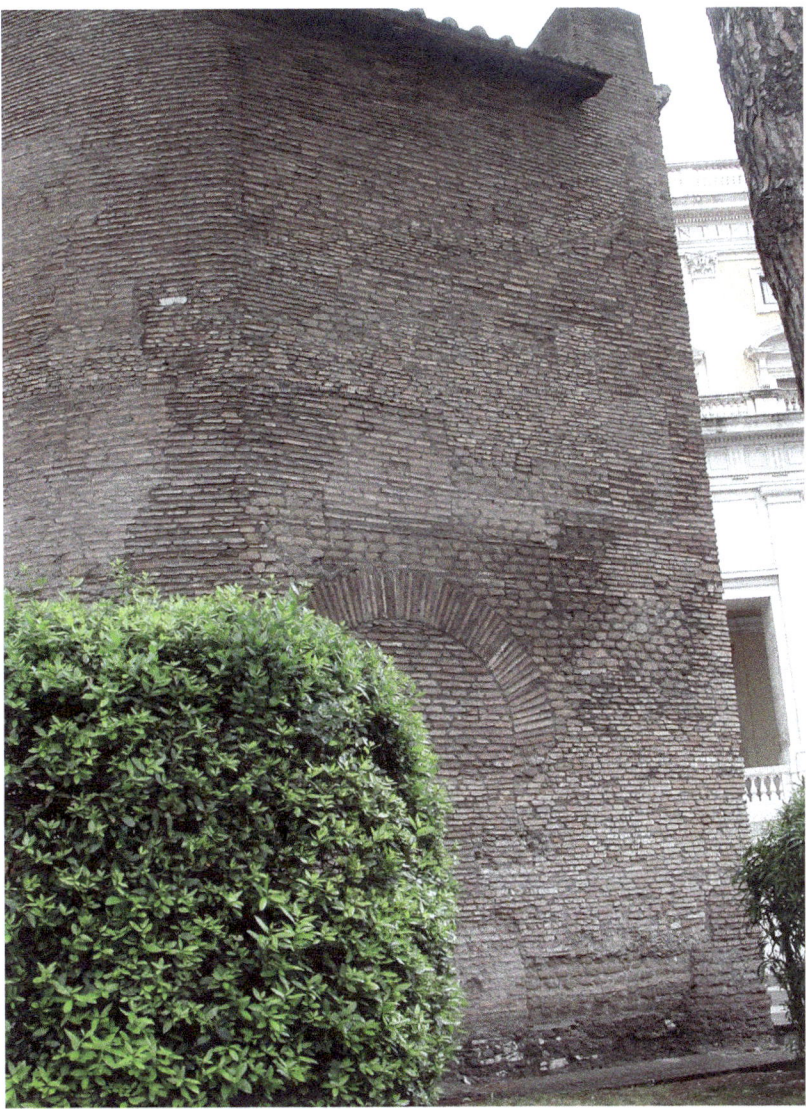

**Fig. 11.13** Outside of the left apse of the vestibule of the Lateran baptistery (By the author).

It seems that the walls of the raised octagon initially ended immediately above the new windows, which means that the deambulatory must have had a flat ceiling. It is possible that the highest part of the outer walls was added in a second (third) phase, in order to add a barrel vault. This would also have consequences for the interpretation of the central octagon above the *baldacchino* and hidden by the seventeenth-century ceiling. This smaller brick octagon has remains of square openings on all sides which are covered by today's roof. It is possible that these openings were originally windows before a barrel vault was added above the octagonal deambulatory.

And, to conclude, I would like to draw the attention to a wall reused in the left apse of the vestibule. It is a wall in *opus vittatum* with a door. The wall is straight, unlike the curved apse of the vestibule, and is aligned with the Via Tusculana. The building technique (Fig. 11.13) seems similar to the pillar in *opus vittatum* which connects the remains of the third-century hall which later became the chapel of San Venanzio to the octagon built under Constantine. The possibility cannot be excluded that this wall with its modest door was part of the original Constantinian arrangement of the area where the vestibule was later built. This wall may give a clue to how to reconstruct this part of the complex and its connection to the structure known as San Venanzio before the construction of the vestibule in the fifth century.

This leads us to a final observation. Much research has been dedicated to the octagon but little to San Venanzio, although it is evident that it preserves traces of phases from the third century to the seventh, when it was transformed into today's chapel.[33] This is where I think further research may give particularly important results.

[33] *LP* 74, 2.

# 12 | The Nymphaeum of Pope Hilarus

PAOLO LIVERANI AND IAN P. HAYNES

Shortly after the middle of the fifth century Pope Hilarus enriched the Lateran baptistery with a series of chapels and oratories of the finest quality: some of these structures were investigated in the 1960s by Giovanni Pelliccioni.[1] They have since been re-examined by Olof Brandt, who identified the remains of the oratory of the Holy Cross.[2] Following recent work by the Lateran Project and a review of the relevant passage of the *Liber Pontificalis* we believe that it is now possible to add to these insights and identify surviving elements of the nymphaeum of Pope Hilarus (Fig. 12.1). The monument was of considerable importance, not only at the time of its creation, but also centuries later when the surviving account was composed. In the life of Hilarus in the *Liber Pontificalis* the pope's work on the complex constitutes his most important architectural achievement, placed as it is at the beginning of the list of papal works and described in rich detail.[3]

The passage concerning the area in front of the oratory reads as follows:

> *Nympheum et triporticum ante oraturium Sanctae Crucis,*
> *ubi sunt columnae mirae magnitudinis quae dicuntur <u>exatonpentaicas</u>,*
> *et concas striatas duas cum columnas purphyreticas raiatas aqua fundentes;*
> *et in medio lacum purphyreticum cum conca raiata in medio aquam*
>     *fundentem,*
> *circumdatam a dextris vel sinistris in medio cancellis aereis et columnis cum*
>     *fastigiis et epistuliis,*

---

[1] G. Pelliccioni, *Le nuove scoperte sulle origini del battistero lateranense* (Memorie della Pontificia Accademia Romana di Archeologia 12.1) (Vatican City, 1973).

[2] O. Brandt, 'Il Battistero lateranense da Costantino a Ilaro: Un riesame degli scavi', *Opuscula Romana* 22–3 (1997–8), 7–65, at pp. 57–60 fig. 82; O. Brandt, 'L'Oratorio della Santa Croce', in P. Liverani (ed.), *Giornata di studio tematica dedicata al Patriarcato Lateranense: Atti della giornata tematica dei Seminari di Archeologia Cristiana (École française de Rome, 10 maggio 2001) (MEFRA* 116, 1) (special issue) (Rome, 2004), 79–93; cf. M. J. Johnson, 'The fifth-century oratory of the Holy Cross at the Lateran in Rome', *Architectura. Zeitschrift für Geschichte der Baukunst* 25, 2 (1995), 128–55; M. Romano, 'L'Oratorio della S. Croce al Laterano: Preliminari di un'indagine archeologica-topografica', *Zeitschrift für Kunstgeschichte* 59, 3 (1996), 337–59; G. Mackie, 'The Santa Croce drawings: A re-examination', *Revue d'art canadienne/Canadian Art Review* 24, 1 (1997), 1–14.

[3] H. Geertman, 'The Builders of the Basilica Maior in Rome', in *Festoen: Opgedragen aan A. N. Zadoks-Josephus Jitta bij haar zeventigste verjaardag* (Scripta archaeologica Groningana 6) (Groningen, 1976), 277–95; repr. in H. Geertman, *Hic fecit basilicam: Studi sul Liber Pontificalis e gli edifici ecclesiastici di Roma da Silvestro a Silverio* (Leuven, 2004), 1–16.

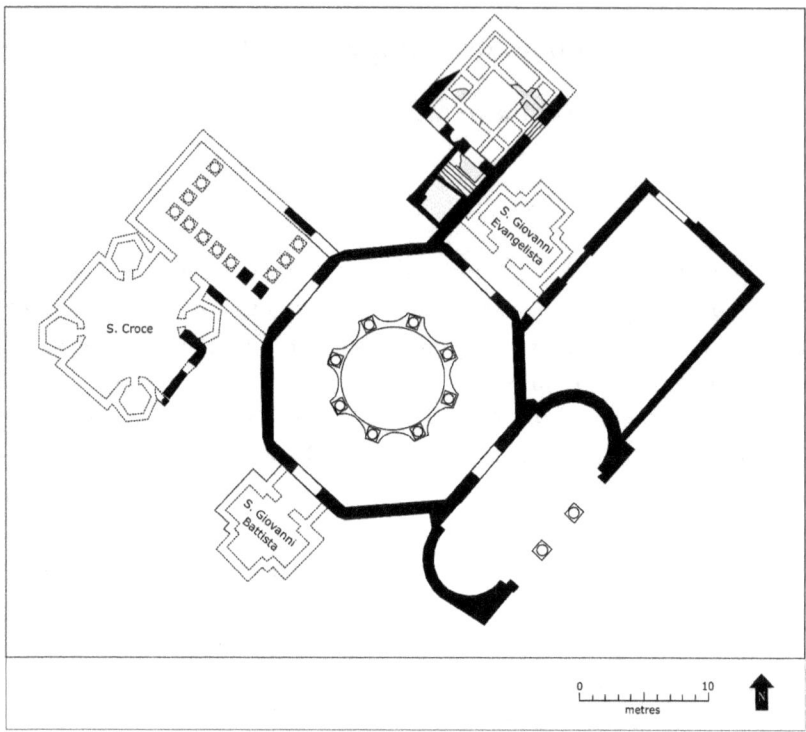

**Fig 12.1** Plan of the area around the baptistery. Intact walls are marked in black. The oratory of Santa Croce lies to the northwest of the baptistery; the area we identify with the nymphaeum of Pope Hilarus lies north-northeast of the baptistery and directly north of the chapel of San Giovanni Evangelista (image: T. Ravasi).

> *undique ornatum ex musibo et columnis Aquitanicis et Tripolitis et purphyreticis.*
>
> In front of the oratory of the Holy Cross, a nymphaeum and a triple portico, where there are columns of marvellous size called hecatonpentaic, and two striated shells, with striped porphyry columns, pouring water; and in the middle a porphyry basin with a striped shell pouring water in the middle, surrounded right, left, and centre by bronze railings and columns with pediments and entablatures, decorated on all sides with mosaics and with Aquitanian, Tripolitan, and porphyry columns.[4]

[4] *LP* 48, 4 according to the text revised by H. Geertman, 'Le biografie del *Liber Pontificalis* dal 311 al 535: Testo e commentario', in H. Geertman (ed.), *Atti del Colloquio Internazionale Il Liber Pontificalis e la storia materiale: Roma, 21–22 febbraio 2002* (Mededelingen van het Nederlands Instituut te Rome, Antiquity 60-1 (2001–2)) (Assen, 2003), 138–355 (repr. in Geertman, *Hic fecit basilicam*, 169–235), trans. in R. Davis, *The Book of Pontiffs (Liber Pontificalis): The Ancient Biographies of the First Ninety Roman Bishops to AD 715* (Liverpool Translated Texts for Historians 6), rev. 3rd edn (Liverpool, 2010), 38, with a few retouches.

A first step in the analysis of this text and its surviving relationship with the archaeology is to distinguish between the nymphaeum and the triple portico.[5] The latter, a little courtyard with porticoes on three sides adjacent to the northwestern side of the baptistery, is documented in views and plans pre-dating the pontificate of Sixtus V, the pope who ordered the destruction of the oratory and the portico remains. The triple portico was connected to the baptistery through the door, which now forms the entrance from Piazza San Giovanni. The importance Hilarus attributed to the oratory was highlighted by an inscription, now lost, that ran on the epistyle of the portico. It was transcribed in the first Sylloge of Lauresham, which is derived from earlier syllogai of the seventh century.[6] Later, the larger part of the inscribed entablature was reused for a kind of *pergula* in the chapel of Saint Thomas, the medieval sacristy of the Lateran basilica, built at the southern end of the entrance portico by Pope John XII in 956.[7]

> *Hic locus olim sordentis cumuli squalore congestus*
> *Sumptu et studio Christi famuli Hilari episcopi, juvante domino*
> *Tanta ruderum mole sublata quantum culminis nunc videtur*
> *ad offerendum Christo Deo munus ornatus et dedicatus est*

> This place, once occupied by the squalor of heap of ruins, with the diligence and at the expense of the servant of Christ, the bishop Hilarus, and with the help of the Lord, after removing an amount of debris as high as the top of the building now you see, was decorated and dedicated to providing a service to Christ God.[8]

Hilarus clearly and emphatically uses the *topos* of the famous inscription on Trajan's Column, celebrating the excavation of the saddle between the Quirinal hill and the Capitol:[9]

> ... ad declarandum quantae altitudinis
> mons et locus tan[tis ope]ribus sit egestus

---

[5] By contrast, R. Valentini and G. Zucchetti, *Codice topografico della città di Roma*, 4 vols. (Fonti per la Storia d'Italia 90) (Rome, 1940–53), II, 241 n. 1 and D. Senekovic, 'S. Giovanni in Fonte und S. Croce in Laterano', in P. C. Claussen, *Die Kirchen der Stadt Rom im Mittelalter 1050-1300, Bd. 2: S. Giovanni in Laterano* (Corpus Cosmatorum II, 2) (Forschungen zur Kunstgeschichte und Christlichen Archäologie 21) (Stuttgart, 2008), 357–93, at p. 357 consider them together as a single structure.

[6] *ICUR* II, 142–3; A. Silvagni, 'Intorno alle più antiche raccolte di iscrizioni classiche e medioevali. I. Nuovo ordinamento delle sillogi epigrafiche di Roma anteriori al secolo XI', *Atti della Pontificia accademia romana di archeologia. Dissertazioni* 15 (1921), 179–229, at pp. 220–3.

[7] Claussen, *Die Kirchen der Stadt Rom*, 62–3.   [8] *ICUR* II, 147–8, no. 12; *ILCV* 977.

[9] *CIL* VI 960; M. Raoss, 'L'iscrizione della colonna Traiana e una epigrafe latina cristiana di Roma del V secolo', in *Seconda miscellanea greca e romana* (Rome, 1968), 399–435.

> ... to declare the height and location of the hill removed for such great structures.

The *topos* of the ruins removed for the new construction has noble models too: we can quote Emperor Honorius' inscription celebrating the restoration of the Aurelian Walls:[10]

> ... ob instauratos urbi(s) aeternae muros portas ac turres egestis inmensis ruderibus.
>
> ... for the restoration of the walls, gates and towers of the eternal city after the removal of immense ruins.

This text should not be understood as mere rhetoric, however; Hilarus built the oratory and portico among the remains of the Severan baths that pre-existed the baptistery, a challenging and technically demanding task.[11]

The decoration of the triple portico and the nymphaeum as described is luxurious and deserves attention. The columns called *exatonpentaicas* (that is, '150 colours') were carved in the rare *Breccia Verde* of Wadi Hammamat from the Egyptian eastern desert. In contemporary Rome, there are very few examples of this marble and no entire columns.[12] Ancient sources offer several names for this marble;[13] all allude to the large number of different colours in its composition. The Aquitanian marble – called *Bianco e Nero antico* – came from the Aubert quarries in the Pyrenees and was also used for imperial burials, as in the case of the sarcophagus of Emperor Athanasius I (491–518) in Constantinople.[14] The *Tripolitis* marble, on the other hand, is never mentioned elsewhere, leading Raniero Gnoli[15] to hypothesise that the text is a mistake for *Hierapolitis*: in which case the marble would be alabaster.[16] This possibility is interesting because we could identify four of these columns with

---

[10] *CIL* VI, 1188 = 31257. Cf. also *AE* 2004, 1798; *AE* 1946, 61; *AE* 1946, 107 = 111.

[11] O. Brandt and F. Guidobaldi, 'Il Battistero lateranense: Nuove interpretazioni delle fasi strutturali', *RAC* 84 (2008), 189–282, at p. 282 attribute the inscription to the baptistery, but the reasons behind this attribution are unclear to us.

[12] F. Corsi, *Delle pietre antiche: trattato*, 3rd edn (Rome, 1845), 199–200.

[13] R. Gnoli, 'Su alcuni marmi e pietre da decorazione usate nell'antichità', *La parola del passato* 21 (1966), 41–55, at pp. 46–8; U. Gnoli, *Marmora Romana* (Rome, 1988), 90, 117–20, 208, 232; J. A. Harrell, V. M. Brown and L. Lazzarini, 'Breccia verde antica: Sources, petrology, and ancient uses', in L. Lazzarini (ed.), *Interdisciplinary Studies on Ancient Stone: Proceedings of the Sixth International Conference of the Association for the Study of Marble and Other Stones in Antiquity: Venice, June 15–18, 2000* (Padua, 2002), 207–18; P. Liverani, 'Marmor', in *Reallexikon für Antike und Christentum* (Stuttgart, 2010), XXIV, 208–46, at pp. 214–15, no. 15.

[14] Const. Porph., *De cerimoniis* 2.42, ed. Reiske and Heinrich 642B; P. Grierson, 'The Tombs and Obits of the Byzantine Emperors (337–1042)', *Dumbarton Oaks Papers* 16 (1962), 1–63, at p. 45; Gnoli, *Marmora Romana*, 197–8; Liverani, 'Marmor', 210 n.2.

[15] Gnoli, *Marmora Romana*, 42–6.  [16] Liverani, 'Marmor', 215–16, no. 18.

those now displayed on the altar of the Colonna chapel in the Lateran basilica with their characteristic bands of cream and brown.[17] They came from the above-mentioned chapel dedicated to Saint Thomas,[18] where they supported the entablature with the inscription of Hilarus.

At the centre of the triple portico was a porphyry basin that Carlo Gasparri thinks could be the one used in a fountain of the gardens of the Quirinal palace.[19] In the early nineteenth century it was brought to the Vatican Museums, and a few years later it arrived at Santa Maria Maggiore, where it was employed by the architect Valadier as a baptismal font (Fig. 12.2).[20] Other features of the description are less clear: probably the 'striped' porphyry columns are fluted or even spiral-fluted columns. It is more difficult to determine what is meant by the striated or 'striped' shells. Nevertheless, a marble vessel now in the Galleria dei Candelabri of the Vatican Museums may, however, offer a clue; it is shaped like a shell and its interior is characterised by pronounced ridges running top to bottom.[21]

Having considered the text of the *Liber Pontificalis* and the decorative elements, it is important to consider the structural archaeology in the area of the baptistery. Following Olof Brandt's proposal, we can identify the structures of the oratory of the Holy Cross. Immediately to the north of the baptistery, there is a structure that is quite difficult to understand but worthy of attention.[22] To aid analysis of this structure, this area has been extensively surveyed as part of the Lateran Project. Laser scanning here with two different systems, a Leica HDS and the Faro Focus, has had the merit of allowing us to record the structural remains with sub-millimetre accuracy in three dimensions. The point cloud generated through this process has been edited to remove later features (Fig. 12.3).

From this it is possible to see that the structure consists of a couple of rooms of the pre-existing Severan bath lying parallel to the chapel of Saint

---

[17] L. Barroero, 'La Basilica dal Cinquecento ai nostri giorni', in C. Pietrangeli (ed.), *San Giovanni in Laterano* (Florence, 1990), 144–255, at pp. 154–5, fig. at p. 203.

[18] Claussen, *Die Kirchen der Stadt Rom*, 62–3.

[19] R. Delbrück, *Antike Porphyrwerke* (Berlin, 1932), 186–8 plate 83; C. Gasparri and L. Guerrini, *Il Palazzo del Quirinale* (Rome, 1985), 14; P. Liverani, 'Dal Quirinale al Vaticano', *Bollettino d'Arte* 83 (1994), 11–26, at p. 16.

[20] A. Valentini, *La Patriarcale Basilica Liberiana* (Rome, 1839), 20; Corsi, *Delle pietre antiche*, 306 L. Barroero, 'La Basilica dal Cinquecento all'Ottocento', in C. Pietrangeli (ed.), *Santa Maria Maggiore a Roma* (Florence, 1988), 214–59, at p. 254, fig. at pp. 310–1.

[21] G. Lippold, *Die Skulpturen des Vatikanischen Museums* (Berlin, 1965), 340 n. 84, plate 148. The vessel was found on the Aventine and has no association with the Lateran site. At 0.585–0.61 m in diameter it is also probably smaller than the shells described in the *Liber Pontificalis* entry.

[22] Some notes in O. Brandt, 'Strutture del IV secolo per la lavanda dei piedi in due battisteri romani', *Arte medievale* 2, 1 (2003), 137–44, at pp. 141–3.

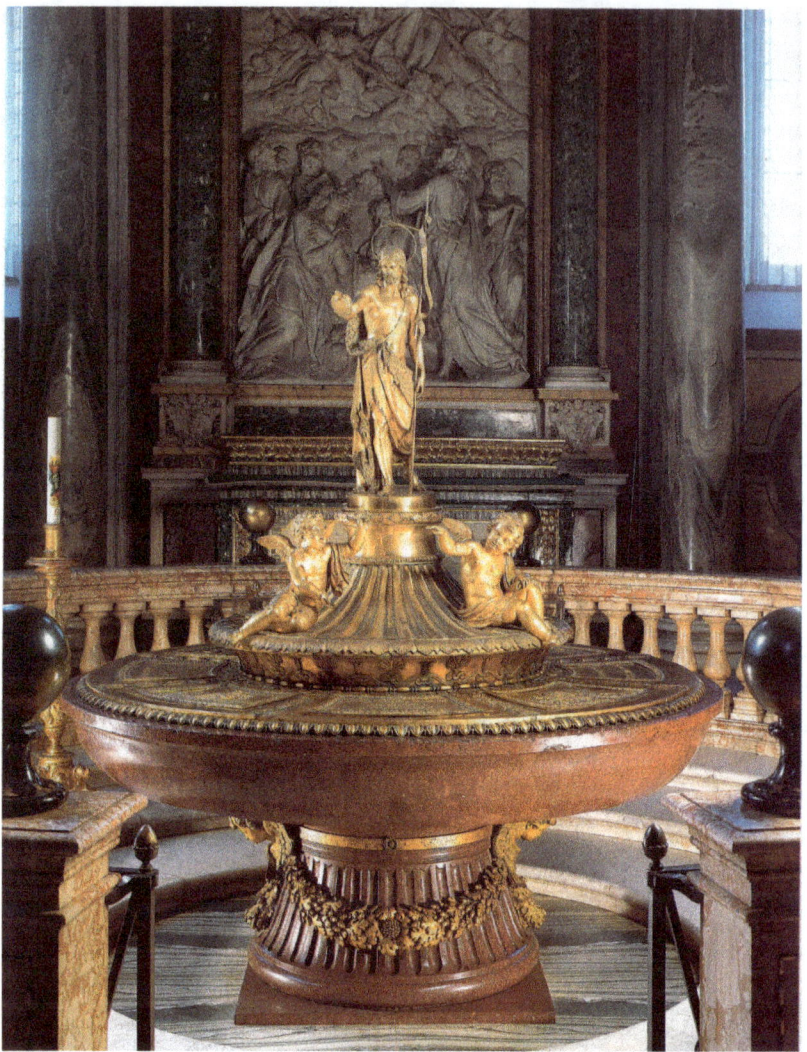

**Fig 12.2** Porphyry basin used as baptismal font, Santa Maria Maggiore (photo P. Liverani).

John the Evangelist. In Late Antiquity the *suspensurae* of the bathrooms were destroyed, thus lowering the floor level. A trapezoidal cistern was built in half of the southwestern room,[23] immediately to the northeast of which is a series of steps ending in a sloping mosaic floor (Fig. 12.4).[24] The mosaic

[23] Pelliccioni, *Le nuove scoperte*, room '*i*'.
[24] Pelliccioni, *Le nuove scoperte*, fig. 56 'stair' *s*; fig. 129 s; fig. 134; at p. 88 n.10, Pelliccioni dedicates only few lines to this structure, with a complete misunderstanding: he interprets it as a stair connecting the rooms to the northeast at the level of the baptistery; furthermore he believes (108) that the cistern (*m*1) destroyed the stair during the Middle Ages.

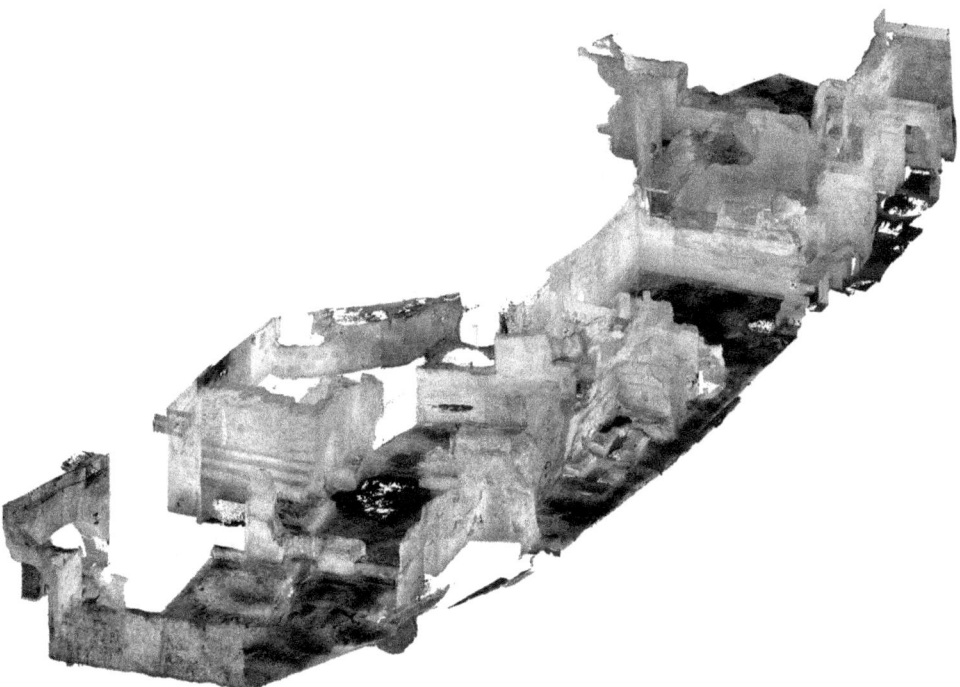

**Fig 12.3** Laser-scan point-cloud data rotated to view from northeast with later intrusive features digitally removed (Alex Turner, Lateran Project).

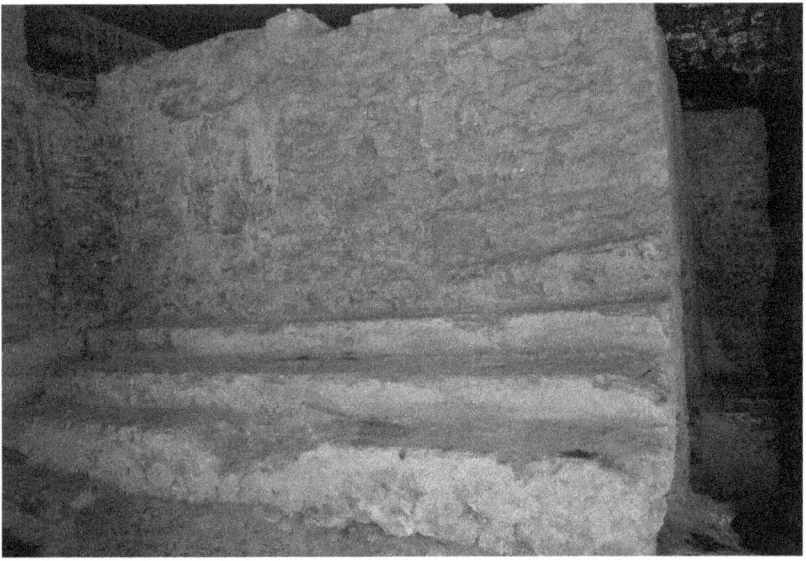

**Fig 12.4** Cistern, fountain and 'steps' viewed from the northeast (Sabrina Amaducci, Lateran Project).

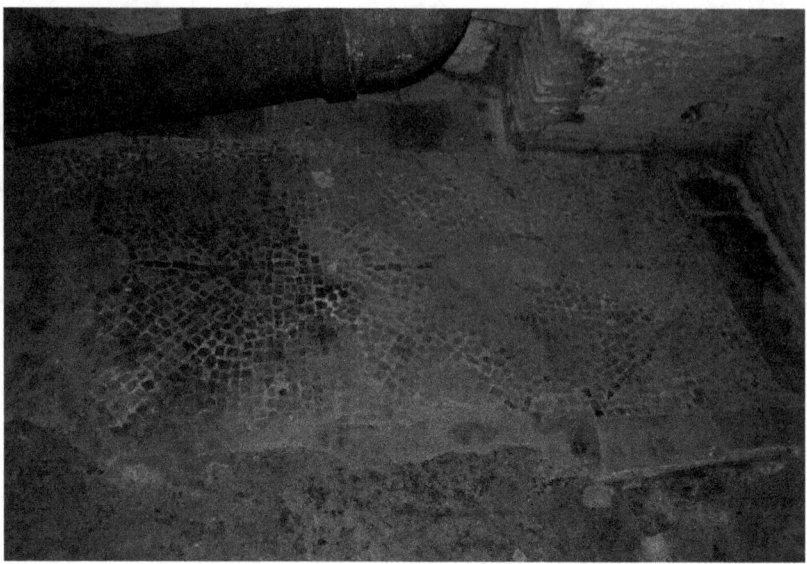

Fig. 12.5 Mosaic floor positioned at base of 'steps' shown in Fig. 12.4 (Sabrina Amaducci, Lateran Project).

(Fig. 12.5)[25] has been dated between the fifth and sixth centuries.[26] If we consider the dimension of treads and risers, it is evident that these are not the steps of a staircase, but of a cascading fountain fed from the tank through a duct passing through its northeastern wall. The second room,[27] however, does not seem to have changed in plan, although its northeastern limit cannot be determined. Its pavement is in *opus sectile*[28] according to a pattern with white marble tile framed in green porphyry strips (to the east) and red porphyry (Fig. 12.6), delimited by bands of white marble. At the centre of the room is a circular masonry foundation,[29] while in the south-western wall is a niche covered with marble[30] between two doors (Fig. 12.7). The southeastern door[31] opens to the sloping mosaic floor of the fountain

---

[25] Pelliccioni, *Le nuove scoperte*, fig. 134b, 135; Brandt, 'Strutture del IV secolo', fig. 9.

[26] F. Guidobaldi and A. Guiglia Guidobaldi, *Pavimenti marmorei di Roma dal IV al IX secolo* (Vatican City, 1983), 356–60 dated it to the fifth century; later, A. Guiglia Guidobaldi, 'Pavimenti marmorei a Roma e nel suburbio nel secoli IV–VII', in M. Cecchelli (ed.), *Materiali e tecniche dell'edilizia paleocristiana a Roma* (Rome, 2001), 191–202, at pp. 198–9 fig. 6 lowered the date to the sixth century.

[27] Pelliccioni, *Le nuove scoperte*, room 'l'.     [28] Pelliccioni, *Le nuove scoperte*, 89.

[29] Pelliccioni, *Le nuove scoperte*, 89.

[30] Pelliccioni, *Le nuove scoperte*, 89 fig. 56 *f*, fig. 129 f, plate V *f*.

[31] Closed at a later, unknown, date.

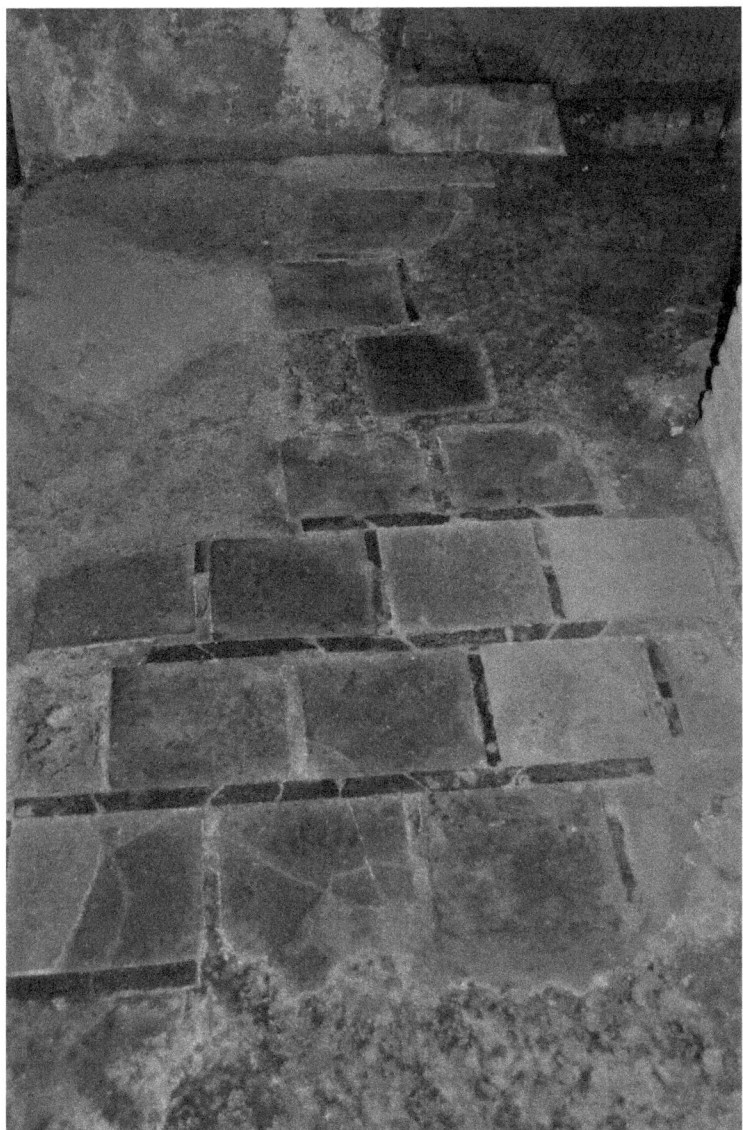

**Fig. 12.6** *Opus sectile* floor (Sabrina Amaducci, Lateran Project).

we have just described. The niche housed a further small fountain: the water flowed through a lead pipe, now lost: only the spoliation trench remains.[32]

It is very tempting to suggest that these features are what is left of the nymphaeum of Hilarus, although the system of drainage for the water of

---

[32] Pelliccioni, *Le nuove scoperte*, 56 fig. 63 O; Brandt, 'Strutture del IV secolo', fig. 10.

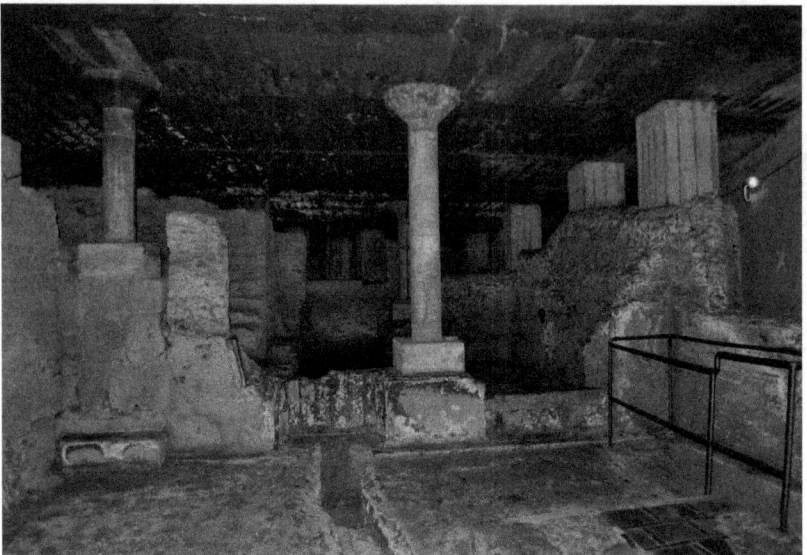

Fig. 12.7 Structures associated with the putative nymphaeum viewed from the northeast. The marble covered niche is immediately left of the modern support column shown in the centre of the picture (Sabrina Amaducci, Lateran Project).

the cascading fountain and the connection of rooms to the higher level of the portico and baptistery are not clear. Here we should acknowledge work done by colleagues in the early stages of the Lateran Project.[33] Ground-penetrating radar survey revealed something of the complexity of features underneath the nymphaeum. Without excavation, it is difficult to ascertain the role or date of all of these anomalies, some of which may be related to engineering for the Severan bath complex, but it is probable that some of them represent changes introduced to serve the later water features here.

Two more details may usefully be considered. The first concerns the circular foundation in the middle of the second room. This could plausibly be interpreted as the base for one of the two *conchas striatas* mentioned by *Liber Pontificalis*. The second concerns the tank that lies in the south-eastern part of the second room. This rests on a body of earth that rises

---

[33] V. Gaffney, S. Piro, I. P. Haynes, M. Watters, S. Wilkes, M. Lobb and D. Zamuner, 'Three-Tier Visualization of San Giovanni in Laterano, Rome, Italy', *12th International Conference on Ground Penetrating Radar, June 16–19, 2008, Birmingham, UK*. Proceedings Expanded Abstract Volume. (2008), http://www.eurogpr.org/vn2/images/documents/members/B2857%20GPR%20brochure%20final.pdf.

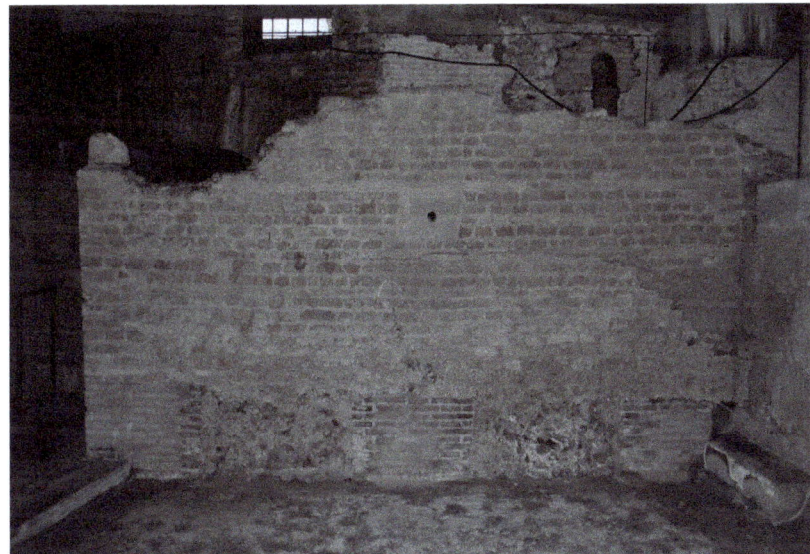

**Fig. 12.8** The northwest wall of the twelfth/thirteenth-century fountain, seen from the northeast (Sabrina Amaducci, Lateran Project).

about 70 cm above the *opus sectile* floor. It also has a duct for a fountain piercing its northwestern wall (Fig. 12.8). This suggests an interesting example of functional and topographical continuity; it is likely that this water feature replaced the putative nymphaeum fountain in or around the twelfth century. The building technique of the later tank is typical for the twelfth–thirteenth centuries, while inside the cistern of the putative nymphaeum a funerary inscription of Theodora, dating between the eleventh and twelfth centuries, was discovered.[34]

---

[34] Pelliccioni, *Le nuove scoperte*, 108 fig. 166; G. Spinola, 'Sculture, rilievi, decorazione, architettonica, iscrizioni e reperti ceramici', in P. Liverani (ed.), *Laterano 1: Scavi sotto la Basilica di S. Giovanni*, vol. I: *Materiali* (Vatican City, 1998), 17–114, 97, no. 466, fig. 343.

## 13 | Examples of Medieval Construction Techniques in the Basilica of San Giovanni in Laterano

LIA BARELLI

We should start this chapter by noting that the study of construction techniques cannot be separated from either the study of the design or the actual construction of the buildings in question, as they are closely related. When considering these two aspects from a historiographical point of view, they both generally require reconstruction, given that the direct evidence of the former rarely survives, while, with regard to the latter, the original state of a building has almost always been modified over time by alterations that are, in some instances, quite radical.

In this particular case, the basilica of San Giovanni in Laterano was altered many times over the course of the Middle Ages, and not all of these alterations are clearly documented and/or recognisable.[1] On this occasion, we have decided to examine two such instances – the portico built by Pope Sergius II (844–7) in front of the east façade, and the two towers placed at the sides of the northern end of the transept – as they can be considered typical examples, from a methodological point of view, of construction techniques. These cases are extremely distant one from the other, so to speak, both in terms of their chronology – with one dating from the early Middle Ages and the other from the late Middle Ages – and in terms of their material state, as the portico has been completely demolished, while the towers remain exceptionally well preserved.

The portico is a perfect example of a hermeneutic circle, where indirect sources – particularly visual representations – demonstrate the use of construction techniques that were typical of the period in which they were carried out, an in-depth knowledge of which allows us, in turn, to interpret those same sources more precisely, resulting in an improved reconstruction of all that has been lost. As far as the towers are concerned, a direct analysis of their material evidence makes it possible to date major

---

[1] For the general chronology, see mainly P. Lauer, *Le palais de Latran: Étude historique et archéologique* (Paris, 1911); R. Krautheimer, S. Corbett and R. Malmstrom, 'S. Giovanni in Laterano', *CBCR* V, 1–96; P. C. Claussen, *Die Kirchen der stadt Rom im Mittelalter 1050–1300, Bd. 2: S. Giovanni in Laterano* (Corpus Cosmatorum II, 2) (Forschungen zur Kunstgeschichte und Christlichen Archäologie 21) (Stuttgart, 2008).

phases of reconstruction that were carried out on the entire basilica more precisely, and to associate them with written sources.

## The Sergian Portico

Evidence of the construction of the Sergian portico[2] is found in the *Liber Pontificalis*:

> [the Pontiff] et aliud quidam opus ante fores huius venerandae ecclesiae valde optimum fecit, quia sacra pridem quae latebant populus limina summo studio omnibus manifesta constituit cum pulchri decoris ibidem arcos a fundamentis construxit; quos etiam variis picturis nitide decoravit.[3]

In other words, Sergius had a portico of arches built in front of the basilica's façade, replacing an earlier structure of which nothing is known, except that it obstructed the view of the entrance doors.[4] This portico – boasting *pulcher decor* and decorated with colourful paintings, as was to be expected given the importance of the building – is consistent with the Carolingian architecture of Rome, when porticoes and *quadriportici* were used to add grandeur to religious buildings, in keeping with an architectural programme that was part of a strategy to assert the papacy's authority.[5]

---

[2] With regard to the eastern façade of the Lateran basilica and its alterations in the Middle Ages, see, in general, V. Hoffmann, 'Die Fassade von S. Giovanni in Laterano 313/14–1649', *Römisches Jahrbuch für Kunstgeschichte* 17 (1978), 1–46); *CBCR* V, 1–96; I. Herklotz, 'Der mittelalterliche Fassadenportikus der Lateranbasilika und seine Mosaiken: Kunst und Propaganda am Ende des 12. Jahrhunderts', *RJBH* 25 (1989): 25–95; Blaauw, *CD*, 170–3, 213–15; I. Herklotz, *Gli eredi di Costantino: Il papato, il Laterano e la propaganda visiva nel XII secolo* (La corte dei papi 6) (Rome, 2000), 159–209, 161–3; Claussen, *Die Kirchen der stadt Rom*, 38–92.

[3] *LP* II, 91.

[4] The existence of a structure in front of the Lateran basilica prior to the work of Pope Sergius II is not addressed on this occasion, apart from some passing mentions. There is no evidence to either confirm or refute the possibility of a quadriporticus having been present in the early Christian age. Only the Lives of Pope Hadrian I (*LP* I, 507) and Leo III (*LP* II, 2) mention 'quadriportici' in the plural, leading Krautheimer, Corbett and Malmstrom, *CBCR* V, 1–96, at p. 89, to attribute them to the Lateran palace. Traces of wall joints (piers?) near the colonnades of the central nave can still be found on the outside of the façade, as shown in Borromini's drawings as well. Hoffmann, 'Die Fassade' and Krautheimer, Corbett and Malmstrom, *CBCR* V, 1–96, at p. 89 suppose that they can be dated to Constantine, while Krautheimer and Corbett, in referring to the same piers, posit that there may have been a cross-vaulted propylon in front of the façade. On the other hand, Blaauw, *CD*, 171 supposes the possibility of a relatively closed-off type of portico, such as the one found in Sant'Andrea in Catabarbara.

[5] See L. Barelli, 'I quadriportici nell'architettura religiosa della Roma carolingia (secoli VIII e IX)', in F. Cantatore, A. Cerutti Fusco and P. Cimbolli Spagnesi (eds.), *Giornate di studio in onore di Claudio Tiberi* (Rome, 2012), 71–80. There were porticoes in front of the following Carolingian churches in Rome: Santa Maria in Cosmedin, Sant'Anastasia, Santi Nereo e Achilleo, Santa

The first major reconstruction programme on the portico took place when Pope John XII (955–64) closed off the southern section to create the chapel of Saint Thomas, to be used as a private sacristy by the pontiff. Luckily, this alteration saved the Sergian walls from demolition, as they ended up being incorporated in the chapel, following an even greater alteration in 1187–98. At this time, the section corresponding to the central nave and the northern aisles was replaced by a portico featuring Ionic columns with architraves, the work of the *marmorarius* Nicolaus de Angelo.[6] The surviving walls dating from the early Middle Ages were brought back to light in 1647 by Francesco Borromini, who eliminated the chapel of Saint Thomas, only to be demolished once and for all in 1732 when Alessandro Galilei's portico was built.

In 1978 Volker Hoffmann became the first to realise that a portion of the Sergian portico had been incorporated in the southern section of the portico, as shown by the drawings done by Borromini and his assistants following the demolition of the chapel walls (see Figs 13.1 and 13.4).[7] This section featured three large arches on two columns and a large pier that separated the arches from the portico built by Nicolaus, all elements that led this scholar to conjecture that the front of the portico consisted of three triple archways separated by large piers. His reconstruction, though not universally accepted,[8] was later corroborated by unmistakable similarities with the portico built, though admittedly on a smaller scale, in the basilica of the Santi Quattro Coronati by the pope who succeeded Sergius II, Leo IV (847–55): a building whose early medieval features were recently reconstructed thanks to historical research and archaeological excavations (Fig. 13.2).[9]

---

Maria in Domnica, San Marco, San Giorgio al Velabro, Santa Francesca Romana, with *quadriportici* in the churches of Santa Prassede, Santi Quattro Coronati (which also had a portico) and possibly San Silvestro in Capite and San Martino ai Monti.

[6] His signature was on the portico's northern pier, as shown by Ciampini's engraving. See Blaauw, *CD*, 214; Herklotz, *Gli eredi di Costantino*, 161; Claussen, *Die Kirchen der stadt Rom*, 77.

[7] Hoffmann, 'Die Fassade'. With regard to this part of the portico, see also Blaauw, *CD*, 170–1, 213–15; Herklotz, *Gli eredi di Costantino*, 161–3, where other contributions by the same author are summarised, as in Herklotz, 'Der mittelalterliche Fassadenportikus'; Claussen, *Die Kirchen der stadt Rom*, 60–9.

[8] Herklotz, 'Der mittelalterliche Fassadenportikus', 28, no. 7 surmises that it consisted of eleven arches, a hypothesis supported by Blaauw, *CD*, 171. In Herklotz, *Gli eredi di Costantino*, however, Hoffmann's proposal is backed.

[9] The similarities between the two porticoes had already been pointed out in Barelli, 'I quadriportici'. The reconstruction of the early medieval portico of the Santi Quattro Coronati, now incorporated in a building that was reconstructed in the seventeenth century, is based primarily on traces that can be observed on the façade thanks to gaps in the plaster, and on arches in the northern area rendered visible inside in 2003: see L. Barelli, 'Note lateranensi e note al testo', in M. Morbidelli, *L'abside di S. Giovanni in Laterano: Una vicenda controversa* (I libri di Viella. Arte) (Rome, 2010), 15–22; L. Barelli, 'Un portico altomedievale fra i disegni di antichità di Alberto Alberti: Confronto tra dati diretti e indiretti', *Palladio* 25, 49 (2012), 5–24. This

Examples of Medieval Construction Techniques 253

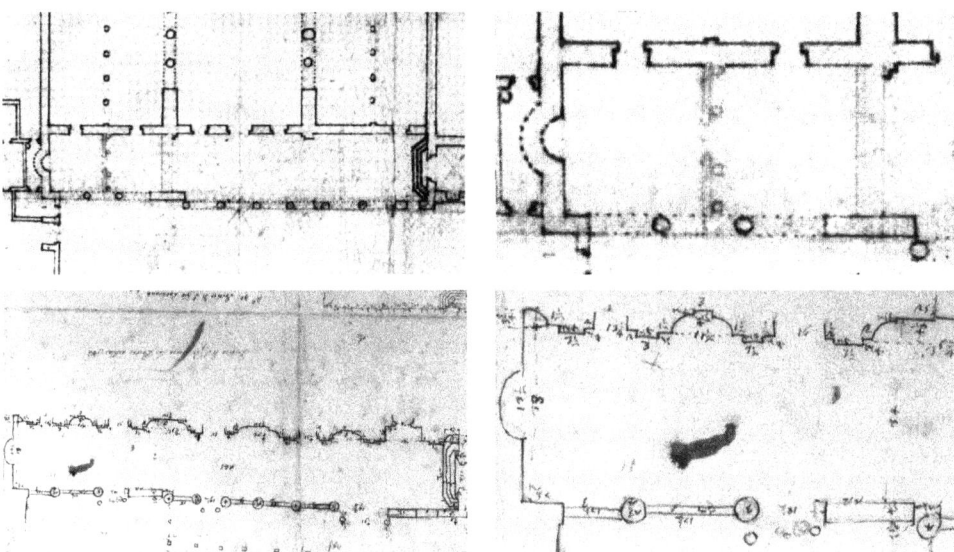

**Fig. 13.1** Above, details with the east portico and south area of the same, from the plan of the Lateran complex of Francesco Borromini, c. 1647, Vienna, Albertina, IT AZ 383a; down, the same details from the plan drawn by Giuseppe Marchetti for the Holy Year 1725, Windsor, Royal Library, inv. RCIN 911005 (Royal Collection Trust/© Her Majesty Queen Elizabeth II 2019).

The portico of the Santi Quattro Coronati basilica – part of a massive reconstruction effort undertaken by Pope Leo on the complex of that name, located on the Caelian hill – led into a grand quadriporticus, which itself led into the basilica. Outside, at the north end, it rested on an imposing substructure of tufa blocks, while a tall and imposing tower soared above it, though the tower actually sat in the middle of the quadriporticus' back wing. It was only one storey high, covered by a mono-pitched roof, approximately 5.5 m deep and 25 m long, while the height was not less than 7 m. The façade featured arches resting on columns that were divided by four large piers into a central triple archway and two side double archways;[10] an arch on the short northern side looked out over the valley below, and there was probably a matching arch on the south side.

arrangement, a hypothetical reconstruction lacking in exact measurements that modifies the hypothesis put forward in R. Krautheimer and S. Corbett, 'SS. Quattro Coronati', *CBCR* IV, 1–34, had already been put forward in 1995 (see L. Barelli and M. Falconi, 'I Ss. Quattro Coronati a Roma: Nuove acquisizioni sugli edifici annessi alla basilica carolingia', *Palladio* 8, 16 (1995), 6–14).

[10] In actual fact, the corner piers consist of the side walls of the portico, which turn in the façade, creating two antae.

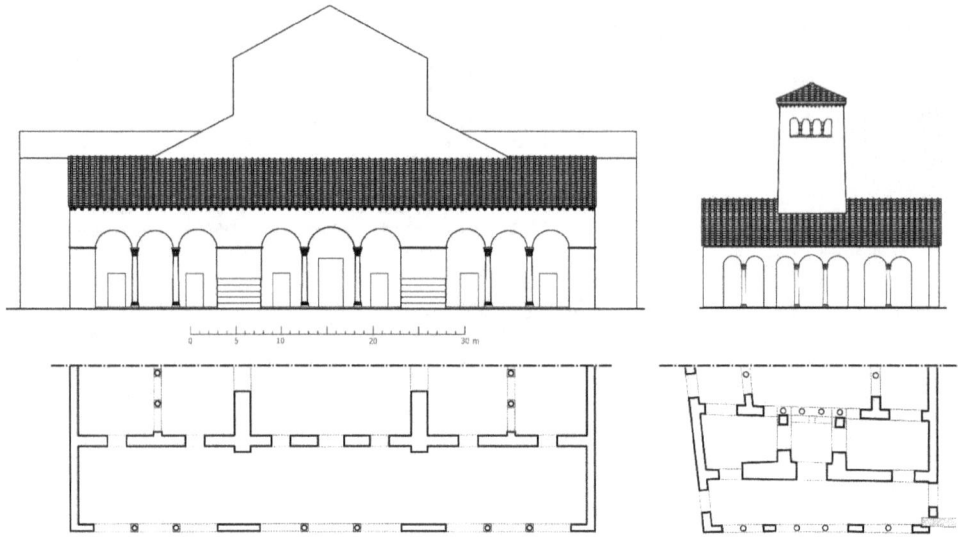

**Fig. 13.2** On the left, hypothetical reconstruction of the portico of Sergius II (844–7) in front of Lateran basilica, plan and elevation; on the right, hypothetical reconstruction of the portico of Leo IV (847–55) in the complex of the Santi Quattro Coronati at Rome (Lia Barelli, 2016).

A drawing by Alberto Alberti, datable to between approximately 1575 and 1579–80, shows that the columns had Corinthian or composite capitals and bases decorated with moulding, all made of marble materials that were almost certainly *spolia*, as was the custom in the early Middle Ages. The northern double archway and the adjacent pier were wider than the matching elements to the south, a difference explained by the need to compensate for asymmetries in the layout caused by the use of earlier structures as foundations. The triple archway's central opening was wider than the two flanking openings which, in turn, were wider than those of the double archways so as to highlight the central axis, in accordance with a design frequently employed both in Late Antiquity and in the early Middle Ages.[11] The portico was designed in Alexandrine feet (1 AF = 30.8 cm), probably using a square module 12.5 AF (385 cm) wide[12]. The

---

[11] See Barelli, 'I quadriportici'.

[12] On the use of the Alexandrine foot in Rome, see, in general *CBCR* I, 2–12, 38; in terms of this structure, and as regards its proportions as well, see L. Barelli, 'Il complesso dei Ss. Quattro Coronati a Roma in età carolingia', in F. Guidobaldi and A. Guiglia Guidobaldi (eds.), *Ecclesiae Urbis: Atti del Congresso internazionale di studi sulle chiese di Roma (IV–X secolo) (Roma 4–10 settembre 2000)* (Studi di antichità cristiana 59) (Vatican City, 2002), 979–92; Barelli, 'Un portico altomedievale'.

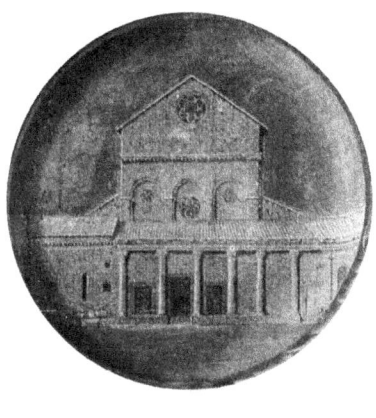
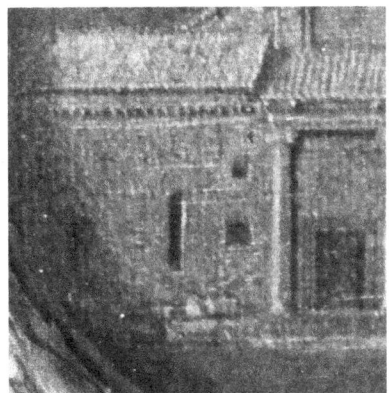
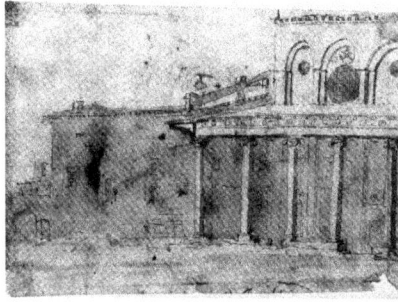
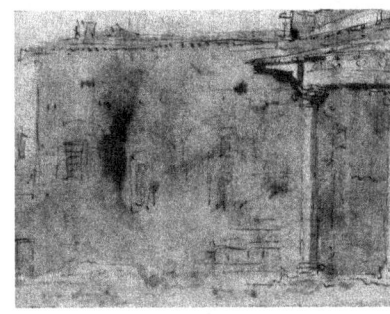

Fig. 13.3 Above, Lateran baptistery. Fresco by Andrea Sacchi depicting the façade of the Lateran basilica (c. 1644) and detail of the same; below, anonymous sketch of the southern section of the east portico of the Lateran basilica during the demolition of the chapel of Saint Thomas in 1647, Düsseldorf, Kunstmuseum, Graphische Sammlung, inv. FP4309 (Kunstpalast – Horst Kolberg/ARTOTHEK).

triple archway, for example, is exactly 2 x 12.5 AF (770 cm) wide. As for the height, the distance from the ground to the point where shafts and capitals met was equal to one module, while there is no certain information on the overall height, though it could have been two modules.

A comparison of the two porticoes not only provides support for Hoffmann's hypothesis; it also makes it possible to strengthen certain points. One can reasonably suppose that the Lateran portico also had openings on its shorter sides and that the apse of the chapel of Saint Thomas (10 feet wide) could have been inserted in the existing gap.[13] One can also assume that the entire triple archway, and particularly the central opening, was wider than the side archways, a supposition supported

---

[13] Evidence of side openings in porticoes of the Carolingian age, though in the form of double archways, can also be found in the churches of Sant'Anastasia and Santi Nereo e Achilleo, which had already been linked to each other in *CBCR* I, 61.

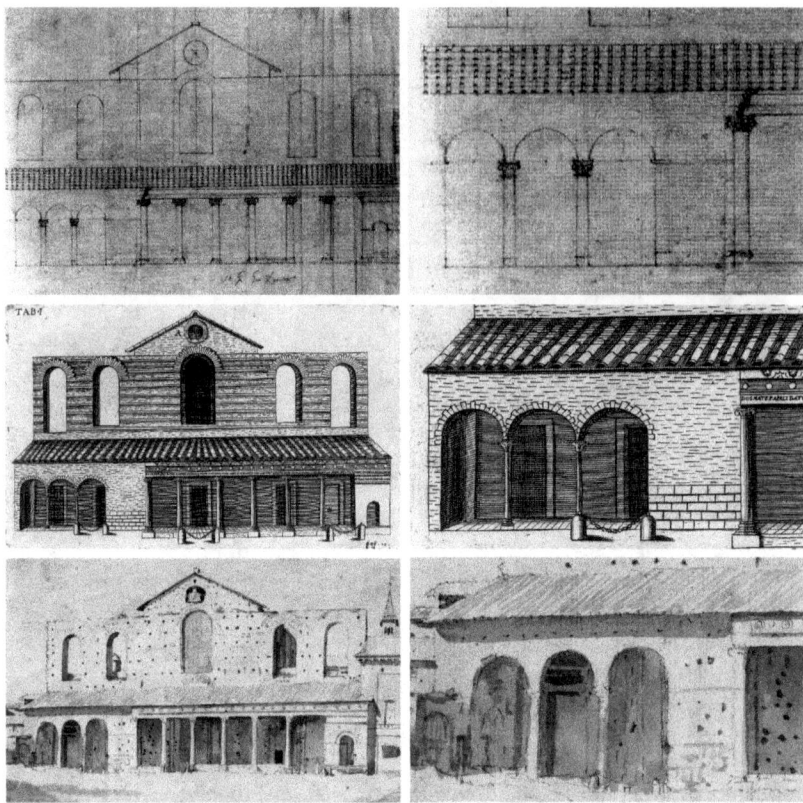

Fig. 13.4 Above, detail of survey of the east façade of the Lateran complex designed by Francesco Righi, *c.* 1647, and detail of the same, Vienna, Albertina, IT AZ 386; in the middle, engraving of the Lateran basilica façade and detail (from Ciampini, *De sacris Aedificiis a Constantino Magno constructis*, table I, p. 10); below, view from east of the Lateran basilica of Hendrik van Lint, datable between 1700 and 1732, and detail, Berlin, Kupferstichkabinett – Staatliche Museen zu Berlin, inv. KdZ 14268 (© 2019. Photo: Scala, Firenze).

by the extremely precise measurements indicated by the architect Giuseppe Marchetti on a plan presented for the Jubilee Year of 1725 (Fig. 13.1). This plan shows the total length of the portico plotted in Roman palms (1 RP = 22.34 cm), 245 RP,[14] and the respective widths of the three arches, moving from south to north, as 17⅔, 17¼ and 18½ RP, the diameters of the columns as 2¾ and 3 RP, the dimensions of the pier as 4 x 22 RP and

---

[14] For Marchetti, the internal width of the portico, given that one Roman palm = 22.34 cm, would be 54.73 m. The size of the façade varies from one author to another. In Krautheimer, Corbett and Malmstrom, *CBCR* V, 1–96, at p. 52, the external measurement is given as 56.05 m, while at p. 76 it is listed as 55.38 m (!), both measurements that prove incompatible with that of Marchetti, once the thickness of the outside walls is subtracted.

the internal width of the southernmost anta/pier as 7½ RP. It follows that the internal length of the preserved section of the Sergian portico was 88⅔ RP; if we apply this measurement symmetrically to the northern section, the space left for the central triple archway (67¾ RP) is significantly greater than that available for the side triple archways (59⅙ RP), as is the case in the basilica of the Santi Quattro Coronati. The module used could be 16 AF, corresponding to the width of the pier (22 RP = 491.5 cm; 16 AF = 492.8 cm). Nevertheless, we will analyse these measurements at a later date.

In terms of the formal differences found at the basilica of the Santi Quattro Coronati, the side triple archways were replaced by double archways, but this can be explained by the smaller size of the façade.

It is interesting to note that the side doors to the quadriporticus of the Santi Quattro Coronati align with the double archways. Perhaps as regards the Lateran portico built by Sergius II, their purpose may not have been to make the doors visible but rather to highlight their position, showing them to be perfectly framed by the openings. Were this the case, then inferences could be drawn for clarifying the positioning and the number of the doors on the façade of the Lateran basilica, something that remains unexplained to this day, though this is another topic that lies outside the scope of this chapter.[15]

The analogies between the two porticos lead us to suppose that they were built using the same construction techniques as well. Information regarding this aspect is provided by visual sources, the most useful of which can be divided into two groups: one dating from before the demolition of the chapel of Saint Thomas in 1647 and a later group that was, however, prior to the demolition of the entire portico in 1732.

The first group (Fig. 13.3) includes: a medallion frescoed in the Lateran baptistery by Andrea Sacchi (c. 1644) and a sketch of the façade by an anonymous hand, preserved in Düsseldorf. It should be noted that the proportions shown in the medallion are altered, while the sketch imprecisely depicts and places the various architectural features.

The second group (Fig. 13.4) includes a survey drawing of the façade by Francesco Righi, an architect who collaborated with Borromini; an engraving published in 1693 by Giovanni Ciampini in his *De Sacris Aedificiis a Constantino Magno Constructis*; and a painting by the Dutch artist Hendrik van Lint, datable to some point in the first thirty years of the

---

[15] The basilica is thought to have had only three doors aligned with the central nave (Hoffmann, 'Die Fassade', 32, 34–5; Krautheimer, Corbett and Malmstrom, *CBCR* V, 1–96, at pp. 80–1, where the hypothesis is not confirmed). In actual fact, the number remains uncertain.

eighteenth century.[16] This last source in particular provides some very important information, given that the underlying pencil drawing was almost certainly done using a *camera obscura*, an optical instrument used to trace actual projected images, meaning that the position, form and size of features depicted in this fashion are reliable. The image was then completed in watercolour, in some cases following the pencil drawing, in others adding details designed to create a pictorial effect as opposed to a rigorously accurate survey.

Though these images have been published many times in the past, a new interpretation of them based on our knowledge of the construction methods used in Carolingian Rome[17] allows us to conclude that the portico is a perfect example of those methods.

To start with, it is important to note that almost all of the materials used were salvaged from ancient buildings, a custom that was already widespread in Classical Antiquity and was by then common practice, though these materials were often chosen inaccurately, despite the abundant supply.

The Sergian portico, as is made clear by Ciampini's engraving, was constructed with a brick facing. This type of wall cladding had well-established characteristics in the period in question. First of all, it was very uneven. As a rule, reused bricks differed significantly in terms of their size, due to the lack of care taken when selecting them; a large number of roof tiles were also used on the wings, as well as *bipedales* and *sesquipedales*, though they were not laid in the types of rows normally found in Roman architecture.

The mortar – made of lime, large-grain red pozzolana and a small quantity of sand – has a typical greyish-purple colour; though very hard and resistant, it had not been mixed well, so that it often contains clots of quicklime.

---

[16] Van Lint (1684–1763) was in Rome from around 1697–1700 until his death: see A. Busiri Vici, *Peter, Hendrik e Giacomo Van Lint: Tre pittori di Anversa del '600 e '700 lavorano a Roma* (Rome, 1987).

[17] On construction techniques in Carolingian Rome, see G. Bertelli, A. Guiglia Guidobaldi and P. Rovigatti Spagnoletti Zeuli, 'Strutture murarie degli edifici religiosi di Roma dal VI al IX secolo', *Rivista dell'Istituto Nazionale di Archeologia e Storia dell'Arte* 23-4 (1976-7), 95–172; L. Barelli, M. Asciutti and M. C. Fabbri, 'Lettura storico-tecnica di una muratura altomedievale: l'*opus quadratum* a Roma nei secoli VIII e IX', in D. Fiorani and D. Esposito (eds.), *Tecniche costruttive dell'edilizia storica: Conoscere per conservare* (Rome, 2005), 59–76; L. Barelli, 'La diffusione e il significato dell'*opus quadratum* a Roma nei secoli VIII e IX', in M. P. Sette, M. Caperna, M. Docci and M. G. Turco (eds.), *Saggi in onore di Gaetano Miarelli Mariani* (Rome, 2007), 67–74; L. Barelli, 'Construction methods in Carolingian Rome (eighth–ninth centuries)', in R. Carvais, A. Guillerme, V. Nègre and J. Sakarovitch (eds.), *Nuts and Bolts of Construction History: Culture, Technology and Society*, 3 vols. (Paris, 2012), II, 135–41.

The bricks were laid in a distinctive fashion: the courses undulate and two rows often merge into one; the surface of the wall is not flat and features protuberances and recesses, and is often off plumb. The mortar joints are handled in different ways, in an apparently haphazard fashion, even on the same surface: they can be flush with the brick wall, or finished in a slightly concave fashion, or may even jut out. The height of the horizontal joints is affected by the lack of uniformity of the materials used, as st mortar served to offset the differences in the sizes of the bricks, meaning that its thickness could vary significantly.

The size of the module (an average height of five rows of mortar and five rows of bricks), one of the criteria used to classify different types of brick walls, varies enormously, ranging from a minimum of 26–7 cm to a maximum of 33–4 cm, even within the same wall. As a result, though an analysis of such a module is not so useful if we want to work out an average size that can be compared to other known examples, it is however helpful in identifying and evaluating the range of variation as a distinctive characteristic of this type of masonry.

Van Lint's illustration clearly shows three rows of small holes along the portico's wall: two on the pier and a third running along the entire wall between the arches and the roof, with features typical of the putlog holes of the early Middle Age; they were small and round (with a diameter of up to 5–6 cm), made by placing thin slats of unfinished wood on top of the wall under construction and surrounding them with spare bricks and copious quantities of mortar, without even a rudimentary architrave. The holes are arranged in undulating lines, and the intervals between the rows can vary as well. Quite often the distances between the holes in a given line vary, nor are the holes always aligned vertically with those in the rows below.

The lower portion of the pier that separated the triple archway from the portico built by Nicolaus was made of blocks of stone, as can be seen in Ciampini's engraving, in van Lint's illustration and, though less distinctly, in the Düsseldorf drawing. This detail is also confirmed by a description of the portico provided by Benedetto Mellini (around 1697): 'verso mezzogiorno, tra esso portico (quello di Nicolò) et un grosso muro di pietra, era un altro portico più piccolo, sopra tre archi con due colonne lisce corinthie, il qual portico serviva all'antico oratorio di S. Tomaso'.[18] The pencil

---

[18] 'To the south, between this portico (that of Nicolò) and a *large stone wall*, was another, smaller portico, atop three arches with two smooth Corinthian columns, which portico lead to the old oratory of St Thomas.' See F. Guidobaldi and C. Angelelli, *La 'Descrittione di Roma' di Benedetto Mellini nel Codice Vat. Lat. 11905*, in collaboration with L. Spadano and G. Tozzi (Sussidi allo studio delle antichità cristiane 23) (Vatican City, 2010), 74.

drawing by van Lint particularly demonstrates how the blocks were worn at their edges, to be expected from a soft variety of stone. It follows that the stonework in question can easily be identified as the *opus quadratum* widely used in Carolingian Rome. This was a surface made of large blocks of tufa stone, mainly used in the lower parts of buildings, and regularly used in foundations, so much so that it became a distinctive trait of that time, meaning that a well-defined construction technique did actually exist. The success of such *opus quadratum* was partly due to technical and economic factors, such as the availability of ancient material, the ease with which it could be salvaged, with the additional advantage that it provided an easily collected source of metal from the inner clamps, and a relatively simple and quick assembly process if high precision was not necessary, with clearly solid results.

Once salvaged, the blocks were not reworked before being reused, as proven by their varying sizes and their often worn out or chipped edges, which were the consequences of having been dismantled and transported, and by the traces of decay they had suffered in their previous location. The installation of such blocks was often imprecise: they were laid out in uneven, undulating lines; more often than not, the blocks were off plumb and were not parallel to the wall surface; the differences in size and the uneven texture created a number of gaps, which were often filled up with wedges of brick, including *bipedales* or *sesquipedales*, which were laid sideways, even vertically. Such a feature was rarely used on its own, and the transition between one kind of wall and the next was solved in different ways: either by simply building one on top of the other along a seamless line, perhaps near a feature of a different width, or by thinning out the blocks in the last few rows, with bricks inserted there in order to act as joining elements.

We can assume that the lower portions of the other piers were also built using this technique. As for the arched lintels, Ciampini's engraving points to the fact that they were most likely made from bricks, as once again knowledge of the technique used at that time makes it possible to hypothesise the construction features involved. The arched lintels around the openings, in fact, as in Classical Antiquity, were made of 'slices' cut lengthwise off bricks (usually *sesquipedales* or *bipedales*), fitted just about 10–15 cm deep into the wall. The bricks were laid out in varying cambers within each arched lintel, and usually the bricks at the impost are much more tilted. The extrados is often frayed, as it was made of reused material of varying lengths and because it was laid down in a seemingly careless way.

In the 1644 fresco, the uppermost part of the Sergian portico has a cornice of stone corbels. In both this painting and the Düsseldorf drawing, the roof of this portion is higher than that of the portico built by Nicolaus. It can thus be assumed that the cornice was destroyed when the level of the roof was evened out during the work done by Borromini.

Given that the cornice's features would have been of noteworthy size, in the light of the portico's grandeur, and that it was most likely built with *spolia*, there is good reason to surmise that it included a decorative element which, based on recent studies, would appear to have been a fairly regular feature of churches of the period, pointing to a conscious reiteration of ancient motifs: a cornice made with corbels decorated with leaf motifs, topped by sculpted slabs, both salvaged from older buildings and found for the first time in the basilica of Santi Nereo e Achilleo, constructed by Pope Leo III (795–816), but also used by none other than Sergius II on the church of San Martino ai Monti and by Leo IV on the basilica of the Santi Quattro Coronati.[19] In these buildings, as with the apses of Santa Cecilia in Trastevere and of Santa Prassede, both dating from the papacy of Paschal I (817–24), and that of San Giorgio in Velabro (Gregory IV, 827–44) – though, in their present state these last are lacking the upper slabs – corbels probably dating from the Severan era were used or that, in any case, dated from the third century AD and hail from one or more Roman monuments.

It is almost certain that the columns used for the portico were salvaged as well, as were the capitals and the bases. This assumption is supported not only by the standard practice of the time but by the lack of uniformity in the materials employed as well. The two granite shafts that survived into the eighteenth century[20] had different diameters, as shown by Marchetti. In Righi's illustration, the capitals, which the written sources refer to as Corinthian – though the term was also used to indicate composite columns – differ from one another.

A moulded cornice on the pier marked the arch's impost as shown in van Lint's drawing, in a more confused manner in the Düsseldorf drawing and in Righi's illustration, where it extended to the corner pier as well. There is no further evidence of this feature from that same period, at least not in Rome, though it was widely used in Late Antiquity and the early medieval

---

[19] Regarding this type of cornice, see A. Guiglia Guidobaldi and P. Pensabene, 'Il recupero dell'antico in età carolingia: La decorazione scultorea absidale delle chiese di Roma', *Rendiconti della Pontificia Accademia Romana di Archeologia* 78 (2005–6), 3–74. See also a work currently in progress by the author and A. Guiglia Guidobaldi for new observations.

[20] See the bill of the master masons Paolo Stambrini and Paolo Ingami for the demolition of the portico, dated 29 February 1732 and cited by Bernacchio and de Strobel, Chapter 14 in this volume (p. 285).

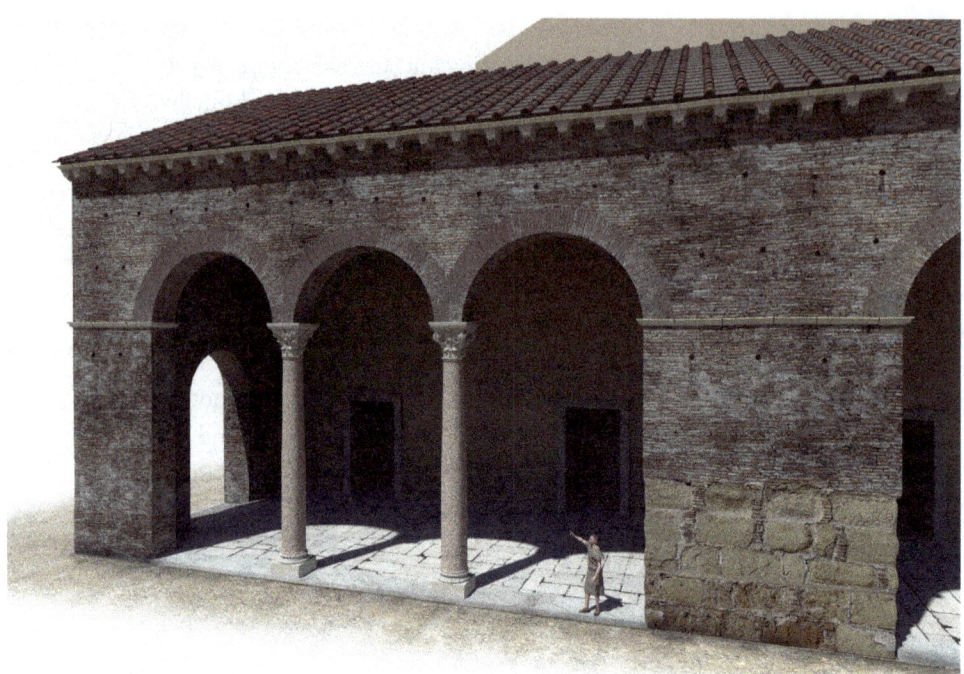

**Fig. 13.5** Southern section of Sergian portico at the conclusion of the construction site, highlighting the construction techniques (hypothetical reconstruction, 3D model, Lia Barelli and Pietro Galifi, 2016).

period (for example, in what is referred to as the palace of Theoderic in Ravenna).

In conclusion, we present a hypothetical 3D reconstruction of the Sergian portico (see Fig 13.5). It should be remembered, however, that the walls were not exposed and were covered with painted plaster instead (*vela*, faux painted blocks, *opus sectile*, figured frescoes), as demonstrated both by the *Liber Pontificalis* ('*variis picturis*') and examples from the same period. The purpose of the image put forward here, therefore, is to illustrate the construction techniques employed and may depict the portico as it appeared when it was first completed.

## The Towers of the Transept

When it comes to the analysis of construction techniques, the towers that flank the northern end of the basilica's transept are an almost undisturbed sample, thanks to the relatively few alterations they have undergone

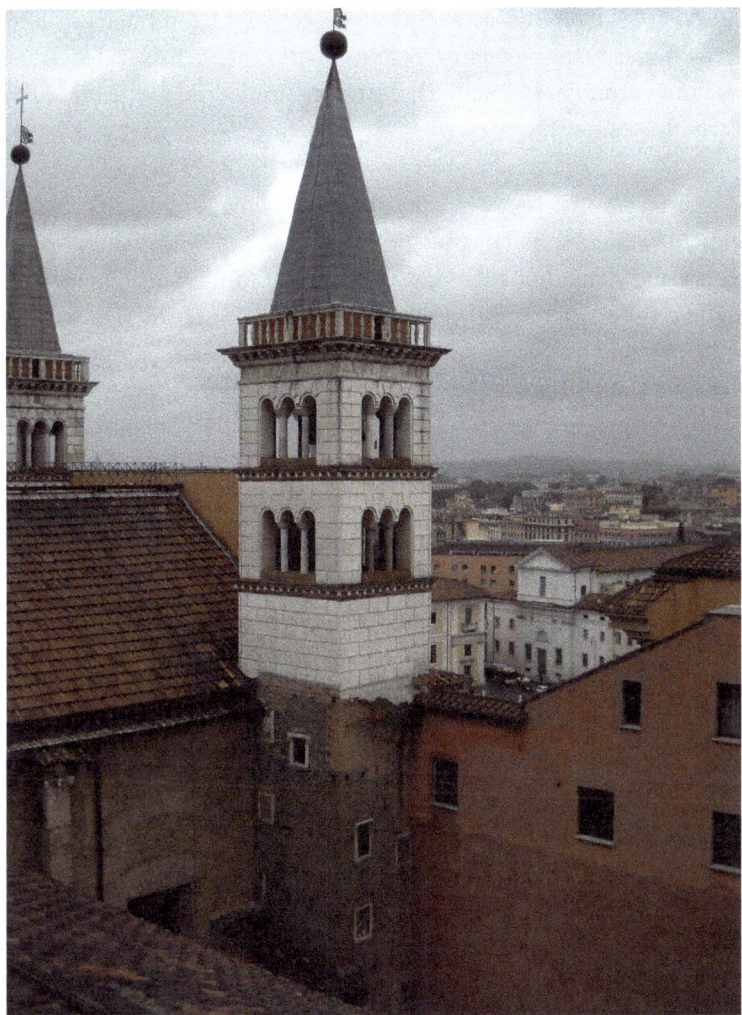

**Fig. 13.6** The east tower view from the roof of the nave.

(Fig. 13.6). In particular, their interiors have never been plastered, so one can clearly see the structure of the walls, which are perfectly preserved.[21] Here too, however, it should be remembered that any study of the construction techniques used to build the towers must also take into account

---

[21] Research under way on the towers for some time now has involved – in addition to myself, Monica Morbidelli and Chiara Musco – Alessandra Guiglia with regard to the study of the marble elements, Laura Sadori and Alessia Masi on materials of vegetable origin and Elisabetta Giorgi on the mortar. A number of results have already been presented by myself and Chiara Musco at the *Architetture e città nel medioevo* Congress, Rome, Museo Nazionale Romano – Terme di Diocleziano, 12 May 2010.

architectural considerations, as well as the larger context of the basilica in its entirety. Indeed, the very first results of the research clarified what structural and chronological ties link the towers to the rest of the building, particularly the transept.

The towers were not designed to be bell towers; their purpose was to serve as stairways, which proved particularly useful for maintenance.[22] Their plans are quadrangular and the stairs, covered with vaults, spiral upwards around a quadrangular-sectioned pier until they reach the cells featuring two orders of trifora windows crowned with cusps. The towers were located behind two wings of masonry that, by widening the front end of the transept, transformed it into a true façade;[23] seen from the front, only the cells emerged from the façade, while the main body of the towers was visible from behind. Today this façade appears very different, due to the addition of the parapet and the faux marble facing of the cells (under Pope Pius IV, 1562–7), as well as the portico, complete with a loggia, built by Domenico Fontana (under Pope Sixtus V, 1586). The medieval features of the façade are illustrated in a well-known drawing by Marten van Heemskerck (1535–6), which shows a horizontal termination with a cavetto cornice, a common architectural element in thirteenth-century Rome,[24] above which rose a tympanum flanked by the tower cells; there are only three openings – a Gothic portal and two rose windows – while painted arms are visible on the wall.[25]

In the light of the above, the architectural survey performed by Chiara Musco – which was limited, for now, to the interiors – proved a key contribution to this study. It highlighted noteworthy differences between the towers, starting with the smaller and slightly more extended plan of the

---

[22] Towers with similar functions, usually built with a circular plan, are found in many large medieval churches, such as by the side of the apse of Santa Maria Maggiore in Rome, as well as in the cathedrals of Orvieto and Palermo.

[23] The purpose of the wings was to emphasise the importance of the northern end of the transept as the preferred side of entry, in that it faced the city centre. Other examples of wings that expand a façade in Rome are found at Santa Maria in Aracoeli and Santa Maria sopra Minerva though, unlike the Lateran wings, their lower portions are aligned with side aisles.

[24] Found on the façades of San Lorenzo fuori le Mura, Santa Maria in Trastevere, Santa Maria Maggiore, Santa Maria in Aracoeli, Santa Maria sopra Minerva, Saint Peter's in the Vatican and San Paolo fuori le Mura.

[25] The sources mention restoration work carried out under Pope Gregory XI (1370–8), though this probably only concerned decorative elements, and in particular the restoration of the portal: Krautheimer, Corbett and Malmstrom, *CBCR* V, 1–96, at p. 13. The tympanum and the rose window are still visible in the attic of the transept, and remains of the painted arms are found in the same area of the loggia (A. Schiavo, 'Vicende della Cattedrale di Roma e del Patriarchio Lateranense', *Studi Romani* 17, 1 (1969), 60–6).

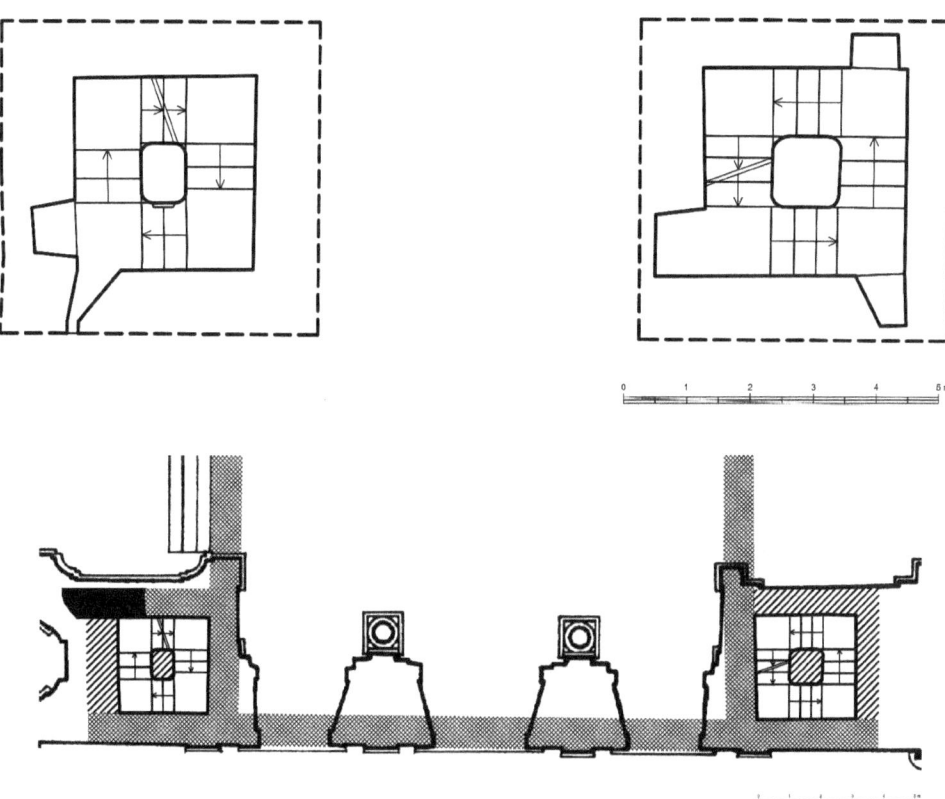

Fig. 13.7 Above, plans of the east and west towers (survey Chiara Musco, 2010); below, plan of the north arm of the transept with the addition of towers between the existing walls: in black Constantinian wall, the dotted lines indicate the walls of medieval transept with wings, in hatched fill walls of the towers (graphical base in Krautheimer, Corbett and Malmstrom, *CBCR* V, plate I).

east tower (approximately 2.85 m x 2.95 m inside, as opposed to the 3.20 m x 3.15 m of the west tower) (Fig. 13.7). This difference is due to the effect on the east tower of the distance between the walls of the side nave and the wing of the transept. As a consequence, the east tower's central pier is more slender, and given that the stairs are supported by the piers, each flight consists of only three steps, whereas those in the west tower have four. This difference, in turn, means that the east tower has more landings, while the west tower's floor slabs are thicker (Fig. 13.8).

The survey also brought to light the fact that the construction techniques used on the towers are identical, and boast considerable regularity and refinement. There are two types of wall facing: one of brick, the other of *tufelli* (Fig. 13.9). The bricks were salvaged from earlier buildings but

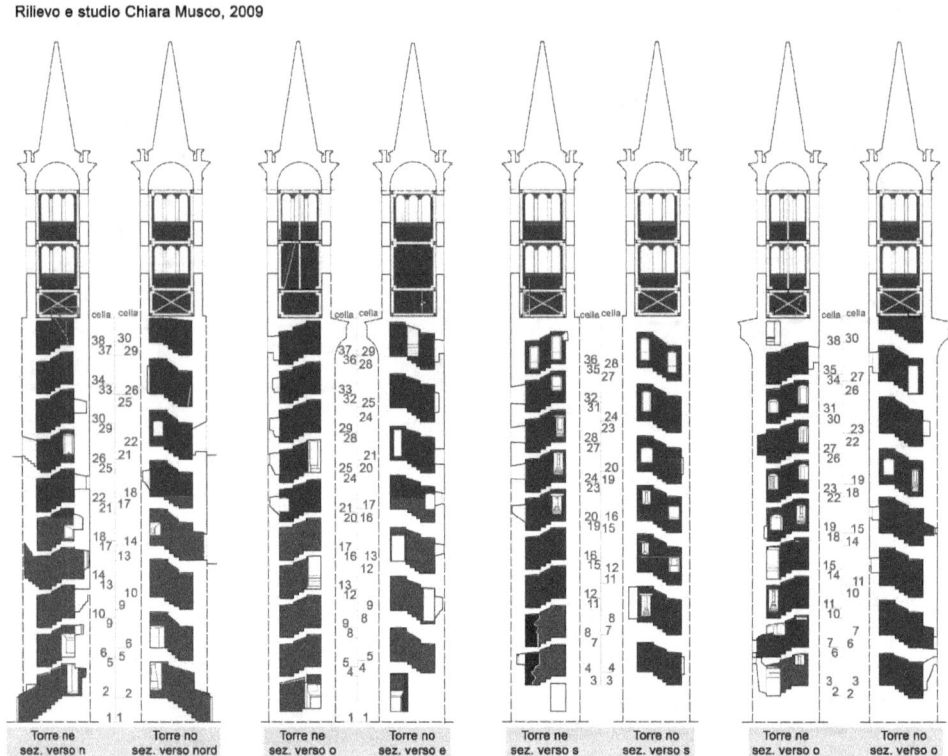

Fig. 13.8 Survey of the inner walls of the towers with indication of materials: in red, bricks of Constantine's courtain; in brown, bricks of the medieval curtain; in grey, *tufelli* (Chiara Musco 2010).

were selected with care; the *tufelli* are small in size and have smooth rectangular faces thanks to the way they were carefully moulded; the rows are horizontal; the mortar is made from lime, sand and finely sifted pozzolana; the module for the brickwork measures approximately 24/25 cm, while that of the *tufelli* measures 35/36 cm. Special care was taken when finishing the mortar joints, both horizontal and vertical, which were either slanted inwards at tallest brick (or *tufello*) or pressed using a flat smooth tool. The central piers, whose edges were rounded off to facilitate the ascent of the stairs, feature joints cut out like a band that jut out a great deal and are geometrically shaped, as required by their structural importance. All these features would support a dating of the masonry to the second half of the thirteenth century.[26]

[26] For the techniques employed, see J. E. Barclay Lloyd, 'Masonry techniques in medieval Rome *c.* 1080–1300', *PBSR* 53 (1985), 225–77; D. Esposito, *Tecniche costruttive murarie medievali*:

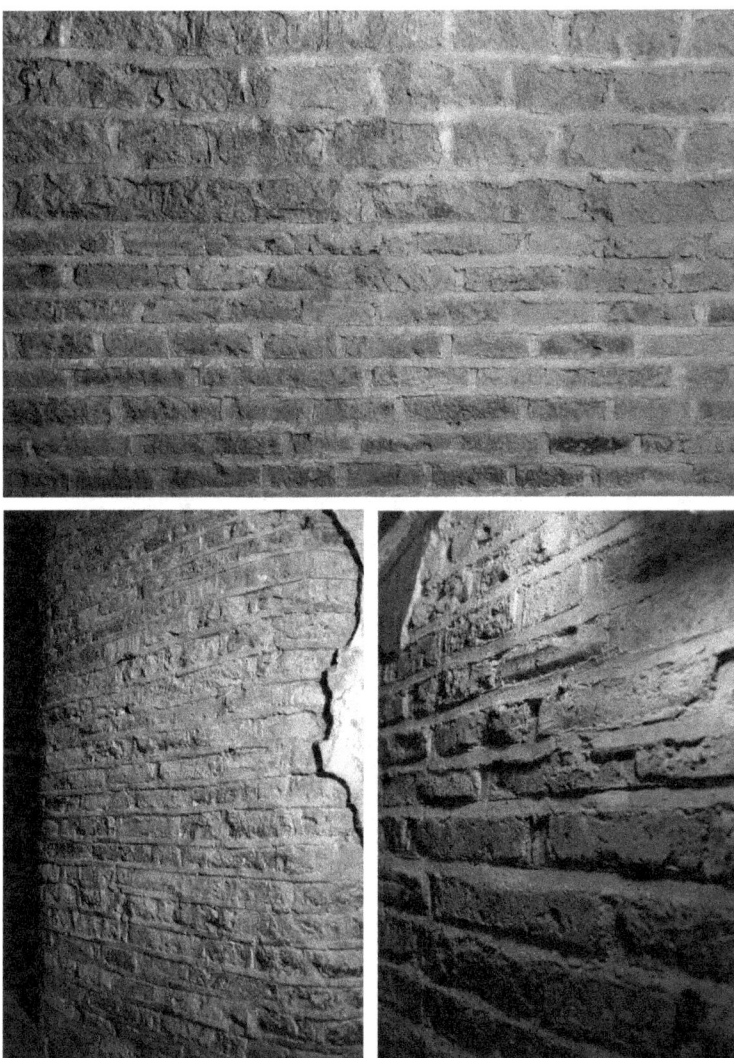

**Fig. 13.9** East tower: above, detail of the transition between the courtain of bricks and the courtain of *tufelli*; below, details of mortar joints of central pier and an inner wall (Lia Barelli, 2016).

The staircase ceilings are particularly interesting, as they consist of small barrel vaults set very low, one for each landing and for each flight of stairs,

*Murature a 'tufelli' in area romana* (Storia della tecnica edilizia e restauro dei monumenti 2) (Rome, 1997); D. Fiorani (ed.), *Finiture murarie e architetture nel medioevo: Una panoramica e tre casi di studio nell'Italia centro-meridionale* (Rome, 2005); E. Montelli, *Tecniche costruttive murarie medievali: Mattoni e laterizi in Roma e nel Lazio fra X e XV secolo* (Storia della tecnica edilizia e restauro dei monumenti 7) (Rome, 2011).

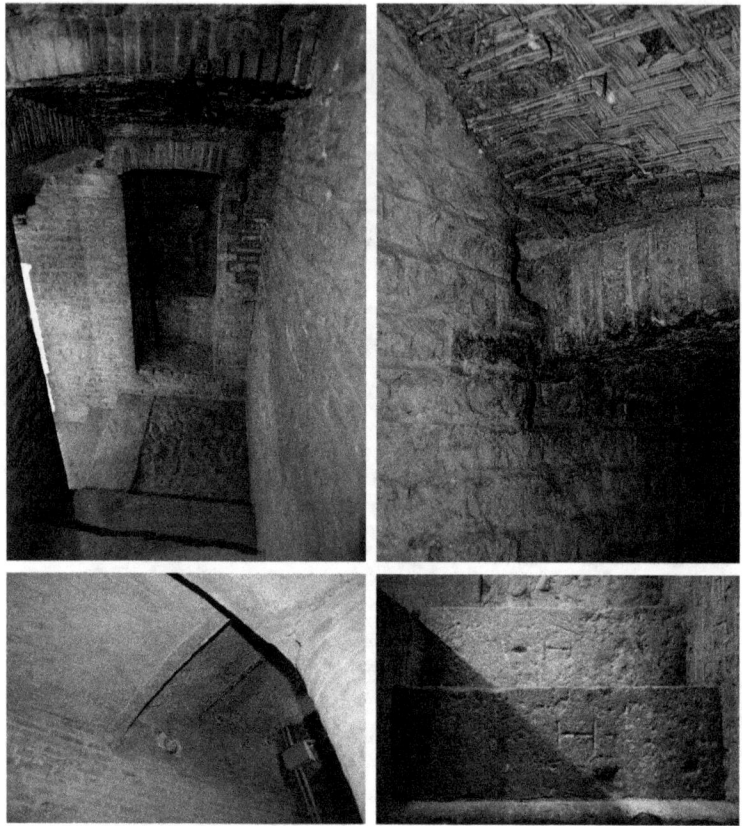

Fig. 13.10 Above, on the left, view of staircase of east tower and, on the right, detail of the vaults of west tower with centring holes; below, on the left, detail of vaults of east tower and, on the right, steps of east tower with marks in the form of an 'H' (Lia Barelli, 2016).

separated by differences in height finished with brick lintels (Fig. 13.10). The ceilings were made from a mix of mortar and stone materials poured onto mats made from interwoven reeds. These mats formed a pattern of small squares which, once the mats were removed, left their mark on the intrados.[27] The mats, in turn, were laid on wooden centrings held up by small joists inserted in the masonry at the height of the impost, leaving holes. The use of this type of mat would seem suddenly to have appeared,

---

[27] Portions of the mats have been preserved here and there, providing an opportunity for analysis: see C. Musco, A. Masi, M. Morbidelli, L. Barelli, and L. Sadori, 'An integrated approach to the study of the bell towers of S. Giovanni in Laterano', in A. Macchia, L. Campanella and E. Borrelli (eds.), *Proceedings of YOCOCU, Youth in the Conservation of Cultural Heritage (Rome, 24th–25th November 2008)* (Rome, 2009), 279. A systematic study of the topic, however, has yet to be done.

and become widespread, at some point between the twelfth and the early fourteenth centuries in Rome (examples of which can be found in the residential portions of the titular complexes of San Lorenzo fuori le Mura, San Clemente and the Santi Quattro Coronati) and in central Italy (for example: residential buildings in Ninfa; the enlargement of the crypt of Santa Maria di Vescovio; the papal palace of Montefiascone; the abbey of Sassovivo in Foligno), only to disappear just as suddenly. Before the mats were introduced, in fact, vaults were poured onto wooden boards, while afterwards they were replaced by bundles of unwoven reeds.

The steps of the stairs are made of thick blocks of marble. At the centre of the tread of almost every step, masons' marks in the form of a cross or an 'H' were engraved with a fine-pointed tool. These could be benchmarks,[28] similar to those found on the ogival windows of the Sancta Sanctorum (Pope Nicholas III, 1277–80).[29]

The original windows of the towers were of two types: the lower portions feature embrasures that allowed light in with a splayed stepped base on the inside; the upper portions have rectangular windows allowing one to look out, with a brick flat arch inside and a rectangular marble frame with a discharging arch on the outside. Both types of windows are among those found most frequently in medieval Rome.[30] A number of the architraves are made from reworked pieces of salvaged marble.

The cells have cornices typical of those found on bell towers in Rome and the rest of the Lazio region,[31] made from rows of bricks that progressively jut out, sawtooth friezes and smooth marble brackets. In this particular case there is a sequence of eight rows, starting from the bottom,

---

[28] It would seem that these banker marks ensured that the stone mason would be paid, but also served as a method of quality control on the part of the client: R. Dionigi, 'I segni dei lapicidi: Evidenze europee', in *I magistri commacini: Mito e realtà del medioevo Lombardo (Atti del XIX Congresso internazionale di studio sull'alto medioevo, Varese – Como, 23-25 ottobre 2008)*, 2 vols. (Spoleto, 2009), I, 341–471, at p. 361. For an overview of this type of mark, see G. Bianchi, 'I segni dei tagliatori di pietre negli edifici medievali: Spunti metodologici ed interpretativi', *Archeologia dell'Architettura* 2 (1997), 25–37.

[29] See the plate in H. Grisar, *Die römische Kapelle Sancta Sanctorum und ihr Schatz: Meine Entdeckungen und Studien in der Palastkapelle der mittelalterlichen Päpste* (Freiburg, 1908), 22. M. Righetti Tosti-Croce, 'L'architettura tra il 1254 e il 1308', in A. M. Romanini (ed.), *Roma nel Duecento: L'arte nella città dei papi da Innocenzo III a Bonifacio VIII* (Turin, 1991), 73–143, at p. 111, points out that similar marks can be found in Cistercian buildings and others built under Frederick II.

[30] For examples, see the illustrations in Romanini (ed.), *Roma nel Duecento*. On thirteenth-century windows, see L. Barelli, 'Architetture altoresidenziali a Roma nel XIII secolo: Alcune osservazioni', in R. M. Dal Mas and R. Mancini (eds.), *Cinte murarie e abitati: Restauro, riuso e valorizzazione* (Beni architettonici e paesaggio 3) (Rome, 2015), 133–43.

[31] For examples of this type of cornice, see A. E. Priester, 'The Belltowers of Medieval Rome and the Architecture of Renovatio', Ph.D. thesis (Princeton University, 1990).

arrayed as follows: bricks, sawtooth friezes, bricks, brackets with the space between them corresponding to two bricks, and then bricks, sawtooth friezes, bricks and bricks. They would have been completed with red plaster on the portions in brick and white on the sections in marble, as shown, for example, by the traces to be found in the cloisters of San Francesca Romana and the Santi Quattro Coronati, as well as those on the southern end of the Lateran basilica's transept.[32]

Marble salvaged from ancient buildings was re-utilised for the trifora windows: the columns are of especially high quality, being made of porphyry or white marble finished either by being strigilated, decorated with a Roman lattice motif, never found on columns, or patterns of intertwined vegetation. Nevertheless, these decorations, given their height, would have been difficult to perceive, as shown by the fact that some of the columns are made of pieces that do not match or are mounted backwards.

It is important to note that the towers feature the same construction techniques of both the north and south ends of the transept. Though there are noteworthy differences in form between them, these are most likely due to the specific function of the northern end within the urban layout. While the southern end, whose entire external brick facing is still visible, has only one wing to the east (the function of which is unclear), it has no cavetto cornice and is topped by a tympanum that corresponds to the actual width of the transept behind it, placing it in an asymmetrical position. A cornice with sawtooth bricks and marble bracket friezes runs around the tympanum, similar to those of the towers. This cornice also runs around the corners, continuing along the back of the wing, and must originally have run along the side walls of the transept as well, finishing to the north, against the towers, where it was replaced by another cornice with late Gothic features.

The study of these construction techniques has clarified once and for all the relationship between the towers and the transept, thanks to the precise determination of the materials used for the facing walls inside the towers, whose arrangement, as shown by the diagram drawn up by Chiara Musco, varies from one to the other (Fig. 13.8).

All that can be seen from surrounding rooftops are the south and east façades of the east tower and the south and west façades of the west tower, which, apart from the cells, appear to be made entirely of *tufelli*. Things are more varied on the inside. The ground floor of the east tower is made

---

[32] L. Barelli, *Il complesso monumentale dei Ss. Quattro Coronati a Roma* (Rome, 2009), 59 and Montelli, *Tecniche costruttive*, plate 8b. Thanks are extended to Enrico Sebastiani, head of the Construction Services Office of the State of the Vatican City, who granted me access to the scaffolding located in the south transept.

entirely of brick: its south wall corresponds to that of the Constantinian side aisle, which is interrupted when it reaches a door and a window,[33] and gives way towards the west to a wall that connects it to the west wall, which constitutes the wall of the medieval transept; its north wall is that of the wing that extends the north end of the transept; its east wall probably served to close off a blind zone between the transept and the structures to the side of the Leonine *triclinium*, though modifications made at later points in time make it difficult to determine exactly what links there were with adjoining walls. At the next highest level, the east wall is made of *tufelli* and is clearly placed against both the Constantinian wall to the south and the wing to the north. Above the roof of the side aisle, the south wall is also made of *tufelli*, so that, at a particular height, there is a mirror-image symmetry in the way the materials of the two towers are arranged. Indeed, from the ground floor on up, the south and west sides of the west tower are made of *tufelli* and placed against the brick walls of the transept and west wing.

However, once they reach a height of 12.97 m to the east and 14.46 m to the west, as calculated from the current floor level of the transept, all the internal façades are made from *tufelli*, without any interruption, so that the south and east walls of the east tower, together with the south and west walls of the west tower, are made entirely of *tufelli*, while the walls corresponding to the transept and the wings are entirely made of *tufelli* on the inside and brick on the outside, as shown by portions of these latter surfaces documented by photographs taken prior to different restorations. None of this should come as a surprise, given that walls built with facings of different materials are nothing out of the ordinary for medieval Rome (as in the case of the Torre Maggiore of the Santi Quattro Coronati complex, 1247). The east pier is made of brick for four-fifths of its length, which then gives way to *tufelli*, the material used throughout the west pier. The cavetto cornice, made entirely of brick, runs along the *tufelli* walls of the towers at the corners. Above the cornice, the walls of the cells are thinner and made of brick both inside and out.

From a construction point of view, there can only be one explanation for these variations: when construction of the new transept began, it was to be built in brick and the north wall was to have two wings. At the same time, it was decided to re-utilise the Constantinian foundations of what can be termed an 'aisle-transept'[34] as much as possible, making the positioning of the

---

[33] E. Josi, R. Krautheimer and S. Corbett, 'Note Lateranensi', *RAC* 34, 1–4 (1958), 59–72; Krautheimer, Corbett and Malmstrom, *CBCR* V, 1–96, at p. 40.

[34] The excavations of 1957–8 showed that the Constantinian basilica had a low type of transept referred to as 'aisle-transepts' (E. Josi, R. Krautheimer and S. Corbett, 'Note Lateranensi', *RAC* 33, 1–4 (1957), 79–98).

northeast and southeast corners of the transept a foregone conclusion, as they had to coincide with the old layout, and so the distance between the east wing and the north side aisle was also a given, dictating the width of the east tower.

Roughly halfway through the construction of the transept, the decision to add the towers was made, with the wings to be used as their north wall. As mentioned earlier, the situation on the two sides differed: to the west, two new walls were needed to complete the square of the plan between the wing and the transept. To the east, apart from the ground floor, it was enough to insert a wall to close the gap between the wall of the wing and that of the side aisle, until construction arrived above the latter, where two new walls had to be built, as was the case on the west side. The new walls were made entirely of *tufelli*.

Once building work reached the height that the transept's construction had reached – which differed slightly between the east and west sides – the towers and the transept were built at the same time, as shown by the fact that, from that point on, the internal walls of the towers were built entirely of *tufelli*, without any interruptions, even when they coincided with those of the transept and wings (Fig. 13.11). The north façade – including the cavetto cornice, the tympanum and the tower cells – was completed in the course of the same construction period, and probably included the south tympanum as well, which was possibly envisaged in the original plan. Indeed, the construction features of all these different parts are practically identical, with variations in the materials employed determined not by distinct phases of construction but by the use of bricks that were stronger (and perhaps considered to be more refined) for the parts that were more structurally delicate or more exposed, or of greater architectural importance. Upon careful analysis, in particular, the perfect joins between the walls, where three bricks correspond to two *tufelli*, demonstrate that the cavetto cornice was built at the same time as the towers.[35]

Once we have established the links between the construction of the transept and the towers, we still need to date them. The studies done up to now have almost completely ignored the towers, which have been labelled as additions,[36] concentrating instead on the transept: the dates put forward vary widely and differences have been observed between its two sides,

---

[35] As opposed to what is stated in Blaauw, *CD*, 227.

[36] Leaving aside the fantastical interpretations of A. Serafini, *Torri campanarie di Roma e del Lazio nel Medioevo* (Rome, 1927), 169–70, and B. M. Apollonj Ghetti, *La basilica del Salvatore poi di S. Giovanni al Laterano cattedrale di Roma: Edizione a cura di Eugenio Russo* (San Marino, 2013), 115–28, scholars date the towers to various times between the twelfth and fourteenth centuries, considering them to be additions to the transept.

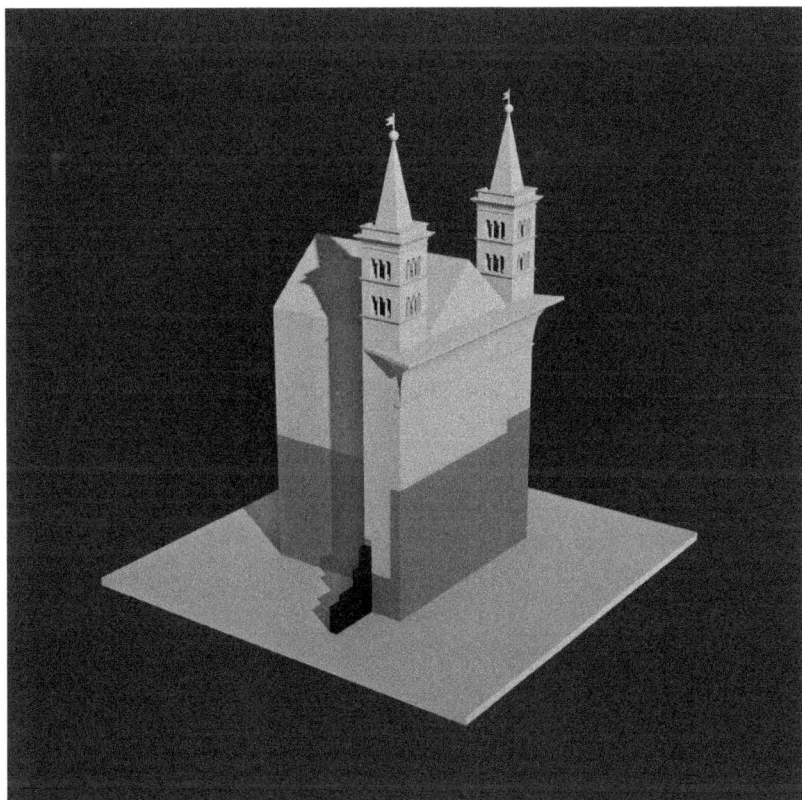

Fig. 13.11 Synthetic model of construction phases of northern end of the transept: in black Constantinian walls, in dark grey, first phase of the medieval transept; in light grey, design change of transept with the inclusion of the towers (3D model by Pietro Galifi, 2016).

though such differences have not been supported by material evidence.[37] What is certain is that it existed in its current dimensions in 1308, the year in

---

[37] For example, G. Rohault de Fleury, *Le Latran au Moyen-âge*, 2 vols. (Paris, 1877), I, 308, identified the northern end with the two-towered façade engraved on the bronze doors that Pope Celestine III (1191-8) commissioned for the Lateran palace and which are now found in the baptistery; J. Toynbee and J. Ward Perkins, *The Shrine of St. Peter and the Vatican Excavations* (New York, 1957), 206; and G. Matthiae, *Le chiese di Roma dal IV al X secolo* (Roma Cristiana 3) (Rome, 1962), 237-8 went so far as to suggest that the transept could be dated to Pope Sergius III (904-11); according to Josi, Krautheimer and Corbett, 'Note Lateranensi' (1957), the south wing was built later, possibly in the fourteenth century, whereas the northern portion may have been constructed as many as 100-200 years earlier. R. E. Malmstrom, 'The building of the nave piers at S. Giovanni in Laterano, after the fire at 1361', *RAC* 434, 2 (1967), 155-64, with the most feasible claim, followed by Krautheimer, Corbett and Malmstrom, *CBCR* V, 1-96, at pp. 19-22, 91 and F. Gandolfo, 'Assisi e il Laterano', *Archivio della Società Romana di Storia Patria* 106 (1983), 63-113, assumed that it was rebuilt under Pope Nicholas IV, who included the same type of structure in Santa Maria Maggiore. According to Blaauw, *CD*, 221-32, the transept is attributable to the influence of Monte Cassino and may date from the 1130s.

which a fire destroyed the roof, given that a document of 1309 lists measurements for the beams that are identical to the current width.[38]

In the light of what has been stated above, the most probable conclusion would appear to be that these structures should be linked to the construction work carried out by Pope Nicholas IV (1288–92) *ante retroque* of the basilica, including a portion built from the foundations up, a fact recorded in two well-known mosaic epigraphs.[39] These efforts most certainly had to do with alterations to the Constantinian apse and the Leonine portico that surrounded it. As already sustained, the old apse was most likely not destroyed, but merely re-faced by curtain walls built by Nicholas,[40] meaning that the work done from the foundations up could indeed correspond to the transept and the towers. The work done on the apse, with the mosaic by Torriti, was completed in approximately 1292 and, given that the high altar was put in place in 1293, the transept and the towers must have been completed in roughly the same period.

As we have seen, such a presumed date is in no way ruled out by the construction or formal features of any of the above elements, which actually share a good many characteristics. Photographs taken prior to the destruction of the apse in 1880, for example, show that it had a cornice, complete with marble brackets and sawtooth friezes, similar to that of the towers and the south tympanum, and which would presumably have run along the entire transept. This cornice differed considerably from that of the walls running lengthwise, which was presumably rebuilt

---

[38] M. Gaglione, '"Lignamina necessaria de Calabria ferenda": Interventi angioini per la ricostruzione di San Giovanni in Laterano (1308)', *Archivio della Società Romana di Storia Patria* 128 (2005), 5–34.

[39] One is found at the bottom of the apse mosaic: '[...] PARTEM POSTERIOREM ET ANTERIOREM RUINOSAS HUIUS SANCTI TEMPLI A FUNDAMENTIS REEDIFICARI FECIT ET ORNARI OPERE MOSYACO NICOLAUS PP. IIII [...] ANNO DOMINI M CC NONAGESI.I'. The other is inscribed in a mosaic panel to the side of the sacristy door that was originally located at the south entrance of the ambulatory: '[...] HYERONIMUS QUARTI NICOLAI NOMINE SURGENS ROMANUS PRESUL PARTES CIRCUMSPICIT HUIUS ECCLESIAE CERTA IAM DEPENDERE RUINA ANTE RETROQUE LEVAT DESTRUCTA REFORMAT ET ORNAT ET FUNDAMENTIS PARTEM COMPONIT AB YMIS [...] ANNO AB INCARNATIONE DOMINI NOSTRI JESU CHRISTI M.CC.XCI [...]'.

[40] L. Barelli and M. Morbidelli, '"Ad imitatione, e somiglianza di quello che v'era anticamente": il restauro dell'abside di San Giovanni in Laterano a Roma al tempo di Nicola IV (1288–1292)', in V. Franchetti Pardo (ed.), *Arnolfo di Cambio e la sua epoca: Costruire, scolpire, dipingere, decorare (Atti del Convegno Internazionale di Studi, Firenze – Colle di Val d'Elsa, 7–10 marzo 2006)* (Rome, 2006), 197–208.

following the fire of 1308 or that of 1361.[41] With regard to another feature of the apse, the semi-circular lesenes at the impost of the blind arches have a semi-circular marble string course, something also found at the top of the lesenes of the transept, which is of the same type as that placed at the impost of the arches outside the Sancta Sanctorum built by Nicholas III just a few years earlier.[42]

In conclusion, it can be assumed fairly reliably that Pope Nicholas IV commissioned a unified set of alterations affecting the entire western portion of the Lateran basilica, comparable in terms of their importance to the effort undertaken by the same pontiff at Santa Maria Maggiore, though in that case the particular conditions of urban layout that led to the creation of a second façade at the Lateran complex, together with the introduction of the towers, were not present.

Though we cannot, on this occasion, go into the reasons for such alterations, it can nevertheless be said that they make of Nicholas IV, the first Franciscan pope, a true restorer of the basilica, just as Saint Francis, in Pope Innocent III's dream, had kept Saint John Lateran from falling down.[43]

---

[41] Presumably the burning beams destroyed the upper portions of the walls as they collapsed, where an original cornice with sawtooth and bracket friezes had been located, whereas the tympana of the transept were practically undamaged. San Paolo fuori le Mura sustained similar damage after the fire of 1823.

[42] J. Gardner, 'L'architettura del Sancta Sanctorum', in C. Pietrangeli (ed.), *Sancta Sanctorum* (Milan, 1995), 19–37.

[43] The episode of the *Dream of Innocent III* first appeared in the *Vita Secunda* by Thomas of Celano (1244–5); for its meaning and ties to Pope Nicholas IV, see M. Andaloro, 'Il sogno di Innocenzi III all'Aracoeli, Niccolò IV e la basilica di S. Giovanni in Laterano', in S. Macchioni and B. Tavassi La Greca (eds.), *Studi in onore di Giulio Carlo Argan*, 2 vols. (Rome, 1984), I, 29–42.

# 14 | The Medieval Portico of Saint John Lateran

ANNA MARIA DE STROBEL AND NICOLETTA BERNACCHIO

In 2009, forty-two fragments of marble slabs (Musei Vaticani, inv. 57919.31.1–31) were found during the compilation of an inventory of the material stored in a storage room under the Cortile Ottagono of the Vatican Museums. Only one side of each slab was decorated, showing bands of Cosmatesque mosaic forming a circles-and-squares motif. The areas framed by these circles and squares were originally covered in mosaics or fragments of stone, as suggested by the analysis of the few fragments of mortar that have been identified. At some point the slabs must have been reused as part of a floor, as several of them had been shaped and their back sides were smooth and worn. Some of the fragments showed remains of short narrative epigraphs or *tituli*, which once described the now lost scenes in the squares on the decorated side. At the time of the discovery, once we had put all the fragments side by side, it became clear that they were part of a monumental marble frieze dating to the Middle Ages. Similar friezes still decorate the portico of the cathedral of Civita Castellana, and, in Rome, the portico of the basilica of San Lorenzo fuori le Mura (Fig. 14.1), and the external galleries of the cloisters of the basilica of San Paolo fuori le Mura and of the archbasilica of Saint John Lateran.

Based on the results of our investigations into the archive of the Vatican Museums, we came to believe that the slabs were originally stored in the depots of the Lateran palace and that they had been brought to the Vatican Museums together with the art collections, which were moved there in the 1970s. At the same time, the *tituli* played a significant role in the identifications of these pieces, and guided our research.

The archbasilica of Saint John Lateran was the obvious place to start our investigation. The texts of the three surviving *tituli*, despite several lacunae, appeared to be identical to those recorded by the antiquarian Giovanni

---

For extended treatment of this topic, see A. M. De Strobel, *Il portico medievale di San Giovanni in Laterano: I frammenti ritrovati* (Vatican City, 2019). The volume includes an *Appendice Documentaria* (ed. N. Bernacchio) and brings together all relevant bibliographical references. Only the most relevant ones are included in this contribution. The authors are grateful to Dr Giacomo Savani for his excellent English translation of this chapter.

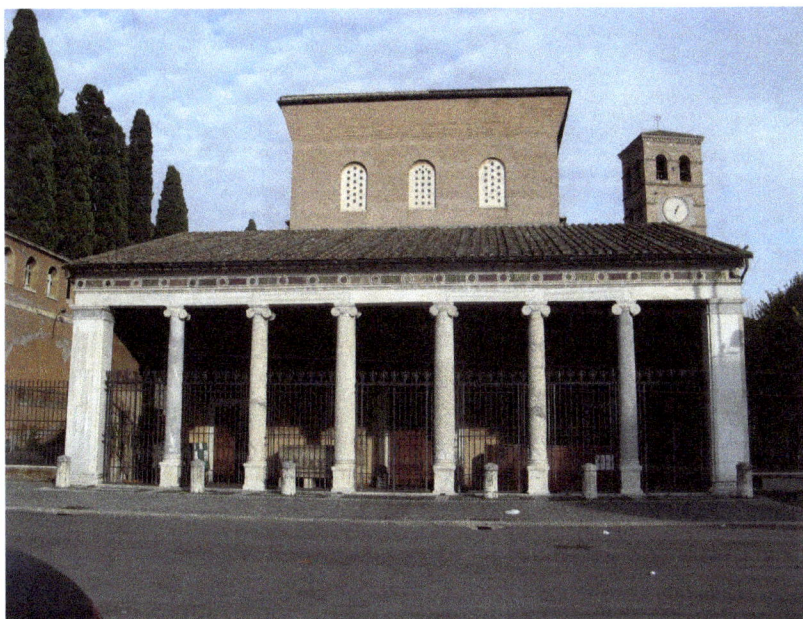

Fig. 14.1 The portico of the basilica of San Lorenzo fuori le Mura.

Giustino Ciampini, who left an extremely detailed description of the medieval façade of the archbasilica in 1693.[1] Among these, the first one began with the words 'Naves Romani', followed by the other two, beginning with 'Rex in scriptura' and 'Rex baptizatur'. The second *titulus*, starting with 'Regia nobilitas', was not preserved. It appeared that we had found three out of four of the *tituli* recorded by Ciampini, and that the marble fragments were part of the mosaic frieze of the medieval portico of the archbasilica of Saint John Lateran, which was demolished in 1731 when the façade was rebuilt by Alessandro Galilei.

The next step was to identify the historical context of our fragments. We then examined the architectonical and structural history of the portico, trying at the same time to discover what happened to its components after it was demolished, in particular its columns and the slabs of its frieze.

The appearance of the main façade of the medieval archbasilica, as planned by Francesco Borromini in the mid-seventeenth century, is documented by written and iconographical sources. These include table I of the

---

[1] G. G. Ciampini, *De sacris aedificiis a Costantino Magno constructis: Synopsis historica* (Rome, 1693), 4–23, in particular 10–14, where he describes the portico and transcribes the *tituli*. According to Ciampini's transcription, they were in this order: (1) 'Naves Romani Ducis hæ sunt Vespasiani'; (2) 'Regia nobilitas hic obsidet Israelitas'; (3) 'Rex in Scriptura Sylvestro dat sua iura'; (4) 'Rex baptizatur & lepræ sorde lavatur'.

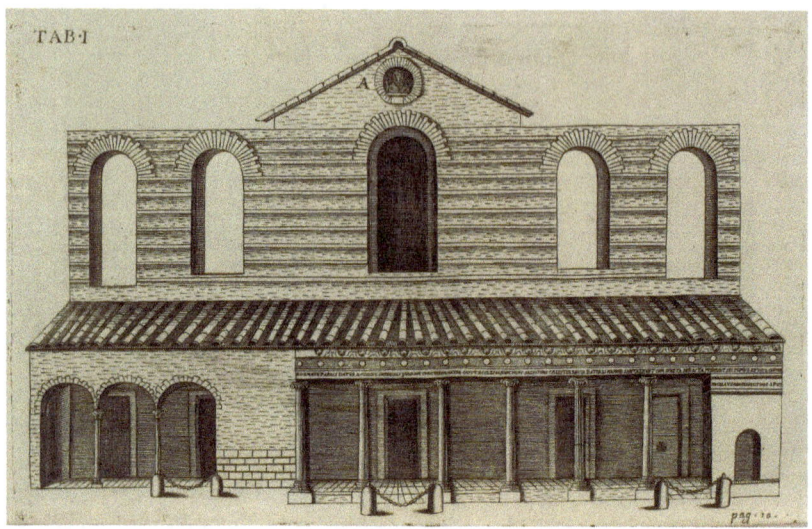

**Fig. 14.2** The main façade of the medieval archbasilica as depicted in Ciampini, *De sacris aedificiis*, table I.

already mentioned antiquarian work by Ciampini (Fig. 14.2) and a slightly later drawing (*c.* 1720) now in Berlin, attributed to Hendrik van Lint.[2] These depictions show that the façade included a six-column portico supporting a trabeation; the portico joined a three-arched bay to the south, the remains of an older portico. Three building phases of the medieval portico can be identified. The first portico was constructed under Pope Sergius II (844–7) and was formed by three large, three-arched bays.[3] During the second phase (*c.* 960), by order of Pope John XII (955–64), the first bay to the left was walled up and transformed into the chapel of Saint Thomas. Finally, at the end of the twelfth century (third phase), the two remaining bays were demolished and substituted by a new structure with six columns supporting an architrave, to the left of the chapel of Saint Thomas.

Thanks to antiquarian descriptions and depictions realised before the demolition of 1731, such as the account by Ciampini (Fig. 14.2) and van Lint's drawing together with an anonymous drawing dating to the seventeenth century and now in Düsseldorf,[4] we know that the architrave was constituted of (from top to bottom): a jutting cornice

---

[2] Berlin, Kupferstichkabinett, n. 14262. See D. Popp, 'Eine unbekannte Ansicht der mittelalterlichen Fassade von S. Giovanni in Laterano', *Römisches Jahrbuch für Bibliotheca Hertziana* 26 (1990), 31–9, with bibliography.

[3] See Barelli, Chapter 13 in this volume.

[4] Kunstmuseum, Graphische Sammlung, Inv. FP 4309. See Popp, 'Eine unbekannte Ansicht'.

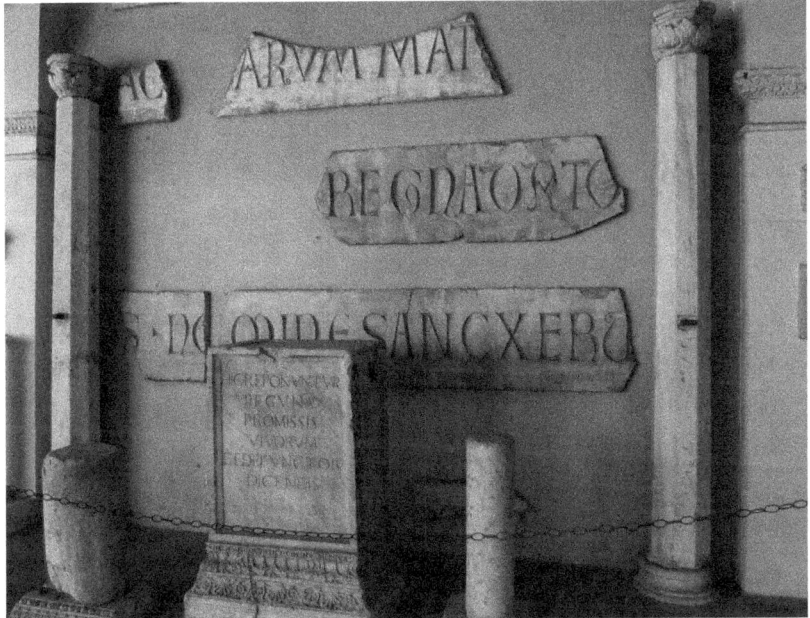

**Fig. 14.3** Fragments of the architrave of the medieval archbasilica, now in the cloister of the complex.

with animal protomes; a frieze with mosaic scenes and *tituli* (including our fragments); another smaller cornice; and the band with the dedicatory inscription of the archbasilica, starting with the words *Dogmate papali* ... (the few surviving fragments are now in the cloister of the complex; see Fig. 14.3).[5]

Thanks to Ciampini, we also know the themes and the sequence of the scenes on the frieze, which were still visible at the end of the seventeenth century (Fig. 14.4). Another important source is the codex Barberinianus Latinus 4423 from the Vatican Library, dating from 1672. We can then reconstruct the sequence of nine scenes: (1) *The Journey of Vespasian towards Judea*; (2) *The Siege of Jerusalem* (we did not find the fragments with the *titulus* relevant to this scene); (3) *The Donation of Constantine*; (4) *The Baptism of Constantine*; (5) *The Beheading of Saint John the Baptist*; (6) *Pope Silvestrus Tethers the Dragon from the Tarpeian Rock*; (7) a poorly preserved scene showing a sitting man, described but not identified by

---

[5] For these and other ancient descriptions of the archbasilica, including Ciampini, *De sacris aedificiis*, see the *Appendice Documentaria* in De Strobel, *Il portico medievale di San Giovanni in Laterano*.

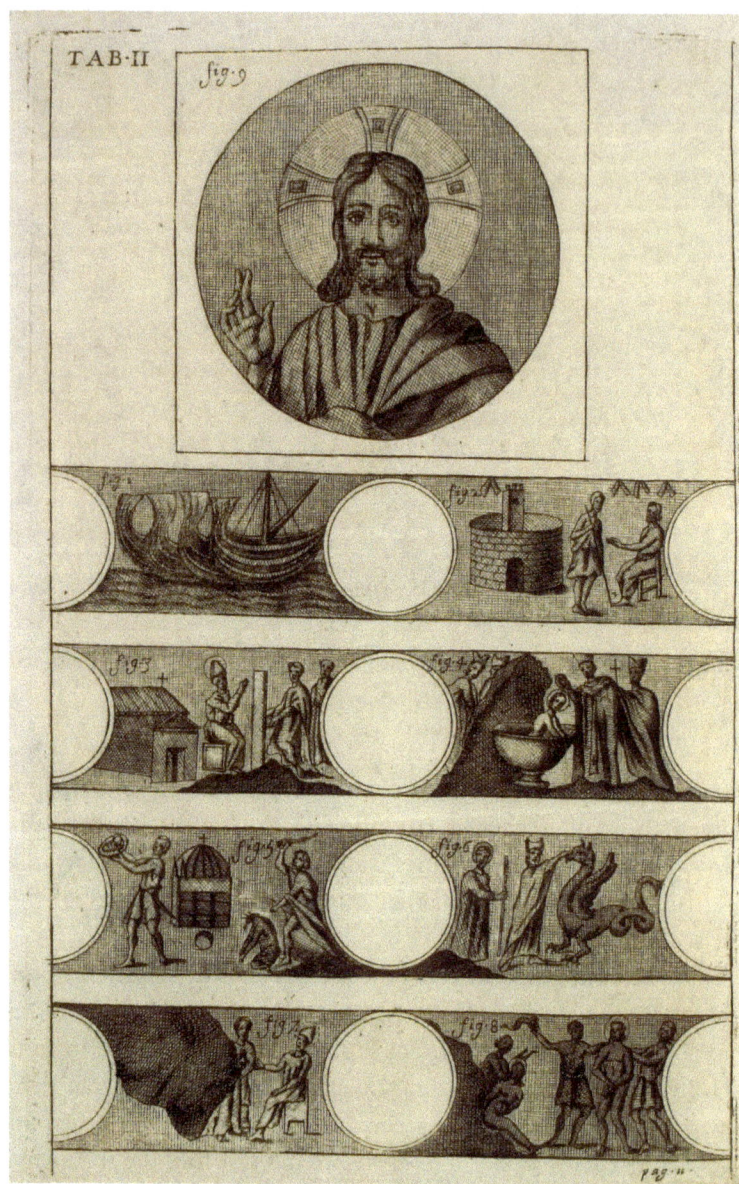

**Fig. 14.4** The frieze of the medieval archbasilica as depicted in Ciampini, *De sacris aedificiis*.

Ciampini;[6] (8) *The Martyrdom of Saint John the Evangelist*; (9) *The Anastasis*, mentioned only in the codex Barberinianus.

---

[6] Ciampini, *De sacris aedificiis*, 13: 'VII. Quæ né dimidia quidem sui parte sana est, atque unicam modò è duabus figuris integram offert, sedentem, ut vides, & diademate insignem, ac superiori in

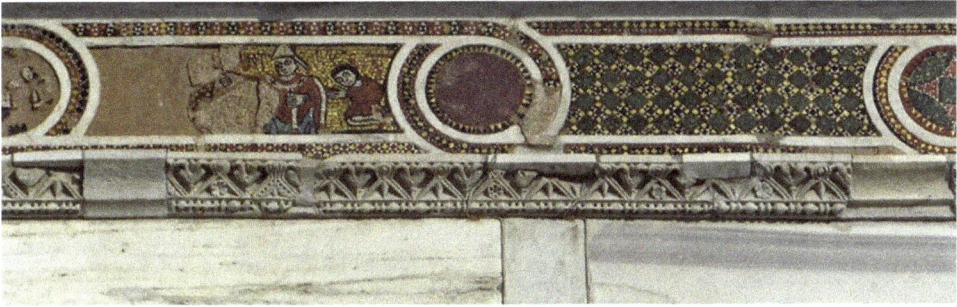

Fig. 14.5 The frieze of the portico of San Lorenzo fuori le Mura.

Considering the size of the frieze (we have calculated approximately 37.3 m long, with 21/22 square frames and the same number of circular frames), not all of the square frames seem to have contained figurative scenes. It is likely that each figurative scene was alternated with geometric or aniconic decorative motifs, similar to those still visible on the frieze of the portico of San Lorenzo fuori le Mura (see Figs 14.1 and 14.5). The same pattern was probably employed for the circular frames, which might have contained busts. This is suggested by the oldest depiction of the portico of the archbasilica, the fresco with the scene of *The Dream of Innocent III* in the upper basilica of Saint Francis of Assisi, painted by Giotto in around 1300.

The architectonic structure of the portico and the iconography of the mosaics as described and depicted in antiquarian sources have been thoroughly investigated by scholars. According to the most recent interpretations, the dating of the Cosmatesque portico ranges between the end of the twelfth and the beginning of the thirteenth centuries, between the pontificates of Pope Alexander III (1159–81) and Pope Honorius III (1216–27).[7] This dating

tertia tabella delineatæ persimilem, Beatum Sylvestrum representare posse coniicio. In hac figura observatione dignam existimo Cathedram, in qua iste Pontifex sedit, quæ persimilis est Cathedræ D. Petri, quæ adhuc in Vaticana asservatur Basilica, de cujus identitate eruditum scripsit Tractatum bon. mem. Franciscus Maria Phœbeus Cæremoniarum Magister, deinde Archiepiscopus Tarsensis. Plura præterire confultius est, cùm nec ab illa quid certum, ac utile haurire valeamus, nec ab aliquo versiculorum qui, si priores quatuor areolas excipias, desiderantur: absumptâ videlicet fasciâ marmoreâ, in in (sic) fuerunt cælati, ac alia simplici, & prorsus levi suffectâ.' See *Appendice Documentaria* in De Strobel, *Il portico medievale di San Giovanni in Laterano*, D41.

[7] I. Herklotz, 'Der mittelalterliche Fassadenportikus der Lateranbasilika und seine Mosaiken: Kunst und Propaganda am Ende des 12. Jahrhunderts', *RJBH* 25 (1989), 27–95; I. Herklotz, *Gli eredi di Costantino: Il papato, il Laterano e la propaganda visiva nel XII secolo* (La corte dei papi 6) (Rome, 2000); S. Maddalo, '*Caput et vertex omnium ecclesiarum*: La cattedrale di Roma tra XII e XIII secolo', in A. C. Quintavalle (ed.), *Medioevo: l'Europa delle Cattedrali. Atti del Convegno Internazionale di Studi (Parma 19–23 settembre 2006)* (I convegni di Parma 9) (Parma,

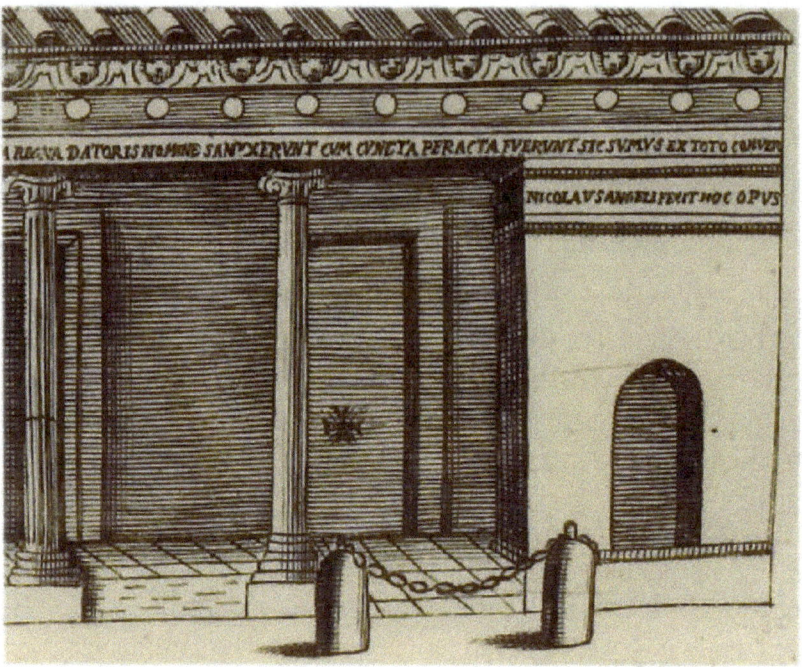

**Fig. 14.6** The inscription-signature of Nicolaus de Angelo in Ciampini's etching (Ciampini, *De sacris aedificiis*, table I).

is suggested by a structural and stylistic comparison with other examples in Rome and Latium. Thanks to the inscription-signature in Ciampini's etching and to other antiquarian sources[8] (Fig. 14.6), the portico is attributed to Nicolaus de Angelo, a sculptor and architect active from the end of the twelfth and the beginning of the thirteenth centuries. Significantly, he, together with Pietro Vassalletto, worked on the *Easter Candlestick* in the basilica of San Paolo fuori le Mura, a sculpture that has explanatory *tituli* associated with figurative scenes just like those included in our fragments (Fig. 14.7).

2007), 424–34; S. Maddalo, 'Immagini e ideologia tra gli *Actus Sylvestri* e il *Constitutum Constantini*: Riflessioni su una duplice tradizione figurativa', in A. C. Quintavalle (ed.), *Medioevo: Arte e storia. Atti del Convegno Internazionale di Studi (Parma, 18–22 settembre 2007)* (I convegni di Parma 10) (Parma, 2008), 481–94; P. C. Claussen, Die Kirchen der Stadt Rom im Mittelalter 1050–1300, Bd. 2: S. Giovanni in Laterano (Corpus Cosmatorum II, 2) (Forschungen zur Kunstgeschichte und Christlichen Archäologie 21) (Stuttgart, 2008).

[8] The signature 'Nicolaus Angelus/ Angeli fecit hoc opus' is transcribed also by Alfonso Ciacconio (preparatory manuscript of the *Historica Descriptio Urbis Romae*, Madrid, Biblioteca National Ms.2008; c. 1570); by Benedetto Mellini (*Roma Descritta da Benedetto Millino. Rione de Monti* in the Archivio Capitolare Lateranense, codex A. XXIX; middle of the seventeenth century); and in *An Account of a Journey* by Philip Skippon, who visited Rome in 1664; see *Appendice Documentaria*, D20, D36, and D40 in De Strobel, *Il portico medievale di San Giovanni in Laterano*.

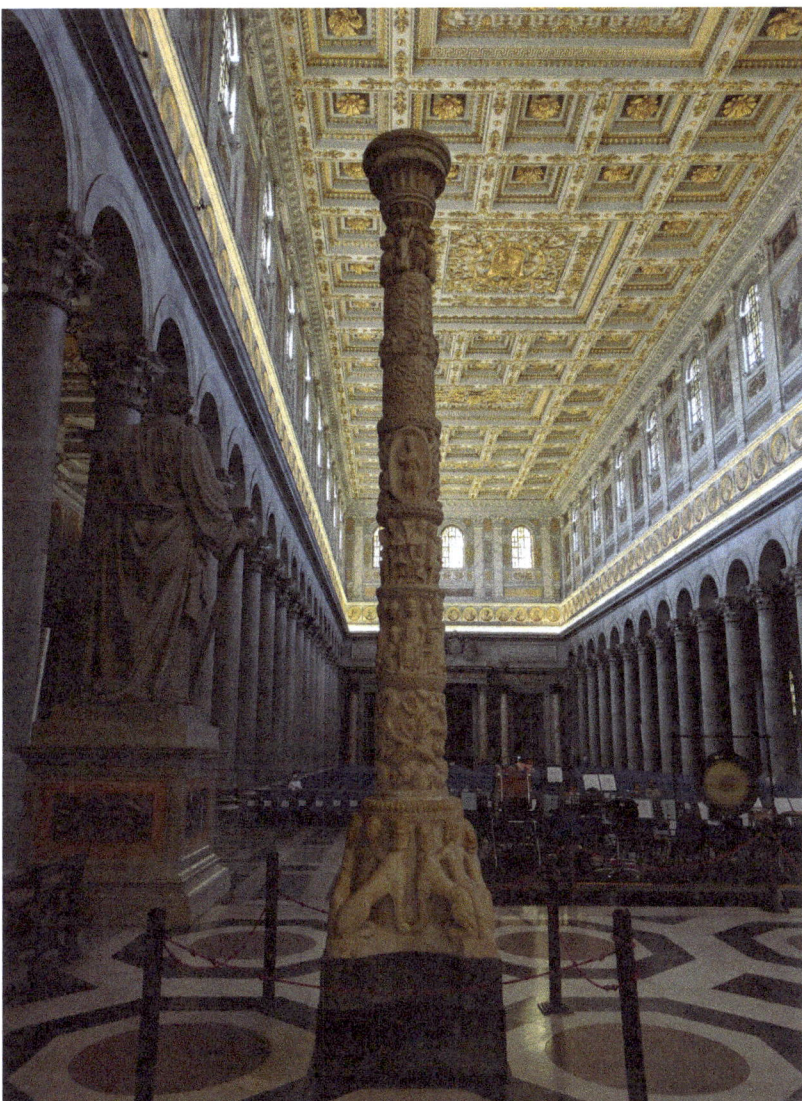

**Fig. 14.7** The *Easter Candlestick* in the basilica of San Paolo fuori le Mura.

After the restoration, Ottavio Bucarelli examined the yet unpublished *tituli* and the large inscription of the portico beginning 'Dogmate papali'. He dated the *tituli* to the last two decades of the twelfth century, while the inscription seems to be later in date, perhaps from the time of Pope Honorius III (1216–27).[9] The evidence suggests that the portico and its

---

[9] O. Bucarelli, 'I frammenti epigrafici del fregio del portico medievale di San Giovanni in Laterano', in De Strobel, *Il portico medievale di San Giovanni in Laterano*, 149–63.

mosaics were made at the end of the twelfth century, probably soon after 1188, when the papal court was restored in Rome after decades of conflict with the Commune. The promoter might have been either Clement III (1187–91), the pope who re-established the Curia in Rome, or his successor Celestine III (1191–8). The iconographic programme of the mosaics, especially The Donation of Constantine, is strongly politicised and exalts the temporal power of the popes in relation to the city of Rome and the Commune. On the other hand, Peter Cornelius Claussen proposes the canons of the archbasilica as the promoters of the construction and decoration of the portico at the end of the twelfth century.[10]

The portico was not significantly modified in the following four centuries. The roof was restored in 1433–4 by Eugenius IV (1431–47) and again in 1573 by Gregory XIII (1572–85). On the other hand, substantial modifications occurred under Pope Clement VIII (1592–1605) and it is worth examining them in details.

At the time of Pope Clement VIII, antiquarian accounts (especially by Onofrio Panvinio and Pompeo Ugonio[11]) tell us that the portico still had three smooth columns and three fluted columns at the front, although they do not mention the type of marble used. Thanks to a series of documents dating from 1597 to 1598 and linked to the large reconstruction of the transept of the archbasilica under Clement VIII, we know that the shafts of two columns in yellow marble were removed and reused, with new capitals, to support the organ of the transept (Fig. 14.8). The marble shafts of the columns of the portico were substituted by shafts in granite, one coming from the Fabbrica di San Pietro and the other bought from Madonna Ginevra di Ciccone Fiorentino, who found it in one of her vineyards near Santa Croce in Gerusalemme.[12] After the works supported by Clement VIII, the portico had five smooth columns in granite and only one fluted column. We have an antiquarian description of them by Benedetto Mellini,[13] confirmed by a very precious document from the Archivio Capitolare Lateranense regarding the dismantling of the medieval

---

[10] Claussen, *Die Kirchen der Stadt Rom*, esp. 84–9.

[11] See *Appendice Documentaria* in De Strobel, *Il portico medievale di San Giovanni in Laterano*, D18 and D19 (Onofrio Panvinio) and D22 (Pompeo Ugonio).

[12] See *Appendice Documentaria* in De Strobel, *Il portico medievale di San Giovanni in Laterano*, D26–30 and D32–3.

[13] Manuscript by Benedetto Mellini, *ROMA Descritta da Benedetto Millino: Rione de Monti*, cc. 33v–34r: 'La facciata ad oriente ha un portico antico, con cinque porte, il quale perché hora si va rinovando, non si può descrivere intieramente. Hoggi è alzato sopra sei colonne. cinque di granito, et una di marmo scannellata, con capitelli d'ordine Ionico, di circonferenza palmi 12 l'una. All'angolo verso settentrione un gran pilastro di marmo ... ' (Archivio Capitolare Lateranense, A. XXIX). An extended version of this document is

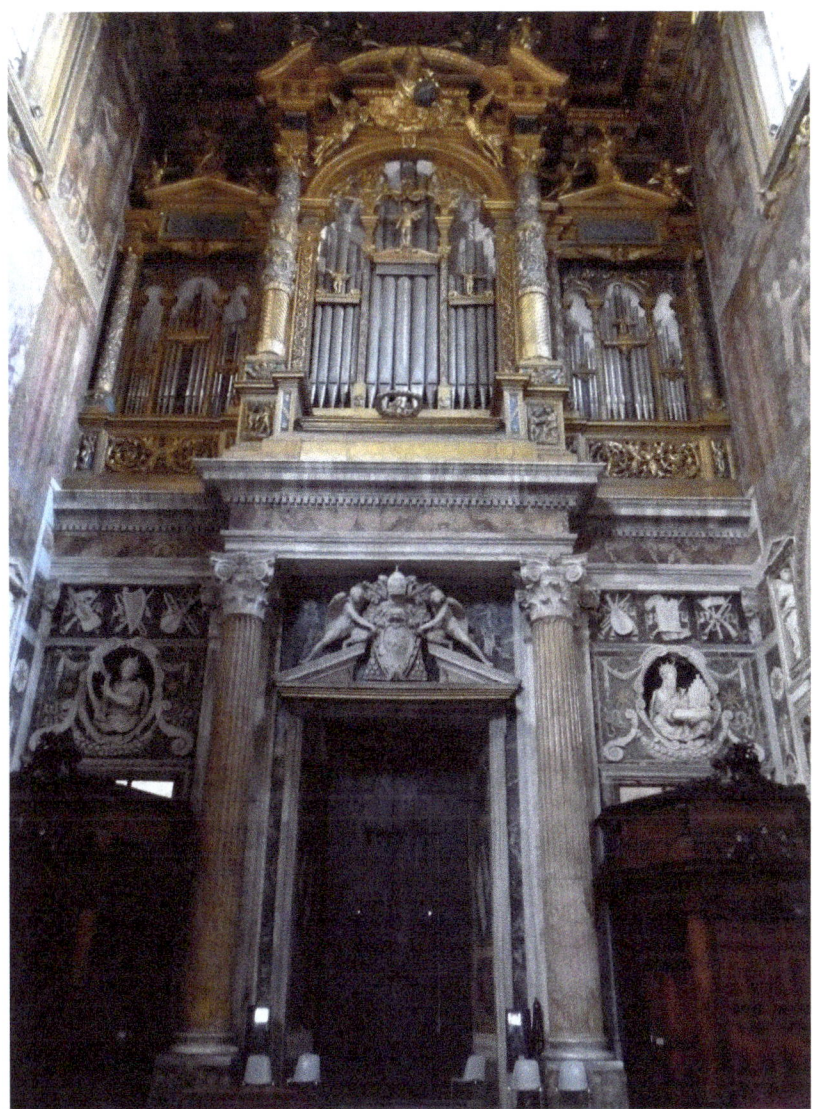

**Fig. 14.8** Two columns in yellow marble supporting the organ of the transept.

portico, dating to 29 February 1732 (*Document of 1732 about the Dismantling*).[14] This is a payment request from the master builders who

> included in the *Appendice Documentaria* in De Strobel, *Il portico medievale di San Giovanni in Laterano*, D36.

[14] Rome, Archivio Capitolare Lateranense, FB. 21, *Fabrica della Facciata Lateranense. Giustificazioni del Libro Mastro. Parte Prima, Dal N.° P.° al N.° 123 (1731–1734)*, doc. no. 28. This document is included in the *Appendice Documentaria* in De Strobel, *Il portico medievale di San Giovanni in Laterano*, D50.

dismantled the medieval portico, and it gives a very detailed account of the materials and of the steps taken by the workers, each of whom had to be compensated. The *Document* confirms that the portico had eight columns, six of which were '31¼ palmi [spans]' high and had a diameter of '3⅔ palmi'. Furthermore, it usefully explicitly states that five of the columns were of granite and one was made of two pieces of marble ('n° 5 di granito intiere et una di marmo di due pezzi'). The other two columns were smaller and were part of the bay of the portico built by Sergius II, later incorporated into the chapel of Saint Thomas and made visible again in 1647 when Borromini was planning a new façade. The *Document* also mentions that the six larger columns of the portico were moved to near the wall of the Ospizio and the other two near the Scala Santa (trasportate addosso il muro dell'Ospizio e l'altre due piccole vicino la Scala Santa ...).[15]

Once again, written accounts are supported by iconographic sources. In particular, the previously mentioned table I in Ciampini's volume shows that the second column from the right was fluted and it is depicted with a horizontal line, possibly indicating that the column was fractured 'in due pezzi' (Figs 14.2 and 14.6).

We will now look at the new building phase promoted by Pope Clement XII Corsini (1730–40) and at the new façade. The medieval façade was abruptly demolished at the beginning of December 1731, as testified by the *Diario di Roma* by Francesco Valesio and the *avvisi* from the Archivio di Stato di Firenze. These documents specify that, when the ancient portico was in the process of being demolished, there was not yet a project in place for its substitution, nor was there an architect to carry it out.[16] However, soon after the demolition in December 1731, the Florentine architect Alessandro Galilei won the bid for the façade of the archbasilica, which was completed in 1735.

The next step was to identify the location of the pieces of the portico, especially the columns, after it was dismantled. As mentioned above, the *Document of 1732 about the Dismantling* mentions that,

---

[15] The Ospizio (hospice) mentioned here is the Lateran palace, at the time used by the Ospizio Apostolico di San Michele. When the Ospizio Apostolico dei Poveri Invalidi was created in 1693, Pope Innocent XII (1691–1700) donated the palace to this institution: A. Ippoliti, *Il Palazzo Apostolico del Laterano* (Monumenta Sanctae Sedis 4) (Rome, 2008), 20–2, 103–4, document 23 (the act of foundation).

[16] These documents are included in the *Appendice Documentaria* in De Strobel, *Il portico medievale di San Giovanni in Laterano*, D47 E and F (*Diario di Roma*), D48 A and B (*Avvisi*).

after being grounded, the large columns were stored in the Lateran palace.[17] About a year later, the white marble column in two pieces is described in a survey dating 7 March 1732: 'an ancient, fluted column of marble fit for statues ... in two pieces ... which was employed in the eastern side of the ancient Portico' (una colonna di marmo statuario antica scannellata ... di due pezzi ... la quale era in opera nel Portico antico verso oriente). According to this text, the column was 31 spans high, corresponding to the 31¼ spans given in the *Document about the Dismantling*. The survey was carried out by the architects of the Lateran Chapter, who evaluated the column worth 100 scudi.[18] The 'fluted column of marble in two pieces' ('la colonna di marmo scannellata di due pezzi') was evaluated once again, this time by the architect of the Municipality of Rome, who decided for a price of 84 scudi.[19]

Another document, a chirograph by Clement XII dated 10 April 1732, explains the reason for these assessments:

> We have been informed that in the ancient Portico of our basilica, founded by Imperator Constantine the Great and lately demolished to rebuild the façade of the aforementioned basilica, was found a fluted column of white marble in two pieces, weighing approximately 10 *carrettate*, that has now been removed and lies in the piazza of the basilica. We have been also informed that this column is believed to be one of those that decorated the so-called Arch of Constantine. We have therefore decided that the column should be returned to the Arch, so that it might be put back in place in its own site ... [20]

---

[17] See above, nn. 14 and 15.
[18] Roma, Biblioteca dell'Accademia Romana dei Lincei e Corsiniana, Codex 32.D.1, c. 504r; in *Appendice Documentaria* in De Strobel, *Il portico medievale di San Giovanni in Laterano*, D51.
[19] Roma, Biblioteca dell'Accademia Romana dei Lincei e Corsiniana, Codex 32.D.1, c. 500r; in *Appendice Documentaria* in De Strobel, *Il portico medievale di San Giovanni in Laterano*, D52.
[20] 'Essendoci stato rappresentato che nell'antico Portico di detta nostra Basilica, la dicui (sic) fondazione provenne da Costantino Imperatore il Magno, et ultimamente demolito per la fabrica della facciata di detta Basilica, ritrovavasi conservata una colonna di marmo bianco scannellata in due pezzi, di misura di dieci carrettate incirca, quale presentemente apparisce asportata, et esistente nella Piazza di detta Basilica, et essendoci stato anche esposto che la predetta colonna si creda l'istessa et una di quelle mancanti che esistevano et servivano d'ornato all'Arco denominato di Constantino ... habbiamo deliberato ordinare che sia risarcito il predetto Arco, et in tal congiuntura riposta in esso et nel suo proprio sito la detta colonna ...': Rome, Archivio di Stato di Roma, Trenta Notai Capitolini, Notai del Vicario, Ufficio 30, J. A. Sfasciamonti, v. 445; in *Appendice Documentaria* in De Strobel, *Il portico medievale di San Giovanni in Laterano*, D53.

Clement XII was told that the fluted column in white marble from the demolished portico of the archbasilica was the one that had been removed from the Arch of Constantine. He thus ordered Cardinal Pietro Ottoboni, archpriest of the archbasilica, to deliver the column to Marquis Alessandro Capponi. He was then to return it to the Arch of Constantine, which at the time was being restored by the pope under the direction of Capponi himself.

The document reflects the erroneous antiquarian idea that a column from the Arch of Constantine had been reused in the archbasilica. The 'informants' of Clement XII believed that this missing element was the 'fluted column of white marble in two pieces'[21] from the medieval portico. According to another hypothesis, the missing column from the arch was of yellow marble and was therefore to be identified with the one reused at the time of Pope Clement VIII to support the organ of the transept of the archbasilica. This theory was supported by Ridolfino Venuti in his *Accurata, e succinta descrizione topografica delle Antichità di Roma*:

> Along the same road, after the church of St Gregory ... one will see the Arch of Constantine not far away, partially built with material from the buildings of the Forum of Trajan ... Together with the beautiful sculpture just described, one should consider the fine ornaments taken from the triumphal Arch of Trajan, and the ornaments under the eight large yellow columns in gold; one of these was removed by Clement VIII and placed to support the organ of the Lateran archbasilica together with another one. The column of the arch was substituted by another one in white marble ... This arch was isolated from other structures and restored by Clement XII.[22]

---

[21] 'di marmo bianco scannellata in due pezzi' (see previous note).

[22] 'Proseguendosi per la detta strada passata la chiesa di S. Gregorio ... si vede poco lontano l'Arco di Costantino, fabbricato in parte con le spoglie degli Edificj del Foro di Trajano; ... Oltre all'eccellenza delle predette sculture si deve considerare il pregio degli altri ornamenti tolti parimente dall'arco trionfale di Trajano, e sotto le otto grosse colonne di giallo in oro; una delle quali tolta da Clemente VIII. e posta per accompagnare altra sotto l'organo della Basilica Lateranense. Vi fu posta in sua vece altra di marmo bianco ... Quest'Arco è stato reso isolato da Clemente XII. e risarcito': *Accurata, e succinta descrizione topografica delle Antichità di Roma dell'Abate Ridolfino Venuti Cortonese Presidente dell'Antichità Romane, E Membro Onorario della Regia Società degli Antiquarj di Londra, Parte Prima* (Rome, 1763), 10–12, in *Appendice Documentaria*, in De Strobel, *Il portico medievale di San Giovanni in Laterano*, D61.

Just before the restoration of the Arch of Constantine by Clement XII, a column was indeed missing from the rightmost side of the northern façade. However, it had gone missing long before the pontificate of Clement VIII, so he was certainly not to blame for removing and reusing it as suggested in Venuti's reconstruction. This is testified by a number of iconographic sources, including a drawing by Giovanni Antonio Dosio dating to around 1560 (Florence, Gabinetto Disegni e Stampe degli Uffizi, 2531/A), which appears not to have been considered in previous academic works concerning the state of the arch during the sixteenth century.

Among the many iconographic sources depicting the arch before Clement XII's restorations, we should mention an etching by Bonaventura van Overbeek (1660–1705), published in 1708 (Fig. 14.9).[23] Here we can see the hollow left by the missing column that the pope intended to fill with the white column from the demolished portico of the archbasilica. The evidence collected so far suggests that the column now located in the rightmost side of the northern façade of the Arch of Constantine indeed came from the medieval portico and was placed there by Clement XII (Fig. 14.10). A brief survey has confirmed this hypothesis: (i) this is the only column in 'white' marble of the arch (the other seven being of yellow marble);[24] (ii) the column is fluted; (iii) it is broken in two; and (iv) it is 7.1 m high, very close to the the '31¼ palmi [spans]' mentioned in our eighteenth-century descriptions.[25]

We have subsequently tried to identify the remaining seven smooth granite columns: five from the Cosmatesque portico and two from the portico of Pope Sergius II. While we do not have any information about the latter, four of the five columns from the Cosmatesque portico seem to have been reused in the Loggia delle Benedizioni of the new façade of the archbasilica, as proposed by Peter Cornelius Claussen in his 2008 volume on the complex (Fig. 14.11).[26] The shafts of the columns in granite of the Loggia are 6.98 m high with a diameter of 82 cm, once again matching the

---

[23] B. van Overbeek, *Reliquiae Antiquae Urbis Romae* ... (Amsterdam, 1708), table b9. Other iconographical sources are discussed in De Strobel, *Il portico medievale di San Giovanni in Laterano*.

[24] The 'white' marble mentioned in the sources is actually *pavonazzetto* marble. We would like to thank Matthias Bruno for this information.

[25] The *Document of 1732 about the Dismantling* reports these measurements (corresponding to 6.98 m) for all the large columns of the portico. These are confirmed by the survey dated 7 March 1732, which gives the measurements of 10½ + 21¼ palmi (see n. 18 above).

[26] Claussen, *Die Kirchen der Stadt Rom*, 73.

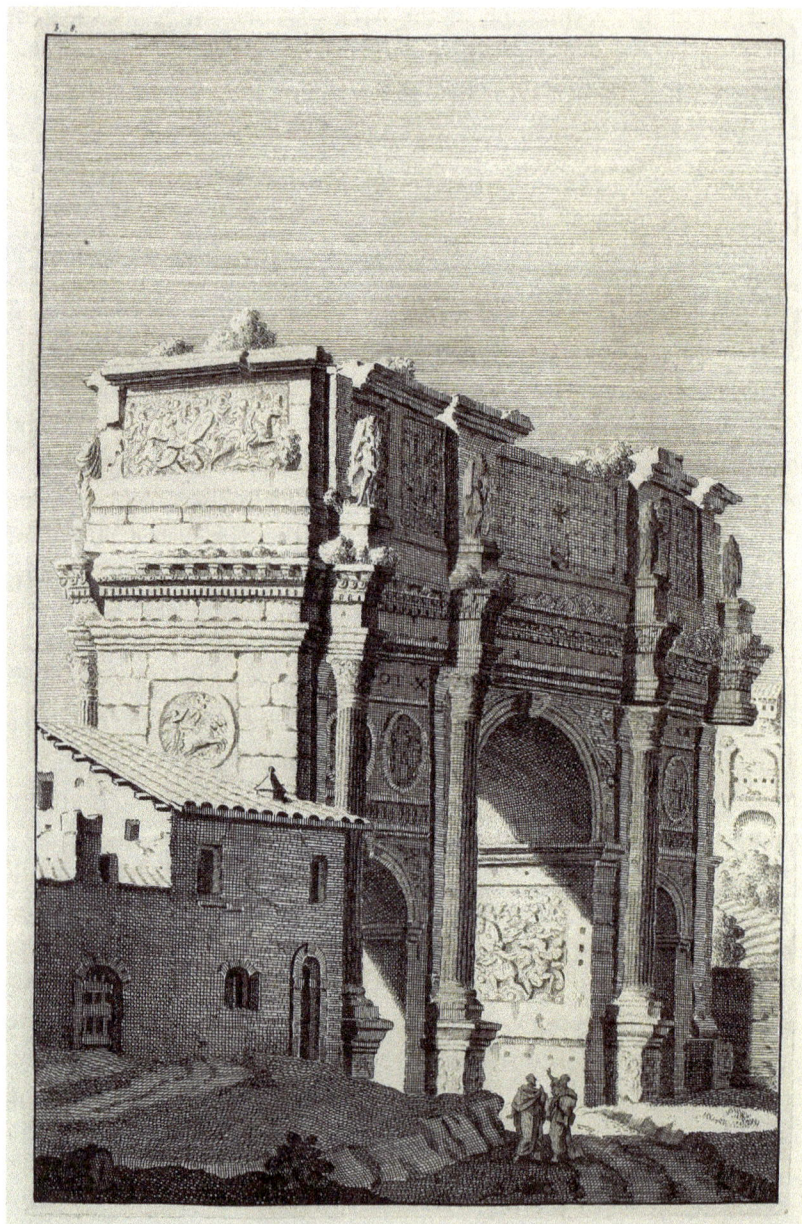

**Fig. 14.9** The Arch of Constantine in an etching by Bonaventura van Overbeek (1660–1705), published in 1708 (van Overbeek, *Reliquiae Antiquae*, table b9).

size given in the eighteenth-century sources. They might have been kept as 'relics' of the ancient archbasilica, together with the mosaic with the *Bust of Christ*.

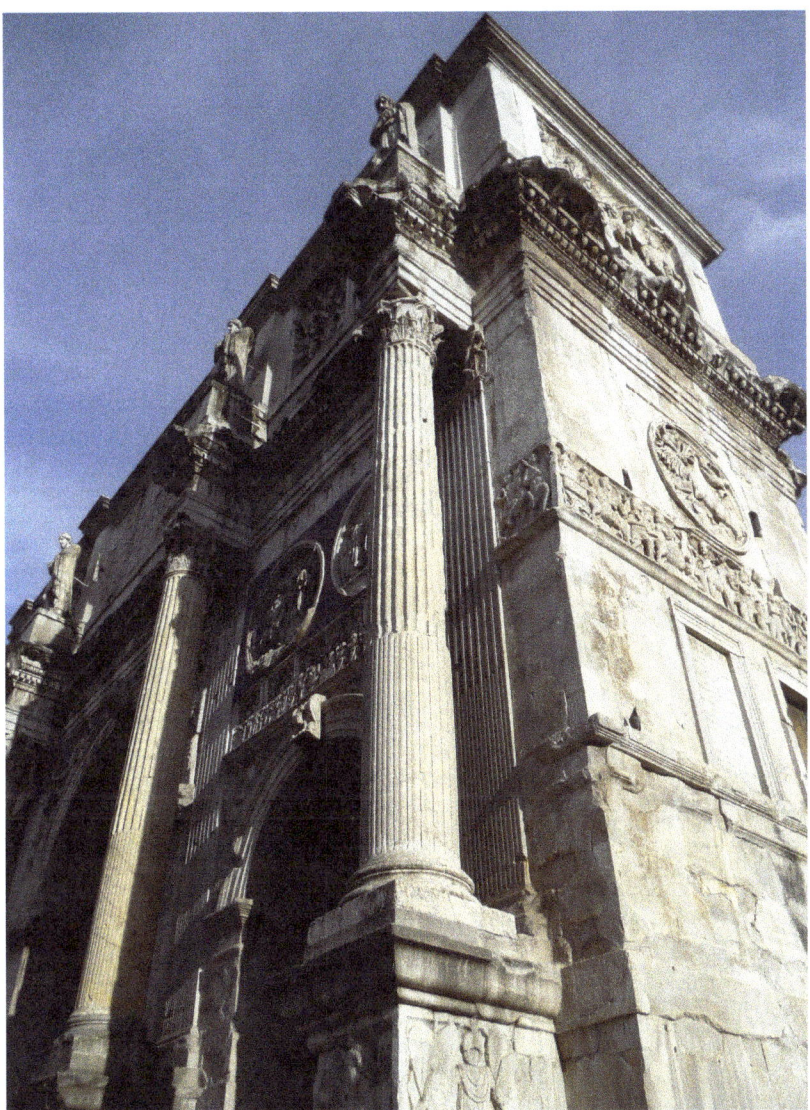

**Fig. 14.10** The column now located in the rightmost side of the northern façade of the Arch of Constantine.

The last aspect to clarify was what happened of the fragments of the frieze after the destruction of the medieval portico, and how they ended up in the storage room of Saint John in Lateran. Once again, archival research has provided important information. A document from the Archivio Capitolare Lateranense states that the central part of the pavement of the Portico Sistino was remade in 1734. This is

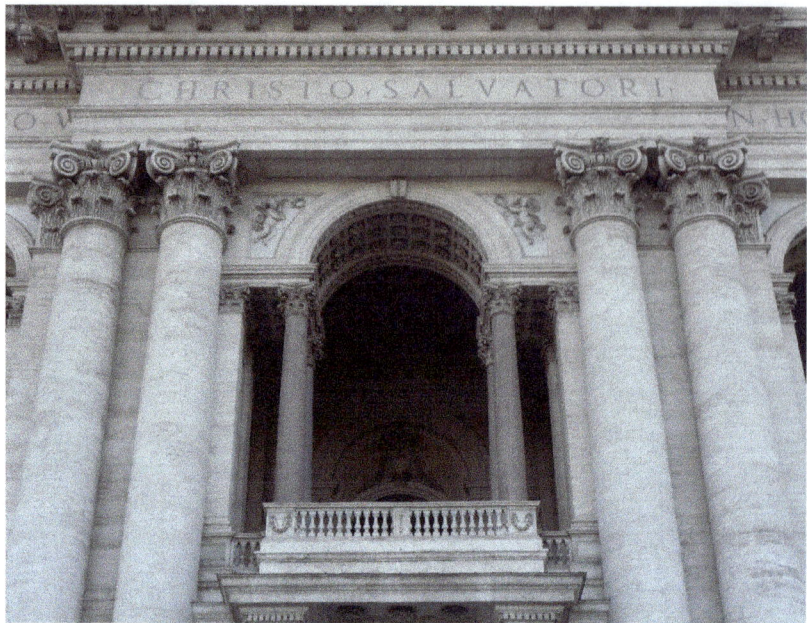

**Fig. 14.11** Four of the five columns from the Cosmatesque portico seem to have been reused in the Loggia delle Benedizioni of the new façade of the archbasilica.

another payment request: it meticulously details the types of marble used and, more importantly, it provides a sketch of the new section of the pavement with the coat of arms of Clement XII at its centre, giving the measures of each component.[27]

Thanks to a series of graphical reconstructions realised by architect Paola Brunori,[28] we have verified that the drawing and measurements of the various parts of the pavement match the measurements of the geometrical shapes of a large number of the surviving fragments. Furthermore, fragment 57919.31.20 shows a moulded incision on its southern side, seemingly carved to fit in the top part of a papal tiara. The latter is indicated as a 'triregno' in the 1734 document. This slab was then probably part of the inlay with Clement XII's coat of arms.

The eighteenth-century pavement was substituted by a new one laid down by the Ditta Medici in 1948 as part of a significant restoration

---

[27] ACL, FB 21 – *Fabrica della Facciata Lateranense. Giustificazioni del Libro Mastro. Parte Prima Dal N° P° al N°123. Angelo Orlandi Computista,* Document 98. The document is published in *Appendice Documentaria* in De Strobel, *Il portico medievale di San Giovanni in Laterano*, D58.

[28] P. Brunori and F. Carboni, 'Il disegno come strumento. Rilievi, ricostruzioni, modelli nello studio del fregio', in De Strobel, *Il portico medievale di San Giovanni in Laterano*, 165–87, at pp. 183–4.

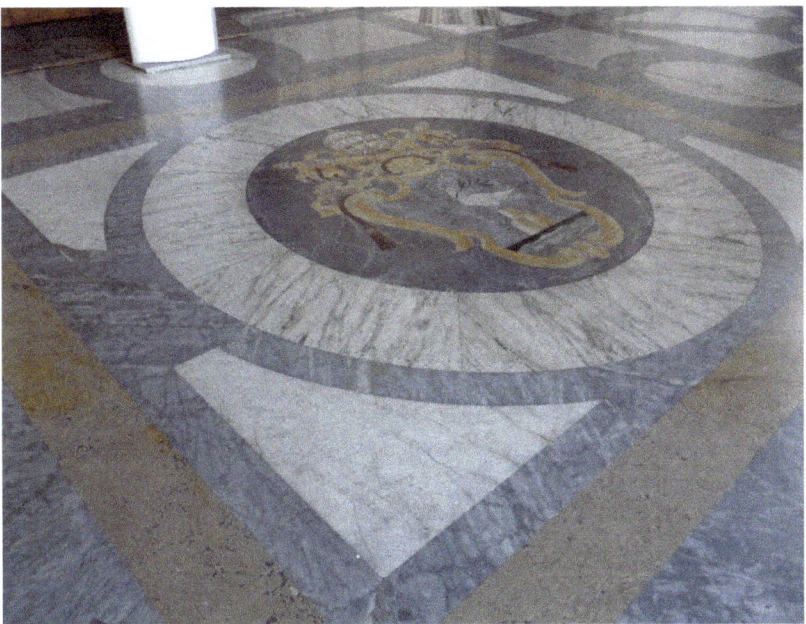

**Fig. 14.12** The coat of arms of Pope Pius XII at the centre of the modern pavement of the archbasilica.

decided by Pope Pius XII (1939–58). The coat of arms of the latter can still be seen at the centre of this modern pavement (Fig. 14.12). As testified by contemporary records, during these works '60 broken frames of marble and bardiglio, 28 × 28 cm in size' (60 riquadri rotti di marmo e bardiglio di cm 28 × 28) were substituted.[29] Clement XII's pavement was probably disassembled at this time, and the fragmentary slabs from the frieze of the portico were found. The fragments were then stored in the Lateran Museums, before being transferred in the storage room of the Vatican Museums, where they were found and identified in 2009.

---

[29] P. Grazioli Medici, *Medici: Marmorari Romani* (Vatican City, 1992), 307.

# 15 | MATER ET CAPUT OMNIUM ECCLESIARUM: Visual Strategies in the Rivalry between San Giovanni in Laterano and San Pietro in Vaticano

CAROLA JÄGGI

*Dedicated to Sible de Blaauw, a bit too late for his sixty-fifth birthday*

In October 2014 a conference was held in Mannheim on 'The Popes and the Unity of the Latin World'. The papers from this conference have recently been published under the title *Die Päpste: Amt und Herrschaft in Antike, Mittelalter und Renaissance*.[1] The book cover shows the silhouette of Saint Peter's basilica combined with Arnolfo di Cambio's statue of Pope Boniface VIII as one of the most famous representatives of the medieval papacy. But why the dome of Saint Peter's? Why not San Giovanni in Laterano, which is still the cathedral of the bishop of Rome and therefore *stricto sensu* the head and mother of all the other churches in Rome and the world? The honorary title OMNIVM VRBIS ET ORBIS ECCLESIARVM MATER ET CAPVT was officially assigned to the Lateran basilica by papal bull in 1372 and can be read still today in an inscription on the eighteenth-century façade of Alessandro Galilei (Fig. 15.1).[2]

The fact that the organisers of the Mannheim conference did not even comment on their choice of Saint Peter's basilica for the conference flyer and the book cover proves the close and unquestioned link between papacy and Saint Peter's in our perception today. The basilica of Saint Peter's actually seems to have turned into a cypher for the pope and for papacy as an institution. It is Saint Peter's that is regarded as the 'most important church in Western Christendom' and the 'most significant religious site in Western Europe', at least in the eyes of those colleagues who in March 2010 held a conference about

---

[1] B. Schneidmüller, S. Weinfurter, M. Matheus and A. Wieczorek (eds.), *Die Päpste: Amt und Herrschaft in Antike, Mittelalter und Renaissance* (Regensburg, 2016).

[2] For the bull of 1372 see Blaauw, *CD* I, 48; A. Rehberg, *Die Kanoniker von S. Giovanni in Laterano und S. Maria Maggiore im 14. Jahrhundert* (Tübingen, 1999), 21. For the history and evolution of the honorary title 'mater et caput omnium ecclesiarum' (and similar versions), see I. Herklotz, 'Der mittelalterliche Fassadenportikus der Lateranbasilika und seine Mosaiken. Kunst und Propaganda am Ende des 12. Jahrhunderts', *RJBH* 25 (1989), 27–95, at pp. 89–92; Blaauw, *CD* I, 204. For the eighteenth-century façade of San Giovanni in Laterano, see L. Barroero, 'La basilica dal cinquecento ai nostri giorni', in C. Pietrangeli (ed.), *San Giovanni in Laterano* (Florence, 1990), 145–255, at pp. 167–71; H. Hyde Minor, *The Culture of Architecture in Enlightenment Rome* (University Park, PA, 2010), 31–58.

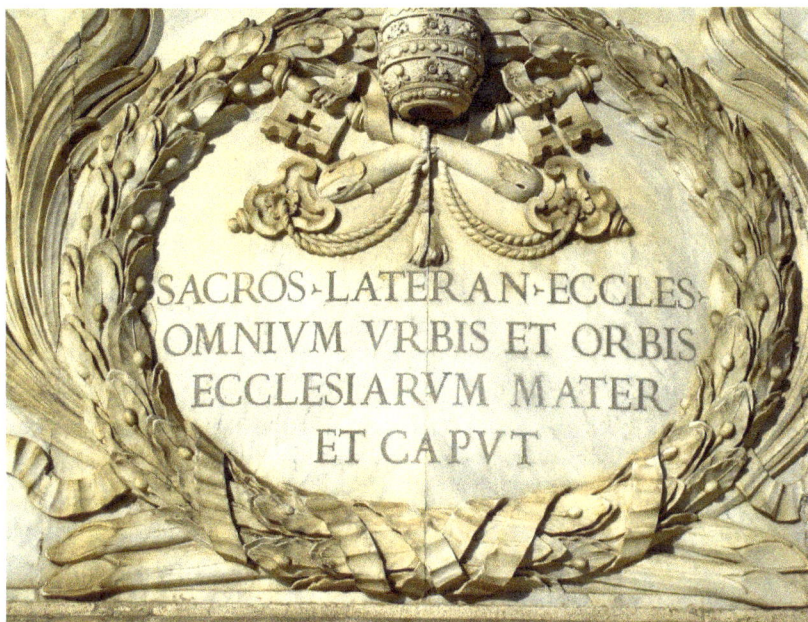

**Fig. 15.1** Cartouche with inscription on the eighteenth-century façade of San Giovanni in Laterano (Photo: C. Jäggi).

Old Saint Peter's at the British School at Rome and therefore in the same location where six years later the Lateran conference took place.[3] Even the sequence of these Roman conferences shows that the Lateran church is considered only second best. But so far nobody seems to have explicitly wondered why this is the case, nor when this process started, by whom it was prompted and which visual (and also non-visual) media were used.[4]

## The Lateran and Saint Peter's: Basic Commonalities and Differences

We all know that the Lateran basilica was founded by Constantine immediately after the battle at the Milvian Bridge in 312.[5] It was erected *intra*

---

[3] R. McKitterick, J. Osborne, C. M. Richardson and J. Story, 'Introduction', in R. McKitterick, J. Osborne, C. M. Richardson and J. Story (eds.), *Old Saint Peter's, Rome* (British School at Rome Monograph Series) (Cambridge, 2013) 1–20 (quotations from pp. 1 and 7).

[4] The topic will be discussed in greater detail by Angela Yorck von Wartenburg in her Ph.D. thesis.

[5] For the early history of the Lateran see *CBCR* V, 10–11 and 25–48; Blaauw, *CD* I, 109–47; S. de Blaauw, 'Le origini e gli inizi dell'architettura cristiana', in S. de Blaauw (ed.), *Storia dell'architettura italiana*, vol. I: *Da Costantino a Carlo Magno* (Milan, 2010), 22–53, esp. pp. 32–5; P. C. Claussen, 'S. Giovanni in Laterano', in P. C. Claussen, *Die Kirchen der Stadt Rom im Mittelalter, 1050–1300,*

*muros*, close to the city walls on the site of the former barracks of the *equites singulares*. It is equally known that the new church at the Lateran was consecrated to Christ the Saviour and given to the bishop of Rome as his cathedral. Saint Peter's basilica at the Vatican, however – and this again is a well-known fact – was also commissioned by Constantine, a few years later, and was destined to preserve the *memoria* for Saint Peter.[6] With the basilica on the Vatican hill, the tomb of the prince of the apostles received a gigantic shrine destined to house additional tombs, funeral repasts and memorial services. The two churches were therefore built with completely different functions and different liturgical purposes: on the one hand there was the Saviour's church at the Lateran, where papal services were held, on the other hand there was Saint Peter's basilica at the Vatican, which was a kind of covered cemetery built around the *memoria* of Saint Peter.

It is evident that the situation today is a completely different one: Saint Peter's is now the pope's church for liturgical services, whereas in the Lateran basilica we find a number of sepulchral monuments. How did this reinterpretation happen? Why was a baptistery added to Saint Peter's in the fourth century (or in the fifth at the latest) while a spacious and richly decorated baptistery for papal baptismal services was available at the Lateran? What is the purpose of a baptistery at a memorial and pilgrimage church like Saint Peter's that – unlike other early Christian pilgrimage churches with proper baptisteries such as Qual'at Sem'an (in Syria) or Abu Mena (in Egypt) – does not lie remote from civilisation but next to a vibrant city with a magnificent cathedral-baptistery and a number of additional baptisteries in the urban titular churches?[7] And – concerning the Lateran – how could a pope even come up with the idea of choosing the intra-mural cathedral as his final resting place when, from the fifth century onwards, the traditional papal burial place had always been Saint Peter's? And how

---

Bd. 2: *S. Giovanni in Laterano* (Corpus Cosmatorum II, 2) (Forschungen zur Kunstgeschichte und Christlichen Archäologie 21) (Stuttgart, 2008), 25–8; B. M. Apollonj Ghetti, *La basilica del Salvatore poi di S. Giovanni al Laterano cattedrale di Roma: Edizione a cura di Eugenio Russo* (San Marino, 2013), 9–42. See also Bosman, Chapter 9 in this volume.

[6] CBCR V, 176–82 and 191–220; Blaauw, *CD* II, *passim*; de Blaauw, 'Le origini e gli inizi', 35–8; F. A. Bauer, 'Saint Peter's as a place of collective memory in Late Antiquity', in R. Behrwald and C. Witschel (eds.), *Rom in der Spätantike: Historische Erinnerung im städtischen Raum* (Stuttgart, 2012), 155–70. See also the respective contributions in McKitterick et al. (eds.), *Old Saint Peter's, Rome*.

[7] On the organisation of baptism in early Christian Rome, see B. Bruderer Eichberg, 'Prolegomena zur frühchristlichen und frühmittelalterlichen Tauforganisation in Rom: Die Baptisterien und die Stifterrolle der Päpste', in N. Bock, P. Kurmann, S. Romano and J.-M. Spieser (eds.), *Art, cérémonial et liturgie au moyen age* (Actes du Colloque de 3e Cycle Romand de Lettres, Lausanne/Fribourg 2000) (Rome, 2002), 321–56.

was it that the Lateran, without containing the tomb of any saint, became the custodian of the holiest reliquary treasure of Rome, the Sancta Sanctorum, and as a consequence surpassed in holiness all the Roman churches that were built over the tombs of martyrs including Saint Peter's?

Questions such as these have rarely been asked with regard to the two main churches of Rome – perhaps because these two churches have hardly ever been compared directly.[8] With such a comparative look at the Lateran and Saint Peter's, however, dynamics become apparent that provide insights into the ecclesiastical and worldly power structure of early Christian and medieval Rome.

## Foundation and Appropriation: Fourth–Ninth Centuries

Let us start in the fourth century, when Constantine initiated and financed the new construction of the Roman episcopal church, and also founded the memorial church over the tomb of Saint Peter. I have already mentioned the fundamentally different functions and liturgical contexts of the two churches. This does not seem to have considerably changed until the fifth century: The Basilica Constantiniana at the Lateran was the papal celebration church, Saint Peter's a memorial and cemeterial basilica that soon became firmly established as the favourite burial place of the Christian upper class of Rome. In Saint Peter's, precious sarcophagi were erected or lowered into the floor, and on the exterior walls family mausoleums were built. In the early fifth century Saint Peter's even advanced to be the burial church of the western Roman emperors, as Honorius built a large mausoleum next to the south transept that followed the pattern of the Severan rotunda located immediately to the east.[9] It is not only Honorius and his

---

[8] Among the rare exceptions, above all Blaauw, *CD* I. See also M. Maccarone, 'L'indulgenza del Giubileo del 1300 e la basilica di San Pietro', in A. M. Romanini (ed.), *Roma anno 1300: Atti della IV Settimana di Studi di Storia dell'Arte Medievale dell'Università di Roma La Sapienza (19–24 maggio 1980)* (Rome 1983), 731–52, esp. 736–7; T. F. X. Noble, 'Topography, celebration and power: The making of papal Rome in the eighth and ninth centuries', in M. De Jong and F. Theuws (eds.), *Topographies of Power in the Early Middle Ages* (Leiden, 2001), 45–91, esp. 51–6; L. Bosman, 'S. Giovanni in Laterano and medieval architecture: The significance of architectural quotations', in M. Verhoeven, L. Bosman and H. van Asperen (eds.), *Monuments and Memory: Christian Cult Buildings and Constructions of the Past: Essays in Honour of Sible de Blaauw* (Architectural Crossroads. Studies in the History of Architecture 3) (Turnhout, 2016), 43–51, at pp. 43–4.

[9] Blaauw, *CD* II, 466–8 (with reference to previous research); J. Niebaum, 'Die spätantiken Rotunden an Alt-St. Peter in Rom', *Marburger Jahrbuch für Kunstwissenschaft* 34 (2007), 101–61; M. J. Johnson, *The Roman Imperial Mausoleum in Late Antiquity* (Cambridge, 2009), 167–75; M. McEvoy, 'The mausoleum of Honorius: Late Roman imperial Christianity and the city of Rome in the fifth century', in McKitterick et al. (eds.), *Old Saint Peter's, Rome*, 119–36.

two wives who appear to have been buried in this mausoleum, but also Galla Placidia, her first son Theodosius and even her second son Valentinian III, who died as emperor in 455.

But it seems as if the function of Saint Peter's had ceased to be merely funerary before the end of the fourth century with the construction of a baptistery under Pope Damasus (366–84); the details, however, are only poorly documented.[10] Anyway, by the middle of the fifth century at the latest a baptistery must have existed at Saint Peter's as Pope Simplicius (468–83) established *ebdomadas* 'ad sanctum Petrum Apostolum', 'ut presbyteri manerent, propter penitentes et baptismum'.[11] In the course of the fifth century Saint Peter's was apparently involved in papal stational service and in pastoral care for the residents of the *suburbium*.[12] And yet, it was not turned into a 'normal' station church or into a titular church, but primarily became a highly political monument.[13]

The imperial character inherent in the building since its Constantinian foundation was reinforced by the construction of the imperial mausoleum by Honorius in the early fifth century, and also prevailed in the course of the following centuries. Consequently, it was Saint Peter's where emperors, kings and other rulers coming to Rome made their first stop. It was Saint Peter to whom they paid reverence in the first place, and it was his church where they were received by the pope and worldly dignitaries.[14] This was the case with Honorius in 404, with Valentinian III in 425, with Theodoric

---

[10] The construction of a baptistery in Saint Peter's by Pope Damasus is documented through inscriptions, but it is not attested in the *Liber Pontificalis*; for the documentary situation, see O. Brandt, 'The early Christian baptistery of Saint Peter's', in McKitterick et al. (eds.), *Old Saint Peter's, Rome*, 81–94, esp. 82–5. See also A. Ferrua, 'Dei primi battisteri Parocchiali e di quello di S. Pietro in particolare', *La Civiltà Cattolica* 90, 2 (1939), 146–57, at pp. 150–7; W. N. Schumacher, 'Das Baptisterium von Alt-St. Peter und seine Probleme', in O. Feld and U. Peschlow (eds.), *Studien zur spätantiken und byzantinischen Kunst: F. W. Deichmann gewidmet*, 3 vols. (Bonn, 1986), I, 215–33, at pp. 224–5; Blaauw, *CD* II, 487–8; H. Brandenburg, 'Das Baptisterium und der Brunnen des Atriums von Alt-St. Peter in Rom', *BOREAS, Münstersche Beiträge zur Archäologie* 26 (2003), 55–71, at pp. 56–7 and 64–5. On the role of the Damasian baptistery, see A. Thacker, 'Popes, emperors and clergy of Old Saint Peter's from the fourth to the eighth century', in McKitterick et al. (eds.), *Old Saint Peter's, Rome*, 137–56, at p. 145.

[11] *LP* I, Life 49, 249 (c. 2); Thacker, 'Popes, emperors and clergy', 151.

[12] For the development of the stational liturgy in early Christian Rome, see S. Diefenbach, *Römische Erinnerungsräume: Heiligenmemoria und kollektive Identitäten im Rom des 3. bis 5. Jahrhunderts n. Chr.* (Berlin, 2007), 232–3, 408–14 and 432.

[13] See Blaauw, *CD* I, 27–31, 52–7 and II, 454–5, 484–5 and 498–503.

[14] This was also for legal reasons, as Saint Peter's was positioned outside the city walls. Before entering the city, the foreign sovereigns had to ask the pope for permission to do so. In the case of Charlemagne's visit in 774, it is documented that the king of the Franks and his entourage had to leave the city every night and spend the night outside the city walls: S. Scholz, *Politik - Selbstverständnis - Selbstdarstellung: Die Päpste in karolingischer und ottonischer Zeit* (Stuttgart, 2006), 82.

in 500, with Constans II in 662 and with Charlemagne in 774, to mention just a few of the most prominent visitors of Rome.[15] For the Carolingians in general, Saint Peter's was an important point of reference: in 781 Carloman, the son of Charlemagne, was baptised and anointed king by Pope Hadrian in Saint Peter's and not in the old episcopal baptistery at the Lateran, and Saint Peter's basilica also represented a very effective backdrop for the imperial coronation of Charlemagne on Christmas day in 800.[16] Moreover, from about 760 the Carolingians used the old imperial mausoleum, now under the patronage of Saint Petronilla, as their private oratory.[17] That they also owned a palace near Saint Peter's and published important political announcements on the church's façade (or rather on its atrium) might round off the picture.[18]

What about the pope? He was always an active protagonist in these performances of political alliances and was very aware of the high symbolic value that Saint Peter's had on these occasions. Sible de Blaauw has rightly called Saint Peter's the 'centro simbolico dal quale il vescovo di Roma esercita la propria autorità'.[19] The fact that the popes claimed Saint Peter's as their own burial site as early as the second half of the fifth century (and therefore just after the last members of the dynasty of the western

---

[15] M. Humphries, 'From emperor to Pope? Ceremonial, space, and authority at Rome from Constantine to Gregory the Great', in K. Cooper and J. Hillner (eds.), *Religion, Dynasty, and Patronage in Early Christian Rome, 300–900* (Cambridge, 2007), 21–58, at p. 47 (Honorius and Valentinian III), 48 (Theoderic), 56 (Constans II); P. Liverani, 'Saint Peter's and the city of Rome between Late Antiquity and the early Middle Ages', in McKitterick et al. (eds.), *Old Saint Peter's, Rome*, 21–34, at pp. 30–3; R. McKitterick, 'The representation of Old Saint Peter's basilica in the *Liber Pontificalis*', in McKitterick et al. (eds.), *Old Saint Peter's, Rome*, 95–118, esp. pp. 100–1. For Theoderic, see Anon. Vales. c. 65–7, in I. König, *Aus der Zeit Theoderichs des Großen: Einleitung, Text, Übersetzung und Kommentar einer anonymen Quelle* (Darmstadt, 1997), 82–5; M. Vitiello, 'Teodorico a Roma: Politica, amministrazione e propaganda nell'adventus dell'anno 500 (considerazioni sull'Anonimo Valesiano II)', *Historia* 53 (2004), 73–120. On the *adventus* of Constans II, see *LP* I, Life 78, 343 (c. 2); on the *adventus* of Charlemagne in the year 774, see *LP* I, Life 97, 497 (c. 37–8); Scholz, *Politik – Selbstverständnis – Selbstdarstellung*, 81–2.

[16] Scholz, *Politik – Selbstverständnis – Selbstdarstellung*, 64 and 89; for the coronation of Charlemagne, see 126–35, esp. 132. See also F. A. Bauer, *Das Bild der Stadt Rom im Frühmittelalter: Papststiftungen im Spiegel des* Liber Pontificalis *von Gregor dem Dritten bis zu Leo dem Dritten* (Wiesbaden, 2004), 91–120; J. Story, 'The Carolingians and the oratory of Saint Peter the Shepherd', in McKitterick et al. (eds.), *Old Saint Peter's, Rome*, 257–73.

[17] On Saint Petronilla, see M. Borgolte, *Petrusnachfolge und Kaiserimitation: Die Grablege der Päpste, ihre Genese und Traditionsbildung* (Göttingen, 1989), 110; Scholz, *Politik – Selbstverständnis – Selbstdarstellung*, 67; McKitterick et al., 'Introduction', 5.

[18] C. R. Brühl, 'Die Kaiserpfalz bei St. Peter und die Pfalz Ottos III. auf dem Palatin', *Quellen und Forschungen aus römischen Archiven und Bibliotheken* 34 (1935), 1–30; Bauer, *Das Bild der Stadt Rom im Frühmittelalter*, 177; Humphries, 'From emperor to Pope?' 48.

[19] Blaauw, *CD* II, 515.

Roman Empire had been buried there) shows that they weren't willing to leave the memorial church above the tomb of their saintly predecessor to the worldly rulers.[20] Their donation policy gives the impression that the popes were keen to keep up with the donations of worldly sovereigns to Saint Peter's in order not to lose control over this highly symbolic place and to be 'present' there in a visible way.[21]

Besides that, the above-mentioned baptistery at Saint Peter's demonstrated papal presence at the Vatican as well. It had probably been founded by Pope Damasus, but it had surely existed since the fifth century and was converted into a replica of the Lateran baptistery by Pope Symmachus in the first years of the sixth century.[22] Thus Saint Peter's was presented as a branch of the Lateran, or rather as a fully adequate replacement for the cathedral. Symmachus, by erecting three oratories annexed to the baptistery in Saint Peter's, reinstalled there exactly the same chapel programme that Pope Hilarus (461–8) had set up at the Lateran baptistery only a few years before.[23] In both Saint Peter's and the Lateran two of the three chapels were dedicated to the two Saint Johns – the Evangelist and the Baptist – whereas the third was dedicated to the Holy Cross and received a corresponding relic.[24] Unfortunately,

---

[20] Borgolte, *Petrusnachfolge und Kaiserimitation*, esp. 49–93; McKitterick, 'The representation of Old Saint Peter's basilica', 105–17.

[21] For the donations of worldly sovereigns to Saint Peter's, see F. A. Bauer, 'Herrschergeschenke an Sankt Peter', *Mitteilungen zur Spätantiken Archäologie und Byzantinischen Kunstgeschichte* 4 (2005), 65–99. On papal donations to Saint Peter's, see Blaauw, *CD* II, 482–5; J. Alchermes, 'Petrine Politics: Pope Symmachus and the Rotunda of St. Andrew at Old St. Peter's', *Catholic Historical Review* 81 (1995), 1–40, at pp. 10–1; Bauer, *Das Bild der Stadt Rom im Frühmittelalter*, passim.

[22] *LP* I, Life 53, 261–2 (c. 7). For the building initiatives of Pope Symmachus in Saint Peter's, especially the *oratoria* of the baptistery, see J. H. Emminghaus, 'Die Taufanlage ad sellam Petri confessionis', *Römische Quartalschrift* 57 (1962), 78–103, esp. 78–82 and 93–5; Blaauw, *CD* II, 485–6; Alchermes, 'Petrine Politics', 15–17; Brandenburg, 'Das Baptisterium und der Brunnen', 67–70; A. Guiglia, 'Il VI secolo: da Simmaco (498–514) a Gregorio Magno (590–604)', in M. D'Onofrio (ed.), *La committenza artistica dei papi a Roma nel Medioevo* (Rome, 2016), 109–43, at p. 111.

[23] For the chapels annexed by Hilarus to the Lateran baptistery, see *LP* I, Life 48, 242–3 (c. 2–5); Blaauw, *CD* I, 135–40; M. J. Johnson, 'The fifth-century oratory of the Holy Cross at the Lateran in Rome', *Architectura. Zeitschrift für die Geschichte der Baukunst* 25, 2 (1995), 128–55; G. Mackie, 'The Sancta Croce drawings: A re-examination', *Revue d'art Canadienne/Canadian Art Review* 24, 1 (1997), 1–14; O. Brandt, 'L'oratorio della Santa Croce', in P. Liverani (ed.), *Giornata di studio tematica dedicata al Patriarcato Lateranense: Atti della giornata tematica dei Seminari di Archeologia Cristiana (École française de Rome, 10 maggio 2001)* (*MEFRA* 116, 1) (special issue) (Rome, 2004), 79–93; O. Brandt, *Battisteri oltre la pianta: Gli alzati di nove battisteri paleocristiani in Italia* (Vatican City, 2012), 33–85; M. Gianandrea, 'Il V secolo: Da Innocenzo I (401–417) ad Anastasio II (496–498)', in D'Onofrio (ed.), *La committenza artistica dei papi*, 73–108, at pp. 93–6. See also Brandt, Chapter 11 in this volume.

[24] See previous two notes. For both constructions see also S. de Blaauw, 'Jerusalem in Rome and the cult of the Cross', in R. Colella and R. Krautheimer (eds.), *Pratum Romanum: Richard Krautheimer zum 100. Geburtstag* (Wiesbaden, 1997), 55–73, esp. 68–9.

how this triad of chapels at the Vatican presented itself is in doubt, and even the position and shape of the baptistery are still disputed.[25] On the late sixteenth-century ground plan designed by Tiberio Alfarano (Fig. 15.2), the *piscina* and the three altars belonging to the three chapels are situated in the north transept, but it is not clear if this situation goes back to the early Middle Ages, or even to the fourth century. Most recently, Olof Brandt assumed that the early Christian baptistery of Saint Peter's was attached to the north transept as a free-standing central-plan building with the annexed chapels. Only when Pope Hadrian IV (1154–9) raised the transept would the baptistery and the annexed chapels have been pulled down and transferred into the transept as shown on Alfarano's plan.[26] Emminghaus and others have argued for locating the baptistery of Saint Peter's in the north transept from the beginning; the *fons* would then initially have been situated in a small apse, and only with Leo III (795–816) would it have been moved to the centre of the transept and remodelled as a free-standing *piscina*, as in the Lateran baptistery.[27] Unfortunately this cannot be finally determined, either through archaeological evidence or through pictures or written sources, as these are contradictory in many respects. For my purpose, however, this does not matter. In the context of my interests it is primarily important that it seems to have been essential to Symmachus – regardless of the final architectural implementation – to have a liturgical disposition at the Vatican that allowed him to celebrate baptisms according to the same rite as in the episcopal baptistery at the Lateran. Probably this project of a functional – if not formal – replica fell into the period 501–6, when Symmachus had no access to the cathedral and its baptistery in the

---

[25] Schumacher, 'Das Baptisterium von Alt-St. Peter' (with localisation of the Damasian baptistery in the Western Rotunda on the south side of the transept of Saint Peter's and its relocation in the northern wing of the transept in the time of Leo III); Blaauw, *CD* II, 485–91 (with localisation of the early Christian baptistery in the northern wing of the transept); Brandenburg, 'Das Baptisterium und der Brunnen' (like de Blaauw). See also n. 22 and 23.

[26] Brandt, 'The early Christian baptistery', 91–4; see Mackie, 'The Sancta Croce drawings', 5–11. From Peter Mallius and other sources of the twelfth century we learn that at this time at the latest the arrangement was the one documented by Alfarano in the sixteenth century: R. Valentini and G. Zucchetti, *Codice topografico della città di Roma*, 4 vols. (Fonti per la Storia d'Italia 90) (Rome, 1940–53), III, 422–3; Schumacher, 'Das Baptisterium von Alt-St. Peter', 231–2. See also the description written in 1452 by Nikolaus Muffel, who verifies the arrangement documented by Alfarano posthumously on the basis of proper inspection; interestingly enough, the disposition in Saint Peter's with the six columns around the *piscina* reminded Muffel of 'Sant Johanns latron': N. Muffel, *Descrizione della città di Roma nel 1452: Delle indulgenze e dei luoghi sacri di Roma (Der ablas und die heiligen stet zu Rom)*, ed. and trans. D. G. Wiedmann (Bologna, 1999), 54–5.

[27] Emminghaus, 'Die Taufanlage'; Blaauw, *CD* II, 491. See also L. Duchesne, in *LP* I, 266, nn. 20–2.

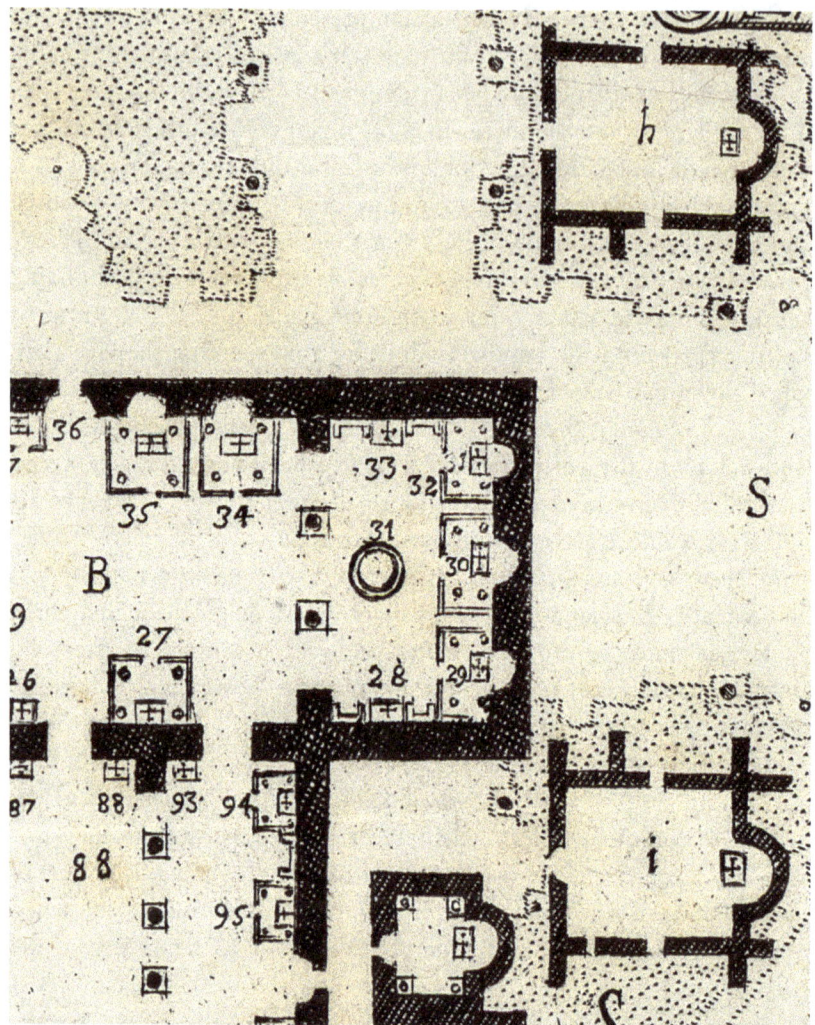

Fig. 15.2 T. Alfarano: Plan of Saint Peter's (detail of the northern part of the transept with the *piscina* of the baptistery and the chapels of Saint John the Evangelist (no. 32), Saint John the Baptist (no. 30) and the Holy Cross (no. 35) (Bibliotheca Hertziana – Max Planck-Institut für Kunstgeschichte, Rome).

aftermath of the conflicts with Laurentius, who was elected pope on the same day as Symmachus himself had been elected, and who occupied the Lateran claiming to be the legitimate pope.[28] It fits with the scenario

---

[28] J. Richards, *The Popes and the Papacy in the Early Middle Ages 476–752* (London, 1979), 80–91; E. Wirbelauer, *Zwei Päpste in Rom: Der Konflikt zwischen Laurentius und Symmachus (498–514): Studien und Texte* (Quellen und Forschungen zur antiken Welt 16) (Munich, 1993), esp. 34–7; C. Laudage, *Kampf um den Stuhl Petri: Die Geschichte der Gegenpäpste* (Freiburg, 2012), 42–6; Thacker, 'Popes, emperors and clergy', 151–3. At the same period, around 500, the

that Symmachus not only structurally optimised the accessibility of Saint Peter's but also built *episcopia* next to the atrium.[29] With these apparently residential and administrative buildings, he actually laid the foundation for today's layout.

Compared with this, the Lateran basilica got remarkably less attention in the first centuries of its existence.[30] The cathedral of Rome did not possess a saint at whose grave people could pray for healing or who could act as an intercessor. Still, we can observe a process of enhancement concerning the Lateran during the early Middle Ages, focused less on the basilica and its liturgical furnishings than on the nearby papal palace.[31] From the sixth century onwards, and especially in the decades after the establishment of the *Patrimonium Petri* by Pippin in 756, the papal palace at the Lateran was modelled after the Byzantine imperial palace of Constantinople, and thus turned into one of the most important residences in Europe.[32] Together with the piazza in front of it, the palace served as the backdrop of the increasingly imperialistic self-representation of the pope. Another part of this enhanced appreciation was the accumulation of sacred assets in the palace in the form of highly potent relics of Christ. Through these relics the papal chapel became styled as the Sancta Sanctorum, the Lateran as a new

---

*Gesta Liberii* were written, which claimed that Pope Liberius, expelled by Constantine from Rome, was prompted by his deacon, Damasus, to install a baptistery at Saint Peter's because he feared not being able to celebrate Pentecost at the Lateran: Schumacher, 'Das Baptisterium von Alt-St. Peter', 225; Blaauw, *CD* II, 489.

[29] *LP* I, Life 53, 262 (c. 7) and 267, n. 25. Pope Leo III extended the Vatican residence: *LP* II, Life 98, 1 (c. 3). A discussion on the position of the Symmachian *episcopia* and the Leonine residence at the Vatican can be found in K. Steinke, *Die mittelalterlichen Vatikanpaläste und ihre Kapellen: Baugeschichtliche Untersuchungen anhand der schriftlichen Quellen* (Vatican City, 1984), 11–32; A. Monciatti, *Il Palazzo Vaticano nel Medioevo* (Florence, 2005), 93–5. See also Bauer, *Das Bild der Stadt Rom im Frühmittelalter*, 174–6.

[30] See Liverani, 'Saint Peter's and the city of Rome', 30–4.

[31] On the early medieval building activities in the Lateran, see *CBCR* V, 11; Claussen, 'S. Giovanni in Laterano', 29–30; Blaauw, *CD* I, 163–9. For the papal residence at the Lateran, its constructive evolution and its political dimensions, see next note.

[32] M. Luchterhandt, 'Vom Haus des Bischofs zum Locus Sanctus: Der Lateranspalast im kulturellen Gedächtnis des römischen Mittelalters', in M. Featherstone, J.-M. Spieser, G. Tanman and U. Wulf-Rheidt (eds.), *The Emperor's House: Palaces from Augustus to the Age of Absolutism* (Berlin, 2015), 73–92; X. Barral i Altet, 'L'VIII secolo: Da Giovanni VI (701–705) ad Adriano I (772–795)', in D'Onofrio (ed.), *La committenza artistica dei papi*, 181–212, at pp. 202–4. See also I. Herklotz, 'Der Campus Lateranense im Mittelalter', *Römisches Jahrbuch für Kunstgeschichte* 22 (1985), 1–43, esp. 36–7 and 41; Bauer, *Das Bild der Stadt Rom im Frühmittelalter*, 61–75; Liverani (ed.), *Giornata di studio*, esp. the chapter by U. Real, at pp. 95–108); Monciatti, *Il Palazzo Vaticano nel Medioevo*, 1–29. For the references to the imperial palace in Constantinople – also in view of the possession of relics and their political instrumentalisation – see H. A. Klein, 'Sacred relics and imperial ceremonies at the great palace of Constantinople', in F. A. Bauer (ed.), *Visualisierungen von Herrschaft: Frühmittelalterliche Residenzen – Gestalt und Zeremoniell* (Istanbul, 2006), 79–99.

Jerusalem, and its guardian, the pope, as the high priest of the Holy of Holies.[33] It was surely not by accident that the *arca* commissioned in the years around 800 by Leo III (795–816) for the papal relic treasure was made of wood (Fig. 15.3) – like the Ark of the Covenant.[34] Compared with the 'super relic' of Saint Peter's, the tomb of Saint Peter, the relics that were kept in the papal chapel had the advantage of being mobile, so they could be carried around in processions. Their holiness was therefore not limited to the Lateran only, but on certain occasions also reached out to the city.[35]

For a long time the Lateran seems to have been mainly the site of encounters between the pope and the Romans.[36] Thus, until the end of Byzantine rule in Italy it was here, in the *patriarchium*, that the Romans acclaimed the new emperor after his election in the form of his effigies that had been sent to Rome.[37] But visits by actual rulers to the Lateran are scarcely documented, either in the palace or in the basilica.[38] Interestingly

---

[33] The name 'Sancta Sanctorum' for the papal chapel in the Lateran palace is not attested earlier than the eleventh century: H. Grisar, *Die römische Kapelle Sancta Sanctorum und ihr Schatz: Meine Entdeckungen und Studien in der Palastkapelle der mittelalterlichen Päpste* (Freiburg 1908), 16 and 57; O. Nussbaum, 'Sancta Sanctorum', *Römische Quartalschrift* 54 (1959), 234–46, at pp. 242–4; S. de Blaauw, 'Il Patriarchio, la Basilica Lateranense e la liturgia', in Liverani (ed.), *Giornata di studio*, 161–71, at p. 171. Some scholars suggest that the papal relic treasure was called 'Santa Sanctorum' as early as the ninth century: Nussbaum, 'Sancta Sanctorum', 243; E. Thunø, *Image and Relic: Mediating the Sacred in Early Medieval Rome* (Analecta Romana Instituti Danici, Supplementum 32) (Rome, 2002), 161 and n. 438. See also G. Cornini, '"Non est in toto sanctior orbe locus": Collecting relics in early medieval Rome', in M. Bagnoli, H. A. Klein, C. Griffith Mann and J. Robinson (eds.), *Treasures of Heaven: Saints, Relics, and Devotion in Medieval Europe* (Baltimore, 2010), 69–78, esp. p. 71. For the chapel and its relics, see also R. Colella, 'Hagiographie und Kirchenpolitik: Stephanus und Laurentius in Rom', in Colella and Krautheimer (eds.), *Pratum Romanum*, 75–96, esp. pp. 87–8; M. Cempanari, *Sancta Santorum Lateranense: Il Santuario della Scala Santa dalle origini ai nostri giorni*, 2 vols. (Rome, 2003); Bauer, *Das Bild der Stadt Rom im Frühmittelalter*, 75–80.

[34] Grisar, *Die römische Kapelle*, 56 f.; Thunø, *Image and Relic*, 160–6 and 168–9; Bauer, *Das Bild der Stadt Rom im Frühmittelalter*, 75 and figs. 26–8 at pp. 72–4; Cornini, '"Non est in toto sanctior orbe locus"', 70–1.

[35] Blaauw, *CD* I, 195–8 and 313–6. This is especially true for the most venerated icon of the Saviour, sixth-seventh century: Grisar, *Die römische Kapelle*, 39–54 and 58–137; G. Wolf, *Salus Populi Romani: Die Geschichte römischer Kultbilder im Mittelalter* (Weinheim, 1990), 29–78; E. Parlato, 'Le icone in processione', in M. Andaloro and S. Romano (eds.), *Arte e iconografia a Roma dal Tardoantico alla fine del Medioevo* (Milan, 2002), 64–8; S. Romano, 'L'icône *acheiropoiete* du Latran: Fonction d'une image absente', in Bock et al. (eds.), *Art, cérémonial et liturgie*, 301–19; Thunø, *Image and Relic*, 15–17; Cornini, '"Non est in toto sanctior orbe locus"', 72–4; A. van Dijk, 'The Veronica, the *Vultus Christi* and the veneration of icons in medieval Rome', in McKitterick et al. (eds.), *Old Saint Peter's, Rome*, 229–56, at pp. 233 and 237; Luchterhandt, 'Vom Haus des Bischofs', 82–6.

[36] Herklotz, 'Der Campus Lateranense', 8.

[37] Herklotz, 'Der Campus Lateranense', 39; Humphries, 'From emperor to Pope?' 21 and 56.

[38] One exception seems to have been the visit of Emperor Constans II in 662; like other sovereigns visiting Rome, Constans resided during his stay in the old imperial palace on the Palatine and

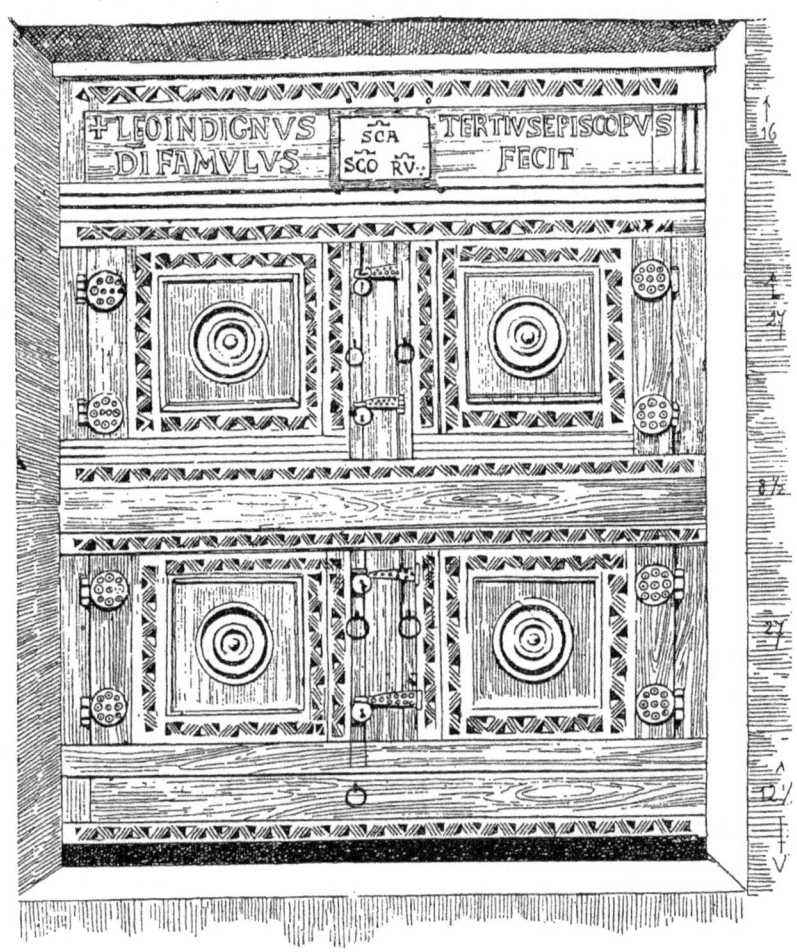

Fig. 15.3 Drawing of the wooden *arca* commissioned by Pope Leo III (795–816) (from Grisar, *Die römische Kapelle*).

enough, the basilica played no role at all in the presentation of the relics in the early Middle Ages – this changed only in the high Middle Ages.[39] In the early Middle Ages the holiness of the Lateran relics was totally focused on

set a high value on his visit to Saint Peter's at the Vatican, but he also was received by Pope Vitalian in the papal palace at the Lateran: *LP* I, Life 78, 343 (c. 3). Even Charlemagne, after having prayed at the tomb of Saint Peter during the Easter festivities in 774, was invited by the pope to join baptismal mass in the Lateran basilica and to dine with him in the Lateran palace: *LP* I, Life 97, 497 (c. 39). See Scholz, *Politik – Selbstverständnis – Selbstdarstellung*, 82.

[39] Herklotz, 'Der mittelalterliche Fassadenportikus', 85; Blaauw, *CD* I, 318–19; L. Burkart, 'Die Aufhebung der Sichtbarkeit: Der Schatz der Sancta Sanctorum und die Modi seiner visuellen Inszenierung', in A. Rathmann-Lutz (ed.), *Visibilität des Unsichtbaren: Sehen und Verstehen in Mittelalter und früher Neuzeit* (Zurich, 2011), 69–82, at p. 73; D. Mondini, 'Reliquie incarnate:

the *patriarchium*, and especially on the papal chapel that was dedicated to Saint Lawrence.[40] On the other hand, the *Liber Pontificalis* documents that Pope Sergius II (844–7) had a *confessio* set up shortly before the middle of the ninth century.[41] He thus established a liturgical disposition in the cathedral that since the time of Gregory the Great had become customary for Roman churches with a saint's tomb or other high-grade body relics. Even though the nature of the relics in the Lateran basilica is unknown, the new *confessio* is evidence of an attempt to rectify the lack of precious relics, which was obviously considered a deficit.[42] However, in view of the claim that the Lateran basilica was the 'head and summit of all churches on earth' (*caput et vertex omnium ecclesiarum in universo orbe terrarum*) – as it was formulated for the first time in the *Constitutum Constantini* around the middle of the eighth century – this attempt appears quite desperate.[43]

## The Situation in the High and Late Middle Ages

In the aftermath of the Investiture Controversy, the Lateran's claim to be the first of all churches grew increasingly explicit.[44] Ingo Herklotz and others have shown in various publications how papacy and Lateran formed an 'inseparable unit' in the high Middle Ages and how the Lateran basilica became the 'material symbol of the Roman church' par excellence; the famous dream vision of Innocent III who saw Saint Francis rescuing the

---

Le "sacre teste" di Pietro e Paolo a San Giovanni in Laterano a Roma', in D. Scotto (ed.), *Del visibile credere: Pellegrinaggi, santuari, miracoli, reliquie* (Florence, 2011), 265–96, at p. 274.

[40] De Blaauw, 'Il Patriarchio', 164–5.  [41] *LP* II, Life 104, 91 (c. 19).

[42] Blaauw, *CD* I, 174–6; Claussen, 'S. Giovanni in Laterano', 186.

[43] *Constitutum Constantini*, c. 13: H. Fuhrmann (ed.), *Das Constitutum Constantini (Konstantinische Schenkung), Text* (MGH Fontes Iuris Germanici Antiqui in usum scholarium ex Monumentis Germaniae Historicis separatim editi 10) (Hanover, 1968), 84–5: 'Interea nosse volumus omnem populum universarum gentium ac nationum per totum orbem terrarum, construxisse nos intro palatium nostrum Lateranense eidem salvatori nostro domino Iesu Christo ecclesiam a fundamentis cum baptisterio … ; quam sacrosanctam ecclesiam caput et verticem omnium ecclesiarum in universo orbe terrarum dici, coli, venerari ac praedicari sancimus, sicut per alia nostra imperialia decreta statuimus'. See Herklotz, 'Der Campus Lateranense', 38; Blaauw, *CD* I, 164–5.

[44] One of the medieval authors quoting the honorary title given to the Lateran basilica in the *Constitutum Constantini* was Pier Damiani († 1072), *Epist.* II 1, 255 (see Blaauw, *CD* I, 204). In official documents of this time (for instance in the bull that Pope Anastasius IV issued in December 1153), the Lateran basilica is mentioned as 'basilica Salvatoris domini, que Constantiniana vocatur, pariterque beati Iohannis baptiste et Iohannis evangeliste': J. von Pflugk-Harttung, *Acta pontificum romanorum inedita*, vol. III: *Urkunden der Päpste 590–1197* (Graz, 1958), 133.

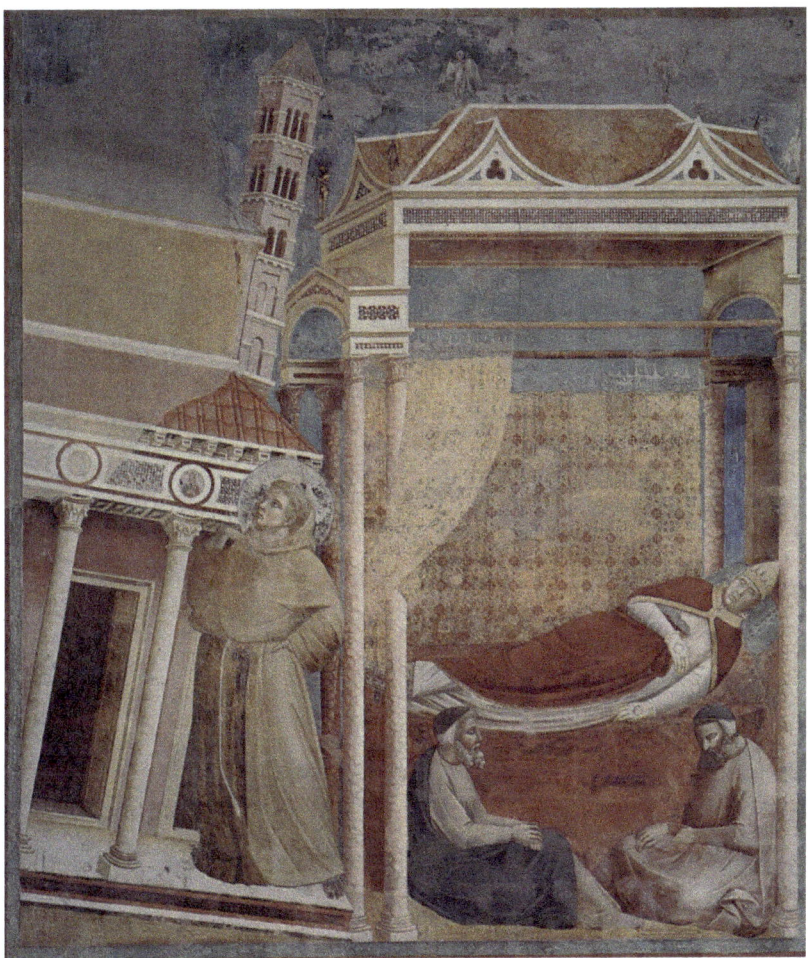

Fig. 15.4 Giotto: Fresco in Saint Francis, Assisi, showing Saint Francis acting as support for the collapsing Lateran basilica (= Roman Church) (commons.wikimedia.org/wiki/File:Giotto_di_Bondone_(und_Werkstatt)_001.jpg).

Church by underpinning the collapsing Lateran basilica (Fig. 15.4) might be the most obvious proof of this.[45]

The new understanding of the old Constantinian cathedral manifested itself in different media. This is particularly the case with the mosaic images and the inscription on the portico that was built in front of the eastern façade in the late twelfth century, but also, and most of all, with the papal tombs.[46]

---

[45] Herklotz, 'Der mittelalterliche Fassadenportikus', 71.
[46] See below. Another interesting element in this context are the murals of the twelfth century in the *patriarchium* with their highly political iconography: C. Walter, 'Papal political imagery in the Medieval Lateran Palace', *Cahiers Archéologiques* 20 (1970), 155–76 (part 1) and *Cahiers*

By the tenth century some popes had chosen the Lateran basilica as their burial place.[47] By doing so, they had broken with the old tradition of papal burials in Saint Peter's, instituted by Leo the Great in the middle of the fifth century.[48] The ban on burying the dead inside the city walls had been flaunted with increasing frequency from around the end of Late Antiquity, and since Carolingian times this practice had been sanctioned by corresponding legislation.[49] In addition, Saint Peter's had lost its *extra-muros* position after 846 when Leo IV included its *borgo* in the fortified area of the city.[50] But all this does not sufficiently explain why John X in 928 and perhaps already Leo V († 903) preferred to be buried in the cathedral instead of the old papal burial place near the tomb of Saint Peter in the Vatican.[51] Was it because in those years, under Pope Sergius III (904–11), the cathedral regained its old splendour after an earthquake had seriously damaged it in 896?[52] Or was it because already then, by the early tenth century, the Lateran

---

*Archéologiques* 21 (1971), 109–36 (part 2); Borgolte, *Petrusnachfolge und Kaiserimitation*, 152–7; I. Herklotz, 'Die Beratungsräume Calixtus' II. im Lateranspalast und ihre Fresken: Kunst und Propaganda am Ende des Investiturstreits', *Zeitschrift für Kunstgeschichte* 52 (1989), 145–214; J. Johrendt, 'Das Innozenzische Schisma aus kurialer Perspektive', in H. Müller and B. Hotz (eds.), *Gegenpäpste: Ein unerwünschtes mittelalterliches Phänomen* (Vienna, 2012), 127–63, at pp. 136–42; D. Kinney, 'Patronage of art and architecture', in J. Doran and D. J. Smith (eds.), *Pope Innocent II (1130–1143): The World vs. the City* (Abingdon, 2016), 352–87, at pp. 381–4.

[47] Borgolte, *Petrusnachfolge und Kaiserimitation*, 127–32 (for the papal tombs of the eleventh and twelfth centuries in the Lateran, see pp. 129–30, 135–6, 152–78); A. Paravicini Bagliani, *Il corpo del Papa* (Turin, 1994), 20–1 and 61–2, n. 57; I. Herklotz, 'Sepulcra' et 'Monumenta' del Medioevo: Studi sull'arte sepolcrale in Italia (Naples, 2001), 136–7.

[48] See above, n. 20.

[49] R. Meneghini and R. Santangeli Valenzani, 'Sepolture intramuranee e paesaggio urbano a Roma tra V e VII secolo', in L. Paroli and P. Delogu (eds.), *La storia economica di Roma nell'alto medioevo alla luce dei recenti scavi archeologici* (Florence, 1993), 89–111; R. Meneghini and R. Santangeli Valenzani, 'Sepolture intramuranee e paesaggio urbano a Roma tra V e VII secolo d.C.: Aggiornamenti e considerazioni', *Archeologia Medievale* 22 (1995), 283–90; M. Costambeys, 'Burial topography and the power of the Church in fifth- and sixth-century Rome', *PBSR* 69 (2001), 169–89. See also G. Cantino Wataghin, 'The ideology of urban burials', in G. P. Brogiolo and B. Ward Perkins (eds.), *The Idea and Ideal of the Town between Late Antiquity and the Early Middle Ages* (Leiden, 1999), 147–80.

[50] For the *civitas Leonina*, see *LP* II, Life 105, 123; Bauer, *Das Bild der Stadt Rom im Frühmittelalter*, 177–8; Scholz, *Politik – Selbstverständnis – Selbstdarstellung*, 175–6; McKitterick et al., 'Introduction', 6.

[51] Blaauw, *CD* I, 258–9; Herklotz, 'Sepulcra' et 'Monumenta', 137; Claussen, 'S. Giovanni in Laterano', 216.

[52] *CBCR* V, 11–12; Claussen, 'S. Giovanni in Laterano', 29–31; G. De Spirito, 'La Basilica Lateranense nel quadro delle vicende del Patriarcato del secolo X', in Liverani (ed.), *Giornata di studio*, 117–39; G. Pollio, 'Il X secolo: Da Benedetto IV (900–903) a Gregorio V (996–999)', in D'Onofrio (ed.), *La committenza artistica dei papi*, 239–54. As the earthquake of 896 is not verified by other sources it does not figure in the list of historically proven earthquakes: R. Budriesi, 'I terremoti e l'edilizia religiosa a Roma e a Ravenna tra VII/X secolo', in

was linked to Mount Sinai as a place of divine legislation?[53] Or because the popes wanted to state their presence at the place of their ministry, 'in sede propria', as we can read in the *Liber Pontificalis* concerning the tomb of Paschal II?[54] Whatever the reason, from this time on many popes chose the Lateran basilica as their final resting place.[55] But as the papal tombs of the tenth and the first half of the eleventh centuries at the Lateran had been placed in the floor near the façade, either in the portico or within the church near the entrances, from the Investiture Controversy onwards the tombs arose self-confidently in the western part of the nave and in the south transept – that is, in the centre of the liturgical activity and in the area of passage towards the chapter's cloister.[56] Antique sarcophagi were reused for many of these papal burials – in the case of Innocent II († 1143) and Anastasius IV († 1154), even imperial sarcophagi from the mausoleums of Hadrian and the empress Helena (Fig. 15.5).[57] Yet by their mere material, the red porphyry with its explicitly imperial connotations, these sarcophagi revealed with whom the popes of that time competed.

The above-mentioned portico of the late twelfth century, however, with its admittedly not very large-format mosaic images on its frieze (Figs 15.6 and 15.7), unequivocally presented subjects that showed quite plainly the papal claim to power.[58] In most of the images this claim was linked to the concrete site, the Lateran, whether by the image of the baptism of Constantine or the *Donatio Constantini*, by the depiction of the heads of the two apostles which the Lateran claimed to have possessed since the second half of the eleventh century, or by the scene with the conquest

E. Guidoboni (ed.), *I terremoti prima del Mille in Italia e nell'area mediterranea: Storia archeologia sismologia* (Bologna, 1989), 364–87.

[53] De Spirito, 'La Basilica Lateranense', 120. See also n. 33 above.
[54] *LP* II, Life 161, 305; Herklotz, *'Sepulcra' et 'Monumenta'*, 146–7. See also Paravicini Bagliani, *Il corpo del Papa*, 20 and 62 n. 58.
[55] Blaauw, *CD* I, 204–5.
[56] For the position of the tombs, see Blaauw, *CD* II, 258–61 and fig. 8; Claussen, 'S. Giovanni in Laterano', 69 and 218–19.
[57] Herklotz, 'Der Campus Lateranense', 3, 11 and 42; Borgolte, *Petrusnachfolge und Kaiserimitation*, 163–5 and 169–71; S. de Blaauw, 'Papst und Purpur. Porphyr in frühen Kirchenausstattungen in Rom', in E. Dassmann and K. Thraede (eds.), *Tesserae. Festschrift für Josef Engemann* (Jahrbuch für Antike und Christentum, Ergänzungsband 18) (Münster, 1991), 36–50, esp. 47; Blaauw, *CD* I, 261–2; Paravicini Bagliani, *Il corpo del Papa*, 21; Herklotz, *'Sepulcra' et 'Monumenta'*, 147–54, 173–6 and 195–203; Claussen, 'S. Giovanni in Laterano', 217–19; most recently, see Kinney, 'Patronage of art and architecture', 384–7.
[58] Nine of the originally more than twenty scenes are known from drawings by Ciampini and others: Herklotz, 'Der mittelalterliche Fassadenportikus', 48–53; Claussen, 'S. Giovanni in Laterano', 78–84. For the construction history of the portico and its dating, see Herklotz, 'Der mittelalterliche Fassadenportikus'; Claussen, 'S. Giovanni in Laterano', 31–2 and 63–77. See also F. Pomarci, 'Medioevo: Architettura', in Pietrangeli (ed.), *San Giovanni in Laterano*, 63–6.

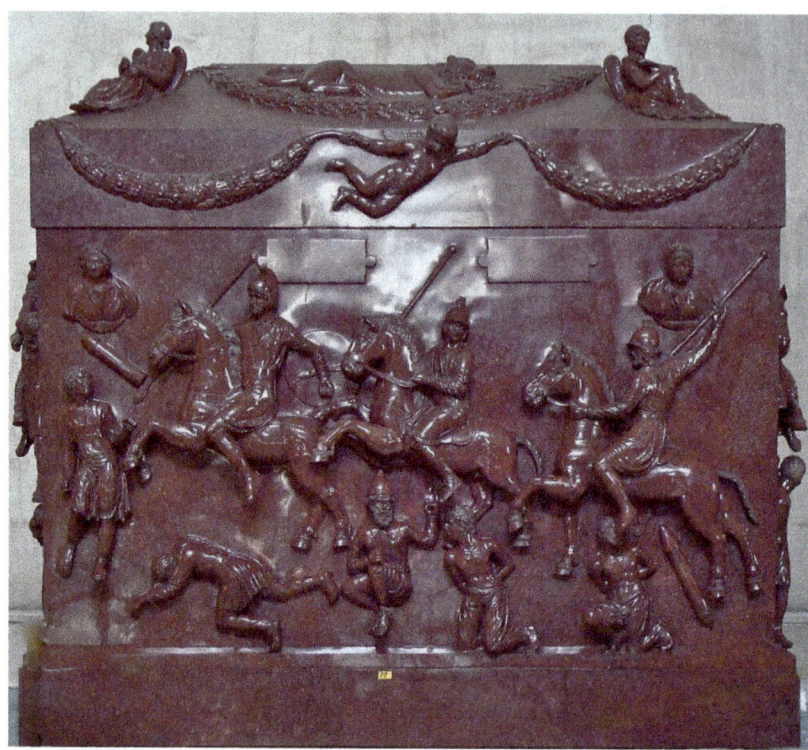

Fig. 15.5 Late Antique porphyry sarcophagus from the mausoleum of Helena, reused in 1154 for the burial of Pope Anastasius IV. In the Lateran basilica (Photo: C. Jäggi).

of Jerusalem by the Romans in AD 70 followed by the transfer of the *spolia* of the Jerusalem Temple to Rome.[59] It is this striking accent on the Lateran in the mosaics, but also the irritating lack of a donor's inscription as well as the silence in the *Liber Pontificalis* concerning the construction of the portico, that led Cornelius Claussen to the intriguing assumption that it was not the pope who commissioned the portico and the design of the mosaic images, but the chapter.[60] After Eugenius III (1149-54) had transformed the papal

---

[59] The scenes from the *vitae* of John the Baptist and John the Evangelist also hint at the Lateran and its (secondary) patrons: Herklotz, 'Der mittelalterliche Fassadenportikus', 73–88; Claussen, 'S. Giovanni in Laterano', 79-82. See also M. Falla Castelfranchi, 'Sull'origine, e la funzione "politica", dell'immagine del battesimo di Costantino nel portico della basilica Lateranense', in G. Bordi, I. Carlettini, M. L. Fobelli, M. R. Menna and P. Pogliani (eds.), *L'officina dello sguardo: Scritti in onore di Maria Andaloro*, 2 vols. (Rome, 2014), I, 375–82.

[60] Claussen, 'S. Giovanni in Laterano', 32 and 85-9. Cf. A. Iacobini, 'La pittura e le arti suntuarie: Da Innocenzo III al Innocenzo IV (1198–1254)', in A. M. Romanini (ed.), *Roma nel Duecento: L'arte nella città dei Papi da Innocenzo III al Bonifacio VIII* (Turin, 1991), 237–319, at p. 272; contra I. Herklotz, *Gli eredi di Costantino: Il papato, il Laterano e la propaganda visiva nel XII secolo* (La corte dei papi 6) (Rome, 2000), 218.

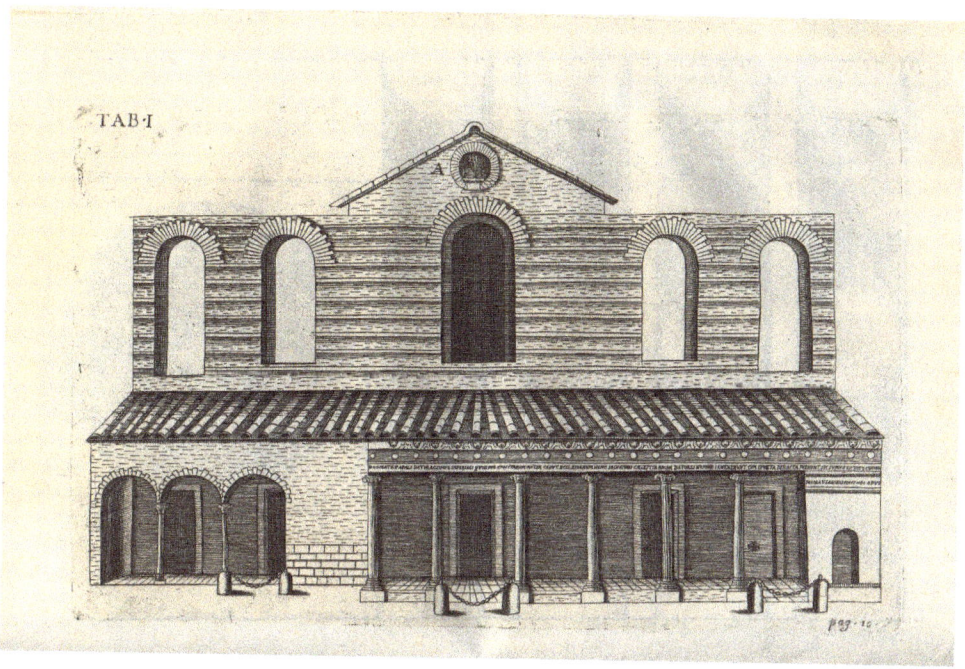

Fig. 15.6 The medieval façade of San Giovanni in Laterano with the twelfth-century portico (from Ciampini, *De sacris aedificiis*, table 1; ETH-Bibliothek Zürich, Rar 1279, doi.org/10.3931/e-rara-13091, Public Domain Mark).

*casa* at Saint Peter's into a proper palace, the popes transferred their residence more and more to the Vatican, while the old *patriarchium* at the Lateran lost its importance.[61] In this situation, the Lateran chapter could have deliberately used the portico and its images to make the popes realise their historically founded responsibility for their cathedral. Claussen appropriately calls the mosaic programme, in which 'the legitimate home basilica (Hausbasilika) of the Roman bishop reminds one of the good old times and its proven dowry of relics', a 'courting [of the Lateran canons] for the favour of the popes who were cheating with Saint Peter's'.[62] This seems to

---

[61] Steinke, *Die mittelalterlichen Vatikanpaläste*, 32–66; Herklotz, 'Der Campus Lateranense', 42; Monciatti, *Il Palazzo Vaticano nel Medioevo*, 96–182; J. Johrendt, *Die Diener des Apostelfürsten: Das Kapitel von St. Peter im Vatikan (11.–13. Jahrhundert)* (Berlin, 2011), 329–35.

[62] Claussen, 'S. Giovanni in Laterano', 87–8: 'Es wird gleichsam eine versteckte Werbung um die Gunst der nach St. Peter "fremd gehende" Päpste sein, wenn die legitime Hausbasilika des römischen Bischofs an gute alte Zeiten und ihre bewährte Mitgift an Heiltümern erinnert. Eine derartige Botschaft ist dezent, sollte aber nachdrücklich wirken, wenn sie vom Klerus der Laterankirche dem jeweiligen Papst ausgelegt wurde und dann als Mahnung präsent bleiben sollte.' See also P. C. Claussen, 'Il XII secolo: Da Pasquale II (1099–1118) a Celestino III (1191–1198), in D'Onofrio (ed.), *La committenza artistica dei papi*, 275–97, at p. 294.

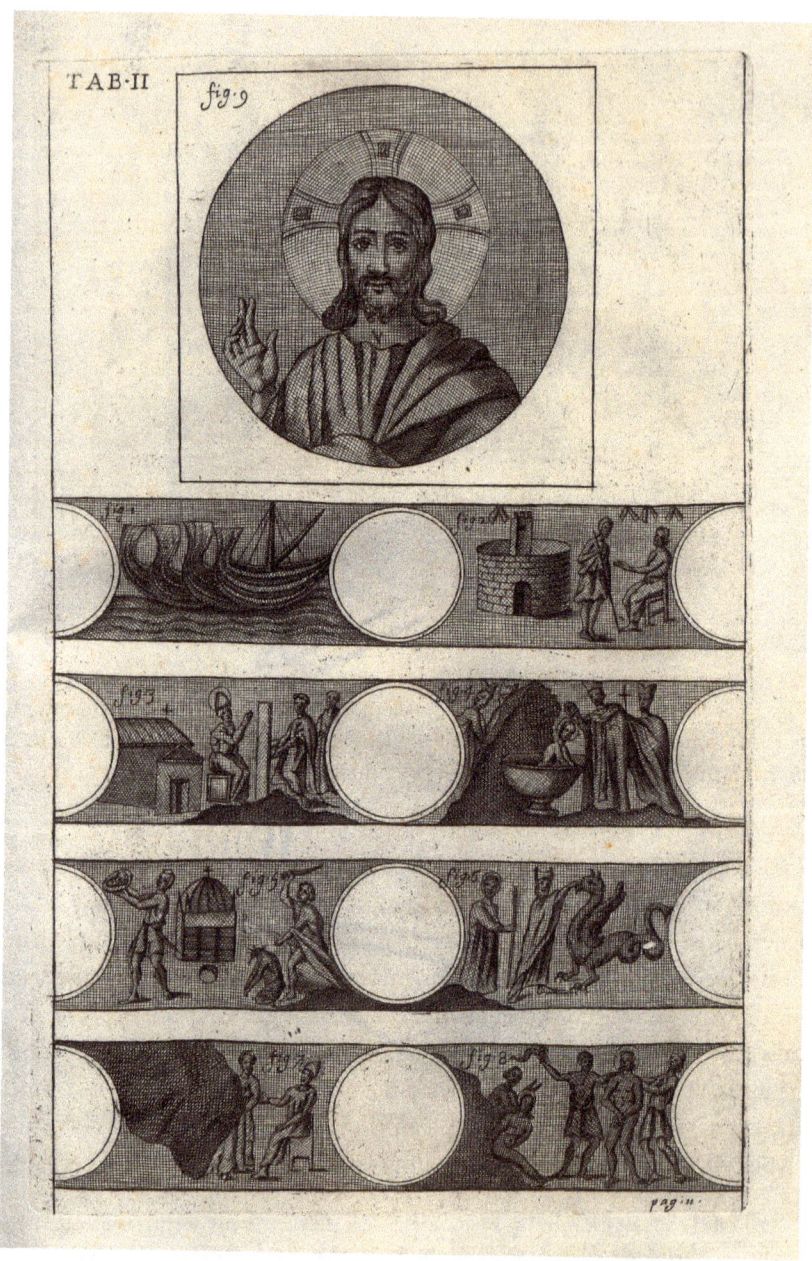

**Fig. 15.7** Seventeenth-century drawings of the twelfth-century mosaics of the Lateran portico (from Ciampini, *De sacris aedificiis*, table 2 (detail); ETH-Bibliothek Zürich, Rar 1279, doi.org/10.3931/e-rara-13091 / Public Domain Mark).

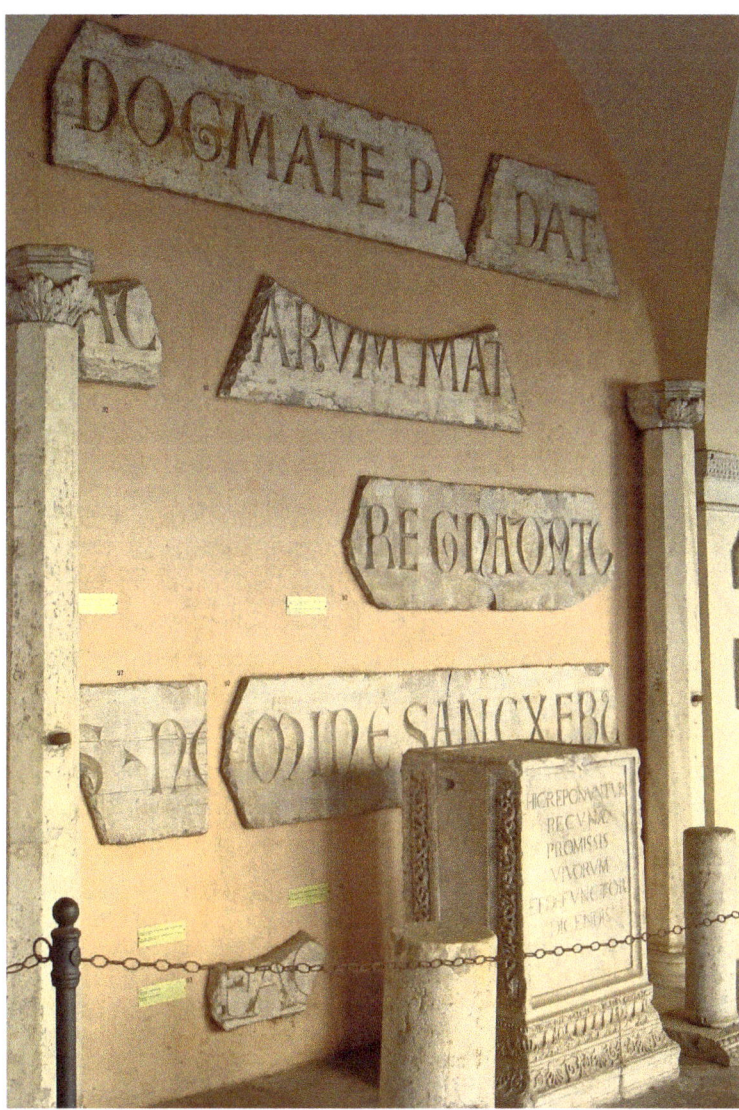

Fig. 15.8 Remaining fragments of the twelfth-century inscription of the Lateran portico, today in the cloister of San Giovanni in Laterano (Photo: C. Jäggi).

apply also to the monumental inscription on the portico (Fig. 15.8) that once again conveyed that it was the Lateran basilica that deserves to use the title 'mater et caput cunctarum ecclesiarum'.[63]

---

[63] 'DOGMATE PAPALI DATUR AC SIMUL IMPERIALI/QUOD SIM CUNCTARUM MATER CAPUT ECCLESIARUM [...]'; for the interpretation of the inscription, see Herklotz, 'Der mittelalterliche Fassadenportikus', 89–95; Claussen, 'S. Giovanni in Laterano', 84–8.

Only a bit later however, Saint Peter's claimed this title for itself as well; at least the inscription beneath its apse mosaic, renewed by Innocent III in the first years of the thirteenth century, speaks of it as 'mater cunctarum, decor et decus ecclesiarum'.[64] The rivalry between the old cathedral and Saint Peter's seems to have been stirred up by the chapters of the two churches. As the Lateran chapter – since its reformation in the early eleventh century – consisted of regulated Augustinian canons until its transformation into a secular canon monastery in 1299, whereas the chapter of Saint Peter's was constituted as a secular canon monastery since its foundation in the middle of the eleventh century, the two communities had different institutional backgrounds (and, based on that, perhaps a certain 'natural' antipathy).[65] It is from among these two chapters that the propagandistic *descriptiones* of both churches emerged; they were clearly formulated interdependently at the time of Alexander III (1159–81), each with the implicit aim of stressing and justifying the primacy of its church. The author of the *Descriptio Lateranensis Ecclesiae* was the cathedral's canon John the Deacon; the author of the Petrinian counterpart, the *Descriptio basilicae Vaticanae*, was Peter Mallius, a canon of Saint Peter's.[66] Yet the heading of the eleventh-century text that was used by John the Deacon as a model for his 'description' of the Lateran gives an idea of what it was all about: 'Scriptum de supremo sanctuario sanctae Dei romanae (ecclesiae)'.[67]

It is interesting that the authors of the two writings primarily list the relics that were kept in their respective basilicas in order to emphasise their claims

---

[64] Herklotz, 'Der mittelalterliche Fassadenportikus', 92; A. Iacobini, 'Il mosaico absidiale di San Pietro in Vaticano', in M. Andaloro and A. Ghidoli (eds.), *Fragmenta Picta: Affreschi e mosaici staccati del Medioevo romano* (Rome, 1989), 119–29; A. Paravicini Bagliani, *Le Chiavi e la Tiara: Immagini e simboli del papato medievale* (La corte dei Papi 3) (Rome, 1998), 43–59; Johrendt, *Die Diener des Apostelfürsten*, 326–8; McKitterick et al., 'Introduction', 6–7; V. Pace, 'Il XIII secolo: Da Innocenzo III (1198–1216) a Bonifacio VIII (1294–1303)', in D'Onofrio (ed.), *La committenza artistica dei papi*, 299–329, at pp. 303–5.

[65] For the history of the Lateran chapter, see T. Schmidt, 'Die Kanonikerreform in Rom und Papst Alexander II. (1061–1073)', *Studi Gregoriani* 9 (1972), 199–221, at pp. 207–21; Blaauw, *CD* I, 208–13; Rehberg, *Die Kanoniker*, esp. 22–3; T. di Calpegna Falconieri, *Il clero di Roma nel medioevo: Istituzioni e politica cittadina (secoli VIII–XIII)* (Rome, 2002), 180–93; Claussen, 'S. Giovanni in Laterano', 30–4, 86–9, 255. For the early history of Saint Peter's chapter, see Johrendt, *Die Diener des Apostelfürsten*, 17–25.

[66] Valentini and Zucchetti, *Codice topografico*, III, 326–73 and 382–442; for the significance of the two sources in the rivalry of the two basilicas, see III, 319–22 and 375–81; Borgolte, *Petrusnachfolge und Kaiserimitation*, 157–9; Herklotz, 'Der mittelalterliche Fassadenportikus', 71–2 and *passim*; Johrendt, *Die Diener des Apostelfürsten*, 316–27. For the redaction criticism of the *Descriptio* of John the Deacon, see C. Vogel, 'La Descriptio Ecclesiae Lateranensis du Diacre Jean: Histoire du texte manuscrit', in *Mélanges en l'honneur du Monseigneur Michel Andrieu* (Strasbourg, 1965), 457–76; Blaauw, *CD* I, 205–7.

[67] D. Giorgi, *De liturgia romani pontificis in solemni celebratione missarum*, 3 vols. (Rome, 1744), III, 542–55; Herklotz, 'Der mittelalterliche Fassadenportikus', 71.

to primacy.[68] For the Lateran basilica, or rather for its main altar, most stress is laid – along with the *mensa* of the Last Supper and the five loaves and two fishes of the Feeding of the Five Thousand – on the Jewish cult objects from the Solomonic Temple in Jerusalem.[69] These (and even the Ark of the Covenant) had allegedly been brought to Rome after the victory of Titus in AD 70, and it was believed to have been Constantine who donated them to the Roman cathedral. Due to the possession of the Jewish cult objects, the Lateran basilica was henceforth qualified as the temple of the new covenant. Even columns from the Solomonic Temple are attested for the Lateran in the twelfth century, perhaps linked to the bronze Hadrianic columns reused around 1600 for the altar of the Holy Sacrament in the south transept.[70] Sible de Blaauw has shown that this self-qualification of the Lateran basilica as the temple of the new covenant met a performative response in the high medieval liturgy of Maundy Thursday. As we have learned, some of the mosaics of the portico described the possession of the precious temple relics, and their transfer to Rome.[71] Thus, the Roman Church had found some very clear and comprehensible arguments for its institutional claim to primacy, which in these very years (of the twelfth century) was increasingly questioned by the patriarchies of Jerusalem, Constantinople and Antioch.[72]

In addition to this, the argument was concerned with matters pertaining to the situation in Rome itself: arguments *pro* Lateran and *contra* Saint Peter's. So it is not surprising that the chapter of Saint Peter's in return felt compelled to not only constantly refer to the tomb of Saint Peter, but also to

---

[68] Blaauw, *CD* I, 206–7. The role of relics for the enforcement of claims of power is discussed by E. Bozóky, *La politique des relics de Constantin à Saint-Louis: Protection collective et légitimation du pouvoir* (Paris, 2007).

[69] Valentini and Zucchetti, *Codice topografico*, III, 83–4, 336–47, 357–8; Herklotz, 'Der mittelalterliche Fassadenportikus', 73–5 and 84–7; S. de Blaauw, 'The solitary celebration of the supreme pontiff: The Lateran basilica as the new Temple in the medieval liturgy of Maundy Thursday', in C. Caspers and M. Schneiders (eds.), *Omnes circumstantes: Contributions Towards a History of the Role of the People in the Liturgy Presented to Herman Wegman* (Kampen, 1990), 120–43.

[70] For instance, by Benjamin of Tudela, who visited Rome and its churches in 1166: Benjamin of Tudela, *The Itinerary of Benjamin of Tudela: Travels in the Middle Ages*, introd. M. A. Signer (Malibu, 1992), 64; de Blaauw, 'The solitary celebration', 136 n. 67; Blaauw, *CD* I, 249–52. See also M.-T. Champagne, '"Treasures of the Temple" and claims of authority in twelfth-century Rome', in B. M. Bolton and C. E. Meek (eds.), *Aspects of Power and Authority in the Middle Ages* (Turnhout, 2007), 107–18, at p. 109; D. Kinney, 'Spolia', in W. Tronzo (ed.), *St Peter's in the Vatican* (Cambridge, 2008), 16–47, at p. 36; A. Infrate, *The Wandering Throne of Solomon: Objects and Tales of Kingship in the Medieval Mediterranean* (Leiden, 2016), 38–41.

[71] De Blaauw, 'The solitary celebration'; Blaauw, *CD* I, 233–46. See Herklotz, 'Der mittelalterliche Fassadenportikus', 46 and 74; Champagne, '"Treasures of the Temple"', 115–18. For the mosaics of the portico, see above, n. 60.

[72] Herklotz, 'Der mittelalterliche Fassadenportikus', 77–8 and 91.

propagate 'new' relics or to revalue old objects in their possession as Petrinian or even Jesuanic contact relics. One of the best known is the Vera Icon, the *sudarium* of Christ, which is first attested in Saint Peter's basilica in the tenth century.[73] In the *Descriptio basilicae Vaticanae* of Peter Mallius it is listed as an unquestionable relic of Jesus.[74] In the late twelfth century it was additionally revalued by a precious ciborium commissioned by Celestine III (1191–8), and, after Innocent III had established a regular procession in 1204, its fame reached out also into the city.[75] Also the wooden throne, presumably brought to Rome by Charles the Bald on the occasion of his coronation in 875 and left to Saint Peter's, gained the status of a relic in the eleventh century, as it was considered then to be the chair of Saint Peter, the *Cathedra Petri*.[76] From that time on the chair was also used in the ceremonial of the papal coronation. From the thirteenth century the *Cathedra Petri* was regularly presented as a relic to the faithful for veneration on the Feast of the Chair of Saint Peter on 22 February. In this context, the Chair was carried by the canons of Saint Peter's in a solemn procession from its depository into the church, where it was initially brought to the main altar; after mass it was placed in front of the *confessio*, where the faithful could approach it, venerate it and give donations.

By that time the Vatican had already won the race against the Lateran.[77] Whenever the pope and the Curia stayed in Rome in the thirteenth century, they mostly resided in the palace that Innocent III had had built in the Vatican.[78] This preference was finally affirmed when the popes returning from Avignon (in 1377) did not move back into the old *patriarchium* at the Lateran but installed themselves permanently at the Vatican.[79] This does not

---

[73] See below, n. 75.   [74] Valentini and Zucchetti, *Codice topografico*, III, 411 and 420.

[75] Maccarone, 'L'indulgenza', 732 and 739–40; Wolf, *Salus Populi Romani*, 83–4; Blaauw, *CD* II, 669 and 724; G. Wolf, '"Or fu sì la sembianza vostra?" Sguardi alla "vera icona" e alle sue copie artistiche', in G. Morello and G. Wolf (eds.), *Il volto di Cristo* (Milan, 2000), 103–14; van Dijk, 'The Veronica', 237–56.

[76] Most recently, C. Jäggi, 'Cathedra Petri und Colonna Santa in St. Peter zu Rom: Überlegungen zu "Produktion" und Konjunktur von Reliquien im Mittelalter', in A. F. Bergmeier, K. Palmberger and J. E. Sanzo (eds.), *Erzeugung und Zerstörung von Sakralität zwischen Antike und Mittelalter* (Distant World Journal Special Issues 1) (Heidelberg, 2016), 109–31, books.ub.uni-heidelberg.de/propylaeum/catalog/book/188.

[77] Maccarone, 'L'indulgenza', 736–40.

[78] Steinke, *Die mittelalterlichen Vatikanpaläste*, 39–47; B. Schimmelpfennig, 'Der Palast als Stadtersatz: Funktionale und zeremonielle Bedeutung der Papstpaläste in Avignon und im Vatikan', in W. Paravicini (ed.), *Zeremoniell und Raum* (Sigmaringen, 1997), 239–56, esp. 239–44; A. Monciatti, 'Funzione e decorazione dell'architettura nel Palazzo di Niccolò III Orsini', in T. Weddigen, S. de Blaauw and B. Kempers (eds.), *Functions and Decorations: Art and Ritual at the Vatican Palace in the Middle Ages and the Renaissance* (Vatican City, 2003), 27–39; V. Brancone, *Le domus dei cardinali nella Roma del Duecento: Gioielli, mobili, libri* (Rome, 2010), 34.

[79] Luchterhandt, 'Vom Haus des Bischofs', 78–80.

mean that the Lateran with its episcopal church now totally declined into insignificance; after all, the bull by which the primacy among the Roman churches was officially conceded to the Lateran basilica dates from 1372 – that is, shortly before the return of the popes to Rome.[80] The reliquaries that were commissioned by Pope Urban V in 1369–70 for the heads of the two princes of the apostles that are attested in the Lateran since the eleventh century (by then however in the papal chapel in the *patriarchium*) are to be seen in this context as well, as is their demonstrative exposition in the high altar ciborium.[81] But by entering into the discourse about relics, and by courting pilgrims and other devout visitors by making its reliquary treasure permanently accessible and visible, just as Saint Peter's and the other pilgrimage churches did, the Lateran basilica gave up its status of exclusiveness and – as one would say today – its unique selling point.[82] By the high Middle Ages the papal private chapel had been styled as a 'centre of Christian hope of salvation'[83] that was staged between visibility and withdrawal by an intelligent management of relics. But now, in the late Middle Ages, the Lateran relics were used to openly woo the public. Since the beginning of the fourteenth century the old cathedral and its relics had been integrated into the official Roman pilgrimage route; even the old papal chapel and the relics that had remained there were now accessible for the masses of pilgrims.[84] However, against the treasure of salvation that was kept in Saint Peter's, the cathedral had drawn the short straw. The lack of a saint's tomb, and hence of a person who stood as a *pars pro toto* for the church, could in the end not be outweighed by anything.

---

[80] See above, n. 2. Mainly in the context of the holy year 1300, we know of new elements of furnishing in the Lateran basilica initiated by members of the chapter. From 1299 onwards the chapter no longer consisted of Augustan canons, but – like the chapter of Saint Peter's – of secular canons. An especially interesting piece of this time is the so-called cross of Constantine: U. Koenen, *Das 'Konstantinskreuz' im Lateran und die Rezeption frühchristlicher Genesiszyklen im 12. und 13. Jahrhundert* (Worms, 1995), esp. 287–9.

[81] Mondini, 'Reliquie incarnate'. See also Claussen, *Die Kirchen der Stadt Rom*, 190–2; Luchterhandt, 'Vom Haus des Bischofs', 77; C. Bolgia, 'Il XIV secolo: Da Benedetto XI (1303–1304) a Bonifacio IX (1389–1404)', in D'Onofrio (ed.), *La committenza artistica dei papi*, 331–59, at pp. 344–8.

[82] Luchterhandt, 'Vom Haus des Bischofs', 84–5, rightly pointed out that the treasure in the medieval *patriarchium* at the Lateran was not in the possession of the pope and therefore was not taken to Avignon or to the Vatican; during the absence of the popes in Avignon in the fourteenth century, care of the papal treasure fell to the clergy of Saint Peter's.

[83] Burkart, 'Die Aufhebung der Sichtbarkeit', 71.

[84] N. R. Miedema, *Die römischen Kirchen im Spätmittelalter nach den 'Indulgentiae ecclesiarum urbis Romae'* (Tübingen, 2001), 200–4; N. R. Miedema, *Rompilgerführer in Spätmittelalter und Früher Neuzeit* (Tübingen, 2003), 93, 159–60, 242–3; Muffel, *Descrizione*, 30–1. See Burkart, 'Die Aufhebung der Sichtbarkeit', 69–70; Luchterhandt, 'Vom Haus des Bischofs', 76–8.

16 | The Remodelling of San Giovanni in Laterano by Pope Nicholas IV: Transept, Apse and Façade

PETER CORNELIUS CLAUSSEN

No pope during the Middle Ages altered the form of the Lateran basilica or disturbed the Constantinian walls and columns, with the exception of necessary repairs after disastrous earthquakes or fires,[1] until Nicolas IV (1288–92), the first pope with a Franciscan background (Fig. 16.1), dared to pull down the Constantinian apse. He erected a new apse and ambulatory, probably built on top of the foundations of a pre-existing structure. He shortened the nave and built a grand transept; and he reinforced and adorned the eastern façade. He also ordered the exact same type of remodelling at Santa Maria Maggiore, where he shifted the new apse further to the west, added a narrow transept, and rebuilt the upper part of the façade.[2] Both venerable basilicas were sanctified by their foundation legends.[3] Still, in the Baroque period, further alterations to these venerated sanctuaries were highly problematic. In 1647 Innocent X rejected a proposal by Borromini for the building of a new cathedral at the Lateran because he did not want to destroy the walls from the time of Constantine and Silvester.[4] The two substantial building campaigns of Nicholas IV should therefore be understood as more than mere repairs. It

---

I have to thank Linda Nolan (Rome) for a revision and correction of my text.

[1] Concerning the medieval building history of the Lateran basilica, including the catastrophic earthquake of 896, see *CBCR* V, 9–12, 91; Blaauw, *CD*, 109–331, esp. 203–265; also P. C. Claussen, *Die Kirchen der Stadt Rom im Mittelalter 1050–1300, Bd. 2: S. Giovanni in Laterano* (Corpus Cosmatorum II, 2) (Forschungen zur Kunstgeschichte und Christlichen Archäologie 21) (Stuttgart, 2008), 29–34.

[2] See P. C. Claussen, 'Nikolaus IV. als Erneuerer von S. Giovanni in Laterano und S. Maria Maggiore', in M. Verhoeven, L. Bosman, H. Van Asperen (eds.), *Monuments and Memory: Rome, Christian Cult Buildings and Constructions of the Past: Essays in Honour of Sible de Blaauw* (Architectural Crossroads. Studies in the History of Architecture 3) (Turnhout, 2016), 53–67.

[3] The Lateran basilica was sanctified by two legends: Constantine himself helped to dig the foundations; and an image of the Saviour appeared on the wall during consecration. On the other hand, the place and plan of Santa Maria Maggiore was outlined miraculously by a snowfall in August, announced and sent by the Virgin Mary.

[4] Borromini's project of 1647 for a new and modernised Lateran basilica with an enlarged choir in the west is inscribed: 'SS.ta disse che piaceva il disegno ma che non voleva variare li fond[amen]ti e sito della chiesa antica fatta da un Papa santo e un imperatore santo e che Iddio non averia [sic: aveva?] mai permesso che nessuno Pontefice havesse variato la pianta di questa SS.ta Basilica e che pero non voleva se non repararla fortificarla e ornarla ma non mai variare li suoi fondamenti e però resto della volta come sta nel sito antico senza trasportarsi come si vede nel

*The Remodelling by Pope Nicholas IV* 319

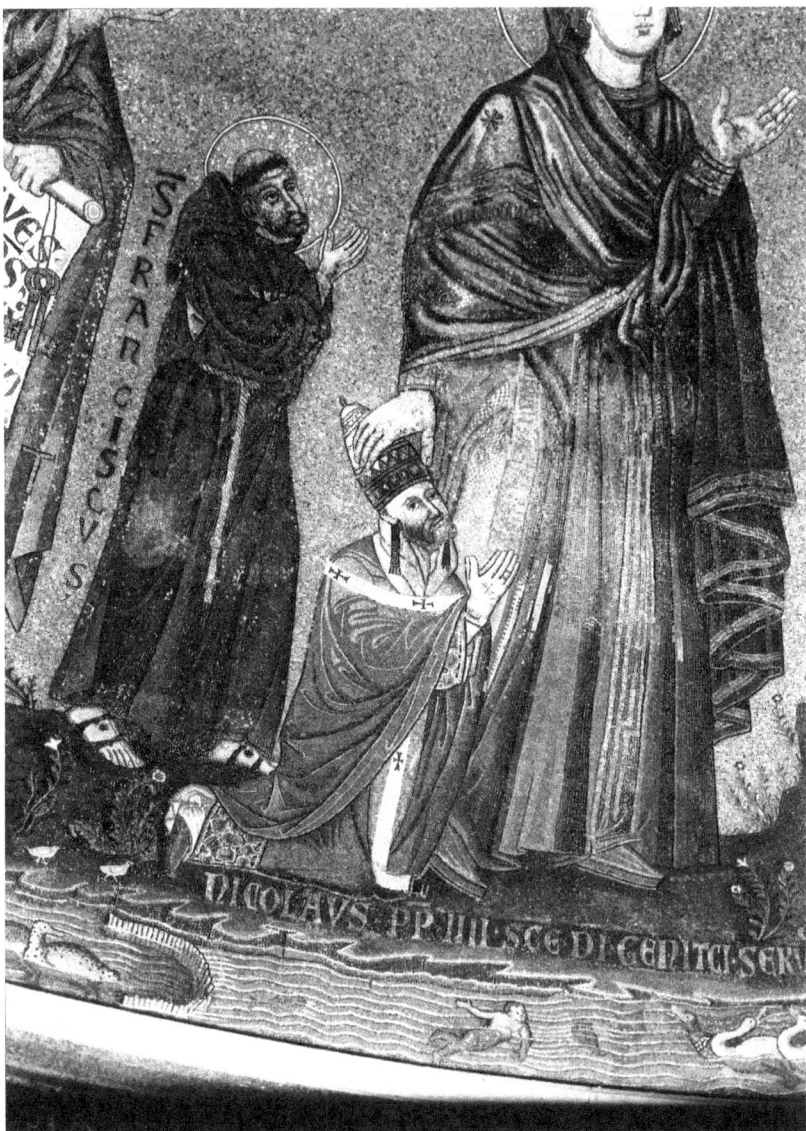

Fig. 16.1 San Giovanni in Laterano: Saint Francis and Nicholas IV, renewed apse mosaic (after Claussen, Die Kirchen der Stadt Rom).

seems that the remodelling was a programme for the renovation of the Roman church, a mighty demonstration of assertiveness that followed the spirit of Saint Francis, who had become a metaphoric embodiment of

presente disegno.' See J. Connors and A. Roca de Amicis, 'A new plan by Borromini for the Lateran basilica, Rome', *Burlington Magazine* 146 (2004), 526–33, at pp. 526, 529 fig. 23.

the cornerstone of the Lateran basilica since the dream of Innocent III (Fig. 16.2).[5]

## Rebuilding the Constantinian Apse

Although two inscriptions of Nicholas IV state that the Constantinian apse was ruined, and thus needed to be replaced in the late thirteenth century, this seems highly unlikely. In the Constantinian period an apse would have been constructed of solid materials – in particular, the characteristic concrete-like brickwork. In fact, the excavated foundation walls are perfectly preserved, and were even reused as the base layer for the new foundation in *tuffo*.[6] Thus, the inscriptions proclaiming the ruined state of the apse seem to be a *topos* to justify the new construction. The new apse was erected with almost the same measurements, but different in design. It was polygonal on the outside and curved on the inside, the walls pierced by four large ogival windows. The mosaic was restored by Jacopo Torriti in a splendid revival of early Christian style.[7] However, the Franciscan pope modified the iconography of the attending saints by adding Saint Francis, who stands behind the kneeling pope (see Fig. 16.1), and Saint Antony of Padua on the other side. A bust of the Saviour, regarded as *acheiropoieton* since at least the eleventh century, was situated at the upper centre of the Constantinian apse. According to legend, the image of the Saviour miraculously appeared on the wall of the basilica during consecration. Nicholas IV had to save the revered miraculous mosaic bust (Fig. 16.3) by integrating the image into the new building. During the destruction of the medieval apse after 1880, it came to light that the icon differs from the surrounding mosaic: the *tesserae* of the icon of the Saviour are bigger and the image is separated from the rest of the mosaic by a travertine frame.[8] As such, the mosaic of the Saviour was inserted by Torriti into the new apse as a relic of the original building. The inscription of Nicolas IV at the bottom of the apse mosaic testifies

---

[5] The famous image of Saint Francis supporting the corner column of the portico of the Lateran façade was created by Giotto, and substantiates the metaphorical dream narration in an architectural setting. See J. Gardner, 'The Louvre stigmatization and the problem of the narrative altarpiece', *Zeitschrift für Kunstgeschichte* 45 (1982), 217–48.

[6] *CBCR* V, 21 fig. 37; Claussen, *Die Kirchen der Stadt Rom*, 92–104.

[7] R. Warland, *Das Brustbild Christi: Studien zur spätantiken und frühbyzantinischen Bildgeschichte* (Rome, 1986); A. Tomei, *Iacobus Torriti pictor: Una vicenda figurativa del tardo Duecento romano* (Rome, 1990), 77–98; V. Pace, 'Per Iacopo Torriti, frate, architetto e "pictor"', *Mitteilungen des Kunsthistorischen Institutes in Florenz* 40 (1996), 212–21.

[8] J. Wilpert, 'La decorazione costantiniana della Basilica Lateranense', *RAC* 6 (1929), 53–150, at p. 110.

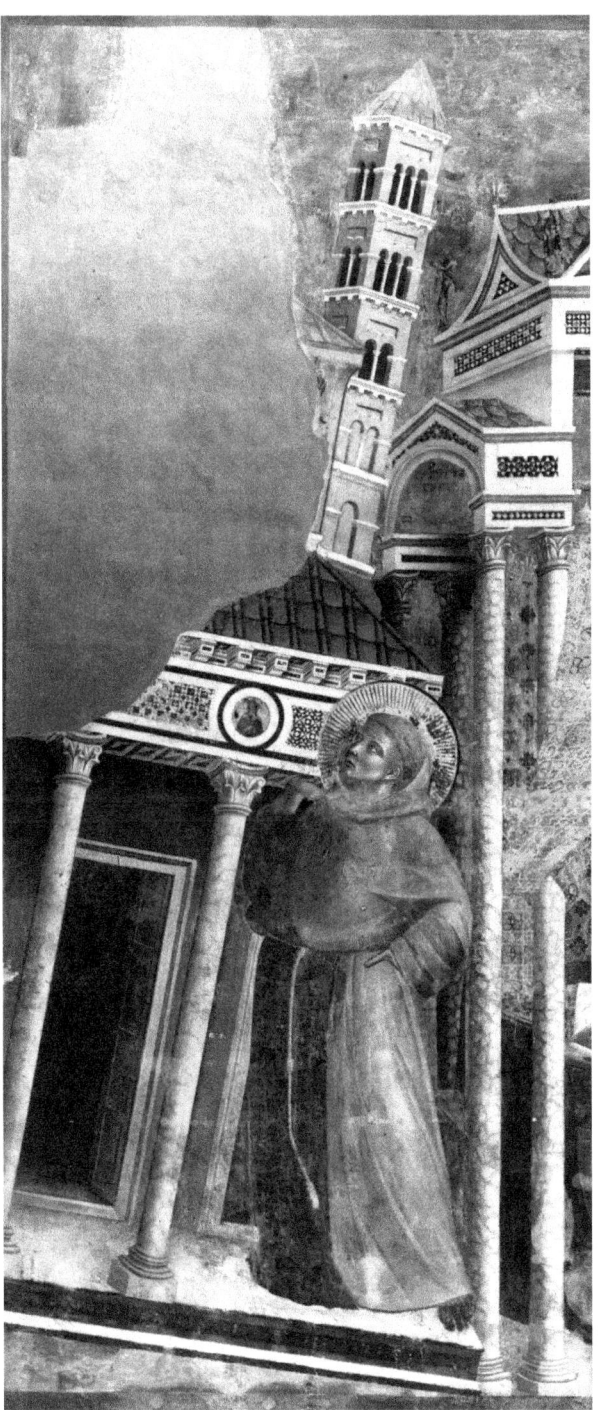

**Fig. 16.2** Assisi, San Francesco, upper church. Saint Francis supports the porch of San Giovanni in Laterano. Detail of the *Dream of Innocent III* scene within the Saint Francis cycle, probably by Giotto (after Claussen, *Die Kirchen der Stadt Rom*).

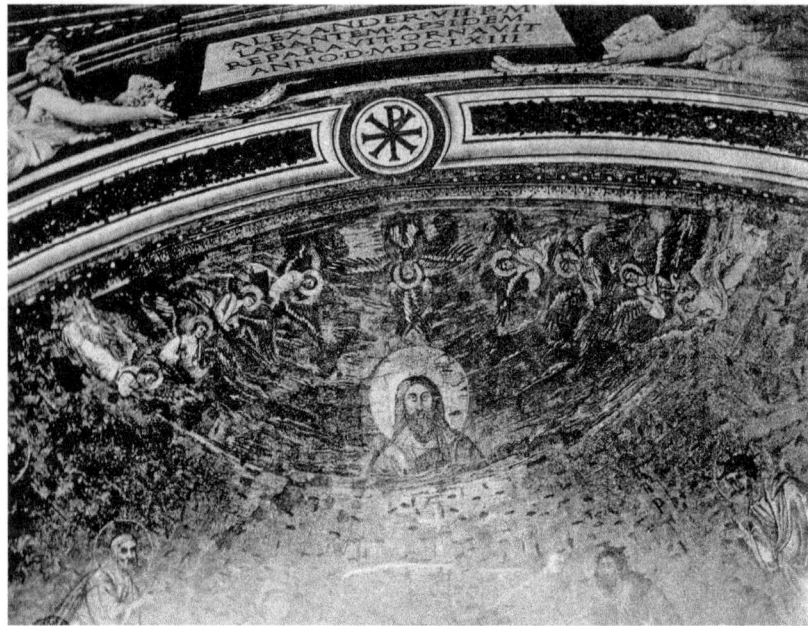

Fig. 16.3 San Giovanni in Laterano, Saviour, apse mosaic. Photo before 1880 of the original mosaic of 1292 (after Armellini and Cecchelli, *Chiese*).

exactly to this: 'sacrum vultum Salvatoris integrum reponi fecit in loco ubi primo miraculose populo romano apparuit quando fuit ista ecclesia consecrata'.[9]

Around the new apse of Nicholas IV, a spacious ambulatory (Fig. 16.4) was erected.[10] It was covered by cross-vaults divided into two half-circular aisles (Fig. 16.5). This was a massive construction, the outer walls of which were more than 140 cm thick with small round-arched windows. Since the 1870s it has been assumed that the ambulatory was a later addition to the medieval apse, because the pointed apse windows were partially covered by the roof of the ambulatory.[11] Yet we know that the ambulatory roof

---

[9] He reinserted the Holy Face of the Saviour in the place where it first appeared to the Roman people during consecration of this church.

[10] S. de Blaauw, 'Deambulatori e transetti: I casi di S. Maria Maggiore e del Laterano', *Rendiconti della Pontificia Accademia Romana di Archeologia* 59 (1986/7), 93–109, at p. 104; Blaauw, *CD*, 219–21; Claussen, *Die Kirchen der Stadt Rom*, 121–9.

[11] A. Busiri Vici, *Il Laterano nel Pontificato di Pio IX, Progetti del nuovo coro, presbiterio e dipendenze dell'Arcibasilica Lateranese, grandi lavori sinora eseguiti scoperta dell'antica casa dei Laterani, rilievi dell'absida e Portico Leoniano, restauro dell'Absida Costantiniana suo trasferimento meccanico e conservazione ideati disegnati e diretti da Andrea Busiri* (Rome, 1868/1878), 18; *CBCR* V, 22, 70–1 follows this argumentation. Claussen, *Die Kirchen der Stadt Rom*, 126–8.

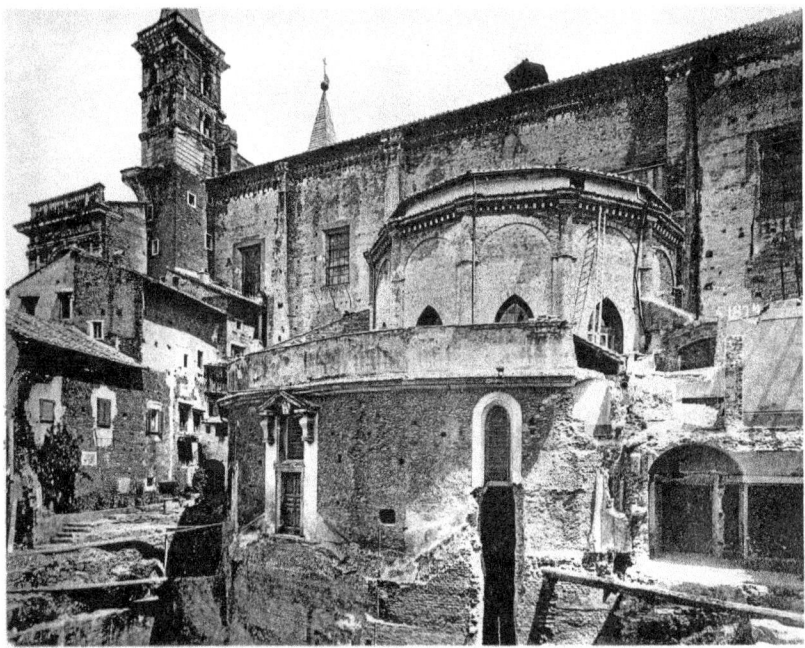

Fig. 16.4 San Giovanni in Laterano, apse with ambulatory before 1875 from the west (after Claussen, Die Kirchen der Stadt Rom).

underwent significant alterations during the restoration phase of Borromini in the seventeenth century, leading me to question Andrea Busiri Vici's argument. Alternate solutions would have left enough space for the entire window openings. Busiri Vici argued for a Constantinian origin of the then extant apse, which he wanted to move to the west of the church by means of steam engines and locomotives to create a spacious choir.[12] This extension was later realised by Virginio Vespignani, without steam, destroying the apse, which had in the meantime been recognised as medieval. The existing apse is a copy made during the late nineteenth century and entirely built of new materials. Nothing remains of either the Constantinian apse or the Torriti mosaics.

As de Blaauw has noted, the ambulatory was multifunctional and primarily served for distribution of the clergy (and perhaps, pilgrims) in the space.[13] Yet a question remains: was it a new idea or a revival of an older structure? Tomei and others have also questioned whether the circular

---

[12] P. C. Claussen and D. Mondini, 'Die Lokomotive des Papstes: Busiris Plan, die Apsis von S. Giovanni in Laterano mit Dampfkraft zu verschieben', in K. Gimmi (ed.), SvM: Die Festschrift für Stanislaus von Moos (Zurich, 2005), 56–72.

[13] Blaauw, CD, 304.

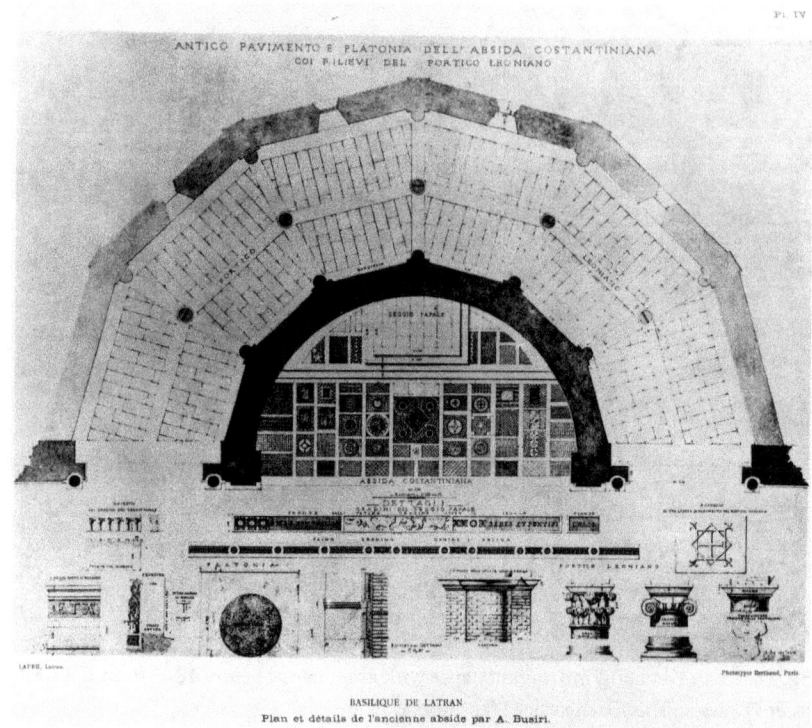

Fig. 16.5 San Giovanni in Laterano, ground plan of apse with ambulatory, before 1880, by Busiri Vici (after Lauer, *Le palais de Latran*)

corridor of the building fabric could date to the early Christian period.[14] However, the foundation consists of the same *tuffo* footings as the apse of Nicholas IV, thus supporting the medieval origin of the project. As Paola Mathis and Lia Barelli observed, there are layers of older walls and foundations underneath the *tuffo* footings of the late thirteenth century.[15] Thus, de Blaauw's thesis that the late medieval ambulatory replaced a similar pre-existing structure seems highly likely,[16] although not from the Constantinian period, but still early Christian in date. The name used since the Renaissance, 'Portico Leoniano', connects it with Leo the Great and could provide the right period for its date.

[14] Tomei, *Iacobus Torriti*, 87–8.
[15] P. Mathis, 'L'antica abside della basilica di S. Giovanni in Laterano e la questione del ambulatorio', *Opus* 7 (2003), 19–38; L. Barelli and M. Morbidelli, '"Ad imitatione, e somiglianza di quello que v'era anticamente": Il restauro dell'abside di San Giovanni in Laterano a Roma al tempo di Nicola IV (1288–92)', in V. Franchetti Pardo (ed.), *Arnolfo di Cambio e la sua epoca. Costruire, scolpire, dipingere, decorare (Atti del Convegno, Firenze-Colle di Val d'Elsa, 7–10 marzo 2006)* (Rome, 2006), 197–208, at pp. 201ff.
[16] Blaauw, *CD*, 219–21.

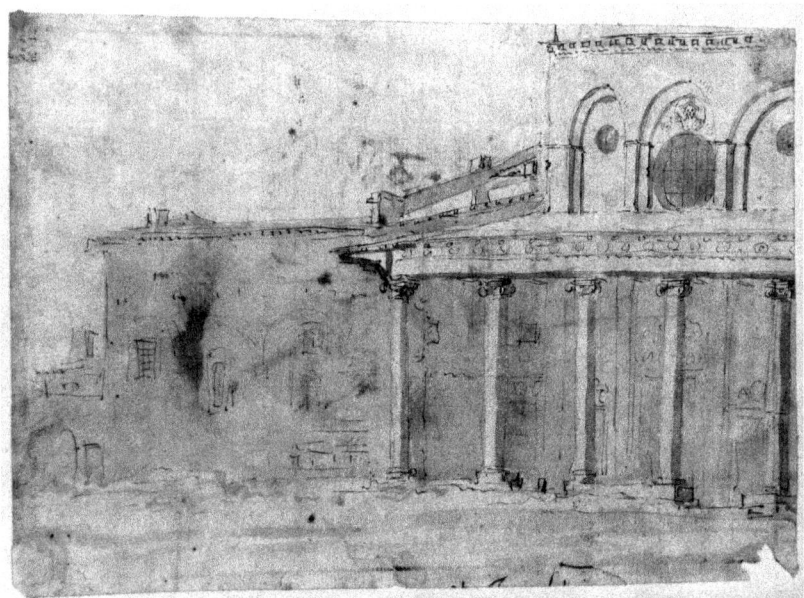

Fig. 16.6 San Giovanni in Laterano, drawing of the eastern façade, seventeenth century (Düsseldorf, Museum Kunstpalast).

As the dedicatory inscription of Nicholas IV indicates, he restored both the ruined western and eastern parts of the basilica.[17] What exactly was his contribution to the east façade? We know that he reinforced the upper structure of the façade by adding buttresses and large arches. The best source for this profound renovation is a seventeenth-century drawing (Fig. 16.6).[18] It shows a mosaic *tondo* with the image of the Saviour, probably by Torriti, which still exists in a new setting at the summit of the eighteenth-century façade. The gable was stepped from a zone of circular windows by a strong and decorated cornice. I provide a reconstruction (Fig. 16.7) of the appearance of the completely destroyed façade at the end of the thirteenth century.[19]

Considering Nicholas' renovation of the Lateran basilica, in particular the new late medieval transept,[20] its possible forerunners and the entrance situation towards the Campus Lateranensis, makes me question the existence of a transept at the Constantinian basilica. The foundation walls of a small

---

[17] Claussen, *Die Kirchen der Stadt Rom*, 96–7, 341–5.
[18] D. Popp, 'Eine unbekannte Ansicht der mittelalterlichen Fassade von S. Giovanni in Laterano', *Römisches Jahrbuch für Kunstgeschichte* 26 (1990), 31–9.
[19] Claussen, *Die Kirchen der Stadt Rom*, 38–58.
[20] Claussen, *Die Kirchen der Stadt Rom*, 140–67.

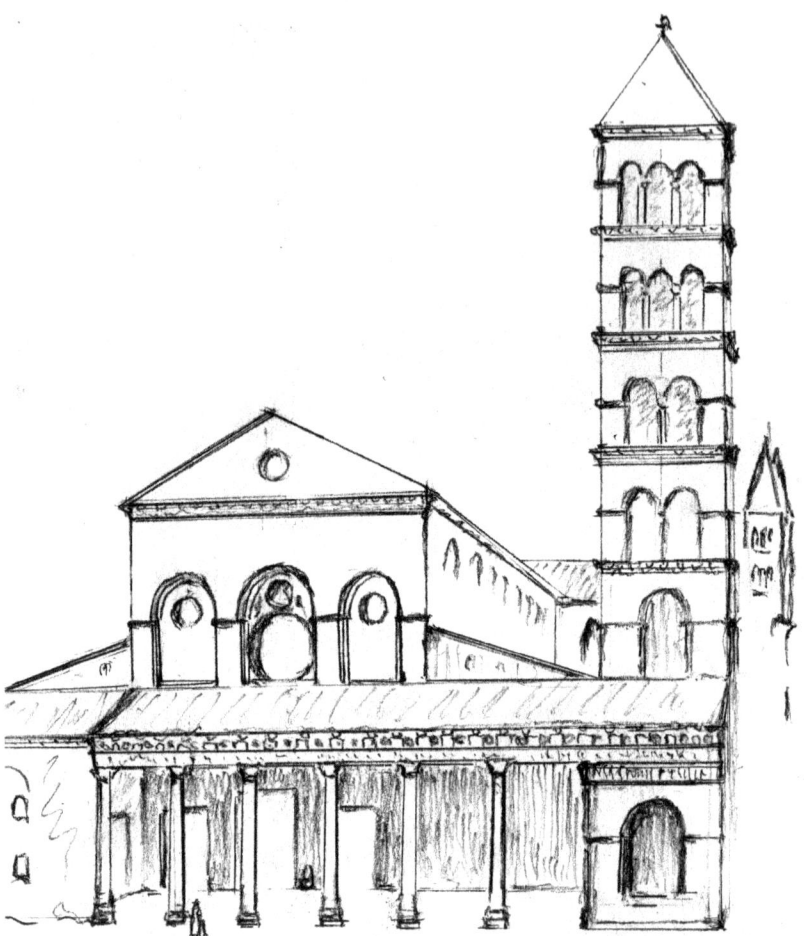

**Fig. 16.7** San Giovanni in Laterano, reconstruction sketch of the eastern façade, *c.* 1300 (P. C. Claussen).

transverse wing were excavated in 1958 in the south transept (Fig. 16.8).[21] Should we take this structure as a type of transept? I am not certain. The wing broadened the width of the basilica by about 4 m and was 8 m wide. It cropped the west end of the outer south aisle, which had the same width. As such, the small wing could be seen as a deviated continuation of the southern aisle. Yet the discussion of this structure does not stop here. Lex Bosman proposes a continuation of the innermost aisles to the west, separated from the outer aisles by a colonnade with marvellous *giallo antico* (and other) columns, thus

---

[21] *CBCR* V, 41 ff., 72ff.

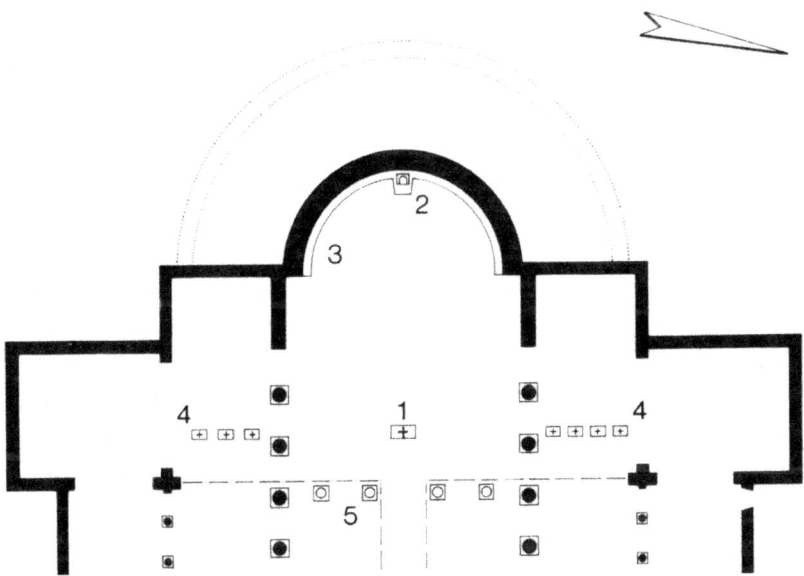

Fig. 16.8 San Giovanni in Laterano, reconstruction of the Constantinian basilica by de Blaauw, apse and western parts (detail from Blaauw, *CD*).

reconstructing a continuation of the colonnade of the side aisles.[22] He seems to favour its separation from the rest of the nave, and at the same time gives it an exceptional position as a side wing, but not necessarily as a transept.

I have followed the distinction between early Roman basilicas with a martyr tomb (such as Saint Peter's and Saint Paul's with transepts) and those without transepts and without *memoria* (such as the Lateran basilica and Santa Maria Maggiore). If we can trust this typological association, the transept is something that could be functionally connected with the cult of the martyr in early Christian times. Whatever the function of the small south wing of the south side-aisle of the Lateran basilica, for the moment we have no proof that it had a counterpart at the north side. The dominance of symmetry in the Roman basilica provides a strong argument, so it is plausible to assume that a second wing was located on the north side.

A drawing in a private collection in Münster, published by Claudia Echinger Maurach for the appearance of the lower part of the tomb of Pope Julius II as it appeared in 1540 inside the church of San Pietro in Vincoli, also includes a view of the late medieval Lateran basilica from the

---

[22] See Bosman, Chapter 9 in this volume.

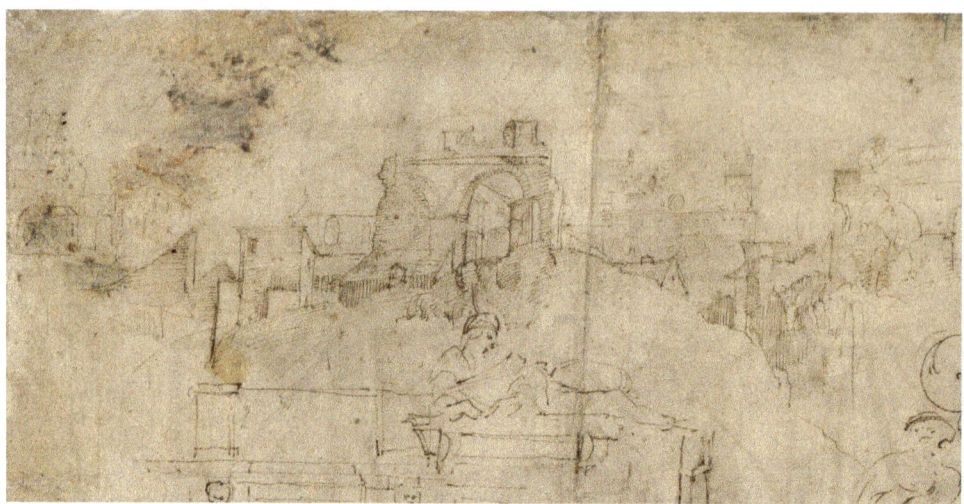

Fig. 16.9 San Giovanni in Laterano, view from the north. Anonymous drawing, c. 1540. Private collection (detail, photo: Claudia Echinger Maurach).

north (Fig. 16.9).[23] The upper part of the drawing gives a panoramic view of the Lateran area, moving from the Sancta Sanctorum at the left to the Annibaldi buildings located in the western part of the Lateran square. Looking through the ruins of the Aqua Claudia, one can recognise parts of the papal palace, and in the background the basilica of San Giovanni in Laterano. Although rather hastily drawn, the view can complete the famous *veduta* of Marten van Heemskerck, dated to a few years earlier. Left of the ruined piers of the aqueduct, the eastern part of the basilica with two clerestory windows (the one next to the façade seems to be much bigger than the other) and the nave roof, ending with the gable of the façade, are both clearly visible. In the lower area there is a high wall pierced by an arcade with a slanted roof. It is not entirely clear if this is the north wall of the side-aisle or the portico, which runs alongside the papal palace. There is no trace of the twelfth-century campanile on the east façade, which was torn down after being hit by lighting in 1411.

To the right of the aqueduct, behind a mound of rubble, arises the north transept façade of the basilica. The western end of the nave with two clerestory windows is visible, although appearing lower than the ridge of the transept in the drawing. The huge block-like appearance of the transept

---

[23] C. Echinger Maurach, 'Michelangelo's monument for Julius II in 1534', *Burlington Magazine* 145 (2003), 336–44. I thank Tatjana Bartsch (Rome) for bringing this drawing to my attention. Claudia Echinger Maurach, who owns the drawing, was so kind to provide me a photo for publication.

façade is terminated by a broad and protruding *cavetto*, which was without doubt the main accent of the façade. In van Heemskerck's drawing (see Fig. 16.12) the left part of the façade is hidden by the Aula Concilii, making only the west bell tower visible. In the drawing in Münster, the east bell tower campanile lacks its upper storey and top, which you can recognise in the west bell tower, the result of a restoration under Sixtus IV. The presence of scaffolds between the bell tower and the roof suggests that the east bell tower was damaged and under reconstruction. The damage was probably the result of lightning that struck the bell tower in 1493.[24] In the middle of the façade there was a rounded window and a second oculus in the roof gable. The large Gothic portal, which van Heemskerck shows, is hidden by rubble in the foreground and some houses in the Lateran square. However, the drawing in Münster gives a better impression of the proportions of the whole façade than van Heemskerck's view (see Fig. 16.12).

Typical disparaging *topoi* about San Giovanni in Laterano note that it is an isolated site far away from the Roman *abitato* and that the main entrance facing the east turned away from the city is impractical.[25] For Krautheimer it was more than logical that a northern entrance was necessary to open the basilica towards the city, and de Blaauw agrees with this point. In fact, formerly there was a doorway in the north aisle. As Krautheimer has shown, there are traces of a Constantinian period door and window (Fig. 16.10).[26] Only a small strip of brickwork remains in the south wall of the staircase in the left transept tower. It shows the start of an entrance arch measuring about 3.5 m in height and less than 3 m in width. This entrance (Fig. 16.11) would have nearly touched the edge of the small north transverse wing discussed earlier. It is not known for how long this portal was in use. However, it seems unlikely that another portal 5 m away pierced the north end of the transept wing.

In the fourteenth century the existing transept façade of 1300 was opened by a grand portal topped by an ogival arch and framed by columns as Marten van Heemskerck represented it around 1536 (Fig. 16.12).[27] Built by Pope Gregory XI as late as 1370–8, the Gothic portal had coloured marble revetment and mosaic incrustations, flanked

---

[24] *CBCR* V, 13; S. Infessura, *Diario della Città di Roma di Stefano Infessura scriba senato*, ed. O. Tommasini (Fonti per la storia d'Italia 5) (Rome, 1890), 292.

[25] Blaauw, *CD*, 233. Beginning with Fra Mariano da Firenze, *Itinerarium urbis Romae (1517)*, ed. E. Bulletti (Studi di antichità cristiana 2) (Rome, 1931 [1518]), 152: 'Ad istam ecclesiam communiter ingreditur per ostium quod est in fronte sinistris lateris crucis ecclesiae, eo quod principalis frons illius ad meridiem tendens, iuxta moenia urbis, non facilis est ita ingressus advenientibus sicut ille.'

[26] *CBCR* V, 39–40.   [27] Marten van Heemskerck, Berlin, Kupferstichkabinett.

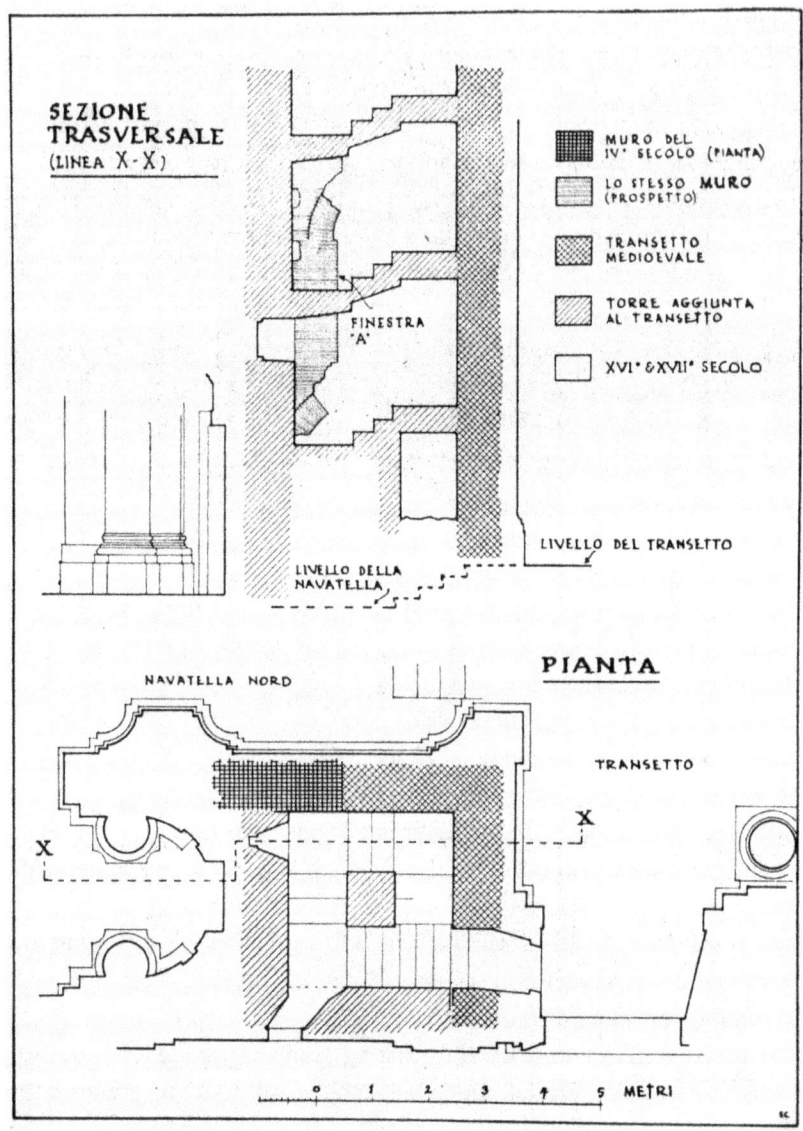

**Fig. 16.10** San Giovanni in Laterano, traces of a Constantinian door and window in the northern aisle (after *CBCR* V).

by two large lions of probable Antique origin.[28] Pope Gregory XI tried to return from Avignon, but did not succeed. One of his aims was the reappraisal of the Lateran basilica. With a papal bull of 1372, issued in

---

[28] R. Lanciani, *Storia degli scavi di Roma e notizie intorno le collezioni romane di antichità*, 4 vols. (Turin, 1902–12), IV, 102; Claussen, *Die Kirchen der Stadt Rom*, 157–60.

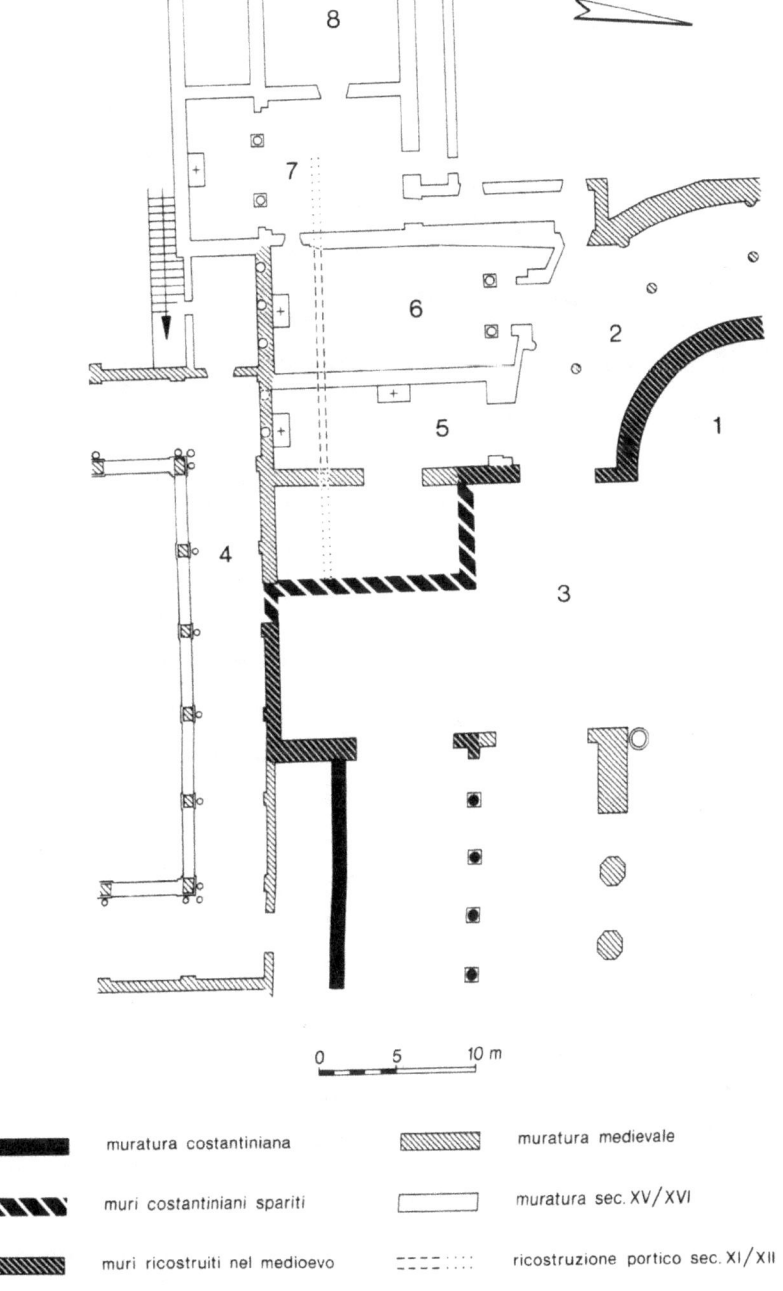

Fig. 16.11 San Giovanni in Laterano, plan of the southwestern parts of the basilica. Black indicates the Constantinian foundations, diagonal black/white indicates the foundations of the transverse wing (after Blaauw, *CD*).

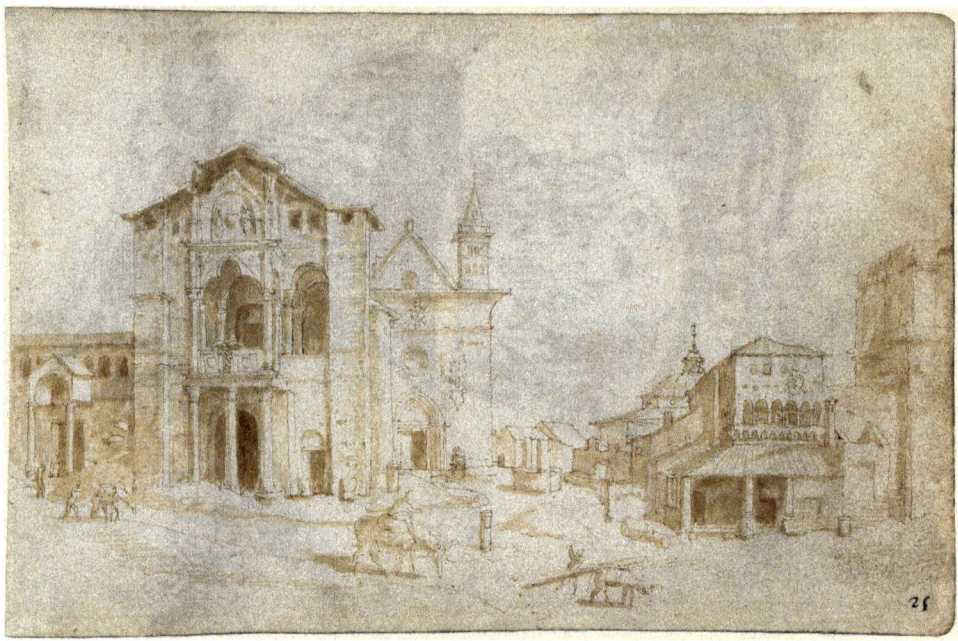

Fig. 16.12 San Giovanni in Laterano, Marten van Heemskerck, view from the Lateran field with the papal palace und the façade of the north transept of the basilica, *c.* 1536 (Berlin, Kupferstichkabinett, Heemskerck-Album I, fol. 12r, detail. Bildagentur für Kunst, Kultur und Geschichte, bpk, Kupferstichkabinett, SMB, J. P. Anders).

Avignon, he tried to re-establish the primacy of the Lateran basilica above all other churches. A marble inscription, almost a reproduction of the papal bull with its seals, is still preserved in the Lateran cloister.[29] Not until the late sixteenth century did the north transept become the face of the basilica with its new double-storeyed loggia by Domenico Fontana, while the old main façade in the east was left to deteriorate until its rebuilding in the eighteenth century by Alessandro Galilei. This is a common narrative of the changes at the Lateran basilica, but is it true? We must ask whether access for people was a major factor for a liturgical space such as the medieval Lateran. What seems to be self-evident for the late Middle Ages (and for us) could be unusual in earlier times. Certainly the new façade of 1300 should have had a doorway, but probably not a grand, ornamental portal for the public. Otherwise, there was no need for the new portal of Gregory XI.

One should not forget that the transepts at the basilicas of Saint Peter and Saint Paul respectively did not have side entrances for the public. An

---

[29] P. Lauer, *Le palais de Latran: Étude historique et archéologique* (Paris, 1911), 268–9 fig. 98.

entrance to the often raised podium of the sanctuary from the outside was not usual in Rome. The reason could be that people entering from the side of the high altar area would disturb the services. Medieval transepts in Rome are quite hermetic. They are closed to the outside, as in the example of the transept of Santa Maria Maggiore, also built under Nicholas IV.

In fact, we have no references to a medieval entrance from the north before 1370. The smaller processions of the twelfth–thirteenth centuries within the Lateran area departed from the basilica through a door in the ambulatory.[30] They proceeded to the baptistery and returned to the basilica by almost the same route. Only the procession on the Saturday before Easter (*Sabato santo*) approached the baptistery by a different path. One way was the just mentioned door of the ambulatory for the cardinals, and the other, which is not very clear, was for the pope. The pope had to walk 'the normal way' through a dark corridor, the *porticum obscurum*, next to the chapel of San Venantius, where a throne was erected. De Blaauw argues that the pope left the basilica through a portal in the north transept and then went through a dark corridor, which has disappeared without a trace. However, there is no clear evidence for a public portal in the area of the later north transept in the twelfth–thirteenth centuries. As de Blaauw has stressed, the starting point of the great processions was always, and was still in the thirteenth century, from the narthex and the portals in the east.[31]

If I understand the 1242 registers of the possessions of the Lateran church correctly, numerous stands (*mense*) for merchants were located in the area of the east portico, yet none are listed for the area of the late medieval north entrance.[32] This suggests that in the thirteenth century, people and pilgrims who wanted to visit the basilica still approached from the main eastern portals. If there was a notable flow of visitors entering the basilica from the Campus Lateranensis, there would have been merchant stands in that neighbourhood. Today it is difficult to imagine when standing in the modern city: a crowded *borgo* in the area east of the basilica situated in the area towards the city walls. Now an open area, it was formerly called the *burgus* (*borgo*) and was filled with as many as three hundred houses, which are listed in the 1242 registers.

The lack of documentary or archaeological evidence of a northern entrance could be the result of unfortunate circumstances. For this reason, an order for an extraordinary procession of the Holy Cross in 1215 to pray for the victory of the Christian army against the Arabs in Spain is of special

---

[30] Blaauw, *CD*, 304.  [31] Blaauw, *CD*, 314.
[32] Arch. Lat. Q. 8. B. 32 (rotulus). P. Pressuti, *Regesta Honorii Papae III* (Rome, 1888–95), ii, cxv–cxvi; Lauer, *Le palais de Latran*, 491–7, esp. 496.

interest. The reference is located in the letters of Innocent III.[33] Nadja Horsch has analysed the order with regard to the topography of the Campus Lateranensis,[34] in which each branch of the procession (women, laymen and clerics) came together after a long march from diverse starting points, and then took positions at diverse locations.[35] The pope gave a sermon sitting on the steps of a palace of the bishop of Albano.[36] In my opinion this palace might be a predecessor of the so-called Loggia of Benediction (better put, malediction) of Boniface VIII. After this sermon Innocent III descended through the palace (Aula Concilii), into the basilica, while the women went to Santa Croce in Gerusalemme, and the clerics entered San Giovanni through the portico from the eastern main portal (they probably took the corridor, which led through the papal palace). The laymen took the way *per burgum* in the church. Horsch interpreted this instruction for the laymen as the direct way from the Campus Lateranensis through a portal in the north transept into the basilica.[37] I do not agree with this. The 1300 form of the north transept with its portal did not exist in

---

[33] *Patrologia Latina*, ed. J. P. Migne, 217 vols. (Paris, 1841–65), CCXVI, 698–9, Innocentii III Romani Pontificis Regestorum sive Epistolarum Liber decimus quintus (1212). N. Horsch, 'Die Nordflanke des mittelalterlichen Lateranpalastes als "Bühne" des Papstes', in S. Albrecht (ed.), *Stadtgestalt und Öffentlichkeit: Die Enstehung politischer Räume in der Stadt der Vormoderne* (Veröffentlichungen des Zentralinstituts für Kunstgeschichte in München 24) (Cologne, 2010), 253–73, at pp. 261–2.

[34] Horsch, 'Die Nordflanke'.

[35] *Patrologia Latina*, CCXVI, 698-9: '... Mulieres ... per Merulanam et ante Sanctum Bartholomaeum veniant in campum Lateranensem et collocent se ante Felloniam (lavandery at the north side of the campus), in silentio permanentes. Clericos ... per via majorem et arcum Basili veniant ante palatium episcopi Albanensis, et ibi directe in medio campi se collocent. Laicos autem ... per Sanctos Joannem et Paulum et ante Sanctum Nicolaum de Formis in Campum veniant, et collocent se ab altera parte. Interim vero Romanus Pontifex cum episcopis et cardinalibus et capellanis ingrediatur basilicam quae dicitur Sancta Sanctorum; et inde reverenter assumpto ligno vivificae crucis, precessionaliter veniat ante palatium episcopi Albanensis, et sedens in scalis exhortatorium faciat sermonem ad populum universum. Quo finito, mulieres ... procedant ad basilicam Sanctae Crucis ... Romanus autem pontifex cum episcopiis et cardinalibus et capellanis per palatium descendat in Lateranensem basilicam. Clerici vero per porticum, et laici per burgum, ingrediantur in illam.'

[36] The palace of the bishop of Albano was an annex of the Aula Concilii. Manfred Luchterhandt kindly called my attention to a document of Gregory IX (1227–41) from his first year, permitting the bishop of Albano to use the upper floor of the *domus major* (=Aula Concilii) next to the bishop's palace (*casa*): '... usum superioris camere palatii nostri quod "Domus Maior" dicitur iuxta domum tuam posite, persone tue tantum duximus concedendum, statuentes ut eadem camera post decessum tuum plene ac libere ad manus Romani pontificis revertatur': ASV, Reg. Vat. 14, fol. 7r (1227, 04–22). L. Auvray, *Les régistres de Grégoire IX: Récueil des bulles de ce pape*, 4 vols. (Paris, 1896), I, 23, no. 48. We can conclude that the bishop of Albano owned a palace attached to the Carolingian *aula* and that its rooms were situated in the upper floor, where a flight of stairs led from the Campus Lateranensis.

[37] Horsch, 'Die Nordflanke', 263.

1215. There was no façade, and probably not even a public portal. In the thirteenth-century registers Burgus is the name of the neighbourhood on the opposite side of the basilica to the east, as noted earlier. I cannot say exactly which path the laymen had to process along, but the phrase *per burgum* seems not to point to the north transept. Probably the laymen had to walk around the papal palace to enter the church from the east, where the *borgo* of the Lateran area was situated.

On the other hand, I cannot exclude a predecessor of the existing transept. De Blaauw, who emphasised the reform efforts since Alexander II (1061–73) to regulate the Lateran clergy, cited Gerhoch von Reichersberg (*c.* 1140) praising the newly reformed churches of Rome, Santa Croce, Santa Maria Nova and San Giovanni in Laterano.[38] Their improved physical state should have been evident in the newly constructed walls. De Blaauw attributed this to building activity in the Lateran area, at the existing transept in particular, suggesting Pope Anacletus II (1130–8) as the most likely patron. De Blaauw published this hypothesis in *Cultus et decor* more than thirty years ago. In the meantime he has changed his mind, and is now convinced that the brickwork and ornamentation of the existing transept is of late thirteenth-century type.[39]

On the other hand, de Blaauw's argument in favour of a transept in the early twelfth century remains quite plausible. I have therefore proposed an intermediate stage, namely a high medieval transept in line with the Constantinian wings but much higher. This hypothetical narrow transept could have been built in the first decades of the twelfth century, and possibly by Anacletus II. But we have no evidence for it. The twelfth-century restoration at San Stefano Rotondo might provide a contemporary project with the Lateran transept. The diaphragm arches supporting the ceiling of the central rotunda are positioned on two slender granite column shafts of 8.70 m. According to the *Liber Pontificalis*, they are part of a restoration by Innocent II (in Rome 1138–43).[40] The original column shafts of the Lateran nave were also of granite. They have been removed or were hidden in the later piers. Only the two columns of the triumphal arch, which were positioned in 1490, are considered to originate from the nave colonnade. Their height was

---

[38] Blaauw, *CD*, 230.
[39] S. de Blaauw, 'Reception and renovation of Early Christian churches in Rome, c. 1050–1300', in C. Bolgia, R. McKitterick and J. Osborne (eds.), *Rome across Time and Space: Cultural Transmission and the Exchange of Ideas c. 500–1400* (Cambridge, 2011), 151–66.
[40] Recent authors have proposed Innocent's predecessor and rival Anacletus II instead. See A. Locke Perchuk, 'Schismatic (re)visions: Sant'Elia near Nepi and Sta. Maria in Trastevere in Rome, 1120–1143', *Gesta* 55 (2016), 179–212, at pp. 211–12.

measured by Lex Bosman as 9.38 m.[41] The difference of about 68 cm from the pair of columns at San Stefano excludes them from coming from the same site. As such, it seems impossible that the two columns of San Stefano came from the Lateran church nearby,[42] unless one could accept a variety of column length in the nave and altar area of the Lateran basilica. To create a continuous transept in line with the Constantinian wings, one would have had to remove two pairs of columns in the west of the nave, which was probably raised in the time of Sergius II (844–7). Only in this case, and with the replacement of the original columns with shorter ones in the altar area, could the repair in San Stefano be connected with the erection of the hypothetical twelfth-century transept of San Giovanni in Laterano, which would then have had to be older than the repairs in San Stefano.

There is a second argument. If you look at the ground plan and elevation of the basilica, you can see that the existing transept and the adjacent cloister is out of axis (Fig. 16.13). Otherwise the axis of the small cross-wing coincides exactly with the central line of the cloister. One can conclude that during the planning and building of the cloister around 1225 the narrow wing or transept still existed and was replaced only in later times by the more prominent structure which still exists today.

The transept of Pope Nicholas IV was the grandest building project during the Middle Ages in Rome, bigger than the naves of San Lorenzo fuori le Mura, Santa Maria in Trastevere or Santa Maria in Aracoeli. It measured 24,300 cubic metres,[43] compared to 7,700 cubic metres for the nave of San Lorenzo. To achieve the expanse of 912 m$^2$, the ground plan had to be augmented only by two small areas of 80 m$^2$ in the south and the north (see Figs 16.13, 16.16), if one can assume that the transverse wings existed. The enormous space was distinguished by its height, 2.80 m higher than the medieval nave.[44] The surface of the inner east transept walls, without windows, seemed to be prepared to receive a monumental pictorial cycle

---

[41] I thank Lex Bosman for his kind help. The cross-section *CBCR* V, plate II (measured and designed by S. Corbett) seems to indicate around 9.10 m. But there is an odd contradiction in the added scale (plate I). The first 5 m are smaller than the following segments.

[42] The two columns of San Giovanni are of red granite, while those in San Stefano Rotondo are grey granite, and seem to be more slender. It is clear that they did not come from the same series.

[43] The height is 26.67 m above the pavement of the transept, the width 1.7 m and length from north to south approximately 62 m. Measurements of the interior taken by Ron Malmstrom and Krautheimer in *CBCR* V, 23. The outer dimensions as given by Blaauw, *CD*, 222: length 64 m, width 16–18 m, and height until the ridge of the roof 35.5 m.

[44] *CBCR* V, 20, 23, 62. The transept walls reached 27.40 m from the pavement of the nave. The pavement of the transept is raised by 0.73 m. Therefore the height of the inner transept walls is 26.67 m.

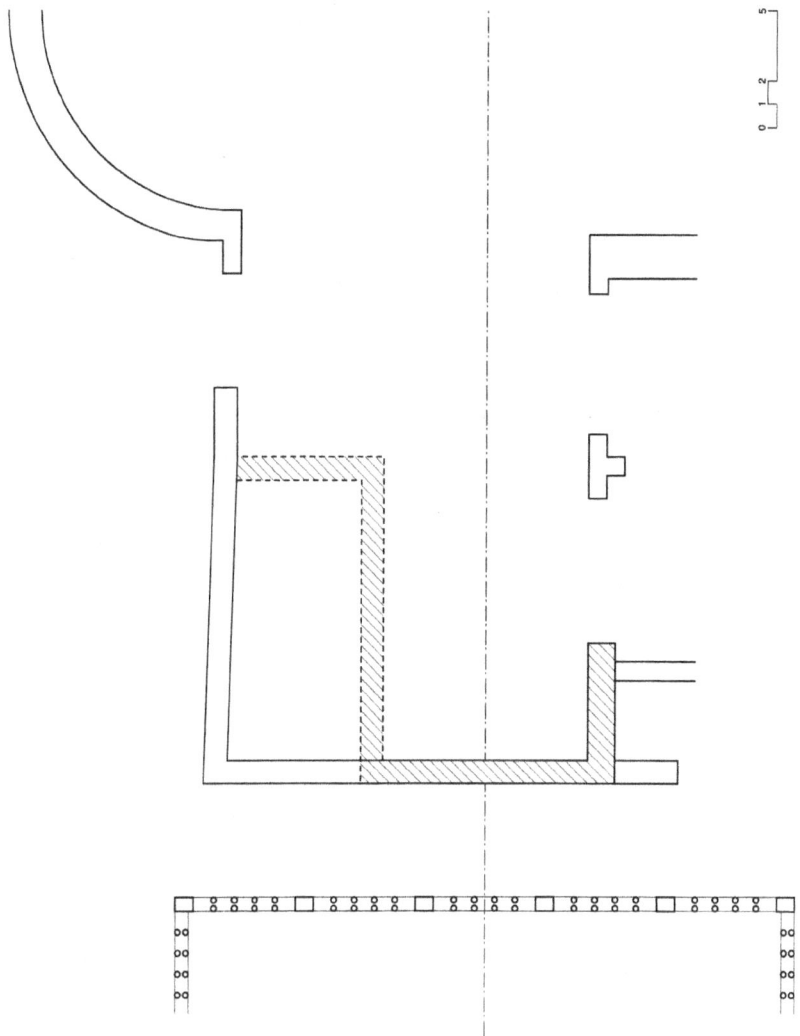

Fig. 16.13 San Giovanni in Laterano, scheme of south transept, transverse wing and cloister (drawing, F. Bächler and P. C. Claussen).

which was never realised. Also, from the outside, the walls are impressive in their vast volume. One can imagine how much a construction site such as this must have disturbed the liturgical services. After erecting the new apse and the walls of the transept a new pavement was laid. All this took more than the lifetime of the pope, who died in 1292 after a brief four-year reign; and the financial support disappeared when his wealthy and powerful supporter, Cardinal Jacopo Colonna, fell from grace under Boniface VIII (1294–1303) and had to leave Rome in 1297. As Krautheimer had already observed, there are formal differences in the discrete parts of the transept, which suggest an extended building history which included the reign of Boniface VIII. The main interest of this pope in San Giovanni was the transformation of the regular canons to a secular status. But Jacopo Colonna returned in the early years of the fourteenth century, and the papal cathedral was completed, but was immediately abandoned because the popes transferred to Avignon.

The huge structure-less south wall (Fig. 16.14) seems to be the oldest part of the transept, penetrated only by a later walled-up oculus and terminated by a brick cornice with marble corbels. The complete set of brick ornamentation can be found in the two rampant rows of the gable, which correlates with the normal type of decorated cornice of the thirteenth century. The wall is extended to the right, broadening the transept asymmetrically eastward (see Fig. 16.19). There is no explanation for this strange feature.

The transept side walls were stabilised by less prominent buttresses. Only at the east side was the wall pierced by ogival windows (Fig. 16.15), closed and altered during the Baroque-period renovations. The cornice differs from that of the south transept, introducing two friezes of pointed arches, one on top of the other. This means that the side walls were built later in addition to the south wall, but not necessarily much later. I do not believe that the crown was totally renewed after the fire of 1308. But there were damages and repairs.

The north side of the transept towards the Lateran field was built as a new façade with two towers (see Fig. 16.12), which were standing over a huge horizontal *cavetto*. Even without mosaics, this *cavetto* gave the façade a dominant, monumental appearance. Here on the north, the extending buttress walls of the façade tending towards both sides, east and west. And that is reasonable, because they are the front walls of square towers behind in the corners, which broaden the width of the transept front considerably (Fig. 16.16). I think this type of expanding front wall with a remarkable strong horizontal emphasis is a highly original concept not easy to fit into the architectural tradition. Without any doubt, this façade tends to impress with its 'wide shoulders', which makes us forget the rather narrow chest of the transept behind. Although in this time a large campanile (see Fig. 16.2) already existed on the east façade, two additional bell towers were added to the north façade: smaller, with three storeys, two of which opened by window arcades. One of the bells was signed and dated 1304, which marks the completion of the towers, later restored by Sixtus IV and Sixtus V. The *cavetto* was built in brick at the same time as the erection of the towers. This may be seen as an invention in the time of the first Holy Year of 1300. Thus,

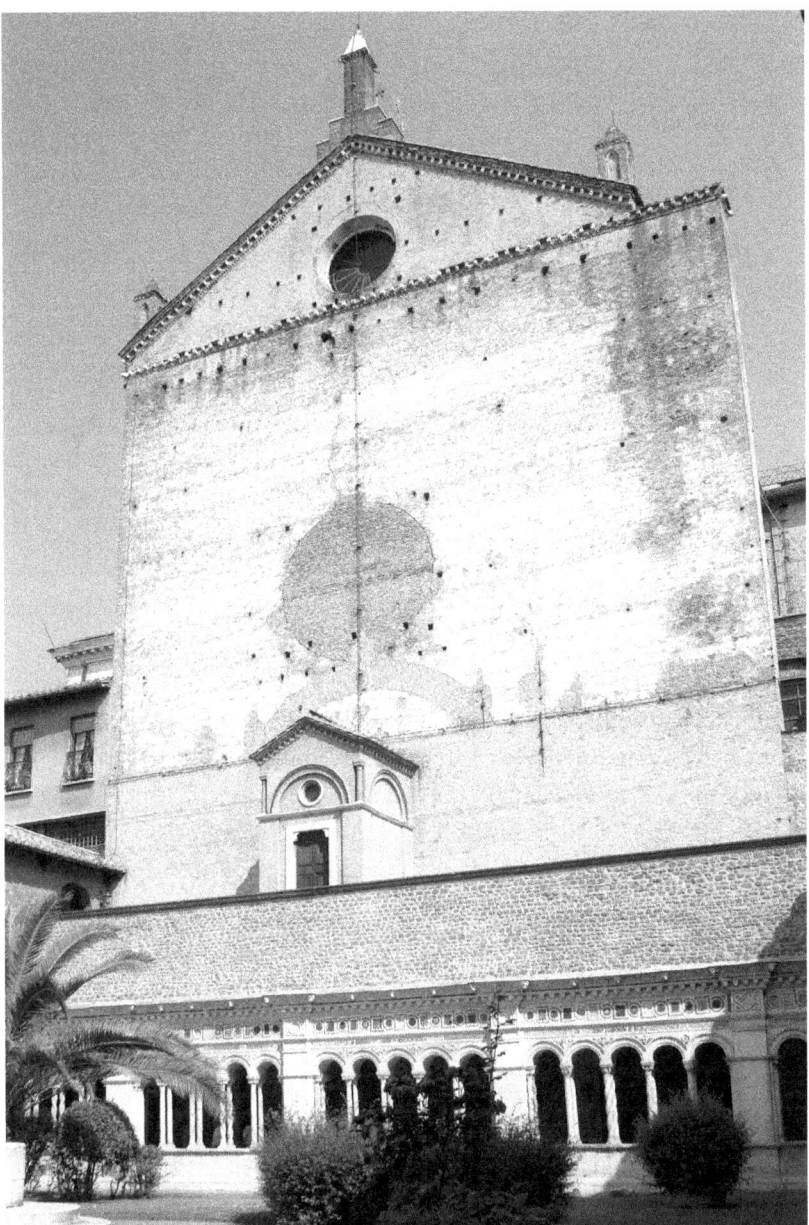

Fig. 16.14 San Giovanni in Laterano, south wall of transept (photo D. Senekovic).

a type of twin tower façade was created. It is a phenomenon so rare in Italy that art historians try to connect the idea with northern building traditions.[45]

---

[45] The comparison with the early Gothic framing relief of the bronze door from the papal palace (now in the portal of the Saint John's chapel in the baptistery) donated in 1195 by Cardinal

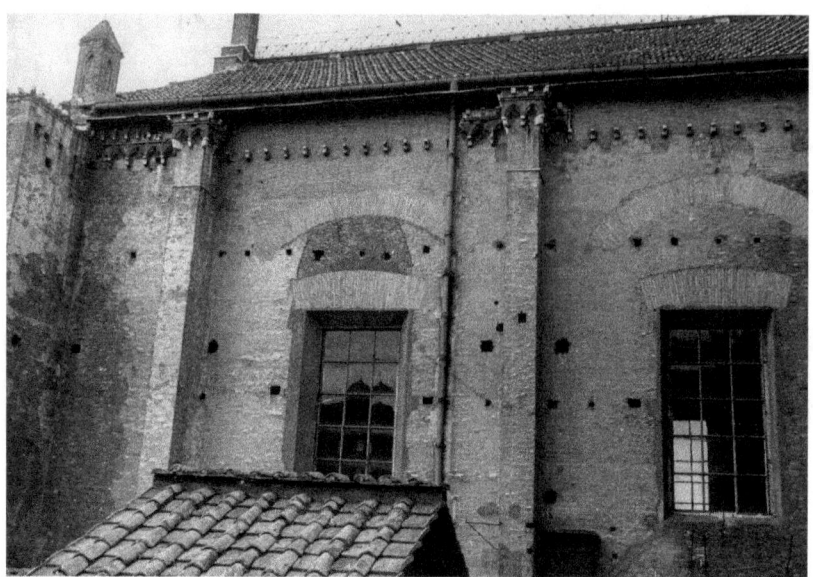

**Fig. 16.15** San Giovanni in Laterano, east wall of south transept (Bibliotheca Hertziana, Rome; photo: R. Malmstrom).

I think the transept façade is an invention of its own, created for the Campus Lateranensis, where the same motif was doubled in the vaulted building of the so-called Loggia of Benediction, probably built before 1300 by Boniface VIII. This loggia was flanked by two slim staircase towers, which create a small façade in front of the north side of the Aula Concilii, square staircase towers like those of the façade of the transept behind.

The interior of the staircases of the towers are nearly 3 m wide, thus quite spacious and easy to use (Fig. 16.17). They are built around a core pillar with rounded corners. The lower storeys of the left tower are built in brick with curved stones specially prepared for this purpose. In contrast, the upper storeys and the right staircase were erected in *tuffo*. This change of building material, first brick, then *tuffo*, is interesting, but does not necessarily indicate a long break in

Cencius Camerarius, later Honorius III, which has a pointed arch with gable and two towers, is problematic. This was without doubt an import from the north, and the artists' signature (Umbertus and Petrus, Magistri Lausenensis) seems to point to a Lausanne origin. Thus, is probably unrelated to the architecture of the Lateran area of the twelfth century. Furthermore, it is unlikely that the architects of the late thirteenth century had this small bronze relief in mind when they designed the new grand façade.

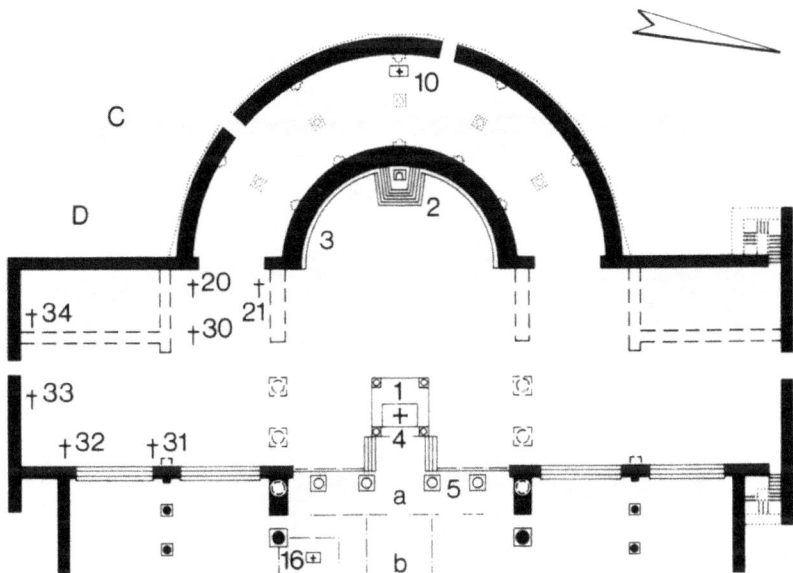

Fig. 16.16 San Giovanni in Laterano, ground plan. Reconstruction of the medieval basilica, detail with transept (from Blaauw, *CD*).

the work. You may ask: why two staircases, and why so ample and functional – only to reach the towers and the roof structure? That is extraordinary. No other bell tower in Rome is built like this. I tried to give an answer by proposing a concept of fire protection: a one-way system up and down for the transport of water buckets. If so, it did not help against the disastrous fires of 1308 and 1361.

For a broader view of the transept fronts with massive extending buttresses, sometimes transformed into tower-like structures, it is helpful to look at the architecture of aristocratic residences in Rome. In particular, one should compare the so-called Torre Magno of the palace of Cardinal Stefano Conti next to Santi Quattro Coronati, built in the middle of the thirteenth century. This high-rising building, which houses the chapel of Silvester and the so-called Aula Gotica,[46] provides a key for the aesthetics of the Lateran transept at the end of the century. In this civil building, the same massive extensions of buttress walls can be found

---

[46] L. Barelli, 'Il palazzo cardinalizio dei Santissimi Quattro Coronati a Roma nel Basso Medioevo', in Z. Mari, M. T. Petrara and M. Sperandio (eds.), *Il Lazio tra antichità e medioevo: Studi in memoria di Jean Coste* (Rome, 1998), 111–24; L. Barelli, *Il complesso monumentale dei Ss. Quattro Coronati a Roma* (Rome, 2009); L. Barelli and R. Pugliese, *Dal cantiere dei SS. Quattro Coronati a Roma: Note di storia e restauro per G. Carbonara* (Rome, 2012).

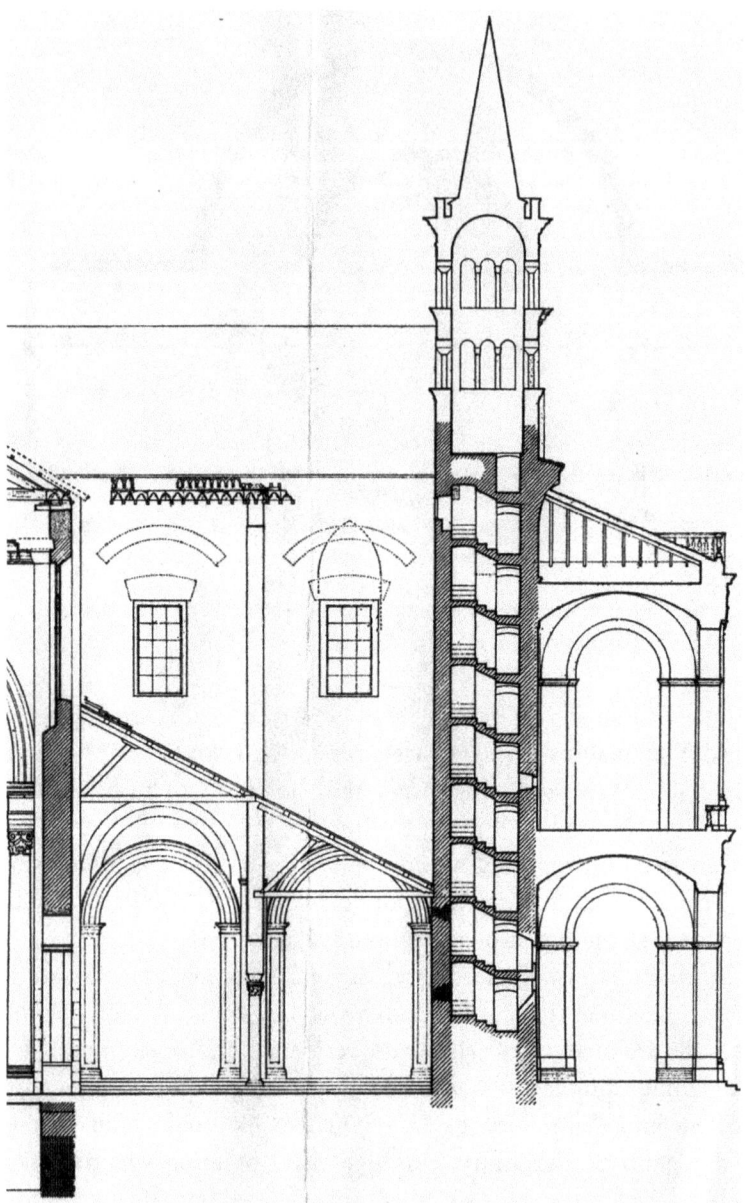

Fig. 16.17 San Giovanni in Laterano, cross-section of the basilica and eastern transept tower (detail from *CBCR* V).

(Fig. 16.18), which are partially used to build tower-like structures in the wall corners of the transept of the basilica (Fig. 16.19).

The project to rebuild and alter parts of the two main basilicas inside the Roman walls is exceptional but not comparable to the *tabula rasa* situation of

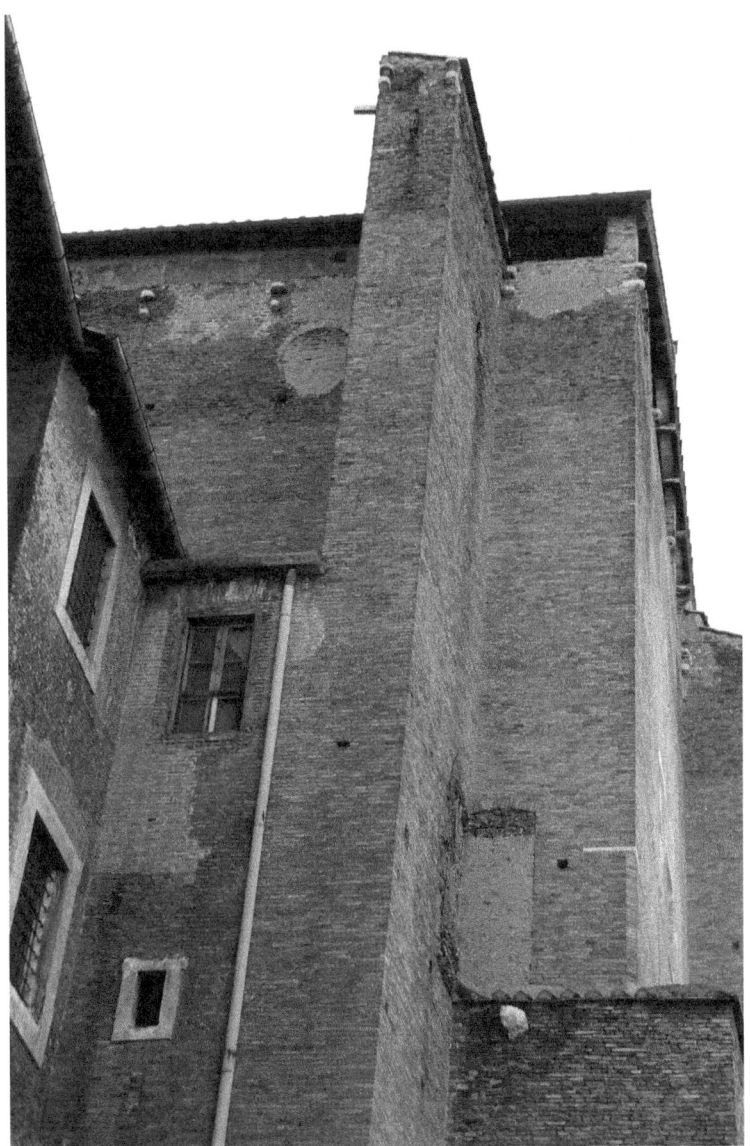

Fig. 16.18 Rome, Santi Quattro Coronati, palace (Torre Magno) from the east with buttress (Photo: T. Bartsch).

the new construction of Saint Peter's in 1506 by Julius II and Bramante.[47] San Giovanni in Laterano and likewise Santa Maria Maggiore were renewed by

[47] More closely comparable with the renovation of the Lateran basilica by Nicolas IV is the project by Nicholas V (1447–55) to enlarge the basilica of Saint Peter's to the west, which included the destruction of the Constantinian apse and transept. The work (1452–5) stopped after the foundations was laid. See C. L. Frommel, 'Il San Pietro di Nicolò V', in G. Spagnesi (ed.), *L'architettura della basilica di San Pietro, Storia e costruzione* (Quaderni dell'Istituto di Storia dell'Architettura 25–30, 1995–7) (Rome, 1997) 103–10.

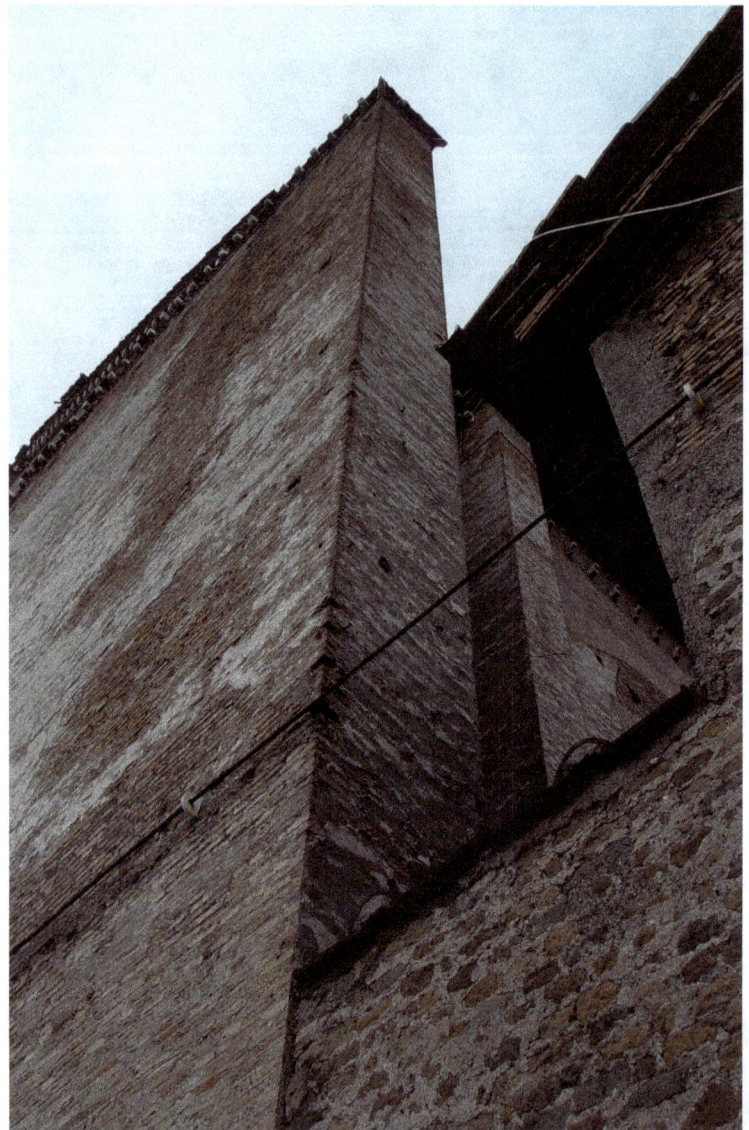

**Fig. 16.19** San Giovanni in Laterano, south wall of transept with buttresses (Photo: author).

Nicholas IV in a spirit of Roman – and likewise Franciscan – assertiveness, but in a careful, conservative manner, which was intended not to do much more than to manifest and preserve the ancient past.

# 17 | *Furtum Sacrilegum*: The 'Holy Heads' of Peter and Paul and Their Reliquaries in the Lateran

DANIELA MONDINI

In what follows here, I shall be outlining the processes involved in the revaluation, 'iconisation' and 'image loss' associated with the Sacred Heads of Peter and Paul.[1] The heads represent an important reliquary complex in the Lateran over a period of several centuries (the basis for the analysis is provided by an extensive range of treatises written by Christian antiquaries, including the main authors Soresini (1673) and Cancellieri (1806)).[2] After a description of the lost late Gothic reliquaries, I shall go on to discuss a little-known, similarly lost fresco cycle in the north transept of the Lateran basilica, which commemorated a notorious event: the theft of several jewels from the reliquaries of Peter and Paul and the punishment assigned to the perpetrators.

To anticipate the conclusion: the two half-length busts that can be seen today in the monumental late Gothic tabernacle above the main altar of Saint John Lateran, in 'constant ostension' (Figs 17.1 and 17.2), are only a modest replacement, dating from the early nineteenth century, for the formerly much more magnificent late Gothic bust reliquaries. These goldsmithing works, made to the highest standards, dated from a joint endowment by the French pope Urban V (Guillaume de Grimoard), who had brought the Curia back from Avignon to Rome for a short period in 1368 (Fig. 17.3). The king of

---

[1] I am grateful to Michel Robertson for his very accurate translation. I have discussed the dynamics of display and concealment in ritual in greater detail in an earlier essay: see D. Mondini, 'Reliquie incarnate: Le "sacre teste" di Pietro e Paolo a San Giovanni in Laterano a Roma', in D. Scotto (ed.), *Del visibile credere: Pellegrinaggi, santuari, miracoli, reliquie* (Florence, 2011), 265–96; see now also C. D'Alberto, *Roma al tempo di Avignone: Sculture nel contesto* (Rome, 2013), 147–97.

[2] J. M. Soresini, *De capitibus sanctorum apostolorum Petri et Pauli in sacrosancta lateranensi ecclesia* (Rome, 1673); see also the shorter Italian edition by the same author, *Compendio istorico cronologico delle cose più cospique concernenti la Scala Santa e le SS. Teste* (Rome, 1674). Later authors who also refer back to Soresini include A. Baldeschi and G. Crescimbeni, *Stato della SS. chiesa papale lateranense nell'anno MDCCXXIII* (Rome, 1723), 96–119; G. Marangoni, *Istoria dell'antichissimo oratorio, o cappella di San Lorenzo nel Patriarchio Lateranense comunemente appellato Sancta Sanctorum* (Rome, 1747), 260–4; [F. Cancellieri], *Memorie istoriche delle sacre teste de' santi Apostoli Pietro e Paolo e della loro solenne ricognizione nella basilica lateranense* (Rome, 1806).

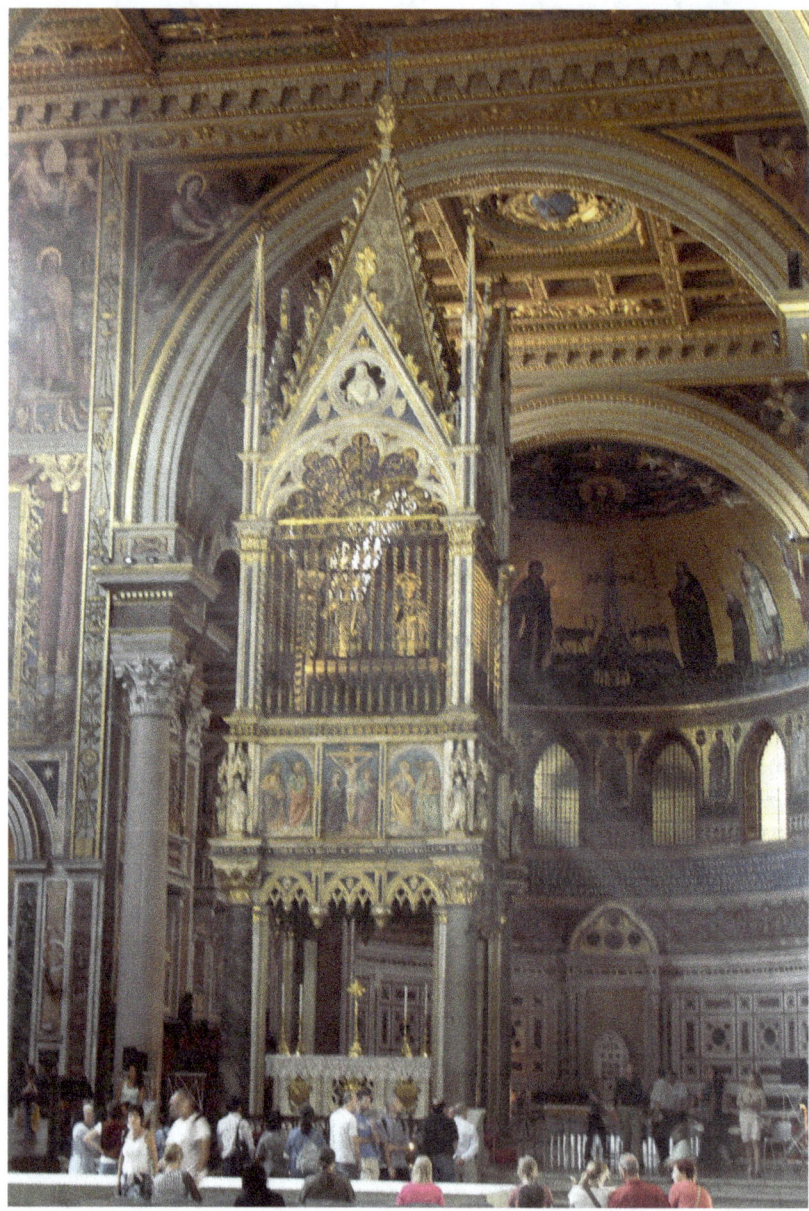

Fig. 17.1 San Giovanni in Laterano, main altar tabernacle by Giovanni di Stefano, 1370 (Photo: author).

France, Charles V, and prominent members of other royal houses also contributed to the endowment (the queen of Naples, Joanna of Anjou (1343–82) and Joan of France (1355–73), sister of the French king and

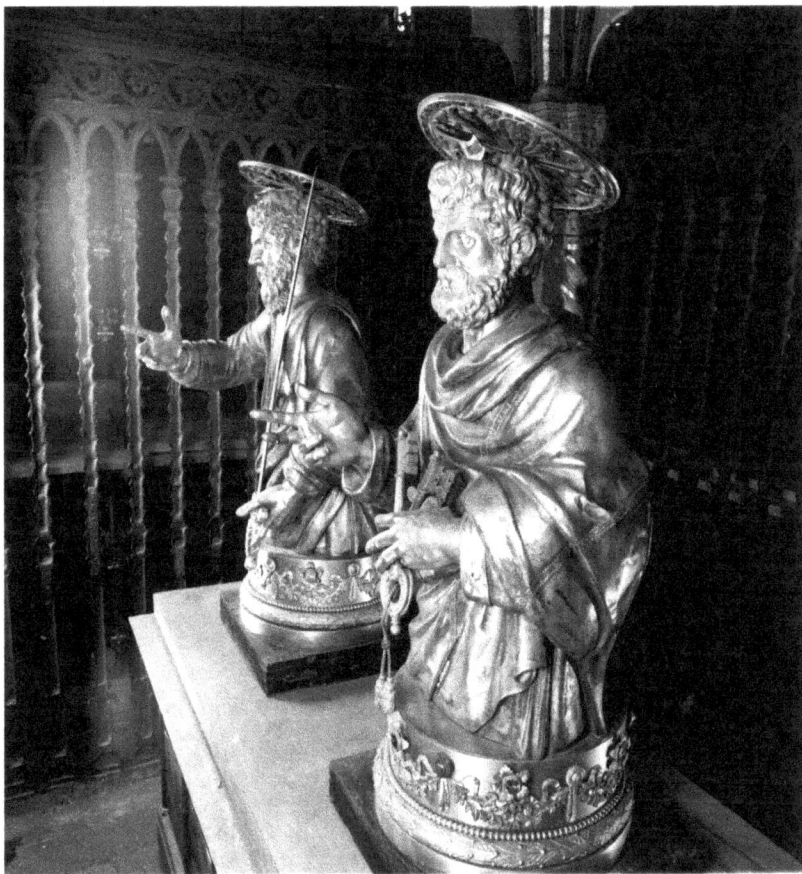

Fig. 17.2 San Giovanni in Laterano, the reliquaries of the 'Holy Heads' of Peter and Paul, enclosed in the tabernacle; Giuseppe Valadier and Workshop, 1804 (Photo: Archivio fotografico Musei Vaticani).

consort of Charles II of Navarre).[3] From 1370 to 1798 the reliquaries remained enclosed in the upper storey of the monumental main altar ciborium, which was specially constructed for the purpose.[4]

---

[3] The collective endowment is mentioned in the files for the unsuccessful canonisation of Urban V (Archivio Segreto Vaticano, fol. 123, cited in Soresini, *De capitibus*, 6 and Cancellieri, *Memorie*, 20; however, this document can now no longer be located and is missing from the document collection by J. H. Albanès and U. Chevalier, *Actes anciens et documents concernant le bienheureux Urbain V pape, sa famille, sa personne, son pontificat, ses miracles et son culte* (Paris, 1897). I have not yet found any evidence in the sources for the possible involvement of Emperor Charles IV of Bohemia, who was staying in Rome in the autumn of 1368 (see J. M. Fritz, *Goldschmiedekunst der Gotik in Mitteleuropa* (Munich, 1982), 222–3 fig. 260); I regard it as a case of mistaken identity.

[4] A. Monferini, 'Il ciborio Lateranense e Giovanni di Stefano', *Commentari. Rivista di Critica e Storia dell'Arte*, n.s., 13, 3.4 (1962), 182–212; D'Alberto, *Roma al tempo di Avignone*, 166–79.

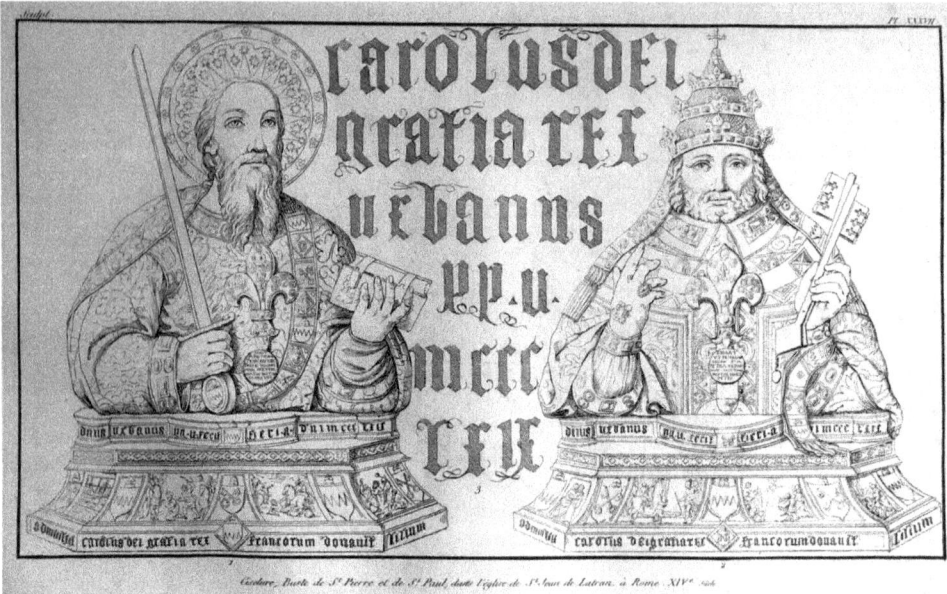

Fig. 17.3 The 'Holy Heads' of Paul and Peter, reliquaries endowed by the French pope Urban V and the French king Charles V, 1369 (Séroux d'Agincourt, Histoire de l'art par les monumens, IV, plate XXXVII (Sculpture); photo: author).

In the 1780s – probably because they featured French insignia – the two late medieval relic receptacles were already included in the text and illustrations of the first comprehensive survey of the history of medieval art, the *Histoire de l'art par les monumens* by the French nobleman Jean-Baptiste Séroux d'Agincourt.[5] And probably again because of the royal fleurs-de-lis appearing on them, the two silver reliquaries were confiscated from the main altar tabernacle of the Lateran at the end of November 1798, during the occupation of Rome by French troops – and were melted down for use as coins in January 1799.

This inglorious end (certainly also representing kind of a state-ordained *furtum sacrilegum*) and the less significant substitute reliquaries in Classicist style from the workshop of Giuseppe Valadier – which were less valuable and notably did not feature the insignia of the French crown – probably contributed to the fact that this major work of late Gothic goldsmithing art came to be forgotten.

---

[5] J. B. L. G. Séroux d'Agincourt, *Histoire de l'art par les monumens depuis sa décadence au IVe siècle jusqu'à son renouvellement au XVIe*, 6 vols. (Paris, 1810–23), II, 69–70, IV, pl. XXXVII (*Sculpture*).

## From Relic to Three-Dimensional Sculpture

But how did the 'Apostles' heads' of Peter and Paul – which might have been expected to be found in the corresponding tombs of the Apostles in San Pietro in Vaticano and San Paolo fuori le Mura on the Via Ostiense – originally find their way to the Lateran? This is not known. The skull relics of Peter and Paul are first mentioned – almost in passing – in an inventory dating from the late eleventh century, as forming part of the most important relic treasury in the chapel of Saint Lawrence in the papal Lateran palace.[6]

Anton de Waal, Pietro Sinthern and Engelbert Kirschbaum consider that the gathering in of the 'Capita Apostolorum' to the Lateran palace took place relatively late, in the second half of the ninth century.[7] Recently, Jörg Bölling has suggested that the relics of the Apostles' heads in the Lateran originated from a place of worship that had been held in traditional memory since the mid-third century, the Basilica Apostolorum on the Via Appia (today San Sebastiano). Depending on the way in which the sources are interpreted, the entire bodies of the Apostles – or only their heads, or only contact relics – were temporarily housed there in the mid-third century.[8] According to Bölling, the precious skull relics were thus removed *before* the 'sealing' of the Apostles' tombs when the basilicas were erected in the Constantinian period.[9] However, the hypothesis of such an

---

[6] *Descriptio Lateranensis Ecclesiae* (*DLE*), in R. Valentini and G. Zucchetti (eds.), *Codice topografico della città di Roma*, 4 vols. (Fonti per la Storia d'Italia 90) (Rome, 1940–53), III, 356–8 (quoted below in n. 12).

[7] In advance of a Saracen attack, Sergius II (844–7) is said to have been warned by the duke of Tuscany, Adalbertus, that he should transfer the bodies of Peter and Paul to the city for safety; this may have taken place immediately before the plundering of the basilicas of San Pietro and San Paolo fuori le Mura by the Saracens in August 846: *LP* II, Life 104, 99. A. de Waal, 'Die Häupter Petri und Pauli im Lateran', *Römische Quartalschrift* 5 (1891), 340–8; P. Sinthern, 'Le teste dei SS. Apostoli Pietro e Paolo', *Civiltà Cattolica* 3 (1907), 444–57, esp. p. 456; E. Kirschbaum, *Die Gräber der Apostelfürsten*, 3rd edn (Frankfurt, 1974), 210–22, esp. p. 214; for a convincingly argued view that this only took place *after* the plundering in 846, see P. Jounel, *Le culte des saints dans les basiliques du Latran et du Vatican au douzième siècle* (Collection de l'École Française de Rome 26) (Rome, 1977), 102. See also Mondini, 'Reliquie incarnate', 271 n. 19.

[8] During the Valerian persecutions of 258. In the sixth century the *Vita* of Pope Cornelius (251–3) reports that he had transferred the bodies of the Apostles from the Via Appia to their present-day location in the Vatican and to the Via Ostiense (*LP* I, 150; Kirschbaum, *Die Gräber*, 207); Gregory the Great writes that they were stolen by Orientals after the martyrdom and temporarily hidden on the Via Appia. For a summary of the positions for and against a translation to the Via Appia, see Kirschbaum, *Die Gräber*, 208.

[9] Based on Josi's hypothesis that according to the contemporary interpretation of the law, the grave is legally located where the head is (Kirschbaum, *Die Gräber*, 209). J. Bölling, 'Die zwei Körper des Apostelfürsten: Der heilige Petrus im Rom des Reformpapsttums', *Römische Quartalschrift für christliche Altertumskunde und Kirchengeschichte* 106, 3–4 (2011), 155–92, esp. p. 161 n. 31 and pp. 178–9. Without further argumentation, Bölling places the translation to the

early translation of such important bodily relics in Rome appears to me to be highly questionable, as it runs counter to the long-persisting ancient custom in Rome of the inviolability of tombs.[10]

By contrast, the fact that the translation of relics as significant as those of the most important saints of the city left no traces in the tradition, and that the relics only become tangible in their new location in sources dating from the eleventh century, raises some doubts regarding their authenticity.[11] In this view, what would be involved would not be a less official translation of relics or a *furtum sacrum* within the city, but rather a matter of relic forgery – pious fraud.

The inventory of the relic treasury of the oratory of Saint Lawrence in the Lateran palace, compiled in 1073, clearly shows the great importance of the relics preserved there: in addition to a concentration of relics of Christ, headed by the Salvator icon, as well as the bodily relics of a large number of martyrs, the mention of four heads in a side altar – those of the Apostles Peter and Paul, along with the martyrs Agnes and Euphemia – is important.[12] The impression is that an effort had been made to concentrate as much salvific power based on Roman martyrs as possible within the papal relic treasury inside the city walls.

In the context of a renovation and 'securing' of the main altar of the chapel, the relics of the Apostles' heads – and only those! – were given a facial appearance in two portrait medallions on the bronze doors of the reliquary altar endowed by Innocent III (1198–1216). It is notable that only the heads

---

Lateran in the tenth century, taking into consideration the origin of the skull relics in the Late Antique *triclia* near San Sebastiano.

[10] On the *triclia* on the Via Appia as a site of transference of worship, rather than translation, of corporeal relics, see H. G. Thümmel, *Die Memorien für Petrus und Paulus in Rom: Die archäologischen Denkmäler und die literarische Tradition* (Berlin, 1999), 99.

[11] I. Herklotz, 'Der mittelalterliche Fassadenportikus der Lateransbasilika und seine Mosaiken: Kunst und Propaganda am Ende des 12. Jahrhunderts in Rom', *RJBH* 25 (1989), 27–95, esp. p. 84.

[12] 'In alio vero altari eiusdem oratori sunt capita sanctorum apostolorum Petri et Pauli, et capita sanctarum Agnetis et Eufemiae virginum': *Descriptio Lateranensis Ecclesiae* (*DLE*), in its first version, written before 1073; I am quoting here from the later edition compiled by Johannes Diaconus for Pope Alexander III (1159–81): Valentini and Zucchetti (eds.), *Codice topografico*, III, 356–8. For a reference to the eleventh-century version of the *DLE*, see S. de Blaauw, 'Il patriarchio, la Basilica lateranense e la liturgia', in P. Liverani (ed.), *Giornata di studio tematica dedicata al Patriarcato Lateranense: Atti della giornata tematica dei Seminari di Archeologia Cristiana (École française de Rome, 10 maggio 2001)* (*MEFRA* 116, 1) (special issue) (Rome, 2004), 161–70, esp. p. 166. Only the authenticity of Saint Euphemia is upheld: 'capud et vestimentum sancte Agnetis, relique et vestimentum sancte Eufemie': B. Galland, *Les authentiques de reliques du Sancta Sanctorum* (Vatican City, 2004), 67 and authentication no. 85. However, the authentication dates from the thirteenth century and was evidently copied when the skull relic of Saint Agnes was transferred to a new shrine under Honorius III.

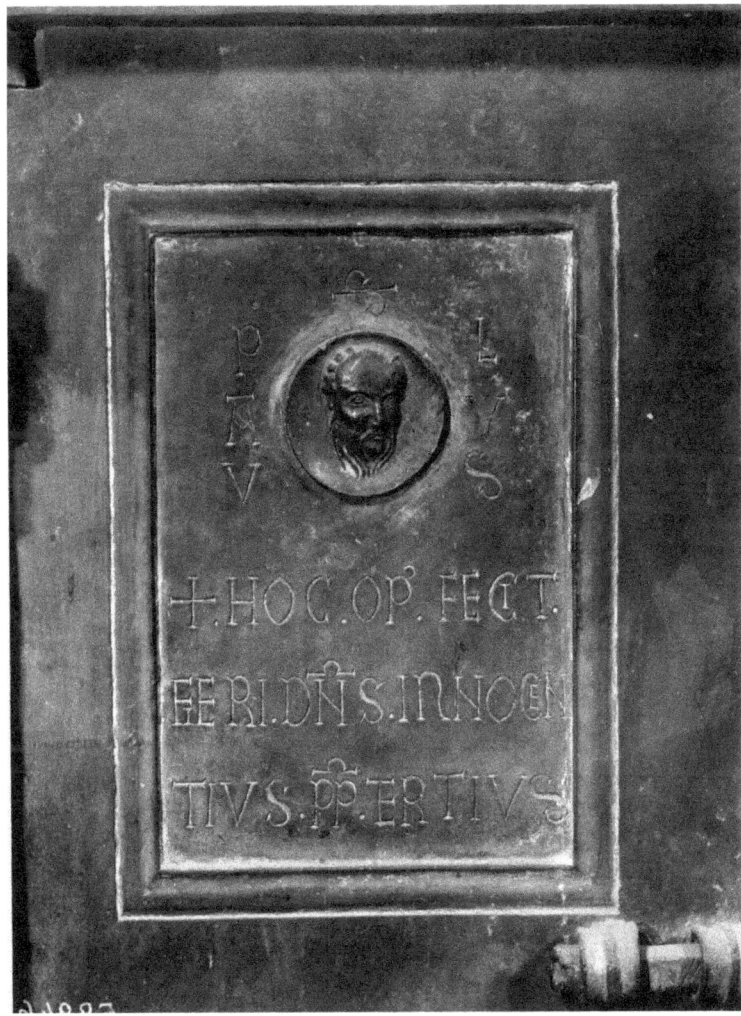

Fig. 17.4 Portrait medallion of Paul on the left bronze door of the reliquary altar endowed by Innocent III in the former chapel of Saint Lawrence in the Lateran Palace (Sancta Sanctorum) (Photo: Bibliotheca Hertziana, Rome. GFN E 59946).

are shown, without necks – probably as a direct reference to the Apostles' skulls secured behind the bronze doors in the altar (Fig. 17.4). This may have followed on from the iconography of the visualisation of the heads of Paul and Peter on papal seals that had been canonical since Paschal II (1099–1118) (Fig. 17.5).[13]

---

[13] I. Herklotz, 'Zur Ikonographie der Papstsiegel im 11. und 12. Jahrhundert', in H.-R. Meier, C. Jäggi and P. Büttner (eds.), *Für irdischen Ruhm und himmlischen Lohn: Stifter und Auftraggeber in der mittelalterlichen Kunst* (Berlin, 1995), 116–30; Bölling, 'Die zwei Körper',

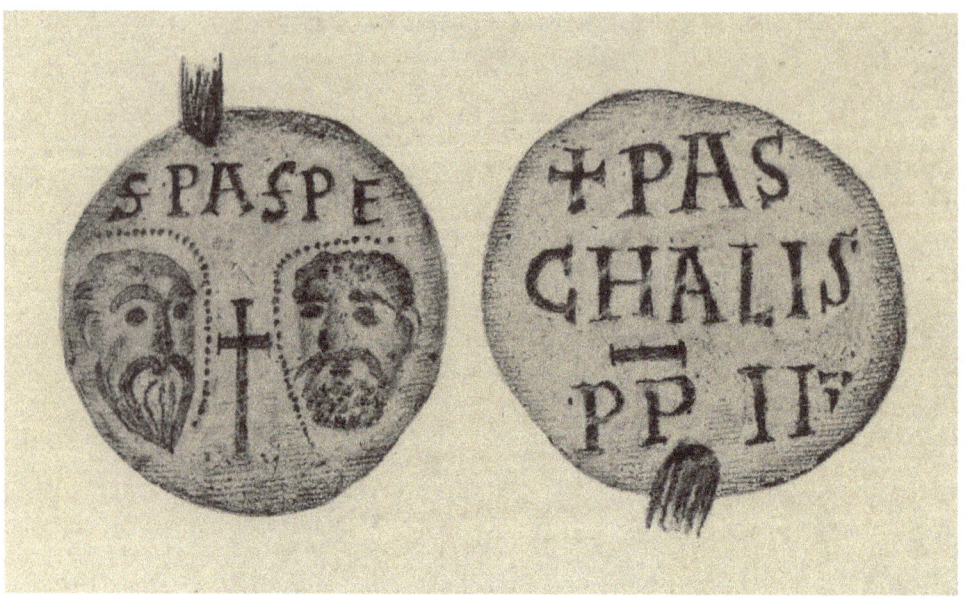

**Fig. 17.5** Papal seal of Paschal II (1099–1118) with the portraits of Paul and Peter (Photo from Julius von Pflugk-Harttung, *Specimina selecta chartarum Pontificum Romanorum, Pars tertia: Sigilla* (Stuttgart, 1887), Tf. IX 9.7; photo © Zentralbibliothek Zürich Aeg 423).

In the late twelfth and early thirteenth centuries the relics of the skulls of the Apostles Peter and Paul began to acquire an 'active' role in state ceremony and ritual, and they were even led in processions through the city by the pope during special political events.[14] For reasons of space alone in the confinement of the reliquary altar, the so-called *arca cipressina*, anthropomorphic head or bust reliquaries – a rare form of reliquary that only became widespread in Rome and Latium in the late Middle Ages – are scarcely to be expected during this period. The skull relics probably rested in simple small chests of precious metal, of the type used for the heads of Saint Agnes and Saint Praxedes – two relic receptacles that belonged to the treasury of the Sancta Sanctorum.[15]

---

177; A. Paravicini Bagliani, 'Grégoire VII et l'excommunication: À propos des figures des apôtres Pierre e Paul sur les bulles pontificales', in F. Elsig (ed.), *L'image en questions: Pour Jean Wirth* (Geneva, 2013), 120–9.

[14] For further references, see Mondini, 'Reliquie incarnate', 272–7.

[15] P. Lauer, *Le trésor du Sancta Sanctorum* (Monuments et mémoires publiés par l'Académie des inscriptions et belles lettres 15) (Paris, 1906), 79–81 (reliquary of Saint Agnes, thirteenth century), 73–8 (reliquary of Saint Praxedes, eleventh century).

Following the rebuilding of the chapel of Sancta Sanctorum under Nicholas III (1277–80), the pope again personally sealed the relics of the Apostles into the reliquary altar that was taken over from the previous building. Ptolemy of Lucca for the first time explicitly describes the reliquaries here as 'thecas argenteas'.[16] These silver vessels had probably not been newly made and would still have been the existing simple old caskets.

The Apostles' heads in their receptacles thus vanished into the altar again along with the other reliquaries. In the chapel newly furnished by Nicholas III, however, bust portraits of Peter and Paul now appeared in the mosaic programme in the lunette above the central bay over the main altar. With their constant presence in the mosaic they represented the precious content held within the altar safe, which was closed with strong bars.

The Apostles' heads made their first truly great appearances in 1368–70, when Pope Urban V (1362–70) wished to set a clear signal on the occasion of his return from Avignon to Rome. In March 1368 the pope ordered a search for the Apostles' relics in the altar of the Sancta Sanctorum. Their rediscovery was at once celebrated with their 'spontaneous display' on the Campus Lateranensis, and the Sienese goldsmith Giovanni di Bartolo completed the new reliquaries in 1369. The official ceremonies celebrating the translation of the Apostles' heads to the Lateran church took place on Easter Monday, 16 April 1370. The new, weighty and anthropomorphic – but as yet still empty! – bust reliquaries were led in procession through the city from the Vatican palace to the Lateran by three cardinals on foot (actually rather a peculiar procedure).[17] In the Sancta Sanctorum the precious relics of the Apostles' skulls were transferred into the new reliquaries before the eyes of 'totius populi'. After that the reliquaries were ceremonially borne to the Lateran basilica and placed on the main altar. Here Urban V is said to have publicly stated that the alleged value of the new reliquaries was 150,000 gold florins.[18] A total value of slightly over 30,000 gold florins, which is mentioned in Urban V's canonisation files, appears more realistic.[19]

---

[16] Soresini, *De capitibus*, 83–5. Soresini quotes reports by Nicola Processi (fourteenth century) and by the Dominican Tolomeo da Lucca (1236–1326).

[17] Garoscus de Ulmoisca, 'Iter italicum Urbani V Romani Pontificis' in S. Baluzius, *Vitae Paparum Avenionesioum [1693], nouvelle édition d'après les manuscrits par G. Mollat*, 4 vols. (Paris, 1916–22), IV, 136.

[18] Garoscus de Ulmoisca, 'Iter italicum'; the text is quoted in Mondini, 'Reliquie incarnate', 279 n. 48.

[19] 'Quae secundum communem aestimationem, excedebant valorem 30. Mila florenorum de Camera': Arch. Secret. Vat. fol. 123, quoted in Soresini, *De capitibus*, 6 and Cancellieri, *Memorie*, 20 n. 1.

The translation of the Apostles' heads represented a tremendous addition to the treasure of the episcopal church of Rome. As the ecclesiastical seat of the pope, the Lateran basilica lacked a saint's tomb, and had previously only been furnished with rather obscure relics such as the inventory of the Temple of Solomon. In comparison with Saint Peter's and other basilicas, it had previously lacked a focus of worship. In addition, the elegant reliquary tabernacle above the Magdalene altar, which was renovated in Gothic style after 1307 – just under 10 m away in the chapters choir – 'stole the show' from the small main altar tabernacle, which probably still dated from the early Middle Ages.[20]

Urban's new *mise-en-scène* restored the visual hierarchy among the altars within the church, and also to some extent established a balance relative to the Vatican with the tomb of Saint Peter. In addition, it initiated a type of relic display that was new in the city of Rome (Fig. 17.6). The visual expectations[21] of pilgrims from north of the Alps, who were accustomed to the Gothic staging of relics, may perhaps thus have been satisfied for the first time in Rome here in the Lateran basilica. Conversely, the Apostles' heads, which had been isolated from the treasury of the Sancta Sanctorum – previously hierarchically subordinate to the relics of Christ and the icon of the Saviour not painted by human hand (*acheiropoietos*) – rose to the status of principal relics of the highest rank. Urban V ordained an indulgence, for a visit to the Lateran basilica on the occasion of the high feast-days of Maundy Thursday, Easter, the church's consecration day, and the saints' days of Peter and Paul, on which the Apostles' heads were displayed. During the other 360 days of the year the magnificent reliquaries were hidden from pious view.

As a final measure taken to secure and increase the value of the reliquary treasure newly safeguarded in the Lateran basilica, Urban V – shortly before his return to Avignon in August 1370 – set out in a papal bull a threat of excommunication against anyone who might remove even the slightest part of the treasure.[22] The document explicitly mentions 'reliquiae et imagines', since also only the precious vessels were in fact capable of arousing unwanted covetousness.

---

[20] P. C. Claussen, *Die Kirchen der Stadt Rom im Mittelalter 1050–1300, vol. 2: S. Giovanni in Laterano* (Corpus Cosmatorum II, 2) (Forschungen zur Kunstgeschichte und Christlichen Archäologie 21) (Stuttgart, 2008), 198–216, figs. 115–16.

[21] H. R. Jauss, 'Literaturgeschichte als Provokation der Literaturwissenschaft', in R. Warning (ed.), *Rezeptionsästhetik: Theorie und Praxis*, 2nd edn (Munich, 1979), 126–62, at p. 127 (where he creates the concept of the horizon of expectations that is fundamental for reception aesthetics).

[22] Bull of excommunication, V. Kal. Augusti 1370: Soresini, *De capitibus*, 47–52; Cancellieri, *Memorie*, 74–5.

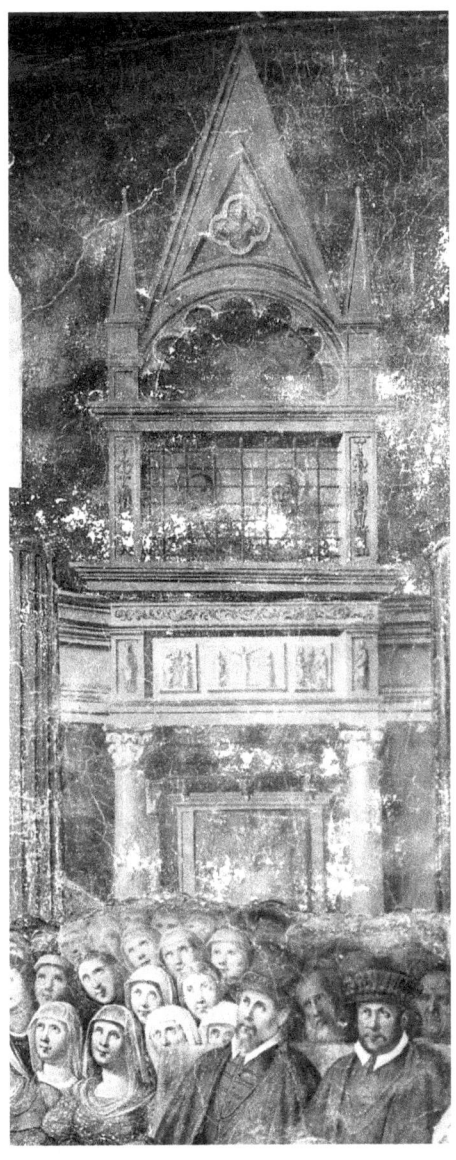

**Fig. 17.6** The Lateran tabernacle during the ostention of the 'Holy Heads', detail from a fresco representing the Encounter of Saint Francis, Dominicus and the Carmelitan Saint Angelus, by Giacomo Ligozzi, *c.* 1600, Florence, Ognissanti, first cloister (Photo: Bibliotheca Hertziana, Rome. Pont. Comm. Arch. Sacra n. 12446).

The relics of the Apostles' heads, which first began to acquire a recognisable appearance in the chapel of Saint Lawrence in the Lateran palace before 1200, approximately at the same time as the Sudarium Christi in Saint Peter's basilica, now after a delay of some 170 years underwent the process of

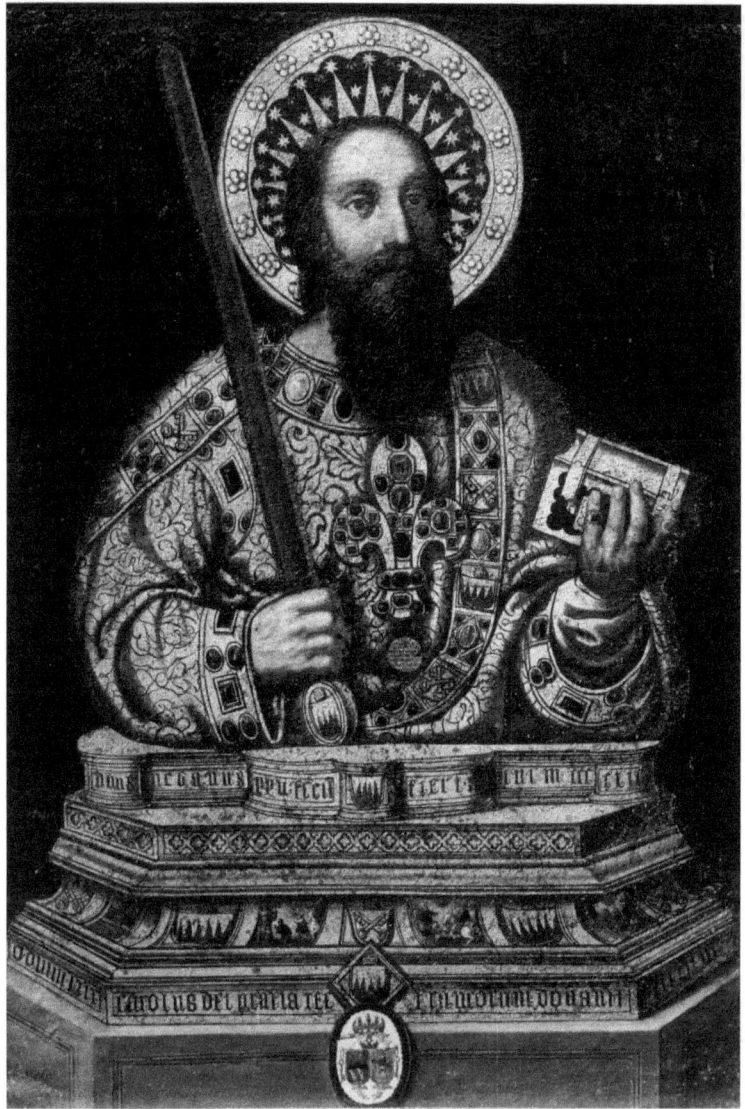

Fig. 17.7 San Giovanni in Laterano, Cappella del Coro, former Colonna chapel, late Gothic reliquary bust of Paul, painting, oil on canvas, *c.* 1585 (Photo: Bibliotheca Hertziana, Rome. GFN C 9028).

iconisation – from relic to image – that had previously turned Christ's *sudarium* (Veronica/Vera Icon) in Saint Peter's into the most popular devotional image of the late Middle Ages. The choice of the bejewelled, three-dimensional medium of the bust reliquaries might perhaps be regarded as an attempt to use their physical presence to outdo the Sudarium Christi.

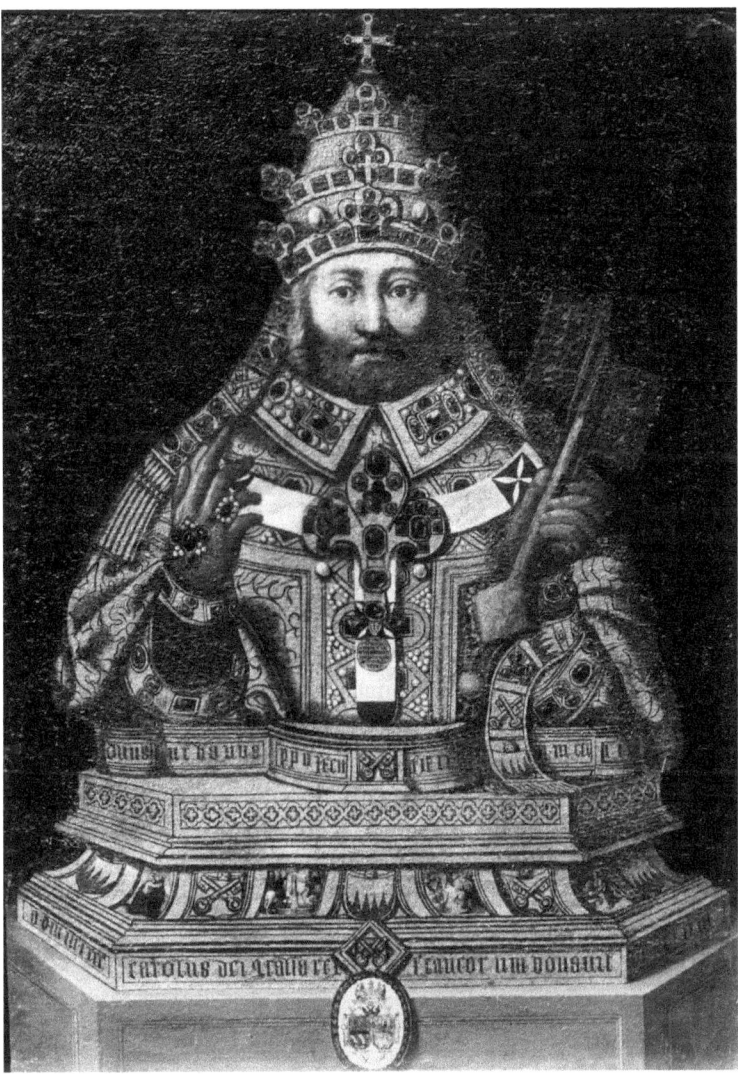

**Fig. 17.8** San Giovanni in Laterano, Cappella del Coro, former Colonna chapel, late Gothic reliquary of Peter, painting, oil on canvas, c. 1585 (Photo: Bibliotheca Hertziana, Rome. GFN C 9027).

Barely a year after the death of Urban V, Gregory XI issued a bull in Avignon that raised the corresponding indulgence to the same level as that applying to the Veronica in Saint Peter's – thereby increasing the power of indulgence of the Capita Apostolorum by a factor of more than 1,000.[23] This

---

[23] Bull of Gregory XI (issued in Avignon, May 1371), in Cancellieri, *Memorie*, 76. In the last quarter of the fourteenth century the indulgence applicable to the ostension of the Veronica

adjustment is perhaps an indication that the indulgence originally set for the newly staged apostolic relics in the Lateran did not correspond to the indulgence expectations that were customary at the time. The Apostles' heads above the high altar of the Lateran basilica had perhaps not immediately established themselves as a magnet for pilgrims, due to this 'undervaluation'.

## Appearance and Material Quality of the Apostolic Reliquaries

Various pictorial and textual sources provide a fairly clear picture of the half-length jewelled silver reliquaries that were destroyed in 1799 (Figs 17.7 and 17.8).[24] The two reliquaries were erected over a two-part base; their height can be estimated as a substantial 156 cm (seven palms).[25] The base had a hexagonal ground plan, and along its fluted central zone it depicted scenes from the lives of the Apostles, alternating with the coat of arms of Urban V. In the lower border of the base, both reliquaries bore the donor inscription of the French king, Charles V, referring to the gold fleur-de-lis: 'Carolus dei gratia Rex Francorum qui coronatus fuit Anno Domini 1364 donavit praesens lilium ad honorem capitis B. Pauli, quod est in pectore eius.'[26] A second, smaller, inscription was incorporated into the band along the second, narrower part of the base, directly underneath the busts of the Apostles. This was the inscription of the principal donor, Urban V: 'Urbanus Papa V. fecit fieri hoc opus ad honorem Beati Pauli anno domini 1369.'[27] The signature of the goldsmith was also included beneath the figure of Saint Peter: 'HOC OPVS FECIT JOANNES BARTOLI DE SENIS AVRIFABER'.[28]

amounted to 3,000 years for Romans, 9,000 years for pilgrims from the vicinity and 12,000 years for travellers from afar (*ultramontanis vel marinijs*): Mirabilia and Indulgentiae ecclesiarum, Sankt Gallen, Stiftsbibliothek, Ms. 1093, Mondini, 'Reliquie incarnate', 283 n. 59.

[24] Of particular interest are two paintings today preserved in the left choir chapel that can be dated to the pontificate of Sixtus V (1585–90) on the basis of the coats of arms (Savelli and Sixtus V) shown on their lower edges. They were probably commissioned by Cardinal Giacomo Savelli (d. 1587), who also arranged for the preservation of the bronze doors of the demolished Lateran palace. For further references, see Mondini, 'Reliquie incarnate', 284 n. 61.

[25] '[S]ono d'argento smaltati d'altezza di sette palmi l'uno, e la spada che tiene in mano S. Paolo è alta cinque palmi': description by Urbano Millini, in Soresini, *De capitibus*, 44.

[26] See also the accurate description of the reliquaries, with copies of all the surviving inscriptions, by S. Riccioni and M. Tomasi, 'Giovanni di Bartolo: Busti reliquiario dei santi Pietro e Paolo (opera perduta)', in M. M. Donato (ed.), *Opere firmate nell'arte italiana/Medioevo: Siena e artisti senesi: maestri orafi* (Opera Nomina Historiae 5/6, 2011–12. Repertorio) (Pisa, 2013), cat. 22.S.1, 219–24 and D'Alberto, *Roma al tempo di Avignone*, 150–5.

[27] Description by Urbano Millini in Soresini, *De capitibus*, 45–6.

[28] D'Alberto suggests that Johannes Bartoli's signature must also have been on the bust of Saint Paul, although it is not mentioned by Millini; she also discovered the bull of payment with the record of the goldsmith's name; a second name, Guglielmo de Frezenthis, is mentioned (ASV,

The way in which the French king figured prominently as a fellow donor alongside the pope is of interest. Although the golden, jewel-studded fleurs-de-lis were explicitly mentioned as his endowment, the location of the inscription on the base and the quantity of jewels on the two busts suggest, however, that the royal endowment, which was estimated at more than 4,000 gold florins, also applied to the figures and their jewelled decoration.[29] Coats of arms of the French king are also found on the ciborium. The supreme saints of Rome – Peter and Paul – are thus presented as bearing the French royal insignia.[30]

The half-length figures of the Apostles had arms and torsos. Paul was bare-headed and set off with a halo; in his right hand he held the sword of his martyrdom and in his left hand a closed codex with a gold binding. Peter, whose head is framed by a heavy tiara, has a considerably stiffer appearance than his counterpart. He held the keys to Paradise in his left hand, while his right hand was raised in blessing.

The accuracy of the depiction in the two paintings is credible, as it can be verified from a slightly later description by Urbano Millini. In 1649 Millini climbed through the only door into the grating-protected high altar tabernacle for a visit and cleaning, and he made a detailed record of the sacred treasures found there under a thick layer of dust.[31] Millini's meticulous inventory of the rubies, diamonds, pearls, cameos and other jewels was made for purposes of establishing their value – the rear of the reliquaries was also set with jewels (Fig. 17.9):[32]

> A mano dritta sta la Testa di S. Paolo, tutta d'argento dorato, mezza figura del naturale con un manto, le fasce del quale sono guarnite di pretiosissime gioie; tra l'altre più cospique è sù la spalla diritta un zaffiro grosso, dov'è intagliato il Salvatore; a mano manca verso il petto una pietra bianca con

---

Cam. Ap. Intr. et Ex., vol. 331, fol. 114r, June 1369). It is known from archival sources that one Johannes Marci *argentarius* was also involved; however, the payment is related to arrangements for the transportation of the busts to the Lateran basilica: E. Müntz, 'Giovanni di Bartolo da Siena: Orafo della corte di Avignone nel XIV secolo', *Archivio storico italiano*, fifth series, 2 (1888), 3–20, esp. p. 8; D'Alberto, *Roma al tempo di Avignone*, 154–5 and n. 73.

[29] *Ex processu canon.* Urbani V. Arch. Secret. Vat. fol. 123, Soresini, *De capitibus*, 6; Cancellieri, *Memorie*, 20 n. 1.

[30] After many years' waiting, a male descendant had been born to the French king on 3 December 1368. It is possible that Charles V's endowment had a votive quality.

[31] Including several gemstones that had fallen out, which were carefully collected in a small box. Report by Urbano Millini on the condition of the reliquaries in the upper storey of the ciborium, 22 December 1649, printed in Soresini, *De capitibus*, 33–42. Reprinted in Baldeschi and Crescimbeni, *Stato della SS. chiese papale lateranense*, 105–11 and Cancellieri, *Memorie*, 86–9.

[32] Collection of drawings and graphic materials by Séroux d'Agincourt (*c.* 1780–90), Vatican Library (BAV), Vat. lat. 9840, fol. 72r.

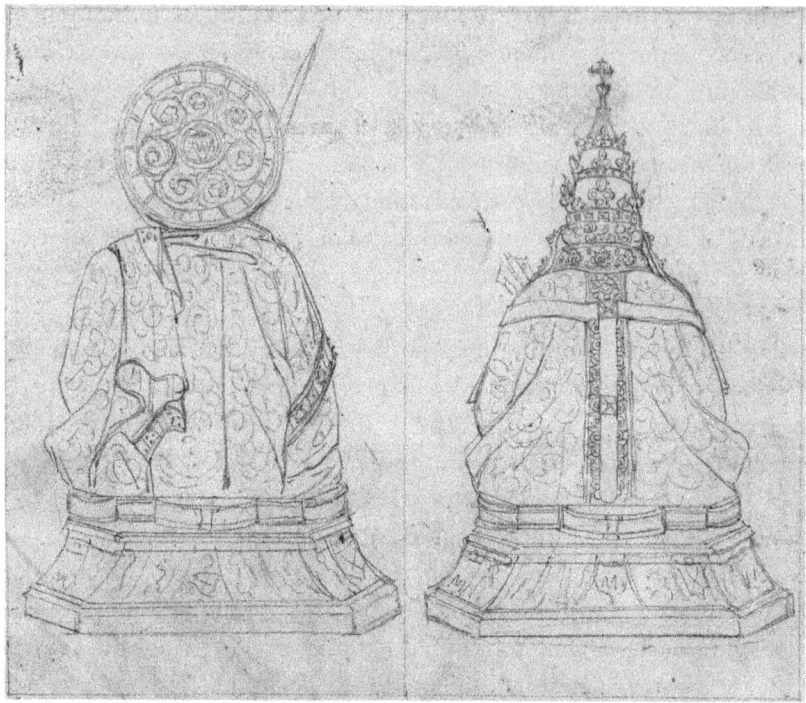

**Fig. 17.9** The reliquary busts of Peter and Paul from behind (Drawing collection of Séroux d'Agincourt, Bibliotheca Apostolica Vaticana, Vat. lat. 9840, fol. 72r; © 2017 Bibliotheca Apostolica Vaticana).

> testa naturale, dicono sia l'effigie di Nerone Imperatore, in mezzo al petto un giglio grande d'oro massiccio con tre rubini grossi, quattro balassi, e certi diamantini tramezzati, e sedici perle grosse tonde introno ...[33]

The written description is probably more reliable here than the reproduction in the paintings, although I think I can identify the 'pietra bianca con testa naturale' and perhaps also the sapphire with an engraved face of the Saviour in the paintings.

Counting only the 'pezzi grossi' among the jewels listed by Millini provides the following 'statistics':

- Four large sapphires and one small one
- Twelve large and five small rubies
- Seven light rubies, 'balasci' (rubino spinello, rubino balascio = rubino roseo/chiaro)
- Many small diamonds

---

[33] Description by Urbano Millini, in Soresini, *De capitibus*, 36; Cancellieri, *Memorie*, 86.

- Thirty-seven large round pearls
- Four large emeralds (in the crucifix at the top of Saint Peter's tiara)

The two silver reliquaries were gilded. On the cloaks of the Apostles, chased work[34] is used to create an impression of the raised pattern of damask material. The 'structural material', silver, only appears in its own (oxidised) material colouring in Saint Peter's two pontifical gloves and keys, as well as on the blade of Saint Paul's sword. By contrast, the two Apostles' faces and Saint Paul's hands were painted in skin colour. The naturalistic flesh tone is also attested to by Millini: 'la Testa di San Paolo oltre l'esser dorata, è la faccia, & il collo di color di carne'.[35]

The flesh tone will have involved painting (with tempera on a ground of gesso or gypsum) applied to the gilded silver surface of the faces. A similar technique is found in a bust of Saint Juliana from the Cistercian convent of Santa Giuliana in Perugia,[36] originating from Giovanni di Bartolo's circle after 1376, and in the more important reliquary bust of Saint Agatha in Catania (Fig. 17.10).[37] The Sienese goldsmith Johannes Bartoli had returned to Avignon along with Urban V in 1370. He made the bust reliquary for Saint Agatha of Catania based on the model of the Apostles' busts in Rome. This bust, around 80 cm tall without its modern base, still survives and is actively in use as an object of worship. The bust, commissioned by the bishops of Catania – Martialis and his successor Elias (depicted in translucent enamel) – in Avignon around 1373 and signed by Johannes Bartoli in 1376, can be regarded as a 'younger sister' of the Roman Apostles' reliquaries and allows some inferences to be drawn regarding their technical execution. Peter and Paul (and their sisters) are presented in their reliquaries as three-dimensional bust portraits almost of

---

[34] Séroux d'Agincourt, who was able to examine the reliquaries from close up, listed the works in his section on 'Sculpture' under the heading 'Cisélure': Séroux d'Agincourt, *Histoire de l'art*.

[35] Description by Urbano Millini, in Soresini, *De capitibus*, 38.

[36] New York, Metropolitan Museum of Art, Cloisters Collection, Inv. Nr. 61.266. The paint layer is approximately 13 mm thick: see R. Palm, 'Reliquienbüste der hl. Juliana von Nikomedia', in A. Legner (ed.), *Die Parler und der Schöne Stil 1350–1400*, 3 vols. (Cologne, 1978), I, 33.

[37] In an earlier essay, I considered the possibility of the use of *email à ronde bosse* as a technique, in view of the quality expected in a commission for the Lateran – which would have made the two reliquaries of the Apostles the earliest examples of this elaborate method of execution (Mondini, 'Reliquie incarnate', 287). This is probably not the case: according to the recently published monograph on the bust reliquary of Saint Agatha of Catania, which is also signed by Giovanni di Bartolo and is later than the Apostle reliquaries, the flesh tone is executed in paint. However, a scientific analysis of the paint layer was not carried out; see F. Pomarici, 'Il reliquiario di Sant'Agata nel contesto della produzione artistica avignonese', in Ufficio Beni Culturali dell' Arcidiocesi di Catania, *Sant'Agata il reliquiario a Busto: Contributi interdisciplinari* (Catania, 2010), 23–41, esp. p. 34.

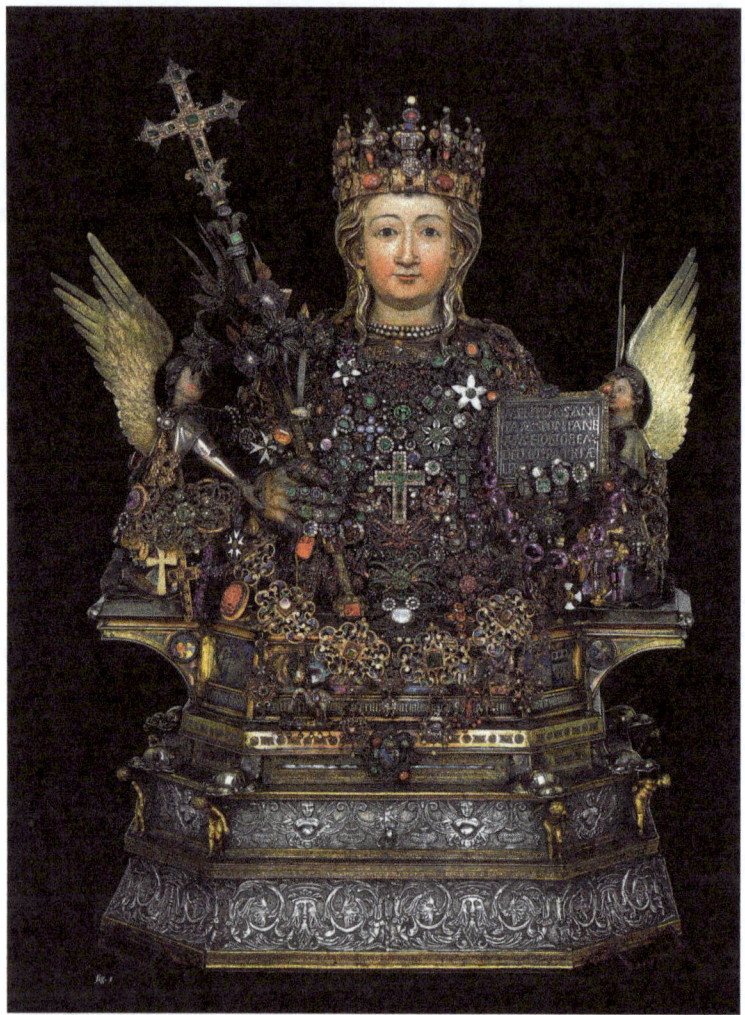

**Fig. 17.10** The reliquary bust of Saint Agatha, Catania Cathedral, signed by Giovanni di Bartolo, 1376 (Photo in *Sant'Agata il reliquiario a Busto*, 10).

'flesh and blood', with more or less individual, amiable features. I agree with Michele Tomasi that this new trend towards the use of flesh tone in bust reliquaries may have been encouraged by the Europe-wide spread of large numbers of colourfully painted wooden busts of Saint Ursula during the fourteenth century.[38] The faces were not transfigured with shining

---

[38] The bust reliquary of Saint Ursula from Castiglione Fiorentino, dated to around 1340, might be a missing link for the spread of this type in Italy, and particularly in Tuscany: see M. Tomasi, 'L'or l'argent et la cher: Remarques sur l'usage de la couleur dans les bustes relquiaires en métal au XIVe siècle', in M. Boudel-Machuel, M. Brock and P. Charron (eds.), *Aux limites de la couleur: Monochromie e polychromie dans les arts (1300–1650)* (Turnhout, 2011), 133–44, esp. p. 139.

gold. The saint in the bust reliquary is no longer shown in the celestial radiance of the shining body he was then thought to have in the afterlife, but instead almost 'reincarnated' as a human, in an image commemorating his earthly, corporeal existence.[39] On the day before Easter 1581, Michel de Montaigne recorded the vivid effect of the two busts and ostension practices in his *Journal du voyage*:

> On Easter eve, I saw at Saint John Lateran the heads of Saint Paul and Saint Peter, which have still some flesh upon them, and are coloured and bearded as in life. The face of Saint Peter is fair, somewhat elongated, with a ruddy, almost sanguine tint on the cheeks, and a forked grey beard, the head being covered with a papal mitre. That of Saint Paul is dark, broad, and fatter; the head altogether being larger and beard thick and grey. They are kept high up in a place devised for them, and the exhibition is made in this wise. The people are summoned by the ringing of bells, then a curtain, stretched before the heads, is let down, and they may be seen side by side. They are left visible long enough to let the spectators say an Ave Maria, and then the curtain is drawn up again. Afterwards they are displayed afresh in the same way, and then for a third time. This exhibition takes place three or four times during the day. The place where they are kept is about the height of a pike from the ground, and a heavy iron grating is in front of them, through which the spectator must peer in order to see them, several candles being lighted outside the grating, but it is difficult to discern clearly the particular features. I saw them three or four times, and found the skin shiny and something like the masks we use.[40]

During ceremonial reliquary displays the ciborium was equipped with a balcony-like stage (Fig. 17.11).[41] Members of the higher nobility were

---

[39] Mondini, 'Reliquie incarnate', 289.

[40] 'La veille de Pasques, je vis à S. Jean de Latran, les Chefs S. Pol & S. Pierre qu'on y montre, qui ont encore leur charnure, teint & barbe, come s'ils vivoint : S. Pierre, un visage blanc un peu longuet, le teint vermeil & tirant sur le sanguin, une barbe grise fourchue, la teste couverte d'une mitre papale ; & S. Pol, noir, le visage large & plus gras, la teste plus grosse, la barbe grise, espesse. Ils sont en haut dans un lieu exprès. La façon de les montrer, c'est qu'on apele le peuple au son des cloches, & que à secousses, on devale contre bas un rideau au derriere duquel sont ces testes, à costé l'une de l'autre. On les laisse voir le tamps de dire un Ave Maria, & soudein on remonte ce rideau : après on le ravale de mesmes, & cela jusques à trois fois : on refaict cete montre quatre ou cinq fois le jour. Le lieu est élevé, de la hautur d'une pique, & puis de grosses grilles de fer, au travers lesqueles on voit. On alume autour par le dehors, plusieurs sierges ; mais est mal aisé de discerner bien cleremant toutes les particularités ; je les vis à deus ou trois fois. La polissure de ces faces avoit quelque rassemblance à nos masques': A. d'Ancona (ed.), *Journal du voyage de Michel Montaigne en Italie par la Suisse et l'Allemagne en 1580 et 1561* (Città di Castello, 1889), 312, trans. in W. G. Waters, *The Journal of Montaigne's Travels in Italy*, 3 vols. (London, 1903), II, 156–8. I am grateful to Ingo Herklotz for this reference.

[41] BAV, Vat. lat. 5479, fol. 12r–v (Visitatio Clementis VIII anno 1592), before the redecoration of the transept: 'Deinde ad principum Apostolorum capita inspicienda et veneranda Clemens accessit, ascendit Pontifex sequentibus illum Cardinalibus quinque, qui aderant, Archiepiscopo, et Episcopo,

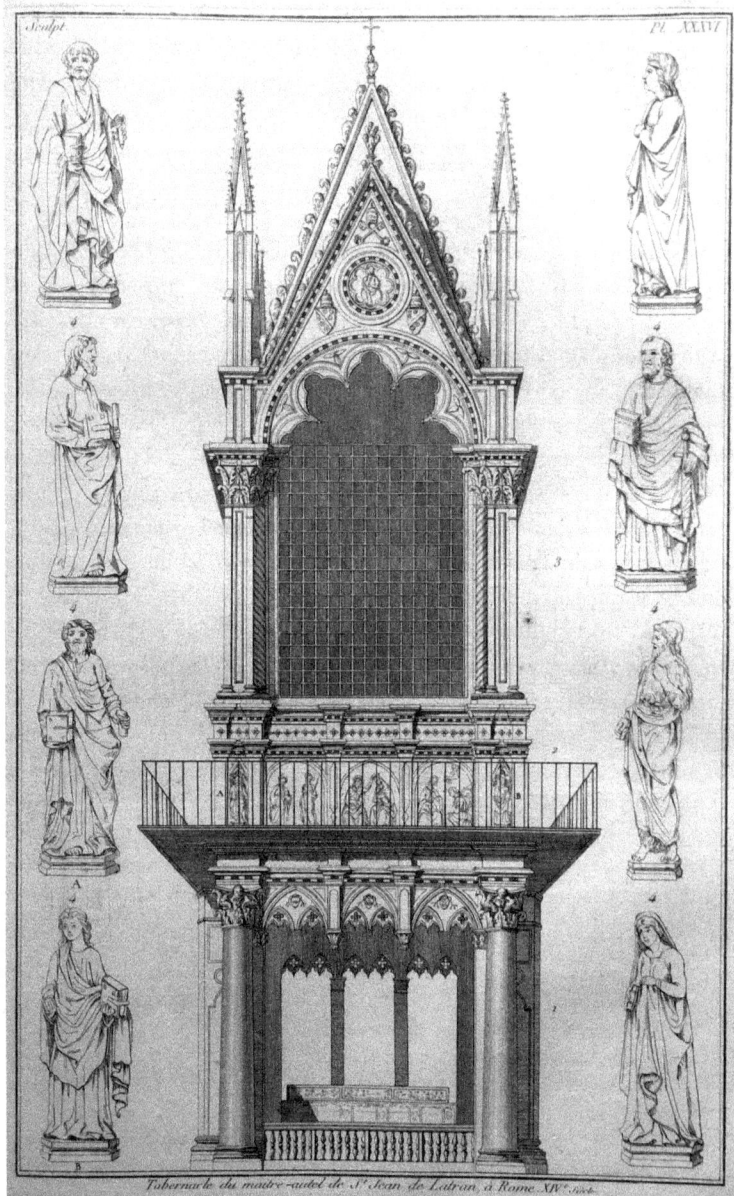

**Fig. 17.11** The Lateran tabernacle with a balcony-like stage (western side) (Séroux d'Agincourt, Histoire de l'art, IV, plate XXXVI (sculpture)).

et perpaucis aliis, per ligneum pontem, qui extructus fuerat ut commode in locum illum conscendi posset, ubi Thesaurus ille pretiosissimus ecclesiae, capita sanctorum Petri et Pauli asservantur, (…). Vidit Pontifex in sacro angusto illo loco, et veneratus est, viderunt et venerati sunt genuflexi cum Pontifice Cardinales principum Petri et Pauli sanctissima capita, quae Vrbanus quintus Pontifex, eximia pietate uir, smaragdis, sapphiris, unionibus, et quamplurimis aliis gemmis pretiosissimis ornanda curavit' (information kindly provided by Darko Senekovic).

permitted to ascend and view the reliquaries from close up. Even ordinary people were allowed at least once, in 1438, to ascend the podium to witness that all of the jewels had been returned to their places following a sacrilegious theft.

## *Furtum Sacrilegum*: A Fresco Cycle of Horror and Deterrence

In order to deter future generations, the archpriest of the Lateran basilica, Cardinal Angelotto Foschi (d. 1444), had the theft recorded in a fresco sequence on the west wall of the north transept between 1438 and 1440, along with details of the subsequent show trial and public execution.[42] (Angelotto's endowment of it also included a host miracle altar erected there, which probably incorporated an earlier fresco showing Maria Advocata).[43] Nothing is known about the artists involved in executing the fresco; they may have been associated with the workshops of Gentile da Fabriano and his successor Pisanello, who left the paintings in the nave of the basilica incomplete under Eugenius IV.[44] Drawings copying the fresco cycle of the historical event – described by Arnold Nesselrath as the earliest known example of a cycle of images depicting events – have survived.[45] Published in full for the first time by Rossella Magrì in 1988, they were lost in the Lateran archives for a long period and have only recently reappeared.[46] The copies also document three scenes from an older cycle recording a theft committed

---

[42] 'Postremus in portico est maximus paries ... (= apse side) paries ipse variis picturis est ornatus et eorum suppliciis qui furto quaedam ex hac Basilica asportarunt': Panvinio, after P. Lauer, *Le palais du Latran: Étude historique et archéologique* (Paris, 1911), 435; Claussen, *Die Kirchen der Stadt Rom*, 146.

[43] The altar is now located in the chapel of Saint John the Evangelist in the Lateran baptistery, and the overpainted fresco fragment dating from the late thirteenth century is in the cloister; on this point, see D. Senekovic, 'S. Giovanni in Fonte und S. Croce in Laterano', in Claussen, *Die Kirchen der Stadt Rom*, 355–93, at pp. 375–7 and G. Bordi and F. Consoli, 'S. Giovanni in Laterano', in M. Andaloro (ed.), *La pittura medievale a Roma 312–1431: Atlante percorsi visivi*, vol. I: *Suburbio, Vaticano, Rione Monti* (Milan, 2006), 193–202, esp. p. 195, fig. at p. 201 (where the Cappella del Santi Sacramento in the Scala Santa building is incorrectly given as the provenance).

[44] A. De Marchi, 'Gentile da Fabriano et Pisanello à Saint-Jean de Latran', in Dominique Cordellier and Bernardette Py (eds.), *Pisanello: Actes du colloque organisé au musée du Louvre 26–28 juin 1996* (La documentation française I) (Paris, 1998), 161–213; See also De Marchi, Chapter 18 in this volume.

[45] A. Nesselrath, 'Bildgeschichte – Geschichtsbilder', in M. Matheus, B. Schneidmüller, S. Weinfurter and A. Wieczorek (eds.), *Die Päpste der Renaissance: Politik, Kunst und Musik* (Regensburg, 2017), 49–67.

[46] Archivio Capitolare Lateranense, Q.8.D.1.; pen on paper, 50 x 235 cm; the sequence of the scenes was confused when the sheets were mounted on card. Basic details in R. Magrí, 'La lupa simbolo di giustizia in Laterano', in A. Nesselrath (ed.), *Da Pisanello alla nascita dei Musei Capitolini: L'Antico a Roma alla vigilia del Rinascimento* (exhibition catalogue) (Milan, 1988), 225–6 (cat. no. 71).

by Andreuccio da Peroscia[47] in 1364 (probably of church property, possibly from the treasury of the Sancta Sanctorum) and his execution by hanging (Figs 17.12, 17.13 and 17.14).[48] It is not clear from the late sixteenth-century copies whether the scenes depicting the theft and the punishment of Andreuccio de Peroscia, who was executed in 1364, date from an earlier period or whether they were also commissioned by Angelotto Foschi so that the updating would doubly maintain awareness of the just and cruel punishments meted out for a *furtum sacrilegum*. It appears probable, however, that they do in fact date from the *trecento* and may even have served as a model for the later cycle – since the name of Ciuccio Jani Catini, a highly influential representative of the 'popolo grasso' ahead of the schism of 1378 (Fig. 17.15), appears below the coat of arms shown on the last sheet (lower row) and *tituli*.[49] In addition, the space in the scene showing the torture of Andreuccio is indicated in inverse perspective, while in the other cycle perspective lines aligned towards the rear can be seen. It is not possible to discuss that cycle in greater depth here; that will require a separate study.[50]

To return to the events of 1438: according to contemporary reports by Stefano Infessura, as well as Paolo di Liello Petrone and Paolo de lo Mastro, the offenders on the night of Easter Monday, 12 April 1438 were insiders.[51]

---

[47] Perhaps not coincidental, in my view, is the fact that the name is the same as that of the protagonist of the fifth story of the second day in Boccaccio's *Decameron* (c. 1350). As is well known, Boccaccio certainly made use of contemporary events and characters in the novellas of the *Decameron*. The simple horse-dealer Andreuccio da Perugia gets caught up in various criminal intrigues in the story. With a bit of luck and innocent cunning, the sympathetic rogue even succeeds in seizing with impunity a ruby worth 500 gold florins from the tomb of the archbishop of Naples, who might be identified with Orso Minutolo (d. 1333) and buried in the Minutolo family chapel (N. Bock, 'I re, i vescovi e la cattedrale: Sepolture e costruzione architettonica', in S. Romano and N. Bock (eds.), *Il Duomo di Napoli dal paleocristiano all'età angioina* (Naples, 2002), 132–47, at p. 139. In view of the incomplete state of the sources for Rome during the *trecento*, this lost fresco perhaps represents the only documentary trace of Andreuccio's inglorious end. One might wonder whether an educated contemporary viewer of the frescos might have recalled Boccaccio's hero when gazing at the hanged Andreuccio; but the link was not made in the antiquarian literature.

[48] Magrí, 'La lupa', 225. The first sheet of the *rotulus* transcribes the *tituli* and inscriptions for the figures and coats of arms: 'lettere sotto le arme. Hoc fuit sub anno dni M.CCC. LXIIII. in mense Magio / (quello che si tenaglia) Andreuccio da Peroscia /(impiccato si chiama) Andreuccio da Peroscia.'

[49] Magrí, 'La lupa', 225. I am grateful to Andreas Rehberg for valuable information here. On Ciuccio Jani Catini, see A. Rehberg, 'Il Rione Trastevere e i suoi abitanti nelle testimonianze raccolte sugli inizi dello Scisma del 1378', in L. Ermini Pani and C. Travaglini (eds.), *Trastevere: Un'analisi di lungo periodo* (Convegno di Studi 2008) (Rome, 2010), 255–317, esp. pp. 283–5.

[50] A more detailed study and heraldic analysis of the *rotulus* and the historical events documented on it is currently in preparation in collaboration with Andreas Rehberg.

[51] Transcripts in Cancellieri, *Memorie*, 77–80, and R. Magrí, 'La mesticanza', in Nesselrath (ed.), *Da Pisanello*, 227–8; S. Infessura, *Diario della città di Roma di Stefano Infessura scriba senato*, ed. O. Tommasini (Fonti per la storia d'Italia 5) (Rome, 1890) 36–8.

Furtum Sacrilegum 367

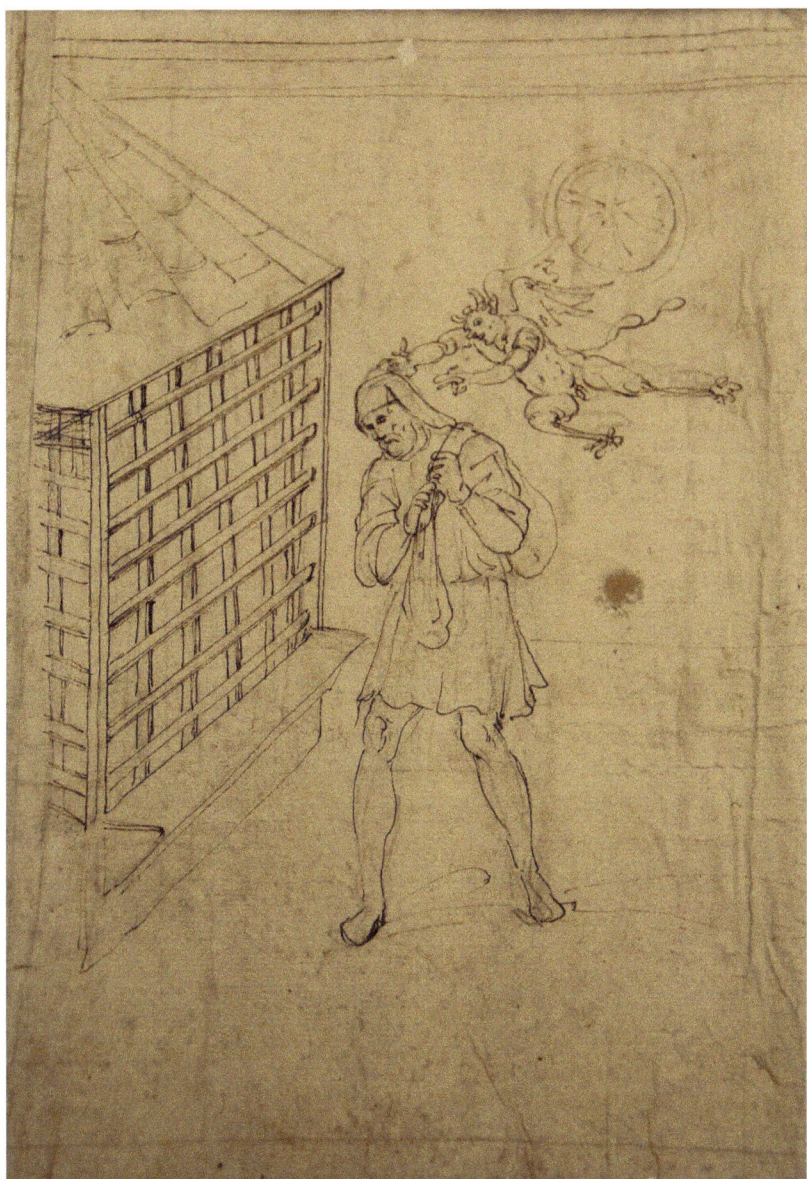

**Fig. 17.12** Andreuccio da Peroscia (?) stealing ecclesiastical goods (?); copy of a lost fresco cycle, dated 1364, formerly in the north transept of the Lateran basilica, roll of pen drawings (end of the sixteenth century) (Archivio Capitolare Lateranense).

Domenico de Tito Capocciola and Cristoforo Garofalo were beneficiates of the Lateran, and may have held the office of supervisor of the Apostles'

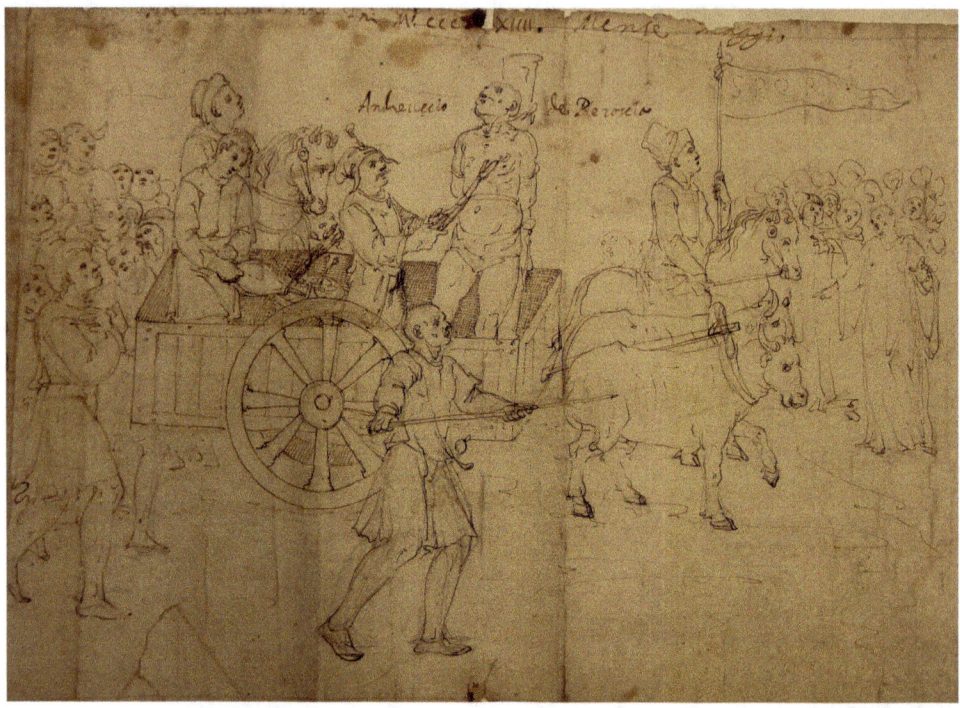

**Fig. 17.13** Andreuccio da Peroscia being punished with incandescent irons; copy of a lost fresco cycle, dated 1364, formerly in the north transept of the Lateran basilica, roll of pen drawings (end of the sixteenth century) (Archivio Capitolare Lateranense).

relics;[52] their uncle, the Lateran canon Nicola di Valmontone, aided and abetted them.[53] They acted a second time in June, on the feast day of Saints Peter and Paul. On each occasion it was thus a day on which the 'sacre teste' were ceremonially displayed and the stage of the ciborium was accessible by

---

[52] The regulation regarding the way in which the 'Custodes Beneficiati, pro Custodia Capitum Beatorum Apsotolorum' were to be selected by the Chapter of the Lateran was already included in the *Constitutiones Lateranensis Ecclesiae* under Urban V in 1370: see Cancellieri, *Memorie*, doc. XII, 76–7.

[53] Soresini, *De capitibus*, pp. 53–4, gives the full names and origins of the perpetrators from an accounts book in the Lateran Archive that can no longer be located at the shelfmark he gives ('liber introit. & exit. Lateran. Eccles. Sign. Litt. E. fol 150'): 'Dominicus de Tito Capocciola Apulus et Iohannes Christophorus Garofalus Castri Vallis montanae'. However, the subsequent mention of 'Nicolaus Andreuccio de Peroscia ex eodem Castro', is incorrect, since this combines the names of two different people – Nicolaus de eodem Castro (= Valmontone) and Andreuccio de Peroscia. The inscription on the *rotulus* gives the former *titulus* of the fresco in Italian: 'Lettere sotto l'historia suddetta sono queste. Come Domenico de Tito de Puglia, et Janni Garofalo di Valle Montone furaro le prete preziose de Santo Pietro et Paolo'. Archivio Capitolare Lateranense, Q.8.D.1; Magrì, 'La lupa', 225. There is no surviving *titulus* which would identify the figure of the Lateran canon Nicolaus de Valmontone on the paintings.

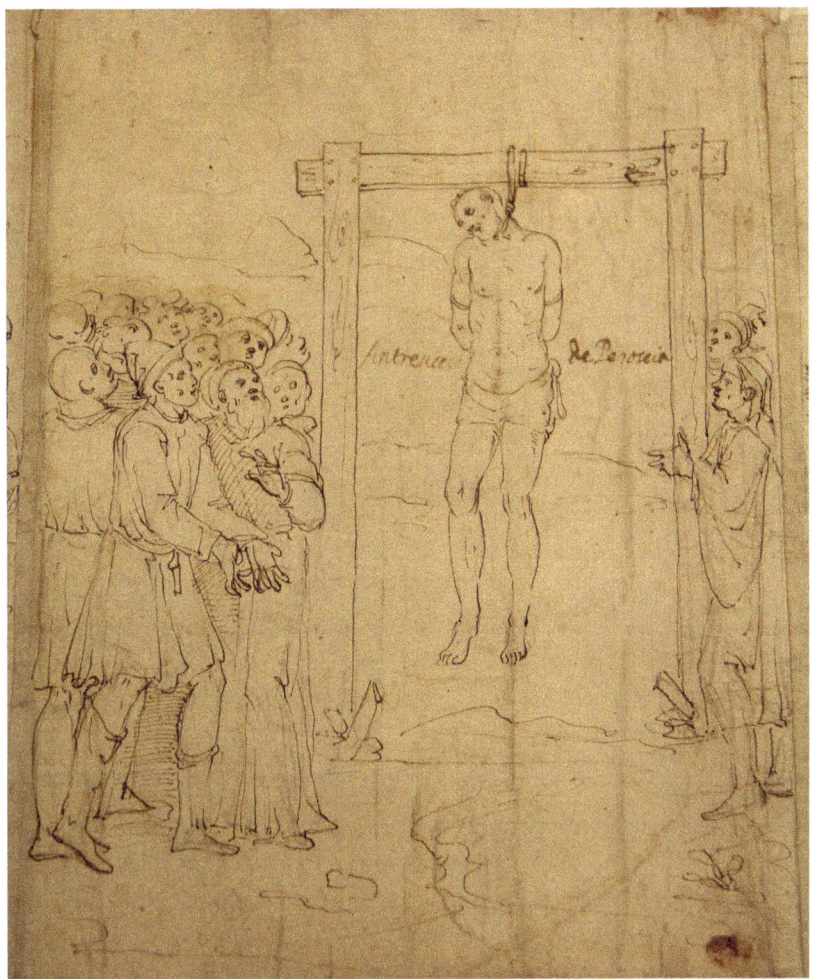

**Fig. 17.14** Execution of Andreuccio da Peroscia; copy of a fresco cycle, dated 1364, formerly in the north transept of the Lateran basilica, roll of pen drawings (end of the sixteenth century) (Archivio Capitolare Lateranense).

ladder. The first scene shows only the upper storey of the Lateran tabernacle, in a kind of 'close-up' (Fig. 17.16). Three moments from the deed are recorded simultaneously: we see the two thieves in the interior of the 'gabbia' of the tabernacle in the act of 'plucking' the jewels – 'molte petre preziose, zafiri, balassi, ametisti et perle'[54] – from the reliquaries; then their

---

[54] Infessura, *Diario*, 37; Cancellieri, *Memorie*, 77. The chronicler Paolo de Lello Petrone discusses the value of the booty in detail: ' ... la notte cavaro dalla mitra che tiene S. Pietro in capo, dui finissimi balasci, un finissimo zaffiro, tre finissimi diamanti, 12 perle grosse, li quali balasci, di poi che vennero alle mano del regimento uno però 48 carati e l'altro 47 et vale la carata 28 ducati

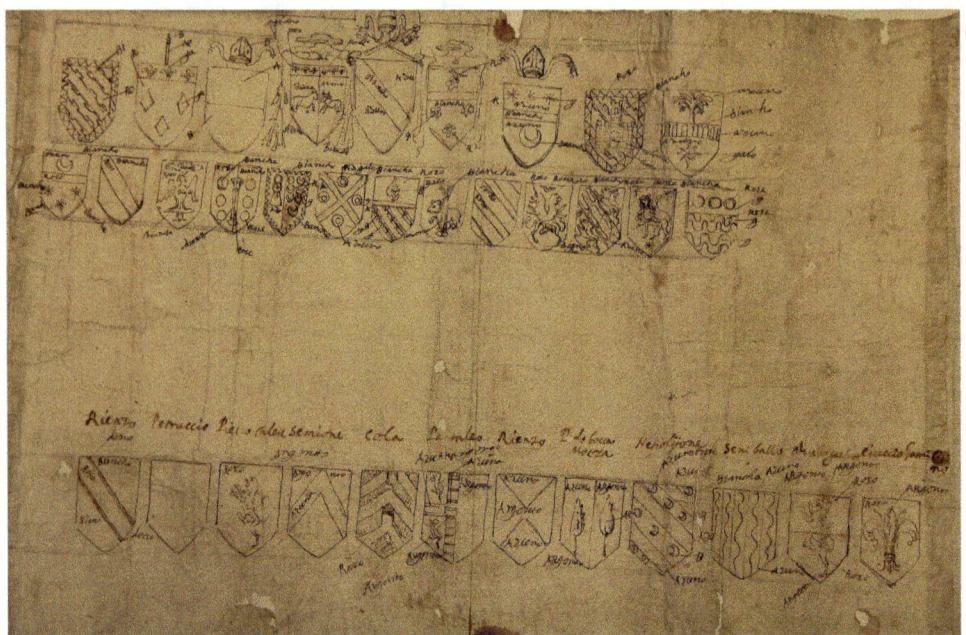

**Fig. 17.15** Coat of arms belonging to the lost fresco cycles in the north transept of the Lateran basilica, roll of pen drawings (end of the sixteenth century) (Archivio Capitolare Lateranense).

flight through the arch opening above the protective bars (the fresco thus also reveals the gap that existed in the 'security arrangements' of the Lateran ciborium). On the right edge of the picture, finally, it is probably their accomplice the Lateran canon Nicola di Valmontone who is shown making contacts for reselling the booty.

According to Infessura, the whole affair came to light because a certain Servestro de Pallone, who had purchased a large pearl for 30 ducats, had a disagreement with his goldsmith that had to be settled publicly. In the process, the trail led back to the pearl's seller, the canon Nicola di Valmontone, and suspicions were aroused. The two thieves were caught near Velletri; all of the jewels were returned to the Lateran on 22 August 'con tutta la processione di Roma e giro lo Senatore di Roma con tutti li Offitiali con tutto lo popolo, et lo

et più hera stimato quanto valevano li balasci, quanto potevano valere li diamanti, il zaffiro et le perle, et non contenti li ribaldi di questo il dì di S. Pietro e S. Paolo il Giugno seguente ne tolsero 18 altre pietre finissime d'infinita valuta, et queste cose furono ritrovate et reposte nelli lochi dove furon tratte . . . ': Paolo di Lello, cited after Magrí, 'La mesticanza', 227.

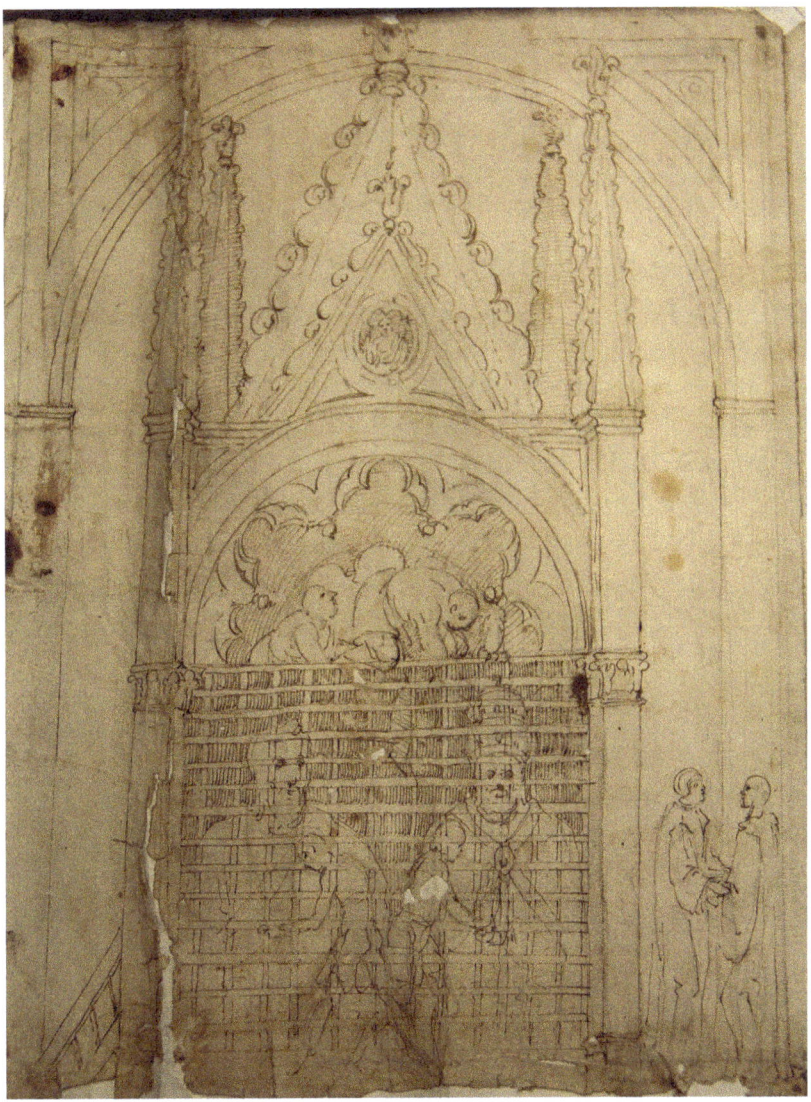

Fig. 17.16 Cappocciola and Garofalo stealing the jewels from the reliquary busts of Peter and Paul in the tabernacle of the Lateran; copy of a fresco cycle (1438–40), formerly in the north transept of the Lateran basilica, roll of pen drawings (end of the sixteenth century) (Archivio Capitolare Lateranense).

Senatore lesse la scommunica che fece papa Urbano V, lo quale pose lì quelle teste e ornolle colle ditte prete'.[55]

---

[55] Infessura, *Diario*, 37.

The coat of arms of the Roman senator who was in office at the time, Francesco de Salimbeni,[56] appears in the upper row of coats of arms, which was probably depicted underneath the cycle. At the sides of the coat of arms of Pope Eugenius IV, the arms of Papal *condottiere* and cardinal Giovanni Maria Vitelleschi (d. 1440) and of the archpriest of the Lateran basilica, Angelotto Foschi, who commissioned the paintings, are also recognizable (Fig. 17.15).[57]

According to a different version of the events recorded by Soresini, it was by contrast the Holy Spirit who provided active assistance in tracing the stolen goods.[58] A Venetian nobleman who was dangerously ill had wanted to offer an extremely valuable pearl, which he had unwittingly purchased from the thieves, to Saints Peter and Paul as a gift, in order to obtain a cure. When the delighted clerics in the Lateran climbed up to the ciborium to add the pearl to the Apostles' reliquaries, it was discovered 'that the ruby, the sapphire, the diamonds, pearls and other jewels were missing, but what caused the greatest astonishment was that both the size and shape of the donated pearl and also a certain empty space there left no doubt that the pearl had previously been set there'. The Romans were able to obtain the name of the seller from the Venetian, who had in the meantime been cured, as well as the time and circumstances of the sale, and they succeeded in convicting the perpetrators.

The deed was regarded as sacrilege (theft of a consecrated object from a consecrated space),[59] and its brutal consequences for the convicted thieves are displayed in the following scenes, documented in the *rotulus*. One scene is

---

[56] C. De Dominicis, *Membri del Senato della Roma pontificia: Senatori, conservatori, caporioni e loro priori e lista d'oro delle famiglie dirigenti (sec. X–XIX)* (Rome, 2009), 171.

[57] Final sheet of the *rotulus*; the coats of arms were probably placed as a frieze underneath or above the cycle of frescos.

[58] Soresini, *De capitibus*, 56–8, gives as his source the custodian of the Vatican Library, Leo Allatius (Leone Allacci), who claimed to have read this report in an old codex – not further specified.

[59] G. Dahm, *Das Strafrecht Italiens im ausgehenden Mittelalter: Untersuchung über die Beziehung von Theorie und Praxis im Strafrecht des Spätmittelalters, namentlich im 14. Jahrhundert* (Beiträge zur Geschichte der deutschen Strafrechtspflege 3) (Berlin, 1931), 476. Urban's bull of excommunication, which was intended to protect the relics and their reliquaries, begins with the words 'Sacrilegorum damnanda praesumptio' (see above, n. 22). For an explanation of this in canon law, see A. Reiffenstuel (OFM), *Jus canonicum universum* (n. p., 1717), titulus 18 (De furtis), nos. 54–5, 234–5. One of the earliest mentions of the concept of *furtum sacrilegum* is found in the autobiography of Guibert de Nogeant in the twelfth century: Guibert de Nogent, *Vie de Guibert de Nogent, par lui-même*, book III (XII to XXI), chap. XV (XVI): 'Secundo quidam Ansellus vulgo urbis oriundus, immanis et rusticus, *infra dies Dominici natalis ante matutinos, cruces, calices, aurea quaeque subripuit*. Cumque post aliquod tempus praerepti auri massulam Suessonico cuidam mercatori venum tulisset, et *furtum sacrilegum quod fecerat, prodidisset*, ac sacramentum ab eo ne se proderet accepisset, ille interim damni illius conscios per Suessorum parochias excommunicari audivit.' E.-R. Labande (ed. and trans.), *Guibert de Nogent, Autographie* (Les classiques de l'histoire de France au moyen âge 34) (Paris, 1981), book III, chap. XV, 418.

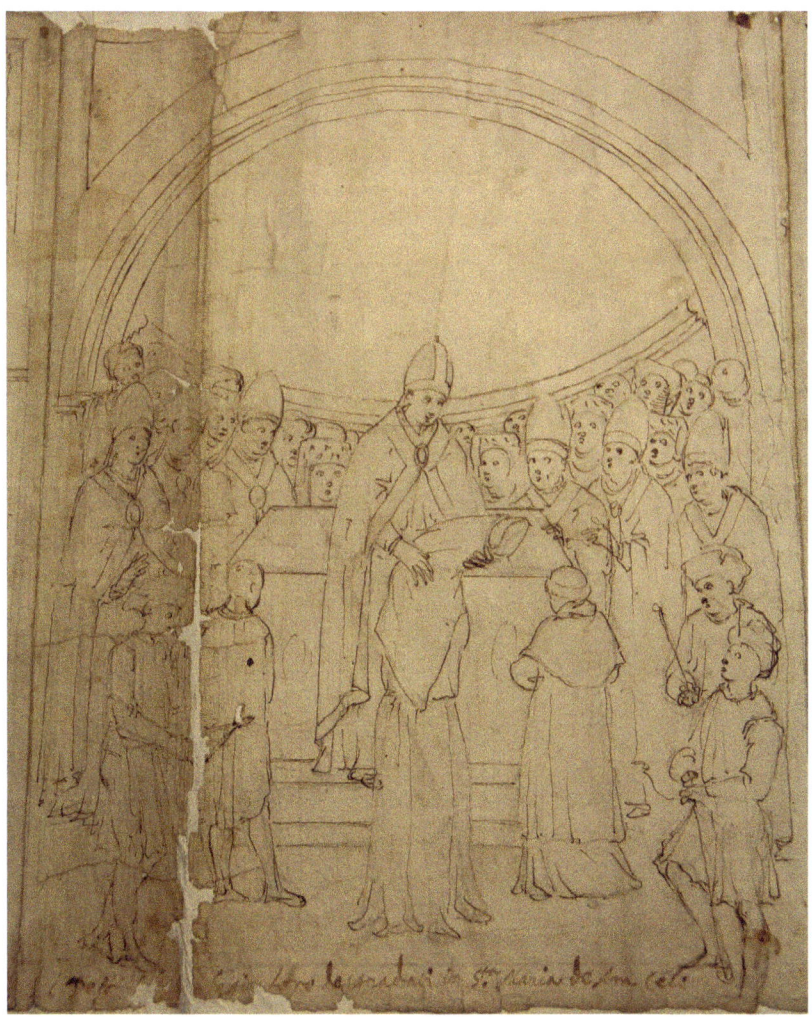

**Fig. 17.17** The public removal from office and degradation of the three clergymen at the main altar of Santa Maria di Aracoeli; copy of a fresco cycle (1438–40), formerly in the north transept of the Lateran basilica, roll of pen drawings (end of the sixteenth century) (Archivio Capitolare Lateranense).

devoted to the public removal from office and degradation of the three clergymen by the papal vicar, Andrea da Montecchio,[60] at the main altar of Santa Maria in Aracoeli (Fig. 17.17).[61] On the left, the canon Nicola, who has

---

[60] Andrea da Montecchio, bishop of Osimo (1434–54) is mentioned by Paolo di Lello Petrone: see Magrí, 'La mesticanza', 227.

[61] The dismissal from office of the Lateran canon and the two beneficiates also went down in the history of the Franciscan church of Santa Maria in Aracoeli. Padre Casimiro quotes the wording of Paolo di Lello Petrone's 'La mesticanza' along with other public events on the Capitol square,

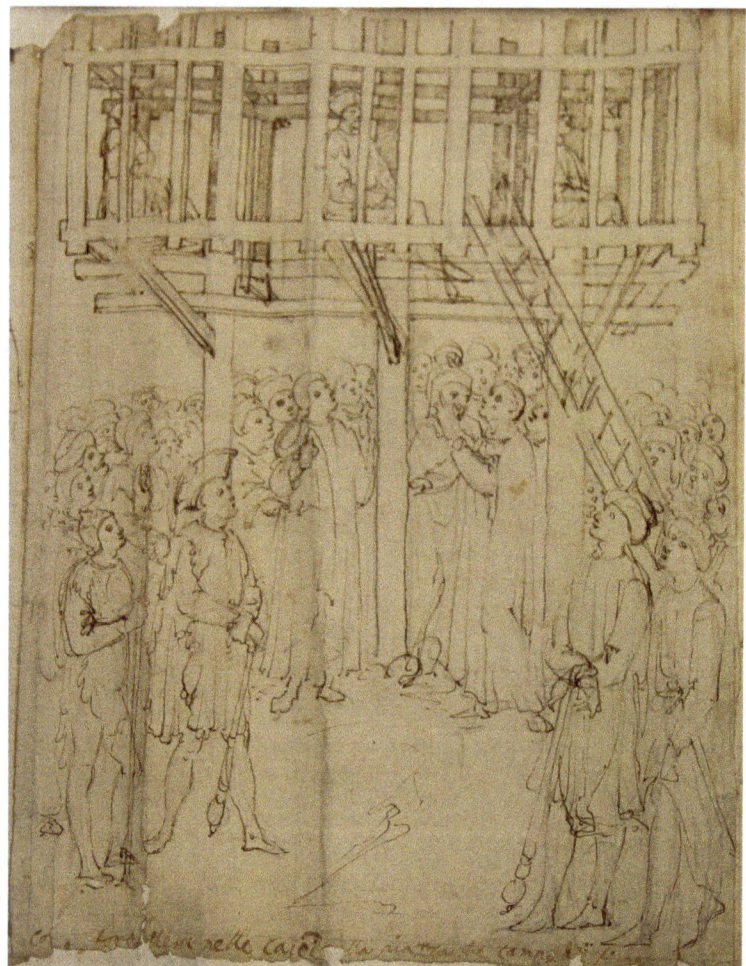

Fig. 17.18 The exposure of the three culprits in the pillory on the Campo dei Fiori; copy of a fresco cycle (1438–40), formerly in the north transept of the Lateran basilica, roll of pen drawings (end of the sixteenth century) (Archivio Capitolare Lateranense).

already had his clerical robes removed, is having the hair of his tonsure cut off; in the centre, one of the two beneficiates is being disrobed, while his partner, on the right with his back towards the viewer, is still awaiting his disrobing and shaving. This is followed by their exposure in the pillory, for

including the burning at the stake of Maria Fenicella, who had been accused of witchcraft, in the period when Bernardino da Siena was preaching in Rome: see P. Casimiro, *Memorie istoriche della chiesa e convento di S. Maria in Araceli di Roma* (Rome, 1736), 416–18, esp. p. 418.

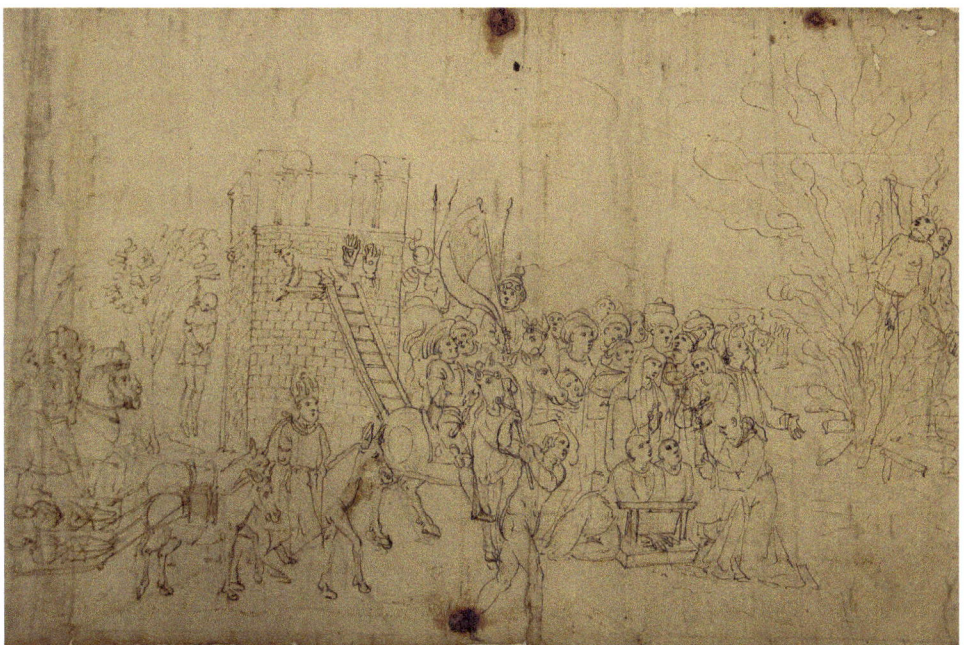

**Fig. 17.19** The dragging and public execution of the sacrilegious thieves on the Lateran square in front of the Annibaldi tower; copy of a fresco cycle (1438–40), formerly in the north transept of the Lateran basilica, roll of pen drawings (end of the sixteenth century) (Archivio Capitolare Lateranense).

four days from 4 to 8 September, set high up in a cage on the Campo dei Fiori, followed by a further day on the Capitol (Fig. 17.18).[62]

The next scene shows the procession of disgrace and the humiliating dragging of the evildoers from the Capitol to the Lateran square (Fig. 17.19): the canon is riding on an ass and wearing a 'mitra di carta depenta con doi diavoli in capo'[63] – according to Paolo di Lello Petrone, the *mitra infamiae*[64] is clearly recognisable in the copy of the fresco. Capocciola and Garofalo, also wearing *mitrae infamiae*, were tied to wooden planks and dragged along the ground behind two donkeys.[65]

The right half of the large pictorial field shows the public execution on the Campus Lateranensis, the cruelty of which is described

---

[62] Paolo di Lello Petrone, cited after Magrí, 'La mesticanza', 227.
[63] Paolo di Lello Petrone, cited after Magrí, 'La mesticanza', 227.
[64] W. J. Connell and G. Constable, 'Sacrilege and redemption in Renaissance Florence: The case of Antonio Rinaldeschi', *Journal of the Warburg and Courtauld Institutes* 61 (1998), 53–92, at p. 75.
[65] '... e li detti Capocciola et Garofalo furon legati in doi tavole et strascinati foro menati dreto a Messer Necola', Paolo di Lello Petrone: see Magrí, 'La mesticanza', 227.

consistently both in contemporary reports and also in the image. The canon, who had initially disputed his involvement and thus also made himself guilty of perjury, received a 'milder' punishment, since he belonged to a higher rank, and perhaps also because he did not 'directly' lay his hands on the reliquaries: he was hanged from the elm tree on the Lateran square.[66] By contrast, the executioner first cut off the right hands of the two thieves;[67] a Capuchin monk in the foreground is holding a cross up in front of the two transgressors to remind them that it was 'an act of penance for the salvation' of their 'sin-stained' souls.[68] The two chopped-off right hands are seen on the wall of the Annibaldi tower alongside the Capitoline *lupa*, which served as a symbol of papal justice during the Middle Ages.[69] Finally, the two evildoers were burnt at the stake, seen on the right edge of the image. According to Dahm, hanging (in contrast to beheading for higher-ranking individuals) was the usual punishment for criminals of the lower ranks or for particularly repellent crimes, while 'burning was rare and tended to be the sentence for extreme heresy or repeated sodomy'.[70]

These narrative images show *sui generis* some of the components of 'pitture infamanti' (images of shame),[71] as they present the names, deeds, degradation and punishment of the evildoers to contemporaries and their descendants in an iconic fashion in a form of 'visual' pillory. As Samuel Edgerton points out, however, there is a fundamental difference: instead of 'defaming portraits, intended as official punishments of individual persons', the Lateran frescoes are 'pictures of infamous incidents,

---

[66] '... Nicola come mero peccatore fu appeso in l'olmo come foro gionti alla Piazza de S. Giovanni': Paolo di Lello Petrone, cited after Magrí, 'La mesticanza', 227. On the hierarchical ranking according to social status and type of offence, see Dahm, *Das Strafrecht Italiens*, 284–317, esp. pp. 299–305.

[67] For the cutting off of the hands, the fresco documents an instrument (*mannaia*) otherwise used in the quattrocento for decapitations – shown for example in an execution scene on the Capitoline attributed to Ciriaco d'Ancona: see S. Y. Edgerton Jr., *Pictures and Punishment: Art and Criminal Prosecution during the Florentine Renaissance* (Ithaca, NY, 1985), 152–5 fig. 38.

[68] Edgerton, *Pictures and Punishment*, 131.

[69] The site with the she-wolf at the Lateran is described as being a place of justice in the chronicle of Benedict of San Andreas de Soracte, as early as the tenth century: 'in iudicali loco ad Lateranis ubi quidam locus dicitur ad lupam, quae mater vocabatur romanorum, ibi iudiciarum legem finiebat': MGH, Pertz, pp. 720–1 and also p. 712. See also J. Corcopino, 'La louve du Capitole', *Bulletin de l'Association Guillaume Budé* 4 (1924), 3–19, esp. pp. 10–12.

[70] Edgerton, *Pictures and Punishment*, 135; Dahm, *Das Strafrecht Italiens*, 301–3.

[71] With reference to the definition by Ortalli, who regards the images of shame as being a constitutive element of an iconic, public, official and lay communication system ('elemento interno e costitutivo di un sistema iconico pubblico, ufficiale e laico'): G. Ortalli, '... *pingatur in palatio* ...': *La pittura infamante nei secoli XIII–XIV* (Rome, 1979), 280.

intended to commemorate notorious events', belonging to the genre and to the early history of (political) history painting.⁷² Elements evocative of the secular practice of 'pittura infamante' on public squares and buildings, which was widespread – and equally widely effective – in late medieval communes in Italy were thus present in the form of a narrative depiction in the interior of the Lateran, the *mater ecclesiarum*.⁷³ The north transept was apparently the location used for this type of image in the Lateran church, as the cycle showing the execution of Andreuccio da Peroscia in 1364 already existed there as a precedent.

As Magrì has rightly emphasised, it was customary in the Middle Ages for blood justice proceedings to be conducted in front of the legal symbol of the *lupa* on the square in front of the north transept façade of the Lateran basilica (until the *lupa* was moved to the Capitol in 1471).⁷⁴ The square was also the place of assembly in which, according to Paravicini Bagliani, the pontifical rite of excommunication (*execrationes in coena Domini*) customarily took place, from the Gothic loggia of the Sala del Concilio of the Lateran palace, built by Pope Boniface VIII.⁷⁵

In the mid-fifteenth century the faithful were faced with a spatially complex referential system on high feast days in the Lateran basilica. On the upper storey of the high altar tabernacle, the curtains and shutters were opened. The richly decorated busts of the Apostle Princes behind the secure bars looked down kindly. If the gaze moved right across the west wall of the north transept, those in the know would be able to view, high up on the wall,⁷⁶ the crimes that had been committed against the Apostles'

---

⁷² Edgerton, *Pictures and Punishment*, 77 n. 65, referring for instance to the early Cinquecento narrative panel (Museo Stibbert, Florence) with the 'story of Renaldeschi's blasphemy' against a picture of the Virgin Mary in the church of Santa Maria de' Ricci al Corso in Florence: see Edgerton, *Pictures and Punishment*, esp. pp. 47–58.

⁷³ The fresco cycle could also be read as a warning to anyone who might attack or insult the papacy, symbolised by the two princes among the Apostles: see J. T. Paoletti and G. M. Radke, *Art in Renaissance Italy*, 3rd edn (London, 2005), 290.

⁷⁴ R. Magrì, 'Lupa capitolina', in Nesselrath (ed.), *Da Pisanello*, 224 (cat. no. 70).

⁷⁵ In connection with the 'Loggia di giustizia' (*lovium*) erected on the Capitoline hill by the senators of Rome at the same time, see A. Paravicini Bagliani, 'Bonifacio VIII, la loggia di giustizia al Laterano e i processi generali di scomunica', *Rivista di storia della Chiesa in Italia* 59 (2005), 377–428, esp. pp. 391–6, 411–13. On the loggia on the Capitoline: G. B. de Rossi, 'La loggia del comune di Roma compiuta nel Campidoglio l'anno 1299', *Bollettino della commissione archeologica comunale di Roma ser. Seconda* 10 (1882), 130–40.

⁷⁶ Located, according to Infessura: 'si vede la memoria penta come s'entra la ecclesia del santo Ianni ad mano ritta su ad alto': Infessura, *Diario*, 38. See also Paolo di Benedetto di Cola dello Mastro, cited after R. Magrì, 'Il Memoriale', in Nesselrath (ed.), *Da Pisanello*, 228.

reliquaries, and thus against Peter and Paul themselves – as well as the 'just' punishments to which the thieves had been condemned. Would it have been clear to pilgrims from more distant places that the men depicted on the wall, martyred by dragging and burning, were not saints, but rather villains? The possibility of misunderstanding can certainly not be ruled out. The fact that these murals were destroyed in the late sixteenth century under Clement VIII, during renovation of the transept, may be connected with the Counter-Reformation goal of banning such images of iniquity from church interiors and instead disseminating clear messages of salvation. At the same time, the desire to have the paintings documented by a professional draughtsman and to keep the copies in the Lateran archives shows that their – judicial – testimonial quality was still being considered seriously.[77]

[77] It can be assumed that an artist working on the redecoration of the transept of the Lateran basilica (directed by Cavalier d'Arpino) was called upon to produce the copies – perhaps Agostino Ciampelli, who worked in Rome on the Lateran baptistery and on the triumphal arch of the Lateran basilica starting from the end of 1594 and in 1596–7: Archivio Storico di Roma (ASR), Camerale I, fabbriche, vol. 1524, S. G. Laterano: 1597 Pagamento a Agostino Ciampelli pittore, 'deve dare a di 25 ottobre scudi 20 di moneta fatto nel mandato al Sg. Gerolamo a Abrusco sono a buon conto delle pitture che fa nell'andito della Cap. S. Giovanni Evangelista .... 20'. I am grateful to Adriano Amendola for this suggestion.

# 18 | Reconsidering the Traces of Gentile da Fabriano and Pisanello in the Lateran Basilica

ANDREA DE MARCHI

'Pisanellus pictor simul et factor. Eius opus picta paries in aede Lateranensi. Fuit in umbris et coloribus diligens.'[1] In Raffaele Maffei from Volterra, the author in 1506 of the massive *Commentariorum Urbanorum libri octo et triginta*, the Veronese painter's fame decidedly surpassed the celebrity of the artist from Fabriano; whereas, not long before, Gentile had been the only one to be named by Bartolomeo Platina, when mentioning his undertaking the decoration of the Lateran basilica for Pope Martin V, who 'picturam, Gentilis opus pictoris egregii, inchoavit'.[2] Later, friar minor Mariano da Firenze[3] and scholar antiquarian Andrea Fulvio[4] mentioned both the popes who promoted the decoration of this church, Martin V and Eugenius IV, but only one painter, Pisanello. Appropriating this already compromised tradition, Giorgio Vasari made Pisanello the leading character in this campaign, and caused great confusion by declaring that he had been summoned from Florence to Rome by Pope Martin V; he also created the idea of a partnership with Gentile, who would have been his collaborator and even his competitor, and who would have painted several stories and also 'tra le finestre in chiaro e scuro alcuni Profeti che sono tenuti la miglior cosa di quella opera'.[5] In sixteenth-century literature the overwhelming enthusiasm of the earliest mentions inevitably dissolved, first of all that of Jean Baudoin de Rosières-aux-Salines: in his poem *Instruction de la vie mortelle* or *Roman de la vie humaine*, written around 1431, immediately after Pope Martin V's death, and therefore when one could only see the work carried out by Gentile from 1426 to his death between

---

[1] R. Maffei, *Commentariorum Urbanorum libri octo et triginta*, 38 vols. (Rome, 1506), XXI, 300r.
[2] B. Platina, *Liber de vita Christi ac omnium pontificum* (Città di Castello, 1479), reproduced in G. Gaida (ed.), *Rerum Italicarum Scriptores III/1* (Bologna, 1913–32), 312, 327.
[3] Fra Mariano da Firenze, *Tractatus de origine, nobilitate et de excellentia Tusciae* (Archivio francescano di Ognissanti, ms. F 16), ed. E. Bulletti (Rome, 1931 [Florence, 1517]), 97r; Fra Mariano da Firenze, *Itinerarium urbis Romae*, ed. E. Bulletti (Studi di antichità cristiana 2) (Rome, 1931 [Rome, 1518]), 148.
[4] A. Fulvio, *Antiquaria Urbis* (Rome, 1514), 50; A. Fulvio, *Antiquitates Urbis* (Rome, 1545 [1527]), 116.
[5] G. Vasari, *Le vite de' più eccellenti pittori, scultori et architetti coll'aggiunta de' vivi et de' morti, dall'anno 1550 al 1567* (Florence, 1550–68), ed. R. Bettarini and P. Barocchi (Florence, 1966–87), III, 365–6.

August and October 1427, he wrote that it was the pope who 'Faire la noble et excellant pointure / Fit pour adonq de couleur haute et pure / A S. Jehan de Latran et portraire / Ou vont mains pointres pour veoir l'exemplaire / Et se le maistre eust vescu longement / Oncques on n'eust veu tel ymaginement.'[6]

The high and pure colour ('couleur haute et pure') was surely blazing at that time, and had certainly made the work, though no more than the *incipit* of a much larger decoration, an eminent *exemplum* that attracted several painters ('mains pointres'); this was also thanks to the exceptional illusionistic expedients of the framework and to the inventive composition of the first stories of Saint John the Baptist. In the middle of the fifteenth century Bartolomeo Facio, a Ligurian humanist at the Aragonese court, admired above all the Major Prophets, 'ita expressi, ut non picti, sed e marmore ficti esse videantur':[7] a work in which Gentile, almost as if foreseeing his own imminent death, outdid himself to the point of earning the unconditional admiration of Rogier van der Weyden, who, when visiting the basilica on the jubilee of 1450, declared that he preferred him above all other Italian painters. Facio himself, however, in his biography of Pisanello, did not abstain from reporting the very serious state of disrepair of this cycle, which 'parietis humectatione pene oblitteratum est'.[8] The zeal that Maffei still commended ('in umbris et coloribus diligens')[9] would soon become in Vasari's lexicon ('diligenza') synonymous with the frustrating limits of the analytical and too well defined painting of the so-called second age. The swift, stylistic obsolescence is ratified by the German traveller Johannes Fichard, who in 1536 considered these paintings no less than 'antiquissimae', and only appreciated, among the wraiths of patchy colour, the intensity of the azure, 'caeruleus color, qui inter obsoletos reliquos antiquissimos colores, ipse tam nitidus est, ac si heri pictus fuisset'.[10] In the Torrentino edition of the *Vite*, in 1550, Vasari had already exalted the quality of that colour, which he considered 'una sorte di azzurro oltramarino donatoli dal detto Papa [Martin V], sì bello e sì colorito che non ha

---

[6] J. Baudoin de Rosières-aux-Salines, *Instruction de la vie mortelle*, or *Roman de la vie humaine* (c. 1431), ed. in P. Meyer, 'L'Instruction de la vie mortelle par Jean Baudoin de Rosières-aux-Salines', *Romania* 35 (1906), 531–54, at p. 552.

[7] B. Facio, *De viris illustribus* (Biblioteca Vaticana, ms.Vat. Lat. 13650) (Rome, 1453–7), ed. in M. Baxandall, *Giotto and the Orators: Humanist Observers of Painting in Italy and the Discovery of Pictorial Composition 1350–1450* (Oxford, 1971), 165.

[8] Facio, *De viris illustribus*, 166.   [9] Maffei, *Commentariorum Urbanorum*, XXI, 300r.

[10] J. Fichard, *Observationes antiquitatum et aliarum rerum magis memorabilium quae Romae videntur* (1536), ed. in A. Schmarsow, 'Excerpte aus Joh. Fichard's "Italia" von 1536', in *Repertorium für Kunstwissenschaft* 14 (1891), 130–9 and 373–83, at p. 133.

avuto ancor paragone'.[11] A year later, on 1 November 1551, Paolo Giovio, when writing to Cosimo I de' Medici, reported that Pisanello had painted the Lateran basilica walls 'con molto azzurro oltramarino, talmente ricco che i pittorelli dell'età nostra si sono più volte sforzati, montando con le scale, a rader via il detto azzurro, il quale per la dignità della sua preciosa natura né s'incorpora con la calcina, né mai si corrompe'.[12]

The azure filled the backgrounds of the stories, but probably also enriched many other backdrops in the illusionistic decoration Gentile had invented in order to frame the prophets of the clerestory and link them to the narrative cycle below. In the fragment of the foliated frieze I had the fortune to discover in 1996 (Figs 18.1–18.4),[13] above the sixteenth-century coffered ceiling, at the left-hand top of the northern wall, the large, fleshy foliage, painted in monochrome to simulate a sculpted relief, stands out against a red background, i.e. the *morellone* of the canonical base for the azurite layer applied *a secco* (on dry plaster, as Giovio also knew!). The surviving section corresponds to a long segment of the upper moulding, for as much as 16.18 m, that also stands out against a band of *morellone*, which curves at the top where the original wooden truss rested (Fig. 18.5). The edge of the mortar that climbed the truss is clearly visible on the opposite southern wall, except for the final section, where the wall appears to have been restructured; we can deduce from these surviving parts that the underlying brickwork had been left visible, as in other large areas – the pillars and the terminal sections – documented in the drawing by Borromini's workshop (Fig. 18.6).[14] Here, on top of the *morellone* layer, we can detect an unmistakable trace of azurite (not lapis lazuli), altered to malachite (Fig. 18.7). The rather thick *intonachino* (*c.* 3–4 cm) was not applied onto the *arriccio*, but on top of a polished, whitened and hacked plaster, following an older practice that is also documented in Gentile's wall paintings in Brescia. In the foliated frieze the last to be applied was the *morellone* background, which outlines the profile of the indented foliage, expertly blended into the monochrome imitating sculpture so that it would emerge in perceptible light. It is possible

[11] Vasari, *Le vite*, III, 365.
[12] P. Giovio, *Lettere volgari di Mons. Paolo Giovio da Como Vescovo di Nocera raccolte per messer Lodovico Domenichi* (Venice, 1560), 59r–v.
[13] A. De Marchi, 'Gentile da Fabriano', *Art Dossier* 136 (1998), 44; A. De Marchi, 'Gentile da Fabriano et Pisanello à Saint-Jean de Latran', in D. Cordellier and B. Py (eds), *Pisanello: Actes du colloque, Musée du Louvre* (La documentation française I) (Paris, 1998), 161–213, at pp. 163–8.
[14] Berlin, Kunstbibliothek, inv. Hdz. 4467, 670 x 484.5 mm (K. Cassirer, 'Zu Borrominis Umbau der Lateransbasilika', *Jahrbuch der Preussischen Kunstsammlungen* 42 (1921), 55–66, at pp. 62–4; R. Bartoli, 'Cerchia di Francesco Borromini, Rilievo della navata destra di San Giovanni in Laterano con gli affreschi di Gentile da Fabriano', in A. De Marchi, L. Laureati and L. Mochi Onori (eds), *Gentile da Fabriano: Studi e ricerche* (Milan, 2006), 306–7, cat. VII.5).

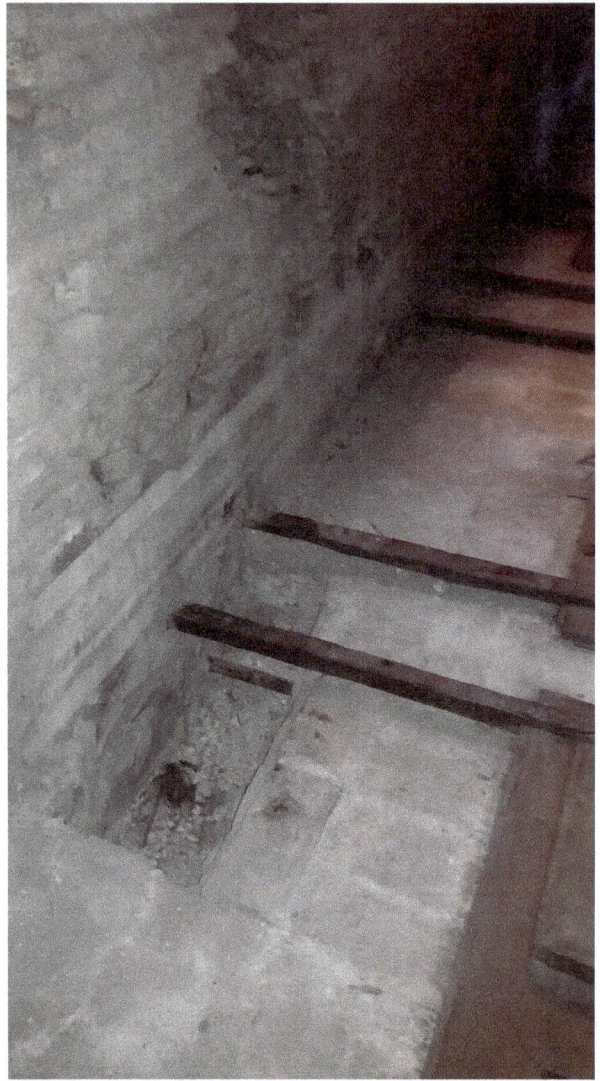

**Fig. 18.1** Saint John Lateran, general view of the fragment of the foliated frieze by Gentile da Fabriano at the top of the northern wall of the nave.

to detect the sinopia pigment of the guiding lines for the horizontal moulding ('linee battute'), while no pounced drawing was used for the foliage, which seems to have been painted directly. On top of a first layer of lime water there are actually incisions of arches intersecting and merging in various ways (Fig. 18.8), from which we may deduce that the original curvature of the scroll was modified when it was painted. The impetuous vitalism ingrained in this giant acanthus foliage, destined to be seen at

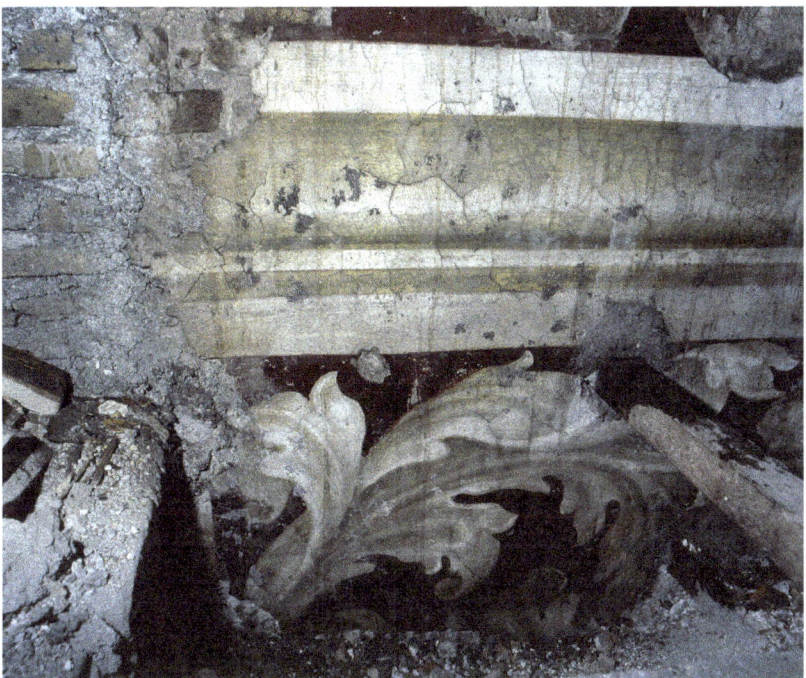

**Fig. 18.2** Saint John Lateran, fragment of the foliated frieze by Gentile da Fabriano, at the top of the northern wall of the nave.

a distance of 20 m from the ground, contrasts with the more mechanical definition of the leaves in the upper friezes of the scenes in the *Foundation of Rome* in Palazzo Trinci in Foligno, which are however comparable for their marked fleshiness: these were painted around 1411–12 by assistants of Gentile, under his guidance, but with a smaller degree of autography.[15]

In 1998, when I published these fragments, in the papers from the Louvre conference on Pisanello,[16] I drew attention to the upper part of the moulding, where a garland of flowers surrounded the pointed profile of the three-light windows and therefore overlapped the aforementioned upper moulding of the horizontal foliated frieze, interrupting it instead of joining it organically as if they were on two different planes (Figs 18.9, 18.10). At the time I highlighted the lavishly theatrical effect of these illusionistic tricks, opposed to the Masaccesque rationalism that even Gentile must have had to deal with in the years he had just spent in Florence, 1420–5. We can hypothesise that the flaming silhouette of the

---

[15] A. De Marchi, 'Gentile e la sua bottega', in De Marchi et al. (eds.), *Gentile da Fabriano*, 9–53, at pp. 18–31.
[16] De Marchi, 'Gentile da Fabriano et Pisanello'.

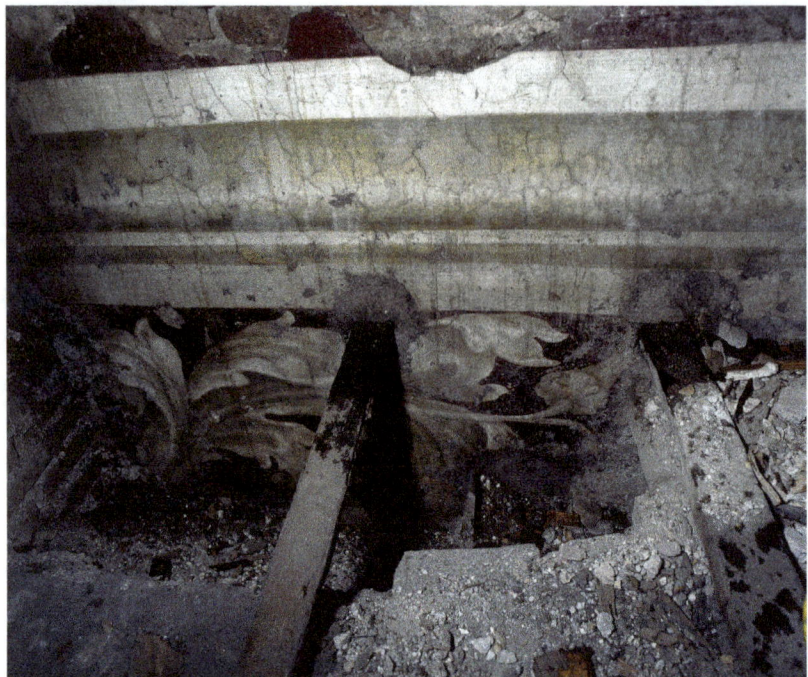

**Fig. 18.3** Saint John Lateran, fragment of the foliated frieze by Gentile da Fabriano at the top of the northern wall of the nave. Rome, St John Lateran.

dossal that includes the niches with the prophets, decorated with pinnacles and gables, also stood out against the azurite; as for the minutely carved, feigned architecture – its monochromatic tone artfully softened to give the illusion of sculpture – of which the Berlin drawing gives us a believable depiction, it must have contrasted intentionally with the dazzling intensity of the azurite, just as in the fragment of foliated frieze (if one mentally replaces the *morellone* with the missing azurite). Lower down, just below the clerestory, the Minor Prophets that looked out from the pointed windows, waving scrolls over the window sill, also stood out against the azurite. Should the head on a block in the Musei Vaticani (Fig. 18.11),[17] traditionally considered to represent Charlemagne, indeed come from one of these arches, this would confirm our hypothesis: in fact, besides being attributable to Gentile for the reddening and the mellow sheen of the flesh tones, it is surrounded by the *morellone*, customary base for the azurite. The

---

[17] Città del Vaticano, Musei Vaticani (Museo Sacro), inv. 41011.2.1, detached fresco, 59 x 47 cm (G. Cornini, 'Gentile da Fabriano, Testa di re (David o Salomone)', in De Marchi et al. (eds.), *Gentile da Fabriano*, 308–9, cat. VII.6).

*Traces of Gentile da Fabriano and Pisanello* 385

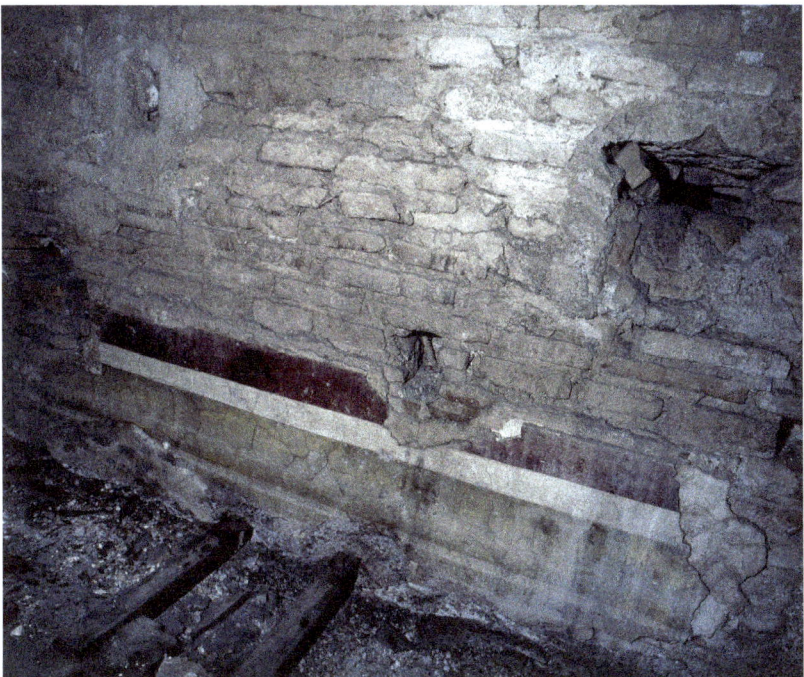

Fig. 18.4 Saint John Lateran, fragment of the foliated frieze by Gentile da Fabriano at the top of the northern wall of the nave.

provenance of this haloed king, which may be David or Solomon, from the walls of the central nave, is supported by the shape of the pointed arch that seems to include the original traces of the *morellone* background, and by the empirical perspective of the halo, seen from below, precisely like the one surrounding the head of Jeremiah in the Berlin drawing (Fig. 18.6). The red mantle hanging from the left shoulder, the neckline decorated with pearls and the fur cape make it clear that this was not a monochromatic figure. Even the drapery with symbols of the Evangelists, which alternated with the half-length prophets in the fake windows, must have been coloured, and brightly too, while the upper part of the wall, between the windows, was on the contrary dominated by the monochromatic tone of the luxuriant mock stone carvings. I am convinced that the fragment of fresco that was detached and walled into the southeastern corner of the cloister (Fig. 18.12),[18] the original parts of which are only the dilated left eye, part of the nose and of the mouth, comes from one of the Major

---

[18] A. De Marchi, *Gentile da Fabriano: Un viaggio nell'arte italiana alla fine del gotico* (Milan, 1992), 207, 209 plate 111.

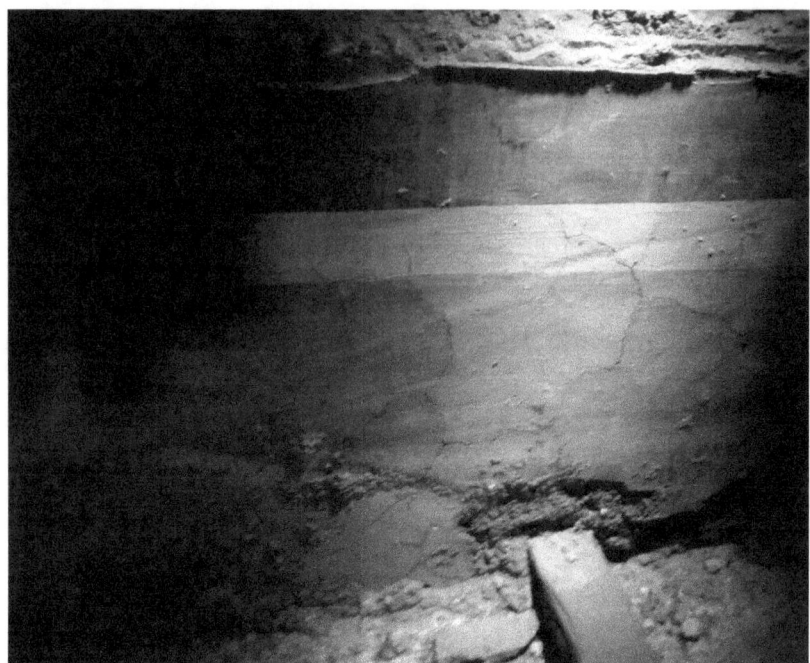

**Fig. 18.5** Saint John Lateran, fragment of the foliated frieze by Gentile da Fabriano (detail of the raised plaster at the top of the northern wall of the nave).

Prophets, that according to the drawing were more than 4 m tall.[19] In 1836 the scholar Luigi Pungileoni from Urbino identified in the detached fresco the remnants of the Redeemer depicted among angels in glory painted by Donato Bramante above the Jubilee door in the narthex of the basilica, which remained in the porch after the seventeenth-century detachment and was demolished in 1736 by Pope Clement XII.[20] The tenuous outlines and the delicate mellow, rosy flesh tones are in no way compatible with this hypothesis, while they easily comply with Gentile's style. The head is exactly double the size of a real head (18 cm from pupil to lip) and therefore tallies with the size of the enormous Major Prophets. Both these heads are characterised by natural flesh tones, and this clashes with Facio's appreciation for the marble-like appearance of the prophets. Moreover, the Ligurian

---

[19] The size of the opening of the niches excluding the pedestal is 465 x 135 cm, calculated on the Berlin sheet.

[20] L. Pungileoni, *Memoria intorno alla vita ed alle opere di Donato o Donnino Bramante* (Rome, 1836), 85. The work was reported to Pungileoni by the abbot Leoni of Urbino. Thanks to the intervention of the artist Carlo Ruspi, on 10 April 1836 the fresco, forgotten in a corner of the ancient cloister ('in un angolo del chiostro dell'antica canonica'), was mounted on a wooden frame 'alto oncie 2 1/2, largo palmi 4 ½ ed alto palmi 4'.

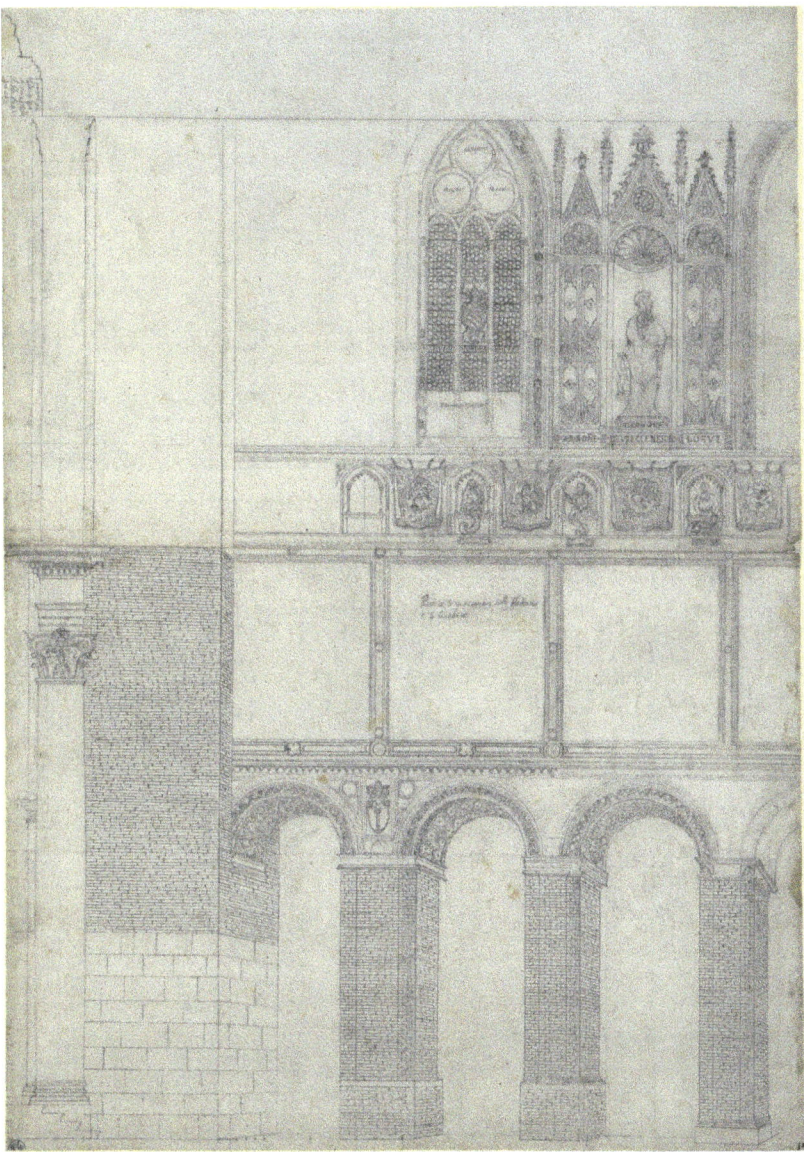

**Fig. 18.6** Saint John Lateran, relief from Gentile da Fabriano's frescos at the top of the northern wall of the nave, workshop of Francesco Borromini (Berlin, Staatsbibliothek).

humanist's opinion on the frescos was not based on a first-hand inspection: his comments on their state of disrepair originated in fact from what Pisanello himself had told him in Naples ('quantum ex eo audivi').[21] The exuberance of the *grisaille* micro-architecture that included the prophets

---

[21] Facio, *De viris illustribus*, 166.

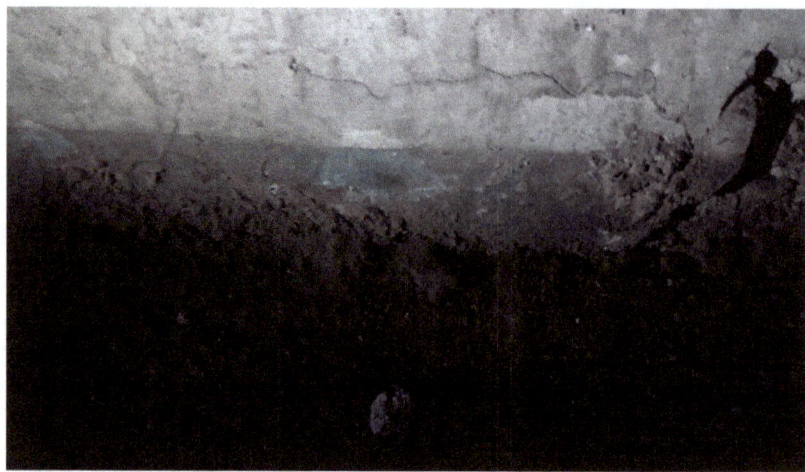

Fig. 18.7 Saint John Lateran, fragment of the foliated frieze by Gentile da Fabriano (detail of the azurite on the layer of red *morellone* altered to malachite).

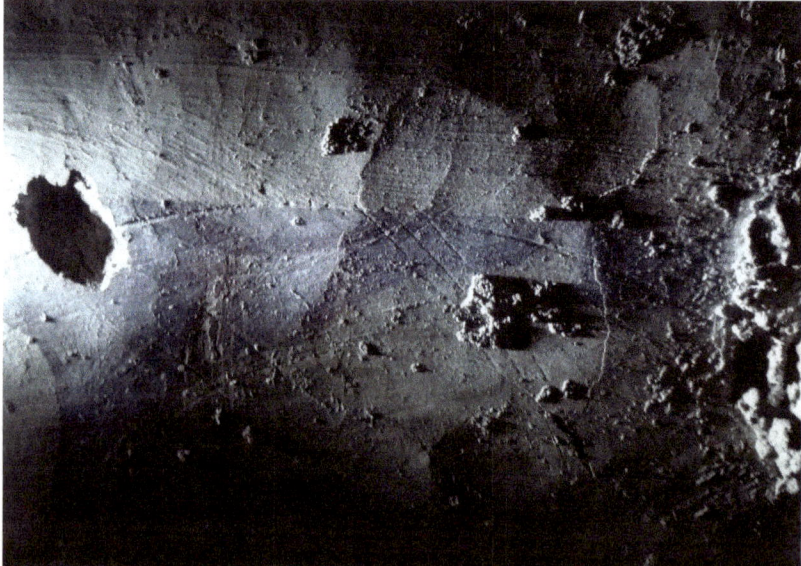

Fig. 18.8 Saint John Lateran, fragment of the foliated frieze by Gentile da Fabriano (detail of the incisions of arches related to the original curvature of the scroll).

was so strikingly illusionistic as to steal the limelight from the figures, which were indeed imagined as statues inside niches, but were probably polychrome.

In the years of the Avignon papacy the basilica endured two serious fires, in 1308 and in 1361. As late as 1527 Andrea Fulvio associated Martin V's

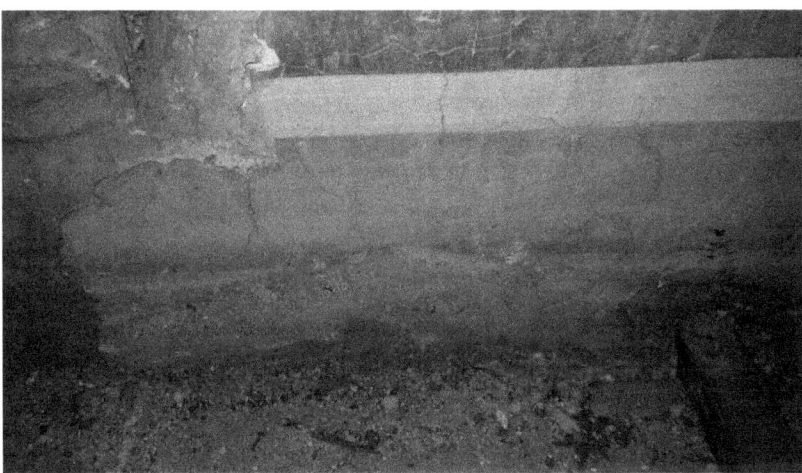

Fig. 18.9 Saint John Lateran, fragment of the foliated frieze by Gentile da Fabriano (detail of the vertex of the moulding surrounding a window and overlapping the horizontal foliated frieze).

restoration, which included the reconstruction of the mosaic floor and of the mural paintings, with the state of disrepair the church was still in, 'ignibus et ruinis deformatam'.[22] The inclusion, or replacement, of the columns inside octagonal brick pillars, which are clearly visible in the Berlin drawing (Fig. 18.6), entailed in Augusto Roca de Amicis's[23] opinion the thickening of the stonework above them: this intervention may date back to a fourteenth-century restoration, following the second fire, to which we may refer the Gothic shape of the sixteen three-light windows of the nave that are also recorded in the drawing. In this way any trace of a most likely pre-existing decoration was concealed. Gentile and Pisanello probably had to invent the cycle of stories of Saint John from scratch, as they couldn't find support in an older palimpsest; if this ever existed, it would have been located in a smaller section between the entablature and the clerestory, as in the Liberian basilica and unlike in the basilicas of Saint Peter or Saint Paul, and it would have already been destroyed with the creation of the system of pillars and brick arches. The only earlier work recalled by later sources was a *Final Judgement* on the counter-façade, mentioned first by Panvinio.[24] It has been hypothesised that the reinforced

[22] Fulvio, *Antiquitates Urbis*, 116.
[23] A. Roca de Amicis, *L'opera di Borromini in San Giovanni in Laterano: Gli anni della fabbrica (1646–1650)* (Rome, 1995), 28.
[24] O. Panvinio, *De sacrosancta basilica baptisterio et patriarchio Lateranensi* (before 1569), ed. in P. Lauer, *Le palais du Latran: Étude historique et archéologique* (Rome, 1911), 410–90, at p. 434.

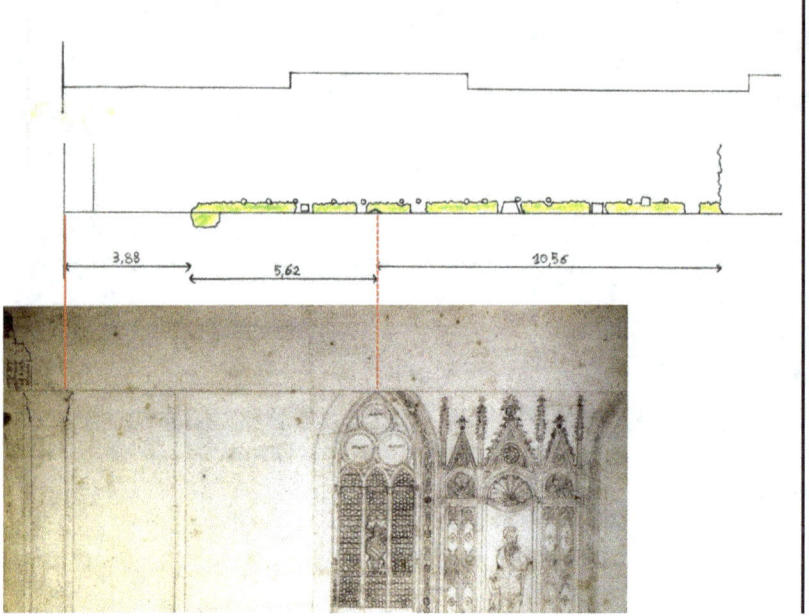

Fig. 18.10 Saint John Lateran, relief of the foliated frieze at the end of the northern wall of the nave.

wall at the end of the nave before the triumphal arch was even older, and datable to the years of Nicholas IV: in the aforementioned drawing (Fig. 18.6) it appears coherent with the new octagonal pillars and the resulting arches. The abrupt interruption to the left of the first scene of the cycle of the Baptist, frameless on this side, reveals however the existence of a fracture and therefore of an intervention that followed that of Gentile: it is possible that the wall in this last section was thickened later on, but we cannot hypothesise that the aforementioned scene was preceded by another, owing to the fact that the second episode listed in the legend is the Visitation ('qui ce la visitazione della Madonna e S. Lisabetta'), which can only be preceded by the Annunciation to Zechariah. We can rely on two inscriptions from 1364 and 1365,[25] once affixed to the brick pillars and recalling the private bequests that contributed to their erection, to date to the time of Urban V, just after the fire of 21 August 1361, the replacement of the tall columns and their entablature with short octagonal pillars and arches. Nevertheless, Martin V marked the new pendentives between the arches with the Colonna coat of arms. Panvinio mistakenly ascribed to

---

[25] Lauer, *Le palais du Latran*, 261; R. E. Malmstrom, 'The building of the nave piers at S. Giovanni in Laterano after the fire of 1361', *RAC* 43, 2 (1967), 155–64.

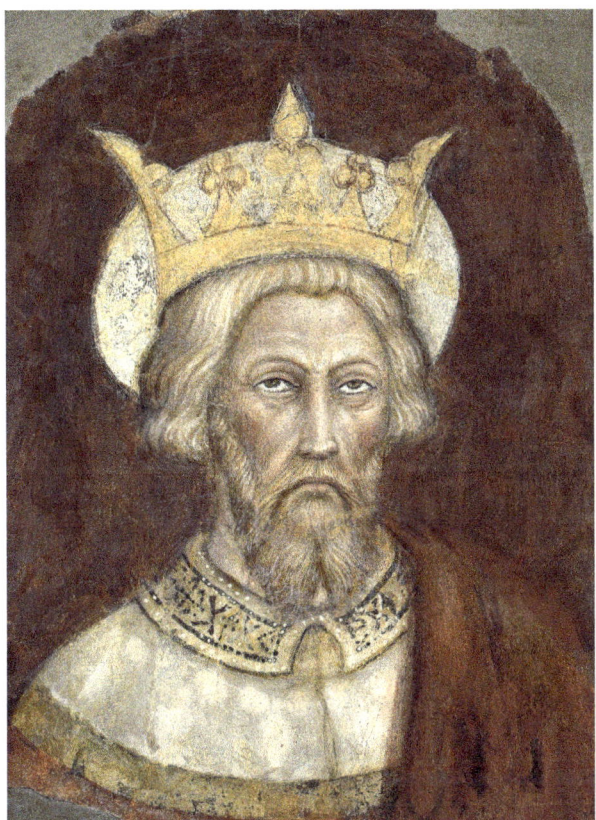

**Fig. 18.11** *Head of a Prophet* (Solomon? Also believed to represent Charlemagne) by Gentile da Fabriano (Vatican City, Vatican Museums (Museo Sacro)).

Eugenius IV the covering of all the columns but seven with bricks, and the consequent creation of the arches.[26] These being much lower than the previous entablature between the columns, it became necessary to decorate the large, bare brick wall above.

We must remember that the cycle embarked on from the end of the right-hand wall by Gentile, who received a monthly salary of 25 florins from 28 January to 2 August 1427 (though the first payments 'super pavimentis et picturis' date back to 17 September of the previous year),[27] and later taken up again by Pisanello in 1431–2, was in the end grossly incomplete; the

---

[26] O. Panvinio, *De praecipuis urbis Romae sanctioribusque; basilicis quas Septem ecclesias vulgo vocant, Liber* (Rome, 1570), 114–15: 'Sed etiam Eugenius columnas fere omnes primae contignationis, maioris videlicet zophori incendio confractas et ruinosas, opere cocto et lateribus vestivit, arcusque inter columnas fecit.'

[27] M. Mazzalupi, 'Regesto', in De Marchi et al. (eds.), *Gentile da Fabriano*, 68–84, at pp. 82–3, documents 85, 86.

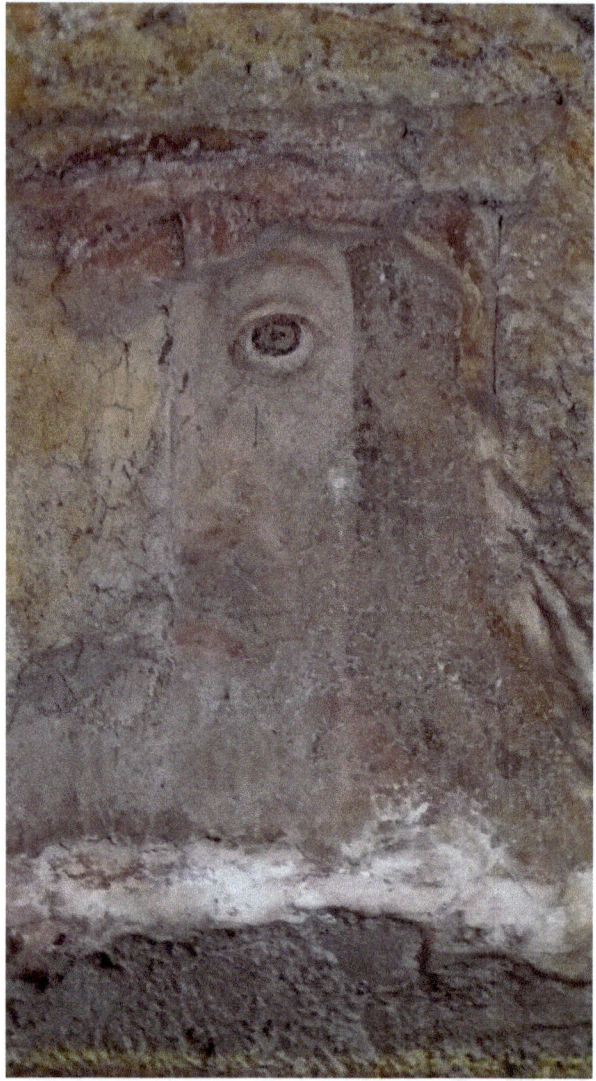

**Fig. 18.12** *Fragment of the Head of a Prophet* by Gentile da Fabriano. Saint John Lateran, cloister.

opposite wall had not even been touched, though it was probably meant to be decorated with stories of Saint John the Evangelist, for which several drawings by Pisanello still survive. There is a significant annotation at the side of the report sent between 1627 and 1630 to Cardinal Francesco Barberini from the Barnabite architect Giovanni Ambrogio Magenta: it tells us that the prelate 'in quel mentre diede ordine che prontamente si facessero i ponti per turar tutte le buche che nelle pareti della nave maggiore si vedevano, le quali erano tante che rendevano deformità, parendo che la chiesa fusse ridotta a colombaia'.[28] We can clearly deduce that large areas of the nave walls still showed open putlog holes and had therefore never been plastered. The fresco by Filippo Gagliardi in San Martino ai Monti (Fig. 8.1), which was executed when the interior of the church was already being transformed by Borromini, is imaginary, not only because it shows shafts of ancient columns located under arcades, and not under the entablature or associated with octagonal brick pillars, but also because it depicts a series of framed mural paintings on the left-hand wall. This dramatic incompleteness, linked to the sudden evolution of figurative taste in the following decades, was an insult to the decorum of the basilica: Cardinal Barberini therefore ordered the putlog holes to be filled up and the integrations to be painted in order to harmonise with the rest of the wall. This was clearly a bare brick wall, as we can easily see by examining the top part of the southern side, where there are still traces of the mortar that goes up to fill the interstice where the wooden roof commissioned by Martin V rested.

In my 1998 essay I had tried for the first time to figure out what would have been the extension of the painted decoration by Gentile and Pisanello, basing my calculations on the sources.[29] In Gentile's biography, Bartolomeo Facio declared he had painted episodes from the life of the Baptist (later completed by Pisanello) 'ac supra eam historiam Prophetae quinque',[30] five large Prophets: if we consider that the first one was located between the triumphal arch and the first three-light window, the frescos would have reached the space between the fourth and the fifth of the eight three-light windows. In his *De sacrosanta basilica baptisterio et patriarchio Lateranensi* (before 1569), Onofrio Panvinio recalled the existence of a work commissioned by Martin V and carried on by Eugenius IV – though he only speaks of Pisanello, who was already active for the former – and mentions eight stories from the life of the saint, that he could obviously see and check with his own eyes, 'octo inter columnarum spatium Sancti Iohannis Baptistae acta'.[31] Eight framed frescoes would have therefore corresponded to eight of the sixteen intercolumns of the nave (Fig. 18.13), hence half the potential extension. In 2004 my reconstruction was duly corrected by Bernhard Degenhart and Annegritt Schmitt,[32] in the light of Augusto Roca de

---

[28] Montpellier, Bibliothèque de l'École de Médicine, ms. H. 267, 51r (in G. Boffitto and F. Fracassetti (eds.), *Il Collegio di San Luigi dei PP. Barnabiti in Bologna 1773–1873–1923* (Florence, 1925), 35; De Marchi, 'Gentile da Fabriano et Pisanello', 194–5, doc. 21).

[29] De Marchi, 'Gentile da Fabriano et Pisanello'. [30] Facio, *De viris illustribus*, 165.

[31] Panvinio, *De sacrosancta basilica*, 434.

[32] B. Degenhart and A. Schmitt, *Corpus der italienischen Zeichnungen 1300–1450, Teil III: Verona. Pisanello und seine Werkstatt. I Band. Text* (Munich, 2004), 126–37.

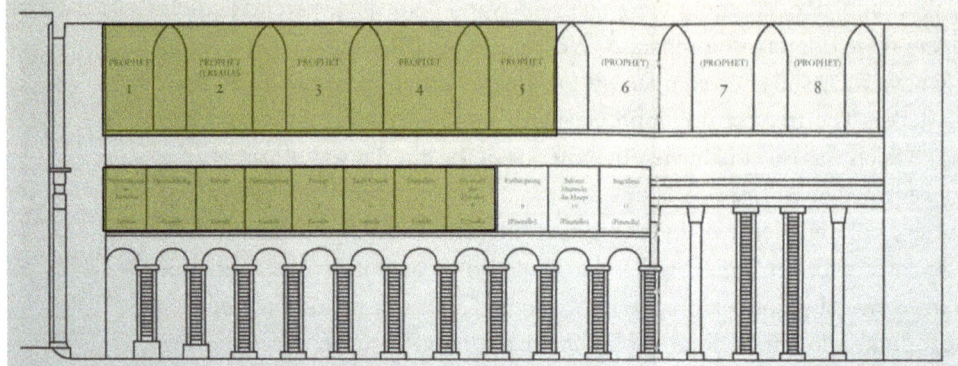

Fig. 18.13 Proposal for the sequence of the episodes painted by Gentile da Fabriano (1427) and Pisanello (1431–2) on the northern wall of the nave in Saint John Lateran (from Degenhart and Schmitt, *Corpus der italienischen*, 136–7, with some corrections by the author).

Amicis's studies:[33] this scholar had suggested that five intercolumns of the northern side and three of the southern, towards the façade, had preserved the entablature and the ancient columns in their full height, as can be deduced by cross-checking Panvinio and the maps by Rainaldi and Borromini. On the right-hand side there were therefore only eleven intercolumns, which, having been lowered by the brick arches, could be decorated with stories. I had therefore wrongly speculated on a particularly detailed cycle divided into sixteen sections, which had to be reduced instead to eleven. Degenhart and Schmitt wanted however to re-state the idea that Pisanello had completed the whole decoration of the northern wall, including the registers of the eight prophets and of the eleven episodes, hence giving no credit to Facio and Panvinio's statements, which on the contrary I consider reliable, especially for their uncommon congruence. If Pisanello had come to a halt just after executing the fifth prophet, then the scene immediately below, the ninth, could have been left undone: given that painters started working from the top and then moved downwards, the interruption could have taken place before lowering the scaffolding to proceed with the ninth episode.

Degenhart had been perceptive in noticing the Gentilesque traits in the composition of the *Baptism of Christ* and of the *Capture of the Baptist*, which are known to us thanks to two pen and metalpoint drawings by Pisanello's workshop, now in the Louvre (inv. RF 420) and in the British

[33] A. Roca de Amicis, 'Considerazioni sulla Basilica Lateranense prima del rifacimento borrominiano', in G. Villetti, R. Bozzoni and G. Carbonara (eds.), *Saggi in onore di Renato Bonelli*, 2 vols. (Rome, 1992), I, 345–54; Roca de Amicis, *L'opera di Borromini*, 28, 35.

Museum (inv. 1947-10-11-20).³⁴ Moreover, a drawing by the school of Peruzzi of the nude figure undressing in the Baptism scene strengthens the hypothesis of its relevance to the Roman cycle. This figure was very much admired, and allows us to definitively confirm the connection between the two drawings in Paris and London and the lost Lateran cycle. As Matteo Mazzalupi pointed out to me, there is a seventeenth-century manuscript from the Marches that supports this theory: in fact, it mentions this exact figure, though wrongly identifying it as Christ – which would have been a heterodox iconography indeed – instead of with a neophyte waiting to be baptised. This mistake was made by Fra Bonaventura Roscetti da Matelica, in 1627, in his *La preclarissima historia fabrianese novamente ricopiata dal p(adre) frà Bonaventura di Matellica,* a source that eluded the summary I published in 1998 of the twenty-four texts that mention the paintings by Gentile and Pisanello, from the origins to the *Relazione dello stato nel quale si trovava la Basilica Lateranense* (1660 circa). The *preclarissima historia* reports that Gentile worked 'et in Roma particolarmente nella chiesa di S. Giovan Laterano; ve fra l'altre è un Christo, il quale sendo al Giordano per battezzarsi da Giovan Battista sta in atto di cavarsi la camiscia, et di maniera, che non è anco fuor della testa, et dell'ultime parti delle braccia, il quale è molto lodato dagl'eccellenti pittori'.³⁵

I myself added other accurate comparisons with works by Gentile in order to confirm this theory.³⁶ Thanks to these, Degenhart and Schmitt hypothesised that Gentile's part went exactly as far as the *Capture of the Baptist*, which could in their opinion have been the seventh scene. Gentile and Pisanello were busy working in the basilica, the former for seven months, and the latter for about a year and a half: hence the necessity to calculate the extent of painted surface more or less according to the payment the artists received (but the partition hypothesised by the two scholars is not in proportion, since Gentile's section would have covered a smaller area than Pisanello's), which would mean that the cycle on the right-hand wall had been completed by the Veronese painter. The clear dependence of Masolino da Panicale's frescos in the Baptistery of Castiglione Olona (1435) on these two compositions was also referred to as further proof of this. Pisanello was paid from 18 March 1431 to

---

[34] B. Degenhart and A. Schmitt, 'Gentile da Fabriano in Rom und die Anfänge des Antikenstudiums', *Münchner Jahrbuch der bildenden Kunst* 11 (1960), 59–151, at pp. 59–60, 142 n. 65; B. Blass-Simmen, 'Pisanellos Tätigkeit in Rom', in B. Degenhart and A. Schmitt (eds), *Pisanello und Bono da Ferrara* (Munich, 1995), 81–117 and 279–80, at pp. 84–8.

[35] B. Roscetti, *La preclarissima Historia fabrianese novamente ricopiata dal p(adre) fra' Roscetti Bonaventura di Matellica* (Fabriano, Biblioteca comunale, ms 159) (1627), c. 90v .

[36] De Marchi, *Gentile da Fabriano*, 203–4; De Marchi, 'Gentile da Fabriano et Pisanello', 176–7.

28 February 1432, and on 26 July 1432 obtained a safe conduct from Eugenius IV in order to leave Rome with his entourage.[37] In 1432 Masolino was still in Rome, as he was completing the *Sala Theatri* in the palace of Cardinal Giordano Orsini before moving to Todi: he may have therefore seen those scenes even if the author had been Pisanello, who might have been called to complete Gentile's work after his death, due to his having been first a pupil then an associate of the artist in Venice. Gentile might have also prepared drawings for the episodes he didn't have time to paint, but this theory cannot be supported by the famous document from April 1433 that informs us that the 'suppellettili' previously purchased by the Lateran chapter for Gentile and later passed on to Pisanello ('pro suppellictibus emptis tunc per capitulum magistro Gentili que postea remanserunt magistro Pisano pictori')[38] were sold by the same chapter to the sacristan and priest Enrico for 10 gold ducats (i.e. 18 florins and 39 *soldi*): the *suppellettili* were in fact working tools (paintbrushes, trowels, floats, straightedges, ropes, etc. and perhaps also colours and scaffolding), and not preparatory drawings. There is however another indirect clue that the artist who continued the work behaved in a similar way: there are in fact two drawings by Pisanello's workshop that can be connected to the Roman phase (one is a bifolio of the 'carnet de voyage', which shows on one side a copy of Giotto's *Navicella* and, on the other, one of the *Dioscuri* of Montecavallo) and therefore to early ideas for the cycle of Saint John the Evangelist for the southern wall, that were definitely never executed (one drawing depicts Saint John giving alms to a pilgrim,[39] another in the Biblioteca Ambrosiana, which I have identified as the *Fall of the temple in Ephesus*).[40] Masolino may also have known the drawings prepared by Gentile that remained, in the absence of heirs, in the possession of the canons after his sudden death. Cordellier pointed out that the first

[37] D. Cordellier, 'Documenti e fonti su Pisanello (1395–1581 circa)', *Verona illustrate* 8 (1995), 45–6, doc. 13.

[38] Cordellier, 'Documenti e fonti', 55, document 18. The proposal of integrating '[a] magistro Gentili' requires the chapter to have bought these tools ('suppellettili') from Gentile, but this is wrong; as remarked by Mazzalupi (M. Mazzalupi, 'Roma', in De Marchi et al. (eds.), *Gentile da Fabriano*, 140–1), the simple dative case 'magistro Gentili' means that these tools have been bought for the master himself.

[39] Paris, Louvre, Département des arts graphiques, inv. 2541 (Cordellier, 'Documenti e fonti', cat. 89).

[40] Milan, Biblioteca Ambrosiana, F. 214 inf. 10 (De Marchi, *Gentile da Fabriano*, 207, 216 n. 120; D. Cordellier, 'Pisanello et atelier (?), Saint Jean l'Évangéliste faisant s'écrouler le temple de Diane à Éphèse. La "Navicella" de Giotto. Verso: Un des Dioscures. Sept etudes de paons. Deuz pieds', in D. Cordellier and P. Marini (eds.), *Pisanello: Le peintre aux sept vertus* (Paris, 1996), 153–4, cat. 84). It was previously thought to represent the *Expulsion of Joachim from the Temple*.

payment to Pisanello on 18 March 1431, in which we also find reference to paintings that had already been executed ('pro picturis per eum factis et fiendis in ecclesia [Sancti] Iohannis Lateranensis'),[41] arrived just fifteen days after Gabriele Condulmer was elected pope (as Eugenius IV), on 3 March: hence Pisanello must have been summoned to Rome not by the new pope, but by his predecessor, Martin V Colonna, who had been Gentile's patron. It seems odd that this decorative campaign was suspended for as long as four years and that no attempt was made to contact other painters, the greatest of whom was no doubt Masolino da Panicale, who was active in that quadrennium in Rome after Masaccio had died a year after Gentile, and who was the favourite artist of great cardinals such as Branda di Castiglione and Giordano Orsini. For this reason, I had even got to the point of hypothesising that he had actually been summoned, and that on that occasion he had been able to observe, and perhaps even copy, Gentile's drawings, and later put the memory of them to use in Castiglione Olona.

The sequence of the episodes proposed by Degenhart and Schmitt for the eleven scenes, based on the subjects painted by Masolino in Castiglione Olona,[42] is by and large plausible, except for some possible variations, such as the infant John the Baptist in the desert (and there also meeting Jesus returning from Egypt) or the Baptist pointing out Jesus to his disciples, also known as the *Ecce Agnus Dei*. If we keep to the German scholars' reasonable hypothesis, I believe it possible that the author of the fifth scene, which was in their opinion the *Preaching of the Baptist* (the fifth among the eight scenes that were actually painted, according to Panvinio), was already Pisanello and not Gentile.

There are very good reasons to believe that the fresco fragment by Pisanello with a woman's head in the Museo di Palazzo Venezia (Fig. 18.14),[43] on the Roman art market in the late nineteenth century, is one of the remains of the Lateran cycle. This is confirmed by its style, halfway between the mural paintings of the Brenzoni monument in the church of San Fermo (1424–6) and those in the Pellegrini chapel (*c.* 1436), and quite close to the Arthurian cycle in the palace in Mantua, which was in my opinion quickly executed prior to leaving for Rome at the beginning of

---

[41] Cordellier, 'Documenti e fonti', 45–6, doc. 13.
[42] Degenhart and Schmitt, *Corpus der italienischen*, 126–37.
[43] Rome, Museo Nazionale di Palazzo Venezia, inv. P. V. 4217, cm 24 x 17,2 (E. Moench, 'Pisanello, Tête de femme', in Cordellier and Marini (eds.), *Pisanello: Le peintre aux sept vertus*, 95, cat. 47; T. Franco, 'Testa femminile, Roma, Museo di Palazzo Venezia', in L. Puppi and D. Battilotti (eds.), *Pisanello: Una poetica* (Milan, 1996), 59–60, cat. 3).

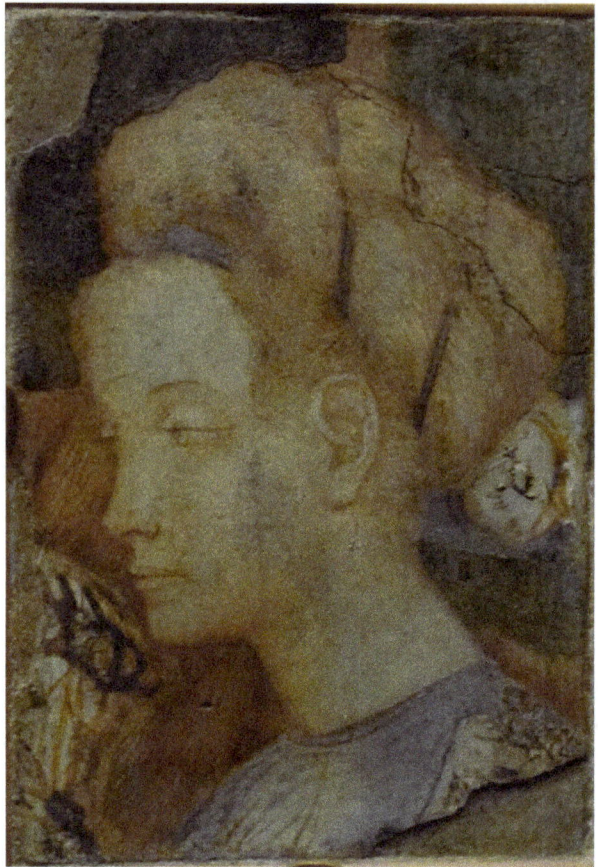

**Fig. 18.14** Pisanello, *Woman's Head* (from a lost fresco with the *Preaching of the Baptist*?) (Rome, Museo Nazionale di Palazzo Venezia).

1431, before the arrival of the future emperor Sigismund in the city of the Gonzaga, whom he would have created imperial vicars and marquesses. The current opinion is that this fragment comes from the *Feast of Herod*, or even that it may represent the wicked Herodias. Its size is quite small if compared to that of the framed scenes, which were about 4x4 m; it is therefore unacceptable for one of the main characters of the episode, while more suitable for a background figure. Even in the *Departure of St George* on the outside of the Pellegrini chapel Pisanello counterposed the foreground characters to the smaller figures of the king of Selena and his court, which is quite surprising if one considers the distance from which these paintings could be seen, which allowed the viewer only to guess, not to actually detect, the accuracy of the details: an impudent exhibition typical of the artist. If we carefully observe this fragment, which was certainly painted by Pisanello himself and which is still admirable despite the impoverishment of the colour applied *a secco*, mostly missing, and of the flesh itself, a little worn, we will notice that at the back of the young woman's neck and her elaborate chignon there is the drawing of two rings belonging to a belt, once decorated with gilded raised gesso motifs of which tiny traces survive; this accessory originally pertained to a green male 'zornea', the bottom of its skirt trimmed with fur, according to a typical fashion between the third and fifth decades of the fifteenth century. At the top left there are traces of cross-hatched silver leaf, part of another fabric, whereas under the young woman's chin we seemingly detect the outline of a large drum-shaped hat. At any rate, this figure was not a commensal lined up next to others, but one of the many richly arrayed male and female figures in the more or less tumultuous crowd. Only one episode from the cycle of the Baptist can offer a similar sight, and that is the *Preaching of the Baptist*, which would be useful to compare with the same scene in the frescos by Jacopo and Lorenzo Salimbeni in the oratory of San Giovanni in Urbino, where however there are only male onlookers.

Despite their technical quality and iconographical originality, the small size of this fragment and of the ones attributable to Gentile cannot but make us mourn for the loss of that display of tirelessly tooled materials, of bold expedients in decoration and illusionism, of inventiveness in the crowded compositions, which had made these paintings sensational, but had soon condemned them to an irreparable incompleteness and a rapid obsolescence.

'The author wishes to thank Raffaella Calamini for translating this paper from the original Italian'.

# 19 | The Rite of the Reconciliation of Penitents at the Lateran Basilica

JOHN F. ROMANO

Because so many complicated questions exist about the physical form of the Lateran basilica, it can be all too easy to overlook the function for which it was designed. It is primarily a house of worship, and its architecture must be read in this context.[1] Because the liturgy itself is sometimes considered esoteric, the natural conclusion is that this basilica was more a museum than a living space. Yet scholars are more fortunate with the Lateran basilica than the vast majority of churches in western Europe, both for the sources that describe the patterns of worship in this building and the foundational research of Sible de Blaauw on this church.[2] A host of questions remain about the liturgy of the Lateran basilica, however. Its sources are more plentiful than those of most churches, but they have their own intractable problems. In addition, modern scholars have not yet fully analysed the sources we have, at least not in a way that would be considered satisfactory by contemporary standards. Past research on aspects of the liturgy of the Lateran has operated under the assumption that its worship was static across a period of centuries, which has only reinforced the consensus that the liturgy can be safely ignored.

In a volume in which the ancient foundation of the basilica receives considerable attention, it may prove frustrating to turn one's attention to the liturgy. In one article that set out to describe liturgical manifestations of Constantine's victory, it becomes only too clear that what we can say about *any* ceremonial in this period is minimal.[3] We know not from liturgical but from legal sources that Constantine set aside Sunday as a legal holiday and

---

[1] For an overview of this question, see A. Doig, *Liturgy and Architecture from the Early Church to the Middle Ages* (Aldershot, 2008).

[2] Blaauw, *CD* I, 292–3, briefly mentions the reconciliation of penitents, but the theme merits greater elaboration. For one example of the interaction between liturgy and architecture, see S. de Blaauw, 'Il patriarchio, la basilica Lateranense e la liturgia', in P. Liverani (ed.), *Giornata di studio tematica dedicata al Patriarcato Lateranense: Atti della giornata tematica dei Seminari di Archeologia Cristiana (École française de Rome, 10 maggio 2001)* (*MEFRA* 116, 1) (special issue) (Rome, 2004), 161–71.

[3] M. H. Sheppard, 'Liturgical expressions of the Constantinian triumph', *Dumbarton Oaks Papers* 21 (1967), 57–78.

a special occasion for corporate or liturgical prayer (*euchas*),[4] but nothing about the form that this worship would assume. This gap is not unique to Constantine's reign, since our sources on ancient liturgy are scarce and incomplete.[5] One is reduced to repeating generalities – for instance, that liturgical forms borrowed from late Roman ceremonial, such as the carrying of candles and incense in front of the emperor and the vestments of late Roman magistrates.[6] Any hope of reconstructing entire worship services in the Lateran basilica appears scant for the fourth to the sixth centuries. The first liturgy that can be understood in any depth is the mid-seventh-century baptism at the Lateran,[7] although this is only one of the many services that it regularly hosted.

In spite of these obstacles, there are indications that from an early stage of its development the Lateran basilica was of central importance to papal liturgy in the city of Rome. Several of the donations to the church listed in the series of papal biographies known as the *Liber Pontificalis* were intended for liturgical purposes.[8] It was a constitutive part of the stational liturgy in the city of Rome until the collapse of this system during the Avignon papacy.[9] From the earliest period we can map out the churches the pope would visit in a regular cycle throughout the ecclesiastical year (*c.* 500), the Lateran basilica held a place of pride.[10] Some of the most solemn moments of the liturgical calendar were assigned to this church, and in particular during the Lenten and Easter seasons, the high time of the calendar. These included the First Sunday in Lent; Palm Sunday; Maundy or Holy Thursday, the Thursday before Easter; the Easter Vigil; the

---

[4] T. Mommsen and P. M. Meyer (eds.), *Theodosiani libri XVI*, 2 vols. (Berlin, 1905), I, 87; Eusebius, *Vita Constantini*, in F. Winkelmann (ed.), *Eusebius Werke*, 2nd edn (Berlin, 2008), 126–7.

[5] P. F. Bradshaw, *The Search for the Origins of Christian Worship: Sources and Methods for the Study of Early Liturgy*, 2nd edn (Oxford, 2002).

[6] A. Alföldi, *Die monarchische Repräsentation im römischen Kaiserreiche* (Darmstadt, 1970), 111–18; and specifically for vestments, T. Klauser, 'Der Ursprung der bischöflichen Insignien und Ehrenrechte', *Bonner Akademische Reden* 1 (1948), 5–44.

[7] Ordo XI, in M. Andrieu (ed.), *Les Ordines Romani du haut moyen âge*, 5 vols. (Louvain, 1931–61) (hereafter *OR*), II, 363–447. For discussion, J. F. Romano, 'Baptizing the Romans', *Acta ad archaeologiam et artium historiam pertinentia* 31 (2019), 43–62.

[8] See for instance F. A. Bauer, *Das Bild der Stadt Rom im Frühmittelalter: Papststiftungen im Spiegel des Liber Pontificalis von Gregor dem Dritten bis zu Leo dem Dritten* (Wiesbaden, 2004), esp. pp. 77, 87–9, 103, 129, 141, 208, but also McKitterick, Chapter 10 in this volume.

[9] J. F. Baldovin, *The Urban Character of Christian Worship: The Origins, Development, and Meaning of Stational Liturgy* (Rome, 1987).

[10] H. Geertman, 'Forze centrifughe e centripete nella Roma cristiana: il Laterano, la "basilica Iulia" e la "basilica Liberiana"', *Atti della Pontificia Accademia Romana di Archeologia. Rendiconti* 59 (1986–7), 63–91, and reprinted in H. Geertman, *Hic fecit basilicam: Studi sul Liber Pontificalis e gli edifici ecclesiastici di Roma da Silvestro a Silverio* (Leuven, 2004), 17–44.

Saturday immediately following Easter; and *Dominica in Albis*, the Sunday immediately following Easter, so named for the white clothing of the faithful who had been recently baptised during the Easter Vigil. Once churches had achieved a certain station, they tended to keep them, since the clergy at any given church tenaciously clung to the honour of hosting the pope's visit.

It is no accident that the Lateran basilica attained a high status in the stational system. The basilica was part of the complex that was the nerve centre of the papacy for much of the Middle Ages, especially the *patriarchium*, which was the primary residence of the pontiff.[11] In addition to its symbolic connection with the papacy, it had the practical advantage of not requiring the pope to travel, unlike far-flung churches such as San Pietro or San Paolo. The Lateran basilica maintained its importance in the stational system because of the political associations it had from its inception. It was well known for its Constantinian foundations. One can easily imagine if not prove that some of the early liturgies in the basilica would have incorporated a papal blessing of the *fastigium*. The imperial connections would only grow in meaning with the composition of the Donation of Constantine, which placed the epochal if fictional handing over of secular power to the pope at the Lateran palace (within which the emperor had the church and baptistery built) after Constantine completed a penance imposed by Pope Sylvester I (314–35).[12] This document may well have been composed originally to promote the Lateran basilica as a site of pilgrimage over San Pietro,[13] and it broadcast the importance of the former site. As the medieval period progressed, new legends of its spiritual authority further reinforced its status. From the thirteenth century on the Lateran basilica was said to possess relics with liturgical significance such as a small wooden altar on which Peter had celebrated Mass, which additionally enclosed wood from the table of the Last Supper.[14] They also had the blood relics of Jesus, which were displayed to the faithful as part of the

---

[11] For the history of the Lateran basilica, see *CBCR* V, 1–92.

[12] For references to the Lateran *palatium* in the Donation of Constantine, see H. Fuhrmann (ed.), *Das Constitutum Constantini: Text* (Monumenta Germaniae Historica, Leges. Fontes Iuris Germanici Antiqui in Usum Scholarum Separatim Editi 10) (Hanover, 1968), 74, 84, 87.

[13] N. Huyghebaert, 'Une légende de foundation: le "Constitutum Constantini"', *Moyen âge* sér. 4, 32 (1979), 177–210.

[14] S. de Blaauw, 'The solitary celebration of the supreme pontiff: The Lateran basilica as the new Temple in the medieval liturgy of Maundy Thursday', in C. Caspers and M. Schneiders (eds.), *Omnes circumstantes: Contributions towards a History of the Role of the People in the Liturgy Presented to Herman Wegman* (Kampen, 1990), 120–43; J. M. Powell, 'Honorius III's "Sermo in dedicatione ecclesie Lateranensis" and the historical–liturgical traditions of the Lateran', *Archivum Historiae Pontificiae* 21 (1983), 195–209.

celebration on Maundy Thursday. The church became defined by Old Testament parallels, through which the pope could be seen as a kind of new Jewish high priest and the basilica as a recreated Temple of Solomon.

Profound source problems confront the scholar wishing to analyse the liturgy held at the Lateran basilica as a whole, apart from issues specific to the rite of the reconciliation of penitents. There exists no medieval *ordo* or liturgical script designed primarily to describe or carry out the Mass at the Lateran basilica. The famed seventh-century papal Mass the First Roman Ordo only explicitly references Santa Maria Maggiore, San Pietro and San Paolo.[15] The same stage directions could with minor modifications be applied to the Lateran basilica, but any unusual features observed at this church could not be found in this document. Outside high liturgical feasts we must proceed with greater caution, and in fact admit to ignorance about how other Masses appeared, papal or otherwise. Because feasts such as Palm Sunday, Maundy Thursday, and the Easter Vigil were significant to the ecclesiastical calendar, it was imperative to get their celebration right; their infrequency meant that they needed to be written down, as opposed to most celebrations which were probably known by heart. Lengthy chronological gaps are encountered in our source material, and so it is difficult to chart when changes in Roman liturgy were introduced. Perhaps most troublingly, standard liturgical sources long believed to reflect Roman tradition have come under renewed scrutiny. The origins of the Romano-German Pontifical at Mainz have been called into question, as well as the extent to which it was understood as a coherent, unified volume; in addition, its manuscript tradition suggests a limited diffusion in the city of Rome.[16] The Roman pontifical of the twelfth century may originate from Monte Cassino rather than Rome, and so may not accurately reflect contemporary Roman practice.[17]

In spite of the challenges presented by the sources, some of the most pivotal and dramatic liturgies occurred at the Lateran basilica, and if we cannot always reconstruct them in detail, we can emphasise some of their

---

[15] For the critical edition of the First Roman Ordo, see *OR*, II, 1–112, and for the specific chapters with the names of the churches, pp. 71–2 (Chapters 15–7). A new presentation and translation of the source appears in J. F. Romano, *Liturgy and Society in Early Medieval Rome* (Farnham, 2014), 229–48, at pp. 231–2.

[16] H. Parkes, *The Making of Liturgy in the Ottonian Church: Books, Music and Ritual in Mainz, 950–1050* (Cambridge, 2015); H. Parkes, 'Questioning the authority of Vogel and Elze's *Pontifical romano-germanique*', in H. Gittos and S. Hamilton (eds.), *Understanding Medieval Liturgy: Essays in Interpretation* (Burlington, VT, 2016), 75–101; and for its spread in Rome, see S. Hamilton, *The Practice of Penance, 900–1050* (Woodbridge, 2001), 211–19.

[17] R. F. Gyug, 'The pontificals of Monte Cassino', in *L'età dell'abate Desiderio*, 3 vols. (Monte Cassino, 1989–92), III, 413–39.

defining moments.[18] On Palm Sunday, either palm fronds or olive branches were blessed and distributed to the faithful in order to imitate those who received Jesus as he entered into Jerusalem. On Maundy Thursday, the three holy oils used throughout the year – the oil of the catechumens, the oil of the sick and chrism – would be blessed. The Roman clergy would also perform the *mandatum*, the washing of feet as commanded by Jesus in the Gospel read during the Mass; two iterations of this ritual would be carried out, the first on the feet of the poor before Mass and the second on the feet of the clergy after Mass. The pope also used this Mass as an occasion to distribute payments to certain members of his clergy, which were known as *presbyterium*. The Easter Vigil was the lengthiest and most solemn liturgical celebration of the entire year. In its course the new Paschal candle would be blessed and lit for the first time, and would continue to be used in the church throughout the Easter season. Twelve readings would be chanted, and until the twelfth century, both in Latin and in Greek; this was one of the rare opportunities to hear any Old Testament pericopes in the Mass at all, and as a result they were well-known readings, such as the creation (Genesis 1:1–2:2), the sacrifice of Isaac (Genesis 22:1–19), and the Jewish departure from Egypt (Exodus 14:24–15:1a).[19] Finally, the vigil was when a number of infants would be baptised in the baptistery, albeit only a small, symbolic number when the vigil ceased to serve as the primary occasion for baptism in the Church.

Because these and similar liturgies on or around Easter can be described as having the same characteristics over the course of centuries, there appears to be no impediment to arguing that there was resistance to any change in the liturgy.[20] It is precisely these liturgies that helped to bolster one of the pseudoscientific liturgical 'laws' of the renowned historian of the liturgy Anton Baumstark (1872–1948).[21] For Baumstark primitive vestiges of the

---

[18] For the liturgy of Holy Week, see H. A. P. Schmidt, *Hebdomada sancta*, 2 vols. (Rome, 1956–7); A. Nocent, 'La semaine sainte dans la liturgie romaine', in A. G. Kollamparampil (ed.), *Hebdomadae sanctae celebratio: Conspectus historicus comparativus* (Rome, 1997), 277–310; and J. W. Tyrer, *Historical Survey of Holy Week, Its Services and Ceremonial* (London, 1932). For the Easter Vigil alone, see R. Amiet, *La veillée pascale dans l'Église latine*, vol. I: *Le rite romain: Histoire et liturgie* (Paris, 1999).

[19] For Roman readings, see G. Morin (ed.), 'Le plus ancien "Comes" ou lectionnaire de l'Église romaine', *Revue bénédictine* 27 (1910), 41–74 and T. Klauser (ed.), *Das römische Capitulare evangeliorum* (Münster, 1935).

[20] M. C. Mansfield, *The Humiliation of Sinners: Public Penance in Thirteenth-Century France* (Ithaca, NY, 1995), 160–8, specifically with reference to penance.

[21] A. Baumstark, *Comparative Liturgy*, rev. B. Botte, trans. F. L. Cross (London, 1958), 27–30; A. Baumstark, 'Das Gesetz der Erhaltung des Alten in liturgisch hochwertiger Zeit', *Jahrbuch für Liturgiewissenschaft* 7 (1927), 1–23.

liturgy emerged during more sacred times of the liturgical calendar, and none more so than in the period leading up to Easter. Of course the papacy is strongly wedded to tradition, much as the liturgy is; these are two conservative forces that reinforce one another's traditionalism. In addition, Baumstark's theory maps seamlessly on to the popular conception that rhythms of worship are ossified. Either directly from Baumstark or from this widespread attitude, scholarship on Holy Week in particular has characterised its worship as static, and methodologically it has been thought possible to draw from scattered sources from across a period of centuries to describe it. While it is true that the clergy may present the liturgy as if it had an air of the eternal, there is no reason for an outside observer to accept this as true. As I have argued elsewhere, there were modest changes and experimentation in the liturgy of the Lateran basilica during Holy Week that can be witnessed between the eighth and twelfth centuries.[22] So for instance on Maundy Thursday, the Kiss of Peace was phased out because of the negative connotations of Judas' kiss of Jesus. Similarly, on Maundy Thursday, in one prayer the term *proditor* (traitor) was inserted in front of Judas' name. On the Easter Vigil we witness a reduction of the canonical number of infants baptised from between four and five to three because of the Trinitarian significance, and the infants started to receive standardised names (John, Peter and Mary). In addition, as the role of cardinals grew in stature, a new blessing for cardinals was given after the baptism of the infants at the Lateran baptistery, after which the cardinals would return to the titular churches and perform their own baptisms. In all of these cases, however, it might be argued that these are minor changes that do not alter anything essential about the liturgical action of the day, leaving an indefinable core as immutable as ever.

To gain a better sense of how and why liturgy as practised at the Lateran could transform itself it is advantageous to focus on one celebration, and it is to this subject that I devote the rest of this chapter. The rite of the reconciliation of penitents was one of the more characteristic elements of Maundy Thursday.[23] It is also one that was already established in Rome by

---

[22] For the changes in this paragraph with references, see J. F. Romano, 'Innocent II and the liturgy', in J. Doran and D. J. Smith (eds.), *Pope Innocent II (1130–43): The World vs. the City* (Abingdon, 2016), 326–51.

[23] For previous scholarly accounts, see especially R. Meßner, 'Feiern der Umkehr und Versöhnung', in R. Meßner (ed.), *Sakramentliche Feiern I/2* (Gottesdienst der Kirche 7) (Regensburg, 1992), 84–134; W. Lentzen-Deis, *Busse als Bekenntnisvollzug* (Freiburg, 1969); A. Nocent, 'La riconciliazione dei penitenti nella Chiesa del VI e X secolo', *Rivista liturgica* 54 (1967), 628–42. A useful discussion of Late Antique penance in the city of Rome is K. Uhalde, 'The sinful subject: Doing penance in Rome', *Studia Patristica* 44 (2010), 405–14. See too the more comprehensive works on penance in n. 26 below.

the fourth century, even if we are not able to reconstruct its form fully for that early date. Although attached to one of the more important days of the ecclesiastical year, it has received little attention in modern scholarship. This neglect is not surprising given that, unlike other ceremonies on and around Holy Week, it has no echo in modern Roman Catholic liturgy. Another stumbling block, and one to which we will return, is the state of the sources that describe it: as a rule, they tend to be brief or unreliable in nature. The difficulties with the sources, and especially their lack, bedevilled one of the great scholars of penance, Cyrille Vogel, in his attempt to comment on this rite in medieval France,[24] but they are no less complicated for the city of Rome. In answering this question, it is essential to incorporate liturgical sources alongside narrative sources, although sometimes the former have been passed over in silence.[25]

To some degree earlier investigations of this subject have been hampered by scholarly conceptions of penance.[26] The previous consensus had determined that the rite of public penance was first stage in the development of penance, now dismissed as the 'grand narrative of penance'. Every plank of this narrative has now been subjected to intense scrutiny, even those pieces that were uncontroversial a generation ago. The rite of reconciliation was seen in this widespread scholarly construct as the only method of absolving one's sins in the Late Antique and early medieval world; it also bore the burden of being a forerunner to sacramental penance, if not fully a sacrament.[27] Increasingly a closer reading of the sources from this period without ideological blinkers has made clear that a spectrum of informal methods of penance were operative even while public penance was at its

---

[24] C. Vogel, 'La discipline pénitentielle en Gaule des origines au IXe siècle: Le dossier hagiographique', *Revue des sciences religieuses* 30 (1956), 1–26, 157–86; reprinted in A. Faivre (ed.), *En rémission des péchés: Recherches sur les systèmes pénitentiels dans l'Église latine* (Aldershot, 1994) as no. VI.

[25] Hamilton, *Practice of Penance*, 16–17; S. Hamilton, 'The unique favor of penance: The Church and the people, c. 800–c.1100', in P. Linehan and J. L. Nelson (eds.), *The Medieval World* (London, 2001), 229–45, at pp. 236–40.

[26] Here I provide some necessarily selective examples of older and newer approaches in the history of penance. Among older approaches, see J. A. Jungmann, *Die lateinischen Bußriten in ihrer geschichtlichen Entwicklung* (Innsbruck, 1932); B. Poschmann, *Die abendländische Kirchenbusse im Ausgang des christlichen Altertums* (Munich, 1928); B. Poschmann, *Die abendländische Kirchenbusse im frühen Mittelalter* (Breslau, 1930); Vogel, 'La discipline pénitentielle'. Among newer approaches, see M. de Jong, 'Transformations of penance', in F. Theuws and J. L. Nelson (eds.), *Rituals of Power: From Late Antiquity to the Early Middle Ages* (Leiden, 2000), 185–224; Hamilton, *Practice of Penance*; Mansfield, *Humiliation of Sinners*; A. Fiery (ed.), *A New History of Penance* (Leiden, 2008), with excellent historiographical overviews; R. Meens, *Penance in Medieval Europe* (Cambridge, 2014).

[27] Meens, *Penance*, 15–25.

height.[28] These included almsgiving, expressing sorrow, reconciling personally with those wronged, taking part in processions, travelling on pilgrimages, prayer, attendance at Masses, and calling on the intercession of angels and saints. It is difficult to see the relative importance of each method of discharging sin, and it appears that public penance may have been reserved for sins that were scandalous and serious, such as idolatry, murder, or certain sexual sins – failings that affected the entire community.[29] The older arguments for the elevated status of public penance left its chronology ambiguous, especially the hazy date of its origin, but also when it was phased out, which was somewhere between the fifth and eighth centuries. At this point tariffed penance or confession, originally from Ireland, supposedly became dominant in western Europe. The chronology for the end of public penance in western Europe must be fully rejected now that examples have emerged in the thirteenth and as late as the sixteenth centuries in northern France.[30] In Konstanz in the fifteenth century hundreds of the faithful were absolved on Maundy Thursday.[31] Some of the latest examples of public penance were still operative in pre-Revolutionary, eighteenth-century France.[32] These were probably not a continuous tradition from Antiquity, but they prove the tenacity of this form of penance even as competing methods circulated; this may stem from a need to publicly shame and forgive sinners.[33] Finally, the distinction between public and private theoretically delineated in penance between this rite and confession has now been called into question; it has been convincingly characterised as anachronistic before the Carolingian age, and uncertain after that point, since most people would have known when their neighbours were engaging in 'private' or 'secret' penance.[34]

---

[28] De Jong, 'Transformations', 209–17; Mansfield, *Humiliation of Sinners*, 157; Meens, *Penance*, 79–80; R. Price, 'Informal penance in early medieval Christendom', in K. Cooper and J. Gregory (eds.), *Retribution, Repentance, and Reconciliation* (Studies in Church History 40) (Woodbridge, 2004), 29–39; Vogel, 'La discipline pénitentielle', 8–12, even if Vogel holds to the traditional framework of penance.

[29] M. de Jong, 'What was public about public penance?' in *La Giustizia nell'alto medioevo, secoli IX–XI: 11–17 aprile 1996* (Settimane di studio del Centro italiano di studi sull'alto Medioevo 44) (Spoleto, 1997), 863–902, at pp. 865–6; Hamilton, 'Unique favor', 232–4.

[30] Mansfield, *Humiliation of Sinners*, 248–87.

[31] F. Neumann, *Öffentliche Sünder in der Kirche des späten Mittelalters: Verfahren, Sanktionen, Rituale* (Cologne, 2008), 28.

[32] J. B. Le Brun des Marettes, *Voyages liturgiques de France* (Paris, 1718), 19–21, 185–6, 222, 231, 255, 297, 299, 329–36. The most elaborate rites for public penance in France at this time were held in Rouen.

[33] Meens, *Penance*, 215–16.

[34] De Jong, 'What was public'; M. de Jong, 'Pollution, penance and sanctity: Ekkehard's *Life* of Iso of St Gall', in J. Hill and M. Swain (eds.), *The Community, the Family and the Saint: Patterns of*

Aside from the broader chronological questions surrounding penance, dating the rite of reconciliation in Rome is vexing. The first time that the rite appears in the sources is in around 399, although it is almost certainly older than this point in time.[35] By the ordinal of Gregory X, written in around 1273–4, the rite had been suppressed.[36] It would go on to become a literary or scholarly tradition, copied but not celebrated. Altogether this would mean that for approximately 900 years the rite was practised in one form or another. At Rome it appears to have been a continuous tradition from Antiquity to the later Middle Ages. In this it deviates from the Carolingian realm, where it was 'rediscovered' in the canons by certain bishops in the eighth and ninth centuries.[37] Though I am primarily interested with the rite as a Roman phenomenon, its influence extended beyond the walls of Rome, and similar public penance rites were imitated in western Europe. This is evident with the Roman rite of public penance in the Gelasian Sacramentary from about 750, which was transcribed into several later eighth-century Gelasian sacramentaries, even if it is impossible to see to what degree they were enacted.[38]

It will prove helpful to provide an outline of the steps of public penance in Rome, only the last of which occurred at the Lateran, however problematic these are given the gaps in our sources. Its normal celebrant was the pope, and as a rule the rite seemed to be an episcopal prerogative.[39] In its most simplified form, it involved a threefold process.[40] The sinners were

---

*Power in Early Medieval Europe* (Turnhout, 1998), 145–58, at pp. 149–50; Meens, *Penance*, 154–7.

[35] In comparison with similar rites elsewhere that were already extant in the third century: Meßner, 'Feiern der Umkehr und Versöhnung', 85–97.

[36] S. J. P. van Dijk and J. Hazelden Walker (eds.), *The Ordinal of the Papal Court from Innocent III to Boniface VIII and Related Documents* (Fribourg, 1975), LVII-LX; M. Dykmans (ed.), *Le cérémonial papal de la fin du moyen âge à la renaissance*, 4 vols. (Brussels 1977–85), I, 13–66.

[37] De Jong, 'What was public', 864.

[38] L. C. Mohlberg, L. Eizenhöfer and P. Siffrin (eds.), *Liber sacramentorum Romanae Aeclesiae ordinis anni circuli: Cod. Vat. Reg. lat. 316/Paris Bibl. Nat. 7193, 41/56 (Sacramentarium Gelasianum)*, 3rd edn (Rome, 1981), 55–60. The formularies for the rite of reconciliation appear in four versions of the eighth-century Gelasian sacramentaries: (1) A. Dumas and J. Deshusses (eds.), *Liber sacramentorum Gellonensis* (CCSL 159A), 2 vols. (Turnhout, 1981), I, 33–4, 76–9; (2) P. Saint-Roch (ed.), *Liber sacramentorum Engolismensis* (CCSL 159C) (Turnhout, 1986), 83–5; (3) L. C. Mohlberg (ed.), *Das fränkische Sacramentarium gelasianum im alamannischer Überlieferung*, 2nd edn (Münster, 1939), 68–73; (4) O. Heiming (ed.), *Liber sacramentorum Augustodunensis* (CCSL 159B) (Turnhout, 1984), 53–6.

[39] Poschmann, *Die abendländische Kirchenbusse im Ausgang*, 28–9, 48–57; J. Longère, 'La pénitence selon le *Repertorium*, les instructions et constitutions, et le pontifical de Guillaume Durand', in P. M. Gy (ed.), *Guillaume Durand: Évêque de Mende (v. 1230–1296): Canoniste, liturgiste et homme politique* (Paris, 1992), 105–33, at pp. 117–20.

[40] Meßner, 'Feiern der Umkehr und Versöhnung', 122–34.

first expelled from the ecclesiastical community, an event imbued with such gravity that one medieval liturgist compared it to the casting out of Adam and Eve from the Garden of Eden.[41] This seems to have started from the beginning of Lent; in Rome approximately from the eighth century this season started on Ash Wednesday, although only around 1000 did ashes start to be distributed to the faithful.[42] Those who became penitents could continue to attend liturgies, but they were excluded from the reception of Eucharist. Once the penitents were incorporated into the order of the penitents they were required to undertake acts of mortification such as wearing sackcloth, putting ashes on their heads, eschewing bodily care, abstaining from meat, and fasting, combined with a steady regimen of prayer.[43] In the final stage of the process the penitents underwent the reconciliation on Maundy Thursday, through which they would be reintegrated into the community of the faithful. In searching for biblical parallels to this rite, one liturgist hit upon various figures known for having completed penitence, such as Adam, the inhabitants of Nineveh, or the 'good thief' crucified with Jesus.[44] The final stage of the rite of reconciliation has also been described as a threefold process. In the first stage, the penitents gathered outside the front portal of the church and mortified their bodies there; they would encounter the bishop and deacon, who entreated the bishop to forgive them. In the second stage, the penitents were reintroduced into the church, by being physically led by the clergy into the building. In the third stage, the penitents had the prayers of absolution said over them and they were blessed with holy water and incense. In all of these stages, music would have been chanted to accompany the actions. Even from this basic outline it can be seen how topography played a symbolic role in expressing the position of the penitents in relation to the Church. When they were still excluded from the ecclesiastical community, they remained outside the church building, but they were welcomed back across its threshold to re-join it.[45]

---

[41] H. Douteil (ed.), *Iohannis Beleth Summa de ecclesiasticis officiis* (CCCM 41–41A), 2 vols. (Turnhout, 1976), I, 159.

[42] Jungmann, *Die lateinischen Bußriten*, 44–62.

[43] P. M. Gy, 'Histoire liturgique du sacrement de pénitence', *La Maison-Dieu* 56 (1958), 5–21, at p. 10; C. Vogel, 'Les rites de la pénitence publique aux Xe et XIe siècle', in P. Gallais and Y. J. Riou (eds.), *Mélanges offerts à René Crozet*, 2 vols. (Poitiers, 1966), I, 137–44, at pp. 141–3; repr. in Faivre (ed.), *En rémission des péchés*, as no. VIII.

[44] Honorius Augustodunensis, *Gemma animae*, PL 172, cols. 541–737, esp. cols. 662–3.

[45] D. Iogna-Prat, 'Topographies of penance in the Latin West', in Fiery (ed.), *A New History of Penance*, 149–72, at pp. 163–5.

The outline I have provided of the rite largely followed the Romano-German Pontifical, which has become the 'classical formulation' within the literature. As will become obvious as we advance through the sources, however, not all of them provide the same level of detail or agree on the same ritual flowchart. For these reasons, it is problematic to describe only the Romano-German Pontifical's version as if that had always been the gold standard. It was not the only game in town in its time for pontificals.[46] As with any ritual, a reconstruction of the reconciliation of the penitents hinges on an understanding of the sources that allow us to discuss it. For a rite that existed for such a lengthy chronological sweep, the issues with its sources will become immediately apparent. A closer look at them provides enough explanation why it is reductive to boil down the rite to one standard set of directions across the centuries.

The first source that mentions the rite is Jerome's epistle 77, written in about 399.[47] In the course of this letter Jerome wrote an encomium to Fabiola, a Christian noblewoman who left her first husband and remarried. Because by doing so Fabiola became guilty of the sin of adultery, upon the death of the first husband she decided to enter what Jerome refers to as the ordo of penitents (*ordo penitentium*) to make amends. This source is particularly strong evidence of the form of the rite, at least to the degree that Jerome understood it, because the point of the letter was not to describe its form at all, but instead to heap praise upon Fabiola. Jerome often focused on the virtues of those who were already traditionally noble in Roman society, but he casts Fabiola as being even nobler for her asceticism and accepting penitence rather than the nobility of her birth.[48] It is striking that now becoming a penitent could win one admiration and status.[49] Jerome's letter described Fabiola as having done mortification in front of the entire city of Rome, appearing dishevelled, without make-up, unwashed, with a bare head, and wearing sackcloth. After this procedure she would be restored to Communion, from which she evidently had been excluded while still living in sin. The text also firmly locates the rite at the

---

[46] N. K. Rasmussen, 'Unité et diversité des pontificaux latins aux VIIIe, IXe et Xe siècles', in *Liturgie de l'Église particulière et liturgie de l'Église universelle* (Rome, 1976), 393–410, at pp. 408–9.

[47] Jer. *Ep.* 77, in I. Hilberg (ed.), *Sancti Eusebii Hieronymi Epistulae*, 2 vols. (CSEL 54–6) (Vienna, 1910–18), II, 37–49.

[48] M. R. Salzman, *The Making of a Christian Aristocracy: Social and Religious Change in the Western Roman Empire* (Cambridge, MA, 2002), 215–16; J. L. Nelson, 'Nobility in the ninth century', in A. J. Duggan (ed.), *Nobles and Nobility in Medieval Europe* (Woodbridge, 2000), 43–51, at pp. 43–5.

[49] Meens, *Penance*, 20–1.

Lateran basilica. Yet even here Jerome did not clarify significant aspects about the nature of the ceremony. From what Jerome reported, Fabiola simply arrived on Maundy Thursday and immediately participated without any previous mortification during the season of Lent.[50] The assumption has been made that somehow Fabiola has taken an abbreviated path to reconciliation,[51] but the letter itself leaves ambiguous the question of how lengthy the penance required was. In addition, Jerome had little to say on the actions of the clergy, since his emphasis was on Fabiola alone.

The next source that made reference to the rite was a letter of Pope Innocent I (401–17) from 416.[52] In the course of the letter, Innocent I mentioned that it was the custom of the Church of Rome to forgive sins on the Thursday before Easter. Since elsewhere in the same letter Innocent I stressed the need for liturgical uniformity, he did seem to view this as the standard time of year to forgive sins. Some flexibility was nevertheless built into the system. The rule could be relaxed for those who were sick, and presumably in fear for their lives. That this brief sentence referred to the rite of reconciliation is apparent, even though he mentions nothing about its form. Innocent I wanted everyone to share in papal liturgy,[53] although there existed no practical way to enforce his liturgical notions more widely.

The rite of reconciliation in Rome appears subsequently in Sozomen's *Ecclesiastical History* from around 450.[54] Sozomen told about a place designated for penitents in the church set apart from other worshippers, where they would stand in the course of the service.[55] He described the rite by which penitents would initially be ritually expelled from the Church. Both penitents and the bishop prostrated themselves; the penitents shed tears; and prayers were said over the penitents. At that point the penitents would fast, stop washing, and abstain from certain foods. Then at a time established by the bishop the penitents were made free from sin and they could attend the liturgy with the rest of the people (*meta tou laou ekklēsiazei*). Sozomen provided a more extensive view of this rite than

---

[50] The term that Jerome used to refer to when this occurred, 'ante diem festum Paschae' (Jer. *Ep.* 77.40), is seemingly taken from John 13:1, and in that context it referred to Maundy Thursday.

[51] Meßner, 'Feiern der Umkehr und Versöhnung', 100–2. The author suggests that the intensity of Fabiola's penance replaced the normally anticipated duration.

[52] R. Cabié (ed.), *La lettre du pape Innocent Ier à Décentius de Gubbio, 19 mars 416* (Louvain, 1973), 28–9.

[53] E. Göller, *Papsttum und Bußgewalt in spätrömischer und frühmittelalterlicher Zeit* (Freiburg, 1933), 35.

[54] Sozomen, *Historia ecclesiastica*, ed. and trans. G. C. Hansen as *Kirchengeschichte*, 4 vols. (Turnhout, 2004), III, 886–9.

[55] For this interpretation of Sozomen, see H. Koch, 'Der Büßerplatz im Abendland', *Theologische Quartalschrift* 85 (1903), 253–70.

anyone previous to him, but it is unclear how well informed he was about Roman liturgy. The standard interpretation of this passage has been that he was referring to Maundy Thursday here, but nowhere did Sozomen insist on this, and in fact he implied that the period for offering the rite was variable and dictated by the bishop. Further, one cannot assume that the liturgy was as ancient as Sozomen asserted.[56]

Another source that handled the rite is a series of three 'sermons' delivered at Rome by a deacon or the archdeacon.[57] These are more rightly viewed as entreaties by the deacon, in which he would intercede on behalf of the Roman penitents with the pope, who would be won over by the deacon's rhetoric and ask God for their forgiveness. Unlike the other sources at this point, these gave some idea of the ideology behind the service. The rite developed on several levels, from God to sinner. God was merciful, desiring the conversion and salvation of sinners, not their damnation. Penance was a kind of medicine for salvation that allowed God's mercy to manifest itself. The pope had the power to bind and loose sin, which positioned him to mediate for the sinner with God. The penitent would need to mourn for his sins, groan, cry and prostrate himself. These acts would facilitate the forgiveness of his sins and reincorporation into the Church. These speeches focused mainly on the words of the deacon, not the actions that surrounded them. They establish that the community was meant to help reconcile fellow Christian sinners, and also that the archdeacon was supposed to simulate convincing the pope to reconcile the sinners, although this was a foregone conclusion.

One source that provides a tantalising clue to the rite of reconciliation of penitents are the canons of Theodore of Tarsus (602–60).[58] Theodore had lived for several years in the city of Rome before travelling to England to become the archbishop of Canterbury, and as a result he knew the tradition of Rome well.[59] One canon from Theodore takes it as a given that the

---

[56] De Jong, 'Transformations', 193–4.

[57] F. Heylen (ed.), *Archidiaconi Romani Sermones tres de reconciliandis paenitentibus* (CCSL 9) (Turnhout, 1957), 349–63. For analysis of this ritual, see F. Bussini, 'L'intervention de l'Assemblée des fidèles au moment de la réconciliation des pénitents, d'après les trois "postulationes" d'un archidiacre romain du Ve–VIe siècle', *Revue des Sciences Religieuses* 41 (1967), 29–38; F. Bussini, 'L'intervention de l'évêque dans la réconciliation des pénitents, d'après les trois "postulationes" d'un archidiacre romain du Ve–VIe siècle', *Revue des sciences religieuses* 42 (1968), 326–38; Meßner, 'Feiern der Umkehr und Versöhnung', 124–5. The earliest text of these sermons only had a generic deacon, though already here it was probably the archdeacon; it was not until the Romano-German Pontifical that the archdeacon was specified.

[58] Meens, *Penance*, 89–96.

[59] M. Lapidge (ed.), *Archbishop Theodore: Commemorative Studies on his Life and Influence* (Cambridge, 1995).

reconciliation of the penitents is executed on Maundy Thursday; the only issue was who should perform it.[60] The normative minister for Theodore was the bishop, but in cases of necessity the priest could also do it. Theodore also allowed a sinner to confess directly to God. A regulation appearing only in one tradition of his canons was that 'Romans' reconcile in the apse, while 'Greeks' do not.[61] The difficulty with this latter regulation was that it appears in a tradition (U) known for inauthentic statements that did not issue from the mouth or pen of Theodore himself.[62] The second problematic element is the term *Romani*, which, rather than being translated by the literal 'Romans', i.e. citizens of the city of Rome, should instead be understood as western European Christians who follow the pope's brand of Christianity.[63] None of the other sources for the rite specified that the final reconciliation was carried out in the apse, although if from Theodore himself, this may be a genuine reminiscence of what he had seen in Rome. They were not reflective of English practice, since one of the canons stated that the rite was not performed in England.[64]

An important stage in the rite's history was its inclusion within the Gelasian Sacramentary, copied in around 750 in the monastery of Chelles or Jouarre, but originally from a Roman source.[65] The formulae for this sacramentary described the penitents assembling on Maundy Thursday in a place where penance was done, presumably meaning mortification, before prayers were said over them. Afterwards they entered the church and prostrated themselves in the nave (*in gremio*). Then the deacon delivered his entreaties, and prayers were pronounced to reconcile the penitents. The final prayers for the penitents would be said either after the reconciliation or after they took the Eucharist. The rubrics provided for this rite were minimal, and raise as many questions as they answer. Although the most logical place for the penitents to gather would be

---

[60] P. W. Finsterwalder (ed.), *Die Canones Theodori Cantuariensis und ihre Überlieferungsgeschichte* (Weimar, 1929), 283 (nos. 190–2, Co. tradition), 306 (nos. 2–3, U tradition).

[61] *Canones Theodori Cantuariensis*, 306 (no. 1, U tradition).

[62] R. Flechner, 'The making of the canons of Theodore', *Peritia* 17–18 (2003–4), 121–43, at pp. 126–9.

[63] W. Ullmann, 'On the use of the term "Romani" in the sources of the earlier Middle Ages', *Studia Patristica* 2 (1957), 155–63.

[64] *Canones Theodori Cantuariensis*, 306 (no. 4, U tradition).

[65] Mohlberg et al. (eds.), *Liber sacramentorum Romanae Aeclesiae ordinis anni circuli*, 55–60. An excellent discussion of these texts as well as a reconstruction of its version of the rite of reconciliation is J. Dyer, 'Reconciliation, blessing and commemoration in the Holy Thursday liturgy of medieval Rome', *Archiv für Liturgiewissenschaft* 56 (2014), 16–48. See also Meens, *Penance*, 29–30; Meßner, 'Feiern der Umkehr und Versöhnung', 123–5.

outside the main portal of the Lateran basilica (so that they could easily enter afterwards), this is never specified. The rubrics consistently employ the singular to describe how many penitents would be present, which seems hard to believe unless this was an unpopular rite. A long list of prayers is provided without much indication of how all of them are to be used, perhaps because they derive from an independent *libellus* for the reconciliation of various classes of penitents.[66] It is not clear that the last part of the rite took place in the course of the Mass, but the Mass formularies given and the prayer said after the penitents would take the Eucharist make this the best suggestion.

The liturgist Amalar of Metz (c. 775–c. 850) was an authority who called attention to the rite of reconciliation of penitents. At first blush he would seem well placed to report because of his love for the Roman liturgy and his having visited Rome to observe it in person and consult with the clergy of the eternal city.[67] Amalar instead betrayed an entirely textual knowledge of the rite: he first cited Jerome's letter on Fabiola and afterwards Innocent I's letter.[68] What Amalar added to the tradition is nothing about the form of the ritual, but instead a typically imaginative link. For him the washing of feet on Maundy Thursday was associated with the cleansing from sin, which was the same reason he claimed that penitents return to the hands of priests. By referring to the priests' hands, Amalar was presumably indicating the step by which they would physically lead penitents back into the church, although he never explicitly drew this connection or otherwise mentioned this act.

One fascinating if puzzling source for the rite is the late ninth- or early tenth-century manuscript known as the 'Pontifical of Poitiers', although it does not meet the definition of what a pontifical is and only became associated with Poitiers in the seventeenth century.[69] The rite of penance described in this manuscript has previously been treated as Roman,[70] but little about its form can sustain this judgement.[71] A Romanising and possibly monastic scribe, likely from St Pierre de Vierzon (northeast of

---

[66] Dyer, 'Reconciliation', 25.   [67] A. Cabaniss, *Amalarius of Metz* (Amsterdam, 1954).
[68] Amalar of Metz: E. Knibbs (ed. and trans.), *On the Liturgy* (Dumbarton Oaks Medieval Library 35–6), 2 vols. (Cambridge, MA, 2014), I, 136–9.
[69] A. Martini (ed.), *Il cosiddetto Pontificale di Poitiers (Paris, Bibliothèque de l'Arsenal, cod. 227)* (Rome, 1979). On this source, see in particular A. Martini, 'L'ordo paenitentiae in feria quarta quinquagesimale del cosiddetto Pontificale di Poitiers', in *Mens concordet voci: Pour Mgr. A. G. Martimort* (Paris, 1983), 629–38.
[70] Jungmann, *Die lateinischen Bußriten*, 83–8; Meßner, 'Feiern der Umkehr und Versöhnung', 125–7; Iogna-Prat, 'Topographies of Penance', 163–5.
[71] S. W. Collins, *The Carolingian Debate over Sacred Space* (New York, 2012), 108–12; Hamilton, *Practice of Penance*, 105–20.

Paris), produced a compilation of liturgical practices based upon Roman prayer books. The anonymous liturgist drew upon genuine Roman prayers and music, but created original rubrics, in some cases seemingly to fill out the terse original documents. In any case, it provides little more than a vantage point to the author's capacious imagination, and probably never served as anything but a reference text. The extravagant level of activity anticipated for Maundy Thursday was such that it would have been impossible to complete it in the course of an entire day!

With all of that being said, in reading over its detailed description of the rite of reconciliation, one can see the temptation of trying to plumb it for authentic but lost Roman traditions if not simply admiring its elegance.[72] The rite of reconciliation on Maundy Thursday, explicitly located at the Lateran basilica,[73] began outside the main portal of the church. As part of this initial ceremony, the archdeacon entreated the pope to forgive the penitents, but the pope then heard the case of each individual penitent before allowing them to join the order of penitents. The pope entered the church, and only after an antiphon was chanted and the deacon called to them could the penitents follow into the church. The penitents prostrated themselves on the ground, where they would be exposed to a series of prayers, chants and readings. At that point an entire votive Mass (*missa specialis*) would be chanted for the penitents, and the enthusiastic scribe allowed for a second Mass to be said for the penitents if too many of them were present. Two more Masses would be celebrated on the same day, one for those about to be baptised and the other to consecrate the oils. After all that, the main Mass for the day would be celebrated, during which the rite of reconciliation would be staged after the Gospel reading. Both the deacon and bishop then gave speeches, and a litany was chanted. The penitents would then prostrate themselves before the bishop, who would say the reconciliation prayer over them; at this point either the bishop or priests touched the right hands of penitents. The formal rite was then completed, but the compiler also allotted special tasks to the penitents for the remainder of the Mass: they would bring up wine and bread during the offertory, take the Eucharist immediately after the clergy but before the rest of the laity, and were invited to the meal after the ceremony with the clergy (or, if there were too many, at least a subsection of them).

The difficulties encountered in the previous sources are scarcely alleviated by the *ordines romani*, the liturgical scripts that contain so much of

---

[72] Martini (ed.), *Cosiddetto Pontificale di Poitiers*, 136–90.
[73] Martini (ed.), *Cosiddetto Pontificale di Poitiers*, 165–6.

the remaining early medieval ritual guidelines. For several of the *ordines* that contain a reference to Maundy Thursday, nothing at all about the reconciliation of the penitents appears.[74] Given how spotty the record of what is left over is, it is not unanticipated that we lack a reference to the rite in these, although it might suggest that it was not viewed as a necessary text to own by the Frankish liturgists who preserved the *ordines*. The lone exception is Ordo XXXI, which was produced in the Carolingian realm around 900, and describes the Divine Office from the fifth Sunday in Lent to the octave of Easter.[75] In Ordo XXXI:20 it has a brief aside (probably inserted from another *libellus*) that after the Gospel was read on Maundy Thursday, 'Here the reconciliation of the penitents is inserted and thereafter the Mass proceeds in its order ... '[76] This text certainly indicates an awareness of the rite at this point in time, although, as with many of the *ordines romani*, questions remain as to how Roman they were or if this text was intermixed with Frankish custom as well.

The most important version of the rite of reconciliation as far as the scholarship is concerned is the mid-tenth-century Romano-German Pontifical.[77] In this description, the penitents assembled in front of the main portal of the church, where the bishop would be sitting. The archdeacon entreated the pope to forgive the penitents, and a psalm was chanted. In the second stage, the penitents were reintroduced into the church. The bishop would first chant an antiphon three times, beginning with Psalm 33:12: 'Venite, filii, audite me; timorem Domini docebo vos'. The penitents prostrated themselves at the feet of the bishop. The bishop would then lead the penitents by the hand back into the church. Once inside the church, they prostrated themselves again. In the third and final stage of the rite, an antiphon and litany would be chanted. At this point, prayers of absolution were pronounced over the penitents, and then they were blessed with holy water and incense. As I indicated earlier, scholars still have not entirely figured how to read this source, although some

---

[74] See with page numbers referring to *OR*: Ordo XXIII (vol. III, 267–73), Ordo XXIV (vol. III, 275–98), Ordo XXV (vol. III, 299–304), Ordo XXVI (vol. III, 307–22), Ordo XXVII (vol. III, 331–72), Ordo XXXA–B (vol. III, 447–77), Ordo XXXII (vol. III, 511–24), Ordo XXXIII (vol. III, 525–32).

[75] *OR*, III, 479–509. For discussion of this *ordo*, see C. Vogel, *Medieval Liturgy: An Introduction to the Sources*, rev. and trans. W. G. Storey and N. K. Rasmussen (Washington, DC, 1986), 173; E. Palazzo, *A History of Liturgical Books from the Beginning to the Thirteenth Century* (Collegeville, MN, 1998), 180.

[76] *OR*, III, 494: 'Hic inserenda est reconciliatio pęnitentium et deinceps peragitur missa ordine suo ... '; Dyer, 'Reconciliation', 27–8.

[77] C. Vogel and R. Elze (eds.), *Le pontifical romano-germanique du dixième siècle*, 3 vols. (Vatican City, 1963–72), II, 59–71.

version of the ritual it contains would later be followed by the Roman pontifical of the twelfth century, albeit only an abbreviated form of the beginning of the ritual.[78] In this pontifical penitents entered the church from the place where they did penance; they would be presented to the pope, accompanied by antiphons and prayers. It does not make any mention of their having been reconciled, either in the course of the Mass or elsewhere. Liturgists such as Bonizo de Sutri (d. c. 1095) and Sicard of Cremona (1155–1215) would similarly draw from the resources of the Romano-German Pontifical in their description of the rite.[79] In the modern period it has become a favourite of scholars, perhaps because of its detail, though also its supposed influence.[80]

One particularly instructive piece of evidence authored by Benedict the canon of San Pietro was the *Liber Politicus*, a liturgical guidebook that reports on the state of the Roman liturgy in the mid-twelfth century.[81] Benedict located the final reconciliation of sin as done by the pope in approximately the same position as in Ordo XXXI: 'After having done the preaching he does the remission to the people, he blesses and descends to the seat, where he announces the *Credo in unum Deum*.'[82] Since Benedict had nothing to say about the ceremony before the Mass started, this is the only indication we are given as to the existence of the rite of reconciliation. We are only told that it is after the sermon but before the *Credo*, but nothing about its form. A potential place to find more on the reconciliation of the penitents in the twelfth century is the contemporary liturgical guidebook of the Lateran written by the canon of the Lateran basilica, Bernard, who normally is well informed about the liturgical practice there. All Bernard did, however, was to provide the passage written

---

[78] M. Andrieu (ed.), *Le Pontifical romain au moyen âge*, 4 vols. (Vatican City, 1938–41), II, 229.

[79] Bonizo of Sutri, *Liber de vita christiana*, ed. E. Perels (Berlin, 1930), 60–2; G. Sarbak and L. Weinrich (eds.), *Sicardi Cremonensis Mitralis de officiis* (CCCM 228) (Turnhout, 2008), 469–70. In form, Sicard's description corresponded with the Romano-German Pontifical, but he was more interested in symbolic readings of the ceremony than straight description.

[80] Hamilton, *Practice of Penance*, 118–22, although Hamilton cautions that the rite in the Romano-German Pontifical cannot be taken as the standard liturgy for all places at the time; Mansfield, *Humiliation of Sinners*, 168–81; Meens, *Penance*, 154–7; Meßner, 'Feiern der Umkehr und Versöhnung', 127–8; Nocent, 'Riconciliazione dei penitenti', 632–41; Vogel, 'Rites de la pénitence publique'.

[81] *Liber Politicus*, in P. Fabre and L. Duchesne (eds.), *Le Liber censuum de l'Église romaine*, 3 vols. (Paris 1910–52), II, cols. 141a–159b. For this source, see J. F. Romano, 'The ceremonies of the Roman pontiff: Rereading Benedict's twelfth-century liturgical script', *Viator* 41 (2010), 133–49.

[82] *Liber Politicus*, col. 151a: 'Peracta predicatione facit remissionem populo, benedicit et descendit ad sedem, ubi nunciat *Credo in unum Deum*.'

by Innocent I, without describing anything about the contemporary ritual, which he could have witnessed.[83]

The last major attempt to reformulate the rite of reconciliation in the Middle Ages came from what some would consider its greatest and most influential liturgist, William Durandus.[84] Durandus had a lively interest in and knowledge of the liturgy of the papacy, as well as a desire to systematise the liturgy in his writings. Judging from his other writings, intellectually he was fascinated by penance, and he had a positive attitude towards retaining a variation of public penitence. Though it is valuable for all of these reasons, scholars have tended to view Durandus' rite of reconciliation of 1296 as being a scholarly or literary project, possibly motivated by antiquarian interests; it does not seem to ever have been performed.[85] His conservatism led him at times to 'reintroduce' offices that had ceased to be celebrated. Possibly the largest innovation in Durandus' method of reconciliation was to collapse confession and public penance together; before penitents were allowed to participate in the rite, they would first have to do confession.[86] This can perhaps be read as an attempt to compromise between maintaining the requirements for confession that were current in his day with a preservation of the long-standing rite; but if this is the case, it was to have no future.

The rest of Durandus' flowchart for the rite follows the pattern of the Romano-German Pontifical, albeit with some new details inserted. The penitents would gather in front of the doors of the church barefoot and prostrate themselves on the ground, while holding extinguished candles. A group of subdeacons would twice emerge with candles, which were first lit and then extinguished, accompanied by the chanting of a litany (that during the second time concluded with the Agnus Dei). At this point, again accompanied by an antiphon and litany, a larger candle was produced, with which the clergy would light the candles of the penitents. The pope then entered into the church, and, sitting on a stool, looked towards the door of the church. The deacon then gave his speech entreating the pope to forgive the penitents, and the schola chanted another antiphon. The pope delivered an exhortation to the penitents on how they were to live their lives. After this point, the *Venite* antiphon was chanted, while the penitents knelt and

---

[83] L. Fischer (ed.), *Bernhardi cardinalis et Lateranensis ecclesiae prioris, Ordo officiorum ecclesiae Lateranensis* (Munich, 1916), 49.

[84] Andrieu (ed.), *Pontifical romain au moyen âge*, III, 559–69. On Durandus, see Gy (ed.), *Guillaume Durand: Évêque de Mende*.

[85] Longère, 'Pénitence', 128–31; Mansfield, *Humiliation of Sinners*, 185–8.

[86] Andrieu (ed.), *Pontifical romain au moyen âge*, III, 560.

rose three times. The penitents were then introduced into the church, and they ran to the feet of the pope, prostrated themselves, and cried. At this point the archpriest requested that the pope reconcile the penitents; the pope had an exchange with the archdeacon, in which he asked if they were worthy to be reconciled. The deacon then ordered them to rise, and the pope took each of the penitents by the hand while the archpriest chanted. The penitents were brought into the middle of the church, where they knelt and prayers and antiphons were chanted. Everyone prostrated themselves, and afterwards the pope rose, chanted, and prayed over the penitents, the last step with responses. Finally the pope blessed the penitents with holy water and incense and gave them indulgences. The entire ceremony was self-contained in Durandus' account; it did not impinge upon the main Mass of Maundy Thursday.

Durandus' recasting of this rite would not prove immediately successful, but it eventually worked itself back into the tradition of Roman pontificals, a liturgical book intended primarily for bishops. Any hint of the rite was omitted in the 1485 version of the Roman Pontifical.[87] In the sixteenth century, what was in essence Durandus' rite would be restored to the pontificals, appearing first in the 1520 Roman pontifical and later in the 1595–6 edition.[88] It was unusual that these liturgical books copied a rite that was never practised into official liturgical books of the Roman Church, and that the papacy sent out these volumes to guide other bishops in a practice they themselves had abandoned. Stranger still is that in each of these sixteenth-century pontificals, the rite appeared with five woodcuts – which effectively illustrated the stages of a ritual that had never taken place the way that Durandus imagined it and surely had never been witnessed by the artist.

The source problems of the rite of the reconciliation, then, are extremely complex and incapable of being easily solved. They occur in a variety of genres, with few providing systematic liturgical scripts. Most do not bother to state the entire rite, because it was irrelevant or unnecessary for the audience. The reliable sources we have tend to be the shortest and most unyielding, whereas the longest sources also tend to be the most questionable to use. At least two of them were academic products never

---

[87] Agostino Patrizi Piccolomini and Giovanni Burcardo, *Il Pontificalis liber (1485)*, ed. M. Sodi (Vatican City, 2006), 457–82.

[88] *Pontificale secundum ritum sacrosancte Romane ecclesie cum multis additionibus* (Venice, 1520), fols. 177v–182r; *Pontificale Romanum: Editio princeps, 1595–1596*, ed. M. Sodi and A. M. Triacca (MLCT) (Vatican City, 1997), 550–68 (original pagination), 555–73 (modern pagination). For the influence of Durandus on these books, see Meßner, 'Feiern der Umkehr und Versöhnung', 129.

implemented at all. A host of details cannot be readily confirmed. Although based upon the description it seems clear that the first part of the rite of reconciliation would have taken place outside the main portal of the church, where the final blessing took place and whether or not the penitents moved into the apse or remained in the nave remain uncertain.[89] That the rite was on Maundy Thursday is similarly well established, with the only source that omits this being the non-Roman Sozomen's history. Whether or not the final part of the rite was incorporated into the Mass for Maundy Thursday remains unclear, although two sources (Ordo XXXI and Benedict) reported this. So far as the version of this rite in the Romano-German pontifical is concerned, it was self-contained, not a part of the Mass. This, combined with this source's placing of the final blessing in the nave rather than the apse, raises the spectre that this description of the rite was never fully implemented in Rome. It is at least possible that the author of the Romano-German Pontifical started with some Roman version of the rite (or one that had at least been influenced by Rome), but that it was then embellished north of the Alps. None of the sources provide a sense of the relative importance of the rite for the Roman clergy or laity.

Furthermore, the brevity of the sources does not resolve the major issue of change. The impossibility of tracing its development obscures what modifications may have been made as it was celebrated across the centuries. Because most scholars are trained to see continuity in worship rather than change, they have neglected to detail the changes or explain them.[90] The alterations in this rite, however, would extended beyond minor details. In time the rite would be transformed from a rite intended to reconcile sinners with the Church to one designed to excommunicate them.[91] Scholars tend to discuss the rite of reconciliation and that of excommunication separately,

---

[89] F. J. Dölger, 'Ante absidem: Der Platz des Büßers beim Akte der Rekonziliation', *Antike und Christentum* 6 (1940–50), 196–201, argues for the apse as the universal spot for reconciliation, but to my mind unconvincingly. Much of his evidence was irrelevant for medieval Rome.

[90] F. Claeys-Boúúaert, 'Bulle in Coena Domini', in R. Naz (ed.), *Dictionnaire de droit canonique*, 7 vols. (Paris, 1935–6), II, cols. 1132–36, esp. col. 1132, attempts to argue without success that excommunication was always a part of the rite, because those who had not been admitted to reconciliation were implicitly excommunicated; this would mean by extension that a majority of Romans would have been excommunicated. A. Paravicini Bagliani, 'Bonifacio VIII, la loggia di giustizia al Laterano e i processi generali di scomunica', *Rivista di storia delle Chiese in Italia* 59 (2005), 377–428, is correct to argue that the traditional rite of reconciliation on Maundy Thursday is a sign of the importance attributed to this day by popes, but it makes little sense to argue that the rite of reconciliation was the 'l'orginario punto di partenza' (p. 409) for the rite of excommunication without taking into consideration the very different nature of the two.

[91] This modification was noted briefly in C. Jaser, *Ecclesia maledicens: Rituelle und zeremonielle Exkommunikationsformen im Mittelalter* (Tübingen, 2013), 375–7.

which makes us lose sight of the fact that excommunication supplanted the previous rite of reconciliation that existed on Maundy Thursday.

Leaving aside the pontifical of William Durandus, whose production was a 'closet liturgy' that was never performed, the turning point for the rite was the thirteenth century. In two important liturgical sources of the Roman liturgy, the ordinal of Innocent III (1213–16) and the missal of Haymo of Faversham (c. 1243–4), the rite was not included at all.[92] When the rite began to change, the rite of reconciliation was relegated to a rump, whereas the centre of the ritual became excommunication. The exact period of time in which this transition occurred cannot be dated with confidence. When the rite appeared in the Roman pontifical of the thirteenth century (which cannot be dated more securely), it was in the midst of a transitional phase.[93] On the one hand, it copied some of the same verbiage in an abbreviated form from the Roman pontifical of the twelfth century. The penitents would enter into the nave of the church from the place where they had done penance, after which they would be presented to the pope and reconciled by him, accompanied by antiphons and prayers. Afterwards, however, the pope would preach a sermon, and then also recite the sentences of excommunication (*sentencie*). He then proceeded to absolve the people who had previously had their confessions heard by a cardinal deacon and also issued them an indulgence. Presumably the penitents are the same people who later receive absolution and an indulgence here, but there is no indication of such in the script, which uses the generic *populus* for the latter part of the rite. Because of the confession – privately heard but publicly absolved – the previous rite of reconciliation was redundant. The way that the two halves of the ceremony are joined together makes it seem as if they had nothing to do with one another; it is possible that the first half was simply carried over from the twelfth-century pontifical whether or not it was in use. Giacomo Stefaneschi (c. 1300–40) later cribbed his description of what had become a defunct rite from this description after the papacy's return from Avignon.[94]

By the time that the ordinal of Gregory X was issued in about 1273–4, the first half of the rite from the Roman pontifical of the thirteenth century had

---

[92] See the ordinal of Innocent III, in van Dijk and Hazelden Walker (eds.), *Ordinal of the Papal Court*, 89–484; and S. J. P. van Dijk (ed.), *Sources of the Modern Roman Liturgy: The Ordinals by Haymo of Faversham and Related Documents (1243–1307)*, 2 vols. (Leiden, 1963). Its absence may be due to the Fourth Lateran Council: Mansfield, *Humiliation of Sinners*, 183.
[93] Andrieu (ed.), *Pontifical romain au moyen âge*, II, 455–6.
[94] Dykmans (ed.), *Cérémonial papal*, II, 363.

fallen away entirely.[95] In this new ceremony there was no initial rite of reconciliation. Instead, the pope first preached a sermon, then performed the excommunications, and finally confession was heard and indulgences were issued. The ordinal broke down the groups of those seeking indulgence into the poor, non-Romans and those who had come from north of the Alps. No indication exists that a group marked off as penitents existed any longer. Confession and absolution were available to all without any previous preparation. Although the confession and absolution may be taken as a vestige of the ancient rite, by this point the major part of the ceremony had become the rite of excommunication. The names would be read out, candles held by the clergy would be cast down to snuff them out, and a bell would ring. Just as the lit candle had to be thrown down and extinguished, 'so the grace of the Holy Spirit, which is symbolized by the light removed from him, is cast out through excommunication'.[96]

The initial temptation upon finding this new rite in the ordinal of Gregory X is to assert that this pope was the one responsible for excising the old rite. This is not an unreasonable position to take, given the interest Gregory X had both in reform of the Church and an engagement with the liturgy.[97] To provide but two examples, during his pontificate he directed that at the Second Council of Lyon (1274), the Creed with the *filioque* was chanted both in Latin and in Greek as part of an attempt to reunite the Western and Eastern Churches, albeit likely with little contribution from the Byzantine attendees.[98] The council also criticised canons who allowed the Mass to go unperformed in cathedrals, and instructed the faithful devote themselves to this worship, taking part in prayers and nodding their heads when Jesus' name was spoken out loud.[99] However, not all of the material found in Gregory X's ordinal can be securely dated to his pontificate,[100] and the ordinal probably represents the first attestation rather than when it was first practised. If I were to suggest a more likely

---

[95] Van Dijk and Hazelden Walker (eds.), *Ordinal of the Papal Court*, 560–3; Dykmans (ed.), *Cérémonial papal*, I, 190–3.

[96] Van Dijk and Hazelden Walker (eds.), *Ordinal of the Papal Court*, 561; Dykmans (ed.), *Cérémonial papal*, I, 192: 'sic per excommunicationem ab ecclesia cum eicitur spiritus sancti gratia. que significatur in lumine. ab eo removetur.'

[97] On Gregory X, see esp. L. Gatto, *Il Pontificato di Gregorio X (1271–1276)*, 2nd edn (Naples, 2007). On Gregory's reform, see S. Kuttner, 'Conciliar law in the making: The Lyonese Constitutions (1274) of Gregory X in a manuscript at Washington', in *Miscellanea Pio Paschini: Studi di Storia Ecclesiastica*, 2 vols. (Rome, 1948–9), II, 39–81.

[98] B. Roberg, *Das Zweite Konzil von Lyon [1274]* (Paderborn, 1990), esp. pp. 231–7.

[99] Roberg, *Zweite Konzil von Lyon*, 321, 324–5.

[100] A. Stroick, 'Zum Zeremoniale Gregors X', *Historisches Jahrbuch* 55 (1935), 305–11, at pp. 305–6.

chronology for the re-creation of this rite, it would be when the pope first started to send out bulls *in Coena Domini*, which were issued from 1226 to 1627, and contained a series of general excommunications only the pope could absolve, which were pronounced on Maundy Thursday.[101] It would make sense for the pope both to condemn excommunicates ritually and send them bulls confirming the ritual at the same time. Yet this still would not tell us when the excommunication was decoupled from the rite.

The only eyewitness account we have of this new rite was the ambassador of the Mongols and priest of the Church of the East Rabban Sauma, who was in Rome in 1288.[102] In many aspects Sauma's record of the liturgies he attended is invaluable, but when it came to this particular rite, one would not know what Sauma was describing without the benefit of Roman liturgical documents. Sauma saw a crowd gathered at the Lateran on Maundy Thursday in a large open space or piazza in front of the façade of the church. The clergy, who stood on a temporary platform, said a prayer; the pope preached; and the people loudly responded 'Amen'. What seems to have attracted Sauma's attention in this case was the first part of the new ceremony. This is when the pope preached, and the 'Amen' was probably said in response to the end of the sermon, while it cannot be excluded that it came after the granting of indulgence. As with Sauma's travelogue more generally, we only have an abbreviated translation in Syriac of the original Persian, and so it is possible in the process of translation or editing that part of the rite was removed.

When the papacy travelled to Avignon, no form of reconciliation, even vestigial, remained. This is attested in the Long Ceremonial of Avignon.[103] This was to be expected, given that most of the curial ceremony in Avignon tended to be performed in the papal palace, and any connection with the laity had been severed.[104] By the time the papacy returned to Rome, as can be seen in the ceremonial of Pierre Ameil from around 1475, the state of affairs was restored to what was contained within the ordinal of

---

[101] Claeys-Boúúaert, 'Bulle'; Paravicini Bagliani, 'Loggia di giustizia', 391–7; Jaser, *Ecclesia maledicens*, 374–524.

[102] P. G. Borbone (ed.), *Storia di Mar Yahballaha e di Rabban Sauma: Cronaca sirica del XIV secolo* (Moncalieri, 2009), 37*. For discussion of the liturgical evidence in this source, see J. F. Romano, 'The travelogue of Rabban Sauma as a source for thirteenth-century liturgy', *Archiv für Liturgiewissenschaft* 58/9 (2016/17), 59–101, at pp. 76–9.

[103] Dykmans (ed.), *Cérémonial papal*, III, 207–13.

[104] B. Schimmelpfennig, 'Die Funktion des Papstpalastes und der kurialen Gesellschaft im päpstlichen Zeremoniell vor und während des Schismas', in *Génèse et débuts du Grand Schisme d'Occident 1362-1394 (Avignon 25-28 septembre 1978)* (Paris, 1980), 317–28.

Gregory X.[105] Reconciliation had definitively disappeared; all that remained was the rite of excommunication followed by the granting of indulgences.

The rite of reconciliation consequently assumed a radically new form in which excommunication became its centre, but we are still left without much of an idea of why this came to pass. Because of the crowds of the faithful, some of them pilgrims, that gathered for the Triduum, it provided an ideal opportunity to publicise excommunications.[106] But this observation lacks any explanatory force as to why this moment in the Triduum was chosen, or why the old rite of reconciliation had to be supplanted. A transformation so fundamental remains a hurdle to be explained. In this case we cannot rely on any medieval sources, none of which is theoretically oriented and recognises that something new was happening, much less provides a rationale. This cannot be reduced to the fact it was staged during a busy liturgical season, or it would have made little sense to replace one ritual with another, rather than simply extricating it entirely.

As far as I envision it, a series of interconnected arguments explain the disappearance of this rite, all of which may have contributed to some degree. The first of these is that since the original creation of this rite, Lent had expanded to become a penitential season for all of the faithful, not only a smaller circle of penitents.[107] Everyone received ashes on Ash Wednesday and everyone was expected to perform acts of mortification. It would have been anomalous to single out anyone as penitents requiring a unique ceremony when everyone was charged with a similar task. A chronologically more proximate event was the Fourth Lateran Council in 1215, which in the twenty-first canon (*Omnis utrisque sexus*) for the first time required individual auricular confession and the performance of penance for all of the faithful at least once a year.[108] Recent scholarship has tended to downplay the importance of this new rule, and it is well established that not everywhere adopted it quickly or seamlessly.[109] While this may be true, in the city of Rome itself at the very basilica where the council had been held and under the watchful eye of the pope, it would have been unusual for the pope to continue to promote what must have envisioned as an archaic holdover instead of private confessions.

---

[105] Dykmans (ed.), *Cérémonial papal*, IV, 129–35.   [106] Jaser, *Ecclesia maledicens*, 375–6.

[107] Jungmann, *Die lateinischen Bußriten*, 59–62; Gy, 'Histoire liturgique', 14.

[108] N. P. Tanner (ed.), *Decrees of the Ecumenical Councils*, 2 vols. (London, 1990), I, 245. For the traditional account, see N. Bériou, 'Autour de Latran IV (1215): La naissance de la confession moderne et sa diffusion', in *Pratiques de la confession: Des Pères du désert à Vatican II: Quinze études d'histoire* (Paris, 1983), 73–93.

[109] See the more recent accounts in the introduction of A. Fiery in *A New History of Penance*, 1–18, esp. pp. 2–3; and Mansfield, *Humiliation of Sinners*, 60–91.

The other two reasons both hinge on the burgeoning status of the papacy in the later Middle Ages. In the early Middle Ages the papacy was first and foremost a local institution and its primary charge was caring for the people of the city, but by the thirteenth century it had emerged as an international player.[110] At this time the pope was far more concerned with punishing foreign potentates whose actions could interfere with the papacy's interests than issues of pastoral care over sinful Romans. As a manifestation of this trend, previously the entreaty of the deacon implied that the entire community would have to be present to intercede on behalf of the penitents.[111] By the time that this had become a rite mainly of excommunication, the crowd had been reduced to the status of spectators who only affirmed the actions of the pope.[112] Finally, it is fair to say that the papacy had moved from what we may term a policy of inclusion to one of exclusion when it came to this rite. The initial point of holding the rite on Maundy Thursday was to reincorporate sinners into the Christian community so that they could partake in the Eucharist with everyone else on Maundy Thursday, the rest of the Triduum, and throughout the Easter season.[113] The explicit reason given in the ordinal of Gregory X, which in this case incorporated some reflection, was to place the excommunication on Maundy Thursday to ensure that sinners were excluded from the reception of the Eucharist, since this day commemorated the beginning of this sacrament and all the faithful took the Eucharist on this day.[114] The social pressure of being excluded from taking Communion when everyone else did would exert

---

[110] C. Morris, *The Papal Monarchy: The Western Church from 1050 to 1250* (Oxford, 1989).

[111] Bussini, 'L'intervention de l'Assemblée'.

[112] This can be seen in the language of the papal bulls of excommunication, starting for instance with the first attested example in a letter of Honorius III from 1226: 'solemniter presente toto populo, qui diversis mundi partibus tunc concurrit', in C. Rodenberg (ed.), *Epistolae saeculi XIII e regestis pontificum Romanorum selectae*, 3 vols. (Berlin, 1883), I, 233–4 (no. 306). For discussion, Paravicini Bagliani, 'Loggia di giustizia', 380.

[113] Gy, 'Histoire liturgique', 13. Some sense of this can be gained from the opening prayers of the reconciliation of the penitents in the Gelasian Sacramentary, which, in asking for the absolution from sin, requests it so that God's servants may enter into all the mysteries of the Paschal feast more fully and more perfectly: Mohlberg et al. (eds.), *Liber sacramentorum Romanae Aeclesiae ordinis anni circuli*, 55: '... plenius adque perfectius omnia festi paschalis introire mysteria ...'

[114] Van Dijk and Hazelden Walker (eds.), *Ordinal of the Papal Court*, 561–2; Dykmans (ed.), *Cérémonial papal*, I, 192–3: 'Primo hac die iovis sacramentum corporis et sanguinis Christi habuit principium. in quo omnes fideles communicant. Ad ostendendum vero quod excommunicationi in hoc non communicant. eo die ab ecclesia exclusi ostenduntur ... Et hoc etiam fit pro utilitate excommunicatorum. ut videntes se a tot bonis tantorum dierum excludi. facilius ad reconciliationis gratiam condescendant. Ad diem vero festum respondentur quod hoc non est sententie prolatio sed exclusionis ostensio et non per viam iudicalem sed admonitionem et correctionem maternalem.'

influence on those excommunicated to submit to confession; this act was justified as an admonition and correction.

Several conclusions can be drawn by an examination of this rite. The first is to emphasise a lesser-known liturgy, one that extended in some form from the Late Antique period into the later Middle Ages, for an institution and a basilica that was shaped by worship. We can only reconstruct how it was carried out to a limited degree, and in fact it is easier to see it towards the end of its existence rather than during most of its history. Nevertheless, we have some idea of its ritual as well as the remarkable transition it underwent. This was a case in which the original form was eliminated and was replaced with excommunication, which neatly turned the ceremony on its head. Methodologically, the process of reconstruction of a defunct liturgy can be difficult to resolve, and historians of the liturgy can only look on with envy when learning about scholars of archaeology and architecture who often have physical structures to examine when doing their reconstruction. When it comes to the liturgy, unless there is a written source, the act of worship disappears immediately. A liturgy like the rite of reconciliation seems to require little specific architecture to be performed, suggesting that it was fairly malleable when it came to which space it could be performed in; nearly any church could be the locus considering its limited rubrics.

The rite of reconciliation also served as a strong example of how much change can occur in the liturgy, as opposed to the common reflex to treat it as immutable or fall to back on Anton Baumstark's theory about its stability at liturgically high times of year. Baumstark accounted for liturgical evolution in another of his laws,[115] but what we have seen with the rite of penitence is not how liturgy should operate during Holy Week according to him. Ultimately, not even this time was immune from liturgical change, which calls into question how much confidence to place in Baumstark's theory. This study also allows us to engage with recent scholarship on the history of penance. Nothing about the sources that discuss the rite of reconciliation could be used as the basis for arguing that it was the only method of gaining forgiveness or that it was a sacrament before the sacrament. The older chronology that suggested an abrupt end to this practice in Rome or elsewhere in western Europe simply cannot be sustained, and a more thorough reading of the evidence would no doubt turn up additional examples of the rite practised long beyond the early Middle Ages. This chapter also supports the movement among scholars to do in-depth

---

[115] Baumstark, *Comparative Liturgy*, 23–7.

study of individual documents in the history of penance, rather than to locate them within an artificial broader scheme that elides their differences.[116] The only way I would differ from the growing consensus is to suggest that, at least in a limited respect, the Fourth Lateran Council may have been more of a watershed than is now thought; whether or not this is true for the rite in Rome lacks definitive proof, but it would provide one convincing reason why the rite would end up changing to the degree that it did.

Finally, the rite of reconciliation of penance provides one concrete example as to the broader reach of the liturgy of the Lateran basilica. As interest in Roman liturgy grew, this rite would evoke interest in western Europe, especially as mediated through the Gelasian Sacramentary and the pontifical of William Durandus. Much as through the Donation of Constantine, the Lateran came alive for a new audience through texts originating in Rome. That the ritual would undergo further modification as it departed the eternal city shows how liturgy worked in a manuscript culture. Eventually even after the rite had effectively been suppressed in Rome, it still was celebrated elsewhere. The shadow of the liturgy of the Lateran basilica extended well beyond its original Roman audience.

---

[116] See de Jong, 'Pollution, penance and sanctity'; Meens, *Penance*.

# 20 | The New Passion Relics at the Lateran, Fifteenth to Sixteenth Centuries: A Translocated Sacred Topography

NADJA HORSCH

Around the Holy Year 1450 an outstanding 'invention of relics' took place at the Lateran, especially in the papal palace and in the baptistery. Several architectural elements – columns, doorframes, stone slabs, and even a whole staircase – were declared monumental relics related to the life of Christ and his saints.[1] The step-by-step appearance of those new relics and of the related legends can be followed in the pilgrim accounts and further sources of the fifteenth and early sixteenth centuries.[2] After the destruction of the medieval palace under Sixtus V in the late 1580s, several of these objects, by then distinguished as a part of the Lateran's pious traditions, were displayed in new contexts. While the most prominent of these objects,

---

[1] Similar creations of new relic identities for older objects can be traced for example at the Vatican basilica. Outstanding examples are the 'Colonna Santa' or the 'Cathedra Petri', analysed recently by Carola Jäggi: C. Jäggi, 'Cathedra Petri und Colonna Santa in St. Peter zu Rom: Überlegungen zu "Produktion" und Konjunktur von Reliquien im Mittelalter', in A. Bergmeier, K. Palmberger and J. E. Sanzo (eds.), *Erzeugung und Zerstörung von Sakralität zwischen Antike und Mittelalter* (Distant World Journal Special Issue 1) (Heidelberg, 2016), 109–31, http://books.ub.uni-heidelberg.de/propylaeum/catalog/book/188.

[2] For this contribution, the following exemplary sources were analysed: pilgrim accounts and guidebooks: Coppart de Velaines (in P. Lauer, *Le palais de Latran: Étude historique et archéologique* (Paris, 1911); G. Rucellai, *Zibaldone quaresimale: Della bellezza e anticaglia di Roma* (1450), in R. Valentini and G. Zucchetti, *Codice topografico della città di Roma*, 4 vols. (Fonti per la Storia d'Italia 90) (Rome, 1940–53), IV, 405–8); J. Capgrave, *Ye solace of pilgrims: A description of Rome, circa AD 1450, by John Capgrave, an Austin Friar of King's Lynn*, ed. C. A. Mills (Oxford, 1911); N. Muffel, *Descrizione della città di Roma nel 1452: Delle indulgenze e dei luoghi sacri di Roma (Der ablas und die heiligen stet zu Rom)*, ed. and trans. G. Wiedmann (Bologna, 1999); Anonymous, *Mirabilia Romae: Ein deutsches Blockbuch vom Ende des XV. Jahrhunderts* (c. 1475), ed. R. Ehwald (Berlin, 1903); G. Dati, *Statione/indulgetie reliqe di Roma scta* (n.p., c. 1500); Fra Mariano da Firenze, *Itinerarium urbis Romae* (1517), ed. E. Bulletti (Studi di antichità cristiana 2) (Rome, 1931 [1518]); A. Palladio, *Descritione de le Chiese, Stationi, Indulgenze et reliquie de Corpi Sancti che sonno in la Città de Roma* (1554), repr., ed. L. Puppi (Vicenza, 2000); Anonymous, *Le cose maravigliose dell'alma città di Roma* ... (Rome, 1575). Ceremonial diaries: J. Burckard, *Johannis Burchardi Argentinensis capelle pontificio sacrorum rituum magistri diarium, sive Rerum urbanarum commentarii (1483–1506): Texte latin publié intégralement pour la primiere fois d'après les manuscrits de Paris, de Rome et de Florence, avec introduction, notes, appendices, tables et index par L. Thuasne* (1484), ed. L. Thuasne, 2 vols. (Paris, 1884), I, 1483–92; P. de Grassis, *Diario di Leone – di Paride de Grassi ... dai volumi manoscritti degli Archivi Vaticani della S. Sede con note di M. Armellini, mons. Pio Delicati*, ed. P. Delicati and M. Armellini (Rome, 1884).

the Scala Santa, was united with the chapel of Sancta Sanctorum in a new building by Domenico Fontana, other objects wandered at first to the eastern portico of the Lateran basilica, then to the choir ambulatory, and finally to the cloister, where they can be visited to this day as part of the 'lapidary' of the Lateran's eventful history.

This chapter will focus on the objects related to the life and Passion of Christ, leaving aside others such as the memorial relics related to the emperor Constantine.[3] I will argue that the 'invention' made use both of the Lateran relic traditions and of contemporaneous devotional trends and that, as a whole, it was meant not only as a series of relics, but also as a veritable translocated Passion topography.

## The New Passion Relics at the Lateran

As can be deduced from the examined pilgrims' accounts, the new Passion relics of the Lateran not only formed a thematic ensemble but were also visited in a particular order (Figs 20.1a, 20.1b). Although this is never specifically mentioned, we may presume that the visitors were guided, most likely by a member of the basilica's chapter, and received explanations about the objects. The same route had probably been used by pilgrims in the Middle Ages since it corresponds with the traditional ceremonial itinerary connecting the Lateran baptistery, the basilica and the palace chapel of San Lorenzo (Sancta Sanctorum).[4] The new relics were placed 'along the way' and were intended to fill up the 'void' between the basilica and the chapel of Sancta Sanctorum, transforming the palace's representational room sequence into a sacred space.

The tour began at the baptistery, the legendary place of the emperor Constantine's baptism and conversion to Christendom. Among a number of memorial relics visualising the Constantinian tradition of the Lateran, the pilgrims were also shown some Holy Land relics: for example, two columns at the altar of the chapel of the Holy Cross believed to come from Mary's house at Nazareth[5] or two octagonal pillars with iron rings placed in the portico of the same chapel, which are displayed today in the basilica's

---

[3] For the Constantinian tradition of the complex and its consequences in relic creation and veneration, see K. L. Bierbaum, *Die Ausstattung des Lateranbaptisteriums unter Urban VIII.* (Petersberg, 2014), esp. 35–48.

[4] See Blaauw, *CD* I, 290–304, explaining the Easter liturgy at the Lateran.

[5] See D. Senekovic, 'S. Giovanni in Fonte und S. Croce in Laterano', in P. C. Claussen, *Die Kirchen der Stadt Rom in Mittelalter 1050–1300, Bd. 2: San Giovanni in Laterano* (Corpus Cosmatorum II, 2) (Forschungen zur Kunstgeschichte und Christlichen Archäologie 21) (Stuttgart, 2008), 355–93, at pp. 389–90.

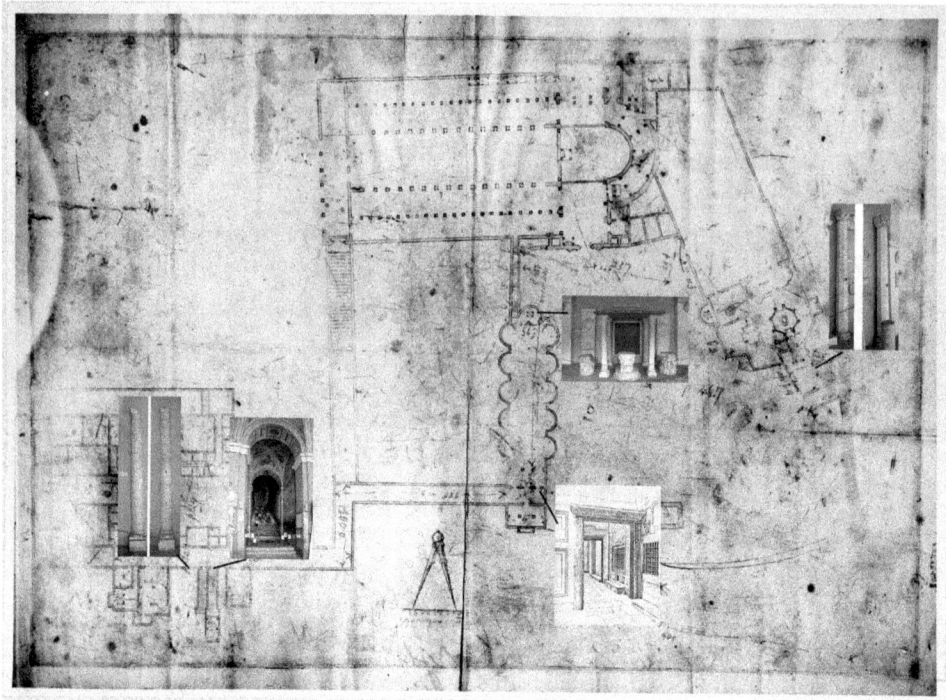

**Fig. 20.1** The 'new relics' marked in the so-called archive plan, workshop of Domenico Fontana (?), 1585-6, etching, Rome, Archivio Capitolare Lateranense (Photo: Bibliotheca Hertziana, Rome, modified by Nadja Horsch).

cloister (Figs 20.2a, 20.2b).[6] These pillars, probably of late medieval origin, were said to come from the entrance of Pilate's palace in Jerusalem. According to the relic list *Tabula Magna Lateranensis*, the rings originally served as flag holders; while the German pilgrim Nikolaus Muffel writes that they were used to tether horses.[7]

After having left the baptistery, the pilgrims entered the basilica of San Giovanni in Laterano. This central part of the pious visit was dedicated to the veneration of the famous relic treasures of the basilica. Via a staircase in the

---

[6] See E. Josi, *Il chiostro lateranense: Cenni storici e illustrazione* (Vatican City, 1970), no. 94; Senekovic, 'S. Giovanni in Fonte', 390–1.

[7] *Tabula Magna Lateranensis* (c. 1518), in Lauer, *Le palais de Latran*, 296–301, at p. 300: 'Item in Porticum ejusdem Capellae duae sunt aliae columnae marmoreae, quae erant ante Domum Pilati, ubi pendebant vexilla, quae se inclinaverunt Christo transeunte.' See also Muffel, *Descrizione*, 28–30: 'zwu seulen von alabaster mit zweyen pleyen kreutzen, daryn zwey lochereten eysen vermacht sind, darein man dye fackelen vor Pylatushauß und stigen zu sehen eingesteckt hat, do Cristus durchgefurt worden bey nacht.' For the location of the octagonal piers, see Senekovic, 'S. Giovanni in Fonte', 390.

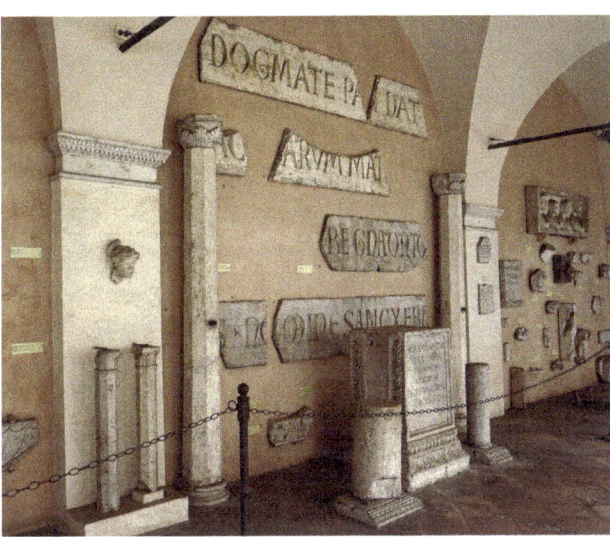

Fig. 20.2a  Two octagonal pillars 'from Pilate's palace', cloister of San Giovanni in Laterano (Photo: N. Horsch).

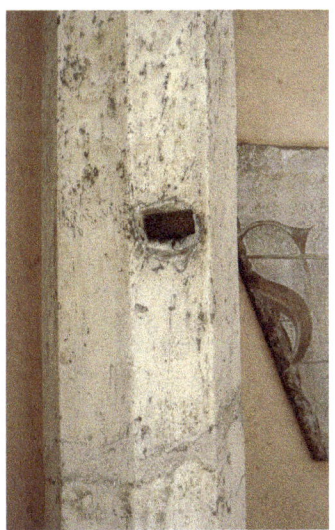

Fig. 20.2b  Detail of a column shaft with iron ring (Photo: N. Horsch).

northern aisle of the basilica, the pilgrims then reached the first floor of the connected palace, continuing with the most important 'new relics'.[8] Visits to

---

[8] See the most recent reconstruction of the palace's complex building history and disposition in M. Luchterhandt, 'Päpstlicher Palastbau und höfisches Zeremoniell unter Leo III.', in C. Stiegemann and M. Wemhoff (eds.), *799: Kunst und Kultur der Karolingerzeit: Karl der Große und Papst Leo III. in Paderborn* (Mainz, 1999), 109–22. In general, see P. Liverani (ed.), *Giornata di studio tematica dedicata al Patriarcato Lateranense: Atti della giornata tematica dei Seminari di*

the palace started in the large Carolingian eleven-conche *aula*, constructed by Pope Leo III (795–816) for ceremonial purposes and later known as Aula Concilii. In front of the main apse of this sumptuous room stood a structure called the *mensura Christi*, the 'measure of Christ', documented by several written sources as well as by a drawing by Pompeo Ugonio (BAV, Cod. Barb. lat. 2160, fol.157v). This object, which could be called a 'multifunctional' relic of Christ and his Passion, can be visited today in the cloister's west aisle (Figs 20.3a, 20.3b).[9] Its four marble columns of uncertain date were believed to indicate the height of Christ's body,[10] while the granite slab on the top was said to be the table on which the thirty pieces of silver were handed over to Judas. Furthermore, the framed porphyry slab placed today on the wall behind the *mensura* is mentioned by Muffel in 1452 as part of the relic ensemble: he locates it 'under' the *mensura* and tells us that this had been the place where the dice were thrown by the soldiers under the Cross to gain the unsewn garment of Christ. According to other sources, both events happened on the granite slab.[11] After the *mensura*'s transfer to the choir ambulatory of the Lateran church in 1646, the porphyry slab bore the image of three dice and was commented by the inscription 'Et super vestem meam miserunt sortes' placed next to the porphyry slab.[12]

---

*Archeologia Cristiana (École française de Rome, 10 maggio 2001)* (*MEFRA* 116, 1) (special issue) (Rome, 2004). One of the most important sources is the description by Onofrio Panvinio (in Lauer, *Le palais de Latran*, 410–90).

[9] See Claussen, *Die Kirchen der Stadt Rom*, 339–40; Josi, *Il chiostro lateranense*, no. 165–8; Lauer, *Le palais de Latran*, 103–4. P. Ugonio, *Historia delle stationi di Roma* (Rome, 1588), 37–9, saw the object after its translocation in the basilica's transept. Some years later, the *mensura* ensemble was shown in the western portico near the chapel of Saint Thomas (see for example Lauer, *Le palais de Latran*, 233, citing the description by the pilgrim Vinchant of 1610, or G. Baglione, *Le nove chiese di Roma*, ed. L. Barroero (Rome, 1990 [1639]). The Lateran canon Carlo Paolucci de Calboli transferred it in 1646 to the apse ambulatory: see Claussen, *Die Kirchen der Stadt Rom*, 349. Under Clement XII, it was finally transferred to the cloister.

[10] The first textual source for this interpretation of the columns seems to be Burckard, *Johannis Burchardi*, 106. Claussen, *Die Kirchen der Stadt Rom*, 341: 'Ob die Säulen mittelalterlich sind, ist schwer zu entscheiden. Die korinthischen Kapitelle wirken so, als seien sie im Quattrocento entstanden.'

[11] See Muffel, *Descrizione*, 38: 'Item als man dieselben stigen hinauf in sal kompt, do stet ein preiter stein auf vier seulen auf dem man die XXX pfennig jude, dem verretter Christi zalt hat, und unter dem stein ligt ein stein, auf dem das gewant Christi geteilt und gelost ist worden.' The legends were merged in the *Tabula Magna Lateranensis*: 'Item in cappella ... est lapis quadratus quatuor columnis marmoreis, sub cujus ... altitudo Domini Nostri Jesu Christi, antequam crucifigeretur, staturam corporisque magnitudinem denotat, supra quem numerati fuerunt triginta denarii a Judaeis Judae traditori, ac etiam a Judaeis super Christi vestem jactae sortes' (in Lauer, *Le palais de Latran*, 298).

[12] See Claussen, *Die Kirchen der Stadt Rom*, 341 n. 1406, citing two texts: Mellini, transcript by Francesco de Vico (ACL, FFXXII): 'v'era ià affissa trà due colonne ottagone di marmo bianco ... una tavola di porfido alta pal. 511, e larga pal. 4.8 col motto sopra: Et super vestem meam

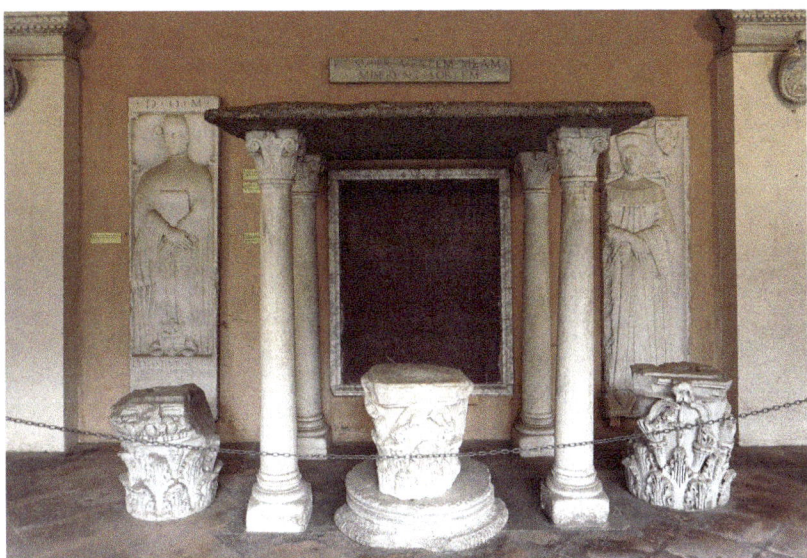

Fig. 20.3a  The *mensura Christi*, cloister of San Giovanni in Laterano (Photo: N. Horsch).

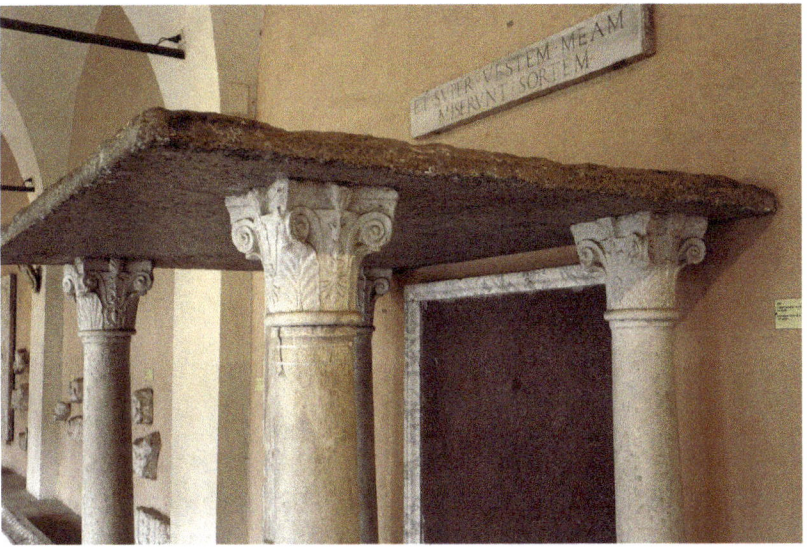

Fig. 20.3b  Close-up of the upper part of the *mensura Christi* (Photo: N. Horsch).

Proceeding to the northern end of the Aula Concilii, the pilgrims visited three antique marble doorframes, which formed part of a twofold screen

miserunt sortem.' Martinelli, ebd.: 'Pietra di porfido, ornata con pittura di tre dadi, con l'iscrittione super vestem meam miserunt sortem.'

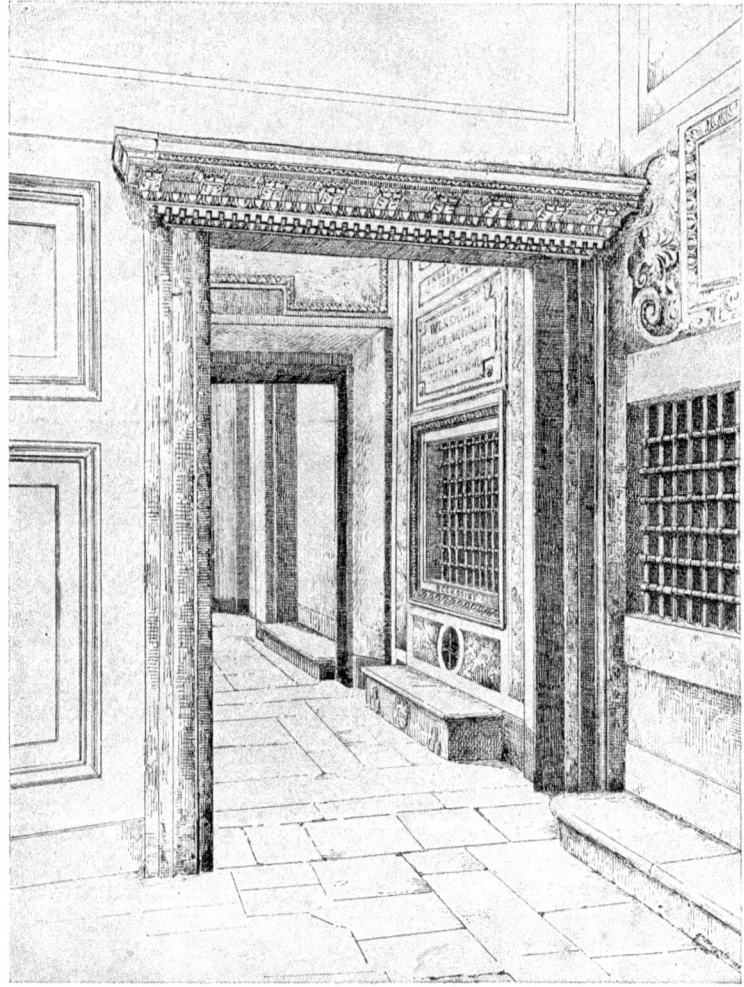

Fig. 20.4 One of the three Pilate doors in the upper corridor of the Scala Santa building (in Grisar, *Die römische Kapelle*, 27).

architecture, formerly the representative entrance to this important ceremonial space. The pilgrims were told that the doors came from Pilate's palace in Jerusalem and that Christ had passed through them during his trial. When Fontana constructed the new building for the Scala Santa in 1587–9, he inserted the three doorframes into the upper corridor of the edifice (Fig. 20.4).[13]

---

[13] See N. Horsch, *Ad astra gradus: Scala Santa und Sancta Sanctorum in Rom unter Sixtus V. (1585–1590)* (Munich, 2014), 80.

Having passed these 'Pilate doors', the pilgrims continued through the long portico of Leo III, the *macrona*, and visited next the chapel of Saint Silvester, where further holy objects were shown. The fifteenth-century sources mention a stone with the cast of Christ's five fingers, while in the sixteenth century the pilgrims were shown a window from Mary's house in Nazareth. Unfortunately, these objects have not survived.[14]

The principal entrance of the palace was next to the chapel of Saint Silvester, where a white marble staircase of twenty-eight steps led down to the Campus Lateranensis. This staircase was associated with Pilate's palace as well; it was called Scala Santa because the Saviour had allegedly walked on it. Under Sixtus V the staircase was joined with the chapel of Sancta Sanctorum in the before-mentioned building by Fontana. The Scala Santa has proved to be by far the most successful of the Lateran's new relics, and is still highly venerated today (Fig. 20.5).[15]

Near the entrance of the palace 'the first bells of the world' were shown (not preserved),[16] as well as the two beautiful antique half-columns today in the cloister, covered with finely sculpted foliage and decorated with relief bands showing dancing maenads (Figs 20.6a, 20.6b). The legend said that they were the two halves of a single column that had stood in Jerusalem (either again in Pilate's palace or in the Temple of Solomon) and split at the moment of Christ's death.[17] The relic tour through the Lateran ended – and reached its second climax – with a visit to (or the view into) the chapel of Sancta Sanctorum with the *acheiropoieton* image of Christ.

## How to Create New Relics (And Why?)

It took about thirty years to complete this new ensemble of relics in the Lateran palace and baptistery. The first source for the process is the description by the French pilgrim Coppart de Velaines who dwelt in Rome in 1424. Coppart mentions a split column, although with a different

---

[14] The stone is described by, among others, Muffel, *Descrizione*, 38; the window is mentioned in Anonymous, *Le cose maravigliose*.

[15] For the history of the Scala Santa, see Horsch, *Ad astra gradus*; L. Donadono, *La Scala Santa a San Giovanni in Laterano* (Rome, 2000); M. Cempanari and T. Amodei, *La Scala Santa* (Le chiese di Roma illustrate, nuova serie 23) (Rome, 1989).

[16] The bells are mentioned e.g. by John Capgrave, *Ye solace of pilgrims*, 74: 'A litil ferther in that cloystir hang the first bellis that euyr wer mad.'

[17] This connection is confirmed by the description by G. A. Brutius (*Theatrum Romanae urbis sive Romanorum sacrae aedes*, BAV, Vat. Lat. 11873, fol. 373r), cited by Claussen, *Die Kirchen der Stadt Rom*, 339, n. 1395. Brutius mentions the inscription 'Et petrae scissae sunt' above the column halves.

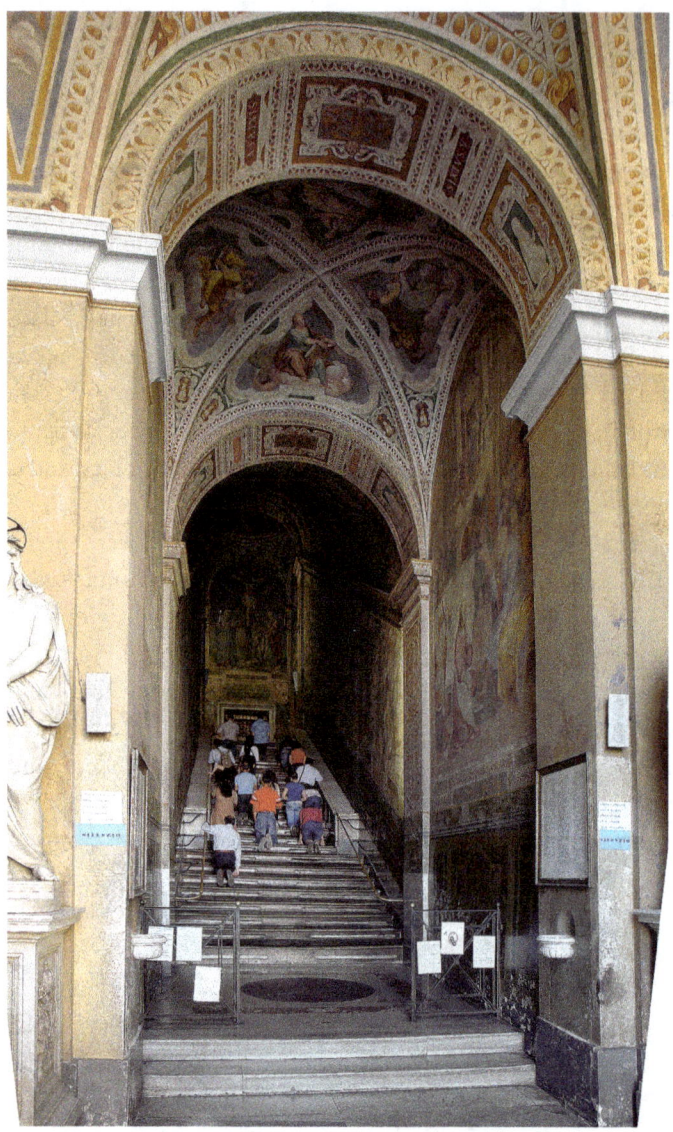

**Fig. 20.5** The Scala Santa with pilgrims (Photo: Michael Imhof).

legend, as well as a stone on which Christ rested during his way to Golgotha. Although the locations given by Coppart are very obscure, the objects are probably identifiable with the described split column and the stone with Christ's fingerprints.[18] By far the greatest number of relic creations can be dated around 1450. Several detailed accounts especially by

---

[18] 'En l'église S. Jehan du Latran est la colonne que Noste [*sic*] Sire fendit a son doit et le pierre sur quoy il se repossa quant il porta le crois': Coppart in Lauer, *Le palais de Latran*, 275–6 (fol. 23).

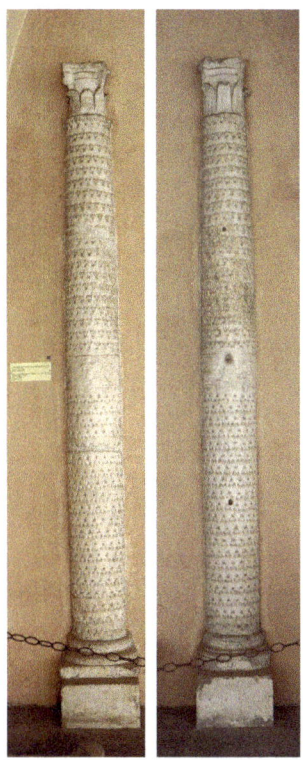

**Fig. 20.6a** The 'split column', cloister of San Giovanni in Laterano (Photo: N. Horsch).

foreign pilgrims such as Nikolaus Muffel from Augsburg or the Englishman John Capgrave already list an impressive range of new relics.[19] The oral origin of the inventions becomes clear considering the differences in the relic lists and explanations given by the authors. For example, Muffel mentions the stone slab on top of the *mensura Christi* and the dice legend, but he does not know the *mensura* legend. Capgrave offers a different explanation for the stone slab.[20] The identification of the columns with Christ's body height appears for the first time in the diary of the papal master of ceremony, Johannes Burckard, describing in 1484 the pope's entry into the Aula Concilii.[21] The wording, however, suggests that he

---

[19] Muffel, *Descrizione*, 28 and 30; Capgrave, *Ye solace of pilgrims*.
[20] Capgrave, *Ye solace of pilgrims*, 73–4.
[21] Burckard, *Johannis Burchardi*, 106: ' ... ascendit per basilicam predictam ad palatium Lateranense, et cum pervenisset ad primam aulam magnam que aula concilii nuncupatur, positum fuit faldistorium ante gradus lapidis, super quatuor columnas positi, qui mensura Christi apellatur ubi Papa sedit'.

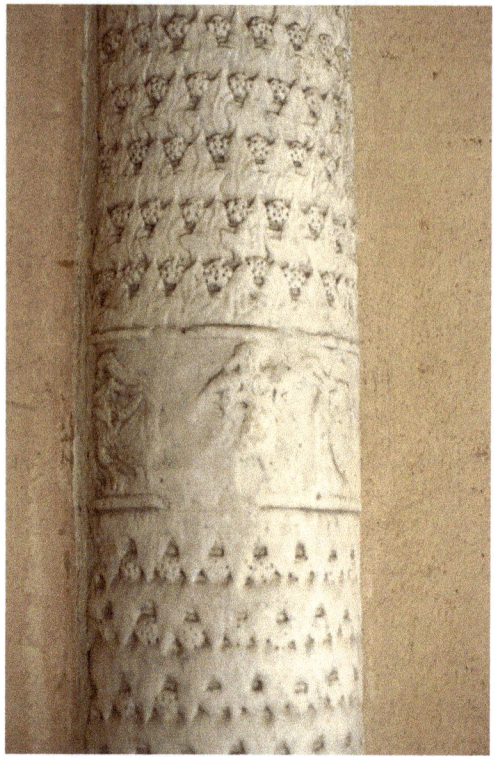

**Fig. 20.6b** Detail of a shaft with foliage and maenad relief (Photo: N. Horsch).

refers to an established tradition.[22] The ensemble of new relics seems to have been complete around 1520, as can be deduced from the actualised version of the *Tabula Magna Lateranensis*, dating from the pontificate of Leo X.[23] The pilgrim guides of the sixteenth century usually mention at least the *mensura*, the three doors, the Scala Santa and the split column.[24]

Of course, it would be very interesting to know whose idea it was to convert the profane palace architecture into an ensemble of Passion relics. Unfortunately, a simple answer to that question is difficult to give, but it seems likely that the inventor(s) must be looked for in the Lateran chapter. On the one hand, the canons, responsible for the pastoral care of the pious visitors, could have created the relic ensemble as an answer to pilgrims' expectations and desires; on the other, the general difficult condition of

---

[22] This can be shown by the analysis of some pictorial sources: see below.
[23] *Tabula Magna Lateranensis*, in Lauer, *Le palais de Latran*, 296–301.
[24] See for example Palladio, *Descritione de le Chiese*, 16–17.

the Lateran in the fifteenth century may somehow have forced the canons to action.

There are mainly two circumstances pointing in that direction and helping to explain the phenomenon. Firstly, the Holy Year of 1450 was expected to bring an unprecedented number of pilgrims to the Holy City, so the Lateran canons looked for strategies to emphasise – and to enhance – the Lateran's importance as an attractive devotional hotspot.[25] Second, the initiative can also be contextualised in the centuries-old competition for primacy between the Lateran and the Vatican. The striving to underline the Lateran's primacy had become even more urgent after the pope's decision to transfer the residence permanently to the Vatican. This choice had been the culmination of the Lateran's gradual loss of importance, which had begun with the Avignon exile of the popes and was aggravated by two major fires in the basilica during the fourteenth century. Although several popes (for example, Eugenius VI and Martin V) had tried to restore the former glory of the complex, it could no longer bear comparison with the new centre of papal power, the Vatican.[26]

We may thus presume that focusing on the Lateran's pious qualities was meant as a compensation for the definitive loss of its residential and representative functions. While during past controversies over the role of 'caput et mater ecclesiarum' the Lateran faction had principally based their argument on the Constantinian foundation of the Lateran and its status as the true seat of the Roman bishop, relics were already being called upon as arguments too. This is manifested, for example, by the long and fantastic relic lists given by John the Deacon in its *Descriptio Lateranensis Ecclesiae*, based on a text of the eleventh century.[27]

Given the experience of the first three 'Holy Years', Rome expected thousands of foreign, especially northern European, pilgrims to come to the city in 1450.[28] It seems very likely that the pious 'relabelling' of the palace furniture was invented primarily with regard to this special audience. The foreign pilgrims were not able – or were not keen – to interpret correctly the heterogeneous building complex attached to the Lateran basilica. Instead of perceiving the walk up from the basilica to the palace as a transition from a sacred to a profane space, the route is described as a continuous whole; the German *Mirabilia* text of around 1475 even refers to the *aula* as a further

---

[25] For the Holy Year of 1450, see M. Miglio, 'Il giubileo di Niccolò V (1450)', in G. Fossi (ed.), *La storia dei giubilei*, 2 vols. (Rome, 1998), II, 56–73.

[26] For a detailed account of the Lateran's history, see Lauer, *Le palais de Latran*.

[27] See below, as well as Jäggi, Chapter 15 in this volume.

[28] See Miglio, 'Il giubileo di Niccolò V'.

'chapel'.²⁹ Only rarely is a specific explanation attempted; Muffel, for example, was told that the *aula* had been Constantine's 'town hall'; Palladio mentions its function as the venue of the Fifth Lateran Council.³⁰

Consequently, the first evidence for the new relics is found in non-Roman sources, both written and visual. For example, an altarpiece by Hans Burgkmair the Elder (1502) – who had never been in Rome but relied on the accounts of his compatriots – shows a fantastic view of Saint John Lateran resembling a collage of the complex's devotional hotspots combined with scenes from the title saints' legends (Fig. 20.7). At the side-aisle of the fictive basilica there is the first more detailed representation of the Scala Santa, venerated by northern European pilgrims.³¹

By contrast, the relics were approved in official Roman sources only gradually from the late 1480s onwards. The first hints of the new relics are found in the ceremonial diaries of Johannes Burckard and Paris de Grassis, mentioning respectively the *mensura Christi* (in 1484) and the Scala Santa (in 1513).³² The relics were officially 'approved' in the above-mentioned version of the *Tabula Magna Lateranensis* relic list, dating from the pontificate of Leo X.³³

In the following I will try to explain how this 'invented tradition' was constructed and why it was able to convince the visitors. I will propose that the devotional success of the 'palace relics' is due to their multifaceted interlinking with older Lateran traditions on the one hand and with popular and 'up-to-date' themes and practices of late medieval piety on the other.

## Lateran Traditions: Passion and Holy Land Relics

The relic traditions of the Lateran differed considerably from Saint Peter's or other martyr basilicas. At the centre of the representational strategies stood the Constantinian foundation, not the gathering at a saint's tomb. The first datable relics – the treasure of the papal palace chapel Sancta Sanctorum and perhaps the Cross relic of the baptistery – date from the

---

[29] Anonymous, *Mirabilia Romae*, without pagination.
[30] Muffel, *Descrizione*, 38: 'den sal, das Constantinus rathauß gewest ist'; Palladio, *Descritione de le Chiese*, 16.
[31] See Horsch, *Ad astra gradus*, 82–3; M. Gärtner, *Römische Basiliken in Augsburg: Nonnenfrömmigkeit und Malerei um 1500* (Augsburg, 2002).
[32] See Horsch, *Ad astra gradus*, 75–83.
[33] See text of the *Tabula Magna* in Lauer, *Le palais de Latran*, 296–301.

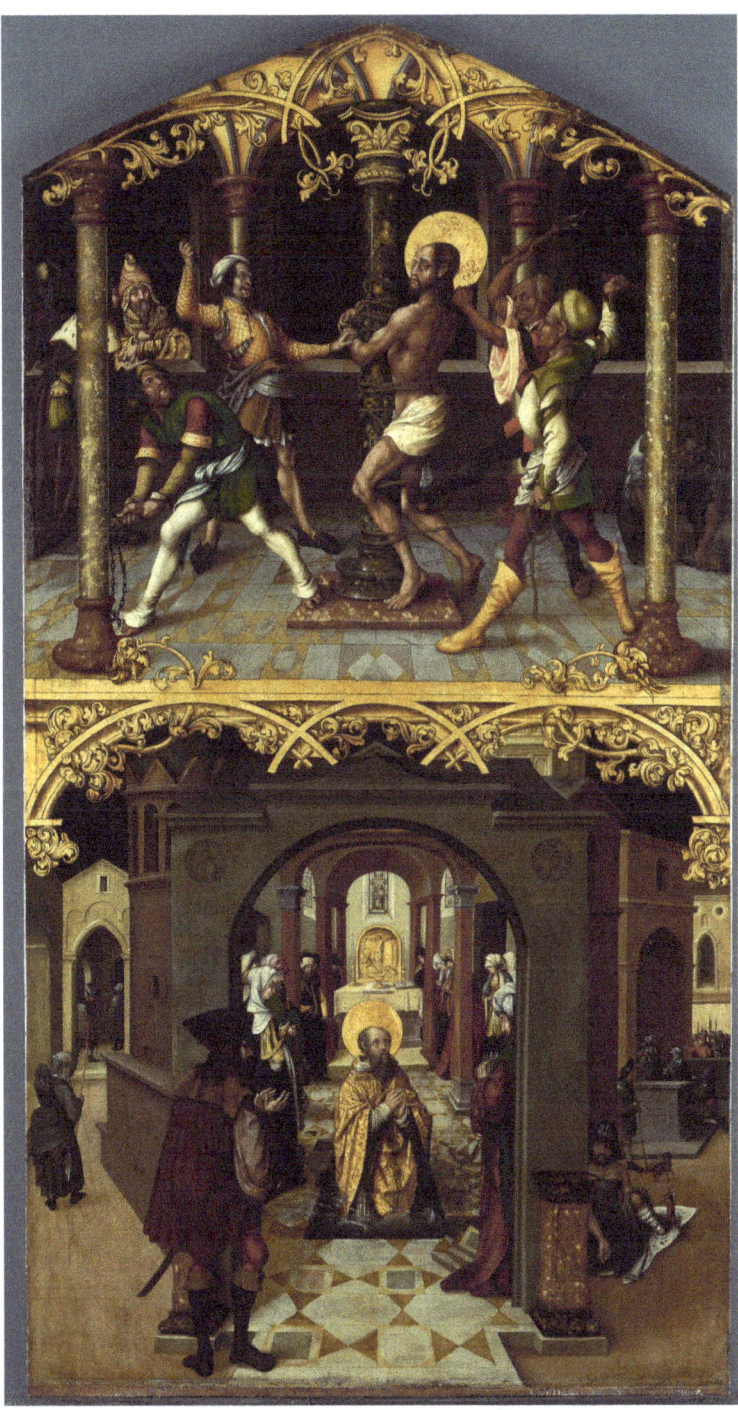

**Fig. 20.7** Hans Burgkmair, central panel of the triptych *San Giovanni in Laterano*, from a series of seven altar pieces dedicated to the principal Roman Churches, oil on wood, 1502. Augsburg, Bayerische Staatsgemäldesammlungen. The Scala Santa is shown on the lower part of the panel on the right side (Photo: ©bpk – Bildagentur für Kunst, Kultur und Geschichte).

sixth, maybe even the fifth, century and already show two focal points: Christological and Holy Land relics.[34]

The basilica, dedicated to Christ the Saviour (Basilica Salvatoris), played an important role in the Holy Week liturgy and possessed an impressive amount of Christological and especially Passion relics. Among them, relics of the Holy Blood, the legendary *praeputium*, fragments of the Holy Cross, the *mensa Domini* of the Last Supper as well as several garments and the 'sandals' of Christ.[35] Moreover, the Lateran claimed to possess two *acheiropoieta*: the famous icon kept in the Sancta Sanctorum chapel and the mosaic image of Christ in the apse of the basilica, believed to have appeared miraculously on the wall during the consecration of the church by Pope Sylvester.[36]

A further *topos* of Lateran relic propaganda, intimately linked with the Christological theme by a typological argumentation,[37] was the traditional claim to possess objects from the Holy Land, especially from the Temple of Jerusalem. While in the palace chapel of San Lorenzo were kept earth, stones and fragments from legendary sites of the Holy Land, partly in the wall behind the altar, partly in a small casket with painted lid,[38] the basilica

---

[34] Blaauw, *CD* I, 163-7 for an overview of the different relic groups at the Lateran, 167 for Sancta Sanctorum. The objects referring to the Constantinian tradition and to the two Saint Johns cannot be discussed here. For the Sancta Sanctorum treasure, see also H. Grisar, *Die römische Kapelle Sancta Sanctorum und ihr Schatz: Meine Entdeckungen und Studien in der Palastkapelle der mittelalterlichen Päpste* (Freiburg, 1908); G. Morello, 'Il tesoro del Sancta Sanctorum', in C. Pietrangeli (ed.), *Il Palazzo Apostolico Lateranense* (Florence, 1991), 91-106; E. Thunø, *Image and Relic: Mediating the Sacred in Medieval Rome* (Analecta Romana Instituti Danici, Supplementum 32) (Rome, 2002).

[35] The denomination 'Basilica Salvatoris' is documented since the seventh century: see Blaauw, *CD* I, 161. For the Lateran's role in Easter liturgy, see Blaauw, *CD* I, 290-308. The relic lists from the twelfth century onwards are reproduced in Lauer, *Le palais de Latran*. For a general discussion of the Christological relics' meaning, See S. de Blaauw, 'The solitary celebration of the supreme pontiff: The Lateran basilica as the new Temple in the medieval liturgy of Maundy Thursday', in C. Caspers and M. Schneiders (eds.), *Omnes circumadstantes: Contributions towards a History of the Role of the People in the Liturgy* (Kampen, 1990), 120-43.

[36] *Descriptio Lateranensis ecclesiae*, cit. after Lauer, *Le palais de Latran*, 395. For the legend's development, see Lauer, *Le palais de Latran*, 216-18.

[37] See J. M. Powell, 'Honorius III's "Sermo in dedicatione ecclesiae Lateranensis" and the historical-liturgical traditions of the Lateran', *Archivium historiae pontificiae* 21 (1983), 195-209; I. Herklotz, 'Der mittelalterliche Fassadenportikus der Lateranbasilika und seine Mosaiken: Kunst und Propaganda am Ende des 12. Jahrhunderts', *RJBH* 25 (1989), 25-95; de Blaauw, 'The solitary celebration'; Horsch, *Ad astra gradus*.

[38] *Descriptio Lateranensis ecclesiae*, cit. after Lauer, *Le palais de Latran*, 403. See Morello, 'Il tesoro del Sancta Sanctorum'; Thunø, *Image and Relic*; B. Reudenbach, 'Reliquien von Orten: Ein frühchristliches Reliquiar als Gedächtnisort', in B. Reudenbach and G. Toussaint (eds.), *Reliquiare im Mittelalter* (Berlin, 2005), 21-42; B. Reudenbach, '"Loca sancta": Zur materiellen Übertragung der heiligen Stätten', in B. Reudenbach (ed.), *Jerusalem, du Schöne: Vorstellungen und Bilder einer heiligen Stadt* (Vestigia Bibliae 28) (Bern, 2008), 9-32, at pp. 21-5.

counted among its most mysterious treasures several objects from the Temple's treasure (the Ark of the Covenant, the rods of Moses and Aaron and others) believed to have been brought to Rome by Titus and Vespasian after the destruction of Jerusalem and to have been given to the Lateran by Constantine.[39] The same provenance was assigned to the four large bronze columns now framing the altar of the Holy Sacrament.[40]

Both traditions can be situated in a larger context; while the basilicas of Saints Peter and Paul were constructed to encompass the Apostles' burial places and reacted to the already existing martyr cults, the Lateran and its environs were instead charged with references to the Holy Sites of Jerusalem.[41] These are documented since the middle of the fourth century, the time when a general interest in the Holy Land topography became manifest among the members of the Christian elite of Rome. The clearest evidence of this tradition is the church of Santa Croce in Gerusalemme, which not only houses a relic of the True Cross, but partly alludes to the topographical setting of the Golgotha sanctuary in Jerusalem.[42] Maybe, also the mention of a 'Pilate's house' near the Lateran in the *Itinerarium Einsidlense* alludes to the topographical analogies between the Lateran area and Jerusalem.[43] It is known that Santa Croce as well as the 'Bethlehem' of Rome, Santa Maria Maggiore, and the church of San Stefano, the first martyr, whose cult was intimately tied to Jerusalem, were linked to the Lateran by stationary masses on the High Feasts of the Easter and Christmas cycle. Relics such as the Cross fragments of Santa Croce and the Lateran have since then been the principal media manifesting the Holy Land allusions and fixing them in Roman topography.[44]

It is evident that these traditions were intimately known and instrumentalised by the relic inventors of the fifteenth century. They refer to already existing relic categories and themes, fill up gaps and sometimes even try to surpass the traditional objects. For example, the bloodstains on the Scala

---

[39] See de Blaauw, 'The solitary celebration', 126–8; Herklotz, 'Der mittelalterliche Fassadenportikus', 71–80.

[40] See Blaauw, *CD* I, 176–7; J. Freiberg, *The Lateran in 1600: Christian Concord in Counter-Reformation Rome* (Cambridge, 1995).

[41] See H. Grisar, *Analecta Romana: Dissertazioni, testi, monumenti dell'arte riguardanti principalmente la storia di Roma e dei papi nel Medio Evo. Volume Primo* (Rome, 1899); C. C. Sahner, 'Hierusalem in Laterano: The translation of sacred space in fifth century Rome', in A. Lidov (ed.), *New Jerusalems: Hierotopy and Iconography of Sacred Spaces* (Moscow, 2009), 103–30, with reference to R. Krautheimer, *Rom: Schicksal einer Stadt, 312–1308* (Munich, 1996), 67–71.

[42] See Grisar, *Analecta Romana*; S. de Blaauw, 'Jerusalem in Rome and the cult of the Cross', in R. L. Colella and R. Krautheimer (eds.), *Pratum Romanum: Richard Krautheimer zum 100. Geburtstag* (Wiesbaden, 1997), 55–73; Sahner, 'Hierusalem in Laterano'.

[43] *Itinerarium Einsidlense*, cit. after C. Hülsen, *La Pianta di Roma dell'Anonimo Einsidlense* (Rome, 1907), at p. 29. See the discussion in Horsch, *Ad astra gradus*, 75, and below.

[44] See Grisar, *Analecta Romana*; de Blaauw, 'Jerusalem in Rome'.

Santa refer to the holy blood relic; the *mensura Christi* or the handprint on the stone are linked to the bodily appearance of Christ and thus to the older *acheiropoieta* tradition; while the architectural fragments of Jerusalem buildings refer to the Passion as well as to the tradition of Holy Land relics at the Lateran. A 'prototype' for the many column relics is clearly offered by the bronze columns of the main altar; they are likewise architectural elements of considerable size believed to have been transported from Jerusalem to Rome.

The attempt to enhance these traditions by the invention of new relics must also be seen in the light of the latent rivalry between the Lateran and the Vatican. Despite the high ranking of several Lateran relics in the hierarchy of relics, and despite the attempt to create a Roman Holy Land topography based on relics, the Lateran obviously could not compete in the pilgrims' favour with Saint Peter's tomb. This problem goes back to Constantinian times when the emperor wished to make the Lateran the centre of a new Christian topography but obviously failed to take into sufficient account the important Christian tradition of gathering at a martyr's tomb.[45] The dedication to Christ the Saviour, the Holy Land allusions and the Constantinian foundation were strong theological and political arguments for the Lateran's role as 'mater ecclesiarum urbis et orbis', but they were too abstract to create an emotional identification by the Christian community of Rome with its cathedral or to attract as many foreign pilgrims as Saint Peter's. Moreover, despite the long relic lists in the descriptions, the exact disposition of the relics remained rather obscure; there was obviously no clear target for the visitors' devotions.[46]

Therefore, different strategies had already been used throughout the Middle Ages at the Lateran to improve the visual reception and thus the emotional impact of the relics. Several of them were involved in mass religious manifestations marking high days in the liturgical calendar of the Holy City. For example, the processions with the True Cross relic from the Lateran to Santa Croce, the ceremonial of Good Thursday during which a blood relic was extracted from the basilica's altar and shown to the people, or the assumption procession with the Salvator icon from Sancta Sanctorum to Santa Maria Maggiore.[47]

---

[45] See e.g. Krautheimer, *Rom*, 68.

[46] For the competition between Lateran and Vatican, see for instance Blaauw, *CD* I, 206–7; Herklotz, 'Der mittelalterliche Fassadenportikus'. For the obscure character of the relics, see de Blaauw, 'The solitary celebration', 126–7.

[47] See de Blaauw, 'The solitary celebration'; G. Wolf, *Salus Populi Romani: Die Geschichte römischer Kultbilder im Mittelalter* (Weinheim, 1990).

The desire to enhance the visualisation of the relics was also essential for some architectural projects. The rebuilding of the San Lorenzo chapel by Nicholas III (1277–80), for example, emphasised its character as a Christian 'Sancta Sanctorum'. The visitors were allowed to look through a grille window in the chapel's west wall into a precious realm of the holy, with hundreds of relics stored in the darkness of grille deposits and the non-handmade icon of Christ enthroned on the altar. Likewise, the outstanding grille ciborium with the new bust reliquaries above the high altar of the basilica, ordered by Pope Urban V (1362–70) and possibly replacing an older precedent, was intended for the presentation of the heads of Saints Peter and Paul, which had formerly been stored in the Sancta Sanctorum. The ciborium 'cage' probably refers to the chapel's grille deposits, but once again it aimed at increasing the visibility and therefore the devotional impact of the holy objects.[48]

## The Palace Relics in the Context of Late Medieval Piety and Devotion

The new relics invented in the fifteenth century went one step further: they were freely accessible to pilgrims; they were not only visible, but touchable; and moreover, they captured the most important theme not only of the Lateran's pious tradition, but of fifteenth-century spirituality in general, the Passion of Christ.

As mentioned above, the concentration of Passion relics at the Lateran can be explained first and foremost by the Christological *patrocinium* of the Basilica Salvatoris, dedicated by Constantine to the victorious Christian God. Beginning with this imperial foundation, Christological relics were traditionally instrumentalised to prove and legitimise the power of sovereigns.[49] But from the twelfth century onwards especially, Passion relics played an increasingly important role for individual piety in western Europe too. Crusaders and pilgrims brought them from Byzantium and the Holy Land; monastic movements such as the Cistercians and later the mendicant orders propagated devotion to the Passion of Christ as the principal means of an emotional approach to God and opened it up

---

[48] See Mondini, Chapter 17 in this volume; Claussen, *Die Kirchen der Stadt Rom*, 190–2.

[49] See A. Grabar, *Martyrium: Recherches sur le culte des reliques et l'art chrétien antique*, 2 vols. (Paris, 1946), I, 561–5; H. A. Klein, 'The Crown of His Kingdom: Imperial ideology, palace ritual, and the relics of Christ's Passion', in M. Featherstone (ed.), *The Emperor's House: Palaces from Augustus to the Age of Absolutism* (Berlin, 2015), 201–12.

gradually for a large lay audience. This broad and partly non-intellectual public requested innovative medialisations of the sacred themes, affecting all fields of religious literature, art and devotional practices.[50]

## Amplification of the Passion Gospels

Alongside the enormous narrative and emotional amplification of the Passion Gospels in late medieval meditational literature (for example, the *Meditationes Vitae Christi*), there can be observed an increasing desire to venerate ever more and ever new relics of Christ's Passion capable of illustrating the details of Christ's sufferings as well as to channel religious emotions. What this could mean for pilgrimage had been shown prominently by the Vatican 'Veronica'.[51] The legend of this most coveted relic of the Middle Ages derived from amplification and merging of two biblical episodes which were connected to a material object. The result of this complex process, the image-relic of the Veronica, was able to physically connect core themes of Christian piety such as compassion, the physical appearance of Christ, the promise of a 'visio beatifica' in heaven and the healing power of Christ's touch – and it was ideally appropriate to receive the veneration of a large pilgrim public. Alongside outstanding examples such as the Veronica, an extreme multiplication of relic 'stock' can be observed all over Europe in the late Middle Ages. In particular, the category of secondary relics offered inexhaustible possibilities for the 'relicisation' of profane objects.

The most important reason for this trend is the increasing desire for materialised, graspable faith. The new Lateran relics were invented to satisfy this desire. Just like the detailed descriptions in Passion literature and iconography, the objects were able to fill some gaps in the canonical gospel texts. They too could be inserted more or less logically into existing, well-known narratives and offered a more concrete idea of some crucial events of

---

[50] See for instance T. A. Kemper, *Die Kreuzigung Christi: Motivgeschichtliche Studien zu lateinischen und deutschen Passionstraktaten des Spätmittelalters* (Münchener Texte und Untersuchungen zur deutschen Literatur des Mittelalters 131) (Tübingen, 2006); A. A. MacDonald, H. N. B. Ridderbos and R. M. Schlusemann (eds.), *The Broken Body: Passion Devotion in Late-Medieval Culture* (Groningen, 1998).

[51] See for instance H. Belting, *Das Bild und sein Publikum im Mittelalter: Form und Funktion früher Bildtafeln der Passion* (Berlin, 1981), 200–10; Wolf, *Salus Populi Romani*, 81–7; G. Wolf, '"Or fu sì fatta la sembianza vostra?" Sguardi alla "vera icona" e alle sue copie artistiche', in G. Morello and G. Wolf (eds.), *Il volto di Cristo* (Milan, 2000), 103–14; A. K. van Dijk, 'The Veronica, the *Vultus Christi* and the veneration of icons in medieval Rome', in R. McKitterick, J. Osborne, C. M. Richardson and J. Story (eds.), *Old Saint Peter's, Rome* (British School at Rome Monograph Series) (Cambridge, 2013), 229–56.

salvation history. This is true for example for the stone slabs placed on top and under the *mensura Christi*, related respectively to the delivery of the thirty pieces of silver to Judas (Matthew 26:15) and to the distribution of Christ's unsewn, seamless robe by the soldiers under the Cross (John 19:23–4). The stone slabs can be thus viewed as complementing the ensemble of the *arma Christi*, the objects involved in the sufferings of Christ. The *arma* had an interesting double identity: as relics and as symbols. Several *arma* had long been venerated as relics. This is true for the Holy Lance or the Crown of Thorns, and also for the unsewn robe, which was claimed not only for the cathedral of Trier, but also for the Lateran's treasure and thus directly related to the local tradition.[52] Furthermore, the *arma* formed an iconographical complex which played an important role in late medieval piety. Often paired with the *imago pietatis* of the suffering Christ, these objects and abbreviated scenes were meant as iconic signs helping the spectator's mind to memorise step by step the whole Passion story;[53] this is how the Lateran relics could be used too. Of course, the strange *mensura* object is not self-explaining like the *arma*, but the link to the Gospel text is made sure by the explanation of the presumed guide – and later by inscriptions and images too.[54]

Still wittier is the legend of the split column which alluded to the Gospel of Matthew (27:51–2): 'At that moment the curtain of the temple was torn in two from top to bottom. The earth shook, the rocks split.' The splitting of the column is thus explained 'logically' by the analogous splitting of the rocks. The Gospels do not mention a column, but the column calls the Bible verse – and thus the dramatic moment of Christ's death – to the pilgrim's mind and gives it a tangible form.[55]

A whole complex of new relics had the palace of Pilate as its presumed origin, a setting referred to very briefly in the Gospels (John 18–19, esp. 19:13) but forming part of the sacred topography of Jerusalem.[56] Not only

---

[52] For example in the *Descriptio Lateranensis Ecclesiae*: 'Tunica inconsultilis, quam fecit virgo Maria filio suo Domino nostro Jesu Christo (quae in morte ipsius a militibus sortita est … ', cit. after Lauer, *Le palais de Latran*, 396.

[53] For the *arma Christi*, see recently L. Cooper and A. Denny-Brown (eds.), *The Arma Christi in Medieval and Modern Material Culture: With a Critical Edition of 'O Vernicle'* (Farnham, 2014); see also Belting, *Das Bild und sein Publikum*, 100–2; R. Suckale, 'Arma Christi: Überlegungen zur Zeichenhaftigkeit mittelalterlicher Andachtsbilder', *Städel-Jahrbuch*, n.s. 6 (1977), 177–208.

[54] See above, note 12.

[55] The direct connection to the Bible verse is confirmed by the description by G. A. Brutius (*Theatrum Romanae urbis sive Romanorum sacrae aedes*, BAV, Vat. Lat. 11873, fol. 373r), cited by Claussen, *Die Kirchen der Stadt Rom*, 339 n. 1395: Brutius mentions the inscription 'Et petrae scissae sunt' above the column halves.

[56] See M. Halbwachs, *Stätten der Verkündigung im Heiligen Land: Eine Studie zum kollektiven Gedächtnis*, ed. S. Egger (Konstanz, 2003), 101–8.

the Scala Santa and the three doorframes, but also the octagonal piers with the iron rings at the baptistery were thought to come from this building. This remarkable issue probably has more than one explanation. First, it seems that the late Middle Ages generally saw an increased interest in the complex and ambiguous personality of the Roman praetor.[57] This interest becomes also evident in a range of newly created 'Pilate relics', not only at the Lateran, but also at Saint Peter's. Muffel, for example, was shown the 'basin of the handwashing' hanging next to the altar of Simon and Judas in the middle of the central nave;[58] a connotation applied also to a fountain basin in the courtyard of San Stefano at Bologna.[59] Moreover, I have already mentioned the tradition involving Pilate that had existed in the Lateran area since at least the ninth century. A *casa Pilati* is mentioned in the *Itinerarium Einsidlense* as well as in a pilgrims' guide of the fourteenth century; the Casa de' Crescenzi, a twelfth-century family palace near the Tiber, was known as 'Casa Pilati' too for some time.[60] A *scala Pilati* existed in the surroundings of the Lateran palace in the thirteenth century, although it cannot be identified convincingly with the later Scala Santa.[61] The reasons underlying the 'Pilate' associations of the area are very difficult to unveil. Most probably they can be explained by the above-mentioned general idea of Holy Land analogies in early Christian and medieval Rome. It is furthermore conceivable that the Lateran relic inventors of the fifteenth century chose the palace of the Roman governor as the pretended

---

[57] For the legends and sites related to Pilate, see A. Hoffmann and G. Wolf, 'Narrative and iconic space: From Pontius to Pilate', in Lidov (ed.), *New Jerusalems*, 395–409.

[58] 'Item darnach [next to the altar of Simon and Judas] hangt in der kirchen mitten das messenpeck [bronze basin], daraus Pylatus wasser nam und Christum darauf verurtelit zum tote von droung wegen der Juden': Muffel, *Descrizione*, 68 (explanations by the author).

[59] See R. Ousterhout, 'Flexible geography and transportable topography', in B. Kühnel (ed.), *The Real and Ideal Jerusalem in Jewish, Christian and Islamic Art: Studies in Honor of Bezalel Narkiss on the Occasion of His Seventieth Birthday* (Jewish Art 23/24) (Jerusalem, 1997/8), 393–404, at p. 397.

[60] *Itinerarium Einsidlense*, in Valentini and Zucchetti, *Codice topografico*, II, 193; the fourteenth-century *Mirabilia* text: Vat. Lat. 4265, fol. 214r. For the identification of the Casa de' Crescenzi with Pilate's palace, see Anonymous, *Le cose maravigliose*, 62. See the discussion in Horsch, *Ad astra gradus*, 72–5.

[61] See Horsch, *Ad astra gradus*, 72–5. The sources are two inventories of 1242 and 1300 documenting the real estates of the Lateran chapter, published in Lauer, *Le palais de Latran*, 491–6 and 505–7 (492 and 505 the 'scala Pilati'). Lauer, *Le palais de Latran*, 185, and C. D'Onofrio, *Scalinate di Roma* (Rome, 1973), 88, tried to identify the *scala Pilati* with the later Scala Santa. See an alternative interpretation in N. Horsch, 'Die Nordflanke des mittelalterlichen Lateranpalastes als "Bühne" des Papstes', in S. Albrecht (ed.), *Stadtgestalt und Öffentlichkeit: Die Entstehung politischer Räume in der Stadt der Vormoderne* (Veröffentlichungen des Zentralinstituts für Kunstgeschichte in München 24) (Cologne, 2010), 253–73.

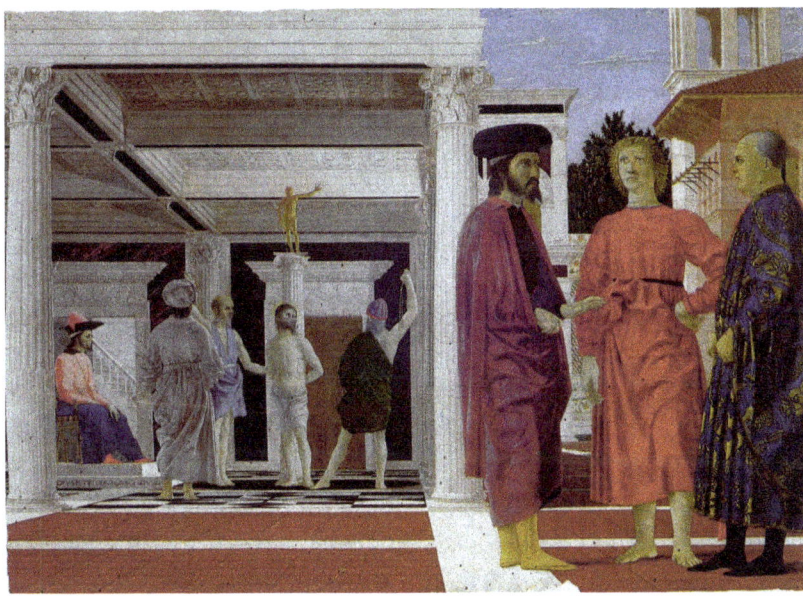

Fig. 20.8 The interior of Pilate's palace with the Scala Santa, the doorframes and a porphyry slab. Detail from Piero della Francesca, *Flagellation of Christ*, c. 1456–7, tempera on wood. Urbino, Galleria Nazionale delle Marche (Photo: Bildarchiv).

place of origin of the new relics just because several objects in question are in fact Antique *spolia* and could be thus associated convincingly with a Roman building.[62]

Interestingly, the Lateran fragments of Pilate's palace seem to have affected Passion iconography immediately, as has been shown for palace's depiction in Piero della Francesca's famous *Flagellation* (Fig. 20.8).[63] The antique doorframes and the stairway in the background of the scene were interpreted by Carlo Ginzburg as the 'Pilate doors' and the Scala Santa. I have added that the porphyry *rota* on which the flagellation takes place may also be a reference to the Lateran palace: comparable *rotae* lay next to the doors in the Aula Concilii as well as at the foot of the Scala Santa.[64]

This pseudo-archaeological (re)construction of Pilate's palace shows how objects were able to enrich the canonical account of the Gospels

---

[62] This has been proposed for the Casa de' Crescenzi by E. Amadei, *Le torri di Roma* (Rome, 1932), 113.

[63] See C. Ginzburg, *Erkundungen über Piero: Piero della Francesca, ein Maler der frühen Renaissance* (Frankfurt, 1991), 152–4; see also below. See Horsch, *Ad astra gradus*, 81–2, for a discussion of Ginzburg and further examples.

[64] See N. Horsch, 'Die Scala Santa im mittelalterlichen Lateranpalast: Eine neue Lektüre der Quellen', *Zeitschrift für Kunstgeschichte* 66 (2003), 524–32, at p. 530; Horsch, *Ad astra gradus*, 81.

with concrete details. Even if the objects were not mentioned in the text, they could be connected logically to specific sites and actions. Their role was to manifest visibly and materially the related site or action in the pilgrim's here and now and thus to fix it firmly in his devotional memory.[65]

## 'Need for Touch'

The new relics fulfilled this purpose not only by their material presence itself, but also by the performative 'dialogue' with the pilgrims that they produced. Compared to the traditional sacred treasures of the Lateran, the new relics offered enormously increased possibilities of multi-sensorial veneration. On the one hand, their absorption into a structured veneration practice distinguished by para-liturgical elements contributed to their transformation into holy objects;[66] on the other hand, they were able to satisfy the pilgrims' desire for 'materialised', graspable faith.

This is due largely to their specific character as 'architectural relics',[67] a subcategory of 'secondary' or 'contact relics'. Compared to bodily relics such as bones or teeth, which were distinguished by their substantial holiness, the secondary relics derived their *virtus* from physical contact with saintly persons. But unlike other secondary Passion relics (the Crown of Thorns, the Holy Lance, Christ's garments, the stones or earth from the Holy Land etc.), the Lateran relics are not small, mobile objects, but entire architectural elements, some of considerable dimensions. As translocated *partes pro toto*, they are able to suggest a very concrete idea of the original settings of Christ's Passion.[68]

This architectural, setting-like character had crucial consequences for the veneration practices too. Other than the 'holy bones' and the 'traditional' secondary relics, wrapped in paper or cloth, stored in chests and coffers and shown to the faithful on rare occasions and often from a safe distance, the new relics were venerated with practices resembling those performed traditionally at Holy Sites: they could be viewed up close; they could be circled, touched, kneeled upon and kissed – they perfectly satisfied the late medieval pilgrim's 'need for touch'.

---

[65] For the memorial function, see below.
[66] See E. Koch and H. Schlie (eds.), *Orte der Imagination – Räume des Affekts: Die mediale Formierung des Sakralen* (Paderborn, 2016), 9–10.
[67] For the term 'architectural relic' (*Architekturreliquie*), see Horsch, *Ad astra gradus*, 87 and 148–9.
[68] This situation is comparable to the cult of the Santa Casa of Loreto, whose legend arose around 1470. See Horsch, *Ad astra gradus*, 89 and 149.

The sources inform us (albeit laconically) about some specific forms of approaching the palace relics. First of all, we can presume that all of them were meant to be touched, perhaps also kissed, by the pilgrims. Giuliano Dati explicitly mentions the touching of the split column: 'la divisa colonna che le persone / diuotamente tochan colle mane(i)'.[69] Other descriptions describe how the stairs of the Scala Santa and the bloodstains shown on three of them were kissed.[70] Circumambulating a holy object is a further pilgrimage practice which was performed at the Lateran. Dealing with the doorframes of Pilate's palace in the Aula Concilii, the pilgrim Fra Mariano da Firenze describes a witty variation of this ritual approach: 'ostia tria ... per quae omnes exeunt et reintrant serpiendo transeuntes' (three doors ... through which everybody exited and entered again, crossing them snakewise).[71] An explanation for this ritual is given by the English pilgrim John Capgrave: 'And be cause no man can telle uerily be whech dor crist went oute for ther be iii dores ther for pilgrimes goo throw all iii dores ... .'[72]

The tradition of ascending the Scala Santa on one's knees is a further special case of corporeal piety.[73] It can be read as a combination between kneeling as a traditional gesture of reverence and self-humiliation and the likewise traditional climbing up to an elevated sanctuary, often metaphorically compared to climbing a series of stairs. Initially, the practice of 'kneeling up' was optional; the 'Holy Stairs' could be venerated by walking up *and* down, *or* by kneeling up – the kneeling was then seen as a sign of peculiar piety.[74] But since the addition of the two lateral stairs by Gregory XIII at the latest, it *had* to be kneeled up: the touching of the holy object by feet was at that time considered sacrilege.

Another interesting practice of physical approach is documented for the so-called *mensura Christi*. Here, the pilgrim could directly compare the length of his own body to the length of the Saviour's; he could experience a proportional relation with Christ. Giuliano Dati rhymes: '[i]n sula sala del concilio santo / la misura di christo trouerrai / in forma d'uno altare posato alquanto / sopra quatro colonne oue potrai / misurare se tu se alto tanto / o forse che piu basso tu sarai'.[75] The *mensura* legend can be interpreted as part of the speculation about the real physical appearance of Christ, another key

---

[69] Dati, *Statione/indulgetie*, 6.  [70] See Muffel, *Descrizione*, 42.
[71] Fra Mariano da Firenze, *Itinerarium urbis Romae*, 156.
[72] Capgrave, *Ye solace of pilgrims*, 74.
[73] See M. Combi, 'Il corpo devoto e la Scala Santa', in L. M. Lombardi Satriani (ed.), *La sacra città: Itinerari antropologico-religiosi nella Roma di fine millennio* (Rome, 1999), 77–105; Horsch, *Ad astra gradus*, 91–3.
[74] See Anonymous, *Mirabilia Romae*; Rucellai, *Zibaldone quaresimale*, 407.
[75] Dati, *Statione/indulgetie*, 28.

theme of Christological piety. It was rooted in Late Antiquity, but became very up-to-date in the late Middle Ages. Like the much more famous and already mentioned *acheiropoieta*, believed to show the true features of Christ's face, the issue of 'holy measures' too was derived from Byzantine devotional traditions. In the Hagia Sophia, a so-called *crux mensuralis* was kept, denoting the height of Christ and the breadth across his shoulders.[76]

This topic had an interesting impact on Western Passion iconography from the eleventh century onwards, and found an expression in diverse categories of devotional objects. The 'length amulets', for example, are rolled-up paper strips corresponding to Christ's body height (Fig. 20.9); the 'true length' or its derivations also appear as part of *arma Christi* depictions.[77]

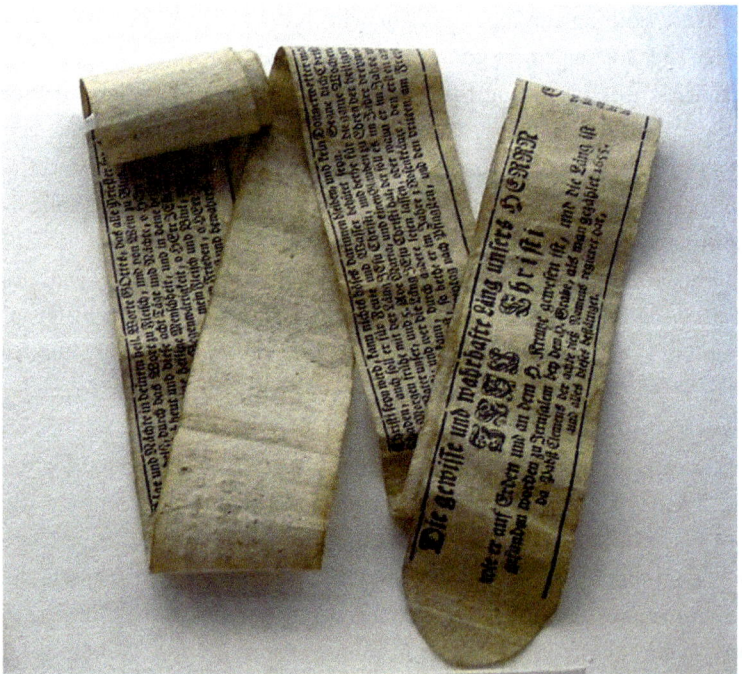

**Fig. 20.9** *Die gewisse und wahrhafte Läng unsers Herrn Jesu Christi* ('the true length of Our Lord Jesus Christ'), paper amulet, Germany, fifteenth century. Freistadt (Upper Austria), Mühlviertler Schlossmuseum (Photo: Wolfgang Sauber).

---

[76] See M. Bacci, 'Vera croce, vero ritratto e vera misura', in J. Durand and B. Flusin (eds.), *Byzance et les reliques du Christ* (Paris, 2004), 235–8.

[77] See T. Lentes, 'Die Vermessung des Christus-Körpers', in C. Geissmar-Brandi and E. Louis (eds.), *Glaube – Liebe – Hoffnung* (Klagenfurt, 1995), 144–7; H. W. Stork, 'Spätmittelalterliche Gebetbücher in Rollenform in Überlieferung und Bild', *Gutenberg-Jahrbuch* 85 (2010), 43–78, at p. 62.

The unusual idea of the Lateran *mensura* to link the theme of the 'holy measure' to a column puts still another association into play: the then highly modern architectural theories on the proportional analogies between man and column. In fact, this idea seems to play an important role for the conception of the already-mentioned *Flagellation* by Piero della Francesca. Based on Carter and Wittkower's thesis that the figure of Christ served as module for the whole picture's proportional system, Carlo Ginzburg has proposed that the system of the measurements was based on the *mensura*, embodied in the picture by the flagellated Christ himself. The figure of Christ in the picture is 17.8 cm high – approximately a tenth of the *mensura* column.[78]

## Passion, Devotion and Memory

All the veneration practices described here responded ideally to the pilgrims' 'need for touch', but they also play a vital role in the active memorisation of the sacred histories. Even if the presumed relics in the Lateran palace rely on an 'invented tradition', the aspiration of each of them is to represent physically a specific *locus* of biblical history. Their function as a relic is not thus limited to their 'holy' identity and the concomitant salvific qualities, but furthermore by their agency as material reminders of specific moments of sacred history. This 'symbolic', referencing property of relics lies at the core of devotional and pilgrimage practices, especially those centred on the Passion of Christ.

Devotional practices of visualisation, structuring and numeric speculation typical for meditational literature are subtly interwoven with the veneration of the new relics. The kneeling up on the Scala Santa for instance is a materialisation of the meditational *topos* of the 'Ladder of virtue' or even 'Ladder of Passion' to climb up step by step; the *mensura* could be the starting point of pious speculations about Christ's physical appearance and the healing power of the holy measures.[79]

But apart from these symbolic associations, the objects per se could act as agents of memory. Architectural and topographical *memoria* were crucial components of the mnemonic arts – not only in form of the well-

---

[78] B. A. R. Carter and R. Wittkower, 'The perspective of Piero della Francesca's "Flagellation"', *Journal of the Warburg and Courtauld Institutes* 16 (1953), 292–302; Ginzburg, *Erkundungen über Piero*, 155.

[79] See Horsch, *Ad astra gradus*, 227–32, for the interpretation of the Scala Santa; see n. 76 and n. 78 for the numeric speculations.

known memory palaces to be built in the mind, but also applied to real-life architecture and sites. On the example of Classical Athens, Cicero stressed how sites contain a great power of memory able to conserve memory over a long period of time.[80]

The encounter between the relic and the pilgrim can be described as such a materialisation of memory, a moment in which the geographical and historical distance between the present of the pilgrim and the site and moment of salvation history he remembers is overridden. This is the experience of *hic et nunc* described especially by pilgrims to the Holy Land.[81]

Thomas Lentes has stressed the general importance of the human body as an instrument of memory in the Middle Ages. The *memoria passionis* described by Bernard of Clairvaux, for example, is not so much to be understood as an intellectual act but as a bodily memorisation aiming at activating the believer's compassion with Christ. This idea is perfectly achieved in the stigmatisation of Saint Francis: the wounds can be interpreted as the outer appearance of the inner identification of the saint with the suffering Christ; his body 'becomes a Memotopos [sic] of the Passion'.[82] Aside from such extreme examples of somatic *imitatio*, becoming engaged with the material reminder of the relic and exploiting its mnemonic power is based on the corporeal presence, and often performance, of the believer. By seeing, touching or kissing a relic, the pilgrim remembers or even re-enacts a specific moment of sacred history and imprints it into his mind.

This phenomenon is also fundamental for the pilgrimage practices at the Lateran. The crossing of the 'Pilate doors' as well as the walking (or kneeling) up the Scala Santa were not only intense forms of physical approach, but also a very concrete 'imitation of Christ', performed by the pilgrim's body. The pilgrim simulated Christ's actions, which had sanctified the doors and the staircase, imprinting them into his body and mind, and in doing so he perpetuated ritually the sanctifying action.[83]

---

[80] 'Tanta vis admonitionis inest in locis': Cic. *Fin.* 5.1–2; see A. Assmann, *Erinnerungsräume: Formen und Wandlungen des kulturellen Gedächtnisses* (Munich, 2010), 303–14, esp. p. 313.

[81] See below.

[82] T. Lentes, 'Der Körper als Ort des Gedächtnisses: Der Körper als Text', in Geissmar-Brandi and Louis (eds.), *Glaube – Liebe – Hoffnung*, 76–9, at p. 76.

[83] Combi, 'Il corpo devoto e la Scala Santa', 95 and 101; Horsch, *Ad astra gradus*, 91–3.

## Passion, Memory and Sacred Topography: The Lateran Palace as a Memorial Space

Site-based *memoria* is not limited to single places, but can attain topographical dimensions. Just as single rooms together form a building and single buildings a city, the memorial connotations of single sites could be combined to form a complex whole, a memorial 'space' or landscape.[84] In the perception of the visitor, the connection between them is established primarily by bodily movement. Regarding the practice of processions, the nature of such ritualised movement has been described as both performative and symbolic. The movement creates a spatio-temporal continuum able to connect past and present, individual and collective as well as presence and memory.[85]

The outstanding example of a Christian memory landscape, the Holy Sites of Jerusalem, had been created step by step, probably on the base of Jewish traditions which had already connected Old Testament events to specific sites.[86] With the large buildings and framing projects of the Constantinian era, Jerusalem had become the principal model for architectural enactment of holy sites as well as for performative veneration practices in Christendom.[87] The veneration of the *loca sancta* of Jerusalem was further improved under Franciscan guidance from the fourteenth century.[88] The sites were framed

---

[84] For the definition of places and spaces and their interaction, see M. De Certeau, *Kunst des Handelns* (Berlin, 1988). These concepts have been applied convincingly to pilgrimage research e.g. by Koch and Schlie (eds.), *Orte der Imagination*; J. Hommers, *Gehen und Sehen in Saint-Lazare in Autun: Bewegung – Betrachtung – Reliquienverehrung* (Cologne, 2015), 210; T. Urban, 'Heilige Orte – Heiliger Raum: Zur Translokation der Sakraltopographie Jerusalems', in D. Dittmeyer, J. Hommers and S. Windmüller (eds.), *Verrückt, Verrutscht, Versetzt: Zur Verschiebung von Gegenständen, Körpern und Orten* (Berlin, 2015), 170–90; H. Schlie, 'Das Mnemotop Jerusalem in der Prozession, in Brügge und im Bild: Die Turiner Passion von Hans Memling', in K. Gvozdeva and H. R. Velten (eds.), *Medialität der Prozession: Performanz ritueller Bewegung in Texten und Bildern der Vormoderne* (Germanisch-romanische Monatsschrift 39) (Heidelberg, 2011), 141–75; C. Kiening, 'Prozessionalität der Passion', in Gvozdeva and Velten (eds.) *Medialität der Prozession*, 177–97.

[85] 'Die Prozession schafft in der Bewegung ein raumzeitliches Kontinuum, in welchem Vergangenheit, Gegenwart und Zukunft, das Individuelle wie das Kollektive, das Normative wie das Transgressive, Präsenz und Gedächtnis aufeinander bezogen werden können': Gvozdeva and Velten (eds.), *Medialität der Prozession*, 12.

[86] See Halbwachs, *Stätten der Verkündigung*, 154–211, esp. pp. 180–7.

[87] See for instance Egeria, *Itinerarium – Reisebericht: Mit Auszügen aus Petrus Diaconus, De locis Sanctis – Die Heiligen Stätten*, ed. and trans. G. Röwekamp (Fontes Christiani 20) (Freiburg, 2000); H. F. M. Prescott, *Felix Fabris Reise nach Jerusalem* (Freiburg, 1960), 127–8, and the summaries in U. Verstegen, 'Im Kontakt mit den Allerheiligsten: Zur frühchristlichen Inszenierung der Heilsorte in der Jerusalemer Grabeskirche', in Koch and Schlie (eds.), *Orte der Imagination*, 31–54; Kiening, 'Prozessionalität der Passion', 182–8; and Reudenbach, '"Loca sancta", 11–18.

[88] See L. Lemmens, *Die Franziskaner auf dem Sion* (Franziskanische Studien 4) (Munich, 1916); see also the accounts of Fra Niccoló di Poggibonsi, *A voyage beyond the seas (1346–1350)*, ed.

visually, approached haptically, and connected to the Bible narrative by lectures and prayers, allowing the visitors to 'reperform' the biblical events actively. The pilgrims were encouraged to imagine each event vividly and to activate their compassion. This staging of the sites and the experience of one's own emotional response to it firmly imprinted this experience into the pilgrims' minds.[89] There was a special focus on the *mise-en-scène* of the Via Dolorosa leading from Pilate's palace to the Church of the Holy Sepulchre. It was established as a more or less fixed processional route structured by 'stations' as benchmarks, each of them dedicated to the memory of a single moment of the Passion.[90] The fragmentary narratives of the Gospels are concentrated, structured and materialised to form a comprehensible and tangible memorial space.

On a smaller scale, the new relics at the Lateran unfold their full power as components of a memorial 'space' established by the pious itinerary involving the whole Lateran complex. As described above, the pilgrim moved along a predetermined route and was probably guided. The different objects that were shown to him were perceived very actively: walking, stopping at an object, seeing, hearing the explanations, and venerating it with the described haptical practices. In this way, the objects were stored one by one in the pilgrim's memory and were connected during the process of the visit. Having completed the whole itinerary, it became clear that several objects belonged to the same thematic context; the fragments could be put together to form a logical whole.

As the visited objects related to corresponding biblical events, the meaning of the whole walk through the Lateran shifted towards a symbolic topography. The profane palace rooms – which carried no evident meaning in the eyes of the pilgrims, especially those coming from abroad – were transformed in their minds into a virtual holy space, a fragmentary topography of Christ's Passion, intimately connected to the Holy Sites of Jerusalem.

## Architectural Relics and Translocated Topography

In modern perception, this situation conveys a paradox. How is it possible to copy the *hic et nunc* experience of Jerusalem at the Lateran palace? It

and trans. Fr T. Bellorini and Fr E. Hoade (Jerusalem, 1945) and Felix Fabri (Prescott, *Felix Fabris*).

[89] See for instance Egeria, *Itinerarium*; Kiening, 'Prozessionalität der Passion', 182–8.
[90] See Halbwachs, *Stätten der Verkündigung*, 109–20.

seems logical to us that the described memory of site and space must refer to a fixed position in topography.[91] After all, the experience of the holy events taking place in the pilgrim's here and now derived essentially from the specific site – at least, this is the impression.

However, the phenomenon of transportable memory spaces is widespread in Christian piety, for several reasons. As Robert Ousterhout has stressed, medieval concepts of geography were in general rather flexible and provided several strategies for transfer phenomena.[92] Still more important is the fact that the concept of 'holy sites' and 'holy spaces' is not really rooted in Christian faith. In contrast with pagan – and Jewish – concepts of the numinous presences in nature, the holy sites of Christendom are not holy in substance, but made holy by a divine or saintly contact – comparable to the above-mentioned contact relics. This idea of the sanctifying of places by the principle of contiguity was propagated successfully only in the age of Constantine.[93]

This concept of attached rather than substantial holiness is fundamental to all site-specific devotions, but it also implied the idea of transfer, and thus allows a series of practices aiming at the multiplication of holy presence on earth. The first possibility was the partial transfer, the extraction of small parts to be distributed; but soon other, less destructive, options were developed. For instance, holy objects and sites were copied or reproduced in other media. These reproductions not only had a memorial function but were believed to carry the *virtus* of the original – or at least a part of it. Furthermore, not only the objects, but also the connected practices could be reproduced. The visit to the Holy Sites was thus adapted to the devotional practice of 'virtual pilgrimage'.

The strategies and techniques of transfer, reproduction and virtual re-enactment are manifold:[94] The Holy Sites of Jerusalem (the Holy Sepulchre or an entire topography) could be 'copied' architecturally.[95]

---

[91] See Assmann, *Erinnerungsräume*, 313, for the difference between 'Gedächtnis der Orte' (memorial sites) and 'Örtern des Gedächtnisses' (mnemonical *loci*).

[92] See Ousterhout, 'Flexible geography', esp. pp. 393–4.

[93] See Verstegen, 'Im Kontakt mit den Allerheiligsten', 31–3; Reudenbach, '"Loca sancta", 11–15; Koch and Schlie (eds.), *Orte der Imagination*, 10–11.

[94] See e.g. the overviews in Kühnel (ed.), *The Real and Ideal Jerusalem*; Lidov (ed.), *New Jerusalems*; Reudenbach, '"Loca sancta"'; L. Donkin and H. Vorholt (eds.), *Imagining Jerusalem in the Medieval West* (Proceedings of the British Academy 175) (Oxford, 2012); H. Aurenhammer and D. Bohde (eds.), *Räume der Passion: Raumvisionen, Erinnerungsorte und Topographien des Leidens Christi in Mittelalter und Früher Neuzeit* (Vestigia Bibliae. Jahrbuch des Deutschen Bibelarchivs Hamburg 32/3) (Bern, 2015).

[95] For the medieval concept of 'copies', see R. Krautheimer, 'Introduction to an "Iconography of Mediaeval Architecture"', *Journal of the Warburg and Courtauld Institutes* 5 (1942), 1–33; G.

Often the reproductions were made holy by the presence of a Passion relic. But there was also the option of a mere imaginative transposition of Jerusalem into a different space, an urban space (in Passion plays and processions, but also as a devotional technique) or the cloister of a monastery, for instance. A similar idea underlies the use of texts, maps or detailed pictorial or sculptural depictions of the Jerusalem memory landscape as a tool for mental pilgrimage.[96] Very often, these different strategies were combined.[97]

The Lateran relic topography obviously belongs to these contexts, but at the same time it represents a very original concept. On one hand, it is a virtual topography because it transfers Jerusalem sites to a completely different situation: the empty rooms of the papal palace. However, compared to other virtual pilgrimages, the Lateran architectural relics allowed – although on a restricted scale – just the same *hic et nunc* experience that made up the principal fascination of the original Jerusalem memory space. Material objects and topographical sites enabled the pilgrim to communicate directly with biblical history and to engage emotionally with its protagonists.

The veneration experiences are thus rather comparable to those practised at Jerusalem itself or at the Holy Sepulchres and 'Holy Landscapes'.[98] Unlike those, however, the Lateran objects were not copies, nor did they merely contain relics (like some Holy Land copies). Instead, they claimed to be 'originals', true relics of the Passion, authentic fragments of the Holy Land topography claimed to have been removed from their original sites. As such, they formed a kind of complementary Passion topography, which could be visited exclusively at the Lateran. This topography distinguished

Bresc-Bautier, 'Les imitations du Saint-Sépulcre de Jérusalem (IXe–XVe siècles)', *Revue d'histoire de la spiritualité* 50 (1974), 319–42; J. Pieper, A. Naujokat and A. Kappler, *Jerusalemskirchen: Mittelalterliche Kleinarchitekturen nach dem Modell des Heiligen Grabes* (Aachen, 2003); B. Kühnel, 'Virtual pilgrimages to real places: the holy landscapes', in Donkin and Vorholt (eds.), *Imagining Jerusalem in the Medieval West*, 243–64.

[96] See for instance K. M. Rudy, *Virtual Pilgrimages in the Convent: Imagining Jerusalem in the Late Middle Ages* (Turnhout, 2011) (about virtual Jerusalems in cloisters); Kemper, *Die Kreuzigung Christi* (about Passion treatises as a devotional means); G. Ehrstine, 'Passion spectatorship between private and public devotion', in E. Gertsman and J. Stevenson (eds.), *Thresholds of Medieval Visual Culture: Liminal Spaces* (Woodbridge, 2012), 302–20 (about the close relations between private and public Passion devotion); Schlie, 'Das Mnemotop Jerusalem' (about the interaction between Jerusalem, the Holy Blood Procession of Brügge and Hans Memling's Passion panorama in Turin).

[97] The Sacri Monti for instance combine topographical and architectural copies with sculptural and/or pictorial representations of the biblical events: see L. Vaccaro and F. Riccardi (eds.), *Sacri Monti: Devozione, arte e cultura della controriforma* (Milan, 1992); Kühnel, 'Virtual pilgrimages to real places'.

[98] See Kühnel, 'Virtual pilgrimages to real places'.

itself by its novelty and originality, while appearing convincing and legitimised just because of its strong interdependence with Jerusalem. Although it offered only a fragmentary picture of the Passion landscape, the gaps could be filled by the pilgrims' knowledge about the biblical events and the topography of Jerusalem – a common procedure in devotional practice.

The fifteenth-century ensemble of Passion relics at the Lateran presents the unusual – and perhaps unique – case of a memory topography consisting of original sites but applied to a totally different space. The former papal palace which had practically forfeited its original function presented itself as a tabula rasa, ready to be rewritten with a new narrative, that of a fragmentary Jerusalem. Moreover, although the relic itinerary can be described as a translocated memory space, it is nevertheless bound back to the *genius loci* of the Lateran. The idea of a *Hierusalem translata* is convincing at this specific site just because it derives its legitimisation from the Lateran's oldest liturgical traditions and relic treasures. The principal argumentation schemes – the Christological patronage, Constantine or Helena as possible donators – had long been established. The actual elaboration of the new relic topography, however, followed the most up-to-date trends of piety.

## The Lateran Relics Completing the Image of Jerusalem

Looking at it the other way around, it becomes evident that the most prominent Lateran fragments had for their part an effect on the perception of the Holy Sites in Jerusalem. This effect can be traced in Passion iconography. For example, in Piero della Francesca's flagellation scene discussed above or – even more clearly – in one of Jeronimo Nadal's *Evangelicae Historiae Imagines* (Fig. 20.10). The architectural fragments displayed at the Lateran are merged here into a detailed reconstruction of Pilate's palace. The Scala Santa leads up to a balcony, where the three doors lead into the interior of the building. Between the doors are the two pillars with the flag holders. Although the Lateran relics are not copied exactly, the short explanations in the margin of the sheet, corresponding to letters in the image, leave no doubt that the representation was inspired by them. Interestingly, the function of the architectural elements as devotional means is adapted too. The small texts connect the single objects with specific parts of the narrative to be considered one by one during the meditation.

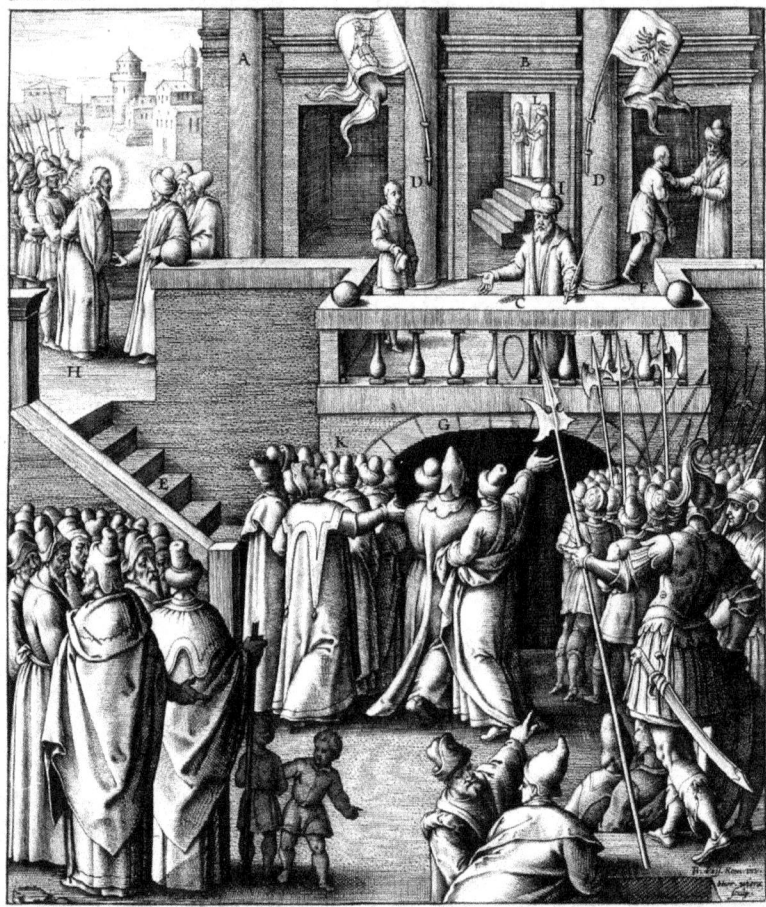

Fig. 20.10 Jeronimo Nadal, *Evangelicae Historiae Imagines*, Antwerp, 1593, p. CXVIII (Photo: Archive N. Horsch).

While Piero and Nadal's architectures are fictions based exclusively on the Lateran fragments, these also influenced the perception of the 'original' palace of Pilate in Jerusalem. The site of this building was one of the most discussed in the holy topography of Jerusalem. Halbwachs has listed the different interpretations concerning the location and identity of the praetor's residence. In the fifteenth century it was identified with the former Herodian fortress Antonia.[99] Reading the descriptions of the presumed palace of Pilate in Jerusalem written after the establishment of the Scala Santa tradition, it becomes clear that the Jerusalem pilgrims began to look for the original site of the translocated staircase. Generally, it was believed to have led up from the Via Dolorosa to the paved courtyard Lithostrathos or Gabbatha.[100] The alleged former site of the Scala Santa was even shown in reconstructing illustrations of Pilate's palace, for example in Bernardino Amico's *Trattato delle piante et imagini dei sacri edifici di Terra Santa* (Fig. 20.11).

The Lateran relics even appear to have influenced the conception of an outstanding late medieval Holy Land copy, the Passion topography of Görlitz in Saxonia, unique in Europe at that time in commemorating not only the Holy Sepulchre but a whole landscape consisting of three buildings and a series of sculptural stations.[101] The chapel of the Holy Cross, the upper chapel of a two-storey edifice, offers a vivid tableau of the Golgotha topography (Figs 20.12a, 20.12b). Three holes in the pavement indicate the position of the crosses, a ditch for Christ's blood and a sculpted INRI table. On the left side, just in front of the chapel's entrance, stands a strange altar-like table (Fig. 20.13a). At the front of the slab, a small grated repository contains three bronze dice as a hint at the sharing of Christ's garments (Fig. 20.13b).[102] The most reliable explanation for the table, proposed by Till Meinert, connects it to the altar's situation in the

---

[99] See Halbwachs, *Stätten der Verkündigung*, 101–8.

[100] See for instance G. Zuallardo, *Il devotissimo Viaggio di Gerusalemme, fatto, & descritto in sei libri dal Sig.r Giovanni Zuallardo, Cavaliero del Santiß. Sepolcro di N.S. l'anno 1586: Aggiontovi i disegni di varij luoghi di Terra Santa & altri paesi Intagliati da Natale Bonifacio Dalmata* (Rome, 1587), 165: 'Dal medesimo lato della detta casa di Pilato, & poco piu inanzi, è ancora il letto della Scala Santa, che avanza sopra la detta strada (del quale li scaloni furono portati à Roma, & posti à S. Giovanni Laterano) che menava al Tribunale del detto Pilato, chiamato, Licostratos ... '.

[101] See T. Meinert, *Die Heilig-Grab-Anlage in Görlitz: Architektur und Geschichte eines spätmittelalterlichen Bauensembles* (Esens, 2004); Pieper et al., *Jerusalemskirchen*; Kühnel, 'Virtual pilgrimages to real places', 252–7; C. Freigang, 'Bildskeptische Nachbildungsmodi der Passionstopographie Christi im Spätmittelalter: der Görlitzer Kalvarienberg', in Aurenhammer and Bohde (eds.), *Räume der Passion*, 117–49.

[102] The dice are dated to the seventeenth century but are supposed to replace older ones. See Freigang, 'Bildskeptische Nachbildungsmodi', 122.

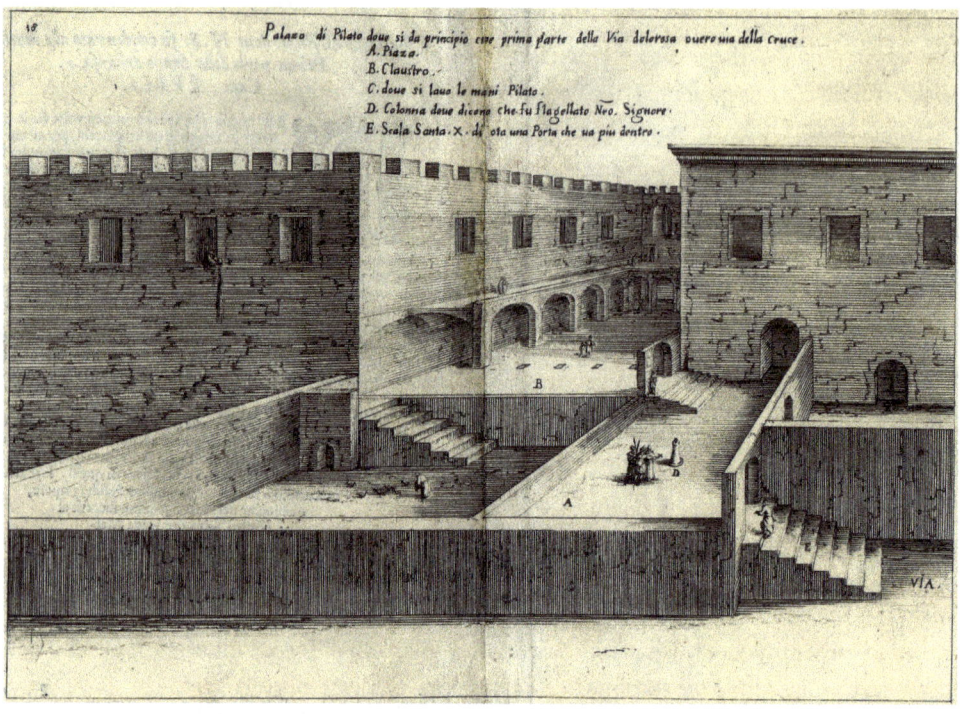

Fig. 20.11 Bernardino Amico, Reconstruction of Pilate's palace in Jerusalem with the Scala Santa, 1620 (Photo: ©Trustees of the British Museum, London).

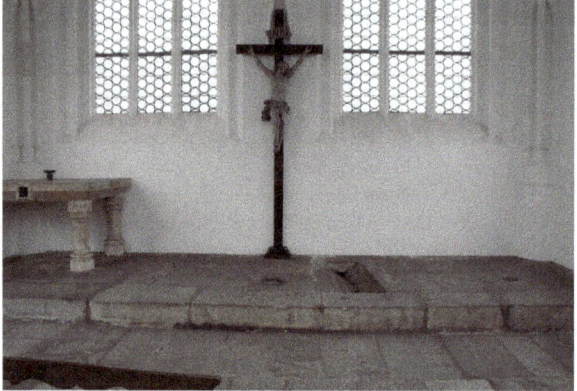

Fig. 20.12a Görlitz (Saxonia), interior of the Holy Cross chapel, before 1520. 'Golgotha' setting with the three holes of the crosses and a ditch for Christ's blood (Photo: Marianne Lutter).

The New Passion Relics at the Lateran 463

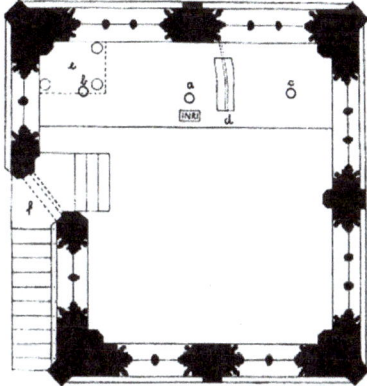

Fig. 20.12b Görlitz, ground plan of the Holy Cross chapel (in Freigang, 'Bildskeptische Nachbildungsmodi', 144).

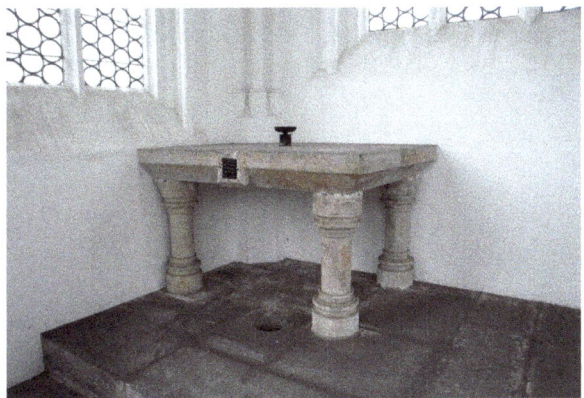

Fig. 20.13a Görlitz, Holy Cross chapel, table with three dice in a repository – an adaptation of the *mensura Christi*? (Photo: Marianne Lutter).

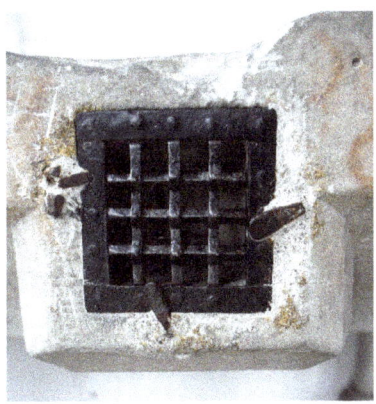

Fig. 20.13b Detail of the repository (Photo: Marianne Lutter).

Golgotha chapel of Jerusalem.[103] However, it does not explain the presence of the dice.

I would like to propose that the Lateran *mensura Christi* is the model for the table: The conception of the altar refers generally to the *mensura*'s construction as a slab on four columns and to the dice legend, an episode located literally 'under the Cross' and therefore logically placed in the upper chapel's *mise-en-scène*. The divergent height of the columns is probably due to the circumstance that the idea of the columns alluding to Christ's height seems to have been diffused exclusively in Italian circles at that time; at least, it appears exclusively in Italian sources. The foreign sources, by contrast, only mention the dice or the silver pieces legends.

This approach is comparable to the insertion of the Scala Santa in the topography of Pilate's palace. It shows likewise how the Lateran relics formed – at least for a period of time – part of the collective memory which reconstructs the sites of Christ's Passion from a number of fragments – at their original site as well as in a translocated topography.

## Closing Remarks

As discussed above, the concept of 'holy sites' is not and has never been a Christian article of faith. As a consequence, even the identity of the most important sites can be discussed and contested. In Jerusalem there are, for example, two possible sites for the Last Supper and two palaces of Pilate,[104] but this paradox obviously did not interfere with their credibility or with their appeal as pilgrim destinations.

Although the Holy Sites derive all their fascination from their supposed authenticity, this authenticity can be – and often is – an open question. Even if we suppose that memory of the biblical settings was handed down in the Christian community, the first notions of pilgrimage to Jerusalem date from around 300, a time when the city's image had substantially changed. The material remnants were diminished and the attribution of an event to an exact site in many cases contested.[105] Nevertheless, the fascination of the *hic et nunc* experience has always

---

[103] Meinert, *Die Heilig-Grab-Anlage in Görlitz*, 339–40.
[104] See Halbwachs, *Stätten der Verkündigung*, 192–3.
[105] See Halbwachs, *Stätten der Verkündigung*, 20–1: 'Wenn, wie wir glauben, das kollektive Gedächtnis wesentlich eine Rekonstruktion der Vergangenheit bedeutet, wenn es dementsprechend sein Bild früherer Tatsachen den religiösen Überzeugungen und spirituellen

been described as the principal issue of the pilgrimage to Jerusalem. What matters is fiction more than fact: the emotional impact effected by the – rediscovered or even newly defined – sites on the pious visitor and their power to activate his religious memory. The sites, however fictitious they might be, were the principal medium that allowed to experience the biblical events with all senses.

The same argumentation is formulated with astonishing clearness in the middle of the seventeenth century by the erudite librarian and Lateran canon Fioravante Martinelli.[106] In an unpublished treatise on our Lateran relics, Martinelli proposes, for instance – quite convincingly – that the *mensura Christi* was built of medieval altar fragments. Nevertheless, he defends those manifestly 'false' relics because of their devotional value. The relics, he argues, which are not only of dubious but of mere 'symbolic' nature, are still precious because they serve the people as a memory of Christ's Passion. Their 'reality' is the reality of the devotion brought to them:

> senza concedersi che alcune delle d[ett]e reliquie, o sacri monumenti, non solo siano dubie, ma simboliche per rappresentare al popolo la memoria della Passione di Christo Signor n[ost]ro, chi ardirà di dire che sia falsa la religione del Popolo, che le bacia, che l'honora, che le venera come Imagini della d[ett]a Passione ... La traslatione delle d[ett]e Reliquie e sacri monumenti fatta con l'autorità Pontificia nella Chiesa che è la Sede Vescovile del Papa in diversi tempi, et ultimam[en]te di Sisto V., di Clemente VIII e d'Innocenzo X.mo è sufficiente argomento della loro realtà .... Gloriandosi tanto la Basilica Lateranense del possesso di d[ett]e Reliquie, e de' sacri monumenti sod[ett]i non deve esserne privata, ancorche non consti con evidenza dell'identità loro ...[107]

Since the eighteenth century the sacred identity of the new relics – with the exception of the Scala Santa – has been irretrievably contested; their meaning changed again. Instead of commemorating as 'sacri monumenti' the events of Christ's Passion, they became part of a diverse, 'modern' memorial topography, the lapidary of the cloister, preserving a large part of the medieval Lateran's surviving material memory.

---

Bedürfnissen der Gegenwart anpaßt, wird das Wissen darum, was ursprünglich war, mindestens zweitrangig, wenn nicht ganz und gar überflüssig ... .'

[106] F. Martinelli, 'Discorso di Fioravanti Martinelli sopra alcune Reliquie della Basilica Lateranense', ACL, A 26.

[107] Martinelli 'Discorso', 43 f.

## 21 | The East Façade of the Complex of Saint John Lateran in the Modern Era

ALESSANDRO IPPOLITI

A central theme in of the history of the Lateran complex is the architectural definition of its eastern façade, to be inserted in the modern era in a defined and extra-urban context, and suitable to the prestige of the basilica itself.

Beginning with the abandonment of the Porta Asinaria in favour of the new Porta San Giovanni, desired by Pope Gregory XIII (1572–85) and designed by Giacomo del Duca, the present text retraces the projects and constructions for this area, examining the choices made by Sixtus V (1585–90) and Domenico Fontana, and by Innocent X (1644–55) and Francesco Borromini, up to the solutions from the 1700s for the new façade of the basilica, the completion of the Apostolic palace and the liberation of the area in front of the remains of the Leonian *triclinium*.

Consequently, I believe that an accurate interpretation of the demolitions and transformations involving the Lateran complex over the centuries requires an examination of the diachronic evolution of the history of the papacy, which presents us with moments of abandonment and renewed phases of intense building activity. The popes continually felt the 'necessity of a direct or indirect confrontation with this site, choosing to promote activities of building but also to abstain from any work at all'.[1]

The structural and symbolic decline of the Lateran, which certainly occurred from the late Middle Ages onward, is not recorded in any specific manner by literary and cartographic sources. They reiterate the importance of its relics, while emphasising its altimetric and archaeological aspects. Iconographic sources privilege the mythical image of the site, home to a collection of relics from Jerusalem and tied to an endless comparison between the empire and the papacy. This is the case of the *Dittamondo* by Fazio degli Uberti[2] and the map by Fra' Paolino of Venice, featuring a schematic representation of the façade and bell tower[3] (Fig. 21.1); the plan of Rome from 1474 by Alessandro Strozzi marks the beginning of

---

[1] L. Donadono, *La Scala Santa a San Giovanni in Laterano* (Rome, 2000), 14.
[2] Florence, 1445. Bibliothèque Nationale de Paris, Manuscrits. Ms. It. n.81, fol. 81.
[3] The miniature was probably based on a plan from the twelfth century, published in 1879 by G. B. de Rossi, *Piante iconografiche e prospettiche di Roma* (Rome, 1879), in which the pre-existing constructions are indicated as 'Palatium Neronis Lateranense'.

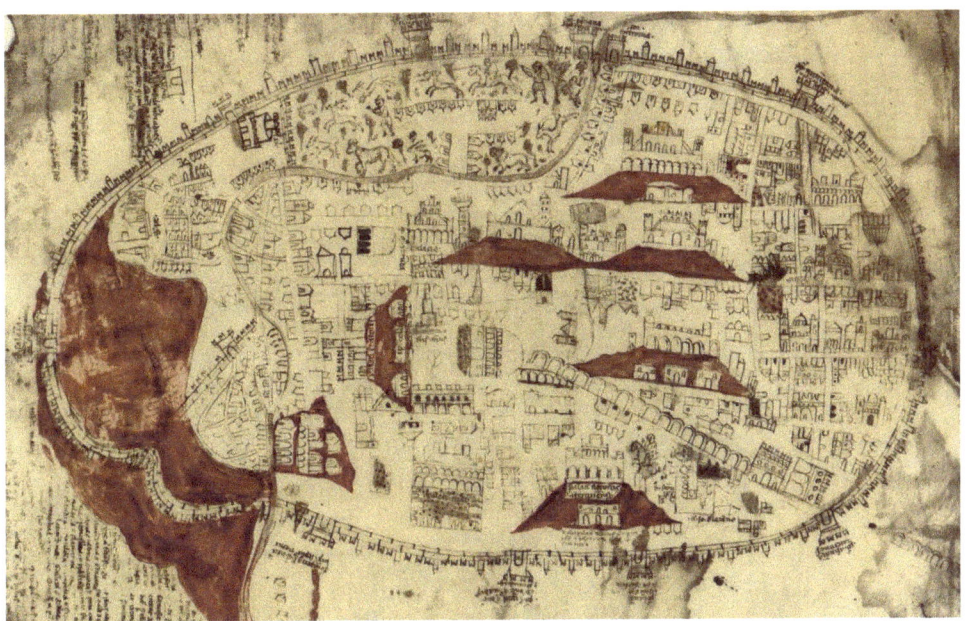

Fig. 21.1 Fra' Paolino da Venezia, *Roma di Fra' Paolino da Venezia*, Rome, 1320.

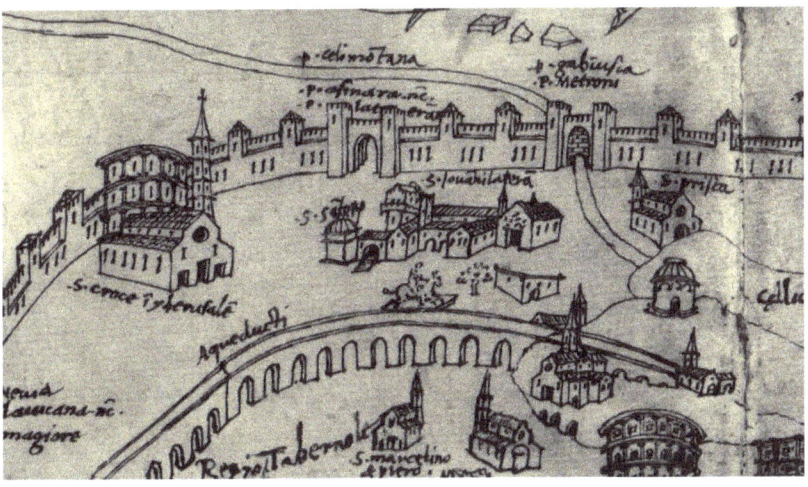

Fig. 21.2 Alessandro Strozzi, *Roma nei secoli IV/V*, detail, Rome, 1474.

representations of the diverse buildings comprising the Lateran complex (Fig. 21.2). They were later depicted with more detail in the archaeological plan of 1551 by Leonardo Bufalini (Fig. 21.3), in which it is possible to make out the plan of the basilica, the baptistery, the *patriarchium* and the Scala Santa. These iconographic sources, together with a reading of the drawing

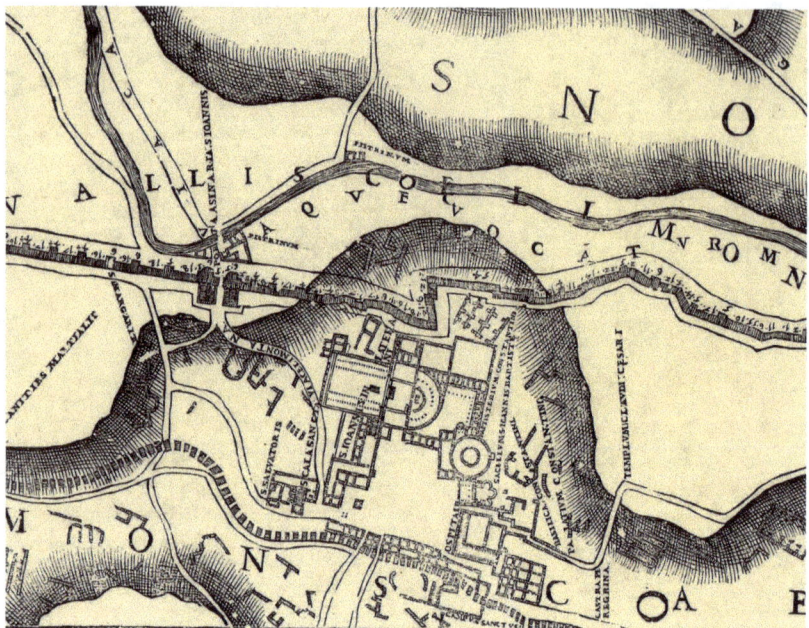

**Fig. 21.3** Leonardo Bufalini, *Roma nei secc. IV/XV: zona del Celio*, Rome, 1551.

from Marten van Heemskerck's notebook[4] (Fig. 21.4) depicting the entry portico to the palace, the Loggia of Benediction and the equestrian statue of Marcus Aurelius, reveal the consistency of the Lateran complex during the Middle Ages as a group of constructions situated primarily to the north of the Constantinian basilica, in an area with a prevalently suburban character and still strongly characterised by remains from imperial Rome. Remains were evident along the Via Celimontana, which, running alongside the basilica, led to the Porta Asinaria, towards which the basilica was oriented, in all likelihood to welcome pilgrims arriving from the south.

In the arrangement of the medieval constructions of the Lateran, the area to the right of the façade of the basilica would seem to define an urban space delimited by these latter elements, the façade and the Aurelian Walls. In reality this area remained 'uninhabited',[5] even when the attention of the popes once again focused on the Lateran, as a relic, and as a unique testimonial to be conserved and instrumentally exploited as part of a project to powerfully affirm the indispensable principles of Christianity.

---

[4] Ink and sepia watercolour, Rome 1535–8. Union of the two plates conserved in Berlin at the Kupferstichkabnet, 79, D2, fols. 71 and 12r.

[5] R. Krautheimer, *Roma: Profilo di una città* (Rome, 1981), 383–402 (originally published in English as *Rome: Profile of a City, 312–1308* (Princeton, 1980).

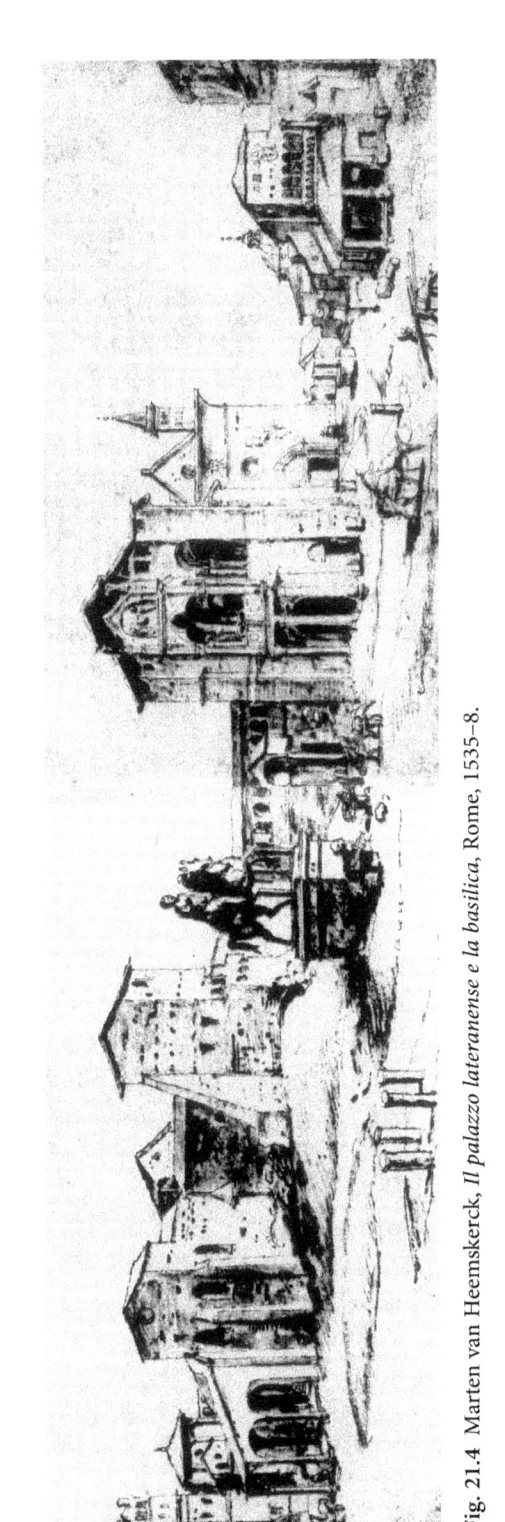

Fig. 21.4 Marten van Heemskerck, *Il palazzo lateranense e la basilica*, Rome, 1535–8.

There is no doubt that the reasons for intervening here are to be sought in the concept of restoration already present under the papacy of Pius IV (1559–65), the first pope to manage the legacy of ideas and prescriptions to come out of the Council of Trent (1545–63), and under Pius V (1566–72), one of the more intransigent defenders of these ideals. In 1562 Pius IV commissioned Pirro Ligorio with the renewal of the façade of the transept, restoring the two bell towers of Pope Gregory XI (1370–8) and adding the attic between them, in addition to restoration works inside the basilica, in particular the coffered ceilings; Pius V dealt primarily with the institutional restoration of the Lateran with the bull issued on 21 December 1569, in which he resolved the conflict with Saint Peter's, confirming Pius IV's privilege over the clergy of the Lateran and declaring, 'che il Jus di precedere, le prerogative d'onore, et il luogo più nobile e supremo nelle Processioni solenni, decreti, et in tutti gli altri atti pubblici, e privati appartenesse al clero Lateranense'.[6] The Lateran was thus revitalised in the thinking of the popes, at a delicate time in the history of the papacy, as the authentic testimonial of Christianity. The ideological matrix 'which had animated the flowering of studies of ancient Christianity was clear: identifying in the history of the early centuries of Christianity the motivations and internal historic necessity of papal majesty, negated by Protestant critics'.[7]

The renewed interest in the Lateran, considered not only as a relic of the early history of the Church, but also as a model for reaffirming the papacy's supremacy, deriving from its foundation by Constantine, also included interest in the grand choices for the city made, above all, by Pope Gregory XIII (1572–85) and Sixtus V (1585–90), who attempted not only to restore the complex, but to coherently insert it within the city. On occasion of the 1575 Jubilee, Gregory XIII connected the basilica of Saint John Lateran with the basilica of Santa Maria Maggiore by rectifying the Via Merulana, whose view was blocked on the one hand by the renewed portico at Santa Maria Maggiore and, on the other, by a new portal for the baptistery of San Giovanni in Fonte, opposite the narthex of Sixtus III (432–40) and facing Piazza San Giovanni (Fig. 21.5). He later regularised the Via della Ferratella to connect the Lateran complex with the urban portion of the Via Appia,

---

[6] 'That the right to precede, the prerogatives of honour, and the most noble and supreme position in solemn processions, decrees and in all other public and private acts belongs to the clergy of the Lateran': Biblioteca Apostolica Vaticana, *Vat. Lat.* 7925, fols. 12–16, *Sacro parallelo della Basilica Lateranense e Vaticana*.

[7] A. Roca de Amicis, *L'Opera di Borromini in San Giovanni in Laterano: Gli anni della fabbrica (1646–1650)* (Rome, 1995), 16.

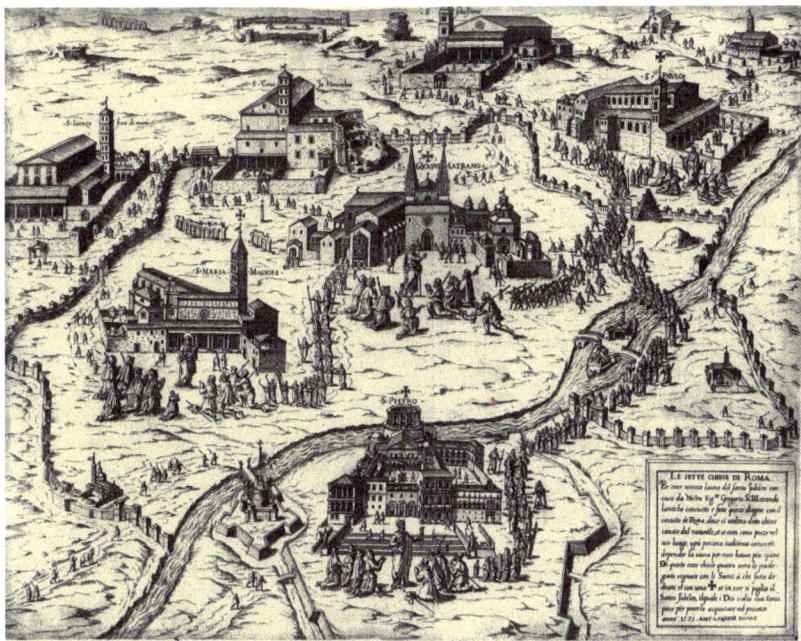

**Fig. 21.5** Antonio Lafrèry, *Veduta delle sette chiese di Roma*, Rome, 1575.

and thus with the church of San Sebastiano fuori le Mura, one of the processional churches. If these interventions aimed at reinserting the Lateran within the urbanised and Christian fabric of Rome, Pope Gregory XIII, in reality, also intervened on a greater scale with the opening in the Aurelian Walls of the Porta San Giovanni, commissioned from the architect Giacomo del Duca. The gate was inaugurated in 1574 and its opening, designed to facilitate traffic to and from southern Italy, necessitated the definitive closure of the nearby Porta Asinaria, rendered almost inaccessible by the progressive elevation of the street level.

The structure of the new gate confirmed the use for which it had been conceived: in fact, it is more akin to that leading into a villa than a defensive construction, wholly devoid as it is of side towers, bastions or crenellations, and instead provided with a marked rustication and a simple ornamentation composed of a large bearded face at the top of the gate itself, on the exterior side. Porta San Giovanni is the first construction from the Middle Ages on the eastern side of the Lateran complex. All the same, it appears to face more towards the exterior of the city, with simple functional objectives, than to have been inserted within a project for the rehabilitation of this part of the Lateran, as shown in the plans drawn up by Mario Cartaro in 1576 (Fig. 21.6) and by Stefano du Pérac in 1577 (Fig. 21.7). On the contrary, it

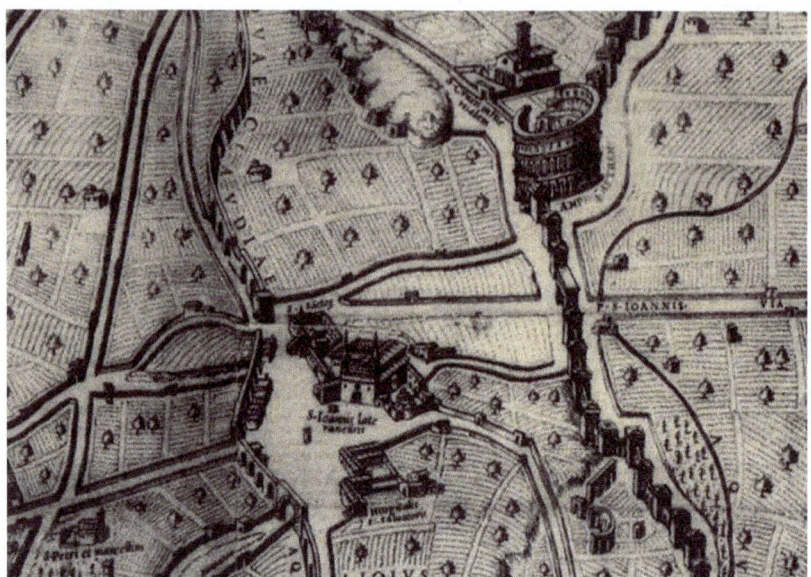

Fig. 21.6 Mario Cartaro, *Roma nel sec. XVI: Zona di Porta Maggiore e del Colosseo*, Rome, 1576.

could be said that the construction of the gate constituted the realisation of a road that, passing in front of the *patriarchium* and the group of medieval buildings, leads into Piazza San Giovanni and that its layout thus contributes to further isolating the area in front of the façade of the basilica, which remains a sort of suburban space divided into two uncultivated areas separated by the Via Celimontana, which leads towards the now abandoned Porta Asinaria.

All of this delineates the context of the project developed by Sixtus V for the Lateran. The architect Domenico Fontana, referring to the state of the area of the Lateran in 1590,[8] when Pope Sixtus V decided to intervene, described it as an 'obscure and formless' site, where, around the Scala Santa, were 'fabbriche antiche, che, minacciando rovina, toglievano in gran parte il decoro di una sì gran devozione' (ancient buildings that, on the verge of collapse, robbed much of the decorum of such a great devotion), while Pirro Ligorio had already written, in 1563, that the seat of the papacy was 'vicina quasi alla rovina et deforme tutta esposta alla pioggia et alle tempeste, senza riparo, senza ornamento alcuno' (near ruin and without form, wholly exposed to rain and storm,

---

[8] D. Fontana, *Della Trasportazione dell'Obelisco Vaticano et delle Fabbriche di Nostro SignorePapa Sixtus V fatte fare dal Cavaliere Domenico Fontana Architetto di Sua Santità* (Rome, 1590), 57–74v.

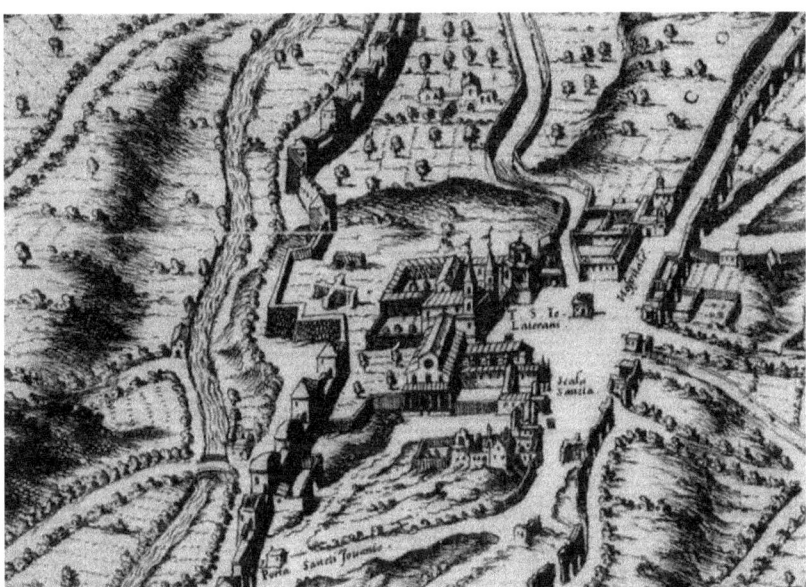

**Fig. 21.7** Stefano du Pèrac, *Roma nel sec. XVI: Zona dell'Anfiteatro Castrense e di Porta Latina*, Rome, 1577.

without shelter, without any form of ornament). The state of abandonment in which the complex lay, and the desire of Pope Sixtus V to intervene as part of his more general programme to restore a historical–political role to Christian Rome, are to be sought in the highly symbolic content of the Lateran, the bearer of a moral or artistic message of enduring value, separate from the duration of the construction itself, and which well lent itself to supporting the authority of the Church and confirming the importance of the Apostolic Seat. The exemplarity and innovative efficacy of the choices implemented, which involved the entire city during his brief papacy, including the reorganisation of infrastructures and monuments, testify to the grandiosity of a programme that saw 'urbanism' as a tool of government that could offer Rome a precise Christian imprint. The Lateran was ideal for this transformation, which pursued the objective of converting the monuments of Antiquity into emblems of faith. The value of the relics acquired over the centuries by the pre-existing elements of the Scala Santa, the Sancta Sanctorum, the baptistery and the *patriarchium*, guided the pope towards the redefinition of the Lateran complex through a project that included the realisation of the new Apostolic palace and the architectural positioning of the Scala Santa. This freed up the baptistery and restored to the faithful a space that is the expression of a pivotal moment in the history of Rome: the foundation by Constantine of the first Christian church. With the project for the Lateran, Sixtus V became the interpreter of a diverse attitude towards the pre-existing elements of the complex of medieval buildings, bending the rigidity of his plan in the face of the versatility of the *patriarchium* in any case, radically modifying its overall appearance with sudden and substantial demolitions. The Constantinian church, 'of venerable beauty',[9] was to be conserved; however, the 'obscure' and 'sordid' *patriarchium*, the public square filled with shacks arranged around the Annibaldi tower, the *triclinium* transformed into a garden, and the other buildings in a state of abandonment, were evident signs of the failure of an operation to define the centrality of the papacy, and could thus be relegated to a different destiny from that of the basilica. Sixtus V entrusted the design and construction of his project for the Lateran to Domenico Fontana, an architect at the pope's side throughout all of his architectural and urban undertakings. The project undoubtedly belongs to a complex situation, and the architectural result offers proof of this complexity. The information that can be inferred from an analysis of the construction budget, conserved in the State Archives of Rome, and documents held in the Secret Vatican Archives, reveal a constantly changing situation in relation to the intentions and aims of the entire operation, which includes at least two clearly distinct phases of design.[10]

The first phase involved the 'eastern' volume adjacent to the façade of the basilica, including the realisation of the volume containing the stair 'amplissima ... la maggiore di quane ne siano in Roma: perché è larga palmi trentadue, di dove tutti I Pontefici, quando vorranno far Cappella, potranno discendere in Pontificale con grandissima comodità per entrare nella porta principle della Chiesa di San Giovanni'.[11]

---

[9] Fontana, *Della Trasportazione dell'Obelisco Vaticano*, 57–74v.

[10] To offer the most reliable recounting of the history of the transformations of the Lateran complex, a process was instituted – shared with the directors of the Vatican Museums professors Pietrangeli, Buranelli and Paolucci, and encouraged by a friend Paolo Liverani, who I thank – beginning with the awareness that any historical study, any synthetic interpretation, cannot but be the in-depth analysis of specific individual events, through a rigorous ascertainment of facts and a consequent analytical reconstruction of the process of construction. The research was thus oriented towards a reflection linked directly to this monumental episode, exploring the individual aspects of the architectural design using the tools of the architect, to be critically evaluated: type, building systems, materials, architectural vocabulary and its syntactic organisation and stylistic characteristics. Only after the objective evaluation of the real conditions of architecture, understood as a historical and building process and the critical interpretation of the design solutions adopted, is it possible, in my opinion, to interpret the historic significances contained in a work of architecture. See A. Bruschi, *Introduzione alla storia dell'architettura: Considerazioni sul metodo e sulla storia degli studi* (Milan, 2009).

[11] '... very ample ... the largest of those in Rome: because it is thirty-two palms wide, where all of the popes, when they wish to go to chapel, can descend in pontifical robes with ease and enter through the main door to the Church of St John': Fontana, *Della Trasportazione dell'Obelisco Vaticano*, 57–74v.

*L'inserimento nel complesso monumentale del Laterano medioevale, attraverso i conti di cantiere riordinati da Giovanni Fontana (1586), del "coritore novo" che si affianca alla preesistente basilica paleocristiana restituita dal rilievo eseguito da Francesco Borromini (1646).*

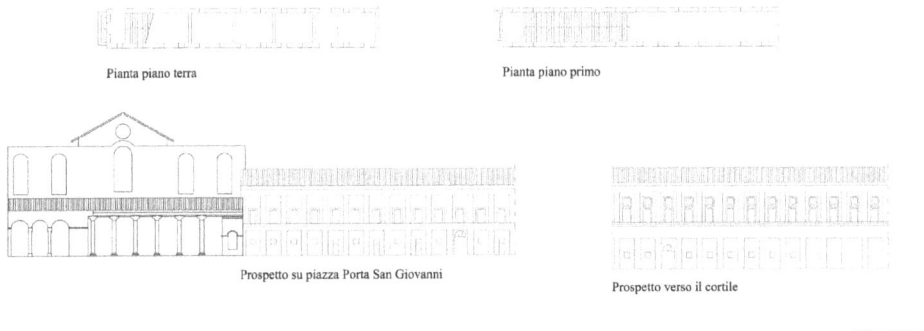

**Fig. 21.8** Historical reconstruction of *coritore novo* through building costs: plans and façades.

The works ordered by Domenico Fontana were carried out by Giovanni Fontana, while the *misuratore* (surveyor) was Prospero Rochi. The accounts are dated 15 March 1586, the sum of the expenses is 8,511.99 scudi, later reduced to 8,100 scudi by the pope and paid in full to the architect on 21 January 1590. The building realised was situated between the *portigale* or old loggia of the Porta Santa and the *logia vechia verso tramontana* (the old loggia towards the west) (Fig. 21.8). The length of the walls for the foundations was the same as those of the façades, both internal at 256 palms, and external at 280.25 palms (Fig. 21.9). The system of foundation walls consists of an alternation of columns and arches. The two perimeter walls are connected by fifteen transversal arches, some of which serve as a foundation for the dividing walls of the rooms on the ground floor. The walls of both façades were built up to a length of 130.5 palms from the portico of the basilica, immediately and for the entire height of the elevation. This first phase of works is identified in the accounts as reaching as far as the 'dritto del pilastro quanto tiene la scala a cordone' (the line of the column where it supports the stepped ramp). The remaining façades, facing the Piazza Porta San Giovanni and the interior courtyard, were constructed in overlapping parts, whose heights mirror the interior divisions: the vault of the ground floor, the vault of the loggia, the cornice and/or spring line, eave and roof. Between the interior and exterior façades there is a level change of 3.30 m, and to calibrate the realisation of the new building to be attached to the façade of the basilica it was necessary to excavate a great deal of earth in front of the portico to reach the threshold of the Porta Santa. The building system used for the walls was for the most part a single width 'de tavolozze

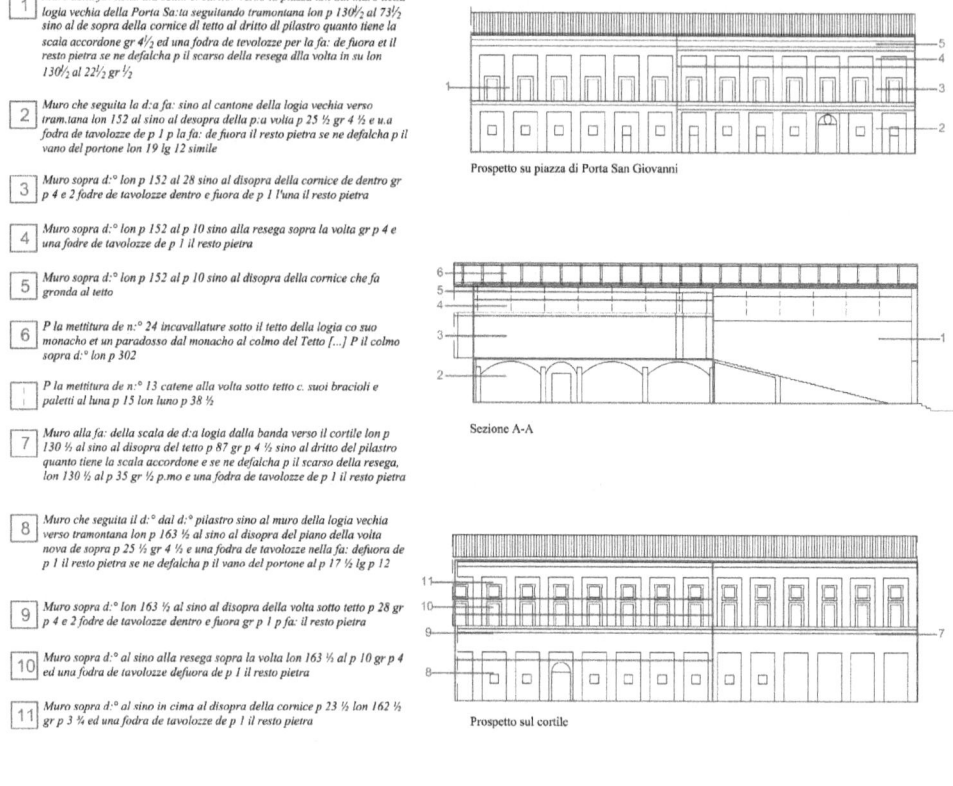

**Fig. 21.9** Historical reconstruction of *coritore novo* through building costs: sections and façade.

e il resto pietra' (of *tavolozze* and the rest in stone), while the vaults were entirely poured and reinforced by chains, four on the ground floor and thirteen on the *piano nobile*. The roof was installed on twenty-four *incavallature* (trusses); the windows of the mezzanine level and *piano nobile* were realised in travertine recovered from the 'piazza dovera il caval de bronzo' (the square once occupied by the bronze horse). The external façade was finished with a 'ricciatura sottile alla genovese' (a thin plaster daubing in the Genoese style), while a greater formal articulation was reserved for the façade facing the courtyard, which features windows at the mezzanine with cornices with ears. This decorative choice to privilege the internal elevation over that facing the Porta San Giovanni explicates the typology of this first intervention, which evidently pursued a functional purpose, with the realisation of a new stair connecting the basilica and the palace, to facilitate the path of papal investiture that, starting from the basilica, crossed the atrium to receive the acclamation of the public and continued into the Council Hall, the oratory of Saint Silvester and, crossing the *macrona*, arrived at the Sancta Sanctorum.[12] Hence, the new connection was to facilitate an easier passage between the various ancient parts of the palace, which was to have gradually lost its elevated position atop a sort of plateau, in the wake of important excavations that were part of the first phase of works.

In terms of the overall image, the Lateran must have resembled to the pope a sum of buildings constructed at different times in history, in the absence of an overall design, which was ill-suited to the idea of a city that privileged an urban condition of perspectival views connoted by focal points, stage sets and backdrops. It is perhaps with this aim that the pope commissioned a second project, again from Domenico Fontana, involving the almost total demolition of the medieval constructions, with the exception of the Christian relics to be conserved and repositioned. After completion of the first phase, the documentation records an interruption to works on site. On 4 July 1586 the accounts record the 'disfattura della Torre ch'era nella piazza di S. Giovanni' (the demolition of the tower that once stood in Piazza San Giovanni), known as the Annibaldi tower, at a cost of 140 scudi. While for the eastern part a 'muraglia bassa ... nella quale facciata non v'è altro che una scala che viene da fuori'[13] was realised, when works recommenced they did so with a notable leap in scale and ambition of construction. In fact, turning towards the city, in line with the interventions of his predecessors, the project of Sixtus V required a greater commitment and work that was ten times more costly than that which preceded it. The grandiosity of the operation was subject to the rapidity of its realisation, imposed by the pope himself. Two *Avvisi*, the first dated 29 August 1587 and the second 21 October 1587, inform us that the pope visited the site and insisted on the rapid completion of the works: 'Sisto V, dopo aver ascoltato la messa in san Giovanni, passò nell'attiguo cantiere e rimproverò i capimastri per la loro pigrizia'[14]; 'Nostro signore a S. G. in Laterano ... si compiacque di vedere minutamente la grande fabbrica, che

---

[12] Lauer, in the registry of documents relative to the ancient *patriarchium*, published the *Ordo di Cencio Camerarius* describing the Cæremoniale of the new pope.

[13] 'A low wall ... whose façade contained nothing more than a stair from the exterior': P. Tomei, *L'architettura a Roma nel Quattrocento* (Rome, 1942), 228.

[14] 'Sixtus V, after attending mass in (the Church of) Sant John, visited the adjacent construction site and scolded the head tradesmen for their laziness': *Avvisi*, 29 August 1587.

*Le trasformazioni apportate al complesso monumentale del Laterano medioevale con la costruzione del nuovo Palazzo Apostolico restituite attraverso i conti di cantiere di Domenico Fontana (1589-1590).*

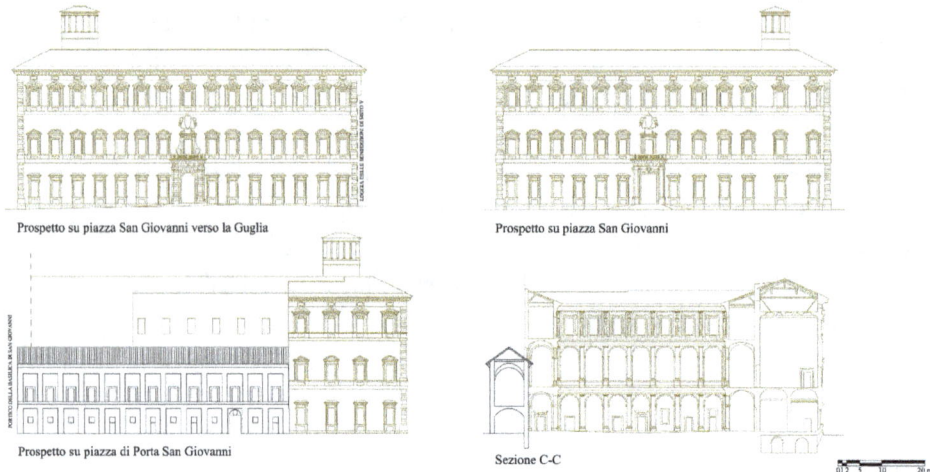

Fig. 21.10 Domenico Fontana's survey of the Palazzo Apostolico: façades.

fa fare unita a quella della Basilica, sollecitandola et salendo per tutte quelle volte et stanze con disposizione giovanile (Dio laudato) ancorché il tempo fosse cattivo'[15] (Fig. 21.10).

All the same, behind this image of efficiency and achievement, there were moments when Sixtus V demonstrated a certain disappointment and dissatisfaction for the progress of the works; on 31 August 1588 'il Papa andò a messa nella chiesa di S. Giovanni in Laterano et da poi volse vedere tutte quelle strutture nove, dicendo parerli, che la guglia sia posta troppo sotto alla fabbrica et palazzo'.[16] In some cases the pope even appeared to question the entire operation, to the point of 'qualche pentimento di aver principiato quella fabbrica di detto S. Giovanni'.[17] Nonetheless, work continued and, as further confirmation of its realisation in two phases, we have evidence of the diverse presence of trades and the fact that the accounts from this second phase include non-sequential measurements. There was also a continual alternation between works involving the internal and external façades, such that their

[15] 'While at Saint John Lateran our Lord ... was pleased to see every detail of the large construction site, that he was having joined to the basilica, asking it be finished soon and visiting all of the vaults and rooms with the sprightliness of youth (God be praised) despite the poor weather': *Avvisi*, 21 October 1587.
[16] 'The pope attended mass at the church of Saint John Lateran and then wished to visit all of the new structures, claiming that in his opinion the spire was located too far below the building and the palace': *Avvisi*, 31 August 1588.
[17] 'Some reconsiderations about having originated the building dedicated to Saint John': *Avvisi*, 31 August 1588.

progress can only be reconstructed using individual plans and not through coherent and successive realisations. Maintaining the stair from the first phase, adjacent to the basilica, but with the new need to reach the new building, raised by one storey, a second ramp of stairs was added to the first, in *mattoni in coltello* (brick laid on end); however, this construction was not inserted within a unitary design of the new palace (Fig. 21.11). This latter, inaugurated on 30 May 1589, after four years of work, presents two uniform three-storey elevations, with a sequence of aedicule windows facing the spire and Piazza San Giovanni, while the elevation facing the Porta San Giovanni remained two storeys in height. The comprehension of the intervention involving the palace can be linked to the entire reorganisation of the side of the Lateran facing the

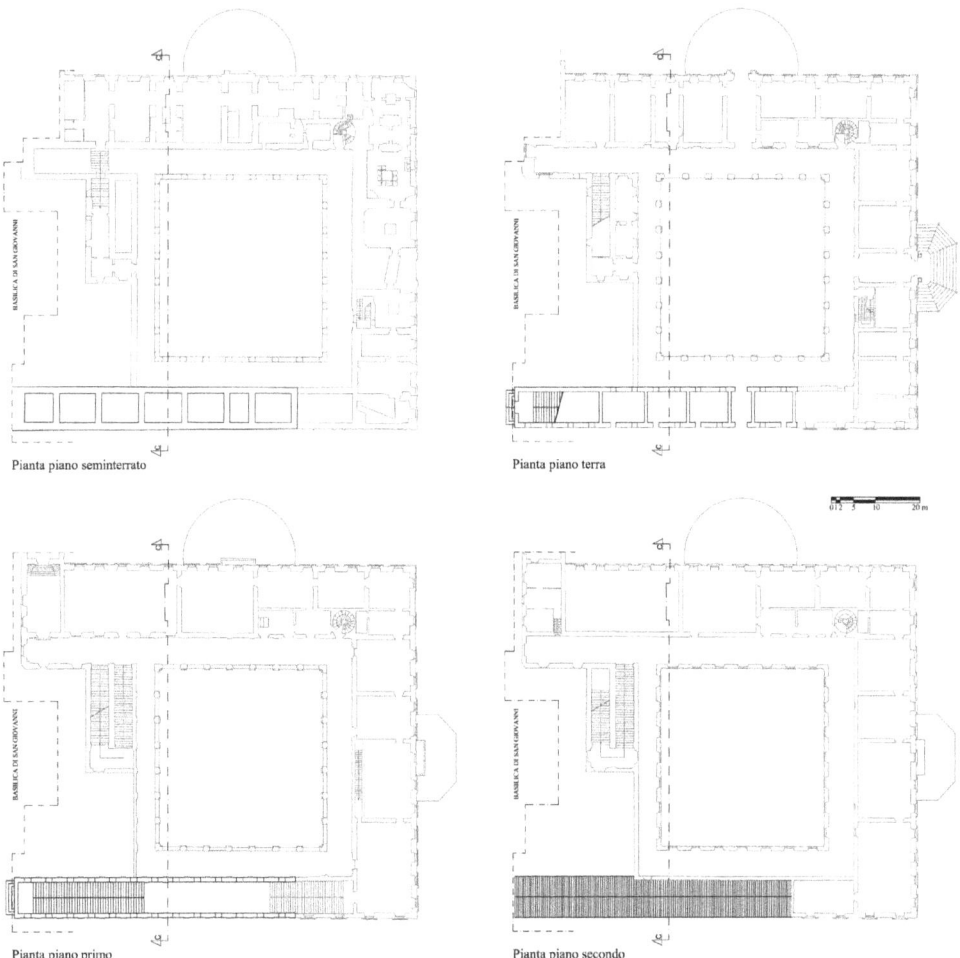

Fig. 21.11 Domenico Fontana's survey of the Palazzo Apostolico: plans.

city. The operation dealt, in fact, with the demolition of the oratory of the Cross, adjacent to the baptistery and the Annibaldi tower, the erection of the Lateran obelisk and the relocation of the Scala Santa, alongside the Sancta Sanctorum. The redesign of the public plaza once again privileged the view at the end of Via San Giovanni, with its two three-storey elevations, the west and the north, and the new Apostolic palace, with the construction of the Loggia of Benediction to the right and the building of the Scala Santa as the backdrop to the entirely redesigned space; a self-contained phase within the greater project for the entire city pursued by Sixtus V from the earliest days of his papacy: the centrality of the basilica of Santa Maria Maggiore with respect to the principal sites of papal and imperial Rome.

Although the book by Domenico Fontana contains a project for connecting Saint John Lateran with the basilica of Santa Croce in Gerusalemme,[18] even the new building that was to have contained the Scala Santa, and which could have presented an opportunity to define this possible new axis, was in any case oriented towards the city. Indeed, 'the destruction of the ancient *patriarchium* inevitably compromised the system of connections between the basilica and the chapel of the Sancta Sanctorum, isolated and profoundly altered by demolitions. Sixtus V decided to valorise the ancient papal chapel by proposing a work of architecture that contained the pre-existing constructions and restored to the faithful a scenographic perspectival vision perceived by pilgrims arriving from Via di San Giovanni in Laterano.'[19]

The beginning of the works for a first phase to erect a building with three bays can be dated to the second half of 1586, while the definitive building with five bays was completed in 1589, with the solemn relocation of the Scala Santa:

> li Canonici di detta Chiesa la sera di notte facendosi devotissime processioni, si tenne questo ordine, che cominciassi a levare l'ultimo scalino di sopra seguendo a basso tenendo il medesimo ordine quando si mettevano in opera, al contrario di quello che ordinariamente far si vuole accioché non vi si dovesse camminar con li piedi sopra, già che i Pontefici istessi divotamente van salendo quelle inginocchione e tutta l'opera fu in una sol notte posta in esecutione.[20]

---

[18] Fontana, *Della Trasportazione dell'Obelisco Vaticano*, 20v.

[19] Donadono, *La Scala Santa*, 21.

[20] 'As the canonical figures of the Church undertook religious processions at night, the order was issued to begin by removing the last stair from the top and to proceed toward the bottom and to proceed in the same order when replacing them, contrary to the normal order of a similar process, in order not to have to walk on the newly laid stairs, as the popes themselves, with great devotion, climb the stairs on their knees, and the entire work was completed in only one night': Donadono, *La Scala Santa*, 23.

*The East Façade in the Modern Era* 481

Despite the difficulties in offering an exact interpretation of the consistency of the medieval buildings of the *patriarchium*, if we observe with attention the fifteenth-century fresco by Filippino Lippi (Fig. 21.12), *The Triumph of Saint Thomas Aquinas over the Heretics*, in the Carafa chapel at Santa Maria Sopra Minerva, and the drawing by Marten van Heemskerck

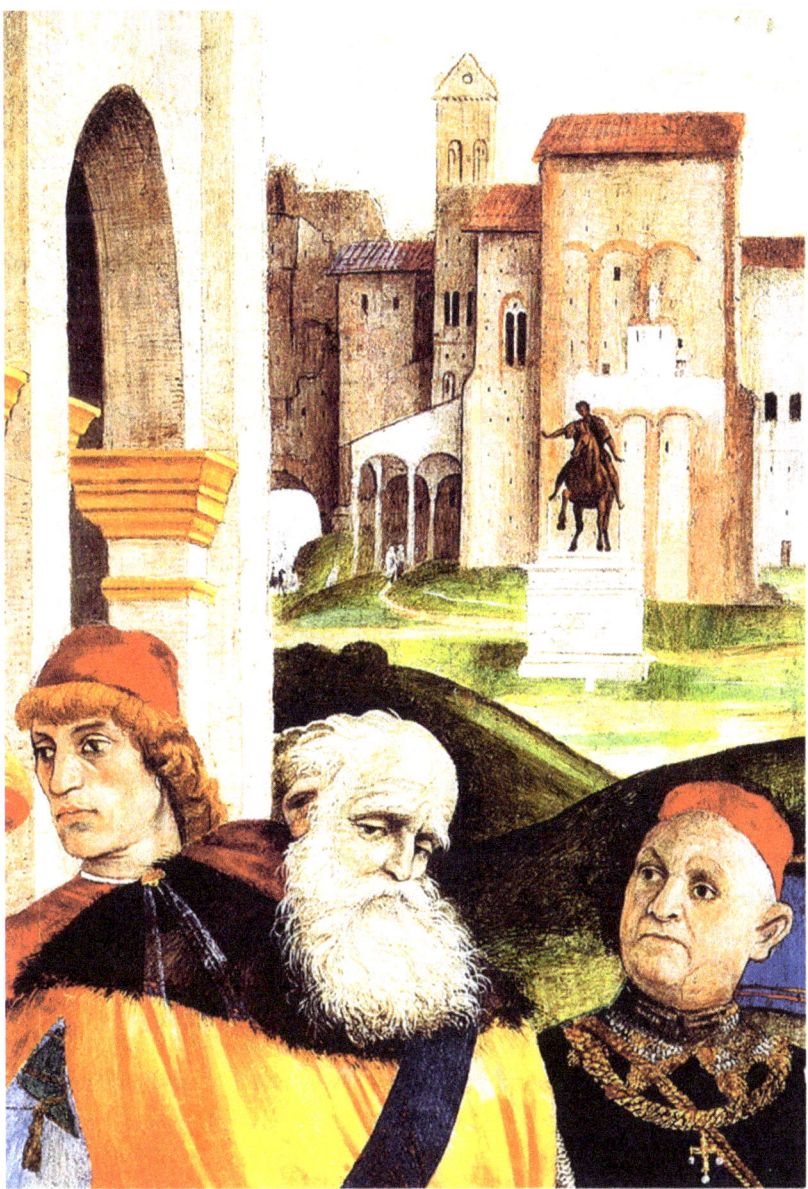

**Fig. 21.12** Filippino Lippi, *Disputa di S. Tommaso d'Aquino con gli eretici*, Rome, 1488.

(Fig. 21.13), it is possible to note that the Scala Santa was oriented ninety degrees with respect to its actual position. This confirms the explicit choice by the pope and his architect to ensure that the new building functioned as a scenographic backdrop to the view of the Lateran from Via San Giovanni, rather than being an element that served to define the eastern elevation of the Lateran complex. Not even the fact that Domenico Fontana had recovered pre-existing masonry structures can be considered to have dictated his choice to modify the orientation of the new building[21] because the architect attributed a purely instrumental value to pre-existing elements in order to favour the rapidity and economy of the construction of the new works, without any intentions of conservation.

The late fifteenth-century construction was thus unable to interpret and transmit the contents of one of the most important and representative sites of Christianity, to the point of establishing the historic premise for the renovation by Borromini desired by Innocent X (1644–55) and the other interventions made during the eighteenth century. The idea of a project involving the Constantinian basilica itself was seen as the anchor for rediscovering a new unity interrupted by the monumental architectural structure of the palace, the rich decoration of the Loggia of Benediction and the value of a container of relics assumed by the Scala Santa. This is precisely the approach required for a reading of the desire expressed by Pope Innocent X to conserve the testimonial significance of the basilica erected by Constantine, the first Christian emperor, with the respect for the pre-existing elements 'no longer symbolically reserved, as with Saint Peter's, to the extension of the perimeter of the ancient complex, but which involved the concreteness of the monument'.[22]

While the intervention promoted by the pope and realised by Borromini involved the entire basilica (1646–9), the death of Innocent X and later of the architect in 1667, impeded the progress of work and the design of the new façade and public plaza imagined by Borromini, as demonstrated in various documents, which reveal the preparation of multiple projects for the Lateran that his heirs Giuseppe and Pietro Antonio Borromini had sold to Antonio Libera for 600 scudi, at the time of Innocent XIII (1721–4). The order refers to a 'pianta ed un alzata della facciata a farsi a San Giovanni in Laterano come anche della pianta come sta presentata la piazza e dell'altra pianta in forma di teatro come voleva ridurre detta piazza il fu Francesco Borromini' (plan and elevation

---

[21] Donadono, *La Scala Santa*, 24.  [22] Roca de Amicis, *L'Opera di Borromini*, 38.

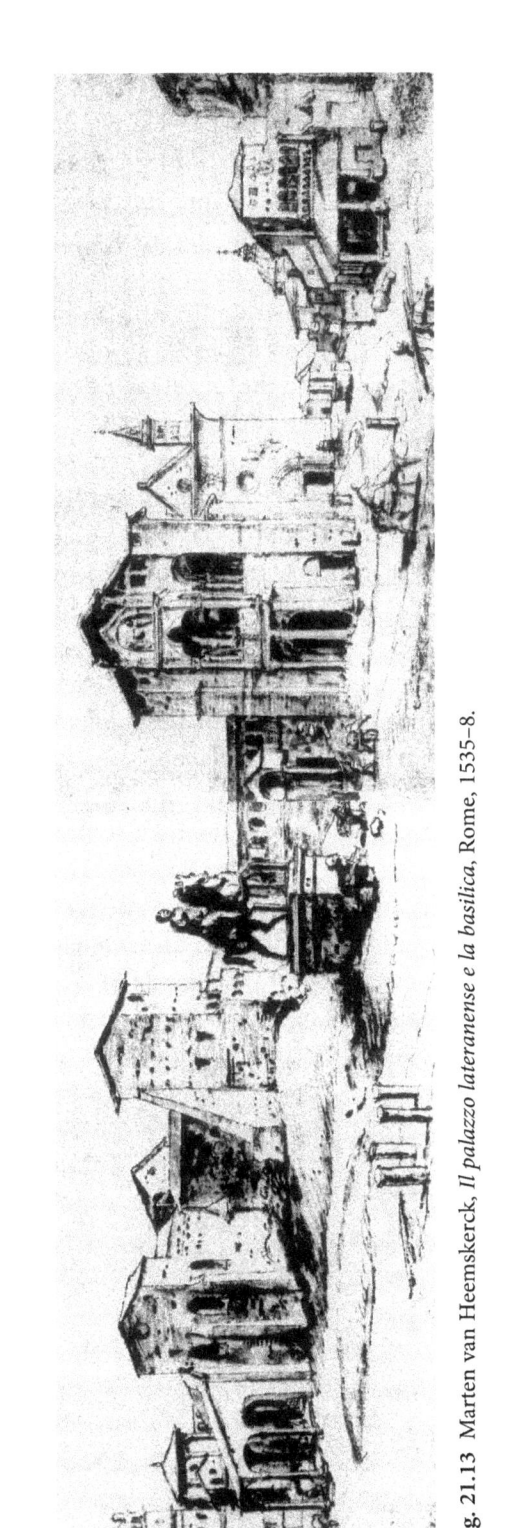

Fig. 21.13 Marten van Heemskerck, *Il palazzo lateranense e la basilica*, Rome, 1535–8.

of the façade to be realised at Saint John Lateran, as well as the plan of the square and the other plan in the form of a theatre as per the plans for the square by the late Francesco Borromini). Unfortunately, the loss of Borromini's drawings does not permit a precise idea of the project imagined by the architect for the elevation and/or the public square in front of it; we can only rely on rather vague written sources or draw indications from what was realised prior to 1667 in the area of the counter-façade and consisting primarily in the consolidation of the existing masonry and the study for the insertion of new structural-decorative elements necessary for the anchoring of the elevation, which can be assumed to have included a first porticoed level and a loggia of benediction on the second level. It is certain that Borromini imagined an upper level, given that Pope Alexander VI (1655–67), when works resumed, had mentioned it in order to advise against it, and that he imagined reusing ancient materials such as columns from other constructions.

All the same, for the present intervention, also of particular interest are the surveys by Borromini or his assistants, not only of the basilica but of the entire complex. Drawing Alb. 386 conserved at the Albertina depicts the eastern elevation of the Lateran complex: the façade of the basilica presents a portico at grade, with the final southern bays filled because they hosted the oratory of Saint Thomas, later opened on 4 April 1647, and at the upper level a wall with five arches set in correspondence with the nave and a tympanum emphasising the sole central nave (Fig. 21.14). Contiguous to the façade of the basilica is the two-storey building by Sixtus V containing the grand stair and, finally,

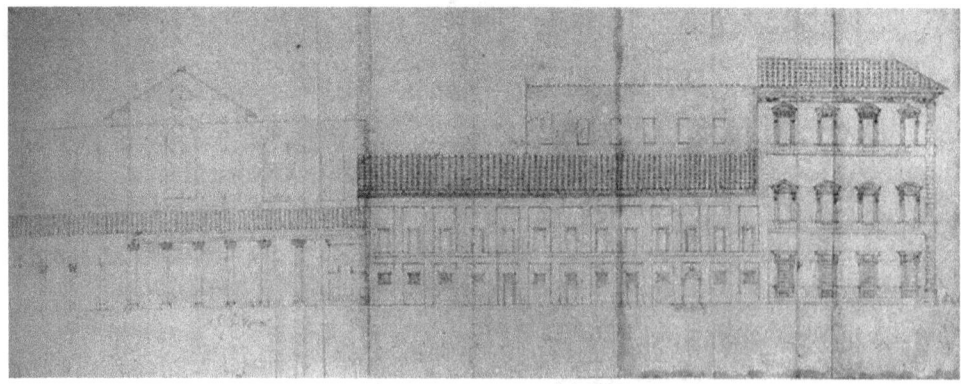

**Fig. 21.14** First scholar of Francesco Borromini, *Alzato di S. Giovanni in Laterano*, Rome, 1647.

the four bays of the northern building of the Apostolic palace. The survey of all of the buildings in a single drawing demonstrates how Borromini's project, unlike all those that preceded it, wished to take into account the pre-existing constructions not exclusively as relics of the Middle Ages, nor as structural elements for new interventions, as with the fountain, but inserting them into a new all-encompassing modern vision that would restore the uniformity of the complex because it would be perceived as the centre of spiritual and administrative power of the Church and no longer as a confused jumble of constructions inherited from the past. Aligned with this principle, a plan survey was made of the entire Lateran, including the area immediately around it (Fig. 21.15). In

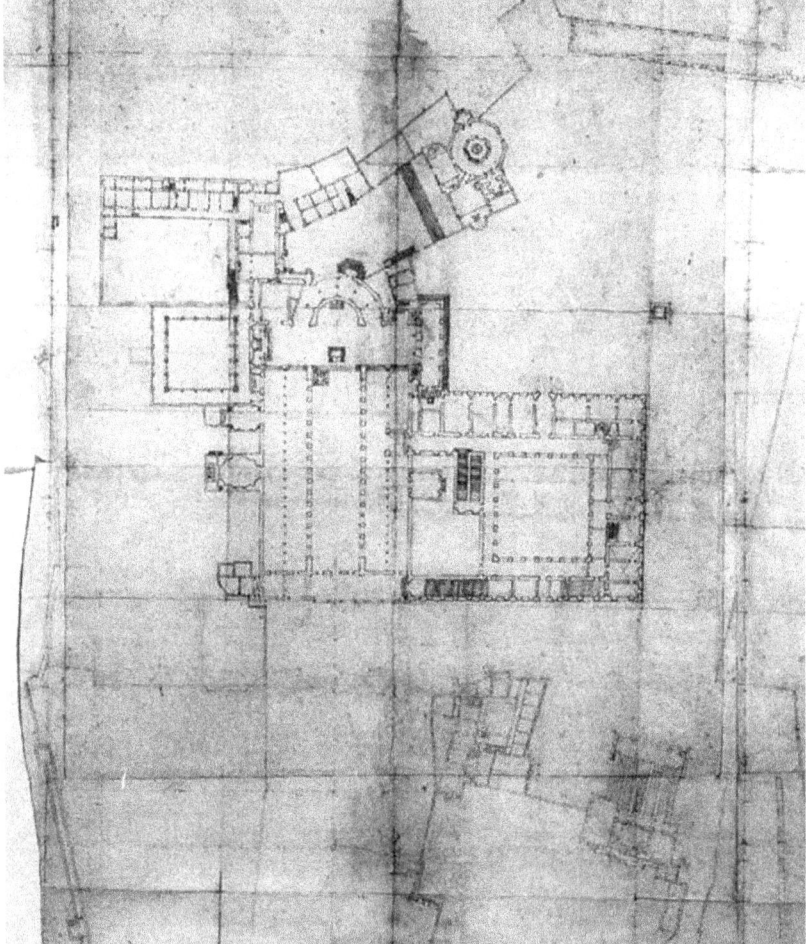

**Fig. 21.15** Francesco Borromini and scholars, *Pianta del complesso di S. Giovanni in Laterano*, Rome, 1646.

the drawing the eastern area is represented beyond the Porta San Giovanni, with hints of the Via Appia, and the varied fabric in front of the walls; it is also possible to observe, beyond the new building of the Scala Santa, the Leonian *triclinium* and the Casa dei Penitenzieri still in their original position. This drawing offers further proof of how the project by Sixtus V for the eastern front was exclusively functional: not only because the façade of the grand stair was not inserted in the project of the Apostolic palace but, what is more, it was not given any value in a possible overall view, leaving the pre-existing structures from the Middle Ages in front of it and partially covering it. The etching by Giovanni Battista Falda, while containing elements that do not respond to the conditions of the site, such as the Loggia of Benediction separated from the Apostolic palace, is one of the few images to depict the irregularity of the eastern front, even after completion of Borromini's project for the basilica (Fig. 21.16).

Hence the eastern façade of the Lateran remained unresolved, above all because, if we exclude the projects by Borromini, it was not considered as such, due also to the failure of Sixtus V to revitalise the Apostolic palace, which practically never served this function but,

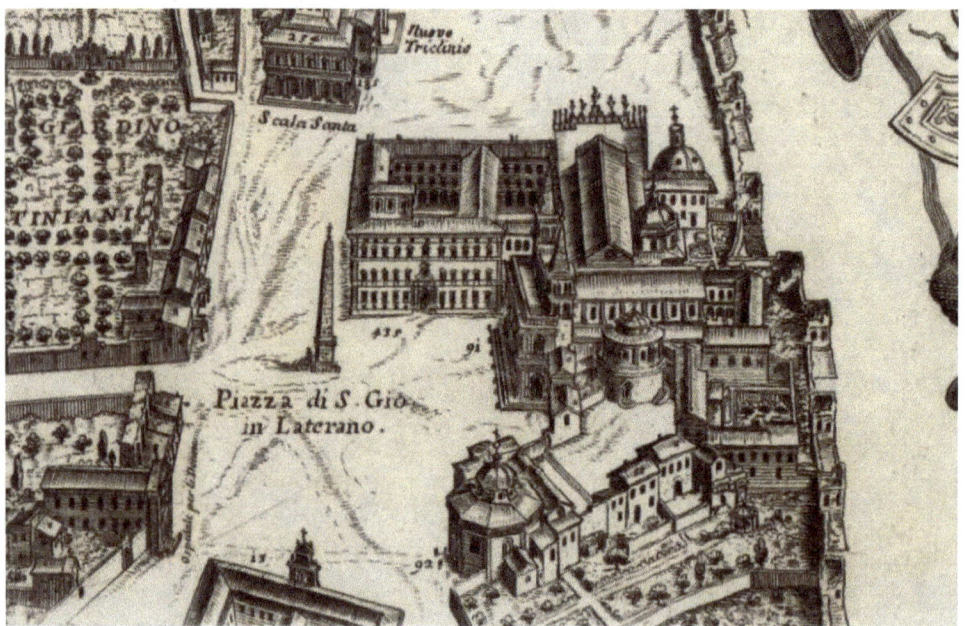

**Fig. 21.16** Giovan Battista Falda, *Roma nel sec. XVII: Zona di S. Giovanni in Laterano e delle Terme di Caracalla*, Rome, 1676.

surprisingly enough, from the papacy of Innocent XII (1691-1700) was utilised as a home for spinsters. The proposals made by architects during the seventeenth and eighteenth centuries concentrated exclusively on projects to complete the façade of the basilica, such as those by Felice della Greca or Andrea Pozzo. Even the Concorso Clementino of 1705 for the second class at the Accademia di San Luca dealt solely with the façade of the basilica and, as pointed out by Elisabeth Kieven,[23] the participants' projects contain all of the motifs encountered in all of the projects for Saint John Lateran: experiments with the colossal or minor orders; the convex or concave curvature of the façade; and the arrangement of the arches. The only architect we know for sure to have expressed a vision for the entire eastern area of the Lateran is Filippo Juvarra, involved on more than one occasion in projects for the elevation of Saint John Lateran, though none of the drawings conserved can be dated with any precision. Juvarra's view from the east, one of the views to have survived, datable in all probability to his time in Rome between 1704 and 1714, depicts a disarticulated urban situation in which, other than the incomplete façade of the basilica, it is also possible to note the *triclinium* and the Casa dei Penitenzieri in front of the Apostolic palace at the centre of an abandoned suburban area, far from the inhabited city. Juvarra's interest in considering the entire urban context before beginning the design of the building, typical of his working method, was also rendered concrete in the sketch of Madrid connected with the Concorso Clementino of 1705, though which Kieven hypothesises as belonging to a possible competition held in 1715-16,[24] which proposed the reorganisation of the entire area (Fig. 21.17). On the basis of this drawing, the scholar also attributes to Juvarra an anonymous text conserved by the Fondo Albani at the Vatican Secret Archives, in which the author proposes dismantling the Penitenzieria, the opening of a road towards Santa Croce in Gerusalemme and the completion of the Apostolic palace. Juvarra's project in any case included a closed church square that, with the curved and straight lines of the colonnades, intelligently concealed the length of the façades of both the basilica and the Apostolic palace. The canvas by Paolo Anesi is another of the few images depicting the Lateran complex from the

---

[23] E. Kieven, 'Il ruolo del disegno: Il concorso per la facciata di S. Giovanni in Laterano', in B. Contardi and G. Curcio (eds.), *Urbe architectus: Modelli. Disegni. Misure: La professione dell'architetto: Roma 1680-1750* (Rome, 1991), 78-123, esp. p. 88.

[24] Kieven, 'Il ruolo del disegno', 88.

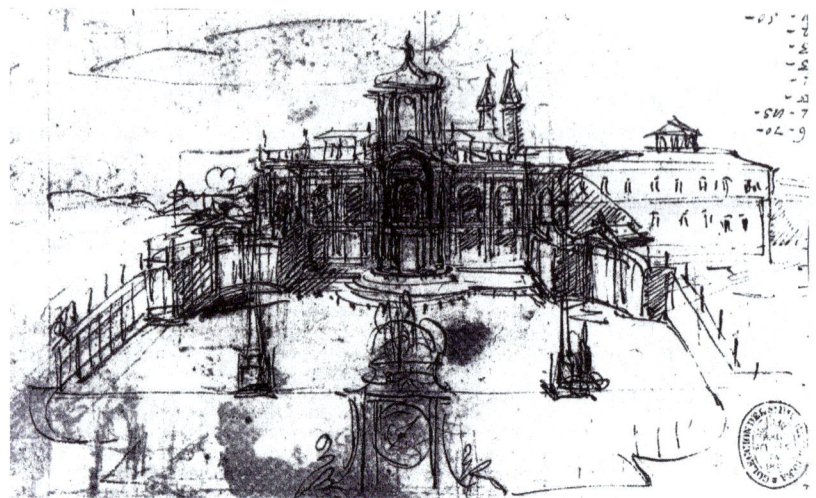

**Fig. 21.17** Filippo Juvarra, *Progetto per la facciata e la piazza di S. Giovanni in Laterano*, Rome, 1715–16?

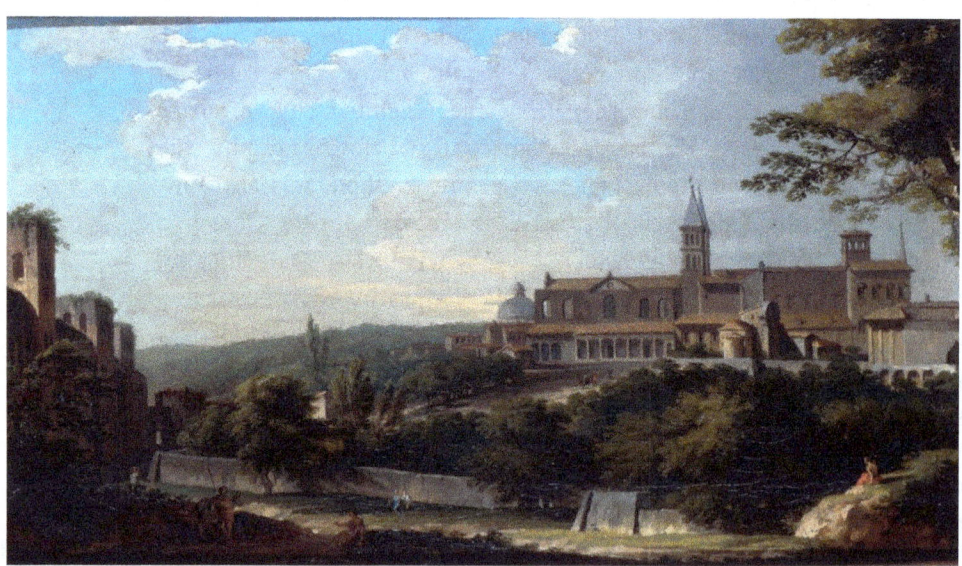

**Fig. 21.18** Paolo Anesi, *Veduta della basilica di S. Giovanni in Laterano*, Rome, 1697–1773.

east (Fig. 21.18). Other than the palaeo-Christian façade of the basilica, the foreground also features the rear elevation of the Scala Santa and the Leonian *triclinium* in its original location, surrounded by low constructions – in other words, the remains of the ancient *patriarchium* and the Casa dei Penitenzieri. The setting of the painting offers further confirmation that the complex was considered, at least from the east, as a suburban monument.

In 1732 Cardinal Benedetto Pamphili, nephew of Innocent X and archpriest of Saint John Lateran, acquired from the heirs of Borromini seven drawings for the façade of the basilica and one for the public square in front of it. He then commissioned Mario Bernardi to construct a model. Based on these drawings, the pope commissioned the architects Tommaso Mattei, Antonio Canevari and Filippo Cremoli with a project 'in elevazione pianta e profilo della facciata fatti a tenore del disegno di Francesco Borromini' (in elevation, plan and section of the façade on the basis of the drawing by Francesco Borromini). When in 1731 these projects arrived at the Congregation headed by Cardinal Ottoboni, charged with evaluating the reconstruction of the façade, no agreement was reached and, some eighty years after Borromini's project had first been developed, its guidelines were abandoned, and the Congregation decided to organise an official competition. On 16 April 1732 a papal edict was published 'to invite the most famous architects to compete [by submitting] their drawings or models' for the reconstruction of the façade. The event, which can be considered the first modern architectural competition, was awarded to the Florentine Alessandro Galilei, the architect of di Neri Corsini, nephew of Pope Clement XII (1730–40). Beyond the controversies that accompanied this victory, and the criticisms of the winning project, the pope commissioned the architect with the completion of the Apostolic palace, concluded by simply replicating the language adopted by Domenico Fontana.[25] An analysis of the twofold project for the church–palace is possible through the reading of the accounts of the construction, conserved at the Archivio del Capitolo di San Giovanni in Laterano, neither transcribed nor published, which conclude with the work of the mosaic tile installer in relation to the relocation of the Leonian *triclinium*. The completion of the palace therefore also appears to meet the desire to intervene in the area in front of it, and precisely from this period are two drawings in plan by an anonymous hand illustrating perhaps the first concrete ideas for the redesign of the eastern part of the Lateran with the creation of a public square and colonnade solely in front of the basilica, ignoring the path of the Aurelian Walls. What is more, it foresaw the demolition of the Casa dei

---

[25] A. Ippoliti, 'Il lato orientale di Alessandro Galilei (1731–1738)', in A. Ippoliti, *Il Palazzo Apostolico del Laterano* (Monumenta Sanctae Sedis 4) (Rome, 2008), 23–4.

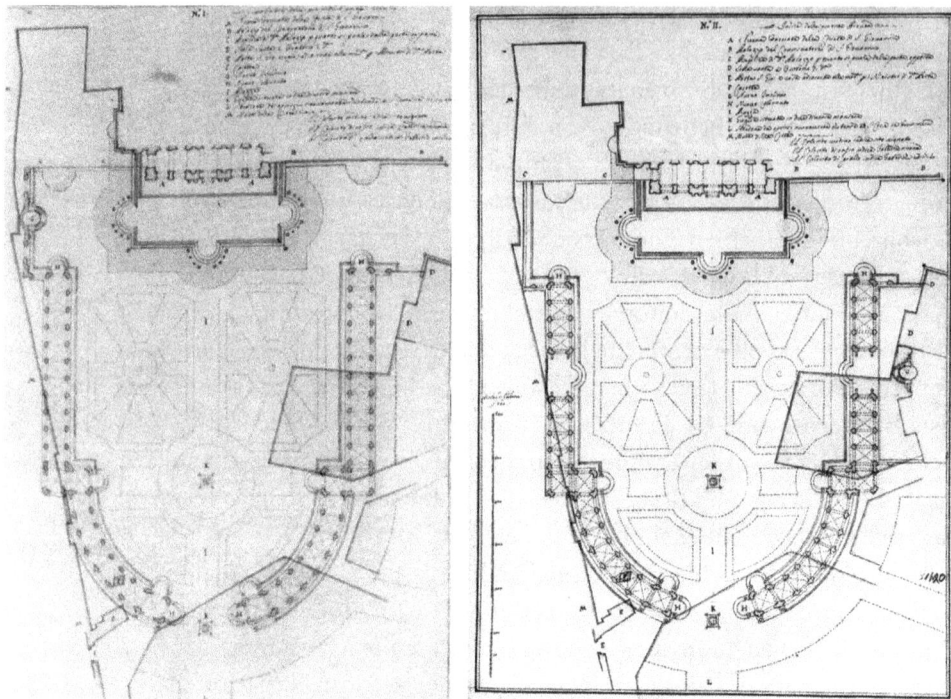

Fig. 21.19 Anonymous, *Pianta di progetto della piazza da realizzare davanti alla Basilica di S. Giovanni in Laterano*, Rome, eighteenth century.

Penitenzieri and the relocation of the *triclinium*, in the first solution to the left after the colonnade towards the Porta San Giovanni and near the elevation of the church and, in the second, near the Scala Santa (Fig. 21.19). It was precisely in this position, facing the basilica, that it would be relocated in the project by Ferdinando Fuga, deliberately freeing up the space between the complex of the Lateran and the Aurelian Walls, though rendering it even more uncertain as an urban space of large dimensions and without any architectural or urban definition. The theme of the redesign of the public square was approached in an anonymous drawing[26] from 1820 proposing a tree-lined boulevard between Saint John Lateran and Santa Croce in Gerusalemme and by Giuseppe Valadier who, in 1831, presented two proposals[27] featuring a hemicycle of regularised avenues and the addition of new constructions serving the guardhouses. Nonetheless, to this day the Piazza Porta San Giovanni in

---

[26] Archivio di Stato di Roma, *Collezione Piante e Disegni*, cart. 81, tav. n. 292, 1820.
[27] Archivio di Stato di Roma, *Collezione Disegni e Mappe*, bob. 27, cart. 78, n. 207 and bob. 29, cart. 81, n. 296.

The East Façade in the Modern Era 491

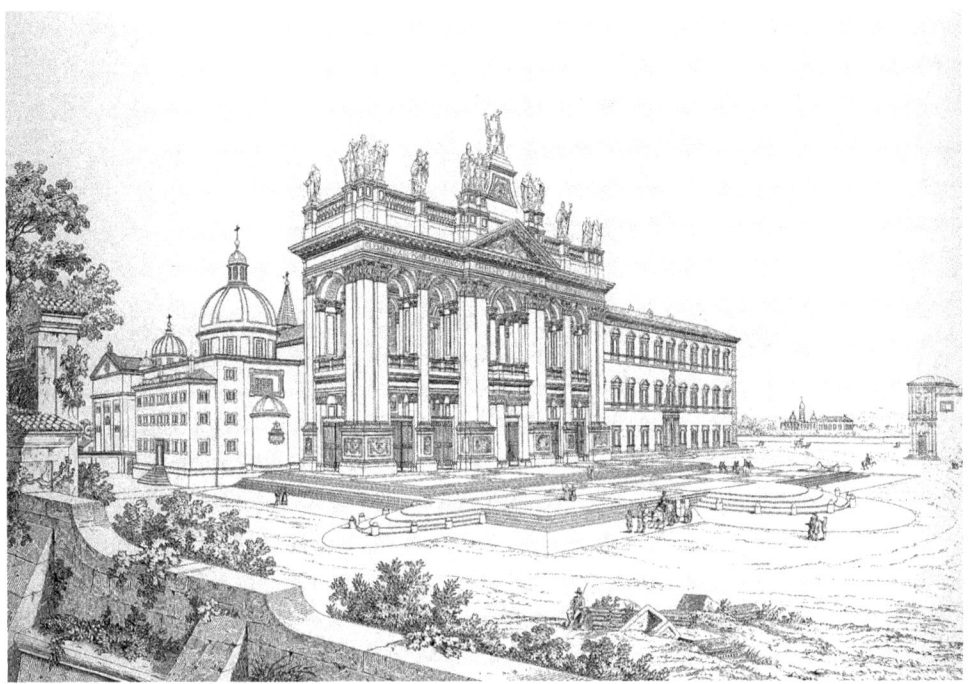

**Fig. 21.20** Paul Marie Letarouilly, *Veduta della facciata principale della Basilica e del Palazzo di S. Giovanni in Laterano*, Rome, 1841.

Laterano, more correctly the area in front of the basilica (Fig. 21.20), represents an unresolved design issue, without a complete definition of urban space, with the exception of its prevalently public use as a space of gathering for large political demonstrations.

# 22 | The Book of Acts in the Constantinian Basilica: Cardinal Cesare Baronio and the *Navata Clementina* in San Giovanni in Laterano

FILIP MALESEVIC

Along with the commissions of the Jesuits for embellishing their own churches in Rome during Gregory XIII's pontificate, a well-known repertoire of Constantinian imagery was reintroduced into church decoration during the Cinquecento. This type of imagery was known before the sixteenth century to have been reserved for church decoration only, but made its way at the beginning of the century even into the pictorial programmes for the Vatican Apostolic palace. One needs only to be reminded of the scenes in Santi Quattro Coronati with the legend of Pope Sylvester I or even Pope Innocent III's commission to paint the presbytery of San Silvestro in Tivoli around 1215 with a frieze of scenes from the emperor Constantine's life. The decoration of the Sala di Costantino in the Vatican Apostolic palace occupies a fundamental place in the evolution of this type of pictorial narrative, as it becomes entangled with the papacy's defence of the powers under attack by Protestants, inspired by Lorenzo Valla's refutation of the *Constitutum Constantini* in the Quattrocento.[1]

The Jesuits sought to frame an appropriate and equivalent response to the claims made by Protestant authors in their martyrologies, such as for instance John Foxe's *Acts and Monuments of These Latter and Perilous Days* (Foxe's *Book of Martyrs*) from 1563, and similar works challenging the Roman Church's fundamental preservation of its ritual practices,

---

[1] Martin Luther himself became well acquainted with Valla's treatise through his correspondence with Georg Spalatin, who was able to obtain a copy of the *De falso credita et ementita Constantini donatione* that Ulrich von Hutten had edited. Luther then used Valla's arguments for refuting the Donation of Constantine and declared its supporting document a fake in order to motivate the German aristocracy to detach itself from the Roman Church's so-called 'Constantinheit' in his tract *An den christlichen Adel deutscher Nation* of 1520. On Luther's use of Valla's treatise, see J. Fried, *'Donation of Constantine' and 'Constitutum Constantini': The Misinterpretation of a Fiction and Its Original Meaning* (Berlin, 2007), 32–6; W. Setz, *Lorenzo Vallas Schrift gegen die konstantinische Schenkung: 'De falso credita et ementita Constantini donatione', zur Interpretation und Wirkungsgeschichte* (Tübingen, 1975). On the reception of Valla's refutation in the Italian peninsula, see G. M. Vian, *La donazione di Costantino: Potere religioso e potere politico in Italia* (L'identità italiana 35) (Bologna, 2004), 129–68; G. Antonazzi, *Lorenzo Valla e la polemica sulla Donazione di Costantino* (Rome, 1985), 105–12.

supported by pictures and images. When Foxe's *Book of Martyrs* appeared on the market again in 1583, the English Catholics responded in a similar manner with their own writings, the most heavily illustrated volume being *A Briefe Historie of the Glorious Martyrdom of Twelve Reverend Priests* by Cardinal William Allen. An Italian version of Allen's treatise was also published in Macerata in 1583 under the patronage of the Venerable English College as *Historia del glorioso martirio di sedici sacerdoti*, including six engravings, each followed by a Latin inscription.[2] William Allen was an English Catholic who founded a college in Douai in France to train English priests for the dangerous pastoral work they would eventually face in their homeland. During Queen Elizabeth I's reign Catholics were so heavily persecuted that England became one of the most dangerous places for missionary work. His book thus confronts Foxe's by recounting the martyrdoms of twelve English Catholic priests, the number echoing the number of the Apostles; one of them was the Jesuit Edmund Campion, executed under Elizabeth I in December 1581.[3]

A closer look at the illustrations in William Allen's treatise shows a considerable resemblance to the fresco cycle painted on the upper part of the nave walls in the chapel of the Venerable English College in Rome. Since 1560 the college, situated near the Piazza Farnese, had functioned as a seminary supported by the English community in Rome for the training of Englishmen as priests.[4] In 1578 Pope Gregory XIII had appointed the Society of Jesus to run the college. The pictorial decoration of the church of San Tommaso di Canterbury, the college's chapel, was entrusted by the Jesuits to a Tuscan painter from Pomarance, Niccolò Circignani, who had

---

[2] See T. Buser, 'Jerome Nadal and early Jesuit art in Rome', *Art Bulletin* 58 (1976), 423–33, at p. 429 n. 30; G. A. Bailey, *Between Renaissance and Baroque: Jesuit Art in Rome, 1565–1610* (Toronto, 2009), 155.

[3] See also R. Parsons, An Epistle of the Persecution of Catholicks in Englande (Douai, 1582) as well as John Gibbons and John Fenn, *Concertation ecclesiae catholicae in Anglia, adversus Calvinopapistas & Puritanos* (Trier, 1583). For Allen's book, Thomas Buser was able to show that the illustrations follow those in Foxe's work very closely: see Buser, 'Jerome Nadal', 429–30.

[4] On the history of the Venerable English College in Rome, see Cardinal Francis Aidan Gasquet, *A History of the Venerable English College, Rome* (London, 1920), 71–8; Bailey, *Between Renaissance and Baroque*, 153–4. In terms of theological training, this college was more like the one Cardinal Allen had founded in Douai, although the Jesuits themselves thought it more similar to their more important German institution, the Collegio Germanico-Hungarico. See William Allen's *Apologie and True Declaration* (Rheims, 1581), where he noted that 'there was no distinction (to Douai) between them as to aim or recruitment. There is similar course of studies, the kinds of sermons preached, the exercises of religion and devotion, are the same' (quoted in Bailey, *Between Renaissance and Baroque*, 154).

already embellished the order's other two churches, Santo Stefano Rotondo and Sant'Apollinare, with a fresco cycle showing various martyrdoms.

The iconographic programme in San Tommaso di Canterbury, executed by Circignani, was lost during a demolition of the church edifice in 1860. However, it had been recorded by the engraver Giovanni Battista Cavalieri in his *Ecclesiae anglicanae trophaea* from 1584.[5] This painting cycle included martyrdoms but, unlike Circignani's other frescoes for Santo Stefano Rotondo, it also presented images that emphasised the legitimacy of the Roman Church in England and thus attempted to refute Foxe's distinction between a spiritual explanation of martyrdom and its material manifestation in pictorial decorations, which Foxe directly associated with the falsity of Constantine's mythical donation.[6] By including the scene of *Constantine the Great's Vision of the True Cross*, which also showed Constantine's baptism in the background of the left half, the fresco cycle in San Tommaso di Canterbury stressed the important ties between Britain and Rome that had already been apparent in Late Antiquity (Fig. 22.1). Niccolò Circignani's iconographic programme in San Tommaso di Canterbury thus enters into a specific dialogue with the revisions carried out on the *Martyrologium Romanum*, when in the case of the *Vision of the True Cross* a well-known pictorial formula was employed to include Constantine the Great in the larger body of the Roman Church's martyrs from early Christianity. Constantine's *Vision* had a famous precedent in Cinquecento pictorial production in Rome: Raphael's workshop included the same scene in the decoration of the Sala di Costantino in the Vatican Apostolic palace. There is, however, a crucial difference between Raphael and Circignani's treatment of the same scene. While the former clearly intended to render the subject through a more accurate setting of the scene in front of a historicised landscape of Late Antique Rome, in Circignani's

---

[5] See G. B. Cavalieri, *Ecclesiae anglicanae trophaea . . . Romae in collegio Anglico per Nicolaum Circinianum depictae* (Rome, 1584). A series of engravings was also produced by Cavalieri around three years after Circignani's completion of the fresco cycle in Santo Stefano Rotondo: see G. B. Cavalieri, *Ecclesiae militantis triumphi . . . in ecclesia S. Stephani Rotundi Romae Nicolai Circiniani pictoris manu visuntur* (Rome, 1585). On the latter iconographic programme, see K. Noreen, '*Ecclesiae militantis triumphi*: Jesuit iconography and the Counter-Reformation', *Sixteenth Century Journal* 29 (1998), 689–716; and C. Behrmann, *Tyrann und Märtyrer: Bild und Ideengeschichte des Rechts um 1600* (Berlin, 2015), 163–86.

[6] See John Foxe, *Actes and Monuments of these Latter and Perillous Days, Touching Matters of the Church* (London, 1563): ' . . . the goodes and ornaments of the Church chiefly . . . consist, not in Donatives and patrimonies, but in the bloud, actes, and lyfe of Martyres, the seekying and settynge foorthe whereof ought to occupie the studie of true Christian Byshoppes' (introduction, n.p.) See also B. S. Gregory, *Salvation at Stake: Christian Martyrdom in Early Modern Europe* (Cambridge, MA, 2001).

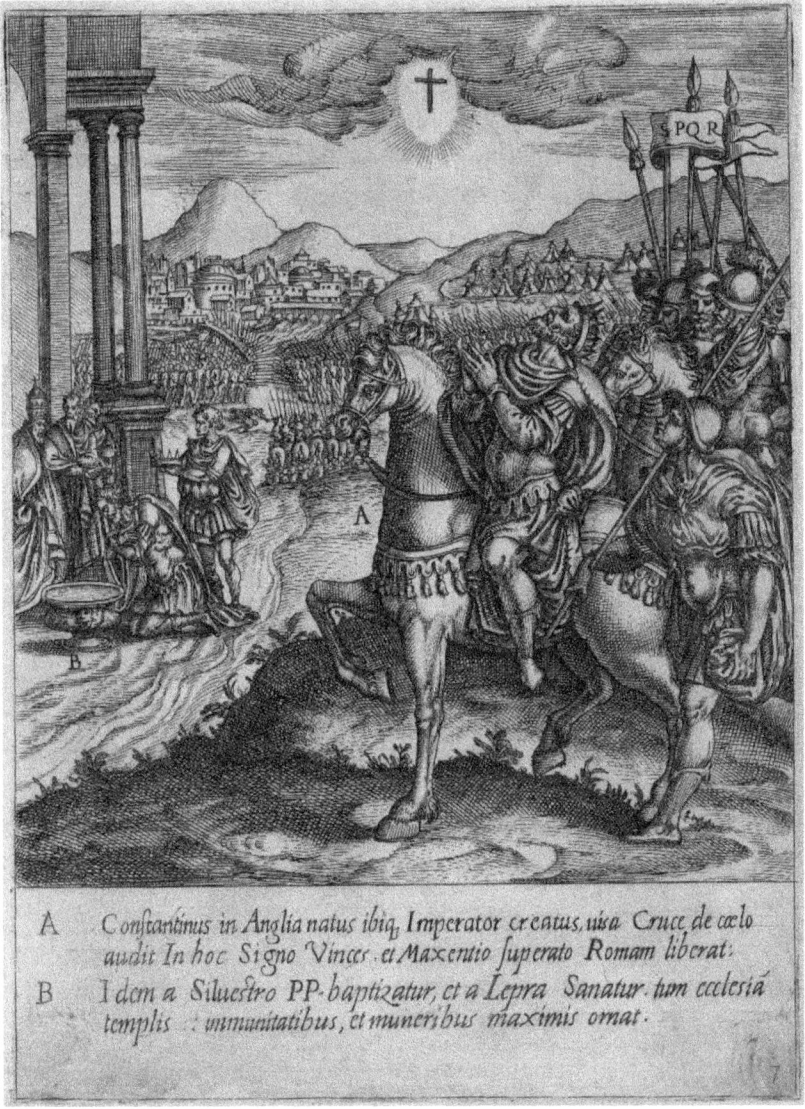

Fig. 22.1 Giovanni Battista de' Cavalieri, *Constantine the Great's Vision of the Cross*, in *Ecclesiae anglicanae trophaea* (1584), c. 7r.

fresco Constantine is presented on horseback, and above him in the upper centre of the picture the True Cross miraculously appears. The pose of Constantine's horse is clearly modelled upon the equestrian statue of the Capitoline Marcus Aurelius. The landscape scenery is considerably larger than Raphael's, and the *veduta* of Rome in San Tommaso di Canterbury is only suggested by the Pantheon in the far left background of the picture.

The apparition of the Cross and Constantine's own gesture of hands folded in prayer suggest a more accentuated miraculous moment. The Constantinian episode in the church of the Venerable English College is thus transferred to a realm almost detached from the historical event, and now confronts the beholder from a sensuous dimension of devotion that could only have been perceived from the perspective of the Roman rite.[7]

This study attempts to analyse how Constantinian imagery in Rome after the Council of Trent expanded into artistic patronage of the Curia that concentrated on the decoration of church interiors in Rome. Beginning with the architectural reorganisation of the complex on the ancient Patriarchium Lateranensis for which the papacy of Sixtus V had commissioned Domenico Fontana to construct a new palace attached to the basilica, the church of San Giovanni in Laterano and its importance for the city of Rome as well as for the Curia in general was gradually acquiring a grandeur commensurate with Pope Pius V's declaration of the Lateran as *Mater et Caput Orbis Ecclesiasrum* expressed in a bull from 1569.[8] Unfortunately, due to the brevity of Sixtus V's five-year pontificate and of the three that followed his death in 1590, only the papacy of Gregory XIV lasting as long as a year, no interventions within the basilica of San Giovanni in Laterano were carried out. It was only with the election of Cardinal Ippolito Aldobrandini in 1592 as Pope Clement VIII that further work on the Lateran could be carried out. Immediately after his election the new pope paid a pastoral visit to San Giovanni in Laterano and decided that not only the basilica, but also its baptistery, would need crucial changes.[9]

---

[7] On the historical accuracy of the Constantinian imagery in the Vatican Sala di Costantino, see P. P. Fehl, 'Raphael as a historian: Poetry and historical accuracy in the Sala di Costantino', *Artibus et Historiae* 28 (1993), 9–76; R. Quednau, *Die Sala di Costantino im Vatikanischen Palast: Zur Dekoration der beiden Medici-Päpste Leo X. und Clemens VII* (Hildesheim, 1979).

[8] For Pius V's bull from 21 December 1569, see *Collectionis bullarum sacrosanctae basilicae vaticanae*, 3 vols. (Rome, 1747–52), III, 72–5. However, the spiritual revival of the Lateran in the sixteenth century can be dated back to Pope Paul IV's impetus to confer custody of the *acheiropoieta* preserved in the Sancta Sanctorum upon the Collegio Capranica in 1558, a detail so far ignored by the scholarship. See J. Freiberg, *The Lateran in 1600: Christian Concord in Counter-Reformation Rome* (New York, 1995), 10. On Pope Sixtus V's restorations carried out by his architect Domenico Fontana at the Lateran complex, see C. Mandel, *Sixtus V and the Lateran Palace* (Rome, 1994); N. Horsch, *Ad astra gradus: Scala Santa und Sancta Sanctorum in Rom unter Sixtus V (1585–1590)* (Munich, 2014).

[9] For Clement's visits of June 1592 and their spiritual compliance with the norms declared by the Council of Trent for pastoral visits, see D. Beggiao, *La visita pastorale di Clemente VIII (1592–1600): Aspetti di riforma post-tridentina a Roma* (Rome, 1978), 24–32, 49–50 n. 11; L. Fiorani, 'Le visite apostoliche del Cinque-Seicento e la società religiosa romana', *Ricerche per la storia religiosa di Roma* 4 (1980), 53–148; Freiberg, *The Lateran in 1600*, 36–8. Clement VIII also issued a bull that emphasised the importance of the so-called *quarant'ore* – Forty Hours' Devotion – which he requested in order to give him divine assistance. See *Bullarium,*

While the baptistery was provided with renovations focusing on the chapels that surround the central octagon, the changes planned for the basilica were far more extensive, and manifested themselves most dramatically in the church's transept. Clement VIII ordered that a new ceiling was to be constructed in order to complement the ceiling of the central nave that Pope Pius IV had already installed around 1563. The organ was then to be transferred from the south transept to the inner façade of the northern entrance and a balcony constructed, which allowed the pope to observe the liturgical services privately. Furthermore, the most crucial intervention concerned the transfer of Gregory XIII's Altar of the Blessed Sacrament to a 'nobler place of the church where it would be most exposed to the eyes of those entering the church'.[10] Another major intervention, ordered by Clement VIII, concerned the Sacristy of Canons that was located at the southern ambulatory encircling the apse. A new sacristy would be constructed that was linked by a passage with the apse.

Finally, Clement VIII's transept would be embellished with an iconographic programme on the lateral walls that constituted eight select episodes from the life of Constantine the Great, above which a series of figures of Apostles would then also be painted. Above the newly erected Altar of the Blessed Sacrament, Cesare d'Arpino would then paint his *Ascension of Christ* (Figs 22.2 and 22.3). This chapter concentrates on the specific programme that employed Constantinian imagery within this church edifice. It argues that the programme was specifically directed at a particular group of prelates belonging to the Roman Curia, not the general public, since it conveyed a particular interpretation and treatment of Constantine's life with respect to its importance for the historical evolution of the Roman Church. This study therefore explores the involvement of specific members of the Curia in the design of the iconographic programme in the Navata Clementina and aims to show how the episodes from Constantine's life were linked to the performance of the liturgy of the Roman rite, especially when it was carried out by the pope in his capacity as the bishop of Rome.

The programme of the western and eastern walls in the Lateran transept begins at the southwestern end with *Constantine the Great's Triumphal Entry into Rome*, immediately followed by *Constantine's Dream of Saints*

*diplomatum et privilegiorum sanctorum romanorum pontificum, Taurinensis editio*, 24 vols. (n.p., 1857–72) (2 supp. vols., 1867–85) (hereafter *Bull. Rom.*), IX, 564–5.

[10] See Beggiao, *La visita pastorale*, 59; Freiberg, *The Lateran in 1600*, 38. See also A. Valier's report regarding the transfer of the Altar of the Blessed Sacrament in ASV, Armadio VII, IV, fol. 7v: 'Tractatum est etiam de trasferendo altari S.ctissimi Sacramenti Eucharistiae, ut nobiliori in loco Ecclesiae poneretur, ubi ingredientium Ecclesiam oculis esset magis expositum, et magnificentius, ut maxime decet, custodiretur'.

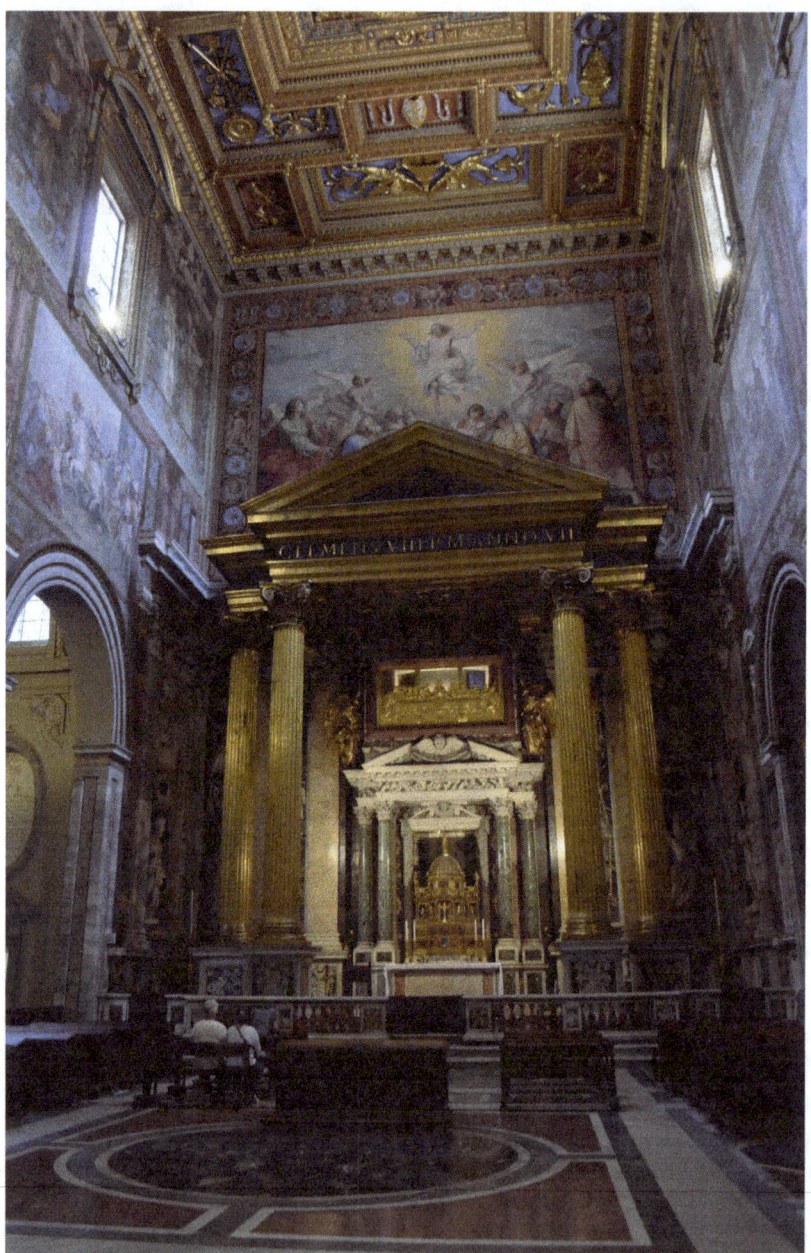

**Fig. 22.2** Pier Paolo Olivieri et al., Altar of the Blessed Sacrament, transept, San Giovanni in Laterano (Photo: F. Malesevic).

*Peter and Paul* (Figs 22.4 and 22.5). This part of the decoration then proceeds on the northeastern wall with the *Finding of Pope Sylvester I on Mount Soratte* and *Constantine's Baptism by Pope Sylvester I* (Figs 22.6 and

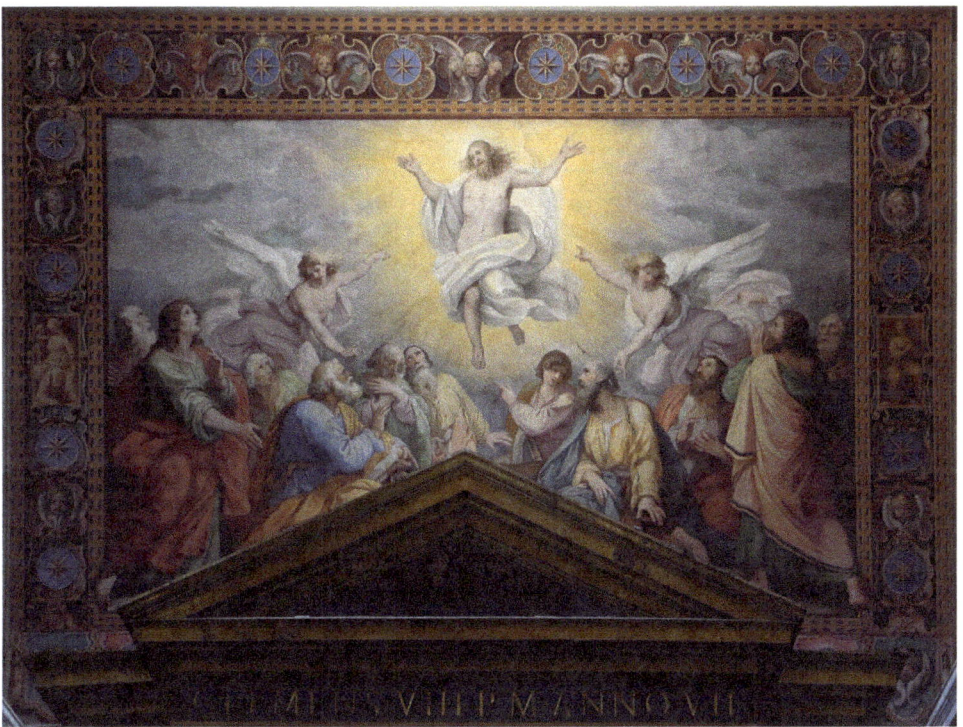

Fig. 22.3 Cesare d'Arpino, *Ascension of Christ*, 1601, transept, San Giovanni in Laterano (Art Resource, New York).

22.7). The last scene thus presents a moment within the progression of the pictorial narrative in which bishop and emperor appear simultaneously. From this point onward these two key figures will be treated inseparably as the western wall compartments unfold several scenes that present the importance of the Lateran for the city of Rome. The cycle opens with the *Foundation of the Lateran* and the *Consecration of the High Altar* at the northern entrance (Figs 22.8 and 22.9). Closing the fresco cycle at the southwestern wall compartment are the *Apparition of Christ's Head in the Lateran's Apse* and Giovanni Baglione's *Donation of Constantine to the Lateran* (Figs 22.10 and 22.11). Above the large scenes that are framed by opened fictive tapestries, also called *arazzi finti*, several figures of apostles and Church Fathers appear between the window openings of the Navata Clementina, painted by the same group of artists who executed the large episodes from Constantine's life.[11] To date, scholarship on Clement VIII's

---

[11] For a reconstruction of the participating painters who were employed under the guidance of Cesare d'Arpino, who was responsible for the *Transfiguration of Christ*, see G. Baglione, *Le vite de' pittori, scultori et architetti: Dal Pontificato di Gregorio XIII del 1572 in fino a' tempi di Papa*

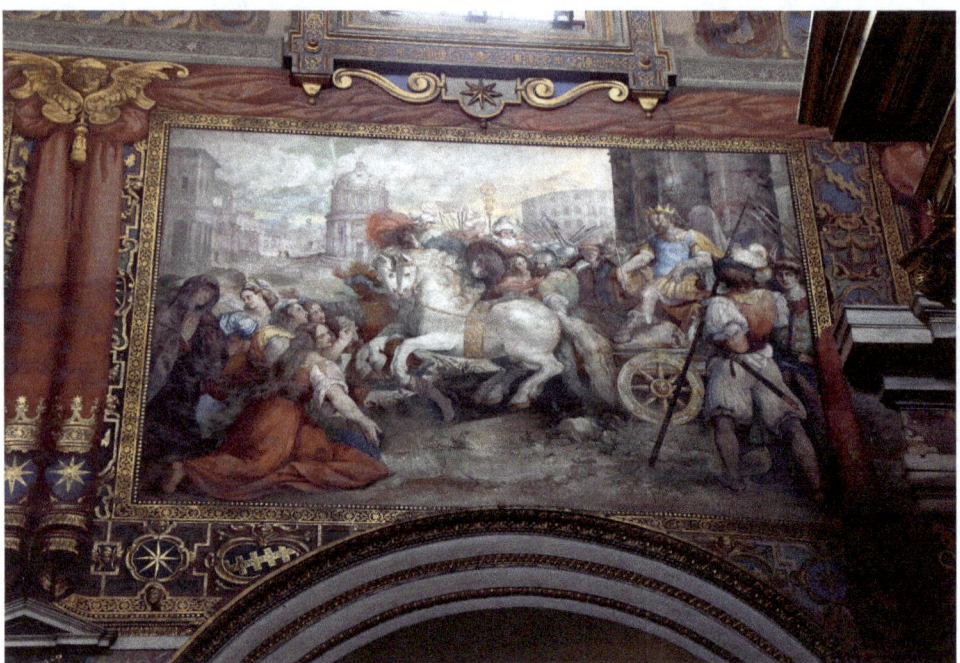

Fig. 22.4 Bernardino Cesari, *Triumphal Entry of Constantine the Great into Rome*, 1598–1600, fresco, transept, San Giovanni in Laterano (Photo: F. Malesevic).

transept decoration in San Giovanni in Laterano has argued that the artists enjoyed a high degree of artistic freedom in the design of the iconographic programme.[12] As we will see, the workshop of artists assembled around Cesare d'Arpino had to follow precisely the intentions expressed by the Curia regarding the specific functions this fresco cycle had to fulfil.

An essential component of the decoration in the Lateran basilica can be found in its narrative of the progression of the scenes outlined above and the way in which its pictorial narration relates to the transept's significance within the architecture of the Lateran basilica. The installation of a new altar at the southern end of the Navata Clementina, where the Holy Sacrament of the Eucharist was to be preserved within a tabernacle, introduced a novelty in respect to church architecture in Rome during the last decade of the

*Urbano Ottavo nel 1642*, ed. Jacob Hess, 3 vols. (Studi e testi, Biblioteca Apostolica Vaticana 367–69) (Vatican City, 1995), 89 (Paris Nogari), 117 (Cesare Nebbia), 147 (Bernardino Cesari), 149 (Giovanni Battista da Novara), 190 (Cristofano Roncalli), 401 (Giovanni Baglione). On d'Arpino Baglione, see also Baglione, *Vite*, 367–57.

[12] See H. Röttgen, 'Repräsentationsstil und Historienbild in der römischen Malerei um 1600', in J. A. Schmoll (ed.), *Beiträge für Hans Gerhard Evers anlässlich seiner Emeritierung im Jahre 1968* (Darmstädter Schriften 22) (Darmstadt, 1968), 71–82; C. Strinati, 'Roma nell'anno 1600: Studio di pittura', *Ricerche di storia dell'arte* 10 (1980), 15–48, at pp. 26–33.

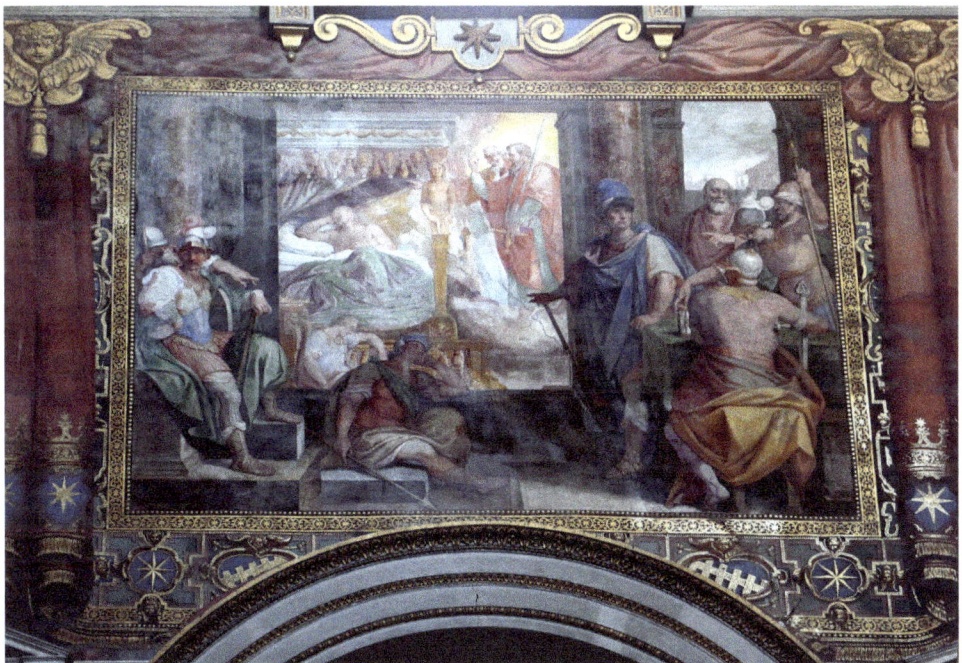

Fig. 22.5 Cesare Nebbia, *Constantine the Great's Dream of the Apostles Peter and Paul*, 1598–1600, transept, San Giovanni in Laterano (Photo: F. Malesevic).

sixteenth century that significantly contributed to devotional practice performed at San Giovanni in Laterano. This decisive modification of outfitting a church interior with two altars is best understood by contrasting Clement VIII's interventions at San Giovanni with Pope Sixtus V's patronage of the construction of his private chapel in Santa Maria Maggiore between 1585 and 1590. Pope Sixtus V's freestanding tabernacle in the Cappella Sistina follows an instruction that Carlo Borromeo suggested in his *Instructiones fabricae et supellectilis ecclesiasticae* (1577). According to Borromeo, tabernacles were to be placed in separate chapels dedicated solely to the Eucharist or upon the high altar so that they would constitute the focal point of the altar's decoration. He further prescribed that sacrament tabernacles should be domed and centrally planned.[13] The centralised architectural plan of the Cappella Sistina emulates the central planning of the Sacrament tabernacle

[13] See C. Borromeo, *Instructiones fabricae et supellectilis ecclesiasticae*, in *Trattati d'arte del Cinquecento: Fra manierismo e controriforma*, ed. P. Barocchi, 3 vols. (Bari, 1960–2), III, 22–4; E. C. Voelker, 'Charles Borromeo's *Instructiones fabricae et suppellectilis ecclesiasticae* 1577: A Translation with Commentary and Analysis', Ph.D. thesis (Syracuse University, 1977), 161–5. The most elaborate study on Sixtus V's Cappella Sistina remains S. F. Ostrow, *L'arte dei papi: La politica delle immagini nella Roma della Controriforma* (Rome, 2002). See also J. M. Beene,

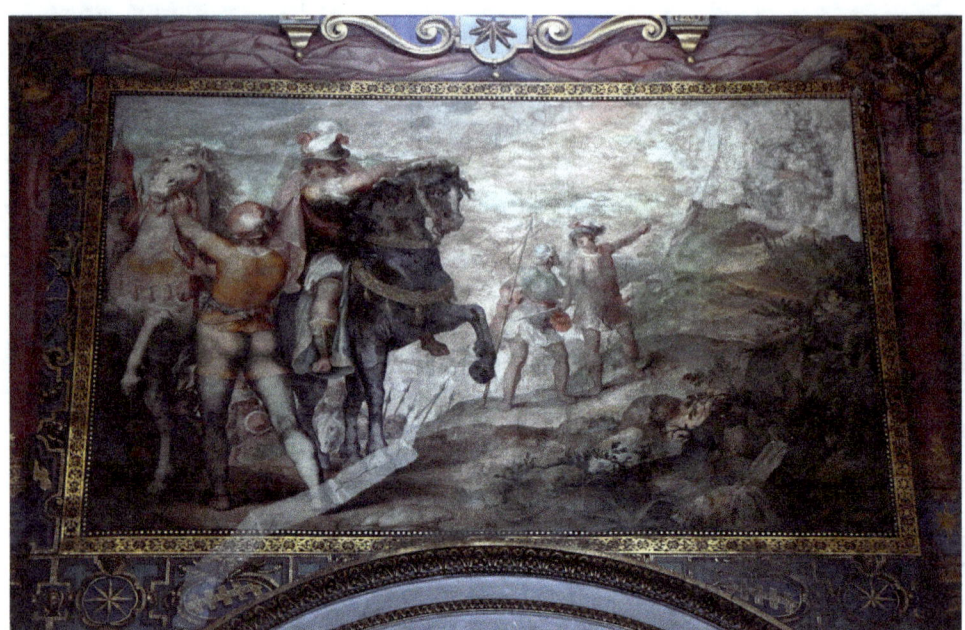

Fig. 22.6 Paris Nogari, *The Discovery of Sylvester on Mount Soratte*, 1598–1600, transept, San Giovanni in Laterano (Photo: F. Malesevic).

and configures the chapel itself in order to establish a focus on the veneration of the Eucharist. Although Pope Clement VIII's Altar of the Blessed Sacrament in San Giovanni in Laterano also presents itself as a chapel, it does not seem to articulate the same intentions as those of Sixtus V's private chapel in Santa Maria Maggiore. It rather establishes a dynamic with the high altar that appears to the beholder immediately upon entering the basilica through the northern entrance. The altar at the southern end of the Navata Clementina is conceived as a pedimented *aedicula* with a ciborium that renders it a chapel-like space. A secondary *aedicula* then shelters the altar and the tabernacle, repeating the form of the outer structure. Jack Freiberg has noted the connection between the altar ciborium as imitating a monumental entrance portico that is physically integrated within the transept.[14] This sheltered architecture in the Lateran's transept

'Hope for Salvation and Salvation Granted: The Burial Chapel and Reburial Ceremony of Pope Sixtus V in Santa Maria Maggiore', Ph. D. thesis (University of Georgia, 2009), 28.

[14] See Freiberg, *The Lateran in 1600*, 133. Such a reinterpretation is valid when considering that the architect of the Altar of the Blessed Sacrament, Pier Paolo Olivieri, had a long-standing relationship with Giacomo della Porta, who introduced a double-aedicular arrangement in his facade of the Gesù. For Olivieri in general, see Baglione, *Vite*, 59–60, 76; H. Hibbard, 'The early history of Sant'Andrea della Valle', *Art Bulletin* 43 (1961), 289–318, at pp. 295–6; E. Borsellino, 'Una nuova acquisizione sulla collezione Corsini: La *Cleopatra* di Pietro Paolo Olivieri',

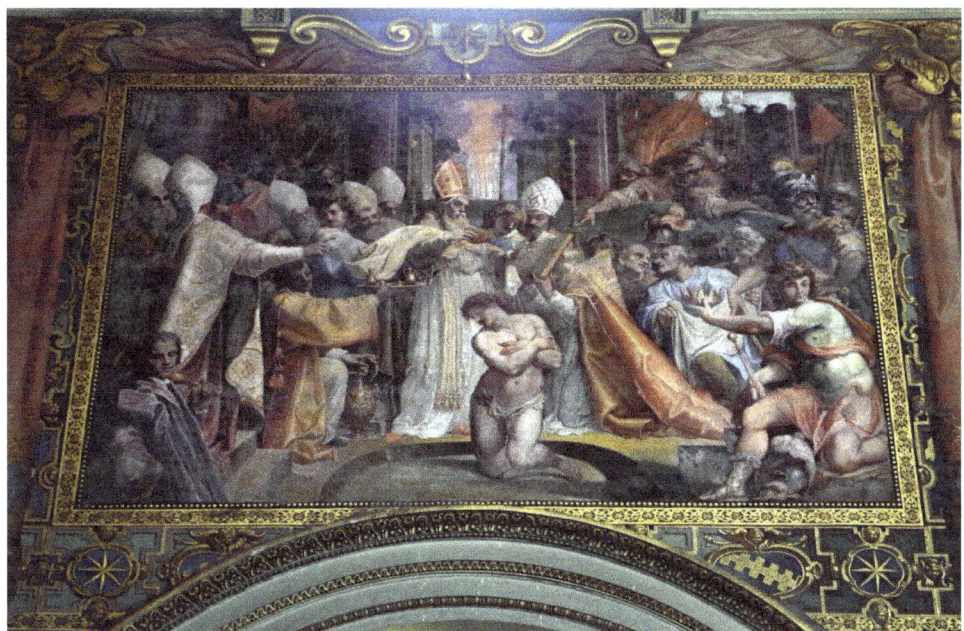

**Fig. 22.7** Cristoforo Roncalli, *Pope Sylvester Baptises Constantine the Great*, 1598–1600, transept, San Giovanni in Laterano (Photo: F. Malesevic).

consequently conveys the functional role this altar had for the Divine Office celebrated at San Giovanni in Laterano on significant feast days during the liturgical calendar, such as the dedication of the basilica on 9 November or during Lent. For the Eastern liturgical festivities in particular, the basilica of San Giovanni in Laterano was seen as constituting an essential part in the stationary liturgical ensemble that Pope Sixtus V had re-enacted during his pontificate for other churches in Rome's urban topography.[15]

The liturgical function of the altar tabernacle was to preserve the Eucharistic Host, which the celebrant would retrieve for the celebration of

*Paragone* n.s. 40 (1989), 3–14. The double-aedicular portico was also a well-known structure during Sixtus V's pontificate and a fresco in the Salone Sistino recalls such a feature for the façade of Saint Peter's. Scholars believe it to have originally been an unexecuted design for Saint Peter's by Michelangelo: see C. Thoenes, 'Bemerkungen zur St. Peter-Fassade Michelangelos', in T. Buddensieg and M. Winner (eds.), *Munuscula discipulorum: Kunsthistorische Studien Hans Kauffmann zum 70. Geburtstag 1966* (Berlin, 1968), 331–41.

[15] For such specific liturgical functionality of San Giovanni Laterano, see P. Ugonio, *Historia delle stationi di Roma* (Rome, 1588) and S. de Blaauw, 'Immagini di liturgia: Sisto V, la traduzione liturgica dei papi e le antiche basiliche di Roma', *RJBH* 33 (2003), 259–302. Regarding the renewal of stational liturgy during Sixtus V's pontificate, see the papal constitution from 13 February 1586, *Egregia populi Romani*, in the diaries of the Masters of Ceremonies Francesco Mucanzio and Paolo Alaleone de Branca in BAV, Vat. lat. 12315, fols. 172r–73; BAV, Barb. lat. 2814, fols. 211v–12r; BAV, Chig.L.II.33, fols 18v–20r.

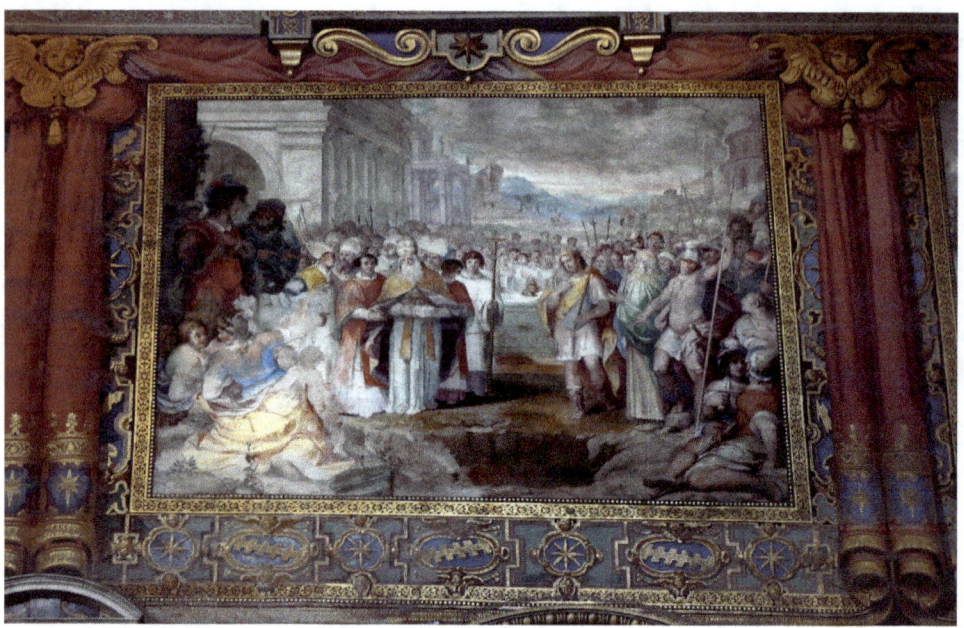

**Fig. 22.8** Paris Nogari, *Foundation of the Lateran*, 1598–1600, transept, San Giovanni in Laterano (Photo: F. Malesevic).

Mass and return to it afterwards. This ceremonial act was performed in commemoration of Christ's burial and resurrection. While in the case of the papal Mass (*cappella papalis*) at the Vatican this celebration was articulated through a spatial distance between the Pauline and Sistine chapels, where the former was specifically used for sheltering the Eucharistic Host separately from the space where the liturgical celebration would take place, the Lateran's disposition of its two altars encapsulated this moment in a single architectural edifice. How does the iconographic programme in Clement VIII's transept relate to such a liturgical function with respect to its narrative progression, since it also encircles the basilica's main altar?

Scholarship in general has so far asserted a primary emphasis on the figure of Constantine the Great, but has failed to take a closer look at how the figure of the emperor interacts with that of the bishop of Rome, Pope Sylvester I, as the narrative cycle progresses. This is due to the assumption that the decorative scheme must have presented a collective effort by the artists involved, resulting in a unified programme.[16] Contributing to this

---

[16] See M. Aronberg Lavin, *The Place of Narrative: Mural Decoration in Italian Churches* (Chicago, 1994), 257. A similarly narrow view of the narrative cycle in the Lateran's transept has been expressed by S. Epp, *Konstantinszyklen in Rom: Die päpstliche Interpretation der Geschichte Konstantins des Grossen bis zur Gegenreformation* (Schriften aus dem Institut für

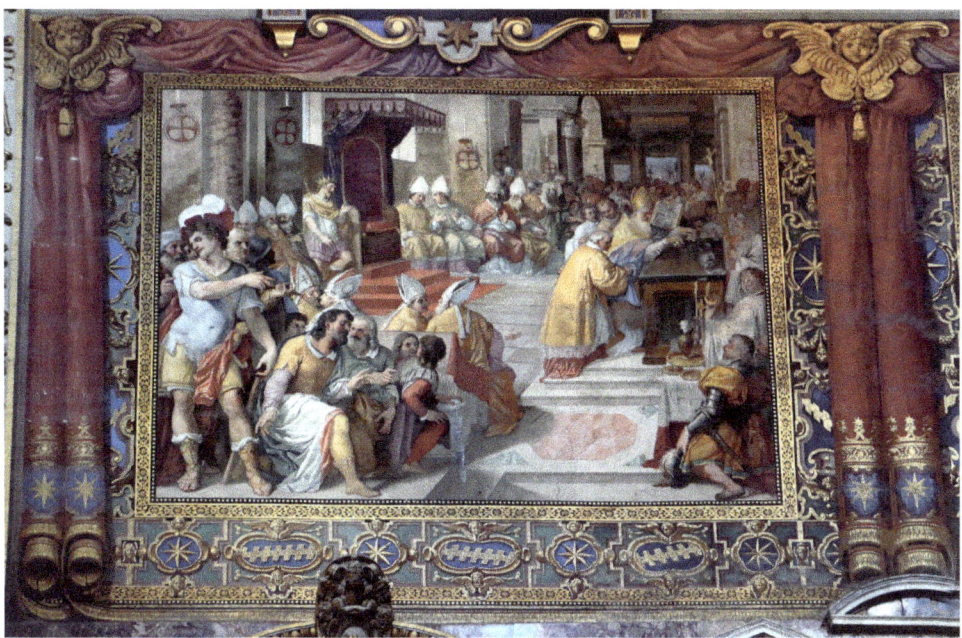

**Fig. 22.9** Giovanni Battista Ricci, *The Consecration of the Main Altar*, 1598–1600, transept, San Giovanni in Laterano (Photo: F. Malesevic).

perception of the iconography in the Navata Clementina is undoubtedly the chronology of execution of the painted decoration. A total of 9,000 scudi was paid to the superintendent Giuseppe Cesari d'Arpino between May 1599 and February 1600.[17] D'Arpino's fresco of Christ's *Ascension*

>  Kunstgeschichte der Universität München 36) (Munich, 1988), 102: 'Zudem ist das Hauptaugenmerk auf die Figur Konstantins gerichtet, er ist der wirkliche Agitator in dieser Darstellung der Geschichte'. Only for the scene of the consecration of the basilica is Epp prepared to take into consideration the important role of Pope Sylvester I. See also See Freiberg, *The Lateran in 1600*, 50, 81. Freiberg sees the cycle as an intertwined narrative between Constantine the Great and the Lateran.

[17] For a reconstruction of the frequency of payments and their individual amounts during that phase of decoration, see A. M. Corbo, *Fonti per la storia artistica al tempo di Clemente VIII* (Ministero per i Beni Culturali e Ambientali, Archivio di Stato di Roma 85) (Rome, 1975), 158–9, 196, 212, 221, 254; M. C. Abromson, *Painting in Rome during the Papacy of Clement VIII (1592–1605): A Documented Study* (New York, 1981), 49–50, 55, 337–8, 340. Abromson published another document dated 17 April 1601 and proposed it as a *terminus ante quem* for the completion of the frescoed programme in the transept. However, this conflicts with the *avviso* from 19 August 1600 that records the pope's visit to the basilica to see d'Arpino's completed fresco, in BAV, Urb. lat. 1068, fol. 538r: 'Dom.ca il Papa andò alle 4 chiese, et à San Gio: Laterano mirò le belliss.e pitture della Assunt.e fatte da Gioseppe d'Artino (sic!), a cui oltra la mercede S. B.ne donò un Cavall.to et una taza d'oro'. This last phrase refers to Clement VIII's elevation of d'Arpino to the status of Cavaliere and not to a gift of a horse, as it has often been believed. See for this Freiberg, *The Lateran in 1600*, 302. A more detailed enquiry into the

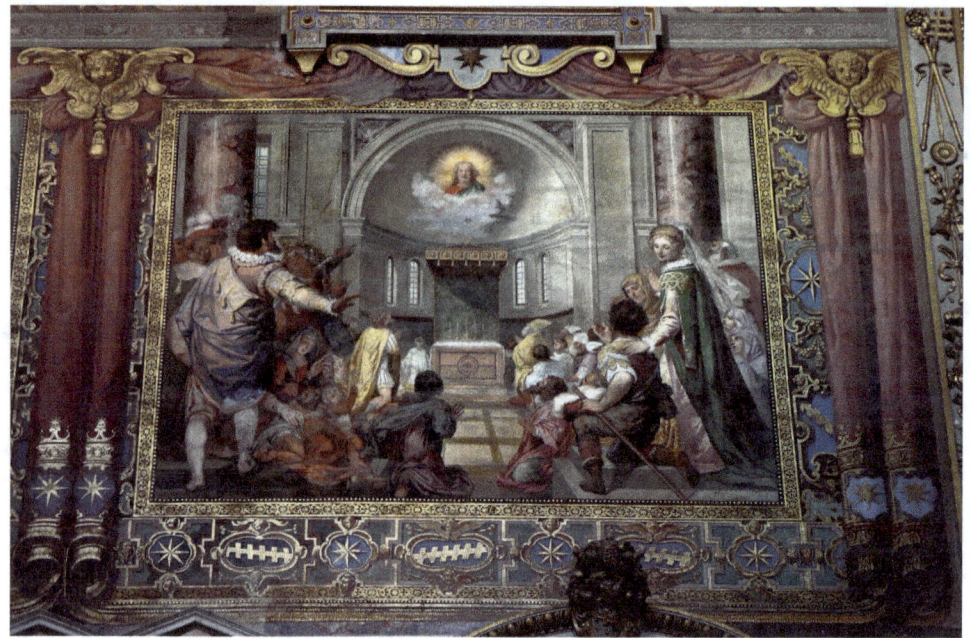

**Fig. 22.10** Paris Nogari, *The Miraculous Apparition of the Volto Santo*, 1598–1600, transept, San Giovanni in Laterano (Photo: F. Malesevic).

above the Altar of the Blessed Sacrament, however, was completed after the lateral walls were decorated with the eight scenes from Constantine the Great's life, between August 1600 and January 1601, when the last disbursement of payments is recorded. D'Arpino's fresco is thus to be regarded as a product of Pope Clement VIII's dissatisfaction with progress on the appearance of the Altar of the Blessed Sacrament, as recorded by the papal Master of ceremonies, Giovanni Paolo Mucanzio, during the pope's visit to San Giovanni in Laterano on 3 January 1599.[18]

The progression of the pictorial narrative must consequently be considered to have a function of its own, detached from the liturgical function that Clement VIII's Altar of the Blessed Sacrament would have inherited

precise dating of d'Arpino's *Ascension* and the criteria for the artists' payment is needed. See F. Malesevic, *Rome Unveiled: Cardinal Cesare Baronio, San Giovanni in Laterano and the Liturgical Spaces of the Roman Curia* (forthcoming).

[18] BAV, Barb. lat. 2809, fol. 5r, and the *avviso* dated 6 January 1599 in BAV, Urb. lat. 1067, fols. 94r–v: 'Arrivato S. B.ne in S. Giovanni Laterano, dove restò à desinare, et à diporto buona parte del giorno per rilatione di persone, che sanno l'intrinseco, si è inteso, che S. S.tà non senti punto di *sodisfat.ne* in veder l'altar grande, fatto far da S. B.ne con tanta spesa in quella basilica, poiche con nulla ò pochiss.a simmetria di architettura è riuscito in modo la fabrica bassa et nana . . . ', quoted in E. Rossi, 'Roma ignorata', *Roma* 12 (1934), 39–40, at p. 40.

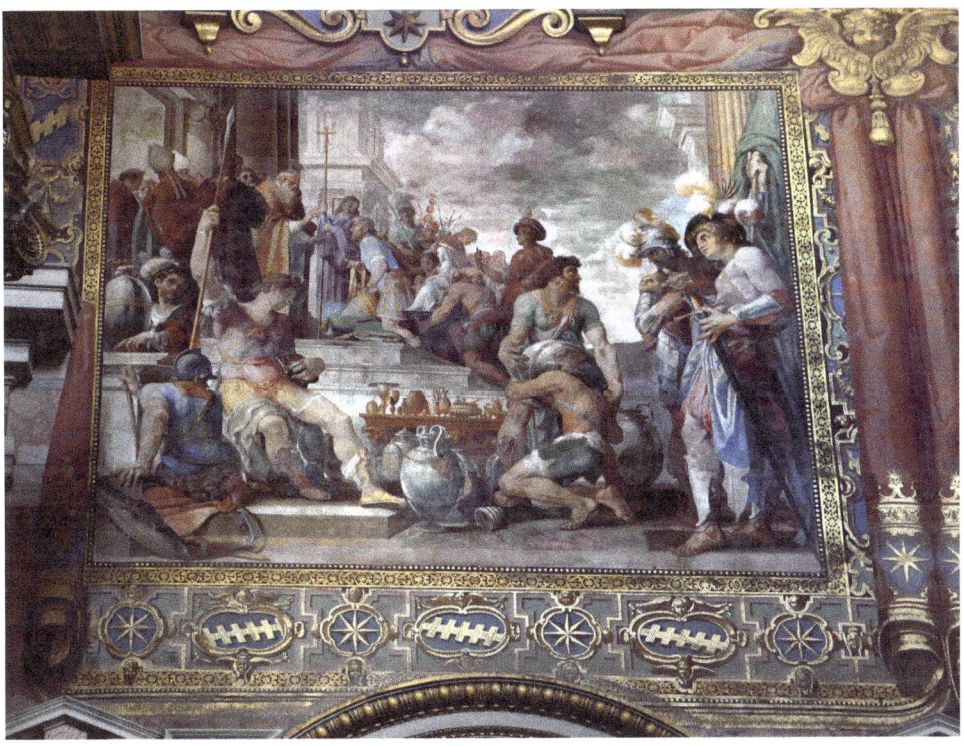

**Fig. 22.11** Giovanni Baglione, *Constantine the Great's Donation to the Lateran*, 1598–1600, transept, San Giovanni in Laterano (Photo: F. Malesevic).

after its completion. The narrative of the scenes unfolds with Constantine the Great's *Triumphal Entry*, immediately followed by his *Dream of Saints Peter and Paul*. One observes in these scenes that they markedly only recount Constantine's relationship to the city of Rome in its physico-topographical and spiritual–imaginative configurations. The figure of the pope as bishop of Rome is completely omitted. He is only revealed in the third scene, where Constantine the Great orders his soldiers to retrieve Sylvester from the mountain near Rome, following the command of Peter and Paul. The inclusion of this scene, which has no precedent in Roman pictorial cycles of the sixteenth century, indicates, together with Constantine's *Dream*, a remarkable shift in the overall selection of episodes when compared to the first fresco of the *Triumphal Entry to Rome*. Whereas this first scene depicts a historical moment of salvation, the subsequent two scenes primarily depict miracles that are now being disclosed in the Lateran and in the immediate vicinity of the main altar. In fact, the episode of *Constantine's Dream of Saints Peter and Paul* makes an explicit reference to the Lateran's most precious relics, the heads of the two Apostles, which were preserved in the ciborium above the high altar. Pope Clement VIII decreed after his visit to San Giovanni in Laterano in 1592 that an image of the two Apostles be placed within the metal grille of the upper range of the ciborium and that an honorific canopy was to hang from the ceiling above it. This image of Saints Peter and Paul was designed by Agostino Ciampelli in October 1598, shortly before work on the transept's lateral walls would commence. Although this work no longer exists, it might be presumed that the saints had been depicted in half-length with Paul on the left side, as an engraving by Giovanni Maggi and Matthias Greuter from their series of etchings entitled *Praecipua urbis Romanae templa* (1650) also indicates.[19] In conjunction with the embroidered canopy, the image of the two Apostles was closely associated with the legend in the *Liber Pontificalis*, according to which Pope Sylvester showed Constantine the Great the two portraits of Peter and Paul.[20]

In this sense, the selection of the episode of Constantine the Great's *Dream*, in which Rome's two primary Apostles appeared, must have been decided as a response to Clement VIII's order to transfer the high altar from its position into the tribune so that its towering ciborium would not obscure the view onto the sacrament altar from the northern entrance to the basilica. Although this project was never carried out, by moving the altar into the tribune not only would Clement VIII have solved an aesthetic problem that he considered most important, but it would also not conflict with the tradition that the Eucharist should not be reserved in the vicinity of relics, as Carlo Borromeo also noted in his *Instructiones*.[21] The emphasis on the

---

[19] For the payments to Ciampelli see Corbo, *Fonti per la storia artistica*, 124–7, 197, 234, 247.

[20] See B. Mombritius, *Sanctuarium seu Vitae Sanctorum*, 2 vols. (Paris, 1910), II, 508–31; K. C. Schüppel, 'The stucco crucifix of Saint Peter's reconsidered: Textual sources and visual evidence for the Renaissance copy of a medieval silver crucifix', in R. McKitterick, J. Osborne, C. M. Richardson and J. Story (eds.), *Old Saint Peter's, Rome* (Cambridge, 2013), 306–23, at p. 318. The diptych, whose dating remains controversial, was conserved in the Sancta Sanctorum and later transferred to the Vatican Museums. I would like to thank Paolo Liverani for this information.

[21] Borromeo, *Instructiones*, III, 36: 'Haec ... aut in gremio ecclesiae, prout loci amplitudo fert, aut in cappella insigniori, praeterquam in ea, ubi sanctissimae Eucharistiae sacramentum asservatur, decentius collocabitur.' On the project of transferring the Lateran's high altar to the tribune, see Freiberg, *The Lateran in 1600*, 52–3 and the *avviso* from 9 January 1599 in BAV, Urb. lat. 1067, fol. 39r: 'Nella visita del Papa delle s(ette) chiese si fermo a desinare a S. Gio. Laterano, dove volse vedere minutamente la capella et li organi che vi si fabricano, et se bene S. S.ta sia molto essausta de danari ordinò agli architetti che tirassero l'opera à fine dovendovisi *rimover quel gran tabernacolo* che contien li corpi delli dui Principi d'Apostoli ... ', quoted in Rossi, 'Roma ignorata', 40. The timely closeness to the beginning of the decoration campaign of the transept with the eight scenes from Constantine's life suggests that the design of the iconographic programme must have had some connection to this project. Another proposal

main altar's designated place in the basilica is also made in Giovanni Battista Ricci's *Consecration of the High Altar*, diagonally juxtaposed to *Constantine's Dream* on the northwestern wall compartment. A preparatory study from the collection of D. C. Miller (Palo Alto, California) allows us to trace important accents in the final execution, although it must be kept in mind that Ricci's fresco was subject to extensive restorations carried out in the 1880s. First and foremost, however, the scene itself establishes the most vital aspect pertaining to the Lateran basilica in its relation to the papal office through the main altar, since the high altar is also known as the episcopal altar per se, where only the pope may celebrate the Divine Office.[22] Giovanni Battista Ricci's drawing, by contrast, had not specified where the consecration is taking place, whereas the site is now clearly identifiable as the Lateran, since it presents the entrance in the form it received during Clement VIII's restorations. The preparatory stage thus solely concentrated on configuring the liturgical scene within a proper historical tradition, a tradition preserved in the *Pontificale Romanum*, the new edition of which had been published in 1595 and approved by Clement VIII in the constitution *Ex quo in Ecclesia Dei* a year later. Indeed, the consecration of a church altar occupies an important place within this liturgical book, since it is regarded as a vital part of the larger ceremony of the dedication of a basilica. A visual tradition that the *Pontificale* consciously follows presents in one illustration the *Consecration of an Altar with Holy Oils* pertaining to the rite of dedication, while another presents the *Consecration of an Altar and its Relics*, performed independently from the consecration of a basilica.[23]

On the level of pictorial production concerning the workshop of artists at the Lateran transept, Ricci's fresco indicates a specific recurrence of already existing *formulae* employed by Cesare Nebbia during his work in the Lateran palace, when Pope Sixtus V renovated it and commissioned

---

was to elevate the bronze ciborium of the Altar of the Blessed Sacrament so that it would be seen when one entered the basilica from the northern entrance.

[22] John the Deacon was also the first to ascribe to the basilica's altar its primacy. See R. Valentini and G. Zucchetti, *Codice topografico della città di Roma*, 4 vols. (Fonti per la Storia d'Italia 90) (Rome, 1940–53), III, 351: '... sacrosanctum altare dominicum quod omnium altarium solum habet principatum ...'. The humanist Flavio Biondo also recognised it as the 'first altar that the religion of Christianity had' ('primum altare quod habuit religio Christiana') in his *Roma instaurata* in Valentini and Zucchetti, *Codice topografico*, IV, 320.

[23] For Clement VIII's bull from 10 February 1596, see *Bull. Rom.*, X, 246–8. That the year of publication proves to be solid for 1595 is indicated by a passage that refers to the parchment to be approved of, in fact, in connection with the descriptions of the dedication of a church as well as the consecration of the altar in *Pontificale Romanum: Editio princeps (1595–1596)*, ed. M. Sodi and A. M. Triacca (MLCT) (Vatican City, 1997), 297 n. 497, 400 n. 719. The pagination corresponds to the printed edition of the *Pontificale Romanum*.

Nebbia and Giovanni Guerra to decorate its interiors. The scene of the *Consecration* is extensively based on Nebbia's *Donation of Constantine* in the Salone di Costantino. Other than the *modello raffaelesco* in the Vatican Sala, Nebbia's pictorial solution interprets Constantine's mythical act towards the Roman Church as being similar to a consecration of the church's altar. Pope Sylvester sits enthroned beneath a baldachin and watches the emperor as he places the *Constitutum Constantini*, the forged document from the eighth century that was held to document Constantine's bestowal of the papacy with the *Patrimonium Petri*, on the facing high altar of San Giovanni in Laterano.[24] However, the episode of the *Consecration* in the Navata Clementina does not necessarily convey the same iconological meaning as the *Donation of Constantine* in the Lateran palace, since Ricci's borrowing of Nebbia's pictorial solution has to a great extent to be put in correlation with its proximity to the high altar, the liturgical place to which the scene mainly refers. Additionally, this fresco reinforces the dignified position of the Lateran's high altar by explicitly presenting its consecration with holy oils stored in the *confessio* chapel of Saint John the Evangelist beneath the altar and consecrated at the Lateran on Holy Thursday by the pope. Pompeo Ugonio recorded in his *Historia delle stationi di Roma* that entrance to the chapel was enabled by a wooden ladder that descended from the level of the nave. Supposedly, according to another account by Pope Gregory the Great, the tunic of Saint John the Evangelist was preserved in the chapel, within which a bare altar (*altare nudo*) was to be found. Its walls were also decorated with floral motifs, and in the centre of the vault a lamb was painted. Furthermore, Ugonio also noted in his treatise a fresco above the altar that showed the miracle of Christ's appearance during Pope Sylvester I's consecration of the high altar with holy oils, thus establishing a vertical axis of apostolic continuity between the heads of Peter and Paul in the ciborium of the high altar and the *confessio* chapel beneath.[25]

---

[24] On Cesare Nebbia's fresco in the Lateran palace's Salone di Costantino, see Epp, *Konstantinszyklen*, 63–7, 99–100; Mandel, *Sixtus V and the Lateran Palace*, 159; M. L. Chappell and W. Chandler Kirwin, 'A Petrine triumph: The decoration of the *Navi Piccole* in San Pietro under Clement VIII', *Storia dell'arte* 21 (1974), 119–70, at pp. 124–5.

[25] Ugonio, *Historia*, 41r–v: 'Sotto le teste dei santi Apostoli nel piano della nave principale, si vede nel muro una fenestra con un cancello di metallo. Per questa si scende una Cappelletta sotterranea che sogliono chiamar la Confessione, dove essendo io entrato per una scaletta di legno, non ho visto altro che un altare accosto al muro con un fenestrino dinanzi, & sopra esso altare dipinto un Salvatore con certi Angeli attorno . . . .' See also Panvinio, 'De sacrosancta basilica', in Lauer, *Le palais de Latran*, 435, where the stage of the holy oils is recorded as well as the remark that after their consecration they were distributed to all other churches of Rome. On this, see also M. A. Serrano, *De septem urbis ecclesiis* (Rome, 1575), 1, 529; C. Rasponi, *De*

When Clement VIII visited San Giovanni in Laterano in 1592 he ordered that this chapel be restored and redecorated with paintings, although their subjects were not specified. Access to the *confessio* was to be facilitated by constructing steps, and the outer wall was to be riveted with marble. Another wish that Clement expressed was to transfer the relics that were preserved in the chapel of Saint Thomas to the *confessio* chapel, where they would then be re-consecrated with the altar in honour of Saint Silvester.[26] It is clear that this ceremony of consecration was conducted independently from the rite of dedication. The altar in the *confessio* chapel was then re-consecrated to its original patron, John the Evangelist, on 10 September 1594.[27] With respect to the location of the *confessio* chapel and the high altar, which clearly pertained to the principal nave of the Lateran basilica, the rite of consecration, as formulated in the *Pontificale Romanum* a year after the altar of the *confessio* was re-sanctified to John the Evangelist, indicates a pivotal moment where the two liturgical orientations regarding this particular celebration come together in the most sacred part of the church. The removal of the high altar to the tribune would therefore have had a detrimental effect on the liturgical importance of this part, which would be clear not only to the faithful attending the Divine service but also to the prelates assisting the pope during the liturgy. Giovanni Battista Ricci's *Consecration of the Lateran's High Altar* and Cesare Nebbia's *Dream of Constantine* thus establish a liturgical core of the transept's iconographic programme that is detached from the historiographical themes that San Giovani in Laterano represented. In the same way, as Nebbia's *Dream of Constantine* isolates itself from Bernardino Cesari's *Triumphal Entry*, so does Giovanni Battista Ricci's scene of the *Consecration* interrupt a historical dynamic of the pictorial narrative in respect to Paris Nogari's *Foundation of the Lateran*. At this point it is

---

*Basilica et Patriarchio Lateranensis libri IV* (Rome, 1656), 49; and Freiberg, *The Lateran in 1600*, 282–3.

[26] See Beggiao, *La visita pastorale*, 114–15. Rasponi, *De basilica et patriarchio IV*, 49, noted the existence of the paintings, but unfortunately no visual record of them survives. At the beginning of the eighteenth century the chapel was redecorated by Giovanni Battista Brughi, for which see F. Gerardi, *La patriarcale basilica lateranense illustrata per cura di Agostino Valentini*, 2 vols. (Rome, 1832–4), I, 49.

[27] The chapel's re-consecration was celebrated by the archbishop of Montreale, Ludovico de Torres, who conducted the service 'ex auctoritate Clementis VIII' (by the authority of Clement VIII) as recorded in a tablet above the altar that was in fact meant to be read from the level of the transept: V. Forcella, *Iscrizioni delle chiese e d'altri edificii di Roma dal secolo XI fino ai giorni nostri*, 14 vols. (Rome, 1869–84), VIII, 46 n. 123. Torres was another member of the commission within the Congregation of Rites and Ceremonies charged with revising the *Pontificale Romanum*.

essential to note that the development of the pictorial narrative in the Lateran's Navata Clementina does not necessarily imply that the selection of the episodes from Constantine's life with respect to their historiographical relevance, such as the *Triumphal Entry* or the *Foundation of the Lateran*, are to be regarded as a matter of chronology. In fact, they were selected based on how the emperor's *Vita*, and to a larger part the anonymous *Actus Silvestri* from the *Liber Pontificalis*, advanced a liturgical view of Constantine's importance for the Roman *Ecclesia* as well as for its bishop (*episcopus*). To view this pictorial programme also from a point of liturgical reference with respect to the celebration of the Divine Offices at San Giovanni in Laterano consequently allows us to isolate several sequences from the overall decoration and to describe them in accordance with Tridentine norms for liturgical celebrations which were being formulated by the newly edited liturgical books.

With these interventions in the *confessio* chapel beneath the high altar, Pope Clement VIII consciously related back to Sixtus V's pre-existing solutions for his own chapel in Santa Maria Maggiore, where a subterranean *confessio* was created by the pope's architect Domenico Fontana to house the Cappella del Presepio, a simulacrum of the grotto of Bethlehem which contained relics of Christ's birth and which was translated from the right side aisle of the basilica to Sixtus V's new chapel.[28] This particular *confessio* chapel is open, however, also containing a semi-circular balustrade that circumscribes the opening at floor level as well as two curving staircases descending to the chapel, while Clement VIII's would remain closed with the chapel's doors. It is again Pompeo Ugonio who noted that 'the entire ancient chapel has been placed below the altar in memory of its venerable antiquity'.[29] A close interrelationship between Clement VIII's restorations of the *confessio* chapel in San Giovanni in Laterano and the editing as well as publication of the *Pontificale*

---

[28] See Ostrow, L'arte dei papi, 37 and O. Panvinio, De praecipuis urbis Romae sanctioribusque; basilicis quas Septem ecclesias vulgo vocant, Liber (Rome, 1570), trans. M. A. Lanfranchi as Le sette chiese principali di Roma (Rome, 1570), 300: '... rintegrata poi da Xisto III & dedicata alla beata vergine fù nominata la chiesa di santa Maria madre del Signore: dapoi, per rispetto della capella del presepio quivi dentra fabricata, fù chiamata santa Maria del presepio'.

[29] Ugonio, *Historia*, 69v: '... esso santo Presepio con tutta la Cappelletta antica per memoria della veneranda antichità è sotto questo altare tra[s]portato'. See also D. Fontana, *Della Trasportatione dell'Obelisco Vaticano et delle Fabriche di Nostro Signore Papa Sisto V (1590)*, ed. A. Carugo and P. Portoghesi (Rome, 1978 [1590]), 50: 'Volle Dunque Nostro Signore dentro alla sopranominata Capella così ricca, & adorna trasportare quella del Presepio tanto devota, & antica, per il che ordinò, ch'io dovessi levare tutta intiera dal luogo proprio, dove prima si ritrovava per mantenere la devozione, e la memoria... Il luogo, dove questa Capella s'haveva da mettere è cavato sotto terra per maggior devotione....'

*Romanum* around 1595 can be discerned by this comparison with architectural solutions that were realised for such a specific place of worship during the pontificate of Sixtus V. From this contrasting juxtaposition regarding the treatment of the *confessio* in Rome during the last two decades of the sixteenth century it has to be asked who it was who inspired Pope Clement VIII to preserve the idea of a closed *confessio* chapel. The Sixtine solution not only had the effect of freeing up the area in front of the chapel's main altar during the celebration of Mass but also had the benefit of giving visitors with direct contact with the ancient and venerable Cappella del Presepio. In fact, this was also the case in the churches of Santa Susanna and San Paolo fuori le Mura, where variations of an open *confessio* were being created during Clement VIII's pontificate, including staircases that facilitated descent to the shrine where the relics were preserved. In Santa Susanna, for instance, the architects Domenico Fontana and Carlo Maderno had begun to install, commissioned by the cardinal and papal *vicarius* Girolamo Rusticucci, an oval-shaped longitudinal crypt before 16 April 1593, which was to be completed, along with the presbytery, in 1595.[30] In San Paolo fuori le Mura an earlier, smaller and minimally accessible *confessio* was replaced with a larger one behind the ciborium facing the apse.[31]

Within this constellation of other renovation campaigns in Rome during Clement VIII's interventions at San Giovanni in Laterano, Cesare Baronio appears to have been instrumental in the pope's ambitions for the renovations carried out at the Lateran basilica, even well before his election to the cardinalate in 1596. Upon the death of Filippo Neri, the founder of the Congregation of the Oratory, Cardinal Ippolito Aldobrandini's confessor, Baronio was elected to succeed him as *praepositus* of the congregation in 1595. Not only would Baronio have been

---

[30] See H. Hibbard, *Carlo Maderno and Roman Architecture: 1580–1630* (London, 1971), 112; E. Hubala, 'Roma sotterranea barocca', *Das Münster* 18 (1965), 157–70, at pp. 161–2. Pompeo Ugonio already remarked in 1588 that Cardinal Rusticucci heightened the architectonical functionality of Santa Susanna: Ugonio, *Historia*, 193v. The crypt was to house Rusticucci's own tomb.

[31] There is still much confusion whether it was Sixtus or Clement who was responsible for creating the open *confessio* in San Paolo fuori le Mura. De Blaauw, 'Immagini di liturgia', *passim* has argued convincingly that it was Clement, while the work on the presbytery had already begun under Sixtus – just as in the case of Santa Susanna. See also Ugonio, *Historia*, 236v–237r: ' ... per commodità delle quali cappelle si è allargato il spatio dietro l'altar dei santi apostoli e sono stati levati tutti gl'impedimenti che ingombravano la vista di esso altare'. On the restoration of the basilica see M. Docci, *San Paolo fuori le Mura: dalle origini alla basilica delle 'origini'* (Rome, 2006), 102–18, 122; *CBCR* V, 106, 134; G. Filippi and S. de Blaauw, 'San Paolo fuori le Mura: La disposizione liturgica fino a Gregorio Magno', *Mededelingen van het Nederlands Instituut te Rome* 59 (2001), 5–25, at p. 10.

highly suitable as the pope's main adviser in the restoration campaigns in San Giovanni in Laterano, as he was also Clement VIII's confessor after 1592, but he would have been well placed to guide the pivotal changes to the architecture and pictorial decoration of the interior in the last decade of the Cinquecento. In the fifth volume of his *Annales Ecclesiastici*, dedicated to Clement VIII, Baronio extensively discussed the issue of the *confessio* in relation to the foundation of various bishoprics in Africa during Late Antiquity.[32] The interpretation of the *confessio* that Baronio conveys in the *Annales* is thus specifically connected with the office of a bishop (*episcopus*) and the liturgical service he performs for dedicating a church. This view corresponds with the decision made by Clement VIII to close off the *confessio* chapel in San Giovanni in Laterano to the faithful, since the Lateran's high altar was thought to be the first altar inaugurated in accordance with sacred ritual, which then provided the model for all later consecrations. Pious belief furthermore held that the altar incorporated the wooden *mensa* used by Saint Peter and his successors. The basilica's *confessio* thus had to be marked by an extraordinary venerability; an appearance achieved by decorating its doors with grey marble with the pope's name and his heraldic stars. In this way, Clement VIII commemorated his place in an apostolic succession that went back to the first Apostle appointed by Christ.[33]

While the Sistine solution of making the *confessio* more accessible to the faithful had gained momentum during Clement VIII's pontificate, it is

[32] C. Baronio, *Annales Ecclesiastici*, 12 vols. (Venice, 1600–12), V, 294. In this passage Baronio describes the relics of Saint Stephen being received by some bishops in Africa, among them Saint Augustine, who then dedicated churches to the proto-martyr and placed the relics therein. See also A. Herz, 'Cardinal Cesare Baronio's restoration of SS. Nereo ed Achilleo and S.Cesareo de' Appia', *Art Bulletin* 70 (1988), 590–620, at p. 600. The entry in the index of this volume of the *Annales* describes the *confessio* as a place 'where relics are preserved, with a small window or opening' ('Confessio, ubi reliquiae conditae sunt, cum fenestella, seu foramine'). Baronio must have thus relied heavily on Gregory of Tours' often-quoted description from around 590, when he visited the shrine of Saint Peter's in Gregory of Tours, *Liber Miraculorum: De Gloria Beatorum Martyrum*, in J.-P. Migne, *Patrologiae cursus completus: Series Latina*, 221 vols. (Paris, 1844–1905), LXXI, cols. 705–800, esp. 728–9: 'Hoc enim sepulcrum sub altari collocatum valde rarum habetur. Sed qui orare desiderat, reseratis cancellis quibus, locus ille ambitur, accedit super sepulcrum; et sic fenestella parvula patefacta, immissio introrsum capite, quae necessitas, promit efflagitat. Nec moratur effectus, si petitionis tantum justa proferatur oratio. Quod si beata auferre desiderat pignora palliolum aliquod momentana pensatum facit intrisecus, deinde vigilans ac jejunans, devotissime deprecatur, ut devotioni suae virtus apostolica suffragetur. Mirum dictu! si fides hominis praevaluerit, a tumulo palliolum elevatum ita imbuitur divina virtute . . . .'

[33] On the decoration of the door, see Mellini's *Descrittioni* in BAV, Barb. lat. 4318, fol. 84r. We mentioned the primacy of the Lateran's altar by John the Deacon in n. 22 above.

possible to discern why the closed *confessio*, the form most ardently supported by Cesare Baronio, was preferred here. His own aspirations and intentions regarding a church's *confessio* can be derived from his propositions to create a *confessio* with a *fenestrella* directly below the altar of Santa Maria in Navicella (Chiesa Nuova), the Oratorian's mother church, in 1595. Unfortunately, Baronio's plans were never carried out, since an open *confessio* was preferred instead.[34] Just as he would later carry out in his own titular church of Santi Nereo e Achilleo after his elevation to the cardinalate in 1596, Baronio thought it important to raise the presbytery in order to place the *confessio* directly below the altar. The altar would then also be flanked with stairs that provided access from the nave. Baronio believed that this type of *confessio* arrangement had been in use since the time of Saint Augustine, although it more closely resembles eighth- and ninth-century examples, such as those in Santa Prassede and San Giorgio al Velabro.[35] Scholars have attempted to argue that Baronio's specific choice of *confessio* was modelled on that of Saint Peter's, dating back to around 600 and preserved in a drawing by Sebastiano Werro from 1581, prior to its dismantling in 1592 under Clement VIII. However, as Steven Ostrow has correctly observed, Baronio's disposition of the *confessio* in relation to the altar neglects one key element, namely the subterranean annular crypt around the tomb of Saint Peter as well as the connecting corridor that enabled the faithful to get closer to the relic (Fig. 22.12).[36] In fact, the difference between the place of a church's sanctified objects and their physical relationship to the believer is emphasised to a greater extent in the arrangement at San Giovanni in Laterano than at Saint Peter's.

---

[34] Baronio's proposal was recorded by the Oratorian's third volume of their Libro dei Decreti as quoted in G. Calenzio, La vita e gli scritti del cardinale Cesare Baronio della Congregazione dell'Oratorio, bibliotecario di Santa Romana Chiesa (Rome, 1907), 398.

[35] Baronio's belief that this type of *confessio* dated back to Saint Augustine is expressed in the already mentioned paragraph from his *Annales*, for which see Herz, 'Cardinal Cesare Baronio's restoration', 600. Santa Prassede had been Carlo Borromeo's *titulus*, but its *confessio* arrangement dated back to Pope Paschal I. See J. J. Emerick, 'Focusing on the celebrant: The column display inside Santa Prassede', *Mededelingen van het Nederlands Instituut te Rome* 59 (2001), 129–59, at pp. 143–5; C. J. Goodson, 'The Basilicas of Pope Paschal I (817–824): Tradition and Transformation in Early Medieval Rome', Ph. D. thesis (Columbia University, 2004). For Baronio's arrangement in Santi Nereo e Achilleo as well as later in San Cesareo de' Appia (1597–1601), see M. G. Turco, *Il 'titulus' dei Santi Nereo e Achilleo: Emblema della riforma cattolica* (Rome, 1997), 74–87, 132.

[36] S. F. Ostrow, 'The confessi in post-tridentine Rome', in P. Tosini (ed.), Arte e committenza nel Lazio nell' età di Cesare Baronio: Atti del convegno internazionale di studi Frosinone, Sora, 16–18 maggio 2007 (Rome, 2009), 19–33, at p. 22. For Saint Peter's as model for Baronio's arrangement, see M. G. Turco, 'Cesare Baronio e i dettami tridentini nelle sistemazioni presbiteriali Romane', in Tosini (ed.), Arte e committenza, 87–107, at p. 99.

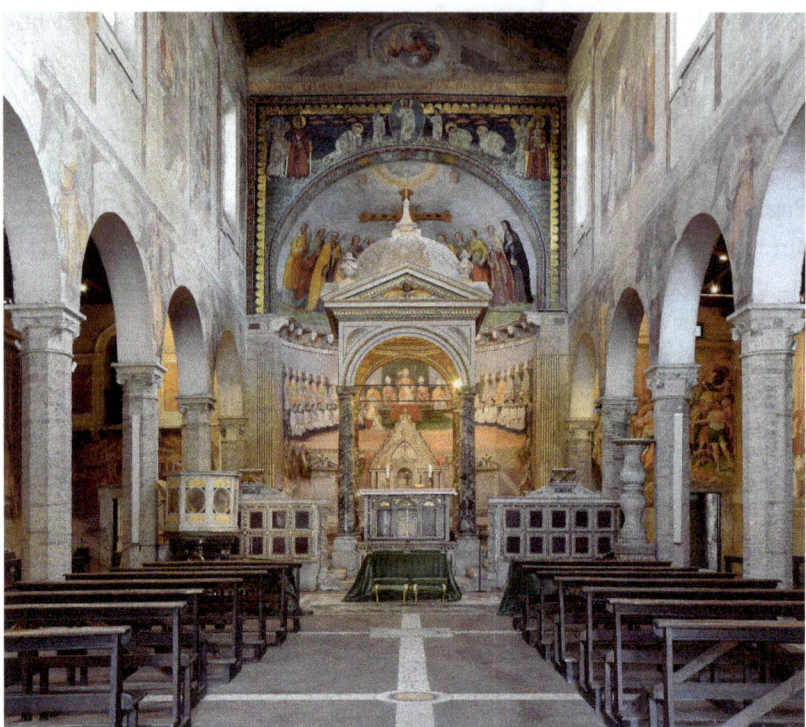

**Fig. 22.12** Altar and *confessio* chapel in Cardinal Baronio's titular church of Santi Nereo e Achilleo (Photo: F. Malesevic).

Another fresco in the Clementine transept of the Lateran basilica also accentuates the venerable sanctity of the place, where salvation is revealed through an *agens historiae*, namely in Paris Nogari's *Miraculous Apparition of Christ's Head in the Lateran's Apse*. The choice for this specific revelatory miracle which supposedly occurred at the Lateran in connection with the basilica's dedication was consciously intended to repeat the monumental thirteenth-century mosaic in the apse. The apse mosaic in turn linked the revelation of the reliquary busts of Saints Peter and Paul on specific liturgical days with Christ himself, and thus lent them their extraordinary status.[37] Indeed, Nogari's pictorial reproduction of the mosaic renders it

---

[37] The Lateran altar establishes, as Freiberg has also observed, not only a very specific symbolic connection with the Ark of the Covenant, but also a material assertion that is encountered in other churches. The Ark itself was claimed as one of the Lateran's most prestigious relics that had formerly been housed in the *confessio*. See Freiberg, *The Lateran in 1600*, 112, for a connection with the Ark of the Covenant. See also John the Deacon's account in Valentini and Zucchetti, *Codice topografico*, III, 336: '... et eiusdem ecclesiae ara principalis est arca foederis Domini, vel ut aiunt, arca est inferius, et altare ad mensuram longitudinis, latitudinis et altitudinis arcae conditum est superius ...'. See also S. de Blaauw, 'The solitary celebration of

yet another precious relic of the Lateran basilica that must have influenced the figural disposition in the fresco. The scene unfolds within an embellished church interior where Christ's head miraculously appears in the curved semicircular space of the church's apse above the main altar. The background is occupied with the emperor Constantine the Great on the left side of the picture field and Pope Sylvester on the right, while other worshippers observe the miraculous appearance in the foreground of the fresco. Again, this scene does not depict a historical event, but rather a specific moment in the rite of the consecration unfolding from the liturgy of the dedication. Through this scene, the church of San Giovanni in Laterano is now definitely dedicated to the Saviour, thus its original designation as Basilica Salvatoris. Nogari's fresco consequently corresponds to the third scene on the opposite lateral wall of the Navata Clementina, since the appearance of Sylvester as bishop of Rome as Saint Peter's successor is then equated with the miraculous revelation of Christ's head in the church's most prominent liturgical place.

Accordingly, the progression of the inner enclosed pictorial cycle around the high altar and its *confessio* emphasises not only the Lateran's venerability through miracles and the church's relic treasure, but also stresses the church's role in the Roman rite of consecration. The overall decoration of the transept appears to have gained momentum after the first phase was concluded in 1596 and required the inclusion of further episodes from Constantine's life which addressed the emperor's importance from a historiographical point of view and expressed the themes depicted in the outer cycle (*Triumphal Entry, Baptism, Foundation, Donation*). The choice of scenes addressing the liturgical sanctity of the Lateran, the preservation of the original *confessio* chapel beneath the high altar as well as the choice of painters for the decoration of the tribune in the Navata Clementina can be regarded as Cesare Baronio's success in convincing Clement VIII to arrange the Lateran's transept as a liturgical space that did not consequently break with the historiographical tradition of the basilica.

---

the supreme pontiff: The Lateran basilica as the new Temple in the medieval liturgy of Maundy Thursday', in C. Caspers and M. Schneiders (eds.), *Omnes Circumadstantes: Contributions towards a History of the Role of the People in the Liturgy Presented to Herman Wegman* (Kampen, 1990), 120–43, at pp. 120–1, who established an important connection between a passage in the medieval Roman *Ordo* and both this precious relic at the Lateran and a specific liturgical celebration, in which the Ark was transported together with the table of the Last Supper into the Sacristy of Canons on Holy Thursday, where it remained until Holy Saturday; see also F. Martinelli, 'Discorso di Fioravante Martinelli sopra alcune reliquie della basilica lateranense', in ACL, FF.XXIII, fols. 4r–24v.

The Tuscan painter Cristoforo Roncalli obtained the commission to execute the *Baptism of Constantine the Great*. Roncalli was one of the artists in d'Arpino's workshop at the Lateran who probably had the closest contact, not only with the Congregation of the Oratory in general, but especially with Cardinal Baronio himself. During the cardinal's renovation campaign in his *titulus* of Santi Nereo e Achilleo, Baronio employed Roncalli to paint an altarpiece of *Saint Domitilla with Nereus and Achilleus* for the southern wall altar. He also had extensive influence on the overall decoration of Baronio's titular church; Roncalli was probably responsible for painting the angelic figures in the pendentives below the clerestory of the main nave, as Alessandro Zuccari has convincingly outlined.[38] The fresco that concludes the transept's pictorial narrative on the eastern lateral wall has so far been regarded as derived from Raphael's *Baptism* in the Vatican Sala di Costantino. Roncalli, however, introduced specific modifications to the overall scene which suggest that the composition had a closer relationship with models produced during the last two decades of the Cinquecento than it did with the one from Raphael's workshop. These specific alterations to an already well-known pictorial prototype furthermore emphasise several liturgical concerns, indicating that Cesare Baronio must have been instrumental in the design as well as in the choice of scenes for the overall iconographic programme in the Lateran's transept.

The most essential alterations in Roncalli's fresco of Constantine the Great's *Baptism* in the Lateran's Navata Clementina concern the treatment of architecture as well as the figural disposition, which is orchestrated by the richness of garments this scene presents to the beholder. That the emperor's baptism is taking place inside the Lateran's baptistery is indicated by the semicircular placing of the four columns in the background. Unlike the fresco in the Vatican Sala di Costantino, the interior here has been deliberately enlarged, reducing the number of figures but enlarging them at the same time. Between the central two columns, the emerging light rays seem to suggest the descent of the Holy Spirit upon Constantine's anointment, lending this episode a more dramatic character. Unlike the Vatican depiction, Cristoforo Roncalli's scene places a clearer accent upon

---

[38] A. Zuccari, 'Cesare Baronio, le immagini, gli artisti', in C. Strinati (ed.), *La regola e la fama: S. Filippo Neri e l'arte* (Rome and Milan, 1995), 80–97, at pp. 88–9; I. Chiappini di Sorio, *Cristoforo Roncalli detto il Pomarancio* (Bergamo, 1975), 136–7. For Roncalli's altarpiece in Santi Nereo e Achilleo, see the most recent studies by B. Treffers in B. L. Brown (ed.), *The Genius of Rome 1592–1623* (London, 2001), 345, no. 131; M. Pupillo in R. Vodrte (ed.), *Roma al tempo di Caravaggio 1600–1630*, 2 vols. (Milan, 2011), II, 48, no. II; S. Schütze in D. Franklin, S. Schü, C. Gasparri and I. D. Rowland (eds.), *From Raphael to Carracci: The Art of Papal Rome* (Ottawa, 2009), 426–7, no. 144.

Pope Sylvester, who is not wearing the papal tiara, but instead a bishop's mitre, along with several other clergymen grouped around the baptismal font, in which the emperor is kneeling. The emperor is depicted with bent elbows, slightly turning his upper body to the left to accentuate the diagonal axis on which the scene unfolds.[39] This specific shift in the emphasis of the pope as bishop of Rome has crucial consequences for the interpretation of this particular episode in the overall progression of the pictorial narrative. As the first scene to present Pope Sylvester in this way, it also transfers the emphasis from the emperor onto the bishop who is performing the rite of baptism, assisted by other church prelates.

Already in Pope Sixtus V's Salone di Costantino inside the new Lateran palace, the scene of Constantine's *Baptism* has placed the figure of the bishop within the centre of the picture field to underline the importance of the Lateran palace as the official residence of the bishop of Rome. But Roncalli's slight de-placement of the figure of Sylvester from the centre of the picture field in his treatment of the subject seems to recur to specific compositions that the Tuscan artist must have encountered since 1578 while working in Niccolò Circignani's workshop in Rome.[40] As was noted above, Circignani included the same scene in his lost fresco for the church of San Tommaso di Canterbury. In his fresco cycle for the Jesuit church of Santo Stefano Rotondo Circignani seems to have been occupied by the relationship between pope and bishop as he also represented it in the fresco that concludes this famous cycle. Roncalli's further modification of treating Pope Sylvester as the bishop of Rome must have been inspired by an ambition for the transept's overall iconographic programme, namely to represent the church of San Giovanni in Laterano as the principal church of the city's bishop. The composition therefore had to correspond with certain requirements that the liturgical book of the *Caeremoniale Episcoporum* also stipulated to sustain the liturgical importance of the office of the *episcopus* in this particular church.

Conformity between the ceremonial importance of the episcopal office for the Roman rite as defined by the directives of the Tridentine council

---

[39] See also Freiberg, *The Lateran in 1600*, 100–2. The figure of Constantine was clearly adapted from Michelangelo's sculpture of the *Risen Christ* in Santa Maria sopra Minerva. See also Chiappini di Sorio, *Cristoforo Roncalli*, 111, where a pictorial derivation from Jacobino del Conte's fresco of Christ's baptism in the oratory of San Giovanni Decollato is also suggested.

[40] Baglione, Vite, 288. For Roncalli's early career in Rome, see J. von Henneberg, L'oratorio dell'arciconfraternita del santissimo crocifisso di San Marcello (Rome, 1974); R. P. Ciardi, Nicolò Circignani, Cristofano Roncalli: Pittori di Pomarance (Volterra, 1992); W. Chandler Kirwin, 'Cristofano Roncalli (1551/2–1626), an Exponent of the Proto-Baroque: His Activity through 1605', Ph.D. thesis (Stanford University, 1972), 24–8.

during its last session and the iconographic programme in the Navata Clementina suggests that a much more sophisticated design was selected for this decorative scheme than simply a basic historical sequence. According to an instruction given in the *Caeremoniale Episcoporum* concerning the decoration of a church on the occasion of a bishop's visit, the exterior of a church edifice should be ornamented with flowers in order to present an enriched and colourful appearance, while the interior should be embellished with colourful vestments, which resemble 'noble curtains appropriate for festivities'.[41] This instruction corresponds to another pictorial element of the frescoes in the transept in so far as each of the eight scenes from Constantine's life is presented on fictive tapestries. These *arazzi finti* suggest manifold dynamics of revelation as each episode is unrolled in front of the faithful as well as in front of the celebrant. The idea of Cesare Baronio in the design of this iconographic programme thus seems unsurprising considering the pictorial criteria that this decoration had to fulfil, since he was employed by Pope Clement VIII immediately after his elevation to the cardinalate in 1596 to work in the Congregazione dei Riti e Cerimonie on revising the *Caeremoniale*, which would see its publication in 1600. In the bull of approbation dated 14 July 1600 it is stated that Clement was advised by 'pious and erudite men' ('piis et eruditis viris') and that the book of the *Caeremoniale* should be based on the work already carried out for the *Pontificale Romanum* that appeared five years earlier. It is therefore possible to discern Baronio as having acted as a major contributor to both the *Pontificale* and the *Caeremoniale*, since he also provided corrections to the *Breviarum* that would ultimately be published, two years after the *Caeremoniale*.[42]

The fact that the Oratorian and Cardinal Cesare Baronio was regarded as an erudite man among the members of the Roman Curia during Clement VIII's pontificate, such as the Jesuit Roberto Bellarmino, gives also a reflection of how his magnum opus, the *Annales Ecclesiastici*, had been

---

[41] *Caeremoniale Episcoporum: Editio Princeps (1600)*, ed. A. M. Triacca and M. Sodi (MLCT 4) (Vatican City, 2000), 52: ' ... de solemnioribus illius Ecclesiae, primum a parte exteriori ornandae erunt valuae ipsius floribus, ramis, & frontibus virentibus, bracteolis, aut fasciis diversi coloris appersis, vel colligatis, quo splendidius pro locorum consuetudine ... inferioris vero ordinis hominum, maxime laicorum, insignia non sunt apponenda. ... quod & in aliis pannis, in apparatu interiori, & exteriori Ecclesiae observandum erit, & maxime ut non ponatur ibidem ullae effigies, nisi Sanctorum, vel summorum Pontificum. Intus quoque, si fieri poterit, parietes Ecclesiae aulaeis ... aut nobilioribus cortinis coloris caeterorum paramentorum pro festi qualitate.'

[42] For Baronio's corrections on the *Breviarum Romanum*, which he must have begun by 1588, see the document in the Biblioteca Vallicelliana (=BV), Q. 33, fols. 27r–28v. Regarding Pope Clement VIII's bull of approving the new *Caeremoniale*, see *Bull. Rom.*, X, 597–8.

received by the Curia upon the publication of the first volume in 1588. With his appointment to the cardinalate in 1596, Baronio's contributions to the artistic production of Clementine Rome became more conspicuous than while he was working on corrections to the *Martyrologium Romanum* during Pope Gregory XIII's pontificate. His influence with respect to Clement VIII's restorations in San Giovanni in Laterano, as argued in the arrangement of the high altar and its *confessio* chapel, seem to have produced a counterpart to what the pope realised, also with Baronio's assistance, at New Saint Peter's. After Bramante's Doric temple, built to house and protect the tomb of the Apostle, was torn down during the construction of the new church, Clement VIII ordered that a new high altar be erected in its place. This altar was consecrated by the pope on 26 June 1594 in the presence of all the cardinals, clergy and pious confraternities of Rome during a solemn ceremony.[43] After work on the high altar was completed, the pope's attention was directed towards the subterranean chapel located directly beneath it that tradition identified as the burial chapel of Saint Peter. The papal architect, Giacomo della Porta, supervised the excavations in the *grotte* that brought two preceding altars to light, both of which lay on a direct axis with the new Clementine altar. Clement VIII descended to view this find in 1594, accompanied by the Cardinals Antoniano, Bellarmino and Sfondrato – and presumably also Baronio – who wanted to recognise this place as the very tomb Constantine the Great had erected for the relics of Saint Peter.[44] As an *avviso* dated 2 June 1593 also reports, Clement VIII's admiration for this place was so great that he had a private passage constructed that connected the

---

[43] For a description of the ceremony, see G. Grimaldi, *Descrizione della Basilica Antica di S. Pietro in Vaticano: Codice Barberini Latino 2733*, ed. R. Niggl (Vatican City, 1972), 204–6. The diary of the master of papal ceremonies, Paolo Alaleona, also contains descriptions of the ceremony in BAV, Barb. lat. 2808, fols. 5r–v. See also the *avvisi* dated 11 and 29 June 1594 that record the consecration just three days before the feast of Saints Peter and Paul in BAV, Urb. lat. 1062. This material was amply discussed in W. Chandler Kirwin, 'Bernini's baldacchino reconsidered', *Römisches Jahrbuch für Kunstgeschichte* 19 (1981), 141–71, at pp. 144 n. 11, 147. See also H. Siebenhüner, 'Umrisse zur Geschichte der Ausstattung von St. Peter in Rom von Paul III. bis Paul V. (1547–1606)', in K. Oettinger and M. Rassem (eds.), *Festschrift für Hans Sedlmayr* (Munich, 1962), 229–320, at pp. 291–2.

[44] For an account of Clement VIII's visit to the *grotte*, see F. Bonanni, *Numismata summorum pontificium templi vaticani fabricam indicantia* (Rome, 1696), 149, also discussed by L. Duchesne, 'Notes sur la topographie de Rome au moyen-âge, XIII. Vaticana', *Mélanges d'archéologie et d'histoire d'École Française de Rome* 35 (1915), 3–13. See also F. M. Torrigio, *Le sacre grotte vaticane* (Viterbo, 1618), 44: 'Questo luoco è stato di varie pietre adornato da Clemente Ottavo, e nella volta fece fare i lavori di stucco indorato, & il pavimento pure di varie pietre, e marmi ... Qui vi si celebra la santa Messa spesse volte da Cardinali, Vescovi, Prelati, & altri gran personaggi con divotione incredibile.'

Apostolic palace with the crypt, enabling him to visit the Apostle's tomb unobserved. Additionally, the pope also built a small chapel in this 'passageway' (*strada*) with walls sheathed with polychrome marble and a vault decorated with stuccoes celebrating Peter's Apostolic Acts.[45]

When viewed from the perspective of the works carried out in Saint Peter's, the Navata Clementina is an important counterpart to the interventions in the Vatican basilica. It seems to have been a renovation campaign with a highly sophisticated iconographic programme that would only be fully comprehensible to members of the Roman Curia, individuals who must have been close to Cardinal Baronio himself. The transept's iconography, as the arguments above have attempted to demonstrate, did not in fact aim to contrast the imperial character of the Lateran with the more apostolic intentions realised at Saint Peter's. Rather, we should see the Navata Clementina as representing a complex interaction between imperial and episcopal history, having primarily been designed according to the reform of the Roman rite as laid down in the *Pontificale Romanum* and the *Caeremoniale Episcoporum*. With respect to his contributions to both these liturgical books, the Oratorian and Cardinal Cesare Baronio was surely instrumental to the conception and articulation of this programme.

---

[45] BAV, Urb. lat. 1061, fol. 306r: ' ... et qui non lasciano di dire delle orationi secrete, che fa il nostro Pastore, havendo a q[ues]to effetto S. B.[ne] fatta fare una strada sotterranea, et secreta nel Vaticano, che va à finire sotto quelle volte, ove sono li corpi degli Apostoli, orando, et vegliando spesso mentro altri dormono.' It is noteworthy that this *avviso* also mentions the forty-hour celebration that took place at San Giovanni in Laterano.

# Bibliography

## Primary Sources

Sources are listed in alphabetical order of author except in the cases of anonymous works by single authors (under Anon.) or multiple authors (under title and also in alphabetical order of editor).

Albanès, J. H. and Chevalier, U., *Actes anciens et documents concernant le bienheureux Urbain V pape, sa famille, sa personne, son pontificat, ses miracles et son culte* (Paris, 1897)

Allen, W., *Apologie and True Declaration* (Rheims, 1581)

Amalar of Metz: E. Knibbs (ed. and trans.), *On the Liturgy*, 2 vols. (Dumbarton Oaks Medieval Library 35–6) (Cambridge, MA, 2014)

Andrieu, M. (ed.), *Le Pontifical romain au moyen âge*, 4 vols. (Vatican City, 1938–41)

Anon., *Le cose maravigliose dell'alma città di Roma* ... (Rome, 1575)

  *Mirabilia Romae: Ein deutsches Blockbuch vom Ende des XV. Jahrhunderts* (*c.* 1475), ed. R. Ehwald (Berlin, 1903)

Auvray, L., *Les régistres de Grégoire IX: Récueil des bulles de ce pape*, 4 vols. (Paris, 1896)

Baglione, G., *Le nove chiese di Roma*, ed. L. Barroero (Rome, 1990 [1639])

  *Le vite de' pittori, scultori et architetti: Dal Pontificato di Gregorio XIII del 1572 in fino a' tempi di Papa Urbano Ottavo nel 1642*, ed. J. Hess, 3 vols. (Studi e testi, Biblioteca Apostolica Vaticana 367–9) (Vatican City, 1995)

Baldeschi, A. and Crescimbeni, G., *Stato della SS. chiesa papale lateranense nell'anno MDCCXXIII* (Rome, 1723)

Baronio, C., *Annales Ecclesiastici*, 12 vols. (Venice, 1600–12)

Baudoin de Rosières-aux-Salines, J., *Instruction de la vie mortelle*, or *Roman de la vie humaine* (*c.* 1431): in P. Meyer (ed.), 'L'Instruction de la vie mortelle par Jean Baudoin de Rosières-aux-Salines', *Romania* 35 (1906), 531–54

Bede, *De temporum ratione*: in C. Jones (ed.), *Bedae Venerabilis Opera. Pars VI: Opera didascalica 2 (De temporum ratione)* (Corpus Christianorum Series Latina 123B) (Turnhout, 1977); ed. and trans. F. Wallis as *Bede: The Reckoning of Time* (Translated Texts for Historians 29) (Liverpool, 1999)

Benjamin of Tudela, *The Itinerary of Benjamin of Tudela: Travels in the Middle Ages*, introd. M. A. Signer (Malibu, 1992)

Bonanni, F., *Numismata summorum pontificium templi vaticani fabricam indicantia* (Rome, 1696)

Bonizo of Sutri, *Liber de vita christiana*, ed. E. Perels (Berlin, 1930)

Borbone, P. G. (ed.), *Storia di Mar Yahballaha e di Rabban Sauma: Cronaca sirica del XIV secolo* (Moncalieri, 2009)

Borromeo, C., *Instructiones fabricae et supellectilis ecclesiasticae*, in *Trattati d'arte del Cinquecento: Fra manierismo e controriforma*, ed. P. Barocchi, 3 vols. (Bari, 1960-2)

*Bullarium, diplomatum et privilegiorum sanctorum romanorum pontificum, Taurinensis editio*, 24 vols. (n.p., 1857-72) (2 supp. vols., 1867-85)

Burckard, J., *Johannis Burchardi Argentinensis capelle pontificio sacrorum rituum magistri diarium, sive Rerum urbanarum commentarii (1483-1506): Texte latin publié intégralement pour la primiere fois d'après les manuscrits de Paris, de Rome et de Florence, avec introduction, notes, appendices, tables et index par L. Thuasne (1484)*, ed. L. Thuasne, 2 vols. (Paris, 1884)

Cabié, R. (ed.), *La lettre du pape Innocent Ier à Décentius de Gubbio, 19 mars 416* (Louvain, 1973)

*Caeremoniale Episcoporum: Editio Princeps (1600)*, ed. A. M. Triacca and M. Sodi (MLCT 4) (Vatican City, 2000)

Calenzio, G., *La vita e gli scritti del cardinale Cesare Baronio della Congregazione dell'Oratorio, bibliotecario di Santa Romana Chiesa* (Rome, 1907)

Cancellieri, F., *Memorie istoriche delle sacre teste de' santi Apostoli Pietro e Paolo e della loro solenne ricognizione nella basilica lateranense* (Rome, 1806)

  *Il mercato, il lago dell'Acqua Vergine ed il palazzo panfiliano nel Circo Agonale detto volgarmente Piazza Navona* (Rome, 1811)

*Canones Theodori Cantuariensis*: P. W. Finsterwalder (ed.), *Die Canones Theodori Cantuariensis und ihre Überlieferungsgeschichte* (Weimar, 1929)

Capgrave, J., *Ye solace of pilgrims: A description of Rome, circa AD 1450, by John Capgrave, an Austin Friar of King's Lynn*, ed. C. A. Mills (Oxford, 1911)

Casimiro, P., *Memorie istoriche della chiesa e convento di S. Maria in Araceli di Roma* (Rome, 1736)

Cavalieri, G. B., *Ecclesiae anglicanae trophaea ... Romae in collegio Anglico per Nicolaum Circinianum depictae* (Rome, 1584)

  *Ecclesiae militantis triumphi ... in ecclesia S. Stephani Rotundi Romae Nicolai Circiniani pictoris manu visuntur* (Rome, 1585)

Ciampini, G. G., *De sacris aedificiis a Costantino Magno constructis: Synopsis historica* (Rome, 1693)

Claeys-Boúúaert, F., 'Bulle in Coena Domini', in R. Naz (ed.), *Dictionnaire de droit canonique*, 7 vols. (Paris, 1935-6), II, cols. 1132-6

*Collectionis bullarum sacrosanctae basilicae vaticanae*, 3 vols. (Rome, 1747-52)

Constantinus Porphyrogentius, *Imperatoris de Ceremoniis Aulae Byzantinae*, ed. J. J. Reiske and J. Heinrich (Corpus Scriptorum Historiae Byzantinae 2) (Bonn, 1830)

*Constitutum Constantini*: H. Fuhrmann (ed.), *Das Constitutum Constantini: Text* (MGH Fontes Iuris Germanici Antiqui in usum scholarium ex Monumentis Germaniae Historicis separatim editi 10) (Hanover, 1968)

Cordellier, D., 'Documenti e fonti su Pisanello (1395–1581 circa)', *Verona illustrate* 8 (1995)

*Corpus Inscriptionum Latinarum*, ed. Deutsche Akademie der Wissenschaften zu Berlin, 17 vols. (Berlin, 1862–93)

Crivello, F., Denoël, C. and Orth, P., *Das Godescalc-Evangelistar: Eine Prachthandschrift für Karl den Großen* (Darmstadt, 2011)

d'Ancona, A. (ed.), *Journal du voyage de Michel Montaigne en Italie par la Suisse et l'Allemagne en 1580 et 1561* (Città di Castello, 1889); trans. W. G. Waters in *The Journal of Montaigne's Travels in Italy*, 3 vols. (London, 1903)

Dati, G., *Statione/indulgetie reliqe di Roma scta* (n.p., *c.* 1500)

Degenhart B. and Schmitt, A., *Corpus der italienischen Zeichnungen 1300–1450, Teil III: Verona. Pisanello und seine Werkstatt. I Band. Text* (Munich, 2004)

de Grassis, P., *Diario di Leone – di Paride de Grassi . . . dai volumi manoscritti degli Archivi Vaticani della S. Sede con note di M. Armellini, mons. Pio Delicati*, ed. P. Delicati and M. Armellini (Rome, 1884)

de Rossi, G. B., *Inscriptiones Christianae Urbis Romae*, 2 vols. (Rome, 1857–88)

'Descriptio Lateranensis Ecclesiae': in Valentini and Zucchetti, *Codice topografico*, III, 356–8

Douteil, H. (ed.), *Iohannis Beleth Summa de ecclesiasticis officiis* (CCCM 41–41A), 2 vols. (Turnhout, 1976)

Dumas, A. and Deshusses, J. (eds.), *Liber sacramentorum Gellonensis* (CCSL 159A), 2 vols. (Turnhout, 1981)

Edwards, M., *Constantine and Christendom. The Oration to the Saints. The Greek and Latin Accounts of the Discovery of the Cross. The Edict of Constantine to Pope Silvester* (Translated Texts for Historians 39) (Liverpool, 2003)

Egeria, *Itinerarium – Reisebericht: Mit Auszügen aus Petrus Diaconus, De locis Sanctis – Die Heiligen Stätten*, ed. and trans. G. Röwekamp (Fontes Christiani 20) (Freiburg, 2000)

Eusebius, *Vita Constantini*: in F. Winkelmann (ed.), *Eusebius Werke*, 2nd edn (Berlin, 2008), 126–7

Facio, B., *De viris illustribus* (Biblioteca Vaticana, ms.Vat. Lat. 13650) (Rome, 1453–7): in M. Baxandall (ed.), *Giotto and the Orators: Humanist Observers of Painting in Italy and the Discovery of Pictorial Composition 1350–1450* (Oxford, 1971)

Fichard, J., *Observationes antiquitatum et aliarum rerum magis memorabilium quae Romae videntur* (1536): in A. August Schmarsow (ed.), 'Excerpte aus Joh. Fichard's "Italia" von 1536', in *Repertorium für Kunstwissenschaft* 14 (1891), 130–9, 373–83

Fischer, L. (ed.), *Bernhardi cardinalis et Laterancensis ecclesiae prioris, Ordo officiorum ecclesiae Lateranensis* (Munich, 1916)

Fontana, D., *Della Trasportazione dell'Obelisco Vaticano et delle Fabbriche di Nostro Signore Papa Sixtus V fatte fare dal Cavaliere Domenico Fontana Architetto di Sua Santità*, Book I (Rome, 1590); ed. A. Carugo and P. Portoghesi as *Della Trasportatione dell'Obelisco Vaticano et delle Fabriche di Nostro Signore Papa Sisto V (1590)* (Rome, 1978)

Forcella, V., *Iscrizioni delle chiese e d'altri edificii di Roma dal secolo XI fino ai giorni nostri*, 14 vols. (Rome, 1869–84)

Foxe, J., *Actes and Monuments of these Latter and Perillous Days, Touching Matters of the Church* (London, 1563)

Fra Mariano da Firenze, *Itinerarium urbis Romae (1517)*, ed. E. Bulletti (Studi di antichità cristiana 2) (Rome, 1931 [1518])

*Tractatus de origine, nobilitate et de excellentia Tusciae*, ed. E. Bulletti (Archivio francescano di Ognissanti, ms. F 16) (Rome, 1931 [Florence, 1518])

Fra Niccoló di Poggibonsi, *A voyage beyond the seas (1346–1350)*, ed. and trans. Fr T. Bellorini and Fr E. Hoade (Jerusalem, 1945)

Francino, G., *Le cose maravigliose dell'alma citta' di Roma* (Venice, 1588)

Fulvio, A., *Antiquaria Urbis* (Rome, 1514)

*Antiquitates Urbis* (Rome, 1545 [1527])

Garoscus de Ulmoisca, 'Iter italicum Urbani V Romani Pontificis': in S. Baluzius, *Vitae Paparum Avenionesioum [1693], nouvelle édition d'après les manuscrits par G. Mollat*, 4 vols. (Paris, 1916–22), IV, 136

Gerardi, F., *La patriarcale basilica lateranense illustrata per cura di Agostino Valentini*, 2 vols. (Rome, 1832–4)

Geyer, P. and Cuntz, O. (eds.), *Itineraria et alia geographica* (Corpus Christianorum Series Latina 175) (Turnhout, 1965)

Gibbons, J. and Fenn, J., *Concertation ecclesiae catholicae in Anglia, adversus Calvinopapistas & Puritanos* (Trier, 1583)

Giorgi, D., *De liturgia romani pontificis in solemni celebratione missarum*, 3 vols. (Rome, 1744)

Giovio, P., *Lettere volgari di Mons. Paolo Giovio da Como Vescovo di Nocera raccolte per messer Lodovico Domenichi* (Venice, 1560)

Gregory of Tours, *Liber Miraculorum: De Gloria Beatorum Martyrum*: in J.-P. Migne, *Patrologiae cursus completus: Series Latina*, 221 vols. (Paris, 1844–1905), LXXI, cols. 705–800

Grimaldi, G., *Descrizione della Basilica Antica di S. Pietro in Vaticano: Codice Barberini Latino 2733*, ed. R. Niggl (Vatican City, 1972)

Halbwachs, M., *Stätten der Verkündigung im Heiligen Land. Eine Studie zum kollektiven Gedächtnis*, ed. S. Egger (Konstanz, 2003)

Heiming, O. (ed.), *Liber sacramentorum Augustodunensis* (CCSL 159B) (Turnhout, 1984)

Heylen, F. (ed.), *Archidiaconi Romani Sermones tres de reconciliandis paenitentibus* (CCSL 9) (Turnhout, 1957)

Honorius Augustodunensis, *Gemma animae*, PL 172, cols. 541–737

Infessura, S., *Diario della città di Roma di Stefano Infessura scriba senato*, ed. O. Tommasini (Fonti per la storia d'Italia 5) (Rome, 1890)

*Itinerarium Einsidlense*: C. Hülsen, *La Pianta di Roma dell'Anonimo Einsidlense* (Rome, 1907)

Jerome, *Epistolae*: I. Hilberg (ed.), *Sancti Eusebii Hieronymi Epistulae*, 2 vols. (CSEL 54–6) (Vienna, 1910–18)

*Epistulae* 77.4: in Liverani, 'L'area lateranense in età tardo antica', 21

John the Deacon, *Epistola ad Senarium* 6: A. Wilmart (ed.), 'Epistola de Iohannis Diaconis ad Senarium', in *Analecta Reginensia, Studi e Testi* 59 (Vatican City, 1933), 170–9

Jones, A. H. M., Martindale, J. R. and Morris, J. (eds.), *The Prosography of the Later Roman Empire*, 3 vols. (Cambridge, 1972–92)

Juvenal, *Saturae*: E. Barelli (ed.), *Satire: Testo latino a fronte*, trans. A. Agostini, 6th edn. (Classici greci e latine) (Milan, 1976); ed. and trans. N. Rudd as *Juvenal: The Satires* (Oxford, 1991)

König, I., *Aus der Zeit Theoderichs des Großen: Einleitung, Text, Übersetzung und Kommentar einer anonymen Quelle* (Darmstadt, 1997)

Labande, E.-R. (ed. and trans.), *Guibert de Nogent, Autographie* (Les classiques de l'histoire de France au moyen âge 34) (Paris, 1981)

Le Brun des Marettes, J. B., *Voyages liturgiques de France* (Paris, 1718)

Leo Magnus, *Sermones*: J. P. Freeland (ed.), *St Leo the Great: Sermons* (Fathers of the Church Patristic Series 93) (Washington, DC, 1996)

*Liber Politicus*: in P. Fabre and L. Duchesne (eds.), *Le Liber censuum de l'Église romaine*, 3 vols. (Paris, 1910–52), II, cols. 141a–159b

*Liber Pontificalius*: L. Duchesne (ed.), *Le Liber Pontificalis: Texte, introduction et commentaire I* (Rome, 1886); L. Duchesne (ed.), *Le Liber Pontificalis: Texte, introduction et commentaire II* (Rome, 1892); Agostino Patrizi Piccolomini and Giovanni Burcardo, *Il Pontificalis liber (1485)*, ed. M. Sodi (Vatican City, 2006); trans. R. Davis as *The Book of Pontiffs (Liber Pontificalis): The Ancient Biographies of the First Ninety Roman Bishops to AD 715* (Liverpool Translated Texts for Historians 6), rev. 3rd edn (Liverpool, 2010); R. Davis (ed.), *The Lives of the Eighth-Century Popes* (Translated Texts for Historians 13) (Liverpool, 1992); R. Davis (ed.), *The Lives of the Ninth-Century Popes (Liber Pontificalis)* (Translated Texts for Historians 20) (Liverpool, 1995)

Geertman, H. 'Le biografie del *Liber Pontificalis* dal 311 al 535: Testo e commentario', in H. Geertman (ed.), *Atti del Colloquio Internazionale Il Liber Pontificalis e la storia materiale. Roma, 21–22 febbraio 2002* (Mededelingen van het Nederlands Instituut te Rome, Antiquity 60–1 (2001–2)) (Assen, 2003), 285–356

'La genesi del *Liber Pontificalis* romano: Un processo di organizzazione della memoria', in Bougard and Sot (eds.), *Liber, gesta, histoire*, 37–107

Loewy, E., *Inschriften Griechischer Bildhauer* (Leipzig, 1885)

Lupus Protospatarius, *Chronicon*: G. H. Pertz (ed.), MGH, SS, 5 (Hanover, 1844)

Maffei, R. *Commentariorum Urbanorum libri octo et triginta*, 38 vols. (Rome, 1506)
Mango, C., *The Art of the Byzantine Empire, 312–1453: Sources and Documents*, 2nd edn (Toronto, 1986)
Mansi, G. D., *Sacrorum conciliorum nova et amplissima collectio 7* (Florence, 1762)
Marangoni, G., *Delle cose gentilesche e profane trasportate ad uso, e adornamento delle chiese* (Rome, 1744)
   *Istoria dell'antichissimo oratorio, o cappella di San Lorenzo nel Patriarchio Lateranense comunemente appellato Sancta Sanctorum* (Rome, 1747)
Martinelli, F., 'Discorso di Fioravanti Martinelli sopra alcune Reliquie della Basilica Lateranense', ACL, A 26
Martini, A. (ed.), *Il cosiddetto Pontificale di Poitiers (Paris, Bibliothèque de l'Arsenal, cod. 227)* (Rome, 1979)
Mattingly, H. and Syndenham, E. A., *The Roman Imperial Coinage*, 10 vols. (London, 1923–94)
Mellini, B., *ROMA Descritta da Benedetto Millino: Rione de Monti* (Archivio Capitolare Lateranense, A. XXIX), *Appendice Documentaria* in A. M. De Strobel, *Il Portico Medievale di San Giovanni in Laterano. I Frammenti Ritrovati* (Vatican City, 2019), D36
Mohlberg, L. C. (ed.), *Das fränkische Sacramentarium gelasianum im alamannischer Überlieferung*, 2nd edn (Münster, 1939)
Mohlberg, L. C., Eizenhöfer, L. and Siffrin, P. (eds.), *Liber sacramentorum Romanae Aeclesiae ordinis anni circuli: Cod. Vat. Reg. lat. 316/Paris Bibl. Nat. 7193, 41/56 (Sacramentarium Gelasianum)*, 3rd edn (Rome, 1981)
Mombritius, B., *Sanctuarium seu Vitae Sanctorum*, 2 vols. (Paris, 1910)
Mommsen, T. (ed.), *Libri Pontificalis* (MGH, Gestorum Pontificum Romanorum 1, 1) (Berlin, 1898)
Mommsen, T. and Meyer, P. M. (eds.), *Theodosiani libri XVI*, 2 vols. (Berlin, 1905)
Montpellier, Bibliothèque de l'École de Médecine, ms. H. 267, 51 r: in G. Boffitto and F. Fracassetti (eds.), *Il Collegio di San Luigi dei PP. Barnabiti in Bologna 1773–1873–1923* (Florence, 1925), 35
Muffel, N., *Descrizione della città di Roma nel 1452: Delle indulgenze e dei luoghi sacri di Roma (Der ablas und die heiligen stet zu Rom)*, ed. and trans. D. G. Wiedmann (Bologna, 1999)
*Ordines*: M. Andrieu (ed.), *Les Ordines Romani du haut moyen âge*, 5 vols. (Louvain, 1931–61); J. F. Romano, *Liturgy and Society in Early Medieval Rome* (Farnham, 2014), 229–48
Palladio, A., *Descritione de le Chiese, Stationi, Indulgenze &t reliquie de Corpi Sancti che sonno in la Città de Roma* (1554), ed. L. Puppi (Vicenza, 2000)
Panvinio, O., *De praecipuis urbis Romae sanctioribusque; basilicis, quas Septem ecclesias vulgo vocant, Liber* (Rome, 1570); trans. M. A. Lanfranchi as *Le sette chiese principali di Roma* (Rome, 1570)
   *De sacrosanta basilica baptisterio et patriarchio Lateranensi* (before 1569): in Lauer, *Le palais du Latran*, 410–90

Parsons, R., *An Epistle of the Persecution of Catholicks in Englande* (Douai, 1582)
*Patrologia Latina*, ed. J.-P. Migne, 217 vols. (Paris, 1841–65)
Platina, B., *Liber de vita Christi ac omnium pontificum* (Città di Castello, 1479); reproduced in G. Gaida (ed.), *Rerum Italicarum Scriptores III/1* (Bologna, 1913–32)
Pliny the Elder, *Naturalis Historia*, ed. H. Rackham (Loeb Classical Library) (Cambridge, MA, 1952)
Pollard, R. M., 'The language and style of the *Codex epistolaris Carolinus*, and their affinities with other papal documents', in R. McKitterick, R. M. Pollard, R. Price and D. van Espelo, *Codex epistolaris carolinus* (Translated Texts for Historians) (Liverpool, 2021)
*Pontificale Romanum: Editio princeps (1595–1596)*, ed. M. Sodi and A. M. Triacca (MLCT) (Vatican City, 1997)
*Pontificale secundum ritum sacrosancte Romane ecclesie cum multis additionibus* (Venice, 1520)
Prescott, H. F. M., *Felix Fabris Reise nach Jerusalem* (Freiburg, 1960)
Pressuti, P., *Regesta Honorii Papae III* (Rome, 1888–95)
Price, R., *The Acts of the Lateran Synod of 649* (Translated Texts for Historians 61) (Liverpool, 2014)
*Prosographia Imperi Romani*, ed. Deutsche Akademie der Wissenschaften zu Berlin, 8 vols. (Berlin, 1933–2015)
Pseudo-Aurelius Victor, *Epitome de Caesaribus*: J.-L. Gauville (ed.), *Abbreviated Histories. The Case of the Epitome de Caesaribus (AD 395)* (Montreal, 1995)
Pungileoni, L., *Memoria intorno alla vita ed alle opere di Donato o Donnino Bramante* (Rome, 1836)
Rasponi, C., *De Basilica et Patriarchio Lateranense libri V* (Rome, 1656)
 *De Basilica et Patriarchio Lateranensis libri IV* (Rome, 1656)
Reiffenstuel, A. (OFM), *Jus canonicum universum* (n. p., 1717)
Rodenberg, C. (ed.), *Epistolae saeculi XIII e regestis pontificum Romanorum selectae*, 3 vols. (Berlin, 1883)
Roscetti, B., *La preclarissima Historia fabrianese novamente ricopiata dal p(adre) fra' Roscetti Bonaventura di Matellica* (Fabriano, Biblioteca comunale, ms 159) (1627)
Rossi, E., 'Roma ignorata', *Roma* 12 (1934), 39–40
Rucellai, G., *Zibaldone quaresimale: Della bellezza e anticaglia di Roma* (1450): in Valentini and Zucchetti, *Codice topografico*, IV, 405–8
Saint-Roch, P. (ed.), *Liber sacramentorum Engolismensis* (CCSL 159C) (Turnhout, 1986)
Sarbak, G. and Weinrich, L. (eds.), *Sicardi Cremonensis Mitralis de officiis* (CCCM 228) (Turnhout, 2008)
Séroux d'Agincourt, J. B. L. G., *Histoire de l'art par les monumens depuis sa décadence au IVe siècle jusqu'à son renouvellement au XVIe*, 6 vols. (Paris, 1810–23)

Serrano, M. A., *De septem urbis ecclesiis* (Rome, 1575)
Severano, G., *Memorie sacre delle sette chiese di Roma*, 2 parts (Rome, 1630)
Soresini, J. M., *De capitibus sanctorum apostolorum Petri et Pauli in sacrosancta lateranensi ecclesia* (Rome, 1673)
*Compendio istorico cronologico delle cose più cospique concernenti la Scala Santa e le SS. Teste* (Rome, 1674)
Sozomen, *Historia ecclesiastica*: G. C. Hansen (ed. and trans.), *Kirchengeschichte*, 4 vols. (Turnhout, 2004)
*Tabula Magna Lateranensis* (c. 1518): in Lauer, *Le palais de Latran*, 296–301
Tacitus, *Annales*: ed. in The Latin Library, www.thelatinlibrary.com/tacitus/tac.ann15.shtml.
Tanner, N. P. (ed.), *Decrees of the Ecumenical Councils*, 2 vols. (London, 1990)
Thurn, H., *Comes Romanus Wirziburgensis: Facsimileausgabe des Codex M.p.th. f.62 der Universitäts-Bibliothek Würzburg* (Graz, 1968)
Torrigio, F. M., *Le sacre grotte vaticane* (Viterbo, 1618)
Trout, D., *Damasus of Rome: The Epigraphic Poetry* (Oxford, 2015)
Ugonio, P., *Historia delle stationi di Roma* (Rome, 1588)
Unterkircher, F. (ed.), *Alkuin-Briefe und andere Traktate: Im Auftrage des Salzburger Erzbischofs Arn um 799 zu einem Sammelband vereinigt: Codex Vindobonensis 795 der Österreichischen Nationalbibliothek* (Codices selecti 20) (Graz, 1969)
Vacca, F., *Memorie di varie antichità trovate in diversi luoghi della città di Roma* (Rome, 1594)
Valesio, F. *Diario di Roma*, 5 vols., ed. G. Scano (Milan, 1979)
Vallo, L., *De falso credita et ementita Constantini donatione* (Rome, 1517)
van Dijk, S. J. P. (ed.), *Sources of the Modern Roman Liturgy: The Ordinals by Haymo of Faversham and Related Documents (1243–1307)*, 2 vols. (Leiden, 1963)
van Dijk, S. J. P. and Hazelden Walker, J. (eds.), *The Ordinal of the Papal Court from Innocent III to Boniface VIII and Related Documents* (Fribourg, 1975)
van Overbeek, B., *Reliquiae Antiquae Urbis Romae . . .* (Amsterdam, 1708)
Vasari, G., *Le vite de' più eccellenti pittori, scultori et architetti coll'aggiunta de' vivi et de' morti, dall'anno 1550 al 1567* (Florence, 1550–68); ed. R. Bettarini and P. Barocchi (Florence, 1966–87)
Venuti, R., *Accurata, e succinta descrizione topografica delle Antichità di Roma dell'Abate Ridolfino Venuti Cortonese Presidente dell'Antichità Romane, E Membro Onorario della Regia Società degli Antiquarj di Londra, Parte Prima* (Rome, 1763); *Appendice Documentaria* in A. M. De Strobel, *Il Portico Medievale di San Giovanni in Laterano. I Frammenti Ritrovati* (Vatican City, 2019), D61
*Osservazioni sopra un'antica iscrizione aggiunta al Museo Corsini* (Rome, 1733).
Vergil the Grammarian, *Epitomae*: in G. Polara (ed.), *Virgilie Marone grammatico: Epitome ed Epistole* (Naples, 1979)

Vogel, C. and Elze, R. (eds.), *Le pontifical romano-germanique du dixième siècle*, 3 vols. (Vatican City, 1963–72)
von Pflugk-Harttung, J., *Acta pontificum romanorum inedita*, vol. III: *Urkunden der Päpste 590–1197* (Graz, 1958)
Walser, G. (ed.), *Die Einsiedler Inschriftsammlung und der Pilgerführer durch Rom (Codex Einsidlensis 326)* (Stuttgart, 1987)
Zuallardo, G., *Il devotissimo Viaggio di Gerusalemme, fatto, & descritto in sei libri dal Sig.r Giovanni Zuallardo, Cavaliero del Santiß. Sepolcro di N.S. l'anno 1586. Aggiontovi i disegni di varij luoghi di Terra Santa & altri paesi Intagliati da Natale Bonifacio Dalmata* (Rome, 1587)

## Secondary Sources

Abromson, M. C., *Painting in Rome during the Papacy of Clement VIII (1592–1605): A Documented Study* (New York, 1981)
Adam, J.-P., *L'arte di costruire presso i Romani* (Milan, 2006)
Adams, J. N., 'The poets of Bu Njem: Language, culture and the centurionate', *Journal of Roman Studies* 89 (1999), 109–34
Adkin, N., 'Jerome, Seneca, Juvenal', *Revue belge d'archéologie et d'histoire de l'art* 78 (2000), 119–28
  'Juvenal and Jerome', *Classical Philology* 89 (1994), 69–72
Albana, M., 'Aspetti della burocrazia militare nell'alto impero', *Annali della Facoltà di Scienze della Formazione, Università degli Studi di Catania* 12 (2013), 3–39
Alchermes, J., 'Petrine Politics: Pope Symmachus and the Rotunda of St. Andrew at Old St. Peter's', *Catholic Historical Review* 81 (1995), 1–40
Alföldi, A., *Die monarchische Repräsentation im römischen Kaiserreiche* (Darmstadt, 1970)
Alonso Alonso, A., 'Fuentes literarias y epigraficas para el estudio de los valetudinaria urbanos en el mundo romano', *Classica et Christiana* 9, 1 (2014), 11–34
Amadei, E., *Le torri di Roma* (Rome, 1932)
Amici, C. M., *Foro di Traiano: Basilica Ulpia e biblioteche* (Rome, 1982)
  'From project to monument', in C. Giavarini (ed.), *The Basilica of Maxentius: The Monument, Its Materials, Construction, and Stability* (Rome, 2005), 21–74
Amiet, R., *La veillée pascale dans l'Église latine*, vol. I: *Le rite romain: Histoire et liturgie* (Paris, 1999)
Andaloro, M., 'Il sogno di Innocenzi III all'Aracoeli, Niccolò IV e la basilica di S. Giovanni in Laterano', in S. Macchioni and B. Tavassi La Greca (eds.), *Studi in onore di Giulio Carlo Argan*, 2 vols. (Rome, 1984), I, 29–42
Antonazzi, G., *Lorenzo Valla e la polemica sulla Donazione di Costantino* (Rome, 1985)
Apollonj Ghetti, B. M., *La basilica del Salvatore poi di S. Giovanni al Laterano cattedrale di Roma: Edizione a cura di Eugenio Russo* (San Marino, 2013)

Aronberg Lavin, M., *The Place of Narrative: Mural Decoration in Italian Churches* (Chicago, 1994)

Asor Rosa, L., Loreti, E. M., Motta, R., Pacetti, F. and Saviane, N., 'Piazza di Porta S. Giovanni: Riscoperta di un tratto di Mura Aureliane (2013–2015)', *Bullettino della Commissione Archeologica Comunale di Roma* 115 (2015), 211–20

Assmann, A., *Erinnerungsräume: Formen und Wandlungen des kulturellen Gedächtnisses* (Munich, 2010)

Aurenhammer, H. and Bohde, D. (eds.), *Räume der Passion: Raumvisionen, Erinnerungsorte und Topographien des Leidens Christi in Mittelalter und Früher Neuzeit* (Vestigia Bibliae. Jahrbuch des Deutschen Bibelarchivs Hamburg, 32/3) (Bern, 2015)

Bacci, M., 'Jacopo Ligozzi e la sua posizione nella pittura fiorentina', *Proporzioni* 4 (1963), 46–84

'Vera croce, vero ritratto e vera misura', in J. Durand and B. Flusin (eds.), *Byzance et les reliques du Christ* (Paris, 2004), 235–8

Bailey, G. A., *Between Renaissance and Baroque: Jesuit Art in Rome, 1565–1610* (Toronto, 2009)

Baldovin, F., *The Urban Character of Christian Worship: The Origins, Development, and Meaning of Stational Liturgy* (Rome, 1987)

Ballardini, A., '"In antiquissimo ac venerabili Lateranensi palatio": La residenza dei pontefici secondo il Liber Pontificalis', in *Le corti nell'alto Medioevo* (Settimane di Studio del Centro italiano di studi sull'alto medioevo 62) (Spoleto, 2014), 889–928

Barbera, M., 'Un anfiteatro di corte: Il Castrense', in A. La Regina (ed.), *Sangue e Arena* (Milan, 2001), 127–45

'Dagli *Horti Spei Veteris* al *Palatium Sessorium*', in S. Ensoli and E. La Rocca (eds.), *Aurea Roma: Dalla città pagana alla città Cristiana* (Florence, 2000), 104–12

Barbera, M., Barrano, S., de Cola, G., Festuccia, S., Giovannetti, L., Menghi, O. and Pales, M., 'La villa di Caligola: Un nuovo settore degli Horti Lamiani scoperto sotto la sede dell'ENPAM a Roma', *Journal of Fasti Online* (2010), 1–59

Barbero, A., *Costantino il vincitore* (Rome, 2016)

Barclay Lloyd, J. E., 'Masonry techniques in medieval Rome c. 1080–1300', *PBSR* 53 (1985), 225–77

Barelli, L., 'Architetture altoresidenziali a Roma nel XIII secolo: Alcune osservazioni', in R. M. Dal Mas and R. Mancini (eds.), *Cinte murarie e abitati: Restauro, riuso e valorizzazione* (Beni architettonici e paesaggio 3) (Rome, 2015), 133–43

*Il complesso monumentale dei Ss. Quattro Coronati a Roma* (Rome, 2009)

'Il complesso dei Ss. Quattro Coronati a Roma in età carolingia', in F. Guidobaldi and A. Guiglia Guidobaldi (eds.), *Ecclesiae Urbis: Atti del Congresso internazionale di studi sulle chiese di Roma (IV–X secolo) (Roma 4–10 settembre 2000)* (Studi di antichità cristiana 59) (Vatican City, 2002), 979–92

'Construction methods in Carolingian Rome (eighth–ninth centuries)', in R. Carvais, A. Guillerme, V. Nègre and J. Sakarovitch (eds.), *Nuts and Bolts of Construction History: Culture, Technology and Society*, 3 vols. (Paris, 2012), II, 135–41

'La diffusione e il significato dell'opus quadratum a Roma nei secoli VIII e IX', in M. P. Sette, M. Caperna, M. Docci and M. G. Turco (eds.), *Saggi in onore di Gaetano Miarelli Mariani* (Rome, 2007), 67–74

'Note lateranensi e note al testo', in M. Morbidelli, *L'abside di S. Giovanni in Laterano: Una vicenda controversa* (I libri di Viella. Arte) (Rome, 2010), 15–22

'Il palazzo cardinalizio dei Santissimi Quattro Coronati a Roma nel Basso Medioevo', in Z. Mari, M. T. Petrara and M. Sperandio (eds.), *Il Lazio tra antichità e medioevo: Studi in memoria di Jean Coste* (Rome, 1998), 111–24

'Un portico altomedievale fra i disegni di antichità di Alberto Alberti: Confronto tra dati diretti e indiretti', *Palladio* 25, 49 (2012), 5–24

'I quadriportici nell'architettura religiosa della Roma carolingia (secoli VIII e IX)', in F. Cantatore, A. Cerutti Fusco and P. Cimbolli Spagnesi (eds.), *Giornate di studio in onore di Claudio Tiberi* (Rome, 2012), 71–80

Barelli, L., Asciutti M. and Fabbri, M. C., 'Lettura storico-tecnica di una muratura altomedievale: L'*Opus quadratum* a Roma nei secoli VIII e IX', in D. Fiorani and D. Esposito (eds.), *Tecniche costruttive dell'edilizia storica: Conoscere per conservare* (Rome, 2005), 59–76

Barelli, L. and Falconi, M., 'I Ss. Quattro Coronati a Roma: Nuove acquisizioni sugli edifice annessi alla basilica carolingia', *Palladio* 8, 16 (1995), 6–14

Barelli, L. and Morbidelli, M., '"Ad imitazione, e somiglianza di quello che v'era anticamente": Il restauro dell'abside di San Giovanni in Laterano a Roma al tempo di Nicola IV (1288-1292)', in V. Franchetti Pardo (ed.), *Arnolfo di Cambio e la sua epoca: Costruire, scolpire, dipingere, decorare (Atti del Convegno, Firenze–Colle di Val d'Elsa, 7–10 marzo 2006)* (Rome, 2006), 197–208

Barelli, L. and Pugliese, R., *Dal cantiere dei SS. Quattro Coronati a Roma: Note di storia e restauro per G. Carbonara* (Rome, 2012)

Barral i Altet, X., 'L'VIII secolo: da Giovanni VI (701–705) ad Adriano I (772–795)', in D'Onofrio (ed.), *La committenza artistica dei papi*, 181–212

Barresi, P., 'Il ruolo delle colonne nel costo degli edifici publici', in M. de Nuccio and L. Ungaro (eds.), *I marmi colorati della Roma imperiale* (Rome, 2002), 69–81

Barroero, L., 'La Basilica dal Cinquecento ai nostri giorni', in Pietrangeli (ed.), *San Giovanni in Laterano*, 145–255

'La Basilica dal Cinquecento all'Ottocento', in C. Pietrangeli (ed.), *Santa Maria Maggiore a Roma* (Florence, 1988), 214–59

Bartoli, R., 'Cerchia di Francesco Borromini, Rilievo della navata destra di San Giovanni in Laterano con gli affreschi di Gentile da Fabriano', in De Marchi et al (eds.), *Gentile da Fabriano*, 306–7

Bauer, F. A., *Das Bild der Stadt Rom im Frühmittelalter: Papststiftungen im Spiegel des Liber Pontificalis von Gregory dem Dritten bis zu Leo dem Dritten* (Wiesbaden, 2004)
  'Herrschergeschenke an Sankt Peter', *Mitteilungen zur Spätantiken Archäologie und Byzantinischen Kunstgeschichte* 4 (2005), 65–99
  'Saint Peter's as a place of collective memory in Late Antiquity', in R. Behrwald and C. Witschel (eds.), *Rom in der Spätantike: Historische Erinnerung im städtischen Raum* (Stuttgart, 2012), 155–70
Baumann, P., 'Ein spätantikes Säulenmonument am Jerusalemer Nordtor? Zu einem Detail auf der Mosaiklandkarte von Madaba/Jordanien', *Das Münster: Zeitschrift für christliche Kunst und Kunstwissenschaft* 53 (2000), 38–46
Baumstark, A., *Comparative Liturgy*, rev. B. Botte, trans. F. L. Cross (London, 1958)
  'Das Gesetz der Erhaltung des Alten in liturgisch hochwertiger Zeit', *Jahrbuch für Liturgiewissenschaft* 7 (1927), 1–23
Becatti, G., *Scavi di Ostia*, vol. IV: *Mosaici e pavimenti marmorei* (Rome, 1961)
Beene, J. M., 'Hope for Salvation and Salvation Granted: The Burial Chapel and Reburial Ceremony of Pope Sixtus V in Santa Maria Maggiore', Ph.D. thesis (University of Georgia, 2009)
Beggiao, D., *La visita pastorale di Clemente VIII (1592–1600): Aspetti di riforma post-tridentina a Roma* (Rome, 1978)
Behrmann, C., *Tyrann und Märtyrer: Bild und Ideengeschichte des Rechts um 1600* (Berlin, 2015)
Behrwald, R., 'Senatoren als Stifter der Kirche im Spätantiken Rom', in Verhoeven et al. (eds.), *Monuments and Memory*, 162–76
Belting, H., *Das Bild und sein Publikum im Mittelalter: Form und Funktion früher Bildtafeln der Passion* (Berlin, 1981)
Bénazeth, D., *L'art du métal au début de l'ère chrétienne* (Paris, 1992)
Bergmeier, A. F., 'Vom Kultbild zur Kirche: Veränderte Materialisierungsformen von Heiligkeit in der Spätantike', in Bergmeier et al. (eds.), *Erzeugung und Zerstörung von Sakralität*, 63–79
Bergmeier, A. F., Palmberger, K. and Sanzo, J. E. (eds.), *Erzeugung und Zerstörung von Sakralität zwischen Antike und Mittelalter* (Distant Worlds Journal Special Issues 1) (Heidelberg, 2016), books.ub.uni-heidelberg.de/propylaeum/catalog/book/188
Bériou, N., 'Autour de Latran IV (1215): La naissance de la confession moderne et sa diffusion', in *Pratiques de la confession: Des Pères du désert à Vatican II: Quinze études d'histoire* (Paris, 1983), 73–93
Bertani, B., 'I sotterranei della sede dell'Arciconfraternita lateranense del Ss. Sacramento', *Alma Roma* 27, 3–4 (1986), 79–96
Bertelli, G., Guiglia Guidobaldi, A. and Rovigatti Spagnoletti Zeuli, P., 'Strutture murarie degli edifici religiosi di Roma dal VI al IX secolo', *Rivista dell'Istituto Nazionale di Archeologia e Storia dell'Arte* 23–4 (1976–7), 95–172

Bianchi, G., 'I segni dei tagliatori di pietre negli edifici medievali: Spunti metodologici ed interpretativi', *Archeologia dell'Architettura* 2 (1997), 25–37

Bierbaum, K. L., *Die Ausstattung des Lateranbaptisteriums unter Urban VIII* (Petersberg, 2014)

Bischoff, B., *Die sudostdeutschen Schreibschulen und Bibliotheken in der Karolingerzeit.2. Die vorwiegend Österreichischen Diözesen* (Wiesbaden, 1980)

Bisconti, F., 'L'affresco del S. Agostino', in Liverani (ed.), *Giornata di studio*, 51–78

'L'iconografia dei battisteri paleocristiani', in *Atti dell'VIII Congresso Nazionale di Archeologia Cristiana* (Bordighera, 2001), 405–40

'Programmi figurativi', in S. Ensoli and E. La Rocca (eds.), *Aurea Roma: Dalla città pagana alla città cristiana* (Rome, 2000), 184–90

Blair-Dixon, K., 'Memory and authority in sixth-century Rome: The *Liber Pontificalis* and the *Collectio Avellana*', in K. Cooper and J. Hillner (eds.), *Religion, Dynasty, and Patronage in Early Christian Rome, 300–900* (Cambridge, 2007), 59–76

Blass-Simmen, B., 'Pisanellos Tätigkeit in Rom', in B. Degenhart and A. Schmitt (eds.), *Pisanello und Bono da Ferrara* (Munich, 1995), 81–117, 279–80

Bock, N., 'I re, i vescovi e la cattedrale: Sepolture e costruzione architettonica', in S. Romano and N. Bock (eds.), *Il Duomo di Napoli dal paleocristiano all'età angioina* (Naples, 2002), 132–47

Bock, N., Kurmann, P., Romano, S. and Spieser, J.-M. (eds.), *Art, cérémonial et liturgie au moyen age* (Actes du Colloque de 3e Cycle Romand de Lettres, Lausanne/Fribourg 2000) (Rome, 2002)

Boisclair, M. N., *Gaspar Dughet, sa vie et son oeuvre (1615–1675)* (Paris, 1986)

Bolgia, C., 'Il XIV secolo: Da Benedetto XI (1303–1304) a Bonifacio IX (1389–1404)', in D'Onofrio (ed.), *La committenza artistica dei papi*, 331–59

Bolgia, C., McKitterick, R. and Osborne, J. (eds.), *Rome across Time and Space: Cultural Transmission and the Exchange of Ideas c. 500–1400* (Cambridge, 2011)

Bölling, J., 'Die zwei Körper des Apostelfürsten: Der heilige Petrus im Rom des Reformpapsttums', *Römische Quartalschrift für christliche Altertumskunde und Kirchengeschichte* 106, 3–4 (2011), 155–92

Bona Castellotti, M. (ed.), *Quadreria dell'Arcivescovado* (Milan, 1999)

Bordi, G. and Consoli, F., 'S. Giovanni in Laterano', in M. Andaloro (ed.), *La pittura medievale a Roma 312–1431: Atlante percorsi visivi*, vol. I: *Suburbio, Vaticano, Rione Monti* (Milan, 2006), 193–202

Borghini, G., *Marmi antichi*, 3rd edn (Rome, 1998)

Borgolte, M., *Petrusnachfolge und Kaiserimitation: Die Grablegen der Päpste, ihre Genese und Traditionsbildung* (Göttingen, 1989)

Borsellino, E., 'Una nuova acquisizione sulla collezione Corsini: La *Cleopatra* di Pietro Paolo Olivieri', *Paragone* n.s. 40 (1989), 3–14

Bosman, L., *The Power of Tradition: Spolia in the architecture of St. Peter's in the Vatican* (Hilversum, 2004)

'S. Giovanni in Laterano and medieval architecture: The significance of architectural quotations', in Verhoeven et al. (eds.), *Monuments and Memory*, 43–51

'Spolia in the fourth-century basilica', in McKitterick et al. (eds.), *Old Saint Peter's, Rome*, 65–80

Bougard, F., 'Composition, diffusion et réception des parties tardives du Liber Pontificalis romain (VIIIe–IXe siècles)', in Bougard and Sot (eds.), *Liber, gesta, histoire*, 127–52

Bougard, F. and Sot, M. (eds.), *Liber, gesta, histoire: Écrire l'histoire des évêques et des papes de l'antiquité au XXe siècle* (Turnhout, 2009)

Bouhot, J. P., *La confirmation, sacrement de la communion ecclésiale* (Lyons, 1968); 1st Italian edn. *La confermazione sacramento della comunione ecclesiale* (Turin, 1970)

Bouras, L. and Parani, M. G., *Lighting in Early Byzantium* (Washington, DC, 2008)

Bowes, K., *Private Worship, Public Values and Religious Change in Late Antiquity* (Cambridge, 2008)

Bozóky, E., *La politique des relics de Constantin à Saint-Louis: Protection collective et légitimation du pouvoir* (Paris, 2007)

Bradshaw, P., *The Search for the Origins of Christian Worship: Sources and Methods for the Study of Early Liturgy*, 2nd edn (Oxford, 2002)

'What do we really know about the earliest Roman liturgy?' in Day and Vinzent (eds.), *Early Roman Liturgy to 600*, 7–20

Brancone, V., *Le domus dei cardinali nella Roma del Duecento: Gioielli, mobili, libri* (Rome, 2010)

Brandenburg, H., 'Das Baptisterium und der Brunnen des Atriums von Alt-St. Peter in Rom', *BOREAS, Münstersche Beiträge zur Archäologie* 26 (2003), 55–71

*Die frühchristlichen Kirchen in Rom vom 4. bis zum 7. Jahrhundert: Der Beginn der abendländischen Kirchenbaukunst* (Regensburg, 2004)

'Prachtentfaltung und Monumentalität als Bauaufgaben frühchristlicher Kirchenbaukunst', in J. Gebauer (ed.), *Bildergeschichte: Festschrift Klaus Stähler* (Möhnesee, 2004), 59–76

*Le prime chiese di Roma IV–VII secolo* (Milan, 2013)

Brandt, O., 'The archaeology of Roman ecclesiastical architecture and the study of early Christian liturgy', in Day and Vinzent (eds.), *Early Roman Liturgy to 600*, 21–52

*Battisteri oltre la pianta: Gli alzati di nove battisteri paleocristiani in Italia* (Vatican City, 2012)

'Il Battistero lateranense da Costantino a Ilaro: Un riesame degli scavi', *Opuscula Romana* 22–3 (1997–8), 7–65

*La Croce e il capitello: Le chiese paleocristiane e la monumentalità* (Vatican City, 2016)

'The early Christian baptistery of Saint Peter's', in McKitterick et al. (eds.), *Old Saint Peter's, Rome*, 81–94

'L'improbabile legame delle colonne di bronzo al Laterano con il *fastigium costantiniano*', *RAC* 92 (2016), 117–36

'L'Oratorio della Santa Croce', in Liverani (ed.), *Giornata di studio*, 79–93

'Strutture del IV secolo per la lavanda dei piedi in due battisteri romani', *Arte medievale* 2, 1 (2003), 137–44

Brandt, O. and Guidobaldi, F., 'Il Battistero Lateranense: Nuove interpretazioni delle fasi strutturali', *RAC* 84 (2008), 189–282

Brenk, B., 'Spolia from Constantine to Charlemagne: Aesthetics versus ideology', *Dumbarton Oaks Papers* 41 (1987), 103–9

'Spolien und ihre Wirkung auf die Ästhetik der *varietas*: Zum Problem alternierender Kapitelltypen', in J. Poeschke (ed.), *Antike Spolien in der Architektur des Mittelalters und der Renaissance* (Munich, 1996), 49–92

Brent, A., *Hippolytus and the Roman Church in the Third Century: Communities in Tension before the Emergence of a Monarch Bishop* (Supplements to *Vigiliae Christianae* 31) (Leiden, 1995)

Bresc-Bautier, G., 'Les imitations du Saint-Sépulcre de Jérusalem (IXe–XVe siècles)', *Revue d'histoire de la spiritualité* 50 (1974), 319–42

Broise, H. and Jolivet, V., *Pincio 1. La villa Médicis et le couvent de la Trinité-des-Monts à Rome: Réinvestir un site antique* (Rome, 2009)

Brown, B. L. (ed.), *The Genius of Rome 1592-1623* (London, 2001)

Bruderer Eichberg, B., 'Prolegomena zur frühchristlichen und frühmittelalterlichen Tauforganisation in Rom: Die Baptisterien und die Stifterrolle der Päpste', in Bock et al. (eds.), *Art, cérémonial et liturgie au moyen age*, 321–56

Brühl, C. R., 'Die Kaiserpfalz bei St. Peter und die Pfalz Ottos III. auf dem Palatin', *Quellen und Forschungen aus römischen Archiven und Bibliotheken* 34 (1935), 1–30

Brunori, P. and Carboni, F., 'Il disegno come strumento: Rilievi, ricostruzioni, modelli nello studio del fregio', in De Strobel, *Il portico medievale di San Giovanni in Laterano*, 165–87

Bruschi, A., *Introduzione alla storia dell'architettura: Considerazioni sul metodo e sulla storia degli studi* (Milan, 2009)

Bucarelli, O., 'I frammenti epigrafici del fregio del portico medievale di San Giovanni in Laterano', in De Strobel, *Il portico medievale di San Giovanni in Laterano*, 149–63

Budriesi, R., 'I terremoti e l'edilizia religiosa a Roma e a Ravenna tra VII/X secolo', in E. Guidoboni (ed.), *I terremoti prima del Mille in Italia e nell'area mediterranea: Storia archeologia sismologia* (Bologna, 1989), 364–87

Buonfiglio, M., 'M. E. Blake e lo sviluppo dell'*opus testaceum* a Roma: Il "caso" del Teatro di Marcello', *Musiva & Sectilia* 7 (2010), 109–22

'L'utilizzo di laterizi nella costruzione augustea del Teatro di Marcello', in E. Bukowiecki, R. Volpe and U. Wulf-Rheidt (eds.), *Il laterizio nei cantieri imperiali: Roma e il Mediterraneo: Atti del I Workshop 'Laterizio' (Roma, 27–28 Novembre 2014), Archeologia dell'Architettura* 20 (special issue) (2015), 13–19

Buranelli, F. and Le Pera Buranelli, S., 'Rinvenimenti arcaici sotto il Palazzo Apostolico Lateranense', in M. Pallottino (ed.), *Etrusca et italica: Scritti in ricordo di Massimo Pallottino I* (Pisa, 1997), 79–115

Burkart, L., 'Die Aufhebung der Sichtbarkeit: Der Schatz der Sancta Sanctorum und die Modi seiner visuellen Inszenierung', in A. Rathmann-Lutz (ed.), *Visibilität des Unsichtbaren: Sehen und Verstehen in Mittelalter und früher Neuzeit* (Zurich, 2011), 69–82

Busch, A. W., *Militär in Rom: Militärische und paramilitärische Einheiten im kaiserzeitlichen Stadtbild* (Palilia 20) (Wiesbaden, 2011)

Buser, T., 'Jerome Nadal and early Jesuit art in Rome', *Art Bulletin* 58 (1976), 423–33

Busiri Vici, A., *Il Laterano nel Pontificato di Pio IX, Progetti del Nuovo Coro, Presbiterio e dipendenze dell'Arcibasilica Lateranense, grandi lavori finora eseguiti, scoperta dell'antica casa dei Laterani, rilievi dell'Absida e Portico leonino, restauro dell'Absida costantiniana, suo trasferimento meccanico e conservazione* (Rome, 1868/78)

*L'obelisco vaticano nel terzo centenario della sua erezione* (Rome, 1886)

*Peter, Hendrik e Giacomo Van Lint: Tre pittori di Anversa del '600 e '700 lavorano a Roma* (Rome, 1987)

Busiri Vici, S., *L'architettura di Saverio Busiri Vici e cenni su alcuni altri architetti della sua famiglia: Volume primo 1651–1974* (Rome, 1974)

Bussini, F., 'L'intervention de l'Assemblée des fidèles au moment de la réconciliation des pénitents, d'après les trois "postulationes" d'un archidiacre romain du Ve–VIe siècle', *Revue des Sciences Religieuses* 41 (1967), 29–38

'L'intervention de l'évêque dans la réconciliation des pénitents, d'après les trois "postulationes" d'un archidiacre romain du Ve–VIe siècle', *Revue des sciences religieuses* 42 (1968), 326–38

Cabaniss, A., *Amalarius of Metz* (Amsterdam, 1954)

Calabi Limentani, I., *Studi sulla società romana: Il lavoro artistico* (Milan, 1958)

Cameron, A. D. E., 'Literary allusions in the *Historia Augusta*', *Hermes* 92 (1964), 363–77

Cantino Wataghin, G., 'The ideology of urban burials', in G. P. Brogiolo and B. Ward-Perkins (eds.), *The Idea and Ideal of the Town between Late Antiquity and the Early Middle Ages* (Leiden, 1999), 147–80

Gasquet, Francis Aidan, *A History of the Venerable English College, Rome* (London, 1920)

Carragáin, E. Ó., 'Interactions between liturgy and politics in Old Saint Peter's, 670–741: John the Archcantor, Sergius I and Gregory III', in McKitterick et al. (eds.), *Old Saint Peter's, Rome*, 177–89

Carter, B. A. R. and Wittkower, R., 'The perspective of Piero della Francesca's "Flagellation"', *Journal of the Warburg and Courtauld Institutes* 16 (1953), 292–302

Cassirer, K., 'Zu Borrominis Umbau der Lateransbasilika', *Jahrbuch der Preussischen Kunstsammlungen* 42 (1921), 55–66

Castagnoli, F., Colini, A. M., Buzzetti, C. and Pisano Sartorio G. (eds.), 'Notiziario di scavi, scoperte e studi intorno alle Antichità di Roma e Campagna Romana 1946–1960: Prima parte', *Bullettino della Commissione archeologica Comunale di Roma* 83 (1972–3), 5–156

Ceci, M., 'La cosidetta Domus Parthorum: Vecchie e nuove ipotesi per l'aula absidata', *Bullettino della Commissione archeologica Comunale di Roma* 115 (2014), 354–9

Cempanari, M., *Sancta Santorum Lateranense: Il Santuario della Scala Santa dalle origini ai nostri giorni*, 2 vols. (Rome, 2003)

Cempanari, M. and Amodei, T., *La Scala Santa* (Le chiese di Roma illustrate, nuova serie 23) (Rome, 1989).

Cerruto, A., 'Oratori ed edifici di culto minori di Roma tra il IV secolo ed primi decenni del V', in F. Guidobaldi and A. Guiglia Guidobaldi (eds.), *Ecclesiae Urbis: Atti del congresso internazionale di studi sulle chiese di Roma (IV–X secolo) (Roma 4–10 settembre 2000)* (Studi di antichità cristiana 59) (Vatican City, 2002), 397–418

Champagne, M.-T., '"Treasures of the Temple" and claims of authority in twelfth-century Rome', in B. M. Bolton and C. E. Meek (eds.), *Aspects of Power and Authority in the Middle Ages* (Turnhout, 2007), 107–18

Chandler Kirwin, W., 'Bernini's baldacchino reconsidered', *Römisches Jahrbuch für Kunstgeschichte* 19 (1981), 141–71

 'Cristofano Roncalli (1551/2–1626), an Exponent of the Proto-Baroque: His Activity through 1605', Ph.D. thesis (Stanford University, 1972)

Chappell, M. L. and Chandler Kirwin, W., 'A Petrine triumph: The decoration of the *Navi Piccole* in San Pietro under Clement VIII', *Storia dell'arte* 21 (1974), 119–70

Chiappini di Sorio, I., *Cristoforo Roncalli detto il Pomarancio* (Bergamo, 1975)

Christern, J. 'Die "Gerichtsbasilika" beim Forum von Tipasa (Neuaufnahme), ihre Funkton und die Frage nach den Vorbildern für den basilikalen Kirchenbau', in O. Feld and U. Peschlow (eds.), *Studien zur spätantiken und byzantinischen Kunst: Friedrich Wilhelm Deichmann gewidmet* (Bonn, 1986), 163–204

Ciardi, R. P., *Nicolò Circignani, Cristofano Roncalli: Pittori di Pomarance* (Volterra, 1992)

Cicerchia, P., 'L'Analisi metrologica', in *Adriano: Architettura e progetto* (Tivoli, 2000), 131–5

 'Considerazioni metrologiche sull'arco', in M. L. Conforto (ed.), *Adriano e Costantino: Le due fasi dell'arco nella valle del Colosseo* (Milan, 2001), 61–77

Claridge, A., *Rome: An Oxford Archaeological Guide* (Oxford, 2010)

Claussen, P. C., 'Il XII secolo: da Pasquale II (1099–1118) a Celestino III (1191–1198)', in D'Onofrio (ed.), *La committenza artistica dei papi*, 275–97

 *Die Kirchen der Stadt Rom im Mittelalter 1050–1300, Bd. 2: S. Giovanni in Laterano* (Corpus Cosmatorum II, 2) (Forschungen zur Kunstgeschichte und Christlichen Archäologie 21) (Stuttgart, 2008)

*Magistri Doctissimi Romani: Die römischen Marmorkünstler des Mittelalters* (Wiesbaden, 1987)

'Nikolaus IV: Als Erneuerer von S. Giovanni in Laterano und S. Maria Maggiore in Rom', in Verhoeven et al. (eds.), *Monuments and Memory*, 53–67

Claussen, P. C. and Mondini, D., 'Die Lokomotive des Papstes: Busiris Plan, die Apsis von S. Giovanni in Laterano mit Dampfkraft zu verschieben', in K. Gimmi (ed.), *SvM: Die Festschrift für Stanislaus von Moos* (Zurich, 2005), 56–72

Coarelli, F., 'Architettura sacra e architettura privata nella tarda repubblica', in École française de Rome (ed.), *Architecture et société: De l'archaïsme grec à la fin de la République. Actes du Colloque international organise par le Centre national de la recherche scientifique et l'École française de Rome (Rome 2–4 décembre 1980)* (Rome, 1983), 191–217

Colella, R., 'Hagiographie und Kirchenpolitik: Stephanus und Laurentius in Rom', in Colella and Krautheimer (eds.), *Pratum Romanum*, 75–96

Colella, R. and Krautheimer, R. (eds.), *Pratum Romanum: Richard Krautheimer zum 100. Geburtstag* (Wiesbaden, 1997)

Colini, A. M., *Storia e topografia del Celio nell'antichità* (Memorie della Pontificia Accademia Romana di Archeologia 7) (Vatican City, 1944)

Colli, D., Martines, M. and Palladino, S., 'Roma: Viale Manzoni, via Emanuele Filiberto. L'ammodernamento della linea A della Metropolitana: Nuovi spunti per la conoscenza della topografia antica', *Journal of Fasti Online* (2009), 1–26

Colli, D., Palladino, S., Paterna, C. and Zisa, F., 'Le campagne di scavo nell'anfiteatro Castrense a Roma: Nuove acquisizioni', *Bullettino della Commissione Archeologica Comunale di Roma* 98 (1997), 249–82

Collins, S. W., *The Carolingian Debate over Sacred Space* (New York, 2012)

Colonna, G., 'Roma arcaica, i suoi sepolcri e le vie per i Colli Albani', in A. Pasqualini (ed.), *Alba Longa: Mito, storia, archeologia. Atti dell'incontro di studi Roma-Albano Laziale 27–29 gennaio 1994* (Rome, 1996), 335–54

Combi, M., 'Il corpo devoto e la Scala Santa', in L. M. Lombardi Satriani (ed.), *La sacra città: Itinerari antropologico-religiosi nella Roma di fine millennio* (Rome, 1999), 77–105

Connell, W. J. and Constable, G., 'Sacrilege and redemption in Renaissance Florence: The case of Antonio Rinaldeschi', *Journal of the Warburg and Courtauld Institutes* 61 (1998), 53–92

Connors, J. and Roca de Amicis, A., 'A new plan by Borromini for the Lateran basilica, Rome', *Burlington Magazine* 146 (2004), 526–33

Consalvi, F., *Il Celio Orientale: Contributi alla carta archeologica di Roma Tav. VI settore H* (Rome, 2009)

Cooper, L. and Denny-Brown, A. (eds.), *The Arma Christi in Medieval and Modern Material Culture: With a Critical Edition of 'O Vernicle'* (Farnham, 2014)

Corbo, A. M., *Fonti per la storia artistica al tempo di Clemente VIII* (Ministero per i Beni Culturali e Ambientali, Archivio di Stato di Roma 85) (Rome, 1975)

Corcopino, J., 'La louve du Capitole', *Bulletin de l'Association Guillaume Budé* 4 (1924), 3–19

Cordellier, D., 'Pisanello et atelier (?), Saint Jean l'Évangéliste faisant s'écrouler le temple de Diane à Éphèse. La "Navicella" de Giotto. Verso: Un des Dioscures. Sept etudes de paons. Deuz pieds', in Cordellier and Marini (eds.), *Pisanello: Le peintre aux sept vertus*, 153–4

Cordellier, D. and Marini, P. (eds.), *Pisanello: Le peintre aux sept vertus* (Paris, 1996)

Cornini, G., 'Gentile da Fabriano, Testa di re (David o Salomone)', in De Marchi et al. (eds.), *Gentile da Fabriano*, 308–9

'"Non est in toto sanctior orbe locus": Collecting relics in early medieval Rome', in M. Bagnoli, H. A. Klein, C. Griffith Mann and J. Robinson (eds.), *Treasures of Heaven: Saints, Relics, and Devotion in Medieval Europe* (Baltimore, 2010), 69–78

Corsi, F., *Delle pietre antiche: Trattato*, 3rd edn (Rome, 1845)

*Delle pietre antiche di Faustino Corsi Romano*, ed. C. Napoleone (Milan, 2001)

Costambeys, M., 'Burial topography and the power of the Church in fifth- and sixth-century Rome', *PBSR* 69 (2001), 169–89

Coulston, J. C. N., '"Armed and Belted Men": The soldiery in imperial Rome', in J. C. N. Coulston and H. Dodge (eds.), *Ancient Rome: The Archaeology of the Eternal City* (Oxford University School of Archaeology Monograph 54) (Oxford, 2000), 76–118

Curran, J. R., *Pagan City and Christian Capital: Rome in the Fourth Century* (Oxford, 2000)

Dahm, G., *Das Strafrecht Italiens im ausgehenden Mittelalter: Untersuchung über die Beziehung von Theorie und Praxis im Strafrecht des Spätmittelalters, namentlich im 14. Jahrhundert* (Beiträge zur Geschichte der deutschen Strafrechtspflege 3) (Berlin, 1931)

D'Alberto, C., *Roma al tempo di Avignone: Sculture nel contesto* (Rome, 2013)

Davison, D. P., *The Barracks of the Roman Army from the 1st to 3rd Centuries A.D.* (British Archaeological Reports International Series 472) (Oxford, 1989)

Day, J. and Vinzent, M. (eds.), *Early Roman Liturgy to 600* (Studia Patristica 71) (Leuven, 2014)

de Blaauw, S., *Cultus et décor: Liturgia e Architettura nella Roma Tardoantica e Medievale. Basilica Salvatoris, Sancatae Mariae, Sancti Petri*, 2 vols. (Studi e testi 355) (Vatican City, 1994)

*Cultus et decor: Liturgie en architectuur in laatantiek en middeleeuws Rome: Basilica Salvatoris, Sanctae Mariae, Sancti Petri* (Delft, 1987)

'Deambulatori e transetti: I casi di S. Maria Maggiore e del Laterano', *Rendiconti della Pontificia Accademia Romana di Archeologia* 59 (1986/7), 93–109

'Das *Fastigium* der Lateranbasilika: Schöpferische Innovation, Unikat oder Paradigma?' in B. Brenk (ed.), *Innovation in der Spätantike (Kolloquium Basel 6.–7. Mai 1994)* (Wiesbaden, 1996), 53–65

'Die Gräber der frühen Päpste', in B. Schneidmüller, S. Weinfurter, M. Mattheus and A. Wieczorek (eds.), *Die Päpste: Amt und Herrschaft in Antike, Mittelalter und Renaissance* (Regensburg, 2016), 77–99

'Immagini di liturgia: Sisto V, la traduzione liturgica dei papi e le antiche basiliche di Roma', *RJBH* 33 (2003), 259–302

'Imperial connotations in Roman church interiors: The significance and effect of the Lateran *fastigium*', in R. J. Brandt and O. Steen (eds.), *Imperial Art as Christian Art–Christian Art as Imperial Art: Expression and Meaning in Art and Architecture from Constantine to Justinian (International Conference Rome 1999)* (Acta ad archaeologiam et artium historiam pertinentia 15) (Rome, 2001), 137–46

'Jerusalem in Rome and the cult of the Cross', in Colella and Krautheimer (eds.), *Pratum Romanum*, 55–73

'Kultgebäude (Kirchenbau)', *Reallexikon für Antike und Christentum* (Stuttgart, 2007), XXII, 227–393

'A mediaeval portico at San Giovanni in Laterano: The basilica and its ancient conventual building', *PBSR* 58 (1990), 299–313

'Le origine e gli inizi dell'architettura cristiana', in S. de Blaauw (ed.), *Storia dell' architettura italiana*, vol. I: *Da Costantino a Carlo Magno* (Milan, 2010), 22–53

'Papst und Purpur: Porphyr in frühen Kirchenausstattungen in Rom', in E. Dassmann and K. Thraede (eds.), *Tesserae: Festschrift für Josef Engemann* (Jahrbuch für Antike und Christentum, Ergänzungsband 18) (Münster, 1991), 36–50

'Il Patriarchio, la Basilica Lateranense e la liturgia', in Liverani (ed.), *Giornata di studio*, 161–71

'Reception and renovation of early Christian churches in Rome, c. 1050–1300', in Bolgia et al. (eds.), *Rome across Time and Space*, 151–66

'The solitary celebration of the supreme pontiff: The Lateran basilica as the new Temple in the medieval liturgy of Maundy Thursday', in C. Caspers and M. Schneiders (eds.), *Omnes circumstantes: Contributions towards a History of the Role of the People in the Liturgy Presented to Herman Wegman* (Kampen, 1990), 120–43

(ed.), *Arredi di culto e disposizioni liturgiche a Roma da Costantino a Sisto IV (Atti del colloquio internazionale - Roma, 3-4 dic. 1999)* (Mededelingen van het Nederlands Instituut te Rome 59) (Rome, 2000)

De Certeau, M., *Kunst des Handelns* (Berlin, 1988)

Deckers, J., 'Die Wandmalerei in Kaiserkultraum von Luxor', *Jahrbuch des Deutschen Archäologischen Instituts* 94 (1979), 600–52

De Dominicis, C., *Membri del Senato della Roma pontificia: Senatori, conservatori, caporioni e loro priori e lista d'oro delle famiglie dirigenti (sec. X–XIX)* (Rome, 2009)

Degenhart, B. and Schmitt, A., 'Gentile da Fabriano in Rom und die Anfänge des Antikenstudiums', *Münchner Jahrbuch der bildenden Kunst* 11 (1960), 59–151

Deichmann, F. W., 'Die Architektur des Konstantinischen Zeitalters', in F. W. Deichmann, *Rom, Ravenna, Konstantinopel, Naher Osten: Gesammelte Studien zur spätantiken Architektur, Kunst und Geschichte* (Wiesbaden, 1982), 117–18

de Jong, M., 'Pollution, penance and sanctity: Ekkehard's *Life* of Iso of St Gall', in J. Hill and M. Swain (eds.), *The Community, the Family and the Saint: Patterns of Power in Early Medieval Europe* (Turnhout, 1998), 145–58

  'Transformations of penance', in F. Theuws and J. L. Nelson (eds.), *Rituals of Power: From Late Antiquity to the Early Middle Ages* (Leiden, 2000), 185–224

  'What was public about public penance?' in *La Giustizia nell'alto medioevo, secoli IX–XI: 11–17 aprile 1996* (Settimane di studio del Centro italiano di studi sull'alto Medioevo 44) (Spoleto, 1997), 863–902

Delbrück, R., *Antike Porphyrwerke* (Berlin, 1932)

De Luca, G., *I monumenti antichi di Palazzo Corsini in Roma* (Rome, 1976)

De Marchi, A., 'Gentile da Fabriano', *Art Dossier* 136 (1998), 44

  *Gentile da Fabriano: Un viaggio nell'arte italiana alla fine del gotico* (Milan, 1992)

  'Gentile da Fabriano et Pisanello à Saint-Jean de Latran', in D. Cordellier and B. Py (eds.), *Pisanello: Actes du colloque, Musée du Louvre* (La documentation française I) (Paris, 1998), 161–213

  'Gentile e la sua bottega', in De Marchi et al. (eds.), *Gentile da Fabriano*, 9–53

De Marchi, A., Laureati, L. and Mochi Onori, L. (eds.), *Gentile da Fabriano: Studi e ricerche* (Milan, 2006)

Denard, H., *The London Charter for the Computer-Based Visualisation of Cultural Heritage*, 2.1 edn (London, 2009)

de Rossi, G. B., 'La loggia del comune di Roma compiuta nel Campidoglio l'anno 1299', *Bollettino della commissione archeologica comunale di Roma ser. Seconda* 10 (1882), 130–40

  *Piante iconografiche e prospettiche di Roma* (Rome, 1879)

  *Roma sotteranea Christiana*, 3 vols. (Rome, 1864)

De Spirito, G. 'La Basilica Lateranense nel quadro delle vicende del Patriarcato del secolo X', in Liverani (ed.), *Giornata di studio*, 117–39

Dessales, H., Ponce, J., Carrive, M., Cavero, J., Dubouloz, J., Letellier, É., Marchand-Beaulieu, F., Monier, F., Péron, A., Tricoche, A. and Ubelmann, Y., 'Pompéi: Villa de Diomède', in *Chronique des activités archéologiques de l'École française de Rome, Les cités vésuviennes, mis en ligne le 02 février 2015* (Rome, 2015), 1–15

De Strobel, A. M., *Il portico medievale di San Giovanni in Laterano: I frammenti ritrovati* (Vatican City, 2019)

de Waal, A., 'Die Häupter Petri und Pauli im Lateran', *Römische Quartalschrift* 5 (1891), 340–8

di Calpegna Falconieri, T., *Il clero di Roma nel medioevo: Istituzioni e politica cittadina (secoli VIII–XIII)* (Rome, 2002)

Diefenbach, S., *Römische Erinnerungsräume: Heiligenmemoria und kollektive Identitäten im Rom des 3. bis 5. Jahrhunderts n. Chr.* (Berlin, 2007)

Diesenberger, M., 'Rom als virtueller Raum der Märtyrer: Zur gedanklichen Aneignung der Roma suburbana in bayerischen Handschriften um 800', in E. Vavra (ed.), *Imaginäre Räume* (Krems, 2004), 43–68

Dionigi, R., 'I segni dei lapicidi: Evidenze europee', in *I magistri commacini: Mito e realtà del medioevo Lombardo (Atti del XIX Congresso internazionale di studio sull'alto medioevo, Varese – Como, 23–25 ottobre 2008)*, 2 vols. (Spoleto, 2009), I, 341–471

Docci, M., *San Paolo fuori le Mura: Dalle origini alla basilica delle 'origini'* (Rome, 2006)

Doig, A., *Liturgy and Architecture from the Early Church to the Middle Ages* (Aldershot, 2008)

Dölger, J., 'Ante absidem: Der Platz des Büßers beim Akte der Rekonziliation', *Antike und Christentum* 6 (1940–50), 196–201

Donadono, L., 'In margine alle celebrazioni sistine: La Scala Santa (1586–1853): Nuove acquisizioni', *Roma Moderna e Contemporanea* 2, 1 (1994), 249–66

*La Scala Santa a San Giovanni in Laterano* (Rome, 2000)

Donkin, L. and Vorholt, H. (eds.), *Imagining Jerusalem in the Medieval West* (Proceedings of the British Academy 175) (Oxford, 2012)

D'Onofrio, M., 'Il Patriarchio nascosto', Liverani (ed.), *Giornata di studio*, 141–60

*Scalinate di Roma* (Rome, 1973)

(ed.), *La committenza artistica dei papi a Roma nel Medioevo* (Rome, 2016)

Dresken Weiland, J., *Bild, Grab und Wort: Untersuchungen zu Jenseitsvorstellungen von Christen des 3. und 4. Jahrhunderts* (Regensburg, 2010)

Drijvers, J.-W., 'Helena Augusta, Cross and myth: Some new reflections', *Millennium* 8 (2011), 125–74

Duchesne, L., *Étude sur le* Liber Pontificalis (Paris, 1877)

'Notes sur la topographie de Rome au moyen-âge, XIII: Vaticana', *Mélanges d'archéologie et d'histoire d'École Française de Rome* 35 (1915), 3–13

Dunn, G. D. (ed.), *The Bishop of Rome in Late Antiquity* (Farnham, 2016)

Dyer, J., 'Reconciliation, blessing and commemoration in the Holy Thursday liturgy of medieval Rome', *Archiv für Liturgiewissenschaft* 56 (2014), 16–48

Dykmans, M. (ed.), *Le cérémonial papal de la fin du moyen âge à la renaissance*, 4 vols. (Brussels 1977–85)

Ebanista, C., 'Il complesso archeologico dei Santi Quaranta: Archeologia e storia', in M. Rotili (ed.), *Benevento nella Tarda Antichità: Dalla diagnostica archeologica in contrada Cellarulo alla ricostruzione dell'assetto urbano* (Naples, 2006), 179–210

Echinger Maurach, C., 'Michelangelo's monument for Julius II in 1534', *Burlington Magazine* 145 (2003), 336–44

Eck, W., 'Domus: L. Lusius Petellinus', in *LTUR* II, 134

Edgerton S. Y., Jr., *Pictures and Punishment: Art and Criminal Prosecution during the Florentine Renaissance* (Ithaca, NY, 1985)

Ehrstine, G., 'Passion spectatorship between private and public devotion', in E. Gertsman and J. Stevenson (eds.), *Thresholds of Medieval Visual Culture: Liminal Spaces* (Woodbridge, 2012), 302–20

Emerick, J. J., 'Focusing on the celebrant: The column display inside Santa Prassede', *Mededelingen van het Nederlands Instituut te Rome* 59 (2001), 129–59

Emminghaus, J. H., 'Die Taufanlage ad sellam Petri confessionis', *Römische Quartalschrift* 57 (1962), 78–103

Engemann, J., 'Der Skulpturenschmuck des "Fastigiums" Konstantins I. nach dem Liber Pontificalis und der "Zufall der Überlieferung"', *RAC* 69 (1993), 179–203

Epp, S., *Konstantinszyklen in Rom: Die päpstliche Interpretation der Geschichte Konstantins des Grossen bis zur Gegenreformation* (Schriften aus dem Institut für Kunstgeschichte der Universität München 36) (Munich, 1988)

Eristov, H., 'Décors méconnus de la Villa de Diomède', in T. Ganschow, M. Steinhart and D. Berges (eds.), *Otium: Festschrift für Volker Michael Strocka* (Remshalden, 2005), 75–86

Esposito, D., *Tecniche costruttive murarie medievali: Murature a 'tufelli' in area romana* (Storia della tecnica edilizia e restauro dei monumenti 2) (Rome, 1997)

Fabricius Hansen, M., *The Eloquence of Appropriation: Prolegomena to an Understanding of Spolia in Early Christian Rome* (Rome, 2003)

Falla Castelfranchi, M., 'Sull'origine, e la funzione "politica", dell'immagine del battesimo di Costantino nel portico della basilica Lateranense', in G. Bordi, I. Carlettini, M. L. Fobelli, M. R. Menna and P. Pogliani (eds.), *L'officina dello sguardo: Scritti in onore di Maria Andaloro*, 2 vols. (Rome, 2014), I, 375–82

Falzone, S., *Scavi di Ostia*, vol. XIV: *Le pitture delle insulae (180–250 circa d.C.)* (Rome, 2004)

Fantozzi, A. (ed.), *Nota d'anticaglie et spoglie et cose maravigliose et grande sono nella cipta de Roma da vederle volentieri*, 2 parts (Rome, 1994)

Fehl, P. P., 'Raphael as a historian: Poetry and historical accuracy in the Sala di Costantino', *Artibus et Historiae* 28 (1993), 9–76

Ferrari, G., *Early Roman Monasteries: Notes for the History of Monasteries and Convents from the V through the X Century* (Studi di antichità cristiana 23) (Vatican City, 1957)

Ferrua, A., 'Dei primi battisteri Parocchiali e di quello di S. Pietro in particolare', *La Civiltà Cattolica* 90, 2 (1939), 146–57

Filippi, G. and de Blaauw, S., 'San Paolo fuori le Mura: La disposizione liturgica fino a Gregorio Magno', *Mededelingen van het Nederlands Instituut te Rome* 59 (2001), 5–25

Fiorani, D. (ed.), *Finiture murarie e architetture nel medioevo: Una panoramica e tre casi di studio nell'Italia centro-meridionale* (Rome, 2005)

Fiorani, L., 'Le visite apostoliche del Cinque-Seicento e la società religiosa romana', *Ricerche per la storia religiosa di Roma* 4 (1980), 53–148

Flechner, R., 'The Making of the Canons of Theodore', *Peritia* 17–18 (2003–4), 121–43

Fobelli, M. L., *Un tempio per Giustiniano: Santa Sofia di Costantinopoli e la descrizione di Paolo Silenziario* (Rome, 2005)

Fraioli, F., 'Regione V: Esquiliae', in A. Carandini (ed.), *Atlante di Roma antica* (Milan, 2012), 232–41

Franco, T., 'Testa femminile, Roma, Museo di Palazzo Venezia', in L. Puppi and D. Battilotti (eds.), *Pisanello: Una poetica* (Milan, 1996), 59–60

Franklin, D., Schü, S., Gasparri, C. and Rowland, I. D. (eds.), *From Raphael to Carracci: The Art of Papal Rome* (Ottawa, 2009)

Freiberg, J., *The Lateran in 1600: Christian Concord in Counter-Reformation Rome* (New York, 1995)

*The Lateran and Clement VIII* (New York, 1988)

Fiery, A. (ed.), *A New History of Penance* (Leiden, 2008)

Freigang, C., 'Bildskeptische Nachbildungsmodi der Passionstopographie Christi im Spätmittelalter: Der Görlitzer Kalvarienberg', in Aurenhammer and Bohde (eds.), *Räume der Passion*, 117–49

Fried, J., *'Donation of Constantine' and 'Constitutum Constantini': The Misinterpretation of a Fiction and Its Original Meaning* (Berlin, 2007)

Fritz, J. M., *Goldschmiedekunst der Gotik in Mitteleuropa* (Munich, 1982)

Frommel, C. L., 'Il San Pietro di Nicolò V', in G. Spagnesi (ed.), *L'architettura della basilica di San Pietro, Storia e costruzione* (Quaderni dell'Istituto di Storia dell'Architettura 25–30, 1995–7) (Rome, 1997) 103–10

Frommel, C. L. and Pentiricci, M. (eds.), *L'antica basilica di San Lorenzo in Damaso: Indagini archeologiche nel Palazzo della Cancelleria (1988–1993)* (Rome, 2009)

Frutaz, A. P., *Le piante di Roma* (Rome, 1962)

Funiciello, R., Praturlon, A. and Giordano, G., *La geologia di Roma dal centro storico alla periferia* (Florence, 2008)

Gaffney, V., Piro, S., Haynes, I. P., Watters, M., Wilkes, S., Lobb, M. and Zamuner, D., 'Three-Tier Visualization of San Giovanni in Laterano, Rome, Italy', *12th International Conference on Ground Penetrating Radar, June 16-19, 2008, Birmingham, UK.* Proceedings Expanded Abstract Volume (2008), http://www.eurogpr.org/vn2/images/documents/mem bers/B2857%20GPR%20brochure%20final.pdf

Gaglione, M., '"Lignamina necessaria de Calabria ferenda": Interventi angioini per la ricostruzione di San Giovanni in Laterano (1308)', *Archivio della Società Romana di Storia Patria* 128 (2005), 5–34

Galland, B., *Les authentiques de reliques du Sancta Sanctorum* (Vatican City, 2004)

Gandolfo, F., 'Assisi e il Laterano', *Archivio della Società Romana di Storia Patria* 106 (1983), 63–113

Gantner, C., 'The Lombard recension of the *Liber Pontificalis*', *Rivista di Storia del cristianesimo* 10 (2013), 65–114

Gardner, J., 'L'architettura del Sancta Sanctorum', in C. Pietrangeli (ed.), *Sancta Sanctorum* (Milan, 1995), 19–37

  'The Louvre stigmatization and the problem of the narrative altarpiece', *Zeitschrift für Kunstgeschichte* 45 (1982), 217–48

Gärtner, M., *Römische Basiliken in Augsburg: Nonnenfrömmigkeit und Malerei um 1500* (Augsburg, 2002)

Gasparri, C. and Guerrini, L., *Il Palazzo del Quirinale* (Rome, 1985)

Gatto, L., *Il Pontificato di Gregorio X (1271–1276)*, 2nd edn (Naples, 2007)

Geertman, H., 'Le biografie del Liber Pontificalis dal 311 al 535: Testo e commentario', *Mededelingen van het Nederlands Instituut te Rome* 60–61 (2001–2), 138–355; repr. in Geertman, *Hic fecit basilicam*, 169–235

  'The Builders of the Basilica Maior in Rome', in *Festoen: Opgedragen aan A. N. Zadoks-Josephus Jitta bij haar zeventigste verjaardag* (Scripta archaeologica Groningana 6) (Groningen, 1976), 277–95; repr. in Geertman, *Hic fecit basilicam*, 1–16

  'Forze centrifughe e centripete nella Roma cristiana: Il Laterano, la "basilica Iulia" e la "basilica Liberiana"', *Atti della Pontificia Accademia Romana di Archeologia. Rendiconti* 59 (1986–7), 63–91; repr. in Geertman, *Hic fecit basilicam*, 17–44

  'Il *fastigium* Lateranense e l'arredo presbiteriale: una lunga storia', in H. Geertman (ed.), *Atti del Colloquio Internazionale Il Liber Pontificalis e la storia material: Roma, 21–22 febbraio 2002* (Mededelingen van het Nederlands Instituut te Rome, Antiquity 60–1 (2001–2)) (Assen, 2003), 29–44; repr. in Geertman, *Hic fecit basilicam*, 133–48

  *Hic fecit basilicam: Studi sul Liber Pontificalis e gli edifici ecclesiastici di Roma da Silvestro a Silverio* (Leuven, 2004)

  'L'illuminazione della basilica paleocristiana secondo il Liber Pontificalis', *RAC* 64 (1988), 135–60

  *More veterum: Il Liber Pontificalis e gli edifice ecclesiastici di Roma nella tarda antichita e nell'alto medioevo* (Archaeologia Traiectina 10) (Groningen, 1975)

  'Nota sul Liber Pontificalis come fonte archeologica', in Geertman, *Hic fecit basilicam* (article first published in 1989), 78–82

Geissmar-Brandi, C. and Louis, E. (eds.), *Glaube – Liebe – Hoffnung* (Klagenfurt, 1995)

Gianandrea, M., 'Il V secolo: Da Innocenzo I (401–417) ad Anastasio II (496–498)', in D'Onofrio (ed.), *La committenza artistica dei papi*, 73–108

Ginzburg, C., *Erkundungen über Piero: Piero della Francesca, ein Maler der frühen Renaissance* (Frankfurt, 1991)

Giovenale, G. B., *Il Battistero Lateranense nelle recenti indagini della Pontificia Commissione di Archeologia Sacra* (Studi di antichità cristiana 1) (Rome, 1929)

Giuliani, C. F. and Verduchi, P., *L'area centrale del Foro Romano* (Florence, 1987)

Gnilka, C., 'Aedes Laterani', *Zeitschrift für Papyrologie und Epigraphik* 188 (2014), 70–80

    *Prudentius. Contra orationem Symmachy, eine kritische Revue.* (Münster, 2017)

Gnoli, R., 'Su alcuni marmi e pietre da decorazione usate nell'antichità', *La parola del passato* 21 (1966), 41–55

Gnoli, U., *Marmora Romana* (Rome, 1988)

Göller, E., *Papsttum und Bußgewalt in spätrömischer und frühmittelalterlicher Zeit* (Freiburg, 1933)

Goodman, D. *GPR-Slice 7.0, Manual* (www.gpr-survey.com, 2016)

Goodman, D. and Piro, S., *GPR Remote Sensing in Archaeology* (Berlin, 2013)

Goodson, C. J., 'The Basilicas of Pope Paschal I (817–824): Tradition and Transformation in Early Medieval Rome', Ph.D. thesis (Columbia University, 2004)

Grabar, A., *Martyrium: Recherches sur le culte des reliques et l'art chrétien antique*, 2 vols. (Paris, 1946)

Grazioli Medici, P., *Medici: Marmorari Romani* (Vatican City, 1992)

Gregory, B. S., *Salvation at Stake: Christian Martyrdom in Early Modern Europe* (Cambridge, MA, 2001)

Grierson, P., 'The Tombs and Obits of the Byzantine Emperors (337–1042)', *Dumbarton Oaks Papers* 16 (1962), 1–63

Grisar, H., *Analecta Romana: Dissertazioni, testi, monumenti dell'arte riguardanti principalmente la storia di Roma e dei papi nel Medio Evo. Volume Primo* (Rome, 1899)

    *Die römische Kapelle Sancta Sanctorum und ihr Schatz: Meine Entdeckungen und Studien in der Palastkapelle der mittelalterlichen Päpste* (Freiburg, 1908)

Guidobaldi, F., 'Caratteri e contenuti della nuova architettura dell'età costantiniana', *RAC* 80 (2004), 233–76

    'Struttura e cronologia delle recinzioni liturgiche nelle chiese di Roma dal VI al IX secolo', in de Blaauw (ed.), *Arredi di culto e disposizioni liturgiche a Roma da Costantino a Sisto IV*, 81–99

    'Il Tempio di Minerva e le strutture adiacenti: Settore privato del *Sessorium* costantiniano', *RAC* 74 (1998), 485–518

Guidobaldi, F. and Angelelli, C., *La 'Descrittione di Roma' di Benedetto Mellini nel Codice Vat. Lat. 11905* (Sussidi allo studio delle antichità cristiane 23) (Vatican City, 2010)

Guidobaldi, F. and Guiglia Guidobaldi, A., *Pavimenti marmorei di Roma dal IV al IX secolo* (Vatican City, 1983)

Guiglia, A., 'Il VI secolo: da Simmaco (498–514) a Gregorio Magno (590–604)', in D'Onofrio (ed.), *La committenza artistica dei papi a Roma nel Medioevo*, 109–43

Guiglia Guidobaldi, A., 'Pavimenti marmorei a Roma e nel suburbio nel secoli IV–VII', in M. Cecchelli (ed.), *Materiali e tecniche dell'edilizia paleocristiana a Roma* (Rome, 2001), 191–202

Guiglia Guidobaldi, A. and Pensabene, P., 'Il recupero dell'antico in età carolingia: La decorazione scultorea absidale delle chiese di Roma', *Rendiconti della Pontificia Accademia Romana di Archeologia* 78 (2005-6), 3–74

Güthlein, K., 'Quellen aus dem Familienarchiv Spada zum römischen Barock. 2. Folge', *Römisches Jahrbuch für Kunstgeschichte* 19 (1981), 179–243

Gvozdeva, K. and Velten, H. R. (eds.), *Medialität der Prozession: Performanz ritueller Bewegung in Texten und Bildern der Vormoderne* (Germanisch-romanische Monatsschrift 39) (Heidelberg, 2011)

Gy, P. M., 'Histoire liturgique du sacrement de pénitence', *La Maison-Dieu* 56 (1958), 5–21

(ed.), *Guillaume Durand: Évêque de Mende (v. 1230-1296): Canoniste, liturgiste et homme politique* (Paris, 1992)

Gyug, R. F., 'The pontificals of Monte Cassino', in *L'età dell'abate Desiderio*, 3 vols. (Monte Cassino, 1989-92), III, 413–39

Hamilton, S., *The Practice of Penance, 900–1050* (Woodbridge, 2001)

'The unique favor of penance: The Church and the people, c. 800–c.1100', in P. Linehan and J. L. Nelson (eds.), *The Medieval World* (London, 2001), 229–45

Harrell, J. A., Brown, V. M. and Lazzarini, L., 'Breccia verde antica: Sources, petrology, and ancient uses', in L. Lazzarini (ed.), *Interdisciplinary Studies on Ancient Stone: Proceedings of the Sixth International Conference of the Association for the Study of Marble and Other Stones in Antiquity: Venice, June 15-18, 2000* (Padua, 2002), 207–18

Haynes, I. P., *Blood of the Provinces: The Roman Auxilia and the Making of Provincial Society from Augustus to the Severans* (Oxford, 2013)

Haynes, I. P., Liverani, P., Heslop, D., Peverett, I., Spinola, G. and Turner, A., 'The Lateran Project: Interim report for the 2016–2017 seasons (Rome)', *PBSR* 85 (2017), 317–20

Haynes, I. P., Liverani, P., Peverett, I., Spinola, G. and Turner, A., 'The Lateran Project: Interim report for 2015–2016 seasons (Rome)', *PBSR* 84 (2016), 311–16

Haynes, I. P., Liverani, P., Piro, S., Peverett, I. and Spinola, G., 'Progetto Laterano: Primi risultati', *Atti della Pontificia Accademia Romana di Archeologia (Serie III)* 86 (2013–14), 125–44

Haynes, I. P., Liverani, P., Piro, S. and Spinola, G., 'The Lateran Project: Interim report on the July 2012 and January 2013 seasons (Rome)', *PBSR* 81 (2013), 360–3

Haynes, I. P., Liverani, P., Piro, S. and Spinola, G., and Peverett, I., 'Progetto Laterano: Primi risultati', *Rendiconti della Pontificia Accademia Romana di Archeologia* 86 (2014), 1–19

Haynes, I. P., Liverani, P., Spinola, G. and Piro, S., 'The Lateran Project', *PBSR* 80 (2012), 369–71

Haynes, I. P., Liverani, P., Spinola, G., Piro, S., Peverett, I. and A. Turner, 'The Lateran Project: Interim report for the January 2014 Season (Rome)', *PBSR* 82 (2014), 331–5

Haynes, I. P., Liverani, P., Turner, A. and Ravasi, T., 'Roma si trasforma: Gli scavi di San Giovanni in Laterano e l'evoluzione della città eterna tra II e VI sec. d. C.', *Forma Urbis* 17, 6 (2011), 36–44

Heidemann, S., 'The evolving representation of the early Islamic Empire and its religion on coin imagery', in A. Neuwirth, N. Sinai and M. Marx (eds.), *The Qur'ān in Context: Historical and Literary Investigations into the Qur'ānic Milieu* (Leiden, 2010), 149–95

Heres, T. L., *A Proposal for a Dating System of Late-Antique Masonry Structures in Rome and Ostia* (Amsterdam, 1982)

Herklotz, I., 'Die Beratungsräume Calixtus' II. im Lateranspalast und ihre Fresken: Kunst und Propaganda am Ende des Investiturstreits', *Zeitschrift für Kunstgeschichte* 52 (1989), 145–214

'Der Campus Lateranense im Mittelalter', *Römisches Jahrbuch für Kunstgeschichte* 22 (1985), 1–43

*Gli eredi di Costantino: Il papato, il Laterano e la propaganda visiva nel XII secolo* (La corte dei papi 6) (Rome, 2000)

'Excavations, collectors and scholars in seventeenth-century Rome', in I. Bignamini (ed.), *Archives and Excavations: Essays on the History of Archaeological Excavations in Rome and Southern Italy from the Renaissance to the Nineteenth Century* (London, 2004), 55–88

'Zur Ikonographie der Papstsiegel im 11. und 12. Jahrhundert', in H.-R. Meier, C. Jäggi and P. Büttner (eds.), *Für irdischen Ruhm und himmlischen Lohn: Stifter und Auftraggeber in der mittelalterlichen Kunst* (Berlin, 1995), 116–30

'Der mittelalterliche Fassadenportikus der Lateranbasilika und seine Mosaiken: Kunst und Propaganda am Ende des 12. Jahrhunderts', *RJBH* 25 (1989), 27–95

*'Sepulcra' et 'Monumenta' del Medioevo: Studi sull'arte sepolcrale in Italia* (Naples, 2001)

Herz, A., 'Cardinal Cesare Baronio's restoration of SS. Nereo ed Achilleo and S. Cesareo de' Appia', *Art Bulletin* 70 (1988), 590–620

Hibbard, H., *Carlo Maderno and Roman Architecture: 1580–1630* (London, 1971)

'The early history of Sant'Andrea della Valle', *Art Bulletin* 43 (1961), 289–318

Hodgson, N. and Bidwell, P. T., 'Auxiliary barracks in a new light: Recent discoveries on Hadrian's Wall', *Britannia* 35 (2004), 121–57

Hoffmann, A. and Wolf, G., 'Narrative and iconic space: From Pontius to Pilate', in Lidov (ed.), *New Jerusalems*, 395–409

Hoffmann, V., 'Die Fassade von S. Giovanni in Laterano 313/14–1649', *Römisches Jahrbuch für Kunstgeschichte* 17 (1978), 1–46

Hommers, J., *Gehen und Sehen in Saint-Lazare in Autun: Bewegung – Betrachtung – Reliquienverehrung* (Cologne, 2015)
Horsch, N., *Ad astra gradus: Scala Santa und Sancta Sanctorum in Rom unter Sixtus V. (1585–1590)* (Munich, 2014)
  'Die Nordflanke des mittelalterlichen Lateranpalastes als "Bühne" des Papstes', in S. Albrecht (ed.), *Stadtgestalt und Öffentlichkeit: Die Enstehung politischer Räume in der Stadt der Vormoderne* (Veröffentlichungen des Zentralinstituts für Kunstgeschichte in München 24) (Cologne, 2010) 253–73
  'Die Scala Santa im mittelalterlichen Lateranpalast: Eine neue Lektüre der Quellen', *Zeitschrift für Kunstgeschichte* 66 (2003), 524–32
Hubala, E., 'Roma sotterranea barocca', *Das Münster* 18 (1965), 157–70
Hug, A., 'Lactarius 2', in *Realencyclopädie der classischen Altertumswissenschaft* (Stuttgart, 1924), XII, 1, col. 361
Hughes, L. A., 'Illusive idols and the Constantinian aesthetic: A note on the Lateran *fastigium*', *Latomus* 70, 2 (2011), 478–92
Humphries, M., 'From emperor to Pope? Ceremonial, space, and authority at Rome from Constantine to Gregory the Great', in K. Cooper and J. Hillner (eds.), *Religion, Dynasty, and Patronage in Early Christian Rome, 300–900* (Cambridge, 2007), 21–58
  'Liturgy and laity in Late Antique Rome: Problems, sources and social dynamics', in Day and Vinzent (eds.), *Early Roman Liturgy to 600*, 171–86
Huyghebaert, N., 'Une légende de foundation: Le "Constitutum Constantini"', *Moyen âge* series 4, 32 (1979), 177–210
Hyde Minor, H., *The Culture of Architecture in Enlightenment Rome* (University Park, PA, 2010)
Iacobini, A., 'Il mosaico absidiale di San Pietro in Vaticano', in M. Andaloro and A. Ghidoli (eds.), *Fragmenta Picta: Affreschi e mosaici staccati del Medioevo romano* (Rome, 1989), 119–29
  'La pittura e le arti suntuarie: Da Innocenzo III al Innocenzo IV (1198–1254)', in Romanini (ed.), *Roma nel Duecento*, 237–319
Infrate, A., *The Wandering Throne of Solomon: Objects and Tales of Kingship in the Medieval Mediterranean* (Leiden, 2016)
Iogna-Prat, D., 'Topographies of penance in the Latin West', in Fiery (ed.), *A New History of Penance*, 149–72
Ippoliti, A., 'Il lato orientale di Alessandro Galilei (1731–1738)', in Ippoliti, *Il Palazzo Apostolico del Laterano*, 23–4
  *Il Palazzo Apostolico del Laterano* (Monumenta Sanctae Sedis 4) (Rome, 2008)
Jäggi, C., 'Cathedra Petri und Colonna Santa in St. Peter zu Rom: Überlegungen zu "Produktion" und Konjunktur von Reliquien im Mittelalter', in Bergmeier et al. (eds.), *Erzeugung und Zerstörung von Sakralität*, 109–31
James, S., *Rome and the Sword* (London, 2011)
Jaser, C., *Ecclesia maledicens: Rituelle und zeremonielle Exkommunikationsformen im Mittelalter* (Tübingen, 2013)

Jauss, H. R., 'Literaturgeschichte als Provokation der Literaturwissenschaft', in R. Warning (ed.), *Rezeptionsästhetik: Theorie und Praxis*, 2nd edn (Munich, 1979), 126–62

Jensen, R. M., 'Saints' relics and the consecration of church buildings in Rome', *Studia Patristica* 71 (2014), 153–70

Johnson, M. J., 'The fifth-century oratory of the Holy Cross at the Lateran in Rome', *Architectura. Zeitschrift für Geschichte der Baukunst* 25, 2 (1995), 128–55

*The Roman Imperial Mausoleum in Late Antiquity* (Cambridge, 2009)

Jordan-Ruwe, M., *Das Säulenmonument: Zur Geschichte der erhöhten Aufstellung antiker Porträtstatuen* (Asia Minor Studien 19) (Bonn, 1995)

Johrendt, J., *Die Diener des Apostelfürsten: Das Kapitel von St. Peter im Vatikan (11.–13. Jahrhundert)* (Berlin, 2011)

'Das Innozenzische Schisma aus kurialer Perspektive', in H. Müller and B. Hotz (eds.), *Gegenpäpste: Ein unerwünschtes mittelalterliches Phänomen* (Vienna, 2012), 127–63

Josi, E., *Il chiostro lateranense: Cenni storici e illustrazione* (Vatican City, 1970)

'Scoperte nella Basilica costantiniana al Laterano, Rome', *RAC* 11 (1934), 335–8

Josi, E., Krautheimer, R. and Corbett, S., 'Note Lateranensi', *RAC* 33, 1–4 (1957), 79–98

'Note Lateranensi', *RAC* 34, 1–4 (1958), 59–72

Jounel, P., *Le culte des saints dans les basiliques du Latran et du Vatican au douzième siècle* (Collection de l'École Française de Rome 26) (Rome, 1977)

Jungmann, J. A., *Die lateinischen Bußriten in ihrer geschichtlichen Entwicklung* (Innsbruck, 1932)

Kalavrezou-Maxeiner, I., 'The Imperial Chamber at Luxor', *Dumbarton Oaks Papers* 29 (1975), 225–51

Kemper, T. A., *Die Kreuzigung Christi: Motivgeschichtliche Studien zu lateinischen und deutschen Passionstraktaten des Spätmittelalters* (Münchener Texte und Untersuchungen zur deutschen Literatur des Mittelalters 131) (Tübingen, 2006)

Kiening, C., 'Prozessionalität der Passion', in Gvozdeva and Velten (eds.), *Medialität der Prozession*, 177–97

Kieven, E., 'Il ruolo del disegno: Il concorso per la facciata di S. Giovanni in Laterano', in B. Contardi and G. Curcio (eds.), *Urbe architectus: Modelli. Disegni. Misure: La professione dell'architetto: Roma 1680–1750* (Rome, 1991), 78–123

Kinney, D., 'Bearers of meaning', *Jahrbuch für Antike und Christentum* 50 (2007), 139–53

'The church basilica', *Acta ad Archaeologiam et Artium Historiarum Pertinentia* 15 (2001), 115–27

'The concept of "spolia"', in C. Rudolph (ed.), *A Companion to Medieval Art: Romanesque and Gothic in Northern Europe* (Malden, 2006), 233–52

'Patronage of art and architecture', in J. Doran and D. J. Smith (eds.), *Pope Innocent II (1130–1143): The World vs. the City* (Abingdon, 2016), 352–87

'Spolia', in W. Tronzo (ed.), *St Peter's in the Vatican* (Cambridge, 2008), 16–47

'Spolia: Damnatio and renovatio memoriae', *Memoirs of the American Academy in Rome* 42 (1997), 117–48

Kirschbaum, E., *Die Gräber der Apostelfürsten*, 3rd edn (Frankfurt, 1974)

Klauser, T. (ed.), *Das römische Capitulare evangeliorum* (Münster, 1935)

'Der Ursprung der bischöflichen Insignien und Ehrenrechte', *Bonner Akademische Reden* 1 (1948), 5–44

Klein, H. A., 'The Crown of His Kingdom: Imperial ideology, palace ritual, and the relics of Christ's Passion', in M. Featherstone (ed.), *The Emperor's House: Palaces from Augustus to the Age of Absolutism* (Berlin, 2015), 201–12

'Sacred relics and imperial ceremonies at the great palace of Constantinople', in F. A. Bauer (ed.), *Visualisierungen von Herrschaft: Frühmittelalterliche Residenzen – Gestalt und Zeremoniell* (Istanbul, 2006), 79–99

Koch, E. and Schlie, H. (eds.), *Orte der Imagination – Räume des Affekts: Die mediale Formierung des Sakralen* (Paderborn, 2016)

Koch, H., 'Der Büßerplatz im Abendland', *Theologische Quartalschrift* 85 (1903), 253–70

Koenen, U., *Das 'Konstantinskreuz' im Lateran und die Rezeption frühchristlicher Genesiszyklen im 12. und 13. Jahrhundert* (Worms, 1995)

Koster, A., Peterse, K. and Swinkels, L., *Romeins Nijmegen boven het maaiveld* (Nijmegen, 2002)

Krautheimer, R., *Architettura paleocristiana e bizantina* (Turin, 1986)

'The building inscriptions and the dates of construction of Old St. Peter's: A reconsideration', *RJBH* 25 (1989), 1–23

'The Constantinian basilica', *Dumbarton Oaks Papers* 21 (1967), 115–40

*Early Christian and Byzantine Architecture* (Harmondsworth, 1965)

'Introduction to an "Iconography of Mediaeval Architecture"', *Journal of the Warburg and Courtauld Institutes* 5 (1942), 1–33

'Die konstantinische Basilika', in R. Krautheimer, *Ausgewählte Aufsätze zur Europäischen Kunstgeschichte* (Cologne, 1988), 40–80

*Roma. Profilo di una città* (Rome, 1981)

*Rom: Schicksal einer Stadt, 312–1308* (Munich, 1996)

*Rome: Profile of a City, 312–1308* (Princeton, 1980)

Krautheimer, R. and Corbett, S., 'The Constantinian basilica of the Lateran', *Antiquity* 34, 135 (1960), 201–6

'SS. Quattro Coronati', in R. Krautheimer, S. Corbett and W. Frankl, *Corpus Basilicarum Christianarum Romae*, IV (Vatican City, 1976), 1–34

Krautheimer, R., Corbett, S., Malmstrom, R. and Stapleford, R., 'La basilica costantiniana al Laterano: Un tentativo di ricostruzione', *RAC* 43 (1967), 125–54

Krautheimer, R. and Pentiricci, M., 'La basilica di S. Lorenzo nei secoli IV–X (periodi 8–9)', in Frommel and Pentiricci (eds.), *L'antica basilica di San Lorenzo in Damaso*, 267–76

Kronberger, M., *Siedlungschronologische Forschungen zu den canabae legionis von Vindobona: Die Gräberfelder* (Monographien der Stadtarchäologie Wien Band 1) (Vienna, 2005)

Kühnel, B., 'Virtual pilgrimages to real places: The holy landscapes', in Donkin and Vorholt (eds.), *Imagining Jerusalem in the Medieval West*, 243–64

(ed.), *The Real and Ideal Jerusalem in Jewish, Christian and Islamic Art: Studies in Honor of Bezalel Narkiss on the Occasion of His Seventieth Birthday* (Jewish Art 23/24) (Jerusalem, 1997/8)

Kuttner, S., 'Conciliar law in the making: The Lyonese Constitutions (1274) of Gregory X in a manuscript at Washington', in *Miscellanea Pio Paschini: Studi di Storia Ecclesiastica*, 2 vols. (Rome, 1948–9), II, 39–81

Lanciani, R., *The Ruins and Excavations of Ancient Rome: A Companion Book for Students and Travellers* (Cambridge, 1897)

*Storia degli scavi di Roma e notizie intorno le collezioni romane di antichità*, 4 vols. (Turin, 1902–12)

Lapidge, M. (ed.), *Archbishop Theodore: Commemorative Studies on his Life and Influence* (Cambridge, 1995)

Laubscher, H. P., *Der Reliefschmuck des Galeriusbogens in Thessaloniki* (Archäologische Forschungen 1) (Berlin, 1975)

Laudage, C., *Kampf um den Stuhl Petri: Die Geschichte der Gegenpäpste* (Freiburg, 2012)

Lauer, P., 'Les fouilles du *Sancta Sanctorum* au Latran', *Mélanges de l'École Française de Rome* 20 (1900), 251–87

*Le palais de Latran: Étude historique et archéologique* (Paris, 1911)

*Le trésor du Sancta Sanctorum* (Monuments et mémoires publiés par l'Académie des inscriptions et belles lettres 15) (Paris, 1906)

Lemmens, L., *Die Franziskaner auf dem Sion* (Franziskanische Studien 4) (Munich, 1916)

Lentes, T., 'Der Körper als Ort des Gedächtnisses: Der Körper als Text', in Geissmar-Brandi and Louis (eds.), *Glaube – Liebe – Hoffnung*, 76–9

'Die Vermessung des Christus-Körpers', in Geissmar-Brandi and Louis (eds.), *Glaube – Liebe – Hoffnung*, 144–7

Lentzen-Deis, W., *Busse als Bekenntnisvollzug* (Freiburg, 1969)

Lidov, A. (ed.), *New Jerusalems: Hierotopy and Iconography of Sacred Spaces* (Moscow, 2009)

Lindros Wohl, B., 'Constantine's use of spolia', in J. Fleischer, J. Lund and M. Nielsen (eds.), *Late Antiquity: Art in Context* (Acta Hyperborea, Danish Studies in Classical Archaeology) (Copenhagen, 2001), 85–115

Lippold, I. G., *Die Skulpturen des Vatikanischen Museums* (Berlin, 1965)

Lissi Caronna, E., 'Terrecotte da una tomba repubblicana in via S. Stefano Rotondo', in Musei Capitolini, *Roma Medio repubblicana: Aspetti culturali di Roma e del Lazio nei secoli IV e III a.C.* (exhibition catalogue, Roma – maggio-giugno 1973) (Rome, 1973), 241–6 nos. 373–7, plates LIII–LV

Liverani, P., 'Dalle *Aedes Laterani* al patriarchio lateranense', *RAC* 75 (1999), 521–49
  'L'area lateranense in età tardo antica e le origini del patriarchio', *MEFRA* 116 (2004), 17–49
  'L'arco di Costantino', in A. Donati and G. Gentili (eds.), *Costantino il Grande: La civiltà antica al bivio tra Occidente e Oriente* (Rimini, 2005), 65–9
  '"Camerae" e coperture delle basiliche paleocristiane', *Mededelingen van het Nederlands Instituut te Rome* 60–61 (2001–2), 13–27
  'Le colonne e il capitello in bronzo d'età romana dell'altare del Ss. Sacramento in Laterano: Analisi archeologica e storica', *Rendiconti: Atti della Pontificia accademia romana di archeologia* 75 (1992–3), 75–99
  'Discoveries at the Scala Santa: The excavations of 1852–54', in I. Bignamini (ed.), *Archives and Excavations: Essays on the History of Archaeological Excavations in Rome and Southern Italy from the Renaissance to the Nineteenth Century* (Archaeological Monographs of the British School at Rome) (London, 2004), 203–220
  'Domus: Laterani', in *LTUR* II, 127
  'Domus: Parthorum', in *LTUR* II 152–3
  'L'episcopio lateranense dalle origini all'Alto Medioevo', In S. Balcon, E. Baratte, J.-P. Caillet and D. Sandron (eds.), *Des 'domus ecclesiae' aux palais épiscopaux: Actes du colloque tenu à Autun du 26 au 28 novembre 2009* (Bibliothèque de l'Antiquité tardive 23) (Turnhout, 2012), 119–31
  'Introduzione topografica', in Liverani (ed.), *Laterano 1*, 6–16
  'Marmor', in *Reallexikon für Antike und Christentum* (Stuttgart, 2010), XXIV, 208–46
  'Il monumento e la voce', in O. Brandt and V. Fiocchi Nicolai (eds.), *Costantino e i Costantinidi: L'Innovazione costantiniana, le sue radici e i suoi sviluppi. Atti del XIV Congresso Internazionale di Archeologia Cristiana* (Vatican City, 2016), 393–405
  'Osservazioni sul libellus delle donazioni costantiniane nel Liber Pontificalis', Athenaeum 107 (2019), 169–217
  'Osservazioni sui rostri del Foro Romano in età tardoantica', in A. Leone, D. Palombi and S. Walker (eds.), *Res bene gestae: Ricerche di storia urbana su Roma antica in onore di Eva Margareta Steinby* (Rome, 2007), 169–93
  'Le proprietà private nell'area lateranense fino all'età di Costantino', *MEFRA* 100, 2 (1988), 891–915
  'Dal Quirinale al Vaticano', *Bollettino d'Arte* 83 (1994), 11–26
  'Reimpiego senza ideologia: La lettura antica degli spolia dall'arco di Costantino all'età carolingia', *Mitteilungen des Deutschen Archäologischen Instituts, Römische Abteilung* 111 (2004), 383–433
  'Saint Peter's and the city of Rome between Late Antiquity and the early Middle Ages', in McKitterick et al. (eds.), *Old Saint Peter's, Rome*, 21–34

'Spätantike Ehrenstatuen zwischen Distanz und Dialog', in D. Boschung and C. Vorster (eds.), *Leibhafte Kunst: Statuen und kulturelle Identität* (Paderborn, 2015), 93–121

(ed.), *Giornata di studio tematica dedicata al Patriarcato Lateranense. Atti della giornata tematica dei Seminari di Archeologia Cristiana (École française de Rome, 10 maggio 2001)* (*MEFRA* 116, 1) (special issue) (Rome, 2004)

*Laterano 1: Scavi sotto la Basilica di S. Giovanni in Laterano*, vol. I: *Materiali* (Vatican City, 1998)

Liverani, P. and Spinola, G., *Mosaici in bianco e nero dal tratto vaticano della necropoli della via Trionfale: Aiscom, Atti del V Colloquio* (Ravenna, 1999)

Locke Perchuk, A., 'Schismatic (re)visions: Sant'Elia near Nepi and Sta. Maria in Trastevere in Rome, 1120–1143', *Gesta* 55 (2016), 179–212

Longère, J., 'La pénitence selon le *Repertorium*, les instructions et constitutions, et le pontifical de Guillaume Durand', in P. M. Gy (ed.), *Guillaume Durand: Évêque de Mende (v. 1230–1296): Canoniste, liturgiste et homme politique* (Paris, 1992), 105–33

Luchterhandt, M., 'Vom Haus des Bischofs zum Locus Sanctus: Der Lateranspalast im kulturellen Gedächtnis des römischen Mittelalters', in M. Featherstone, J.-M. Spieser, G. Tanman and U. Wulf-Rheidt (eds.), *The Emperor's House: Palaces from Augustus to the Age of Absolutism* (Berlin, 2015), 73–92

'Päpstlicher Palastbau und höfisches Zeremoniell unter Leo III', in C. Stiegemann and M. Wemhoff (eds.), *799: Kunst und Kultur der Karolingerzeit: Karl der Große und Leo III. in Paderborn* (Mainz,1999), 109–22

'Rom und Aachen: Die Karolinger und der päpstliche Hof um 800', in F. Pohle (ed.), *Karl der Grose/Charlemagne: Orte der Macht* (Aachen, 2014), 104–13

Lugli, G., *La tecnica edilizia romana* (Rome, 1957)

Lusnia, S. S., *Creating Severan Rome: The Architecture and Self-Image of L. Septimius Severus (AD 193–211)* (Collection Latomus 345) (Leuven, 2014)

Macaulay Lewis, E., 'The role of *ollae perforatae* in understanding horticulture, planting techniques, garden design, and plant trade in the Roman world', in J.-P. Morel, J. Tesserras and J. C. Matamala (eds.), *The Archaeology of Crop Fields and Gardens* (Bari, 2006), 207–19

Maccarone, M., 'L'indulgenza del Giubileo del 1300 e la basilica di San Pietro', in A. M. Romanini (ed.), *Roma anno 1300: Atti della IV Settimana di Studi di Storia dell'Arte Medievale dell'Università di Roma La Sapienza (19–24 maggio 1980)* (Rome 1983), 731–52

MacDonald, A. A., Ridderbos, H. N. B. and Schlusemann, R. B. (eds.), *The Broken Body: Passion Devotion in Late-Medieval Culture* (Groningen, 1998)

Mackie, G., 'The Santa Croce drawings: A re-examination', *Revue d'art canadienne/ Canadian Art Review* 24, 1 (1997), 1–14

Maddalo, S., '*Caput et vertex omnium ecclesiarum*: La cattedrale di Roma tra XII e XIII secolo', in A. C. Quintavalle (ed.), *Medioevo: l'Europa delle Cattedrali.*

*Atti del Convegno Internazionale di Studi (Parma 19-23 settembre 2006)* (I convegni di Parma 9) (Parma, 2007), 424-34

'Immagini e ideologia tra gli *Actus Sylvestri* e il *Constitutum Constantini*: Riflessioni su una duplice tradizione figurativa', in A. C. Quintavalle (ed.), *Medioevo: Arte e storia. Atti del Convegno Internazionale di Studi (Parma, 18-22 settembre 2007)* (I convegni di Parma 10) (Parma, 2008), 481-94

Magrí, R., 'Lupa capitolina', in Nesselrath (ed.), *Da Pisanello*, 224

'La lupa simbolo di giustizia in Laterano', in Nesselrath (ed.), *Da Pisanello*, 225-6

'Il Memoriale', in Nesselrath (ed.), *Da Pisanello*, 228

'La mesticanza', in Nesselrath (ed.), *Da Pisanello*, 227-8

Maiuri, A. and Pane, R., *La casa di Loreio Tiburtino e la villa di Diomede in Pompei* (Rome, 1947)

Malesevic, F., *Rome Unveiled: Cardinal Cesare Baronio and San Giovanni in Laterano during the Post-Tridentine Papacy* (forthcoming)

Malmstrom, R. E., 'The building of the nave piers at S. Giovanni in Laterano after the fire of 1361', *RAC* 43, 2 (1967), 155-64

Manacorda, D., 'Il Laterano e la produzione ceramica a Roma: Aspetti del paesaggio urbano', in A. Leone, D. Palombi and S. Walker (eds.), *Res Bene Gestae: Ricerche di storia urbana su Roma antica in onore di Eva Margareta Steinby* (Rome, 2007), 195-204

Mancioli, D., 'Horti Torquatiani', in *LTUR* III, 85-6

Mandel, C., *Sixtus V and the Lateran Palace* (Rome, 1994)

Mansfield, M. C., *The Humiliation of Sinners: Public Penance in Thirteenth-Century France* (Ithaca, NY, 1995)

Marcattili, F., 'Tetrastyl: Ipotesi sull'origine del ciborio d'altare', *RAC* 87-8 (2011-14), 147-74

Martines, M., 'Un laboratorio di marmi fuori Porta Asinaria. Scavi Metro C 2006-2007', *Bollettino di Archeologia Online* 6 (2015), 1-24

Martini, A., 'L'ordo paenitentiae in feria quarta quinquagesimale del cosiddetto Pontificale di Poitiers', in *Mens concordet voci: Pour Mgr. A. G. Martimort* (Paris, 1983), 629-38

Mathis, P., 'L'antica abside della basilica di S. Giovanni in Laterano e la questione del ambulatorio', *Opus* 7 (2003), 19-38

Matthiae, G., *Le chiese di Roma dal IV al X secolo* (Roma Cristiana 3) (Rome, 1962)

Mauskopf Deliyannis, D., 'The Roman *Liber Pontificalis*, papal primacy and the Acacian Schism', *Viator* 45 (2014), 1-16

Mazzalupi, M., 'Regesto', in De Marchi et al. (eds.), *Gentile da Fabriano*, 68-84

'Roma', in De Marchi et al. (eds.), *Gentile da Fabriano*, 140-1

McEvoy, M., 'The mausoleum of Honorius: Late Roman imperial Christianity and the city of Rome in the fifth century', in McKitterick et al. (eds.), *Old Saint Peter's, Rome,* 119-36

McFadden, S., 'The Luxor temple paintings in context: Roman visual culture in Late Antiquity', in M. Jones and S. McFadden (eds.), *Art of Empire: The*

*Roman Frescoes and Imperial Cult Chamber in Luxor Temple* (New Haven, 2015), 105–33

McKitterick, R., 'The *damnatio memoriae* of Pope Constantine II (767–768)', in R. Balzaretti, J. Barrow and P. Skinner (eds.), *Italy and Medieval Europe: Papers for Chris Wickham on the Occasion of His 65th Birthday* (Past and Present Supplementary series) (Oxford: 2018), 231–49

'The *Liber Pontificalis* and the transformation of Rome from pagan to Christian city in the early Middle Ages', in M. Kahlos, K. Ritari and J. Stenger (eds.), *Being Pagan, Being Christian in Late Antiquity and the Early Middle Ages* (London, forthcoming)

'Liturgy and history in the early Middle Ages', in M. Fassler, K. Bugyis and A. Kraebel (eds.), *Music, Liturgy, and the Shaping of History (800–1500)* (York, 2017), 23–40

'Narrative strategies in the *Liber Pontificalis*: The case of St Paul, *doctor mundi, doctor gentium*, and San Paolo fuori le Mura', *Rivista di Storia del Cristianesimo* 10 (2013), 115–30

'The papacy and Byzantium in the seventh and early eighth-century sections of the *Liber Pontificalis*', *PBSR* 84 (2016), 241–73

*Perceptions of the Past in the Early Middle Ages* (Notre Dame, IN, 2006)

'La place du Liber Pontificalis dans les genres historiographiques du haut moyen âge', in Bougard and Sot (eds.), *Liber, gesta, histoire*, 23–36

'The representation of Old Saint Peter's basilica in the Liber Pontificalis', in McKitterick et al. (eds.), *Old Saint Peter's, Rome*, 95–118

'Roman texts and Roman history in the early Middle Ages', in Bolgia et al. (eds.), *Rome across Time and Space*, 19–34

*Rome and the Invention of the Papacy: The Liber Pontificalis* (Cambridge, 2020)

'Transformations of the Roman past and Roman identity in the early Middle Ages', in C. Gantner, R. McKitterick and S. Meeder (eds.), *The Resources of the Past in Early Medieval Europe* (Cambridge, 2015), 225–44

'Die Überlieferung eines bestimmten Bildes der Stadt Rom im frühen Mittelalter: der *Liber Pontificalis*', in H. Finger (ed.), *Gedenkschrift Josef Semmler* (Cologne, 2012), 33–46

McKitterick, R., Osborne, J., Richardson, C. M. and Story, J., 'Introduction', in McKitterick et al. (eds.), *Old Saint Peter's, Rome*, 1–20

McKitterick, R., Osborne, J., Richardson C. M. and Story, J. (eds.), *Old Saint Peter's, Rome* (British School at Rome Monograph Series) (Cambridge, 2013)

Meens, R., *Penance in Medieval Europe* (Cambridge, 2014)

Meinert, T., *Die Heilig-Grab-Anlage in Görlitz: Architektur und Geschichte eines spätmittelalterlichen Bauensembles* (Esens, 2004)

Meneghini, R., 'La Forma Urbis severiana: Storia e nuove scoperte', in R. Meneghini and R. Rea (eds.), *La biblioteca infinita* (Milan, 2014), 327–36

Meneghini, R. and Santangeli Valenzani, R., 'Sepolture intramuranee e paesaggio urbano a Roma tra V e VII secolo', in L. Paroli and P. Delogu (eds.), *La storia economica di Roma nell'alto medioevo alla luce dei recenti scavi archeologici* (Florence, 1993), 89–111

'Sepolture intramuranee e paesaggio urbano a Roma tra V e VII secolo d.C.: Aggiornamenti e considerazioni', *Archeologia Medievale* 22 (1995), 283–90

Messineo, G., 'Ville a Tor di Quinto e nelle tenute di Grottarossa e Acquatraversa', in B. S. Frizell and A. Klynne (eds.), *Roman Villas around the Urbs: Interaction with Landscape and Environment. Proceedings of a Conference Held at the Swedish Institute in Rome, September 17–18, 2004* (Rome, 2005), 1–5

Meßner, R., 'Feiern der Umkehr und Versöhnung', in R. Meßner (ed.), *Sakramentliche Feiern I/2* (Gottesdienst der Kirche 7) (Regensburg, 1992), 84–134

Miedema, N. R., *Die römischen Kirchen im Spätmittelalter nach den 'Indulgentiae ecclesiarum urbis Romae'* (Tübingen, 2001)

*Rompilgerführer in Spätmittelalter und Früher Neuzeit* (Tübingen, 2003)

Miglio, M., 'Il giubileo di Niccolò V (1450)', in G. Fossi (ed.), *La storia dei giubilei*, 2 vols. (Rome, 1998), II, 56–73

Moench, E., 'Pisanello, Tête de femme', in Cordellier and Marini (eds.), *Pisanello: Le peintre aux sept vertus*, 95

Mols, S. T. A. M. and Moormann, E. M., 'L'edificio romano sotto S. Maria Maggiore a Roma e le sue pitture: Proposta per una nuova lettura', *Mitteilungen des Deutschen Archäologischen Instituts. Römische Abteilung* 116 (2010), 469–506

Monciatti, A., 'Funzione e decorazione dell'architettura nel Palazzo di Niccolò III Orsini', in T. Weddigen, S. de Blaauw and B. Kempers (eds.), *Functions and Decorations: Art and Ritual at the Vatican Palace in the Middle Ages and the Renaissance* (Vatican City, 2003), 27–39

*Il Palazzo Vaticano nel Medioevo* (Florence, 2005)

Mondini, D., 'Reliquie incarnate: Le "sacre teste" di Pietro e Paolo a San Giovanni in Laterano a Roma', in D. Scotto (ed.), *Del visibile credere: Pellegrinaggi, santuari, miracoli, reliquie* (Florence, 2011), 265–96

Monferini, A., 'Il ciborio Lateranense e Giovanni di Stefano', *Commentari. Rivista di Critica e Storia dell'Arte*, n.s. 13, 3.4 (1962), 182–212

Montella, F., 'Via Latina: Quartiere Metronio. Insediamenti abitativi a nord della via Latina', *Bullettino della Commissione Archeologica Comunale di Roma* 109 (2008), 281–99

Montelli, E., *Tecniche costruttive murarie medievali: Mattoni e laterizi in Roma e nel Lazio fra X e XV secolo* (Storia della tecnica edilizia e restauro dei monumenti 7) (Rome, 2011)

Montinaro, F., 'Les fausses donations de Constantin dans le *Liber Pontificalis*', *Millennium* 12 (2015), 203–29

Moormann, E. M. and Mols, S. T. A. M., 'Le pitture romane: Frammenti e resti in situ', in Liverani (ed.), *Laterano 1*, 115–32

Morbidelli, M., *L'Abside di S. Giovanni in Laterano: Una vicenda controversa* (Rome, 2010)

Morello, G., 'Il tesoro del Sancta Sanctorum', in C. Pietrangeli (ed.), *Il Palazzo Apostolico Lateranense* (Florence, 1991), 91–106

Morin, G. (ed.), 'Le plus ancien "Comes" ou lectionnaire de l'Église romaine', *Revue bénédictine* 27 (1910), 41–74

Morris, C., *The Papal Monarchy: The Western Church from 1050 to 1250* (Oxford, 1989)

Motta, R. 'Il canale della Marana o Acqua Mariana', in D. Mancioli and G. Pisani Sartorio (eds.), *Gli Acquedotti Claudio e Aniene Nuovo nell'area della Banca d'Italia in via Tuscolana* (Rome, 2001), 91–101

Müntz, E., 'Giovanni di Bartolo da Siena: Orafo della corte di Avignone nel XIV secolo', *Archivio storico italiano*, fifth series, 2 (1888), 3–20

Musco, C., Masi, A., Morbidelli, M., Barelli, L. and Sadori, L., 'An integrated approach to the study of the bell towers of S. Giovanni in Laterano', In A. Macchia, L. Campanella and E. Borrelli (eds.), *Proceedings of YOCOCU, Youth in the Conservation of Cultural Heritage (Rome, 24th–25th November 2008)* (Rome, 2009), 279

Nash, E. T., '*Convenerunt in domum Faustae in Laterano*: Optati Milevitani 1.23', *Römische Quartalschrift für Altertumskunde und für Kirchengeschichte* 71 (1976), 1–21

Nelson, J. L., 'Nobility in the ninth century', in A. J. Duggan (ed.), *Nobles and Nobility in Medieval Europe* (Woodbridge, 2000), 43–51

Nesbitt, C., 'Space, Light and Experience in Middle Byzantine Churches', Ph.D. thesis (Newcastle University, 2007)

Nesselrath, A., 'Bildgeschichte – Geschichtsbilder', in M. Matheus, B. Schneidmüller, S. Weinfurter and A. Wieczorek (eds.), *Die Päpste der Renaissance: Politik, Kunst und Musik* (Regensburg, 2017), 49–67

(ed.), *Da Pisanello alla nascita dei Musei Capitolini: L'Antico a Roma alla vigilia del Rinascimento* (exhibition catalogue) (Milan, 1988)

Neumann, F., *Öffentliche Sünder in der Kirche des späten Mittelalters: Verfahren, Sanktionen, Rituale* (Cologne, 2008)

Niebaum, J., 'Die spätantiken Rotunden an Alt-St. Peter in Rom', *Marburger Jahrbuch für Kunstwissenschaft* 34 (2007), 101–61

Nieddu, A. M., *La Basilica Apostolorum sulla via Appia e l'area cimiteriale circostante* (Vatican City, 2009)

Nilgen, U., 'Das *Fastigium* in der Basilica Constantiniana und vier Bronzesäulen des Lateran', *Römische Quartalschrift für christliche Altertumskunde und Kirchengeschichte* 72 (1977), 1–31

Noble, T. F. X., 'A new look at the *Liber Pontificalis*', *Archivium Historiae Pontificiae* 23 (1985), 347–58

'Topography, celebration and power: The making of papal Rome in the eighth and ninth centuries', in M. de Jong and F. Theuws (eds.), *Topographies of Power in the Early Middle Ages* (Leiden, 2001), 45–91

Nocent, A., 'La riconciliazione dei penitenti nella Chiesa del VI e X secolo', *Rivista liturgica* 54 (1967), 628–42
  'La semaine sainte dans la liturgie romaine', in A. G. Kollamparampil (ed.), *Hebdomadae sanctae celebratio: Conspectus historicus comparativus* (Rome, 1997), 277–310
Noreen, K., '*Ecclesiae militantis triumphi*: Jesuit iconography and the Counter-Reformation', *Sixteenth Century Journal* 29 (1998), 689–716
Nota Santi, M., 'La zona del Laterano', *Archeologia Laziale* 1 (1978), 2–5
Nussbaum, O., 'Sancta Sanctorum', *Römische Quartalschrift* 54 (1959), 234–46
Odahl, C., 'The Christian basilicas of Constantinian Rome', *The Ancient World* 1 (1995), 3–28
Oosten, D., 'The mausoleum of Helena and the adjoining basilica Ad duos lauros: construction, evolution and reception', in Verhoeven et al. (eds.), *Monuments and Memory*, 137–43
Ortalli, G., '... *pingatur in palatio* ...': *La pittura infamante nei secoli XIII–XIV* (Rome, 1979)
Ostrow, S. F., *L'arte dei papi: La politica delle immagini nella Roma della Controriforma* (Rome, 2002)
  'The confessio in post-tridentine Rome', in Tosini (ed.), *Arte e committenza*, 19–33
Ousterhout, R., 'Flexible geography and transportable topography', in Kühnel (ed.), *The Real and Ideal Jerusalem*, 393–404
Pace, V., 'Il XIII secolo: Da Innocenzo III (1198-1216) a Bonifacio VIII (1294–1303)', in D'Onofrio (ed.), *La committenza artistica dei papi*, 299–329
  'Per Iacopo Torriti, frate, architetto e "pictor"', *Mitteilungen des Kunsthistorischen Institutes in Florenz* 40 (1996), 212–21
Padovese, L., *La cristologia di Aurelio Clemente Prudenzio* (Analecta Gregoriana 219) (Rome, 1980)
Page, C., *The Christian West and Its Singers: The First Thousand Years* (New Haven, 2010)
Palazzo, E., *A History of Liturgical Books from the Beginning to the Thirteenth Century* (Collegeville, MN, 1998)
Palm, R., 'Reliquienbüste der hl. Juliana von Nikomedia', in A. Legner (ed.), *Die Parler und der Schöne Stil 1350–1400*, 3 vols. (Cologne, 1978), I, 33
Palombi, D., 'Columnae rostratae Augusti', in *LTUR* I, 308
Paoletti, J. T. and Radke, G. M., *Art in Renaissance Italy*, 3rd edn (London, 2005)
Paravicini Bagliani, A., 'Bonifacio VIII, la loggia di giustizia al Laterano e i processi generali di scomunica', *Rivista di storia della Chiesa in Italia* 59 (2005), 377–428
  *Le Chiavi e la Tiara: Immagini e simboli del papato medievale* (La corte dei Papi 3) (Rome, 1998)
  *Il corpo del Papa* (Turin, 1994)
  'Grégoire VII et l'excommunication: À propos des figures des apôtres Pierre e Paul sur les bulles pontificales', in F. Elsig (ed.), *L'image en questions: Pour Jean Wirth* (Geneva, 2013), 120–9

Parkes, H., *The Making of Liturgy in the Ottonian Church: Books, Music and Ritual in Mainz, 950–1050* (Cambridge, 2015)

'Questioning the authority of Vogel and Elze's *Pontifical romano-germanique*', in H. Gittos and S. Hamilton (eds.), *Understanding Medieval Liturgy: Essays in Interpretation* (Burlington, VT, 2016), 75–101

Parlato, E., 'Le icone in processione', in M. Andaloro and S. Romano (eds.), *Arte e iconografia a Roma dal Tardoantico alla fine del Medioevo* (Milan, 2002), 64–8

Pavolini, C., *Archeologia e Topografia della regione II (Celio): un aggiornamento sessant'anni dopo Colini* (*LTUR*, Supplementum III) (Rome, 2006)

Pavolini, C., Carignani, A., Pacetti, F., Spinola, G. and Vitti, M., 'La topografia antica della sommità del Celio', *Mitteilungen des Deutschen Archäologischen Instituts Römische Abteilung* 100 (1993), 443–505

Pelliccioni, G., *Le nuove scoperte sulle origini del battistero lateranense* (Memorie della Pontificia Accademia Romana di Archeologia 12.1) (Vatican City, 1973)

Pensabene, P., *Roma su Roma: Reimpiego architettonico, recupero dell'antico e trasformazioni urbane tra il III e il XIII secolo* (Monumenti di antichità cristiana ser. II, vol. XXII) (Vatican City, 2015)

Pensabene, P. and Panella, C., 'Reimpiego e progettazione architettonica nei monumenti tardo-antichi di Roma', *Atti della Pontificia accademia romana di archeologia: Rendiconti* 66 (1993–4), 111–283

Pentiricci, M., 'Lo scavo: Periodi 8–9', in Frommel and Pentiricci (eds.), *L'antica basilica di San Lorenzo in Damaso*, 235–65

Picard, J.-C., 'Étude sur l'emplacement des tombes des papes du IIIe au Xe siècle', *Mélanges d'archéologie et d'histoire* 81 (1960), 725–82

Pieper, J., Naujokat, A. and Kappler, A., *Jerusalemskirchen: Mittelalterliche Kleinarchitekturen nach dem Modell des Heiligen Grabes* (Aachen, 2003)

Pietrangeli, C. (ed.), *San Giovanni in Laterano* (Florence, 1990)

Pietri, C., *Roma christiana: Recherches sur l'Église de Rome, son organisation, sa politique, son idéologie de Miltiade à Sixte III (311–440)* (Rome, 1976)

Piro, S., Haynes, I. P., Liverani, P. and Zamuner, D., 'GPR investigation to map the subsoil of the St John Lateran Basilica (Rome)', *Bollettino di Geofisica Teorica ed Applicata* 58, 4 (2018), 431–44

'Integrated archaeological and geophysical investigations to study the area of S. Giovanni in Laterano basilica (Rome, Italy)', in C. Einwogerer, W. Neubauer, R. B. Salisbury and I. Trinks (eds.), *Archaeological Prospection: Proceedings of the 10th International Conference* (Vienna, 2013), 203–5

Platner, S. B. and Ashby, T., *A Topographical Dictionary of Ancient Rome* (London, 1929)

Pohlkamp, W., '*Privilegium ecclesiae romanae pontifici contulit*: Zur Vorgeschichte der Konstantinischen Schenkung', in H. Fuhrmann (ed.), *Fälschungen im Mittelalter*, 5 vols. (Hanover, 1988), II, 413–90

'Textfassungen, literarische Formen und geschichtliche Funktionen der römischen Silvester-Akten', *Francia* 19 (1992), 115–96
Pollio, G., 'Il X secolo: Da Benedetto IV (900–903) a Gregorio V (996–999)', in D'Onofrio (ed.), *La committenza artistica dei papi*, 239–54
Pomarci, F., 'Medioevo: Architettura', in Pietrangeli (ed.), *San Giovanni in Laterano*, 63–6
'Il reliquiario di Sant'Agata nel contesto della produzione artistica avignonese', in Ufficio Beni Culturali dell' Arcidiocesi di Catania, *Sant'Agata il reliquiario a Busto: Contributi interdisciplinari* (Catania, 2010), 23–41
Popp, D., 'Eine unbekannte Ansicht der mittelalterlichen Fassade von S. Giovanni in Laterano', *Römisches Jahrbuch für Bibliotheca Hertziana* 26 (1990), 31–9
Poschmann, B., *Die abendländische Kirchenbusse im Ausgang des christlichen Altertums* (Munich, 1928)
*Die abendländische Kirchenbusse im frühen Mittelalter* (Breslau, 1930)
Powell, J. M., 'Honorius III's "Sermo in dedicatione ecclesie Lateranensis" and the historical–liturgical traditions of the Lateran', *Archivum Historiae Pontificiae* 21 (1983), 195–209
Price, R., 'Informal penance in early medieval Christendom', in K. Cooper and J. Gregory (eds.), *Retribution, Repentance, and Reconciliation* (Studies in Church History 40) (Woodbridge, 2004), 29–39
Priester, A. E., 'The Belltowers of Medieval Rome and the Architecture of Renovatio', Ph.D. thesis (Princeton University, 1990)
Prosperi Valenti Rodinò, S., *L'immagine di San Francesco nella Controriforma* (Rome, 1982)
Quednau, R., *Die Sala di Costantino im Vatikanischen Palast: Zur Dekoration der beiden Medici-Päpste Leo X. und Clemens VII* (Hildesheim, 1979)
Racine, F., 'Review of Lusnia 2014 Creating Severan Rome', *Bryn Mawr Classical Review* Blog 2015.06.23 (2015) (http://bmcr.brynmawr.edu/2015/2015-06-23.html)
Raoss, M., 'L'iscrizione della colonna Traiana e una epigrafe latina cristiana di Roma del V secolo', in *Seconda miscellanea greca e romana* (Rome, 1968), 399–435
Rasmussen, N. K., 'Unité et diversité des pontificaux latins aux VIIIe, IXe et Xe siècles', in *Liturgie de l'Église particulière et liturgie de l'Église universelle* (Rome, 1976), 393–410
Raspi Serra, J. (ed.), *Il primo incontro di Winckelmann con le collezioni romane: Ville e Palazzi di Roma, 1756* (Quaderni di Eutopia 6.2) (Rome, 2003)
Raspi Serra, J., de Polignac, F. and Themelly, A., 'Cronologia: 1726–1732', in J. Raspi Serra (ed.), *Idea e Scienza dell'antichità: Roma e l'Europa 1700–1770* (Eutopia II, 1) (Rome, 1993), 105–50
Rea, R., 'Archeologia nel suburbio di Roma: La stazione S. Giovanni della Linea C della Metropolitana', in A. F. Ferrandes and G. Pardini (eds.), *Le regole del gioco: Tracce archeologi racconti: Studi in onore di Clementina Panella* (Rome, 2016), 425–42

'Indagini archeologiche 1999-2009 lungo le Mura Aureliane: Da via Casilina vecchia a Porta Metronia. L'evoluzione del paesaggio', in R. Egidi, F. Filippi and S. Martone (eds.), *Archeologia e infrastrutture: Il tracciato fondamentale della linea C della metropolitana di Roma: Prime indagini archeologiche* (Bollettino d'Arte Serie 7) (Rome, 2010), 221-42

'Roma: Progettazione e realizzazione della Linea "C" della metropolitana', in *Arqueologia, Patrimonio y Desarrollo Urbano: Problematica y Soluciones* (Girona, 2010), 181-98

(ed.), *Cantieristica archeologica e opere pubbliche: La linea C della metropolitana di Roma* (Rome, 2011)

Rehberg, A., *Die Kanoniker von S. Giovanni in Laterano und S. Maria Maggiore im 14. Jahrhundert* (Tübingen, 1999)

'Il Rione Trastevere e i suoi abitanti nelle testimonianze raccolte sugli inizi dello Scisma del 1378', in L. Ermini Pani and C. Travaglini (eds.), *Trastevere: Un'analisi di lungo periodo* (Convegno di Studi 2008) (Rome, 2010), 255-317

Reudenbach, B., '"Loca sancta": Zur materiellen Übertragung der heiligen Stätten', in B. Reudenbach (ed.), *Jerusalem, du Schöne: Vorstellungen und Bilder einer heiligen Stadt* (Vestigia Bibliae 28) (Bern, 2008), 9-32

'Reliquien von Orten: Ein frühchristliches Reliquiar als Gedächtnisort', in B. Reudenbach and G. Toussaint (eds.), *Reliquiare im Mittelalter* (Berlin, 2005), 21-42

Ricci, C., 'Il principe in villa: Residenze imperiali in Italia e servizi di sicurezza', *Cahiers du Centre Gustave Glotz* 15 (2004), 317-41

'*Pro bona valetudine*: Considerazioni sul personale addetto all'infermeria e sui valetudinaria a Roma', *Humanitas* 70, 3 (2015), 355-66

Riccioni, S. and Tomasi, M., 'Giovanni di Bartolo: Busti reliquiario dei santi Pietro e Paolo (opera perduta)', in M. M. Donato (ed.), *Opere firmate nell'arte italiana/Medioevo: Siena e artisti senesi: maestri orafi* (Opera Nomina Historiae 5/6, 2011-12. Repertorio) (Pisa, 2013), cat. 22.S.1, 219-24

Richards, J., *The Popes and the Papacy in the Early Middle Ages 476-752* (London, 1979)

Righetti Tosti-Croce, M., 'L'architettura tra il 1254 e il 1308', in Romanini (ed.) *Roma nel Duecento*, 73-143

Roberg, B., *Das Zweite Konzil von Lyon [1274]* (Paderborn, 1990)

Roca de Amicis, A., 'Considerazioni sulla basilica Lateranense prima del rifacimento borrominiano', in G. Villetti, R. Bozzoni and G. Carbonara (eds.), *Saggi in onore di Renato Bonelli*, 2 vols. (Rome, 1992), I, 345-54

*L'Opera di Borromini in San Giovanni in Laterano: Gli anni della fabbrica (1646-1650)* (Rome, 1995)

Rohault de Fleury, G., *Le Latran au Moyen-âge*, 2 vols. (Paris, 1877)

Romanini, A. M. (ed.), *Roma nel Duecento: L'arte nella città dei Papi da Innocenzo III al Bonifacio VIII* (Turin, 1991)

Romano, J. F., 'Baptizing the Romans', *Acta ad archaeologiam et artium historiam pertinentia* 31 (2019), 43–62

'The ceremonies of the Roman pontiff: Rereading Benedict's twelfth-century liturgical script', *Viator* 41 (2010), 133–49

'Innocent II and the liturgy', in J. Doran and D. J. Smith (eds.), *Pope Innocent II (1130–43): The World vs. the City* (Abingdon, 2016), 326–51

*Liturgy and Society in Early Medieval Rome* (Farnham, 2014)

'The travelogue of Rabban Sauma as a source for thirteenth-century liturgy', *Archiv für Liturgiewissenschaft* 58/9 (2016/17), 59–101

Romano, M., 'L'Oratorio della S. Croce al Laterano: Preliminari di un'indagine archeologica-topografica', *Zeitschrift für Kunstgeschichte* 59, 3 (1996), 337–59

Romano, S., 'L'icône acheiropoiete du Latran: Fonction d'une image absente', in Bock et al. (eds.), *Art, cérémonial et liturgie*, 301–19

Röttgen, H., 'Repräsentationsstil und Historienbild in der römischen Malerei um 1600', in J. A. Schmoll (ed.), *Beiträge für Hans Gerhard Evers anlässlich seiner Emeritierung im Jahre 1968* (Darmstädter Schriften 22) (Darmstadt, 1968), 71–82

Rudy, K. M., *Virtual Pilgrimages in the Convent: Imagining Jerusalem in the Late Middle Ages* (Turnhout, 2011)

Sahner, C. C., 'Hierusalem in Laterano: The translation of sacred space in fifth century Rome', in Lidov (ed.), *New Jerusalems*, 103–30

Salzman, M. R., *The Making of a Christian Aristocracy: Social and Religious Change in the Western Roman Empire* (Cambridge, MA, 2002)

Sannibale, M., 'Le colonne e il capitello in bronzo d'età romana dell'altare del SS. Sacramento in Laterano: Analisi tecnica', *Rendiconti: Atti della Pontificia accademia romana di archeologia* 75 (1992–3), 101–25

Saxer, V., 'Recinzioni liturgiche secondo le fonti letterarie', in de Blaauw (ed.), *Arredi di culto e disposizioni liturgiche a Roma da Costantino a Sisto IV*, 71–9

*Les rites de l'initiation chrétienne du IIe au VIe siècle: Esquisse historique et signification d'après leurs principaux témoins* (Spoleto, 1988)

Schiavo, A., *Restauri e nuove opera nella zona extraterritoriale lateranense (1961–1968)*. (Vatican City, 1968)

'Vicende della Cattedrale di Roma e del Patriarchio Lateranense', *Studi Romani* 17, 1 (1969), 60–6

Schimmelpfennig, B., 'Die Funktion des Papstpalastes und der kurialen Gesellschaft im päpstlichen Zeremoniell vor und während des Schismas', in *Gènese et débuts du Grand Schisme d'Occident 1362–1394 (Avignon 25–28 septembre 1978)* (Paris, 1980), 317–28

'Der Palast als Stadtersatz: Funktionale und zeremonielle Bedeutung der Papstpaläste in Avignon und im Vatikan', in W. Paravicini (ed.), *Zeremoniell und Raum* (Sigmaringen, 1997), 239–56

Schlie, H., 'Das Mnemotop Jerusalem in der Prozession, in Brügge und im Bild: Die Turiner Passion von Hans Memling', in Gvozdeva and Velten (eds.), *Medialität der Prozession*, 141–75

Schmidt, H. A. P., *Hebdomada sancta*, 2 vols. (Rome, 1956–7)

Schmidt, T., 'Die Kanonikerreform in Rom und Papst Alexander II. (1061–1073), *Studi Gregoriani* 9 (1972), 199–221

Schneidmüller, B., Weinfurter, S., Matheus, M. and Wieczorek, A. (eds.), *Die Päpste: Amt und Herrschaft in Antike, Mittelalter und Renaissance* (Regensburg, 2016)

Scholz, S., *Politik – Selbstverständnis – Selbstdarstellung: Die Päpste in karolingischer und ottonischer Zeit* (Stuttgart, 2006)

Schumacher, W. N., 'Das Baptisterium von Alt-St. Peter und seine Probleme', in O. Feld and U. Peschlow (eds.), *Studien zur spätantiken und byzantinischen Kunst: F. W. Deichmann gewidmet*, 3 vols. (Bonn, 1986), I, 215–33

Schüppel, K. C, 'The stucco crucifix of Saint Peter's reconsidered: Textual sources and visual evidence for the Renaissance copy of a medieval silver crucifix', in McKitterick et al. (eds.), *Old Saint Peter's, Rome*, 306–23

Scrinari, V. S. M., 'Contributo all'urbanistica tardo antica sul Campo Laterano', in N. Duval (ed.), *Actes du XIe congrès International d'archéologie chrétienne* (Rome, 1989), 2201–20

  *Il Laterano imperiale I: Dalle 'Aedes Laterani' alla 'Domus Faustae'* (Vatican City, 1991)

  *Il Laterano imperiale II: Dagli 'horti Domitiae' alla cappella cristiana* (Vatican City, 1995)

  'Tombe a camera sotto via S. Stefano Rotondo', *Bullettino della Commissione archeologica comunale di Roma* 81 (1968–9), 17–24

Senekovic, D., 'S. Giovanni in Fonte und S. Croce in Laterano', in Claussen, *Die Kirchen der Stadt Rom*, 355–93

Serafini, A., *Torri campanarie di Roma e del Lazio nel Medioevo* (Rome, 1927)

Setz, W., *Lorenzo Vallas Schrift gegen die konstantinische Schenkung: 'De falso credita et ementita Constantini donatione', zur Interpretation und Wirkungsgeschichte* (Tübingen, 1975)

Sheppard, M. H., 'Liturgical expressions of the Constantinian triumph', *Dumbarton Oaks Papers* 21 (1967), 57–78

Siebenhüner, H., 'Umrisse zur Geschichte der Ausstattung von St. Peter in Rom von Paul III. bis Paul V. (1547–1606)', in K. Oettinger and M. Rassem (eds.), *Festschrift für Hans Sedlmayr* (Munich, 1962), 229–320

Silvagni, A., 'Intorno alle più antiche raccolte di iscrizioni classiche e medioevali. I. Nuovo ordinamento delle sillogi epigrafiche di Roma anteriori al secolo XI', *Atti della Pontificia accademia romana di archeologia. Dissertazioni* 15 (1921), 179–229

Simoncini, G., *Roma: Le trasformazioni urbane nel quattrocento*, 2 vols. (Florence, 2004)

Simperl, M., 'Ein gallischer *Liber Pontificalis*: Bermerkungen zur text- und Überlieferungsgeschichte des sogeanannten Caralogus Felicianus', *Römische Quartalschrift* 111 (2016), 272–87

Sinthern, P., 'Le teste dei SS. Apostoli Pietro e Paolo', *Civiltà Cattolica* 3 (1907), 444–57

Smith, J. M. H., 'Care of relics in early medieval Rome', in O. Phelan and V. Garver (eds.), *Rome and Religion in the Medieval World: Studies in Honor of Thomas F. X. Noble* (Farnham, 2014), 179–207

Sommer, C. S., '"Where did they put the horses?" Überlegungen zu Aufbau und Starke römischer Auxiliartruppen und deren Unterbringung in den Kastellen', in W. Czysz, C. M. Hüssen, H. P. Kuhnen, C. S. Sommer and G. Weber (eds.), *Provincialrömische Forschungen: Festschrift für Günter Ulbert zum 65. Geburtstag* (Rahden, 1995), 149–68

Speidel, M. P., *Die Denkmäler der Kaiserreiter: Equites Singulares Augusti* (Beihefte der Bonner Jahrbücher 50) (Cologne, 1994)

  *Die Equites Singulares Augusti: Begleit-truppe der römischen Kaiser des 2. und 3. Jahrhunderts* (Antiquitas I, 11) (Bonn, 1965)

  'Lebensbeschreibungen traianisch-hadrianischer Gardereiter', in K. Vössing (ed.), *Biographie und Prosopographie: Internationales Kolloquium zum 65. Geburtstag von Anthony R. Birley* (Historia Einzelschrift 178) (Stuttgart, 2005), 73–89

  'Maxentius and his "equites singulares" in the battle of the Milvian Bridge', *Classical Antiquity* 5, 2 (1986), 253–62

  *Riding for Caesar: The Roman Emperors' Horse Guards* (Boston, 1994)

Spinola, G., 'Alcune sculture egittizzanti nell'area lateranense: Nuove testimonianze dell'Iseum Metellinum?' *Bollettino dei Monumenti, Musei e Gallerie Pontificie* 21 (2001), 75–101

  'Il dominus Gaudentius e l'Antinoo Casali: Alcuni aspetti della fine del paganesimo da una piccola domus sul Celio?' *MEFRA* 104, 2 (1992), 953–79

  'Nuove ipotesi per l'area sotto la basilica lateranense: La *villa suburbana* e il possible *valetudinarium* dei *Castra Nova Equitum Singularium*', *Bolletino dei Monumenti, Musei e Gallerie Pontificie* 35 (2017), 61–92

  'Sculture, rilievi, decorazione, architettonica, iscrizioni e reperti ceramici', in Liverani (ed.), *Laterano 1*, 17–114

Stasolla, F. R., 'Dal tramonto all'alba: strumenti e tecniche di illuminazione nell'alto medioevo', in *Il fuoco nell'Alto Medioevo* (Settimane di studio del Centro italiano di studi sull'alto medioevo 60) (Spoleto, 2013), 857–8

Steinby, E. M., 'I bolli laterizi dell'Area sacra di Largo Argentina', in F. Coarelli, I. Kajanto, U. Nyberg and M. Steinby (eds.), *L'Area sacra di Largo Argentina I* (Rome, 1981), 298–332

  'La cronologia delle figlinae doliari urbane dalla fine dell'età repubblicana fino all'inizio del III sec', *Bollettino della Commissione Archeologica Comunale di Roma* 84 (1974-5), 7–132

Steinke, K., *Die mittelalterlichen Vatikanpaläste und ihre Kapellen: Baugeschichtliche Untersuchungen anhand der schriftlichen Quellen* (Vatican City, 1984)

Stevenson, E. 'Scoperte di antichi edifizi al Laterano', *Annali dell'Istituto di corrispondenza Archeologica* 49 (1877), 332–84

Stewart, P., *The Social History of Roman Art* (Cambridge, 2008)

Stork, H. W., 'Spätmittelalterliche Gebetbücher in Rollenform in Überlieferung und Bild', *Gutenberg-Jahrbuch* 85 (2010), 43–78

Story, J., 'The Carolingians and the oratory of Saint Peter the Shepherd', in McKitterick et al. (eds.), *Old Saint Peter's, Rome*, 257–73

Strinati, C., 'Roma nell'anno 1600: Studio di pittura', *Ricerche di storia dell'arte* 10 (1980), 15–48

Ströger, J., *Rethinking Ostia: A Spatial Enquiry into the Urban Society of Rome's Imperial Port-Town* (Leiden, 2011)

Stroick, A., 'Zum Zeremoniale Gregors X', *Historisches Jahrbuch* 55 (1935), 305–11

Suckale, R., 'Arma Christi: Überlegungen zur Zeichenhaftigkeit mittelalterlicher Andachtsbilder', *Städel-Jahrbuch*, n.s. 6 (1977), 177–208

Swinkels, L. and Koster, A., *Nijmegen, oudste Stad van Nederland* (Nijmegen, 2005)

Taffetani, C., 'Il complesso della c.d. *Domus Parthorum*: Nuova interpretazione delle fasi costruttive', in D. Manacorda and R. Santangeli Valenzani (eds.), *Il primo miglio della via Appia a Roma* (Rome, 2011), 39–45

Tamburini, F., *Andrea Busiri Vici (1818-1911): Architetto-ingegnere del Capitolo Lateranense: Le sue scoperte, i suoi progetti e le polemiche* (Archivium Historiae Pontificiae 34) (Rome, 1996)

Teasdale Smith, M., 'The Lateran *fastigium*: A gift of Constantine the Great', *RAC* 46 (1970), 149–75

Thacker, A., 'Popes, emperors and clergy of Old Saint Peter's from the fourth to the eighth century', in McKitterick et al. (eds.), *Old Saint Peter's, Rome*, 137–56

  'Rome: The pilgrim's city in the seventh century', in F. Tinti (ed.), *England and Rome in the Early Middle Ages: Pilgrimage, Art, and Politics* (Turnhout, 2014), 89–139

Thiel, W., 'Die "Pompeius-Säule" in Alexandria und die Vier-Säulen-Monumente Ägyptens: Überlegungen zur tetrarchischen Repräsentationskultur in Nordafrika', in D. Boschung and W. Eck (eds.), *Die Tetrarchie: Ein neues Regierungssystem und seine mediale Präsentation* (Wiesbaden, 2006), 249–322

  'Tetrakiona: Überlegungen zu einem Denkmaltypus tetrarchischer Zeit im Osten des römischen Reiches', *Antiquité tardive* 10 (2002), 299–326

Thoenes, C., 'Bemerkungen zur St. Peter-Fassade Michelangelos', in T. Buddensieg and M. Winner (eds.), *Munuscula discipulorum: Kunsthistorische Studien Hans Kauffmann zum 70. Geburtstag 1966* (Berlin, 1968), 331–41

Thümmel, H. G., *Die Memorien für Petrus und Paulus in Rom: Die archäologischen Denkmäler und die literarische Tradition* (Berlin, 1999)

Thunø, E., *Image and Relic: Mediating the Sacred in Early Medieval Rome* (Analecta Romana Instituti Danici, Supplementum 32) (Rome, 2002)

Tomasi, M., 'L'or l'argent et la cher: Remarques sur l'usage de la couleur dans les bustes relquiaires en métal au XIVe siècle', in M. Boudel-Machuel, M. Brock and P. Charron (eds.), *Aux limites de la couleur: Monochromie e polychromie dans les arts (1300–1650)* (Turnhout, 2011), 133–44

Tomassini, P., '"Scavare" negli Archivi: La domus tardo-repubblicana e giulio-claudia sotto al Caseggiato delle Tabernae Finestrate di Ostia (IV, V, 18): Nuove e vecchie scoperte', *Journal of Fasti Online* (2016), 1–12

Tomei, A., *Iacobus Torriti pictor: Una vicenda figurativa del tardo Duecento romano* (Rome, 1990)

Tomei, M. A., '*Domus* oppure *lupanar*? I materiali dallo scavo Boni della "casa repubblicana" a ovest dell'Arco di Tito', *MEFRA* 107 (1995), 549–619

Tomei, P., *L'architettura a Roma nel Quattrocento* (Rome, 1942)

Tomlin, R. S. O., 'Castra Nova Graffiti Report', Lateran Project, unpublished working document (2017)

Tonbrägel, M., 'Considerazioni sull'origine dell'opus incertum: il caso delle ville repubblicane di Tivoli', in F. M. Cifarelli (ed.), *Tecniche costruttive del tardo ellenismo nel Lazio e in Campania: Atti del Convegno (Segni, 3 dicembre 2011)* (Rome, 2013), 33–42

Torelli, M., 'La "Sedia Corsini", monumento della genealogia etrusca dei Plautii', in M.-M. Mactoux and E. Geny (eds.), *Mélanges Pierre Lévêque*, vol. V: *Anthropologie et société* (Besançon, 1990), 355–67

Tosini, P. (ed.), *Arte e committenza nel Lazio nell' età di Cesare Baronio: Atti del convegno internazionale di studi Frosinone, Sora, 16–18 maggio 2007* (Rome, 2009)

Toynbee, J. and Ward-Perkins, J., *The Shrine of St. Peter and the Vatican Excavations* (New York, 1957)

Turco, M. G., 'Cesare Baronio e i dettami tridentini nelle sistemazioni presbiteriali Romane', in Tosini (ed.), *Arte e committenza*, 87–107

   Il *'titulus' dei Santi Nereo e Achilleo: Emblema della riforma cattolica* (Rome, 1997)

Tyrer, J. W., *Historical Survey of Holy Week, Its Services and Ceremonial* (London, 1932)

Uhalde, K., 'The sinful subject: Doing penance in Rome', *Studia Patristica* 44 (2010), 405–14

Ullmann, W., 'On the use of the term "Romani" in the sources of the earlier Middle Ages', *Studia Patristica* 2 (1957), 155–63

Urban, T., 'Heilige Orte – Heiliger Raum: Zur Translokation der Sakraltopographie Jerusalems', in D. Dittmeyer, J. Hommers and S. Windmüller (eds.), *Verrückt, Verrutscht, Versetzt: Zur Verschiebung von Gegenständen, Körpern und Orten* (Berlin, 2015), 170–90

Vaccaro, L. and Riccardi, F. (eds.), *Sacri Monti: Devozione, arte e cultura della controriforma* (Milan, 1992)

Valentini, A., *La Patriarcale Basilica Liberiana* (Rome, 1839)

Valentini, R. and Zucchetti, G., *Codice topografico della città di Roma*, 4 vols. (Fonti per la Storia d'Italia 90) (Rome, 1940–53)

van Dijk, A., 'The Veronica, the *Vultus Christi* and the veneration of icons in medieval Rome', in McKitterick et al. (eds.), *Old Saint Peter's, Rome*, 229–56

van Dijk, S. J. P. and Hazelden Walker, J. (eds.), *The Ordinal of the Papal Court from Innocent III to Boniface VIII and Related Documents* (Fribourg, 1975)

Verardi, A. A., 'La genesi del *Liber Pontificalis* alla luce delle vicende della città di Roma tra la fine del V e gli inizi del VI secolo: Una proposta', *Rivista di Storia del cristianesimo* 10 (2013), 7–28

  *La memoria legittimante: Il* Liber Pontificalis *e la chiesa di Roma del secolo VI* (Nuovi Studi Storici 99) (Rome, 2016)

Verduchi, P., 'Colonne onorarie (Forum Romanum)', *LTUR* I, 294–5

  'Columna Phocae', *LTUR* I, 307

  'Lavori ai rostri del Foro Romano: L'esempio dell'Umbilicus', *Rendiconti: Atti della Pontificia accademia romana di archeologia* 55–6 (1982–3), 329–40

  'Rostra Augusti', *LTUR* IV, 214–17

  'Rostra Diocletiani', *LTUR* IV, 217–18

  'Le tribune rostrate', in A. M. Bietti Sestieri (ed.), *Roma: Archeologia nel centro 1: L'area archeologica centrale* (Rome, 1985), 29–33

Verhoeven, M., Bosman, L. and van Asperen, H. (eds.), *Monuments and Memory: Christian Cult Buildings and Constructions of the Past: Essays in Honour of Sible de Blaauw* (Architectural Crossroads. Studies in the History of Architecture 3) (Turnhout, 2016)

Verstegen, U., 'Im Kontakt mit den Allerheiligsten: Zur frühchristlichen Inszenierung der Heilsorte in der Jerusalemer Grabeskirche', in Koch and Schlie (eds.), *Orte der Imagination*, 31–54

Vian, G. M., *La donazione di Costantino: Potere religioso e potere politico in Italia* (L'identità italiana 35) (Bologna, 2004)

Vinzent, M., 'Rome', in M. M. Mitchell and F. M. Young (eds.), *Cambridge History of Christianity*, vol. I: *Origins to Constantine* (Cambridge, 2006), 397–414

Vitiello, M., 'Teodorico a Roma: Politica, amministrazione e propaganda nell'adventus dell'anno 500 (considerazioni sull'Anonimo Valesiano II)', *Historia* 53 (2004), 73–120

Vodrte, R. (ed.), *Roma al tempo di Caravaggio 1600–1630*, 2 vols. (Milan, 2011)

Voelker, E. C., 'Charles Borromeo's *Instructiones fabricae et suppellectilis ecclesiasticae* 1577: A Translation with Commentary and Analysis', Ph.D. thesis (Syracuse University, 1977)

Vogel, C., 'La Descriptio Ecclesiae Lateranensis du Diacre Jean: Histoire du texte manuscrit', in *Mélanges en l'honneur du Monseigneur Michel Andrieu* (Strasbourg, 1965), 457–76

  'La discipline pénitentielle en Gaule des origines au IXe siècle: Le dossier hagiographique', *Revue des sciences religieuses* 30 (1956), 1–26, 157–86; repr. in A. Faivre (ed.), *En rémission des péchés: Recherches sur les systèmes pénitentiels dans l'Église latine* (Aldershot, 1994), as no. VI

*Medieval Liturgy: An Introduction to the Sources*, rev. and trans. W. G. Storey and N. K. Rasmussen (Washington, DC, 1986)

'Les rites de la pénitence publique aux Xe et XIe siècle', in P. Gallais and Y. J. Riou (eds.), *Mélanges offerts à René Crozet*, 2 vols. (Poitiers, 1966), I, 137–44; repr. in A. Faivre (ed.), *En rémission des péchés: Recherches sur les systèmes pénitentiels dans l'Église latine* (Aldershot, 1994), as no. VIII

von Henneberg, J., *L'oratorio dell'arciconfraternita del santissimo crocifisso di San Marcello* (Rome, 1974)

von Petrikovits, H., *Das Handwerk in vor- und frühgeschichtlicher Zeit I.* (Abhandlungen der Akademie der Wissenschaften zu Göttingen, Philologisch-Historische Klasse 122) (Göttingen, 1981)

Walter, C., 'Papal political imagery in the medieval Lateran palace', *Cahiers Archéologiques* 20 (1970), 155–76 (part 1)

'Papal political imagery in the medieval Lateran palace', *Cahiers Archéologiques* 21 (1971), 109–36 (part 2)

Ward-Perkins, B., 'Constantinople: A city and its ideological territory', in G. P. Brogiolo, N. Gauthier and N. Christie (eds.), *Towns and their Territories between Late Antiquity and the Early Middles Ages* (Leiden, 2000), 325–46

Ward-Perkins, J. B., 'Constantine and the origins of the Christian basilica', in J. B. Ward-Perkins (ed.), *Studies in Roman and Early Christian Architecture* (London, 1994), 447–68

Warland, R., *Das Brustbild Christi: Studien zur spätantiken und frühbyzantinischen Bildgeschichte* (Rome, 1986)

Werner, K., *Mosaiken aus Rom: Polychrome Mosaikpavimente und Emblemata aus Rom und Umgebung* (Würzburg, 1994)

Wilpert, J., 'La decorazione costantiniana della Basilica Lateranense', *RAC* 6 (1929), 53–150

Wilson Jones, M., 'Genesis and mimesis: The design of the Arch of Constantine in Rome', *Journal of the Society of Architectural Historians* 59 (2000), 50–77

*Principles of Roman Architecture* (New Haven, 2000)

Wirbelauer, E., *Zwei Päpste in Rom: Der Konflikt zwischen Laurentius und Symmachus (498–514): Studien und Texte* (Quellen und Forschungen zur antiken Welt 16) (Munich, 1993)

Wolf, G., '"Or fu sì la sembianza vostra?" Sguardi alla "vera icona" e alle sue copie artistiche', in G. Morello and G. Wolf (eds.), *Il volto di Cristo* (Milan, 2000), 103–14

*Salus Populi Romani: Die Geschichte römischer Kultbilder im Mittelalter* (Weinheim, 1990)

Zollikofer, K., *Berninis Grabmal für Alexander VII: Fiktion und Repräsentation* (Worms, 1994)

Zuccari, A., 'Cesare Baronio, le immagini, gli artisti', in C. Strinati (ed.), *La regola e la fama: S. Filippo Neri e l'arte* (Rome and Milan, 1995), 80–97

# Index

Aalen, Germany, 104
Abu Mena, 296
Accademia di San Luca, 118, 487
Acqua Mariana, 41
*Actus Silvestri*, 512
*Aedes Parthorum*, 43, 82, 83, 86
Africa, 205, 206, 514
Agrippina Minor, empress, 86
Albano, 35, 97, 204, 211, 334
Alberti, Alberto, 254
Aldobrandini, Ippolito, cardinal, 496
Alexander II, pope, 335
Alexander III, pope, 281, 314
Alexander VI, pope, 484
Alexandria, *farus*, 154
Alfarano, Tiberio, 301
Allen, William, cardinal, 493
Amphitheatrum Castrensis, 39
Anacletus II, pope, 191, 335
Anastasius IV, pope, xvi, 309
Andrea da Montecchio, 373
Andreuccio da Peroscia, 366, 377
Anesi, Paolo, 9, 64, 487
Anicetus, pope, 200
Anicia family, 19
*Annales Ecclesiastici*, 514, 520
Anteros, pope, 200
Antioch, patriarchy, 315
Antonelli, Giacomo, cardinal, 114
Antoniano, Silvio, cardinal, 521
Aqua Claudia (Claudio-Neroniano), 100, 328
*aqua Crabra*, 25, 41
*Aquincum*, 39
Ara Pacis, 161
Arch of Constantine, 184, 185, 195, 287, 288, 289
Archive
    Archivio Capitolare Lateranense, 284, 291
    Archivio del Capitolo di San Giovanni in Laterano, 489
    Archivio di Stato di Firenze, 286
    Secret Vatican Archives (also Vatican Secret Archives), 474, 487
    State Archives of Rome, 474

Ark of the Covenant, 304, 443
*arma Christi*, 447, 452
Arnolfo di Cambio, 294
Assisi, basilica of St Francis, 281
Athanasius I, emperor, 242
Athens, 454
Auditorium of Maecenas, 78
Augsburg, 437
Augustine, 19, 20
Augustus, emperor, 51
Aurelian Walls, 6, 7, 25, 26, 28, 33, 41, 83, 106, 109, 242, 468, 489, 490
    Porta Asinaria, 25, 466, 468, 471, 472
    Porta Maggiore, 39, 109
    Porta Metronia, 25
    Porta San Giovanni, 466, 471, 476, 479
Aurelius Bithus, Marcus, 108
Aurelius Mestrius, 101
Avignon, 1, 330, 338, 345, 353, 354, 357, 361, 421, 423
    Papacy, 388, 401, 439

Baglione, Giovanni, 181, 499
Baldo, scribe, 218
Barelli, Lia, 324
Baronio, Cesare, cardinal, 513, 515, 517, 518, 520, 521, 522
barracks, 33, 36
Basilica Apostolorum, 349
Basilica of Julius, 211
Basilica of Maxentius, 148
Basilica Ulpia, 148
Bede, 4, 217
Behrwald, Ralf, 206
Bellarmino, Roberto, cardinal, 520, 521
Benedict III, pope, 209, 215
Berlin, 217, 278, 384, 385, 389
Bernard de Clairvaux, 454
Bernardi, Mario, 489
Bernardino Amico, 461
Bethlehem, 186, 443, 512
Bisconti, Fabrizio, 233
Bölling, Jörg, 349

Bologna
  Santo Stefano, 448
Boniface I, 210
Boniface I, pope, 210
Boniface II, 211
Boniface VIII, pope, 377
Borromeo, Carlo, cardinal, 501, 508
Borromini, Francesco, 2, 66, 69, 70, 92, 484
Borromini, Giuseppe, 482
Borromini, Pietro Antonio, 482
Bosman, Lex, 68, 138, 326, 336
Bramante, Donato, 343, 386, 521
Brandenburg, Hugo, 136, 147, 234
Brandt, Olof, 239, 243, 301
Brenk, Beat, 148
Brunori, Paola, 292
Bucarelli, Ottavio, 283
Bufalini, Leonardo, 467
Burckard, Johannes (also Burckhard), 437, 440
Burgkmair the Elder, Hans, 440
Busiri Vici, Andrea, 73, 87, 114, 115, 116, 117, 118, 120, 121, 123, 125, 126, 130, 131, 132, 133
Byzantium, 198, 445

Caelian hill, 6, 7, 28, 33, 37, 64, 91, 96, 98, 100, 106, 108
*Caeremoniale Episcoporum*, 519, 520, 522
Callistus, pope, 200, 201, 202
Callixtus II, pope, 41
Calpurni Pisoni, 51, 81, 84
Campania, 150
Campion, Edmund, 493
Campo dei Fiori, 375
Campus Caelemontanus, 39, 58
Campus Lateranensis, 39, 58, 325, 333, 334, 340, 353, 375, 435
*Campus Martialis*, 39
Cancellieri, Francesco, 12, 345
Canevari, Antonio, 489
Capgrave, John, 437, 451
Capitol, 241, 375, 377
Capitoline 'lupa', 376
Capocciola, 367, 375
Capponi, Alessandro, 288
Capua, 204
Caracalla, emperor, 109, 110
*Carnuntum*, 39
Cartaro, Mario, 471
Casa de' Crescenzi, 448
Casa della Farnesina, 78
*Casa Pilati*, 448
*Castra Albana*, 102

*Castra Nova Equitum Singularium* (also Equites Singulares, *castra*), 4, 6, 8, 11, 14, 37, 43, 52, 55, 59, 60, 61, 69, 70, 71, 74, 80, 81, 83, 84, 86, 87, 88, 89, 90, 91, 92, 93, 94, 95, 96, 97, 98, 99, 100, 101, 102, 103, 104, 105, 106, 107, 108, 109, 110, 112, 118, 121, 123, 125, 130, 132, 158, 169, 170, 194
  *principia*, 11, 71, 86, 88, 94, 95, 99, 102, 103, 106, 111
  *schola*, 88, 94
  *valetudinarium*, 72, 89
  *via principalis*, 112
*Castra Peregrina*, 6, 37, 108
*Castra Praetoria*, 107, 109
*Castra Priora Equitum Singularium*, 6, 39, 90, 101, 103, 106, 107, 108, 109
Cavalieri, Giovanni Battista, 494
Celestinus III, pope (also Celestine III), 284, 316
Cesari, Bernardino, 511
Charlemagne, 63
Charles II of Navarre, king, 347
Charles the Bald, 316
Charles V, king, 346, 358
Ciambelli, Agostino, 508
Ciampini, Giovanni Giustino, 182, 257, 258, 259, 260, 277, 278, 279, 282, 286
Cicero, 41, 454
Circignani, Niccolò, 494, 519
Circus Maximus, 109
Ciuccio Jani Catini, 366
Civita Castellana, 276
Claudius Gothicus, emperor, 160
Claudius, emperor, 50
Claussen, Peter Cornelius, 173, 189, 190, 289, 311
Clement I, pope, 200
Clement III, pope, 284
Clement VIII, pope, 2, 181, 284, 288, 289, 378, 496, 497, 499, 501, 504, 506, 508, 509, 511, 512, 513, 514, 515, 520, 521
Clement XII, pope, 286, 288, 289, 292, 386, 489
Cletus, pope, 200
Colini, Antonio Maria, 7, 11, 94
College of San Tommaso di Canterbury, 493, 494, 519
Colonna, Jacopo, cardinal, 337
Commodus, emperor, 11, 80
Constans II, emperor, 210, 299
Constantine II, papal candidate, 212
Constantine, emperor, 2, 6, 14, 18, 19, 91, 109, 110, 112, 134, 136, 137, 138, 144, 167, 168, 169, 171, 183, 186, 196, 199, 202, 203, 204,

205, 206, 207, 216, 217, 219, 222, 223, 224,
279, 287, 295, 297, 309, 315, 318, 400, 429,
440, 443, 445, 457, 459, 470, 473, 482, 492,
494, 497, 498, 504, 506, 507, 508, 509, 510,
512, 517, 518, 520, 521
  Donation of, 206, 207, 219, 220, 224, 284,
306, 309, 427, 492, 494, 499, 510, 517
Constantinople, 242
  Hagia Sophia, 153, 452
  patriarchy, 315
*Constitutum Constantini.* See Constantine,
  emperor, Donation of
Contini, Francesco, 158
Coppart de Velaines, 435
Corbett, Spencer, 67
Corsi, Faustino, 185
Corsini Throne, 11
Corsini, Neri, 489
Council of Trent, 470, 496
Cremoli, Filippo, 489
Crown of Thorns, 447, 450

d'Arpino, Cesare, 497, 500, 505
Dahm, Georg, 376
Dalmatia, 201, 216
Damasus, pope, 14, 199, 300
Dati, Giuliano, 451
Davison, David P., 35, 36
De Blaauw, Sible, 5, 136, 147, 157, 162, 165,
  186, 191, 299, 315, 324, 329, 333, 335, 400
de Grassis, Paris, 440
de Montaigne, Michel, 363
De Rossi, Giovanni Battista, 218
De Waal, Anton, 349
degli Uberti, Fazio, 466
del Duca, Giacomo, 466, 471
della Greca, Felice, 487
della Porta, Giacomo, 521
*Descriptio Lateranensis Ecclesiae*, 157, 314, 439
Diacono, Giovanni, 439
Dio Cassius, 108
Diocletian, emperor, 95
Dionysius, pope, 201
*Domus Parthorum*, 86
*Donatio Constantini.* See Constantine,
  emperor, Donation of
Donatism, 1
Donatist schism, 18
Dosio, Giovanni Antonio, 289
Douai, 493
Du Pérac, Stefano, 471
Duchesne, Louis, 199, 203, 207
Düsseldorf, 257, 259, 261

earthquake, 2
Echinger Maurach, Claudia, 327
Edgerton, Samuel, 376
Elagabalus, emperor, 39
Elizabeth I, queen, 493
Ephesus, council, 229
Equitius, priest, 203
Eugen III, pope, 310
Eugen VI, pope, 439
Eugene IV, pope, 365, 372
Eulalius, antipope, 210
Eusebius of Caesarea, 165, 200, 203
Eutropia, empress, 19
Eutychian, pope, 200
Evaristus, pope, 200
Eventius, pope, 200

Fabian, pope, 200, 201
Falda, Giovanni Battista, 486
Faro Focus 3D scanner, 94, 140, 243
Fausta, empress, 18, 19
Felix I, pope, 202
Felix II, pope, 202, 210
*figlinae Sulpicianae*, 31
Fobelli, Maria Luigia, 153
Foligno, 269, 383
Fontana, Domenico, 264, 332, 429, 466, 472,
  474, 475, 477, 480, 482, 489, 496, 512, 513
Fontana, Francesco, 114
Fontana, Giovanni, 475
Forum of Augustus, 185
Forum of Trajan, 185, 288
Foschi, Angelotto, cardinal, 365, 366, 372
Foxe, John, 492, 493, 494
Fra Mariano da Firenze, 379, 451
Fra' Paolino of Venice, 466
Francesco de Salimbeni, 372
Francia, 203, 217
Francino, Girolamo, 59
Freiberg, Jack, 2, 502
Frontinus, 41
Fuga, Ferdinando, 490

Gagliardi, Filippo, 134, 147, 148, 179, 393
Gaius, pope, 200, 201
Galilei, Alessandro, 252, 277, 286, 294, 332, 489
Galla Placidia, 210, 229, 298
Garofalo, 367, 375
Gasparri, Carlo, 243
Geertman, Herman, 152, 154
Gelasius. pope, 208, 211
Gentile da Fabriano, 365
Gerhoch von Reichersberg, 335

Ginzburg, Carlo, 449, 453
Giovanni di Bartolo, 353, 361
Giovenale, Giovanni Battista, 222, 226, 228
Gnilka, Christian, 13, 14, 15, 16, 17, 18, 19
Gnoli, Raniero, 242
Görlitz, 461
Greece, 205
Gregory I, pope, 306, 510
Gregory II, pope, 215
Gregory III, pope, 213
Gregory IV, pope, 261
Gregory XI, pope, 1, 357, 470
Gregory XIII, pope, 284, 451, 466, 470, 471, 492, 493, 497, 521
Gregory XIV, pope, 496
Greuter, Matthias, 508
Ground Penetrating Radar (GPR), 52, 53, 57, 69, 91, 102, 138, 140, 248
Guidobaldi, Federico, 39, 224, 229

Hadrian I, pope, 209, 214, 299
Hadrian II, pope, 215
Hadrian IV, pope, 301
Hadrian, emperor, 39
Halbwachs, Maurice, 461
Helen, empress, 459
Herklotz, Ingo, 306
Hilarus, pope, 239, 241, 242, 243, 247, 300
Hoffmann, Volker, 252, 255
Holy Cross, 204, 205, 216, 333, 442
Holy Lance, 447, 450
Holy Land, 429, 442, 443, 444, 445, 448, 450, 454, 458, 461
Honorius I, pope, 214
Honorius III, pope, 281, 283
Honorius, emperor, 41, 210, 242, 297, 298
Hormisdas, pope, 211
*Horti Calyclani*, 85
*Horti Lamiani*, 85
*Horti* of Caius Sallustius Crispus Passienus, 86
Horti of Maecenas, 85
*Horti Pallantiani*, 86
*Horti Sallustiani*, 85
*Horti Tauriani*, 85
*Horti Torquatiani*, 51
Hospital of St John, 10

Infessura, Stefano, 370
Innocent I, pope, 17
Innocent II, pope, 309, 335
Innocent III, pope, 281, 314, 316, 320, 334, 350, 421, 492
Innocent X, pope, 66, 172, 173, 318, 466, 482, 489

Innocent XII, pope, 487
Innocent XIII, pope, 482
Italy, 35, 114, 205, 206, 269, 304, 339, 377, 471
*Itinerarium Einsidlense*, 443, 448
Iunius Torquatus Silanus, Decius, 51

Jerome, 13, 14, 16, 85
Jerusalem, 304, 310, 315, 404, 430, 434, 435, 442, 443, 444, 447, 455, 456, 457, 458, 459, 461, 464, 465, 466
   fortress Antonia, 461
   Golgotha, 436, 443, 461
   Holy Sepulchre, 456, 461
   Lithostrathos (also Gabbatha), 461
   palace of Pilate, 430, 434, 435, 447, 449, 451, 456, 459, 461, 464
   patriarchy, 315
   Temple of Solomon, 354, 403, 435
   Via Dolorosa, 456, 461
Joan of France, Queen, 346
Joanna of Anjou, Queen, 346
John IV, pope, 209, 216
John the Deacon, 17, 18
John X, pope, 308
John XII, pope, 241
Josi, Enrico, 10, 67, 79, 93, 94
Judas, 405, 432, 447
Julius II, pope, 327, 343
Juvarra, Filippo, 487
Juvenal, 12, 16, 51, 83

Kieven, Elisabeth, 487
Kirschbaum, Engelbert, 349
Krautheimer, Richard, 4, 67, 69, 134, 136, 139, 146, 147, 148, 171, 174, 176, 177, 178, 179, 189, 190, 218, 221, 224, 226, 231, 329, 337

Lafrery, Antoine, 59
Lampl, Paul, 134
Lanciani, Rodolfo, 106, 107, 117
Lateran
   *acheiropoieta*, 320, 442, 444, 452
   *Aedes Laterani*, 13, 14, 15, 16, 17, 18, 19, 20, 43
   *Aedes Lateranorum*, 12, 15, 51, 83, 84
   Altar of the Holy Sacrament, 174, 183, 315, 443
   Annibaldi Tower, 376, 474, 477, 480
   apse, 8, 17, 63, 71, 87, 102, 110, 114, 115, 116, 118, 121, 126, 127, 131, 132, 133, 136, 147, 155, 158, 159, 170, 187, 190, 192, 194, 238, 274, 301, 318, 320, 322, 323, 324, 337, 413, 420, 432, 442, 497, 513, 516, 517

Lateran (cont.)
  baptistery, 6, 8, 17, 52, 78, 110, 202, 203, 204, 205, 206, 208, 209, 211, 213, 216, 217, 219, 221, 222, 224, 226, 227, 229, 231, 233, 236, 239, 241, 242, 243, 248, 257, 299, 300, 301, 333, 402, 405, 428, 429, 430, 435, 440, 448, 467, 473, 480, 497, 518
  baptistery, Oratory of St Stephen, 213
  basilica, 1, 4, 6, 8, 52, 82, 83, 84, 92, 112, 134, 136, 138, 147, 148, 152, 162, 167, 192, 202, 204, 211, 219, 221, 236, 241, 243, 257, 270, 275, 294, 295, 296, 303, 306, 308, 309, 313, 315, 317, 318, 320, 325, 327, 332, 336, 345, 353, 354, 358, 365, 372, 377, 379, 381, 400, 401, 402, 403, 405, 411, 414, 415, 417, 427, 429, 439, 496, 500, 509, 511, 513, 516, 517
  basilica, *Basilica Aurea* (also Golden Basilica), 4
  basilica, Basilica Constantiniana (also Constantinian Basilica), 4, 8, 52, 91, 102, 105, 106, 108, 112, 119, 138, 139, 143, 146, 168, 169, 170, 171, 185, 186, 194, 195, 196, 197, 200, 203, 206, 207, 208, 209, 210, 211, 212, 213, 214, 216, 217, 218, 219, 220, 236, 297, 325, 468, 482
  basilica, *Basilica Lateranensis*, 14
  basilica, Basilica Salvatoris (also Saviour's Church), 179, 194, 213, 296, 442, 445, 517
  baths, 51, 61, 82, 102, 242
  bell towers, 264, 338, 470
  *Casa dei Penitenzieri*, 65, 486, 487, 489, 490
  cavetto, 329, 338
  Chapel of St John the Baptist, 208, 213, 217, 219, 229, 300
  Chapel of St John the Evangelist, 208, 213, 216, 217, 219, 229, 244, 300
  Chapel of St Silvester, 435
  Chapel of St Thomas, 241, 252, 255, 257, 286, 484
  Chapel of St Venanzio, 110
  Chapel of the Holy Cross, 52, 208, 213, 217, 229, 240, 243, 300, 429, 461
  choir ambulatory, 429, 432
  cloister, 9, 279, 309, 332, 336, 385, 429, 430, 432, 435, 458, 465
  Colonna Chapel, 243
  Corsini chapel, 11, 92, 95, 107
  *Domus Faustae*, 1, 4, 204
  eastern façade, 1, 186, 250, 307, 318, 466, 486
  equestrian statue of Marcus Aurelius, 468, 495
  *fastigium*, 136, 139, 150, 151, 155, 158, 160, 161, 162, 165, 183, 186, 187, 192, 196, 208, 216, 236, 402

  Fifth Council, 440
  Fourth Council, 424, 427
  *fullonica*, 88, 89
  Galilei's façade, 11
  High Altar, 274, 317, 333, 358, 359, 377, 445, 501, 502, 508, 509, 510, 511, 512, 514, 517, 521
  lapidary, 429, 465
  Loggia of Benediction (also Loggia of the Blessings), 334, 340, 468, 480, 482, 484, 486
  *macellum*, 72, 87, 88
  *Macrona*, 435, 477
  main altar, 170, 187, 191, 192, 196, 315, 345, 347, 348, 350, 353, 444, 504, 507, 509, 517
  *mensura Christi*, 432, 437, 440, 444, 447, 451, 464, 465
  monastery of the Passionist Fathers, 20
  *Navata Clementina*, 497, 499, 500, 502, 510, 512, 517, 518, 520, 522
  nymphaeum, 2, 239, 240, 241, 242, 248
  obelisk, 480
  Oratory of Santa Croce (also Oratory of the Holy Cross. *See* Lateran, Chapel of the Holy Cross
  Oratory of Santissimo Sacramento, 19
  Oratory of St John the Baptist. *See* Lateran, Chapel of St John the Baptist
  Oratory of St John the Evangelist. *See* Lateran, Chapel of St John the Evangelist
  Oratory of St Thomas. *See* Lateran, Chapel of St Thomas
  palace, 5, 9, 59, 63, 78, 173, 198, 210, 211, 215, 219, 276, 287, 349, 350, 355, 377, 402, 428, 435, 448, 449, 453, 456, 496, 509, 510, 519
  palace, *Aula Concilii* (also Sala del Concilio), 329, 334, 340, 377, 432, 433, 437, 449, 451
  palace, Chapel of St Lawrence (also Oratory of St Lawrence), 306, 349, 350, 355, 429, 442
  palace, Sala di Costantino, 510, 519
  palace, Salvator icon (also Icon of the Saviour), 320, 350, 354, 444
  *patriarchium*, 1, 5, 6, 17, 22, 53, 55, 61, 64, 65, 70, 304, 311, 316, 317, 402, 467, 472, 473, 474, 480, 481, 489, 496
  Pilate doors, 449, 454
  Pilate's house, 443
  *Portico Leoniano*, 114, 116, 117, 121, 274, 324, 435
  *posterula*, 7
  reliquaries of Peter and Paul, 345
  Sacrisrty of Canons, 497

Sancta Sanctorum, 19, 64, 269, 275, 297, 303, 328, 353, 354, 366, 429, 435, 440, 442, 445, 477, 480
*scala Pilati*, 448
*scrinium*, 19
*solea*, 136, 138, 139, 150, 155, 162, 165
southern ambulatory, 497
suburban villa, 71, 72, 83, 123
synod, 1, 212, 216
transept, 2, 54, 56, 67, 68, 69, 171, 172, 176, 181, 183, 189, 190, 191, 192, 194, 250, 262, 264, 265, 270, 271, 272, 274, 275, 284, 288, 297, 301, 309, 315, 318, 325, 328, 329, 332, 333, 334, 335, 336, 337, 338, 340, 341, 345, 365, 377, 378, 470, 497, 500, 502, 504, 508, 509, 511, 516, 517, 518, 519, 520, 522
Trapezoidal Building, 71, 73, 79, 86, 88, 89, 90, 99, 100, 102, 111, 115, 117, 118, 120, 122, 123, 125, 127, 128
Triclinium of Pope Leo III, 63, 64, 65, 70, 271, 466, 474, 486, 487, 488, 489
Lateran Chapter, 114, 138, 311, 314, 396, 438
Lateran hill, 43, 46, 47, 51
Lateran Project, 6, 52, 61, 67, 91, 92, 94, 98, 101, 138, 140, 142, 239, 243, 248
Latium, 352
Lauer, Philippe, 19
Laurence, antipope, 211
*Legio II Parthica*, 97
Leica scan stations, 140, 243
Lentes, Thomas, 454
Leo III, pope, 63, 64, 301
Leo IV, pope, 212, 215, 252, 261, 308
Leo V, pope, 308
Leo X, pope, 438, 440
Leo XIII, pope, 114
*Liber Pontificalis*, 17, 63, 136, 138, 144, 150, 154, 155, 156, 158, 160, 186, 187, 197, 198, 199, 200, 202, 203, 204, 205, 206, 207, 209, 210, 211, 212, 213, 216, 219, 220, 222, 224, 228, 229, 234, 236, 239, 243, 248, 251, 262, 306, 309, 310, 335, 401, 508, 512
Libera, Antonio, 482
Liberius, pope, 210
Licinian Rogations, 16
Licinius Calvus Stolo, Caius, 16
Ligorio, Pirro, 470, 472
Linus, pope, 200
Lippi, Filippino, 481
Liverani, Paolo, 92
Lloyd, Joan Barclay, 134, 136
London Charter, 138, 167
Luchterhandt, Manfred, 64

Lucius, pope, 200
Lund University, 224, 231
Lusius Petellinus, Lucius, 81
Lusnia, Susann S., 108

Macerata, 493
Maderno, Carlo, 513
Madonna Ginevra di Ciccone Fiorentino, 284
Madrid, 487
Maecenas, 39
Maggi, Giovanni, 508
Magrì, Rossella, 365, 377
Mallius, Peter, 314, 316
Malmstrom, Rickard E., 172, 190
Mannheim, 294
Marangoni, Giovanni, 176
Marcellinus, pope, 200
Marcellus, pope, 200
Marchetti, Giuseppe, 256, 261
Marcus Aurelius, emperor, 20
Martin I, pope, 212
Martin V, pope, 164, 379, 388, 390, 393, 397, 439
Martinelli, Fioravante, 465
*Martyrologium Romanum*, 494, 521
Mathis, Paola, 324
Mattei, Tommaso, 489
Maurice the Cartularius, 211
mausoleum of Hadrian, 309
mausoleum of St Helena, xvi, 106, 204, 309
Maxentius, 168
Maximian, emperor, 19, 95
*Meditationes Vitae Christi*, 446
Meinert, Till, 461
Mellini, Benedetto, 259, 284
*mensa Domini*, 442
Metro Line C., 25, 39, 46
Milan, 210
Miller, Dayton C., collection, 509
Millini, Benedetto. *See* Mellini, Benedetto
Millini, Urbano, 359, 360, 361
Miltiades, pope, 204
Milvian Bridge, battle of, 4, 110, 168, 295
*Mirabilia*, 439
Mithras, 20
Mols, Stephan, 225
monastery of SS Andrew and Bartholomew, 214
monastery of SS John the Evangelist, John the Baptist and St Pancras, 213
monastery of St Pancras, 214
Montinaro, Federico, 206, 207
Moormann, Eric, 225

Mount Soratte, 498
Mucanzio, Giovanni Paolo, 506
Muffel, Nikolaus, 430, 432, 437, 440, 448
Münster, 327, 329
Musco, Chiara, 264, 270
Myron, 11

Nadal, Jeronimo, 459, 461
Nash, Ernest, 18
Nazareth
    Mary's house, 429, 435
Nebbia, Cesare, 509, 511
Neri, Filippo, 513
Nero, emperor, 12, 15, 22, 51, 81, 83, 84, 85, 86
Nesselrath, Arnold, 365
Nicaea, synod, 203
Nicholas I, pope, 212, 215, 217
Nicholas III, pope, 269, 275, 353
Nicholas IV, pope (also Nicolas IV), 172, 274, 275, 322, 390
Nicola di Valmontone, 368, 370, 373
Nicolaus de Angelo (also Nicolò d'Angelo), 183
Nijmegen
    castrum, 34
Ninfa, 269
Nogari, Paris, 516, 517

*ollae perforatae*, 43
Optatus of Milevi, 18, 19, 204
Ostia, 35, 204
Ostrow, Steven, 515
Ottoboni, Pietro, cardinal, 288, 489
Ousterhout, Robert, 457

palace of Cardinal Stefano Conti, 341
    Aula Gotica, 341
    Chapel of Silvester, 341
Palladio, 440
Pamphili, Benedetto, cardinal, 489
Pantheon, 185, 495
Panvinio, Onofrio, 284, 389, 393, 394, 397
Panzera, Battista, 158
Paolo de lo Mastro, 366
Paolo di Lello Petrone, 366, 375
Paravicini Bagliani, Agostino, 377
Paris, 395
    Louvre, 383, 394
Paschal I, pope, 212, 214, 215, 261
Paschal II, pope, 309, 351
*Patrimonium Petri*, 303, 510
Paul I, pope, 215
Paul the Silentiary, 153
Pelliccioni, Giovanni, 239

Piazza di Porta San Giovanni, 475, 491
Piazza Farnese, 493
Piazza Giovanni Paolo II, 55
Piazza San Giovanni, 39, 55, 241, 470, 479
Piazzale Metronio, 28
Piero della Francesca, 449, 453, 459
Pippin, father of Charlemagne, 303
Pippin, son of Charlemagne, 212
Piro, Salvatore, 189
Pisanello, 365
Pisonian conspiracy, 12, 51, 85
Pius IV, pope, 470, 497
Pius V, pope, 470, 496
Pius IX, pope, 114
Pius XII, pope, 293
Plautius Lateranus, 12, 14, 16, 22, 51, 82, 85
Plautius Lateranus, Sextius, 15
Pliny the Elder, 154
Pompeii
    House of the Bracciale d'Oro, 78
    House of the Cubicoli Floreali, 78
    House of the Frutteto, 78
    House of the Menandro, 78
    Villa of Diomedes, 74
Pontian, pope, 200
Pontifical Commission of Sacred Archaeology, 94
*Pontificale Romanum*, 509, 511, 513, 520, 522
Porto, 211
Pozzo, Andrea, 487
Praetorian Guard, 97
Procopius, 41
Prudentius, 16, 17, 18
Ptolemy of Lucca, 203, 353
Pyrenees, 242

Qual'at Sem'an, 296
Quirinal hill, 241
Quirinal Palace, 243

Raphael, 494, 495, 518
Ravenna, 210, 212, 232
    San Giovanni Evangelista, 229
Regionary Catalogues, 36
Ricci, Giovanni Battista, 509, 511
Righi, Francesco, 257, 261
Roca de Amicis, Augusto, 173, 389, 393
Rochi, Prospero, 475
Roman Forum, 113, 160, 162
    Rostra, 162
Roman pilgrims route, 317
Romano, John, 213
Roncalli, Cristoforo, 518

Rufinus, 203
Rusticucci, Girolamo, cardinal, 513

San Clemente, 269
San Giorgio al Velabro, 261, 515
San Lorenzo fuori le Mura, 269, 276, 281, 336
San Lorenzo in Damaso, 162
San Martino ai Monti, 134, 179, 261, 393
San Paolo fuori le mura, 197, 203, 205, 208, 210, 221, 276, 282, 332, 349, 443, 513
San Pietro in Vaticano. *See* St Peter's basilica
San Pietro in Vincoli, 327
San Sebastiano, 349
San Sebastiano fuori le mura, 471
Sancta Sanctorum, 473
Sangallo, Giuliano da, 232
Sant'Apollinare, 494
Santa Cecilia in Trastevere, 261
Santa Costanza, 221
Santa Croce in Gerusalemme, 284, 334, 443, 444, 480, 487, 490
Santa Francesca Romana, 270
Santa Giuliana in Perugia, 361
Santa Maria in Aracoeli, 373
Santa Maria in Navicella, 515
Santa Maria in Trastevere, 210, 336
Santa Maria Maggiore, 211, 214, 225, 243, 275, 318, 327, 333, 343, 403, 443, 444, 470, 480, 502, 512
    Capella Sistina, 501
    Cappella del Presepio, 512
Santa Maria Nova, 335
Santa Maria Sopra Minerva
    Carafa Chapel, 481
Santa Prassede, 261, 515
Santa Susanna, 173, 513
Sant'Agnese, 173, 203, 221
Santi Nereo e Achilleo, 261, 515, 518
Santi Quattro Coronati, 252, 253, 257, 261, 269, 270, 271, 341, 492
Santo Stefano, 443
Santo Stefano Rotondo, 6, 335, 494, 519
sarcophagus, 242, 297, 309
Sarti, Antonio, 114
Scala Sancta (also Scala Santa), 20, 64, 78, 82, 286, 429, 434, 435, 438, 440, 444, 448, 449, 451, 453, 454, 459, 461, 464, 465, 467, 472, 473, 480, 482, 486, 488, 490
Scrinari, Valnea, 9
Septimius Severus, emperor, 4, 8, 13, 15, 16, 22, 24, 43, 81, 82, 84, 91, 95, 97, 103, 108, 109, 110
Sergius I, pope, 216
Sergius II, pope, 209, 215, 250, 252, 257, 261, 278, 286, 289, 306, 336
Sergius III, pope, 137, 308
Séroux d'Agincourt, Jean-Baptiste, 348
Servestro de Pallone, 370
Servian Walls, 83
Sessorian palace, 4, 106, 109, 110, 113, 202, 204, 205
Severano, Giovanni, 181
Severinus, pope, 211
Sextius Lateranus, 15, 16
Sextius Lateranus, Sextius, 43
Sextius Lateranus, Titus, 13, 22, 43, 82, 84, 86
Sextius Sextinus Lateranus, 16
Sicily, 205
Silverius, pope, 199
Silvester, pope, 4, 200, 202, 203, 204, 219, 318, 402, 442, 492, 498, 504, 507, 508, 510, 511, 517, 519,
Simplicius, pope, 298
Sinthern, Pietro, 349
Sixtus I, pope, 200
Sixtus II, pope, 200
Sixtus III, pope, 208, 216, 223, 228, 229, 234, 470
Sixtus IV, pope, 329, 338
Sixtus V, pope, 53, 59, 63, 65, 173, 181, 229, 241, 264, 338, 428, 435, 466, 470, 472, 473, 477, 478, 480, 484, 486, 496, 501, 503, 509, 512, 513, 519
Soresini, Giuseppe Maria, 345, 372
Spinola, Giandomenico, 102
*spolia*, 2, 134, 137, 138, 143, 144, 171, 184, 194, 195, 254, 261, 449
St Antony of Padua, 320
St Francis, 275, 306, 319, 320, 454
St Peter and St Marcellinus, 106, 204
St Peter, pope, 197, 200, 201, 204, 205, 236, 304, 315, 354, 358, 372, 378, 444
St Peter's basilica, 1, 110, 147, 171, 179, 185, 186, 194, 196, 197, 203, 204, 205, 208, 210, 211, 214, 216, 221, 294, 296, 297, 298, 299, 300, 301, 303, 304, 308, 311, 314, 315, 316, 317, 332, 343, 349, 354, 355, 361, 440, 443, 444, 470, 482, 522
    Altar of Simon and Judas, 448
    *Cathedra Petri*, 316
    Oratory of Petronilla, 218, 299
Stephen I, pope, 200
Stephen II, pope, 215, 219
Stephen III, pope, 212, 215
Stephen V, pope, 215
Stevenson, Enrico, 123, 126

Strozzi, Alessandro, 466
*suspensurae*, 44
sylloge of Lauresham, 241
Sylvester I, pope. *See* Silvester, pope
Symmachus, pope, 16, 300, 301
synod of 313, 1, 18, 204

*Tabula Magna Lateranensis*, 430, 438, 440
Tacitus, 16, 84, 85
Telesphorus, pope, 200
Temple of Castor, 174
Temple of Divus Julius, 174
Temple of the Palatine Apollo, 154
Theoderich, king, 16
Theodosius, son of Galla Placidia, 298
Theodulus, deacon, 200
Thessaloniki
   Arch of Galerius, 161
Tiber, 46, 202, 448
Titus, emperor, 315, 443
Tivoli
   San Silvestro, 492
Tizzani, Vincenzo, 114
Tomasi, Michele, 362
tomb, chamber, 9
Tomlin, Roger S. O., 98
Torriti, Jacopo, 115, 116, 274, 320, 323, 325
Trajan, emperor, 39, 108
Trajan's Column, 241
Trier, 447
   basilica, 226

Ugonio, Pompeo, 174, 180, 284, 432, 510, 512
Urban I, pope, 201
Urban V, pope, 317, 345, 353, 354, 357, 358, 361, 371, 390, 445

Valadier, Giuseppe, 243, 348, 490
Valentine, pope, 215
Valentinian III, emperor, 210, 298
Valla, Lorenzo, 492
van Heemskerck, Martin (also Maarten van Heemskerck), 59, 264, 328, 329, 468, 481
van Lint, Hendrik, 257, 259, 261, 278
van Overbeek, Bonaventura, 289
Vassalletto, Pietro, 282
Vatican, 354, 439, 444, 518
   *grotte*, 521
   palace, 353, 492, 494, 522
   Pauline Chapel, 504
   Sala di Costantino, 492, 494, 518
   Sistine Chapel, 504, 514
Vatican Apostolic Library, 131

Vatican hill, 196, 296
Vatican Museums, 20, 224, 243, 276, 293, 384
   Galleria dei Candelabri, 243
   Raphael Rooms, 20
Venuti, Ridolfino, 288, 289
Vera Icon, 316
Veronica (also Vera Icon), 356, 446
Vespasian, emperor, 279, 443
Vespignani, Virginio, 116, 125, 126, 127, 128, 323
Via Amba Aradam, 51, 81
Via Appia, 201, 349, 470, 486
Via Asinaria, 7, 51, 71, 77, 83, 84
Via Aurelia, basilica, 202
Via Casilina Vecchia, 25
Via Celimontana, 468, 472
Via della Ferratella, 470
Via di San Giovanni, 480, 482
Via Emanuele Filiberto, 39
Via Farsalo, 28
Via Illiria, 28
Via La Spezia, 25, 28
Via Merulana, 470
Via Ostiense, 349
Via Sacra, 14
Via Sannio, 25, 27, 28, 39, 42, 51
Via Statilia, 39
Via Tasso, 39, 106, 108
Via Tuscolana, 7, 8, 9, 51, 59, 60, 70, 71, 73, 74, 76, 79, 80, 82, 83, 84, 85, 86, 87, 88, 100
Viale Carlo Felice, 25
Viale Ipponio, 28, 36, 39
Victor, pope, 200
Vienna
   Albertina, 179
*Vigiles*, 97
   fifth cohort, 37
Villa of Livia at Prima Porta, 78
Villa of Valerius Asiaticus, 86
Vitalian, pope, 210
Vitelleschi, Giovanni Maria, cardinal, 372
Votive offerings, 9

Waddy, Patricia, 134, 136
Wadi Hammamat, 242
Werro, Sebastiano, 515
Wilson Jones, Mark, 185

Xystus II, pope, 200

Zacharias, pope, 217
Zagotto, Natalino, xxiii, 138
Zephyrinus, pope, 201
Zuccari, Alessandro, 518

For EU product safety concerns, contact us at Calle de José Abascal, 56–1°, 28003 Madrid, Spain or eugpsr@cambridge.org.

www.ingramcontent.com/pod-product-compliance
Lightning Source LLC
LaVergne TN
LVHW080928290425
809882LV00005B/366